Core Rulebook

Core Rulebook

CREDITS

Lead Designer: Jason Bulmahn
Design Consultant: Monte Cook
Additional Design: James Jacobs, Sean K Reynolds, and F. Wesley Schneider
Additional Contributions: Tim Connors, Elizabeth Courts, Adam Daigle, David A. Eitelbach, Greg Oppedisano, and Hank Woon

Cover Artist: Wayne Reynolds
Interior Artists: Abrar Ajmal, Concept Art House, Vincent Dutrait, Jason Engle, Andrew Hou, Imaginary Friends,
Steve Prescott, Wayne Reynolds, Sarah Stone, Franz Vohwinkel, Tyler Walpole, Eva Widermann, Ben Wootten,
Svetlin Velinov, Kevin Yan, Kieran Yanner, and Serdar Yildiz

Creative Director: James Jacobs
Editing and Development: Christopher Carey, Erik Mona, Sean K Reynolds,
Lisa Stevens, James L. Sutter, and Vic Wertz
Editorial Assistance: Jeffrey Alvarez and F. Wesley Schneider
Editorial Interns: David A. Eitelbach and Hank Woon
Art Director: Sarah E. Robinson
Senior Art Director: James Davis

Publisher: Erik Mona
Paizo CEO: Lisa Stevens
Vice President of Operations: Jeffrey Alvarez
Corporate Accountant: Dave Erickson
Director of Sales: Pierce Watters
Sales Manager: Christopher Self
Technical Director: Vic Wertz
Events Manager: Joshua J. Frost

Special Thanks: The Paizo Customer Service and Warehouse Teams, Ryan Dancey, Clark Peterson, and the proud participants of the Open Gaming Movement.

This game is dedicated to Gary Gygax and Dave Arneson.

Based on the original roleplaying game rules designed by Gary Gygax and Dave Arneson and inspired by the third edition of the game designed by Monte Cook, Jonathan Tweet, Skip Williams, Richard Baker, and Peter Adkison.

This game would not be possible without the passion and dedication of the thousands of gamers who helped playtest and develop it. Thank you for all of your time and effort.

Paizo Publishing, LLC
7120 185th Ave NE
Ste 120
Redmond, WA 98052-0577
paizo.com

TABLE OF CONTENTS

It started in early 1997. Steve Winter, Creative Director at TSR, told a few of us designers and editors that we should start thinking about a new edition of the world's most popular roleplaying game. For almost three years, a team of us worked on developing a new rules set that built upon the foundation of the 25 years prior. Released in 2000, 3rd Edition started a new era. A few years later, a different set of designers made updates to the game in the form of 3.5.

Today, the Pathfinder Roleplaying Game carries on that same tradition as the next step in the progression. Now, that might seem inappropriate, controversial, or even a little blasphemous, but it's still true. The Pathfinder RPG uses the foundations of the game's long history to offer something new and fresh. It's loyal to its roots, even if those roots are—in a fashion—borrowed.

The game's designer, Jason Bulmahn, did an amazing job creating innovative new mechanics for the game, but he started with the premise that he already had a pretty good game to build upon. He didn't wipe the slate clean and start over. Jason had no desire to alienate the countless fans who had invested equally countless hours playing the game for the last 35 years. Rather, he wanted to empower them with the ability to build on what they'd already created, played, and read. He didn't want to take anything away from them—only to give them even more.

One of the best things about the Pathfinder RPG is that it really necessitates no "conversion" of your existing books and magazines. That shelf you have full of great adventures and sourcebooks (many of them very likely from Paizo)? You can still use everything on it with the Pathfinder RPG. In fact, that was what convinced me to come on board the Pathfinder RPG ship. I didn't want to see all the great stuff that had been produced thus far swept under the rug.

Now, my role as "design consultant" was a relatively small one. Make no mistake: the Pathfinder RPG is Jason's baby. While my role was to read over material and give feedback, mostly I just chatted with Jason, relating old 3rd Edition design process stories. Jason felt it valuable to know why things were done the way they were. What was the thinking behind the magic item creation feats? Had we ever considered doing experience points a different way? How did the Treasure Value per Encounter chart evolve? And so on.

It was an interesting time. Although I sometimes feel I have gone on at length about every facet of 3rd Edition design in forums, in interviews, and at conventions, Jason managed to ask questions I'd never been asked before. Together, we really probed the ins and outs of the game, which I think is important to do before you start making changes. You've got to know where you've been before you can figure out where you're going. This is particularly true when you start messing around with a game as robust and tightly woven as 3rd Edition. The game's design is an intricate enough matrix that once you change one thing, other aspects of the game that you never even suspected were related suddenly change as well. By the time we were done hashing things out, we'd really put the original system through its paces and conceived of some interesting new ideas. Jason used that as a springboard and then went and did all the hard work while I sat back and watched with a mix of awe and excitement as the various playtest and preview versions of the game came out.

The Pathfinder RPG offers cool new options for characters. Rogues have talents. Sorcerers have bloodline powers. It fixes a few areas that proved troublesome over the last few years. Spells that turn you into something else are restructured. Grappling is simplified and rebalanced. But it's also still the game that you love, and have loved for so long, even if it was called by a different name.

I trust the gang at Paizo to bear the game's torch well. They respect the game's past as much as its future. They understand its traditions. It was my very distinct and sincere pleasure to play a small role in the Pathfinder RPG's development. You hold in your hands a truly great game that I've no doubt will provide you with hours and hours of fun.

Enjoy!

Monte Cook

ADVENTURE AWAITS!

Welcome to a world where noble warriors battle mighty dragons and powerful wizards explore long-forgotten tombs. This is a world of fantasy, populated by mysterious elves and savage orcs, wise dwarves and wily gnomes. In this game, your character can become a master swordsman who has never lost a duel, or a skilled thief capable of stealing the crown from atop the king's head. You can play a pious cleric wielding the power of the gods, or unravel the mysteries of magic as an enigmatic sorcerer. The world is here for you to explore, and your actions will have a profound influence in shaping its history. Who will rescue the king from the clutches of a powerful vampire? Who will thwart the vengeful giants who have come from the mountains to enslave the common folk? These stories wait for your character to take center stage. With this rulebook, a few friends, and a handful of dice, you can begin your epic quest.

The Pathfinder Roleplaying Game did not start out as a standalone game. The first draft was designed as a series of house rules for the 3.5 version of the world's oldest roleplaying game. In the fall of 2007, with a new edition of that game on the horizon, it seemed only natural that some gamers would prefer to stick with the rules they already owned. It also made sense that those same gamers would like some updates to their rules, to make the game easier to use and more fun to play. When design of this game first began, compatibility with existing products was one of my primary goals, but I also wanted to make sure that all of the classes, races, and other elements were balanced and fun to play. In other words, I endeavored to keep all of the great, iconic parts of the game, while fixing up the clunky rules that slowed down play and caused more than one heated argument at the game table.

As the rules grew in size, it became apparent that the changes were growing beyond a simple update into a full-fledged rules system. So while the Pathfinder RPG is compatible with the 3.5 rules, it can be used without any other books. In the coming months, you can expect to see a number of brand-new products, made specifically to work with this version of the rules, from Paizo and a host of other publishers through the Pathfinder Roleplaying Game Compatibility License. This license allows publishers to use a special logo to indicate that their product works with the rules in this book.

Making an already successful game system better is not a simple task. To accomplish this lofty goal, we turned to fans of the 3.5 rules, some of whom had been playing the game for over eight years. Since the spring of 2008, these rules have undergone some of the most stringent and extensive playtesting in gaming history. More than 50,000 gamers have downloaded and used these rules. Moving through a number of playtest drafts, the final game that you now hold in your hands slowly started to come together. There were plenty of missteps, and more than one angry debate, but I believe that we ended up with a better game as a result. This would not be the game you now hold without the passion and inspiration of our playtesters. Thank you.

In closing, this game belongs to you and all the fans of fantasy gaming. I hope that you find this system to be fun and simple to use, while still providing the same sort of depth and variety of options you've come to expect from a fantasy roleplaying game.

There is a world of adventure waiting for you to explore. It's a world that needs brave and powerful heroes. Countless others have come before, but their time is over. Now it's your turn.

Jason Bulmahn
Lead Designer

1 GETTING STARTED

The dragon roared in triumph as Valeros collapsed into the snow, blood spurting from the terrible wound in his belly. Kyra rushed to his side, praying that she wasn't too late to save his life.

"I'll hold the beast off!" Seoni cried as she stepped up to the dragon, her staff flaring with defensive fire. Merisiel looked to the hulking dragon, then at the delicate sorcerer, and shook her head sadly.

The adventure had just barely begun, and judging by this fight alone, they weren't getting paid enough for the job.

The Pathfinder Roleplaying Game is a tabletop fantasy game in which the players take on the roles of heroes who form a group (or party) to set out on dangerous adventures. Helping them tell this story is the Game Master (or GM), who decides what threats the player characters (or PCs) face and what sorts of rewards they earn for succeeding at their quest. Think of it as a cooperative storytelling game, where the players play the protagonists and the Game Master acts as the narrator, controlling the rest of the world.

If you are a player, you make all of the decisions for your character, from what abilities your character has to the type of weapon he carries. Playing a character, however, is more than just following the rules in this book. You also decide your character's personality. Is he a noble knight, set on vanquishing a powerful evil, or is he a conniving rogue who cares more about gold than glory? The choice is up to you.

If you are a Game Master, you control the world that the players explore. Your job is to bring the setting to life and to present the characters with challenges that are both fair and exciting. From the local merchant prince to the rampaging dragon, you control all of the characters that are not being played by the players. Paizo's *Pathfinder Adventure Path* series, Pathfinder Modules, and Pathfinder Chronicles world guides provide everything you need to run a game, or you can invent your own, using the rules in this book as well as the monsters found in the *Pathfinder RPG Bestiary*.

What You Need: In addition to this book, you will need a number of special dice to play the Pathfinder Roleplaying Game. The dice that come with most board games have six sides, but the Pathfinder Roleplaying Game uses dice with four sides, six sides, eight sides, ten sides, twelve sides, and twenty sides. Dice of this sort can be found at your local game store or online at **paizo.com**.

In addition to dice, if you are a player, you will need a character sheet (which can be photocopied from the back of this book) and, if the Game Master uses a map to represent the adventure, a small figurine to represent your character. These figurines, or miniatures, can also be found at most game stores. They come in a wide variety of styles, so you can probably find a miniature that relatively accurately depicts your character.

If you are the Game Master, you will need a copy of the *Pathfinder RPG Bestiary*, which contains the rules for a whole spectrum of monsters, from the mighty dragon to the lowly goblin. While many of these monsters can be used to fight against the players, others might provide useful information or become powerful allies. Some might even join the group, with one of the players taking on the role of a monstrous character. In addition, you should have your own set of dice and some sort of screen you can use to hide your notes, maps, and dice rolls behind. (Although you should be honest about the results of your dice rolls, sometimes the results are not evident, and openly rolling the dice might give away too much information.) Combat in the Pathfinder RPG can be resolved in one of two ways: you can describe the situation to the characters and allow them to interact based on the description you provide, or you can draw the situation on a piece of paper or a specially made battle mat and allow the characters to move their miniatures around to more accurately represent their position during the battle. While both ways have their advantages, if you choose the latter, you will need a mat to draw on, such as Paizo's line of GameMastery Flip-Mats, as well as miniatures to represent the monsters or other adversaries. These can also be found at your local game shop, or at **paizo.com**.

Playing the Game: While playing the Pathfinder RPG, the Game Master describes the events that occur in the game world, and the players take turns describing what their characters do in response to those events. Unlike storytelling, however, the actions of the players and the characters controlled by the Game Master (frequently called non-player characters, or NPCs) are not certain. Most actions require dice rolls to determine success, with some tasks being more difficult than others. Each character is better at some things than he is at other things, granting him bonuses based on his skills and abilities.

Whenever a roll is required, the roll is noted as "d#," with the "#" representing the number of sides on the die. If you need to roll multiple dice of the same type, there will be a number before the "d." For example, if you are required to roll 4d6, you should roll four six-sided dice and add the results together. Sometimes there will be a + or – after the notation, meaning that you add that number to, or subtract it from, the total results of the dice (not to each individual die rolled). Most die rolls in the game use a d20 with a number of modifiers based on the character's skills, his or her abilities, and the situation. Generally speaking, rolling high is better than rolling low. Percentile rolls are a special case, indicated as rolling d%. You can generate a random number in this range by rolling two differently colored ten-sided dice (2d10). Pick one color to represent the tens digit, then roll both dice. If the die chosen to be the tens digit rolls a "4" and the other d10 rolls a "2," then you've generated a 42. A zero on the tens digit die indicates a result from 1 to 9, or 100 if both dice result in a zero. Some d10s are printed with "10," "20," "30," and so on in order to make reading d% rolls easier. Unless otherwise noted, whenever you must round a number, always round down.

As your character goes on adventures, he earns gold, magic items, and experience points. Gold can be used to purchase better equipment, while magic items possess powerful abilities that enhance your character.

Experience points are awarded for overcoming challenges and completing major storylines. When your character has earned enough experience points, he increases his character level by one, granting him new powers and abilities that allow him to take on even greater challenges. While a 1st-level character might be up to saving a farmer's daughter from rampaging goblins, defeating a terrifying red dragon might require the powers of a 20th-level hero. It is the Game Master's duty to provide challenges for your character that are engaging, but not so deadly as to leave you with no hope of success. For more information on the duties of being a Game Master, see Chapter 12.

Above all, have fun. Playing the Pathfinder RPG is supposed to be exciting and rewarding for both the Game Master and the players. Adventure awaits!

The Most Important Rule

The rules in this book are here to help you breathe life into your characters and the world they explore. While they are designed to make your game easy and exciting, you might find that some of them do not suit the style of play that your gaming group enjoys. Remember that these rules are yours. You can change them to fit your needs. Most Game Masters

have a number of "house rules" that they use in their games. The Game Master and players should always discuss any rules changes to make sure that everyone understands how the game will be played. Although the Game Master is the final arbiter of the rules, the Pathfinder RPG is a shared experience, and all of the players should contribute their thoughts when the rules are in doubt.

USING THIS BOOK

This book is divided into 15 chapters, along with a host of appendices. Chapters 1 through 11 cover all of the rules needed by players to create characters and play the game. Chapters 12 through 15 contain information intended to help a Game Master run the game and adjudicate the world. Generally speaking, if you are a player, you do not need to know the information in these later chapters, but you might be asked to reference them occasionally. The following synopses are presented to give you a broad overview of the rules encompassed within this book.

Chapter 1 (Getting Started): This chapter covers the basics of the Pathfinder RPG, including information on how to reference the rest of the book, rules for generating player characters (PCs), and rules for determining a character's ability scores. Ability scores are the most basic attributes possessed by a character, describing his raw potential and ability.

Chapter 2 (Races): The Pathfinder RPG contains seven core races that represent the most common races in the game world. They are dwarves, elves, gnomes, half-elves, half-orcs, halflings, and humans. This chapter covers all of the rules needed to play a member of one of these races. When creating a PC, you should choose one of the races from this chapter.

Chapter 3 (Classes): There are 11 core classes in the Pathfinder RPG. Classes represent a character's basic profession, and each one grants a host of special abilities. A character's class also determines a wide variety of other statistics used by the character, including hit points, saving throw bonuses, weapon and armor proficiencies, and skill ranks. This chapter also covers the rules for advancing your character as he grows in power (gaining levels). Gaining additional levels in a class grants additional abilities and increases other statistics. When creating a PC, you should choose one class from this chapter and put one level into that class (for example, if you choose your starting class to be wizard, you would be a 1st-level wizard).

Chapter 4 (Skills): This chapter covers skills and how to use them during the game. Skills represent a wide variety of simple tasks that a character can perform, from climbing a wall to sneaking past a guard. Each character receives a number of skill ranks, which can be used to make the character better at using some skills. As a character gains levels, he receives additional skill ranks, which can be used to improve existing skills possessed by the character or to become proficient in the use of new skills. A character's class determines how many skill ranks a character can spend.

Chapter 5 (Feats): Each character possesses a number of feats, which allow the character to perform some special action or grant some other capability that would otherwise not be allowed. Each character begins play with at least one feat, and new feat choices are awarded as a character advances in level.

Chapter 6 (Equipment): This chapter covers the basic gear and equipment that can be purchased, from armor and weapons to torches and backpacks. Here you will also find listed the cost for common services, such as staying in an inn or booking passage on a boat. Starting characters receive an amount of gold based on their respective classes which they can spend on equipment at 1st level.

Chapter 7 (Additional Rules): The rules in this chapter cover several miscellaneous rules that are important to playing the Pathfinder RPG, including alignment, encumbrance, movement, and visibility. Alignment tells you whether your character is an irredeemable villain, a virtuous hero, or anywhere in between. Encumbrance

deals with how much weight your character can carry without being hindered. Movement describes the distance your character can travel in a minute, hour, or day, depending upon his race and the environment. Visibility deals with how far your character can see, based on race and the prevailing light conditions.

Chapter 8 (Combat): All characters eventually end up in life-or-death struggles against fearsome monsters and dangerous villains. This chapter covers how to deal with combat in the Pathfinder RPG. During combat, each character acts in turn (determined by initiative), with the order repeating itself until one side has perished or is otherwise defeated. In this chapter, you will find rules for taking a turn in combat, covering all of the various actions that you can perform. This chapter also includes rules for adjudicating special combat maneuvers (such as attempting to trip your enemy or trying to disarm his weapon) and character injury and death.

Chapter 9 (Magic): A number of classes (and some monsters) can cast spells, which can do nearly anything, from bringing the dead back to life to roasting your enemies with a ball of fire. This chapter deals with the rules for casting spells and learning new spells to cast. If your character can cast spells, you should become familiar with these rules.

Chapter 10 (Spells): Whereas the magic chapter describes how to cast a spell, this chapter deals with the individual spells themselves, starting with the lists of which spells are available to characters based on their classes. This is followed up by an extensive listing of every spell in the game, including its effects, range, duration, and other important variables. A character that can cast spells should read up on all the spells that are available to him.

Chapter 11 (Prestige Classes): Although the core classes in Chapter 3 allow for a wide variety of character types, prestige classes allow a character to become a master of one select theme. These advanced classes grant a specialized list of abilities that make a character very powerful in one area. A character must meet specific prerequisites before deciding to take levels in a prestige class. These prerequisites vary depending upon the prestige class. If you plan on taking levels in a prestige class, you should familiarize yourself with the prerequisites to ensure that your character can eventually meet them.

Chapter 12 (Gamemastering): This chapter covers the basics of running the Pathfinder RPG. It includes guidelines for creating a game, using a published adventure, adjudicating matters at the table, and awarding experience points and treasure. If you are the GM, you should become familiar with the concepts presented in this chapter.

Chapter 13 (Environment): Aside from fighting against monsters, a host of other dangers and challenges await the PCs as they play the Pathfinder RPG. This chapter covers the rules for adjudicating the environment, from cunning traps to bubbling lava, and is broken down by environment type, including dungeons, deserts, mountains, forests, swamps, aquatic, urban, and other dimensions and planes beyond reality. Finally, this chapter also includes information on weather and its effects on the game.

Chapter 14 (Creating NPCs): In addition to characters and monsters, the world is populated by countless nonplayer characters (NPCs). These characters are created and controlled by the GM and represent every other person that exists in the game world, from the local shopkeep to the greedy king. This chapter includes simple classes used by most NPCs (although some can possess levels in the core classes and prestige classes) and a system for generating an NPC's statistics quickly.

Chapter 15 (Magic Items): As a character goes on adventures, he often finds magic items to help him in his struggles. This chapter covers these magic items in detail, including weapons, armor, potions, rings, rods, scrolls, staves, and wondrous items (a generic category that covers everything else). In addition, you will find cursed items (which hinder those who wield them), intelligent items, artifacts (items of incredible power), and the rules for creating new magic items in this chapter.

Appendices: The appendices at the back of the book gather a number of individual rules concerning special abilities and conditions. This section also includes a list of recommended reading and a discussion of other tools and products that you can use for a more enjoyable Pathfinder RPG experience.

COMMON TERMS

The Pathfinder RPG uses a number of terms, abbreviations, and definitions in presenting the rules of the game. The following are among the most common.

Ability Score: Each creature has six ability scores: Strength, Dexterity, Constitution, Intelligence, Wisdom, and Charisma. These scores represent a creature's most basic attributes. The higher the score, the more raw potential and talent your character possesses.

Action: An action is a discrete measurement of time during a round of combat. Using abilities, casting spells, and making attacks all require actions to perform. There are a number of different kinds of actions, such as a standard action, move action, swift action, free action, and full-round action (see Chapter 8).

Alignment: Alignment represents a creature's basic moral and ethical attitude. Alignment has two components: one describing whether a creature is lawful, neutral, or chaotic, followed by another that describes whether a character is good, neutral, or evil. Alignments

are usually abbreviated using the first letter of each alignment component, such as LN for lawful neutral or CE for chaotic evil. Creatures that are neutral in both components are denoted by a single "N."

Armor Class (AC): All creatures in the game have an Armor Class. This score represents how hard it is to hit a creature in combat. As with other scores, higher is better.

Base Attack Bonus (BAB): Each creature has a base attack bonus and it represents its skill in combat. As a character gains levels or Hit Dice, his base attack bonus improves. When a creature's base attack bonus reaches +6, +11, or +16, he receives an additional attack in combat when he takes a full-attack action (which is one type of full-round action—see Chapter 8).

Bonus: Bonuses are numerical values that are added to checks and statistical scores. Most bonuses have a type, and as a general rule, bonuses of the same type are not cumulative (do not "stack")—only the greater bonus granted applies.

Caster Level (CL): Caster level represents a creature's power and ability when casting spells. When a creature casts a spell, it often contains a number of variables, such as range or damage, that are based on the caster's level.

Class: Classes represent chosen professions taken by characters and some other creatures. Classes give a host of bonuses and allow characters to take actions that they otherwise could not, such as casting spells or changing shape. As a creature gains levels in a given class, it gains new, more powerful abilities. Most PCs gain levels in the core classes or prestige classes, since these are the most powerful (see Chapters 3 and 11). Most NPCs gain levels in NPC classes, which are less powerful (see Chapter 14).

Check: A check is a d20 roll which may or may not be modified by another value. The most common types are attack rolls, skill checks, ability checks, and saving throws.

Combat Maneuver: This is an action taken in combat that does not directly cause harm to your opponent, such as attempting to trip him, disarm him, or grapple with him (see Chapter 8).

Combat Maneuver Bonus (CMB): This value represents how skilled a creature is at performing a combat maneuver. When attempting to perform a combat maneuver, this value is added to the character's d20 roll.

Combat Maneuver Defense (CMD): This score represents how hard it is to perform a combat maneuver against this creature. A creature's CMD is used as the difficulty class when performing a maneuver against that creature.

Concentration Check: When a creature is casting a spell, but is disrupted during the casting, he must make a concentration check or fail to cast the spell (see Chapter 9).

Creature: A creature is an active participant in the story or world. This includes PCs, NPCs, and monsters.

Damage Reduction (DR): Creatures that are resistant to harm typically have damage reduction. This amount is subtracted from any damage dealt to them from a physical source. Most types of DR can be bypassed by certain types of weapons. This is denoted by a "/" followed by the type, such as "10/cold iron." Some types of DR apply to all physical attacks. Such DR is denoted by the "—" symbol. See Appendix 1 for more information.

Difficulty Class (DC): Whenever a creature attempts to perform an action whose success is not guaranteed, he must make some sort of check (usually a skill check). The result of that check must meet or exceed the Difficulty Class of the action that the creature is attempting to perform in order for the action to be successful.

Extraordinary Abilities (Ex): Extraordinary abilities are unusual abilities that do not rely on magic to function.

Experience Points (XP): As a character overcomes challenges, defeats monsters, and completes quests, he gains experience points. These points accumulate over time, and when they reach or surpass a specific value, the character gains a level.

Feat: A feat is an ability a creature has mastered. Feats often allow creatures to circumvent rules or restrictions. Creatures receive a number of feats based off their Hit Dice, but some classes and other abilities grant bonus feats.

Game Master (GM): A Game Master is the person who adjudicates the rules and controls all of the elements of the story and world that the players explore. A GM's duty is to provide a fair and fun game.

Hit Dice (HD): Hit Dice represent a creature's general level of power and skill. As a creature gains levels, it gains additional Hit Dice. Monsters, on the other hand, gain racial Hit Dice, which represent the monster's general prowess and ability. Hit Dice are represented by the number the creature possesses followed by a type of die, such as "3d8." This value is used to determine a creature's total hit points. In this example, the creature has 3 Hit Dice. When rolling for this creature's hit points, you would roll a d8 three times and add the results together, along with other modifiers.

Hit Points (hp): Hit points are an abstraction signifying how robust and healthy a creature is at the current moment. To determine a creature's hit points, roll the dice indicated by its Hit Dice. A creature gains maximum hit points if its first Hit Die roll is for a character class level. Creatures whose first Hit Die comes from an NPC class or from his race roll their first Hit Die normally. Wounds subtract hit points, while healing (both natural and magical) restores hit points. Some abilities and spells grant temporary hit points that disappear after a specific duration. When a creature's hit points drop below 0, it becomes unconscious. When a creature's hit points reach a negative total equal to its Constitution score, it dies.

Initiative: Whenever combat begins, all creatures involved in the battle must make an initiative check to determine the order in which creatures act during combat. The higher the result of the check, the earlier a creature gets to act.

Level: A character's level represents his overall ability and power. There are three types of levels. Class level is the number of levels of a specific class possessed by a character. Character level is the sum of all of the levels possessed by a character in all of his classes. In addition, spells have a level associated with them numbered from 0 to 9. This level indicates the general power of the spell. As a spellcaster gains levels, he learns to cast spells of a higher level.

Monster: Monsters are creatures that rely on racial Hit Dice instead of class levels for their powers and abilities (although some possess class levels as well). PCs are usually not monsters.

Multiplying: When you are asked to apply more than one multiplier to a roll, the multipliers are not multiplied by one another. Instead, you combine them into a single multiplier, with each extra multiple adding 1 less than its value to the first multiple. For example, if you are asked to apply a ×2 multiplier twice, the result would be ×3, not ×4.

Nonplayer Character (NPC): These are characters controlled by the GM.

Penalty: Penalties are numerical values that are subtracted from a check or statistical score. Penalties do not have a type and most penalties stack with one another.

Player Character (Character, PC): These are the characters portrayed by the players.

Round: Combat is measured in rounds. During an individual round, all creatures have a chance to take a turn to act, in order of initiative. A round represents 6 seconds in the game world.

Rounding: Occasionally the rules ask you to round a result or value. Unless otherwise stated, always round down. For example, if you are asked to take half of 7, the result would be 3.

Saving Throw: When a creature is the subject of a dangerous spell or effect, it often receives a saving throw to mitigate the damage or result. Saving throws are passive, meaning that a character does not need to take an action to make a saving throw—they are made automatically. There are three types of saving throws: Fortitude (used to resist poisons, diseases, and other bodily ailments), Reflex (used to avoid effects that target an entire area, such as *fireball*), and Will (used to resist mental attacks and spells).

Skill: A skill represents a creature's ability to perform an ordinary task, such as climb a wall, sneak down a hallway, or spot an intruder. The number of ranks possessed by a creature in a given skill represents its proficiency in that skill. As a creature gains Hit Dice, it also gains additional skill ranks that can be added to its skills.

Spell: Spells can perform a wide variety of tasks, from harming enemies to bringing the dead back to life. Spells specify what they can target, what their effects are, and how they can be resisted or negated.

Spell-Like Abilities (Sp): Spell-like abilities function just like spells, but are granted through a special racial ability or by a specific class ability (as opposed to spells, which are gained by spellcasting classes as a character gains levels).

Spell Resistance (SR): Some creatures are resistant to magic and gain spell resistance. When a creature with spell resistance is targeted by a spell, the caster of the spell must make a caster level check to see if the spell affects the target. The DC of this check is equal to the target creature's SR (some spells do not allow SR checks).

Stacking: Stacking refers to the act of adding together bonuses or penalties that apply to one particular check or statistic. Generally speaking, most bonuses of the same type do not stack. Instead, only the highest bonus applies. Most penalties do stack, meaning that their values are added together. Penalties and bonuses generally stack with one another, meaning that the penalties might negate or exceed part or all of the bonuses, and vice versa.

Supernatural Abilities (Su): Supernatural abilities are magical attacks, defenses, and qualities. These abilities can be always active or they can require a specific action to utilize. The supernatural ability's description includes information on how it is used and its effects.

Turn: In a round, a creature receives one turn, during which it can perform a wide variety of actions. Generally in the course of one turn, a character can perform one standard action, one move action, one swift action, and a number of free actions. Less-common combinations of actions are permissible as well, see Chapter 8 for more details.

EXAMPLE OF PLAY

The GM is running a group of four players through their latest adventure. They are playing Seelah (a human paladin), Ezren (a human wizard), Harsk (a dwarf ranger) and Lem (a halfling bard). The four adventurers are exploring the ruins of an ancient keep, after hearing rumors that there are great treasures to be found in its musty vaults. As the adventurers make their way toward the crumbling edifice, they cross an ancient stone bridge. After describing the scene, the GM asks the players what they want to do.

Harsk: Let's keep moving. I don't like the look of this place. I draw my crossbow and load it.

Seelah: Agreed. I draw my sword, just in case.

Ezren: I'm going to cast *light* so that we can see where we're going.

GM: Alright, a flickering glow springs up from your hand, illuminating the area.

Lem: I'd like to keep a lookout, just to make sure there are no monsters nearby.

The GM consults his notes about this part of the adventure and realizes that there are indeed some monsters nearby, and that the PCs have walked into their trap.

GM: Lem, could you roll a Perception check?

Lem rolls a d20 and gets a 12. He then consults his character sheet to find his bonus on Perception skill checks, which turns out to be a +6.

Lem: I got an 18. What do I see?

GM: As you turn around, you spot six dark shapes moving up behind you. As they enter the light from Ezren's spell, you can tell that they're skeletons, marching onto the bridge wearing rusting armor and waving ancient swords.

Lem: Guys, I think we have a problem.

GM: You do indeed. Can I get everyone to roll initiative?

To determine the order of combat, each one of the players rolls a d20 and adds his or her initiative bonus. The GM rolls once for the skeletons and one additional time for their hidden leader. Seelah gets an 18, Harsk a 16, Ezren a 12, and Lem a 5. The skeletons get an 11, and their leader rolled an 8.

GM: Seelah, you have the highest initiative. It's your turn.

Seelah: Since they're skeletons, I'm going to attempt to destroy them using the power of my goddess Iomedae. I channel positive energy.

Seelah rolls 2d6 and gets a 7.

Seelah: The skeletons take 7 points of damage, but they get to make a DC 15 Will save to only take half damage.

The GM rolls the Will saving throws for the skeletons and gets an 18, two 17s, a 15, an 8, and a 3. Since four of the skeletons made their saving throws, they only take half damage (3 points), while the other two take the full 7 points of damage.

GM: Two of the skeletons burst into flames and crumble as the power of your deity washes over them. The other four continue their advance. Harsk, it's your turn.

Harsk: Great. I'm going to fire my crossbow at the nearest skeleton.

Harsk rolls a d20 and gets a 13. He adds that to his bonus on attack rolls with his crossbow and announces a total of 22. The GM checks the skeleton's armor class, which is only a 14.

GM: That's a hit. Roll for damage.

Harsk rolls a d10 and gets an 8. The GM realizes that the skeletons have damage reduction that can only be overcome by bludgeoning weapons. Since crossbow bolts deal piercing damage, the skeleton's damage reduction reduces the damage from 8 to 3, but this is still enough to reduce that skeleton's hit points to below 0.

GM: Although the crossbow bolt seemed to do less damage against the skeleton's ancient bones, the hit was hard enough to cause that skeleton to break apart. Ezren, it's your turn.

Ezren: I'm going to cast *magic missile* at the skeleton that's closest to me.

Magic missile creates a number of glowing darts that always hit their target. Ezren rolls 1d4+1 for each missile and gets a

total of 6. *Since this is magic, it automatically bypasses the skeleton's DR, causing another one to fall.*

GM: There are only two skeletons left, and it's their turn. One of them charges up to Seelah and takes a swing at her, while the other moves up to Harsk and attacks.

The GM rolls a d20 for both attacks. The attack against Seelah is only an 8, which is not equal to or higher than her AC of 18. The attack against Harsk is a 17, which beats his AC of 16. The GM rolls damage for the skeleton's attack.

GM: The skeleton hits you, Harsk, leaving a nasty cut on your upper arm. Take 7 points of damage.

Harsk: Ouch. I have 22 hit points left.

GM: That's not all. Charging out of the fog onto the bridge is a skeleton dressed like a knight, riding the bones of a long-dead horse. The heads of the warrior's previous victims are mounted atop its deadly lance. Lem, it's your turn. What do you do?

Lem: Run!

The combat continues in order, starting over with Seelah, until one side or the other is defeated. If the PCs survive the fight, they can continue on to the ancient castle to see what treasures and perils lie within.

GENERATING A CHARACTER

From the sly rogue to the stalwart paladin, the Pathfinder RPG allows you to make the character you want to play.

When generating a character, start with your character's concept. Do you want a character who goes toe-to-toe with terrible monsters, matching sword and shield against claws and fangs? Or do you want a mystical seer who draws his powers from the great beyond to further his own ends? Nearly anything is possible.

Once you have a general concept worked out, use the following steps to bring your idea to life, recording the resulting information and statistics on your Pathfinder RPG character sheet, which can be found at the back of this book and photocopied for your convenience.

Step 1—Determine Ability Scores: Start by generating your character's ability scores (see page 15). These six scores determine your character's most basic attributes and are used to decide a wide variety of details and statistics. Some class selections require you to have better than average scores for some of your abilities.

Step 2—Pick Your Race: Next, pick your character's race, noting any modifiers to your ability scores and any other racial traits (see Chapter 2). There are seven basic races to choose from, although your GM might have others to add to the list. Each race lists the languages your character automatically knows, as well as a number of bonus languages. A character knows a number of additional bonus languages equal to his or her Intelligence modifier (see page 17).

Step 3—Pick Your Class: A character's class represents a profession, such as fighter or wizard. If this is a new character, he starts at 1st level in his chosen class. As he gains experience points (XP) for defeating monsters, he goes up in level, granting him new powers and abilities.

Step 4—Pick Skills and Select Feats: Determine the number of skill ranks possessed by your character, based on his class and Intelligence modifier (and any other bonuses, such as the bonus received by humans). Then spend these ranks on skills, but remember that you cannot have more ranks than your level in any one skill (for a starting character, this is usually one). After skills, determine how many feats your character receives, based on his class and level, and select them from those presented in Chapter 5.

Step 5—Buy Equipment: Each new character begins the game with an amount of gold, based on his class, that can be spent on a wide range of equipment and gear, from chainmail armor to leather backpacks. This gear helps your character survive while adventuring. Generally speaking, you cannot use this starting money to buy magic items without the consent of your GM.

Step 6—Finishing Details: Finally, you need to determine all of a character's details, including his starting hit points (hp), Armor Class (AC), saving throws, initiative modifier, and attack values. All of these numbers are determined by the decisions made in previous steps. A level 1 character begins with maximum hit points for its Hit Die roll. Aside from these, you need to decide on your character's name, alignment, and physical appearance. It is best to jot down a few personality traits as well, to help you play the character during the game. Additional rules (like age and alignment) are described in Chapter 7.

ABILITY SCORES

Each character has six ability scores that represent his character's most basic attributes. They are his raw talent and prowess. While a character rarely rolls an ability check (using just an ability score), these scores, and the modifiers they create, affect nearly every aspect of a character's skills and abilities. Each ability score generally ranges from 3 to 18, although racial bonuses and penalties can alter this; an average ability score is 10.

Generating Ability Scores

There are a number of different methods used to generate ability scores. Each of these methods gives a different level of flexibility and randomness to character generation.

Racial modifiers (adjustments made to your ability scores due to your character's race—see Chapter 2) are applied after the scores are generated.

Standard: Roll 4d6, discard the lowest die result, and add the three remaining results together. Record this total and repeat the process until six numbers are generated.

Assign these totals to your ability scores as you see fit. This method is less random than Classic and tends to create characters with above-average ability scores.

Classic: Roll 3d6 and add the dice together. Record this total and repeat the process until you generate six numbers. Assign these results to your ability scores as you see fit. This method is quite random, and some characters will have clearly superior abilities. This randomness can be taken one step further, with the totals applied to specific ability scores in the order they are rolled. Characters generated using this method are difficult to fit to predetermined concepts, as their scores might not support given classes or personalities, and instead are best designed around their ability scores.

Heroic: Roll 2d6 and add 6 to the sum of the dice. Record this total and repeat the process until six numbers are generated. Assign these totals to your ability scores as you see fit. This is less random than the Standard method and generates characters with mostly above-average scores.

Dice Pool: Each character has a pool of 24d6 to assign to his statistics. Before the dice are rolled, the player selects the number of dice to roll for each score, with a minimum of 3d6 for each ability. Once the dice have been assigned, the player rolls each group and totals the result of the three highest dice. For more high-powered games, the GM should increase the total number of dice to 28. This method generates characters of a similar power to the Standard method.

Purchase: Each character receives a number of points to spend on increasing his basic attributes. In this method, all attributes start at a base of 10. A character can increase an individual score by spending some of his points. Likewise, he can gain more points to spend on other scores by decreasing one or more of his ability scores. No score can be reduced below 7 or raised above 18 using this method. See Table 1–1 on the next page for the costs of each score. After all the points are spent, apply any racial modifiers the character might have.

The number of points you have to spend using the purchase method depends on the type of campaign you are playing. The standard value for a character is 15 points. Average nonplayer characters (NPCs) are typically built using as few as 3 points. See Table 1–2 on the next page for a number of possible point values depending on the style of campaign. The purchase method emphasizes player choice and creates equally balanced characters. This system is typically used for organized play events, such as the Pathfinder Society (visit **paizo.com/pathfinderSociety** for more details on this exciting campaign).

Determine Bonuses

Each ability, after changes made because of race, has a modifier ranging from −5 to +5. Table 1–3 shows the modifier for each score. The modifier is the number you apply to the die roll when your character tries to do something related to that ability. You also use the modifier with some numbers that aren't die rolls. A positive modifier is called a bonus, and a negative modifier is called a penalty. The table also shows bonus spells, which you'll need to know about if your character is a spellcaster.

Abilities and Spellcasters

The ability that governs bonus spells depends on what type of spellcaster your character is: Intelligence for wizards; Wisdom for clerics, druids, and rangers; and Charisma for bards, paladins, and sorcerers. In addition to having a high ability score, a spellcaster must be of a high enough class level to be able to cast spells or use spell slots of a given spell level. See the class descriptions in Chapter 3 for details.

The Abilities

Each ability partially describes your character and affects some of his actions.

Strength (Str)

Strength measures muscle and physical power. This ability is important for those who engage in hand-to-hand (or "melee") combat, such as fighters, monks, paladins, and some rangers. Strength also sets the maximum amount of weight your character can carry. A character with a Strength score of 0 is too weak to move in any way and is unconscious. Some creatures do not possess a Strength score and have no modifier at all to Strength-based skills or checks.

You apply your character's Strength modifier to:
- Melee attack rolls.
- Damage rolls when using a melee weapon or a thrown weapon, including a sling. (Exceptions: Off-hand attacks receive only half the character's Strength bonus, while

two-handed attacks receive 1–1/2 times the Strength bonus. A Strength penalty, but not a bonus, applies to attacks made with a bow that is not a composite bow.)
- Climb and Swim checks.
- Strength checks (for breaking down doors and the like).

Dexterity (Dex)

Dexterity measures agility, reflexes, and balance. This ability is the most important one for rogues, but it's also useful for characters who wear light or medium armor or no armor at all. This ability is vital for characters seeking to excel with ranged weapons, such as the bow or sling. A character with a Dexterity score of 0 is incapable of moving and is effectively immobile (but not unconscious).

You apply your character's Dexterity modifier to:
- Ranged attack rolls, including those for attacks made with bows, crossbows, throwing axes, and many ranged spell attacks like *scorching ray* or *searing light*.
- Armor Class (AC), provided that the character can react to the attack.
- Reflex saving throws, for avoiding *fireballs* and other attacks that you can escape by moving quickly.
- Acrobatics, Disable Device, Escape Artist, Fly, Ride, Sleight of Hand, and Stealth checks.

Constitution (Con)

Constitution represents your character's health and stamina. A Constitution bonus increases a character's hit points, so the ability is important for all classes. Some creatures, such as undead and constructs, do not have a Constitution score. Their modifier is +0 for any Constitution-based checks. A character with a Constitution score of 0 is dead.

You apply your character's Constitution modifier to:
- Each roll of a Hit Die (though a penalty can never drop a result below 1—that is, a character always gains at least 1 hit point each time he advances in level).
- Fortitude saving throws, for resisting poison, disease, and similar threats.

If a character's Constitution score changes enough to alter his or her Constitution modifier, the character's hit points also increase or decrease accordingly.

Intelligence (Int)

Intelligence determines how well your character learns and reasons. This ability is important for wizards because it affects their spellcasting ability in many ways. Creatures of animal-level instinct have Intelligence scores of 1 or 2. Any creature capable of understanding speech has a score of at least 3. A character with an Intelligence score of 0 is comatose. Some creatures do not possess an Intelligence score. Their modifier is +0 for any Intelligence-based skills or checks.

TABLE 1–1: ABILITY SCORE COSTS

Score	Points	Score	Points
7	−4	13	3
8	−2	14	5
9	−1	15	7
10	0	16	10
11	1	17	13
12	2	18	17

TABLE 1–2: ABILITY SCORE POINTS

Campaign Type	Points
Low Fantasy	10
Standard Fantasy	15
High Fantasy	20
Epic Fantasy	25

TABLE 1-3: ABILITY MODIFIERS AND BONUS SPELLS

Ability Score	Modifier	Bonus Spells per Day (by Spell Level)									
		0	1st	2nd	3rd	4th	5th	6th	7th	8th	9th
1	−5	Can't cast spells tied to this ability									
2–3	−4	Can't cast spells tied to this ability									
4–5	−3	Can't cast spells tied to this ability									
6–7	−2	Can't cast spells tied to this ability									
8–9	−1	Can't cast spells tied to this ability									
10–11	0	—	—	—	—	—	—	—	—	—	—
12–13	+1	—	1	—	—	—	—	—	—	—	—
14–15	+2	—	1	1	—	—	—	—	—	—	—
16–17	+3	—	1	1	1	—	—	—	—	—	—
18–19	+4	—	1	1	1	1	—	—	—	—	—
20–21	+5	—	2	1	1	1	1	—	—	—	—
22–23	+6	—	2	2	1	1	1	1	—	—	—
24–25	+7	—	2	2	2	1	1	1	1	—	—
26–27	+8	—	2	2	2	2	1	1	1	1	—
28–29	+9	—	3	2	2	2	2	1	1	1	1
30–31	+10	—	3	3	2	2	2	2	1	1	1
32–33	+11	—	3	3	3	2	2	2	2	1	1
34–35	+12	—	3	3	3	3	2	2	2	2	1
36–37	+13	—	4	3	3	3	3	2	2	2	2
38–39	+14	—	4	4	3	3	3	3	2	2	2
40–41	+15	—	4	4	4	3	3	3	3	2	2
42–43	+16	—	4	4	4	4	3	3	3	3	2
44–45	+17	—	5	4	4	4	4	3	3	3	3

etc. ...

You apply your character's Intelligence modifier to:

- The number of bonus languages your character knows at the start of the game. These are in addition to any starting racial languages and Common. If you have a penalty, you can still read and speak your racial languages unless your Intelligence is lower than 3.
- The number of skill points gained each level, though your character always gets at least 1 skill point per level.
- Appraise, Craft, Knowledge, Linguistics, and Spellcraft checks.

A wizard gains bonus spells based on his Intelligence score. The minimum Intelligence score needed to cast a wizard spell is 10 + the spell's level.

Wisdom (Wis)

Wisdom describes a character's willpower, common sense, awareness, and intuition. Wisdom is the most important ability for clerics and druids, and it is also important for paladins and rangers. If you want your character to have acute senses, put a high score in Wisdom. Every creature has a Wisdom score. A character with a Wisdom score of 0 is incapable of rational thought and is unconscious.

You apply your character's Wisdom modifier to:

- Will saving throws (for negating the effects of *charm person* and other spells).
- Heal, Perception, Profession, Sense Motive, and Survival checks.

Clerics, druids, and rangers get bonus spells based on their Wisdom scores. The minimum Wisdom score needed to cast a cleric, druid, or ranger spell is 10 + the spell's level.

Charisma (Cha)

Charisma measures a character's personality, personal magnetism, ability to lead, and appearance. It is the most important ability for paladins, sorcerers, and bards. It is also important for clerics, since it affects their ability to channel energy. For undead creatures, Charisma is a measure of their unnatural "lifeforce." Every creature has a Charisma score. A character with a Charisma score of 0 is not able to exert himself in any way and is unconscious.

You apply your character's Charisma modifier to:

- Bluff, Diplomacy, Disguise, Handle Animal, Intimidate, Perform, and Use Magic Device checks.
- Checks that represent attempts to influence others.
- Channel energy DCs for clerics and paladins attempting to harm undead foes.

Bards, paladins, and sorcerers gain a number of bonus spells based on their Charisma scores. The minimum Charisma score needed to cast a bard, paladin, or sorcerer spell is 10 + the spell's level.

2 RACES

With a small army of merciless dark elf warriors fast on their heels, escape from the drow city seemed unlikely. While the human Sajan and gnome Lini might survive as slaves, Seltyiel knew the drow would only keep him, a half-elf, alive long enough to boast over while they tortured him. Cursing his mixed blood again, he sneered and turned abruptly, instantly summoning to mind the words of his most devastating arcane fire.

"Come on, you fungus-eating freaks!" he shouted at the relentless drow. "Let me show you how elves from the surface world dance!"

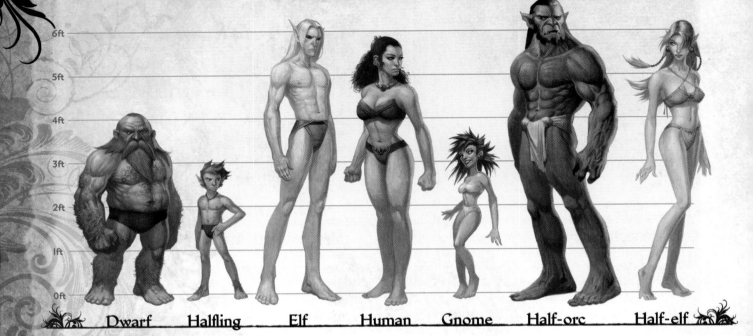

| Dwarf | Halfling | Elf | Human | Gnome | Half-orc | Half-elf |

From the stout dwarf to the noble elf, the races of the Pathfinder Roleplaying Game are a diverse mix of cultures, sizes, attitudes, and appearances. After you've generated your character's basic ability scores, the next step in the character creation process is to select your character's race; this chapter presents seven different options from which to choose. These seven races comprise the most commonly encountered civilized races in the Pathfinder RPG.

Choosing your character's race is one of the more important decisions you'll need to make. As your character grows more powerful, you'll be able to diversify his or her abilities by selecting different classes, skills, and feats, but you only get to pick your race once (unless some unusual magic, like *reincarnation*, comes into play). Of course, each race is best suited to a specific type of role—dwarves make better fighters than they do sorcerers, while halflings aren't as good as half-orcs at being barbarians. Keep each race's advantages and disadvantages in mind when making your choice. While it can be fun to play a race against its assumed role, it's not as fun to get three levels into a character before realizing that the character you wanted to play would have been better off as a different race entirely.

Each of the seven races in this chapter is presented in the same format, starting with a generalized description of the race's role in the world. This is followed by a physical description of an average member of that race, a brief overview of the race's society, and a few words about the race's relations with the other six. Although your race doesn't force you to choose one religion or alignment over another, the typical choices for each race are mentioned. Next is a discussion of why a member of the race in question might decide to take on the peril-filled life of an adventurer. Finally, we list a few sample names for males and females of each race.

Each of the seven races also has a suite of special abilities, bonuses, and other adjustments that apply to all members of that race. These are your character's "racial traits."

Each race also has ability score modifiers that are applied after you've generated your ability scores, as described in the previous chapter. These modifiers can raise an ability score above 18 or reduce a score below 3—although having such a low score in any of your abilities is something you should avoid, as there's no surer route to character death than a low Constitution, and no swifter route to frustration than a PC who can't talk since his Intelligence is lower than 3. You should seek your GM's approval before playing a character with any ability score of less than 3.

The seven races presented in this chapter have wildly different abilities, personalities, and societies, but at the same time, all seven races are quite similar—none of the races here deviate too far from humanity, and all of their abilities are roughly equal and balanced. Other races, more powerful and more exotic, exist in the game world as well, but the Pathfinder RPG is built and balanced with the expectation that all players start on roughly equal footing. Rules and guidelines for playing more powerful or more unusual races can be found in Chapter 12.

DWARVES

Dwarves are a stoic but stern race, ensconced in cities carved from the hearts of mountains and fiercely determined to repel the depredations of savage races like orcs and goblins. More than any other race, the dwarves have acquired a reputation as dour and humorless craftsmen of the earth. It could be said that dwarven history shapes the dark disposition of many dwarves, for they reside in high mountains and dangerous realms below the earth, constantly at war with giants, goblins, and other such horrors.

Physical Description: Dwarves are a short and stocky race, and stand about a foot shorter than most humans, with wide, compact bodies that account for their burly appearance. Male and female dwarves pride themselves on the length of their hair, and men often decorate their beards with a variety of clasps and intricate braids. A clean-shaven male dwarf is a sure sign of madness, or worse—no one familiar with their race trusts a beardless dwarf.

Society: The great distances between their mountain citadels account for many of the cultural differences that exist within dwarven society. Despite these schisms, dwarves throughout the world are characterized by their love of stonework, their passion for stone- and metal-based craftsmanship and architecture, and a fierce hatred of giants, orcs, and goblinoids.

Relations: Dwarves and orcs have long dwelt in proximity, theirs a history of violence as old as both their races. Dwarves generally distrust and shun half-orcs. They find halflings, elves, and gnomes to be too frail, flighty, or "pretty" to be worthy of proper respect. It is with humans that dwarves share the strongest link, for humans' industrious nature and hearty appetites come closest to matching those of the dwarven ideal.

Alignment and Religion: Dwarves are driven by honor and tradition, and while they are often satirized as standoffish, they have a strong sense of friendship and justice, and those who win their trust understand that, while they work hard, they play even harder—especially when good ale is involved. Most dwarves are lawful good. They prefer to worship deities whose tenets match these traits, and Torag is a favorite among dwarves, though Abadar and Gorum are common choices as well.

Adventurers: Although dwarven adventurers are rare compared to humans, they can be found in most regions of the world. Dwarves often leave the confines of their redoubts to seek glory for their clans, to find wealth with which to enrich the fortress-homes of their birth, or to reclaim fallen dwarven citadels from racial enemies. Dwarven warfare is often characterized by tunnel fighting and melee combat, and as such most dwarves tend toward classes such as fighters and barbarians.

Male Names: Dolgrin, Grunyar, Harsk, Kazmuk, Morgrym, Rogar.

Female Names: Agna, Bodill, Ingra, Kotri, Rusilka, Yangrit.

DWARF RACIAL TRAITS

+2 Constitution, +2 Wisdom, −2 Charisma: Dwarves are both tough and wise, but also a bit gruff.

Medium: Dwarves are Medium creatures and have no bonuses or penalties due to their size.

Slow and Steady: Dwarves have a base speed of 20 feet, but their speed is never modified by armor or encumbrance.

Darkvision: Dwarves can see in the dark up to 60 feet.

Defensive Training: Dwarves get a +4 dodge bonus to AC against monsters of the giant subtype.

Greed: Dwarves receive a +2 racial bonus on Appraise skill checks made to determine the price of nonmagical goods that contain precious metals or gemstones.

Hatred: Dwarves receive a +1 bonus on attack rolls against humanoid creatures of the orc and goblinoid subtypes due to special training against these hated foes.

Hardy: Dwarves receive a +2 racial bonus on saving throws against poison, spells, and spell-like abilities.

Stability: Dwarves receive a +4 racial bonus to their Combat Maneuver Defense when resisting a bull rush or trip attempt while standing on the ground.

Stonecunning: Dwarves receive a +2 bonus on Perception checks to potentially notice unusual stonework, such as traps and hidden doors located in stone walls or floors. They receive a check to notice such features whenever they pass within 10 feet of them, whether or not they are actively looking.

Weapon Familiarity: Dwarves are proficient with battleaxes, heavy picks, and warhammers, and treat any weapon with the word "dwarven" in its name as a martial weapon.

Languages: Dwarves begin play speaking Common and Dwarven. Dwarves with high Intelligence scores can choose from the following: Giant, Gnome, Goblin, Orc, Terran, and Undercommon.

ELVES

The long-lived elves are children of the natural world, similar in many superficial ways to fey creatures, yet different as well. Elves value their privacy and traditions, and while they are often slow to make friends, at both the personal and national levels, once an outsider is accepted as a comrade, such alliances can last for generations. Elves have a curious attachment to their surroundings, perhaps as a result of their incredibly long lifespans or some deeper, more mystical reason. Elves who dwell in a region for long find themselves physically adapting to match their surroundings, most noticeably taking on coloration reflecting the local environment. Those elves that spend their lives among the short-lived races, on the other hand, often develop a skewed perception of mortality and become morose, the result of watching wave after wave of companions age and die before their eyes.

Physical Description: Although generally taller than humans, elves possess a graceful, fragile physique that is accentuated by their long, pointed ears. Their eyes are wide and almond-shaped, and filled with large, vibrantly colored pupils. While elven clothing often plays off the beauty of the natural world, those elves that live in cities tend to bedeck themselves in the latest fashion.

Society: Many elves feel a bond with nature and strive to live in harmony with the natural world. Most, however, find manipulating earth and stone to be distasteful, and prefer instead to indulge in the finer arts, with their inborn patience making them particularly suited to wizardry.

Relations: Elves are prone to dismissing other races, writing them off as rash and impulsive, yet they are excellent judges of character. An elf might not want a dwarf neighbor, but would be the first to acknowledge that dwarf's skill at smithing. They regard gnomes as strange (and sometimes dangerous) curiosities, and halflings with a measure of pity, for these small folk seem to the elves to be adrift, without a traditional home. Elves are fascinated with humans, as evidenced by the number of half-elves in the world, even if they usually disown such offspring. They regard half-orcs with distrust and suspicion.

Alignment and Religion: Elves are emotional and capricious, yet value kindness and beauty. Most elves are chaotic good. They prefer deities that share their love of the mystic qualities of the world—Desna and Nethys are particular favorites, the former for her wonder and love of the wild places, and the latter for his mastery of magic. Calistria is perhaps the most notorious of elven deities, for she represents elven ideals taken to an extreme.

Adventurers: Many elves embark on adventures out of a desire to explore the world, leaving their secluded forest realms to reclaim forgotten elven magic or search out lost kingdoms established millennia ago by their forefathers. For those raised among humans, the ephemeral and unfettered life of an adventurer holds natural appeal. Elves generally eschew melee because of their frailty, preferring instead to pursue classes such as wizards and rangers.

Male Names: Caladrel, Heldalel, Lanliss, Meirdrarel, Seldlon, Talathel, Variel, Zordlon.

Female Names: Amrunelara, Dardlara, Faunra, Jathal, Merisiel, Oparal, Soumral, Tessara, Yalandlara.

ELF RACIAL TRAITS

+2 Dexterity, +2 Intelligence, –2 Constitution: Elves are nimble, both in body and mind, but their form is frail.

Medium: Elves are Medium creatures and have no bonuses or penalties due to their size.

Normal Speed: Elves have a base speed of 30 feet.

Low-Light Vision: Elves can see twice as far as humans in conditions of dim light. See Chapter 7.

Elven Immunities: Elves are immune to magic sleep effects and get a +2 racial saving throw bonus against enchantment spells and effects.

Elven Magic: Elves receive a +2 racial bonus on caster level checks made to overcome spell resistance. In addition, elves receive a +2 racial bonus on Spellcraft skill checks made to identify the properties of magic items.

Keen Senses: Elves receive a +2 racial bonus on Perception skill checks.

Weapon Familiarity: Elves are proficient with longbows (including composite longbows), longswords, rapiers, and shortbows (including composite shortbows), and treat any weapon with the word "elven" in its name as a martial weapon.

Languages: Elves begin play speaking Common and Elven. Elves with high Intelligence scores can choose from the following: Celestial, Draconic, Gnoll, Gnome, Goblin, Orc, and Sylvan.

GNOMES

Gnomes trace their lineage back to the mysterious realm of the fey, a place where colors are brighter, the wildlands wilder, and emotions more primal. Unknown forces drove the ancient gnomes from that realm long ago, forcing them to seek refuge in this world; despite this, the gnomes have never completely abandoned their fey roots or adapted to mortal culture. As a result, gnomes are widely regarded by the other races as alien and strange.

Physical Description: Gnomes are one of the smallest of the common races, generally standing just over 3 feet in height. Their hair tends toward vibrant colors such as the fiery orange of autumn leaves, the verdant green of forests at springtime, or the deep reds and purples of wildflowers in bloom. Similarly, their flesh tones range from earthy browns to floral pinks, frequently with little regard for heredity. Gnomes possess highly mutable facial characteristics, and many have overly large mouths and eyes, an effect which can be both disturbing and stunning, depending on the individual.

Society: Unlike most races, gnomes do not generally organize themselves within classic societal structures. Whimsical creatures at heart, they typically travel alone or with temporary companions, ever seeking new and more exciting experiences. They rarely form enduring relationships among themselves or with members of other races, instead pursuing crafts, professions, or collections with a passion that borders on zealotry. Male gnomes have a strange fondness for unusual hats and headgear, while females often proudly wear elaborate and eccentric hairstyles.

Relations: Gnomes have difficulty interacting with the other races, on both emotional and physical levels. Gnome humor is hard to translate and often comes across as malicious or senseless to other races, while gnomes in turn tend to think of the taller races as dull and lumbering giants. They get along well with halflings and humans, but are overly fond of playing jokes on dwarves and half-orcs, whom most gnomes feel need to lighten up. They respect elves, but often grow frustrated with the comparatively slow pace at which members of the long-lived race make decisions. To the gnomes, action is always better than inaction, and many gnomes carry several highly involved projects with them at all times to keep themselves entertained during rest periods.

Alignment and Religion: Although gnomes are impulsive tricksters, with sometimes inscrutable motives and equally confusing methods, their hearts are generally in the right place. They are prone to powerful fits of emotion, and find themselves most at peace within the natural world. Gnomes are usually neutral good, and prefer to worship deities who value individuality and nature, such as Shelyn, Gozreh, Desna, and increasingly Cayden Cailean.

Adventurers: Gnomes' propensity for wanderlust makes them natural adventurers. They often become wanderers to experience new aspects of life, for nothing is as novel as the uncounted dangers facing adventurers. Gnomes make up for their weakness with a proclivity for sorcery or bardic music.

Male Names: Abroshtor, Bastargre, Halungalom, Krolmnite, Poshment, Zarzuket, Zatqualmie.

Female Names: Besh, Fijit, Lini, Neji, Majet, Pai, Queck, Trig.

GNOME RACIAL TRAITS

+2 Constitution, +2 Charisma, –2 Strength: Gnomes are physically weak but surprisingly hardy, and their attitude makes them naturally agreeable.

Small: Gnomes are Small creatures and gain a +1 size bonus to their AC, a +1 size bonus on attack rolls, a –1 penalty to their Combat Maneuver Bonus and Combat Maneuver Defense, and a +4 size bonus on Stealth checks.

Slow Speed: Gnomes have a base speed of 20 feet.

Low-Light Vision: Gnomes can see twice as far as humans in conditions of dim light. See Chapter 7.

Defensive Training: Gnomes get a +4 dodge bonus to AC against monsters of the giant subtype.

Gnome Magic: Gnomes add +1 to the DC of any saving throws against illusion spells that they cast. Gnomes with a Charisma of 11 or higher also gain the following spell-like abilities: 1/day—*dancing lights, ghost sound, prestidigitation,* and *speak with animals.* The caster level for these effects is equal to the gnome's level. The DC for these spells is equal to 10 + the spell's level + the gnome's Charisma modifier.

Hatred: Gnomes receive a +1 bonus on attack rolls against humanoid creatures of the reptilian and goblinoid subtypes due to special training against these hated foes.

Illusion Resistance: Gnomes get a +2 racial saving throw bonus against illusion spells and effects.

Keen Senses: Gnomes receive a +2 racial bonus on Perception skill checks.

Obsessive: Gnomes receive a +2 racial bonus on a Craft or Profession skill of their choice.

Weapon Familiarity: Gnomes treat any weapon with the word "gnome" in its name as a martial weapon.

Languages: Gnomes begin play speaking Common, Gnome, and Sylvan. Gnomes with high Intelligence scores can choose from the following: Draconic, Dwarven, Elven, Giant, Goblin, and Orc.

HALF-ELVES

Elves have long drawn the covetous gazes of other races. Their generous life spans, magical affinity, and inherent grace each contribute to the admiration or bitter envy of their neighbors. Of all their traits, however, none so entrance their human associates as their beauty. Since the two races first came into contact with each other, the humans have held up elves as models of physical perfection, seeing in the fair folk idealized versions of themselves. For their part, many elves find humans attractive despite their comparatively barbaric ways, drawn to the passion and impetuosity with which members of the younger race play out their brief lives.

Sometimes this mutual infatuation leads to romantic relationships. Though usually short-lived, even by human standards, these trysts commonly lead to the birth of half-elves, a race descended of two cultures yet inheritor of neither. Half-elves can breed with one another, but even these "pureblood" half-elves tend to be viewed as bastards by humans and elves alike.

Physical Description: Half-elves stand taller than humans but shorter than elves. They inherit the lean build and comely features of their elven lineage, but their skin color is dictated by their human side. While half-elves retain the pointed ears of elves, theirs are more rounded and less pronounced. A half-elf's human-like eyes tend to range a spectrum of exotic colors running from amber or violet to emerald green and deep blue.

Society: The lack of a unified homeland and culture forces half-elves to remain versatile, able to conform to nearly any environment. While often attractive to both races for the same reasons as their parents, half-elves rarely fit in with either humans or elves, as both races see too much evidence of the other in them. This lack of acceptance weighs heavily on many half-elves, yet others are bolstered by their unique status, seeing in their lack of a formalized culture the ultimate freedom. As a result, half-elves are incredibly adaptable, capable of adjusting their mindsets and talents to whatever societies they find themselves in.

Relations: A half-elf understands loneliness, and knows that character is often less a product of race than of life experience. As such, half-elves are often open to friendships and alliances with other races, and less likely to rely on first impressions when forming opinions of new acquaintances.

Alignment and Religion: Half-elves' isolation strongly influences their characters and philosophies. Cruelty does not come naturally to them, nor does blending in and bending to societal convention—as a result, most half-elves are chaotic good. Half-elves' lack of a unified culture makes them less likely to turn to religion, but those who do generally follow the common faiths of their homeland.

Adventurers: Half-elves tend to be itinerants, wandering the lands in search of a place they might finally call home. The desire to prove oneself to the community and establish a personal identity—or even a legacy—drives many half-elf adventurers to lives of bravery.

Male Names: Calathes, Encinal, Kyras, Narciso, Quiray, Satinder, Seltyiel, Zirul.

Female Names: Cathran, Elsbeth, Iandoli, Kieyanna, Lialda, Maddela, Reda, Tamarie.

HALF-ELF RACIAL TRAITS

+2 to One Ability Score: Half-elf characters get a +2 bonus to one ability score of their choice at creation to represent their varied nature.

Medium: Half-elves are Medium creatures and have no bonuses or penalties due to their size.

Normal Speed: Half-elves have a base speed of 30 feet.

Low-Light Vision: Half-elves can see twice as far as humans in conditions of dim light. See Chapter 7.

Adaptability: Half-elves receive Skill Focus as a bonus feat at 1st level.

Elf Blood: Half-elves count as both elves and humans for any effect related to race.

Elven Immunities: Half-elves are immune to magic sleep effects and get a +2 racial saving throw bonus against enchantment spells and effects.

Keen Senses: Half-elves receive a +2 racial bonus on Perception skill checks.

Multitalented: Half-elves choose two favored classes at first level and gain +1 hit point or +1 skill point whenever they take a level in either one of those classes. See Chapter 3 for more information about favored classes.

Languages: Half-elves begin play speaking Common and Elven. Half-elves with high Intelligence scores can choose any languages they want (except secret languages, such as Druidic).

HALF-ORCS

Half-orcs are monstrosities, their tragic births the result of perversion and violence—or at least, that's how other races see them. It's true that half-orcs are rarely the result of loving unions, and as such are usually forced to grow up hard and fast, constantly fighting for protection or to make names for themselves. Feared, distrusted, and spat upon, half-orcs still consistently manage to surprise their detractors with great deeds and unexpected wisdom—though sometimes it's easier just to crack a few skulls.

Physical Description: Both genders of half-orc stand between 6 and 7 feet tall, with powerful builds and greenish or grayish skin. Their canines often grow long enough to protrude from their mouths, and these "tusks," combined with heavy brows and slightly pointed ears, give them their notoriously bestial appearance. While half-orcs may be impressive, few ever describe them as beautiful.

Society: Unlike half-elves, where at least part of society's discrimination is born out of jealousy or attraction, half-orcs get the worst of both worlds: physically weaker than their orc kin, they also tend to be feared or attacked outright by the legions of humans who don't bother making the distinction between full orcs and halfbloods. Still, while not exactly accepted, half-orcs in civilized societies tend to be valued for their martial prowess, and orc leaders have actually been known to spawn them intentionally, as the halfbreeds regularly make up for their lack of physical strength with increased cunning and aggression, making them natural chieftains and strategic advisors.

Relations: A lifetime of persecution leaves the average half-orc wary and quick to anger, yet those who break through his savage exterior might find a well-hidden core of empathy. Elves and dwarves tend to be the least accepting of half-orcs, seeing in them too great a resemblance to their racial enemies, but other races aren't much more understanding. Human societies with few orc problems

tend to be the most accommodating, and there half-orcs make natural mercenaries and enforcers.

Alignment & Religion: Forced to live either among brutish orcs or as lonely outcasts in civilized lands, most half-orcs are bitter, violent, and reclusive. Evil comes easily to them, but they are not evil by nature—rather, most half-orcs are chaotic neutral, having been taught by long experience that there's no point doing anything but that which directly benefits themselves. When they bother to worship the gods, they tend to favor deities who promote warfare or individual strength, such as Gorum, Cayden Cailean, Lamashtu, and Rovagug.

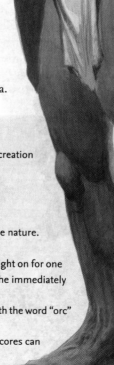

Adventurers: Staunchly independent, many half-orcs take to lives of adventure out of necessity, seeking to escape their painful pasts or improve their lot through force of arms. Others, more optimistic or desperate for acceptance, take up the mantle of crusaders in order to prove their worth to the world.

Male Names: Ausk, Davor, Hakak, Kizziar, Makoa, Nesteruk, Tsadok.

Female Names: Canan, Drogheda, Goruza, Mazon, Shirish, Tevaga, Zeljka.

HALF-ORC RACIAL TRAITS

+2 to One Ability Score: Half-orc characters get a +2 bonus to one ability score of their choice at creation to represent their varied nature.

Medium: Half-orcs are Medium creatures and have no bonuses or penalties due to their size.

Normal Speed: Half-orcs have a base speed of 30 feet.

Darkvision: Half-orcs can see in the dark up to 60 feet.

Intimidating: Half-orcs receive a +2 racial bonus on Intimidate skill checks due to their fearsome nature.

Orc Blood: Half-orcs count as both humans and orcs for any effect related to race.

Orc Ferocity: Once per day, when a half-orc is brought below 0 hit points but not killed, he can fight on for one more round as if disabled. At the end of his next turn, unless brought to above 0 hit points, he immediately falls unconscious and begins dying.

Weapon Familiarity: Half-orcs are proficient with greataxes and falchions and treat any weapon with the word "orc" in its name as a martial weapon.

Languages: Half-orcs begin play speaking Common and Orc. Half-orcs with high Intelligence scores can choose from the following: Abyssal, Draconic, Giant, Gnoll, and Goblin.

HALFLINGS

Optimistic and cheerful by nature, blessed with uncanny luck and driven by a powerful wanderlust, halflings make up for their short stature with an abundance of bravado and curiosity. At once excitable and easy-going, halflings like to keep an even temper and a steady eye on opportunity, and are not as prone as some of the more volatile races to violent or emotional outbursts. Even in the jaws of catastrophe, a halfling almost never loses his sense of humor.

Halflings are inveterate opportunists. Unable to physically defend themselves from the rigors of the world, they know when to bend with the wind and when to hide away. Yet a halfling's curiosity often overwhelms his good sense, leading to poor decisions and narrow escapes.

Though their curiosity drives them to travel and seek new places and experiences, halflings possess a strong sense of house and home, often spending above their means to enhance the comforts of home life.

Physical Description: Halflings rise to a humble height of 3 feet. They prefer to walk barefoot, leading to the bottoms of their feet being roughly calloused. Tufts of thick, curly hair warm the tops of their broad, tanned feet. Their skin tends toward a rich almond color and their hair toward light shades of brown. A halfling's ears are pointed, but proportionally not much larger than those of a human.

Society: Halflings claim no cultural homeland and control no settlements larger than rural assemblies of free towns. Far more often, they dwell at the knees of their human cousins in human cities, eking out livings as they can from the scraps of larger societies. Many halflings lead perfectly fulfilling lives in the shadow of their larger neighbors, while some prefer more nomadic lives on the road, traveling the world and experiencing all it has to offer.

Relations: A typical halfling prides himself on his ability to go unnoticed by other races—it is this trait that allows so many halflings to excel at thievery and trickery. Most halflings, knowing full well the stereotyped view other races take of them as a result, go out of their way to be forthcoming and friendly to the bigger races when they're not trying to go unnoticed. They get along fairly well with gnomes, although most halflings regard these eccentric creatures with a hefty dose of caution. Halflings coexist well with humans as a general rule, but since some of the more aggressive human societies value halflings as slaves, halflings try not to grow too complacent when dealing with them. Halflings respect elves and dwarves, but these races generally live in remote regions far from the comforts of civilization that halflings enjoy, thus limiting opportunities for interaction. Only half-orcs are generally shunned by halflings, for their great size and violent natures are a bit too intimidating for most halflings to cope with.

Alignment and Religion: Halflings are loyal to their friends and families, but since they dwell in a world dominated by races twice as large as themselves, they've come to grips with the fact that sometimes they'll need to scrap and scrounge for survival. Most halflings are neutral as a result. Halflings favor gods that encourage small, tight-knit communities, be they for good (like Erastil) or evil (like Norgorber).

Adventurers: Their inherent luck coupled with their insatiable wanderlust makes halflings ideal for lives of adventure. Other such vagabonds tend to put up with the curious race in hopes that some of their mystical luck will rub off.

Male Names: Antal, Boram, Evan, Jamir, Kaleb, Lem, Miro, Sumak.

Female Names: Anafa, Bellis, Etune, Filiu, Lissa, Marra, Rillka, Sistra, Yamyra.

HALFLING RACIAL TRAITS

+2 Dexterity, +2 Charisma, –2 Strength: Halflings are nimble and strong-willed, but their small stature makes them weaker than other races.

Small: Halflings are Small creatures and gain a +1 size bonus to their AC, a +1 size bonus on attack rolls, a –1 penalty to their Combat Maneuver Bonus and Combat Maneuver Defense, and a +4 size bonus on Stealth checks.

Slow Speed: Halflings have a base speed of 20 feet.

Fearless: Halflings receive a +2 racial bonus on all saving throws against fear. This bonus stacks with the bonus granted by halfling luck.

Halfling Luck: Halflings receive a +1 racial bonus on all saving throws.

Keen Senses: Halflings receive a +2 racial bonus on Perception skill checks.

Sure-Footed: Halflings receive a +2 racial bonus on Acrobatics and Climb skill checks.

Weapon Familiarity: Halflings are proficient with slings and treat any weapon with the word "halfling" in its name as a martial weapon.

Languages: Halflings begin play speaking Common and Halfling. Halflings with high Intelligence scores can choose from the following: Dwarven, Elven, Gnome, and Goblin.

HUMANS

Humans possess exceptional drive and a great capacity to endure and expand, and as such are currently the dominant race in the world. Their empires and nations are vast, sprawling things, and the citizens of these societies carve names for themselves with the strength of their sword arms and the power of their spells. Humanity is best characterized by its tumultuousness and diversity, and human cultures run the gamut from savage but honorable tribes to decadent, devil-worshiping noble families in the most cosmopolitan cities. Human curiosity and ambition often triumph over their predilection for a sedentary lifestyle, and many leave their homes to explore the innumerable forgotten corners of the world or lead mighty armies to conquer their neighbors, simply because they can.

Physical Description: The physical characteristics of humans are as varied as the world's climes. From the dark-skinned tribesmen of the southern continents to the pale and barbaric raiders of the northern lands, humans possess a wide variety of skin colors, body types, and facial features. Generally speaking, humans' skin color assumes a darker hue the closer to the equator they live.

Society: Human society comprises a multitude of governments, attitudes, and lifestyles. Though the oldest human cultures trace their histories thousands of years into the past, when compared to the societies of common races like elves and dwarves, human society seems to be in a state of constant flux as empires fragment and new kingdoms subsume the old. In general, humans are known for their flexibility, ingenuity, and ambition.

Relations: Humans are fecund, and their drive and numbers often spur them into contact with other races during bouts of territorial expansion and colonization. In many cases, this leads to violence and war, yet humans are also swift to forgive and forge alliances with races who do not try to match or exceed them in violence. Proud, sometimes to the point of arrogance, humans might look upon dwarves as miserly drunkards, elves as flighty fops, halflings as craven thieves, gnomes as twisted maniacs, and half-elves and half-orcs as embarrassments—but the race's diversity among its own members also makes humans quite adept at accepting others for what they are.

Alignment and Religion: Humanity is perhaps the most heterogeneous of all the common races, with a capacity for great evil and boundless good. Some assemble into vast barbaric hordes, while others build sprawling cities that cover miles. Taken as a whole, most humans are neutral, yet they generally tend to congregate in nations and civilizations with specific alignments. Humans also have the widest range in gods and religion, lacking other races' ties to tradition and eager to turn to anyone offering them glory or protection. They have even adopted gods like Torag or Calistria, who for millennia were more identified with older races, and as humanity continues to grow and prosper, new gods have begun emerging from their ever-expanding legends.

Adventurers: Ambition alone drives countless humans, and for many, adventuring serves as a means to an end, whether it be wealth, acclaim, social status, or arcane knowledge. A few pursue adventuring careers simply for the thrill of danger. Humans hail from myriad regions and backgrounds, and as such can fill any role within an adventuring party.

Names: Unlike other races, who generally cleave to specific traditions and shared histories, humanity's diversity has resulted in a near-infinite set of names. The humans of a northern barbarian tribe have much different names than those hailing from a subtropical nation of sailors and tradesmen. Throughout most of the world humans speak Common, yet their names are as varied as their beliefs and appearances.

HUMAN RACIAL TRAITS

+2 to One Ability Score: Human characters get a +2 bonus to one ability score of their choice at creation to represent their varied nature.

Medium: Humans are Medium creatures and have no bonuses or penalties due to their size.

Normal Speed: Humans have a base speed of 30 feet.

Bonus Feat: Humans select one extra feat at 1st level.

Skilled: Humans gain an additional skill rank at 1st level and one additional rank whenever they gain a level.

Languages: Humans begin play speaking Common. Humans with high Intelligence scores can choose any languages they want (except secret languages, such as Druidic).

3 Classes

The crumbling walkway atop the ancient dam shook with the force of water cascading through skull-shaped flumes, then shook more as the ogre barbarians strode forth.

"Looks like we've got a few tons of ugly in the way," Valeros roared. "With faces like that, it's no wonder they're afraid to come out in the light." The lead ogre's eyes bulged as it realized it had been insulted, and it shrieked in anger as it flew into a battle rage.

Seoni cursed under her breath. One of these days, Valeros's bravery was going to get them all killed.

A character's class is one of his most defining features. It's the source of most of his abilities, and gives him a specific role in any adventuring party. The following eleven classes represent the core classes of the game.

Barbarian: The barbarian is a brutal berserker from beyond the edge of civilized lands.

Bard: The bard uses skill and spell alike to bolster his allies, confound his enemies, and build upon his fame.

Cleric: A devout follower of a deity, the cleric can heal wounds, raise the dead, and call down the wrath of the gods.

Druid: The druid is a worshiper of all things natural—a spellcaster, a friend to animals, and a skilled shapechanger.

Fighter: Brave and stalwart, the fighter is a master of all manner of arms and armor.

Monk: A student of martial arts, the monk trains his body to be his greatest weapon and defense.

Paladin: The paladin is the knight in shining armor, a devoted follower of law and good.

Ranger: A tracker and hunter, the ranger is a creature of the wild and of tracking down his favored foes.

Rogue: The rogue is a thief and a scout, an opportunist capable of delivering brutal strikes against unwary foes.

Sorcerer: The spellcasting sorcerer is born with an innate knack for magic and has strange, eldritch powers.

Wizard: The wizard masters magic through constant study that gives him incredible magical power.

Table 3–1: Character Advancement and Level-Dependent Bonuses

Character Level	Experience Point Total			Feats	Ability Score
	Slow	Medium	Fast		
1st	—	—	—	1st	—
2nd	3,000	2,000	1,300	—	—
3rd	7,500	5,000	3,300	2nd	—
4th	14,000	9,000	6,000	—	1st
5th	23,000	15,000	10,000	3rd	—
6th	35,000	23,000	15,000	—	—
7th	53,000	35,000	23,000	4th	—
8th	77,000	51,000	34,000	—	2nd
9th	115,000	75,000	50,000	5th	—
10th	160,000	105,000	71,000	—	—
11th	235,000	155,000	105,000	6th	—
12th	330,000	220,000	145,000	—	3rd
13th	475,000	315,000	210,000	7th	—
14th	665,000	445,000	295,000	—	—
15th	955,000	635,000	425,000	8th	—
16th	1,350,000	890,000	600,000	—	4th
17th	1,900,000	1,300,000	850,000	9th	—
18th	2,700,000	1,800,000	1,200,000	—	—
19th	3,850,000	2,550,000	1,700,000	10th	—
20th	5,350,000	3,600,000	2,400,000	—	5th

CHARACTER ADVANCEMENT

As player characters overcome challenges, they gain experience points. As these points accumulate, PCs advance in level and power. The rate of this advancement depends on the type of game that your group wants to play. Some prefer a fast-paced game, where characters gain levels every few sessions, while others prefer a game where advancement occurs less frequently. In the end, it is up to your group to decide what rate fits you best. Characters advance in level according to Table 3–1.

Advancing Your Character

A character advances in level as soon as he earns enough experience points to do so—typically, this occurs at the end of a game session, when your GM hands out that session's experience point awards.

The process of advancing a character works in much the same way as generating a character, except that your ability scores, race, and previous choices concerning class, skills, and feats cannot be changed. Adding a level generally gives you new abilities, additional skill points to spend, more hit points, possibly a permanent +1 increase to one ability score of your choice, or an additional feat (see Table 3–1). Over time, as your character rises to higher levels, he becomes a truly powerful force in the game world, capable of ruling nations or bringing them to their knees.

When adding new levels of an existing class or adding levels of a new class (see Multiclassing, below), make sure to take the following steps in order. First, select your new class level. You must be able to qualify for this level before any of the following adjustments are made. Second, apply any ability score increases due to gaining a level. Third, integrate all of the level's class abilities and then roll for additional hit points. Finally, add new skills and feats. For more information on when you gain new feats and ability score increases, see Table 3–1.

Multiclassing

Instead of gaining the abilities granted by the next level in your character's current class, he can instead gain the 1st-level abilities of a new class, adding all of those abilities to his existing ones. This is known as "multiclassing."

For example, let's say a 5th-level fighter decides to dabble in the arcane arts, and adds one level of wizard when he advances to 6th level. Such a character would have the powers and abilities of both a 5th-level fighter and a 1st-level wizard, but would still be considered a 6th-level character. (His class levels would be 5th and 1st, but his total character level is 6th.) He keeps all of his bonus feats gained from 5 levels of fighter, but can now also cast 1st-level spells and picks an arcane school. He adds all of the hit points, base attack bonuses, and saving throw bonuses from a 1st-level wizard on top of those gained from being a 5th-level fighter.

Note that there are a number of effects and prerequisites that rely on a character's level or Hit Dice. Such effects are always based on the total number of levels or Hit Dice a character possesses, not just those from one class. The exception to this is class abilities, most of which are based on the total number of class levels that a character possesses of that particular class.

Favored Class

Each character begins play with a single favored class of his choosing—typically, this is the same class as the one he chooses at 1st level. Whenever a character gains a level in his favored class, he receives either + 1 hit point or + 1 skill rank. The choice of favored class cannot be changed once the character is created, and the choice of gaining a hit point or a skill rank each time a character gains a level (including his first level) cannot be changed once made for a particular level. Prestige classes (see Chapter 11) can never be a favored class.

BARBARIAN

For some, there is only rage. In the ways of their people, in the fury of their passion, in the howl of battle, conflict is all these brutal souls know. Savages, hired muscle, masters of vicious martial techniques, they are not soldiers or professional warriors—they are the battle possessed, creatures of slaughter and spirits of war. Known as barbarians, these warmongers know little of training, preparation, or the rules of warfare; for them, only the moment exists, with the foes that stand before them and the knowledge that the next moment might hold their death. They possess a sixth sense in regard to danger and the endurance to weather all that might entail. These brutal warriors might rise from all walks of life, both civilized and savage, though whole societies embracing such philosophies roam the wild places of the world. Within barbarians storms the primal spirit of battle, and woe to those who face their rage.

Role: Barbarians excel in combat, possessing the martial prowess and fortitude to take on foes seemingly far superior to themselves. With rage granting them boldness and daring beyond that of most other warriors, barbarians charge furiously into battle and ruin all who would stand in their way.

Alignment: Any nonlawful.

Hit Die: d12.

Class Skills

The barbarian's class skills are Acrobatics (Dex), Climb (Str), Craft (Int), Handle Animal (Cha), Intimidate (Cha), Knowledge (nature) (Int), Perception (Wis), Ride (Dex), Survival (Wis), and Swim (Str).

Skill Ranks per Level: 4 + Int modifier.

Class Features

All of the following are class features of the barbarian.

Weapon and Armor Proficiency: A barbarian is proficient with all simple and martial weapons, light armor, medium armor, and shields (except tower shields).

Fast Movement (Ex): A barbarian's base speed is faster than the norm for her race by +10 feet. This benefit applies only when she is wearing no armor, light armor, or medium armor, and not carrying a heavy load. Apply this bonus before modifying the barbarian's speed because of any load carried or armor worn. This bonus stacks with any other bonuses to the barbarian's base speed.

Table 3–2: Barbarian

Level	Base Attack Bonus	Fort Save	Ref Save	Will Save	Special
1st	+1	+2	+0	+0	Fast movement, rage
2nd	+2	+3	+0	+0	Rage power, uncanny dodge
3rd	+3	+3	+1	+1	Trap sense +1
4th	+4	+4	+1	+1	Rage power
5th	+5	+4	+1	+1	Improved uncanny dodge
6th	+6/+1	+5	+2	+2	Rage power, Trap sense +2
7th	+7/+2	+5	+2	+2	Damage reduction 1/—
8th	+8/+3	+6	+2	+2	Rage power
9th	+9/+4	+6	+3	+3	Trap sense +3
10th	+10/+5	+7	+3	+3	Damage reduction 2/—, Rage power
11th	+11/+6/+1	+7	+3	+3	Greater rage
12th	+12/+7/+2	+8	+4	+4	Rage power, Trap sense +4
13th	+13/+8/+3	+8	+4	+4	Damage reduction 3/—
14th	+14/+9/+4	+9	+4	+4	Indomitable will, Rage power
15th	+15/+10/+5	+9	+5	+5	Trap sense +5
16th	+16/+11/+6/+1	+10	+5	+5	Damage reduction 4/—, Rage power
17th	+17/+12/+7/+2	+10	+5	+5	Tireless rage
18th	+18/+13/+8/+3	+11	+6	+6	Rage power, Trap sense +6
19th	+19/+14/+9/+4	+11	+6	+6	Damage reduction 5/—
20th	+20/+15/+10/+5	+12	+6	+6	Mighty rage, Rage power

Rage (Ex): A barbarian can call upon inner reserves of strength and ferocity, granting her additional combat prowess. Starting at 1st level, a barbarian can rage for a number of rounds per day equal to 4 + her Constitution modifier. At each level after 1st, she can rage for 2 additional rounds. Temporary increases to Constitution, such as those gained from rage and spells like *bear's endurance*, do not increase the total number of rounds that a barbarian can rage per day. A barbarian can enter rage as a free action. The total number of rounds of rage per day is renewed after resting for 8 hours, although these hours do not need to be consecutive.

While in rage, a barbarian gains a +4 morale bonus to her Strength and Constitution, as well as a +2 morale bonus on Will saves. In addition, she takes a –2 penalty to Armor Class. The increase to Constitution grants the barbarian 2 hit points per Hit Dice, but these disappear when the rage ends and are not lost first like temporary hit points. While in rage, a barbarian cannot use any Charisma-, Dexterity-, or Intelligence-based skills (except Acrobatics, Fly, Intimidate, and Ride) or any ability that requires patience or concentration.

A barbarian can end her rage as a free action and is fatigued after rage for a number of rounds equal to 2 times the number of rounds spent in the rage. A barbarian cannot enter a new rage while fatigued or exhausted but can otherwise enter rage multiple times during a single encounter or combat. If a barbarian falls unconscious, her rage immediately ends, placing her in peril of death.

Rage Powers (Ex): As a barbarian gains levels, she learns to use her rage in new ways. Starting at 2nd level, a barbarian gains a rage power. She gains another rage power for every two levels of barbarian attained after 2nd level. A barbarian gains the benefits of rage powers only while raging, and some of these powers require the barbarian to take an action first. Unless otherwise noted, a barbarian cannot select an individual power more than once.

Animal Fury (Ex): While raging, the barbarian gains a bite attack. If used as part of a full attack action, the bite attack is made at the barbarian's full base attack bonus –5. If the bite hits, it deals 1d4 points of damage (assuming the barbarian is Medium; 1d3 points of damage if Small) plus half the barbarian's Strength modifier. A barbarian can make a bite attack as part of the action to maintain or break free from a grapple. This attack is resolved before the grapple check is made. If the bite attack hits, any grapple checks made by the barbarian against the target this round are at a +2 bonus.

Clear Mind (Ex): A barbarian may reroll a Will save. This power is used as an immediate action after the first save is attempted, but before the results are revealed by the GM. The barbarian must take the second result, even if it is worse. A barbarian must be at least 8th level before selecting this power. This power can only be used once per rage.

Fearless Rage (Ex): While raging, the barbarian is immune to the shaken and frightened conditions. A barbarian must be at least 12th level before selecting this rage power.

Guarded Stance (Ex): The barbarian gains a +1 dodge bonus to her Armor Class against melee attacks for a number of rounds equal to the barbarian's current Constitution modifier (minimum 1). This bonus increases by +1 for every 6 levels the barbarian has attained. Activating this ability is a move action that does not provoke an attack of opportunity.

Increased Damage Reduction (Ex): The barbarian's damage reduction increases by 1/—. This increase is always active while the barbarian is raging. A barbarian can select this rage power up to three times. Its effects stack. A barbarian must be at least 8th level before selecting this rage power.

Internal Fortitude (Ex): While raging, the barbarian is immune to the sickened and nauseated conditions. A barbarian must be at least 8th level before selecting this rage power.

Intimidating Glare (Ex): The barbarian can make an Intimidate check against one adjacent foe as a move action. If the barbarian successfully demoralizes her opponent, the foe is shaken for 1d4 rounds + 1 round for every 5 points by which the barbarian's check exceeds the DC.

Knockback (Ex): Once per round, the barbarian can make a bull rush attempt against one target in place of a melee attack. If successful, the target takes damage equal to the barbarian's Strength modifier and is moved back as normal. The barbarian does not need to move with the target if successful. This does not provoke an attack of opportunity.

Low-Light Vision (Ex): The barbarian's senses sharpen and she gains low-light vision while raging.

Mighty Swing (Ex): The barbarian automatically confirms a critical hit. This power is used as an immediate action once a critical threat has been determined. A barbarian must be at least 12th level before selecting this power. This power can only be used once per rage.

Moment of Clarity (Ex): The barbarian does not gain any benefits or take any of the penalties from rage for 1 round. Activating this power is a swift action. This includes the penalty to Armor Class and the restriction on what actions can be performed. This round still counts against her total number of rounds of rage per day. This power can only be used once per rage.

Night Vision (Ex): The barbarian's senses grow incredibly sharp while raging and she gains darkvision 60 feet. A barbarian must have low-light vision as a rage power or a racial trait to select this rage power.

No Escape (Ex): The barbarian can move up to double her base speed as an immediate action but she can only use this ability when an adjacent foe uses a withdraw action to move away from her. She must end her movement adjacent to the enemy that used the withdraw action. The barbarian provokes attacks of opportunity as normal during this movement. This power can only be used once per rage.

Powerful Blow (Ex): The barbarian gains a +1 bonus on a single damage roll. This bonus increases by +1 for every 4 levels the barbarian has attained. This power is used as a swift action before the roll to hit is made. This power can only be used once per rage.

Quick Reflexes (Ex): While raging, the barbarian can make one additional attack of opportunity per round.

Raging Climber (Ex): When raging, the barbarian adds her level as an enhancement bonus on all Climb skill checks.

Raging Leaper (Ex): When raging, the barbarian adds her level as an enhancement bonus on all Acrobatics skill checks made to jump. When making a jump in this way, the barbarian is always considered to have a running start.

Raging Swimmer (Ex): When raging, the barbarian adds her level as an enhancement bonus on all Swim skill checks.

Renewed Vigor (Ex): As a standard action, the barbarian heals 1d8 points of damage + her Constitution modifier. For every four levels the barbarian has attained above 4th, this amount of damage healed increases by 1d8, to a maximum of 5d8 at 20th level. A barbarian must be at least 4th level before selecting this power. This power can be used only once per day and only while raging.

Rolling Dodge (Ex): The barbarian gains a +1 dodge bonus to her Armor Class against ranged attacks for a number of rounds equal to the barbarian's current Constitution modifier (minimum 1). This bonus increases by +1 for every 6 levels the barbarian has attained. Activating this ability is a move action that does not provoke an attack of opportunity.

Roused Anger (Ex): The barbarian may enter a rage even if fatigued. While raging after using this ability, the barbarian is immune to the fatigued condition. Once this rage ends, the barbarian is exhausted for 10 minutes per round spent raging.

Scent (Ex): The barbarian gains the scent ability while raging and can use this ability to locate unseen foes (see Appendix 1 for rules on the scent ability).

Strength Surge (Ex): The barbarian adds her barbarian level on one Strength check or combat maneuver check, or to her Combat Maneuver Defense when an opponent attempts a maneuver against her. This power is used as an immediate action. This power can only be used once per rage.

Superstition (Ex): The barbarian gains a +2 morale bonus on saving throws made to resist spells, supernatural abilities, and spell-like abilities. This bonus increases by +1 for every 4 levels the barbarian has attained. While raging, the barbarian cannot be a willing target of any spell and must make saving throws to resist all spells, even those cast by allies.

Surprise Accuracy (Ex): The barbarian gains a +1 morale bonus on one attack roll. This bonus increases by +1 for every 4 levels the barbarian has attained. This power is used as a swift action before the roll to hit is made. This power can only be used once per rage.

Swift Foot (Ex): The barbarian gains a 5-foot enhancement bonus to her base speed. This increase is always active while the barbarian is raging. A barbarian can select this rage power up to three times. Its effects stack.

Terrifying Howl (Ex): The barbarian unleashes a terrifying howl as a standard action. All shaken enemies within 30 feet must make a Will save (DC equal to 10 + 1/2 the barbarian's level + the barbarian's Strength modifier) or be panicked for 1d4+1 rounds. Once an enemy has made a save versus terrifying howl (successful or not), it is immune to this power for 24 hours. A barbarian must have the intimidating glare rage power to select this rage power. A barbarian must be at least 8th level before selecting this power.

Unexpected Strike (Ex): The barbarian can make an attack of opportunity against a foe that moves into any square threatened by the barbarian, regardless of whether or not that movement would normally provoke an attack of opportunity. This power can only be used once per rage. A barbarian must be at least 8th level before selecting this power.

Uncanny Dodge (Ex): At 2nd level, a barbarian gains the ability to react to danger before her senses would normally allow her to do so. She cannot be caught flat-footed, nor does she lose her Dex bonus to AC if the attacker is invisible. She still loses her Dexterity bonus to AC if immobilized. A barbarian with this ability can still lose her Dexterity bonus to AC if an opponent successfully uses the feint action against her.

If a barbarian already has uncanny dodge from a different class, she automatically gains improved uncanny dodge (see below) instead.

Trap Sense (Ex): At 3rd level, a barbarian gains a +1 bonus on Reflex saves made to avoid traps and a +1 dodge bonus to AC against attacks made by traps. These bonuses increase by +1 every three barbarian levels thereafter (6th, 9th, 12th, 15th, and 18th level). Trap sense bonuses gained from multiple classes stack.

Improved Uncanny Dodge (Ex): At 5th level and higher, a barbarian can no longer be flanked. This defense denies a rogue the ability to sneak attack the barbarian by flanking her, unless the attacker has at least four more rogue levels than the target has barbarian levels.

If a character already has uncanny dodge (see above) from another class, the levels from the classes that grant uncanny dodge stack to determine the minimum rogue level required to flank the character.

Damage Reduction (Ex): At 7th level, a barbarian gains damage reduction. Subtract 1 from the damage the barbarian takes each time she is dealt damage from a weapon or a natural attack. At 10th level, and every three barbarian levels thereafter (13th, 16th, and 19th level), this damage reduction rises by 1 point. Damage reduction can reduce damage to 0 but not below 0.

Greater Rage (Ex): At 11th level, when a barbarian enters rage, the morale bonus to her Strength and Constitution increases to +6 and the morale bonus on her Will saves increases to +3.

Indomitable Will (Ex): While in rage, a barbarian of 14th level or higher gains a +4 bonus on Will saves to resist enchantment spells. This bonus stacks with all other modifiers, including the morale bonus on Will saves she also receives during her rage.

Tireless Rage (Ex): Starting at 17th level, a barbarian no longer becomes fatigued at the end of her rage.

Mighty Rage (Ex): At 20th level, when a barbarian enters rage, the morale bonus to her Strength and Constitution increases to +8 and the morale bonus on her Will saves increases to +4.

Ex-Barbarians

A barbarian who becomes lawful loses the ability to rage and cannot gain more levels in barbarian. She retains all other benefits of the class.

BARD

Untold wonders and secrets exist for those skillful enough to discover them. Through cleverness, talent, and magic, these cunning few unravel the wiles of the world, becoming adept in the arts of persuasion, manipulation, and inspiration. Typically masters of one or many forms of artistry, bards possess an uncanny ability to know more than they should and use what they learn to keep themselves and their allies ever one step ahead of danger. Bards are quick-witted and captivating, and their skills might lead them down many paths, be they gamblers or jacks-of-all-trades, scholars or performers, leaders or scoundrels, or even all of the above. For bards, every day brings its own opportunities, adventures, and challenges, and only by bucking the odds, knowing the most, and being the best might they claim the treasures of each.

Role: Bards capably confuse and confound their foes while inspiring their allies to ever-greater daring. While accomplished with both weapons and magic, the true strength of bards lies outside melee, where they can support their companions and undermine their foes without fear of interruptions to their performances.

Alignment: Any.

Hit Die: d8.

Class Skills

The bard's class skills are Acrobatics (Dex), Appraise (Int), Bluff (Cha), Climb (Str), Craft (Int), Diplomacy (Cha), Disguise (Cha), Escape Artist (Dex), Intimidate (Cha), Knowledge (all) (Int), Linguistics (Int), Perception (Wis), Perform (Cha), Profession (Wis), Sense Motive (Wis), Sleight of Hand (Dex), Spellcraft (Int), Stealth (Dex), and Use Magic Device (Cha).

Skill Ranks per Level: 6 + Int modifier.

Class Features

All of the following are class features of the bard.

Weapon and Armor Proficiency: A bard is proficient with all simple weapons, plus the longsword, rapier, sap, short sword, shortbow, and whip. Bards are also proficient with light armor and shields (except tower shields). A bard can cast bard spells while wearing light armor and use a shield without incurring the normal arcane spell failure chance. Like any other arcane spellcaster, a bard wearing medium or heavy armor incurs a chance of arcane spell failure if the spell in question has a somatic component. A multiclass bard still incurs the normal arcane spell failure chance for arcane spells received from other classes.

Spells: A bard casts arcane spells drawn from the bard spell list presented in Chapter 10. He can cast any spell he knows without preparing it ahead of time. Every bard spell has a verbal component (song, recitation, or music). To learn or cast a spell, a bard must have a Charisma score equal to at least 10 + the spell level. The Difficulty Class for a saving throw against a bard's spell is 10 + the spell level + the bard's Charisma modifier.

Like other spellcasters, a bard can cast only a certain number of spells of each spell level per day. His base daily spell allotment is given on Table 3–3. In addition, he receives bonus spells per day if he has a high Charisma score (see Table 1–3).

The bard's selection of spells is extremely limited. A bard begins play knowing four 0-level spells and two 1st-level spells of the bard's choice. At each new bard level, he gains one or more new spells, as indicated on Table 3–4. (Unlike spells per day, the number of spells a bard knows is not affected by his Charisma score. The numbers on Table 3–4 are fixed.)

Upon reaching 5th level, and at every third bard level after that (8th, 11th, and so on), a bard can choose to learn a new spell in place of one he already knows. In effect, the bard "loses" the old spell in exchange for the new one. The new spell's level must be the same as that of the spell being exchanged, and it must be at least one level lower than the highest-level bard spell the bard can cast. A bard may swap only a single spell at any given level and must choose whether or not to swap the spell at the same time that he gains new spells known for the level.

A bard need not prepare his spells in advance. He can cast any spell he knows at any time, assuming he has not yet used up his allotment of spells per day for the spell's level.

Bardic Knowledge (Ex): A bard adds half his class level (minimum 1) on all Knowledge skill checks and may make all Knowledge skill checks untrained.

Bardic Performance: A bard is trained to use the Perform skill to create magical effects on those around him, including himself if desired. He can use this ability for a number of rounds per day equal to 4 + his Charisma modifier. At each level after 1st a bard can use bardic performance for 2 additional rounds per day. Each round, the bard can produce any one of the types of bardic performance that he has mastered, as indicated by his level.

Starting a bardic performance is a standard action, but it can be maintained each round as a free action. Changing a bardic performance from one effect to another requires the bard to stop the previous performance and start a new one as a standard action. A bardic performance cannot be disrupted, but it ends immediately if the bard is killed, paralyzed, stunned, knocked unconscious, or otherwise prevented from taking a free action to maintain it each round. A bard cannot have more than one bardic performance in effect at one time.

TABLE 3-3: BARD

Level	Base Attack Bonus	Fort Save	Ref Save	Will Save	Special	Spells per Day 1st	2nd	3rd	4th	5th	6th
1st	+0	+0	+2	+2	Bardic knowledge, bardic performance, cantrips, countersong, distraction, fascinate, inspire courage +1	1	—	—	—	—	—
2nd	+1	+0	+3	+3	Versatile performance, well-versed	2	—	—	—	—	—
3rd	+2	+1	+3	+3	Inspire competence +2	3	—	—	—	—	—
4th	+3	+1	+4	+4		3	1	—	—	—	—
5th	+3	+1	+4	+4	inspire courage +2, lore master 1/day	4	2	—	—	—	—
6th	+4	+2	+5	+5	Suggestion, Versatile performance	4	3	—	—	—	—
7th	+5	+2	+5	+5	Inspire competence +3	4	3	1	—	—	—
8th	+6/+1	+2	+6	+6	Dirge of doom	4	4	2	—	—	—
9th	+6/+1	+3	+6	+6	Inspire greatness	5	4	3	—	—	—
10th	+7/+2	+3	+7	+7	Jack-of-all-trades, Versatile performance	5	4	3	1	—	—
11th	+8/+3	+3	+7	+7	Inspire competence +4, inspire courage +3, lore master 2/day	5	4	4	2	—	—
12th	+9/+4	+4	+8	+8	Soothing performance	5	5	4	3	—	—
13th	+9/+4	+4	+8	+8		5	5	4	3	1	—
14th	+10/+5	+4	+9	+9	Frightening tune, Versatile performance	5	5	4	4	2	—
15th	+11/+6/+1	+5	+9	+9	Inspire competence +5, inspire heroics	5	5	5	4	3	—
16th	+12/+7/+2	+5	+10	+10		5	5	5	4	3	1
17th	+12/+7/+2	+5	+10	+10	inspire courage +4, lore master 3/day	5	5	5	4	4	2
18th	+13/+8/+3	+6	+11	+11	Mass suggestion, Versatile performance	5	5	5	5	4	3
19th	+14/+9/+4	+6	+11	+11	Inspire competence +6	5	5	5	5	5	4
20th	+15/+10/+5	+6	+12	+12	Deadly performance	5	5	5	5	5	5

At 7th level, a bard can start a bardic performance as a move action instead of a standard action. At 13th level, a bard can start a bardic performance as a swift action.

Each bardic performance has audible components, visual components, or both.

If a bardic performance has audible components, the targets must be able to hear the bard for the performance to have any effect, and many such performances are language dependent (as noted in the description). A deaf bard has a 20% chance to fail when attempting to use a bardic performance with an audible component. If he fails this check, the attempt still counts against his daily limit. Deaf creatures are immune to bardic performances with audible components.

If a bardic performance has a visual component, the targets must have line of sight to the bard for the performance to have any effect. A blind bard has a 50% chance to fail when attempting to use a bardic performance with a visual component. If he fails this check, the attempt still counts against his daily limit. Blind creatures are immune to bardic performances with visual components.

Countersong (Su): At 1st level, a bard learns to counter magic effects that depend on sound (but not spells that have verbal components). Each round of the countersong he makes a Perform (keyboard, percussion, wind, string, or sing) skill check. Any creature within 30 feet of the bard (including the bard himself) that is affected by a sonic or language-dependent magical attack may use the bard's Perform check result in place of its saving throw if, after the saving throw is rolled, the Perform check result proves to be higher. If a creature within range of the countersong is already under the effect of a noninstantaneous sonic or language-dependent magical attack, it gains another saving throw against the effect each round it hears the countersong, but it must use the bard's Perform skill check result for the save. Countersong does not work on effects that don't allow saves. Countersong relies on audible components.

Distraction (Su): At 1st level, a bard can use his performance to counter magic effects that depend on sight. Each round of the distraction, he makes a Perform (act, comedy, dance, or oratory) skill check. Any creature within 30 feet of the bard (including the bard himself) that is affected by an illusion (pattern) or illusion (figment) magical attack may use the bard's Perform check result in place of its saving throw if, after the saving throw is rolled, the Perform skill check proves to be higher. If a creature within range of the distraction is already under the effect of a noninstantaneous illusion (pattern) or illusion (figment) magical attack, it gains another saving throw against the effect each round it sees the distraction, but it must use the bard's Perform skill check result for the save. Distraction does not work on effects that don't allow saves. Distraction relies on visual components.

Fascinate (Su): At 1st level, a bard can use his performance to cause one or more creatures to become fascinated with him. Each creature to be fascinated must be within 90 feet, able to see and hear the bard, and capable of paying attention to him. The bard must also be able to see the creatures affected. The distraction of a nearby combat or other dangers prevents this ability from working. For every three levels the bard has attained beyond 1st, he can target one additional creature with this ability.

Each creature within range receives a Will save (DC 10 + 1/2 the bard's level + the bard's Cha modifier) to negate the effect. If a creature's saving throw succeeds, the bard cannot attempt to fascinate that creature again for 24 hours. If its saving throw fails, the creature sits quietly and observes the performance for as long as the bard continues to maintain it. While fascinated, a target takes a −4 penalty on all skill checks made as reactions, such as Perception checks. Any potential threat to the target allows the target to make a new saving throw against the effect. Any obvious threat, such as someone drawing a weapon, casting a spell, or aiming a weapon at the target, automatically breaks the effect.

Fascinate is an enchantment (compulsion), mind-affecting ability. Fascinate relies on audible and visual components in order to function.

Inspire Courage (Su): A 1st-level bard can use his performance to inspire courage in his allies (including himself), bolstering them against fear and improving their combat abilities. To be affected, an ally must be able to perceive the bard's performance. An affected ally receives a +1 morale bonus on saving throws against charm and fear effects and a +1 competence bonus on attack and weapon damage rolls. At 5th level, and every six bard levels thereafter, this bonus increases by +1, to a maximum of +4 at 17th level. Inspire courage is a mind-affecting ability. Inspire courage can use audible or visual components. The bard must choose which component to use when starting his performance.

Inspire Competence (Su): A bard of 3rd level or higher can use his performance to help an ally succeed at a task. That ally must be within 30 feet and be able to hear the bard. The ally gets a +2 competence bonus on skill checks with a particular skill as long as she continues to hear the bard's performance. This bonus increases by +1 for every four levels the bard has attained beyond 3rd (+3 at 7th, +4 at 11th, +5 at 15th, and +6 at 19th). Certain uses of this ability are infeasible, such as Stealth, and may be disallowed at the GM's discretion. A bard can't inspire competence in himself. Inspire competence relies on audible components.

TABLE 3-4: BARD SPELLS KNOWN

Level	\ 0	1st	2nd	3rd	4th	5th	6th
1st	4	2	—	—	—	—	—
2nd	5	3	—	—	—	—	—
3rd	6	4	—	—	—	—	—
4th	6	4	2	—	—	—	—
5th	6	4	3	—	—	—	—
6th	6	4	4	—	—	—	—
7th	6	5	4	2	—	—	—
8th	6	5	4	3	—	—	—
9th	6	5	4	4	—	—	—
10th	6	5	5	4	2	—	—
11th	6	6	5	4	3	—	—
12th	6	6	5	4	4	—	—
13th	6	6	5	5	4	2	—
14th	6	6	6	5	4	3	—
15th	6	6	6	5	4	4	—
16th	6	6	6	5	5	4	2
17th	6	6	6	6	5	4	3
18th	6	6	6	6	5	4	4
19th	6	6	6	6	5	5	4
20th	6	6	6	6	6	5	5

Suggestion (Sp): A bard of 6th level or higher can use his performance to make a *suggestion* (as per the spell) to a creature he has already fascinated (see above). Using this ability does not disrupt the fascinate effect, but it does require a standard action to activate (in addition to the free action to continue the fascinate effect). A bard can use this ability more than once against an individual creature during an individual performance.

Making a *suggestion* does not count against a bard's total rounds per day of bardic performance. A Will saving throw (DC 10 + 1/2 the bard's level + the bard's Cha modifier) negates the effect. This ability affects only a single creature. *Suggestion* is an enchantment (compulsion), mind affecting, language-dependent ability and relies on audible components.

Dirge of Doom (Su): A bard of 8th level or higher can use his performance to foster a sense of growing dread in his enemies, causing them to become shaken. To be affected, an enemy must be within 30 feet and able to see and hear the bard's performance. The effect persists for as long as the enemy is within 30 feet and the bard continues his performance. This performance cannot cause a creature to become frightened or panicked, even if the targets are already shaken from another effect. Dirge of doom is a mind-affecting fear effect, and it relies on audible and visual components.

Inspire Greatness (Su): A bard of 9th level or higher can use his performance to inspire greatness in himself or a single willing ally within 30 feet, granting extra fighting capability. For every three levels the bard attains beyond 9th, he can target an additional ally while using this performance (up to a maximum of four targets at 18th level). To inspire greatness, all of the targets must be able to see and hear the bard. A creature inspired with greatness gains 2 bonus Hit Dice (d10s), the commensurate number of temporary hit points (apply the target's Constitution modifier, if any, to these bonus Hit Dice), a +2 competence bonus on attack rolls, and a +1 competence bonus on Fortitude saves. The bonus Hit Dice count as regular Hit Dice for determining the effect of spells that are Hit Dice dependent. Inspire greatness is a mind-affecting ability and it relies on audible and visual components.

Soothing Performance (Su): A bard of 12th level or higher can use his performance to create an effect equivalent to a *mass cure serious wounds,* using the bard's level as the caster level. In addition, this performance removes the fatigued, sickened, and shaken conditions from all those affected. Using this ability requires 4 rounds of continuous performance, and the targets must be able to see and hear the bard throughout the performance. Soothing performance affects all targets that remain within 30 feet throughout the performance. Soothing performance relies on audible and visual components.

Frightening Tune (Sp): A bard of 14th level or higher can use his performance to cause fear in his enemies. To be affected, an enemy must be able to hear the bard perform and be within 30 feet. Each enemy within range receives a Will save (DC 10 + 1/2 the bard's level + the bard's Cha modifier) to negate the effect. If the save succeeds, the creature is immune to this ability for 24 hours. If the save fails, the target becomes frightened and flees for as long as the target can hear the bard's performance. Frightening tune relies on audible components.

Inspire Heroics (Su): A bard of 15th level or higher can inspire tremendous heroism in himself or a single ally within 30 feet. For every three bard levels the character attains beyond 15th, he can inspire heroics in an additional creature. To inspire heroics, all of the targets must be able to see and hear the bard. Inspired creatures gain a +4 morale bonus on saving throws and a +4 dodge bonus to AC. This effect lasts for as long as the targets are able to witness the performance. Inspire heroics is a mind-affecting ability that relies on audible and visual components.

Mass Suggestion (Sp): This ability functions just like *suggestion,* but allows a bard of 18th level or higher to make a *suggestion* simultaneously to any number of creatures that he has already fascinated. *Mass suggestion* is an enchantment (compulsion), mind-affecting, language-dependent ability that relies on audible components.

Deadly Performance (Su): A bard of 20th level or higher can use his performance to cause one enemy to die from joy or sorrow. To be affected, the target must be able to see

and hear the bard perform for 1 full round and be within 30 feet. The target receives a Will save (DC 10 + 1/2 the bard's level + the bard's Cha modifier) to negate the effect. If a creature's saving throw succeeds, the target is staggered for 1d4 rounds, and the bard cannot use deadly performance on that creature again for 24 hours. If a creature's saving throw fails, it dies. Deadly performance is a mind-affecting death effect that relies on audible and visual components.

Cantrips: Bards learn a number of cantrips, or 0-level spells, as noted on Table 3–4 under "Spells Known." These spells are cast like any other spell, but they do not consume any slots and may be used again.

Versatile Performance (Ex): At 2nd level, a bard can choose one type of Perform skill. He can use his bonus in that skill in place of his bonus in associated skills. When substituting in this way, the bard uses his total Perform skill bonus, including class skill bonus, in place of its associated skill's bonus, whether or not he has ranks in that skill or if it is a class skill. At 6th level, and every 4 levels thereafter, the bard can select an additional type of Perform to substitute.

The types of Perform and their associated skills are: Act (Bluff, Disguise), Comedy (Bluff, Intimidate), Dance (Acrobatics, Fly), Keyboard Instruments (Diplomacy, Intimidate), Oratory (Diplomacy, Sense Motive), Percussion (Handle Animal, Intimidate), Sing (Bluff, Sense Motive), String (Bluff, Diplomacy), and Wind (Diplomacy, Handle Animal).

Well-Versed (Ex): At 2nd level, the bard becomes resistant to the bardic performance of others, and to sonic effects in general. The bard gains a +4 bonus on saving throws made against bardic performance, sonic, and language-dependent effects.

Lore Master (Ex): At 5th level, the bard becomes a master of lore and can take 10 on any Knowledge skill check that he has ranks in. A bard can choose not to take 10 and can instead roll normally. In addition, once per day, the bard can take 20 on any Knowledge skill check as a standard action. He can use this ability one additional time per day for every six levels he possesses beyond 5th, to a maximum of three times per day at 17th level.

Jack-of-All-Trades (Ex): At 10th level, the bard can use any skill, even if the skill normally requires him to be trained. At 16th level, the bard considers all skills to be class skills. At 19th level, the bard can take 10 on any skill check, even if it is not normally allowed.

CLERIC

In faith and the miracles of the divine, many find a greater purpose. Called to serve powers beyond most mortal understanding, all priests preach wonders and provide for the spiritual needs of their people. Clerics are more than mere priests, though; these emissaries of the divine work the will of their deities through strength of arms and the magic of their gods. Devoted to the tenets of the religions and philosophies that inspire them, these ecclesiastics quest to spread the knowledge and influence of their faith. Yet while they might share similar abilities, clerics prove as different from one another as the divinities they serve, with some offering healing and redemption, others judging law and truth, and still others spreading conflict and corruption. The ways of the cleric are varied, yet all who tread these paths walk with the mightiest of allies and bear the arms of the gods themselves.

Role: More than capable of upholding the honor of their deities in battle, clerics often prove stalwart and capable combatants. Their true strength lies in their capability to draw upon the power of their deities, whether to increase their own and their allies' prowess in battle, to vex their foes with divine magic, or to lend healing to companions in need.

As their powers are influenced by their faith, all clerics must focus their worship upon a divine source. While the vast majority of clerics revere a specific deity, a small number dedicate themselves to a divine concept worthy of devotion—such as battle, death, justice, or knowledge—free of a deific abstraction. (Work with your GM if you prefer this path to selecting a specific deity.)

Alignment: A cleric's alignment must be within one step of her deity's, along either the law/chaos axis or the good/evil axis (see Chapter 7).

Hit Die: d8.

Class Skills

The cleric's class skills are Appraise (Int), Craft (Int), Diplomacy (Cha), Heal (Wis), Knowledge (arcana) (Int), Knowledge (history) (Int), Knowledge (nobility) (Int), Knowledge (planes) (Int), Knowledge (religion) (Int), Linguistics (Int), Profession (Wis), Sense Motive (Wis), and Spellcraft (Int).

Skill Ranks per Level: 2 + Int modifier.

Class Features

The following are class features of the cleric.

Weapon and Armor Proficiency: Clerics are proficient with all simple weapons, light armor, medium armor, and shields (except tower shields). Clerics are also proficient with the favored weapon of their deity.

Aura (Ex): A cleric of a chaotic, evil, good, or lawful deity has a particularly powerful aura corresponding to the deity's alignment (see the *detect evil* spell for details).

Spells: A cleric casts divine spells which are drawn from the cleric spell list presented in Chapter 10. Her alignment, however, may restrict her from casting certain spells opposed to her moral or ethical beliefs; see chaotic,

evil, good, and lawful spells on page 41. A cleric must choose and prepare her spells in advance.

To prepare or cast a spell, a cleric must have a Wisdom score equal to at least 10 + the spell level. The Difficulty Class for a saving throw against a cleric's spell is 10 + the spell level + the cleric's Wisdom modifier.

Like other spellcasters, a cleric can cast only a certain number of spells of each spell level per day. Her base daily spell allotment is given on Table 3–5. In addition, she receives bonus spells per day if she has a high Wisdom score (see Table 1–3).

TABLE 3-5: CLERIC

Level	Base Attack Bonus	Fort Save	Ref Save	Will Save	Special	Spells per Day									
						0	1st	2nd	3rd	4th	5th	6th	7th	8th	9th
1st	+0	+2	+0	+2	Aura, channel energy 1d6, domains, orisons	3	1+1	—	—	—	—	—	—	—	—
2nd	+1	+3	+0	+3		4	2+1	—	—	—	—	—	—	—	—
3rd	+2	+3	+1	+3	Channel energy 2d6	4	2+1	1+1	—	—	—	—	—	—	—
4th	+3	+4	+1	+4		4	3+1	2+1	—	—	—	—	—	—	—
5th	+3	+4	+1	+4	Channel energy 3d6	4	3+1	2+1	1+1	—	—	—	—	—	—
6th	+4	+5	+2	+5		4	3+1	3+1	2+1	—	—	—	—	—	—
7th	+5	+5	+2	+5	Channel energy 4d6	4	4+1	3+1	2+1	1+1	—	—	—	—	—
8th	+6/+1	+6	+2	+6		4	4+1	3+1	3+1	2+1	—	—	—	—	—
9th	+6/+1	+6	+3	+6	Channel energy 5d6	4	4+1	4+1	3+1	2+1	1+1	—	—	—	—
10th	+7/+2	+7	+3	+7		4	4+1	4+1	3+1	3+1	2+1	—	—	—	—
11th	+8/+3	+7	+3	+7	Channel energy 6d6	4	4+1	4+1	4+1	3+1	2+1	1+1	—	—	—
12th	+9/+4	+8	+4	+8		4	4+1	4+1	4+1	3+1	3+1	2+1	—	—	—
13th	+9/+4	+8	+4	+8	Channel energy 7d6	4	4+1	4+1	4+1	4+1	3+1	2+1	1+1	—	—
14th	+10/+5	+9	+4	+9		4	4+1	4+1	4+1	4+1	3+1	3+1	2+1	—	—
15th	+11/+6/+1	+9	+5	+9	Channel energy 8d6	4	4+1	4+1	4+1	4+1	4+1	3+1	2+1	1+1	—
16th	+12/+7/+2	+10	+5	+10		4	4+1	4+1	4+1	4+1	4+1	4+1	3+1	3+1	2+1
17th	+12/+7/+2	+10	+5	+10	Channel energy 9d6	4	4+1	4+1	4+1	4+1	4+1	4+1	3+1	2+1	1+1
18th	+13/+8/+3	+11	+6	+11		4	4+1	4+1	4+1	4+1	4+1	4+1	3+1	3+1	2+1
19th	+14/+9/+4	+11	+6	+11	Channel energy 10d6	4	4+1	4+1	4+1	4+1	4+1	4+1	4+1	3+1	3+1
20th	+15/+10/+5	+12	+6	+12		4	4+1	4+1	4+1	4+1	4+1	4+1	4+1	4+1	4+1

Note: "+1" represents the domain spell slot

Clerics meditate or pray for their spells. Each cleric must choose a time when she must spend 1 hour each day in quiet contemplation or supplication to regain her daily allotment of spells. A cleric may prepare and cast any spell on the cleric spell list, provided that she can cast spells of that level, but she must choose which spells to prepare during her daily meditation.

Channel Energy (Su): Regardless of alignment, any cleric can release a wave of energy by channeling the power of her faith through her holy (or unholy) symbol. This energy can be used to cause or heal damage, depending on the type of energy channeled and the creatures targeted.

A good cleric (or one who worships a good deity) channels positive energy and can choose to deal damage to undead creatures or to heal living creatures. An evil cleric (or one who worships an evil deity) channels negative energy and can choose to deal damage to living creatures or to heal undead creatures. A neutral cleric who worships a neutral deity (or one who is not devoted to a particular deity) must choose whether she channels positive or negative energy. Once this choice is made, it cannot be reversed. This decision also determines whether the cleric casts spontaneous cure or inflict spells (see spontaneous casting).

Channeling energy causes a burst that affects all creatures of one type (either undead or living) in a 30-foot radius centered on the cleric. The amount of damage dealt or healed is equal to 1d6 points of damage plus 1d6 points of damage for every two cleric levels beyond 1st (2d6 at 3rd, 3d6 at 5th, and so on). Creatures that take damage from channeled energy receive a Will save to halve the damage. The DC of this save is equal to 10 + 1/2 the cleric's level + the cleric's Charisma modifier. Creatures healed by channeled energy cannot exceed their maximum hit point total—all excess healing is lost. A cleric may channel energy a number of times per day equal to 3 + her Charisma modifier. This is a standard action that does not provoke an attack of opportunity. A cleric can choose whether or not to include herself in this effect. A cleric must be able to present her holy symbol to use this ability.

Domains: A cleric's deity influences her alignment, what magic she can perform, her values, and how others see her. A cleric chooses two domains from among those belonging to her deity. A cleric can select an alignment domain (Chaos, Evil, Good, or Law) only if her alignment matches that domain. If a cleric is not devoted to a particular deity, she still selects two domains to represent her spiritual inclinations and abilities (subject to GM approval). The restriction on alignment domains still applies.

Each domain grants a number of domain powers, dependent upon the level of the cleric, as well as a number of bonus spells. A cleric gains one domain spell slot for each level of cleric spell she can cast, from 1st on up. Each day, a cleric can prepare one of the spells from her two domains in that slot. If a domain spell is not on the cleric spell list, a cleric can prepare it only in her domain spell slot. Domain spells cannot be used to cast spells spontaneously.

In addition, a cleric gains the listed powers from both of her domains, if she is of a high enough level. Unless otherwise noted, using a domain power is a standard action. Cleric domains are listed at the end of this class entry.

Orisons: Clerics can prepare a number of orisons, or 0-level spells, each day, as noted on Table 3–5 under "Spells per Day." These spells are cast like any other spell, but they are not expended when cast and may be used again.

Spontaneous Casting: A good cleric (or a neutral cleric of a good deity) can channel stored spell energy into healing spells that she did not prepare ahead of time. The cleric can "lose" any prepared spell that is not an orison or domain spell in order to cast any cure spell of the same spell level or lower (a cure spell is any spell with "cure" in its name).

An evil cleric (or a neutral cleric who worships an evil deity) can't convert prepared spells to cure spells but can convert them to inflict spells (an inflict spell is one with "inflict" in its name).

A cleric who is neither good nor evil and whose deity is neither good nor evil can convert spells to either cure spells or inflict spells (player's choice). Once the player makes this choice, it cannot be reversed. This choice also determines whether the cleric channels positive or negative energy (see Channel Energy).

Chaotic, Evil, Good, and Lawful Spells: A cleric can't cast spells of an alignment opposed to her own or her deity's (if she has one). Spells associated with particular alignments are indicated by the chaotic, evil, good, and lawful descriptors in their spell descriptions.

Bonus Languages: A cleric's bonus language options include Celestial, Abyssal, and Infernal (the languages of good, chaotic evil, and lawful evil outsiders, respectively). These choices are in addition to the bonus languages available to the character because of her race.

Ex-Clerics

A cleric who grossly violates the code of conduct required by her god loses all spells and class features, except for armor and shield proficiencies and proficiency with simple weapons. She cannot thereafter gain levels as a cleric of that god until she atones for her deeds (see the *atonement* spell description).

Domains

Clerics may select any two of the domains granted by their deity. Clerics without a deity may select any two domains (choice are subject to GM approval).

Air Domain

Deities: Gozreh, Shelyn.

Granted Powers: You can manipulate lightning, mist, and wind, traffic with air creatures, and are resistant to electricity damage.

Lightning Arc (Sp): As a standard action, you can unleash an arc of electricity targeting any foe within 30 feet as a ranged touch attack. This arc of electricity deals 1d6 points of electricity damage + 1 point for every two cleric levels you possess. You can use this ability a number of times per day equal to 3 + your Wisdom modifier.

Electricity Resistance (Ex): At 6th level, you gain resist electricity 10. This resistance increases to 20 at 12th level. At 20th level, you gain immunity to electricity.

Domain Spells: 1st—*obscuring mist,* 2nd—*wind wall,* 3rd—*gaseous form,* 4th—*air walk,* 5th—*control winds,* 6th—*chain lightning,* 7th—*elemental body IV* (air only), 8th—*whirlwind,* 9th—*elemental swarm* (air spell only).

Animal Domain

Deities: Erastil, Gozreh.

Granted Powers: You can speak with and befriend animals with ease. In addition, you treat Knowledge (nature) as a class skill.

Speak with Animals (Sp): You can *speak with animals,* as per the spell, for a number of rounds per day equal to 3 + your cleric level.

Animal Companion (Ex): At 4th level, you gain the service of an animal companion. Your effective druid level for this animal companion is equal to your cleric level – 3. (Druids who take this ability through their nature bond class feature use their druid level – 3 to determine the abilities of their animal companions).

Domain Spells: 1st—*calm animals,* 2nd—*hold animal,* 3rd—*dominate animal,* 4th—*summon nature's ally IV* (animals only), 5th—*beast shape III* (animals only), 6th—*antilife shell,* 7th—*animal shapes,* 8th—*summon nature's ally VIII* (animals only), 9th—*shapechange.*

Artifice Domain

Deity: Torag.

Granted Powers: You can repair damage to objects, animate objects with life, and create objects from nothing.

Artificer's Touch (Sp): You can cast *mending* at will, using your cleric level as the caster level to repair damaged objects. In addition, you can cause damage to objects and construct creatures by striking them with a melee touch attack. Objects and constructs take 1d6 points of damage +1 for every two cleric levels you possess. This attack bypasses an amount of damage reduction and hardness equal to your cleric level. You can use this ability a number of times per day equal to 3 + your Wisdom modifier.

Dancing Weapons (Su): At 8th level, you can give a weapon touched the *dancing* special weapon quality for 4 rounds. You can use this ability once per day at 8th level, and an additional time per day for every four levels beyond 8th.

Domain Spells: 1st—*animate rope*, 2nd—*wood shape*, 3rd—*stone shape*, 4th—*minor creation*, 5th—*fabricate*, 6th—*major creation*, 7th—*wall of iron*, 8th—*statue*, 9th—*prismatic sphere*.

Chaos Domain

Deities: Calistria, Cayden Cailean, Desna, Gorum, Lamashtu, Rovagug.

Granted Powers: Your touch infuses life and weapons with chaos, and you revel in all things anarchic.

Touch of Chaos (Sp): You can imbue a target with chaos as a melee touch attack. For the next round, anytime the target rolls a d20, he must roll twice and take the less favorable result. You can use this ability a number of times per day equal to 3 + your Wisdom modifier.

Chaos Blade (Su): At 8th level, you can give a weapon touched the *anarchic* special weapon quality for a number of rounds equal to 1/2 your cleric level. You can use this ability once per day at 8th level, and an additional time per day for every four levels beyond 8th.

Domain Spells: 1st—*protection from law*, 2nd—*align weapon* (chaos only), 3rd—*magic circle against law*, 4th—*chaos hammer*, 5th—*dispel law*, 6th—*animate objects*, 7th—*word of chaos*, 8th—*cloak of chaos*, 9th—*summon monster IX* (chaos spell only).

Charm Domain

Deities: Calistria, Cayden Cailean, Norgorber, Shelyn.

Granted Powers: You can baffle and befuddle foes with a touch or a smile, and your beauty and grace are divine.

Dazing Touch (Sp): You can cause a living creature to become dazed for 1 round as a melee touch attack. Creatures with more Hit Dice than your cleric level are unaffected. You can use this ability a number of times per day equal to 3 + your Wisdom modifier.

Charming Smile (Sp): At 8th level, you can cast *charm person* as a swift action, with a DC of 10 + 1/2 your cleric level + your Wisdom modifier. You can only have one creature charmed in this way at a time. The total number of rounds of this effect per day is equal to your cleric level. The rounds do not need to be consecutive, and you can dismiss the charm at any time as a free action. Each attempt to use this ability consumes 1 round of its duration, whether or not the creature succeeds on its save to resist the effect.

Domain Spells: 1st—*charm person*, 2nd—*calm emotions*, 3rd—*suggestion*, 4th—*heroism*, 5th—*charm monster*, 6th—*geas/quest*, 7th—*insanity*, 8th—*demand*, 9th—*dominate monster*.

Community Domain

Deity: Erastil.

Granted Powers: Your touch can heal wounds, and your presence instills unity and strengthens emotional bonds.

Calming Touch (Sp): You can touch a creature as a standard action to heal it of 1d6 points of nonlethal damage + 1 point per cleric level. This touch also removes the fatigued, shaken, and sickened conditions (but has no effect on more severe conditions). You can use this ability a number of times per day equal to 3 + your Wisdom modifier.

Unity (Su): At 8th level, whenever a spell or effect targets you and one or more allies within 30 feet, you can use this ability to allow your allies to use your saving throw against the effect in place of their own. Each ally must decide individually before the rolls are made. Using this ability is an immediate action. You can use this ability once per day at 8th level, and one additional time per day for every four cleric levels beyond 8th.

Domain Spells: 1st—*bless*, 2nd—*shield other*, 3rd—*prayer*, 4th—*imbue with spell ability*, 5th—*telepathic bond*, 6th—*heroes' feast*, 7th—*refuge*, 8th—*mass cure critical wounds*, 9th—*miracle*.

Darkness Domain

Deity: Zon-Kuthon.

Granted Power: You manipulate shadows and darkness. In addition, you receive Blind-Fight as a bonus feat.

Touch of Darkness (Sp): As a melee touch attack, you can cause a creature's vision to be fraught with shadows and darkness. The creature touched treats all other creatures as if they had concealment, suffering a 20% miss chance on all attack rolls. This effect lasts for a number of rounds equal to 1/2 your cleric level (minimum 1). You can use this ability a number of times per day equal to 3 + your Wisdom modifier.

Eyes of Darkness (Su): At 8th level, your vision is not impaired by lighting conditions, even in absolute darkness and magic darkness. You can use this ability for a number of rounds per day equal to 1/2 your cleric level. These rounds do not need to be consecutive.

Domain Spells: 1st—*obscuring mist*, 2nd—*blindness/deafness* (only to cause blindness), 3rd—*deeper darkness*, 4th—*shadow conjuration*, 5th—*summon monster V* (summons 1d3 shadows), 6th—*shadow walk*, 7th—*power word blind*, 8th—*greater shadow evocation*, 9th—*shades*.

Death Domain

Deities: Norgorber, Pharasma, Urgathoa, Zon-Kuthon.

Granted Powers: You can cause the living to bleed at a touch, and find comfort in the presence of the dead.

Bleeding Touch (Sp): As a melee touch attack, you can cause a living creature to take 1d6 points of damage per round. This effect persists for a number of rounds equal to 1/2 your cleric level (minimum 1) or until stopped with a DC 15 Heal check or any spell or effect that heals damage.

TABLE 3-6: DEITIES OF THE PATHFINDER CHRONICLES

Deity	AL	Portfolios	Domains	Favored Weapon
Erastil	LG	God of farming, hunting, trade, family	Animal, Community, Good, Law, Plant	longbow
Iomedae	LG	Goddess of valor, rulership, justice, honor	Glory, Good, Law, Sun, War	longsword
Torag	LG	God of the forge, protection, strategy	Artifice, Earth, Good, Law, Protection	warhammer
Sarenrae	NG	Goddess of the sun, redemption, honesty, healing	Fire, Glory, Good, Healing, Sun	scimitar
Shelyn	NG	Goddess of beauty, art, love, music	Air, Charm, Good, Luck, Protection	glaive
Desna	CG	Goddess of dreams, stars, travelers, luck	Chaos, Good, Liberation, Luck, Travel	starknife
Cayden Cailean	CG	God of freedom, ale, wine, bravery	Chaos, Charm, Good, Strength, Travel	rapier
Abadar	LN	God of cities, wealth, merchants, law	Earth, Law, Nobility, Protection, Travel	light crossbow
Irori	LN	God of history, knowledge, self-perfection	Healing, Knowledge, Law, Rune, Strength	unarmed strike
Gozreh	N	Deity of nature, weather, the sea	Air, Animal, Plant, Water, Weather	trident
Pharasma	N	Goddess of fate, death, prophecy, birth	Death, Healing, Knowledge, Repose, Water	dagger
Nethys	N	God of magic	Destruction, Knowledge, Magic, Protection, Rune	quarterstaff
Gorum	CN	God of strength, battle, weapons	Chaos, Destruction, Glory, Strength, War	greatsword
Calistria	CN	Goddess of trickery, lust, revenge	Chaos, Charm, Knowledge, Luck, Trickery	whip
Asmodeus	LE	God of tyranny, slavery, pride, contracts	Evil, Fire, Law, Magic, Trickery	mace
Zon-Kuthon	LE	God of envy, pain, darkness, loss	Darkness, Death, Destruction, Evil, Law	spiked chain
Urgathoa	NE	Goddess of gluttony, disease, undeath	Death, Evil, Magic, Strength, War	scythe
Norgorber	NE	God of greed, secrets, poison, murder	Charm, Death, Evil, Knowledge, Trickery	short sword
Lamashtu	CE	Goddess of madness, monsters, nightmares	Chaos, Evil, Madness, Strength, Trickery	falchion
Rovagug	CE	God of wrath, disaster, destruction	Chaos, Destruction, Evil, War, Weather	greataxe

You can use this ability a number of times per day equal to 3 + your Wisdom modifier.

Death's Embrace (Ex): At 8th level, you heal damage instead of taking damage from channeled negative energy. If the channeled negative energy targets undead, you heal hit points just like undead in the area.

Domain Spells: 1st—*cause fear,* 2nd—*death knell,* 3rd—*animate dead,* 4th—*death ward,* 5th—*slay living,* 6th—*create undead,* 7th—*destruction,* 8th—*create greater undead,* 9th—*wail of the banshee.*

Destruction Domain
Deities: Gorum, Nethys, Rovagug, Zon-Kuthon.

Granted Powers: You revel in ruin and devastation, and can deliver particularly destructive attacks.

Destructive Smite (Su): You gain the destructive smite power: the supernatural ability to make a single melee attack with a morale bonus on damage rolls equal to 1/2 your cleric level (minimum 1). You must declare the destructive smite before making the attack. You can use this ability a number of times per day equal to 3 + your Wisdom modifier.

Destructive Aura (Su): At 8th level, you can emit a 30-foot aura of destruction for a number of rounds per day equal to your cleric level. All attacks made against creatures in this aura (including you) gain a morale bonus on damage equal to 1/2 your cleric level and all critical threats are automatically confirmed. These rounds do not need to be consecutive.

Domain Spells: 1st—*true strike,* 2nd—*shatter,* 3rd—*rage,* 4th—*inflict critical wounds,* 5th—*shout,* 6th—*harm,* 7th—*disintegrate,* 8th—*earthquake,* 9th—*implosion.*

Earth Domain
Deities: Abadar, Torag.

Granted Powers: You have mastery over earth, metal, and stone, can fire darts of acid, and command earth creatures.

Acid Dart (Sp): As a standard action, you can unleash an acid dart targeting any foe within 30 feet as a ranged touch attack. This acid dart deals 1d6 points of acid damage + 1 point for every two cleric levels you possess. You can use this ability a number of times per day equal to 3 + your Wisdom modifier.

Acid Resistance (Ex): At 6th level, you gain resist acid 10. This resistance increases to 20 at 12th level. At 20th level, you gain immunity to acid.

Domain Spells: 1st—*magic stone,* 2nd—*soften earth and stone,* 3rd—*stone shape,* 4th—*spike stones,* 5th—*wall of stone,* 6th—*stoneskin,* 7th—*elemental body IV* (earth only), 8th—*earthquake,* 9th—*elemental swarm* (earth spell only).

Evil Domain
Deities: Asmodeus, Lamashtu, Norgorber, Rovagug, Urgathoa, Zon-Kuthon.

Granted Powers: You are sinister and cruel, and have wholly pledged your soul to the cause of evil.

Touch of Evil (Sp): You can cause a creature to become sickened as a melee touch attack. Creatures sickened by your touch count as good for the purposes of spells with the evil descriptor. This ability lasts for a number of rounds equal to 1/2 your cleric level (minimum 1). You can use this ability a number of times per day equal to 3 + your Wisdom modifier.

Scythe of Evil (Su): At 8th level, you can give a weapon touched the *unholy* special weapon quality for a number of rounds equal to 1/2 your cleric level. You can use this ability once per day at 8th level, and an additional time per day for every four levels beyond 8th.

Domain Spells: 1st—*protection from good*, 2nd—*align weapon* (evil only), 3rd—*magic circle against good*, 4th—*unholy blight*, 5th—*dispel good*, 6th—*create undead*, 7th—*blasphemy*, 8th—*unholy aura*, 9th—*summon monster IX* (evil spell only).

Fire Domain

Deity: Asmodeus, Sarenrae.

Granted Powers: You can call forth fire, command creatures of the inferno, and your flesh does not burn.

Fire Bolt (Sp): As a standard action, you can unleash a scorching bolt of divine fire from your outstretched hand. You can target any single foe within 30 feet as a ranged touch attack with this bolt of fire. If you hit the foe, the fire bolt deals 1d6 points of fire damage + 1 point for every two cleric levels you possess. You can use this ability a number of times per day equal to 3 + your Wisdom modifier.

Fire Resistance (Ex): At 6th level, you gain resist fire 10. This resistance increases to 20 at 12th level. At 20th level, you gain immunity to fire.

Domain Spells: 1st—*burning hands*, 2nd—*produce flame*, 3rd—*fireball*, 4th—*wall of fire*, 5th—*fire shield*, 6th—*fire seeds*, 7th—*elemental body IV* (fire only), 8th—*incendiary cloud*, 9th—*elemental swarm* (fire spell only).

Glory Domain

Deities: Gorum, Iomedae, Sarenrae.

Granted Powers: You are infused with the glory of the divine, and are a true foe of the undead. In addition, when you channel positive energy to harm undead creatures, the save DC to halve the damage is increased by 2.

Touch of Glory (Sp): You can cause your hand to shimmer with divine radiance, allowing you to touch a creature as a standard action and give it a bonus equal to your cleric level on a single Charisma-based skill check or Charisma ability check. This ability lasts for 1 hour or until the creature touched elects to apply the bonus to a roll. You can use this ability to grant the bonus a number of times per day equal to 3 + your Wisdom modifier.

Divine Presence (Su): At 8th level, you can emit a 30-foot aura of divine presence for a number of rounds per day equal to your cleric level. All allies within this aura are treated as if under the effects of a *sanctuary* spell with a DC equal to 10 + 1/2 your cleric level + your Wisdom modifier. These rounds do not need to be consecutive. Activating this ability is a standard action. If an ally leaves the area or makes an attack, the effect ends for that ally. If you make an attack, the effect ends for you and your allies.

Domain Spells: 1st—*shield of faith*, 2nd—*bless weapon*, 3rd—*searing light*, 4th—*holy smite*, 5th—*righteous might*, 6th—*undeath to death*, 7th—*holy sword*, 8th—*holy aura*, 9th—*gate*.

Good Domain

Deities: Cayden Cailean, Desna, Erastil, Iomedae, Sarenrae, Shelyn, Torag.

Granted Powers: You have pledged your life and soul to goodness and purity.

Touch of Good (Sp): You can touch a creature as a standard action, granting a sacred bonus on attack rolls, skill checks, ability checks, and saving throws equal to half your cleric level (minimum 1) for 1 round. You can use this ability a number of times per day equal to 3 + your Wisdom modifier.

Holy Lance (Su): At 8th level, you can give a weapon you touch the *holy* special weapon quality for a number of rounds equal to 1/2 your cleric level. You can use this ability once per day at 8th level, and an additional time per day for every four levels beyond 8th.

Domain Spells: 1st—*protection from evil*, 2nd—*align weapon* (good only), 3rd—*magic circle against evil*, 4th—*holy smite*, 5th—*dispel evil*, 6th—*blade barrier*, 7th—*holy word*, 8th—*holy aura*, 9th—*summon monster IX* (good spell only).

Healing Domain

Deities: Irori, Pharasma, Sarenrae.

Granted Powers: Your touch staves off pain and death, and your healing magic is particularly vital and potent.

Rebuke Death (Sp): You can touch a living creature as a standard action, healing it for 1d4 points of damage plus 1 for every two cleric levels you possess. You can only use this ability on a creature that is below 0 hit points. You can use this ability a number of times per day equal to 3 + your Wisdom modifier.

Healer's Blessing (Su): At 6th level, all of your cure spells are treated as if they were empowered, increasing the amount of damage healed by half (+50%). This does not apply to damage dealt to undead with a cure spell. This does not stack with the Empower Spell metamagic feat.

Domain Spells: 1st—*cure light wounds*, 2nd—*cure moderate wounds*, 3rd—*cure serious wounds*, 4th—*cure critical wounds*, 5th—*breath of life*, 6th—*heal*, 7th—*regenerate*, 8th—*mass cure critical wounds*, 9th—*mass heal*.

Knowledge Domain

Deities: Calistria, Irori, Nethys, Norgorber, Pharasma.

Granted Powers: You are a scholar and a sage of legends. In addition, you treat all Knowledge skills as class skills.

Lore Keeper (Sp): You can touch a creature to learn about its abilities and weaknesses. With a successful touch attack, you gain information as if you made the appropriate Knowledge skill check with a result equal to 15 + your cleric level + your Wisdom modifier.

Remote Viewing (Sp): Starting at 6th level, you can use *clairvoyance/clairaudience* as a spell-like ability using your cleric level as the caster level. You can use this ability for a number of rounds per day equal to your cleric level. These rounds do not need to be consecutive.

Domain Spells: 1st—*comprehend languages*, 2nd—*detect thoughts*, 3rd—*speak with dead*, 4th—*divination*, 5th—*true seeing*, 6th—*find the path*, 7th—*legend lore*, 8th—*discern location*, 9th—*foresight*.

Law Domain

Deities: Abadar, Asmodeus, Erastil, Iomedae, Irori, Torag, Zon-Kuthon.

Granted Powers: You follow a strict and ordered code of laws, and in so doing, achieve enlightenment.

Touch of Law (Sp): You can touch a willing creature as a standard action, infusing it with the power of divine order and allowing it to treat all attack rolls, skill checks, ability checks, and saving throws for 1 round as if the natural d20 roll resulted in an 11. You can use this ability a number of times per day equal to 3 + your Wisdom modifier.

Staff of Order (Su): At 8th level, you can give a weapon touched the *axiomatic* special weapon quality for a number of rounds equal to 1/2 your cleric level. You can use this ability once per day at 8th level, and an additional time per day for every four levels beyond 8th.

Domain Spells: 1st—*protection from chaos*, 2nd—*align weapon* (law only), 3rd—*magic circle against chaos*, 4th—*order's wrath*, 5th—*dispel chaos*, 6th—*hold monster*, 7th—*dictum*, 8th—*shield of law*, 9th—*summon monster IX* (law spell only).

Liberation Domain

Deity: Desna.

Granted Powers: You are a spirit of freedom and a staunch foe against all who would enslave and oppress.

Liberation (Su): You have the ability to ignore impediments to your mobility. For a number of rounds per day equal to your cleric level, you can move normally regardless of magical effects that impede movement, as if you were affected by *freedom of movement*. This effect occurs automatically as soon as it applies. These rounds do not need to be consecutive.

Freedom's Call (Su): At 8th level, you can emit a 30-foot aura of freedom for a number of rounds per day equal to

your cleric level. Allies within this aura are not affected by the confused, grappled, frightened, panicked, paralyzed, pinned, or shaken conditions. This aura only suppresses these effects, and they return once a creature leaves the aura or when the aura ends, if applicable. These rounds do not need to be consecutive.

Domain Spells: 1st—*remove fear*, 2nd—*remove paralysis*, 3rd—*remove curse*, 4th—*freedom of movement*, 5th—*break enchantment*, 6th—*greater dispel magic*, 7th—*refuge*, 8th—*mind blank*, 9th—*freedom*.

Luck Domain

Deities: Calistria, Desna, Shelyn.

Granted Powers: You are infused with luck, and your mere presence can spread good fortune.

Bit of Luck (Sp): You can touch a willing creature as a standard action, giving it a bit of luck. For the next round, any time the target rolls a d20, he may roll twice and take the more favorable result. You can use this ability a number of times per day equal to 3 + your Wisdom modifier.

Good Fortune (Ex): At 6th level, as an immediate action, you can reroll any one d20 roll you have just made before the results of the roll are revealed. You must take the result of the reroll, even if it's worse than the original roll. You can use this ability once per day at 6th level, and one additional time per day for every six cleric levels beyond 6th.

Domain Spells: 1st—*true strike*, 2nd—*aid*, 3rd—*protection from energy*, 4th—*freedom of movement*, 5th—*break enchantment*, 6th—*mislead*, 7th—*spell turning*, 8th—*moment of prescience*, 9th—*miracle*.

Madness Domain

Deity: Lamashtu.

Granted Powers: You embrace the madness that lurks deep in your heart, and can unleash it to drive your foes insane or to sacrifice certain abilities to hone others.

Vision of Madness (Sp): You can give a creature a *vision of madness* as a melee touch attack. Choose one of the following: attack rolls, saving throws, or skill checks. The target receives a bonus to the chosen rolls equal to 1/2 your cleric level (minimum +1) and a penalty to the other two types of rolls equal to 1/2 your cleric level (minimum –1). This effect fades after 3 rounds. You can use this ability a number of times per day equal to 3 + your Wisdom modifier.

Aura of Madness (Su): At 8th level, you can emit a 30-foot aura of madness for a number of rounds per day equal to your cleric level. Enemies within this aura are affected by *confusion* unless they make a Will save with a DC equal to 10 + 1/2 your cleric level + your Wisdom modifier. The *confusion* effect ends immediately when the creature leaves the area or the aura expires. Creatures that succeed on their saving throw are immune to this aura for 24 hours. These rounds do not need to be consecutive.

Domain Spells: 1st—*lesser confusion*, 2nd—*touch of idiocy*, 3rd—*rage*, 4th—*confusion*, 5th—*nightmare*, 6th—*phantasmal killer*, 7th—*insanity*, 8th—*scintillating pattern*, 9th—*weird*.

Magic Domain

Deities: Asmodeus, Nethys, Urgathoa.

Granted Powers: You are a true student of all things mystical, and see divinity in the purity of magic.

Hand of the Acolyte (Su): You can cause your melee weapon to fly from your grasp and strike a foe before instantly returning. As a standard action, you can make a single attack using a melee weapon at a range of 30 feet. This attack is treated as a ranged attack with a thrown weapon, except that you add your Wisdom modifier to the attack roll instead of your Dexterity modifier (damage still relies on Strength). This ability cannot be used to perform a combat maneuver. You can use this ability a number of times per day equal to 3 + your Wisdom modifier.

Dispelling Touch (Sp): At 8th level, you can use a targeted *dispel magic* effect as a melee touch attack. You can use this ability once per day at 8th level and one additional time per day for every four cleric levels beyond 8th.

Domain Spells: 1st—*identify*, 2nd—*magic mouth*, 3rd—*dispel magic*, 4th—*imbue with spell ability*, 5th—*spell resistance*, 6th—*antimagic field*, 7th—*spell turning*, 8th—*protection from spells*, 9th—*mage's disjunction*.

Nobility Domain

Deity: Abadar.

Granted Powers: You are a great leader, an inspiration to all who follow the teachings of your faith.

Inspiring Word (Sp): As a standard action, you can speak an inspiring word to a creature within 30 feet. That creature receives a +2 morale bonus on attack rolls, skill checks, ability checks, and saving throws for a number of rounds equal to 1/2 your cleric level (minimum 1). You can use this power a number of times per day equal to 3 + your Wisdom modifier.

Leadership (Ex): At 8th level, you receive Leadership as a bonus feat. In addition, you gain a +2 bonus on your leadership score as long as you uphold the tenets of your deity (or divine concept if you do not venerate a deity).

Domain Spells: 1st—*divine favor*, 2nd—*enthrall*, 3rd—*magic vestment*, 4th—*discern lies*, 5th—*greater command*, 6th—*geas/quest*, 7th—*repulsion*, 8th—*demand*, 9th—*storm of vengeance*.

Plant Domain

Deities: Erastil, Gozreh.

Granted Powers: You find solace in the green, can grow defensive thorns, and can communicate with plants.

Wooden Fist (Su): As a free action, your hands can become as hard as wood, covered in tiny thorns. While you have wooden fists, your unarmed strikes do not provoke attacks of opportunity, deal lethal damage, and gain a bonus on

damage rolls equal to 1/2 your cleric level (minimum +1). You can use this ability for a number of rounds per day equal to 3 + your Wisdom modifier. These rounds do not need to be consecutive.

Bramble Armor (Su): At 6th level, you can cause a host of wooden thorns to burst from your skin as a free action. While bramble armor is in effect, any foe striking you with an unarmed strike or a melee weapon without reach takes 1d6 points of piercing damage + 1 point per two cleric levels you possess. You can use this ability for a number of rounds per day equal to your cleric level. These rounds do not need to be consecutive.

Domain Spells: 1st—*entangle*, 2nd—*barkskin*, 3rd—*plant growth*, 4th—*command plants*, 5th—*wall of thorns*, 6th—*repel wood*, 7th—*animate plants*, 8th—*control plants*, 9th—*shambler*.

Protection Domain

Deities: Abadar, Nethys, Shelyn, Torag.

Granted Powers: Your faith is your greatest source of protection, and you can use that faith to defend others. In addition, you receive a +1 resistance bonus on saving throws. This bonus increases by 1 for every 5 levels you possess.

Resistant Touch (Sp): As a standard action, you can touch an ally to grant him your resistance bonus for 1 minute. When you use this ability, you lose your resistance bonus granted by the Protection domain for 1 minute. You can use this ability a number of times per day equal to 3 + your Wisdom modifier.

Aura of Protection (Su): At 8th level, you can emit a 30-foot aura of protection for a number of rounds per day equal to your cleric level. You and your allies within this aura gain a +1 deflection bonus to AC and resistance 5 against all elements (acid, cold, electricity, fire, and sonic). The deflection bonus increases by +1 for every four cleric levels you possess beyond 8th. At 14th level, the resistance against all elements increases to 10. These rounds do not need to be consecutive.

Domain Spells: 1st—*sanctuary*, 2nd—*shield other*, 3rd—*protection from energy*, 4th—*spell immunity*, 5th—*spell resistance*, 6th—*antimagic field*, 7th—*repulsion*, 8th—*mind blank*, 9th—*prismatic sphere*.

Repose Domain

Deity: Pharasma.

Granted Powers: You see death not as something to be feared, but as a final rest and reward for a life well spent. The taint of undeath is a mockery of what you hold dear.

Gentle Rest (Sp): Your touch can fill a creature with lethargy, causing a living creature to become staggered for 1 round as a melee touch attack. If you touch a staggered living creature, that creature falls asleep for 1 round instead. Undead creatures touched are staggered for a number of rounds equal to your Wisdom modifier.

You can use this ability a number of times per day equal to 3 + your Wisdom modifier.

Ward Against Death (Su): At 8th level, you can emit a 30-foot aura that wards against death for a number of rounds per day equal to your cleric level. Living creatures in this area are immune to all death effects, energy drain, and effects that cause negative levels. This ward does not remove negative levels that a creature has already gained, but the negative levels have no effect while the creature is inside the warded area. These rounds do not need to be consecutive.

Domain Spells: 1st—*deathwatch*, 2nd—*gentle repose*, 3rd—*speak with dead*, 4th—*death ward*, 5th—*slay living*, 6th—*undeath to death*, 7th—*destruction*, 8th—*waves of exhaustion*, 9th—*wail of the banshee*.

Rune Domain

Deities: Irori, Nethys.

Granted Powers: In strange and eldritch runes you find potent magic. You gain Scribe Scroll as a bonus feat.

Blast Rune (Sp): As a standard action, you can create a blast rune in any adjacent square. Any creature entering this square takes 1d6 points of damage + 1 point for every two cleric levels you possess. This rune deals either acid, cold, electricity, or fire damage, decided when you create the rune. The rune is invisible and lasts a number of rounds equal to your cleric level or until discharged. You cannot create a blast rune in a square occupied by another creature. This rune counts as a 1st-level spell for the purposes of dispelling. It can be discovered with a DC 26 Perception skill check and disarmed with a DC 26 Disable Device skill check. You can use this ability a number of times per day equal to 3 + your Wisdom modifier.

Spell Rune (Sp): At 8th level, you can attach another spell that you cast to one of your blast runes, causing that spell to affect the creature that triggers the rune, in addition to the damage. This spell must be of at least one level lower than the highest-level cleric spell you can cast and it must target one or more creatures. Regardless of the number of targets the spell can normally affect, it only affects the creature that triggers the rune.

Domain Spells: 1st—*erase*, 2nd—*secret page*, 3rd—*glyph of warding*, 4th—*explosive runes*, 5th—*lesser planar binding*, 6th—*greater glyph of warding*, 7th—*instant summons*, 8th—*symbol of death*, 9th—*teleportation circle*.

Strength Domain

Deities: Cayden Cailean, Gorum, Irori, Lamashtu, Urgathoa.

Granted Powers: In strength and brawn there is truth—your faith gives you incredible might and power.

Strength Surge (Sp): As a standard action, you can touch a creature to give it great strength. For 1 round, the target gains an enhancement bonus equal to 1/2 your cleric level (minimum +1) to melee attacks, combat maneuver checks that rely on Strength, Strength-based skills, and Strength checks. You can use this ability a number of times per day equal to 3 + your Wisdom modifier.

Might of the Gods (Su): At 8th level, you can add your cleric level as an enhancement bonus to your Strength score for a number of rounds per day equal to your cleric level. This bonus only applies on Strength checks and Strength-based skill checks. These rounds do not need to be consecutive.

Domain Spells: 1st—*enlarge person*, 2nd—*bull's strength*, 3rd—*magic vestment*, 4th—*spell immunity*, 5th—*righteous might*, 6th—*stoneskin*, 7th—*grasping hand*, 8th—*clenched fist*, 9th—*crushing hand*.

Sun Domain

Deities: Iomedae, Sarenrae.

Granted Powers: You see truth in the pure and burning light of the sun, and can call upon its blessing or wrath to work great deeds.

Sun's Blessing (Su): Whenever you channel positive energy to harm undead creatures, add your cleric level to the damage dealt. Undead do not add their channel resistance to their saves when you channel positive energy.

Nimbus of Light (Su): At 8th level, you can emit a 30-foot nimbus of light for a number of rounds per day equal to your cleric level. This acts as a *daylight* spell. In addition, undead within this radius take an amount of damage equal to your cleric level each round that they remain inside the nimbus. Spells and spell-like abilities with the darkness descriptor are automatically dispelled if brought inside this nimbus. These rounds do not need to be consecutive.

Domain Spells: 1st—*endure elements*, 2nd—*heat metal*, 3rd—*searing light*, 4th—*fire shield*, 5th—*flame strike*, 6th—*fire seeds*, 7th—*sunbeam*, 8th—*sunburst*, 9th—*prismatic sphere*.

Travel Domain

Deities: Abadar, Cayden Cailean, Desna.

Granted Powers: You are an explorer and find enlightenment in the simple joy of travel, be it by foot or conveyance or magic. Increase your base speed by 10 feet.

Agile Feet (Su): As a free action, you can gain increased mobility for 1 round. For the next round, you ignore all difficult terrain and do not take any penalties for moving through it. You can use this ability a number of times per day equal to 3 + your Wisdom modifier.

Dimensional Hop (Sp): At 8th level, you can teleport up to 10 feet per cleric level per day as a move action. This teleportation must be used in 5-foot increments and such movement does not provoke attacks of opportunity. You must have line of sight to your destination to use this ability. You can bring other willing creatures with you, but you must expend an equal amount of distance for each creature brought.

Domain Spells: 1st—*longstrider*, 2nd—*locate object*, 3rd—*fly*, 4th—*dimension door*, 5th—*teleport*, 6th—*find the path*, 7th—*greater teleport*, 8th—*phase door*, 9th—*astral projection*.

Trickery Domain

Deities: Asmodeus, Calistria, Lamashtu, Norgorber.

Granted Powers: You are a master of illusions and deceptions. Bluff, Disguise, and Stealth are class skills.

Copycat (Sp): You can create an illusory double of yourself as a move action. This double functions as a single *mirror image* and lasts for a number of rounds equal to your cleric level, or until the illusory duplicate is dispelled or destroyed. You can have no more than one copycat at a time. This ability does not stack with the *mirror image* spell. You can use this ability a number of times per day equal to 3 + your Wisdom modifier.

Master's Illusion (Sp): At 8th level, you can create an illusion that hides the appearance of yourself and any number of allies within 30 feet for 1 round per cleric level. The save DC to disbelieve this effect is equal to 10 + 1/2 your cleric level + your Wisdom modifier. This ability otherwise functions like the spell *veil*. The rounds do not need to be consecutive.

Domain Spells: 1st—*disguise self*, 2nd—*invisibility*, 3rd—*nondetection*, 4th—*confusion*, 5th—*false vision*, 6th—*mislead*, 7th—*screen*, 8th—*mass invisibility*, 9th—*time stop*.

War Domain

Deities: Gorum, Iomedae, Rovagug, Urgathoa.

Granted Powers: You are a crusader for your god, always ready and willing to fight to defend your faith.

Battle Rage (Sp): You can touch a creature as a standard action to give it a bonus on melee damage rolls equal to 1/2 your cleric level (minimum +1) for 1 round. You can do so a number of times per day equal to 3 + your Wisdom modifier.

Weapon Master (Su): At 8th level, as a swift action, you gain the use of one combat feat for a number of rounds per day equal to your cleric level. These rounds do not need to be consecutive and you can change the feat chosen each time you use this ability. You must meet the prerequisites to use this feat.

Domain Spells: 1st—*magic weapon*, 2nd—*spiritual weapon*, 3rd—*magic vestment*, 4th—*divine power*, 5th—*flame strike*, 6th—*blade barrier*, 7th—*power word blind*, 8th—*power word stun*, 9th—*power word kill*.

Water Domain

Deities: Gozreh, Pharasma.

Granted Powers: You can manipulate water and mist and ice, conjure creatures of water, and resist cold.

Icicle (Sp): As a standard action, you can fire an icicle from your finger, targeting any foe within 30 feet as a ranged touch attack. The icicle deals 1d6 points of cold damage + 1 point for every two cleric levels you possess. You can use this ability a number of times per day equal to 3 + your Wisdom modifier.

Cold Resistance (Ex): At 6th level, you gain resist cold 10. This resistance increases to 20 at 12th level. At 20th level, you gain immunity to cold.

Domain Spells: 1st—*obscuring mist*, 2nd—*fog cloud*, 3rd—*water breathing*, 4th—*control water*, 5th—*ice storm*, 6th—*cone of cold*, 7th—*elemental body IV* (water only), 8th—*horrid wilting*, 9th—*elemental swarm* (water spell only).

Weather Domain

Deities: Gozreh, Rovagug.

Granted Powers: With power over storm and sky, you can call down the wrath of the gods upon the world below.

Storm Burst (Sp): As a standard action, you can create a storm burst targeting any foe within 30 feet as a ranged touch attack. The storm burst deals 1d6 points of nonlethal damage + 1 point for every two cleric levels you possess. In addition, the target is buffeted by winds and rain, causing it to take a –2 penalty on attack rolls for 1 round. You can use this ability a number of times per day equal to 3 + your Wisdom modifier.

Lightning Lord (Sp): At 8th level, you can call down a number of bolts of lightning per day equal to your cleric level. You can call down as many bolts as you want with a single standard action, but no creature can be the target of more than one bolt and no two targets can be more than 30 feet apart. This ability otherwise functions as *call lightning*.

Domain Spells: 1st—*obscuring mist*, 2nd—*fog cloud*, 3rd—*call lightning*, 4th—*sleet storm*, 5th—*ice storm*, 6th—*control winds*, 7th—*control weather*, 8th—*whirlwind*, 9th—*storm of vengeance*.

DRUID

Within the purity of the elements and the order of the wilds lingers a power beyond the marvels of civilization. Furtive yet undeniable, these primal magics are guarded over by servants of philosophical balance known as druids. Allies to beasts and manipulators of nature, these often misunderstood protectors of the wild strive to shield their lands from all who would threaten them and prove the might of the wilds to those who lock themselves behind city walls. Rewarded for their devotion with incredible powers, druids gain unparalleled shape-shifting abilities, the companionship of mighty beasts, and the power to call upon nature's wrath. The mightiest temper powers akin to storms, earthquakes, and volcanoes with primeval wisdom long abandoned and forgotten by civilization.

Role: While some druids might keep to the fringe of battle, allowing companions and summoned creatures to fight while they confound foes with the powers of nature, others transform into deadly beasts and savagely wade into combat. Druids worship personifications of elemental forces, natural powers, or nature itself. Typically this means devotion to a nature deity, though druids are just as likely to revere vague spirits, animalistic demigods, or even specific awe-inspiring natural wonders.

Alignment: Any neutral.

Hit Die: d8.

Class Skills

The druid's class skills are Climb (Str), Craft (Int), Fly (Dex), Handle Animal (Cha), Heal (Wis), Knowledge (geography) (Int), Knowledge (nature) (Int), Perception (Wis), Profession (Wis), Ride (Dex), Spellcraft (Int), Survival (Wis), and Swim (Str).

Skill Ranks per Level: 4 + Int modifier.

Class Features

All of the following are class features of the druid.

Weapon and Armor Proficiency: Druids are proficient with the following weapons: club, dagger, dart, quarterstaff, scimitar, scythe, sickle, shortspear, sling, and spear. They are also proficient with all natural attacks (claw, bite, and so forth) of any form they assume with wild shape (see below).

Druids are proficient with light and medium armor but are prohibited from wearing metal armor; thus, they may wear only padded, leather, or hide armor. A druid may also wear wooden armor that has been altered by the *ironwood* spell so that it functions as though it were steel. Druids are proficient with shields (except tower shields) but must use only those crafted from wood.

A druid who wears prohibited armor or uses a prohibited shield is unable to cast druid spells or use any of her supernatural or spell-like class abilities while doing so and for 24 hours thereafter.

Spells: A druid casts divine spells which are drawn from the druid spell list presented in Chapter 10. Her alignment may restrict her from casting certain spells opposed to her moral or ethical beliefs; see Chaotic, Evil, Good, and Lawful Spells. A druid must choose and prepare her spells in advance.

To prepare or cast a spell, the druid must have a Wisdom score equal to at least 10 + the spell level. The Difficulty Class for a saving throw against a druid's spell is 10 + the spell level + the druid's Wisdom modifier.

Like other spellcasters, a druid can cast only a certain number of spells of each spell level per day. Her base daily spell allotment is given on Table 3–7. In addition, she receives bonus spells per day if she has a high Wisdom score (see Table 1–3).

A druid must spend 1 hour each day in a trance-like meditation on the mysteries of nature to regain her daily allotment of spells. A druid may prepare and cast any spell on the druid spell list, provided that she can cast spells of that level, but she must choose which spells to prepare during her daily meditation.

Spontaneous Casting: A druid can channel stored spell energy into summoning spells that she hasn't prepared ahead of time. She can "lose" a prepared spell in order to cast any *summon nature's ally* spell of the same level or lower.

Chaotic, Evil, Good, and Lawful Spells: A druid can't cast spells of an alignment opposed to her own or her deity's (if she has one). Spells associated with particular alignments are indicated by the chaos, evil, good, and law descriptors in their spell descriptions.

Orisons: Druids can prepare a number of orisons, or 0-level spells, each day, as noted on Table 3–7 under "Spells per Day." These spells are cast like any other spell, but they are not expended when cast and may be used again.

TABLE 3-7: DRUID

Level	Base Attack Bonus	Fort Save	Ref Save	Will Save	Special	0	1st	2nd	3rd	4th	5th	6th	7th	8th	9th
											Spells per Day				
1st	+0	+2	+0	+2	Nature bond, nature sense, orisons, wild empathy	3	1	—	—	—	—	—	—	—	—
2nd	+1	+3	+0	+3	Woodland stride	4	2	—	—	—	—	—	—	—	—
3rd	+2	+3	+1	+3	Trackless step	4	2	1	—	—	—	—	—	—	—
4th	+3	+4	+1	+4	Resist nature's lure, Wild shape (1/day)	4	3	2	—	—	—	—	—	—	—
5th	+3	+4	+1	+4		4	3	2	1	—	—	—	—	—	—
6th	+4	+5	+2	+5	Wild shape (2/day)	4	3	3	2	—	—	—	—	—	—
7th	+5	+5	+2	+5		4	4	3	2	1	—	—	—	—	—
8th	+6/+1	+6	+2	+6	Wild shape (3/day)	4	4	3	3	2	—	—	—	—	—
9th	+6/+1	+6	+3	+6	Venom immunity	4	4	4	3	2	1	—	—	—	—
10th	+7/+2	+7	+3	+7	Wild shape (4/day)	4	4	4	3	3	2	—	—	—	—
11th	+8/+3	+7	+3	+7		4	4	4	4	3	2	1	—	—	—
12th	+9/+4	+8	+4	+8	Wild shape (5/day)	4	4	4	4	3	3	2	—	—	—
13th	+9/+4	+8	+4	+8	A thousand faces	4	4	4	4	4	3	2	1	—	—
14th	+10/+5	+9	+4	+9	Wild shape (6/day)	4	4	4	4	4	3	3	2	—	—
15th	+11/+6/+1	+9	+5	+9	Timeless body	4	4	4	4	4	4	3	2	1	—
16th	+12/+7/+2	+10	+5	+10	Wild shape (7/day)	4	4	4	4	4	4	3	3	2	—
17th	+12/+7/+2	+10	+5	+10		4	4	4	4	4	4	4	3	2	1
18th	+13/+8/+3	+11	+6	+11	Wild shape (8/day)	4	4	4	4	4	4	4	3	3	2
19th	+14/+9/+4	+11	+6	+11		4	4	4	4	4	4	4	4	3	3
20th	+15/+10/+5	+12	+6	+12	Wild shape (at will)	4	4	4	4	4	4	4	4	4	4

Bonus Languages: A druid's bonus language options include Sylvan, the language of woodland creatures. This choice is in addition to the bonus languages available to the character because of her race.

A druid also knows Druidic, a secret language known only to druids, which she learns upon becoming a 1st-level druid. Druidic is a free language for a druid; that is, she knows it in addition to her regular allotment of languages and it doesn't take up a language slot. Druids are forbidden to teach this language to nondruids.

Druidic has its own alphabet.

Nature Bond (Ex): At 1st level, a druid forms a bond with nature. This bond can take one of two forms. The first is a close tie to the natural world, granting the druid one of the following cleric domains: Air, Animal, Earth, Fire, Plant, Water, or Weather. When determining the powers and bonus spells granted by this domain, the druid's effective cleric level is equal to her druid level. A druid that selects this option also receives additional domain spell slots, just like a cleric. She must prepare the spell from her domain in this slot and this spell cannot be used to cast a spell spontaneously.

The second option is to form a close bond with an animal companion. A druid may begin play with any of the animals listed in the Animal Companions section

beginning on page 51. This animal is a loyal companion that accompanies the druid on her adventures.

Unlike normal animals of its kind, an animal companion's Hit Dice, abilities, skills, and feats advance as the druid advances in level. If a character receives an animal companion from more than one source, her effective druid levels stack for the purposes of determining the statistics and abilities of the companion. Most animal companions increase in size when their druid reaches 4th or 7th level, depending on the companion. If a druid releases her companion from service, she may gain a new one by performing a ceremony requiring 24 uninterrupted hours of prayer in the environment where the new companion typically lives. This ceremony can also replace an animal companion that has perished.

Nature Sense (Ex): A druid gains a +2 bonus on Knowledge (nature) and Survival checks.

Wild Empathy (Ex): A druid can improve the attitude of an animal. This ability functions just like a Diplomacy check made to improve the attitude of a person (see Chapter 4). The druid rolls 1d20 and adds her druid level and her Charisma modifier to determine the wild empathy check result. The typical domestic animal has a starting attitude of indifferent, while wild animals are usually unfriendly.

To use wild empathy, the druid and the animal must be within 30 feet of one another under normal conditions. Generally, influencing an animal in this way takes 1 minute but, as with influencing people, it might take more or less time.

A druid can also use this ability to influence a magical beast with an Intelligence score of 1 or 2, but she takes a –4 penalty on the check.

Woodland Stride (Ex): Starting at 2nd level, a druid may move through any sort of undergrowth (such as natural thorns, briars, overgrown areas, and similar terrain) at her normal speed and without taking damage or suffering any other impairment. Thorns, briars, and overgrown areas that have been magically manipulated to impede motion, however, still affect her.

Trackless Step (Ex): Starting at 3rd level, a druid leaves no trail in natural surroundings and cannot be tracked. She may choose to leave a trail if so desired.

Resist Nature's Lure (Ex): Starting at 4th level, a druid gains a +4 bonus on saving throws against the spell-like and supernatural abilities of fey. This bonus also applies to spells and effects that utilize or target plants, such as *blight, entangle, spike growth,* and *warp wood.*

Wild Shape (Su): At 4th level, a druid gains the ability to turn herself into any Small or Medium animal and back again once per day. Her options for new forms include all creatures with the animal type. This ability functions like the *beast shape I* spell, except as noted here. The effect lasts for 1 hour per druid level, or until she changes back. Changing form (to animal or back) is a standard action and doesn't provoke an attack of opportunity. The form chosen must be that of an animal with which the druid is familiar.

A druid loses her ability to speak while in animal form because she is limited to the sounds that a normal, untrained animal can make, but she can communicate normally with other animals of the same general grouping as her new form. (The normal sound a wild parrot makes is a squawk, so changing to this form does not permit speech.)

A druid can use this ability an additional time per day at 6th level and every two levels thereafter, for a total of eight times at 18th level. At 20th level, a druid can use wild shape at will. As a druid gains levels, this ability allows the druid to take on the form of larger and smaller animals, elementals, and plants. Each form expends one daily use of this ability, regardless of the form taken.

At 6th level, a druid can also use wild shape to change into a Large or Tiny animal or a Small elemental. When taking the form of an animal, a druid's wild shape now functions as *beast shape II.* When taking the form of an elemental, the druid's wild shape functions as *elemental body I.*

At 8th level, a druid can also use wild shape to change into a Huge or Diminutive animal, a Medium elemental, or a Small or Medium plant creature. When taking the form of animals, a druid's wild shape now functions as *beast shape III.* When taking the form of an elemental, the druid's wild shape now functions as *elemental body II.* When taking the form of a plant creature, the druid's wild shape functions as *plant shape I.*

At 10th level, a druid can also use wild shape to change into a Large elemental or a Large plant creature. When taking the form of an elemental, the druid's wild shape now functions as *elemental body III.* When taking the form of a plant, the druid's wild shape now functions as *plant shape II.*

At 12th level, a druid can also use wild shape to change into a Huge elemental or a Huge plant creature. When taking the form of an elemental, the druid's wild shape now functions as *elemental body IV.* When taking the form of a plant, the druid's wild shape now functions as *plant shape III.*

Venom Immunity (Ex): At 9th level, a druid gains immunity to all poisons.

A Thousand Faces (Su): At 13th level, a druid gains the ability to change her appearance at will, as if using the *alter self* spell, but only while in her normal form.

Timeless Body (Ex): After attaining 15th level, a druid no longer takes ability score penalties for aging and cannot be magically aged. Any penalties she may have already incurred, however, remain in place. Bonuses still accrue, and the druid still dies of old age when her time is up.

Ex-Druids

A druid who ceases to revere nature, changes to a prohibited alignment, or teaches the Druidic language to a nondruid loses all spells and druid abilities (including her animal companion, but not including weapon, armor, and shield proficiencies). She cannot thereafter gain levels as a druid until she atones (see the *atonement* spell description).

Animal Companions

An animal companion's abilities are determined by the druid's level and its animal racial traits. Table 3–8 determines many of the base statistics of the animal companion. They remain creatures of the animal type for purposes of determining which spells can affect them.

Class Level: This is the character's druid level. The druid's class levels stack with levels of any other classes that are entitled to an animal companion for the purpose of determining the companion's statistics.

HD: This is the total number of eight-sided (d8) Hit Dice the animal companion possesses, each of which gains a Constitution modifier, as normal.

BAB: This is the animal companion's base attack bonus. An animal companion's base attack bonus is the same as

TABLE 3-8: ANIMAL COMPANION BASE STATISTICS

Class Level	HD	BAB	Fort	Ref	Will	Skills	Feats	Natural Armor Bonus	Str/Dex Bonus	Bonus Tricks	Special
1st	2	+1	+3	+3	+0	2	1	+0	+0	1	Link, share spells
2nd	3	+2	+3	+3	+1	3	2	+0	+0	1	—
3rd	3	+2	+3	+3	+1	3	2	+2	+1	2	Evasion
4th	4	+3	+4	+4	+1	4	2	+2	+1	2	Ability score increase
5th	5	+3	+4	+4	+1	5	3	+2	+1	2	—
6th	6	+4	+5	+5	+2	6	3	+4	+2	3	Devotion
7th	6	+4	+5	+5	+2	6	3	+4	+2	3	—
8th	7	+5	+5	+5	+2	7	4	+4	+2	3	—
9th	8	+6	+6	+6	+2	8	4	+6	+3	4	Ability score increase, Multiattack
10th	9	+6	+6	+6	+3	9	5	+6	+3	4	—
11th	9	+6	+6	+6	+3	9	5	+6	+3	4	—
12th	10	+7	+7	+7	+3	10	5	+8	+4	5	—
13th	11	+8	+7	+7	+3	11	6	+8	+4	5	—
14th	12	+9	+8	+8	+4	12	6	+8	+4	5	Ability score increase
15th	12	+9	+8	+8	+4	12	6	+10	+5	6	Improved evasion
16th	13	+9	+8	+8	+4	13	7	+10	+5	6	—
17th	14	+10	+9	+9	+4	14	7	+10	+5	6	—
18th	15	+11	+9	+9	+5	15	8	+12	+6	7	—
19th	15	+11	+9	+9	+5	15	8	+12	+6	7	—
20th	16	+12	+10	+10	+5	16	8	+12	+6	7	Ability score increase

that of a druid of a level equal to the animal's HD. Animal companions do not gain additional attacks using their natural weapons for a high base attack bonus.

Fort/Ref/Will: These are the animal companion's base saving throw bonuses. An animal companion has good Fortitude and Reflex saves.

Skills: This lists the animal's total skill ranks. Animal companions can assign skill ranks to any skill listed under Animal Skills. If an animal companion increases its Intelligence to 10 or higher, it gains bonus skill ranks as normal. Animal companions with an Intelligence of 3 or higher can purchase ranks in any skill. An animal companion cannot have more ranks in a skill than it has Hit Dice.

Feats: This is the total number of feats possessed by an animal companion. Animal companions should select their feats from those listed under Animal Feats. Animal companions can select other feats, although they are unable to utilize some feats (such as Martial Weapon Proficiency). Note that animal companions cannot select a feat with a requirement of base attack bonus +1 until they gain their second feat at 3 Hit Dice.

Natural Armor Bonus: The number noted here is an improvement to the animal companion's existing natural armor bonus.

Str/Dex Bonus: Add this modifier to the animal companion's Strength and Dexterity scores.

Bonus Tricks: The value given in this column is the total number of "bonus" tricks that the animal knows in addition to any that the druid might choose to teach it (see the Handle Animal skill for more details on how to teach an animal tricks). These bonus tricks don't require any training time or Handle Animal checks, and they don't count against the normal limit of tricks known by the animal. The druid selects these bonus tricks, and once selected, they can't be changed.

Special: This includes a number of abilities gained by animal companions as they increase in power. Each of these bonuses is described below.

Link (Ex): A druid can handle her animal companion as a free action, or push it as a move action, even if she doesn't have any ranks in the Handle Animal skill. The druid gains a +4 circumstance bonus on all wild empathy checks and Handle Animal checks made regarding an animal companion.

Share Spells (Ex): The druid may cast a spell with a target of "You" on her animal companion (as a spell with a range of touch) instead of on herself. A druid may cast spells on her animal companion even if the spells normally do not affect creatures of the companion's type (animal). Spells cast in this way must come from a class that grants an animal companion. This ability does not allow the animal to share abilities that are not spells, even if they function like spells.

Evasion (Ex): If an animal companion is subjected to an attack that normally allows a Reflex save for half damage, it takes no damage if it makes a successful saving throw.

Ability Score Increase (Ex): The animal companion adds +1 to one of its ability scores.

Devotion (Ex): An animal companion gains a +4 morale bonus on Will saves against enchantment spells and effects.

Multiattack: An animal companion gains Multiattack as a bonus feat if it has three or more natural attacks and does not already have that feat. If it does not have the requisite three or more natural attacks, the animal companion instead gains a second attack with one of its natural weapons, albeit at a –5 penalty.

Improved Evasion (Ex): When subjected to an attack that allows a Reflex saving throw for half damage, an animal companion takes no damage if it makes a successful saving throw and only half damage if the saving throw fails.

Animal Skills

Animal companions can have ranks in any of the following skills: Acrobatics* (Dex), Climb* (Str), Escape Artist (Dex), Fly* (Dex), Intimidate (Cha), Perception* (Wis), Stealth* (Dex), Survival (Wis), and Swim* (Str). All of the skills marked with an (*) are class skills for animal companions. Animal companions with an Intelligence of 3 or higher can put ranks into any skill.

Animal Feats

Animal companions can select from the following feats: Acrobatic, Agile Maneuvers, Armor Proficiency (light, medium, and heavy), Athletic, Blind-Fight, Combat Reflexes, Diehard, Dodge, Endurance, Great Fortitude, Improved Bull Rush, Improved Initiative, Improved Natural Armor (see the *Pathfinder RPG Bestiary*), Improved Natural Attack (see the *Pathfinder RPG Bestiary*), Improved Overrun, Intimidating Prowess, Iron Will, Lightning Reflexes, Mobility, Power Attack, Run, Skill Focus, Spring Attack, Stealthy, Toughness, Weapon Finesse, and Weapon Focus. Animal companions with an Intelligence of 3 or higher can select any feat they are physically capable of using. GMs might expand this list to include feats from other sources.

Animal Choices

Each animal companion has different starting sizes, speed, attacks, ability scores, and special qualities. All animal attacks are made using the creature's full base attack bonus unless otherwise noted. Animal attacks add the animal's Strength modifier to the damage roll, unless it is its only attack, in which case it adds 1-1/2 its Strength modifier. Some have special abilities, such as scent. See Appendix 1 for more information on these abilities. As you gain levels, your animal companion

improves as well, usually at 4th or 7th level, in addition to the standard bonuses noted on Table 3–8. Instead of taking the listed benefit at 4th or 7th level, you can instead choose to increase the companion's Dexterity and Constitution by 2.

The animal companions listed here are by no means the only ones available—additional animal companion types can be found in the *Pathfinder RPG Bestiary*. Some of the special attacks and qualities possessed by animals are covered in more detail there as well.

Ape

Starting Statistics: Size Medium; **Speed** 30 ft., Climb 30 ft.; **AC** +1 natural armor; **Attack** bite (1d4), 2 claws (1d4); **Ability Scores** Str 13, Dex 17, Con 10, Int 2, Wis 12, Cha 7; **Special Qualities** low-light vision, scent.

4th-Level Advancement: Size Large; **AC** +2 natural armor; **Attack** bite (1d6), 2 claws (1d6); **Ability Scores** Str +8, Dex –2, Con +4.

Badger (Wolverine)

Starting Statistics: Size Small; **Speed** 30 ft., burrow 10 ft., climb 10 ft.; **AC** +2 natural armor; **Attack** bite (1d4), 2 claws (1d3); **Ability Scores** Str 10, Dex 17, Con 15, Int 2, Wis 12, Cha 10; **Special Attacks** rage (as a barbarian for 6 rounds per day); **Special Qualities** low-light vision, scent.

4th-Level Advancement: Size Medium; **Attack** bite (1d6), 2 claws (1d4); **Ability Scores** Str +4, Dex –2, Con +2.

Bear

Starting Statistics: Size Small; **Speed** 40 ft.; **AC** +2 natural armor; **Attack** bite (1d4), 2 claws (1d3); **Ability Scores** Str 15, Dex 15, Con 13, Int 2, Wis 12, Cha 6; **Special Qualities** low-light vision, scent.

4th-Level Advancement: Size Medium; **Attack** bite (1d6), 2 claws (1d4); **Ability Scores** Str +4, Dex –2, Con +2.

Bird (Eagle/Hawk/Owl)

Starting Statistics: Size Small; **Speed** 10 ft., fly 80 ft. (average); **AC** +1 natural armor; **Attack** bite (1d4), 2 talons (1d4); **Ability Scores** Str 10, Dex 15, Con 12, Int 2, Wis 14, Cha 6; **Special Qualities** low-light vision.

4th-Level Advancement: Ability Scores Str +2, Con +2.

Boar

Starting Statistics: Size Small; **Speed** 40 ft.; **AC** +6 natural armor; **Attack** gore (1d6); **Ability Scores** Str 13, Dex 12, Con 15, Int 2, Wis 13, Cha 4; **Special Qualities** low-light vision, scent.

4th-Level Advancement: Size Medium; **Attack** gore (1d8); **Ability Scores** Str +4, Dex –2, Con +2; **Special Attacks** ferocity (see the *Pathfinder RPG Bestiary* for more details).

Camel

Starting Statistics: Size Large; **Speed** 50 ft.; **AC** +1 natural armor; **Attack** bite (1d4) or spit (ranged touch attack, target is sickened for 1d4 rounds, range 10 feet); **Ability Scores** Str 18, Dex 16, Con 14, Int 2, Wis 11, Cha 4; **Special Qualities** low-light vision, scent.

4th-Level Advancement: Ability Scores Str +2, Con +2.

Cat, Big (Lion, Tiger)

Starting Statistics: Size Medium; **Speed** 40 ft.; **AC** +1 natural armor; **Attack** bite (1d6), 2 claws (1d4); **Ability Scores** Str 13, Dex 17, Con 13, Int 2, Wis 15, Cha 10; **Special Attacks** rake (1d4); **Special Qualities** low-light vision, scent.

7th-Level Advancement: Size Large; **AC** +2 natural armor; **Attack** bite (1d8), 2 claws (1d6); **Ability Scores** Str +8, Dex −2, Con +4; **Special Attacks** grab, pounce, rake (1d6) (see the *Pathfinder RPG Bestiary* for more details for these attacks).

Cat, Small (Cheetah, Leopard)

Starting Statistics: Size Small; **Speed** 50 ft.; **AC** +1 natural armor; **Attack** bite (1d4 plus trip), 2 claws (1d2); **Ability Scores** Str 12, Dex 21, Con 13, Int 2, Wis 12, Cha 6; **Special Qualities** low-light vision, scent.

4th-Level Advancement: Size Medium; **Attack** bite (1d6 plus trip), 2 claws (1d3); **Ability Scores** Str +4, Dex −2, Con +2; **Special Qualities** sprint (see the *Pathfinder RPG Bestiary*).

Crocodile (Alligator)

Starting Statistics: Size Small; **Speed** 20 ft., swim 30 ft.; **AC** +4 natural armor; **Attack** bite (1d6); **Ability Scores** Str 15, Dex 14, Con 15, Int 1, Wis 12, Cha 2; **Special Qualities** hold breath (see the *Pathfinder RPG Bestiary*), low-light vision.

4th-Level Advancement: Size Medium; **Attack** bite (1d8) or tail slap (1d12); **Ability Scores** Str +4, Dex −2, Con +2; **Special Attacks** death roll, grab, sprint (see the *Pathfinder RPG Bestiary*).

Dinosaur (Deinonychus, Velociraptor)

Starting Statistics: Size Small; **Speed** 60 ft.; **AC** +1 natural armor; **Attack** 2 talons (1d6), bite (1d4); **Ability Scores** Str 11, Dex 17, Con 17, Int 2, Wis 12, Cha 14; **Special Qualities** low-light vision, scent.

7th-Level Advancement: Size Medium; **AC** +2 natural armor; **Attack** 2 talons (1d8), bite (1d6), 2 claws (1d4) **Ability Scores** Str +4, Dex −2, Con +2; **Special Attacks** pounce (see the *Pathfinder RPG Bestiary*).

Dog

Starting Statistics: Size Small; **Speed** 40 ft.; **AC** +2 natural armor; **Attack** bite (1d4); **Ability Scores** Str 13, Dex 17, Con 15, Int 2, Wis 12, Cha 6; **Special Qualities** low-light vision, scent.

4th-Level Advancement: Size Medium; **Attack** bite (1d6); **Ability Scores** Str +4, Dex −2, Con +2.

Horse

Starting Statistics: Size Large; **Speed** 50 ft.; **AC** +4 natural armor; **Attack** bite (1d4), 2 hooves* (1d6); **Ability Scores** Str 16, Dex 13, Con 15, Int 2, Wis 12, Cha 6; **Special Qualities** low-light vision, scent. *This is a secondary natural attack, see Chapter 8 for more information on how secondary attacks work.

4th-Level Advancement: Ability Scores Str +2, Con +2; **Special Qualities** combat trained (see the Handle Animal skill).

Pony

Starting Statistics: Size Medium; **Speed** 40 ft.; **AC** +2 natural armor; **Attack** 2 hooves (1d3); **Ability Scores** Str 13, Dex 13, Con 12, Int 2, Wis 11, Cha 4; **Special Qualities** low-light vision, scent.

4th-Level Advancement: Ability Scores Str +2, Con +2; **Special Qualities** combat trained (see the Handle Animal skill).

Shark

Starting Statistics: Size Small; **Speed** swim 60 ft.; **AC** +4 natural armor; **Attack** bite (1d4); **Ability Scores** Str 13, Dex 15, Con 15, Int 1, Wis 12, Cha 2; **Special Qualities** low-light vision, scent.

4th-Level Advancement: Size Medium; **Attack** bite (1d6); **Ability Scores** Str +4, Dex −2, Con +2; **Special Qualities** blindsense.

Snake, Constrictor

Starting Statistics: Size Medium; **Speed** 20 ft., climb 20 ft., swim 20 ft.; **AC** +2 natural armor; **Attack** bite (1d3); **Ability Scores** Str 15, Dex 17, Con 13, Int 1, Wis 12, Cha 2; **Special Attacks** grab; **Special Qualities** low-light vision, scent.

4th-Level Advancement: Size Large; **AC** +1 natural armor; **Attack** bite (1d4); **Ability Scores** Str +8, Dex −2, Con +4; **Special Attacks** constrict 1d4 (see the *Pathfinder RPG Bestiary*).

Snake, Viper

Starting Statistics: Size Small; **Speed** 20 ft., climb 20 ft., swim 20 ft.; **AC** +2 natural armor; **Attack** bite (1d3 plus poison); **Ability Scores** Str 8, Dex 17, Con 11, Int 1, Wis 12, Cha 2; **Special Attacks** poison (*Frequency* 1 round (6), *Effect* 1 Con damage, *Cure* 1 save, Con-based DC); **Special Qualities** low-light vision, scent.

4th-Level Advancement: Size Medium; **Attack** bite (1d4 plus poison); **Ability Scores** Str +4, Dex −2, Con +2.

Wolf

Starting Statistics: Size Medium; **Speed** 50 ft.; **AC** +2 natural armor; **Attack** bite (1d6 plus trip); **Ability Scores** Str 13, Dex 15, Con 15, Int 2, Wis 12, Cha 6; **Special Qualities** low-light vision, scent.

7th-Level Advancement: Size Large; **AC** +2 natural armor; **Attack** bite (1d8 plus trip); **Ability Scores** Str +8, Dex −2, Con +4.

FIGHTER

Some take up arms for glory, wealth, or revenge. Others do battle to prove themselves, to protect others, or because they know nothing else. Still others learn the ways of weaponcraft to hone their bodies in battle and prove their mettle in the forge of war. Lords of the battlefield, fighters are a disparate lot, training with many weapons or just one, perfecting the uses of armor, learning the fighting techniques of exotic masters, and studying the art of combat, all to shape themselves into living weapons. Far more than mere thugs, these skilled warriors reveal the true deadliness of their weapons, turning hunks of metal into arms capable of taming kingdoms, slaughtering monsters, and rousing the hearts of armies. Soldiers, knights, hunters, and artists of war, fighters are unparalleled champions, and woe to those who dare stand against them.

Role: Fighters excel at combat—defeating their enemies, controlling the flow of battle, and surviving such sorties themselves. While their specific weapons and methods grant them a wide variety of tactics, few can match fighters for sheer battle prowess.

Alignment: Any.

Hit Die: d10.

Class Skills

The fighter's class skills are Climb (Str), Craft (Int), Handle Animal (Cha), Intimidate (Cha), Knowledge (dungeoneering) (Int), Knowledge (engineering) (Int), Profession (Wis), Ride (Dex), Survival (Wis), and Swim (Str).

Skill Ranks per Level: 2 + Int modifier.

Class Features

The following are class features of the fighter.

Weapon and Armor Proficiency: A fighter is proficient with all simple and martial weapons and with all armor (heavy, light, and medium) and shields (including tower shields).

Bonus Feats: At 1st level, and at every even level thereafter, a fighter gains a bonus feat in addition to those gained from normal advancement (meaning that the fighter gains a feat at every level). These bonus feats must be selected from those listed as combat feats, sometimes also called "fighter bonus feats."

Upon reaching 4th level, and every four levels thereafter (8th, 12th, and so on), a fighter can choose to learn a new bonus feat in place of a bonus feat he has already learned. In effect, the fighter loses the bonus feat in exchange for the new one. The old feat cannot be one that was used as a prerequisite for another feat, prestige class, or other ability. A fighter can only change one feat at any given level and must choose whether or not to swap the feat at the time he gains a new bonus feat for the level.

Bravery (Ex): Starting at 2nd level, a fighter gains a +1 bonus on Will saves against fear. This bonus increases by +1 for every four levels beyond 2nd.

Armor Training (Ex): Starting at 3rd level, a fighter learns to be more maneuverable while wearing armor. Whenever he is wearing armor, he reduces the armor check penalty by 1 (to a minimum of 0) and increases the maximum Dexterity bonus allowed by his armor by 1. Every four levels thereafter (7th, 11th, and 15th), these bonuses increase by +1 each time, to a maximum –4 reduction of the armor check penalty and a +4 increase of the maximum Dexterity bonus allowed.

Table 3–9: Fighter

Level	Base Attack Bonus	Fort Save	Ref Save	Will Save	Special
1st	+1	+2	+0	+0	Bonus feat
2nd	+2	+3	+0	+0	Bonus feat, bravery +1
3rd	+3	+3	+1	+1	Armor training 1
4th	+4	+4	+1	+1	Bonus feat
5th	+5	+4	+1	+1	Weapon training 1
6th	+6/+1	+5	+2	+2	Bonus feat, bravery +2
7th	+7/+2	+5	+2	+2	Armor training 2
8th	+8/+3	+6	+2	+2	Bonus feat
9th	+9/+4	+6	+3	+3	Weapon training 2
10th	+10/+5	+7	+3	+3	Bonus feat, bravery +3
11th	+11/+6/+1	+7	+3	+3	Armor training 3
12th	+12/+7/+2	+8	+4	+4	Bonus feat
13th	+13/+8/+3	+8	+4	+4	Weapon training 3
14th	+14/+9/+4	+9	+4	+4	Bonus feat, bravery +4
15th	+15/+10/+5	+9	+5	+5	Armor training 4
16th	+16/+11/+6/+1	+10	+5	+5	Bonus feat
17th	+17/+12/+7/+2	+10	+5	+5	Weapon training 4
18th	+18/+13/+8/+3	+11	+6	+6	Bonus feat, bravery +5
19th	+19/+14/+9/+4	+11	+6	+6	Armor mastery
20th	+20/+15/+10/+5	+12	+6	+6	Bonus feat, weapon mastery

In addition, a fighter can also move at his normal speed while wearing medium armor. At 7th level, a fighter can move at his normal speed while wearing heavy armor.

Weapon Training (Ex): Starting at 5th level, a fighter can select one group of weapons, as noted below. Whenever he attacks with a weapon from this group, he gains a +1 bonus on attack and damage rolls.

Every four levels thereafter (9th, 13th, and 17th), a fighter becomes further trained in another group of weapons. He gains a +1 bonus on attack and damage rolls when using a weapon from this group. In addition, the bonuses granted by previous weapon groups increase by +1 each. For example, when a fighter reaches 9th level, he receives a +1 bonus on attack and damage rolls with one weapon group and a +2 bonus on attack and damage rolls with the weapon group selected at 5th level. Bonuses granted from overlapping groups do not stack. Take the highest bonus granted for a weapon if it resides in two or more groups.

A fighter also adds this bonus to any combat maneuver checks made with weapons from this group. This bonus also applies to the fighter's Combat Maneuver Defense when defending against disarm and sunder attempts made against weapons from this group.

Weapon groups are defined as follows (GMs may add other weapons to these groups, or add entirely new groups):

Axes: battleaxe, dwarven waraxe, greataxe, handaxe, heavy pick, light pick, orc double axe, and throwing axe.

Blades, Heavy: bastard sword, elven curve blade, falchion, greatsword, longsword, scimitar, scythe, and two-bladed sword.

Blades, Light: dagger, kama, kukri, rapier, short sword, sickle, and starknife.

Bows: composite longbow, composite shortbow, longbow, and shortbow.

Close: gauntlet, heavy shield, light shield, punching dagger, sap, spiked armor, spiked gauntlet, spiked shield, and unarmed strike.

Crossbows: hand crossbow, heavy crossbow, light crossbow, heavy repeating crossbow, and light repeating crossbow.

Double: dire flail, dwarven urgrosh, gnome hooked hammer, orc double axe, quarterstaff, and two-bladed sword.

Flails: dire flail, flail, heavy flail, morningstar, nunchaku, spiked chain, and whip.

Hammers: club, greatclub, heavy mace, light hammer, light mace, and warhammer.

Monk: kama, nunchaku, quarterstaff, sai, shuriken, siangham, and unarmed strike.

Natural: unarmed strike and all natural weapons, such as bite, claw, gore, tail, and wing.

Polearms: glaive, guisarme, halberd, and ranseur.

Spears: javelin, lance, longspear, shortspear, spear, and trident.

Thrown: blowgun, bolas, club, dagger, dart, halfling sling staff, javelin, light hammer, net, shortspear, shuriken, sling, spear, starknife, throwing axe, and trident.

Armor Mastery (Ex): At 19th level, a fighter gains DR 5/— whenever he is wearing armor or using a shield.

Weapon Mastery (Ex): At 20th level, a fighter chooses one weapon, such as the longsword, greataxe, or longbow. Any attacks made with that weapon automatically confirm all critical threats and have their damage multiplier increased by 1 (×2 becomes ×3, for example). In addition, he cannot be disarmed while wielding a weapon of this type.

MONK

For the truly exemplary, martial skill transcends the battlefield—it is a lifestyle, a doctrine, a state of mind. These warrior-artists search out methods of battle beyond swords and shields, finding weapons within themselves just as capable of crippling or killing as any blade. These monks (so called since they adhere to ancient philosophies and strict martial disciplines) elevate their bodies to become weapons of war, from battle-minded ascetics to self-taught brawlers. Monks tread the path of discipline, and those with the will to endure that path discover within themselves not what they are, but what they are meant to be.

Role: Monks excel at overcoming even the most daunting perils, striking where it's least expected, and taking advantage of enemy vulnerabilities. Fleet of foot and skilled in combat, monks can navigate any battlefield with ease, aiding allies wherever they are needed most.

Alignment: Any lawful.

Hit Die: d8.

Class Skills

The monk's class skills are Acrobatics (Dex), Climb (Str), Craft (Int), Escape Artist (Dex), Intimidate (Cha), Knowledge (history) (Int), Knowledge (religion) (Int), Perception (Wis), Perform (Cha), Profession (Wis), Ride (Dex), Sense Motive (Wis), Stealth (Dex), and Swim (Str).

Skill Ranks per Level: 4 + Int modifier.

Class Features

All of the following are class features of the monk.

Weapon and Armor Proficiency: Monks are proficient with the club, crossbow (light or heavy), dagger, handaxe, javelin, kama, nunchaku, quarterstaff, sai, shortspear, short sword, shuriken, siangham, sling, and spear.

Monks are not proficient with any armor or shields.

When wearing armor, using a shield, or carrying a medium or heavy load, a monk loses his AC bonus, as well as his fast movement and flurry of blows abilities.

AC Bonus (Ex): When unarmored and unencumbered, the monk adds his Wisdom bonus (if any) to his AC and his CMD. In addition, a monk gains a +1 bonus to AC and CMD at 4th level. This bonus increases by 1 for every four monk levels thereafter, up to a maximum of +5 at 20th level.

These bonuses to AC apply even against touch attacks or when the monk is flat-footed. He loses these bonuses when he is immobilized or helpless, when he wears any armor, when he carries a shield, or when he carries a medium or heavy load.

Flurry of Blows (Ex): Starting at 1st level, a monk can make a flurry of blows as a full-attack action. When doing so, he may make one additional attack, taking a –2 penalty on all of his attack rolls, as if using the Two-Weapon Fighting feat. These attacks can be any combination of unarmed strikes and attacks with a monk special weapon (he does not need to use two weapons to utilize this ability). For the purpose of these attacks, the monk's base attack bonus from his monk class levels is equal to his monk level. For all other purposes, such as qualifying for a feat or a prestige class, the monk uses his normal base attack bonus.

At 8th level, the monk can make two additional attacks when he uses flurry of blows, as if using Improved Two-Weapon Fighting (even if the monk does not meet the prerequisites for the feat).

At 15th level, the monk can make three additional attacks using flurry of blows, as if using Greater Two-Weapon Fighting (even if the monk does not meet the prerequisites for the feat).

A monk applies his full Strength bonus to his damage rolls for all successful attacks made with flurry of blows, whether the attacks are made with an off-hand or with a weapon wielded in both hands. A monk may substitute disarm, sunder, and trip combat maneuvers for unarmed attacks as part of a flurry of blows. A monk cannot use any weapon other than an unarmed strike or a special monk weapon as part of a flurry of blows. A monk with natural

TABLE 3–10: MONK

Level	Base Attack Bonus	Fort Save	Ref Save	Will Save	Special	Flurry of Blows Attack Bonus	Unarmed Damage*	AC Bonus	Fast Movement
1st	+0	+2	+2	+2	Bonus feat, flurry of blows, stunning fist, unarmed strike	−1/−1	1d6	+0	+0 ft.
2nd	+1	+3	+3	+3	Bonus feat, evasion	+0/+0	1d6	+0	+0 ft.
3rd	+2	+3	+3	+3	Fast movement, maneuver training, still mind	+1/+1	1d6	+0	+10 ft.
4th	+3	+4	+4	+4	Ki pool (magic), slow fall 20 ft.	+2/+2	1d8	+1	+10 ft.
5th	+3	+4	+4	+4	High jump, purity of body	+3/+3	1d8	+1	+10 ft.
6th	+4	+5	+5	+5	Bonus feat, slow fall 30 ft.	+4/+4/−1	1d8	+1	+20 ft.
7th	+5	+5	+5	+5	Ki pool (cold iron/silver), wholeness of body	+5/+5/+0	1d8	+1	+20 ft.
8th	+6/+1	+6	+6	+6	Slow fall 40 ft.	+6/+6/+1/+1	1d10	+2	+20 ft.
9th	+6/+1	+6	+6	+6	Improved evasion	+7/+7/+2/+2	1d10	+2	+30 ft.
10th	+7/+2	+7	+7	+7	Bonus feat, ki pool (lawful), slow fall 50 ft.	+8/+8/+3/+3	1d10	+2	+30 ft.
11th	+8/+3	+7	+7	+7	Diamond body	+9/+9/+4/+4/−1	1d10	+2	+30 ft.
12th	+9/+4	+8	+8	+8	Abundant step, slow fall 60 ft.	+10/+10/+5/+5/+0	2d6	+3	+40 ft.
13th	+9/+4	+8	+8	+8	Diamond soul	+11/+11/+6/+6/+1	2d6	+3	+40 ft.
14th	+10/+5	+9	+9	+9	Bonus feat, slow fall 70 ft.	+12/+12/+7/+7/+2	2d6	+3	+40 ft.
15th	+11/+6/+1	+9	+9	+9	Quivering palm	+13/+13/+8/+8/+3/+3	2d6	+3	+50 ft.
16th	+12/+7/+2	+10	+10	+10	Ki pool (adamantine), slow fall 80 ft.	+14/+14/+9/+9/+4/+4/−1	2d8	+4	+50 ft.
17th	+12/+7/+2	+10	+10	+10	Timeless body, tongue of the sun and moon	+15/+15/+10/+10/+5/+5/+0	2d8	+4	+50 ft.
18th	+13/+8/+3	+11	+11	+11	Bonus feat, slow fall 90 ft.	+16/+16/+11/+11/+6/+6/+1	2d8	+4	+60 ft.
19th	+14/+9/+4	+11	+11	+11	Empty body	+17/+17/+12/+12/+7/+7/+2	2d8	+4	+60 ft.
20th	+15/+10/+5	+12	+12	+12	Perfect self, slow fall any distance	+18/+18/+13/+13/+8/+8/+3	2d10	+5	+60 ft.

*The value shown is for Medium monks. See below for Small or Large monk damage.

weapons cannot use such weapons as part of a flurry of blows, nor can he make natural attacks in addition to his flurry of blows attacks.

Unarmed Strike: At 1st level, a monk gains Improved Unarmed Strike as a bonus feat. A monk's attacks may be with fist, elbows, knees, and feet. This means that a monk may make unarmed strikes with his hands full. There is no such thing as an off-hand attack for a monk striking unarmed. A monk may thus apply his full Strength bonus on damage rolls for all his unarmed strikes.

Usually a monk's unarmed strikes deal lethal damage, but he can choose to deal nonlethal damage instead with no penalty on his attack roll. He has the same choice to deal lethal or nonlethal damage while grappling.

A monk's unarmed strike is treated as both a manufactured weapon and a natural weapon for the purpose of spells and effects that enhance or improve either manufactured weapons or natural weapons.

A monk also deals more damage with his unarmed strikes than a normal person would, as shown above on

Table 3–10. The unarmed damage values listed on Table 3–10 is for Medium monks. A Small monk deals less damage than the amount given there with his unarmed attacks, while a Large monk deals more damage; see Small or Large Monk Unarmed Damage on the table given below.

SMALL OR LARGE MONK UNARMED DAMAGE

Level	Damage (Small Monk)	Damage (Large Monk)
1st–3rd	1d4	1d8
4th–7th	1d6	2d6
8th–11th	1d8	2d8
12th–15th	1d10	3d6
16th–19th	2d6	3d8
20th	2d8	4d8

Bonus Feat: At 1st level, 2nd level, and every 4 levels thereafter, a monk may select a bonus feat. These feats must be taken from the following list: Catch Off-Guard, Combat Reflexes, Deflect Arrows, Dodge, Improved Grapple, Scorpion Style, and Throw Anything. At 6th level, the following feats are added to the list: Gorgon's Fist, Improved Bull Rush, Improved Disarm, Improved Feint, Improved Trip, and Mobility. At 10th level, the following feats are added to the list: Improved Critical, Medusa's Wrath, Snatch Arrows, and Spring Attack. A monk need not have any of the prerequisites normally required for these feats to select them.

Stunning Fist (Ex): At 1st level, the monk gains Stunning Fist as a bonus feat, even if he does not meet the prerequisites. At 4th level, and every 4 levels thereafter, the monk gains the ability to apply a new condition to the target of his Stunning Fist. This condition replaces stunning the target for 1 round, and a successful saving throw still negates the effect. At 4th level, he can choose to make the target fatigued. At 8th level, he can make the target sickened for 1 minute. At 12th level, he can make the target staggered for 1d6+1 rounds. At 16th level, he can permanently blind or deafen the target. At 20th level, he can paralyze the target for 1d6+1 rounds. The monk must choose which condition will apply before the attack roll is made. These effects do not stack with themselves (a creature sickened by Stunning Fist cannot become nauseated if hit by Stunning Fist again), but additional hits do increase the duration.

Evasion (Ex): At 2nd level or higher, a monk can avoid even magical and unusual attacks with great agility. If a monk makes a successful Reflex saving throw against an attack that normally deals half damage on a successful save, he instead takes no damage. Evasion can be used only if a monk is wearing light armor or no armor. A helpless monk does not gain the benefit of evasion.

Fast Movement (Ex): At 3rd level, a monk gains an enhancement bonus to his base speed, as shown on Table 3–10. A monk in armor or carrying a medium or heavy load loses this extra speed.

Maneuver Training (Ex): At 3rd level, a monk uses his monk level in place of his base attack bonus when calculating his Combat Maneuver Bonus. Base attack bonuses granted from other classes are unaffected and are added normally.

Still Mind (Ex): A monk of 3rd level or higher gains a +2 bonus on saving throws against enchantment spells and effects.

Ki Pool (Su): At 4th level, a monk gains a pool of ki points, supernatural energy he can use to accomplish amazing feats. The number of points in a monk's ki pool is equal to 1/2 his monk level + his Wisdom modifier. As long as he has at least 1 point in his ki pool, he can make a ki strike. At 4th level, ki strike allows his unarmed attacks to be treated as magic weapons for the purpose of overcoming damage reduction. At 7th level, his unarmed attacks are also treated as cold iron and silver for the purpose of overcoming damage reduction.

At 10th level, his unarmed attacks are also treated as lawful weapons for the purpose of overcoming damage reduction. At 16th level, his unarmed attacks are treated as adamantine weapons for the purpose of overcoming damage reduction and bypassing hardness.

By spending 1 point from his ki pool, a monk can make one additional attack at his highest attack bonus when making a flurry of blows attack. In addition, he can spend 1 point to increase his base speed by 20 feet for 1 round. Finally, a monk can spend 1 point from his ki pool to give himself a +4 dodge bonus to AC for 1 round. Each of these powers is activated as a swift action. A monk gains additional powers that consume points from his ki pool as he gains levels.

The ki pool is replenished each morning after 8 hours of rest or meditation; these hours do not need to be consecutive.

Slow Fall (Ex): At 4th level or higher, a monk within arm's reach of a wall can use it to slow his descent. When first gaining this ability, he takes damage as if the fall were 20 feet shorter than it actually is. The monk's ability to slow his fall (that is, to reduce the effective distance of the fall when next to a wall) improves with his monk level until at 20th level he can use a nearby wall to slow his descent and fall any distance without harm.

High Jump (Ex): At 5th level, a monk adds his level to all Acrobatics checks made to jump, both for vertical jumps and horizontal jumps. In addition, he always counts as having a running start when making jump checks using Acrobatics. By spending 1 point from his ki pool as a swift action, a monk gains a +20 bonus on Acrobatics checks made to jump for 1 round.

Purity of Body (Ex): At 5th level, a monk gains immunity to all diseases, including supernatural and magical diseases.

Wholeness of Body (Su): At 7th level or higher, a monk can heal his own wounds as a standard action. He can heal a number of hit points of damage equal to his monk level by using 2 points from his ki pool.

Improved Evasion (Ex): At 9th level, a monk's evasion ability improves. He still takes no damage on a successful Reflex saving throw against attacks, but henceforth he takes only half damage on a failed save. A helpless monk does not gain the benefit of improved evasion.

Diamond Body (Su): At 11th level, a monk gains immunity to poisons of all kinds.

Abundant Step (Su): At 12th level or higher, a monk can slip magically between spaces, as if using the spell *dimension door*. Using this ability is a move action that consumes 2 points from his ki pool. His caster level for this effect is equal to his monk level. He cannot take other creatures with him when he uses this ability.

Diamond Soul (Ex): At 13th level, a monk gains spell resistance equal to his current monk level + 10. In order to affect the monk with a spell, a spellcaster must get a result on a caster level check (1d20 + caster level) that equals or exceeds the monk's spell resistance.

Quivering Palm (Su): Starting at 15th level, a monk can set up vibrations within the body of another creature that can thereafter be fatal if the monk so desires. He can use this quivering palm attack once per day, and he must announce his intent before making his attack roll. Creatures immune to critical hits cannot be affected. Otherwise, if the monk strikes successfully and the target takes damage from the blow, the quivering palm attack succeeds. Thereafter, the monk can try to slay the victim at any later time, as long as the attempt is made within a number of days equal to his monk level. To make such an attempt, the monk merely wills the target to die (a free action), and unless the target makes a Fortitude saving throw (DC 10 + 1/2 the monk's level + the monk's Wis modifier), it dies. If the saving throw is successful, the target is no longer in danger from that particular quivering palm attack, but it may still be affected by another one at a later time. A monk can have no more than 1 quivering palm in effect at one time. If a monk uses quivering palm while another is still in effect, the previous effect is negated.

Timeless Body (Ex): At 17th level, a monk no longer takes penalties to his ability scores for aging and cannot be magically aged. Any such penalties that he has already taken, however, remain in place. Age bonuses still accrue, and the monk still dies of old age when his time is up.

Tongue of the Sun and Moon (Ex): A monk of 17th level or higher can speak with any living creature.

Empty Body (Su): At 19th level, a monk gains the ability to assume an ethereal state for 1 minute as though using the spell *etherealness*. Using this ability is a move action that consumes 3 points from his ki pool. This ability only affects the monk and cannot be used to make other creatures ethereal.

Perfect Self: At 20th level, a monk becomes a magical creature. He is forevermore treated as an outsider rather than as a humanoid (or whatever the monk's creature type was) for the purpose of spells and magical effects. Additionally, the monk gains damage reduction 10/chaotic, which allows him to ignore the first 10 points of damage from any attack made by a nonchaotic weapon or by any natural attack made by a creature that doesn't have similar damage reduction. Unlike other outsiders, the monk can still be brought back from the dead as if he were a member of his previous creature type.

Ex-Monks

A monk who becomes nonlawful cannot gain new levels as a monk but retains all monk abilities.

 **PALADIN**

Through a select, worthy few shines the power of the divine. Called paladins, these noble souls dedicate their swords and lives to the battle against evil. Knights, crusaders, and lawbringers, paladins seek not just to spread divine justice but to embody the teachings of the virtuous deities they serve. In pursuit of their lofty goals, they adhere to ironclad laws of morality and discipline. As reward for their righteousness, these holy champions are blessed with boons to aid them in their quests: powers to banish evil, heal the innocent, and inspire the faithful. Although their convictions might lead them into conflict with the very souls they would save, paladins weather endless challenges of faith and dark temptations, risking their lives to do right and fighting to bring about a brighter future.

Role: Paladins serve as beacons for their allies within the chaos of battle. While deadly opponents of evil, they can also empower goodly souls to aid in their crusades. Their magic and martial skills also make them well suited to defending others and blessing the fallen with the strength to continue fighting.

Alignment: Lawful good.

Hit Die: d10.

Class Skills

The paladin's class skills are Craft (Int), Diplomacy (Cha), Handle Animal (Cha), Heal (Wis), Knowledge (nobility) (Int), Knowledge (religion) (Int), Profession (Wis), Ride (Dex), Sense Motive (Wis), and Spellcraft (Int).

Skill Ranks per Level: 2 + Int modifier.

Class Features

All of the following are class features of the paladin.

Weapon and Armor Proficiency: Paladins are proficient with all simple and martial weapons, with all types of armor (heavy, medium, and light), and with shields (except tower shields).

Aura of Good (Ex): The power of a paladin's aura of good (see the *detect good* spell) is equal to her paladin level.

Detect Evil (Sp): At will, a paladin can use *detect evil*, as the spell. A paladin can, as a move action, concentrate on a single item or individual within 60 feet and determine if it is evil, learning the strength of its aura as if having studied it for 3 rounds. While focusing on one individual or object, the paladin does not detect evil in any other object or individual within range.

Smite Evil (Su): Once per day, a paladin can call out to the powers of good to aid her in her struggle against evil. As a swift action, the paladin chooses one target within sight to smite. If this target is evil, the paladin adds her Charisma bonus (if any) to her attack rolls and adds her paladin level to all damage rolls made against the target of her smite. If the target of smite evil is an outsider with the evil subtype, an evil-aligned dragon, or an undead creature, the bonus to damage on the first successful attack increases to 2 points of damage per level the paladin possesses. Regardless of the target, smite evil attacks automatically bypass any DR the creature might possess.

In addition, while smite evil is in effect, the paladin gains a deflection bonus equal to her Charisma modifier (if any) to her AC against attacks made by the target of the smite. If the paladin targets a creature that is not evil, the smite is wasted with no effect.

The smite evil effect remains until the target of the smite is dead or the next time the paladin rests and regains her uses of this ability. At 4th level, and at every three levels thereafter, the paladin may smite evil one additional time per day, as indicated on Table 3–11, to a maximum of seven times per day at 19th level.

Divine Grace (Su): At 2nd level, a paladin gains a bonus equal to her Charisma bonus (if any) on all saving throws.

Lay On Hands (Su): Beginning at 2nd level, a paladin can heal wounds (her own or those of others) by touch. Each day she can use this ability a number of times equal to 1/2 her paladin level plus her Charisma modifier. With one use of this ability, a paladin can heal 1d6 hit points of damage for every two paladin levels she possesses. Using this ability is a standard action, unless the paladin targets herself, in which case it is a swift action. Despite the name of this ability, a paladin only needs one free hand to use this ability.

Alternatively, a paladin can use this healing power to deal damage to undead creatures, dealing 1d6 points of damage for every two levels the paladin possesses. Using lay on hands in this way requires a successful melee touch attack and doesn't provoke an attack of opportunity. Undead do not receive a saving throw against this damage.

Aura of Courage (Su): At 3rd level, a paladin is immune to fear (magical or otherwise). Each ally within 10 feet of her gains a +4 morale bonus on saving throws against fear effects. This ability functions only while the paladin is conscious, not if she is unconscious or dead.

Divine Health (Ex): At 3rd level, a paladin is immune to all diseases, including supernatural and magical diseases, including mummy rot.

Mercy (Su): At 3rd level, and every three levels thereafter, a paladin can select one mercy. Each mercy adds an effect to the paladin's lay on hands ability. Whenever the paladin uses lay on hands to heal damage to one target, the target also receives the additional effects from all of the mercies possessed by the paladin. A mercy can remove a condition caused by a curse, disease, or poison without curing the affliction. Such conditions return after 1 hour unless the mercy actually removes the affliction that causes the condition.

At 3rd level, the paladin can select from the following initial mercies.
- *Fatigued:* The target is no longer fatigued.
- *Shaken:* The target is no longer shaken.
- *Sickened:* The target is no longer sickened.

At 6th level, a paladin adds the following mercies to the list of those that can be selected.
- *Dazed:* The target is no longer dazed.
- *Diseased:* The paladin's lay on hands ability also acts as *remove disease*, using the paladin's level as the caster level.
- *Staggered:* The target is no longer staggered, unless the target is at exactly 0 hit points.

TABLE 3–11: PALADIN

Level	Base Attack Bonus	Fort Save	Ref Save	Will Save	Special	Spells per Day			
						1st	2nd	3rd	4th
1st	+1	+2	+0	+2	Aura of good, detect evil, smite evil 1/day	—	—	—	—
2nd	+2	+3	+0	+3	Divine grace, lay on hands	—	—	—	—
3rd	+3	+3	+1	+3	Aura of courage, divine health, mercy	—	—	—	—
4th	+4	+4	+1	+4	Channel positive energy, smite evil 2/day	0	—	—	—
5th	+5	+4	+1	+4	Divine bond	1	—	—	—
6th	+6/+1	+5	+2	+5	Mercy	1	—	—	—
7th	+7/+2	+5	+2	+5	Smite evil 3/day	1	0	—	—
8th	+8/+3	+6	+2	+6	Aura of resolve	1	1	—	—
9th	+9/+4	+6	+3	+6	Mercy	2	1	—	—
10th	+10/+5	+7	+3	+7	Smite evil 4/day	2	1	0	—
11th	+11/+6/+1	+7	+3	+7	Aura of justice	2	1	1	—
12th	+12/+7/+2	+8	+4	+8	Mercy	2	2	1	—
13th	+13/+8/+3	+8	+4	+8	Smite evil 5/day	3	2	1	0
14th	+14/+9/+4	+9	+4	+9	Aura of faith	3	2	1	1
15th	+15/+10/+5	+9	+5	+9	Mercy	3	2	2	1
16th	+16/+11/+6/+1	+10	+5	+10	Smite evil 6/day	3	3	2	1
17th	+17/+12/+7/+2	+10	+5	+10	Aura of righteousness	4	3	2	1
18th	+18/+13/+8/+3	+11	+6	+11	Mercy	4	3	2	2
19th	+19/+14/+9/+4	+11	+6	+11	Smite evil 7/day	4	3	3	2
20th	+20/+15/+10/+5	+12	+6	+12	Holy champion	4	4	3	3

At 9th level, a paladin adds the following mercies to the list of those that can be selected.

- *Cursed*: The paladin's lay on hands ability also acts as *remove curse*, using the paladin's level as the caster level.
- *Exhausted*: The target is no longer exhausted. The paladin must have the fatigue mercy before selecting this mercy.
- *Frightened*: The target is no longer frightened. The paladin must have the shaken mercy before selecting this mercy.
- *Nauseated*: The target is no longer nauseated. The paladin must have the sickened mercy before selecting this mercy.
- *Poisoned*: The paladin's lay on hands ability also acts as *neutralize poison*, using the paladin's level as the caster level.

At 12th level, a paladin adds the following mercies to the list of those that can be selected.

- *Blinded*: The target is no longer blinded.
- *Deafened*: The target is no longer deafened.
- *Paralyzed*: The target is no longer paralyzed.
- *Stunned*: The target is no longer stunned.

These abilities are cumulative. For example, a 12th-level paladin's lay on hands ability heals 6d6 points of damage and might also cure fatigued and exhausted conditions as well as removing diseases and neutralizing poisons. Once a condition or spell effect is chosen, it can't be changed.

Channel Positive Energy (Su): When a paladin reaches 4th level, she gains the supernatural ability to channel positive energy like a cleric. Using this ability consumes two uses of her lay on hands ability. A paladin uses her level as her effective cleric level when channeling positive energy. This is a Charisma-based ability.

Spells: Beginning at 4th level, a paladin gains the ability to cast a small number of divine spells which are drawn from the paladin spell list presented in Chapter 10. A paladin must choose and prepare her spells in advance.

To prepare or cast a spell, a paladin must have a Charisma score equal to at least 10 + the spell level. The Difficulty Class for a saving throw against a paladin's spell is 10 + the spell level + the paladin's Charisma modifier.

Like other spellcasters, a paladin can cast only a certain number of spells of each spell level per day. Her base daily spell allotment is given on Table 3–11. In addition, she receives bonus spells per day if she has a high Charisma score (see Table 1–3). When Table 3–11 indicates that the paladin gets 0 spells per day of a given spell level, she gains only the bonus spells she would be entitled to based on her Charisma score for that spell level.

A paladin must spend 1 hour each day in quiet prayer and meditation to regain her daily allotment of spells. A paladin may prepare and cast any spell on the paladin spell list, provided that she can cast spells of that level, but she must choose which spells to prepare during her daily meditation.

Through 3rd level, a paladin has no caster level. At 4th level and higher, her caster level is equal to her paladin level – 3.

Divine Bond (Sp): Upon reaching 5th level, a paladin forms a divine bond with her god. This bond can take one of two forms. Once the form is chosen, it cannot be changed.

The first type of bond allows the paladin to enhance her weapon as a standard action by calling upon the aid of a celestial spirit for 1 minute per paladin level. When called, the spirit causes a held weapon to shed light as a torch. At 5th level, this spirit grants the weapon a +1 enhancement bonus. For every three levels beyond 5th, the weapon gains another +1 enhancement bonus, to a maximum of +6 at 20th level. These bonuses can be added to the weapon, stacking with existing weapon bonuses to a maximum of +5, or they can be used to add any of the following weapon properties: *axiomatic, brilliant energy, defending, disruption, flaming, flaming burst, holy, keen, merciful,* and *speed.* Adding these properties consumes an amount of bonus equal to the property's cost (see Table 15–9). These bonuses are added to any properties the weapon already has, but duplicate abilities do not stack. If the weapon is not magical, at least a +1 enhancement bonus must be added before any other properties can be added. The bonus and properties granted by the spirit are determined when the spirit is called and cannot be changed until the spirit is called again. The celestial spirit imparts no bonuses if the weapon is held by anyone other than the paladin but resumes giving bonuses if returned to the paladin. These bonuses apply to only one end of a double weapon. A paladin can use this ability once per day at 5th level, and one additional time per day for every four levels beyond 5th, to a total of four times per day at 17th level.

If a weapon bonded with a celestial spirit is destroyed, the paladin loses the use of this ability for 30 days, or until she gains a level, whichever comes first. During this 30-day period, the paladin takes a –1 penalty on attack and weapon damage rolls.

The second type of bond allows a paladin to gain the service of an unusually intelligent, strong, and loyal steed to serve her in her crusade against evil. This mount is usually a horse (for a Medium paladin) or a pony (for a Small paladin), although more exotic mounts, such as a boar, camel, or dog are also suitable. This mount functions as a druid's animal companion, using the paladin's level as her effective druid level. Bonded mounts have an Intelligence of at least 6.

Once per day, as a full-round action, a paladin may magically call her mount to her side. This ability is the equivalent of a spell of a level equal to one-third the paladin's level. The mount immediately appears adjacent to the paladin. A paladin can use this ability once per day at 5th level, and one additional time per day for every 4 levels thereafter, for a total of four times per day at 17th level.

At 11th level, the mount gains the celestial template (see the *Pathfinder RPG Bestiary*) and becomes a magical beast for the purposes of determining which spells affect it. At 15th level, a paladin's mount gains spell resistance equal to the paladin's level + 11.

Should the paladin's mount die, the paladin may not summon another mount for 30 days or until she gains a paladin level, whichever comes first. During this 30-day period, the paladin takes a –1 penalty on attack and weapon damage rolls.

Aura of Resolve (Su): At 8th level, a paladin is immune to charm spells and spell-like abilities. Each ally within 10 feet of her gains a +4 morale bonus on saving throws against charm effects.

This ability functions only while the paladin is conscious, not if she is unconscious or dead.

Aura of Justice (Su): At 11th level, a paladin can expend two uses of her smite evil ability to grant the ability to smite evil to all allies within 10 feet, using her bonuses. Allies must use this smite evil ability by the start of the paladin's next turn and the bonuses last for 1 minute. Using this ability is a free action. Evil creatures gain no benefit from this ability.

Aura of Faith (Su): At 14th level, a paladin's weapons are treated as good-aligned for the purposes of overcoming damage reduction. Any attack made against an enemy within 10 feet of her is treated as good-aligned for the purposes of overcoming damage reduction.

This ability functions only while the paladin is conscious, not if she is unconscious or dead.

Aura of Righteousness (Su): At 17th level, a paladin gains DR 5/evil and immunity to compulsion spells and spell-like abilities. Each ally within 10 feet of her gains a +4 morale bonus on saving throws against compulsion effects.

This ability functions only while the paladin is conscious, not if she is unconscious or dead.

Holy Champion (Su): At 20th level, a paladin becomes a conduit for the power of her god. Her DR increases to 10/evil. Whenever she uses smite evil and successfully strikes an evil outsider, the outsider is also subject to a *banishment,* using her paladin level as the caster level (her weapon and holy symbol automatically count as objects that the subject hates). After the *banishment* effect and the damage from the attack is resolved, the smite immediately ends. In addition, whenever she channels positive energy or uses lay on hands to heal a creature, she heals the maximum possible amount.

Code of Conduct: A paladin must be of lawful good alignment and loses all class features except proficiencies if she ever willingly commits an evil act.

Additionally, a paladin's code requires that she respect legitimate authority, act with honor (not lying, not

cheating, not using poison, and so forth), help those in need (provided they do not use the help for evil or chaotic ends), and punish those who harm or threaten innocents.

Associates: While she may adventure with good or neutral allies, a paladin avoids working with evil characters or with anyone who consistently offends her moral code. Under exceptional circumstances, a paladin can ally with evil associates, but only to defeat what she believes to be a greater evil. A paladin should seek an *atonement* spell periodically during such an unusual alliance, and should end the alliance immediately should she feel it is doing more harm than good. A paladin may accept only henchmen, followers, or cohorts who are lawful good.

Ex-Paladins

A paladin who ceases to be lawful good, who willfully commits an evil act, or who violates the code of conduct loses all paladin spells and class features (including the service of the paladin's mount, but not weapon, armor, and shield proficiencies). She may not progress any further in levels as a paladin. She regains her abilities and advancement potential if she atones for her violations (see the *atonement* spell description in Chapter 10), as appropriate.

RANGER

For those who relish the thrill of the hunt, there are only predators and prey. Be they scouts, trackers, or bounty hunters, rangers share much in common: unique mastery of specialized weapons, skill at stalking even the most elusive game, and the expertise to defeat a wide range of quarries. Knowledgeable, patient, and skilled hunters, these rangers hound man, beast, and monster alike, gaining insight into the way of the predator, skill in varied environments, and ever more lethal martial prowess. While some track man-eating creatures to protect the frontier, others pursue more cunning game— even fugitives among their own people.

Role: Rangers are deft skirmishers, either in melee or at range, capable of skillfully dancing in and out of battle. Their abilities allow them to deal significant harm to specific types of foes, but their skills are valuable against all manner of enemies.

Alignment: Any.

Hit Die: d10.

Class Skills

The ranger's class skills are Climb (Str), Craft (Int), Handle Animal (Cha), Heal (Wis), Intimidate (Cha), Knowledge (dungeoneering) (Int), Knowledge (geography) (Int), Knowledge (nature) (Int), Perception (Wis), Profession (Wis), Ride (Dex), Spellcraft (Int), Stealth (Dex), Survival (Wis), and Swim (Str).

Skill Ranks per Level: 6 + Int modifier.

Class Features

All of the following are class features of the ranger.

Weapon and Armor Proficiency: A ranger is proficient with all simple and martial weapons and with light armor, medium armor, and shields (except tower shields).

Favored Enemy (Ex): At 1st level, a ranger selects a creature type from the ranger favored enemies table. He gains a +2 bonus on Bluff, Knowledge, Perception, Sense Motive, and Survival checks against creatures of his selected type. Likewise, he gets a +2 bonus on weapon attack and damage rolls against them. A ranger may make Knowledge skill checks untrained when attempting to identify these creatures.

At 5th level and every five levels thereafter (10th, 15th, and 20th level), the ranger may select an additional favored enemy. In addition, at each such interval, the bonus against any one favored enemy (including the one just selected, if so desired) increases by +2.

If the ranger chooses humanoids or outsiders as a favored enemy, he must also choose an associated subtype, as indicated on the table below. (Note that there are other types of humanoid to choose from in the *Pathfinder RPG Bestiary*—those called out specifically on the table below are merely the most common.) If a specific creature falls into more than one category of favored enemy, the ranger's bonuses do not stack; he simply uses whichever bonus is higher.

RANGER FAVORED ENEMIES

Type (Subtype)	Type (Subtype)
Aberration	Humanoid (other subtype)
Animal	Magical beast
Construct	Monstrous humanoid
Dragon	Ooze
Fey	Outsider (air)
Humanoid (aquatic)	Outsider (chaotic)
Humanoid (dwarf)	Outsider (earth)
Humanoid (elf)	Outsider (evil)
Humanoid (giant)	Outsider (fire)
Humanoid (goblinoid)	Outsider (good)
Humanoid (gnoll)	Outsider (lawful)
Humanoid (gnome)	Outsider (native)
Humanoid (halfling)	Outsider (water)
Humanoid (human)	Plant
Humanoid (orc)	Undead
Humanoid (reptilian)	Vermin

Track (Ex): A ranger adds half his level (minimum 1) to Survival skill checks made to follow tracks.

Wild Empathy (Ex): A ranger can improve the initial attitude of an animal. This ability functions just like a Diplomacy check to improve the attitude of a person (see Chapter 4). The ranger rolls 1d20 and adds his ranger level and his Charisma bonus to determine the wild empathy check result. The typical domestic animal has a starting attitude of indifferent, while wild animals are usually unfriendly.

To use wild empathy, the ranger and the animal must be within 30 feet of one another under normal visibility conditions. Generally, influencing an animal in this way takes 1 minute, but, as with influencing people, it might take more or less time.

The ranger can also use this ability to influence a magical beast with an Intelligence score of 1 or 2, but he takes a –4 penalty on the check.

Combat Style Feat (Ex): At 2nd level, a ranger must select one of two combat styles to pursue: archery or two-weapon combat. The ranger's expertise manifests in the form of bonus feats at 2nd, 6th, 10th, 14th, and 18th level. He can choose feats from his selected combat style, even if he does not have the normal prerequisites.

If the ranger selects archery, he can choose from the following list whenever he gains a combat style feat: Far Shot, Point Blank Shot, Precise Shot, and Rapid Shot. At 6th level, he adds Improved Precise Shot and Manyshot to the list. At 10th level, he adds Pinpoint Targeting and Shot on the Run to the list.

If the ranger selects two-weapon combat, he can choose from the following list whenever he gains a combat style feat: Double Slice, Improved Shield Bash, Quick Draw, and Two-Weapon Fighting. At 6th level, he adds Improved Two-Weapon Fighting and Two-Weapon Defense to the list. At 10th level, he adds Greater Two-Weapon Fighting and Two-Weapon Rend to the list.

The benefits of the ranger's chosen style feats apply only when he wears light, medium, or no armor. He loses all benefits of his combat style feats when wearing heavy armor. Once a ranger selects a combat style, it cannot be changed.

Endurance: A ranger gains Endurance as a bonus feat at 3rd level.

Favored Terrain (Ex): At 3rd level, a ranger may select a type of terrain from the Favored Terrains table. The ranger gains a +2 bonus on initiative checks and Knowledge (geography), Perception, Stealth, and Survival skill checks when he is in this terrain. A ranger traveling through his favored terrain normally leaves no trail and cannot be tracked (though he may leave a trail if he so chooses).

At 8th level and every five levels thereafter, the ranger may select an additional favored terrain.

In addition, at each such interval, the skill bonus and initiative bonus in any one favored terrain (including the one just selected, if so desired), increases by +2.

If a specific terrain falls into more than one category of favored terrain, the ranger's bonuses do not stack; he simply uses whichever bonus is higher.

FAVORED TERRAINS

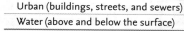

Favored Terrains
Cold (ice, glaciers, snow, and tundra)
Desert (sand and wastelands)
Forest (coniferous and deciduous)
Jungle
Mountain (including hills)
Plains
Planes (pick one, other than Material Plane)
Swamp
Underground (caves and dungeons)
Urban (buildings, streets, and sewers)
Water (above and below the surface)

TABLE 3-12: RANGER

Level	Base Attack Bonus	Fort Save	Ref Save	Will Save	Special	Spells per Day			
						1st	2nd	3rd	4th
1st	+1	+2	+2	+0	1st favored enemy, track, wild empathy	—	—	—	—
2nd	+2	+3	+3	+0	Combat style feat	—	—	—	—
3rd	+3	+3	+3	+1	Endurance, 1st favored terrain	—	—	—	—
4th	+4	+4	+4	+1	Hunter's bond	0	—	—	—
5th	+5	+4	+4	+1	2nd favored enemy	1	—	—	—
6th	+6/+1	+5	+5	+2	Combat style feat	1	—	—	—
7th	+7/+2	+5	+5	+2	Woodland stride	1	0	—	—
8th	+8/+3	+6	+6	+2	Swift tracker, 2nd favored terrain	1	1	—	—
9th	+9/+4	+6	+6	+3	Evasion	2	1	—	—
10th	+10/+5	+7	+7	+3	3rd favored enemy, combat style feat	2	1	0	—
11th	+11/+6/+1	+7	+7	+3	Quarry	2	1	1	—
12th	+12/+7/+2	+8	+8	+4	Camouflage	2	2	1	—
13th	+13/+8/+3	+8	+8	+4	3rd favored terrain	3	2	1	0
14th	+14/+9/+4	+9	+9	+4	Combat style feat	3	2	1	1
15th	+15/+10/+5	+9	+9	+5	4th favored enemy	3	2	2	1
16th	+16/+11/+6/+1	+10	+10	+5	Improved evasion	3	3	2	1
17th	+17/+12/+7/+2	+10	+10	+5	Hide in plain sight	4	3	2	1
18th	+18/+13/+8/+3	+11	+11	+6	4th favored terrain, combat style feat	4	3	2	2
19th	+19/+14/+9/+4	+11	+11	+6	Improved quarry	4	3	3	2
20th	+20/+15/+10/+5	+12	+12	+6	5th favored enemy, master hunter	4	4	3	3

Hunter's Bond (Ex): At 4th level, a ranger forms a bond with his hunting companions. This bond can take one of two forms. Once the form is chosen, it cannot be changed. The first is a bond to his companions. This bond allows him to spend a move action to grant half his favored enemy bonus against a single target of the appropriate type to all allies within 30 feet who can see or hear him. This bonus lasts for a number of rounds equal to the ranger's Wisdom modifier (minimum 1). This bonus does not stack with any favored enemy bonuses possessed by his allies; they use whichever bonus is higher.

The second option is to form a close bond with an animal companion. A ranger who selects an animal companion can choose from the following list: badger, bird, camel, cat (small), dire rat (see the *Pathfinder RPG Bestiary*), dog, horse, pony, snake (viper or constrictor), or wolf. If the campaign takes place wholly or partly in an aquatic environment, the ranger may choose a shark instead. This animal is a loyal companion that accompanies the ranger on his adventures as appropriate for its kind. A ranger's animal companion shares his favored enemy and favored terrain bonuses.

This ability functions like the druid animal companion ability (which is part of the Nature Bond class feature), except that the ranger's effective druid level is equal to his ranger level – 3.

Spells: Beginning at 4th level, a ranger gains the ability to cast a small number of divine spells, which are drawn from the ranger spell list presented in Chapter 10. A ranger must choose and prepare his spells in advance.

To prepare or cast a spell, a ranger must have a Wisdom score equal to at least 10 + the spell level. The Difficulty Class for a saving throw against a ranger's spell is 10 + the spell level + the ranger's Wisdom modifier.

Like other spellcasters, a ranger can cast only a certain number of spells of each spell level per day. His base daily spell allotment is given on Table 3–12. In addition, he receives bonus spells per day if he has a high Wisdom score (see Table 1–3). When Table 3–12 indicates that the ranger gets 0 spells per day of a given spell level, he gains only the bonus spells he would be entitled to based on his Wisdom score for that spell level.

A ranger must spend 1 hour per day in quiet meditation to regain his daily allotment of spells. A ranger may prepare and cast any spell on the ranger spell list, provided that he can cast spells of that level, but he must choose which spells to prepare during his daily meditation.

Through 3rd level, a ranger has no caster level. At 4th level and higher, his caster level is equal to his ranger level – 3.

Woodland Stride (Ex): Starting at 7th level, a ranger may move through any sort of undergrowth (such as natural thorns, briars, overgrown areas, and similar terrain) at his normal speed and without taking damage or suffering any other impairment.

Thorns, briars, and overgrown areas that are enchanted or magically manipulated to impede motion, however, still affect him.

Swift Tracker (Ex): Beginning at 8th level, a ranger can move at his normal speed while using Survival to follow tracks without taking the normal –5 penalty. He takes only a –10 penalty (instead of the normal –20) when moving at up to twice normal speed while tracking.

Evasion (Ex): When he reaches 9th level, a ranger can avoid even magical and unusual attacks with great agility. If he makes a successful Reflex saving throw against an attack that normally deals half damage on a successful save, he instead takes no damage. Evasion can be used only if the ranger is wearing light armor, medium armor, or no armor. A helpless ranger does not gain the benefit of evasion.

Quarry (Ex): At 11th level, a ranger can, as a standard action, denote one target within his line of sight as his quarry. Whenever he is following the tracks of his quarry, a ranger can take 10 on his Survival skill checks while moving at normal speed, without penalty. In addition, he receives a +2 insight bonus on attack rolls made against his quarry, and all critical threats are automatically confirmed. A ranger can have no more than one quarry at a time and the creature's type must correspond to one of his favored enemy types. He can dismiss this effect at any time as a free action, but he cannot select a new quarry for 24 hours. If the ranger sees proof that his quarry is dead, he can select a new quarry after waiting 1 hour.

Camouflage (Ex): A ranger of 12th level or higher can use the Stealth skill to hide in any of his favored terrains, even if the terrain doesn't grant cover or concealment.

Improved Evasion (Ex): At 16th level, a ranger's evasion improves. This ability works like evasion, except that while the ranger still takes no damage on a successful Reflex saving throw against attacks, he henceforth takes only half damage on a failed save. A helpless ranger does not gain the benefit of improved evasion.

Hide in Plain Sight (Ex): While in any of his favored terrains, a ranger of 17th level or higher can use the Stealth skill even while being observed.

Improved Quarry (Ex): At 19th level, the ranger's ability to hunt his quarry improves. He can now select a quarry as a free action, and can now take 20 while using Survival to track his quarry, while moving at normal speed without penalty. His insight bonus to attack his quarry increases to +4. If his quarry is killed or dismissed, he can select a new one after 10 minutes have passed.

Master Hunter (Ex): A ranger of 20th level becomes a master hunter. He can always move at full speed while using Survival to follow tracks without penalty. He can, as a standard action, make a single attack against a favored enemy at his full attack bonus. If the attack hits, the target takes damage normally and must make a Fortitude save or die. The DC of this save is equal to 10 + 1/2 the ranger's level + the ranger's Wisdom modifier. A ranger can choose instead to deal an amount of nonlethal damage equal to the creature's current hit points. A successful save negates this damage. A ranger can use this ability once per day against each favored enemy type he possesses, but not against the same creature more than once in a 24-hour period.

ROGUE

Life is an endless adventure for those who live by their wits. Ever just one step ahead of danger, rogues bank on their cunning, skill, and charm to bend fate to their favor. Never knowing what to expect, they prepare for everything, becoming masters of a wide variety of skills, training themselves to be adept manipulators, agile acrobats, shadowy stalkers, or masters of any of dozens of other professions or talents. Thieves and gamblers, fast talkers and diplomats, bandits and bounty hunters, and explorers and investigators all might be considered rogues, as well as countless other professions that rely upon wits, prowess, or luck. Although many rogues favor cities and the innumerable opportunities of civilization, some embrace lives on the road, journeying far, meeting exotic people, and facing fantastic danger in pursuit of equally fantastic riches. In the end, any who desire to shape their fates and live life on their own terms might come to be called rogues.

Role: Rogues excel at moving about unseen and catching foes unaware, and tend to avoid head-to-head combat. Their varied skills and abilities allow them to be highly versatile, with great variations in expertise existing between different rogues. Most, however, excel in overcoming hindrances of all types, from unlocking doors and disarming traps to outwitting magical hazards and conning dull-witted opponents.

Alignment: Any.

Hit Die: d8.

Class Skills

The rogue's class skills are Acrobatics (Dex), Appraise (Int), Bluff (Cha), Climb (Str), Craft (Int), Diplomacy (Cha), Disable Device (Dex), Disguise (Cha), Escape Artist (Dex), Intimidate (Cha), Knowledge (dungeoneering) (Int), Knowledge (local) (Int), Linguistics (Int), Perception (Wis), Perform (Cha), Profession (Wis), Sense Motive (Wis), Sleight of Hand (Dex), Stealth (Dex), Swim (Str), and Use Magic Device (Cha).

Skill Ranks per Level: 8 + Int modifier.

Class Features

The following are class features of the rogue.

Weapon and Armor Proficiency: Rogues are proficient with all simple weapons, plus the hand crossbow, rapier, sap, shortbow, and short sword. They are proficient with light armor, but not with shields.

Sneak Attack: If a rogue can catch an opponent when he is unable to defend himself effectively from her attack, she can strike a vital spot for extra damage.

The rogue's attack deals extra damage anytime her target would be denied a Dexterity bonus to AC (whether the target actually has a Dexterity bonus or not), or when the rogue flanks her target. This extra damage is 1d6 at 1st level, and increases by 1d6 every two rogue levels thereafter. Should the rogue score a critical hit with a sneak attack, this extra damage is not multiplied. Ranged attacks can count as sneak attacks only if the target is within 30 feet.

With a weapon that deals nonlethal damage (like a sap, whip, or an unarmed strike), a rogue can make a sneak attack that deals nonlethal damage instead of lethal damage. She cannot use a weapon that deals lethal damage to deal nonlethal damage in a sneak attack, not even with the usual –4 penalty.

The rogue must be able to see the target well enough to pick out a vital spot and must be able to reach such a spot. A rogue cannot sneak attack while striking a creature with concealment.

Trapfinding: A rogue adds 1/2 her level to Perception skill checks made to locate traps and to Disable Device skill checks (minimum +1). A rogue can use Disable Device to disarm magic traps.

Evasion (Ex): At 2nd level and higher, a rogue can avoid even magical and unusual attacks with great agility. If she makes a successful Reflex saving throw against an attack that normally deals half damage on a successful save, she instead takes no damage. Evasion can be used only if the rogue is wearing light armor or no armor. A helpless rogue does not gain the benefit of evasion.

Rogue Talents: As a rogue gains experience, she learns a number of talents that aid her and confound her foes. Starting at 2nd level, a rogue gains one rogue talent. She gains an additional rogue talent for every 2 levels of rogue attained after 2nd level. A rogue cannot select an individual talent more than once.

Talents marked with an asterisk add effects to a rogue's sneak attack. Only one of these talents can be applied to an individual attack and the decision must be made before the attack roll is made.

Bleeding Attack* (Ex): A rogue with this ability can cause living opponents to bleed by hitting them with a sneak attack. This attack causes the target to take 1 additional point of damage each round for each die of the rogue's sneak attack (e.g., 4d6 equals 4 points of bleed). Bleeding creatures take that amount of damage every round at the start of each of their turns. The bleeding can be stopped by a DC 15 Heal check or the application of any effect that heals hit point damage. Bleeding damage from this ability does not stack with itself. Bleeding damage bypasses any damage reduction the creature might possess.

Combat Trick: A rogue that selects this talent gains a bonus combat feat (see Chapter 5).

Fast Stealth (Ex): This ability allows a rogue to move at full speed using the Stealth skill without penalty.

Finesse Rogue: A rogue that selects this talent gains Weapon Finesse as a bonus feat.

Ledge Walker (Ex): This ability allows a rogue to move along narrow surfaces at full speed using the Acrobatics skill without penalty. In addition, a rogue with this talent is not flat-footed when using Acrobatics to move along narrow surfaces.

Major Magic (Sp): A rogue with this talent gains the ability to cast a 1st-level spell from the sorcerer/wizard spell list two times a day as a spell-like ability. The caster level for this ability is equal to the rogue's level. The save DC for this spell is 11 + the rogue's Intelligence modifier. The rogue must have an Intelligence of at least 11 to select this talent. A rogue must have the minor magic rogue talent before choosing this talent.

Minor Magic (Sp): A rogue with this talent gains the ability to cast a 0-level spell from the sorcerer/wizard spell list. This spell can be cast three times a day as a spell-like ability. The caster level for this ability is equal to the rogue's level. The save DC for this spell is 10 + the rogue's Intelligence modifier. The rogue must have an Intelligence of at least 10 to select this talent.

Quick Disable (Ex): It takes a rogue with this ability half the normal amount of time to disable a trap using the Disable Device skill (minimum 1 round).

Resiliency (Ex): Once per day, a rogue with this ability can gain a number of temporary hit points equal to the rogue's level. Activating this ability is an immediate action that can only be performed when she is brought to below 0 hit points. This ability can be used to prevent her from dying. These temporary hit points last for 1 minute. If the rogue's hit points drop below 0 due to the loss of these temporary hit points, she falls unconscious and is dying as normal.

Rogue Crawl (Ex): While prone, a rogue with this ability can move at half speed. This movement provokes attacks of opportunity as normal. A rogue with this talent can take a 5-foot step while crawling.

Slow Reactions* (Ex): Opponents damaged by the rogue's sneak attack can't make attacks of opportunity for 1 round.

Stand Up (Ex): A rogue with this ability can stand up from a prone position as a free action. This still provokes attacks of opportunity for standing up while threatened by a foe.

Surprise Attack (Ex): During the surprise round, opponents are always considered flat-footed to a rogue with this ability, even if they have already acted.

Trap Spotter (Ex): Whenever a rogue with this talent comes within 10 feet of a trap, she receives an immediate Perception skill check to notice the trap. This check should be made in secret by the GM.

Weapon Training: A rogue that selects this talent gains Weapon Focus as a bonus feat.

Trap Sense (Ex): At 3rd level, a rogue gains an intuitive sense that alerts her to danger from traps, giving her a +1 bonus on Reflex saves made to avoid traps and a +1 dodge bonus to AC against attacks made by traps. These bonuses rise to +2 when the rogue reaches 6th level, to +3 when she reaches 9th level, to +4 when she reaches 12th level, to +5 at 15th, and to +6 at 18th level.

Trap sense bonuses gained from multiple classes stack.

Uncanny Dodge (Ex): Starting at 4th level, a rogue can react to danger before her senses would normally allow her to do so. She cannot be caught flat-footed, nor does she lose her Dex bonus to AC if the attacker is invisible. She still loses her Dexterity bonus to AC if immobilized. A rogue with this ability can still lose her Dexterity bonus to AC if an opponent successfully uses the feint action (see Chapter 8) against her.

If a rogue already has uncanny dodge from a different class, she automatically gains improved uncanny dodge (see below) instead.

Improved Uncanny Dodge (Ex): A rogue of 8th level or higher can no longer be flanked.

This defense denies another rogue the ability to sneak attack the character by flanking her, unless the attacker has at least four more rogue levels than the target does.

If a character already has uncanny dodge (see above) from another class, the levels from the classes that grant uncanny dodge stack to determine the minimum rogue level required to flank the character.

Advanced Talents: At 10th level, and every two levels thereafter, a rogue can choose one of the following advanced talents in place of a rogue talent.

Crippling Strike* (Ex): A rogue with this ability can sneak attack opponents with such precision that her blows weaken and hamper them. An opponent damaged by one of her sneak attacks also takes 2 points of Strength damage.

Defensive Roll (Ex): With this advanced talent, the rogue can roll with a potentially lethal blow to take less damage from it than she otherwise would. Once per day, when she would be reduced to 0 or fewer hit points by damage in combat (from a weapon

TABLE 3-13: ROGUE

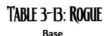

Level	Base Attack Bonus	Fort Save	Ref Save	Will Save	Special
1st	+0	+0	+2	+0	Sneak attack +1d6, trapfinding
2nd	+1	+0	+3	+0	Evasion, rogue talent
3rd	+2	+1	+3	+1	Sneak attack +2d6, trap sense +1
4th	+3	+1	+4	+1	Rogue talent, uncanny dodge
5th	+3	+1	+4	+1	Sneak attack +3d6
6th	+4	+2	+5	+2	Rogue talent, trap sense +2
7th	+5	+2	+5	+2	Sneak attack +4d6
8th	+6/+1	+2	+6	+2	Improved uncanny dodge, rogue talent
9th	+6/+1	+3	+6	+3	Sneak attack +5d6, trap sense +3
10th	+7/+2	+3	+7	+3	Advanced talents, rogue talent
11th	+8/+3	+3	+7	+3	Sneak attack +6d6
12th	+9/+4	+4	+8	+4	Rogue talent, trap sense +4
13th	+9/+4	+4	+8	+4	Sneak attack +7d6
14th	+10/+5	+4	+9	+4	Rogue talent
15th	+11/+6/+1	+5	+9	+5	Sneak attack +8d6, trap sense +5
16th	+12/+7/+2	+5	+10	+5	Rogue talent
17th	+12/+7/+2	+5	+10	+5	Sneak attack +9d6
18th	+13/+8/+3	+6	+11	+6	Rogue talent, trap sense +6
19th	+14/+9/+4	+6	+11	+6	Sneak attack +10d6
20th	+15/+10/+5	+6	+12	+6	Master strike, rogue talent

or other blow, not a spell or special ability), the rogue can attempt to roll with the damage. To use this ability, the rogue must attempt a Reflex saving throw (DC = damage dealt). If the save succeeds, she takes only half damage from the blow; if it fails, she takes full damage. She must be aware of the attack and able to react to it in order to execute her defensive roll—if she is denied her Dexterity bonus to AC, she can't use this ability. Since this effect would not normally allow a character to make a Reflex save for half damage, the rogue's evasion ability does not apply to the defensive roll.

Dispelling Attack (Su)*: Opponents that are dealt sneak attack damage by a rogue with this ability are affected by a targeted *dispel magic*, targeting the lowest-level spell effect active on the target. The caster level for this ability is equal to the rogue's level. A rogue must have the major magic rogue talent before choosing dispelling attack.

Improved Evasion (Ex): This works like evasion, except that while the rogue still takes no damage on a successful Reflex saving throw against attacks, she henceforth takes only half damage on a failed save. A helpless rogue does not gain the benefit of improved evasion.

Opportunist (Ex): Once per round, the rogue can make an attack of opportunity against an opponent who has just been struck for damage in melee by another character. This attack counts as an attack of opportunity for that round. Even a rogue with the Combat Reflexes feat can't use the opportunist ability more than once per round.

Skill Mastery: The rogue becomes so confident in the use of certain skills that she can use them reliably even under adverse conditions.

Upon gaining this ability, she selects a number of skills equal to 3 + her Intelligence modifier. When making a skill check with one of these skills, she may take 10 even if stress and distractions would normally prevent her from doing so. A rogue may gain this special ability multiple times, selecting additional skills for skill mastery to apply to each time.

Slippery Mind (Ex): This ability represents the rogue's ability to wriggle free from magical effects that would otherwise control or compel her. If a rogue with slippery mind is affected by an enchantment spell or effect and fails her saving throw, she can attempt it again 1 round later at the same DC. She gets only this one extra chance to succeed on her saving throw.

Feat: A rogue may gain any feat that she qualifies for in place of a rogue talent.

Master Strike (Ex): Upon reaching 20th level, a rogue becomes incredibly deadly when dealing sneak attack damage. Each time the rogue deals sneak attack damage, she can choose one of the following three effects: the target can be put to sleep for 1d4 hours, paralyzed for 2d6 rounds, or slain. Regardless of the effect chosen, the target receives a Fortitude save to negate the additional effect. The DC of this save is equal to 10 + 1/2 the rogue's level + the rogue's Intelligence modifier. Once a creature has been the target of a master strike, regardless of whether or not the save is made, that creature is immune to that rogue's master strike for 24 hours. Creatures that are immune to sneak attack damage are also immune to this ability.

SORCERER

Scions of innately magical bloodlines, the chosen of deities, the spawn of monsters, pawns of fate and destiny, or simply flukes of fickle magic, sorcerers look within themselves for arcane prowess and draw forth might few mortals can imagine. Emboldened by lives ever threatening to be consumed by their innate powers, these magic-touched souls endlessly indulge in and refine their mysterious abilities, gradually learning how to harness their birthright and coax forth ever greater arcane feats. Just as varied as these innately powerful spellcasters' abilities and inspirations are the ways in which they choose to utilize their gifts. While some seek to control their abilities through meditation and discipline, becoming masters of their fantastic birthright, others give in to their magic, letting it rule their lives with often explosive results. Regardless, sorcerers live and breathe that which other spellcasters devote their lives to mastering, and for them magic is more than a boon or a field of study; it is life itself.

Role: Sorcerers excel at casting a selection of favored spells frequently, making them powerful battle mages. As they become familiar with a specific and ever-widening set of spells, sorcerers often discover new and versatile ways of making use of magics other spellcasters might overlook. Their bloodlines also grant them additional abilities, assuring that no two sorcerers are ever quite alike.

Alignment: Any.

Hit Die: d6.

Class Skills

The sorcerer's class skills are Appraise (Int), Bluff (Cha), Craft (Int), Fly (Dex), Intimidate (Cha), Knowledge (arcana) (Int), Profession (Wis), Spellcraft (Int), and Use Magic Device (Cha).

Skill Ranks per Level: 2 + Int modifier.

Class Features

All of the following are class features of the sorcerer.

Weapon and Armor Proficiency: Sorcerers are proficient with all simple weapons. They are not proficient with any type of armor or shield. Armor interferes with a sorcerer's gestures, which can cause her spells with somatic components to fail (see Arcane Spells and Armor on page 83).

Spells: A sorcerer casts arcane spells drawn primarily from the sorcerer/wizard spell list presented in Chapter 10. She can cast any spell she knows without preparing it ahead of time. To learn or cast a spell, a sorcerer must have a Charisma score equal to at least 10 + the spell level. The Difficulty Class for a saving throw against a sorcerer's spell is 10 + the spell level + the sorcerer's Charisma modifier.

Like other spellcasters, a sorcerer can cast only a certain number of spells of each spell level per day. Her base daily spell allotment is given on Table 3–14. In addition, she receives bonus spells per day if she has a high Charisma score (see Table 1–3).

A sorcerer's selection of spells is extremely limited. A sorcerer begins play knowing four 0-level spells and two 1st-level spells of her choice. At each new sorcerer level, she gains one or more new spells, as indicated on Table 3–15. (Unlike spells per day, the number of spells a sorcerer knows is not affected by her Charisma score; the numbers on Table 3–15 are fixed.) These new spells can be common spells chosen from the sorcerer/wizard spell list, or they can be unusual spells that the sorcerer has gained some understanding of through study.

Upon reaching 4th level, and at every even-numbered sorcerer level after that (6th, 8th, and so on), a sorcerer can choose to learn a new spell in place of one she already knows. In effect, the sorcerer loses the old spell in exchange for the new one. The new spell's level must be the same as that of the spell being exchanged. A sorcerer may swap only a single spell at any given level, and must choose whether or not to swap the spell at the same time that she gains new spells known for the level.

Unlike a wizard or a cleric, a sorcerer need not prepare her spells in advance. She can cast any spell she knows at any time, assuming she has not yet used up her spells per day for that spell level.

Bloodline: Each sorcerer has a source of magic somewhere in her heritage that grants her spells, bonus feats, an additional class skill, and other special abilities. This source can represent a blood relation or an extreme event involving a creature somewhere in the family's past. For example, a sorcerer might have a dragon as a distant relative or her grandfather might have signed a terrible contract with a devil. Regardless of the source, this influence manifests in a number of ways as the sorcerer gains levels. A sorcerer must pick one bloodline upon taking her first level of sorcerer. Once made, this choice cannot be changed.

At 3rd level, and every two levels thereafter, a sorcerer learns an additional spell, derived from her bloodline. These spells are in addition to the number of spells given on Table 3–15. These spells cannot be exchanged for different spells at higher levels.

At 7th level, and every six levels thereafter, a sorcerer receives one bonus feat, chosen from a list specific to each bloodline. The sorcerer must meet the prerequisites for these bonus feats.

Cantrips: Sorcerers learn a number of cantrips, or 0-level spells, as noted on Table 3–15 under "Spells Known." These spells are cast like any other spell, but they do not consume any slots and may be used again.

Eschew Materials: A sorcerer gains Eschew Materials as a bonus feat at 1st level.

Sorcerer Bloodlines

The following bloodlines represent only some of the possible sources of power that a sorcerer can draw upon. Unless otherwise noted, most sorcerers are assumed to have the arcane bloodline.

Table 3-14: Sorcerer

Level	Base Attack Bonus	Fort Save	Ref Save	Will Save	Special	Spells per Day								
						1st	2nd	3rd	4th	5th	6th	7th	8th	9th
1st	+0	+0	+0	+2	Bloodline power, cantrips, eschew materials	3	—	—	—	—	—	—	—	—
2nd	+1	+0	+0	+3		4	—	—	—	—	—	—	—	—
3rd	+1	+1	+1	+3	Bloodline power, bloodline spell	5	—	—	—	—	—	—	—	—
4th	+2	+1	+1	+4		6	3	—	—	—	—	—	—	—
5th	+2	+1	+1	+4	Bloodline spell	6	4	—	—	—	—	—	—	—
6th	+3	+2	+2	+5		6	5	3	—	—	—	—	—	—
7th	+3	+2	+2	+5	Bloodline feat, bloodline spell	6	6	4	—	—	—	—	—	—
8th	+4	+2	+2	+6		6	6	5	3	—	—	—	—	—
9th	+4	+3	+3	+6	Bloodline power, bloodline spell	6	6	6	4	—	—	—	—	—
10th	+5	+3	+3	+7		6	6	6	5	3	—	—	—	—
11th	+5	+3	+3	+7	Bloodline spell	6	6	6	6	4	—	—	—	—
12th	+6/+1	+4	+4	+8		6	6	6	6	5	3	—	—	—
13th	+6/+1	+4	+4	+8	Bloodline feat, bloodline spell	6	6	6	6	6	4	—	—	—
14th	+7/+2	+4	+4	+9		6	6	6	6	6	5	3	—	—
15th	+7/+2	+5	+5	+9	Bloodline power, bloodline spell	6	6	6	6	6	6	4	—	—
16th	+8/+3	+5	+5	+10		6	6	6	6	6	6	5	3	—
17th	+8/+3	+5	+5	+10	Bloodline spell	6	6	6	6	6	6	6	4	—
18th	+9/+4	+6	+6	+11		6	6	6	6	6	6	6	5	3
19th	+9/+4	+6	+6	+11	Bloodline feat, bloodline spell	6	6	6	6	6	6	6	6	4
20th	+10/+5	+6	+6	+12	Bloodline power	6	6	6	6	6	6	6	6	6

Aberrant

There is a taint in your blood, one that is alien and bizarre. You tend to think in odd ways, approaching problems from an angle that most would not expect. Over time, this taint manifests itself in your physical form.

Class Skill: Knowledge (dungeoneering).

Bonus Spells: *enlarge person* (3rd), *see invisibility* (5th), *tongues* (7th), *black tentacles* (9th), *feeblemind* (11th), *veil* (13th), *plane shift* (15th), *mind blank* (17th), *shapechange* (19th).

Bonus Feats: Combat Casting, Improved Disarm, Improved Grapple, Improved Initiative, Improved Unarmed Strike, Iron Will, Silent Spell, Skill Focus (Knowledge [dungeoneering]).

Bloodline Arcana: Whenever you cast a spell of the polymorph subschool, increase the duration of the spell by 50% (minimum 1 round). This bonus does not stack with the increase granted by the Extend Spell feat.

Bloodline Powers: Aberrant sorcerers show increasing signs of their tainted heritage as they increase in level, although they are only visible when used.

Acidic Ray (Sp): Starting at 1st level, you can fire an acidic ray as a standard action, targeting any foe within 30 feet as a ranged touch attack. The acidic ray deals 1d6 points of acid damage + 1 for every two sorcerer levels you possess. You can use this ability a number of times per day equal to 3 + your Charisma modifier.

Long Limbs (Ex): At 3rd level, your reach increases by 5 feet whenever you are making a melee touch attack. This ability does not otherwise increase your threatened area. At 11th level, this bonus to your reach increases to 10 feet. At 17th level, this bonus to your reach increases to 15 feet.

Unusual Anatomy (Ex): At 9th level, your anatomy changes, giving you a 25% chance to ignore any critical hit or sneak attack scored against you, treating it as a normal hit instead. This chance increases to 50% at 13th level.

Alien Resistance (Su): At 15th level, you gain spell resistance equal to your sorcerer level + 10.

Aberrant Form (Ex): At 20th level, your body becomes truly unnatural. You are immune to critical hits and sneak attacks. In addition, you gain blindsight with a range of 60 feet and damage reduction 5/—.

Abyssal

Generations ago, a demon spread its filth into your heritage. While it does not manifest in all of your kin, for you it is particularly strong. You might sometimes have urges to chaos or evil, but your destiny (and alignment) is up to you.

Class Skill: Knowledge (planes).

Bonus Spells: *cause fear* (3rd), *bull's strength* (5th), *rage* (7th), *stoneskin* (9th), *dismissal* (11th), *transformation* (13th), *greater teleport* (15th), *unholy aura* (17th), *summon monster IX* (19th).

Bonus Feats: Augment Summoning, Cleave, Empower Spell, Great Fortitude, Improved Bull Rush, Improved Sunder, Power Attack, Skill Focus (Knowledge [planes]).

Bloodline Arcana: Whenever you cast a spell of the summoning subschool, the creatures summoned gain DR/good equal to 1/2 your sorcerer level (minimum 1). This does not stack with any DR the creature might have.

Bloodline Powers: While some would say that you are possessed, you know better. The demonic influence in your blood grows as you gain power.

Claws (Su): At 1st level, you can grow claws as a free action. These claws are treated as natural weapons, allowing you to make two claw attacks as a full attack action using your full base attack bonus. These attacks deal 1d4 points of damage each (1d3 if you are Small) plus your Strength modifier. At 5th level, these claws are considered magic weapons for the purpose of overcoming DR. At 7th level, the damage increases by one step to 1d6 points of damage (1d4 if you are Small). At 11th level, these claws become *flaming weapons*, each dealing an additional 1d6 points of fire damage on a successful hit. You can use your claws for a number of rounds per day equal to 3 + your Charisma modifier. These rounds do not need to be consecutive.

Demon Resistances (Ex): At 3rd level, you gain resist electricity 5 and a +2 bonus on saving throws made against poison. At 9th level, your resistance to electricity increases to 10 and your bonus on poison saving throws increases to +4.

Strength of the Abyss (Ex): At 9th level, you gain a +2 inherent bonus to your Strength. This bonus increases to +4 at 13th level, and to +6 at 17th level.

Added Summonings (Su): At 15th level, whenever you summon a creature with the demon subtype or the fiendish template using a *summon monster* spell, you summon one additional creature of the same kind.

Demonic Might (Su): At 20th level, the power of the Abyss flows through you. You gain immunity to electricity and poison. You also gain resistance to acid 10, cold 10, and fire 10, and gain telepathy with a range of 60 feet (allowing you to communicate with any creature that can speak a language).

Arcane

Your family has always been skilled in the eldritch art of magic. While many of your relatives were accomplished wizards, your powers developed without the need for study and practice.

Class Skill: Knowledge (any one).

Bonus Spells: *identify* (3rd), *invisibility* (5th), *dispel magic* (7th), *dimension door* (9th), *overland flight* (11th), *true seeing* (13th), *greater teleport* (15th), *power word stun* (17th), *wish* (19th).

Bonus Feats: Combat Casting, Improved Counterspell, Improved Initiative, Iron Will, Scribe Scroll, Skill Focus (Knowledge [arcana]), Spell Focus, Still Spell.

TABLE 3-15: SORCERER SPELLS KNOWN

Level	Spells Known								
	0	1st	2nd	3rd	4th	5th	6th	7th	8th	9th
1st	4	2	—	—	—	—	—	—	—	—
2nd	5	2	—	—	—	—	—	—	—	—
3rd	5	3	—	—	—	—	—	—	—	—
4th	6	3	1	—	—	—	—	—	—	—
5th	6	4	2	—	—	—	—	—	—	—
6th	7	4	2	1	—	—	—	—	—	—
7th	7	5	3	2	—	—	—	—	—	—
8th	8	5	3	2	1	—	—	—	—	—
9th	8	5	4	3	2	—	—	—	—	—
10th	9	5	4	3	2	1	—	—	—	—
11th	9	5	5	4	3	2	—	—	—	—
12th	9	5	5	4	3	2	1	—	—	—
13th	9	5	5	4	4	3	2	—	—	—
14th	9	5	5	4	4	3	2	1	—	—
15th	9	5	5	4	4	4	3	2	—	—
16th	9	5	5	4	4	4	3	2	1	—
17th	9	5	5	4	4	4	3	3	2	—
18th	9	5	5	4	4	4	3	3	2	1
19th	9	5	5	4	4	4	3	3	3	2
20th	9	5	5	4	4	4	3	3	3	3

Bloodline Arcana: Whenever you apply a metamagic feat to a spell that increases the slot used by at least one level, increase the spell's DC by +1. This bonus does not stack with itself and does not apply to spells modified by the Heighten Spell feat.

Bloodline Powers: Magic comes naturally to you, but as you gain levels you must take care to prevent the power from overwhelming you.

Arcane Bond (Su): At 1st level, you gain an arcane bond, as a wizard equal to your sorcerer level. Your sorcerer levels stack with any wizard levels you possess when determining the powers of your familiar or bonded object. This ability does not allow you to have both a familiar and a bonded item. Rules for arcane bonds appear on page 78. Once per day, your bonded item allows you to cast any one of your spells known (unlike a wizard's bonded item, which allows him to cast any one spell in his spellbook).

Metamagic Adept (Ex): At 3rd level, you can apply any one metamagic feat you know to a spell you are about to cast without increasing the casting time. You must still expend a higher-level spell slot to cast this spell. You can use this ability once per day at 3rd level and one additional time per day for every four sorcerer levels you possess beyond 3rd, up to five times per day at 19th level. At 20th level, this ability is replaced by arcane apotheosis.

New Arcana (Ex): At 9th level, you can add any one spell from the sorcerer/wizard spell list to your list of spells

known. This spell must be of a level that you are capable of casting. You can also add one additional spell at 13th level and 17th level.

School Power (Ex): At 15th level, pick one school of magic. The DC for any spells you cast from that school increases by +2. This bonus stacks with the bonus granted by Spell Focus.

Arcane Apotheosis (Ex): At 20th level, your body surges with arcane power. You can add any metamagic feats that you know to your spells without increasing their casting time, although you must still expend higher-level spell slots. Whenever you use magic items that require charges, you can instead expend spell slots to power the item. For every three levels of spell slots that you expend, you consume one less charge when using a magic item that expends charges.

Celestial

Your bloodline is blessed by a celestial power, either from a celestial ancestor or through divine intervention. Although this power drives you along the path of good, your fate (and alignment) is your own to determine.

Class Skill: Heal.

Bonus Spells: *bless* (3rd), *resist energy* (5th), *magic circle against evil* (7th), *remove curse* (9th), *flame strike* (11th), *greater dispel magic* (13th), *banishment* (15th), *sunburst* (17th), *gate* (19th).

Bonus Feats: Dodge, Extend Spell, Iron Will, Mobility, Mounted Combat, Ride-By Attack, Skill Focus (Knowledge [religion]), Weapon Finesse.

Bloodline Arcana: Whenever you cast a spell of the summoning subschool, the creatures summoned gain DR/evil equal to 1/2 your sorcerer level (minimum 1). This does not stack with any DR the creature might have.

Bloodline Powers: Your celestial heritage grants you a great many powers, but they come at a price. The lords of the higher planes are watching you and your actions closely.

Heavenly Fire (Sp): Starting at 1st level, you can unleash a ray of heavenly fire as a standard action, targeting any foe within 30 feet as a ranged touch attack. Against evil creatures, this ray deals 1d4 points of damage + 1 for every two sorcerer levels you possess. This damage is divine and not subject to energy resistance or immunity. This ray heals good creatures of 1d4 points of damage + 1 for every two sorcerer levels you possess. A good creature cannot benefit from your heavenly fire more than once per day. Neutral creatures are neither harmed nor healed by this effect. You can use this ability a number of times per day equal to 3 + your Charisma modifier.

Celestial Resistances (Ex): At 3rd level, you gain resist acid 5 and resist cold 5. At 9th level, your resistances increase to 10.

Wings of Heaven (Su): At 9th level, you can sprout feathery wings and fly for a number of minutes per day equal to your sorcerer level, with a speed of 60 feet and good maneuverability. This duration does not need to be consecutive, but it must be used in 1 minute increments.

Conviction (Su): At 15th level, you can reroll any one ability check, attack roll, skill check, or saving throw you just made. You must decide to use this ability after the die is rolled, but before the results are revealed by the GM. You must take the second result, even if it is worse. You can use this ability once per day.

Ascension (Su): At 20th level, you become infused with the power of the heavens. You gain immunity to acid, cold, and petrification. You also gain resist electricity 10, resist fire 10, and a +4 racial bonus on saves against poison. You also gain unlimited use of the wings of heaven ability. Finally, you gain the ability to speak with any creature that has a language (as per the *tongues* spell).

Destined

Your family is destined for greatness in some way. Your birth could have been foretold in prophecy, or perhaps it occurred during an especially auspicious event, such as a solar eclipse. Regardless of your bloodline's origin, you have a great future ahead.

Class Skill: Knowledge (history).

Bonus Spells: *alarm* (3rd), *blur* (5th), *protection from energy* (7th), *freedom of movement* (9th), *break enchantment* (11th), *mislead* (13th), *spell turning* (15th), *moment of prescience* (17th), *foresight* (19th).

Bonus Feats: Arcane Strike, Diehard, Endurance, Leadership, Lightning Reflexes, Maximize Spell, Skill Focus (Knowledge [history]), Weapon Focus.

Bloodline Arcana: Whenever you cast a spell with a range of "personal," you gain a luck bonus equal to the spell's level on all your saving throws for 1 round.

Bloodline Powers: You are destined for great things, and the powers that you gain serve to protect you.

Touch of Destiny (Sp): At 1st level, you can touch a creature as a standard action, giving it an insight bonus on attack rolls, skill checks, ability checks, and saving throws equal to 1/2 your sorcerer level (minimum 1) for 1 round. You can use this ability a number of times per day equal to 3 + your Charisma modifier.

Fated (Su): Starting at 3rd level, you gain a +1 luck bonus on all of your saving throws and to your AC during surprise rounds (see Chapter 8) and when you are otherwise unaware of an attack. At 7th level and every four levels thereafter, this bonus increases by +1, to a maximum of +5 at 19th level.

It Was Meant To Be (Su): At 9th level, you may reroll any one attack roll, critical hit confirmation roll, or level check made to overcome spell resistance. You must decide to use this ability after the first roll is made but before the results are revealed by the GM. You must take the second result, even if it is worse. At 9th level, you can use this ability once per day. At 17th level, you can use this ability twice per day.

Within Reach (Su): At 15th level, your ultimate destiny is drawing near. Once per day, when an attack or spell that causes damage would result in your death, you may attempt a DC 20 Will save. If successful, you are instead reduced to –1 hit points and are automatically stabilized. The bonus from your fated ability applies to this save.

Destiny Realized (Su): At 20th level, your moment of destiny is at hand. Any critical threats made against you only confirm if the second roll results in a natural 20 on the die. Any critical threats you score with a spell are automatically confirmed. Once per day, you can automatically succeed at one caster level check made to overcome spell resistance. You must use this ability before making the roll.

Draconic

At some point in your family's history, a dragon interbred with your bloodline, and now its ancient power flows through your veins.

Class Skill: Perception.

Bonus Spells: *mage armor* (3rd), *resist energy* (5th), *fly* (7th), *fear* (9th), *spell resistance* (11th), *form of the dragon I* (13th), *form of the dragon II* (15th), *form of the dragon III* (17th), *wish* (19th).

Bonus Feats: Blind-Fight, Great Fortitude, Improved Initiative, Power Attack, Quicken Spell, Skill Focus (Fly), Skill Focus (Knowledge [arcana]), Toughness.

Bloodline Arcana: Whenever you cast a spell with an energy descriptor that matches your draconic bloodline's energy type, that spell deals +1 point of damage per die rolled.

Bloodline Powers: The power of dragons flows through you and manifests in a number of ways. At 1st level, you must select one of the chromatic or metallic dragon types (see the *Pathfinder RPG Bestiary*). This choice cannot be changed. A number of your abilities grant resistances and deal damage based on your dragon type, as noted on the following table.

Dragon Type	Energy Type	Breath Shape
Black	Acid	60-foot line
Blue	Electricity	60-foot line
Green	Acid	30-foot cone
Red	Fire	30-foot cone
White	Cold	30-foot cone
Brass	Fire	60-foot line
Bronze	Electricity	60-foot line
Copper	Acid	60-foot line
Gold	Fire	30-foot cone
Silver	Cold	30-foot cone

Claws (Su): Starting at 1st level, you can grow claws as a free action. These claws are treated as natural weapons, allowing you to make two claw attacks as a full attack action using your full base attack bonus. Each of these attacks deals 1d4 points of damage plus your Strength modifier (1d3 if you are Small). At 5th level, these claws are considered magic weapons for the purpose of overcoming DR. At 7th level, the damage increases by one step to 1d6 points of damage (1d4 if you are Small). At 11th level, these claws deal an additional 1d6 points of damage of your energy type on a successful hit. You can use your claws for a number of rounds per day equal to 3 + your Charisma modifier. These rounds do not need to be consecutive.

Dragon Resistances (Ex): At 3rd level, you gain resist 5 against your energy type and a +1 natural armor bonus. At 9th level, your energy resistance increases to 10 and natural armor bonus increases to +2. At 15th level, your natural armor bonus increases to +4.

Breath Weapon (Su): At 9th level, you gain a breath weapon. This breath weapon deals 1d6 points of damage of your energy type per sorcerer level. Those caught in the area of the breath receive a Reflex save for half damage. The DC of this save is equal to 10 + 1/2 your sorcerer level + your Charisma modifier. The shape of the breath weapon depends on your dragon type (as indicated on the above chart). At 9th level, you can use this ability once per day. At 17th level, you can use this ability twice per day. At 20th level, you can use this ability three times per day.

Wings (Su): At 15th level, leathery dragon wings grow from your back as a standard action, giving you a fly speed of 60 feet with average maneuverability. You can dismiss the wings as a free action.

Power of Wyrms (Su): At 20th level, your draconic heritage becomes manifest. You gain immunity to paralysis, sleep, and damage of your energy type. You also gain blindsense 60 feet.

Elemental

The power of the elements resides in you, and at times you can hardly control its fury. This influence comes from an elemental outsider in your family history or a time when you or your relatives were exposed to a powerful elemental force.

Class Skill: Knowledge (planes).

Bonus Spells: *burning hands** (3rd), *scorching ray** (5th), *protection from energy* (7th), *elemental body I* (9th), *elemental body II* (11th), *elemental body III* (13th), *elemental body IV* (15th), *summon monster VIII* (elementals only) (17th), *elemental swarm* (19th).

*These spells always deal a type of damage determined by your element. In addition, the subtype of these spells changes to match the energy type of your element.

Bonus Feats: Dodge, Empower Spell, Great Fortitude, Improved Initiative, Lightning Reflexes, Power Attack, Skill Focus (Knowledge [planes]), Weapon Finesse.

Bloodline Arcana: Whenever you cast a spell that deals energy damage, you can change the type of damage to match the type of your bloodline. This also changes the spell's type to match the type of your bloodline.

Bloodline Powers: One of the four elements infuses your being, and you can draw upon its power in times of need. At first level, you must select one of the four elements: air, earth, fire, or water. This choice cannot be changed. A number of your abilities grant resistances and deal damage based on your element, as noted below.

Element	Energy Type	Elemental Movement
Air	Electricity	Fly 60 feet (average)
Earth	Acid	Burrow 30 feet
Fire	Fire	+30 feet base speed
Water	Cold	Swim 60 feet

Elemental Ray (Sp): Starting at 1st level, you can unleash an elemental ray as a standard action, targeting any foe within 30 feet as a ranged touch attack. This ray deals 1d6 points of damage of your energy type + 1 for every two sorcerer levels you possess. You can use this ability a number of times per day equal to 3 + your Charisma modifier.

Elemental Resistance (Ex): At 3rd level, you gain energy resistance 10 against your energy type. At 9th level, your energy resistance increases to 20.

Elemental Blast (Sp): At 9th level, you can unleash a blast of elemental power once per day. This 20-foot-radius burst does 1d6 points of damage of your energy type per sorcerer level. Those caught in the area of your blast receive a Reflex save for half damage. Creatures that fail their saves gain vulnerability to your energy type until the end of your next turn. The DC of this save is equal to 10 + 1/2 your sorcerer level + your Charisma modifier. At 9th level, you can use this ability once per day. At 17th level, you can use this ability twice per day. At 20th level, you can use this ability three times per day. This power has a range of 60 feet.

Elemental Movement (Su): At 15th level, you gain a special movement type or bonus. This ability is based on your chosen element, as indicated on the above chart.

Elemental Body (Su): At 20th level, elemental power surges through your body. You gain immunity to sneak attacks, critical hits, and damage from your energy type.

Fey

The capricious nature of the fey runs in your family due to some intermingling of fey blood or magic. You are more emotional than most, prone to bouts of joy and rage.

Class Skill: Knowledge (nature).

Bonus Spells: *entangle* (3rd), *hideous laughter* (5th), *deep slumber* (7th), *poison* (9th), *tree stride* (11th), *mislead* (13th), *phase door* (15th), *irresistible dance* (17th), *shapechange* (19th).

Bonus Feats: Dodge, Improved Initiative, Lightning Reflexes, Mobility, Point Blank Shot, Precise Shot, Quicken Spell, Skill Focus (Knowledge [nature]).

Bloodline Arcana: Whenever you cast a spell of the compulsion subschool, increase the spell's DC by +2.

Bloodline Powers: You have always had a tie to the natural world, and as your power increases, so does the influence of the fey over your magic.

Laughing Touch (Sp): At 1st level, you can cause a creature to burst out laughing for 1 round as a melee touch attack. A laughing creature can only take a move action but can defend itself normally. Once a creature has been affected by laughing touch, it is immune to its effects for 24 hours. You can use this ability a number of times per day equal to 3 + your Charisma modifier. This is a mind-affecting effect.

Woodland Stride (Ex): At 3rd level, you can move through any sort of undergrowth (such as natural thorns, briars, overgrown areas, and similar terrain) at your normal speed and without taking damage or suffering any other impairment. Thorns, briars, and overgrown areas that have been magically manipulated to impede motion, however, still affect you.

Fleeting Glance (Sp): At 9th level, you can turn invisible for a number of rounds per day equal to your sorcerer level. This ability functions as *greater invisibility*. These rounds need not be consecutive.

Fey Magic (Su): At 15th level, you may reroll any caster level check made to overcome spell resistance. You must decide to use this ability before the results are revealed by the GM. You must take the second result, even if it is worse. You can use this ability at will.

Soul of the Fey (Su): At 20th level, your soul becomes one with the world of the fey. You gain immunity to poison and DR 10/cold iron. Creatures of the animal type do not attack you unless compelled to do so through magic. Once per day, you can cast *shadow walk* as a spell-like ability using your sorcerer level as your caster level.

Infernal

Somewhere in your family's history, a relative made a deal with a devil, and that pact has influenced your family line ever since. In you, it manifests in direct and obvious ways, granting you powers and abilities. While your fate is still your own, you can't help but wonder if your ultimate reward is bound to the Pit.

Class Skill: Diplomacy.

Bonus Spells: *protection from good* (3rd), *scorching ray* (5th), *suggestion* (7th), *charm monster* (9th), *dominate person* (11th), *planar binding* (devils and creatures with the fiendish template only) (13th), *greater teleport* (15th), *power word stun* (17th), *meteor swarm* (19th).

Bonus Feats: Blind-Fight, Combat Expertise, Deceitful, Extend Spell, Improved Disarm, Iron Will, Skill Focus (Knowledge [planes]), Spell Penetration.

Bloodline Arcana: Whenever you cast a spell of the charm subschool, increase the spell's DC by +2.

Bloodline Powers: You can draw upon the power of Hell, although you must be wary of its corrupting influence. Such power does not come without a price.

Corrupting Touch (Sp): At 1st level, you can cause a creature to become shaken (see page 568) as a melee touch attack. This effect persists for a number of rounds equal to 1/2 your sorcerer level (minimum 1). Creatures shaken by this ability radiate an aura of evil, as if they were an evil outsider (see *detect evil*). Multiple touches do not stack, but they do add to the duration. You can use this ability a number of times per day equal to 3 + your Charisma modifier.

Infernal Resistances (Ex): At 3rd level, you gain resist fire 5 and a +2 bonus on saving throws made against poison. At 9th level, your resistance to fire increases to 10 and your bonus on poison saving throws increases to +4.

Hellfire (Sp): At 9th level, you can call down a column of hellfire. This 10-foot-radius burst does 1d6 points of fire damage per sorcerer level. Those caught in the area of your blast receive a Reflex save for half damage. Good creatures that fail their saves are shaken for a number of rounds equal to your sorcerer level. The DC of this save is equal to 10 + 1/2 your sorcerer level + your Charisma modifier. At 9th level, you can use this ability once per day. At 17th level, you can use this ability twice per day. At 20th level, you can use this ability three times per day. This power has a range of 60 feet.

On Dark Wings (Su): At 15th level, you can grow fearsome bat wings as a standard action, giving you a fly speed of 60 feet with average maneuverability. The wings can be dismissed as a free action.

Power of the Pit (Su): At 20th level, your form becomes infused with vile power. You gain immunity to fire and poison. You also gain resistance to acid 10 and cold 10, and the ability to see perfectly in darkness of any kind to a range of 60 feet.

Undead

The taint of the grave runs through your family. Perhaps one of your ancestors became a powerful lich or vampire, or maybe you were born dead before suddenly returning to life. Either way, the forces of death move through you and touch your every action.

Class Skill: Knowledge (religion).

Bonus Spells: *chill touch* (3rd), *false life* (5th), *vampiric touch* (7th), *animate dead* (9th), *waves of fatigue* (11th), *undeath to death* (13th), *finger of death* (15th), *horrid wilting* (17th), *energy drain* (19th).

Bonus Feats: Combat Casting, Diehard, Endurance, Iron Will, Skill Focus (Knowledge [religion]), Spell Focus, Still Spell, Toughness.

Bloodline Arcana: Some undead are susceptible to your mind-affecting spells. Corporeal undead that were once humanoids are treated as humanoids for the purposes of determining which spells affect them.

Bloodline Powers: You can call upon the foul powers of the afterlife. Unfortunately, the more you draw upon them, the closer you come to joining them.

Grave Touch (Sp): Starting at 1st level, you can make a melee touch attack as a standard action that causes a living creature to become shaken for a number of rounds equal to 1/2 your sorcerer level (minimum 1). If you touch a shaken creature with this ability, it becomes frightened (see page 567) for 1 round if it has fewer Hit Dice than your sorcerer level. You can use this ability a number of times per day equal to 3 + your Charisma modifier.

Death's Gift (Su): At 3rd level, you gain resist cold 5 and DR 5/— against nonlethal damage. At 9th level, your resistance to cold increases to 10 and your DR increases to 10/— against nonlethal damage.

Grasp of the Dead (Sp): At 9th level, you can cause a swarm of skeletal arms to burst from the ground to rip and tear at your foes. The skeletal arms erupt from the ground in a 20-foot-radius burst. Anyone in this area takes 1d6 points of slashing damage per sorcerer level. Those caught in the area receive a Reflex save for half damage. Those who fail the save are unable to move for 1 round. The DC of this save is equal to 10 + 1/2 your sorcerer level + your Charisma modifier. The skeletal arms disappear after 1 round. The arms must burst up from a solid surface. At 9th level, you can use this ability once per day. At 17th level, you can use this ability twice per day. At 20th level, you can use this ability three times per day. This power has a range of 60 feet.

Incorporeal Form (Sp): At 15th level, you can become incorporeal for 1 round per sorcerer level. While in this form, you gain the incorporeal subtype. You only take half damage from corporeal sources as long as they are magic (you take no damage from non-magic weapons and objects). Likewise, your spells deal only half damage to corporeal creatures. Spells and other effects that do not deal damage function normally. You can use this ability once per day.

One of Us (Ex): At 20th level, your form begins to rot (the appearance of this decay is up to you) and undead see you as one of them. You gain immunity to cold, nonlethal damage, paralysis, and sleep. You also gain DR 5/—. Unintelligent undead do not notice you unless you attack them. You receive a +4 morale bonus on saving throws made against spells and spell-like abilities cast by undead.

WIZARD

Beyond the veil of the mundane hide the secrets of absolute power. The works of beings beyond mortals, the legends of realms where gods and spirits tread, the lore of creations both wondrous and terrible—such mysteries call to those with the ambition and the intellect to rise above the common folk to grasp true might. Such is the path of the wizard. These shrewd magic-users seek, collect, and covet esoteric knowledge, drawing on cultic arts to work wonders beyond the abilities of mere mortals. While some might choose a particular field of magical study and become masters of such powers, others embrace versatility, reveling in the unbounded wonders of all magic. In either case, wizards prove a cunning and potent lot, capable of smiting their foes, empowering their allies, and shaping the world to their every desire.

Role: While universalist wizards might study to prepare themselves for any manner of danger, specialist wizards research schools of magic that make them exceptionally skilled within a specific focus. Yet no matter their specialty, all wizards are masters of the impossible and can aid their allies in overcoming any danger.

Alignment: Any.

Hit Die: d6.

Class Skills

The wizard's class skills are Appraise (Int), Craft (Int), Fly (Dex), Knowledge (all) (Int), Linguistics (Int), Profession (Wis), and Spellcraft (Int).

Skill Ranks per Level: 2 + Int modifier.

Class Features

The following are the class features of the wizard.

Weapon and Armor Proficiency: Wizards are proficient with the club, dagger, heavy crossbow, light crossbow, and quarterstaff, but not with any type of armor or shield. Armor interferes with a wizard's movements, which can cause his spells with somatic components to fail.

Spells: A wizard casts arcane spells drawn from the sorcerer/wizard spell list presented in Chapter 10. A wizard must choose and prepare his spells ahead of time.

To learn, prepare, or cast a spell, the wizard must have an Intelligence score equal to at least 10 + the spell level. The Difficulty Class for a saving throw against a wizard's spell is 10 + the spell level + the wizard's Intelligence modifier.

A wizard can cast only a certain number of spells of each spell level per day. His base daily spell allotment is given on Table 3–16. In addition, he receives bonus spells per day if he has a high Intelligence score (see Table 1–3).

A wizard may know any number of spells. He must choose and prepare his spells ahead of time by getting 8 hours of sleep and spending 1 hour studying his spellbook. While studying, the wizard decides which spells to prepare.

Bonus Languages: A wizard may substitute Draconic for one of the bonus languages available to the character because of his race.

Arcane Bond (Ex or Sp): At 1st level, wizards form a powerful bond with an object or a creature. This bond can take one of two forms: a familiar or a bonded object. A familiar is a magical pet that enhances the wizard's skills and senses and can aid him in magic, while a bonded object is an item a wizard can use to cast additional spells or to serve as a magical item. Once a wizard makes this choice, it is permanent and cannot be changed. Rules for familiars appear on page 82, while rules for bonded items are given below.

Wizards who select a bonded object begin play with one at no cost. Objects that are the subject of an arcane bond must fall into one of the following categories: amulet, ring, staff, wand, or weapon. These objects are always masterwork quality. Weapons acquired at 1st level are not made of any special material. If the object is an amulet or ring, it must be worn to have effect, while staves, wands, and weapons must be held in one hand. If a wizard attempts to cast a spell without his bonded object worn or in hand, he must make a concentration check or lose the spell. The DC for this check is equal to 20 + the spell's level. If the object is a ring or amulet, it occupies the ring or neck slot accordingly.

A bonded object can be used once per day to cast any one spell that the wizard has in his spellbook and is capable of casting, even if the spell is not prepared. This spell is treated like any other spell cast by the wizard, including casting time, duration, and other effects dependent on the wizard's level. This spell cannot be modified by metamagic feats or other abilities. The bonded object cannot be used to cast spells from the wizard's opposition schools (see arcane school).

A wizard can add additional magic abilities to his bonded object as if he has the required item creation feats and if he meets the level prerequisites of the feat. For example, a wizard with a bonded dagger must be at least 5th level to add magic abilities to the dagger (see the Craft Magic Arms and Armor feat in Chapter 5). If the bonded object is a wand, it loses its wand abilities when its last charge is consumed, but it is not destroyed and it retains all of its bonded object properties and can be used to craft a new wand. The magic properties of a bonded object, including any magic abilities added to the object, only function for the wizard who owns it. If a bonded object's owner dies, or the item is replaced, the object reverts to being an ordinary masterwork item of the appropriate type.

If a bonded object is damaged, it is restored to full hit points the next time the wizard prepares his spells. If the object of an arcane bond is lost or destroyed, it can be replaced after 1 week in a special ritual that costs 200 gp per wizard level plus the cost of the masterwork item. This ritual takes 8 hours to complete. Items replaced in this way do not possess any of the additional enchantments of the previous bonded item. A wizard can designate an existing magic item as his bonded item. This functions in the same way as replacing a lost or destroyed item except that the new magic item retains its abilities while gaining the benefits and drawbacks of becoming a bonded item.

Arcane School: A wizard can choose to specialize in one school of magic, gaining additional spells and powers based on that school. This choice must be made at 1st level, and once made, it cannot be changed. A wizard that does not select a school receives the universalist school instead.

A wizard that chooses to specialize in one school of magic must select two other schools as his opposition schools, representing knowledge sacrificed in one area of arcane lore to gain mastery in another. A wizard who prepares spells from his opposition schools must use two spell slots of that level to prepare the spell. For example, a wizard with evocation as an opposition school must expend two of his available 3rd-level spell slots to prepare a *fireball*. In addition, a specialist takes a −4 penalty on any skill checks made when crafting a magic item that has a spell from one of his opposition schools as a prerequisite. A universalist wizard can prepare spells from any school without restriction.

Each arcane school gives the wizard a number of school powers. In addition, specialist wizards receive an additional spell slot of each spell level he can cast, from 1st on up. Each day, a wizard can prepare a spell from his specialty school in that slot. This spell must be in the wizard's spellbook. A wizard can select a spell modified by a metamagic feat to prepare in his school slot, but it uses up a higher-level spell slot. Wizards with the universalist school do not receive a school slot.

Cantrips: Wizards can prepare a number of cantrips, or 0-level spells, each day, as noted on Table 3–16 under "Spells per Day." These spells are cast like any other spell, but they are not expended when cast and may be used again. A wizard can prepare a cantrip from an opposed school, but it uses up two of his available slots (see below).

Scribe Scroll: At 1st level, a wizard gains Scribe Scroll as a bonus feat.

Bonus Feats: At 5th, 10th, 15th, and 20th level, a wizard gains a bonus feat. At each such opportunity, he can choose a metamagic feat, an item creation feat, or Spell Mastery. The wizard must still meet all prerequisites for a bonus feat, including caster level minimums. These bonus feats are in addition to the feats that a character of any class gets from advancing levels. The wizard is not limited to the categories of item creation feats, metamagic feats, or Spell Mastery when choosing those feats.

Spellbooks: A wizard must study his spellbook each day to prepare his spells. He cannot prepare any spell not recorded in his spellbook, except for *read magic*, which all wizards can prepare from memory.

A wizard begins play with a spellbook containing all 0-level wizard spells (except those from his opposed schools, if any; see Arcane Schools) plus three 1st-level spells of his choice. The wizard also selects a number of additional 1st-level spells equal to his Intelligence modifier to add to the spellbook. At each new wizard level, he gains two new spells of any spell level or levels that he can cast (based on his new wizard level) for his spellbook. At any time, a wizard can also add spells found in other wizards' spellbooks to his own (see Chapter 9).

Arcane Schools

The following descriptions detail each arcane school and its corresponding powers.

Abjuration School

The abjurer uses magic against itself, and masters the art of defensive and warding magics.

Resistance (Ex): You gain resistance 5 to an energy type of your choice, chosen when you prepare spells. This resistance can be changed each day. At 11th level, this

TABLE 3-16: WIZARD

Level	Base Attack Bonus	Fort Save	Ref Save	Will Save	Special	0	1st	2nd	3rd	4th	5th	6th	7th	8th	9th
1st	+0	+0	+0	+2	Arcane bond, arcane school, cantrips, Scribe Scroll	3	1	—	—	—	—	—	—	—	—
2nd	+1	+0	+0	+3		4	2	—	—	—	—	—	—	—	—
3rd	+1	+1	+1	+3		4	2	1	—	—	—	—	—	—	—
4th	+2	+1	+1	+4		4	3	2	—	—	—	—	—	—	—
5th	+2	+1	+1	+4	Bonus feat	4	3	2	1	—	—	—	—	—	—
6th	+3	+2	+2	+5		4	3	3	2	—	—	—	—	—	—
7th	+3	+2	+2	+5		4	4	3	2	1	—	—	—	—	—
8th	+4	+2	+2	+6		4	4	3	3	2	—	—	—	—	—
9th	+4	+3	+3	+6		4	4	4	3	2	1	—	—	—	—
10th	+5	+3	+3	+7	Bonus feat	4	4	4	3	3	2	—	—	—	—
11th	+5	+3	+3	+7		4	4	4	4	3	2	1	—	—	—
12th	+6/+1	+4	+4	+8		4	4	4	4	3	3	2	—	—	—
13th	+6/+1	+4	+4	+8		4	4	4	4	4	3	2	1	—	—
14th	+7/+2	+4	+4	+9		4	4	4	4	4	3	3	2	—	—
15th	+7/+2	+5	+5	+9	Bonus feat	4	4	4	4	4	4	3	2	1	—
16th	+8/+3	+5	+5	+10		4	4	4	4	4	4	3	3	2	—
17th	+8/+3	+5	+5	+10		4	4	4	4	4	4	4	3	2	1
18th	+9/+4	+6	+6	+11		4	4	4	4	4	4	4	3	3	2
19th	+9/+4	+6	+6	+11		4	4	4	4	4	4	4	4	3	3
20th	+10/+5	+6	+6	+12	Bonus feat	4	4	4	4	4	4	4	4	4	4

resistance increases to 10. At 20th level, this resistance changes to immunity to the chosen energy type.

Protective Ward (Su): As a standard action, you can create a 10-foot-radius field of protective magic centered on you that lasts for a number of rounds equal to your Intelligence modifier. All allies in this area (including you) receive a +1 deflection bonus to their AC. This bonus increases by +1 for every five wizard levels you possess. You can use this ability a number of times per day equal to 3 + your Intelligence modifier.

Energy Absorption (Su): At 6th level, you gain an amount of energy absorption equal to 3 times your wizard level per day. Whenever you take energy damage, apply immunity, vulnerability (if any), and resistance first and apply the rest to this absorption, reducing your daily total by that amount. Any damage in excess of your absorption is applied to you normally.

Conjuration School

The conjurer focuses on the study of summoning monsters and magic alike to bend to his will.

Summoner's Charm (Su): Whenever you cast a conjuration (summoning) spell, increase the duration by a number of rounds equal to 1/2 your wizard level (minimum 1). This increase is not doubled by Extend Spell. At 20th level, you can change the duration of all *summon monster* spells

to permanent. You can have no more than one *summon monster* spell made permanent in this way at one time. If you designate another *summon monster* spell as permanent, the previous spell immediately ends.

Acid Dart (Sp): As a standard action you can unleash an acid dart targeting any foe within 30 feet as a ranged touch attack. The acid dart deals 1d6 points of acid damage + 1 for every two wizard levels you possess. You can use this ability a number of times per day equal to 3 + your Intelligence modifier. This attack ignores spell resistance.

Dimensional Steps (Sp): At 8th level, you can use this ability to teleport up to 30 feet per wizard level per day as a standard action. This teleportation must be used in 5-foot increments and such movement does not provoke an attack of opportunity. You can bring other willing creatures with you, but you must expend an equal amount of distance for each additional creature brought with you.

Divination School

Diviners are masters of remote viewing, prophecies, and using magic to explore the world.

Forewarned (Su): You can always act in the surprise round even if you fail to make a Perception roll to notice a foe, but you are still considered flat-footed until you take an action. In addition, you receive a bonus on initiative checks equal to 1/2 your wizard level (minimum +1). At 20th level, anytime you roll initiative, assume the roll resulted in a natural 20.

Diviner's Fortune (Sp): When you activate this school power, you can touch any creature as a standard action to give it an insight bonus on all of its attack rolls, skill checks, ability checks, and saving throws equal to 1/2 your wizard level (minimum +1) for 1 round. You can use this ability a number of times per day equal to 3 + your Intelligence modifier.

Scrying Adept (Su): At 8th level, you are always aware when you are being observed via magic, as if you had a permanent *detect scrying*. In addition, whenever you scry on a subject, treat the subject as one step more familiar to you. Very familiar subjects get a –10 penalty on their save to avoid your scrying attempts.

Enchantment School

The enchanter uses magic to control and manipulate the minds of his victims.

Enchanting Smile (Su): You gain a +2 enhancement bonus on Bluff, Diplomacy, and Intimidate skill checks. This bonus increases by +1 for every five wizard levels you possess, up to a maximum of +6 at 20th level. At 20th level, whenever you succeed at a saving throw against a spell of the enchantment school, that spell is reflected back at its caster, as per *spell turning*.

Dazing Touch (Sp): You can cause a living creature to become dazed for 1 round as a melee touch attack. Creatures with more Hit Dice than your wizard level are unaffected. You can use this ability a number of times per day equal to 3 + your Intelligence modifier.

Aura of Despair (Su): At 8th level, you can emit a 30-foot aura of despair for a number of rounds per day equal to your wizard level. Enemies within this aura take a –2 penalty on ability checks, attack rolls, damage rolls, saving throws, and skill checks. These rounds do not need to be consecutive. This is a mind-affecting effect.

Evocation School

Evokers revel in the raw power of magic, and can use it to create and destroy with shocking ease.

Intense Spells (Su): Whenever you cast an evocation spell that deals hit point damage, add 1/2 your wizard level to the damage (minimum +1). This bonus damage is not increased by Empower Spell or similar effects. This bonus only applies once to a spell, not once per missile or ray, and cannot be split between multiple missiles or rays. This damage is of the same type as the spell. At 20th level, whenever you cast an evocation spell you can roll twice to penetrate a creature's spell resistance and take the better result.

Force Missile (Sp): As a standard action you can unleash a force missile that automatically strikes a foe, as *magic missile*. The force missile deals 1d4 points of damage plus the damage from your intense spells evocation power. This is a force effect. You can use this ability a number of times per day equal to 3 + your Intelligence modifier.

Elemental Wall (Sp): At 8th level, you can create a wall of energy that lasts for a number of rounds per day equal to your wizard level. These rounds do not need to be consecutive. This wall deals acid, cold, electricity, or fire damage, determined when you create it. The elemental wall otherwise functions like *wall of fire*.

Illusion School

Illusionists use magic to weave confounding images, figments, and phantoms to baffle and vex their foes.

Extended Illusions (Su): Any illusion spell you cast with a duration of "concentration" lasts a number of additional rounds equal to 1/2 your wizard level after you stop maintaining concentration (minimum +1 round). At 20th level, you can make one illusion spell with a duration of "concentration" become permanent. You can have no more than one illusion made permanent in this way at one time. If you designate another illusion as permanent, the previous permanent illusion ends.

Blinding Ray (Sp): As a standard action you can fire a shimmering ray at any foe within 30 feet as a ranged touch attack. The ray causes creatures to be blinded for 1 round. Creatures with more Hit Dice than your wizard level are dazzled for 1 round instead. You can use this ability a number of times per day equal to 3 + your Intelligence modifier.

Invisibility Field (Sp): At 8th level, you can make yourself invisible as a swift action for a number of rounds per day equal to your wizard level. These rounds do not need to be consecutive. This otherwise functions as *greater invisibility*.

Necromancy School

The dread and feared necromancer commands undead and uses the foul power of unlife against his enemies.

Power over Undead (Su): You receive Command Undead or Turn Undead as a bonus feat. You can channel energy a number of times per day equal to 3 + your Intelligence modifier, but only to use the selected feat. You can take other feats to add to this ability, such as Extra Channel and Improved Channel, but not feats that alter this ability, such as Elemental Channel and Alignment Channel. The DC to save against these feats is equal to 10 + 1/2 your wizard level + your Charisma modifier. At 20th level, undead cannot add their channel resistance to the save against this ability.

Grave Touch (Sp): As a standard action, you can make a melee touch attack that causes a living creature to become shaken for a number of rounds equal to 1/2 your wizard level (minimum 1). If you touch a shaken creature with this ability, it becomes frightened for 1 round if it

has fewer Hit Dice than your wizard level. You can use this ability a number of times per day equal to 3 + your Intelligence modifier.

Life Sight (Su): At 8th level, you gain blindsight to a range of 10 feet for a number of rounds per day equal to your wizard level. This sight only allows you to detect living creatures and undead creatures. This sight also tells you whether a creature is living or undead. Constructs and other creatures that are neither living nor undead cannot be seen with this ability. The range of this ability increases by 10 feet at 12th level, and by an additional 10 feet for every four levels beyond 12th. These rounds do not need to be consecutive.

Transmutation School

Transmuters use magic to change the world around them.

Physical Enhancement (Su): You gain a +1 enhancement bonus to one physical ability score (Strength, Dexterity, or Constitution). This bonus increases by +1 for every five wizard levels you possess to a maximum of +5 at 20th level. You can change this bonus to a new ability score when you prepare spells. At 20th level, this bonus applies to two physical ability scores of your choice.

Telekinetic Fist (Sp): As a standard action you can strike with a telekinetic fist, targeting any foe within 30 feet as a ranged touch attack. The telekinetic fist deals 1d4 points of bludgeoning damage + 1 for every two wizard levels you possess. You can use this ability a number of times per day equal to 3 + your Intelligence modifier.

Change Shape (Sp): At 8th level, you can change your shape for a number of rounds per day equal to your wizard level. These rounds do not need to be consecutive. This ability otherwise functions like *beast shape II* or *elemental body I*. At 12th level, this ability functions like *beast shape III* or *elemental body II*.

Universalist School

Wizards who do not specialize (known as as universalists) have the most diversity of all arcane spellcasters.

Hand of the Apprentice (Su): You cause your melee weapon to fly from your grasp and strike a foe before instantly returning to you. As a standard action, you can make a single attack using a melee weapon at a range of 30 feet. This attack is treated as a ranged attack with a thrown weapon, except that you add your Intelligence modifier on the attack roll instead of your Dexterity modifier (damage still relies on Strength). This ability cannot be used to perform a combat maneuver. You can use this ability a number of times per day equal to 3 + your Intelligence modifier.

Metamagic Mastery (Su): At 8th level, you can apply any one metamagic feat that you know to a spell you are about to cast. This does not alter the level of the spell or the casting time. You can use this ability once per day at 8th level and one additional time per day for every

two wizard levels you possess beyond 8th. Any time you use this ability to apply a metamagic feat that increases the spell level by more than 1, you must use an additional daily usage for each level above 1 that the feat adds to the spell. Even though this ability does not modify the spell's actual level, you cannot use this ability to cast a spell whose modified spell level would be above the level of the highest-level spell that you are capable of casting.

Familiars

A familiar is an animal chosen by a spellcaster to aid him in his study of magic. It retains the appearance, Hit Dice, base attack bonus, base save bonuses, skills, and feats of the normal animal it once was, but is now a magical beast for the purpose of effects that depend on its type. Only a normal, unmodified animal may become a familiar. An animal companion cannot also function as a familiar.

A familiar grants special abilities to its master, as given on the table below. These special abilities apply only when the master and familiar are within 1 mile of each other.

Levels of different classes that are entitled to familiars stack for the purpose of determining any familiar abilities that depend on the master's level.

If a familiar is dismissed, lost, or dies, it can be replaced 1 week later through a specialized ritual that costs 200 gp per wizard level. The ritual takes 8 hours to complete.

Familiar	Special Ability
Bat	Master gains a +3 bonus on Fly checks
Cat	Master gains a +3 bonus on Stealth checks
Hawk	Master gains a +3 bonus on sight-based and opposed Perception checks in bright light
Lizard	Master gains a +3 bonus on Climb checks
Monkey	Master gains a +3 bonus on Acrobatics checks
Owl	Master gains a +3 bonus on sight-based and opposed Perception checks in shadows or darkness
Rat	Master gains a +2 bonus on Fortitude saves
Raven*	Master gains a +3 bonus on Appraise checks
Viper	Master gains a +3 bonus on Bluff checks
Toad	Master gains +3 hit points
Weasel	Master gains a +2 bonus on Reflex saves

*A raven familiar can speak one language of its master's choice as a supernatural ability.

Familiar Basics: Use the basic statistics for a creature of the familiar's kind as described in the *Pathfinder RPG Bestiary*, but with the following changes.

Hit Dice: For the purpose of effects related to number of Hit Dice, use the master's character level or the familiar's normal HD total, whichever is higher.

Hit Points: The familiar has half the master's total hit points (not including temporary hit points), rounded down, regardless of its actual Hit Dice.

Attacks: Use the master's base attack bonus, as calculated from all his classes. Use the familiar's Dexterity or Strength modifier, whichever is greater, to calculate the familiar's melee attack bonus with natural weapons.

Damage equals that of a normal creature of the familiar's kind.

Saving Throws: For each saving throw, use either the familiar's base save bonus (Fortitude +2, Reflex +2, Will +0) or the master's (as calculated from all his classes), whichever is better. The familiar uses its own ability modifiers to saves, and it doesn't share any of the other bonuses that the master might have on saves.

Skills: For each skill in which either the master or the familiar has ranks, use either the normal skill ranks for an animal of that type or the master's skill ranks, whichever is better. In either case, the familiar uses its own ability modifiers. Regardless of a familiar's total skill modifiers, some skills may remain beyond the familiar's ability to use. Familiars treat Acrobatics, Climb, Fly, Perception, Stealth, and Swim as class skills.

Familiar Ability Descriptions: All familiars have special abilities (or impart abilities to their masters) depending on the master's combined level in classes that grant familiars, as shown on the table below. The abilities are cumulative.

Master Class Level	Natural Armor Adj.	Int	Special
1st–2nd	+1	6	Alertness, improved evasion, share spells, empathic link
3rd–4th	+2	7	Deliver touch spells
5th–6th	+3	8	Speak with master
7th–8th	+4	9	Speak with animals of its kind
9th–10th	+5	10	—
11th–12th	+6	11	Spell resistance
13th–14th	+7	12	Scry on familiar
15th–16th	+8	13	—
17th–18th	+9	14	—
19th–20th	+10	15	—

Natural Armor Adj.: The number noted here is in addition to the familiar's existing natural armor bonus.

Int: The familiar's Intelligence score.

Alertness (Ex): While a familiar is within arm's reach, the master gains the Alertness feat.

Improved Evasion (Ex): When subjected to an attack that normally allows a Reflex saving throw for half damage, a familiar takes no damage if it makes a successful saving throw and half damage even if the saving throw fails.

Share Spells: The wizard may cast a spell with a target of "You" on his familiar (as a touch spell) instead of on himself. A wizard may cast spells on his familiar even if the spells do not normally affect creatures of the familiar's type (magical beast).

Empathic Link (Su): The master has an empathic link with his familiar to a 1 mile distance. The master can communicate emphatically with the familiar, but cannot see through its eyes. Because of the link's limited nature, only general emotions can be shared. The master has the same connection to an item or place that his familiar does.

Deliver Touch Spells (Su): If the master is 3rd level or higher, a familiar can deliver touch spells for him. If the master and the familiar are in contact at the time the master casts a touch spell, he can designate his familiar as the "toucher." The familiar can then deliver the touch spell just as the master would. As usual, if the master casts another spell before the touch is delivered, the touch spell dissipates.

Speak with Master (Ex): If the master is 5th level or higher, a familiar and the master can communicate verbally as if they were using a common language. Other creatures do not understand the communication without magical help.

Speak with Animals of Its Kind (Ex): If the master is 7th level or higher, a familiar can communicate with animals of approximately the same kind as itself (including dire varieties): bats with bats, cats with felines, hawks and owls and ravens with birds, lizards and snakes with reptiles, monkeys with other simians, rats with rodents, toads with amphibians, and weasels with ermines and minks. Such communication is limited by the Intelligence of the conversing creatures.

Spell Resistance (Ex): If the master is 11th level or higher, a familiar gains spell resistance equal to the master's level + 5. To affect the familiar with a spell, another spellcaster must get a result on a caster level check (1d20 + caster level) that equals or exceeds the familiar's spell resistance.

Scry on Familiar (Sp): If the master is 13th level or higher, he may scry on his familiar (as if casting the *scrying* spell) once per day.

Arcane Spells and Armor

Armor restricts the complicated gestures required while casting any spell that has a somatic component. The armor and shield descriptions list the arcane spell failure chance for different armors and shields (see page 151).

If a spell doesn't have a somatic component, an arcane spellcaster can cast it with no arcane spell failure chance while wearing armor. Such spells can also be cast even if the caster's hands are bound or he is grappling (although concentration checks still apply normally). The metamagic feat Still Spell allows a spellcaster to prepare or cast a spell without the somatic component at one spell level higher than normal. This also provides a way to cast a spell while wearing armor without risking arcane spell failure.

4 Skills

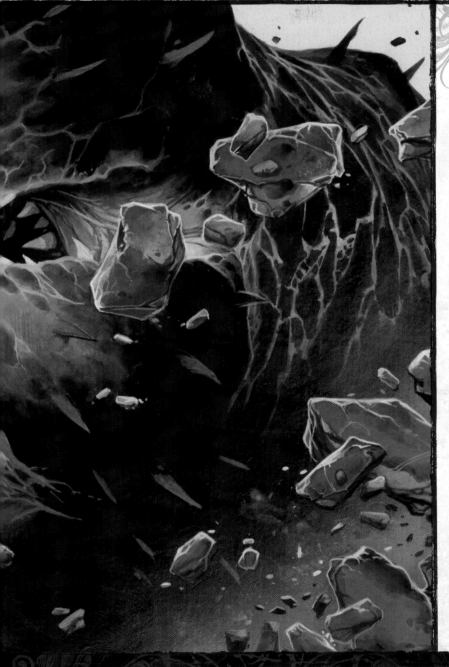

Seelah had faced many tests in her life: tests of faith, tests of valor, tests of prowess. Now, though, with the maw of the massive desert worm driving toward her—as dark and ominous as the death it promised— she faced another test: not of courage, but of knowledge. While a hide like stone girded the monstrosity's titanic form, within it seemed as soft and vulnerable as her own skin. Standing tall before the beast, Seelah acted before she could think better, taking but an instant to whisper a quick prayer: "Iomedae, goddess of valor, please give me the skill to survive!"

Skills represent some of the most basic and yet most fundamental abilities your character possesses. As your character advances in level, he can gain new skills and improve his existing skills dramatically.

ACQUIRING SKILLS

Each level, your character gains a number of skill ranks dependent upon your class plus your Intelligence modifier. Investing a rank in a skill represents a measure of training in that skill. You can never have more ranks in a skill than your total number of Hit Dice. In addition, each class has a number of favored skills, called class skills. It is easier for your character to become more proficient in these skills, as they represent part of his professional training and constant practice. You gain a +3 bonus on all class skills that you put ranks into. If you have more than one class and both grant you a class skill bonus, these bonuses do not stack.

The number of skill ranks you gain when taking a level in one of the base classes is shown on Table 4–1. Humans gain 1 additional skill rank per class level. Characters who take a level in a favored class have the option of gaining 1 additional skill rank or an additional hit point (see page 31). If you select a level in a new class, all of its class skills are automatically added to your list of class skills, and you gain a +3 bonus on these skills if you have ranks in them.

Skill Checks

When your character uses a skill, he isn't guaranteed success. In order to determine success, whenever you attempt to use a skill, you must make a skill check.

Each skill rank grants a +1 bonus on checks made using that skill. When you make a skill check, you roll 1d20 and then add your ranks and the appropriate ability score modifier to the result of this check. If the skill you're using is a class skill (and you have invested ranks into that skill), you gain a +3 bonus on the check. If you are not trained in the skill (and if the skill may be used untrained), you may still attempt the skill, but you use only the bonus (or penalty) provided by the associated ability score modifier to modify the check. Skills can be further modified by a wide variety of sources—by your race, by a class ability, by equipment, by spell effects or magic items, and so on. See Table 4–2 for a summary of skill check bonuses.

If the result of your skill check is equal to or greater than the difficulty class (or DC) of the task you are attempting to accomplish, you succeed. If it is less than the DC, you fail. Some tasks have varying levels of success and failure depending on how much your check is above or below the required DC. Some skill checks are opposed by the target's skill check. When making an opposed skill check, the attempt is successful if your check result exceeds the result of the target.

Taking 10 and Taking 20

A skill check represents an attempt to accomplish some goal, usually while under some sort of time pressure or distraction. Sometimes, though, a character can use a skill under more favorable conditions, increasing the odds of success.

Taking 10: When your character is not in immediate danger or distracted, you may choose to take 10. Instead of rolling 1d20 for the skill check, calculate your result as if you had rolled a 10. For many routine tasks, taking 10 makes them automatically successful. Distractions or threats (such as combat) make it impossible for a character to take 10. In most cases, taking 10 is purely a safety measure—you know (or expect) that an average roll will succeed but fear that a poor roll might fail, so you elect to settle for the average roll (a 10). Taking 10 is especially useful in situations where a particularly high roll wouldn't help.

Taking 20: When you have plenty of time, you are faced with no threats or distractions, and the skill being attempted carries no penalties for failure, you can take 20. In other words, if you roll a d20 enough times, eventually you will get a 20. Instead of rolling 1d20 for the skill check, just calculate your result as if you had rolled a 20.

Taking 20 means you are trying until you get it right, and it assumes that you fail many times before succeeding. Taking 20 takes 20 times as long as making a single check would take (usually 2 minutes for a skill that takes 1 round or less to perform).

Since taking 20 assumes that your character will fail many times before succeeding, your character would automatically incur any penalties for failure before he or she could complete the task (hence why it is generally not allowed with skills that carry such penalties). Common "take 20" skills include Disable Device (when used to open locks), Escape Artist, and Perception (when attempting to find traps).

Ability Checks and Caster Level Checks: The normal take 10 and take 20 rules apply for ability checks. Neither rule applies to concentration checks or caster level checks.

Aid Another

You can help someone achieve success on a skill check by making the same kind of skill check in a cooperative effort. If you roll a 10 or higher on your check, the character you're helping gets a +2 bonus on his or her check. (You can't take 10 on a skill check to aid another.) In many cases, a character's help won't be beneficial, or only a limited number of characters can help at once.

In cases where the skill restricts who can achieve certain results, such as trying to open a lock using Disable Device, you can't aid another to grant a bonus to a task that your character couldn't achieve alone. The GM might impose further restrictions to aiding another on a case-by-case basis as well.

SKILL DESCRIPTIONS

This section describes each skill, including common uses and typical modifiers. Characters can sometimes use skills for purposes other than those noted here, at the GM's discretion. For a complete summary of all of the skills, see Table 4–3.

Skill descriptions adhere to the following guidelines.

Skill Name: The skill name line includes (in addition to the name of the skill) the following information.

Key Ability: The abbreviation of the ability whose modifier applies to the skill check.

Trained Only: If this notation is included in the skill name line, you must have at least 1 rank in the skill to use it. If this notation is omitted, the skill can be used untrained (with a rank of 0). If any special notes apply to trained or untrained use, they are covered in the Untrained section (see below).

Armor Check Penalty: If this notation is included in the skill name line, an armor check penalty applies (see Chapter 6) to checks using this skill. If this entry is absent, an armor check penalty does not apply.

Description: The skill name line is followed by a general description of what using the skill represents.

Check: What a character ("you" in the skill description) can do with a successful skill check and the check's Difficulty Class (DC).

Action: The type of action using the skill requires, or the amount of time required for a check.

Try Again: Any conditions that apply to successive attempts to use the skill successfully. If the skill doesn't allow you to attempt the same task more than once, or if failure carries an inherent penalty (such as with the Climb skill), you can't take 20. If this paragraph is omitted, the skill can be retried without any inherent penalty other than the additional time required.

Special: Any extra facts that apply to the skill, such as special effects deriving from its use or bonuses that certain characters receive because of class, feat choices, or race.

Restriction: The full utility of certain skills is restricted to characters of certain classes. This entry indicates whether any such restrictions exist for the skill.

Untrained: This entry indicates what a character without at least 1 rank in the skill can do with it. If this entry doesn't appear, it means that the skill functions normally for untrained characters (if it can be used untrained) or that an untrained character can't attempt checks with this skill (for skills that are designated "Trained Only").

ACROBATICS
(Dex; Armor Check Penalty)

You can keep your balance while traversing narrow or treacherous surfaces. You can also dive, flip, jump, and roll to avoid attacks and overcome obstacles.

TABLE 4-1: SKILL RANKS

Class	Skill Ranks per Level
Barbarian	4 + Int modifier
Bard	6 + Int modifier
Cleric	2 + Int modifier
Druid	4 + Int modifier
Fighter	2 + Int modifier
Monk	4 + Int modifier
Paladin	2 + Int modifier
Ranger	6 + Int modifier
Rogue	8 + Int modifier
Sorcerer	2 + Int modifier
Wizard	2 + Int modifier

TABLE 4-2: SKILL CHECK BONUSES

Skill	Skill Check is Equal To*
Untrained	1d20 + ability modifier + racial modifier
Trained	1d20 + skill ranks + ability modifier + racial modifier
Trained Class Skill	1d20 + skill ranks + ability modifier + racial modifier + 3

* Armor check penalty applies to all Strength- and Dexterity-based skill checks.

Check: You can use Acrobatics to move on narrow surfaces and uneven ground without falling. A successful check allows you to move at half speed across such surfaces—only one check is needed per round. Use the following table to determine the base DC, which is then modified by the Acrobatics skill modifiers noted on page 89. While you are using Acrobatics in this way, you are considered flat-footed and lose your Dexterity bonus to your AC (if any). If you take damage while using Acrobatics, you must immediately make another Acrobatics check at the same DC to avoid falling or being knocked prone.

Surface Width	Base Acrobatics DC
Greater than 3 feet wide	0*
1–3 feet wide	5*
7–11 inches wide	10
2–6 inches wide	15
Less than 2 inches wide	20

* No Acrobatics check is needed to move across these surfaces unless the modifiers to the surface (see page 89) increase the DC to 10 or higher.

In addition, you can move through a threatened square without provoking an attack of opportunity from an enemy by using Acrobatics. When moving in this way, you move at

half speed. You can move at full speed by increasing the DC of the check by 10. You cannot use Acrobatics to move past foes if your speed is reduced due to carrying a medium or heavy load or wearing medium or heavy armor. If an ability allows you to move at full speed under such conditions, you can use Acrobatics to move past foes. You can use Acrobatics in this way while prone, but doing so requires a full-round action to move 5 feet, and the DC is increased by 5. If you attempt to move through an enemy's space and fail the check, you lose the move action and provoke an attack of opportunity.

Situation	Base Acrobatics DC*
Move through a threatened area	Opponent's Combat Maneuver Defense
Move through an enemy's space	5 + opponent's Combat Maneuver Defense

* This DC is used to avoid an attack of opportunity due to movement. This DC increases by 2 for each additional opponent avoided in 1 round.

Finally, you can use the Acrobatics skill to make jumps or to soften a fall. The base DC to make a jump is equal to the distance to be crossed (if horizontal) or four times the height to be reached (if vertical). These DCs double if you do not have at least 10 feet of space to get a running start. The only Acrobatics modifiers that apply are those concerning the surface you are jumping from. If you fail this check by 4 or less, you can attempt a DC 20 Reflex save to grab hold of the other side after having missed the jump. If you fail by 5 or more, you fail to make the jump and fall (or land prone, in the case of a vertical jump). Creatures with a base land speed above 30 feet receive a +4 racial bonus on Acrobatics checks made to jump for every 10 feet of their speed above 30 feet. Creatures with a base land speed below 30 feet receive a −4 racial penalty on Acrobatics checks made to jump for every 10 feet of their speed below 30 feet. No jump can allow you to exceed your maximum movement for the round. For a running jump, the result of your Acrobatics check indicates the distance traveled in the jump (and if the check fails, the distance at which you actually land and fall prone). Halve this result for a standing long jump to determine where you land.

When you deliberately fall any distance, even as a result of a missed jump, a DC 15 Acrobatics skill check allows you to ignore the first 10 feet fallen, although you still end up prone if you take damage from a fall. See the falling rules on page 443 for further details.

Long Jump	Acrobatics DC
5 feet	5
10 feet	10
15 feet	15
Greater than 15 feet	+5 per 5 feet

TABLE 4-3: SKILL SUMMARY

Skill	Bbn	Brd	Clr	Drd	Ftr	Mnk	Pal	Rgr	Rog	Sor	Wiz	Untrained	Ability
Acrobatics	C	C	—	—	—	C	—	—	C	—	—	Yes	Dex*
Appraise	—	C	C	—	—	—	—	—	C	C	C	Yes	Int
Bluff	—	C	—	—	—	—	—	—	C	C	—	Yes	Cha
Climb	C	C	—	C	C	C	—	C	C	—	—	Yes	Str*
Craft	C	C	C	C	C	C	C	C	C	C	C	Yes	Int
Diplomacy	—	C	C	—	—	—	C	—	C	—	—	Yes	Cha
Disable Device	—	—	—	—	—	—	—	—	C	—	—	No	Dex*
Disguise	—	C	—	—	—	—	—	—	C	—	—	Yes	Cha
Escape Artist	—	C	—	—	—	C	—	—	C	—	—	Yes	Dex*
Fly	—	—	—	C	—	—	—	—	—	C	C	Yes	Dex*
Handle Animal	C	—	—	C	C	—	C	C	—	—	—	No	Cha
Heal	—	—	C	C	—	—	C	C	—	—	—	Yes	Wis
Intimidate	C	C	—	—	C	C	—	C	C	C	—	Yes	Cha
Knowledge (arcana)	—	C	C	—	—	—	—	—	—	C	C	No	Int
Knowledge (dungeoneering)	—	C	—	—	C	—	—	C	C	—	C	No	Int
Knowledge (engineering)	—	C	—	—	C	—	—	—	—	—	C	No	Int
Knowledge (geography)	—	C	—	C	—	—	—	C	—	—	C	No	Int
Knowledge (history)	—	C	C	—	—	C	—	—	—	—	C	No	Int
Knowledge (local)	—	C	—	—	—	—	—	—	C	—	C	No	Int
Knowledge (nature)	C	C	—	C	—	—	—	C	—	—	C	No	Int
Knowledge (nobility)	—	C	C	—	—	—	C	—	—	—	C	No	Int
Knowledge (planes)	—	C	C	—	—	—	—	—	—	—	C	No	Int
Knowledge (religion)	—	C	C	—	—	C	C	—	—	—	C	No	Int
Linguistics	—	C	C	—	—	—	—	—	C	—	C	No	Int
Perception	C	C	—	C	—	C	—	C	C	—	—	Yes	Wis
Perform	—	C	—	—	—	C	—	—	C	—	—	Yes	Cha
Profession	—	C	C	C	C	C	C	C	C	C	C	No	Wis
Ride	C	—	—	C	C	C	C	C	—	—	—	Yes	Dex*
Sense Motive	—	C	C	—	—	C	C	—	C	—	—	Yes	Wis
Sleight of Hand	—	C	—	—	—	—	—	—	C	—	—	No	Dex*
Spellcraft	—	C	C	C	—	—	C	C	—	C	C	No	Int
Stealth	—	C	—	—	—	C	—	C	C	—	—	Yes	Dex*
Survival	C	—	—	C	C	—	—	C	—	—	—	Yes	Wis
Swim	C	—	—	C	C	C	—	C	C	—	—	Yes	Str*
Use Magic Device	—	C	—	—	—	—	—	—	C	C	—	No	Cha

C = Class Skill; * Armor check penalty applies

High Jump	Acrobatics DC
1 foot	4
2 feet	8
3 feet	12
4 feet	16
Greater than 4 feet	+4 per foot

Acrobatics Modifiers	DC Modifier
Slightly obstructed (gravel, sand)	+2
Severely obstructed (cavern, rubble)	+5
Slightly slippery (wet)	+2
Severely slippery (icy)	+5
Slightly sloped (<45°)	+2
Severely sloped (>45°)	+5
Slightly unsteady (boat in rough water)	+2
Moderately unsteady (boat in a storm)	+5
Severely unsteady (earthquake)	+10
Move at full speed on narrow or uneven surfaces	+5*

* This does not apply to checks made to jump.

Many conditions can affect your chances of success with Acrobatics checks. The following modifiers to target DCs apply to all Acrobatics skill checks. The modifiers stack with one another, but only the most severe modifier for any one condition applies.

Action: None. An Acrobatics check is made as part of another action or as a reaction to a situation.

Special: If you have 3 or more ranks in Acrobatics, you gain a +3 dodge bonus to AC when fighting defensively instead of the usual +2, and a +6 dodge bonus to AC when taking the total defense action instead of the usual +4.

If you have the Acrobatic feat, you get a bonus on Acrobatics checks (see Chapter 5).

APPRAISE (Int)

You can evaluate the monetary value of an object.

Check: A DC 20 Appraise check determines the value of a common item. If you succeed by 5 or more, you also determine if the item has magic properties, although this success does not grant knowledge of the magic item's abilities. If your fail the check by less than 5, you determine the price of that item to within 20% of its actual value. If you fail this check by 5 or more, the price is wildly inaccurate, subject to GM discretion. Particularly rare or exotic items might increase the DC of this check by 5 or more.

You can also use this check to determine the most valuable item visible in a treasure hoard. The DC of this check is generally 20 but can increase to as high as 30 for a particularly large hoard.

Action: Appraising an item takes 1 standard action. Determining the most valuable object in a treasure hoard takes 1 full-round action.

Try Again: Additional attempts to Appraise an item reveal the same result.

Special: A spellcaster with a raven familiar gains a +3 bonus on Appraise checks.

BLUFF (Cha)

You know how to tell a lie.

Check: Bluff is an opposed skill check against your opponent's Sense Motive skill. If you use Bluff to fool someone, with a successful check you convince your opponent that what you are saying is true. Bluff checks are modified depending upon the believability of the lie. The following modifiers are applied to the roll of the creature attempting to tell the lie. Note that some lies are so improbable that it is impossible to convince anyone that they are true (subject to GM discretion).

Circumstances	Bluff Modifier
The target wants to believe you	+5
The lie is believable	+0
The lie is unlikely	–5
The lie is far-fetched	–10
The lie is impossible	–20
The target is drunk or impaired	+5
You possess convincing proof	up to +10

Feint: You can use Bluff to feint in combat, causing your opponent to be denied his Dexterity bonus to his AC against your next attack. The DC of this check is equal to 10 + your opponent's base attack bonus + your opponent's Wisdom modifier. If your opponent is trained in Sense Motive, the DC is instead equal to 10 + your opponent's Sense Motive bonus, if higher. For more information on feinting in combat, see Chapter 8.

Secret Messages: You can use Bluff to pass hidden messages along to another character without others understanding your true meaning by using innuendo to cloak your actual message. The DC of this check is 15 for simple messages and 20 for complex messages. If you are successful, the target automatically understands you, assuming you are communicating in a language that it understands. If your check fails by 5 or more, you deliver the wrong message. Other creatures that receive the message can decipher it by succeeding at an opposed Sense Motive check against your Bluff result.

Action: Attempting to deceive someone takes at least 1 round, but can possibly take longer if the lie is elaborate (as determined by the GM on a case-by-case basis).

Feinting in combat is a standard action.

Using Bluff to deliver a secret message takes twice as long as the message would otherwise take to relay.

Try Again: If you fail to deceive someone, further attempts to deceive them are at a –10 penalty and may be impossible (GM discretion).

You can attempt to feint against someone again if you fail. Secret messages can be relayed again if the first attempt fails.

Special: A spellcaster with a viper familiar gains a +3 bonus on Bluff checks.

If you have the Deceitful feat, you get a bonus on Bluff checks (see Chapter 5).

CLIMB (Str; Armor Check Penalty)

You are skilled at scaling vertical surfaces, from smooth city walls to rocky cliffs.

Check: With a successful Climb check, you can advance up, down, or across a slope, wall, or other steep incline (or even across a ceiling, provided it has handholds) at one-quarter your normal speed. A slope is considered to be any incline at an angle measuring less than 60 degrees; a wall is any incline at an angle measuring 60 degrees or more.

A Climb check that fails by 4 or less means that you make no progress, and one that fails by 5 or more means that you fall from whatever height you have already attained.

The DC of the check depends on the conditions of the climb. Compare the task with those on the following table to determine an appropriate DC.

Climb

DC	Example Surface or Activity
0	A slope too steep to walk up, or a knotted rope with a wall to brace against.
5	A rope with a wall to brace against, or a knotted rope, or a rope affected by the *rope trick* spell.
10	A surface with ledges to hold on to and stand on, such as a very rough wall or a ship's rigging.
15	Any surface with adequate handholds and footholds (natural or artificial), such as a very rough natural rock surface or a tree, or an unknotted rope, or pulling yourself up when dangling by your hands.
20	An uneven surface with narrow handholds and footholds, such as a typical wall in a dungeon.
25	A rough surface, such as a natural rock wall or a brick wall.
30	An overhang or ceiling with handholds only.
—	A perfectly smooth, flat vertical (or inverted) surface cannot be climbed.

Climb DC Modifier*	Example Surface or Activity
−10	Climbing a chimney (artificial or natural) or other location where you can brace against two opposite walls.
−5	Climbing a corner where you can brace against perpendicular walls.
+5	Surface is slippery.

* These modifiers are cumulative; use all that apply.

You need both hands free to climb, but you may cling to a wall with one hand while you cast a spell or take some other action that requires only one hand. While climbing, you can't move to avoid a blow, so you lose your Dexterity bonus to AC (if any). You also can't use a shield while climbing. Anytime you take damage while climbing, make a Climb check against the DC of the slope or wall. Failure means you fall from your current height and sustain the appropriate falling damage.

Accelerated Climbing: You try to climb more quickly than normal. By accepting a −5 penalty, you can move half your speed (instead of one-quarter your speed).

Make Your Own Handholds and Footholds: You can make your own handholds and footholds by pounding pitons into a wall. Doing so takes 1 minute per piton, and one piton is needed per 5 feet of distance. As with any surface that offers handholds and footholds, a wall with pitons in it has a DC of 15. In the same way, a climber with a handaxe or similar implement can cut handholds in an ice wall.

Catch Yourself When Falling: It's practically impossible to catch yourself on a wall while falling, yet if you wish to attempt such a difficult task, you can make a Climb check

(DC = wall's DC + 20) to do so. It's much easier to catch yourself on a slope (DC = slope's DC + 10).

Catch a Falling Character While Climbing: If someone climbing above you or adjacent to you falls, you can attempt to catch the falling character if he or she is within your reach. Doing so requires a successful melee touch attack against the falling character (though he or she can voluntarily forego any Dexterity bonus to AC if desired). If you hit, you must immediately attempt a Climb check (DC = wall's DC + 10). Success indicates that you catch the falling character, but his total weight, including equipment, cannot exceed your heavy load limit or you automatically fall. If you fail your Climb check by 4 or less, you fail to stop the character's fall but don't lose your grip on the wall. If you fail by 5 or more, you fail to stop the character's fall and begin falling as well.

Action: Climbing is part of movement, so it's generally part of a move action (and may be combined with other types of movement in a move action). Each move action that includes any climbing requires a separate Climb check. Catching yourself or another falling character doesn't take an action.

Special: You can use a rope to haul a character upward (or lower a character) through sheer strength. You can lift double your maximum load in this manner.

A creature with a climb speed has a +8 racial bonus on all Climb checks. The creature must make a Climb check to climb any wall or slope with a DC higher than 0, but it can always choose to take 10, even if rushed or threatened while climbing. If a creature with a climb speed chooses an accelerated climb (see above), it moves at double its climb speed (or at its land speed, whichever is slower) and makes a single Climb check at a −5 penalty. Such a creature retains its Dexterity bonus to Armor Class (if any) while climbing, and opponents get no special bonus to their attacks against it. It cannot, however, use the run action while climbing.

If you have the Athletic feat, you get a bonus on Climb checks (see Chapter 5).

CRAFT (Int)

You are skilled in the creation of a specific group of items, such as armor or weapons. Like Knowledge, Perform, and Profession, Craft is actually a number of separate skills. You could have several Craft skills, each with its own ranks. The most common Craft skills are alchemy, armor, baskets, books, bows, calligraphy, carpentry, cloth, clothing, glass, jewelry, leather, locks, paintings, pottery, sculptures, ships, shoes, stonemasonry, traps, and weapons.

A Craft skill is specifically focused on creating something. If nothing is created by the endeavor, it probably falls under the heading of a Profession skill.

Check: You can practice your trade and make a decent living, earning half your check result in gold pieces per

week of dedicated work. You know how to use the tools of your trade, how to perform the craft's daily tasks, how to supervise untrained helpers, and how to handle common problems. (Untrained laborers and assistants earn an average of 1 silver piece per day.)

The basic function of the Craft skill, however, is to allow you to make an item of the appropriate type. The DC depends on the complexity of the item to be created. The DC, your check result, and the price of the item determine how long it takes to make a particular item. The item's finished price also determines the cost of raw materials.

In some cases, the *fabricate* spell can be used to achieve the results of a Craft check with no actual check involved. You must still make an appropriate Craft check when using the spell to make articles requiring a high degree of craftsmanship.

A successful Craft check related to woodworking in conjunction with the casting of the *ironwood* spell enables you to make wooden items that have the strength of steel.

When casting the spell *minor creation*, you must succeed on an appropriate Craft check to make a complex item.

All crafts require artisan's tools to give the best chance of success. If improvised tools are used, the check is made with a −2 penalty. On the other hand, masterwork artisan's tools provide a +2 circumstance bonus on the check.

To determine how much time and money it takes to make an item, follow these steps.

1. Find the item's price in silver pieces (1 gp = 10 sp).
2. Find the item's DC from Table 4–4.
3. Pay 1/3 of the item's price for the raw material cost.
4. Make an appropriate Craft check representing one week's worth of work. If the check succeeds, multiply your check result by the DC. If the result × the DC equals the price of the item in sp, then you have completed the item. (If the result × the DC equals double or triple the price of the item in silver pieces, then you've completed the task in one-half or one-third of the time. Other multiples of the DC reduce the time in the same manner.) If the result × the DC doesn't equal the price, then it represents the progress you've made this week. Record the result and make a new Craft check for the next week. Each week, you make more progress until your total reaches the price of the item in silver pieces.

TABLE 4-4: CRAFT SKILLS

Item	Craft Skill	Craft DC
Acid	Alchemy	15
Alchemist's fire, smokestick, or tindertwig	Alchemy	20
Antitoxin, sunrod, tanglefoot bag, or thunderstone	Alchemy	25
Armor or shield	Armor	10 + AC bonus
Longbow, shortbow, or arrows	Bows	12
Composite longbow or composite shortbow	Bows	15
Composite longbow or composite shortbow with high strength rating	Bows	15 + (2 × rating)
Mechanical trap	Traps	Varies*
Crossbow, or bolts	Weapons	15
Simple melee or thrown weapon	Weapons	12
Martial melee or thrown weapon	Weapons	15
Exotic melee or thrown weapon	Weapons	18
Very simple item (wooden spoon)	Varies	5
Typical item (iron pot)	Varies	10
High-quality item (bell)	Varies	15
Complex or superior item (lock)	Varies	20

* Traps have their own rules for construction (see Chapter 13).

If you fail a check by 4 or less, you make no progress this week. If you fail by 5 or more, you ruin half the raw materials and have to pay half the original raw material cost again.

Progress by the Day: You can make checks by the day instead of by the week. In this case your progress (check result × DC) should be divided by the number of days in a week.

Create Masterwork Items: You can make a masterwork item: a weapon, suit of armor, shield, or tool that conveys a bonus on its use through its exceptional craftsmanship. To create a masterwork item, you create the masterwork component as if it were a separate item in addition to the standard item. The masterwork component has its own price (300 gp for a weapon or 150 gp for a suit of armor or a shield, see Chapter 6 for the price of other masterwork tools) and a Craft DC of 20. Once both the standard component and the masterwork component are completed, the masterwork item is finished. The cost you pay for the masterwork component is one-third of the given amount, just as it is for the cost in raw materials.

Repair Items: You can repair an item by making checks against the same DC that it took to make the item in the first place. The cost of repairing an item is one-fifth of the item's price.

Action: Does not apply. Craft checks are made by the day or week (see above).

Try Again: Yes, but each time you fail by 5 or more, you ruin half the raw materials and have to pay half the original raw material cost again.

Special: You may voluntarily add +10 to the indicated DC to craft an item. This allows you to create the item more quickly (since you'll be multiplying this higher DC

by your Craft check result to determine progress). You must decide whether to increase the DC before you make each weekly or daily check.

To make an item using Craft (alchemy), you must have alchemical equipment. If you are working in a city, you can buy what you need as part of the raw materials cost to make the item, but alchemical equipment is difficult or impossible to come by in some places. Purchasing and maintaining an alchemist's lab grants a +2 circumstance bonus on Craft (alchemy) checks because you have the perfect tools for the job, but it does not affect the cost of any items made using the skill.

A gnome receives a +2 bonus on a Craft or Profession skill of her choice.

DIPLOMACY (Cha)

You can use this skill to persuade others to agree with your arguments, to resolve differences, and to gather valuable information or rumors from people. This skill is also used to negotiate conflicts by using the proper etiquette and manners suitable to the problem.

Check: You can change the initial attitudes of nonplayer characters with a successful check. The DC of this check depends on the creature's starting attitude toward you, adjusted by its Charisma modifier. If you succeed, the character's attitude toward you is improved by one step. For every 5 by which your check result exceeds the DC, the character's attitude toward you increases by one additional step. A creature's attitude cannot be shifted more than two steps up in this way, although the GM can override this rule in some situations. If you fail the check by 4 or less, the character's attitude toward you is unchanged. If you fail by

5 or more, the character's attitude toward you is decreased by one step.

You cannot use Diplomacy against a creature that does not understand you or has an Intelligence of 3 or less. Diplomacy is generally ineffective in combat and against creatures that intend to harm you or your allies in the immediate future. Any attitude shift caused through Diplomacy generally lasts for 1d4 hours but can last much longer or shorter depending upon the situation (GM discretion).

Starting Attitude	Diplomacy DC
Hostile	25 + creature's Cha modifier
Unfriendly	20 + creature's Cha modifier
Indifferent	15 + creature's Cha modifier
Friendly	10 + creature's Cha modifier
Helpful	0 + creature's Cha modifier

If a creature's attitude toward you is at least indifferent, you can make requests of the creature. This is an additional Diplomacy check, using the creature's current attitude to determine the base DC, with one of the following modifiers. Once a creature's attitude has shifted to helpful, the creature gives in to most requests without a check, unless the request is against its nature or puts it in serious peril. Some requests automatically fail if the request goes against the creature's values or its nature, subject to GM discretion.

Request	Diplomacy DC Modifier
Give simple advice or directions	−5
Give detailed advice	+0
Give simple aid	+0
Reveal an unimportant secret	+5
Give lengthy or complicated aid	+5
Give dangerous aid	+10
Reveal an important secret	+10 or more
Give aid that could result in punishment	+15 or more
Additional requests	+5 per request

Gather Information: You can also use Diplomacy to gather information about a specific topic or individual. To do this, you must spend at least 1d4 hours canvassing people at local taverns, markets, and gathering places. The DC of this check depends on the obscurity of the information sought, but for most commonly known facts or rumors it is 10. For obscure or secret knowledge, the DC might increase to 20 or higher. The GM might rule that some topics are simply unknown to common folk.

Action: Using Diplomacy to influence a creature's attitude takes 1 minute of continuous interaction. Making a request of a creature takes 1 or more rounds of interaction,

depending upon the complexity of the request. Using Diplomacy to gather information takes 1d4 hours of work searching for rumors and informants.

Try Again: You cannot use Diplomacy to influence a given creature's attitude more than once in a 24-hour period. If a request is refused, the result does not change with additional checks, although other requests might be made. You can retry Diplomacy checks made to gather information.

Special: If you have the Persuasive feat, you gain a bonus on Diplomacy checks (see Chapter 5).

DISABLE DEVICE
(Dex; Armor Check Penalty; Trained Only)

You are skilled at disarming traps and opening locks. In addition, this skill lets you sabotage simple mechanical devices, such as catapults, wagon wheels, and doors.

Check: When disarming a trap or other device, the Disable Device check is made secretly, so that you don't necessarily know whether you've succeeded.

The DC depends on how tricky the device is. If the check succeeds, you disable the device. If it fails by 4 or less, you have failed but can try again. If you fail by 5 or more, something goes wrong. If the device is a trap, you trigger it. If you're attempting some sort of sabotage, you think the device is disabled, but it still works normally.

You also can rig simple devices such as saddles or wagon wheels to work normally for a while and then fail or fall off some time later (usually after 1d4 rounds or minutes of use).

Device	Time	Disable Device DC*	Example
Simple	1 round	10	Jam a lock
Tricky	1d4 rounds	15	Sabotage a wagon wheel
Difficult	2d4 rounds	20	Disarm a trap, reset a trap
Extreme	2d4 rounds	25	Disarm a complex trap, cleverly sabotage a clockwork device

* If you attempt to leave behind no trace of your tampering, add 5 to the DC.

Open Locks: The DC for opening a lock depends on its quality. If you do not have a set of thieves' tools, these DCs increase by 10.

Lock Quality	Disable Device DC
Simple	20
Average	25
Good	30
Superior	40

Action: The amount of time needed to make a Disable Device check depends on the task, as noted above.

Disabling a simple device takes 1 round and is a full-round action. A tricky or difficult device requires 1d4 or 2d4 rounds. Attempting to open a lock is a full-round action.

Try Again: Varies. You can retry checks made to disable traps if you miss the check by 4 or less. You can retry checks made to open locks.

Special: If you have the Deft Hands feat, you get a bonus on Disable Device checks (see Chapter 5).

A rogue who beats a trap's DC by 10 or more can study the trap, figure out how it works, and bypass it without disarming it. A rogue can rig a trap so her allies can bypass it as well.

Restriction: Characters with the trapfinding ability (like rogues) can disarm magic traps. A magic trap generally has a DC of 25 + the level of the spell used to create it.

The spells *fire trap*, *glyph of warding*, *symbol*, and *teleportation circle* also create traps that a rogue can disarm with a successful Disable Device check. *Spike growth* and *spike stones*, however, create magic hazards against which Disable Device checks do not succeed. See the individual spell descriptions for details.

DISGUISE (Cha)

You are skilled at changing your appearance.

Check: Your Disguise check result determines how good the disguise is, and it is opposed by others' Perception check results. If you don't draw any attention to yourself, others do not get to make Perception checks. If you come to the attention of people who are suspicious (such as a guard who is watching commoners walking through a city gate), it can be assumed that such observers are taking 10 on their Perception checks.

You get only one Disguise check per use of the skill, even if several people make Perception checks against it. The Disguise check is made secretly, so that you can't be sure how good the result is.

The effectiveness of your disguise depends on how much you're changing your appearance. Disguise can be used to make yourself appear like a creature that is one size category larger or smaller than your actual size. This does not change your actual size or reach, should you enter combat while wearing such a disguise.

Disguise	Check Modifier
Minor details only	+5
Disguised as different gender[1]	−2
Disguised as different race[1]	−2
Disguised as different age category[1]	−2[2]
Disguised as different size category[1]	−10

1 These modifiers are cumulative; use all that apply.
2 Per step of difference between your actual age category and your disguised age category. The steps are: young (younger than adulthood), adulthood, middle age, old, and venerable.

If you are impersonating a particular individual, those who know what that person looks like get a bonus on their Perception checks according to the table below. Furthermore, they are automatically considered to be suspicious of you, so opposed checks are always called for.

Familiarity	Viewer's Perception Check Bonus
Recognizes on sight	+4
Friends or associates	+6
Close friends	+8
Intimate	+10

An individual makes a Perception check to see through your disguise immediately upon meeting you and again every hour thereafter. If you casually meet a large number of different creatures, each for a short time, check once per day or hour, using an average Perception modifier for the group.

Action: Creating a disguise requires 1d3 × 10 minutes of work. Using magic (such as the *disguise self* spell) reduces this action to the time required to cast the spell or trigger the effect.

Try Again: Yes. You may try to redo a failed disguise, but once others know that a disguise was attempted, they'll be more suspicious.

Special: Magic that alters your form, such as *alter self*, *disguise self*, *polymorph*, or *shapechange*, grants you a +10 bonus on Disguise checks (see the individual spell descriptions). Divination magic that allows people to see through illusions (such as *true seeing*) does not penetrate a mundane disguise, but it can negate the magical component of a magically enhanced one.

You must make a Disguise check when you cast a *simulacrum* spell to determine how good the likeness is.

If you have the Deceitful feat, you gain a bonus on Disguise checks (see Chapter 5).

ESCAPE ARTIST (Dex; Armor Check Penalty)

Your training allows you to slip out of bonds and escape from grapples.

Check: The table below gives the DCs needed to escape various forms of restraints.

Ropes: The DC of your Escape Artist check is equal to the binder's Combat Maneuver Bonus +20.

Manacles and Masterwork Manacles: The DC for manacles is set by their construction (see the table below).

Tight Space: The DC noted is for getting through a space through which your head fits but your shoulders don't. If the space is long, you may need to make multiple checks. You can't squeeze through a space that your head does not fit through.

Grappler: You can make an Escape Artist check in place of a combat maneuver check to escape a grapple (see Chapter 8) or a pin.

Restraint	Escape Artist DC
Rope/bindings	Binder's CMB +20
Net, *animate rope, command plants, control plants,* or *entangle*	20
Snare spell	23
Manacles	30
Tight space	30
Masterwork manacles	35
Grappler	Grappler's CMD

Action: Making an Escape Artist check to escape from rope bindings, manacles, or other restraints (except a grappler) requires 1 minute of work. Escaping from a net or an *animate rope, command plants, control plants,* or *entangle* spell is a full-round action. Escaping from a grapple or pin is a standard action. Squeezing through a tight space takes at least 1 minute, maybe longer, depending on how long the space is.

Try Again: Varies. You can make another check after a failed check if you're squeezing your way through a tight space, making multiple checks. If the situation permits, you can make additional checks, or even take 20, as long as you're not being actively opposed. If the DC to escape from rope or bindings is higher than 20 + your Escape Artist skill bonus, you cannot escape from the bonds using Escape Artist.

Special: If you have the Stealthy feat, you gain a bonus on Escape Artist checks (see Chapter 5).

FLY
(Dex; Armor Check Penalty)

You are skilled at flying, through either the use of wings or magic, and can perform daring or complex maneuvers while airborne. Note that this skill does not give you the ability to fly.

Check: You generally need only make a Fly check when you are attempting a complex maneuver. Without making a check, a flying creature can remain flying at the end of its turn so long as it moves a distance greater than half its speed. It can also turn up to 45 degrees by sacrificing 5 feet of movement, can rise at half speed at an angle of 45 degrees, and can descend at any angle at normal speed. Note that these restrictions only apply to movement taken during your current turn. At the beginning of the next turn, you can move in a different direction than you did the previous turn without making a check. Taking any action that violates these rules requires a Fly check. The difficulty of these maneuvers varies depending upon the maneuver you are attempting, as noted on the following chart.

Flying Maneuver	Fly DC
Move less than half speed and remain flying	10
Hover	15
Turn greater than 45° by spending 5 feet of movement	15
Turn 180° by spending 10 feet of movement	20
Fly up at greater than 45° angle	20

Attacked While Flying: You are not considered flat-footed while flying. If you are flying using wings and you take damage while flying, you must make a DC 10 Fly check to avoid losing 10 feet of altitude. This descent does not provoke an attack of opportunity and does not count against a creature's movement.

Collision While Flying: If you are using wings to fly and you collide with an object equal to your size or larger, you must immediately make a DC 25 Fly check to avoid plummeting to the ground, taking the appropriate falling damage.

Avoid Falling Damage: If you are falling and have the ability to fly, you can make a DC 10 Fly check to negate the damage. You cannot make this check if you are falling due to a failed Fly check or a collision.

High Wind Speeds: Flying in high winds adds penalties on your Fly checks as noted on Table 4–5. "Checked" means that creatures of that size or smaller must succeed on a DC 20 Fly check to move at all so long as the wind persists. "Blown away" means that creatures of that size or smaller must make a DC 25 Fly check or be blown back 2d6 × 10 feet and take 2d6 points of nonlethal damage. This check must be made every round the creature remains airborne. A creature that is blown away must still make a DC 20 Fly check to move due to also being checked.

Action: None. A Fly check doesn't require an action; it is made as part of another action or as a reaction to a situation.

Try Again: Varies. You can attempt a Fly check to perform the same maneuver on subsequent rounds. If you are using wings and you fail a Fly check by 5 or more, you plummet to the ground, taking the appropriate falling damage (see Chapter 13).

Special: A spellcaster with a bat familiar gains a +3 bonus on Fly checks.

Creatures with a fly speed treat the Fly skill as a class skill. A creature with a natural fly speed receives a bonus (or penalty) on Fly skill checks depending on its maneuverability: Clumsy –8, Poor –4, Average +0, Good +4, Perfect +8. Creatures without a listed maneuverability rating are assumed to have average maneuverability.

A creature larger or smaller than Medium takes a size bonus or penalty on Fly checks depending on its size category: Fine +8, Diminutive +6, Tiny +4, Small +2, Large –2, Huge –4, Gargantuan –6, Colossal –8.

You cannot take ranks in this skill without a natural means of flight or gliding. Creatures can also take ranks

TABLE 4-5: WIND EFFECTS ON FLIGHT

Wind Force	Wind Speed	Checked Size	Blown Away Size	Fly Penalty
Light	0–10 mph	—	—	—
Moderate	11–20 mph	—	—	—
Strong	21–30 mph	Tiny	—	–2
Severe	31–50 mph	Small	Tiny	–4
Windstorm	51–74 mph	Medium	Small	–8
Hurricane	75–174 mph	Large	Medium	–12
Tornado	175+ mph	Huge	Large	–16

in Fly if they possess a reliable means of flying every day (either through a spell or other special ability).

If you have the Acrobatic feat, you get a bonus on Fly checks (see Chapter 5).

HANDLE ANIMAL
(Cha: Trained Only)

You are trained at working with animals, and can teach them tricks, get them to follow your simple commands, or even domesticate them.

Check: The DC depends on what you are trying to do.

Task	Handle Animal DC
Handle an animal	10
"Push" an animal	25
Teach an animal a trick	15 or 20*
Train an animal for a general purpose	15 or 20*
Rear a wild animal	15 + HD of animal

* See the specific trick or purpose below.

Handle an Animal: This task involves commanding an animal to perform a task or trick that it knows. If the animal is wounded or has taken any nonlethal damage or ability score damage, the DC increases by 2. If your check succeeds, the animal performs the task or trick on its next action.

"Push" an Animal: To push an animal means to get it to perform a task or trick that it doesn't know but is physically capable of performing. This category also covers making an animal perform a forced march or forcing it to hustle for more than 1 hour between sleep cycles. If the animal is wounded or has taken any nonlethal damage or ability score damage, the DC increases by 2. If your check succeeds, the animal performs the task or trick on its next action.

Teach an Animal a Trick: You can teach an animal a specific trick with 1 week of work and a successful Handle Animal check against the indicated DC. An animal with an Intelligence score of 1 can learn a maximum of three tricks, while an animal with an Intelligence score of 2 can learn a maximum of six tricks. Possible tricks (and their associated DCs) include, but are not necessarily limited to, the following.

- Attack (DC 20): The animal attacks apparent enemies. You may point to a particular creature that you wish the animal to attack, and it will comply if able. Normally, an animal will attack only humanoids, monstrous humanoids, or other animals. Teaching an animal to attack all creatures (including such unnatural creatures as undead and aberrations) counts as two tricks.
- Come (DC 15): The animal comes to you, even if it normally would not do so.
- Defend (DC 20): The animal defends you (or is ready to defend you if no threat is present), even without any command being given. Alternatively, you can command the animal to defend another specific character.
- Down (DC 15): The animal breaks off from combat or otherwise backs down. An animal that doesn't know this trick continues to fight until it must flee (due to injury, a fear effect, or the like) or its opponent is defeated.
- Fetch (DC 15): The animal goes and gets something. If you do not point out a specific item, the animal fetches a random object.
- Guard (DC 20): The animal stays in place and prevents others from approaching.
- Heel (DC 15): The animal follows you closely, even to places where it normally wouldn't go.
- Perform (DC 15): The animal performs a variety of simple tricks, such as sitting up, rolling over, roaring or barking, and so on.
- Seek (DC 15): The animal moves into an area and looks around for anything that is obviously alive or animate.
- Stay (DC 15): The animal stays in place, waiting for you to return. It does not challenge other creatures that come by, though it still defends itself if it needs to.
- Track (DC 20): The animal tracks the scent presented to it. (This requires the animal to have the scent ability.)
- Work (DC 15): The animal pulls or pushes a medium or heavy load.

Train an Animal for a General Purpose: Rather than teaching an animal individual tricks, you can simply train it for a general purpose. Essentially, an animal's purpose represents a preselected set of known tricks that fit into a common scheme, such as guarding or heavy labor. The animal must meet all the normal prerequisites for all tricks included in the training package. If the package includes more than three tricks, the animal must have an Intelligence score of 2 or higher.

An animal can be trained for only one general purpose, though if the creature is capable of learning additional tricks (above and beyond those included in its general purpose), it may do so. Training an animal for a purpose requires fewer checks than teaching individual tricks does, but no less time.

- Combat Training (DC 20): An animal trained to bear a rider into combat knows the tricks attack, come, defend, down, guard, and heel. Training an animal for combat riding takes 6 weeks. You may also "upgrade" an animal trained for riding to one trained for combat by spending 3 weeks and making a successful DC 20 Handle Animal check. The new general purpose and tricks completely replace the animal's previous purpose and any tricks it once knew. Many horses and riding dogs are trained in this way.
- Fighting (DC 20): An animal trained to engage in combat knows the tricks attack, down, and stay. Training an animal for fighting takes 3 weeks.
- Guarding (DC 20): An animal trained to guard knows the tricks attack, defend, down, and guard. Training an animal for guarding takes 4 weeks.
- Heavy Labor (DC 15): An animal trained for heavy labor knows the tricks come and work. Training an animal for heavy labor takes 2 weeks.
- Hunting (DC 20): An animal trained for hunting knows the tricks attack, down, fetch, heel, seek, and track. Training an animal for hunting takes 6 weeks.
- Performance (DC 15): An animal trained for performance knows the tricks come, fetch, heel, perform, and stay. Training an animal for performance takes 5 weeks.
- Riding (DC 15): An animal trained to bear a rider knows the tricks come, heel, and stay. Training an animal for riding takes 3 weeks.

Rear a Wild Animal: To rear an animal means to raise a wild creature from infancy so that it becomes domesticated. A handler can rear as many as three creatures of the same kind at once.

A successfully domesticated animal can be taught tricks at the same time it's being raised, or it can be taught as a domesticated animal later.

Action: Varies. Handling an animal is a move action, while "pushing" an animal is a full-round action. (A druid or ranger can handle an animal companion as a free action or push it as a move action.) For tasks with specific time frames noted above, you must spend half this time (at the rate of 3 hours per day per animal being handled) working toward completion of the task before you attempt the Handle Animal check. If the check fails, your attempt to teach, rear, or train the animal fails and you need not

complete the teaching, rearing, or training time. If the check succeeds, you must invest the remainder of the time to complete the teaching, rearing, or training. If the time is interrupted or the task is not followed through to completion, the attempt to teach, rear, or train the animal automatically fails.

Try Again: Yes, except for rearing an animal.

Special: You can use this skill on a creature with an Intelligence score of 1 or 2 that is not an animal, but the DC of any such check increases by 5. Such creatures have the same limit on tricks known as animals do.

A druid or ranger gains a +4 circumstance bonus on Handle Animal checks involving an animal companion.

In addition, a druid's or ranger's animal companion knows one or more bonus tricks, which don't count against the normal limit on tricks known and don't require any training time or Handle Animal checks to teach.

If you have the Animal Affinity feat, you get a bonus on Handle Animal checks (see Chapter 5).

Untrained: If you have no ranks in Handle Animal, you can use a Charisma check to handle and push domestic animals, but you can't teach, rear, or train animals. A druid or ranger with no ranks in Handle Animal can use a Charisma check to handle and push her animal companion, but she can't teach, rear, or train other nondomestic animals.

HEAL (Wis)

You are skilled at tending to wounds and ailments.

Check: The DC and effect of a Heal check depend on the task you attempt.

Task	DC
First aid	15
Long-term care	15
Treat wounds from caltrops, *spike growth*, or *spike stones*	15
Treat deadly wounds	20
Treat poison	Poison's save DC
Treat disease	Disease's save DC

First Aid: You usually use first aid to save a dying character. If a character has negative hit points and is losing hit points (at the rate of 1 per round, 1 per hour, or 1 per day), you can make him stable. A stable character regains no hit points but stops losing them. First aid also stops a character from losing hit points due to effects that cause bleed (see Appendix 2 for rules on bleed damage).

Long-Term Care: Providing long-term care means treating a wounded person for a day or more. If your Heal check is successful, the patient recovers hit points or ability score points lost to ability damage at twice the normal rate: 2 hit points per level for a full 8 hours of rest in a day, or 4 hit points per level for each full day of complete rest; 2 ability score points for a full 8 hours of rest in a day, or 4 ability score points for each full day of complete rest.

You can tend to as many as six patients at a time. You need a few items and supplies (bandages, salves, and so on) that are easy to come by in settled lands. Giving long-term care counts as light activity for the healer. You cannot give long-term care to yourself.

Treat Wounds from Caltrops, Spike Growth, or Spike Stones: A creature wounded by stepping on a caltrop moves at half normal speed. A successful Heal check removes this movement penalty.

A creature wounded by a *spike growth* or *spike stones* spell must succeed on a Reflex save or take injuries that reduce his speed by one-third. Another character can remove this penalty by taking 10 minutes to dress the victim's injuries and succeeding on a Heal check against the spell's save DC.

Treat Deadly Wounds: When treating deadly wounds, you can restore hit points to a damaged creature. Treating deadly wounds restores 1 hit point per level of the creature. If you exceed the DC by 5 or more, add your Wisdom modifier (if positive) to this amount. A creature can only benefit from its deadly wounds being treated within 24 hours of being injured and never more than once per day. You must expend two uses from a healer's kit to perform this task. You take a –2 penalty on your Heal skill check for each use from the healer's kit that you lack.

Treat Poison: To treat poison means to tend to a single character who has been poisoned and who is going to take more damage from the poison (or suffer some other effect). Every time the poisoned character makes a saving throw against the poison, you make a Heal check. If your Heal check exceeds the DC of the poison, the character receives a +4 competence bonus on his saving throw against the poison.

Treat Disease: To treat a disease means to tend to a single diseased character. Every time the diseased character makes a saving throw against disease effects, you make a Heal check. If your Heal check exceeds the DC of the disease, the character receives a +4 competence bonus on his saving throw against the disease.

Action: Providing first aid, treating a wound, or treating poison is a standard action. Treating a disease or tending a creature wounded by a *spike growth* or *spike stones* spell takes 10 minutes of work. Treating deadly wounds takes 1 hour of work. Providing long-term care requires 8 hours of light activity.

Try Again: Varies. Generally speaking, you can't try a Heal check again without witnessing proof of the original check's failure. You can always retry a check to provide

first aid, assuming the target of the previous attempt is still alive.

Special: A character with the Self-Sufficient feat gets a bonus on Heal checks (see Chapter 5).

A healer's kit gives you a +2 circumstance bonus on Heal checks.

INTIMIDATE (Cha)

You can use this skill to frighten your opponents or to get them to act in a way that benefits you. This skill includes verbal threats and displays of prowess.

Check: You can use Intimidate to force an opponent to act friendly toward you for 1d6 × 10 minutes with a successful check. The DC of this check is equal to 10 + the target's Hit Dice + the target's Wisdom modifier. If successful, the target gives you the information you desire, takes actions that do not endanger it, or otherwise offers limited assistance. After the Intimidate expires, the target treats you as unfriendly and may report you to local authorities. If you fail this check by 5 or more, the target attempts to deceive you or otherwise hinder your activities.

Demoralize: You can use this skill to cause an opponent to become shaken for a number of rounds. The DC of this check is equal to 10 + the target's Hit Dice + the target's Wisdom modifier. If you are successful, the target is shaken for 1 round. This duration increases by 1 round for every 5 by which you beat the DC. You can only threaten an opponent in this way if it is within 30 feet and can clearly see and hear you. Using demoralize on the same creature only extends the duration; it does not create a stronger fear condition.

Action: Using Intimidate to change an opponent's attitude requires 1 minute of conversation. Demoralizing an opponent is a standard action.

Try Again: You can attempt to Intimidate an opponent again, but each additional check increases the DC by +5. This increase resets after 1 hour has passed.

Special: You also gain a +4 bonus on Intimidate checks if you are larger than your target and a –4 penalty on Intimidate checks if you are smaller than your target.

If you have the Persuasive feat, you get a bonus on Intimidate checks (see Chapter 5).

A half-orc gets a +2 bonus on Intimidate checks.

KNOWLEDGE (Int : Trained Only)

You are educated in a field of study and can answer both simple and complex questions. Like the Craft, Perform, and Profession skills, Knowledge actually encompasses a number of different specialties. Below are listed typical fields of study.

- Arcana (ancient mysteries, magic traditions, arcane symbols, constructs, dragons, magical beasts)
- Dungeoneering (aberrations, caverns, oozes, spelunking)
- Engineering (buildings, aqueducts, bridges, fortifications)

- Geography (lands, terrain, climate, people)
- History (wars, colonies, migrations, founding of cities)
- Local (legends, personalities, inhabitants, laws, customs, traditions, humanoids)
- Nature (animals, fey, monstrous humanoids, plants, seasons and cycles, weather, vermin)
- Nobility (lineages, heraldry, personalities, royalty)
- Planes (the Inner Planes, the Outer Planes, the Astral Plane, the Ethereal Plane, outsiders, planar magic)
- Religion (gods and goddesses, mythic history, ecclesiastic tradition, holy symbols, undead)

Check: Answering a question within your field of study has a DC of 10 (for really easy questions), 15 (for basic questions), or 20 to 30 (for really tough questions).

You can use this skill to identify monsters and their special powers or vulnerabilities. In general, the DC of

such a check equals 10 + the monster's CR. For common monsters, such as goblins, the DC of this check equals 5 + the monster's CR. For particularly rare monsters, such as the tarrasque, the DC of this check equals 15 + the monster's CR, or more. A successful check allows you to remember a bit of useful information about that monster. For every 5 points by which your check result exceeds the DC, you recall another piece of useful information. Many of the Knowledge skills have specific uses as noted on Table 4–6.

Action: Usually none. In most cases, a Knowledge check doesn't take an action (but see "Untrained," below).

Try Again: No. The check represents what you know, and thinking about a topic a second time doesn't let you know something that you never learned in the first place.

Untrained: You cannot make an untrained Knowledge check with a DC higher than 10. If you have access to an extensive library that covers a specific skill, this limit is removed. The time to make checks using a library, however, increases to 1d4 hours. Particularly complete libraries might even grant a bonus on Knowledge checks in the fields that they cover.

LINGUISTICS (Int; Trained Only)

You are skilled at working with language, in both its spoken and written forms. You can speak multiple languages, and can decipher nearly any tongue given enough time. Your skill in writing allows you to create and detect forgeries as well.

Check: You can decipher writing in an unfamiliar language or a message written in an incomplete or archaic form. The base DC is 20 for the simplest messages, 25 for standard texts, and 30 or higher for intricate, exotic, or very old writing. If the check succeeds, you understand the general content of a piece of writing about one page long (or the equivalent). If the check fails, make a DC 5 Wisdom check to see if you avoid drawing a false conclusion about the text. (Success means that you do not draw a false conclusion; failure means that you do.)

Both the Linguistics check and (if necessary) the Wisdom check are made secretly by the GM, so that you can't tell whether the conclusion you draw is true or false.

Condition	Linguistics Check Modifier
Type of document unknown to reader	–2
Type of document somewhat known to reader	+0
Type of document well known to reader	+2
Handwriting not known to reader	–2
Handwriting somewhat known to reader	+0
Handwriting intimately known to reader	+2
Reader only casually reviews the document	–2
Document contradicts orders or knowledge	+2

TABLE 4-6: KNOWLEDGE SKILL DCS

Task	Knowledge Skill	DC
Identify auras while using *detect magic*	Arcana	15 + spell level
Identify a spell effect that is in place	Arcana	20 + spell level
Identify materials manufactured by magic	Arcana	20 + spell level
Identify a spell that just targeted you	Arcana	25 + spell level
Identify the spells cast using a specific material component	Arcana	20
Identify underground hazard	Dungeoneering	15 + hazard's CR
Identify mineral, stone, or metal	Dungeoneering	10
Determine slope	Dungeoneering	15
Determine depth underground	Dungeoneering	20
Identify dangerous construction	Engineering	10
Determine a structure's style or age	Engineering	15
Determine a structure's weakness	Engineering	20
Identify a creature's ethnicity or accent	Geography	10
Recognize regional terrain features	Geography	15
Know location of nearest community or noteworthy site	Geography	20
Know recent or historically significant event	History	10
Determine approximate date of a specific event	History	15
Know obscure or ancient historical event	History	20
Know local laws, rulers, and popular locations	Local	10
Know a common rumor or local tradition	Local	15
Know hidden organizations, rulers, and locations	Local	20
Identify natural hazard	Nature	15 + hazard's CR
Identify a common plant or animal	Nature	10
Identify unnatural weather phenomenon	Nature	15
Determine artificial nature of feature	Nature	20
Know current rulers and their symbols	Nobility	10
Know proper etiquette	Nobility	15
Know line of succession	Nobility	20
Know the names of the planes	Planes	10
Recognize current plane	Planes	15
Identify a creature's planar origin	Planes	20
Recognize a common deity's symbol or clergy	Religion	10
Know common mythology and tenets	Religion	15
Recognize an obscure deity's symbol or clergy	Religion	20
Identify a monster's abilities and weaknesses	Varies	10 + monster's CR

Create or Detect Forgeries: Forgery requires writing materials appropriate to the document being forged. To forge a document on which the handwriting is not specific to a person, you need only to have seen a similar document before, and you gain a +8 bonus on your check. To forge a signature, you need an autograph of that person to copy, and you gain a +4 bonus on the check. To forge a longer document written in the hand of some particular person, a large sample of that person's handwriting is needed.

The Linguistics check is made secretly, so that you're not sure how good your forgery is. As with Disguise, you don't make a check until someone examines the work. Your Linguistics check is opposed by the Linguistics check of the person who examines the document to verify its authenticity.

The examiner gains modifiers if any of the conditions are listed on the table found on the previous page.

Learn a Language: Whenever you put a rank into this skill, you learn to speak and read a new language. Common languages (and their typical speakers) include the following.

- Abyssal (demons and other chaotic evil outsiders)
- Aklo (derros, inhuman or otherworldly monsters, evil fey)
- Aquan (aquatic creatures, water-based creatures)
- Auran (flying creatures, air-based creatures)
- Celestial (angels and other good outsiders)
- Common (humans and the core races from Chapter 2)
- Draconic (dragons, reptilian humanoids)
- Druidic (druids only)
- Dwarven (dwarves)

- Elven (elves, half-elves)
- Giant (cyclopses, ettins, giants, ogres, trolls)
- Gnome (gnomes)
- Goblin (bugbears, goblins, hobgoblins)
- Gnoll (gnolls)
- Halfling (halflings)
- Ignan (fire-based creatures)
- Infernal (devils and other lawful evil outsiders)
- Orc (orcs, half-orcs)
- Sylvan (centaurs, fey creatures, plant creatures, unicorns)
- Terran (earth-based creatures)
- Undercommon (drow, duergar, morlocks, svirfneblin)

Action: Varies. Deciphering a page of ordinary text takes 1 minute (10 consecutive rounds). Creating a forgery can take anywhere from 1 minute to 1d4 minutes per page. Detecting a forgery using Linguistics takes 1 round of examination per page.

Try Again: Yes.

Special: You must be trained to use this skill, but you can always attempt to read archaic and strange forms of your own racial bonus languages. In addition, you can also always attempt to detect a forgery.

PERCEPTION (Wis)

Your senses allow you to notice fine details and alert you to danger. Perception covers all five senses, including sight, hearing, touch, taste, and smell.

Check: Perception has a number of uses, the most common of which is an opposed check versus an opponent's Stealth check to notice the opponent and avoid being surprised. If you are successful, you notice the opponent and can react accordingly. If you fail, your opponent can take a variety of actions, including sneaking past you and attacking you.

Perception is also used to notice fine details in the environment. The DC to notice such details varies depending upon distance, the environment, and how noticeable the detail is. The following table gives a number of guidelines.

Detail	Perception DC
Hear the sound of battle	–10
Notice the stench of rotting garbage	–10
Detect the smell of smoke	0
Hear the details of a conversation	0
Notice a visible creature	0
Determine if food is spoiled	5
Hear the sound of a creature walking	10
Hear the details of a whispered conversation	15
Find the average concealed door	15
Hear the sound of a key being turned in a lock	20
Find the average secret door	20
Hear a bow being drawn	25
Sense a burrowing creature underneath you	25

Notice a pickpocket	Opposed by Sleight of Hand
Notice a creature using Stealth	Opposed by Stealth
Find a hidden trap	Varies by trap
Identify the powers of a potion through taste	15 + the potion's caster level

Perception Modifiers	DC Modifier
Distance to the source, object, or creature	+1/10 feet
Through a closed door	+5
Through a wall	+10/foot of thickness
Favorable conditions[1]	–2
Unfavorable conditions[1]	+2
Terrible conditions[2]	+5
Creature making the check is distracted	+5
Creature making the check is asleep	+10
Creature or object is invisible	+20

1 Favorable and unfavorable conditions depend upon the sense being used to make the check. For example, bright light might decrease the DC of checks involving sight, while torchlight or moonlight might increase the DC. Background noise might increase a DC involving hearing, while competing odors might increase the DC of a check involving scent.

2 As for unfavorable conditions, but more extreme. For example, candlelight for DCs involving sight, a roaring dragon for DCs involving hearing, and an overpowering stench covering the area for DCs involving scent.

Action: Most Perception checks are reactive, made in response to observable stimulus. Intentionally searching for stimulus is a move action.

Try Again: Yes. You can try to sense something you missed the first time, so long as the stimulus is still present.

Special: Elves, half-elves, gnomes, and halflings receive a +2 racial bonus on Perception checks. Creatures with the scent special quality have a +8 bonus on Perception checks made to detect a scent. Creatures with the tremorsense special quality have a +8 bonus on Perception checks against creatures touching the ground and automatically make any such checks within their range. For more on special qualities, see Appendix 1.

A spellcaster with a hawk or owl familiar gains a +3 bonus on Perception checks. If you have the Alertness feat, you get a bonus on Perception checks (see Chapter 5).

PERFORM (Cha)

You are skilled at one form of entertainment, from singing to acting to playing an instrument. Like Craft, Knowledge, and Profession, Perform is actually a number of separate skills. You could have several Perform skills, each with its own ranks.

Each of the nine categories of the Perform skill includes a variety of methods, instruments, or techniques, a small sample of which is provided for each category below.

- Act (comedy, drama, pantomime)
- Comedy (buffoonery, limericks, joke-telling)
- Dance (ballet, waltz, jig)
- Keyboard instruments (harpsichord, piano, pipe organ)
- Oratory (epic, ode, storytelling)
- Percussion instruments (bells, chimes, drums, gong)
- String instruments (fiddle, harp, lute, mandolin)
- Wind instruments (flute, pan pipes, recorder, trumpet)
- Sing (ballad, chant, melody)

Check: You can impress audiences with your talent and skill in your chosen performance type.

Perform DC	Performance
10	Routine performance. Trying to earn money by playing in public is akin to begging. You can earn 1d10 cp/day.
15	Enjoyable performance. In a prosperous city, you can earn 1d10 sp/day.
20	Great performance. In a prosperous city, you can earn 3d10 sp/day. In time, you may be invited to join a professional troupe and may develop a regional reputation.
25	Memorable performance. In a prosperous city, you can earn 1d6 gp/day. In time, you may come to the attention of noble patrons and develop a national reputation.
30	Extraordinary performance. In a prosperous city, you can earn 3d6 gp/day. In time, you may draw attention from distant patrons, or even from extraplanar beings.

A masterwork musical instrument gives you a +2 circumstance bonus on all Perform checks that involve its use.

Action: Varies. Trying to earn money by playing in public requires anywhere from an evening's work to a full day's performance. The bard's special Perform-based abilities are described in that class's description.

Try Again: Yes. Retries are allowed, but they don't negate previous failures, and an audience that has been unimpressed in the past is likely to be prejudiced against future performances. (Increase the DC by 2 for each previous failure.)

Special: A bard must have ranks in specific Perform categories to use some of his Bardic Performance abilities. Consult the Bardic Performance section of the bard class description in Chapter 3 for more details.

PROFESSION (Wis; Trained Only)

You are skilled at a specific job. Like Craft, Knowledge, and Perform, Profession is actually a number of separate skills. You could have several Profession skills, each with its own ranks. While a Craft skill represents ability in creating an item, a Profession skill represents an aptitude in a vocation requiring a broader range of less specific knowledge. The most common Profession skills are architect, baker, barrister, brewer, butcher, clerk, cook, courtesan, driver, engineer, farmer, fisherman, gambler, gardener, herbalist, innkeeper, librarian, merchant, midwife, miller, miner, porter, sailor, scribe, shepherd, stable master, soldier, tanner, trapper, and woodcutter.

Check: You can earn half your Profession check result in gold pieces per week of dedicated work. You know how to use the tools of your trade, how to perform the profession's daily tasks, how to supervise helpers, and how to handle common problems. You can also answer questions about your Profession. Basic questions are DC 10, while more complex questions are DC 15 or higher.

Action: Not applicable. A single check generally represents a week of work.

Try Again: Varies. An attempt to use a Profession skill to earn income cannot be retried. You are stuck with whatever weekly wage your check result brought you. Another check may be made after a week to determine a new income for the next period of time. An attempt to accomplish some specific task can usually be retried.

Untrained: Untrained laborers and assistants (that is, characters without any ranks in Profession) earn an average of 1 silver piece per day.

Special: A gnome gets a +2 bonus on a Craft or Profession skill of her choice.

RIDE (Dex; Armor Check Penalty)

You are skilled at riding mounts, usually a horse, but possibly something more exotic, like a griffon or pegasus. If you attempt to ride a creature that is ill suited as a mount, you take a –5 penalty on your Ride checks.

Check: Typical riding actions don't require checks. You can saddle, mount, ride, and dismount from a mount without a problem. The following tasks do require checks.

Task	Ride DC
Guide with knees	5
Stay in saddle	5
Fight with a combat-trained mount	10
Cover	15
Soft fall	15
Leap	15
Spur mount	15
Control mount in battle	20
Fast mount or dismount	20

Guide with Knees: You can guide your mount with your knees so you can use both hands in combat. Make your Ride check at the start of your turn. If you fail, you can use only one hand this round because you need to use the other to control your mount. This does not take an action.

Stay in Saddle: You can react instantly to try to avoid falling when your mount rears or bolts unexpectedly or when you take damage. This usage does not take an action.

Fight with a Combat-Trained Mount: If you direct your war-trained mount to attack in battle, you can still make your own attack or attacks normally. This usage is a free action.

Cover: You can react instantly to drop down and hang alongside your mount, using it as cover. You can't attack or cast spells while using your mount as cover. If you fail your Ride check, you don't get the cover benefit. Using this option is an immediate action, but recovering from this position is a move action (no check required).

Soft Fall: You negate damage when you fall off a mount. If you fail the Ride check, you take 1d6 points of damage and are prone. This usage does not take an action.

Leap: You can get your mount to leap obstacles as part of its movement. If the ride check to make the leap succeeds, make a check using your Ride modifier or the mount's jump modifier, whichever is lower, to see how far the creature can jump. If you fail your Ride check to make the leap, you fall off the mount when it leaps and take the appropriate falling damage (at least 1d6 points). This usage does not take an action but is part of the mount's movement.

Spur Mount: You can spur your mount to greater speed with a move action. A successful Ride check increases the mount's speed by 10 feet for 1 round but deals 1d3 points of damage to the creature. You can use this ability every round, but the mount becomes fatigued after a number of rounds equal to its Constitution score. This ability cannot be used on a fatigued mount.

Control Mount in Battle: As a move action, you can attempt to control a light horse, pony, heavy horse, or other mount not trained for combat riding while in battle. If you fail the Ride check, you can do nothing else in that round. You do not need to roll for horses or ponies trained for combat.

Fast Mount or Dismount: You can attempt to mount or dismount from a mount of up to one size category larger than yourself as a free action, provided that you still have a move action available that round. If you fail the Ride check, mounting or dismounting is a move action. You can't use fast mount or dismount on a mount more than one size category larger than yourself.

Action: Varies. Mounting or dismounting normally is a move action. Other checks are a move action, a free action, or no action at all, as noted above.

Special: If you are riding bareback, you take a –5 penalty on Ride checks.

If you have the Animal Affinity feat, you get a bonus on Ride checks (see Chapter 5).

If you use a military saddle you get a +2 circumstance bonus on Ride checks related to staying in the saddle.

Ride is a prerequisite for Mounted Archery, Mounted Combat, Ride-By Attack, Spirited Charge, and Trample.

SENSE MOTIVE (Wis)

You are skilled at detecting falsehoods and true intentions.

Check: A successful check lets you avoid being bluffed (see the Bluff skill). You can also use this skill to determine when "something is up" (that is, something odd is going on) or to assess someone's trustworthiness.

Task	Sense Motive DC
Hunch	20
Sense enchantment	25 or 15
Discern secret message	Varies

Hunch: This use of the skill involves making a gut assessment of the social situation. You can get the feeling from another's behavior that something is wrong, such as when you're talking to an impostor. Alternatively, you can get the feeling that someone is trustworthy.

Sense Enchantment: You can tell that someone's behavior is being influenced by an enchantment effect even if that person isn't aware of it. The usual DC is 25, but if the target is dominated (see *dominate person*), the DC is only 15 because of the limited range of the target's activities.

Discern Secret Message: You may use Sense Motive to detect that a hidden message is being transmitted via the Bluff skill. In this case, your Sense Motive check is opposed by the Bluff check of the character transmitting the message. For each piece of information relating to the message that you are missing, you take a –2 penalty on your Sense Motive check. If you succeed by 4 or less, you know that something hidden is being communicated, but you can't learn anything specific about its content. If you beat the DC by 5 or more, you intercept and understand the message. If you fail by 4 or less, you don't detect any hidden communication. If you fail by 5 or more, you might infer false information.

Action: Trying to gain information with Sense Motive generally takes at least 1 minute, and you could spend a whole evening trying to get a sense of the people around you.

Try Again: No, though you may make a Sense Motive check for each Bluff check made against you.

Special: A ranger gains a bonus on Sense Motive checks when using this skill against a favored enemy.

If you have the Alertness feat, you get a bonus on Sense Motive checks (see Chapter 5).

SLEIGHT OF HAND
(Dex; Armor Check Penalty; Trained Only)

Your training allows you to pick pockets, draw hidden weapons, and take a variety of actions without being noticed.

Check: A DC 10 Sleight of Hand check lets you palm a coin-sized, unattended object. Performing a minor feat of legerdemain, such as making a coin disappear, also has a DC of 10 unless an observer is determined to note where the item went.

When you use this skill under close observation, your skill check is opposed by the observer's Perception check. The observer's success doesn't prevent you from performing the action, just from doing it unnoticed.

You can hide a small object (including a light weapon or an easily concealed ranged weapon, such as a dart, sling, or hand crossbow) on your body. Your Sleight of Hand check is opposed by the Perception check of anyone observing you or of anyone frisking you. In the latter case, the searcher gains a +4 bonus on the Perception check, since it's generally easier to find such an object than to hide it. A dagger is easier to hide than most light weapons, and grants you a +2 bonus on your Sleight of Hand check to conceal it. An extraordinarily small object, such as a coin, shuriken, or ring, grants you a +4 bonus on your Sleight of Hand check to conceal it, and heavy or baggy clothing (such as a cloak) grants you a +2 bonus on the check.

Drawing a hidden weapon is a standard action and doesn't provoke an attack of opportunity.

If you try to take something from a creature, you must make a DC 20 Sleight of Hand check. The opponent makes a Perception check to detect the attempt, opposed by the Sleight of Hand check result you achieved when you tried to grab the item. An opponent who succeeds on this check notices the attempt, regardless of whether you got the item. You cannot use this skill to take an object from another creature during combat if the creature is aware of your presence.

You can also use Sleight of Hand to entertain an audience as though you were using the Perform skill. In such a case, your "act" encompasses elements of legerdemain, juggling, and the like.

Sleight of Hand DC	Task
10	Palm a coin-sized object, make a coin disappear
20	Lift a small object from a person

Action: Any Sleight of Hand check is normally a standard action. However, you may perform a Sleight of Hand check as a move action by taking a –20 penalty on the check.

Try Again: Yes, but after an initial failure, a second Sleight of Hand attempt against the same target (or while you are being watched by the same observer who noticed your previous attempt) increases the DC for the task by 10.

Untrained: An untrained Sleight of Hand check is simply a Dexterity check. Without actual training, you can't succeed on any Sleight of Hand check with a DC higher than 10, except for hiding an object on your body.

Special: If you have the Deft Hands feat, you get a bonus on Sleight of Hand checks (see Chapter 5).

SPELLCRAFT (Int; Trained Only)

You are skilled at the art of casting spells, identifying magic items, crafting magic items, and identifying spells as they are being cast.

Check: Spellcraft is used whenever your knowledge and skill of the technical art of casting a spell or crafting a magic item comes into question. This skill is also used to identify the properties of magic items in your possession through the use of spells such as *detect magic* and *identify*. The DC of this check varies depending upon the task at hand.

Action: Identifying a spell as it is being cast requires no action, but you must be able to clearly see the spell as it is being cast, and this incurs the same penalties as a Perception skill check due to distance, poor conditions, and other factors. Learning a spell from a spellbook takes 1 hour per level of the spell (0-level spells take 30 minutes). Preparing a spell from a borrowed spellbook does not add any time to your spell preparation. Making a Spellcraft check to craft a magic item is made as part of the creation process. Attempting to ascertain the properties of a magic item takes 3 rounds per item to be identified and you must be able to thoroughly examine the object.

Retry: You cannot retry checks made to identify a spell. If you fail to learn a spell from a spellbook or scroll, you must wait at least 1 week before you can try again. If you fail to prepare a spell from a borrowed spellbook, you cannot try again until the next day. When using *detect magic* or *identify* to learn the properties of magic items, you can only attempt to ascertain the properties of an individual item once per day. Additional attempts reveal the same results.

Special: If you are a specialist wizard, you get a +2 bonus on Spellcraft checks made to identify, learn, and prepare spells from your chosen school. Similarly, you take a –5 penalty on similar checks made concerning spells from your opposition schools.

An elf gets a +2 racial bonus on Spellcraft checks to identify the properties of magic items.

If you have the Magical Aptitude feat, you gain a bonus on Spellcraft checks (see Chapter 5).

STEALTH (Dex; Armor Check Penalty)

You are skilled at avoiding detection, allowing you to slip past foes or strike from an unseen position. This skill covers hiding and moving silently.

Check: Your Stealth check is opposed by the Perception check of anyone who might notice you. Creatures that fail to beat your Stealth check are not aware of you and treat you as if you had total concealment. You can move up to half your normal speed and use Stealth at no penalty. When moving at a speed greater than half but less than your normal speed, you take a –5 penalty. It's impossible to use Stealth while attacking, running, or charging.

Creatures gain a bonus or penalty on Stealth checks based on their size: Fine +16, Diminutive +12, Tiny +8, Small +4, Medium +0, Large –4, Huge –8, Gargantuan –12, Colossal –16.

If people are observing you using any of their senses (but typically sight), you can't use Stealth. Against most creatures, finding cover or concealment allows you to use Stealth. If your observers are momentarily distracted (such as by a Bluff check), you can attempt to use Stealth. While the others turn their attention from you, you can attempt a Stealth check if you can get to an unobserved place of some kind. This check, however, is made at a –10 penalty because you have to move fast.

Breaking Stealth: When you start your turn using Stealth, you can leave cover or concealment and remain unobserved as long as you succeed at a Stealth check and end your turn in cover or concealment. Your Stealth immediately ends after you make an attack roll, whether or not the attack is successful (except when sniping as noted below).

Sniping: If you've already successfully used Stealth at least 10 feet from your target, you can make one ranged attack and then immediately use Stealth again. You take a –20 penalty on your Stealth check to maintain your obscured location.

Creating a Diversion to Hide: You can use Bluff to allow you to use Stealth. A successful Bluff check opposed by the viewer's

TABLE 4-7: SPELLCRAFT DCS

Task	Spellcraft DC
Identify a spell as it is being cast	15 + spell level
Learn a spell from a spellbook or scroll	15 + spell level
Prepare a spell from a borrowed spellbook	15 + spell level
Identify the properties of a magic item using *detect magic*	15 + item's caster level
Decipher a scroll	20 + spell level
Craft a magic item	Varies by item

Sense Motive can give you the momentary diversion you need to attempt a Stealth check while people are aware of you.

Action: Usually none. Normally, you make a Stealth check as part of movement, so it doesn't take a separate action. However, using Stealth immediately after a ranged attack (see Sniping, above) is a move action.

Special: If you are invisible, you gain a +40 bonus on Stealth checks if you are immobile, or a +20 bonus on Stealth checks if you're moving.

If you have the Stealthy feat, you get a bonus on Stealth checks (see Chapter 5).

SURVIVAL (Wis)

You are skilled at surviving in the wild and at navigating in the wilderness. You also excel at following trails and tracks left by others.

Check: You can keep yourself and others safe and fed in the wild. The table below gives the DCs for various tasks that require Survival checks.

Survival DC	Task
10	Get along in the wild. Move up to half your overland speed while hunting and foraging (no food or water supplies needed). You can provide food and water for one other person for every 2 points by which your check result exceeds 10.
15	Gain a +2 bonus on all Fortitude saves against severe weather while moving up to half your overland speed, or gain a +4 bonus if you remain stationary. You may grant the same bonus to one other character for every 1 point by which your Survival check result exceeds 15.
15	Keep from getting lost or avoid natural hazards, such as quicksand.
15	Predict the weather up to 24 hours in advance. For every 5 points by which your Survival check result exceeds 15, you can predict the weather for one additional day in advance.

Follow Tracks: To find tracks or to follow them for 1 mile requires a successful Survival check. You must make another Survival check every time the tracks become difficult to follow. If you are not trained in this skill, you can make untrained checks to find tracks, but you can follow them only if the DC for the task is 10 or lower. Alternatively, you can use the Perception skill to find a footprint or similar sign of a creature's passage using the same DCs, but you can't use Perception to follow tracks, even if someone else has already found them.

You move at half your normal speed while following tracks (or at your normal speed with a −5 penalty on the check, or at up to twice your normal speed with a −20 penalty on the check). The DC depends on the surface and the prevailing conditions, as given on the table.

Surface	Survival DC
Very soft ground	5
Soft ground	10
Firm ground	15
Hard ground	20

Very Soft Ground: Any surface (fresh snow, thick dust, wet mud) that holds deep, clear impressions of footprints.

Soft Ground: Any surface soft enough to yield to pressure, but firmer than wet mud or fresh snow, in which a creature leaves frequent but shallow footprints.

Firm Ground: Most normal outdoor surfaces (such as lawns, fields, woods, and the like) or exceptionally soft or dirty indoor surfaces (thick rugs and very dirty or dusty floors). The creature might leave some traces (broken branches or tufts of hair), but it leaves only occasional or partial footprints.

Hard Ground: Any surface that doesn't hold footprints at all, such as bare rock or an indoor floor. Most streambeds fall into this category, since any footprints left behind are obscured or washed away. The creature leaves only traces (scuff marks or displaced pebbles).

Condition	Survival DC Modifier
Every three creatures in the group being tracked	−1
Size of creature or creatures being tracked:[1]	
Fine	+8
Diminutive	+4
Tiny	+2
Small	+1
Medium	+0
Large	−1
Huge	−2
Gargantuan	−4
Colossal	−8
Every 24 hours since the trail was made	+1
Every hour of rain since the trail was made	+1
Fresh snow since the trail was made	+10
Poor visibility:[2]	
Overcast or moonless night	+6
Moonlight	+3
Fog or precipitation	+3
Tracked party hides trail (and moves at half speed)	+5

1 For a group of mixed sizes, apply only the modifier for the largest size category.

2 Apply only the largest modifier from this category.

Several modifiers may apply to the Survival check, as given on the table above.

Action: Varies. A single Survival check may represent activity over the course of hours or a full day. A Survival check made to find tracks is at least a full-round action, and it may take even longer.

Try Again: Varies. For getting along in the wild or for gaining the Fortitude save bonus noted in the first table on page 107, you make a Survival check once every 24 hours. The result of that check applies until the next check is made. To avoid getting lost or avoid natural hazards, you make a Survival check whenever the situation calls for one. Retries to avoid getting lost in a specific situation or to avoid a specific natural hazard are not allowed. For finding tracks, you can retry a failed check after 1 hour (outdoors) or 10 minutes (indoors) of searching.

Special: If you are trained in Survival, you can automatically determine where true north lies in relation to yourself.

A ranger gains a bonus on Survival checks when using this skill to find or follow the tracks of a favored enemy.

If you have the Self-Sufficient feat, you get a bonus on Survival checks (see Chapter 5).

SWIM (Str; Armor Check Penalty)

You know how to swim and can do so even in stormy water.

Check: Make a Swim check once per round while you are in the water. Success means you may swim at up to half your speed (as a full-round action) or at a quarter of your speed (as a move action). If you fail by 4 or less, you make no progress. If you fail by 5 or more, you go underwater.

If you are underwater, either because you failed a Swim check or because you are swimming underwater intentionally, you must hold your breath. You can hold your breath for a number of rounds equal to twice your Constitution score, but only if you do nothing other than take move actions or free actions. If you take a standard action or a full-round action (such as making an attack), the remainder of the duration for which you can hold your breath is reduced by 1 round. (Effectively, a character in combat can hold his breath only half as long as normal.) After that period of time, you must make a DC 10 Constitution check every round to continue holding your breath. Each round, the DC for that check increases by 1. If you fail the Constitution check, you begin to drown. The DC for the Swim check depends on the water, as given on the table below.

Water	Swim DC
Calm water	10
Rough water	15
Stormy water	20*

* You can't take 10 on a Swim check in stormy water, even if you aren't otherwise being threatened or distracted.

Each hour that you swim, you must make a DC 20 Swim check or take 1d6 points of nonlethal damage from fatigue.

Action: A successful Swim check allows you to swim a quarter of your speed as a move action or half your speed as a full-round action.

Special: A creature with a swim speed can move through water at its indicated speed without making Swim checks. It gains a +8 racial bonus on any Swim check to perform a special action or avoid a hazard. The creature can always choose to take 10 on a Swim check, even if distracted or endangered when swimming. Such a creature can use the run action while swimming, provided that it swims in a straight line.

If you have the Athletic feat, you get a bonus on Swim checks (see Chapter 5).

USE MAGIC DEVICE (Cha; Trained Only)

You are skilled at activating magic items, even if you are not otherwise trained in their use.

Check: You can use this skill to read a spell or to activate a magic item. Use Magic Device lets you use a magic item as if you had the spell ability or class features of another class, as if you were a different race, or as if you were of a different alignment.

You make a Use Magic Device check each time you activate a device such as a wand. If you are using the check to emulate an alignment or some other quality in an ongoing manner, you need to make the relevant Use Magic Device check once per hour.

You must consciously choose which requirement to emulate. That is, you must know what you are trying to emulate when you make a Use Magic Device check for that purpose. The DCs for various tasks involving Use Magic Device checks are summarized on the table below.

Task	Use Magic Device DC
Activate blindly	25
Decipher a written spell	25 + spell level
Use a scroll	20 + caster level
Use a wand	20
Emulate a class feature	20
Emulate an ability score	See text
Emulate a race	25
Emulate an alignment	30

Activate Blindly: Some magic items are activated by special words, thoughts, or actions. You can activate such an item as if you were using the activation word, thought, or action, even when you're not and even if you don't know it. You do have to perform some equivalent activity in order to make the check. That is, you must speak, wave the item around, or otherwise attempt to get it to activate. You get a +2 bonus on your Use Magic Device check if you've activated the item in question at least once before. If you fail by 9 or less, you can't activate the device. If you fail by 10 or more, you suffer a mishap. A mishap means that magical energy gets released but doesn't do what you wanted it to do. The default mishaps are that the item affects the wrong target or that uncontrolled magical energy is released, dealing 2d6 points of damage to you. This mishap is in addition to the chance for a mishap that you normally risk when you cast a spell from a scroll that you could not otherwise cast yourself.

Decipher a Written Spell: This usage works just like deciphering a written spell with the Spellcraft skill, except that the DC is 5 points higher. Deciphering a written spell requires 1 minute of concentration.

Emulate an Ability Score: To cast a spell from a scroll, you need a high score in the appropriate ability (Intelligence for wizard spells, Wisdom for divine spells, or Charisma for sorcerer or bard spells). Your effective ability score (appropriate to the class you're emulating when you try to cast the spell from the scroll) is your Use Magic Device check result minus 15. If you already have a high enough score in the appropriate ability, you don't need to make this check.

Emulate an Alignment: Some magic items have positive or negative effects based on the user's alignment. Use Magic Device lets you use these items as if you were of an alignment of your choice. You can emulate only one alignment at a time.

Emulate a Class Feature: Sometimes you need to use a class feature to activate a magic item. In this case, your effective level in the emulated class equals your Use Magic Device check result minus 20. This skill does not let you actually use the class feature of another class. It just lets you activate items as if you had that class feature. If the class whose feature you are emulating has an alignment requirement, you must meet it, either honestly or by emulating an appropriate alignment with a separate Use Magic Device check (see above).

Emulate a Race: Some magic items work only for members of certain races, or work better for members of those races. You can use such an item as if you were a member of a race of your choice. You can emulate only one race at a time.

Use a Scroll: Normally, to cast a spell from a scroll, you must have the scroll's spell on your class spell list. Use Magic Device allows you to use a scroll as if you had a particular spell on your class spell list. The DC is equal to 20 + the caster level of the spell you are trying to cast from the scroll. In addition, casting a spell from a scroll requires a minimum score (10 + spell level) in the appropriate ability. If you don't have a sufficient score in that ability, you must emulate the ability score with a separate Use Magic Device check.

This use of the skill also applies to other spell completion magic items.

Use a Wand, Staff, or Other Spell Trigger Item: Normally, to use a wand, you must have the wand's spell on your class spell list. This use of the skill allows you to use a wand as if you had a particular spell on your class spell list. Failing the roll does not expend a charge.

Action: None. The Use Magic Device check is made as part of the action (if any) required to activate the magic item.

Try Again: Yes, but if you ever roll a natural 1 while attempting to activate an item and you fail, then you can't try to activate that item again for 24 hours.

Special: You cannot take 10 with this skill. You can't aid another on Use Magic Device checks. Only the user of the item may attempt such a check.

If you have the Magical Aptitude feat, you gain a bonus on Use Magic Device checks (see Chapter 5).

5 FEATS

Harsk glanced upward as he felt something wet spatter across the top of his head. He hadn't noticed the enormous cobra before—his attention had been focused on the fiend that stood before him, and the stealthy snake had slithered out of the shadows with barely a whisper.

"I'll get to your pets later," he muttered, as he calmly turned back to the rakshasa priest. At point-blank range like this, he could hardly miss. He raised his crossbow, the blessed bolt loaded and ready, and took careful aim.

"Now open wide, kitty. Uncle Harsk's got a tasty treat for you!"

ome abilities are not tied to your race, class, or skill—things like particularly quick reflexes that allow you to react to danger more swiftly, the ability to craft magic items, the training to deliver powerful strikes with melee weapons, or the knack for deflecting arrows fired at you. These abilities are represented as feats. While some feats are more useful to certain types of characters than others, and many of them have special prerequisites that must be met before they are selected, as a general rule feats represent abilities outside of the normal scope of your character's race and class. Many of them alter or enhance class abilities or soften class restrictions, while others might apply bonuses to your statistics or grant you the ability to take actions otherwise prohibited to you. By selecting feats, you can customize and adapt your character to be uniquely yours.

PREREQUISITES

Some feats have prerequisites. Your character must have the indicated ability score, class feature, feat, skill, base attack bonus, or other quality designated in order to select or use that feat. A character can gain a feat at the same level at which he gains the prerequisite.

A character can't use a feat if he loses a prerequisite, but he does not lose the feat itself. If, at a later time, he regains the lost prerequisite, he immediately regains full use of the feat that prerequisite enables.

TYPES OF FEATS

Some feats are general, meaning that no special rules govern them as a group. Others are item creation feats, which allow characters to create magic items of all sorts. A metamagic feat lets a spellcaster prepare and cast a spell with greater effect, albeit as if the spell were of a higher spell level than it actually is.

Combat Feats

Any feat designated as a combat feat can be selected as a fighter's bonus feat. This designation does not restrict characters of other classes from selecting these feats, assuming that they meet the prerequisites.

Critical Feats

Critical feats modify the effects of a critical hit by inflicting an additional condition on the victim of the critical hit. Characters without the Critical Mastery feat can only apply the effects of one critical feat to an individual critical hit. Characters with multiple critical feats can decide which feat to apply after the critical hit has been confirmed.

Item Creation Feats

An item creation feat lets a character create a magic item of a certain type. Regardless of the type of item each involves, the various item creation feats all have certain features in common.

Raw Materials Cost: The cost of creating a magic item equals half the base price of the item.

Using an item creation feat also requires access to a laboratory or magical workshop, special tools, and so on. A character generally has access to what he needs unless unusual circumstances apply.

Time: The time to create a magic item depends on the feat and the cost of the item.

Item Cost: Brew Potion, Craft Staff, Craft Wand, and Scribe Scroll create items that directly reproduce spell effects, and the power of these items depends on their caster level—that is, a spell from such an item has the power it would have if cast by a spellcaster of that level. The price of these items (and thus the cost of the raw materials) also depends on the caster level. The caster level must be low enough that the spellcaster creating the item can cast the spell at that level. To find the final price in each case, multiply the caster level by the spell level, then multiply the result by a constant, as shown below:

Scrolls: **Base price = spell level × caster level × 25 gp.**
Potions: **Base price = spell level × caster level × 50 gp.**
Wands: **Base price = spell level × caster level × 750 gp.**

Staves: The price for staves is calculated using more complex formulas (see Chapter 15).

A 0-level spell is considered to have a spell level of 1/2 for the purpose of this calculation.

Extra Costs: Any potion, scroll, or wand that stores a spell with a costly material component also carries a commensurate cost. For potions and scrolls, the creator must expend the material component cost when creating the item. For a wand, the creator must expend 50 units of the material component. Some magic items similarly incur extra costs in material components, as noted in their descriptions.

Skill Check: Successfully creating a magic item requires a Spellcraft check with a DC equal to 5 + the item's caster level. Alternatively, you can use an associated Craft or Profession skill to attempt this check instead, depending upon the item being crafted. See pages 550–553 in Chapter 15 for more details on which Craft and Profession checks may be substituted in this manner. The DC of this check can increase if the crafter is rushed or does not meet all of the prerequisites. A failed check ruins the materials used, while a check that fails by 5 or more results in a cursed item. See Chapter 15 for more details.

Metamagic Feats

As a spellcaster's knowledge of magic grows, he can learn to cast spells in ways slightly different from the norm. Preparing and casting a spell in such a way is harder than normal but, thanks to metamagic feats, is at least possible. Spells modified by a metamagic feat use a spell slot higher than normal. This does not change the level of the spell, so the DC for saving throws against it does not go up. Metamagic feats do not affect spell-like abilities.

Wizards and Divine Spellcasters: Wizards and divine spellcasters must prepare their spells in advance. During preparation, the character chooses which spells to prepare with metamagic feats (and thus which ones take up higher-level spell slots than normal).

Sorcerers and Bards: Sorcerers and bards choose spells as they cast them. They can choose when they cast their spells whether to apply their metamagic feats to improve them. As with other spellcasters, the improved spell uses up a higher-level spell slot. Because the sorcerer or bard has not prepared the spell in a metamagic form in advance, he must apply the metamagic feat on the spot. Therefore, such a character must also take more time to cast a metamagic spell (one enhanced by a metamagic feat) than he does to cast a regular spell. If the spell's normal casting time is a standard action, casting a metamagic version is a full-round action for a sorcerer or bard. (This isn't the same as a 1-round casting time.) The only exception is for spells modified by the Quicken Spell metamagic feat, which can be cast as normal using the feat.

For a spell with a longer casting time, it takes an extra full-round action to cast the spell.

Spontaneous Casting and Metamagic Feats: A cleric spontaneously casting a cure or inflict spell, or a druid spontaneously casting a *summon nature's ally* spell, can cast a metamagic version of it instead. Extra time is also required in this case. Casting a standard action metamagic spell spontaneously is a full-round action, and a spell with a longer casting time takes an extra full-round action to cast. The only exception is for spells modified by the Quicken Spell feat, which can be cast as a swift action.

Effects of Metamagic Feats on a Spell: In all ways, a metamagic spell operates at its original spell level, even though it is prepared and cast using a higher-level spell slot. Saving throw modifications are not changed unless stated otherwise in the feat description.

The modifications made by these feats only apply to spells cast directly by the feat user. A spellcaster can't use a metamagic feat to alter a spell being cast from a wand, scroll, or other device.

Metamagic feats that eliminate components of a spell don't eliminate the attack of opportunity provoked by casting a spell while threatened. Casting a spell modified by Quicken Spell does not provoke an attack of opportunity.

Metamagic feats cannot be used with all spells. See the specific feat descriptions for the spells that a particular feat can't modify.

Multiple Metamagic Feats on a Spell: A spellcaster can apply multiple metamagic feats to a single spell. Changes to its level are cumulative. You can't apply the same metamagic feat more than once to a single spell.

Magic Items and Metamagic Spells: With the right item creation feat, you can store a metamagic version of a spell in a scroll, potion, or wand. Level limits for potions and wands apply to the spell's higher spell level (after the application of the metamagic feat). A character doesn't need the metamagic feat to activate an item storing a metamagic version of a spell.

Counterspelling Metamagic Spells: Whether or not a spell has been enhanced by a metamagic feat does not affect its vulnerability to counterspelling or its ability to counterspell another spell (see Chapter 9).

FEAT DESCRIPTIONS

Feats are summarized on Table 5–1 on the pages following. Note that the prerequisites and benefits of the feats on this table are abbreviated for ease of reference. See the feats description for full details.

The following format is used for all feat descriptions.

Feat Name: The feat's name also indicates what subcategory, if any, the feat belongs to, and is followed by a basic description of what the feat does.

Prerequisite: A minimum ability score, another feat or feats, a minimum base attack bonus, a minimum number of ranks in one or more skills, or anything else required in order to take the feat. This entry is absent if a feat has no prerequisite. A feat may have more than one prerequisite.

Benefit: What the feat enables the character ("you" in the feat description) to do. If a character has the same feat more than once, its benefits do not stack unless indicated otherwise in the description.

Normal: What a character who does not have this feat is limited to or restricted from doing. If not having the feat causes no particular drawback, this entry is absent.

Special: Additional unusual facts about the feat.

Acrobatic

You are skilled at leaping, jumping, and flying.

Benefit: You get a +2 bonus on all Acrobatics and Fly skill checks. If you have 10 or more ranks in one of these skills, the bonus increases to +4 for that skill.

Acrobatic Steps

You can easily move over and through obstacles.

Prerequisites: Dex 15, Nimble Moves.

Benefit: Whenever you move, you may move through up to 15 feet of difficult terrain each round as if it were normal terrain. The effects of this feat stack with those provided by Nimble Moves (allowing you to move normally through a total of 20 feet of difficult terrain each round).

TABLE 5-1: FEATS

Feats	Prerequisites	Benefits
Acrobatic	—	+2 bonus on Acrobatics and Fly checks
Agile Maneuvers*	—	Use your Dex bonus when calculating your CMB
Alertness	—	+2 bonus on Perception and Sense Motive checks
Alignment Channel	Channel energy class feature	Channel energy can heal or harm outsiders
Animal Affinity	—	+2 bonus on Handle Animal and Ride checks
Arcane Armor Training*	Armor Proficiency, Light, caster level 3rd	Reduce your arcane spell failure chance by 10%
Arcane Armor Mastery*	Arcane Armor Training, Armor Proficiency, Medium, caster level 7th	Reduce your arcane spell failure chance by 20%
Arcane Strike*	Ability to cast arcane spells	+1 damage and weapons are considered magic
Armor Proficiency, Light*	—	No penalties on attack rolls while wearing light armor
Armor Proficiency, Medium*	Armor Proficiency, Light	No penalties on attack rolls while wearing medium armor
Armor Proficiency, Heavy*	Armor Proficiency, Medium	No penalties on attack rolls while wearing heavy armor
Athletic	—	+2 bonus on Climb and Swim checks
Augment Summoning	Spell Focus (conjuration)	Summoned creatures gain +4 Str and Con
Blind-Fight*	—	Reroll miss chances for concealment
Catch Off-Guard*	—	No penalties for improvised melee weapons
Channel Smite*	Channel energy class feature	Channel energy through your attack
Combat Casting	—	+4 bonus on concentration checks for defensive casting
Combat Expertise*	Int 13	Trade attack bonus for AC bonus
Improved Disarm*	Combat Expertise	+2 bonus on disarm attempts, no attack of opportunity
Greater Disarm*	Improved Disarm, base attack bonus +6	Disarmed weapons are knocked away from your enemy
Improved Feint*	Combat Expertise	Feint as a move action
Greater Feint*	Improved Feint, base attack bonus +6	Enemies you feint lose their Dex bonus for 1 round
Improved Trip*	Combat Expertise	+2 bonus on trip attempts, no attack of opportunity
Greater Trip*	Improved Trip, base attack bonus +6	Enemies you trip provoke attacks of opportunity
Whirlwind Attack*	Dex 13, Combat Expertise, Spring Attack, base attack bonus +4	Make one melee attack against all foes within reach
Combat Reflexes*	—	Make additional attacks of opportunity
Stand Still*	Combat Reflexes	Stop enemies from moving past you
Command Undead	Channel negative energy class feature	Channel energy can be used to control undead
Critical Focus*	Base attack bonus +9	+4 bonus on attack rolls made to confirm critical hits
Bleeding Critical*	Critical Focus, base attack bonus +11	Whenever you score a critical hit, the target takes 2d6 bleed
Blinding Critical*	Critical Focus, base attack bonus +15	Whenever you score a critical hit, the target is blinded
Critical Mastery*	Any two critical feats, 14th-level fighter	Apply two effects to your critical hits
Deafening Critical*	Critical Focus, base attack bonus +13	Whenever you score a critical hit, the target is deafened
Sickening Critical*	Critical Focus, base attack bonus +11	Whenever you score a critical hit, the target is sickened
Staggering Critical*	Critical Focus, base attack bonus +13	Whenever you score a critical hit, the target is staggered
Stunning Critical*	Staggering Critical, base attack bonus +17	Whenever you score a critical hit, the target is stunned
Tiring Critical*	Critical Focus, base attack bonus +13	Whenever you score a critical hit, the target is fatigued
Exhausting Critical*	Tiring Critical, base attack bonus +15	Whenever you score a critical hit, the target is exhausted
Deadly Aim*	Dex 13, base attack bonus +1	Trade ranged attack bonus for damage
Deceitful	—	+2 bonus on Bluff and Disguise checks
Defensive Combat Training*	—	Use your total Hit Dice as your base attack bonus for CMD
Deft Hands	—	+2 bonus on Disable Device and Sleight of Hand checks
Disruptive*	6th-level fighter	Increases the DC to cast spells adjacent to you
Spellbreaker*	Disruptive, 10th-level fighter	Enemies provoke attacks if their spells fail
Dodge*	Dex 13	+1 dodge bonus to AC
Mobility*	Dodge	+4 AC against attacks of opportunity from movement
Spring Attack*	Mobility, base attack bonus +4	Move before and after melee attack
Wind Stance*	Dex 15, Dodge, base attack bonus +6	Gain 20% concealment if you move
Lightning Stance*	Dex 17, Wind Stance, base attack bonus +11	Gain 50% concealment if you move

Feat	Prerequisites	Benefits
Elemental Channel	Channel energy class feature	Channel energy can harm or heal elementals
Endurance	—	+4 bonus on checks to avoid nonlethal damage
Diehard	Endurance	Automatically stabilize and remain conscious below 0 hp
Eschew Materials	—	Cast spells without material components
Exotic Weapon Proficiency*	Base attack bonus +1	No penalty on attacks made with one exotic weapon
Extra Channel	Channel energy class feature	Channel energy two additional times per day
Extra Ki	Ki pool class feature	Increase your ki pool by 2 points
Extra Lay On Hands	Lay on hands class feature	Use lay on hands two additional times per day
Extra Mercy	Mercy class feature	Your lay on hands benefits from one additional mercy
Extra Performance	Bardic performance class feature	Use bardic performance for 6 additional rounds per day
Extra Rage	Rage class feature	Use rage for 6 additional rounds per day
Fleet	—	Your base speed increases by 5 feet
Great Fortitude	—	+2 on Fortitude saves
Improved Great Fortitude	Great Fortitude	Once per day, you may reroll a Fortitude save
Improved Channel	Channel energy class feature	+2 bonus on channel energy DC
Improved Counterspell	—	Counterspell with spell of the same school
Improved Critical*	Proficiency with weapon, base attack bonus +8	Double the threat range of one weapon
Improved Familiar	Ability to acquire a familiar, see feat	Gain a more powerful familiar
Improved Initiative*	—	+4 bonus on initiative checks
Improved Unarmed Strike*	—	Always considered armed
Deflect Arrows*	Dex 13, Improved Unarmed Strike	Avoid one ranged attack per round
Snatch Arrows*	Dex 15, Deflect Arrows	Catch one ranged attack per round
Improved Grapple*	Dex 13, Improved Unarmed Strike	+2 bonus on grapple attempts, no attack of opportunity
Greater Grapple*	Improved Grapple, base attack bonus +6	Maintain your grapple as a move action
Scorpion Style*	Improved Unarmed Strike	Reduce target's speed to 5 ft.
Gorgon's Fist*	Scorpion Style, base attack bonus +6	Stagger a foe whose speed is reduced
Medusa's Wrath*	Gorgon's Fist, base attack bonus +11	Make 2 extra attacks against a hindered foe
Stunning Fist*	Dex 13, Wis 13, Improved Unarmed Strike, base attack bonus +8	Stun opponent with an unarmed strike
Improvised Weapon Mastery*	Catch Off-Guard or Throw Anything, base attack bonus +8	Make an improvised weapon deadly
Intimidating Prowess*	—	Add Str to Intimidate in addition to Cha
Iron Will	—	+2 bonus on Will saves
Improved Iron Will	Iron Will	Once per day, you may reroll a Will save
Leadership	Character level 7th	Gain a cohort and followers
Lightning Reflexes	—	+2 bonus on Reflex saves
Improved Lightning Reflexes	Lightning Reflexes	Once per day, you may reroll a Reflex save
Lunge*	Base attack bonus +6	Take a −2 penalty to your AC to attack with reach
Magical Aptitude	—	+2 bonus on Spellcraft and Use Magic Device checks
Martial Weapon Proficiency*	—	No penalty on attacks made with one martial weapon
Master Craftsman	5 ranks in any Craft or Profession skill	You can craft magic items without being a spellcaster
Mounted Combat*	Ride 1 rank	Avoid attacks on mount with Ride check
Mounted Archery*	Mounted Combat	Halve the penalty for ranged attacks while mounted
Ride-By Attack*	Mounted Combat	Move before and after a charge attack while mounted
Spirited Charge*	Ride-By Attack	Double damage on a mounted charge
Trample*	Mounted Combat	Overrun targets while mounted
Unseat*	Improved Bull Rush, Mounted Combat	Knock opponents from their mounts
Natural Spell	Wis 13, wild shape class feature	Cast spells while using wild shape
Nimble Moves	Dex 13	Ignore 5 feet of difficult terrain when you move
Acrobatic Steps	Dex 15, Nimble Moves	Ignore 20 feet of difficult terrain when you move
Persuasive	—	+2 bonus on Diplomacy and Intimidate checks

Feat	Prerequisites	Benefits
Point-Blank Shot*	—	+1 attack and damage on targets within 30 feet
Far Shot*	Point-Blank Shot	Decrease ranged penalties by half
Precise Shot*	Point-Blank Shot	No penalty for shooting into melee
Improved Precise Shot*	Dex 19, Precise Shot, base attack bonus +11	No cover or concealment chance on ranged attacks
Pinpoint Targeting*	Improved Precise Shot, base attack bonus +16	No armor or shield bonus on one ranged attack
Shot on the Run*	Dex 13, Mobility, Point-Blank Shot, base attack bonus +4	Make ranged attack at any point during movement
Rapid Shot*	Dex 13, Point-Blank Shot	Make one extra ranged attack
Manyshot*	Dex 17, Rapid Shot, base attack bonus +6	Shoot two arrows simultaneously
Power Attack*	Str 13, base attack bonus +1	Trade melee attack bonus for damage
Cleave*	Power Attack	Make an additional attack if the first one hits
Great Cleave*	Cleave, base attack bonus +4	Make an additional attack after each attack hits
Improved Bull Rush*	Power Attack	+2 bonus on bull rush attempts, no attack of opportunity
Greater Bull Rush*	Improved Bull Rush, base attack bonus +6	Enemies you bull rush provoke attacks of opportunity
Improved Overrun*	Power Attack	+2 bonus on overrun attempts, no attack of opportunity
Greater Overrun*	Improved Overrun, base attack bonus +6	Enemies you overrun provoke attacks of opportunity
Improved Sunder*	Power Attack	+2 bonus on sunder attempts, no attack of opportunity
Greater Sunder*	Improved Sunder, base attack bonus +6	Damage from sunder attempts transfers to your enemy
Quick Draw*	Base attack bonus +1	Draw weapon as a free action
Rapid Reload*	Weapon proficiency (crossbow)	Reload crossbow quickly
Run	—	Run at 5 times your normal speed
Selective Channeling	Cha 13, channel energy class feature	Choose whom to affect with channel energy
Self-Sufficient	—	+2 bonus on Heal and Survival checks
Shield Proficiency*	—	No penalties on attack rolls when using a shield
Improved Shield Bash*	Shield Proficiency	Keep your shield bonus when shield bashing
Shield Slam*	Improved Shield Bash, Two-Weapon Fighting, base attack bonus +6	Free bull rush with a bash attack
Shield Master*	Shield Slam, base attack bonus +11	No two-weapon penalties when attacking with a shield
Shield Focus*	Shield Proficiency, base attack bonus +1	Gain a +1 bonus to your AC when using a shield
Greater Shield Focus*	Shield Focus, 8th-level fighter	Gain a +1 bonus to your AC when using a shield
Tower Shield Proficiency*	Shield Proficiency	No penalties on attack rolls when using a tower shield
Simple Weapon Proficiency*	—	No penalty on attacks made with simple weapons
Skill Focus	—	+3 bonus on one skill (+6 at 10 ranks)
Spell Focus	—	+1 bonus on save DCs for one school
Greater Spell Focus	Spell Focus	+1 bonus on save DCs for one school
Spell Mastery	1st-level Wizard	Prepare some spells without a spellbook
Spell Penetration	—	+2 bonus on level checks to beat spell resistance
Greater Spell Penetration	Spell Penetration	+2 bonus on level checks to beat spell resistance
Stealthy	—	+2 bonus on Escape Artist and Stealth checks
Step Up*	Base attack bonus +1	Take a 5-foot step as an immediate action
Strike Back*	Base attack bonus +11	Attack foes that strike you while using reach
Throw Anything*	—	No penalties for improvised ranged weapons
Toughness	—	+3 hit points, +1 per Hit Die beyond 3
Turn Undead	Channel positive energy class feature	Channel energy can be used to make undead flee
Two-Weapon Fighting*	Dex 15	Reduce two-weapon fighting penalties
Double Slice*	Two-Weapon Fighting	Add your Str bonus to off-hand damage rolls
Two-Weapon Rend*	Double Slice, Improved Two-Weapon Fighting, base attack bonus +11	Rend a foe hit by both your weapons
Improved Two-Weapon Fighting*	Dex 17, Two-Weapon Fighting, base attack bonus +6	Gain additional off-hand attack
Greater Two-Weapon Fighting	Dex 19, Improved Two-Weapon Fighting, base attack bonus +11	Gain a third off-hand attack
Two-Weapon Defense*	Two-Weapon Fighting	Gain +1 shield bonus when fighting with two weapons

Feat	Prerequisites	Benefits
Vital Strike*	Base attack bonus +6	Deal twice the normal damage on a single attack
Improved Vital Strike*	Vital Strike, base attack bonus +11	Deal three times the normal damage on a single attack
Greater Vital Strike*	Improved Vital Strike, base attack bonus +16	Deal four times the normal damage on a single attack
Weapon Finesse*	—	Use Dex instead of Str on attack rolls with light weapons
Weapon Focus*	Proficiency with weapon, base attack bonus +1	+1 bonus on attack rolls with one weapon
Dazzling Display*	Weapon Focus	Intimidate all foes within 30 feet
Shatter Defenses*	Dazzling Display, base attack bonus +6	Hindered foes are flat-footed
Deadly Stroke*	Greater Weapon Focus, Shatter Defenses, base attack bonus +11	Deal double damage plus 1 Con bleed
Greater Weapon Focus*	Weapon Focus, 8th-level fighter	+1 bonus on attack rolls with one weapon
Penetrating Strike*	Weapon Focus, 12th-level fighter	Your attacks ignore 5 points of damage reduction
Greater Penetrating Strike*	Penetrating Strike, 16th-level fighter	Your attacks ignore 10 points of damage reduction
Weapon Specialization*	Weapon Focus, 4th-level fighter	+2 bonus on damage rolls with one weapon
Greater Weapon Specialization*	Weapon Specialization, 12th-level fighter	+2 bonus on damage rolls with one weapon

Item Creation Feats	Prerequisites	Benefits
Brew Potion	Caster level 3rd	Create magic potions
Craft Magic Arms and Armor	Caster level 5th	Create magic armors, shields, and weapons
Craft Rod	Caster level 9th	Create magic rods
Craft Staff	Caster level 11th	Create magic staves
Craft Wand	Caster level 5th	Create magic wands
Craft Wondrous Item	Caster level 3rd	Create magic wondrous items
Forge Ring	Caster level 7th	Create magic rings
Scribe Scroll	Caster level 1st	Create magic scrolls

Metamagic Feats	Prerequisites	Benefits
Empower Spell	—	Increase spell variables by 50%
Enlarge Spell	—	Double spell range
Extend Spell	—	Double spell duration
Heighten Spell	—	Treat spell as a higher level
Maximize Spell	—	Maximize spell variables
Quicken Spell	—	Cast spell as a swift action
Silent Spell	—	Cast spell without verbal components
Still Spell	—	Cast spell without somatic components
Widen Spell	—	Double spell area

* This is a combat feat and can be selected as a fighter bonus feat

Agile Maneuvers (Combat)

You've learned to use your quickness in place of brute force when performing combat maneuvers.

Benefit: You add your Dexterity bonus to your base attack bonus and size bonus when determining your Combat Maneuver Bonus (see Chapter 8) instead of your Strength bonus.

Normal: You add your Strength bonus to your base attack bonus and size bonus when determining your Combat Maneuver Bonus.

Alertness

You often notice things that others might miss.

Benefit: You get a +2 bonus on Perception and Sense Motive skill checks. If you have 10 or more ranks in one of these skills, the bonus increases to +4 for that skill.

Alignment Channel

Choose chaos, evil, good, or law. You can channel divine energy to affect outsiders that possess this subtype.

Prerequisites: Ability to channel energy.

Benefit: Instead of its normal effect, you can choose to have your ability to channel energy heal or harm outsiders of the chosen alignment subtype. You must make this choice each time you channel energy. If you choose to heal or harm creatures of the chosen alignment subtype,

your channel energy has no effect on other creatures. The amount of damage healed or dealt and the DC to halve the damage is otherwise unchanged.

Special: You can gain this feat multiple times. Its effects do not stack. Each time you take this feat, it applies to a new alignment subtype. Whenever you channel energy, you must choose which type to effect.

Animal Affinity

You are skilled at working with animals and mounts.

Benefit: You get a +2 bonus on all Handle Animal and Ride skill checks. If you have 10 or more ranks in one of these skills, the bonus increases to +4 for that skill.

Arcane Armor Mastery (Combat)

You have mastered the ability to cast spells while wearing armor.

Prerequisites: Arcane Armor Training, Medium Armor Proficiency, caster level 7th.

Benefit: As a swift action, reduce the arcane spell failure chance due to the armor you are wearing by 20% for any spells you cast this round. This bonus replaces, and does not stack with, the bonus granted by Arcane Armor Training.

Arcane Armor Training (Combat)

You have learned how to cast spells while wearing armor.

Prerequisites: Light Armor Proficiency, caster level 3rd.

Benefit: As a swift action, reduce the arcane spell failure chance due to the armor you are wearing by 10% for any spells you cast this round.

Arcane Strike (Combat)

You draw upon your arcane power to enhance your weapons with magical energy.

Prerequisite: Ability to cast arcane spells.

Benefit: As a swift action, you can imbue your weapons with a fraction of your power. For 1 round, your weapons deal +1 damage and are treated as magic for the purpose of overcoming damage reduction. For every five caster levels you possess, this bonus increases by +1, to a maximum of +5 at 20th level.

Armor Proficiency, Heavy (Combat)

You are skilled at wearing heavy armor.

Prerequisites: Light Armor Proficiency, Medium Armor Proficiency.

Benefit: See Armor Proficiency, Light.

Normal: See Armor Proficiency, Light.

Special: Fighters and paladins automatically have Heavy Armor Proficiency as a bonus feat. They need not select it.

Armor Proficiency, Light (Combat)

You are skilled at wearing light armor.

Benefit: When you wear a type of armor with which you are proficient, the armor check penalty for that armor applies only to Dexterity- and Strength-based skill checks.

Normal: A character who is wearing armor with which he is not proficient applies its armor check penalty to attack rolls and to all skill checks that involve moving.

Special: All characters except monks, sorcerers, and wizards automatically have Light Armor Proficiency as a bonus feat. They need not select it.

Armor Proficiency, Medium (Combat)

You are skilled at wearing medium armor.

Prerequisite: Light Armor Proficiency.

Benefit: See Armor Proficiency, Light.

Normal: See Armor Proficiency, Light.

Special: Barbarians, clerics, druids, fighters, paladins, and rangers automatically have Medium Armor Proficiency as a bonus feat. They need not select it.

Athletic

You possess inherent physical prowess.

Benefit: You get a +2 bonus on Climb and Swim skill checks. If you have 10 or more ranks in one of these skills, the bonus increases to +4 for that skill.

Augment Summoning

Your summoned creatures are more powerful and robust.

Prerequisite: Spell Focus (conjuration).

Benefit: Each creature you conjure with any *summon* spell gains a +4 enhancement bonus to Strength and Constitution for the duration of the spell that summoned it.

Bleeding Critical (Combat, Critical)

Your critical hits cause opponents to bleed profusely.

Prerequisites: Critical Focus, base attack bonus +11.

Benefit: Whenever you score a critical hit with a slashing or piercing weapon, your opponent takes 2d6 points of bleed damage (see Appendix 2) each round on his turn, in addition to the damage dealt by the critical hit. Bleed damage can be stopped by a DC 15 Heal skill check or through any magical healing. The effects of this feat stack.

Special: You can only apply the effects of one critical feat to a given critical hit unless you possess Critical Mastery.

Blind-Fight (Combat)

You are skilled at attacking opponents that you cannot clearly perceive.

Benefit: In melee, every time you miss because of concealment (see Chapter 8), you can reroll your miss chance percentile roll one time to see if you actually hit.

An invisible attacker gets no advantages related to hitting you in melee. That is, you don't lose your Dexterity bonus to Armor Class, and the attacker doesn't get the usual +2 bonus for being invisible. The invisible attacker's bonuses do still apply for ranged attacks, however.

You do not need to make Acrobatics skill checks to move at full speed while blinded.

Normal: Regular attack roll modifiers for invisible attackers trying to hit you apply, and you lose your Dexterity bonus to AC. The speed reduction for darkness and poor visibility also applies.

Special: The Blind-Fight feat is of no use against a character who is the subject of a *blink* spell.

Blinding Critical (Combat, Critical)

Your critical hits blind your opponents.

Prerequisites: Critical Focus, base attack bonus +15.

Benefit: Whenever you score a critical hit, your opponent is permanently blinded. A successful Fortitude save reduces this to dazzled for 1d4 rounds. The DC of this Fortitude save is equal to 10 + your base attack bonus. This feat has no effect on creatures that do not rely on eyes for sight or creatures with more than two eyes (although multiple critical hits might cause blindness, at the GM's discretion). Blindness can be cured by *heal, regeneration, remove blindness,* or similar abilities.

Special: You can only apply the effects of one critical feat to a given critical hit unless you possess Critical Mastery.

Brew Potion (Item Creation)

You can create magic potions.

Prerequisite: Caster level 3rd.

Benefit: You can create a potion of any 3rd-level or lower spell that you know and that targets one or more creatures or objects. Brewing a potion takes 2 hours if its base price is 250 gp or less, otherwise brewing a potion takes 1 day for each 1,000 gp in its base price. When you create a potion, you set the caster level, which must be sufficient to cast the spell in question and no higher than your own level. To brew a potion, you must use up raw materials costing one half this base price. See the magic item creation rules in Chapter 15 for more information.

When you create a potion, you make any choices that you would normally make when casting the spell. Whoever drinks the potion is the target of the spell.

Catch Off-Guard (Combat)

Foes are surprised by your skilled use of unorthodox and improvised weapons.

Benefit: You do not suffer any penalties for using an improvised melee weapon. Unarmed opponents are flat-footed against any attacks you make with an improvised melee weapon.

Normal: You take a –4 penalty on attack rolls made with an improvised weapon.

Channel Smite (Combat)

You can channel your divine energy through a melee weapon you wield.

Prerequisite: Channel energy class feature.

Benefit: Before you make a melee attack roll, you can choose to spend one use of your channel energy ability as a swift action. If you channel positive energy and you hit an undead creature, that creature takes an amount of additional damage equal to the damage dealt by your channel positive energy ability. If you channel negative energy and you hit a living creature, that creature takes an amount of additional damage equal to the damage dealt by your channel negative energy ability. Your target can make a Will save, as normal, to halve this additional damage. If your attack misses, the channel energy ability is still expended with no effect.

Cleave (Combat)

You can strike two adjacent foes with a single swing.

Prerequisites: Str 13, Power Attack, base attack bonus +1.

Benefit: As a standard action, you can make a single attack at your full base attack bonus against a foe within reach. If you hit, you deal damage normally and can make an additional attack (using your full base attack bonus) against a foe that is adjacent to the first and also within reach. You can only make one additional attack per round with this feat. When you use this feat, you take a –2 penalty to your Armor Class until your next turn.

Combat Casting

You are adept at spellcasting when threatened or distracted.

Benefit: You get a +4 bonus on concentration checks made to cast a spell or use a spell-like ability when casting on the defensive or while grappled.

Combat Expertise (Combat)

You can increase your defense at the expense of your accuracy.

Prerequisite: Int 13.

Benefit: You can choose to take a –1 penalty on melee attack rolls and combat maneuver checks to gain a +1 dodge bonus to your Armor Class. When your base attack bonus reaches +4, and every +4 thereafter, the penalty increases by –1 and the dodge bonus increases by +1. You can only choose to use this feat when you declare that you are making an attack or a full-attack action with a melee weapon. The effects of this feat last until your next turn.

Combat Reflexes (Combat)

You can make additional attacks of opportunity.

Benefit: You may make a number of additional attacks of opportunity per round equal to your Dexterity bonus. With this feat, you may also make attacks of opportunity while flat-footed.

Normal: A character without this feat can make only one attack of opportunity per round and can't make attacks of opportunity while flat-footed.

Special: The Combat Reflexes feat does not allow a rogue to use her opportunist ability more than once per round.

Command Undead

Using foul powers of necromancy, you can command undead creatures, making them into your servants.

Prerequisites: Channel negative energy class feature.

Benefit: As a standard action, you can use one of your uses of channel negative energy to enslave undead within 30 feet. Undead receive a Will save to negate the effect. The DC for this Will save is equal to 10 + 1/2 your cleric level + your Charisma modifier. Undead that fail their saves fall under your control, obeying your commands to the best of their ability, as if under the effects of *control undead*. Intelligent undead receive a new saving throw each day to resist your command. You can control any number of undead, so long as their total Hit Dice do not exceed your cleric level. If you use channel energy in this way, it has no other effect (it does not heal or harm nearby creatures). If an undead creature is under the control of another creature, you must make an opposed Charisma check whenever your orders conflict.

Craft Magic Arms and Armor (Item Creation)

You can create magic armor, shields, and weapons.

Prerequisite: Caster level 5th.

Benefit: You can create magic weapons, armor, or shields. Enhancing a weapon, suit of armor, or shield takes 1 day for each 1,000 gp in the price of its magical features. To enhance a weapon, suit of armor, or shield, you must use up raw materials costing half of this total price. See the magic item creation rules in Chapter 15 for more information.

The weapon, armor, or shield to be enhanced must be a masterwork item that you provide. Its cost is not included in the above cost.

You can also mend a broken or destroyed magic weapon, suit of armor, or shield if it is one that you could make. Doing so costs half the raw materials and half the time it would take to craft that item in the first place.

Craft Rod (Item Creation)

You can create magic rods.

Prerequisite: Caster level 9th.

Benefit: You can create magic rods. Crafting a rod takes 1 day for each 1,000 gp in its base price. To craft a rod, you must use up raw materials costing half of its base price. See the magic item creation rules in Chapter 15 for more information.

Craft Staff (Item Creation)

You can create magic staves.

Prerequisite: Caster level 11th.

Benefit: You can create any staff whose prerequisites you meet. Crafting a staff takes 1 day for each 1,000 gp in its base price. To craft a staff, you must use up raw materials costing half of its base price. A newly created staff has 10 charges. See the magic item creation rules in Chapter 15 for more information.

Craft Wand (Item Creation)

You can create magic wands.

Prerequisite: Caster level 5th.

Benefit: You can create a wand of any 4th-level or lower spell that you know. Crafting a wand takes 1 day for each 1,000 gp in its base price. To craft a wand, you must use up raw materials costing half of this base price. A newly created wand has 50 charges. See the magic item creation rules in Chapter 15 for more information.

Craft Wondrous Item (Item Creation)

You can create wondrous items, a type of magic item.

Prerequisite: Caster level 3rd.

Benefit: You can create a wide variety of magic wondrous items. Crafting a wondrous item takes 1 day for each 1,000 gp in its price. To create a wondrous item, you must use up raw materials costing half of its base price. See the magic item creation rules in Chapter 15 for more information.

You can also mend a broken or destroyed wondrous item if it is one that you could make. Doing so costs half the raw materials and half the time it would take to craft that item.

Critical Focus (Combat)

You are trained in the art of causing pain.

Prerequisites: Base attack bonus +9.

Benefit: You receive a +4 circumstance bonus on attack rolls made to confirm critical hits.

Critical Mastery (Combat)

Your critical hits cause two additional effects.

Prerequisites: Critical Focus, any two critical feats, 14th-level fighter.

Benefit: When you score a critical hit, you can apply the effects of two critical feats in addition to the damage dealt.

Normal: You can only apply the effects of one critical feat to a given critical hit in addition to the damage dealt.

Dazzling Display (Combat)

Your skill with your favored weapon can frighten enemies.

Prerequisite: Weapon Focus, proficiency with the selected weapon.

Benefit: While wielding the weapon in which you have Weapon Focus, you can perform a bewildering show of prowess as a full-round action. Make an Intimidate check to demoralize all foes within 30 feet who can see your display.

Deadly Aim (Combat)

You can make exceptionally deadly ranged attacks by pinpointing a foe's weak spot, at the expense of making the attack less likely to succeed.

Prerequisites: Dex 13, base attack bonus +1.

Benefit: You can choose to take a –1 penalty on all ranged attack rolls to gain a +2 bonus on all ranged damage rolls. When your base attack bonus reaches +4, and every +4 thereafter, the penalty increases by –1 and the bonus to damage increases by +2. You must choose to use this feat before making an attack roll and its effects last until your next turn. The bonus damage does not apply to touch attacks or effects that do not deal hit point damage.

Deadly Stroke (Combat)

With a well-placed strike, you can bring a swift and painful end to most foes.

Prerequisites: Dazzling Display, Greater Weapon Focus, Shatter Defenses, Weapon Focus, proficiency with the selected weapon, base attack bonus +11.

Benefit: As a standard action, make a single attack with the weapon for which you have Greater Weapon Focus against a stunned or flat-footed opponent. If you hit, you deal double the normal damage and the target takes 1 point of Constitution bleed (see Appendix 2). The additional damage and bleed is not multiplied on a critical hit.

Deafening Critical (Combat, Critical)

Your critical hits cause enemies to lose their hearing.

Prerequisites: Critical Focus, base attack bonus +13.

Benefit: Whenever you score a critical hit against an opponent, the victim is permanently deafened. A successful Fortitude save reduces the deafness to 1 round. The DC of this Fortitude save is equal to 10 + your base attack bonus. This feat has no effect on deaf creatures. This deafness can be cured by *heal, regeneration, remove deafness,* or a similar ability.

Special: You can only apply the effects of one critical feat to a given critical hit unless you possess Critical Mastery.

Deceitful

You are skilled at deceiving others, both with the spoken word and with physical disguises.

Benefit: You get a +2 bonus on all Bluff and Disguise skill checks. If you have 10 or more ranks in one of these skills, the bonus increases to +4 for that skill.

Defensive Combat Training (Combat)

You excel at defending yourself from all manner of combat maneuvers.

Benefit: You treat your total Hit Dice as your base attack bonus when calculating your Combat Maneuver Defense (see Chapter 8).

Deflect Arrows (Combat)

You can knock arrows and other projectiles off course, preventing them from hitting you.

Prerequisites: Dex 13, Improved Unarmed Strike.

Benefit: You must have at least one hand free (holding nothing) to use this feat. Once per round when you would normally be hit with an attack from a ranged weapon, you may deflect it so that you take no damage from it. You must be aware of the attack and not flat-footed. Attempting to deflect a ranged attack doesn't count as an action. Unusually massive ranged weapons (such as boulders or ballista bolts) and ranged attacks generated by natural attacks or spell effects can't be deflected.

Deft Hands

You have exceptional manual dexterity.

Benefit: You get a +2 bonus on Disable Device and Sleight of Hand skill checks. If you have 10 or more ranks in one of these skills, the bonus increases to +4 for that skill.

Diehard

You are especially hard to kill. Not only do your wounds automatically stabilize when grievously injured, but you can remain conscious and continue to act even at death's door.

Prerequisite: Endurance.

Benefit: When your hit point total is below 0, but you are not dead, you automatically stabilize. You do not need to make a Constitution check each round to avoid losing additional hit points. You may choose to act as if you were disabled, rather than dying. You must make this decision as soon as you are reduced to negative hit points (even if it isn't your turn). If you do not choose to act as if you were disabled, you immediately fall unconscious.

When using this feat, you are staggered. You can take a move action without further injuring yourself, but if you perform any standard action (or any other action deemed as strenuous, including some swift actions, such as casting a quickened spell) you take 1 point of damage after completing the act. If your negative hit points are equal to or greater than your Constitution score, you immediately die.

Normal: A character without this feat who is reduced to negative hit points is unconscious and dying.

Disruptive (Combat)

Your training makes it difficult for enemy spellcasters to safely cast spells near you.

Prerequisites: 6th-level fighter.

Benefit: The DC to cast spells defensively increases by +4 for all enemies that are within your threatened area. This increase to casting spells defensively only applies if you are aware of the enemy's location and are capable of taking an attack of opportunity. If you can only take one attack of opportunity per round and have already used that attack, this increase does not apply.

Dodge (Combat)

Your training and reflexes allow you to react swiftly to avoid an opponents' attacks.

Prerequisite: Dex 13.

Benefit: You gain a +1 dodge bonus to your AC. A condition that makes you lose your Dex bonus to AC also makes you lose the benefits of this feat.

Double Slice (Combat)

Your off-hand weapon while dual-wielding strikes with greater power.

Prerequisite: Dex 15, Two-Weapon Fighting.

Benefit: Add your Strength bonus to damage rolls made with your off-hand weapon.

Normal: You normally add only half of your Strength modifier to damage rolls made with a weapon wielded in your off-hand.

Elemental Channel

Choose one elemental subtype, such as air, earth, fire, or water. You can channel your divine energy to harm or heal outsiders that possess your chosen elemental subtype.

Prerequisites: Channel energy class feature.

Benefit: Instead of its normal effect, you can choose to have your ability to channel energy heal or harm outsiders of your chosen elemental subtype. You must make this choice each time you channel energy. If you choose to heal or harm creatures of your elemental subtype, your channel energy has no affect on other creatures. The amount of damage healed or dealt and the DC to halve the damage is otherwise unchanged.

Special: You can gain this feat multiple times. Its effects do not stack. Each time you take this feat, it applies to a new elemental subtype.

Empower Spell (Metamagic)

You can increase the power of your spells, causing them to deal more damage.

Benefit: All variable, numeric effects of an empowered spell are increased by half, including bonuses to those dice rolls.

Saving throws and opposed rolls are not affected, nor are spells without random variables. An empowered spell uses up a spell slot two levels higher than the spell's actual level.

Endurance

Harsh conditions or long exertions do not easily tire you.

Benefit: You gain a +4 bonus on the following checks and saves: Swim checks made to resist nonlethal damage from exhaustion; Constitution checks made to continue running; Constitution checks made to avoid nonlethal damage from a forced march; Constitution checks made to hold your breath; Constitution checks made to avoid nonlethal damage from starvation or thirst; Fortitude saves made to avoid nonlethal damage from hot or cold environments; and Fortitude saves made to resist damage from suffocation.

You may sleep in light or medium armor without becoming fatigued.

Normal: A character without this feat who sleeps in medium or heavier armor is fatigued the next day.

Enlarge Spell (Metamagic)

You can increase the range of your spells.

Benefit: You can alter a spell with a range of close, medium, or long to increase its range by 100%. An enlarged spell with a range of close now has a range of 50 ft. + 5 ft./level, while medium-range spells have a range of 200 ft. + 20 ft./level and long-range spells have a range of 800 ft. + 80 ft./level. An enlarged spell uses up a spell slot one level higher than the spell's actual level.

Spells whose ranges are not defined by distance, as well as spells whose ranges are not close, medium, or long, do not benefit from this feat.

Eschew Materials
You can cast many spells without needing to utilize minor material components.

Benefit: You can cast any spell with a material component costing 1 gp or less without needing that component. The casting of the spell still provokes attacks of opportunity as normal. If the spell requires a material component that costs more than 1 gp, you must have the material component on hand to cast the spell, as normal.

Exhausting Critical (Combat, Critical)
Your critical hits cause opponents to become exhausted.

Prerequisites: Critical Focus, Tiring Critical, base attack bonus +15.

Benefit: When you score a critical hit on a foe, your target immediately becomes exhausted. This feat has no effect on exhausted creatures.

Special: You can only apply the effects of one critical feat to a given critical hit unless you possess the Critical Mastery feat.

Exotic Weapon Proficiency (Combat)
Choose one type of exotic weapon, such as the spiked chain or whip. You understand how to use that type of exotic weapon in combat, and can utilize any special tricks or qualities that exotic weapon might allow.

Prerequisite: Base attack bonus +1.

Benefit: You make attack rolls with the weapon normally.

Normal: A character who uses a weapon with which he is not proficient takes a –4 penalty on attack rolls.

Special: You can gain Exotic Weapon Proficiency multiple times. Each time you take the feat, it applies to a new type of exotic weapon.

Extend Spell (Metamagic)
You can make your spells last twice as long.

Benefit: An extended spell lasts twice as long as normal. A spell with a duration of concentration, instantaneous, or permanent is not affected by this feat. An extended spell uses up a spell slot one level higher than the spell's actual level.

Extra Channel
You can channel divine energy more often.

Prerequisite: Channel energy class feature.

Benefit: You can channel energy two additional times per day.

Special: If a paladin with the ability to channel positive energy takes this feat, she can use lay on hands four additional times a day, but only to channel positive energy.

Extra Ki

You can use your ki pool more times per day than most.

Prerequisite: Ki pool class feature.

Benefit: Your ki pool increases by 2.

Special: You can gain Extra Ki multiple times. Its effects stack.

Extra Lay On Hands

You can use your lay on hands ability more often.

Prerequisite: Lay on hands class feature.

Benefit: You can use your lay on hands ability two additional times per day.

Special: You can gain Extra Lay On Hands multiple times. Its effects stack.

Extra Mercy

Your lay on hands ability adds an additional mercy.

Prerequisites: Lay on hands class feature, mercy class feature.

Benefit: Select one additional mercy for which you qualify. When you use lay on hands to heal damage to one target, it also receives the additional effects of this mercy.

Special: You can gain this feat multiple times. Its effects do not stack. Each time you take this feat, select a new mercy.

Extra Performance

You can use your bardic performance ability more often than normal.

Prerequisite: Bardic performance class feature.

Benefit: You can use bardic performance for 6 additional rounds per day.

Special: You can gain Extra Performance multiple times. Its effects stack.

Extra Rage

You can use your rage ability more than normal.

Prerequisite: Rage class feature.

Benefit: You can rage for 6 additional rounds per day.

Special: You can gain Extra Rage multiple times. Its effects stack.

Far Shot (Combat)

You are more accurate at longer ranges.

Prerequisites: Point-Blank Shot.

Benefit: You only suffer a –1 penalty per full range increment between you and your target when using a ranged weapon.

Normal: You suffer a –2 penalty per full range increment between you and your target.

Fleet

You are faster than most.

Benefit: While you are wearing light or no armor, your base speed increases by 5 feet. You lose the benefits of this feat if you carry a medium or heavy load.

Special: You can take this feat multiple times. The effects stack.

Forge Ring (Item Creation)

You can create magic rings.

Prerequisite: Caster level 7th.

Benefit: You can create magic rings. Crafting a ring takes 1 day for each 1,000 gp in its base price. To craft a ring, you must use up raw materials costing half of the base price. See the magic item creation rules in Chapter 15 for more information.

You can also mend a broken ring if it is one that you could make. Doing so costs half the raw materials and half the time it would take to forge that ring in the first place.

Gorgon's Fist (Combat)

With one well-placed blow, you leave your target reeling.

Prerequisites: Improved Unarmed Strike, Scorpion Style, base attack bonus +6.

Benefit: As a standard action, make a single unarmed melee attack against a foe whose speed is reduced (such as from Scorpion Style). If the attack hits, you deal damage normally and the target is staggered until the end of your next turn unless it makes a Fortitude saving throw (DC 10 + 1/2 your character level + your Wis modifier). This feat has no effect on targets that are staggered.

Great Cleave (Combat)

You can strike many adjacent foes with a single blow.

Prerequisites: Str 13, Cleave, Power Attack, base attack bonus +4.

Benefit: As a standard action, you can make a single attack at your full base attack bonus against a foe within reach. If you hit, you deal damage normally and can make an additional attack (using your full base attack bonus) against a foe that is adjacent to the previous foe and also within reach. If you hit, you can continue to make attacks against foes adjacent to the previous foe, so long as they are within your reach. You cannot attack an individual foe more than once during this attack action. When you use this feat, you take a –2 penalty to your Armor Class until your next turn.

Great Fortitude

You are resistant to poisons, diseases, and other maladies.

Benefit: You get a +2 bonus on all Fortitude saving throws.

Greater Bull Rush (Combat)

Your bull rush attacks throw enemies off balance.

Prerequisites: Improved Bull Rush, Power Attack, base attack bonus +6, Str 13.

Benefit: You receive a +2 bonus on checks made to bull rush a foe. This bonus stacks with the bonus granted by Improved Bull Rush. Whenever you bull rush an opponent, his movement provokes attacks of opportunity from all of your allies (but not you).

Normal: Creatures moved by bull rush do not provoke attacks of opportunity.

Greater Disarm (Combat)

You can knock weapons far from an enemy's grasp.

Prerequisites: Combat Expertise, Improved Disarm, base attack bonus +6, Int 13.

Benefit: You receive a +2 bonus on checks made to disarm a foe. This bonus stacks with the bonus granted by Improved Disarm. Whenever you successfully disarm an opponent, the weapon lands 15 feet away from its previous wielder, in a random direction.

Normal: Disarmed weapons and gear land at the feet of the disarmed creature.

Greater Feint (Combat)

You are skilled at making foes overreact to your attacks.

Prerequisites: Combat Expertise, Improved Feint, base attack bonus +6, Int 13.

Benefit: Whenever you use feint to cause an opponent to lose his Dexterity bonus, he loses that bonus until the beginning of your next turn, in addition to losing his Dexterity bonus against your next attack.

Normal: A creature you feint loses its Dexterity bonus against your next attack.

Greater Grapple (Combat)

Maintaining a grapple is second nature to you.

Prerequisites: Improved Grapple, Improved Unarmed Strike, base attack bonus +6, Dex 13.

Benefit: You receive a +2 bonus on checks made to grapple a foe. This bonus stacks with the bonus granted by Improved Grapple. Once you have grappled a creature, maintaining the grapple is a move action. This feat allows you to make two grapple checks each round (to move, harm, or pin your opponent), but you are not required to make two checks. You only need to succeed at one of these checks to maintain the grapple.

Normal: Maintaining a grapple is a standard action.

Greater Overrun (Combat)

Enemies must dive to avoid your dangerous move.

Prerequisites: Improved Overrun, Power Attack, base attack bonus +6, Str 13.

Benefit: You receive a +2 bonus on checks made to overrun a foe. This bonus stacks with the bonus granted by Improved Overrun. Whenever you overrun opponents, they provoke attacks of opportunity if they are knocked prone by your overrun.

Normal: Creatures knocked prone by your overrun do not provoke an attack of opportunity.

Greater Penetrating Strike (Combat)

Your attacks penetrate the defenses of most foes.

Prerequisites: Penetrating Strike, Weapon Focus, 16th-level fighter.

Benefit: Your attacks made with weapons selected with Weapon Focus ignore up to 10 points of damage reduction. This amount is reduced to 5 points for damage reduction without a type (such as DR 10/—).

Greater Shield Focus (Combat)

You are skilled at deflecting blows with your shield.

Prerequisites: Shield Focus, Shield Proficiency, 8th-level fighter.

Benefit: Increase the AC bonus granted by any shield you are using by 1. This bonus stacks with the bonus granted by Shield Focus.

Greater Spell Focus

Choose a school of magic to which you have already applied the Spell Focus feat. Any spells you cast of this school are very hard to resist.

Prerequisite: Spell Focus.

Benefit: Add +1 to the Difficulty Class for all saving throws against spells from the school of magic you select. This bonus stacks with the bonus from Spell Focus.

Special: You can gain this feat multiple times. Its effects do not stack. Each time you take the feat, it applies to a new school to which you already have applied the Spell Focus feat.

Greater Spell Penetration

Your spells break through spell resistance much more easily than most.

Prerequisite: Spell Penetration.

Benefit: You get a +2 bonus on caster level checks (1d20 + caster level) made to overcome a creature's spell resistance. This bonus stacks with the one from Spell Penetration.

Greater Sunder (Combat)

Your devastating strikes cleave through weapons and armor and into their wielders, damaging both item and wielder alike in a single terrific strike.

Prerequisites: Improved Sunder, Power Attack, base attack bonus +6, Str 13.

Benefit: You receive a +2 bonus on checks made to sunder an item. This bonus stacks with the bonus granted by Improved Sunder. Whenever you sunder to destroy a weapon, shield, or suit of armor, any excess damage is applied to the item's wielder. No damage is transferred if you decide to leave the item with 1 hit point.

Greater Trip (Combat)

You can make free attacks on foes that you knock down.

Prerequisites: Combat Expertise, Improved Trip, base attack bonus +6, Int 13.

Benefit: You receive a +2 bonus on checks made to trip a foe. This bonus stacks with the bonus granted by Improved Trip. Whenever you successfully trip an opponent, that opponent provokes attacks of opportunity.

Normal: Creatures do not provoke attacks of opportunity from being tripped.

Greater Two-Weapon Fighting (Combat)

You are incredibly skilled at fighting with two weapons at the same time.

Prerequisites: Dex 19, Improved Two-Weapon Fighting, Two-Weapon Fighting, base attack bonus +11.

Benefit: You get a third attack with your off-hand weapon, albeit at a –10 penalty.

Greater Vital Strike (Combat)

You can make a single attack that deals incredible damage.

Prerequisites: Improved Vital Strike, Vital Strike, base attack bonus +16.

Benefit: When you use the attack action, you can make one attack at your highest base attack bonus that deals additional damage. Roll the weapon's damage dice for the attack four times and add the results together before adding bonuses from Strength, weapon abilities (such as *flaming*), precision-based damage (such as sneak attack), and other damage bonuses. These extra weapon damage dice are not multiplied on a critical hit, but are added to the total.

Greater Weapon Focus (Combat)

Choose one type of weapon (including unarmed strike or grapple) for which you have already selected Weapon Focus. You are a master at your chosen weapon.

Prerequisites: Proficiency with selected weapon, Weapon Focus with selected weapon, 8th-level fighter.

Benefit: You gain a +1 bonus on attack rolls you make using the selected weapon. This bonus stacks with other bonuses on attack rolls, including those from Weapon Focus.

Special: You can gain Greater Weapon Focus multiple times. Its effects do not stack. Each time you take the feat, it applies to a new type of weapon.

Greater Weapon Specialization (Combat)

Choose one type of weapon (including unarmed strike or grapple) for which you possess the Weapon Specialization feat. Your attacks with the chosen weapon are more devastating than normal.

Prerequisites: Proficiency with selected weapon, Greater Weapon Focus with selected weapon, Weapon Focus with selected weapon, Weapon Specialization with selected weapon, 12th-level fighter.

Benefit: You gain a +2 bonus on all damage rolls you make using the selected weapon. This bonus to damage stacks with other damage roll bonuses, including any you gain from Weapon Specialization.

Special: You can gain Greater Weapon Specialization multiple times. Its effects do not stack. Each time you take the feat, it applies to a new type of weapon.

Heighten Spell (Metamagic)

You can cast spells as if they were a higher level.

Benefit: A heightened spell has a higher spell level than normal (up to a maximum of 9th level). Unlike other metamagic feats, Heighten Spell actually increases the effective level of the spell that it modifies. All effects dependent on spell level (such as saving throw DCs and ability to penetrate a *lesser globe of invulnerability*) are calculated according to the heightened level. The heightened spell is as difficult to prepare and cast as a spell of its effective level.

Improved Bull Rush (Combat)

You are skilled at pushing your foes around.

Prerequisite: Str 13, Power Attack, base attack bonus +1.

Benefit: You do not provoke an attack of opportunity when performing a bull rush combat maneuver. In addition, you receive a +2 bonus on checks made to bull rush a foe. You also receive a +2 bonus to your Combat Maneuver Defense whenever an opponent tries to bull rush you.

Normal: You provoke an attack of opportunity when performing a bull rush combat maneuver.

Improved Channel

Your channeled energy is harder to resist.

Prerequisite: Channel energy class feature.

Benefit: Add 2 to the DC of saving throws made to resist the effects of your channel energy ability.

Improved Counterspell

You are skilled at countering the spells of others using similar spells.

Benefit: When counterspelling, you may use a spell of the same school that is one or more spell levels higher than the target spell.

Normal: Without this feat, you may counter a spell only with the same spell or with a spell specifically designated as countering the target spell.

Improved Critical (Combat)

Attacks made with your chosen weapon are quite deadly.

Prerequisite: Proficient with weapon, base attack bonus +8.

Benefit: When using the weapon you selected, your threat range is doubled.

Special: You can gain Improved Critical multiple times. The effects do not stack. Each time you take the feat, it applies to a new type of weapon.

This effect doesn't stack with any other effect that expands the threat range of a weapon.

Improved Disarm (Combat)

You are skilled at knocking weapons from a foe's grasp.

Prerequisite: Int 13, Combat Expertise.

Benefit: You do not provoke an attack of opportunity when performing a disarm combat maneuver. In addition, you receive a +2 bonus on checks made to disarm a foe. You also receive a +2 bonus to your Combat Maneuver Defense whenever an opponent tries to disarm you.

Normal: You provoke an attack of opportunity when performing a disarm combat maneuver.

Improved Familiar

This feat allows you to acquire a powerful familiar, but only when you could normally acquire a new familiar.

Prerequisites: Ability to acquire a new familiar, compatible alignment, sufficiently high level (see below).

Benefit: When choosing a familiar, the creatures listed below are also available to you (see the *Pathfinder RPG Bestiary* for statistics on these creatures). You may choose a familiar with an alignment up to one step away on each alignment axis (lawful through chaotic, good through evil).

Familiar	Alignment	Arcane Spellcaster Level
Celestial hawk[1]	Neutral good	3rd
Dire rat	Neutral	3rd
Fiendish viper[2]	Neutral evil	3rd
Elemental, Small (any type)	Neutral	5th
Stirge	Neutral	5th
Homunculus[3]	Any	7th
Imp	Lawful evil	7th
Mephit (any type)	Neutral	7th
Pseudodragon	Neutral good	7th
Quasit	Chaotic evil	7th

1 Or other celestial animal from the standard familiar list.
2 Or other fiendish animal from the standard familiar list.
3 The master must first create the homunculus.

Improved familiars otherwise use the rules for regular familiars, with two exceptions: if the creature's type is something other than animal, its type does not change; and improved familiars do not gain the ability to speak with other creatures of their kind (although many of them already have the ability to communicate).

Improved Feint (Combat)

You are skilled at fooling your opponents in combat.

Prerequisites: Int 13, Combat Expertise.

Benefit: You can make a Bluff check to feint in combat as a move action.

Normal: Feinting in combat is a standard action.

Improved Grapple (Combat)

You are skilled at grappling opponents.

Prerequisite: Dex 13, Improved Unarmed Strike.

Benefit: You do not provoke an attack of opportunity when performing a grapple combat maneuver. In addition, you receive a +2 bonus on checks made to grapple a foe. You also receive a +2 bonus to your Combat Maneuver Defense whenever an opponent tries to grapple you.

Normal: You provoke an attack of opportunity when performing a grapple combat maneuver.

Improved Great Fortitude

You can draw upon an inner reserve to resist diseases, poisons, and other grievous harm.

Prerequisites: Great Fortitude.

Benefit: Once per day, you may reroll a Fortitude save. You must decide to use this ability before the results are revealed. You must take the second roll, even if it is worse.

Improved Initiative (Combat)

Your quick reflexes allow you to react rapidly to danger.

Benefit: You get a +4 bonus on initiative checks.

Improved Iron Will

Your clarity of thought allows you to resist mental attacks.

Prerequisites: Iron Will.

Benefit: Once per day, you may reroll a Will save. You must decide to use this ability before the results are revealed. You must take the second roll, even if it is worse.

Improved Lightning Reflexes

You have a knack for avoiding danger all around you.

Prerequisites: Lightning Reflexes.

Benefit: Once per day, you may reroll a Reflex save. You must decide to use this ability before the results are revealed. You must take the second roll, even if it is worse.

Improved Overrun (Combat)

You are skilled at running down your foes.

Prerequisite: Str 13, Power Attack, base attack bonus +1.

Benefit: You do not provoke an attack of opportunity when performing an overrun combat maneuver. In addition, you receive a +2 bonus on checks made to overrrun a foe. You also receive a +2 bonus to your Combat Maneuver Defense whenever an opponent tries to overrun you. Targets of your overrun attempt may not choose to avoid you.

Normal: You provoke an attack of opportunity when performing an overrun combat maneuver.

Improved Precise Shot (Combat)

Your ranged attacks ignore anything but total concealment and cover.

Prerequisites: Dex 19, Point-Blank Shot, Precise Shot, base attack bonus +11.

Benefit: Your ranged attacks ignore the AC bonus granted to targets by anything less than total cover, and the miss chance granted to targets by anything less than total concealment. Total cover and total concealment provide their normal benefits against your ranged attacks.

Normal: See the normal rules on the effects of cover and concealment in Chapter 8.

Improved Shield Bash (Combat)

You can protect yourself with your shield, even if you use it to attack.

Prerequisite: Shield Proficiency.

Benefit: When you perform a shield bash, you may still apply the shield's shield bonus to your AC.

Normal: Without this feat, a character that performs a shield bash loses the shield's shield bonus to AC until his next turn (see Chapter 6).

Improved Sunder (Combat)

You are skilled at damaging your foes' weapons and armor.

Prerequisite: Str 13, Power Attack, base attack bonus +1.

Benefit: You do not provoke an attack of opportunity when performing a sunder combat maneuver. In addition, you receive a +2 bonus on checks made to sunder an item. You also receive a +2 bonus to your Combat Maneuver Defense whenever an opponent tries to sunder your gear.

Normal: You provoke an attack of opportunity when performing a sunder combat maneuver.

Improved Trip (Combat)

You are skilled at sending your opponents to the ground.

Prerequisite: Int 13, Combat Expertise.

Benefit: You do not provoke an attack of opportunity when performing a trip combat maneuver. In addition, you receive a +2 bonus on checks made to trip a foe. You also receive a +2 bonus to your Combat Maneuver Defense whenever an opponent tries to trip you.

Normal: You provoke an attack of opportunity when performing a trip combat maneuver.

Improved Two-Weapon Fighting (Combat)

You are skilled at fighting with two weapons.

Prerequisites: Dex 17, Two-Weapon Fighting, base attack bonus +6.

Benefit: In addition to the standard single extra attack you get with an off-hand weapon, you get a second attack with it, albeit at a –5 penalty.

Normal: Without this feat, you can only get a single extra attack with an off-hand weapon.

Improved Unarmed Strike (Combat)

You are skilled at fighting while unarmed.

Benefit: You are considered to be armed even when unarmed—you do not provoke attacks of opportunity when you attack foes while unarmed. Your unarmed strikes can deal lethal or nonlethal damage, at your choice.

Normal: Without this feat, you are considered unarmed when attacking with an unarmed strike, and you can deal only nonlethal damage with such an attack.

Improved Vital Strike (Combat)

You can make a single attack that deals a large amount of damage.

Prerequisites: Vital Strike, base attack bonus +11.

Benefit: When you use the attack action, you can make one attack at your highest base attack bonus that deals additional damage. Roll the weapon's damage dice for the attack three times and add the results together before adding bonuses from Strength, weapon special abilities (such as *flaming*), precision-based damage, and other damage bonuses. These extra weapon damage dice are not multiplied on a critical hit, but are added to the total.

Improvised Weapon Mastery (Combat)

You can turn nearly any object into a deadly weapon, from a razor-sharp chair leg to a sack of flour.

Prerequisites: Catch Off-Guard or Throw Anything, base attack bonus +8.

Benefit: You do not suffer any penalties for using an improvised weapon. Increase the amount of damage dealt by the improvised weapon by one step (for example, 1d4 becomes 1d6) to a maximum of 1d8 (2d6 if the improvised weapon is two-handed). The improvised weapon has a critical threat range of 19–20, with a critical multiplier of ×2.

Intimidating Prowess (Combat)

Your physical might is intimidating to others.

Benefit: Add your Strength modifier to Intimidate skill checks in addition to your Charisma modifier.

Iron Will

You are more resistant to mental effects.

Benefit: You get a +2 bonus on all Will saving throws.

Leadership

You attract followers to your cause and a companion to join you on your adventures.

Prerequisite: Character level 7th.

Benefits: This feat enables you to attract a loyal cohort and a number of devoted subordinates who assist you. A cohort is generally an NPC with class levels, while followers are typically lower level NPCs. See Table 5–2 for what level of cohort and how many followers you can recruit.

Leadership Modifiers: Several factors can affect your Leadership score, causing it to vary from the base score (character level + Cha modifier). Your reputation (from the point of view of the cohort or follower you are trying to attract) raises or lowers your Leadership score:

Leader's Reputation	Modifier
Great renown	+2
Fairness and generosity	+1
Special power	+1
Failure	−1
Aloofness	−1
Cruelty	−2

Other modifiers may apply when you try to attract a cohort, as listed below.

The Leader...	Modifier
Has a familiar, special mount, or animal companion	−2
Recruits a cohort of a different alignment	−1
Caused the death of a cohort	−2*

*Cumulative per cohort killed.

Followers have different priorities from cohorts. When you try to attract a follower, use the following modifiers.

The Leader...	Modifier
Has a stronghold, base of operations, guildhouse, etc.	+2
Moves around a lot	−1
Caused the death of other followers	−1

Leadership Score: Your base Leadership score equals your level plus your Charisma modifier. In order to take into account negative Charisma modifiers, this table allows for very low Leadership scores, but you must still be 7th level or higher in order to gain the Leadership feat. Outside factors can affect your Leadership score, as detailed above.

TABLE 5-2: LEADERSHIP

Leadership Score	Cohort Level	Number of Followers by Level					
		1st	2nd	3rd	4th	5th	6th
1 or lower	—	—	—	—	—	—	—
2	1st	—	—	—	—	—	—
3	2nd	—	—	—	—	—	—
4	3rd	—	—	—	—	—	—
5	3rd	—	—	—	—	—	—
6	4th	—	—	—	—	—	—
7	5th	—	—	—	—	—	—
8	5th	—	—	—	—	—	—
9	6th	—	—	—	—	—	—
10	7th	5	—	—	—	—	—
11	7th	6	—	—	—	—	—
12	8th	8	—	—	—	—	—
13	9th	10	1	—	—	—	—
14	10th	15	1	—	—	—	—
15	10th	20	2	1	—	—	—
16	11th	25	2	1	—	—	—
17	12th	30	3	1	1	—	—
18	12th	35	3	1	1	—	—
19	13th	40	4	2	1	1	—
20	14th	50	5	3	2	1	—
21	15th	60	6	3	2	1	1
22	15th	75	7	4	2	2	1
23	16th	90	9	5	3	2	1
24	17th	110	11	6	3	2	1
25 or higher	17th	135	13	7	4	2	2

Cohort Level: You can attract a cohort of up to this level. Regardless of your Leadership score, you can only recruit a cohort who is two or more levels lower than yourself. The cohort should be equipped with gear appropriate for its level (see Chapter 14). A cohort can be of any race or class. The cohort's alignment may not be opposed to your alignment on either the law/chaos or good/evil axis, and you take a −1 penalty to your Leadership score if you recruit a cohort of an alignment different from your own.

A cohort does not count as a party member when determining the party's XP. Instead, divide the cohort's level by your level. Multiply this result by the total XP awarded to you, then add that number of experience points to the cohort's total.

If a cohort gains enough XP to bring it to a level one lower than your level, the cohort does not gain the new level—its new XP total is 1 less than the amount needed to attain the next level.

Number of Followers by Level: You can lead up to the indicated number of characters of each level. Followers are similar to cohorts, except they're generally low-level NPCs. Because they're usually 5 or more levels behind you, they're rarely effective in combat.

Followers don't earn experience and thus don't gain levels. When you gain a new level, consult Table 5–2 to determine if you acquire more followers, some of whom may be higher level than the existing followers. Don't consult the table to see if your cohort gains levels, however, because cohorts earn experience on their own.

Lightning Reflexes

You have faster reflexes than normal.

Benefit: You get a +2 bonus on all Reflex saving throws.

Lightning Stance (Combat)

The speed at which you move makes it nearly impossible for opponents to strike you.

Prerequisites: Dex 17, Dodge, Wind Stance, base attack bonus +11.

Benefit: If you take two actions to move or a withdraw action in a turn, you gain 50% concealment for 1 round.

Lunge (Combat)

You can strike foes that would normally be out of reach.

Prerequisites: Base attack bonus +6.

Benefit: You can increase the reach of your melee attacks by 5 feet until the end of your turn by taking a –2 penalty to your AC until your next turn. You must decide to use this ability before any attacks are made.

Magical Aptitude

You are skilled at spellcasting and using magic items.

Benefit: You get a +2 bonus on all Spellcraft checks and Use Magic Device checks. If you have 10 or more ranks in one of these skills, the bonus increases to +4 for that skill.

Manyshot (Combat)

You can fire multiple arrows at a single target.

Prerequisites: Dex 17, Point-Blank Shot, Rapid Shot, base attack bonus +6.

Benefit: When making a full-attack action with a bow, your first attack fires two arrows. If the attack hits, both arrows hit. Apply precision-based damage (such as sneak attack) and critical hit damage only once for this attack. Damage bonuses from using a composite bow with a high Strength bonus apply to each arrow, as do other damage bonuses, such as a ranger's favored enemy bonus. Damage reduction and resistances apply separately to each arrow.

Martial Weapon Proficiency (Combat)

Choose a type of martial weapon. You understand how to use that type of martial weapon in combat.

Benefit: You make attack rolls with the selected weapon normally (without the non-proficient penalty).

Normal: When using a weapon with which you are not proficient, you take a –4 penalty on attack rolls.

Special: Barbarians, fighters, paladins, and rangers are proficient with all martial weapons. They need not select this feat.

You can gain Martial Weapon Proficiency multiple times. Each time you take the feat, it applies to a new type of weapon.

Master Craftsman

Your superior crafting skills allow you to create simple magic items.

Prerequisites: 5 ranks in any Craft or Profession skill.

Benefit: Choose one Craft or Profession skill in which you possess at least 5 ranks. You receive a +2 bonus on your chosen Craft or Profession skill. Ranks in your chosen skill count as your caster level for the purposes of qualifying for the Craft Magic Arms and Armor and Craft Wondrous Item feats. You can create magic items using these feats, substituting your ranks in the chosen skill for your total caster level. You must use the chosen skill for the check to create the item. The DC to create the item still increases for any necessary spell requirements (see the magic item creation rules in Chapter 15). You cannot use this feat to create any spell-trigger or spell-activation item.

Normal: Only spellcasters can qualify for the Craft Magic Arms and Armor and Craft Wondrous Item feats.

Maximize Spell (Metamagic)

Your spells have the maximum possible effect.

Benefit: All variable, numeric effects of a spell modified by this feat are maximized. Saving throws and opposed rolls are not affected, nor are spells without random variables. A maximized spell uses up a spell slot three levels higher than the spell's actual level.

An empowered, maximized spell gains the separate benefits of each feat: the maximum result plus half the normally rolled result.

Medusa's Wrath (Combat)

You can take advantage of your opponent's confusion, delivering multiple blows.

Prerequisites: Improved Unarmed Strike, Gorgon's Fist, Scorpion Style, base attack bonus +11.

Benefit: Whenever you use the full-attack action and make at least one unarmed strike, you can make two additional unarmed strikes at your highest base attack bonus. These bonus attacks must be made against a dazed, flat-footed, paralyzed, staggered, stunned, or unconscious foe.

Mobility (Combat)

You can easily move through a dangerous melee.

Prerequisites: Dex 13, Dodge.

Benefit: You get a +4 dodge bonus to Armor Class against attacks of opportunity caused when you move out of or within a threatened area. A condition that makes you lose your Dexterity bonus to Armor Class (if any) also makes you lose dodge bonuses.

Dodge bonuses stack with each other, unlike most types of bonuses.

Mounted Archery (Combat)
You are skilled at making ranged attacks while mounted.

Prerequisites: Ride 1 rank, Mounted Combat.

Benefit: The penalty you take when using a ranged weapon while mounted is halved: –2 instead of –4 if your mount is taking a double move, and –4 instead of –8 if your mount is running.

Mounted Combat (Combat)
You are adept at guiding your mount through combat.

Prerequisite: Ride 1 rank.

Benefit: Once per round when your mount is hit in combat, you may attempt a Ride check (as an immediate action) to negate the hit. The hit is negated if your Ride check result is greater than the opponent's attack roll.

Natural Spell
You can cast spells even while in a form that cannot normally cast spells.

Prerequisites: Wis 13, wild shape class feature.

Benefit: You can complete the verbal and somatic components of spells while using wild shape. You substitute various noises and gestures for the normal verbal and somatic components of a spell.

You can also use any material components or focuses you possess, even if such items are melded within your current form. This feat does not permit the use of magic items while you are in a form that could not ordinarily use them, and you do not gain the ability to speak while using wild shape.

Nimble Moves
You can move across a single obstacle with ease.

Prerequisites: Dex 13.

Benefit: Whenever you move, you may move through 5 feet of difficult terrain each round as if it were normal terrain. This feat allows you to take a 5-foot step into difficult terrain.

Penetrating Strike (Combat)
Your attacks are capable of penetrating the defenses of some creatures.

Prerequisites: Weapon Focus, 12th-level fighter, proficiency with weapon.

Benefit: Your attacks made with weapons selected with Weapon Focus ignore up to 5 points of damage reduction. This feat does not apply to damage reduction without a type (such as DR 10/—).

Persuasive
You are skilled at swaying attitudes and intimidating others into your way of thinking.

Benefit: You get a +2 bonus on Diplomacy and Intimidate skill checks. If you have 10 or more ranks in one of these skills, the bonus increases to +4 for that skill.

Pinpoint Targeting (Combat)
You can target the weak points in your opponent's armor.

Prerequisites: Dex 19, Improved Precise Shot, Point-Blank Shot, Precise Shot, base attack bonus +16.

Benefit: As a standard action, make a single ranged attack. The target does not gain any armor, natural armor, or shield bonuses to its Armor Class. You do not gain the benefit of this feat if you move this round.

Point-Blank Shot (Combat)
You are especially accurate when making ranged attacks against close targets.

Benefit: You get a +1 bonus on attack and damage rolls with ranged weapons at ranges of up to 30 feet.

Power Attack (Combat)
You can make exceptionally deadly melee attacks by sacrificing accuracy for strength.

Prerequisites: Str 13, base attack bonus +1.

Benefit: You can choose to take a –1 penalty on all melee attack rolls and combat maneuver checks to gain a +2 bonus on all melee damage rolls. This bonus to damage is increased by half (+50%) if you are making an attack with a two-handed weapon, a one handed weapon using two hands, or a primary natural weapon that adds 1-1/2 times your Strength modifier on damage rolls. This bonus to damage is halved (–50%) if you are making an attack with an off-hand weapon or secondary natural weapon. When your base attack bonus reaches +4, and every 4 points thereafter, the penalty increases by –1 and the bonus to damage increases by +2. You must choose to use this feat before making an attack roll, and its effects last until your next turn. The bonus damage does not apply to touch attacks or effects that do not deal hit point damage.

Precise Shot (Combat)
You are adept at firing ranged attacks into melee.

Prerequisite: Point-Blank Shot.

Benefit: You can shoot or throw ranged weapons at an opponent engaged in melee without taking the standard –4 penalty on your attack roll.

Quick Draw (Combat)
You can draw weapons faster than most.

Prerequisite: Base attack bonus +1.

Benefit: You can draw a weapon as a free action instead of as a move action. You can draw a hidden weapon (see the Sleight of Hand skill) as a move action.

A character who has selected this feat may throw weapons at his full normal rate of attacks (much like a character with a bow).

Alchemical items, potions, scrolls, and wands cannot be drawn quickly using this feat.

Normal: Without this feat, you may draw a weapon as a move action, or (if your base attack bonus is +1 or higher) as a free action as part of movement. Without this feat, you can draw a hidden weapon as a standard action.

Quicken Spell (Metamagic)

You can cast spells in a fraction of the normal time.

Benefit: Casting a quickened spell is a swift action. You can perform another action, even casting another spell, in the same round as you cast a quickened spell. A spell whose casting time is more than 1 round or 1 full-round action cannot be quickened.

A quickened spell uses up a spell slot four levels higher than the spell's actual level. Casting a quickened spell doesn't provoke an attack of opportunity.

Special: You can apply the effects of this feat to a spell cast spontaneously, so long as it has a casting time that is not more than 1 full-round action, without increasing the spell's casting time.

Rapid Reload (Combat)

Choose a type of crossbow (hand, light, or heavy). You can reload such weapons quickly.

Prerequisite: Weapon Proficiency (crossbow type chosen).

Benefit: The time required for you to reload your chosen type of crossbow is reduced to a free action (for a hand or light crossbow) or a move action (for a heavy crossbow). Reloading a crossbow still provokes an attack of opportunity.

If you have selected this feat for hand crossbow or light crossbow, you may fire that weapon as many times in a full-attack action as you could attack if you were using a bow.

Normal: A character without this feat needs a move action to reload a hand or light crossbow, or a full-round action to reload a heavy crossbow.

Special: You can gain Rapid Reload multiple times. Each time you take the feat, it applies to a new type of crossbow.

Rapid Shot (Combat)

You can make an additional ranged attack.

Prerequisites: Dex 13, Point-Blank Shot.

Benefit: When making a full-attack action with a ranged weapon, you can fire one additional time this round at your highest bonus. All of your attack rolls take a −2 penalty when using Rapid Shot.

Ride-By Attack (Combat)

While mounted and charging, you can move, strike at a foe, and then continue moving.

Prerequisites: Ride 1 rank, Mounted Combat. **Benefit:** When you are mounted and use the charge action, you may move and attack as if with a standard charge and then move again (continuing the straight line of the charge). Your total movement for the round can't exceed double your mounted speed. You and your mount do not provoke an attack of opportunity from the opponent that you attack.

Run

You are swift of foot.

Benefit: When running, you move five times your normal speed (if wearing medium, light, or no armor and carrying no more than a medium load) or four times your speed (if wearing heavy armor or carrying a heavy load). If you make a jump after a running start (see the Acrobatics skill description), you gain a +4 bonus on your Acrobatics check. While running, you retain your Dexterity bonus to your Armor Class.

Normal: You move four times your speed while running (if wearing medium, light, or no armor and carrying no more than a medium load) or three times your speed (if wearing heavy armor or carrying a heavy load), and you lose your Dexterity bonus to AC.

Scorpion Style (Combat)

You can perform an unarmed strike that greatly hampers your target's movement.

Prerequisite: Improved Unarmed Strike.

Benefit: To use this feat, you must make a single unarmed attack as a standard action. If this unarmed attack hits, you deal damage normally, and the target's base land speed is reduced to 5 feet for a number of rounds equal to your Wisdom modifier unless it makes a Fortitude saving throw (DC 10 + 1/2 your character level + your Wis modifier).

Scribe Scroll (Item Creation)

You can create magic scrolls.

Prerequisite: Caster level 1st.

Benefit: You can create a scroll of any spell that you know. Scribing a scroll takes 2 hours if its base price is 250 gp or less, otherwise scribing a scroll takes 1 day for each 1,000 gp in its base price. To scribe a scroll, you must use up raw materials costing half of this base price. See the magic item creation rules in Chapter 15 for more information.

Selective Channeling

You can choose whom to affect when you channel energy.

Prerequisite: Cha 13, channel energy class feature.

Benefit: When you channel energy, you can choose a number of targets in the area up to your Charisma modifier. These targets are not affected by your channeled energy.

Normal: All targets in a 30-foot burst are affected when you channel energy. You can only choose whether or not you are affected.

Self-Sufficient

You know how to get along in the wild and how to effectively treat wounds.

Benefit: You get a +2 bonus on all Heal checks and Survival checks. If you have 10 or more ranks in one of these skills, the bonus increases to +4 for that skill.

Shatter Defenses (Combat)

Your skill with your chosen weapon leaves opponents unable to defend themselves if you strike them when their defenses are already compromised.

Prerequisites: Weapon Focus, Dazzling Display, base attack bonus +6, proficiency with weapon.

Benefit: Any shaken, frightened, or panicked opponent hit by you this round is flat-footed to your attacks until the end of your next turn. This includes any additional attacks you make this round.

Shield Focus (Combat)

You are skilled at deflecting blows with your shield.

Prerequisites: Shield Proficiency, base attack bonus +1.

Benefit: Increase the AC bonus granted by any shield you are using by 1.

Shield Master (Combat)

Your mastery of the shield allows you to fight with it without hindrance.

Prerequisites: Improved Shield Bash, Shield Proficiency, Shield Slam, Two-Weapon Fighting, base attack bonus +11.

Benefit: You do not suffer any penalties on attack rolls made with a shield while you are wielding another weapon. Add your shield's enhancement bonus to attacks and damage rolls made with the shield as if it was a weapon enhancement bonus.

Shield Proficiency (Combat)

You are trained in how to properly use a shield.

Benefit: When you use a shield (except a tower shield), the shield's armor check penalty only applies to Strength- and Dexterity-based skills.

Normal: When you are using a shield with which you are not proficient, you take the shield's armor check penalty on attack rolls and on all skill checks that involve moving.

Special: Barbarians, bards, clerics, druids, fighters, paladins, and rangers all automatically have Shield Proficiency as a bonus feat. They need not select it.

Shield Slam (Combat)

In the right position, your shield can be used to send opponents flying.

Prerequisites: Improved Shield Bash, Shield Proficiency, Two-Weapon Fighting, base attack bonus +6.

Benefit: Any opponents hit by your shield bash are also hit with a free bull rush attack, substituting your attack roll for the combat maneuver check (see Chapter 8). This bull rush does not provoke an attack of opportunity. Opponents who cannot move back due to a wall or other surface are knocked prone after moving the maximum possible distance. You may choose to move with your target if you are able to take a 5-foot step or to spend an action to move this turn.

Shot on the Run (Combat)

You can move, fire a ranged weapon, and move again before your foes can react.

Prerequisites: Dex 13, Dodge, Mobility, Point-Blank Shot, base attack bonus +4.

Benefit: As a full-round action, you can move up to your speed and make a single ranged attack at any point during your movement.

Normal: You cannot move before and after an attack with a ranged weapon.

Sickening Critical (Combat, Critical)

Your critical hits cause opponents to become sickened.

Prerequisites: Critical Focus, base attack bonus +11.

Benefit: Whenever you score a critical hit, your opponent becomes sickened for 1 minute. The effects of this feat do not stack. Additional hits instead add to the effect's duration.

Special: You can only apply the effects of one critical feat to a given critical hit unless you possess Critical Mastery.

Silent Spell (Metamagic)

You can cast your spells without making any sound.

Benefit: A silent spell can be cast with no verbal components. Spells without verbal components are not affected. A silent spell uses up a spell slot one level higher than the spell's actual level.

Special: Bard spells cannot be enhanced by this feat.

Simple Weapon Proficiency (Combat)

You are trained in the use of basic weapons.

Benefit: You make attack rolls with simple weapons without penalty.

Normal: When using a weapon with which you are not proficient, you take a −4 penalty on attack rolls.

Special: All characters except for druids, monks, and wizards are automatically proficient with all simple weapons. They need not select this feat.

Skill Focus

Choose a skill. You are particularly adept at that skill.

Benefit: You get a +3 bonus on all checks involving the chosen skill. If you have 10 or more ranks in that skill, this bonus increases to +6.

Special: You can gain this feat multiple times. Its effects do not stack. Each time you take the feat, it applies to a new skill.

Snatch Arrows (Combat)

Instead of knocking an arrow or ranged attack aside, you can catch it in mid-flight.

Prerequisites: Dex 15, Deflect Arrows, Improved Unarmed Strike.

Benefit: When using the Deflect Arrows feat you may choose to catch the weapon instead of just deflecting it. Thrown weapons can immediately be thrown back as an attack against the original attacker (even though it isn't your turn) or kept for later use.

You must have at least one hand free (holding nothing) to use this feat.

Spell Focus

Choose a school of magic. Any spells you cast of that school are more difficult to resist.

Benefit: Add +1 to the Difficulty Class for all saving throws against spells from the school of magic you select.

Special: You can gain this feat multiple times. Its effects do not stack. Each time you take the feat, it applies to a new school of magic.

Spell Mastery

You have mastered a small handful of spells, and can prepare these spells without referencing your spellbooks at all.

Prerequisite: 1st-level wizard.

Benefit: Each time you take this feat, choose a number of spells that you already know equal to your Intelligence modifier. From that point on, you can prepare these spells without referring to a spellbook.

Normal: Without this feat, you must use a spellbook to prepare all your spells, except *read magic*.

Spell Penetration

Your spells break through spell resistance more easily than most.

Benefit: You get a +2 bonus on caster level checks (1d20 + caster level) made to overcome a creature's spell resistance.

Spellbreaker (Combat)

You can strike at enemy spellcasters who fail to cast defensively when you threaten them.

Prerequisites: Disruptive, 10th-level fighter.

Benefit: Enemies in your threatened area that fail their checks to cast spells defensively provoke attacks of opportunity from you.

Normal: Enemies that fail to cast spells defensively do not provoke attacks of opportunity.

Spirited Charge (Combat)

Your mounted charge attacks deal a tremendous amount of damage.

Prerequisites: Ride 1 rank, Mounted Combat, Ride-By Attack.

Benefit: When mounted and using the charge action, you deal double damage with a melee weapon (or triple damage with a lance).

Spring Attack (Combat)

You can deftly move up to a foe, strike, and withdraw before he can react.

Prerequisites: Dex 13, Dodge, Mobility, base attack bonus +4.

Benefit: As a full-round action, you can move up to your speed and make a single melee attack without provoking any attacks of opportunity from the target of your attack. You can move both before and after the attack, but you must move at least 10 feet before the attack and the total distance that you move cannot be greater than your speed. You cannot use this ability to attack a foe that is adjacent to you at the start of your turn.

Normal: You cannot move before and after an attack.

Staggering Critical (Combat, Critical)

Your critical hits cause opponents to slow down.

Prerequisites: Critical Focus, base attack bonus +13.

Benefit: Whenever you score a critical hit, your opponent becomes staggered for 1d4+1 rounds. A successful Fortitude save reduces the duration to 1 round. The DC of this Fortitude save is equal to 10 + your base attack bonus. The effects of this feat do not stack. Additional hits instead add to the duration.

Special: You can only apply the effects of one critical feat to a given critical hit unless you possess Critical Mastery.

Stand Still (Combat)

You can stop foes that try to move past you.

Prerequisites: Combat Reflexes.

Benefit: When a foe provokes an attack of opportunity due to moving through your adjacent squares, you can make a combat maneuver check as your attack of opportunity. If successful, the enemy cannot move for the rest of his turn. An enemy can still take the rest of his action, but cannot move. This feat also applies to any creature that attempts to move from a square that is adjacent to you if such movement provokes an attack of opportunity.

Stealthy

You are good at avoiding unwanted attention and slipping out of bonds.

Benefit: You get a +2 bonus on all Escape Artist and Stealth skill checks. If you have 10 or more ranks in one of these skills, the bonus increases to +4 for that skill.

Step Up (Combat)

You can close the distance when a foe tries to move away.

Prerequisite: Base attack bonus +1.

Benefit: Whenever an adjacent foe attempts to take a 5-foot step away from you, you may also make a 5-foot step as an immediate action so long as you end up adjacent to the foe that triggered this ability. If you take this step, you cannot take a 5-foot step during your next turn. If you take an action to move during your next turn, subtract 5 feet from your total movement.

Still Spell (Metamagic)

You can cast spells without moving.

Benefit: A stilled spell can be cast with no somatic components. Spells without somatic components are not affected. A stilled spell uses up a spell slot one level higher than the spell's actual level.

Strike Back (Combat)

You can strike at foes that attack you using their superior reach, by targeting their limbs or weapons as they come at you.

Prerequisite: Base attack bonus +11.

Benefit: You can ready an action to make a melee attack against any foe that attacks you in melee, even if the foe is outside of your reach.

Stunning Critical (Combat, Critical)

Your critical hits cause opponents to become stunned.

Prerequisites: Critical Focus, Staggering Critical, base attack bonus +17.

Benefit: Whenever you score a critical hit, your opponent becomes stunned for 1d4 rounds. A successful Fortitude save reduces this to staggered for 1d4 rounds. The DC of this Fortitude save is equal to 10 + your base attack bonus. The effects of this feat do not stack. Additional hits instead add to the duration.

Special: You can only apply the effects of one critical feat to a given critical hit unless you possess Critical Mastery.

Stunning Fist (Combat)

You know just where to strike to temporarily stun a foe.

Prerequisites: Dex 13, Wis 13, Improved Unarmed Strike, base attack bonus +8.

Benefit: You must declare that you are using this feat before you make your attack roll (thus, a failed attack roll ruins the attempt). Stunning Fist forces a foe damaged by your unarmed attack to make a Fortitude saving throw (DC 10 + 1/2 your character level + your Wis modifier), in addition to dealing damage normally. A defender who fails this saving throw is stunned for 1 round (until just before your next turn). A stunned character drops everything held, can't take actions, loses any Dexterity bonus to AC, and takes a –2 penalty to AC. You may attempt a stunning attack once per day for every four levels you have attained (but see Special), and no more than once per round. Constructs, oozes, plants, undead, incorporeal creatures, and creatures immune to critical hits cannot be stunned.

Special: A monk receives Stunning Fist as a bonus feat at 1st level, even if he does not meet the prerequisites. A monk may attempt a stunning attack a number of times per day equal to his monk level, plus one more time per day for every four levels he has in classes other than monk.

Throw Anything (Combat)

You are used to throwing things you have on hand.

Benefit: You do not suffer any penalties for using an improvised ranged weapon. You receive a +1 circumstance bonus on attack rolls made with thrown splash weapons.

Normal: You take a –4 penalty on attack rolls made with an improvised weapon.

Tiring Critical (Combat, Critical)

Your critical hits cause opponents to become fatigued.

Prerequisites: Critical Focus, base attack bonus +13.

Benefit: Whenever you score a critical hit, your opponent becomes fatigued. This feat has no additional effect on a fatigued or exhausted creature.

Special: You can only apply the effects of one critical feat to a given critical hit unless you possess Critical Mastery.

Toughness

You have enhanced physical stamina.

Benefit: You gain +3 hit points. For every Hit Die you possess beyond 3, you gain an additional +1 hit point. If you have more than 3 Hit Dice, you gain +1 hit points whenever you gain a Hit Die (such as when you gain a level).

Tower Shield Proficiency (Combat)

You are trained in how to properly use a tower shield.

Prerequisite: Shield Proficiency.

Benefit: When you use a tower shield, the shield's armor check penalty only applies to Strength and Dexterity-based skills.

Normal: A character using a shield with which he is not proficient takes the shield's armor check penalty on attack rolls and on all skill checks that involve moving, including Ride.

Special: Fighters automatically have Tower Shield Proficiency as a bonus feat. They need not select it.

Trample (Combat)

While mounted, you can ride down opponents and trample them under your mount.

Prerequisites: Ride 1 rank, Mounted Combat.

Benefit: When you attempt to overrun an opponent while mounted, your target may not choose to avoid you. Your mount may make one hoof attack against any target you knock down, gaining the standard +4 bonus on attack rolls against prone targets.

Turn Undead

Calling upon higher powers, you cause undead to flee from the might of your unleashed divine energy.

Prerequisites: Channel positive energy class feature.

Benefit: You can, as a standard action, use one of your uses of channel positive energy to cause all undead within 30 feet of you to flee, as if panicked. Undead receive a Will save to negate the effect. The DC for this Will save is equal to 10 + 1/2 your cleric level + your Charisma modifier. Undead that fail their save flee for 1 minute. Intelligent undead receive a new saving throw each round to end the effect. If you use channel energy in this way, it has no other effect (it does not heal or harm nearby creatures).

Two-Weapon Defense (Combat)

You are skilled at defending yourself while dual-wielding.

Prerequisites: Dex 15, Two-Weapon Fighting.

Benefit: When wielding a double weapon or two weapons (not including natural weapons or unarmed strikes), you gain a +1 shield bonus to your AC.

When you are fighting defensively or using the total defense action, this shield bonus increases to +2.

Two-Weapon Fighting (Combat)

You can fight with a weapon wielded in each of your hands. You can make one extra attack each round with the secondary weapon.

Prerequisite: Dex 15.

Benefit: Your penalties on attack rolls for fighting with two weapons are reduced. The penalty for your primary hand lessens by 2 and the one for your off hand lessens by 6. See Two-Weapon Fighting in Chapter 8.

Normal: If you wield a second weapon in your off hand, you can get one extra attack per round with that weapon. When fighting in this way you suffer a –6 penalty with your regular attack or attacks with your primary hand and a –10 penalty to the attack with your off hand. If your off-hand weapon is light, the penalties are reduced by 2 each. An unarmed strike is always considered light.

Two-Weapon Rend (Combat)

Striking with both of your weapons simultaneously, you can use them to deliver devastating wounds.

Prerequisites: Dex 17, Double Slice, Improved Two-Weapon Fighting, Two-Weapon Fighting, base attack bonus +11.

Benefit: If you hit an opponent with both your primary hand and your off-hand weapon, you deal an additional 1d10 points of damage plus 1-1/2 times your Strength modifier. You can only deal this additional damage once each round.

Unseat (Combat)

You are skilled at unseating your mounted opponents.

Prerequisites: Str 13, Ride 1 rank, Mounted Combat, Power Attack, Improved Bull Rush, base attack bonus +1.

Benefits: When charging an opponent while mounted and wielding a lance, resolve the attack as normal. If it hits, you may immediately make a free bull rush attempt in addition to the normal damage. If successful, the target is knocked off his horse and lands prone in a space adjacent to his mount that is directly away from you.

Vital Strike (Combat)

You make a single attack that deals significantly more damage than normal.

Prerequisites: Base attack bonus +6.

Benefit: When you use the attack action, you can make one attack at your highest base attack bonus that deals additional damage. Roll the weapon's damage dice for the attack twice and add the results together before adding bonuses from Strength, weapon abilities (such as *flaming*), precision-based damage, and other damage bonuses. These extra weapon damage dice are not multiplied on a critical hit, but are added to the total.

Weapon Finesse (Combat)

You are trained in using your agility in melee combat, as opposed to brute strength.

Benefit: With a light weapon, elven curve blade, rapier, whip, or spiked chain made for a creature of your size category, you may use your Dexterity modifier instead of your Strength modifier on attack rolls. If you carry a shield, its armor check penalty applies to your attack rolls.

Special: Natural weapons are considered light weapons.

Weapon Focus (Combat)

Choose one type of weapon. You can also choose unarmed strike or grapple (or ray, if you are a spellcaster) as your weapon for the purposes of this feat.

Prerequisites: Proficiency with selected weapon, base attack bonus +1.

Benefit: You gain a +1 bonus on all attack rolls you make using the selected weapon.

Special: You can gain this feat multiple times. Its effects do not stack. Each time you take the feat, it applies to a new type of weapon.

Weapon Specialization (Combat)

You are skilled at dealing damage with one weapon. Choose one type of weapon (including unarmed strike or grapple) for which you have already selected the Weapon Focus feat. You deal extra damage when using this weapon.

Prerequisites: Proficiency with selected weapon, Weapon Focus with selected weapon, fighter level 4th.

Benefit: You gain a +2 bonus on all damage rolls you make using the selected weapon.

Special: You can gain this feat multiple times. Its effects do not stack. Each time you take the feat, it applies to a new type of weapon.

Whirlwind Attack (Combat)

You can strike out at every foe within reach.

Prerequisites: Dex 13, Int 13, Combat Expertise, Dodge, Mobility, Spring Attack, base attack bonus +4.

Benefit: When you use the full-attack action, you can give up your regular attacks and instead make one melee attack at your highest base attack bonus against each opponent within reach. You must make a separate attack roll against each opponent.

When you use the Whirlwind Attack feat, you also forfeit any bonus or extra attacks granted by other feats, spells, or abilities.

Widen Spell (Metamagic)

You can cast your spells so that they occupy a larger space.

Benefit: You can alter a burst, emanation, or spread-shaped spell to increase its area. Any numeric measurements of the spell's area increase by 100%. A widened spell uses up a spell slot three levels higher than the spell's actual level.

Spells that do not have an area of one of these four sorts are not affected by this feat.

Wind Stance (Combat)

Your erratic movements make it difficult for enemies to pinpoint your location.

Prerequisites: Dex 15, Dodge, base attack bonus +6.

Benefit: If you move more than 5 feet this turn, you gain 20% concealment for 1 round against ranged attacks.

6 EQUIPMENT

Their plates of strange armor shrieking with each titanic lunge, blades massive enough to cleave mountain peaks hefted high and ready to strike, the giants came like avalanches upon their puny foes. Valeros glanced down at the chipped sword that had long been his companion, its length appearing hopelessly feeble in comparison. Through all his adventures, he'd never been one for talking to his sword, but now, standing before these foes, he whispered gravely, "Come on, old gal, see me through just one more time and I'll finally give you that polishing I've been promising."

A well-equipped character can take on nearly any challenge, from surviving in the wilderness to making an impression at the king's banquet. This chapter presents all manner of mundane and exotic equipment for the PCs to purchase and use, from weapons to armor, alchemical items to masterwork tools, fine wines to trail rations. The equipment presented here should be relatively easy to find and purchase in most towns and cities, although GMs might wish to restrict the availability of some of the more expensive and exotic items. Magic items are much more difficult to purchase (see Chapter 15).

WEALTH AND MONEY

Each character begins play with a number of gold pieces that he can spend on weapons, armor, and other equipment. As a character adventures, he accumulates more wealth that can be spent on better gear and magic items. Table 6–1 lists the starting gold piece values by class. In addition, each character begins play with an outfit worth 10 gp or less. For characters above 1st level, see Table 12–4.

TABLE 6-1: STARTING CHARACTER WEALTH

Class	Starting Wealth	Average
Barbarian	3d6 × 10 gp	105 gp
Bard	3d6 × 10 gp	105 gp
Cleric	4d6 × 10 gp	140 gp
Druid	2d6 × 10 gp	70 gp
Fighter	5d6 × 10 gp	175 gp
Monk	1d6 × 10 gp	35 gp
Paladin	5d6 × 10 gp	175 gp
Ranger	5d6 × 10 gp	175 gp
Rogue	4d6 × 10 gp	140 gp
Sorcerer	2d6 × 10 gp	70 gp
Wizard	2d6 × 10 gp	70 gp

Coins

The most common coin is the gold piece (gp). A gold piece is worth 10 silver pieces (sp). Each silver piece is worth 10 copper pieces (cp). In addition to copper, silver, and gold coins, there are also platinum pieces (pp), which are each worth 10 gp.

The standard coin weighs about a third of an ounce (50 to the pound).

TABLE 6-2: COINS

Exchange Value	cp	sp	gp	pp
Copper piece (cp)	1	1/10	1/100	1/1,000
Silver piece (sp)	10	1	1/10	1/100
Gold piece (gp)	100	10	1	1/10
Platinum piece (pp)	1,000	100	10	1

Other Wealth

Merchants commonly exchange trade goods without using currency. As a means of comparison, some trade goods are detailed on Table 6–3.

TABLE 6-3: TRADE GOODS

Cost	Item
1 cp	One pound of wheat
2 cp	One pound of flour, or one chicken
1 sp	One pound of iron
5 sp	One pound of tobacco or copper
1 gp	One pound of cinnamon, or one goat
2 gp	One pound of ginger or pepper, or one sheep
3 gp	One pig
4 gp	One square yard of linen
5 gp	One pound of salt or silver
10 gp	One square yard of silk, or one cow
15 gp	One pound of saffron or cloves, or one ox
50 gp	One pound of gold
500 gp	One pound of platinum

Selling Treasure

In general, a character can sell something for half its listed price, including weapons, armor, gear, and magic items. This also includes character-created items.

Trade goods are the exception to the half-price rule. A trade good, in this sense, is a valuable good that can be easily exchanged almost as if it were cash itself.

WEAPONS

From the common longsword to the exotic dwarven urgrosh, weapons come in a wide variety of shapes and sizes.

All weapons deal hit point damage. This damage is subtracted from the current hit points of any creature struck by the weapon. When the result of the die roll to make an attack is a natural 20 (that is, the die actually shows a 20), this is known as a critical threat (although some weapons can score a critical threat on a roll of less than 20). If a critical threat is scored, another attack roll is made, using the same modifiers as the original attack roll. If this second attack roll is equal to or greater than the target's AC, the hit becomes a critical hit, dealing additional damage.

Weapons are grouped into several interlocking sets of categories. These categories pertain to what training is needed to become proficient in a weapon's use (simple, martial, or exotic), the weapon's usefulness either in close combat (melee) or at a distance (ranged, which includes both thrown and projectile weapons), its relative encumbrance (light, one-handed, or two-handed), and its size (Small, Medium, or Large).

Simple, Martial, and Exotic Weapons: Anybody but a druid, monk, or wizard is proficient with all simple weapons. Barbarians, fighters, paladins, and rangers are proficient with all simple and all martial weapons. Characters of other classes are proficient with an assortment of simple weapons and possibly some martial or even exotic weapons. All characters are proficient with unarmed strikes and any natural weapons possessed by their race. A character who uses a weapon with which he is not proficient takes a –4 penalty on attack rolls.

Melee and Ranged Weapons: Melee weapons are used for making melee attacks, though some of them can be thrown as well. Ranged weapons are thrown weapons or projectile weapons that are not effective in melee.

Reach Weapons: Glaives, guisarmes, lances, longspears, ranseurs, and whips are reach weapons. A reach weapon is a melee weapon that allows its wielder to strike at targets that aren't adjacent to him. Most reach weapons double the wielder's natural reach, meaning that a typical Small or Medium wielder of such a weapon can attack a creature 10 feet away, but not a creature in an adjacent square. A typical Large character wielding a reach weapon of the appropriate size can attack a creature 15 or 20 feet away, but not adjacent creatures or creatures up to 10 feet away.

Double Weapons: Dire flails, dwarven urgroshes, gnome hooked hammers, orc double axes, quarterstaves, and two-bladed swords are double weapons. A character can fight with both ends of a double weapon as if fighting with two weapons, but he incurs all the normal attack penalties associated with two-weapon combat, just as though the character were wielding a one-handed weapon and a light weapon (see page 202).

The character can also choose to use a double weapon two-handed, attacking with only one end of it. A creature wielding a double weapon in one hand can't use it as a double weapon—only one end of the weapon can be used in any given round.

Thrown Weapons: Daggers, clubs, shortspears, spears, darts, javelins, throwing axes, light hammers, tridents, shuriken, and nets are thrown weapons. The wielder applies his Strength modifier to damage dealt by thrown weapons (except for splash weapons). It is possible to throw a weapon that isn't designed to be thrown (that is, a melee weapon that doesn't have a numeric entry in the Range column on Table 6–4), and a character who does so takes a –4 penalty on the attack roll. Throwing a light or one-handed weapon is a standard action, while throwing a two-handed weapon is a full-round action. Regardless of the type of weapon, such an attack scores a threat only on a natural roll of 20 and deals double damage on a critical hit. Such a weapon has a range increment of 10 feet.

Projectile Weapons: Blowguns, light crossbows, slings, heavy crossbows, shortbows, composite shortbows, longbows, composite longbows, halfling sling staves, hand crossbows, and repeating crossbows are projectile weapons. Most projectile weapons require two hands to use (see specific weapon descriptions). A character gets no Strength bonus on damage rolls with a projectile weapon unless it's a specially built composite shortbow or longbow, or a sling. If the character has a penalty for low Strength, apply it to damage rolls when he uses a bow or a sling.

Ammunition: Projectile weapons use ammunition: arrows (for bows), bolts (for crossbows), darts (for blowguns), or sling bullets (for slings and halfling sling staves). When using a bow, a character can draw ammunition as a free action; crossbows and slings require an action for reloading (as noted in their descriptions). Generally speaking, ammunition that hits its target is destroyed or rendered useless, while ammunition that misses has a 50% chance of being destroyed or lost.

Although they are thrown weapons, shuriken are treated as ammunition for the purposes of drawing them, crafting masterwork or otherwise special versions of them (see Masterwork Weapons on page 149), and what happens to them after they are thrown.

Light, One-Handed, and Two-Handed Melee Weapons: This designation is a measure of how much effort it takes to wield a weapon in combat. It indicates whether a melee weapon, when wielded by a character of the weapon's size category, is considered a light weapon, a one-handed weapon, or a two-handed weapon.

Light: A light weapon is used in one hand. It is easier to use in one's off hand than a one-handed weapon is, and can be used while grappling (see Chapter 8). Add the wielder's Strength modifier to damage rolls for melee attacks with a light weapon if it's used in the primary hand, or half the wielder's Strength bonus if it's used in the off hand. Using two hands to wield a light weapon gives no advantage on damage; the Strength bonus applies as though the weapon were held in the wielder's primary hand only.

An unarmed strike is always considered a light weapon.

One-Handed: A one-handed weapon can be used in either the primary hand or the off hand. Add the wielder's Strength bonus to damage rolls for melee attacks with a one-handed weapon if it's used in the primary hand, or 1/2 his Strength bonus if it's used in the off hand. If a one-handed weapon is wielded with two hands during melee combat, add 1-1/2 times the character's Strength bonus to damage rolls.

Two-Handed: Two hands are required to use a two-handed melee weapon effectively. Apply 1-1/2 times the character's Strength bonus to damage rolls for melee attacks with such a weapon.

Weapon Size: Every weapon has a size category. This designation indicates the size of the creature for which the weapon was designed.

A weapon's size category isn't the same as its size as an object. Instead, a weapon's size category is keyed to the size of the intended wielder. In general, a light weapon is an

TABLE 6-4: WEAPONS

Simple Weapons	Cost	Dmg (S)	Dmg (M)	Critical	Range	Weight[1]	Type[2]	Special
Unarmed Attacks								
Gauntlet	2 gp	1d2	1d3	×2	—	1 lb.	B	—
Unarmed strike	—	1d2	1d3	×2	—	—	B	nonlethal
Light Melee Weapons								
Dagger	2 gp	1d3	1d4	19–20/×2	10 ft.	1 lb.	P or S	—
Dagger, punching	2 gp	1d3	1d4	×3	—	1 lb.	P	—
Gauntlet, spiked	5 gp	1d3	1d4	×2	—	1 lb.	P	—
Mace, light	5 gp	1d4	1d6	×2	—	4 lbs.	B	—
Sickle	6 gp	1d4	1d6	×2	—	2 lbs.	S	trip
One-Handed Melee Weapons								
Club	—	1d4	1d6	×2	10 ft.	3 lbs.	B	—
Mace, heavy	12 gp	1d6	1d8	×2	—	8 lbs.	B	—
Morningstar	8 gp	1d6	1d8	×2	—	6 lbs.	B and P	—
Shortspear	1 gp	1d4	1d6	×2	20 ft.	3 lbs.	P	—
Two-Handed Melee Weapons								
Longspear	5 gp	1d6	1d8	×3	—	9 lbs.	P	brace, reach
Quarterstaff	—	1d4/1d4	1d6/1d6	×2	—	4 lbs.	B	double, monk
Spear	2 gp	1d6	1d8	×3	20 ft.	6 lbs.	P	brace
Ranged Weapons								
Blowgun	2 gp	1	1d2	×2	20 ft.	1 lb.	P	—
Darts, blowgun (10)	5 sp	—	—	—	—	—	—	—
Crossbow, heavy	50 gp	1d8	1d10	19–20/×2	120 ft.	8 lbs.	P	—
Bolts, crossbow (10)	1 gp	—	—	—	—	1 lb.	—	—
Crossbow, light	35 gp	1d6	1d8	19–20/×2	80 ft.	4 lbs.	P	—
Bolts, crossbow (10)	1 gp	—	—	—	—	1 lb.	—	—
Dart	5 sp	1d3	1d4	×2	20 ft.	1/2 lb.	P	—
Javelin	1 gp	1d4	1d6	×2	30 ft.	2 lbs.	P	—
Sling	—	1d3	1d4	×2	50 ft.	—	B	—
Bullets, sling (10)	1 sp	—	—	—	—	5 lbs.	—	—

Martial Weapons	Cost	Dmg (S)	Dmg (M)	Critical	Range	Weight[1]	Type[2]	Special
Light Melee Weapons								
Axe, throwing	8 gp	1d4	1d6	×2	10 ft.	2 lbs.	S	—
Hammer, light	1 gp	1d3	1d4	×2	20 ft.	2 lbs.	B	—
Handaxe	6 gp	1d4	1d6	×3	—	3 lbs.	S	—
Kukri	8 gp	1d3	1d4	18–20/×2	—	2 lbs.	S	—
Pick, light	4 gp	1d3	1d4	×4	—	3 lbs.	P	—
Sap	1 gp	1d4	1d6	×2	—	2 lbs.	B	nonlethal
Shield, light	special	1d2	1d3	×2	—	special	B	—
Spiked armor	special	1d4	1d6	×2	—	special	P	—
Spiked shield, light	special	1d3	1d4	×2	—	special	P	—
Starknife	24 gp	1d3	1d4	×3	20 ft.	3 lbs.	P	—
Sword, short	10 gp	1d4	1d6	19–20/×2	—	2 lbs.	P	—
One-Handed Melee Weapons								
Battleaxe	10 gp	1d6	1d8	×3	—	6 lbs.	S	—
Flail	8 gp	1d6	1d8	×2	—	5 lbs.	B	disarm, trip
Longsword	15 gp	1d6	1d8	19–20/×2	—	4 lbs.	S	—
Pick, heavy	8 gp	1d4	1d6	×4	—	6 lbs.	P	—
Rapier	20 gp	1d4	1d6	18–20/×2	—	2 lbs.	P	—
Scimitar	15 gp	1d4	1d6	18–20/×2	—	4 lbs.	S	—
Shield, heavy	special	1d3	1d4	×2	—	special	B	—
Spiked shield, heavy	special	1d4	1d6	×2	—	special	P	—
Trident	15 gp	1d6	1d8	×2	10 ft.	4 lbs.	P	brace
Warhammer	12 gp	1d6	1d8	×3	—	5 lbs.	B	—

Martial Weapons (cont.)	Cost	Dmg (S)	Dmg (M)	Critical	Range	Weight[1]	Type[2]	Special
Two-Handed Melee Weapons								
Falchion	75 gp	1d6	2d4	18–20/×2	—	8 lbs.	S	—
Glaive	8 gp	1d8	1d10	×3	—	10 lbs.	S	reach
Greataxe	20 gp	1d10	1d12	×3	—	12 lbs.	S	—
Greatclub	5 gp	1d8	1d10	×2	—	8 lbs.	B	—
Flail, heavy	15 gp	1d8	1d10	19–20/×2	—	10 lbs.	B	disarm, trip
Greatsword	50 gp	1d10	2d6	19–20/×2	—	8 lbs.	S	—
Guisarme	9 gp	1d6	2d4	×3	—	12 lbs.	S	reach, trip
Halberd	10 gp	1d8	1d10	×3	—	12 lbs.	P or S	brace, trip
Lance	10 gp	1d6	1d8	×3	—	10 lbs.	P	reach
Ranseur	10 gp	1d6	2d4	×3	—	12 lbs.	P	disarm, reach
Scythe	18 gp	1d6	2d4	×4	—	10 lbs.	P or S	trip
Ranged Weapons								
Longbow	75 gp	1d6	1d8	×3	100 ft.	3 lbs.	P	—
Arrows (20)	1 gp	—	—	—	—	3 lbs.	—	—
Longbow, composite	100 gp	1d6	1d8	×3	110 ft.	3 lbs.	P	—
Arrows (20)	1 gp	—	—	—	—	3 lbs.	—	—
Shortbow	30 gp	1d4	1d6	×3	60 ft.	2 lbs.	P	—
Arrows (20)	1 gp	—	—	—	—	3 lbs.	—	—
Shortbow, composite	75 gp	1d4	1d6	×3	70 ft.	2 lbs.	P	—
Arrows (20)	1 gp	—	—	—	—	3 lbs.	—	—

Exotic Weapons	Cost	Dmg (S)	Dmg (M)	Critical	Range	Weight[1]	Type[2]	Special
Light Melee Weapons								
Kama	2 gp	1d4	1d6	×2	—	2 lbs.	S	monk, trip
Nunchaku	2 gp	1d4	1d6	×2	—	2 lbs.	B	disarm, monk
Sai	1 gp	1d3	1d4	×2	—	1 lb.	B	disarm, monk
Siangham	3 gp	1d4	1d6	×2	—	1 lb.	P	monk
One-Handed Melee Weapons								
Sword, bastard	35 gp	1d8	1d10	19–20/×2	—	6 lbs.	S	—
Waraxe, dwarven	30 gp	1d8	1d10	×3	—	8 lbs.	S	—
Whip	1 gp	1d2	1d3	×2	—	2 lbs.	S	disarm, nonlethal, reach, trip
Two-Handed Melee Weapons								
Axe, orc double	60 gp	1d6/1d6	1d8/1d8	×3	—	15 lbs.	S	double
Chain, spiked	25 gp	1d6	2d4	×2	—	10 lbs.	P	disarm, trip
Curve blade, elven	80 gp	1d8	1d10	18–20/×2	—	7 lbs.	S	—
Flail, dire	90 gp	1d6/1d6	1d8/1d8	×2	—	10 lbs.	B	disarm, double, trip
Hammer, gnome hooked	20 gp	1d6/1d4	1d8/1d6	×3/×4	—	6 lbs.	B or P	double, trip
Sword, two-bladed	100 gp	1d6/1d6	1d8/1d8	19–20/×2	—	10 lbs.	S	double
Urgrosh, dwarven	50 gp	1d6/1d4	1d8/1d6	×3	—	12 lbs.	P or S	brace, double
Ranged Weapons								
Bolas	5 gp	1d3	1d4	×2	10 ft.	2 lbs.	B	nonlethal, trip
Crossbow, hand	100 gp	1d3	1d4	19–20/×2	30 ft.	2 lbs.	P	—
Bolts (10)	1 gp	—	—	—	—	1 lb.	—	—
Crossbow, repeating heavy	400 gp	1d8	1d10	19–20/×2	120 ft.	12 lbs.	P	—
Bolts (5)	1 gp	—	—	—	—	1 lb.	—	—
Crossbow, repeating light	250 gp	1d6	1d8	19–20/×2	80 ft.	6 lbs.	P	—
Bolts (5)	1 gp	—	—	—	—	1 lb.	—	—
Net	20 gp	—	—	—	10 ft.	6 lbs.	—	—
Shuriken (5)	1 gp	1	1d2	×2	10 ft.	1/2 lb.	P	monk
Sling staff, halfling	20 gp	1d6	1d8	×3	80 ft.	3 lbs.	B	—
Bullets, sling (10)	1 sp	—	—	—	—	5 lbs.	—	—

1 Weight figures are for Medium weapons. A Small weapon weighs half as much, and a Large weapon weighs twice as much.

2 A weapon with two types is both types if the entry specifies "and," or either type (wielder's choice) if the entry specifies "or."

object two size categories smaller than the wielder, a one-handed weapon is an object one size category smaller than the wielder, and a two-handed weapon is an object of the same size category as the wielder.

Inappropriately Sized Weapons: A creature can't make optimum use of a weapon that isn't properly sized for it. A cumulative –2 penalty applies on attack rolls for each size category of difference between the size of its intended wielder and the size of its actual wielder. If the creature isn't proficient with the weapon, a –4 nonproficiency penalty also applies.

The measure of how much effort it takes to use a weapon (whether the weapon is designated as a light, one-handed, or two-handed weapon for a particular wielder) is altered by one step for each size category of difference between the wielder's size and the size of the creature for which the weapon was designed. For example, a Small creature would wield a Medium one-handed weapon as a two-handed weapon. If a weapon's designation would be changed to something other than light, one-handed, or two-handed by this alteration, the creature can't wield the weapon at all.

Improvised Weapons: Sometimes objects not crafted to be weapons nonetheless see use in combat. Because such objects are not designed for this use, any creature that uses an improvised weapon in combat is considered to be nonproficient with it and takes a –4 penalty on attack rolls made with that object. To determine the size category and appropriate damage for an improvised weapon, compare its relative size and damage potential to the weapon list to find a reasonable match. An improvised weapon scores a threat on a natural roll of 20 and deals double damage on a critical hit. An improvised thrown weapon has a range increment of 10 feet.

Weapon Qualities

Here is the format for weapon entries (given as column headings on Table 6–4).

Cost: This value is the weapon's cost in gold pieces (gp) or silver pieces (sp). The cost includes miscellaneous gear that goes with the weapon, such as a scabbard or quiver.

This cost is the same for a Small or Medium version of the weapon. A Large version costs twice the listed price.

Dmg: These columns give the damage dealt by the weapon on a successful hit. The column labeled "Dmg (S)" is for Small weapons. The column labeled "Dmg (M)" is for Medium weapons. If two damage ranges are given, then the weapon is a double weapon. Use the second damage figure given for the double weapon's extra attack. Table 6–5 gives weapon damage values for Tiny and Large weapons.

Critical: The entry in this column notes how the weapon is used with the rules for critical hits. When your character scores a critical hit, roll the damage two, three, or four times, as indicated by its critical multiplier (using all applicable modifiers on each roll), and add all the results together.

Extra damage over and above a weapon's normal damage is not multiplied when you score a critical hit.

×2: The weapon deals double damage on a critical hit.

×3: The weapon deals triple damage on a critical hit.

×3/×4: One head of this double weapon deals triple damage on a critical hit. The other head deals quadruple damage on a critical hit.

×4: The weapon deals quadruple damage on a critical hit.

19–20/×2: The weapon scores a threat on a natural roll of 19 or 20 (instead of just 20) and deals double damage on a critical hit.

18–20/×2: The weapon scores a threat on a natural roll of 18, 19, or 20 (instead of just 20) and deals double damage on a critical hit.

Range: Any attack at more than this distance is penalized for range. Beyond this range, the attack takes a cumulative –2 penalty for each full range increment (or fraction thereof) of distance to the target. For example, a dagger (with a range of 10 feet) thrown at a target that is 25 feet away would incur a –4 penalty. A thrown weapon has a maximum range of five range increments. A projectile weapon can shoot to 10 range increments.

Weight: This column gives the weight of a Medium version of the weapon. Halve this number for Small weapons and double it for Large weapons. Some weapons have a special weight. See the weapon's description for details.

Type: Weapons are classified according to the type of damage they deal: B for bludgeoning, P for piercing, or S for slashing. Some monsters may be resistant or immune to attacks from certain types of weapons.

Some weapons deal damage of multiple types. If a weapon causes two types of damage, the type it deals is not half one type and half another; all damage caused is of both types. Therefore, a creature would have to be immune to both types of damage to ignore any of the damage caused by such a weapon.

In other cases, a weapon can deal either of two types of damage. In a situation where the damage type is significant, the wielder can choose which type of damage to deal with such a weapon.

Special: Some weapons have special features in addition to those noted in their descriptions.

Brace: If you use a readied action to set a brace weapon against a charge, you deal double damage on a successful hit against a charging character (see Chapter 8).

Disarm: When you use a disarm weapon, you get a +2 bonus on Combat Maneuver Checks to disarm an enemy.

Double: You can use a double weapon to fight as if fighting with two weapons, but if you do, you incur all the normal attack penalties associated with fighting with two weapons, just as if you were using a one-handed weapon and a light weapon. You can choose to wield one end of a double weapon two-handed, but it cannot be used as a double weapon when wielded in this way—only one end of the weapon can be used in any given round.

Monk: A monk weapon can be used by a monk to perform a flurry of blows (see Chapter 3).

Nonlethal: These weapons deal nonlethal damage (see Chapter 8).

Reach: You use a reach weapon to strike opponents 10 feet away, but you can't use it against an adjacent foe.

Trip: You can use a trip weapon to make trip attacks. If you are tripped during your own trip attempt, you can drop the weapon to avoid being tripped.

Weapon Descriptions

Weapons found on Table 6–4 are described below. Splash weapons are described under Special Substances and Items on page 160.

Arrows: An arrow used as a melee weapon is treated as a light improvised weapon (–4 penalty on attack rolls) and deals damage as a dagger of its size (critical multiplier ×2). Arrows come in a leather quiver that holds 20 arrows.

Axe, Orc Double: A cruel weapon with blades placed at opposite ends of a long haft, an orc double axe is a double weapon.

Blowgun: Blowguns are generally used to deliver debilitating (but rarely fatal) poisons from a distance. They are nearly silent when fired. For a list of appropriate poisons, see page 559.

Bolas: A bolas is a pair of weights, connected by a thin rope or cord. You can use this weapon to make a ranged trip attack against an opponent. You can't be tripped during your own trip attempt when using a bolas.

Bolts: A crossbow bolt used as a melee weapon is treated as a light improvised weapon (–4 penalty on attack rolls) and deals damage as a dagger of its size (crit ×2). Bolts come in a case or quiver that holds 10 bolts (or 5, for a repeating crossbow).

Bullets, Sling: Bullets are shaped metal balls, designed to be used by a sling or halfling sling staff. Bullets come in a leather pouch that holds 10 bullets.

Chain, Spiked: A spiked chain is about 4 feet in length, covered in wicked barbs. You can use the Weapon Finesse feat to apply your Dexterity modifier instead of your Strength modifier to attack rolls with a spiked chain sized for you, even though it isn't a light weapon.

Crossbow, Hand: You can draw a hand crossbow back by hand. Loading a hand crossbow is a move action that provokes attacks of opportunity.

You can shoot, but not load, a hand crossbow with one hand at no penalty. You can shoot a hand crossbow with each hand, but you take a penalty on attack rolls as if attacking with two light weapons (see page 202).

Crossbow, Heavy: You draw a heavy crossbow back by turning a small winch. Loading a heavy crossbow is a full-round action that provokes attacks of opportunity.

TABLE 6-5: TINY AND LARGE WEAPON DAMAGE

Medium Weapon Damage	Tiny Weapon Damage	Large Weapon Damage
1d2	—	1d3
1d3	1	1d4
1d4	1d2	1d6
1d6	1d3	1d8
1d8	1d4	2d6
1d10	1d6	2d8
1d12	1d8	3d6
2d4	1d4	2d6
2d6	1d8	3d6
2d8	1d10	3d8
2d10	2d6	4d8

Normally, operating a heavy crossbow requires two hands. However, you can shoot, but not load, a heavy crossbow with one hand at a –4 penalty on attack rolls. You can shoot a heavy crossbow with each hand, but you take a penalty on attack rolls as if attacking with two one-handed weapons (see page 202). This penalty is cumulative with the penalty for one-handed firing.

Crossbow, Light: You draw a light crossbow back by pulling a lever. Loading a light crossbow is a move action that provokes attacks of opportunity.

Normally, operating a light crossbow requires two hands. However, you can shoot, but not load, a light crossbow with one hand at a –2 penalty on attack rolls. You can shoot a light crossbow with each hand, but you take a penalty on attack rolls as if attacking with two light weapons (see page 202). This penalty is cumulative with the penalty for one-handed firing.

Crossbow, Repeating: The repeating crossbow (whether heavy or light) holds 5 crossbow bolts. As long as it holds bolts, you can reload it by pulling the reloading lever (a free action). Loading a new case of 5 bolts is a full-round action that provokes attacks of opportunity.

You can fire a repeating crossbow with one hand or fire a repeating crossbow in each hand in the same manner as you would a normal crossbow of the same size. However, you must fire the weapon with two hands in order to use the reloading lever, and you must use two hands to load a new case of bolts.

Curve Blade, Elven: Essentially a longer version of a scimitar, but with a thinner blade, the elven curve blade is exceptionally rare. You receive a +2 circumstance bonus to your Combat Maneuver Defense whenever a foe attempts to sunder your elven curve blade due to its flexible metal.

You can use the Weapon Finesse feat to apply your Dexterity modifier instead of your Strength modifier to attack rolls with an elven curve blade sized for you, even though it isn't a light weapon.

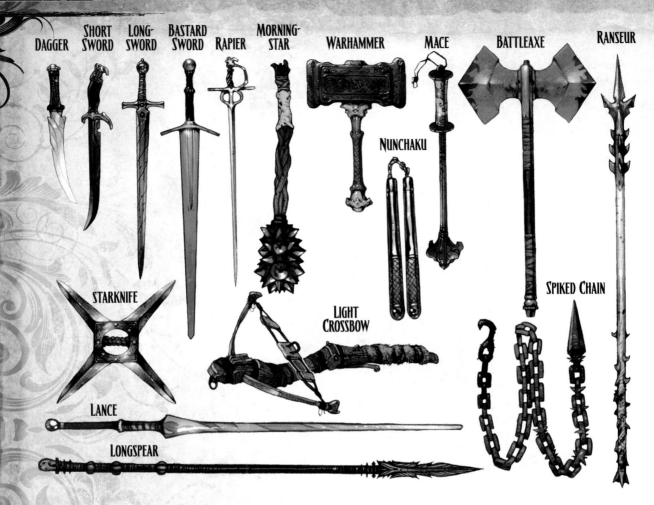

Dagger — Short Sword — Long-sword — Bastard Sword — Rapier — Morning-star — Warhammer — Mace — Battleaxe — Ranseur

Nunchaku

Starknife

Light Crossbow

Spiked Chain

Lance

Longspear

Dagger: A dagger has a blade that is about 1 foot in length. You get a +2 bonus on Sleight of Hand skill checks made to conceal a dagger on your body (see Chapter 4).

Dagger, Punching: A punching dagger's blade is attached to a horizontal handle that projects out from the fist when held.

Flail: A flail consists of a spiked metal ball, connected to a handle by a sturdy chain.

Flail, Dire: A dire flail consists of two spheres of spiked iron dangling from chains at opposite ends of a long haft.

Flail, Heavy: Similar to a flail, a heavy flail has a larger metal ball and a longer handle.

Gauntlet: This metal glove lets you deal lethal damage rather than nonlethal damage with unarmed strikes. A strike with a gauntlet is otherwise considered an unarmed attack. The cost and weight given are for a single gauntlet. Medium and heavy armors (except breastplate) come with gauntlets. Your opponent cannot use a disarm action to disarm you of gauntlets.

Gauntlet, Spiked: The cost and weight given are for a single gauntlet. An attack with a spiked gauntlet is considered an armed attack. Your opponent cannot use a disarm action to disarm you of spiked gauntlets.

Glaive: A glaive is a simple blade, mounted to the end of a pole about 7 feet in length.

Greatsword: This immense two-handed sword is about 5 feet in length.

Guisarme: A guisarme is an 8-foot-long shaft with a blade and a hook mounted at the tip.

Halberd: A halberd is similar to a 5-foot-long spear, but it also has a small, axe-like head mounted near the tip.

Hammer, Gnome Hooked: A gnome hooked hammer is a double weapon—an ingenious tool with a hammer head at one end of its haft and a long, curved pick at the other. The hammer's blunt head is a bludgeoning weapon that deals 1d6 points of damage (crit ×3). Its hook is a piercing weapon that deals 1d4 points of damage (crit ×4). You can use either head as the primary weapon. Gnomes treat hooked hammers as martial weapons.

Javelin: A javelin is a thin throwing spear. Since it is not designed for melee, you are treated as nonproficient with it and take a –4 penalty on attack rolls if you use a javelin as a melee weapon.

Kama: Similar to a sickle, a kama is a short, curved blade attached to a simple handle.

Kukri: A kukri is a curved blade, about 1 foot in length.

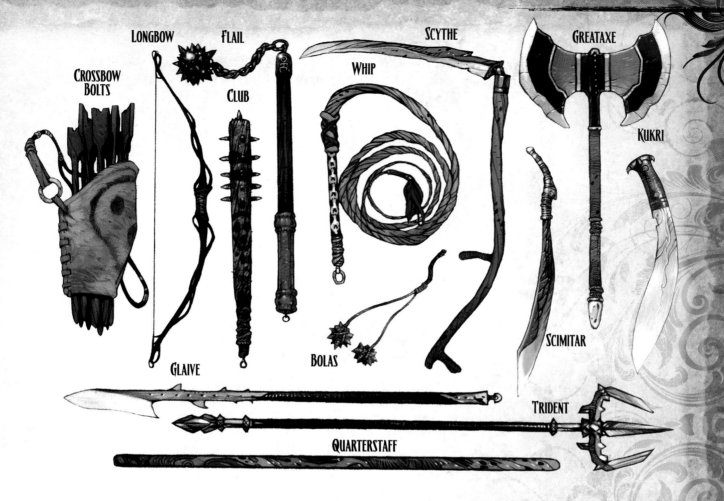

Lance: A lance deals double damage when used from the back of a charging mount. While mounted, you can wield a lance with one hand.

Longbow: At almost 5 feet in height, a longbow is made up of one solid piece of carefully curved wood. You need two hands to use a bow, regardless of its size. A longbow is too unwieldy to use while you are mounted. If you have a penalty for low Strength, apply it to damage rolls when you use a longbow. If you have a Strength bonus, you can apply it to damage rolls when you use a composite longbow (see below), but not when you use a regular longbow.

Longbow, Composite: You need at least two hands to use a bow, regardless of its size. You can use a composite longbow while mounted. All composite bows are made with a particular strength rating (that is, each requires a minimum Strength modifier to use with proficiency). If your Strength bonus is less than the strength rating of the composite bow, you can't effectively use it, so you take a −2 penalty on attacks with it. The default composite longbow requires a Strength modifier of +0 or higher to use with proficiency. A composite longbow can be made with a high strength rating to take advantage of an above-average Strength score; this feature allows you to add your Strength bonus to damage, up to the maximum bonus indicated for the bow. Each point of Strength bonus granted by the bow adds 100 gp to its cost. If you have a penalty for low Strength, apply it to damage rolls when you use a composite longbow.

For purposes of Weapon Proficiency and similar feats, a composite longbow is treated as if it were a longbow.

Longspear: A longspear is about 8 feet in length.

Longsword: This sword is about 3-1/2 feet in length.

Mace, Light: A mace is made up of an ornate metal head attached to a simple wooden or metal shaft.

Mace, Heavy: A heavy mace has a larger head and a longer handle than a normal mace.

Morningstar: A morningstar is a spiked metal ball, affixed to the top of a long handle.

Net: A net is used to entangle enemies. When you throw a net, you make a ranged touch attack against your target. A net's maximum range is 10 feet. If you hit, the target is entangled. An entangled creature takes a −2 penalty on attack rolls and a −4 penalty on Dexterity, can move at only half speed, and cannot charge or run. If you control the trailing rope by succeeding on an opposed Strength check while holding it, the entangled creature can move only within the limits that the rope allows. If the entangled creature attempts to cast a spell, it must make a concentration check with a DC of 15 + the spell's level or be unable to cast the spell.

An entangled creature can escape with a DC 20 Escape Artist check (a full-round action). The net has 5 hit points and can be burst with a DC 25 Strength check (also a full-round action). A net is useful only against creatures within one size category of you.

A net must be folded to be thrown effectively. The first time you throw your net in a fight, you make a normal ranged touch attack roll. After the net is unfolded, you take a –4 penalty on attack rolls with it. It takes 2 rounds for a proficient user to fold a net and twice that long for a nonproficient one to do so.

Nunchaku: A nunchaku is made up of two wooden or metal bars connected by a small length of rope or chain.

Quarterstaff: A quarterstaff is a simple piece of wood, about 5 feet in length.

Ranseur: Similar in appearance to a trident, a ranseur has a single spear at its tip, flanked by a pair of short, curving blades.

Rapier: You can use the Weapon Finesse feat to apply your Dexterity modifier instead of your Strength modifier to attack rolls with a rapier sized for you, even though it isn't a light weapon. You can't wield a rapier in two hands in order to apply 1-1/2 times your Strength bonus to damage.

Sai: A sai is a metal spike flanked by a pair of prongs used to trap an enemy's weapon. With a sai, you get a +2 bonus on Combat Maneuver Checks to sunder an enemy's weapon. Though pointed, a sai is used primarily to bludgeon foes and to disarm weapons.

Shield, Heavy or Light: You can bash with a shield instead of using it for defense. See page 152 for details.

Shortbow: A shortbow is made up of one piece of wood, about 3 feet in length. You need two hands to use a bow, regardless of its size. You can use a shortbow while mounted. If you have a penalty for low Strength, apply it to damage rolls when you use a shortbow. If you have a bonus for high Strength, you can apply it to damage rolls when you use a composite shortbow (see below), but not a regular shortbow.

Shortbow, Composite: You need at least two hands to use a bow, regardless of its size. You can use a composite shortbow while mounted. All composite bows are made with a particular strength rating (that is, each requires a minimum Strength modifier to use with proficiency). If your Strength bonus is lower than the strength rating of the composite bow, you can't effectively use it, so you take a –2 penalty on attacks with it. The default composite shortbow requires a Strength modifier of +0 or higher to use with proficiency. A composite shortbow can be made with a high strength rating to take advantage of an above-average Strength score; this feature allows you to add your Strength bonus to damage, up to the maximum

bonus indicated for the bow. Each point of Strength bonus granted by the bow adds 75 gp to its cost. If you have a penalty for low Strength, apply it to damage rolls when you use a composite shortbow.

For purposes of Weapon Proficiency, Weapon Focus, and similar feats, a composite shortbow is treated as if it were a shortbow.

Shortspear: A shortspear is about 3 feet in length, making it a suitable thrown weapon.

Shortsword: This sword is about 2 feet in length.

Shuriken: A shuriken is a small piece of metal with sharpened edges, designed for throwing. A shuriken can't be used as a melee weapon. Although they are thrown weapons, shuriken are treated as ammunition for the purposes of drawing them, crafting masterwork or otherwise special versions of them, and what happens to them after they are thrown.

Siangham: This weapon is a handheld shaft fitted with a pointed tip for stabbing foes.

Sling: A sling is little more than a leather cup attached to a pair of strings. Your Strength modifier applies to damage rolls when you use a sling, just as it does for thrown weapons. You can fire, but not load, a sling with one hand. Loading a sling is a move action that requires two hands and provokes attacks of opportunity.

You can hurl ordinary stones with a sling, but stones are not as dense or as round as bullets. Thus, such an attack deals damage as if the weapon were designed for a creature one size category smaller than you and you take a –1 penalty on attack rolls.

Sling Staff, Halfling: Made from a specially designed sling attached to a short club, a halfling sling staff can be used by a proficient wielder to devastating effect. Your Strength modifier applies to damage rolls when you use a halfling sling staff, just as it does for thrown weapons. You can fire, but not load, a halfling sling staff with one hand. Loading a halfling sling staff is a move action that requires two hands and provokes attacks of opportunity.

You can hurl ordinary stones with a halfling sling staff, but stones are not as dense or as round as bullets. Thus, such an attack deals damage as if the weapon were designed for a creature one size category smaller than you and you take a –1 penalty on attack rolls.

A halfling sling staff can be used as a simple weapon that deals bludgeoning damage equal to that of a club of its size. Halflings treat halfling sling staves as martial weapons.

Spear: A spear is 5 feet in length and can be thrown.

Spiked Armor: You can outfit your armor with spikes, which can deal damage in a grapple or as a separate attack. See Armor, below, for details.

Spiked Shield, Heavy or Light: You can bash with a spiked shield instead of using it for defense. See page 152 for details.

Starknife: From a central metal ring, four tapering metal blades extend like points on a compass rose. A wielder can stab with the starknife or throw it.

Strike, Unarmed: A Medium character deals 1d3 points of nonlethal damage with an unarmed strike. A Small character deals 1d2 points of nonlethal damage. A monk or any character with the Improved Unarmed Strike feat can deal lethal or nonlethal damage with unarmed strikes, at his discretion. The damage from an unarmed strike is considered weapon damage for the purposes of effects that give you a bonus on weapon damage rolls.

An unarmed strike is always considered a light weapon. Therefore, you can use the Weapon Finesse feat to apply your Dexterity modifier instead of your Strength modifier to attack rolls with an unarmed strike. Unarmed strikes do not count as natural weapons (see Chapter 8).

Sword, Bastard: A bastard sword is about 4 feet in length, making it too large to use in one hand without special training; thus, it is an exotic weapon. A character can use a bastard sword two-handed as a martial weapon.

Sword, Two-Bladed: A two-bladed sword is a double weapon—twin blades extend from either side of a central, short haft, allowing the wielder to attack with graceful but deadly flourishes.

Trident: A trident has three metal prongs at end of a 4-foot-long shaft. This weapon can be thrown.

Urgrosh, Dwarven: A dwarven urgrosh is a double weapon—an axe head and a spear point on opposite ends of a long haft. The urgrosh's axe head is a slashing weapon that deals 1d8 points of damage. Its spear head is a piercing weapon that deals 1d6 points of damage. You can use either head as the primary weapon. The other becomes the off-hand weapon. If you use an urgrosh against a charging character, the spear head is the part of the weapon that deals damage. Dwarves treat dwarven urgroshes as martial weapons.

Waraxe, Dwarven: A dwarven waraxe has a large, ornate head mounted to a thick handle, making it too large to use in one hand without special training; thus, it is an exotic weapon. A Medium character can use a dwarven waraxe two-handed as a martial weapon, or a Large creature can use it one-handed in the same way. A dwarf treats a dwarven waraxe as a martial weapon even when using it in one hand.

Whip: A whip deals no damage to any creature with an armor bonus of +1 or higher or a natural armor bonus of +3 or higher. The whip is treated as a melee weapon with 15-foot reach, though you don't threaten the area into which you can make an attack. In addition, unlike most other weapons with reach, you can use it against foes anywhere within your reach (including adjacent foes).

Using a whip provokes an attack of opportunity, just as if you had used a ranged weapon.

You can use the Weapon Finesse feat to apply your Dexterity modifier instead of your Strength modifier to attack rolls with a whip sized for you, even though it isn't a light weapon.

Masterwork Weapons

A masterwork weapon is a finely crafted version of a normal weapon. Wielding it provides a +1 enhancement bonus on attack rolls.

You can't add the masterwork quality to a weapon after it is created; it must be crafted as a masterwork weapon (see the Craft skill). The masterwork quality adds 300 gp to the cost of a normal weapon (or 6 gp to the cost of a single unit of ammunition). Adding the masterwork quality to a double weapon costs twice the normal increase (+600 gp).

Masterwork ammunition is damaged (effectively destroyed) when used. The enhancement bonus of masterwork ammunition does not stack with any enhancement bonus of the projectile weapon firing it.

All magic weapons are automatically considered to be of masterwork quality. The enhancement bonus granted by the masterwork quality doesn't stack with the enhancement bonus provided by the weapon's magic.

Even though some types of armor and shields can be used as weapons, you can't create a masterwork version of such an item that confers an enhancement bonus on attack rolls. Instead, masterwork armor and shields have lessened armor check penalties.

ARMOR

For most, armor is the simplest way to protect oneself in a world of rampant threats and dangers. Many characters can wear only the simplest of armors, and only some can use shields. To wear heavier armor effectively, a character can select the Armor Proficiency feats, but most classes are automatically proficient with the armors that work best for them.

Here is the format for armor entries (given as column headings on Table 6–6).

Cost: The cost in gold pieces of the armor for Small or Medium humanoid creatures. See Table 6–8 for armor prices for other creatures.

Armor/Shield Bonus: Each type of armor grants an armor bonus to AC, while shields grant a shield bonus to AC. The armor bonus from a suit of armor doesn't stack with other effects or items that grant an armor bonus. Similarly, the shield bonus from a shield doesn't stack with other effects that grant a shield bonus.

Maximum Dex Bonus: This number is the maximum Dexterity bonus to AC that this type of armor allows. Dexterity bonuses in excess of this number are reduced to this number for the purposes of determining the wearer's AC. Heavier armors limit mobility, reducing the wearer's ability to dodge blows. This restriction doesn't affect any other Dexterity-related abilities.

Even if a character's Dexterity bonus to AC drops to 0 because of armor, this situation does not count as losing his Dexterity bonus to AC.

A character's encumbrance (the amount of gear carried, including armor) may also restrict the maximum Dexterity bonus that can be applied to his Armor Class.

Shields: Shields do not affect a character's maximum Dexterity bonus, except for tower shields.

Armor Check Penalty: Any armor heavier than leather, as well as any shield, hurts a character's ability to use Dexterity- and Strength-based skills. An armor check penalty applies to all Dexterity- and Strength-based skill checks. A character's encumbrance may also incur an armor check penalty.

Shields: If a character is wearing armor and using a shield, both armor check penalties apply.

Nonproficient with Armor Worn: A character who wears armor and/or uses a shield with which he is not proficient takes the armor's (and/or shield's) armor check penalty on attack rolls as well as on all Dexterity- and Strength-based ability and skill checks. The penalty for nonproficiency with armor stacks with the penalty for shields.

Sleeping in Armor: A character who sleeps in medium or heavy armor is automatically fatigued the next day. He takes a –2 penalty on Strength and Dexterity and can't charge or run. Sleeping in light armor does not cause fatigue.

Arcane Spell Failure Chance: Armor interferes with the gestures that a spellcaster must make to cast an arcane spell that has a somatic component. Arcane spellcasters face the possibility of arcane spell failure if they're wearing armor. Bards can wear light armor and use shields without incurring any arcane spell failure chance for their bard spells.

Casting an Arcane Spell in Armor: A character who casts an arcane spell while wearing armor must usually make an arcane spell failure check. The number in the Arcane Spell Failure Chance column on Table 6–6 is the percentage chance that the spell fails and is ruined. If the spell lacks a somatic component, however, it can be cast with no chance of arcane spell failure.

Shields: If a character is wearing armor and using a shield, add the two numbers together to get a single arcane spell failure chance.

Speed: Medium or heavy armor slows the wearer down. The number on Table 6–6 is the character's speed while wearing the armor. Humans, elves, half-elves, and half-orcs have an unencumbered speed of 30 feet. They use the first column. Dwarves, gnomes, and halflings have an unencumbered speed of 20 feet. They use the second column. Remember, however, that a dwarf's land speed remains 20 feet even in medium or heavy armor or when carrying a medium or heavy load.

Shields: Shields do not affect a character's speed.

Weight: This column gives the weight of the armor sized for a Medium wearer. Armor fitted for Small characters weighs half as much, and armor for Large characters weighs twice as much.

Armor Descriptions

Any special benefits or accessories to the types of armor found on Table 6–6 are described below.

Armor Spikes: You can have spikes added to your armor, which allow you to deal extra piercing damage (see "spiked armor" on Table 6–4) on a successful grapple attack. The spikes count as a martial weapon. If you are not proficient with them, you take a –4 penalty on grapple checks when you try to use them. You can also make a regular melee attack (or off-hand attack) with the spikes, and they count as a light weapon in this case. (You can't also make an attack with armor spikes if you have already made an attack with another off-hand weapon, and vice versa.) An enhancement bonus to a suit of armor does not improve the spikes' effectiveness, but the spikes can be made into magic weapons in their own right.

Banded Mail: Banded mail is made up of overlapping strips of metal, fastened to a leather backing. The suit includes gauntlets.

Breastplate: Covering only the torso, a breastplate is made up of a single piece of sculpted metal.

Buckler: This small metal shield is worn strapped to your forearm. You can use a bow or crossbow without penalty while carrying it. You can also use your shield arm to wield a weapon (whether you are using an off-hand weapon or using your off hand to help wield a two-handed weapon), but you take a –1 penalty on attack rolls while doing so. This penalty stacks with those that may apply for fighting with your off hand and for fighting with two weapons. In any case, if you use a weapon in your off hand, you lose the buckler's AC bonus until your next turn. You can cast a spell with somatic components using your shield arm, but you lose the buckler's AC bonus until your next turn. You can't make a shield bash with a buckler.

Chain Shirt: Covering the torso, this shirt is made up of thousands of interlocking metal rings.

Chainmail: Unlike a chain shirt, chainmail covers the legs and arms of the wearer. The suit includes gauntlets.

Full Plate: This metal suit includes gauntlets, heavy leather boots, a visored helmet, and a thick layer of padding that is worn underneath the armor. Each suit of full plate must be individually fitted to its owner by a master armorsmith, although a captured suit can be resized to fit a new owner at a cost of 200 to 800 (2d4 × 100) gold pieces.

Gauntlet, Locked: This armored gauntlet has small chains and braces that allow the wearer to attach a weapon to the gauntlet so that it cannot be dropped easily.

TABLE 6-6: ARMOR AND SHIELDS

Armor	Cost	Armor/Shield Bonus	Maximum Dex Bonus	Armor Check Penalty	Arcane Spell Failure Chance	Speed 30 ft.	Speed 20 ft.	Weight[1]
Light armor								
Padded	5 gp	+1	+8	0	5%	30 ft.	20 ft.	10 lbs.
Leather	10 gp	+2	+6	0	10%	30 ft.	20 ft.	15 lbs.
Studded leather	25 gp	+3	+5	−1	15%	30 ft.	20 ft.	20 lbs.
Chain shirt	100 gp	+4	+4	−2	20%	30 ft.	20 ft.	25 lbs.
Medium armor								
Hide	15 gp	+4	+4	−3	20%	20 ft.	15 ft.	25 lbs.
Scale mail	50 gp	+5	+3	−4	25%	20 ft.	15 ft.	30 lbs.
Chainmail	150 gp	+6	+2	−5	30%	20 ft.	15 ft.	40 lbs.
Breastplate	200 gp	+6	+3	−4	25%	20 ft.	15 ft.	30 lbs.
Heavy armor								
Splint mail	200 gp	+7	+0	−7	40%	20 ft.[2]	15 ft.[2]	45 lbs.
Banded mail	250 gp	+7	+1	−6	35%	20 ft.[2]	15 ft.[2]	35 lbs.
Half-plate	600 gp	+8	+0	−7	40%	20 ft.[2]	15 ft.[2]	50 lbs.
Full plate	1,500 gp	+9	+1	−6	35%	20 ft.[2]	15 ft.[2]	50 lbs.
Shields								
Buckler	5 gp	+1	—	−1	5%	—	—	5 lbs.
Shield, light wooden	3 gp	+1	—	−1	5%	—	—	5 lbs.
Shield, light steel	9 gp	+1	—	−1	5%	—	—	6 lbs.
Shield, heavy wooden	7 gp	+2	—	−2	15%	—	—	10 lbs.
Shield, heavy steel	20 gp	+2	—	−2	15%	—	—	15 lbs.
Shield, tower	30 gp	+4[3]	+2	−10	50%	—	—	45 lbs.
Extras								
Armor spikes	+50 gp	—	—	—	—	—	—	+10 lbs.
Gauntlet, locked	8 gp	—	—	special	n/a[4]	—	—	+5 lbs.
Shield spikes	+10 gp	—	—	—	—	—	—	+5 lbs.

1 Weight figures are for armor sized to fit Medium characters. Armor fitted for Small characters weighs half as much, and armor fitted for Large characters weighs twice as much.

2 When running in heavy armor, you move only triple your speed, not quadruple.

3 A tower shield can instead grant you cover. See the description.

4 Hand not free to cast spells.

It provides a +10 bonus to your Combat Maneuver Defense to keep from being disarmed in combat. Removing a weapon from a locked gauntlet or attaching a weapon to a locked gauntlet is a full-round action that provokes attacks of opportunity.

The price given is for a single locked gauntlet. The weight given applies only if you're wearing a breastplate, light armor, or no armor. Otherwise, the locked gauntlet replaces a gauntlet you already have as part of the armor.

While the gauntlet is locked, you can't use the hand wearing it for casting spells or employing skills. (You can still cast spells with somatic components, provided that your other hand is free.)

Like a normal gauntlet, a locked gauntlet lets you deal lethal damage rather than nonlethal damage with an unarmed strike.

Half-Plate: Combining elements of full plate and chainmail, half-plate includes gauntlets and a helm.

Hide: Hide armor is made up of the tanned and preserved skin of any thick-hided beast.

Leather: Leather armor is made up of pieces of hard boiled leather carefully sewn together.

Padded: Little more than heavy, quilted cloth, this armor provides only the most basic protection.

Scale Mail: Scale mail is made up of dozens of small overlapping metal plates. The suit includes gauntlets.

Shield, Heavy; Wooden or Steel: You strap a shield to your forearm and grip it with your hand. A heavy shield is so heavy that you can't use your shield hand for anything else.

Wooden or Steel: Wooden and steel shields offer the same basic protection, though they respond differently to spells and effects.

PADDED ARMOR	LEATHER ARMOR	STUDDED LEATHER	CHAIN SHIRT	HIDE ARMOR
SCALE MAIL	CHAINMAIL	BREASTPLATE	SPLINT MAIL	BANDED MAIL
FULL PLATE	HALF-PLATE	BUCKLER	STEEL SHIELD	TOWER SHIELD

Shield Bash Attacks: You can bash an opponent with a heavy shield. See "shield, heavy" on Table 6–4 for the damage dealt by a shield bash. Used this way, a heavy shield is a martial bludgeoning weapon. For the purpose of penalties on attack rolls, treat a heavy shield as a one-handed weapon. If you use your shield as a weapon, you lose its AC bonus until your next turn. An enhancement bonus on a shield does not improve the effectiveness of a shield bash made with it, but the shield can be made into a magic weapon in its own right.

Shield, Light; Wooden or Steel: You strap a shield to your forearm and grip it with your hand. A light shield's weight lets you carry other items in that hand, although you cannot use weapons with it.

Wooden or Steel: Wooden and steel shields offer the same basic protection, though they respond differently to some spells and effects.

Shield Bash Attacks: You can bash an opponent with a light shield. See "shield, light" on Table 6–4 for the damage dealt by a shield bash. Used this way, a light shield is a martial bludgeoning weapon. For the purpose of penalties on attack rolls, treat a light shield as a light weapon. If you use your shield as a weapon, you lose its AC bonus until your next turn. An enhancement bonus on a shield does not improve the effectiveness of a shield bash made with it, but the shield can be made into a magic weapon in its own right.

TABLE 6-7: DONNING ARMOR

Armor Type	Don	Don Hastily	Remove
Shield (any)	1 move action	n/a	1 move action
Padded, leather, hide, studded leather, or chain shirt	1 minute	5 rounds	1 minute[1]
Breastplate, scale mail, chainmail, banded mail, or splint mail	4 minutes[1]	1 minute	1 minute[1]
Half-plate or full plate	4 minutes[2]	4 minutes[1]	1d4+1 minutes[1]

1 If the character has some help, cut this time in half. A single character doing nothing else can help one or two adjacent characters. Two characters can't help each other don armor at the same time.

2 The wearer must have help to don this armor. Without help, it can be donned only hastily.

Shield, Tower: This massive wooden shield is nearly as tall as you are. In most situations, it provides the indicated shield bonus to your AC. As a standard action, however, you can use a tower shield to grant you total cover until the beginning of your next turn. When using a tower shield in this way, you must choose one edge of your space. That edge is treated as a solid wall for attacks targeting you only. You gain total cover for attacks that pass through this edge and no cover for attacks that do not pass through this edge (see Chapter 8). The shield does not, however, provide cover against targeted spells; a spellcaster can cast a spell on you by targeting the shield you are holding. You cannot bash with a tower shield, nor can you use your shield hand for anything else.

When employing a tower shield in combat, you take a –2 penalty on attack rolls because of the shield's encumbrance.

Shield Spikes: These spikes turn a shield into a martial piercing weapon and increase the damage dealt by a shield bash as if the shield were designed for a creature one size category larger than you (see "spiked shields" on Table 6–4). You can't put spikes on a buckler or a tower shield. Otherwise, attacking with a spiked shield is like making a shield bash attack.

An enhancement bonus on a spiked shield does not improve the effectiveness of a shield bash made with it, but a spiked shield can be made into a magic weapon in its own right.

Splint Mail: Splint mail is made up of metal strips, like banded mail. The suit includes gauntlets.

Studded Leather: Similar to leather armor, this suit is reinforced with small metal studs.

Masterwork Armor

Just as with weapons, you can purchase or craft masterwork versions of armor or shields. Such a well-made item functions like the normal version, except that its armor check penalty is lessened by 1.

A masterwork suit of armor or shield costs an extra 150 gp over and above the normal cost for that type of armor or shield.

TABLE 6-8: ARMOR FOR UNUSUAL CREATURES

Size	Humanoid		Nonhumanoid	
	Cost	Weight	Cost	Weight
Tiny or smaller*	×1/2	×1/10	×1	×1/10
Small	×1	×1/2	×2	×1/2
Medium	×1	×1	×2	×1
Large	×2	×2	×4	×2
Huge	×4	×5	×8	×5
Gargantuan	×8	×8	×16	×8
Colossal	×16	×12	×32	×12

*Divide armor bonus by 2.

The masterwork quality of a suit of armor or shield never provides a bonus on attack or damage rolls, even if the armor or shield is used as a weapon.

All magic armors and shields are automatically considered to be of masterwork quality.

You can't add the masterwork quality to armor or a shield after it is created; it must be crafted as a masterwork item.

Armor for Unusual Creatures

Armor and shields for unusually big creatures, unusually little creatures, and nonhumanoid creatures (such as horses) have different costs and weights from those given on Table 6–6. Refer to the appropriate line on Table 6–8 and apply the multipliers to cost and weight for the armor type in question.

Getting Into and Out of Armor

The time required to don armor depends on its type; see Table 6–7.

Don: This column tells how long it takes a character to put the armor on. (One minute is 10 rounds.) Readying (strapping on) a shield is only a move action.

Don Hastily: This column tells how long it takes to put the armor on in a hurry. The armor check penalty and armor bonus for hastily donned armor are each 1 point worse than normal.

Remove: This column tells how long it takes to get the armor off. Removing a shield from the arm and dropping it is only a move action.

SPECIAL MATERIALS

Weapons and armor can be crafted using materials that possess innate special properties. If you make a suit of armor or weapon out of more than one special material, you get the benefit of only the most prevalent material. However, you can build a double weapon with each head made of a different special material.

Each of the special materials described below has a definite game effect. Some creatures have damage reduction making them resistant to all but a special type of damage, such as that dealt by evil-aligned weapons or bludgeoning weapons. Others are vulnerable to weapons of a particular material. Characters may choose to carry several different types of weapons, depending upon the types of creatures they most commonly encounter.

Adamantine: Mined from rocks that fell from the heavens, this ultrahard metal adds to the quality of a weapon or suit of armor. Weapons fashioned from adamantine have a natural ability to bypass hardness when sundering weapons or attacking objects, ignoring hardness less than 20 (see Chapter 7). Armor made from adamantine grants its wearer damage reduction of 1/— if it's light armor, 2/— if it's medium armor, and 3/— if it's heavy armor. Adamantine is so costly that weapons and armor made from it are always of masterwork quality; the masterwork cost is included in the prices given below. Thus, adamantine weapons and ammunition have a +1 enhancement bonus on attack rolls, and the armor check penalty of adamantine armor is lessened by 1 compared to ordinary armor of its type. Items without metal parts cannot be made from adamantine. An arrow could be made of adamantine, but a quarterstaff could not.

Weapons and armor normally made of steel that are made of adamantine have one-third more hit points than normal. Adamantine has 40 hit points per inch of thickness and hardness 20.

Type of Adamantine Item	Item Cost Modifier
Ammunition	+60 gp per missile
Light armor	+5,000 gp
Medium armor	+10,000 gp
Heavy armor	+15,000 gp
Weapon	+3,000 gp

Darkwood: This rare magic wood is as hard as normal wood but very light. Any wooden or mostly wooden item (such as a bow or spear) made from darkwood is considered a masterwork item and weighs half as much as a normal wooden item of that type. Items not normally made of wood or only partially of (such as a battleaxe or a mace) either cannot be made from darkwood or do not gain any special benefit from being made of darkwood. The armor check penalty of a darkwood shield is lessened by 2 compared to

an ordinary shield of its type. To determine the price of a darkwood item, use the original weight but add 10 gp per pound to the price of a masterwork version of that item.

Darkwood has 10 hit points per inch of thickness and hardness 5.

Dragonhide: Armorsmiths can work with the hides of dragons to produce armor or shields of masterwork quality. One dragon produces enough hide for a single suit of masterwork hide armor for a creature one size category smaller than the dragon. By selecting only choice scales and bits of hide, an armorsmith can produce one suit of masterwork banded mail for a creature two sizes smaller, one suit of masterwork half-plate for a creature three sizes smaller, or one masterwork breastplate or suit of full plate for a creature four sizes smaller. In each case, enough hide is available to produce a light or heavy masterwork shield in addition to the armor, provided that the dragon is Large or larger. If the dragonhide comes from a dragon that had immunity to an energy type, the armor is also immune to that energy type, although this does not confer any protection to the wearer. If the armor or shield is later given the ability to protect the wearer against that energy type, the cost to add such protection is reduced by 25%.

Because dragonhide armor isn't made of metal, druids can wear it without penalty.

Dragonhide armor costs twice as much as masterwork armor of that type, but it takes no longer to make than ordinary armor of that type (double all Craft results).

Dragonhide has 10 hit points per inch of thickness and hardness 10. The hide of a dragon is typically between 1/2 inch and 1 inch thick.

Iron, Cold: This iron, mined deep underground and known for its effectiveness against demons and fey creatures, is forged at a lower temperature to preserve its delicate properties. Weapons made of cold iron cost twice as much to make as their normal counterparts (not counting masterwork costs). Also, adding any magical enhancements to a cold iron weapon increases its price by 2,000 gp. This increase is applied the first time the item is enhanced, not once per ability added.

Items without metal parts cannot be made from cold iron. An arrow could be made of cold iron, but a quarterstaff could not. A double weapon with one cold iron half costs 50% more than normal.

Cold iron has 30 hit points per inch of thickness and hardness 10.

Mithral: Mithral is a very rare silvery, glistening metal that is lighter than steel but just as hard. When worked like steel, it becomes a wonderful material from which to create armor, and is occasionally used for other items as well. Most mithral armors are one category lighter than normal for purposes of movement and other limitations. Heavy armors are treated as medium, and medium armors are treated as light, but light armors are still treated as light. This decrease does not apply to proficiency in wearing the armor. A character wearing mithral full plate must be proficient in wearing heavy armor to avoid adding the armor's check penalty to all his attack rolls and skill checks that involve moving. Spell failure chances for armors and shields made from mithral are decreased by 10%, maximum Dexterity bonuses are increased by 2, and armor check penalties are decreased by 3 (to a minimum of 0).

An item made from mithral weighs half as much as the same item made from other metals. In the case of weapons, this lighter weight does not change a weapon's size category or the ease with which it can be wielded (whether it is light, one-handed, or two-handed). Items not primarily of metal are not meaningfully affected by being partially made of mithral. (A longsword can be a mithral weapon, while a quarterstaff cannot.) Mithral weapons count as silver for the purpose of overcoming damage reduction.

Weapons or armors fashioned from mithral are always masterwork items as well; the masterwork cost is included in the prices given below.

Mithral has 30 hit points per inch of thickness and hardness 15.

Type of Mithral Item	Item Cost Modifier
Light armor	+1,000 gp
Medium armor	+4,000 gp
Heavy armor	+9,000 gp
Shield	+1,000 gp
Other items	+500 gp/lb.

Silver, Alchemical: A complex process involving metallurgy and alchemy can bond silver to a weapon made of steel so that it bypasses the damage reduction of creatures such as lycanthropes.

On a successful attack with a silvered slashing or piercing weapon, the wielder takes a –1 penalty on the damage roll (with a minimum of 1 point of damage). The alchemical silvering process can't be applied to nonmetal items, and it doesn't work on rare metals such as adamantine, cold iron, and mithral.

Alchemical silver has 10 hit points per inch of thickness and hardness 8.

Type of Alchemical Silver Item	Item Cost Modifier
Ammunition	+2 gp
Light weapon	+20 gp
One-handed weapon, or one head of a double weapon	+90 gp
Two-handed weapon, or both heads of a double weapon	+180 gp

GOODS AND SERVICES

Beyond armor and weapons, a character can carry a whole variety of gear, from rations (to sustain him on long travels), to rope (which is useful in countless circumstances). Most of the common gear carried by adventurers is summarized on Table 6–9.

Adventuring Gear

Some of the pieces of adventuring gear found on Table 6–9 are described below, along with any special benefits they confer on the user ("you").

Caltrops: A caltrop is a four-pronged metal spike crafted so that one prong faces up no matter how the caltrop comes to rest. You scatter caltrops on the ground in the hope that your enemies step on them or are at least forced to slow down to avoid them. One 2-pound bag of caltrops covers an area 5 feet square.

Each time a creature moves into an area covered by caltrops (or spends a round fighting while standing in such an area), it runs the risk of stepping on one. Make an attack roll for the caltrops (base attack bonus +0) against the creature. For this attack, the creature's shield, armor, and deflection bonuses do not count. If the creature is wearing shoes or other footwear, it gets a +2 armor bonus to AC. If the attack succeeds, the creature has stepped on a caltrop. The caltrop deals 1 point of damage, and the creature's speed is reduced by half because its foot is wounded. This movement penalty lasts for 24 hours, until the creature is successfully treated with a DC 15 Heal check, or until it receives at least 1 point of magical healing. A charging or running creature must immediately stop if it steps on a caltrop. Any creature moving at half speed or slower can pick its way through a bed of caltrops with no trouble.

Caltrops may not work against unusual opponents.

Candle: A candle dimly illuminates a small area, increasing the light level (see page 172) in a 5-foot radius by one step (darkness becomes dim light and dim light becomes normal light). A candle cannot increase the light level above normal light. A candle burns for 1 hour.

Chain: Chain has hardness 10 and 5 hit points. It can be burst with a DC 26 Strength check.

Crowbar: A crowbar grants a +2 circumstance bonus on Strength checks made to force open a door or chest. If used in combat, treat a crowbar as a one-handed improvised weapon that deals bludgeoning damage equal to that of a club of its size.

Flint and Steel: Lighting a torch with flint and steel is a full-round action, and lighting any other fire with them takes at least that long.

Grappling Hook: Throwing a grappling hook requires a ranged attack roll, treating the hook as a thrown weapon with a range increment of 10 feet. Objects with ample places to catch the hook are AC 5.

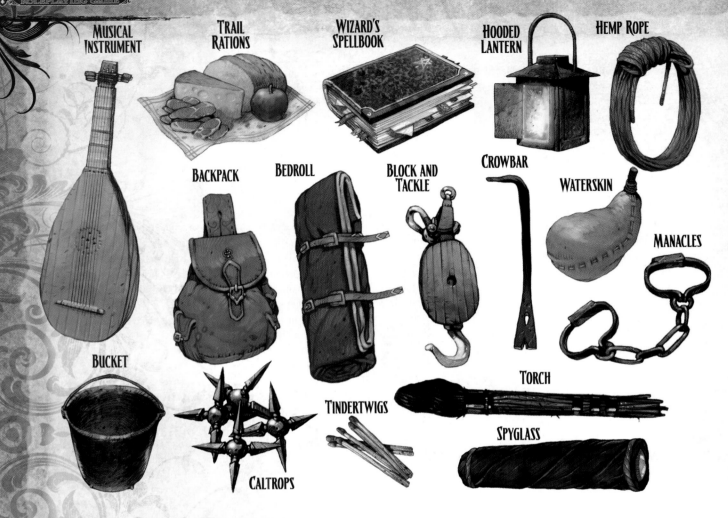

MUSICAL INSTRUMENT

TRAIL RATIONS

WIZARD'S SPELLBOOK

HOODED LANTERN

HEMP ROPE

BACKPACK

BEDROLL

BLOCK AND TACKLE

CROWBAR

WATERSKIN

MANACLES

BUCKET

TORCH

TINDERTWIGS

SPYGLASS

CALTROPS

Hammer: If a hammer is used in combat, treat it as a one-handed improvised weapon that deals bludgeoning damage equal to that of a spiked gauntlet of its size.

Ink: Ink in colors other than black costs twice as much.

Jug, Clay: This basic jug is fitted with a stopper and holds 1 gallon of liquid.

Lamp, Common: A lamp illuminates a small area, providing normal light in a 15-foot radius and increasing the light level (see page 172) by one step for an additional 15 feet beyond that area (darkness becomes dim light and dim light becomes normal light). A lamp does not increase the light level in normal light or bright light. A lamp burns for 6 hours on one pint of oil. You can carry a lamp in one hand.

Lantern, Bullseye: A bullseye lantern provides normal light in a 60-foot cone and increases the light level (see page 172) by one step in the area beyond that, out to a 120-foot cone (darkness becomes dim light and dim light becomes normal light). A bullseye lantern does not increase the light level in normal light or bright light. A lantern burns for 6 hours on one pint of oil. You can carry a lantern in one hand.

Lantern, Hooded: A hooded lantern sheds normal light in a 30-foot radius and increases the light level (see page 172) by one step for an additional 30 feet beyond that area (darkness becomes dim light and dim light becomes normal light). A hooded lantern does not increase the light level in normal light or bright light. A lantern burns for 6 hours on one pint of oil. You can carry a lantern in one hand.

Lock: The DC to open a lock with the Disable Device skill depends on the lock's quality: simple (DC 20), average (DC 25), good (DC 30), or superior (DC 40).

Manacles, Standard and Masterwork: Manacles can bind a Medium creature. A manacled creature can use the Escape Artist skill to slip free (DC 30, or DC 35 for masterwork manacles). Breaking the manacles requires a Strength check (DC 26, or DC 28 for masterwork manacles). Manacles have hardness 10 and 10 hit points.

Most manacles have locks; add the cost of the lock you want to the cost of the manacles.

For the same cost, you can buy manacles for a Small creature. For a Large creature, manacles cost 10 times the indicated amount, and for a Huge creature, 100 times the indicated

amount. Gargantuan, Colossal, Tiny, Diminutive, and Fine creatures can be held only by specially made manacles, which cost at least 100 times the indicated amount.

Oil: A pint of oil burns for 6 hours in a lantern or lamp. You can also use a flask of oil as a splash weapon. Use the rules for alchemist's fire (see Special Substances and Items on Table 6–9), except that it takes a full-round action to prepare a flask with a fuse. Once it is thrown, there is a 50% chance of the flask igniting successfully.

You can pour a pint of oil on the ground to cover an area 5 feet square, provided that the surface is smooth. If lit, the oil burns for 2 rounds and deals 1d3 points of fire damage to each creature in the area.

Pick, Miner's: If a miner's pick is used in combat, treat it as a two-handed improvised weapon that deals piercing damage equal to that of a heavy pick of its size.

Ram, Portable: This iron-shod wooden beam gives you a +2 circumstance bonus on Strength checks made to break open a door and allows a second person to help, automatically increasing your bonus by 2.

Rope, Hemp: This rope has 2 hit points and can be burst with a DC 23 Strength check.

Rope, Silk: This rope has 4 hit points and can be burst with a DC 24 Strength check.

Shovel: If a shovel is used in combat, treat it as a one-handed improvised weapon that deals bludgeoning damage equal to that of a club of its size.

Spyglass: Objects viewed through a spyglass are magnified to twice their size. Characters using a spyglass take a –1 penalty on Perception skill checks per 20 feet of distance to the target, if the target is visible.

Torch: A torch burns for 1 hour, shedding normal light in a 20-foot radius and increasing the light level by one step for an additional 20 feet beyond that area (darkness becomes dim light and dim light becomes normal light). A torch does not increase the light level in normal light or bright light. If a torch is used in combat, treat it as a one-handed improvised weapon that deals bludgeoning damage equal to that of a gauntlet of its size, plus 1 point of fire damage.

Vial: A vial is made out of glass or steel and holds 1 ounce of liquid.

Water Clock: This large, bulky contrivance gives the time accurately to within half an hour per day since it

TABLE 6-9: GOODS AND SERVICES

Adventuring Gear

Item	Cost	Weight
Backpack (empty)	2 gp	2 lbs.[1]
Barrel (empty)	2 gp	30 lbs.
Basket (empty)	4 sp	1 lb.
Bedroll	1 sp	5 lbs.[1]
Bell	1 gp	—
Blanket, winter	5 sp	3 lbs.[1]
Block and tackle	5 gp	5 lbs.
Bottle, glass	2 gp	1 lb.
Bucket (empty)	5 sp	2 lbs.
Caltrops	1 gp	2 lbs.
Candle	1 cp	—
Canvas (sq. yd.)	1 sp	1 lb.
Case, map or scroll	1 gp	1/2 lb.
Chain (10 ft.)	30 gp	2 lbs.
Chalk, 1 piece	1 cp	—
Chest (empty)	2 gp	25 lbs.
Crowbar	2 gp	5 lbs.
Firewood (per day)	1 cp	20 lbs.
Fishhook	1 sp	—
Fishing net, 25 sq. ft.	4 gp	5 lbs.
Flask (empty)	3 cp	1-1/2 lbs.
Flint and steel	1 gp	—
Grappling hook	1 gp	4 lbs.
Hammer	5 sp	2 lbs.
Hourglass	25 gp	1 lb.
Ink (1 oz. vial)	8 gp	—
Inkpen	1 sp	—
Jug, clay	3 cp	9 lbs.
Ladder, 10-foot	2 sp	20 lbs.
Lamp, common	1 sp	1 lb.
Lantern, bullseye	12 gp	3 lbs.
Lantern, hooded	7 gp	2 lbs.
Lock		
Simple	20 gp	1 lb.
Average	40 gp	1 lb.
Good	80 gp	1 lb.
Superior	150 gp	1 lb.
Manacles	15 gp	2 lbs.
Manacles, masterwork	50 gp	2 lbs.
Mirror, small steel	10 gp	1/2 lb.
Mug/Tankard, clay	2 cp	1 lb.
Oil (1-pint flask)	1 sp	1 lb.
Paper (sheet)	4 sp	—
Parchment (sheet)	2 sp	—
Pick, miner's	3 gp	10 lbs.
Pitcher, clay	2 cp	5 lbs.
Piton	1 sp	1/2 lb.
Pole, 10-foot	5 cp	8 lbs.
Pot, iron	8 sp	4 lbs.
Pouch, belt (empty)	1 gp	1/2 lb.[1]
Ram, portable	10 gp	20 lbs.
Rations, trail (per day)	5 sp	1 lb.[1]
Rope, hemp (50 ft.)	1 gp	10 lbs.
Rope, silk (50 ft.)	10 gp	5 lbs.
Sack (empty)	1 sp	1/2 lb.[1]
Sealing wax	1 gp	1 lb.
Sewing needle	5 sp	—
Shovel or spade	2 gp	8 lbs.
Signal whistle	8 sp	—
Signet ring	5 gp	—
Sledge	1 gp	10 lbs.
Soap (per lb.)	5 sp	1 lb.
Spyglass	1,000 gp	1 lb.
Tent	10 gp	20 lbs.[1]
Torch	1 cp	1 lb.
Vial, ink or potion	1 gp	—
Water clock	1,000 gp	200 lbs.
Waterskin	1 gp	4 lbs.[1]
Whetstone	2 cp	1 lb.

Special Substances and Items

Item	Cost	Weight
Acid (flask)	10 gp	1 lb.
Alchemist's fire (flask)	20 gp	1 lb.
Antitoxin (vial)	50 gp	—
Everburning torch	110 gp	1 lb.
Holy water (flask)	25 gp	1 lb.
Smokestick	20 gp	1/2 lb.
Sunrod	2 gp	1 lb.
Tanglefoot bag	50 gp	4 lbs.
Thunderstone	30 gp	1 lb.
Tindertwig	1 gp	—

Tools and Skill Kits

Item	Cost	Weight
Alchemist's lab	200 gp	40 lbs.
Artisan's tools	5 gp	5 lbs.
Artisan's tools, masterwork	55 gp	5 lbs.
Climber's kit	80 gp	5 lbs.[1]
Disguise kit	50 gp	8 lbs.[1]
Healer's kit	50 gp	1 lb.
Holly and mistletoe	—	—
Holy symbol, wooden	1 gp	—
Holy symbol, silver	25 gp	1 lb.
Magnifying glass	100 gp	—
Musical instrument, common	5 gp	3 lbs.[1]
Musical instrument, masterwork	100 gp	3 lbs.[1]
Scale, merchant's	2 gp	1 lb.
Spell component pouch	5 gp	2 lbs.
Spellbook, wizard's (blank)	15 gp	3 lbs.
Thieves' tools	30 gp	1 lb.
Thieves' tools, masterwork	100 gp	2 lbs.
Tool, masterwork	50 gp	1 lb.

Clothing

Item	Cost	Weight
Artisan's outfit	1 gp	4 lbs.[1]
Cleric's vestments	5 gp	6 lbs.[1]
Cold-weather outfit	8 gp	7 lbs.[1]
Courtier's outfit	30 gp	6 lbs.[1]
Entertainer's outfit	3 gp	4 lbs.[1]
Explorer's outfit	10 gp	8 lbs.[1]
Monk's outfit	5 gp	2 lbs.[1]
Noble's outfit	75 gp	10 lbs.[1]
Peasant's outfit	1 sp	2 lbs.[1]
Royal outfit	200 gp	15 lbs.[1]
Scholar's outfit	5 gp	6 lbs.[1]
Traveler's outfit	1 gp	5 lbs.[1]

Food, Drink, and Lodging

Item	Cost	Weight
Ale		
Gallon	2 sp	8 lbs.
Mug	4 cp	1 lb.
Banquet (per person)	10 gp	—
Bread, loaf of	2 cp	1/2 lb.
Cheese, hunk of	1 sp	1/2 lb.
Inn stay (per day)		
Good	2 gp	—
Common	5 sp	—
Poor	2 sp	—
Meals (per day)		
Good	5 sp	—
Common	3 sp	—
Poor	1 sp	—
Meat, chunk of	3 sp	1/2 lb.
Wine		
Common (pitcher)	2 sp	6 lbs.
Fine (bottle)	10 gp	1-1/2 lbs.

Mounts and Related Gear

Item	Cost	Weight
Barding		
Medium creature	×2[2]	×1[2]
Large creature	×4[2]	×2[2]
Bit and bridle	2 gp	1 lb.
Dog, guard	25 gp	—
Dog, riding	150 gp	—
Donkey or mule	8 gp	—
Feed (per day)	5 cp	10 lbs.
Horse		
Horse, heavy	200 gp	—
Horse, heavy (combat trained)	300 gp	—
Horse, light	75 gp	—
Horse, light (combat trained)	110 gp	—
Pony	30 gp	—
Pony (combat trained)	45 gp	—

Saddle	Cost	Weight
Military	20 gp	30 lbs.
Pack	5 gp	15 lbs.
Riding	10 gp	25 lbs.
Saddle, Exotic		
Military	60 gp	40 lbs.
Pack	15 gp	20 lbs.
Riding	30 gp	30 lbs.
Saddlebags	4 gp	8 lbs.
Stabling (per day)	5 sp	—

Transport

Item	Cost	Weight
Carriage	100 gp	600 lbs.
Cart	15 gp	200 lbs.
Galley	30,000 gp	—
Keelboat	3,000 gp	—
Longship	10,000 gp	—
Rowboat	50 gp	100 lbs.
Oar	2 gp	10 lbs.
Sailing ship	10,000 gp	—
Sled	20 gp	300 lbs.
Wagon	35 gp	400 lbs.
Warship	25,000 gp	—

Spellcasting and Services

Service	Cost
Coach cab	3 cp per mile
Hireling, trained	3 sp per day
Hireling, untrained	1 sp per day
Messenger	2 cp per mile
Road or gate toll	1 cp
Ship's passage	1 sp per mile
Spellcasting	Caster level × spell level × 10 gp[3]

— No weight, or no weight worth noting.

1 These items weigh one-quarter this amount when made for Small characters. Containers for Small characters also carry one-quarter the normal amount.

2 Relative to similar armor made for a Medium humanoid.

3 See spell description for additional costs. If the additional costs put the spell's total cost above 3,000 gp, that spell is not generally available. Use a spell level of 1/2 for 0-level spells to calculate the cost.

was last set. It requires a source of water, and it must be kept still because it marks time by the regulated flow of droplets of water.

Special Substances and Items

Any of these substances except for the everburning torch and holy water can be made by a character with the Craft (alchemy) skill.

Acid: You can throw a flask of acid as a splash weapon (see page 202). Treat this attack as a ranged touch attack with a range increment of 10 feet. A direct hit deals 1d6 points of acid damage. Every creature within 5 feet of the point where the acid hits takes 1 point of acid damage from the splash.

Alchemist's Fire: You can throw a flask of alchemist's fire as a splash weapon (see page 202). Treat this attack as a ranged touch attack with a range increment of 10 feet.

A direct hit deals 1d6 points of fire damage. Every creature within 5 feet of the point where the flask hits takes 1 point of fire damage from the splash. On the round following a direct hit, the target takes an additional 1d6 points of damage. If desired, the target can use a full-round action to attempt to extinguish the flames before taking this additional damage. Extinguishing the flames requires a DC 15 Reflex save. Rolling on the ground provides the target a +2 bonus on the save. Leaping into a lake or magically extinguishing the flames automatically smothers the fire.

Antitoxin: If you drink a vial of antitoxin, you get a +5 alchemical bonus on Fortitude saving throws against poison for 1 hour.

Everburning Torch: This otherwise normal torch has a *continual flame* spell cast on it. This causes it to shed light like an ordinary torch, but it does not emit heat or deal fire damage if used as a weapon.

Holy Water: Holy water damages undead creatures and evil outsiders almost as if it were acid. A flask of holy water can be thrown as a splash weapon.

Treat this attack as a ranged touch attack with a range increment of 10 feet. A flask breaks if thrown against the body of a corporeal creature, but to use it against an incorporeal creature, you must open the flask and pour the holy water out onto the target. Thus, you can douse an incorporeal creature with holy water only if you are adjacent to it. Doing so is a ranged touch attack that does not provoke attacks of opportunity.

A direct hit by a flask of holy water deals 2d4 points of damage to an undead creature or an evil outsider. Each such creature within 5 feet of the point where the flask hits takes 1 point of damage from the splash.

Temples to good deities sell holy water at cost (making no profit). Holy water is made using the *bless water* spell.

Smokestick: This alchemically treated wooden stick instantly creates thick, opaque smoke when burned. The smoke fills a 10-foot cube (treat the effect as a *fog cloud*

spell, except that a moderate or stronger wind dissipates the smoke in 1 round). The stick is consumed after 1 round, and the smoke dissipates naturally after 1 minute.

Sunrod: This 1-foot-long, gold-tipped, iron rod glows brightly when struck as a standard action. It sheds normal light in a 30-foot radius and increases the light level by one step for an additional 30 feet beyond that area (darkness becomes dim light and dim light becomes normal light). A sunrod does not increase the light level in normal light or bright light. It glows for 6 hours, after which the gold tip is burned out and worthless.

Tanglefoot Bag: A tanglefoot bag is a small sack filled with tar, resin, and other sticky substances. When you throw a tanglefoot bag at a creature (as a ranged touch attack with a range increment of 10 feet), the bag comes apart and goo bursts out, entangling the target and then becoming tough and resilient upon exposure to air. An entangled creature takes a –2 penalty on attack rolls and a –4 penalty to Dexterity and must make a DC 15 Reflex save or be glued to the floor, unable to move. Even on a successful save, it can move only at half speed. Huge or larger creatures are unaffected by a tanglefoot bag. A flying creature is not stuck to the floor, but it must make a DC 15 Reflex save or be unable to fly (assuming it uses its wings to fly) and fall to the ground. A tanglefoot bag does not function underwater.

A creature that is glued to the floor (or unable to fly) can break free by making a DC 17 Strength check or by dealing 15 points of damage to the goo with a slashing weapon. A creature trying to scrape goo off itself, or another creature assisting, does not need to make an attack roll; hitting the goo is automatic, after which the creature that hit makes a damage roll to see how much of the goo was scraped off. Once free, the creature can move (including flying) at half speed. If the entangled creature attempts to cast a spell, it must make concentration check with a DC of 15 + the spell's level or be unable to cast the spell. The goo becomes brittle and fragile after 2d4 rounds, cracking apart and losing its effectiveness. An application of *universal solvent* to a stuck creature dissolves the alchemical goo immediately.

Thunderstone: You can throw this stone as a ranged attack with a range increment of 20 feet. When it strikes a hard surface (or is struck hard), it creates a deafening bang that is treated as a sonic attack. Each creature within a 10-foot-radius spread must make a DC 15 Fortitude save or be deafened for 1 hour. A deafened creature, in addition to the obvious effects, takes a –4 penalty on initiative and has a 20% chance to miscast and lose any spell with a verbal component that it tries to cast.

Since you don't need to hit a specific target, you can simply aim at a particular 5-foot square. Treat the target square as AC 5.

Tindertwig: The alchemical substance on the end of this small, wooden stick ignites when struck against a rough surface. Creating a flame with a tindertwig is much faster than creating a flame with flint and steel (or a magnifying glass) and tinder. Lighting a torch with a tindertwig is a standard action (rather than a full-round action), and lighting any other fire with one is at least a standard action.

Tools and Skill Kits

These items are particularly useful to characters with certain skills and class abilities.

Alchemist's Lab: This lab is used for making alchemical items, and provides a +2 circumstance bonus on Craft (alchemy) checks. It has no bearing on the costs related to the Craft (alchemy) skill. Without this lab, a character with the Craft (alchemy) skill is assumed to have enough tools to use the skill but not enough to get the +2 bonus that the lab provides.

Artisan's Tools: These special tools include the items needed to pursue any craft. Without them, you have to use improvised tools (–2 penalty on Craft checks), if you can do the job at all.

Artisan's Tools, Masterwork: These tools serve the same purpose as artisan's tools, but masterwork artisan's tools are the perfect tools for the job, so you get a +2 circumstance bonus on Craft checks made with them.

Climber's Kit: These crampons, pitons, ropes, and tools give you a +2 circumstance bonus on Climb checks.

Disguise Kit: The kit is the perfect tool for disguise and provides a +2 circumstance bonus on Disguise checks. A disguise kit is exhausted after 10 uses.

Healer's Kit: This collection of bandages and herbs provides a +2 circumstance bonus on Heal checks. A healer's kit is exhausted after 10 uses.

Holly and Mistletoe: Druids commonly use these plants as divine focuses when casting spells.

Holy Symbol, Silver or Wooden: A holy symbol focuses positive energy and is used by good clerics and paladins (or by neutral clerics who want to cast good spells or channel positive energy). Each religion has its own holy symbol.

Unholy Symbols: An unholy symbol is like a holy symbol except that it focuses negative energy and is used by evil clerics (or by neutral clerics who want to cast evil spells or channel negative energy).

Magnifying Glass: This simple lens allows a closer look at small objects. It is also useful as a substitute for flint and steel when starting fires. Lighting a fire with a magnifying glass requires bright light, such as sunlight to focus, tinder to ignite, and at least a full-round action. A magnifying glass grants a +2 circumstance bonus on Appraise checks involving any item that is small or highly detailed.

Musical Instrument, Common or Masterwork: A masterwork instrument grants a +2 circumstance bonus on Perform checks involving its use.

Scale, Merchant's: A merchant's scale grants a +2 circumstance bonus on Appraise checks involving items that are valued by weight, including anything made of precious metals.

Spell Component Pouch: A spellcaster with a spell component pouch is assumed to have all the material components and focuses needed for spellcasting, except for those components that have a specific cost, divine focuses, and focuses that wouldn't fit in a pouch.

Spellbook, Wizard's: A spellbook has 100 pages of parchment, and each spell takes up one page per spell level (one page each for 0-level spells).

Thieves' Tools: This kit contains lockpicks and other tools you need to use the Disable Device skill. Without these tools, you must use improvised tools, and you take a –2 circumstance penalty on Disable Device checks.

Thieves' Tools, Masterwork: This kit contains extra tools and tools of better make, which grant a +2 circumstance bonus on Disable Device checks.

Tool, Masterwork: This well-made item is the perfect tool for the job. It grants a +2 circumstance bonus on a related skill check (if any). Bonuses provided by multiple masterwork items do not stack.

Clothing

All characters begin play with one outfit, valued at 10 gp or less. Additional outfits can be purchased normally.

Artisan's Outfit: This outfit includes a shirt with buttons, a skirt or pants with a drawstring, shoes, and perhaps a cap or hat. It may also include a belt or a leather or cloth apron for carrying tools.

Cleric's Vestments: These clothes are for performing priestly functions, not for adventuring. Cleric's vestments typically include a cassock, stole, and surplice.

Cold-Weather Outfit: This outfit includes a wool coat, linen shirt, wool cap, heavy cloak, thick pants or skirt, and boots. This outfit grants a +5 circumstance bonus on Fortitude saving throws against exposure to cold weather.

Courtier's Outfit: This outfit includes fancy, tailored clothes in whatever fashion happens to be the current style in the courts of the nobles. Anyone trying to influence nobles or courtiers while wearing street dress will have a hard time of it (–2 penalty on Charisma-based skill checks to influence such individuals). If you wear this outfit without jewelry (costing an additional 50 gp), you look like an out-of-place commoner.

Entertainer's Outfit: This set of flashy—perhaps even gaudy—clothes is for entertaining. While the outfit looks whimsical, its practical design lets you tumble, dance, walk a tightrope, or just run (if the audience turns ugly).

Explorer's Outfit: This set of clothes is for someone who never knows what to expect. It includes sturdy boots, leather breeches or a skirt, a belt, a shirt (perhaps with a vest or jacket), gloves, and a cloak. Rather than a leather skirt, a leather overtunic may be worn over a cloth skirt. The clothes have plenty of pockets (especially the cloak). The outfit also includes any extra accessories you might need, such as a scarf or a wide-brimmed hat.

Monk's Outfit: This simple outfit includes sandals, loose breeches, and a loose shirt, and is bound together with sashes. The outfit is designed to give you maximum mobility, and it's made of high-quality fabric. You can conceal small weapons in pockets hidden in the folds, and the sashes are strong enough to serve as short ropes.

Noble's Outfit: These clothes are designed specifically to be expensive and gaudy. Precious metals and gems are worked into the clothing. A would-be noble also needs a signet ring and jewelry (worth at least 100 gp) to accessorize this outfit.

Peasant's Outfit: This set of clothes consists of a loose shirt and baggy breeches, or a loose shirt and skirt or overdress. Cloth wrappings are used for shoes.

Royal Outfit: This is just the clothing, not the royal scepter, crown, ring, and other accoutrements. Royal clothes are ostentatious, with gems, gold, silk, and fur in abundance.

Scholar's Outfit: Perfect for a scholar, this outfit includes a robe, a belt, a cap, soft shoes, and possibly a cloak.

Traveler's Outfit: This set of clothes consists of boots, a wool skirt or breeches, a sturdy belt, a shirt (perhaps with a vest or jacket), and an ample cloak with a hood.

Food, Drink, and Lodging

These prices are for meals and accommodations at establishments in an average city.

Inn: Poor accommodations at an inn amount to a place on the floor near the hearth. Common accommodations consist of a place on a raised, heated floor and the use of a blanket and a pillow. Good accommodations consist of a small, private room with one bed, some amenities, and a covered chamber pot in the corner.

Meals: Poor meals might be composed of bread, baked turnips, onions, and water. Common meals might consist of bread, chicken stew, carrots, and watered-down ale or wine. Good meals might be composed of bread and pastries, beef, peas, and ale or wine.

Mounts and Related Gear

These are the common mounts available in most cities. Some markets might have additional creatures available, such as camels or even griffons, depending on the terrain. Such additional choices are up to GM discretion, and rules for the creatures can be found in the *Pathfinder RPG Bestiary*.

Barding, Medium Creature and Large Creature: Barding is a type of armor that covers the head, neck, chest, body, and possibly legs of a horse or other mount. Barding made of medium or heavy armor provides better protection than light barding, but at the expense of speed. Barding can be made of any of the armor types found on Table 6–6.

Armor for a horse (a Large nonhumanoid creature) costs four times as much as human armor (a Medium humanoid creature) and also weighs twice as much (see Table 6–8). If the barding is for a pony or other Medium mount, the cost is only double, and the weight is the same as for Medium armor worn by a humanoid. Medium or heavy barding slows a mount that wears it, as shown on the table below.

Flying mounts can't fly in medium or heavy barding.

Removing and fitting barding takes five times as long as the figures given on Table 6–7. A barded animal cannot be used to carry any load other than a rider and normal saddlebags.

	Base Speed		
Barding	**(40 ft.)**	**(50 ft.)**	**(60 ft.)**
Medium	30 ft.	35 ft.	40 ft.
Heavy	30 ft.*	35 ft.*	40 ft.*

* A mount wearing heavy armor moves at only triple its normal speed when running instead of quadruple.

Dog, Riding: This Medium dog is specially trained to carry a Small humanoid rider. It is brave in combat like a combat-trained horse. Due to its smaller stature, you take no damage when you fall from a riding dog.

Donkey or Mule: Donkeys and mules are stolid in the face of danger, hardy, surefooted, and capable of carrying heavy loads over vast distances. Unlike a horse, a donkey or a mule is willing (though not eager) to enter dungeons and other strange or threatening places.

Feed: Horses, donkeys, mules, and ponies can graze to sustain themselves, but providing feed for them is better. If you have a riding dog, you have to feed it meat.

Horse: A horse is suitable as a mount for a human, dwarf, elf, half-elf, or half-orc. A pony is smaller than a horse and is a suitable mount for a gnome or halfling.

A war-trained horse can be ridden into combat without danger. See the Handle Animal skill for a list of tricks known by horses and ponies with combat training.

Saddle, Exotic: An exotic saddle is designed for an unusual mount. Exotic saddles come in military, pack, and riding styles.

Saddle, Military: This saddle braces the rider, providing a +2 circumstance bonus on Ride checks related to staying in the saddle. If you're knocked unconscious while in a military saddle, you have a 75% chance to stay in the saddle.

Saddle, Pack: A pack saddle holds gear and supplies, but not a rider. It holds as much gear as the mount can carry.

Saddle, Riding: If you are knocked unconscious while in a riding saddle, you have a 50% chance to stay in the saddle.

Transport

The prices listed are to purchase the vehicle. These prices generally exclude crew or animals.

Carriage: This four-wheeled vehicle can transport as many as four people within an enclosed cab, plus two drivers. In general, two horses (or other beasts of burden) draw it. A carriage comes with the harness needed to pull it.

Cart: This two-wheeled vehicle can be drawn by a single horse (or other beast of burden). It comes with a harness.

Galley: This three-masted ship has 70 oars on either side and requires a total crew of 200. A galley is 130 feet long and 20 feet wide, and can carry 150 tons of cargo or 250 soldiers. For 8,000 gp more, it can be fitted with a ram and castles with firing platforms fore, aft, and amidships. This ship cannot make sea voyages and sticks to the coast. It moves about 4 miles per hour when being rowed or under sail.

Keelboat: This 50- to 75-foot-long ship is 15 to 20 feet wide and has a few oars to supplement its single mast with a square sail. It has a crew of 8 to 15 and can carry 40 to 50 tons of cargo or 100 soldiers. It can make sea voyages, as well as sail down rivers (thanks to its flat bottom). It moves about 1 mile per hour.

Longship: This 75-foot-long ship with 40 oars requires a total crew of 50. It has a single mast and a square sail, and it can carry 50 tons of cargo or 120 soldiers. A longship can make sea voyages. It moves about 3 miles per hour when being rowed or under sail.

Rowboat: This 8- to 12-foot-long boat with two oars holds two or three Medium passengers. It moves about 1-1/2 miles per hour.

Sailing Ship: This large, seaworthy ship is 75 to 90 feet long and 20 feet wide, and has a crew of 20. It can carry 150 tons of cargo. It has square sails on its two masts and can make sea voyages. It moves about 2 miles per hour.

Sled: This is a wagon on runners for snow and ice travel. In general, two horses (or other beasts of burden) draw it. A sled comes with the harness needed to pull it.

Wagon: A four-wheeled, open vehicle for transporting heavy loads. Two horses (or other beasts of burden) must draw it. A wagon comes with the harness needed to pull it.

Warship: This 100-foot-long ship has a single mast, although oars can also propel it. It has a crew of 60 to 80 rowers. This ship can carry 160 soldiers, but not for long distances, since there isn't room for supplies to support that many people. The warship cannot make sea voyages and sticks to the coast. It is not used for cargo. It moves about 2-1/2 miles per hour when being rowed or under sail.

Spellcasting and Services

Sometimes the best solution to a problem is to hire someone else to take care of it.

Coach Cab: The price given is for a ride in a coach that transports people (and light cargo) between towns. For a ride in a cab that transports passengers within a city, 1 copper piece usually takes you anywhere you need to go.

Hireling, Trained: The amount given is the typical daily wage for mercenary warriors, masons, craftsmen, cooks, scribes, teamsters, and other trained hirelings. This value represents a minimum wage; many such hirelings require significantly higher pay.

Hireling, Untrained: The amount shown is the typical daily wage for laborers, maids, and other menial workers.

Messenger: This includes horse-riding messengers and runners. Those willing to carry a message to a place they were going anyway may ask for only half the indicated amount.

Road or Gate Toll: A toll is sometimes charged to cross a well-kept and well-guarded road to pay for patrols on it and for its upkeep. Occasionally, a large, walled city charges a toll to enter or exit (or sometimes just to enter).

Ship's Passage: Most ships do not specialize in passengers, but many have the capability to take a few along when transporting cargo. Double the given cost for creatures larger than Medium or creatures that are otherwise difficult to bring aboard a ship.

Spellcasting: The indicated amount is how much it costs to get a spellcaster to cast a spell for you. This cost assumes that you can go to the spellcaster and have the spell cast at his convenience (generally at least 24 hours later, so that the spellcaster has time to prepare the spell in question). If you want to bring the spellcaster somewhere to cast a spell you need to negotiate with him, and the default answer is no.

The cost given is for any spell that does not require a costly material component. If the spell includes a material component, add the cost of that component to the cost of the spell. If the spell has a focus component (other than a divine focus), add 1/10 the cost of that focus to the cost of the spell.

Furthermore, if a spell has dangerous consequences, the spellcaster will certainly require proof that you can and will pay for dealing with any such consequences (that is, assuming that the spellcaster even agrees to cast such a spell, which isn't certain). In the case of spells that transport the caster and characters over a distance, you will likely have to pay for two castings of the spell, even if you aren't returning with the caster.

In addition, not every town or village has a spellcaster of sufficient level to cast any spell. In general, you must travel to a small town (or larger settlement) to be reasonably assured of finding a spellcaster capable of casting 1st-level spells, a large town for 2nd-level spells, a small city for 3rd- or 4th-level spells, a large city for 5th- or 6th-level spells, and a metropolis for 7th- or 8th-level spells. Even a metropolis isn't guaranteed to have a local spellcaster able to cast 9th-level spells.

7 Additional Rules

Merisiel cursed as she flung a dagger at yet another cat-sized cockroach. Ahead, Valeros was plowing steadfastly through the hip-deep water—Merisiel didn't want to think about what was under that water, or what was seeping into her boots as she slogged along behind him. Judging from the smell of the place, there were more than derelict ships rotting in the filthy morass.

"Tell me again why we're doing this, Val?" she asked.

"What's the problem, Merisiel?" Valeros replied as a trio of wererats skittered into view. "Afraid of getting a reputation as a do-gooder?"

This chapter presents rules for many miscellaneous parts of the game, such as alignment, character age, and encumbrance. This chapter also covers the rules for exploration, including overland travel, light sources, and breaking objects.

ALIGNMENT

A creature's general moral and personal attitudes are represented by its alignment: lawful good, neutral good, chaotic good, lawful neutral, neutral, chaotic neutral, lawful evil, neutral evil, or chaotic evil.

Alignment is a tool for developing your character's identity—it is not a straitjacket for restricting your character. Each alignment represents a broad range of personality types or personal philosophies, so two characters of the same alignment can still be quite different from each other. In addition, few people are completely consistent.

All creatures have an alignment. Alignment determines the effectiveness of some spells and magic items.

Animals and other creatures incapable of moral action are neutral. Even deadly vipers and tigers that eat people are neutral because they lack the capacity for morally right or wrong behavior. Dogs may be obedient and cats free-spirited, but they do not have the moral capacity to be truly lawful or chaotic.

Good Versus Evil

Good characters and creatures protect innocent life. Evil characters and creatures debase or destroy innocent life, whether for fun or profit.

Good implies altruism, respect for life, and a concern for the dignity of sentient beings. Good characters make personal sacrifices to help others.

Evil implies hurting, oppressing, and killing others. Some evil creatures simply have no compassion for others and kill without qualms if doing so is convenient. Others actively pursue evil, killing for sport or out of duty to some evil deity or master.

People who are neutral with respect to good and evil have compunctions against killing the innocent, but may lack the commitment to make sacrifices to protect or help others.

Law Versus Chaos

Lawful characters tell the truth, keep their word, respect authority, honor tradition, and judge those who fall short of their duties. Chaotic characters follow their consciences, resent being told what to do, favor new ideas over tradition, and do what they promise if they feel like it.

Law implies honor, trustworthiness, obedience to authority, and reliability. On the downside, lawfulness can include closed-mindedness, reactionary adherence to tradition, self-righteousness, and a lack of adaptability. Those who consciously promote lawfulness say that only

lawful behavior creates a society in which people can depend on each other and make the right decisions in full confidence that others will act as they should.

Chaos implies freedom, adaptability, and flexibility. On the downside, chaos can include recklessness, resentment toward legitimate authority, arbitrary actions, and irresponsibility. Those who promote chaotic behavior say that only unfettered personal freedom allows people to express themselves fully and lets society benefit from the potential that its individuals have within them.

Someone who is neutral with respect to law and chaos has some respect for authority and feels neither a compulsion to obey nor a compulsion to rebel. She is generally honest, but can be tempted into lying or deceiving others.

Alignment Steps

Occasionally the rules refer to "steps" when dealing with alignment. In this case, "steps" refers to the number of alignment shifts between the two alignments, as shown on the following diagram. Note that diagonal "steps" count as two steps. For example, a lawful neutral character is one step away from a lawful good alignment, and three steps away from a chaotic evil alignment. A cleric's alignment must be within one step of the alignment of her deity.

	Lawful	**Neutral**	**Chaotic**
Good	Lawful Good	Neutral Good	Chaotic Good
Neutral	Lawful Neutral	Neutral	Chaotic Neutral
Evil	Lawful Evil	Neutral Evil	Chaotic Evil

The Nine Alignments

Nine distinct alignments define the possible combinations of the lawful-chaotic axis with the good-evil axis. Each description below depicts a typical character of that alignment. Remember that individuals vary from this norm, and that a given character may act more or less in accord with his alignment from day to day. Use these descriptions as guidelines, not as scripts.

The first six alignments, lawful good through chaotic neutral, are standard alignments for player characters. The three evil alignments are usually for monsters and villains. With the GM's permission, a player may assign an evil alignment to his PC, but such characters are often a source of disruption and conflict with good and neutral party members. GMs are encouraged to carefully consider how evil PCs might affect the campaign before allowing them.

Lawful Good: A lawful good character acts as a good person is expected or required to act. She combines a commitment to oppose evil with the discipline to fight relentlessly. She tells the truth, keeps her word, helps those in need, and speaks out against injustice. A lawful good character hates to see the guilty go unpunished.

Lawful good combines honor with compassion.

Neutral Good: A neutral good character does the best that a good person can do. He is devoted to helping others. He works with kings and magistrates but does not feel beholden to them.

Neutral good means doing what is good and right without bias for or against order.

Chaotic Good: A chaotic good character acts as his conscience directs him with little regard for what others expect of him. He makes his own way, but he's kind and benevolent. He believes in goodness and right but has little use for laws and regulations. He hates it when people try to intimidate others and tell them what to do. He follows his own moral compass, which, although good, may not agree with that of society.

Chaotic good combines a good heart with a free spirit.

Lawful Neutral: A lawful neutral character acts as law, tradition, or a personal code directs her. Order and organization are paramount. She may believe in personal order and live by a code or standard, or she may believe in order for all and favor a strong, organized government.

Lawful neutral means you are reliable and honorable without being a zealot.

Neutral: A neutral character does what seems to be a good idea. She doesn't feel strongly one way or the other when it comes to good vs. evil or law vs. chaos (and thus neutral is sometimes called "true neutral"). Most neutral characters exhibit a lack of conviction or bias rather than a commitment to neutrality. Such a character probably thinks of good as better than evil—after all, she would rather have good neighbors and rulers than evil ones. Still, she's not personally committed to upholding good in any abstract or universal way.

Some neutral characters, on the other hand, commit themselves philosophically to neutrality. They see good, evil, law, and chaos as prejudices and dangerous extremes. They advocate the middle way of neutrality as the best, most balanced road in the long run.

Neutral means you act naturally in any situation, without prejudice or compulsion.

Chaotic Neutral: A chaotic neutral character follows his whims. He is an individualist first and last. He values his own liberty but doesn't strive to protect others' freedom. He avoids authority, resents restrictions, and challenges traditions. A chaotic neutral character does not intentionally disrupt organizations as part of a campaign of anarchy. To do so, he would have to be motivated either by good (and a desire to liberate others) or evil (and a desire to make those others suffer). A chaotic neutral character may be unpredictable, but his behavior is not totally random. He is not as likely to jump off a bridge as he is to cross it.

Chaotic neutral represents freedom from both society's restrictions and a do-gooder's zeal.

Lawful Evil: A lawful evil villain methodically takes what he wants within the limits of his code of conduct without regard for whom it hurts. He cares about tradition,

loyalty, and order, but not about freedom, dignity, or life. He plays by the rules but without mercy or compassion. He is comfortable in a hierarchy and would like to rule, but is willing to serve. He condemns others not according to their actions but according to race, religion, homeland, or social rank. He is loath to break laws or promises.

This reluctance comes partly from his nature and partly because he depends on order to protect himself from those who oppose him on moral grounds. Some lawful evil villains have particular taboos, such as not killing in cold blood (but having underlings do it) or not letting children come to harm (if it can be helped). They imagine that these compunctions put them above unprincipled villains.

Some lawful evil people and creatures commit themselves to evil with a zeal like that of a crusader committed to good. Beyond being willing to hurt others for their own ends, they take pleasure in spreading evil as an end unto itself. They may also see doing evil as part of a duty to an evil deity or master.

Lawful evil represents methodical, intentional, and organized evil.

Neutral Evil: A neutral evil villain does whatever she can get away with. She is out for herself, pure and simple. She sheds no tears for those she kills, whether for profit, sport, or convenience. She has no love of order and holds no illusions that following laws, traditions, or codes would make her any better or more noble. On the other hand, she doesn't have the restless nature or love of conflict that a chaotic evil villain has.

Some neutral evil villains hold up evil as an ideal, committing evil for its own sake. Most often, such villains are devoted to evil deities or secret societies.

Neutral evil represents pure evil without honor and without variation.

Chaotic Evil: A chaotic evil character does what his greed, hatred, and lust for destruction drive him to do. He is vicious, arbitrarily violent, and unpredictable. If he is simply out for whatever he can get, he is ruthless and brutal. If he is committed to the spread of evil and chaos, he is even worse. Thankfully, his plans are haphazard, and any groups he joins or forms are likely to be poorly organized. Typically, chaotic evil people can be made to work together only by force, and their leader lasts only as long as he can thwart attempts to topple or assassinate him.

Chaotic evil represents the destruction not only of beauty and life, but also of the order on which beauty and life depend.

Changing Alignments

Alignment is a tool, a convenient shorthand you can use to summarize the general attitude of an NPC, region, religion, organization, monster, or even magic item.

Certain character classes in Chapter 3 list repercussions for those who don't adhere to a specific alignment, and some spells and magic items have different effects on targets depending on alignment, but beyond that it's generally not necessary to worry too much about whether someone is behaving differently from his stated alignment. In the end, the Game Master is the one who gets to decide if something's in accordance with its indicated alignment, based on the descriptions given previously and his own opinion and interpretation—the only thing the GM needs to strive for is to be consistent as to what constitutes the difference between alignments like chaotic neutral and chaotic evil. There's no hard and fast mechanic by which you can measure alignment—unlike hit points or skill ranks or Armor Class, alignment is solely a label the GM controls.

It's best to let players play their characters as they want. If a player is roleplaying in a way that you, as the GM, think doesn't fit his alignment, let him know that he's acting out of alignment and tell him why—but do so in a friendly manner. If a character wants to change his alignment, let him—in most cases, this should amount to little more than a change of personality, or in some cases, no change at all if the alignment change was more of an adjustment to more accurately summarize how a player, in your opinion, is portraying his character. In some cases, changing alignments can impact a character's abilities—see the class write-ups in Chapter 3 for details. An *atonement* spell may be necessary to repair damage done by alignment changes arising from involuntary sources or momentary lapses in personality.

Players who frequently have their characters change alignment should in all likelihood be playing chaotic neutral characters.

VITAL STATISTICS

The following section determines a character's starting age, height, and weight. The character's race and class influence these statistics. Consult your GM before making a character that does not conform to these statistics.

Age

You can choose or randomly generate your character's age. If you choose it, it must be at least the minimum age for the character's race and class (see Table 7–1). Alternatively, roll the dice indicated for your class on Table 7–1 and add the result to the minimum age of adulthood for your race to determine how old your character is.

With age, a character's physical ability scores decrease and his mental ability scores increase (see Table 7–2). The effects of each aging step are cumulative. However, none of a character's ability scores can be reduced below 1 in this way.

When a character reaches venerable age, secretly roll his maximum age (on Table 7–2) and record the result, which the player does not know. A character who reaches his maximum age dies of old age sometime during the following year.

The maximum ages are for player characters. Most people in the world at large die from pestilence, accidents, infections, or violence before getting to venerable age.

Height and Weight

To determine a character's height, roll the modifier dice indicated on Table 7–3 and add the result, in inches, to the base height for your character's race and gender. To determine a character's weight, multiply the result of the modifier dice by the weight multiplier and add the result to the base weight for your character's race and gender.

Carrying Capacity

These carrying capacity rules determine how much a character's equipment slows him down. Encumbrance comes in two parts: encumbrance by armor and encumbrance by total weight.

Encumbrance by Armor: A character's armor determines his maximum Dexterity bonus to AC, armor check penalty, speed, and running speed (see Table 6–6). Unless your character is weak or carrying a lot of gear, that's all you need to know; the extra gear your character carries won't slow him down any more than the armor already does.

If your character is weak or carrying a lot of gear, however, then you'll need to calculate encumbrance by weight. Doing so is most important when your character is trying to carry some heavy object.

Encumbrance by Weight: If you want to determine whether your character's gear is heavy enough to slow him down more than his armor already does, total the weight of all the character's items, including armor, weapons, and gear (see appropriate tables in Chapter 6). Compare this total to the character's Strength on Table 7–4. Depending on the character's carrying capacity, he or

Table 7-1: Random Starting Ages

Race	Adulthood	Barbarian, Rogue, Sorcerer	Bard, Fighter, Paladin, Ranger	Cleric, Druid, Monk, Wizard
Human	15 years	+1d4	+1d6	+2d6
Dwarf	40 years	+3d6	+5d6	+7d6
Elf	110 years	+4d6	+6d6	+10d6
Gnome	40 years	+4d6	+6d6	+9d6
Half-elf	20 years	+1d6	+2d6	+3d6
Half-orc	14 years	+1d4	+1d6	+2d6
Halfling	20 years	+2d4	+3d6	+4d6

she may be carrying a light, medium, or heavy load. Like armor, a character's load affects his maximum Dexterity bonus to AC, carries a check penalty (which works like an armor check penalty), reduces the character's speed, and affects how fast the character can run, as shown on Table 7–5. A medium or heavy load counts as medium or heavy armor for the purpose of abilities or skills that are restricted by armor. Carrying a light load does not encumber a character.

If your character is wearing armor, use the worse figure (from armor or from load) for each category. Do not stack the penalties.

Lifting and Dragging: A character can lift as much as his maximum load over his head. A character's maximum load is the highest amount of weight listed for a character's Strength in the heavy load column of Table 7–4.

A character can lift as much as double his maximum load off the ground, but he or she can only stagger around with it. While overloaded in this way, the character loses any Dexterity bonus to AC and can move only 5 feet per round (as a full-round action).

A character can generally push or drag along the ground as much as five times his maximum load. Favorable conditions can double these numbers, and bad circumstances can reduce them by half or more.

Table 7-2: Aging Effects

Race	Middle Age[1]	Old[2]	Venerable[3]	Maximum Age
Human	35 years	53 years	70 years	70 + 2d20 years
Dwarf	125 years	188 years	250 years	250 + 2d% years
Elf	175 years	263 years	350 years	350 + 4d% years
Gnome	100 years	150 years	200 years	200 + 3d% years
Half-elf	62 years	93 years	125 years	125 + 3d20 years
Half-orc	30 years	45 years	60 years	60 + 2d10 years
Halfling	50 years	75 years	100 years	100 + 5d20 years

1 At middle age, −1 to Str, Dex, and Con; +1 to Int, Wis, and Cha.

2 At old age, −2 to Str, Dex, and Con; +1 to Int, Wis, and Cha.

3 At venerable age, −3 to Str, Dex, and Con; +1 to Int, Wis, and Cha.

TABLE 7-3: RANDOM HEIGHT AND WEIGHT

Race	Base Height	Base Weight	Modifier	Weight Multiplier
Human, male	4 ft. 10 in.	120 lbs.	2d10	×5 lbs.
Human, female	4 ft. 5 in.	85 lbs.	2d10	×5 lbs.
Dwarf, male	3 ft. 9 in.	150 lbs.	2d4	×7 lbs.
Dwarf, female	3 ft. 7 in.	120 lbs.	2d4	×7 lbs.
Elf, male	5 ft. 4 in.	100 lbs.	2d8	×3 lbs.
Elf, female	5 ft. 4 in.	90 lbs.	2d6	×3 lbs.
Gnome, male	3 ft. 0 in.	35 lbs.	2d4	×1 lb.
Gnome, female	2 ft. 10 in.	30 lbs.	2d4	×1 lb.
Half-elf, male	5 ft. 2 in.	110 lbs.	2d8	×5 lbs.
Half-elf, female	5 ft. 0 in.	90 lbs.	2d8	×5 lbs.
Half-orc, male	4 ft. 10 in.	150 lbs.	2d12	×7 lbs.
Half-orc, female	4 ft. 5 in.	110 lbs.	2d12	×7 lbs.
Halfling, male	2 ft. 8 in.	30 lbs.	2d4	×1 lb.
Halfling, female	2 ft. 6 in.	25 lbs.	2d4	×1 lb.

Bigger and Smaller Creatures: The figures on Table 7–4 are for Medium bipedal creatures. A larger bipedal creature can carry more weight depending on its size category, as follows: Large ×2, Huge ×4, Gargantuan ×8, Colossal ×16. A smaller creature can carry less weight depending on its size category, as follows: Small ×3/4, Tiny ×1/2, Diminutive ×1/4, Fine ×1/8.

Quadrupeds can carry heavier loads than bipeds can. Multiply the values corresponding to the creature's Strength score from Table 7–4 by the appropriate modifier, as follows: Fine ×1/4, Diminutive ×1/2, Tiny ×3/4, Small ×1, Medium ×1-1/2, Large ×3, Huge ×6, Gargantuan ×12, Colossal ×24.

Tremendous Strength: For Strength scores not shown on Table 7–4, find the Strength score between 20 and 29 that has the same number in the "ones" digit as the creature's Strength score does and multiply the numbers in that row by 4 for every 10 points the creature's Strength is above the score for that row.

Armor and Encumbrance for Other Base Speeds
The table below provides reduced speed figures for all base speeds from 5 feet to 120 feet (in 5-foot increments).

Base Speed	Reduced Speed	Base Speed	Reduced Speed
5 ft.	5 ft.	65 ft.	45 ft.
10 ft.–15 ft.	10 ft.	70 ft.–75 ft.	50 ft.
20 ft.	15 ft.	80 ft.	55 ft.
25 ft.–30 ft.	20 ft.	85 ft.–90 ft.	60 ft.
35 ft.	25 ft.	95 ft.	65 ft.
40 ft.–45 ft.	30 ft.	100 ft.–105 ft.	70 ft.
50 ft.	35 ft.	110 ft.	75 ft.
55 ft.–60 ft.	40 ft.	115 ft.–120 ft.	80 ft.

MOVEMENT

There are three movement scales, as follows:
- Tactical, for combat, measured in feet (or 5-foot squares) per round.
- Local, for exploring an area, measured in feet per minute.
- Overland, for getting from place to place, measured in miles per hour or miles per day.

Modes of Movement: While moving at the different movement scales, creatures generally walk, hustle, or run.

Walk: A walk represents unhurried but purposeful movement (3 miles per hour for an unencumbered adult human).

Hustle: A hustle is a jog (about 6 miles per hour for an unencumbered human). A character moving his speed twice in a single round, or moving that speed in the same round that he or she performs a standard action or another move action, is hustling when he or she moves.

Run (×3): Moving three times speed is a running pace for a character in heavy armor (about 7 miles per hour for a human in full plate).

Run (×4): Moving four times speed is a running pace for a character in light, medium, or no armor (about 12 miles per hour for an unencumbered human, or 9 miles per hour for a human in chainmail). See Table 7–6 for details.

Tactical Movement
Tactical movement is used for combat. Characters generally don't walk during combat, for obvious reasons—they hustle or run instead. A character who moves his speed and takes some action is hustling for about half the round and doing something else the other half.

Hampered Movement: Difficult terrain, obstacles, and poor visibility can hamper movement (see Table 7–7 for details). When movement is hampered, each square moved into usually counts as two squares, effectively reducing the distance that a character can cover in a move.

If more than one hampering condition applies, multiply all additional costs that apply. This is a specific exception to the normal rule for doubling.

In some situations, your movement may be so hampered that you don't have sufficient speed even to move 5 feet (1 square). In such a case, you may use a full-round action to move 5 feet (1 square) in any direction, even diagonally. Even though this looks like a 5-foot step, it's not, and thus it provokes attacks of opportunity normally. (You can't take advantage of this rule to move through impassable terrain or to move when all movement is prohibited to you.)

You can't run or charge through any square that would hamper your movement.

Local Movement
Characters exploring an area use local movement, measured in feet per minute.

Walk: A character can walk without a problem on the local scale.

Hustle: A character can hustle without a problem on the local scale. See Overland Movement, below, for movement measured in miles per hour.

Run: A character can run for a number of rounds equal to his Constitution score on the local scale without needing to rest. See Chapter 8 for rules covering extended periods of running.

Overland Movement

Characters covering long distances cross-country use overland movement. Overland movement is measured in miles per hour or miles per day. A day represents 8 hours of actual travel time. For rowed watercraft, a day represents 10 hours of rowing. For a sailing ship, it represents 24 hours.

Walk: A character can walk 8 hours in a day of travel without a problem. Walking for longer than that can wear him out (see Forced March, below).

Hustle: A character can hustle for 1 hour without a problem. Hustling for a second hour in between sleep cycles deals 1 point of nonlethal damage, and each additional hour deals twice the damage taken during the previous hour of hustling. A character who takes any nonlethal damage from hustling becomes fatigued.

A fatigued character can't run or charge and takes a penalty of –2 to Strength and Dexterity. Eliminating the nonlethal damage also eliminates the fatigue.

Run: A character can't run for an extended period of time. Attempts to run and rest in cycles effectively work out to a hustle.

Terrain: The terrain through which a character travels affects the distance he can cover in an hour or a day (see Table 7–8). A highway is a straight, major, paved road. A road is typically a dirt track. A trail is like a road, except that it allows only single-file travel and does not benefit a party traveling with vehicles. Trackless terrain is a wild area with no paths.

Forced March: In a day of normal walking, a character walks for 8 hours. The rest of the daylight time is spent making and breaking camp, resting, and eating.

A character can walk for more than 8 hours in a day by making a forced march. For each hour of marching beyond 8 hours, a Constitution check (DC 10, +2 per extra hour) is required. If the check fails, the character takes 1d6 points of nonlethal damage. A character who takes any nonlethal damage from a forced march becomes fatigued. Eliminating the nonlethal damage also eliminates the fatigue. It's possible for a character to march into unconsciousness by pushing himself too hard.

Mounted Movement: A mount bearing a rider can move at a hustle. The damage it takes when doing so, however, is lethal damage, not nonlethal damage. The creature

TABLE 7-4: CARRYING CAPACITY

Strength Score	Light Load	Medium Load	Heavy Load
1	3 lbs. or less	4–6 lbs.	7–10 lbs.
2	6 lbs. or less	7–13 lbs.	14–20 lbs.
3	10 lbs. or less	11–20 lbs.	21–30 lbs.
4	13 lbs. or less	14–26 lbs.	27–40 lbs.
5	16 lbs. or less	17–33 lbs.	34–50 lbs.
6	20 lbs. or less	21–40 lbs.	41–60 lbs.
7	23 lbs. or less	24–46 lbs.	47–70 lbs.
8	26 lbs. or less	27–53 lbs.	54–80 lbs.
9	30 lbs. or less	31–60 lbs.	61–90 lbs.
10	33 lbs. or less	34–66 lbs.	67–100 lbs.
11	38 lbs. or less	39–76 lbs.	77–115 lbs.
12	43 lbs. or less	44–86 lbs.	87–130 lbs.
13	50 lbs. or less	51–100 lbs.	101–150 lbs.
14	58 lbs. or less	59–116 lbs.	117–175 lbs.
15	66 lbs. or less	67–133 lbs.	134–200 lbs.
16	76 lbs. or less	77–153 lbs.	154–230 lbs.
17	86 lbs. or less	87–173 lbs.	174–260 lbs.
18	100 lbs. or less	101–200 lbs.	201–300 lbs.
19	116 lbs. or less	117–233 lbs.	234–350 lbs.
20	133 lbs. or less	134–266 lbs.	267–400 lbs.
21	153 lbs. or less	154–306 lbs.	307–460 lbs.
22	173 lbs. or less	174–346 lbs.	347–520 lbs.
23	200 lbs. or less	201–400 lbs.	401–600 lbs.
24	233 lbs. or less	234–466 lbs.	467–700 lbs.
25	266 lbs. or less	267–533 lbs.	534–800 lbs.
26	306 lbs. or less	307–613 lbs.	614–920 lbs.
27	346 lbs. or less	347–693 lbs.	694–1,040 lbs.
28	400 lbs. or less	401–800 lbs.	801–1,200 lbs.
29	466 lbs. or less	467–933 lbs.	934–1,400 lbs.
+10	×4	×4	×4

TABLE 7-5: ENCUMBRANCE EFFECTS

Load	Max Dex	Check Penalty	Speed (30 ft.)	(20 ft.)	Run
Medium	+3	–3	20 ft.	15 ft.	×4
Heavy	+1	–6	20 ft.	15 ft.	×3

can also be ridden in a forced march, but its Constitution checks automatically fail, and the damage it takes is lethal damage. Mounts also become fatigued when they take any damage from hustling or forced marches.

See Table 7–9: Mounts and Vehicles for mounted speeds and speeds for vehicles pulled by draft animals.

Waterborne Movement: See Table 7–9: Mounts and Vehicles for speeds for water vehicles.

Evasion and Pursuit

In round-by-round movement, when simply counting off squares, it's impossible for a slow character to get away

Table 7-6: Movement and Distance

Speed	15 feet	20 feet	30 feet	40 feet
One Round (Tactical)*				
Walk	15 ft.	20 ft.	30 ft.	40 ft.
Hustle	30 ft.	40 ft.	60 ft.	80 ft.
Run (×3)	45 ft.	60 ft.	90 ft.	120 ft.
Run (×4)	60 ft.	80 ft.	120 ft.	160 ft.
One Minute (Local)				
Walk	150 ft.	200 ft.	300 ft.	400 ft.
Hustle	300 ft.	400 ft.	600 ft.	800 ft.
Run (×3)	450 ft.	600 ft.	900 ft.	1,200 ft.
Run (×4)	600 ft.	800 ft.	1,200 ft.	1,600 ft.
One Hour (Overland)				
Walk	1-1/2 miles	2 miles	3 miles	4 miles
Hustle	3 miles	4 miles	6 miles	8 miles
Run	—	—	—	—
One Day (Overland)				
Walk	12 miles	16 miles	24 miles	32 miles
Hustle	—	—	—	—
Run	—	—	—	—

* Tactical movement is often measured in squares on the battle grid (1 square = 5 feet) rather than feet.

Table 7-7: Hampered Movement

Condition	Additional Movement Cost
Difficult terrain	×2
Obstacle*	×2
Poor visibility	×2
Impassable	—

* May require a skill check

Table 7-8: Terrain and Overland Movement

Terrain	Highway	Road or Trail	Trackless
Desert, sandy	×1	×1/2	×1/2
Forest	×1	×1	×1/2
Hills	×1	×3/4	×1/2
Jungle	×1	×3/4	×1/4
Moor	×1	×1	×3/4
Mountains	×3/4	×3/4	×1/2
Plains	×1	×1	×3/4
Swamp	×1	×3/4	×1/2
Tundra, frozen	×1	×3/4	×3/4

from a determined fast character without mitigating circumstances. Likewise, it's no problem for a fast character to get away from a slower one.

When the speeds of the two concerned characters are equal, there's a simple way to resolve a chase: If one creature is pursuing another, both are moving at the same speed, and the chase continues for at least a few rounds, have them make opposed Dexterity checks to see who is the faster over those rounds. If the creature being chased wins, it escapes. If the pursuer wins, it catches the fleeing creature.

Sometimes a chase occurs overland and could last all day, with the two sides only occasionally getting glimpses of each other at a distance. In the case of a long chase, an opposed Constitution check made by all parties determines which can keep pace the longest. If the creature being chased rolls the highest, it gets away. If not, the chaser runs down its prey, outlasting it with stamina.

EXPLORATION

Few rules are as vital to the success of adventurers than those pertaining to vision, lighting, and how to break things. Rules for each of these are explained below.

Vision and Light

Dwarves and half-orcs have darkvision, but the other races presented in Chapter 2 need light to see by. See Table 7–10 for the radius that a light source illuminates and how long it lasts. The increased entry indicates an area outside the lit radius in which the light level is increased by one step (from darkness to dim light, for example).

In an area of bright light, all characters can see clearly. Some creatures, such as those with light sensitivity and light blindness, take penalties while in areas of bright light. A creature can't use Stealth in an area of bright light unless it is invisible or has cover. Areas of bright light include outside in direct sunshine and inside the area of a *daylight* spell.

Normal light functions just like bright light, but characters with light sensitivity and light blindness do not take penalties. Areas of normal light include underneath a forest canopy during the day, within 20 feet of a torch, and inside the area of a *light* spell.

In an area of dim light, a character can see somewhat. Creatures within this area have concealment (20% miss chance in combat) from those without darkvision or the ability to see in darkness. A creature within an area of dim light can make a Stealth check to conceal itself. Areas of dim light include outside at night with a moon in the sky, bright starlight, and the area between 20 and 40 feet from a torch.

In areas of darkness, creatures without darkvision are effectively blinded. In addition to the obvious effects, a blinded creature has a 50% miss chance in combat (all opponents have total concealment), loses any Dexterity bonus to AC, takes a –2 penalty to AC, and takes a –4 penalty on Perception checks that rely on sight and most Strength- and Dexterity-based skill checks. Areas of darkness include an unlit dungeon chamber, most caverns, and outside on a cloudy, moonless night.

Characters with low-light vision (elves, gnomes, and half-elves) can see objects twice as far away as the given radius. Double the effective radius of bright light, normal light, and dim light for such characters.

Characters with darkvision (dwarves and half-orcs) can see lit areas normally as well as dark areas within 60 feet. A creature can't hide within 60 feet of a character with darkvision unless it is invisible or has cover.

Breaking and Entering

When attempting to break an object, you have two choices: smash it with a weapon or break it with sheer strength.

Smashing an Object

Smashing a weapon or shield with a slashing or bludgeoning weapon is accomplished with the sunder combat maneuver (see Chapter 8). Smashing an object is like sundering a weapon or shield, except that your combat maneuver check is opposed by the object's AC. Generally, you can smash an object only with a bludgeoning or slashing weapon.

Armor Class: Objects are easier to hit than creatures because they don't usually move, but many are tough enough to shrug off some damage from each blow. An object's Armor Class is equal to 10 + its size modifier (see Table 7–11) + its Dexterity modifier. An inanimate object has not only a Dexterity of 0 (–5 penalty to AC), but also an additional –2 penalty to its AC. Furthermore, if you take a full-round action to line up a shot, you get an automatic hit with a melee weapon and a +5 bonus on attack rolls with a ranged weapon.

Hardness: Each object has hardness—a number that represents how well it resists damage. When an object is damaged, subtract its hardness from the damage. Only damage in excess of its hardness is deducted from the object's hit points (see Table 7–12, Table 7–13, and Table 7–14).

Hit Points: An object's hit point total depends on what it is made of and how big it is (see Table 7–12, Table 7–13, and Table 7–14). Objects that take damage equal to or greater than half their total hit points gain the broken condition (see Appendix 2). When an object's hit points reach 0, it's ruined.

Very large objects have separate hit point totals for different sections.

Energy Attacks: Energy attacks deal half damage to most objects. Divide the damage by 2 before applying the object's hardness. Some energy types might be

Table 7–9: Mounts and Vehicles

Mount/Vehicle	Per Hour	Per Day
Mount (carrying load)		
Light horse	5 miles	40 miles
Light horse (175–525 lbs.)[1]	3-1/2 miles	28 miles
Heavy horse	5 miles	40 miles
Heavy horse (229–690 lbs.)[1]	3-1/2 miles	28 miles
Pony	4 miles	32 miles
Pony (151–450 lbs.)[1]	3 miles	24 miles
Dog, riding	4 miles	32 miles
Dog, riding (101–300 lbs.)[1]	3 miles	24 miles
Cart or wagon	2 miles	16 miles
Ship		
Raft or barge (poled or towed)[2]	1/2 mile	5 miles
Keelboat (rowed)[2]	1 mile	10 miles
Rowboat (rowed)[2]	1-1/2 miles	15 miles
Sailing ship (sailed)	2 miles	48 miles
Warship (sailed and rowed)	2-1/2 miles	60 miles
Longship (sailed and rowed)	3 miles	72 miles
Galley (rowed and sailed)	4 miles	96 miles

1 Quadrupeds, such as horses, can carry heavier loads than characters can. See Carrying Capacity on page 171 for more information.

2 Rafts, barges, keelboats, and rowboats are most often used on lakes and rivers. If going downstream, add the speed of the current (typically 3 miles per hour) to the speed of the vehicle. In addition to 10 hours of being rowed, the vehicle can also float an additional 14 hours, if someone can guide it, adding an additional 42 miles to the daily distance traveled. These vehicles can't be rowed against any significant current, but they can be pulled upstream by draft animals on the shores.

Table 7–10: Light Sources and Illumination

Object	Normal	Increased	Duration
Candle	n/a[1]	5 ft.	1 hr.
Everburning torch	20 ft.	40 ft.	Permanent
Lamp, common	15 ft.	30 ft.	6 hr./pint
Lantern, bullseye	60-ft. cone	120-ft. cone	6 hr./pint
Lantern, hooded	30 ft.	60 ft.	6 hr./pint
Sunrod	30 ft.	60 ft.	6 hr.
Torch	20 ft.	40 ft.	1 hr.

Spell	Normal	Increase	Duration
Continual flame	20 ft.	40 ft.	Permanent
Dancing lights (torches)	20 ft. (each)	40 ft. (each)	1 min.
Daylight	60 ft.[2]	120 ft.	10 min./level
Light	20 ft.	40 ft.	10 min./level

1 A candle does not provide normal illumination, only dim light.

2 The light for a daylight spell is bright light.

Table 7–11: Size and Armor Class of Objects

Size	AC Modifier
Colossal	–8
Gargantuan	–4
Huge	–2
Large	–1
Medium	+0
Small	+1
Tiny	+2
Diminutive	+4
Fine	+8

particularly effective against certain objects, subject to GM discretion. For example, fire might do full damage against parchment, cloth, and other objects that burn easily. Sonic might do full damage against glass and crystal objects.

Ranged Weapon Damage: Objects take half damage from ranged weapons (unless the weapon is a siege engine or something similar—see page 434). Divide the damage dealt by 2 before applying the object's hardness.

Ineffective Weapons: Certain weapons just can't effectively deal damage to certain objects. Likewise, most melee weapons have little effect on stone walls and doors, unless they are designed for breaking up stone, such as a pick or hammer.

Immunities: Objects are immune to nonlethal damage and to critical hits.

Magic Armor, Shields, and Weapons: Each +1 of enhancement bonus adds 2 to the hardness of armor, a weapon, or a shield, and +10 to the item's hit points.

Vulnerability to Certain Attacks: Certain attacks are especially successful against some objects. In such cases, attacks deal double their normal damage and may ignore the object's hardness.

Damaged Objects: A damaged object remains functional with the broken condition until the item's hit points are reduced to 0, at which point it is destroyed.

Damaged (but not destroyed) objects can be repaired with the Craft skill and a number of spells.

Saving Throws: Nonmagical, unattended items never make saving throws. They are considered to have failed their saving throws, so they are always fully affected by spells and other attacks that allow saving throws to resist or negate. An item attended by a character (being grasped, touched, or worn) makes saving throws as the character (that is, using the character's saving throw bonus).

Magic items always get saving throws. A magic item's Fortitude, Reflex, and Will save bonuses are equal to 2 + half its caster level. An attended magic item either makes

TABLE 7-12: COMMON ARMOR, WEAPON, AND SHIELD HARDNESS AND HIT POINTS

Weapon or Shield	Hardness[1]	Hit Points[2, 3]
Light blade	10	2
One-handed blade	10	5
Two-handed blade	10	10
Light metal-hafted weapon	10	10
One-handed metal-hafted weapon	10	20
Light hafted weapon	5	2
One-handed hafted weapon	5	5
Two-handed hafted weapon	5	10
Projectile weapon	5	5
Armor	special[4]	armor bonus × 5
Buckler	10	5
Light wooden shield	5	7
Heavy wooden shield	5	15
Light steel shield	10	10
Heavy steel shield	10	20
Tower shield	5	20

1   Add +2 for each +1 enhancement bonus of magic items.
2   The hp value given is for Medium armor, weapons, and shields. Divide by 2 for each size category of the item smaller than Medium, or multiply it by 2 for each size category larger than Medium.
3   Add 10 hp for each +1 enhancement bonus of magic items.
4   Varies by material; see Table 7–13: Substance Hardness and Hit Points.

saving throws as its owner or uses its own saving throw bonus, whichever is better.

Animated Objects: Animated objects count as creatures for purposes of determining their Armor Class (do not treat them as inanimate objects).

Breaking Items

When a character tries to break or burst something with sudden force rather than by dealing damage, use a Strength check (rather than an attack roll and damage roll, as with the sunder special attack) to determine whether he succeeds. Since hardness doesn't affect an object's break DC, this value depends more on the construction of the item than on the material the item is made of. Consult Table 7–15 for a list of common break DCs.

If an item has lost half or more of its hit points, the item gains the broken condition (see Appendix 2) and the DC to break it drops by 2.

Larger and smaller creatures get size bonuses and size penalties on Strength checks to break open doors as follows: Fine –16, Diminutive –12, Tiny –8, Small –4, Large +4, Huge +8, Gargantuan +12, Colossal +16.

A crowbar or portable ram improves a character's chance of breaking open a door (see Chapter 6).

TABLE 7-13: SUBSTANCE HARDNESS AND HIT POINTS

Substance	Hardness	Hit Points
Glass	1	1/in. of thickness
Paper or cloth	0	2/in. of thickness
Rope	0	2/in. of thickness
Ice	0	3/in. of thickness
Leather or hide	2	5/in. of thickness
Wood	5	10/in. of thickness
Stone	8	15/in. of thickness
Iron or steel	10	30/in. of thickness
Mithral	15	30/in. of thickness
Adamantine	20	40/in. of thickness

TABLE 7-14: OBJECT HARDNESS AND HIT POINTS

Object	Hardness	Hit Points	Break DC
Rope (1 in. diameter)	0	2	23
Simple wooden door	5	10	13
Small chest	5	1	17
Good wooden door	5	15	18
Treasure chest	5	15	23
Strong wooden door	5	20	23
Masonry wall (1 ft. thick)	8	90	35
Hewn stone (3 ft. thick)	8	540	50
Chain	10	5	26
Manacles	10	10	26
Masterwork manacles	10	10	28
Iron door (2 in. thick)	10	60	28

TABLE 7-15: DCs TO BREAK OR BURST ITEMS

Strength Check to:	DC
Break down simple door	13
Break down good door	18
Break down strong door	23
Burst rope bonds	23
Bend iron bars	24
Break down barred door	25
Burst chain bonds	26
Break down iron door	28
Condition	**DC Adjustment***
Hold portal	+5
Arcane lock	+10

* If both apply, use the larger number.

8 Combat

rashing down the ancient stairs in a shower of weathered stone, the onyx-scaled dragon and its crimson-cloaked rider exulted in their impending triumph, ready to finally bring an end to the upstarts who had long vexed their mistress.

Their resources and resolve already stretched to the limit, Seelah, Ezren, Harsk, and Lem readied sword and spell once more. They had bested countless foes and endured seemingly impossible trials thus far, but never had they faced so fearsome a challenge as a true dragon. Yet in that moment, each of them knew they faced a simple choice: victory or death.

In the wild parts of the world where monsters hold dominion, a sharp sword and sturdy shield are a far more effective means of communication than words. Combat is a common part of the Pathfinder Roleplaying Game, and the following rules explain this crucial process.

HOW COMBAT WORKS

Combat is cyclical; everybody acts in turn in a regular cycle of rounds. Combat follows this sequence:

1. When combat begins, all combatants roll initiative.
2. Determine which characters are aware of their opponents. These characters can act during a surprise round. If all the characters are aware of their opponents, proceed with normal rounds. See the surprise section for more information.
3. After the surprise round (if any), all combatants are ready to begin the first normal round of combat.
4. Combatants act in initiative order (highest to lowest).
5. When everyone has had a turn, the next round begins with the combatant with the highest initiative, and steps 4 and 5 repeat until combat ends.

The Combat Round

Each round represents 6 seconds in the game world; there are 10 rounds in a minute of combat. A round normally allows each character involved in a combat situation to act.

Each round's activity begins with the character with the highest initiative result and then proceeds in order. When a character's turn comes up in the initiative sequence, that character performs his entire round's worth of actions. (For exceptions, see Attacks of Opportunity on page 180 and Special Initiative Actions on page 202.)

When the rules refer to a "full round", they usually mean a span of time from a particular initiative count in one round to the same initiative count in the next round. Effects that last a certain number of rounds end just before the same initiative count that they began on.

Initiative

At the start of a battle, each combatant makes an initiative check. An initiative check is a Dexterity check. Each character applies his or her Dexterity modifier to the roll, as well as other modifiers from feats, spells, and other effects. Characters act in order, counting down from the highest result to the lowest. In every round that follows, the characters act in the same order (unless a character takes an action that results in his or her initiative changing; see Special Initiative Actions on page 202).

If two or more combatants have the same initiative check result, the combatants who are tied act in order of total initiative modifier (highest first). If there is still a tie, the tied characters should roll to determine which one of them goes before the other.

Flat-Footed: At the start of a battle, before you have had a chance to act (specifically, before your first regular turn in the initiative order), you are flat-footed. You can't use your Dexterity bonus to AC (if any) while flat-footed. Barbarians and rogues of high enough level have the uncanny dodge extraordinary ability, which means that they cannot be caught flat-footed. Characters with uncanny dodge retain their Dexterity bonus to their AC and can make attacks of opportunity before they have acted in the first round of combat. A flat-footed character can't make attacks of opportunity, unless he has the Combat Reflexes feat.

Inaction: Even if you can't take actions, you retain your initiative score for the duration of the encounter.

Surprise

When a combat starts, if you are not aware of your opponents and they are aware of you, you're surprised.

Sometimes all the combatants on a side are aware of their opponents, sometimes none are, and sometimes only some of them are. Sometimes a few combatants on each side are aware and the other combatants on each side are unaware. Determining awareness may call for Perception checks or other checks.

The Surprise Round: If some but not all of the combatants are aware of their opponents, a surprise round happens before regular rounds begin. In initiative order (highest to lowest), combatants who started the battle aware of their opponents each take a standard or move action during the surprise round. You can also take free actions during the surprise round. If no one or everyone is surprised, no surprise round occurs.

Unaware Combatants: Combatants who are unaware at the start of battle don't get to act in the surprise round. Unaware combatants are flat-footed because they have not acted yet, so they lose any Dexterity bonus to AC.

COMBAT STATISTICS

This section summarizes the statistics that determine success in combat, then details how to use them.

Attack Roll

An attack roll represents your attempt to strike your opponent on your turn in a round. When you make an attack roll, you roll a d20 and add your attack bonus. (Other modifiers may also apply to this roll.) If your result equals or beats the target's Armor Class, you hit and deal damage.

Automatic Misses and Hits: A natural 1 (the d20 comes up 1) on an attack roll is always a miss. A natural 20 (the d20 comes up 20) is always a hit. A natural 20 is also a threat—a possible critical hit (see the attack action on page 182).

Attack Bonus

Your attack bonus with a melee weapon is the following:

Base attack bonus + Strength modifier + size modifier

With a ranged weapon, your attack bonus is the following:

Base attack bonus + Dexterity modifier
+ size modifier + range penalty

Armor Class

Your Armor Class (AC) represents how hard it is for opponents to land a solid, damaging blow on you. It's the attack roll result that an opponent needs to achieve to hit you. Your AC is equal to the following:

10 + armor bonus + shield bonus + Dexterity modifier +
other modifiers

Note that armor limits your Dexterity bonus, so if you're wearing armor, you might not be able to apply your whole Dexterity bonus to your AC (see Table 6–6).

Sometimes you can't use your Dexterity bonus (if you have one). If you can't react to a blow, you can't use your Dexterity bonus to AC. If you don't have a Dexterity bonus, your AC does not change.

Other Modifiers: Many other factors modify your AC.

Enhancement Bonuses: Enhancement bonuses apply to your armor to increase the armor bonus it provides.

Deflection Bonus: Magical deflection effects ward off attacks and improve your AC.

Natural Armor: If your race has a tough hide, scales, or thick skin you receive a bonus to your AC.

Dodge Bonuses: Dodge bonuses represent actively avoiding blows. Any situation that denies you your Dexterity bonus also denies you dodge bonuses. (Wearing armor, however, does not limit these bonuses the way it limits a Dexterity bonus to AC.) Unlike most sorts of bonuses, dodge bonuses stack with each other.

Size Modifier: You receive a bonus or penalty to your AC based on your size. See Table 8–1.

Touch Attacks: Some attacks completely disregard armor, including shields and natural armor—the aggressor need only touch a foe for such an attack to take full effect. In these cases, the attacker makes a touch attack roll (either ranged or melee). When you are the target of a touch attack, your AC doesn't include any armor bonus, shield bonus, or natural armor bonus. All other modifiers, such as your size modifier, Dexterity modifier, and deflection bonus (if any) apply normally. Some creatures have the ability to make incorporeal touch attacks. These attacks bypass solid objects, such as armor and shields, by passing through them. Incorporeal touch attacks work similarly to normal touch attacks except that they also ignore cover bonuses. Incorporeal touch attacks do not ignore armor bonuses granted by force effects, such as *mage armor* and *bracers of armor*.

TABLE 8–1: SIZE MODIFIERS

Size	Size Modifier
Colossal	–8
Gargantuan	–4
Huge	–2
Large	–1
Medium	+0
Small	+1
Tiny	+2
Diminutive	+4
Fine	+8

Damage

If your attack succeeds, you deal damage. The type of weapon used determines the amount of damage you deal.

Damage reduces a target's current hit points.

Minimum Damage: If penalties reduce the damage result to less than 1, a hit still deals 1 point of nonlethal damage (see page 191).

Strength Bonus: When you hit with a melee or thrown weapon, including a sling, add your Strength modifier to the damage result. A Strength penalty, but not a bonus, applies on damage rolls made with a bow that is not a composite bow.

Off-Hand Weapon: When you deal damage with a weapon in your off hand, you add only 1/2 your Strength bonus. If you have a Strength penalty, the entire penalty applies.

Wielding a Weapon Two-Handed: When you deal damage with a weapon that you are wielding two-handed, you add 1-1/2 times your Strength bonus (Strength penalties are not multiplied). You don't get this higher Strength bonus, however, when using a light weapon with two hands.

Multiplying Damage: Sometimes you multiply damage by some factor, such as on a critical hit. Roll the damage (with all modifiers) multiple times and total the results.

Note: When you multiply damage more than once, each multiplier works off the original, unmultiplied damage. So if you are asked to double the damage twice, the end result is three times the normal damage.

Exception: Extra damage dice over and above a weapon's normal damage are never multiplied.

Ability Damage: Certain creatures and magical effects can cause temporary or permanent ability damage (a reduction to an ability score). Rules covering ability damage are found on page 554.

Hit Points

When your hit point total reaches 0, you're disabled. When it reaches –1, you're dying. When it gets to a negative amount equal to your Constitution score, you're dead. See Injury and Death (page 189), for more information.

Attacks of Opportunity

Sometimes a combatant in a melee lets her guard down or takes a reckless action. In this case, combatants near her can take advantage of her lapse in defense to attack her for free. These free attacks are called attacks of opportunity. See the Attacks of Opportunity diagram for an example of how they work.

Threatened Squares: You threaten all squares into which you can make a melee attack, even when it is not your turn. Generally, that means everything in all squares adjacent to your space (including diagonally). An enemy that takes certain actions while in a threatened square provokes an attack of opportunity from you. If you're unarmed, you don't normally threaten any squares and thus can't make attacks of opportunity.

Reach Weapons: Most creatures of Medium or smaller size have a reach of only 5 feet. This means that they can make melee attacks only against creatures up to 5 feet (1 square) away. However, Small and Medium creatures wielding reach weapons threaten more squares than a typical creature. In addition, most creatures larger than Medium have a natural reach of 10 feet or more.

Provoking an Attack of Opportunity: Two kinds of actions can provoke attacks of opportunity: moving out of a threatened square and performing certain actions within a threatened square.

Moving: Moving out of a threatened square usually provokes attacks of opportunity from threatening opponents. There are two common methods of avoiding such an attack—the 5-foot step and the withdraw action.

Performing a Distracting Act: Some actions, when performed in a threatened square, provoke attacks of opportunity as you divert your attention from the battle. Table 8–2 notes many of the actions that provoke attacks of opportunity.

Remember that even actions that normally provoke attacks of opportunity may have exceptions to this rule.

Making an Attack of Opportunity: An attack of opportunity is a single melee attack, and most characters can only make one per round. You don't have to make an attack of opportunity if you don't want to. You make your attack of opportunity at your normal attack bonus, even if you've already attacked in the round.

An attack of opportunity "interrupts" the normal flow of actions in the round. If an attack of opportunity is provoked, immediately resolve the attack of opportunity, then continue with the next character's turn (or complete the current turn, if the attack of opportunity was provoked in the midst of a character's turn).

Combat Reflexes and Additional Attacks of Opportunity: If you have the Combat Reflexes feat, you can add your Dexterity bonus to the number of attacks of opportunity you can make in a round. This feat does not let you make more than one attack for a given opportunity, but if the same opponent provokes two attacks of opportunity from you, you could make two separate attacks of opportunity (since each one represents a different opportunity). Moving out of more than one square threatened by the same opponent in the same round doesn't count as more than one opportunity for that opponent. All these attacks are at your full normal attack bonus.

Speed

Your speed tells you how far you can move in a round and still do something, such as attack or cast a spell. Your speed depends mostly on your size and your armor.

Dwarves, gnomes, and halflings have a speed of 20 feet (4 squares), or 15 feet (3 squares) when wearing medium or heavy armor (except for dwarves, who move 20 feet in any armor).

Humans, elves, half-elves, half-orcs, and most humanoid monsters have a speed of 30 feet (6 squares), or 20 feet (4 squares) in medium or heavy armor.

If you use two move actions in a round (sometimes called a "double move" action), you can move up to double your speed. If you spend the entire round running, you can move up to quadruple your speed (or triple if you are in heavy armor).

Saving Throws

Generally, when you are subject to an unusual or magical attack, you get a saving throw to avoid or reduce the effect. Like an attack roll, a saving throw is a d20 roll plus a bonus based on your class and level (see Chapter 3), and an associated ability score. Your saving throw modifier is:

Base save bonus + ability modifier

Saving Throw Types: The three different kinds of saving throws are Fortitude, Reflex, and Will:

Fortitude: These saves measure your ability to stand up to physical punishment or attacks against your vitality and health. Apply your Constitution modifier to your Fortitude saving throws.

Reflex: These saves test your ability to dodge area attacks and unexpected situations. Apply your Dexterity modifier to your Reflex saving throws.

Will: These saves reflect your resistance to mental influence as well as many magical effects. Apply your Wisdom modifier to your Will saving throws.

Saving Throw Difficulty Class: The DC for a save is determined by the attack itself.

Automatic Failures and Successes: A natural 1 (the d20 comes up 1) on a saving throw is always a failure (and may cause damage to exposed items; see Items Surviving after a Saving Throw on page 217). A natural 20 (the d20 comes up 20) is always a success.

ATTACKS OF OPPORTUNITY

In this combat, Valeros and Seoni fight an ogre and his goblin buddy.

#1: Valeros can safely approach this way without provoking an attack of opportunity, as he does not pass through a square threatened by the ogre (who has 10 feet of reach) or the goblin.

#2: If Valeros approaches this way, he provokes two attacks of opportunity since he passes through a square both creatures threaten.

#3: Seoni moves away using a withdraw action. The first square she leaves is not threatened as a result, and she can thus move away from the goblin safely, but when she leaves the second square, she provokes an attack of opportunity from the ogre (who has 10 feet of reach). She could instead limit her movement to a 5-foot step, as a free action, and not provoke any attacks of opportunity.

ACTIONS IN COMBAT

During one turn, there are a wide variety of actions that your character can perform, from swinging a sword to casting a spell.

Action Types

An action's type essentially tells you how long the action takes to perform (within the framework of the 6-second combat round) and how movement is treated. There are six types of actions: standard actions, move actions, full-round actions, swift actions, immediate actions, and free actions.

In a normal round, you can perform a standard action and a move action, or you can perform a full-round action. You can also perform one swift action and one or more free actions. You can always take a move action in place of a standard action.

In some situations (such as in a surprise round), you may be limited to taking only a single move action or standard action.

Standard Action: A standard action allows you to do something, most commonly to make an attack or cast a spell. See Table 8–2 for other standard actions.

Move Action: A move action allows you to move up to your speed or perform an action that takes a similar amount of time. See Table 8–2 for other move actions.

You can take a move action in place of a standard action. If you move no actual distance in a round (commonly because you have swapped your move action for one or more equivalent actions), you can take one 5-foot step either before, during, or after the action.

Full-Round Action: A full-round action consumes all your effort during a round. The only movement you can take during a full-round action is a 5-foot step before, during, or after the action. You can also perform free actions and swift actions (see below). See Table 8–2 for a list of full-round actions.

Some full-round actions do not allow you to take a 5-foot step.

Some full-round actions can be taken as standard actions, but only in situations when you are limited to performing only a standard action during your round. The descriptions of specific actions detail which actions allow this option.

Free Action: Free actions consume a very small amount of time and effort. You can perform one or more free actions while taking another action normally. However, there are

reasonable limits on what you can really do for free, as decided by the GM.

Swift Action: A swift action consumes a very small amount of time, but represents a larger expenditure of effort and energy than a free action. You can perform only a single swift action per turn.

Immediate Action: An immediate action is very similar to a swift action, but can be performed at any time—even if it's not your turn.

Not an Action: Some activities are so minor that they are not even considered free actions. They literally don't take any time at all to do and are considered an inherent part of doing something else, such as nocking an arrow as part of an attack with a bow.

Restricted Activity: In some situations, you may be unable to take a full round's worth of actions. In such cases, you are restricted to taking only a single standard action or a single move action (plus free and swift actions as normal). You can't take a full-round action (though you can start or complete a full-round action by using a standard action; see below).

Standard Actions

Most of the common actions characters take, aside from movement, fall into the realm of standard actions.

Attack

Making an attack is a standard action.

Melee Attacks: With a normal melee weapon, you can strike any opponent within 5 feet. (Opponents within 5 feet are considered adjacent to you.) Some melee weapons have reach, as indicated in their descriptions. With a typical reach weapon, you can strike opponents 10 feet away, but you can't strike adjacent foes (those within 5 feet).

Unarmed Attacks: Striking for damage with punches, kicks, and head butts is much like attacking with a melee weapon, except for the following:

Attacks of Opportunity: Attacking unarmed provokes an attack of opportunity from the character you attack, provided she is armed. The attack of opportunity comes before your attack. An unarmed attack does not provoke attacks of opportunity from other foes, nor does it provoke an attack of opportunity from an unarmed foe.

An unarmed character can't take attacks of opportunity (but see "Armed" Unarmed Attacks, below).

"Armed" Unarmed Attacks: Sometimes a character's or creature's unarmed attack counts as an armed attack. A monk, a character with the Improved Unarmed Strike feat, a spellcaster delivering a touch attack spell, and a creature with natural physical weapons all count as being armed (see natural attacks).

Note that being armed counts for both offense and defense (the character can make attacks of opportunity).

Unarmed Strike Damage: An unarmed strike from a Medium character deals 1d3 points of bludgeoning damage (plus your Strength modifier, as normal). A Small character's unarmed strike deals 1d2 points of bludgeoning damage, while a Large character's unarmed strike deals 1d4 points of bludgeoning damage. All damage from unarmed strikes is nonlethal damage. Unarmed strikes count as light weapons (for purposes of two-weapon attack penalties and so on).

Dealing Lethal Damage: You can specify that your unarmed strike will deal lethal damage before you make your attack roll, but you take a –4 penalty on your attack roll. If you have the Improved Unarmed Strike feat, you can deal lethal damage with an unarmed strike without taking a penalty on the attack roll.

Ranged Attacks: With a ranged weapon, you can shoot or throw at any target that is within the weapon's maximum range and in line of sight. The maximum range for a thrown weapon is five range increments. For projectile weapons, it is 10 range increments. Some ranged weapons have shorter maximum ranges, as specified in their descriptions.

Natural Attacks: Attacks made with natural weapons, such as claws and bites, are melee attacks that can be made against any creature within your reach (usually 5 feet). These attacks are made using your full attack bonus and deal an amount of damage that depends on their type (plus your Strength modifier, as normal). You do not receive additional natural attacks for a high base attack bonus. Instead, you receive additional attack rolls for multiple limb and body parts capable of making the attack (as noted by the race or ability that grants the attacks). If you possess only one natural attack (such as a bite—two claw attacks do not qualify), you add 1–1/2 times your Strength bonus on damage rolls made with that attack.

Some natural attacks are denoted as secondary natural attacks, such as tails and wings. Attacks with secondary natural attacks are made using your base attack bonus minus 5. These attacks deal an amount of damage depending on their type, but you only add half your Strength modifier on damage rolls.

You can make attacks with natural weapons in combination with attacks made with a melee weapon and unarmed strikes, so long as a different limb is used for each attack. For example, you cannot make a claw attack and also use that hand to make attacks with a longsword. When you make additional attacks in this way, all of your natural attacks are treated as secondary natural attacks, using your base attack bonus minus 5 and adding only 1/2 of your Strength modifier on damage rolls. Feats such as Two-Weapon Fighting and Multiattack (see the *Pathfinder RPG Bestiary*) can reduce these penalties.

TABLE 8-2: ACTIONS IN COMBAT

Standard Action	Attack of Opportunity[1]
Attack (melee)	No
Attack (ranged)	Yes
Attack (unarmed)	Yes
Activate a magic item other than a potion or oil	No
Aid another	Maybe[2]
Cast a spell (1 standard action casting time)	Yes
Channel energy	No
Concentrate to maintain an active spell	No
Dismiss a spell	No
Draw a hidden weapon (see Sleight of Hand skill)	No
Drink a potion or apply an oil	Yes
Escape a grapple	No
Feint	No
Light a torch with a tindertwig	Yes
Lower spell resistance	No
Read a scroll	Yes
Ready (triggers a standard action)	No
Stabilize a dying friend (see Heal skill)	Yes
Total defense	No
Use extraordinary ability	No
Use skill that takes 1 action	Usually
Use spell-like ability	Yes
Use supernatural ability	No

Move Action	Attack of Opportunity[1]
Move	Yes
Control a frightened mount	Yes
Direct or redirect an active spell	No
Draw a weapon[3]	No
Load a hand crossbow or light crossbow	Yes
Open or close a door	No
Mount/dismount a steed	No
Move a heavy object	Yes
Pick up an item	Yes
Sheathe a weapon	Yes
Stand up from prone	Yes
Ready or drop a shield[3]	No
Retrieve a stored item	Yes

Full-Round Action	Attack of Opportunity[1]
Full attack	No
Charge[4]	No
Deliver coup de grace	Yes
Escape from a net	Yes
Extinguish flames	No
Light a torch	Yes
Load a heavy or repeating crossbow	Yes
Lock or unlock weapon in locked gauntlet	Yes
Prepare to throw splash weapon	Yes
Run	Yes
Use skill that takes 1 round	Usually
Use a touch spell on up to six friends	Yes
Withdraw[4]	No

Free Action	Attack of Opportunity[1]
Cease concentration on a spell	No
Drop an item	No
Drop to the floor	No
Prepare spell components to cast a spell[5]	No
Speak	No

Swift Action	Attack of Opportunity[1]
Cast a quickened spell	No

Immediate Action	Attack of Opportunity[1]
Cast *feather fall*	No

No Action	Attack of Opportunity[1]
Delay	No
5-foot step	No

Action Type Varies	Attack of Opportunity[1]
Perform a combat maneuver[6]	Yes
Use feat[7]	Varies

1 Regardless of the action, if you move out of a threatened square, you usually provoke an attack of opportunity. This column indicates whether the action itself, not moving, provokes an attack of opportunity.

2 If you aid someone performing an action that would normally provoke an attack of opportunity, then the act of aiding another provokes an attack of opportunity as well.

3 If you have a base attack bonus of +1 or higher, you can combine one of these actions with a regular move. If you have the Two-Weapon Fighting feat, you can draw two light or one-handed weapons in the time it would normally take you to draw one.

4 May be taken as a standard action if you are limited to taking only a single action in a round.

5 Unless the component is an extremely large or awkward item.

6 Some combat maneuvers substitute for a melee attack, not an action. As melee attacks, they can be used once in an attack or charge action, one or more times in a full-attack action, or even as an attack of opportunity. Others are used as a separate action.

7 The description of a feat defines its effect.

Multiple Attacks: A character who can make more than one attack per round must use the full-attack action (see Full-Round Actions) in order to get more than one attack.

Shooting or Throwing into a Melee: If you shoot or throw a ranged weapon at a target engaged in melee with a friendly character, you take a –4 penalty on your attack roll. Two characters are engaged in melee if they are enemies of each other and either threatens the other. (An unconscious or otherwise immobilized character is not considered engaged unless he is actually being attacked.)

If your target (or the part of your target you're aiming at, if it's a big target) is at least 10 feet away from the nearest friendly character, you can avoid the –4 penalty, even if the creature you're aiming at is engaged in melee with a friendly character.

If your target is two size categories larger than the friendly characters it is engaged with, this penalty is reduced to –2. There is no penalty for firing at a creature that is three size categories larger than the friendly characters it is engaged with.

Precise Shot: If you have the Precise Shot feat, you don't take this penalty.

Fighting Defensively as a Standard Action: You can choose to fight defensively when attacking. If you do so, you take a –4 penalty on all attacks in a round to gain a +2 dodge bonus to AC until the start of your next turn.

Critical Hits: When you make an attack roll and get a natural 20 (the d20 shows 20), you hit regardless of your target's Armor Class, and you have scored a "threat," meaning the hit might be a critical hit (or "crit"). To find out if it's a critical hit, you immediately make an attempt to "confirm" the critical hit—another attack roll with all the same modifiers as the attack roll you just made. If the confirmation roll also results in a hit against the target's AC, your original hit is a critical hit. (The critical roll just needs to hit to give you a crit, it doesn't need to come up 20 again.) If the confirmation roll is a miss, then your hit is just a regular hit.

A critical hit means that you roll your damage more than once, with all your usual bonuses, and add the rolls together. Unless otherwise specified, the threat range for a critical hit on an attack roll is 20, and the multiplier is ×2.

Exception: Precision damage (such as from a rogue's sneak attack class feature) and additional damage dice from weapon special abilities (such as *flaming*) are not multiplied when you score a critical hit.

Increased Threat Range: Sometimes your threat range is greater than 20. That is, you can score a threat on a lower number. In such cases, a roll of lower than 20 is not an automatic hit. Any attack roll that doesn't result in a hit is not a threat.

Increased Critical Multiplier: Some weapons deal better than double damage on a critical hit (see Chapter 6).

Spells and Critical Hits: A spell that requires an attack roll can score a critical hit. A spell attack that requires no attack roll cannot score a critical hit. If a spell causes ability damage or drain (see Appendix 1), the damage or drain is doubled on a critical hit.

Activate Magic Item

Many magic items don't need to be activated. Certain magic items, however, do need to be activated, especially potions, scrolls, wands, rods, and staves. Unless otherwise noted, activating a magic item is a standard action.

Spell Completion Items: Activating a spell completion item (see page 458) is the equivalent of casting a spell. It requires concentration and provokes attacks of opportunity. You lose the spell if your concentration is broken, and you can attempt to activate the item while on the defensive, as with casting a spell.

Spell Trigger, Command Word, or Use-Activated Items: Activating any of these kinds of items does not require concentration and does not provoke attacks of opportunity.

Cast a Spell

Most spells require 1 standard action to cast. You can cast such a spell either before or after you take a move action.

Note: You retain your Dexterity bonus to AC while casting.

Spell Components: To cast a spell with a verbal (V) component, your character must speak in a firm voice. If you're gagged or in the area of a *silence* spell, you can't cast such a spell. A spellcaster who has been deafened has a 20% chance to spoil any spell he tries to cast if that spell has a verbal component.

To cast a spell with a somatic (S) component, you must gesture freely with at least one hand. You can't cast a spell of this type while bound, grappling, or with both your hands full or occupied.

To cast a spell with a material (M), focus (F), or divine focus (DF) component, you have to have the proper materials, as described by the spell. Unless these components are elaborate, preparing them is a free action. For material components and focuses whose costs are not listed in the spell description, you can assume that you have them if you have your spell component pouch.

Concentration: You must concentrate to cast a spell. If you can't concentrate, you can't cast a spell. If you start casting a spell but something interferes with your concentration, you must make a concentration check or lose the spell. The check's DC depends on what is threatening your concentration (see Chapter 9). If you fail, the spell fizzles with no effect. If you prepare spells, it is lost from preparation. If you cast at will, it counts against your daily limit of spells even though you did not cast it successfully.

Concentrating to Maintain a Spell: Some spells require continued concentration to keep them going. Concentrating to maintain a spell is a standard action that doesn't provoke an attack of opportunity. Anything that could break your concentration when casting a spell can keep you from concentrating to maintain a spell. If your concentration breaks, the spell ends.

Casting Time: Most spells have a casting time of 1 standard action. A spell cast in this manner immediately takes effect.

Attacks of Opportunity: Generally, if you cast a spell, you provoke attacks of opportunity from threatening enemies. If you take damage from an attack of opportunity, you must make a concentration check (DC 10 + points of damage taken + the spell's level) or lose the spell. Spells that require only a swift action to cast don't provoke attacks of opportunity.

Casting on the Defensive: Casting a spell while on the defensive does not provoke an attack of opportunity. It does, however, require a concentration check (DC 15 + double the spell's level) to successfully cast the spell. Failure means that you lose the spell.

Touch Spells in Combat: Many spells have a range of touch. To use these spells, you cast the spell and then touch the subject. In the same round that you cast the spell, you may also touch (or attempt to touch) as a free action. You may take your move before casting the spell, after touching the target, or between casting the spell and touching the target. You can automatically touch one friend or use the spell on yourself, but to touch an opponent, you must succeed on an attack roll.

Touch Attacks: Touching an opponent with a touch spell is considered to be an armed attack and therefore does not provoke attacks of opportunity. The act of casting a spell, however, does provoke an attack of opportunity. Touch attacks come in two types: melee touch attacks and ranged touch attacks. You can score critical hits with either type of attack as long as the spell deals damage. Your opponent's AC against a touch attack does not include any armor bonus, shield bonus, or natural armor bonus. His size modifier, Dexterity modifier, and deflection bonus (if any) all apply normally.

Holding the Charge: If you don't discharge the spell in the round when you cast the spell, you can hold the charge indefinitely. You can continue to make touch attacks round after round. If you touch anything or anyone while holding a charge, even unintentionally, the spell discharges. If you cast another spell, the touch spell dissipates. You can touch one friend as a standard action or up to six friends as a full-round action. Alternatively, you may make a normal unarmed attack (or an attack with a natural weapon) while holding a charge. In this case, you aren't considered armed and you provoke attacks of opportunity as normal for the attack. If your unarmed attack or natural weapon attack normally doesn't provoke attacks of opportunity, neither does this attack. If the attack hits, you deal normal damage for your unarmed attack or natural weapon and the spell discharges. If the attack misses, you are still holding the charge.

Ranged Touch Spells in Combat: Some spells allow you to make a ranged touch attack as part of the casting of the spell. These attacks are made as part of the spell and do not require a separate action. Ranged touch attacks provoke an attack of opportunity, even if the spell that causes the attacks was cast defensively. Unless otherwise noted, ranged touch attacks cannot be held until a later turn.

Dismiss a Spell: Dismissing an active spell is a standard action that doesn't provoke attacks of opportunity.

Start/Complete Full-Round Action

The "start full-round action" standard action lets you start undertaking a full-round action, which you can complete in the following round by using another standard action. You can't use this action to start or complete a full attack, charge, run, or withdraw.

Total Defense

You can defend yourself as a standard action. You get a +4 dodge bonus to your AC for 1 round. Your AC improves at the start of this action. You can't combine total defense with fighting defensively or with the benefit of the Combat Expertise feat. You can't make attacks of opportunity while using total defense.

Use Special Ability

Using a special ability is usually a standard action, but whether it is a standard action, a full-round action, or not an action at all is defined by the ability.

Spell-Like Abilities (Sp): Using a spell-like ability works like casting a spell in that it requires concentration and provokes attacks of opportunity. Spell-like abilities can be disrupted. If your concentration is broken, the attempt to use the ability fails, but the attempt counts as if you had used the ability. The casting time of a spell-like ability is 1 standard action, unless the ability description notes otherwise.

Using a Spell-Like Ability on the Defensive: You may attempt to use a spell-like ability on the defensive, just as with casting a spell. If the concentration check (DC 15 + double the spell's level) fails, you can't use the ability, but the attempt counts as if you had used the ability.

Supernatural Abilities (Su): Using a supernatural ability is usually a standard action (unless defined otherwise by the ability's description). Its use cannot be disrupted, does not require concentration, and does not provoke attacks of opportunity.

Extraordinary Abilities (Ex): Using an extraordinary ability is usually not an action because most extraordinary abilities automatically happen in a reactive fashion. Those extraordinary abilities that are actions are usually standard actions that cannot be disrupted, do not require concentration, and do not provoke attacks of opportunity.

Move Actions

With the exception of specific movement-related skills, most move actions don't require a check.

Move

The simplest move action is moving your speed. If you take this kind of move action during your turn, you can't also take a 5-foot step.

Many nonstandard modes of movement are covered under this category, including climbing (up to one-quarter of your speed) and swimming (up to one-quarter of your speed).

Accelerated Climbing: You can climb at half your speed as a move action by accepting a –5 penalty on your Climb check.

Crawling: You can crawl 5 feet as a move action. Crawling incurs attacks of opportunity from any attackers who threaten you at any point of your crawl. A crawling character is considered prone and must take a move action to stand up, provoking an attack of opportunity.

Direct or Redirect a Spell

Some spells allow you to redirect the effect to new targets or areas after you cast the spell. Redirecting a spell requires a move action and does not provoke attacks of opportunity or require concentration.

Draw or Sheathe a Weapon

Drawing a weapon so that you can use it in combat, or putting it away so that you have a free hand, requires a move action. This action also applies to weapon-like objects carried in easy reach, such as wands. If your weapon or weapon-like object is stored in a pack or otherwise out of easy reach, treat this action as retrieving a stored item.

If you have a base attack bonus of +1 or higher, you may draw a weapon as a free action combined with a regular move. If you have the Two-Weapon Fighting feat, you can draw two light or one-handed weapons in the time it would normally take you to draw one.

Drawing ammunition for use with a ranged weapon (such as arrows, bolts, sling bullets, or shuriken) is a free action.

Manipulate an Item

Moving or manipulating an item is usually a move action.

This includes retrieving or putting away a stored item, picking up an item, moving a heavy object, and opening a door. Examples of this kind of action, along with whether they incur an attack of opportunity, are given in Table 8–2.

Mount/Dismount a Steed

Mounting or dismounting a steed requires a move action.

Fast Mount or Dismount: You can mount or dismount as a free action with a DC 20 Ride check. If you fail the check, mounting or dismounting is a move action instead. You can't attempt a fast mount or fast dismount unless you can perform the mount or dismount as a move action in the current round.

Ready or Drop a Shield

Strapping a shield to your arm to gain its shield bonus to your AC, or unstrapping and dropping a shield so you can use your shield hand for another purpose, requires a move action. If you have a base attack bonus of +1 or higher, you can ready or drop a shield as a free action combined with a regular move.

Dropping a carried (but not worn) shield is a free action.

Stand Up

Standing up from a prone position requires a move action and provokes attacks of opportunity.

Full-Round Actions

A full-round action requires an entire round to complete. Thus, it can't be coupled with a standard or a move action, though if it does not involve moving any distance, you can take a 5-foot step.

Full Attack

If you get more than one attack per round because your base attack bonus is high enough (see Base Attack Bonus in Chapter 3), because you fight with two weapons or a double weapon, or for some special reason, you must use a full-round action to get your additional attacks. You do not need to specify the targets of your attacks ahead of time. You can see how the earlier attacks turn out before assigning the later ones.

The only movement you can take during a full attack is a 5-foot step. You may take the step before, after, or between your attacks.

If you get multiple attacks because your base attack bonus is high enough, you must make the attacks in order from highest bonus to lowest. If you are using two weapons, you can strike with either weapon first. If you are using a double weapon, you can strike with either part of the weapon first.

Deciding between an Attack or a Full Attack: After your first attack, you can decide to take a move action instead of making your remaining attacks, depending on how the first attack turns out and assuming you have not already taken a move action this round. If you've already taken a 5-foot step, you can't use your move action to move any distance, but you could still use a different kind of move action.

Fighting Defensively as a Full-Round Action: You can choose to fight defensively when taking a full-attack action. If you do so, you take a −4 penalty on all attacks in a round to gain a +2 dodge bonus to AC until the start of your next turn.

Cast a Spell

A spell that takes one round to cast is a full-round action. It comes into effect just before the beginning of your turn in the round after you began casting the spell. You then act normally after the spell is completed.

A spell that takes 1 minute to cast comes into effect just before your turn 1 minute later (and for each of those 10 rounds, you are casting a spell as a full-round action). These actions must be consecutive and uninterrupted, or the spell automatically fails.

When you begin a spell that takes 1 round or longer to cast, you must continue the invocations, gestures, and concentration from 1 round to just before your turn in the next round (at least). If you lose concentration after starting the spell and before it is complete, you lose the spell.

You only provoke attacks of opportunity when you begin casting a spell, even though you might continue casting for at least 1 full round. While casting a spell, you don't threaten any squares around you.

This action is otherwise identical to the cast a spell action described under Standard Actions.

Casting a Metamagic Spell: Sorcerers and bards must take more time to cast a metamagic spell (one enhanced by a metamagic feat) than a regular spell. If a spell's normal casting time is 1 standard action, casting a metamagic version of the spell is a full-round action for a sorcerer or bard (except for spells modified by the Quicken Spell feat, which take 1 swift action to cast). Note that this isn't the same as a spell with a 1-round casting time. Spells that take a full-round action to cast take effect in the same round that you begin casting, and you are not required to continue the

invocations, gestures, and concentration until your next turn. For spells with a longer casting time, it takes an extra full-round action to cast the metamagic spell.

Clerics and druids must take more time to spontaneously cast a metamagic version of a cure, inflict, or summon spell. Spontaneously casting a metamagic version of a spell with a casting time of 1 standard action is a full-round action, and spells with longer casting times take an extra full-round action to cast.

Move 5 Feet through Difficult Terrain

In some situations, your movement may be so hampered that you don't have sufficient speed even to move 5 feet (a single square). In such a case, you may spend a full-round action to move 5 feet (1 square) in any direction, even diagonally. Even though this looks like a 5-foot step, it's not, and thus it provokes attacks of opportunity normally.

Run

You can run as a full-round action. If you do, you do not also get a 5-foot step. When you run, you can move up to four times your speed in a straight line (or three times your speed if you're in heavy armor). You lose any Dexterity bonus to AC unless you have the Run feat.

You can run for a number of rounds equal to your Constitution score, but after that you must make a DC 10 Constitution check to continue running. You must check again each round in which you continue to run, and the DC of this check increases by 1 for each check you have made. When you fail this check, you must stop running. A character who has run to his limit must rest for 1 minute (10 rounds) before running again. During a rest period, a character can move no faster than a normal move action.

You can't run across difficult terrain or if you can't see where you're going.

A run represents a speed of about 13 miles per hour for an unencumbered human.

Use Special Ability

Using a special ability is usually a standard action, but some may be full-round actions, as defined by the ability.

Withdraw

Withdrawing from melee combat is a full-round action. When you withdraw, you can move up to double your speed. The square you start out in is not considered threatened by any opponent you can see, and therefore visible enemies do not get attacks of opportunity against you when you move from that square. Invisible enemies still get attacks of opportunity against you, and you can't withdraw from combat if you're blinded. You can't take a 5-foot step during the same round in which you withdraw.

If, during the process of withdrawing, you move out of a threatened square (other than the one you started in), enemies get attacks of opportunity as normal.

You may not withdraw using a form of movement for which you don't have a listed speed.

Note that despite the name of this action, you don't actually have to leave combat entirely.

Restricted Withdraw: If you are limited to taking only a standard action each round you can withdraw as a standard action. In this case, you may move up to your speed.

Free Actions

Free actions don't take any time at all, though there may be limits to the number of free actions you can perform in a turn. Free actions rarely incur attacks of opportunity. Some common free actions are described below.

Cease Concentration on Spell

You can stop concentrating on a spell as a free action.

Drop an Item

Dropping an item in your space or into an adjacent square is a free action.

Drop Prone

Dropping to a prone position in your space is a free action.

Speak

In general, speaking is a free action that you can perform even when it isn't your turn. Speaking more than a few sentences is generally beyond the limit of a free action.

Swift Actions

A swift action consumes a very small amount of time, but represents a larger expenditure of effort than a free action. You can perform one swift action per turn without affecting your ability to perform other actions. In that regard, a swift action is like a free action. You can, however, perform only one single swift action per turn, regardless of what other actions you take. You can take a swift action anytime you would normally be allowed to take a free action. Swift actions usually involve spellcasting, activating a feat, or the activation of magic items.

Cast a Quickened Spell

You can cast a quickened spell (see the Quicken Spell feat), or any spell whose casting time is designated as a free or swift action, as a swift action. Only one such spell can be cast in any round, and such spells don't count toward your normal limit of one spell per round. Casting a spell as a swift action doesn't incur an attack of opportunity.

Immediate Actions

Much like a swift action, an immediate action consumes a very small amount of time but represents a larger expenditure of time and energy than a free action. However, unlike a swift action, an immediate action can be performed at any time—even if it's not your turn. Casting *feather fall* is an immediate action, since the spell can be cast at any time.

Using an immediate action on your turn is the same as using a swift action and counts as your swift action for that turn. You cannot use another immediate action or a swift action until after your next turn if you have used an immediate action when it is not currently your turn (effectively, using an immediate action before your turn is equivalent to using your swift action for the coming turn). You also cannot use an immediate action if you are flat-footed.

Miscellaneous Actions

The following actions take a variable amount of time to accomplish or otherwise work differently than other actions.

Take 5-Foot Step

You can move 5 feet in any round when you don't perform any other kind of movement. Taking this 5-foot step never provokes an attack of opportunity. You can't take more than one 5-foot step in a round, and you can't take a 5-foot step in the same round that you move any distance.

You can take a 5-foot step before, during, or after your other actions in the round.

You can only take a 5-foot-step if your movement isn't hampered by difficult terrain or darkness. Any creature with a speed of 5 feet or less can't take a 5-foot step, since moving even 5 feet requires a move action for such a slow creature.

You may not take a 5-foot step using a form of movement for which you do not have a listed speed.

Use Feat

Certain feats let you take special actions in combat. Other feats do not require actions themselves, but they give you a bonus when attempting something you can already do. Some feats are not meant to be used within the framework of combat. The individual feat descriptions tell you what you need to know about them.

Use Skill

Most skill uses are standard actions, but some might be move actions, full-round actions, free actions, or something else entirely.

The individual skill descriptions in Chapter 4 tell you what sorts of actions are required to perform skills.

INJURY AND DEATH

Your hit points measure how hard you are to kill. No matter how many hit points you lose, your character isn't hindered in any way until your hit points drop to 0 or lower.

Loss of Hit Points

The most common way that your character gets hurt is to take lethal damage and lose hit points.

What Hit Points Represent: Hit points mean two things in the game world: the ability to take physical punishment and keep going, and the ability to turn a serious blow into a less serious one.

Effects of Hit Point Damage: Damage doesn't slow you down until your current hit points reach 0 or lower. At 0 hit points, you're disabled.

If your hit point total is negative, but not equal to or greater than your Constitution score, you are unconscious and dying.

When your negative hit point total is equal to your Constitution, you're dead.

Massive Damage (Optional Rule): If you ever sustain a single attack that deals an amount of damage equal to half your total hit points (minimum 50 points of damage) or more and it doesn't kill you outright, you must make a DC 15 Fortitude save. If this saving throw fails, you die regardless of your current hit points. If you take half your total hit points or more in damage from multiple attacks, no one of which dealt more than half your total hit points (minimum 50), the massive damage rule does not apply.

Disabled (0 Hit Points)

When your current hit point total drops to exactly 0, you are disabled.

You gain the staggered condition and can only take a single move or standard action each turn (but not both, nor can you take full-round actions). You can take move actions without further injuring yourself, but if you perform any standard action (or any other strenuous action) you take 1 point of damage after completing the act. Unless your activity increased your hit points, you are now at –1 hit points and dying.

Healing that raises your hit points above 0 makes you fully functional again, just as if you'd never been reduced to 0 or fewer hit points.

You can also become disabled when recovering from dying. In this case, it's a step toward recovery, and you can have fewer than 0 hit points (see Stable Characters and Recovery).

Dying (Negative Hit Points)

If your hit point total is negative, but not equal to or greater than your Constitution score, you're dying.

A dying character immediately falls unconscious and can take no actions.

A dying character loses 1 hit point every round. This continues until the character dies or becomes stable.

Dead

When your character's current hit points drop to a negative amount equal to his Constitution score or lower, or if he succumbs to massive damage, he's dead. A character can also die from taking ability damage or suffering an ability drain that reduces his Constitution score to 0 (see Appendix 1).

Certain types of powerful magic, such as *raise dead* and *resurrection*, can restore life to a dead character. See Chapter 9 for more information.

Stable Characters and Recovery

On the character's next turn, after being reduced to negative hit points (but not dead), and on all subsequent turns, the character must make a DC 10 Constitution check to become stable. The character takes a penalty on this roll equal to his negative hit point total. A character that is stable does not need to make this check. A natural 20 on this check is an automatic success. If the character fails this check, he loses 1 hit point. An unconscious or dying character cannot use any special action that changes the initiative count on which his action occurs.

Characters taking continuous damage, such as from an *acid arrow* or a bleed effect, automatically fail all Constitution checks made to stabilize. Such characters lose 1 hit point per round in addition to the continuous damage.

You can keep a dying character from losing any more hit points and make him stable with a DC 15 Heal check.

If any sort of healing cures the dying character of even 1 point of damage, he becomes stable and stops losing hit points.

Healing that raises the dying character's hit points to 0 makes him conscious and disabled. Healing that raises his hit points to 1 or more makes him fully functional again, just as if he'd never been reduced to 0 or lower. A spellcaster retains the spellcasting capability she had before dropping below 0 hit points.

A stable character who has been tended by a healer or who has been magically healed eventually regains consciousness and recovers hit points naturally. If the character has no one to tend him, however, his life is still in danger, and he may yet slip away.

Recovering with Help: One hour after a tended, dying character becomes stable, the character must make a DC 10 Constitution check to become conscious. The character takes a penalty on this roll equal to his negative hit point total. Conscious characters with negative hit point totals are treated as disabled characters (see page 189). If the character remains unconscious, he receives another check every hour to regain consciousness. A natural 20 on this check is an automatic success. Even if unconscious, the character recovers hit points naturally. He automatically regains consciousness when his hit points rise to 1 or higher.

Recovering without Help: A severely wounded character left alone usually dies. He has a small chance of recovering on his own. Treat such characters as those attempting to recover with help, but every failed Constitution check to regain consciousness results in the loss of 1 hit point. An unaided character does not recover hit points naturally. Once conscious, the character can make a DC 10 Constitution check once per day, after resting for 8 hours, to begin recovering hit points naturally. The character takes a penalty on this roll equal to his negative hit point total. Failing this check causes the character to lose 1 hit point, but this does not cause the character to become unconscious. Once a character makes this check, he continues to heal naturally and is no longer in danger of losing hit points naturally.

Healing

After taking damage, you can recover hit points through natural healing or through magical healing. In any case, you can't regain hit points past your full normal hit point total.

Natural Healing: With a full night's rest (8 hours of sleep or more), you recover 1 hit point per character level. Any significant interruption during your rest prevents you from healing that night.

If you undergo complete bed rest for an entire day and night, you recover twice your character level in hit points.

Magical Healing: Various abilities and spells can restore hit points.

Healing Limits: You can never recover more hit points than you lost. Magical healing won't raise your current hit points higher than your full normal hit point total.

Healing Ability Damage: Temporary ability damage returns at the rate of 1 point per night of rest (8 hours) for each affected ability score. Complete bed rest restores 2 points per day (24 hours) for each affected ability score.

Temporary Hit Points

Certain effects give a character temporary hit points. These hit points are in addition to the character's current hit point total and any damage taken by the character is subtracted from these hit points first. Any damage in excess of a character's temporary hit points is applied to his current hit points as normal. If the effect that grants the temporary hit points ends or is dispelled, any remaining temporary hit points go away. The damage they sustained is not transferred to the character's current hit points.

When temporary hit points are lost, they cannot be restored as real hit points can be, even by magic.

Increases in Constitution Score and Current Hit Points: An increase in a character's Constitution score, even a temporary one, can give her more hit points (an effective hit point increase), but these are not temporary hit points. They can be restored, and they are not lost first as temporary hit points are.

Nonlethal Damage

Nonlethal damage represents harm to a character that is not life-threatening. Unlike normal damage, nonlethal damage is healed quickly with rest.

Dealing Nonlethal Damage: Certain attacks deal nonlethal damage. Other effects, such as heat or being exhausted, also deal nonlethal damage. When you take nonlethal damage, keep a running total of how much you've accumulated. Do not deduct the nonlethal damage number from your current hit points. It is not "real" damage. Instead, when your nonlethal damage equals your current hit points, you're staggered (see below), and when it exceeds your current hit points, you fall unconscious.

Nonlethal Damage with a Weapon that Deals Lethal Damage: You can use a melee weapon that deals lethal damage to deal nonlethal damage instead, but you take a –4 penalty on your attack roll.

Lethal Damage with a Weapon that Deals Nonlethal Damage: You can use a weapon that deals nonlethal damage, including an unarmed strike, to deal lethal damage instead, but you take a –4 penalty on your attack roll.

Staggered and Unconscious: When your nonlethal damage equals your current hit points, you're staggered. You can only take a standard action or a move action in each round (in addition to free, immediate, and swift actions). You cease being staggered when your current hit points once again exceed your nonlethal damage.

When your nonlethal damage exceeds your current hit points, you fall unconscious. While unconscious, you are helpless (see page 567).

Spellcasters who fall unconscious retain any spellcasting ability they had before going unconscious.

If a creature's nonlethal damage is equal to his total maximum hit points (not his current hit points), all further nonlethal damage is treated as lethal damage.

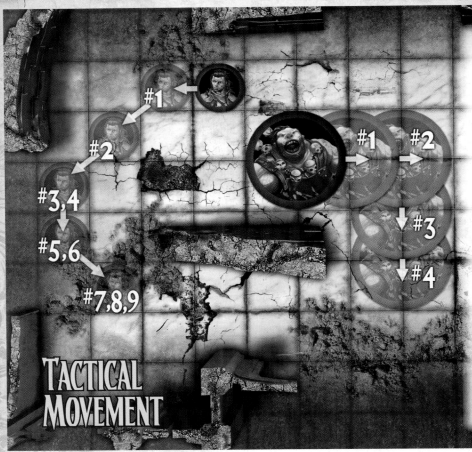

TACTICAL MOVEMENT

This does not apply to creatures with regeneration. Such creatures simply accrue additional nonlethal damage, increasing the amount of time they remain unconscious.

Healing Nonlethal Damage: You heal nonlethal damage at the rate of 1 hit point per hour per character level. When a spell or ability cures hit point damage, it also removes an equal amount of nonlethal damage.

MOVEMENT, POSITION, AND DISTANCE

Miniatures are on the 30mm scale—a miniature of a 6-foot-tall man is approximately 30mm tall. A square on the battle grid is 1 inch across, representing a 5-foot-by-5-foot area.

Tactical Movement

Your speed is determined by your race and your armor (see Table 8–3). Your speed while unarmored is your base land speed.

Encumbrance: A character encumbered by carrying treasure. a large amount of gear, or fallen comrades may move slower than normal (see Chapter 7).

Hampered Movement: Difficult terrain, obstacles, or poor visibility can hamper movement.

Movement in Combat: Generally, you can move your speed in a round and still do something (take a move action and a standard action).

If you do nothing but move (that is, if you use both of your actions in a round to move your speed), you can move double your speed.

If you spend the entire round running, you can move quadruple your speed (or three times your speed in heavy armor). If you do something that requires a full round, you can only take a 5-foot step.

Bonuses to Speed: A barbarian has a +10-foot bonus to her speed (unless she's wearing heavy armor). Experienced monks also have higher speed (unless they're wearing armor of any sort). In addition, many spells and magic items can affect a character's speed. Always apply any modifiers to a character's speed before adjusting the character's speed based on armor or encumbrance, and remember that multiple bonuses of the same type to a character's speed don't stack.

Measuring Distance

As a general rule, distance is measured assuming that 1 square equals 5 feet.

TABLE 8-3: TACTICAL SPEED

Race	No Armor or Light Armor	Medium or Heavy Armor
Human, elf, half-elf, half-orc	30 ft. (6 squares)	20 ft. (4 squares)
Dwarf	20 ft. (4 squares)	20 ft. (4 squares)
Halfling, gnome	20 ft. (4 squares)	15 ft. (3 squares)

Diagonals: When measuring distance, the first diagonal counts as 1 square, the second counts as 2 squares, the third counts as 1, the fourth as 2, and so on.

You can't move diagonally past a corner (even by taking a 5-foot step). You can move diagonally past a creature, even an opponent.

You can also move diagonally past other impassable obstacles, such as pits.

Closest Creature: When it's important to determine the closest square or creature to a location, if two squares or creatures are equally close, randomly determine which one counts as closest by rolling a die.

Moving Through a Square

You can move through an unoccupied square without difficulty in most circumstances. Difficult terrain and a number of spell effects might hamper your movement through open spaces.

Friend: You can move through a square occupied by a friendly character, unless you are charging. When you move through a square occupied by a friendly character, that character doesn't provide you with cover (see page 195).

Opponent: You can't move through a square occupied by an opponent unless the opponent is helpless. You can move through a square occupied by a helpless opponent without penalty. Some creatures, particularly very large ones, may present an obstacle even when helpless. In such cases, each square you move through counts as 2 squares.

Ending Your Movement: You can't end your movement in the same square as another creature unless it is helpless.

Overrun: During your movement, you can attempt to move through a square occupied by an opponent (see page 201).

Tumbling: A trained character can attempt to use Acrobatics to move through a square occupied by an opponent (see the Acrobatics skill).

Very Small Creature: A Fine, Diminutive, or Tiny creature can move into or through an occupied square. The creature provokes attacks of opportunity when doing so.

Square Occupied by Creature Three Sizes Larger or Smaller: Any creature can move through a square occupied by a creature three size categories larger than itself.

A big creature can move through a square occupied by a creature three size categories smaller than it is. Creatures moving through squares occupied by other creatures provoke attacks of opportunity from those creatures.

Designated Exceptions: Some creatures break the above rules. A creature that completely fills the squares it occupies cannot be moved past, even with the Acrobatics skill or similar special abilities.

Terrain and Obstacles

From tangled plants to broken stone, there are a number of terrain features that can affect your movement.

Difficult Terrain: Difficult terrain, such as heavy undergrowth, broken ground, or steep stairs, hampers movement. Each square of difficult terrain counts as 2 squares of movement. Each diagonal move into a difficult terrain square counts as 3 squares. You can't run or charge across difficult terrain.

If you occupy squares with different kinds of terrain, you can move only as fast as the most difficult terrain you occupy will allow.

Flying and incorporeal creatures are not hampered by difficult terrain.

Obstacles: Like difficult terrain, obstacles can hamper movement. If an obstacle hampers movement but doesn't completely block it, each obstructed square or obstacle between squares counts as 2 squares of movement. You must pay this cost to cross the obstacle, in addition to the cost to move into the square on the other side. If you don't have sufficient movement to cross the obstacle and move into the square on the other side, you can't cross it. Some obstacles may also require a skill check to cross.

On the other hand, some obstacles block movement entirely. A character can't move through a blocking obstacle.

Flying and incorporeal creatures are able to avoid most obstacles.

Squeezing: In some cases, you may have to squeeze into or through an area that isn't as wide as the space you take up. You can squeeze through or into a space that is at least half as wide as your normal space. Each move into or through a narrow space counts as if it were 2 squares, and while squeezed in a narrow space, you take a –4 penalty on attack rolls and a –4 penalty to AC.

When a Large creature (which normally takes up 4 squares) squeezes into a space that's 1 square wide, the creature's miniature figure occupies 2 squares, centered on the line between the 2 squares. For a bigger creature, center the creature likewise in the area it squeezes into.

A creature can squeeze past a creature while moving but it can't end its movement in an occupied square.

COVER

#1: Valeros is adjacent to the ogre, and nothing blocks him from reaching it. The ogre does not have cover against Valeros.

#2: Merisiel is adjacent to the ogre, but lines from the corners of her square to the corners of the ogre's square cross through a wall. The ogre has melee cover from her, but if it attacks her, Merisiel does not have cover from it, as the ogre has reach (so it figures attacks as if attacking with a ranged weapon).

#3: Kyra attacks at range, and must pick one of the corners of her square to determine cover. Some of these lines pass through a solid surface, meaning that the ogre has cover.

#4: Seoni attacks at range as well, but her lines reveal that she can clearly see more than half of the ogre. This gives the ogre partial cover.

To squeeze through or into a space less than half your space's width, you must use the Escape Artist skill. You can't attack while using Escape Artist to squeeze through or into a narrow space, you take a –4 penalty to AC, and you lose any Dexterity bonus to AC.

Special Movement Rules

These rules cover special movement situations.

Accidentally Ending Movement in an Illegal Space: Sometimes a character ends its movement while moving through a space where it's not allowed to stop. When that happens, put your miniature in the last legal position you occupied, or the closest legal position, if there's a legal position that's closer.

Double Movement Cost: When your movement is hampered in some way, your movement usually costs double. For example, each square of movement through difficult terrain counts as 2 squares, and each diagonal move through such terrain counts as 3 squares (just as two diagonal moves normally do).

If movement cost is doubled twice, then each square counts as 4 squares (or as 6 squares if moving diagonally). If movement cost is doubled three times, then each square

counts as 8 squares (12 if diagonal) and so on. This is an exception to the general rule that two doublings are equivalent to a tripling.

Minimum Movement: Despite whatever penalties to movement you might have, you can take a full-round action to move 5 feet (1 square) in any direction, even diagonally. This rule doesn't allow you to move through impassable terrain or to move when all movement is prohibited. Such movement provokes attacks of opportunity as normal (despite the distance covered, this move isn't a 5-foot step).

BIG AND LITTLE CREATURES IN COMBAT

Creatures smaller than Small or larger than Medium have special rules relating to position.

Tiny, Diminutive, and Fine Creatures: Very small creatures take up less than 1 square of space. This means that more than one such creature can fit into a single square. A Tiny creature typically occupies a space only 2-1/2 feet across, so four can fit into a single square. 25 Diminutive creatures or 100 Fine creatures can fit into a single square. Creatures that take up less than 1 square of space typically have a natural reach of 0 feet, meaning they can't reach into adjacent squares. They must enter an opponent's square to attack in melee. This provokes an attack of opportunity from the opponent. You can attack into your own square if you need to, so you can attack such creatures normally. Since they have no natural reach, they do not threaten the squares around them. You can move past them without provoking attacks of opportunity. They also can't flank an enemy.

Large, Huge, Gargantuan, and Colossal Creatures: Very large creatures take up more than 1 square.

Creatures that take up more than 1 square typically have a natural reach of 10 feet or more, meaning that they can reach targets even if they aren't in adjacent squares.

Unlike when someone uses a reach weapon, a creature with greater than normal natural reach (more than 5 feet) still threatens squares adjacent to it. A creature with greater than normal natural reach usually gets an attack of opportunity against you if you approach it, because you must enter and move within the range of its reach before you can attack it. This attack of opportunity is not provoked if you take a 5-foot step.

Large or larger creatures using reach weapons can strike up to double their natural reach but can't strike at their natural reach or less.

COMBAT MODIFIERS

A number of factors and conditions can influence an attack roll. Many of these situations grant a bonus or penalty on attack rolls or to a defender's Armor Class.

Cover

To determine whether your target has cover from your ranged attack, choose a corner of your square. If any line from this corner to any corner of the target's square passes through a square or border that blocks line of effect or provides cover, or through a square occupied by a creature, the target has cover (+4 to AC).

When making a melee attack against an adjacent target, your target has cover if any line from any corner of your square to the target's square goes through a wall (including a low wall). When making a melee attack against a target that isn't adjacent to you (such as with a reach weapon), use the rules for determining cover from ranged attacks.

Low Obstacles and Cover: A low obstacle (such as a wall no higher than half your height) provides cover, but only to creatures within 30 feet (6 squares) of it. The attacker can ignore the cover if he's closer to the obstacle than his target.

Cover and Attacks of Opportunity: You can't execute an attack of opportunity against an opponent with cover relative to you.

Cover and Reflex Saves: Cover grants you a +2 bonus on Reflex saves against attacks that originate or burst out

TABLE 8-4: CREATURE SIZE AND SCALE

Creature Size	Space*	Natural Reach*
Fine	1/2 ft.	0
Diminutive	1 ft.	0
Tiny	2-1/2 ft.	0
Small	5 ft.	5 ft.
Medium	5 ft.	5 ft.
Large (tall)	10 ft.	10 ft.
Large (long)	10 ft.	5 ft.
Huge (tall)	15 ft.	15 ft.
Huge (long)	15 ft.	10 ft.
Gargantuan (tall)	20 ft.	20 ft.
Gargantuan (long)	20 ft.	15 ft.
Colossal (tall)	30 ft.	30 ft.
Colossal (long)	30 ft.	20 ft.

* These values are typical for creatures of the indicated size. Some exceptions exist.

TABLE 8-5: ATTACK ROLL MODIFIERS

Attacker is...	Melee	Ranged
Dazzled	−1	−1
Entangled	−2[1]	−2[1]
Flanking defender	+2	—
Invisible	+2[2]	+2[2]
On higher ground	+1	+0
Prone	−4	—[3]
Shaken or frightened	−2	−2
Squeezing through a space	−4	−4

1 An entangled character also takes a −4 penalty to Dexterity, which may affect his attack roll.
2 The defender loses any Dexterity bonus to AC.
3 Most ranged weapons can't be used while the attacker is prone, but you can use a crossbow or shuriken while prone at no penalty.

TABLE 8-6: ARMOR CLASS MODIFIERS

Defender is...	Melee	Ranged
Behind cover	+4	+4
Blinded	−2[1]	−2[1]
Concealed or invisible	See Concealment	
Cowering	−2[1]	−2[1]
Entangled	+0[2]	+0[2]
Flat-footed	+0[1]	+0[1]
Grappling (but attacker is not)	+0	+0
Helpless	−4[3]	+0[3]
Kneeling or sitting	−2	+2
Pinned	−4[3]	+0[3]
Prone	−4	+4
Squeezing through a space	−4	−4
Stunned	−2[1]	−2[1]

1 The defender loses any Dexterity bonus to AC.
2 An entangled character takes a −4 penalty to Dexterity.
3 The defender is denied his Dexterity bonus to his Armor Class.

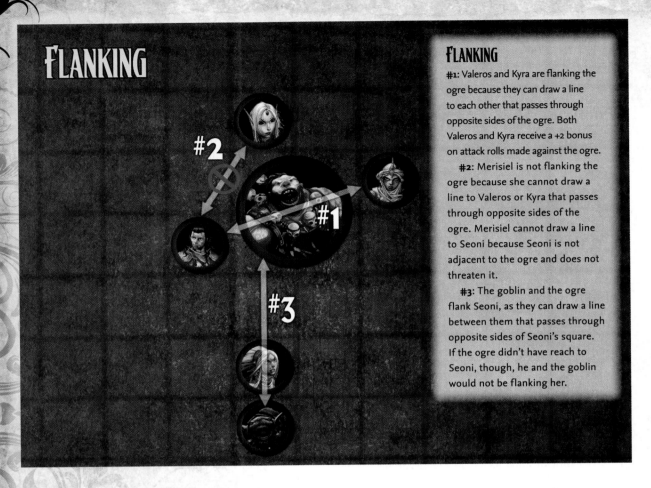

FLANKING

FLANKING

#1: Valeros and Kyra are flanking the ogre because they can draw a line to each other that passes through opposite sides of the ogre. Both Valeros and Kyra receive a +2 bonus on attack rolls made against the ogre.

#2: Merisiel is not flanking the ogre because she cannot draw a line to Valeros or Kyra that passes through opposite sides of the ogre. Merisiel cannot draw a line to Seoni because Seoni is not adjacent to the ogre and does not threaten it.

#3: The goblin and the ogre flank Seoni, as they can draw a line between them that passes through opposite sides of Seoni's square. If the ogre didn't have reach to Seoni, though, he and the goblin would not be flanking her.

from a point on the other side of the cover from you. Note that spread effects can extend around corners and thus negate this cover bonus.

Cover and Stealth Checks: You can use cover to make a Stealth check. Without cover, you usually need concealment (see below) to make a Stealth check.

Soft Cover: Creatures, even your enemies, can provide you with cover against ranged attacks, giving you a +4 bonus to AC. However, such soft cover provides no bonus on Reflex saves, nor does soft cover allow you to make a Stealth check.

Big Creatures and Cover: Any creature with a space larger than 5 feet (1 square) determines cover against melee attacks slightly differently than smaller creatures do. Such a creature can choose any square that it occupies to determine if an opponent has cover against its melee attacks. Similarly, when making a melee attack against such a creature, you can pick any of the squares it occupies to determine if it has cover against you.

Partial Cover: If a creature has cover, but more than half the creature is visible, its cover bonus is reduced to a +2 to AC and a +1 bonus on Reflex saving throws. This partial cover is subject to the GM's discretion.

Total Cover: If you don't have line of effect to your target (that is, you cannot draw any line from your square to your target's square without crossing a solid barrier), he is considered to have total cover from you. You can't make an attack against a target that has total cover.

Improved Cover: In some cases, such as attacking a target hiding behind an arrowslit, cover may provide a greater bonus to AC and Reflex saves. In such situations, the normal cover bonuses to AC and Reflex saves can be doubled (to +8 and +4, respectively). A creature with this improved cover effectively gains improved evasion against any attack to which the Reflex save bonus applies. Furthermore, improved cover provides a +10 bonus on Stealth checks.

Concealment

To determine whether your target has concealment from your ranged attack, choose a corner of your square. If any line from this corner to any corner of the target's square passes through a square or border that provides concealment, the target has concealment.

When making a melee attack against an adjacent target, your target has concealment if his space is entirely within an effect that grants concealment. When making a melee attack against a target that isn't adjacent to you, use the rules for determining concealment from ranged attacks.

In addition, some magical effects provide concealment against all attacks, regardless of whether any intervening concealment exists.

Concealment Miss Chance: Concealment gives the subject of a successful attack a 20% chance that the attacker missed because of the concealment. Make the attack normally—if the attacker hits, the defender must make a miss chance d% roll to avoid being struck. Multiple concealment conditions do not stack.

Concealment and Stealth Checks: You can use concealment to make a Stealth check. Without concealment, you usually need cover to make a Stealth check.

Total Concealment: If you have line of effect to a target but not line of sight, he is considered to have total concealment from you. You can't attack an opponent that has total concealment, though you can attack into a square that you think he occupies. A successful attack into a square occupied by an enemy with total concealment has a 50% miss chance (instead of the normal 20% miss chance for an opponent with concealment).

You can't execute an attack of opportunity against an opponent with total concealment, even if you know what square or squares the opponent occupies.

Ignoring Concealment: Concealment isn't always effective. An area of dim lighting or darkness doesn't provide any concealment against an opponent with darkvision. Characters with low-light vision can see clearly for a greater distance than other characters with the same light source. Although *invisibility* provides total concealment, sighted opponents may still make Perception checks to notice the location of an invisible character. An invisible character gains a +20 bonus on Stealth checks if moving, or a +40 bonus on Stealth checks when not moving (even though opponents can't see you, they might be able to figure out where you are from other visual or auditory clues).

Varying Degrees of Concealment: Certain situations may provide more or less than typical concealment, and modify the miss chance accordingly.

Flanking

When making a melee attack, you get a +2 flanking bonus if your opponent is threatened by another enemy character or creature on its opposite border or opposite corner.

When in doubt about whether two characters flank an opponent in the middle, trace an imaginary line between the two attackers' centers. If the line passes through opposite borders of the opponent's space (including corners of those borders), then the opponent is flanked.

Exception: If a flanker takes up more than 1 square, it gets the flanking bonus if any square it occupies counts for flanking.

Only a creature or character that threatens the defender can help an attacker get a flanking bonus.

Creatures with a reach of 0 feet can't flank an opponent.

Helpless Defenders

A helpless opponent is someone who is bound, sleeping, paralyzed, unconscious, or otherwise at your mercy.

Regular Attack: A helpless character takes a −4 penalty to AC against melee attacks. In addition, a helpless character is treated as having a Dexterity of 0, giving him a −5 penalty to AC against both melee and ranged attacks (for a total of −9 against melee and −5 against ranged). A helpless character is also flat-footed.

Coup de Grace: As a full-round action, you can use a melee weapon to deliver a coup de grace (pronounced "coo day grahs") to a helpless opponent. You can also use a bow or crossbow, provided you are adjacent to the target.

You automatically hit and score a critical hit. If the defender survives the damage, he must make a Fortitude save (DC 10 + damage dealt) or die. A rogue also gets her extra sneak attack damage against a helpless opponent when delivering a coup de grace.

Delivering a coup de grace provokes attacks of opportunity from threatening opponents.

You can't deliver a coup de grace against a creature that is immune to critical hits. You can deliver a coup de grace against a creature with total concealment, but doing this requires two consecutive full-round actions (one to "find" the creature once you've determined what square it's in, and one to deliver the coup de grace).

SPECIAL ATTACKS

This section discusses all of the various standard maneuvers you can perform during combat other than normal attacks, casting spells, or using other class abilities. Some of these special attacks can be made as part of another action (such as an attack) or as a attack of opportunity.

Aid Another

In melee combat, you can help a friend attack or defend by distracting or interfering with an opponent. If you're in position to make a melee attack on an opponent that is engaging a friend in melee combat, you can attempt to aid your friend as a standard action. You make an attack roll against AC 10. If you succeed, your friend gains either a +2 bonus on his next attack roll against that opponent or a +2 bonus to AC against that opponent's next attack (your choice), as long as that attack comes before the beginning of your next turn. Multiple characters can aid the same friend, and similar bonuses stack.

You can also use this standard action to help a friend in other ways, such as when he is affected by a spell, or to assist another character's skill check.

Charge

Charging is a special full-round action that allows you to move up to twice your speed and attack during the action. Charging, however, carries tight restrictions on how you can move.

Movement During a Charge: You must move before your attack, not after. You must move at least 10 feet (2 squares) and may move up to double your speed directly toward the designated opponent. If you move a distance equal to your speed or less, you can also draw a weapon during a charge attack if your base attack bonus is at least +1.

You must have a clear path toward the opponent, and nothing can hinder your movement (such as difficult terrain or obstacles). You must move to the closest space from which you can attack the opponent. If this space is occupied or otherwise blocked, you can't charge. If any line from your starting space to the ending space passes through a square that blocks movement, slows movement, or contains a creature (even an ally), you can't charge. Helpless creatures don't stop a charge.

If you don't have line of sight to the opponent at the start of your turn, you can't charge that opponent.

You can't take a 5-foot step in the same round as a charge.

If you are able to take only a standard action on your turn, you can still charge, but you are only allowed to move up to your speed (instead of up to double your speed) and you cannot draw a weapon unless you possess the Quick Draw feat. You can't use this option unless you are restricted to taking only a standard action on your turn.

Attacking on a Charge: After moving, you may make a single melee attack. You get a +2 bonus on the attack roll and take a –2 penalty to your AC until the start of your next turn.

A charging character gets a +2 bonus on combat maneuver attack rolls made to bull rush an opponent (see Bull Rush on page 199).

Even if you have extra attacks, such as from having a high enough base attack bonus or from using multiple weapons, you only get to make one attack during a charge.

Lances and Charge Attacks: A lance deals double damage if employed by a mounted character in a charge.

Weapons Readied against a Charge: Spears, tridents, and other weapons with the brace feature deal double damage when readied (set) and used against a charging character.

Combat Maneuvers

During combat, you can attempt to perform a number of maneuvers that can hinder or even cripple your foe, including bull rush, disarm, grapple, overrun, sunder, and trip. Although these maneuvers have vastly different results, they all use a similar mechanic to determine success.

Combat Maneuver Bonus: Each character and creature has a Combat Maneuver Bonus (or CMB) that represents its skill at performing combat maneuvers. A creature's CMB is determined using the following formula:

$$\text{CMB} = \text{Base attack bonus} + \text{Strength modifier} + \text{special size modifier}$$

Creatures that are size Tiny or smaller use their Dexterity modifier in place of their Strength modifier to determine their CMB. The special size modifier for a creature's Combat Maneuver Bonus is as follows: Fine –8, Diminutive –4, Tiny –2, Small –1, Medium +0, Large +1, Huge +2, Gargantuan +4, Colossal +8. Some feats and abilities grant a bonus to your CMB when performing specific maneuvers.

Performing a Combat Maneuver: When performing a combat maneuver, you must use an action appropriate to the maneuver you are attempting to perform. While many combat maneuvers can be performed as part of an attack action, full-attack action, or attack of opportunity (in place of a melee attack), others require a specific action. Unless otherwise noted, performing a combat maneuver provokes an attack of opportunity from the target of the maneuver. If you are hit by the target, you take the damage normally and apply that amount as a penalty to the attack roll to perform the maneuver. If your target is immobilized, unconscious, or otherwise incapacitated, your maneuver automatically succeeds (treat as if you rolled a natural 20 on the attack roll). If your target is stunned, you receive a +4 bonus on your attack roll to perform a combat maneuver against it.

When you attempt to perform a combat maneuver, make an attack roll and add your CMB in place of your normal attack bonus. Add any bonuses you currently have on attack rolls due to spells, feats, and other effects. These bonuses must be applicable to the weapon or attack used to perform the maneuver. The DC of this maneuver is your target's Combat Maneuver Defense. Combat maneuvers are attack rolls, so you must roll for concealment and take any other penalties that would normally apply to an attack roll.

Combat Maneuver Defense: Each character and creature has a Combat Maneuver Defense (or CMD) that represents its ability to resist combat maneuvers. A creature's CMD is determined using the following formula:

$$\text{CMD} = 10 + \text{Base attack bonus} + \text{Strength modifier}$$
$$+ \text{Dexterity modifier} + \text{special size modifier}$$

The special size modifier for a creature's Combat Maneuver Defense is as follows: Fine −8, Diminutive −4, Tiny −2, Small −1, Medium +0, Large +1, Huge +2, Gargantuan +4, Colossal +8. Some feats and abilities grant a bonus to your CMD when resisting specific maneuvers. A creature can also add any circumstance, deflection, dodge, insight, luck, morale, profane, and sacred bonuses to AC to its CMD. Any penalties to a creature's AC also apply to its CMD. A flat-footed creature does not add its Dexterity bonus to its CMD.

Determine Success: If your attack roll equals or exceeds the CMD of the target, your maneuver is a success and has the listed effect. Some maneuvers, such as bull rush, have varying levels of success depending on how much your attack roll exceeds the target's CMD. Rolling a natural 20 while attempting a combat maneuver is always a success (except when attempting to escape from bonds), while rolling a natural 1 is always a failure.

Bull Rush

You can make a bull rush as a standard action or as part of a charge, in place of the melee attack. You can only bull rush an opponent who is no more than one size category larger than you. A bull rush attempts to push an opponent straight back without doing any harm. If you do not have the Improved Bull Rush feat, or a similar ability, initiating a bull rush provokes an attack of opportunity from the target of your maneuver.

If your attack is successful, your target is pushed back 5 feet. For every 5 by which your attack exceeds your opponent's CMD you can push the target back an additional 5 feet. You can move with the target if you wish but you must have the available movement to do so. If your attack fails, your movement ends in front of the target.

An enemy being moved by a bull rush does not provoke an attack of opportunity because of the movement unless you possess the Greater Bull Rush feat. You cannot bull rush a creature into a square that is occupied by a solid object or obstacle. If there is another creature in the way of your bull rush, you must immediately make a combat maneuver check to bull rush that creature. You take a −4 penalty on this check for each creature being pushed beyond the first. If you are successful, you can continue to push the creatures a distance equal to the lesser result. For example, if a fighter bull rushes a goblin for a total of 15 feet, but there is another goblin 5 feet behind the first, he must make another combat maneuver check against the second goblin after having pushed the first 5 feet. If his check reveals that he can push the second goblin a total of 20 feet, he can continue to push both goblins another 10 feet (since the first goblin will have moved a total of 15 feet).

Disarm

You can attempt to disarm your opponent in place of a melee attack. If you do not have the Improved Disarm feat, or a similar ability, attempting to disarm a foe provokes an attack of opportunity from the target of your maneuver. Attempting to disarm a foe while unarmed imposes a −4 penalty on the attack.

If your attack is successful, your target drops one item it is carrying of your choice (even if the item is wielded with two hands). If your attack exceeds the CMD of the target by 10 or more, the target drops the items it is carrying in both hands (maximum two items if the target has more than two hands). If your attack fails by 10 or more, you drop the weapon that you were using to attempt the disarm. If you successfully disarm your opponent without using a weapon, you may automatically pick up the item dropped.

Grapple

As a standard action, you can attempt to grapple a foe, hindering his combat options. If you do not have Improved Grapple, grab,

or a similar ability, attempting to grapple a foe provokes an attack of opportunity from the target of your maneuver. Humanoid creatures without two free hands attempting to grapple a foe take a –4 penalty on the combat maneuver roll. If successful, both you and the target gain the grappled condition (see the Appendices). If you successfully grapple a creature that is not adjacent to you, move that creature to an adjacent open space (if no space is available, your grapple fails). Although both creatures have the grappled condition, you can, as the creature that initiated the grapple, release the grapple as a free action, removing the condition from both you and the target. If you do not release the grapple, you must continue to make a check each round, as a standard action, to maintain the hold. If your target does not break the grapple, you get a +5 circumstance bonus on grapple checks made against the same target in subsequent rounds. Once you are grappling an opponent, a successful check allows you to continue grappling the foe, and also allows you to perform one of the following actions (as part of the standard action spent to maintain the grapple).

Move: You can move both yourself and your target up to half your speed. At the end of your movement, you can place your target in any square adjacent to you. If you attempt to place your foe in a hazardous location, such as in a *wall of*

fire or over a pit, the target receives a free attempt to break your grapple with a +4 bonus.

Damage: You can inflict damage to your target equal to your unarmed strike, a natural attack, or an attack made with armor spikes or a light or one-handed weapon. This damage can be either lethal or nonlethal.

Pin: You can give your opponent the pinned condition (see Appendix 2). Despite pinning your opponent, you still only have the grappled condition, but you lose your Dexterity bonus to AC.

Tie Up: If you have your target pinned, otherwise restrained, or unconscious, you can use rope to tie him up. This works like a pin effect, but the DC to escape the bonds is equal to 20 + your Combat Maneuver Bonus (instead of your CMD). The ropes do not need to make a check every round to maintain the pin. If you are grappling the target, you can attempt to tie him up in ropes, but doing so requires a combat maneuver check at a –10 penalty. If the DC to escape from these bindings is higher than 20 + the target's CMB, the target cannot escape from the bonds, even with a natural 20 on the check.

If You Are Grappled: If you are grappled, you can attempt to break the grapple as a standard action by making a combat maneuver check (DC equal to your opponent's CMD; this does not provoke an attack of opportunity) or Escape Artist check (with a DC equal to your opponent's CMD). If you succeed, you break the grapple and can act normally. Alternatively, if you succeed, you can become the grappler, grappling the other creature (meaning that the other creature cannot freely release the grapple without making a combat maneuver check, while you can). Instead of attempting to break or reverse the grapple, you can take any action that doesn't require two hands to perform, such as cast a spell or make an attack or full attack with a light or one-handed weapon against any creature within your reach, including the creature that is grappling you. See the grappled condition for additional details. If you are pinned, your actions are very limited. See the pinned condition in Appendix 2 for additional details.

Multiple Creatures: Multiple creatures can attempt to grapple one target. The creature that first initiates the grapple is the only one that makes a check, with a +2 bonus for each creature that assists in the grapple (using the Aid Another action). Multiple creatures can also assist another creature in breaking free from a grapple, with each creature that assists (using the Aid Another action) granting a +2 bonus on the grappled creature's combat maneuver check.

Overrun

As a standard action, taken during your move or as part of a charge, you can attempt to overrun your target, moving through its square. You can only overrun an opponent who is no more than one size category larger than you. If you do not have the Improved Overrun feat, or a similar ability, initiating an overrun provokes an attack of opportunity from the target of your maneuver. If your overrun attempt fails, you stop in the space directly in front of the opponent, or the nearest open space in front of the creature if there are other creatures occupying that space.

When you attempt to overrun a target, it can choose to avoid you, allowing you to pass through its square without requiring an attack. If your target does not avoid you, make a combat maneuver check as normal. If your maneuver is successful, you move through the target's space. If your attack exceeds your opponent's CMD by 5 or more, you move through the target's space and the target is knocked prone. If the target has more than two legs, add +2 to the DC of the combat maneuver attack roll for each additional leg it has.

Sunder

You can attempt to sunder an item held or worn by your opponent as part of an attack action in place of a melee attack. If you do not have the Improved Sunder feat, or a similar ability, attempting to sunder an item provokes an attack of opportunity from the target of your maneuver.

If your attack is successful, you deal damage to the item normally. Damage that exceeds the object's Hardness is subtracted from its hit points. If an object has equal to or less than half its total hit points remaining, it gains the broken condition (see Appendix 2). If the damage you deal would reduce the object to less than 0 hit points, you can choose to destroy it. If you do not choose to destroy it, the object is left with only 1 hit point and the broken condition.

Trip

You can attempt to trip your opponent in place of a melee attack. You can only trip an opponent who is no more than one size category larger than you. If you do not have the Improved Trip feat, or a similar ability, initiating a trip provokes an attack of opportunity from the target of your maneuver.

If your attack exceeds the target's CMD, the target is knocked prone. If your attack fails by 10 or more, you are knocked prone instead. If the target has more than two legs, add +2 to the DC of the combat maneuver attack roll for each additional leg it has. Some creatures—such as oozes, creatures without legs, and flying creatures—cannot be tripped.

Feint

Feinting is a standard action. To feint, make a Bluff skill check. The DC of this check is equal to 10 + your opponent's base attack bonus + your opponent's Wisdom modifier. If your opponent is trained in Sense Motive, the DC is instead equal to 10 + your opponent's Sense Motive bonus, if higher. If successful, the next melee attack you make against the target does not allow him to use his Dexterity bonus to AC (if any). This attack must be made on or before your next turn.

When feinting against a nonhumanoid you take a –4 penalty. Against a creature of animal Intelligence (1 or 2), you take a –8 penalty. Against a creature lacking an Intelligence score, it's impossible. Feinting in combat does not provoke attacks of opportunity.

Feinting as a Move Action: With the Improved Feint feat, you can attempt a feint as a move action.

Mounted Combat

These rules cover being mounted on a horse in combat but can also be applied to more unusual steeds, such as a griffon or dragon.

Mounts in Combat: Horses, ponies, and riding dogs can serve readily as combat steeds. Mounts that do not possess combat training (see the Handle Animal skill) are frightened by combat. If you don't dismount, you must make a DC 20 Ride check each round as a move action to control such a mount. If you succeed, you can perform a standard action after the move action. If you fail, the move action becomes a full-round action, and you can't do anything else until your next turn.

Your mount acts on your initiative count as you direct it. You move at its speed, but the mount uses its action to move.

A horse (not a pony) is a Large creature and thus takes up a space 10 feet (2 squares) across. For simplicity, assume that you share your mount's space during combat.

Combat while Mounted: With a DC 5 Ride check, you can guide your mount with your knees so as to use both hands to attack or defend yourself. This is a free action.

When you attack a creature smaller than your mount that is on foot, you get the +1 bonus on melee attacks for being on higher ground. If your mount moves more than 5 feet, you can only make a single melee attack. Essentially, you have to wait until the mount gets to your enemy before attacking, so you can't make a full attack. Even at your mount's full speed, you don't take any penalty on melee attacks while mounted.

If your mount charges, you also take the AC penalty associated with a charge. If you make an attack at the end of the charge, you receive the bonus gained from the charge. When charging on horseback, you deal double damage with a lance (see Charge).

You can use ranged weapons while your mount is taking a double move, but at a –4 penalty on the attack roll. You can use ranged weapons while your mount is running (quadruple speed) at a –8 penalty. In either case, you make the attack roll when your mount has completed half its movement. You can make a full attack with a ranged weapon while your mount is moving. Likewise, you can take move actions normally.

Casting Spells While Mounted: You can cast a spell normally if your mount moves up to a normal move (its speed) either before or after you cast. If you have your mount move both before and after you cast a spell, then you're casting the spell while the mount is moving, and you have to make a concentration check due to the vigorous motion (DC 10 + spell level) or lose the spell. If the mount is running (quadruple speed), you can cast a spell when your mount has moved up to twice its speed, but your concentration check is more difficult due to the violent motion (DC 15 + spell level).

If Your Mount Falls in Battle: If your mount falls, you have to succeed on a DC 15 Ride check to make a soft fall and take no damage. If the check fails, you take 1d6 points of damage.

If You Are Dropped: If you are knocked unconscious, you have a 50% chance to stay in the saddle (75% if you're in a military saddle). Otherwise you fall and take 1d6 points of damage. Without you to guide it, your mount avoids combat.

Throw Splash Weapon

A splash weapon is a ranged weapon that breaks on impact, splashing or scattering its contents over its target and nearby creatures or objects. To attack with a splash weapon, make a ranged touch attack against the target. Thrown splash weapons require no weapon proficiency, so you don't take the –4 nonproficiency penalty. A hit deals direct hit damage to the target and splash damage to all creatures within 5 feet of the target. If the target is Large or larger, you choose one of its squares and the splash damage affects creatures within 5 feet of that square. Splash weapons cannot deal precision-based damage (such as sneak attack).

You can instead target a specific grid intersection. Treat this as a ranged attack against AC 5. However, if you target a grid intersection, creatures in all adjacent squares are dealt the splash damage, and the direct hit damage is not dealt to any creature. You can't target a grid intersection occupied by a creature, such as a Large or larger creature; in this case, you're aiming at the creature.

If you miss the target (whether aiming at a creature or a grid intersection), roll 1d8. This determines the misdirection of the throw, with 1 falling short (off-target in a straight line toward the thrower), and 2 through 8 rotating around the target creature or grid intersection in a clockwise direction. Then, count a number of squares in the indicated direction equal to the range increment of the throw. After you determine where the weapon landed, it deals splash damage to all creatures in that square and in all adjacent squares.

Two-Weapon Fighting

If you wield a second weapon in your off hand, you can get one extra attack per round with that weapon. You suffer a –6 penalty with your regular attack or attacks with your primary hand and a –10 penalty to the attack with your off hand when you fight this way. You can reduce these penalties in two ways. First, if your off-hand weapon is light, the penalties are reduced by 2 each. An unarmed strike is always considered light. Second, the Two-Weapon Fighting feat lessens the primary hand penalty by 2, and the off-hand penalty by 6.

Table 8–7 summarizes the interaction of all these factors.

Double Weapons: You can use a double weapon to make an extra attack with the off-hand end of the weapon as if you were fighting with two weapons. The penalties apply as if the off-hand end of the weapon was a light weapon.

Thrown Weapons: The same rules apply when you throw a weapon from each hand. Treat a dart or shuriken as a light weapon when used in this manner, and treat a bolas, javelin, net, or sling as a one-handed weapon.

TABLE 8–7: TWO-WEAPON FIGHTING PENALTIES

Circumstances	Primary Hand	Off Hand
Normal penalties	–6	–10
Off-hand weapon is light	–4	–8
Two-Weapon Fighting feat	–4	–4
Off-hand weapon is light and Two-Weapon Fighting feat	–2	–2

SPECIAL INITIATIVE ACTIONS

Here are ways to change when you act during combat by altering your place in the initiative order.

Delay

By choosing to delay, you take no action and then act normally on whatever initiative count you decide to act. When you delay, you voluntarily reduce your own initiative result for the rest of the combat. When your new, lower initiative count comes up later in the same round, you can act normally. You can specify this new initiative result or just wait until some time later in the round and act then, thus fixing your new initiative count at that point.

You never get back the time you spend waiting to see what's going to happen. You also can't interrupt anyone else's action (as you can with a readied action).

Initiative Consequences of Delaying: Your initiative result becomes the count on which you took the delayed action. If you come to your next action and have not yet performed an action, you don't get to take a delayed action (though you can delay again).

If you take a delayed action in the next round, before your regular turn comes up, your initiative count rises to that new point in the order of battle, and you do not get your regular action that round.

Ready

The ready action lets you prepare to take an action later, after your turn is over but before your next one has begun. Readying is a standard action. It does not provoke an attack of opportunity (though the action that you ready might do so).

Readying an Action: You can ready a standard action, a move action, a swift action, or a free action. To do so, specify the action you will take and the conditions under which you will take it. Then, anytime before your next action, you may take the readied action in response to that condition. The action occurs just before the action that triggers it. If the triggered action is part of another character's activities, you interrupt the other character. Assuming he is still capable of doing so, he continues his actions once you complete your readied action. Your initiative result changes. For the rest of the encounter, your initiative result is the count on which you took the readied action, and you act immediately ahead of the character whose action triggered your readied action.

You can take a 5-foot step as part of your readied action, but only if you don't otherwise move any distance during the round.

Initiative Consequences of Readying: Your initiative result becomes the count on which you took the readied action. If you come to your next action and have not yet performed your readied action, you don't get to take the readied action (though you can ready the same action again). If you take your readied action in the next round, before your regular turn comes up, your initiative count rises to that new point in the

order of battle, and you do not get your regular action that round.

Distracting Spellcasters: You can ready an attack against a spellcaster with the trigger "if she starts casting a spell." If you damage the spellcaster, she may lose the spell she was trying to cast (as determined by her concentration check result).

Readying to Counterspell: You may ready a counterspell against a spellcaster (often with the trigger "if she starts casting a spell"). In this case, when the spellcaster starts a spell, you get a chance to identify it with a Spellcraft check (DC 15 + spell level). If you do, and if you can cast that same spell (and are able to cast it and have it prepared, if you prepare spells), you can cast the spell as a counterspell and automatically ruin the other spellcaster's spell. Counterspelling works even if one spell is divine and the other arcane.

A spellcaster can use *dispel magic* to counterspell another spellcaster, but it doesn't always work.

Readying a Weapon against a Charge: You can ready weapons with the brace feature, setting them to receive charges. A readied weapon of this type deals double damage if you score a hit with it against a charging character.

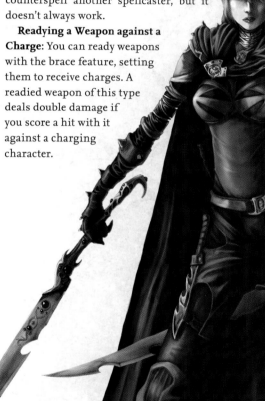

9 Magic

Seelah stood defiantly before the vampiric minions, and as the first undead leapt at her, she cut it in two with a single blow. Yet there were two more to replace their fallen kin. Worse, she could sense more of their sinister auras all around them.

"Hope you've got something left, Ezren," she muttered. Behind her, the elderly wizard finished his spell, and suddenly a blast of heat engulfed the creatures. Their shrieks carried a satisfying note of pain, and as the vampires frantically sought escape from the cleansing fires, Ezren snorted.

"That do the trick for you?"

From creating a wisp of light to causing the ground itself to shatter and break, spells are a source of immense power. A spell is a one-time magical effect. Spells come in two types: arcane (cast by bards, sorcerers, and wizards) and divine (cast by clerics, druids, and experienced paladins and rangers). Some spellcasters select their spells from a limited list of spells known, while others have access to a wide variety of options.

Most spellcasters prepare spells in advance—whether from a spellbook or through prayers—while some cast spells spontaneously without preparation. Despite these different ways characters use to learn or prepare their spells, when it comes to casting them, the spells are very much alike.

CASTING SPELLS

Whether a spell is arcane or divine, and whether a character prepares spells in advance or chooses them on the spot, casting a spell works the same way.

Choosing a Spell

First you must choose which spell to cast. If you're a cleric, druid, experienced paladin, experienced ranger, or wizard, you select from among spells prepared earlier in the day and not yet cast (see Preparing Wizard Spells and Preparing Divine Spells).

If you're a bard or sorcerer, you can select any spell you know, provided you are capable of casting spells of that level or higher.

To cast a spell, you must be able to speak (if the spell has a verbal component), gesture (if it has a somatic component), and manipulate the material components or focus (if any). Additionally, you must concentrate to cast a spell.

If a spell has multiple versions, you choose which version to use when you cast it. You don't have to prepare (or learn, in the case of a bard or sorcerer) a specific version of the spell.

Once you've cast a prepared spell, you can't cast it again until you prepare it again. (If you've prepared multiple copies of a single spell, you can cast each copy once.) If you're a bard or sorcerer, casting a spell counts against your daily limit for spells of that spell level, but you can cast the same spell again if you haven't reached your limit.

Concentration

To cast a spell, you must concentrate. If something interrupts your concentration while you're casting, you must make a concentration check or lose the spell. When you make a concentration check, you roll d20 and add your caster level and the ability score modifier used to determine bonus spells of the same type. Clerics, druids, and rangers add their Wisdom modifier. Bards, paladins, and sorcerers add their Charisma modifier. Finally,

wizards add their Intelligence modifier. The more distracting the interruption and the higher the level of the spell you are trying to cast, the higher the DC (see Table 9–1). If you fail the check, you lose the spell just as if you had cast it to no effect.

Injury: If you take damage while trying to cast a spell, you must make a concentration check with a DC equal to 10 + the damage taken + the level of the spell you're casting. If you fail the check, you lose the spell without effect. The interrupting event strikes during spellcasting if it comes between the time you started and the time you complete a spell (for a spell with a casting time of 1 full round or more) or if it comes in response to your casting the spell (such as an attack of opportunity provoked by the spell or a contingent attack, such as a readied action).

If you are taking continuous damage, such as from an *acid arrow* or by standing in a lake of lava, half the damage is considered to take place while you are casting a spell. You must make a concentration check with a DC equal to 10 + 1/2 the damage that the continuous source last dealt + the level of the spell you're casting. If the last damage dealt was the last damage that the effect could deal, then the damage is over and does not distract you.

Spell: If you are affected by a spell while attempting to cast a spell of your own, you must make a concentration check or lose the spell you are casting. If the spell affecting you deals damage, the DC is 10 + the damage taken + the level of the spell you're casting.

If the spell interferes with you or distracts you in some other way, the DC is the spell's saving throw DC + the level of the spell you're casting. For a spell with no saving throw, it's the DC that the spell's saving throw would have if a save were allowed (10 + spell level + caster's ability score).

Grappled or Pinned: Casting a spell while you have the grappled or pinned condition is difficult and requires a concentration check (DC 10 + the grappler's CMB + the level of the spell you're casting). Pinned creatures can only cast spells that do not have somatic components.

Vigorous Motion: If you are riding on a moving mount, taking a bouncy ride in a wagon, on a small boat in rough water, belowdecks in a storm-tossed ship, or simply being jostled in a similar fashion, you must make a concentration check (DC 10 + the level of the spell you're casting) or lose the spell.

Violent Motion: If you are on a galloping horse, taking a very rough ride in a wagon, on a small boat in rapids or in a storm, on deck in a storm-tossed ship, or being pitched roughly about in a similar fashion, you must make a concentration check (DC 15 + the level of the spell you're casting) or lose the spell. If the motion is extremely violent, such as that caused by an earthquake, the DC is equal to 20 + the level of the spell you're casting.

TABLE 9-1: CONCENTRATION CHECK DCS

Situation	Concentration Check DC
Cast defensively	15 + double spell level
Injured while casting	10 + damage dealt + spell level
Continuous damage while casting	10 + 1/2 damage dealt + spell level
Affected by a non-damaging spell while casting	DC of the spell + spell level
Grappled or pinned while casting	10 + grappler's CMB + spell level
Vigorous motion while casting	10 + spell level
Violent motion while casting	15 + spell level
Extremely violent motion while casting	20 + spell level
Wind with rain or sleet while casting	5 + spell level
Wind with hail and debris while casting	10 + spell level
Weather caused by spell	see spell
Entangled while casting	15 + spell level

Violent Weather: You must make a concentration check if you try to cast a spell in violent weather. If you are in a high wind carrying blinding rain or sleet, the DC is 5 + the level of the spell you're casting. If you are in wind-driven hail, dust, or debris, the DC is 10 + the level of the spell you're casting. In either case, you lose the spell if you fail the concentration check. If the weather is caused by a spell, use the rules as described in the spell's description.

Casting Defensively: If you want to cast a spell without provoking any attacks of opportunity, you must make a concentration check (DC 15 + double the level of the spell you're casting) to succeed. You lose the spell if you fail.

Entangled: If you want to cast a spell while entangled in a net or by a tanglefoot bag or while you're affected by a spell with similar effects, you must make a concentration check to cast the spell (DC 15 + the level of the spell you're casting). You lose the spell if you fail.

Counterspells

It is possible to cast any spell as a counterspell. By doing so, you are using the spell's energy to disrupt the casting of the same spell by another character. Counterspelling works even if one spell is divine and the other arcane.

How Counterspells Work: To use a counterspell, you must select an opponent as the target of the counterspell. You do this by choosing to ready an action (see Combat on page 203). In doing so, you elect to wait to complete your action until your opponent tries to cast a spell. You may still move at your normal speed, since ready is a standard action.

If the target of your counterspell tries to cast a spell, make a Spellcraft check (DC 15 + the spell's level). This

check is a free action. If the check succeeds, you correctly identify the opponent's spell and can attempt to counter it. If the check fails, you can't do either of these things.

To complete the action, you must then cast an appropriate spell. As a general rule, a spell can only counter itself. If you are able to cast the same spell and you have it prepared (or have a slot of the appropriate level available), you cast it, creating a counterspell effect. If the target is within range, both spells automatically negate each other with no other results.

Counterspelling Metamagic Spells: Metamagic feats are not taken into account when determining whether a spell can be countered.

Specific Exceptions: Some spells can counter other specific spells, often those with diametrically opposed effects.

Dispel Magic **as a Counterspell:** You can usually use *dispel magic* to counterspell another spell being cast without needing to identify the spell being cast. *Dispel magic* doesn't always work as a counterspell (see the spell description).

Caster Level

A spell's power often depends on its caster level, which for most spellcasting characters is equal to her class level in the class she's using to cast the spell.

You can cast a spell at a lower caster level than normal, but the caster level you choose must be high enough for you to cast the spell in question, and all level-dependent features must be based on the same caster level.

In the event that a class feature or other special ability provides an adjustment to your caster level, that adjustment applies not only to effects based on caster level (such as range, duration, and damage dealt), but also to your caster level check to overcome your target's spell resistance and to the caster level used in dispel checks (both the dispel check and the DC of the check).

Spell Failure

If you ever try to cast a spell in conditions where the characteristics of the spell cannot be made to conform, the casting fails and the spell is wasted.

Spells also fail if your concentration is broken and might fail if you're wearing armor while casting a spell with somatic components.

The Spell's Result

Once you know which creatures (or objects or areas) are affected, and whether those creatures have made successful saving throws (if any were allowed), you can apply whatever results a spell entails.

Special Spell Effects

Many special spell effects are handled according to the school of the spells in question. Certain other special spell features are found across spell schools.

Attacks: Some spell descriptions refer to attacking. All offensive combat actions, even those that don't damage opponents, are considered attacks. Attempts to channel energy count as attacks if it would harm any creatures in the area. All spells that opponents resist with saving throws, that deal damage, or that otherwise harm or hamper subjects are attacks. Spells that summon monsters or other allies are not attacks because the spells themselves don't harm anyone.

Bonus Types: Usually, a bonus has a type that indicates how the spell grants the bonus. The important aspect of bonus types is that two bonuses of the same type don't

generally stack. With the exception of dodge bonuses, most circumstance bonuses, and racial bonuses, only the better bonus of a given type works (see Combining Magical Effects). The same principle applies to penalties—a character taking two or more penalties of the same type applies only the worst one, although most penalties have no type and thus always stack. Bonuses without a type always stack, unless they are from the same source.

Bringing Back the Dead: Several spells have the power to restore slain characters to life.

When a living creature dies, its soul departs its body, leaves the Material Plane, travels through the Astral Plane, and goes to abide on the plane where the creature's deity resides. If the creature did not worship a deity, its soul departs to the plane corresponding to its alignment. Bringing someone back from the dead involves magically retrieving his soul and returning it to his body. For more information on the planes, see Chapter 13.

Negative Levels: Any creature brought back to life usually gains one or more permanent negative levels (see Appendix 1). These levels apply a penalty to most rolls until removed through spells such as *restoration*. If the character was 1st level at the time of death, he loses 2 points of Constitution instead of gaining a negative level.

Preventing Revivification: Enemies can take steps to make it more difficult for a character to be returned from the dead. Keeping the body prevents others from using *raise dead* or *resurrection* to restore the slain character to life. Casting *trap the soul* prevents any sort of revivification unless the soul is first released.

Revivification against One's Will: A soul can't be returned to life if it doesn't wish to be. A soul knows the name, alignment, and patron deity (if any) of the character attempting to revive it and may refuse to return on that basis.

Combining Magic Effects

Spells or magical effects usually work as described, no matter how many other spells or magical effects happen to be operating in the same area or on the same recipient. Except in special cases, a spell does not affect the way another spell operates. Whenever a spell has a specific effect on other spells, the spell description explains that effect. Several other general rules apply when spells or magical effects operate in the same place:

Stacking Effects: Spells that provide bonuses or penalties on attack rolls, damage rolls, saving throws, and other attributes usually do not stack with themselves. More generally, two bonuses of the same type don't stack even if they come from different spells (or from effects other than spells; see Bonus Types, above).

Different Bonus Types: The bonuses or penalties from two different spells stack if the modifiers are of different types. A bonus that doesn't have a type stacks with any bonus.

Same Effect More than Once in Different Strengths: In cases when two or more identical spells are operating in the same area or on the same target, but at different strengths, only the one with the highest strength applies.

Same Effect with Differing Results: The same spell can sometimes produce varying effects if applied to the same recipient more than once. Usually the last spell in the series trumps the others. None of the previous spells are actually removed or dispelled, but their effects become irrelevant while the final spell in the series lasts.

One Effect Makes Another Irrelevant: Sometimes, one spell can render a later spell irrelevant. Both spells are still active, but one has rendered the other useless in some fashion.

Multiple Mental Control Effects: Sometimes magical effects that establish mental control render each other irrelevant, such as spells that remove the subject's ability to act. Mental controls that don't remove the recipient's ability to act usually do not interfere with each other. If a creature is under the mental control of two or more creatures, it tends to obey each to the best of its ability, and to the extent of the control each effect allows. If the controlled creature receives conflicting orders simultaneously, the competing controllers must make opposed Charisma checks to determine which one the creature obeys.

Spells with Opposite Effects: Spells with opposite effects apply normally, with all bonuses, penalties, or changes accruing in the order that they apply. Some spells negate or counter each other. This is a special effect that is noted in a spell's description.

Instantaneous Effects: Two or more spells with instantaneous durations work cumulatively when they affect the same target.

SPELL DESCRIPTIONS

The description of each spell is presented in a standard format. Each category of information is explained and defined below.

Name

The first line of every spell description gives the name by which the spell is generally known.

School (Subschool)

Beneath the spell name is a line giving the school of magic (and the subschool, if any) to which the spell belongs.

Almost every spell belongs to one of eight schools of magic. A school of magic is a group of related spells that work in similar ways. A small number of spells (*arcane mark*, *limited wish*, *permanency*, *prestidigitation*, and *wish*) are universal, belonging to no school.

Abjuration

Abjurations are protective spells. They create physical or magical barriers, negate magical or physical abilities, harm trespassers, or even banish the subject of the spell to another plane of existence.

If one abjuration spell is active within 10 feet of another for 24 hours or more, the magical fields interfere with each other and create barely visible energy fluctuations. The DC to find such spells with the Perception skill drops by 4.

If an abjuration creates a barrier that keeps certain types of creatures at bay, that barrier cannot be used to push away those creatures. If you force the barrier against such a creature, you feel a discernible pressure against the barrier. If you continue to apply pressure, you end the spell.

Conjuration

Each conjuration spell belongs to one of five subschools. Conjurations transport creatures from another plane of existence to your plane (calling); create objects or effects on the spot (creation); heal (healing); bring manifestations of objects, creatures, or forms of energy to you (summoning); or transport creatures or objects over great distances (teleportation). Creatures you conjure usually—but not always—obey your commands.

A creature or object brought into being or transported to your location by a conjuration spell cannot appear inside another creature or object, nor can it appear floating in an empty space. It must arrive in an open location on a surface capable of supporting it.

The creature or object must appear within the spell's range, but it does not have to remain within the range.

Calling: A calling spell transports a creature from another plane to the plane you are on. The spell grants the creature the one-time ability to return to its plane of origin, although the spell may limit the circumstances under which this is possible. Creatures who are called actually die when they are killed; they do not disappear and reform, as do those brought by a summoning spell (see below). The duration of a calling spell is instantaneous, which means that the called creature can't be dispelled.

Creation: A creation spell manipulates matter to create an object or creature in the place the spellcaster designates. If the spell has a duration other than instantaneous, magic holds the creation together, and when the spell ends, the conjured creature or object vanishes without a trace. If the spell has an instantaneous duration, the created object or creature is merely assembled through magic. It lasts indefinitely and does not depend on magic for its existence.

Healing: Certain divine conjurations heal creatures or even bring them back to life.

Summoning: A summoning spell instantly brings a creature or object to a place you designate. When the spell ends or is dispelled, a summoned creature is instantly sent back to where it came from, but a summoned object is not sent back unless the spell description specifically indicates this. A summoned creature also goes away if it is killed or if its hit points drop to 0 or lower, but it is not really dead. It takes 24 hours for the creature to reform, during which time it can't be summoned again.

When the spell that summoned a creature ends and the creature disappears, all the spells it has cast expire. A summoned creature cannot use any innate summoning abilities it may have.

Teleportation: A teleportation spell transports one or more creatures or objects a great distance. The most powerful of these spells can cross planar boundaries. Unlike summoning spells, the transportation is (unless otherwise noted) one-way and not dispellable.

Teleportation is instantaneous travel through the Astral Plane. Anything that blocks astral travel also blocks teleportation.

Divination

Divination spells enable you to learn secrets long forgotten, predict the future, find hidden things, and foil deceptive spells.

Many divination spells have cone-shaped areas. These move with you and extend in the direction you choose. The cone defines the area that you can sweep each round. If you study the same area for multiple rounds, you can often gain additional information, as noted in the descriptive text for the spell.

Scrying: A scrying spell creates an invisible magical sensor that sends you information. Unless noted otherwise, the sensor has the same powers of sensory acuity that you possess. This level of acuity includes any spells or effects that target you, but not spells or effects that emanate from you. The sensor, however, is treated as a separate, independent sensory organ of yours, and thus functions normally even if you have been blinded or deafened, or otherwise suffered sensory impairment.

A creature can notice the sensor by making a Perception check with a DC 20 + the spell level. The sensor can be dispelled as if it were an active spell.

Lead sheeting or magical protection blocks a scrying spell, and you sense that the spell is blocked.

Enchantment

Enchantment spells affect the minds of others, influencing or controlling their behavior.

All enchantments are mind-affecting spells. Two subschools of enchantment spells grant you influence over a subject creature.

Charm: A charm spell changes how the subject views you, typically making it see you as a good friend.

Compulsion: A compulsion spell forces the subject to act in some manner or changes the way its mind works. Some compulsion spells determine the subject's actions or the effects on the subject, others allow you to determine the subject's actions when you cast the spell, and still others give you ongoing control over the subject.

Evocation

Evocation spells manipulate magical energy or tap an unseen source of power to produce a desired end. In effect, an evocation draws upon magic to create something out of nothing. Many of these spells produce spectacular effects, and evocation spells can deal large amounts of damage.

Illusion

Illusion spells deceive the senses or minds of others. They cause people to see things that are not there, not see things that are there, hear phantom noises, or remember things that never happened.

Figment: A figment spell creates a false sensation. Those who perceive the figment perceive the same thing, not their own slightly different versions of the figment. It is not a personalized mental impression. Figments cannot make something seem to be something else. A figment that includes audible effects cannot duplicate intelligible speech unless the spell description specifically says it can. If intelligible speech is possible, it must be in a language you can speak. If you try to duplicate a language you cannot speak, the figment produces gibberish. Likewise, you cannot make a visual copy of something unless you know what it looks like (or copy another sense exactly unless you have experienced it).

Because figments and glamers are unreal, they cannot produce real effects the way that other types of illusions can. Figments and glamers cannot cause damage to objects or creatures, support weight, provide nutrition, or provide protection from the elements. Consequently, these spells are useful for confounding foes, but useless for attacking them directly.

A figment's AC is equal to 10 + its size modifier.

Glamer: A glamer spell changes a subject's sensory qualities, making it look, feel, taste, smell, or sound like something else, or even seem to disappear.

Pattern: Like a figment, a pattern spell creates an image that others can see, but a pattern also affects the minds of those who see it or are caught in it. All patterns are mind-affecting spells.

Phantasm: A phantasm spell creates a mental image that usually only the caster and the subject (or subjects) of the spell can perceive. This impression is totally in

the minds of the subjects. It is a personalized mental impression, all in their heads and not a fake picture or something that they actually see. Third parties viewing or studying the scene don't notice the phantasm. All phantasms are mind-affecting spells.

Shadow: A shadow spell creates something that is partially real from extradimensional energy. Such illusions can have real effects. Damage dealt by a shadow illusion is real.

Saving Throws and Illusions (Disbelief): Creatures encountering an illusion usually do not receive saving throws to recognize it as illusory until they study it carefully or interact with it in some fashion.

A successful saving throw against an illusion reveals it to be false, but a figment or phantasm remains as a translucent outline.

A failed saving throw indicates that a character fails to notice something is amiss. A character faced with proof that an illusion isn't real needs no saving throw. If any viewer successfully disbelieves an illusion and communicates this fact to others, each such viewer gains a saving throw with a +4 bonus.

Necromancy

Necromancy spells manipulate the power of death, unlife, and the life force. Spells involving undead creatures make up a large part of this school.

Transmutation

Transmutation spells change the properties of some creature, thing, or condition.

Polymorph: A polymorph spell transforms your physical body to take on the shape of another creature. While these spells make you appear to be the creature, granting you a +10 bonus on Disguise skill checks, they do not grant you all of the abilities and powers of the creature. Each polymorph spell allows you to assume the form of a creature of a specific type, granting you a number of bonuses to your ability scores and a bonus to your natural armor. In addition, each polymorph spell can grant you a number of other benefits, including movement types, resistances, and senses. If the form you choose grants these benefits, or a greater ability of the same type, you gain the listed benefit. If the form grants a lesser ability of the same type, you gain the lesser ability instead. Your base speed changes to match that of the form you assume.

If the form grants a swim or burrow speed, you maintain the ability to breathe if you are swimming or burrowing. The DC for any of these abilities equals your DC for the polymorph spell used to change you into that form.

In addition to these benefits, you gain any of the natural attacks of the base creature, including proficiency in those attacks. These attacks are based on your base attack bonus, modified by your Strength or Dexterity as appropriate, and use your Strength modifier for determining damage bonuses.

If a polymorph spell causes you to change size, apply the size modifiers appropriately, changing your armor class, attack bonus, Combat Maneuver Bonus, and Stealth skill modifiers. Your ability scores are not modified by this change unless noted by the spell.

Unless otherwise noted, polymorph spells cannot be used to change into specific individuals. Although many of the fine details can be controlled, your appearance is always that of a generic member of that creature's type. Polymorph spells cannot be used to assume the form of a creature with a template or an advanced version of a creature.

When you cast a polymorph spell that changes you into a creature of the animal, dragon, elemental, magical beast, plant, or vermin type, all of your gear melds into your body. Items that provide constant bonuses and do not need to be activated continue to function while melded in this way (with the exception of armor and shield bonuses, which cease to function). Items that require activation cannot be used while you maintain that form. While in such a form, you cannot cast any spells that require material components (unless you have the Eschew Materials or Natural Spell feat), and can only cast spells with somatic or verbal components if the form you choose has the capability to make such movements or speak, such as a dragon. Other polymorph spells might be subject to this restriction as well, if they change you into a form that is unlike your original form (subject to GM discretion). If your new form does not cause your equipment to meld into your form, the equipment resizes to match your new size.

While under the effects of a polymorph spell, you lose all extraordinary and supernatural abilities that depend on your original form (such as keen senses, scent, and darkvision), as well as any natural attacks and movement types possessed by your original form. You also lose any class features that depend upon form, but those that allow you to add features (such as sorcerers that can grow claws) still function. While most of these should be obvious, the GM is the final arbiter of what abilities depend on form and are lost when a new form is assumed. Your new form might restore a number of these abilities if they are possessed by the new form.

You can only be affected by one polymorph spell at a time. If a new polymorph spell is cast on you (or you activate a polymorph effect, such as wild shape), you can decide whether or not to allow it to affect you, taking the place of the old spell. In addition, other spells that change your size have no effect on you while you are under the effects of a polymorph spell.

If a polymorph spell is cast on a creature that is smaller than Small or larger than Medium, first adjust its ability scores to one of these two sizes using the following table before applying the bonuses granted by the polymorph spell.

Creature's Original Size	Str	Dex	Con	Adjusted Size
Fine	+6	−6	—	Small
Diminutive	+6	−4	—	Small
Tiny	+4	−2	—	Small
Large	−4	+2	−2	Medium
Huge	−8	+4	−4	Medium
Gargantuan	−12	+4	−6	Medium
Colossal	−16	+4	−8	Medium

[Descriptor]

Appearing on the same line as the school and subschool, when applicable, is a descriptor that further categorizes the spell in some way. Some spells have more than one descriptor.

The descriptors are acid, air, chaotic, cold, darkness, death, earth, electricity, evil, fear, fire, force, good, language-dependent, lawful, light, mind-affecting, sonic, and water.

Most of these descriptors have no game effect by themselves, but they govern how the spell interacts with other spells, with special abilities, with unusual creatures, with alignment, and so on.

A language-dependent spell uses intelligible language as a medium for communication. If the target cannot understand or cannot hear what the caster of a language-dependant spell says, the spell fails.

A mind-affecting spell works only against creatures with an Intelligence score of 1 or higher.

Level

The next line of a spell description gives the spell's level, a number between 0 and 9 that defines the spell's relative power. This number is preceded by a list of classes whose members can cast the spell. A spell's level affects the DC for any save allowed against its effects.

Components

A spell's components explain what you must do or possess to cast the spell. The components entry in a spell description includes abbreviations that tell you what type of components it requires. Specifics for material and focus components are given at the end of the descriptive text. Usually you don't need to worry about components, but when you can't use a component for some reason or when a material or focus component is expensive, then the components are important.

Verbal (V): A verbal component is a spoken incantation. To provide a verbal component, you must be able to speak in a strong voice. A *silence* spell or a gag spoils the incantation (and thus the spell). A spellcaster who has been deafened has a 20% chance of spoiling any spell with a verbal component that he tries to cast.

Somatic (S): A somatic component is a measured and precise movement of the hand. You must have at least one hand free to provide a somatic component.

Material (M): A material component consists of one or more physical substances or objects that are annihilated by the spell energies in the casting process. Unless a cost is given for a material component, the cost is negligible. Don't bother to keep track of material components with negligible cost. Assume you have all you need as long as you have your spell component pouch.

Focus (F): A focus component is a prop of some sort. Unlike a material component, a focus is not consumed when the spell is cast and can be reused. As with material components, the cost for a focus is negligible unless a price is given. Assume that focus components of negligible cost are in your spell component pouch.

Divine Focus (DF): A divine focus component is an item of spiritual significance. The divine focus for a cleric or a paladin is a holy symbol appropriate to the character's faith. The divine focus for a druid or a ranger is a sprig of holly, or some other sacred plant.

If the Components line includes F/DF or M/DF, the arcane version of the spell has a focus component or a material component (the abbreviation before the slash) and the divine version has a divine focus component (the abbreviation after the slash).

Casting Time

Most spells have a casting time of 1 standard action. Others take 1 round or more, while a few require only a swift action.

A spell that takes 1 round to cast is a full-round action. It comes into effect just before the beginning of your turn in the round after you began casting the spell. You then act normally after the spell is completed.

A spell that takes 1 minute to cast comes into effect just before your turn 1 minute later (and for each of those 10 rounds, you are casting a spell as a full-round action, just as noted above for 1-round casting times). These actions must be consecutive and uninterrupted, or the spell automatically fails.

When you begin a spell that takes 1 round or longer to cast, you must continue the concentration from the current round to just before your turn in the next round (at least). If you lose concentration before the casting is complete, you lose the spell.

A spell with a casting time of 1 swift action doesn't count against your normal limit of one spell per round. However, you may cast such a spell only once per round. Casting a spell with a casting time of 1 swift action doesn't provoke attacks of opportunity.

You make all pertinent decisions about a spell (range, target, area, effect, version, and so forth) when the spell comes into effect.

Range

A spell's range indicates how far from you it can reach, as defined in the range entry of the spell description. A spell's range is the maximum distance from you that the spell's effect can occur, as well as the maximum distance at which you can designate the spell's point of origin. If any portion of the spell's area would extend beyond this range, that area is wasted. Standard ranges include the following.

Personal: The spell affects only you.

Touch: You must touch a creature or object to affect it. A touch spell that deals damage can score a critical hit just as a weapon can. A touch spell threatens a critical hit on a natural roll of 20 and deals double damage on a successful critical hit. Some touch spells allow you to touch multiple targets. You can touch up to 6 willing targets as part of the casting, but all targets of the spell must be touched in the same round that you finish casting the spell. If the spell allows you to touch targets over multiple rounds, touching 6 creatures is a full-round action.

Close: The spell reaches as far as 25 feet away from you. The maximum range increases by 5 feet for every two full caster levels.

Medium: The spell reaches as far as 100 feet + 10 feet per caster level.

Long: The spell reaches as far as 400 feet + 40 feet per caster level.

Unlimited: The spell reaches anywhere on the same plane of existence.

Range Expressed in Feet: Some spells have no standard range category, just a range expressed in feet.

Aiming a Spell

You must make choices about whom a spell is to affect or where an effect is to originate, depending on a spell's type. The next entry in a spell description defines the spell's target (or targets), its effect, or its area, as appropriate.

Target or Targets: Some spells have a target or targets. You cast these spells on creatures or objects, as defined by the spell itself. You must be able to see or touch the target, and you must specifically choose that target. You do not have to select your target until you finish casting the spell.

If the target of a spell is yourself (the Target line of the spell description includes "You"), you do not receive a saving throw, and spell resistance does not apply. The saving throw and spell resistance lines are omitted from such spells.

Some spells restrict you to willing targets only. Declaring yourself as a willing target is something that can be done at any time (even if you're flat-footed or it isn't your turn). Unconscious creatures are automatically considered willing, but a character who is conscious but immobile or helpless (such as one who is bound, cowering, grappling, paralyzed, pinned, or stunned) is not automatically willing.

Some spells allow you to redirect the effect to new targets or areas after you cast the spell. Redirecting a spell is a move action that does not provoke attacks of opportunity.

Effect: Some spells create or summon things rather than affecting things that are already present.

You must designate the location where these things are to appear, either by seeing it or defining it. Range determines how far away an effect can appear, but if the effect is mobile, after it appears it can move regardless of the spell's range.

Ray: Some effects are rays. You aim a ray as if using a ranged weapon, though typically you make a ranged touch attack rather than a normal ranged attack. As with a ranged weapon, you can fire into the dark or at an invisible creature and hope you hit something. You don't have to see the creature you're trying to hit, as you do with a targeted spell. Intervening creatures and obstacles, however, can block your line of sight or provide cover for the creature at which you're aiming.

If a ray spell has a duration, it's the duration of the effect that the ray causes, not the length of time the ray itself persists.

If a ray spell deals damage, you can score a critical hit just as if it were a weapon. A ray spell threatens a critical hit on a natural roll of 20 and deals double damage on a successful critical hit.

Spread: Some effects, notably clouds and fogs, spread out from a point of origin, which must be a grid intersection. The effect can extend around corners and into areas that you can't see. Figure distance by actual distance traveled, taking into account turns the spell effect takes. When determining distance for spread effects, count around walls, not through them. As with movement, do not trace diagonals across corners. You must designate the point of origin for such an effect, but you need not have line of effect (see below) to all portions of the effect.

Area: Some spells affect an area. Sometimes a spell description specifies a specially defined area, but usually an area falls into one of the categories defined below.

Regardless of the shape of the area, you select the point where the spell originates, but otherwise you don't control which creatures or objects the spell affects. The point of origin of a spell is always a grid intersection. When determining whether a given creature is within the area of a spell, count out the distance from the point of origin in squares just as you do when moving a character or when determining the range for a ranged attack. The only difference is that instead of counting from the center of one square to the center of the next, you count from intersection to intersection.

You can count diagonally across a square, but remember that every second diagonal counts as 2 squares of distance. If the far edge of a square is within the spell's area, anything within that square is within the spell's area. If the spell's area only touches the near edge of a square, however, anything within that square is unaffected by the spell.

Burst, Emanation, or Spread: Most spells that affect an area function as a burst, an emanation, or a spread. In each case, you select the spell's point of origin and measure its effect from that point.

A burst spell affects whatever it catches in its area, including creatures that you can't see. It can't affect creatures with total cover from its point of origin (in other words, its effects don't extend around corners). The default shape for a burst effect is a sphere, but some burst spells are specifically described as cone-shaped. A burst's area defines how far from the point of origin the spell's effect extends.

An emanation spell functions like a burst spell, except that the effect continues to radiate from the point of origin for the duration of the spell. Most emanations are cones or spheres.

A spread spell extends out like a burst but can turn corners. You select the point of origin, and the spell spreads out a given distance in all directions. Figure the area the spell effect fills by taking into account any turns the spell effect takes.

Cone, Cylinder, Line, or Sphere: Most spells that affect an area have a particular shape.

A cone-shaped spell shoots away from you in a quarter-circle in the direction you designate. It starts from any corner of your square and widens out as it goes. Most cones are either bursts or emanations (see above), and thus won't go around corners.

When casting a cylinder-shaped spell, you select the spell's point of origin. This point is the center of a horizontal circle, and the spell shoots down from the circle, filling a cylinder. A cylinder-shaped spell ignores any obstructions within its area.

A line-shaped spell shoots away from you in a line in the direction you designate. It starts from any corner of your square and extends to the limit of its range or until it strikes a barrier that blocks line of effect. A line-shaped spell affects all creatures in squares through which the line passes.

A sphere-shaped spell expands from its point of origin to fill a spherical area. Spheres may be bursts, emanations, or spreads.

Creatures: A spell with this kind of area affects creatures directly (like a targeted spell), but it affects all creatures in an area of some kind rather than individual creatures you select. The area might be a spherical burst, a cone-shaped burst, or some other shape.

Many spells affect "living creatures," which means all creatures other than constructs and undead. Creatures in the spell's area that are not of the appropriate type do not count against the creatures affected.

Objects: A spell with this kind of area affects objects within an area you select (as Creatures, but affecting objects instead).

Other: A spell can have a unique area, as defined in its description.

(S) Shapeable: If an area or effect entry ends with "(S)," you can shape the spell. A shaped effect or area can have no dimension smaller than 10 feet. Many effects or areas are given as cubes to make it easy to model irregular shapes. Three-dimensional volumes are most often needed to define aerial or underwater effects and areas.

Line of Effect: A line of effect is a straight, unblocked path that indicates what a spell can affect. A line of effect is canceled by a solid barrier. It's like line of sight for ranged weapons, except that it's not blocked by fog, darkness, and other factors that limit normal sight.

You must have a clear line of effect to any target that you cast a spell on or to any space in which you wish to create an effect. You must have a clear line of effect to the point of origin of any spell you cast.

A burst, cone, cylinder, or emanation spell affects only an area, creature, or object to which it has line of effect from its origin (a spherical burst's center point, a cone-shaped burst's starting point, a cylinder's circle, or an emanation's point of origin).

An otherwise solid barrier with a hole of at least 1 square foot through it does not block a spell's line of effect. Such an opening means that the 5-foot length of wall containing the hole is no longer considered a barrier for purposes of a spell's line of effect.

Duration

A spell's duration entry tells you how long the magical energy of the spell lasts.

Timed Durations: Many durations are measured in rounds, minutes, hours, or other increments. When the

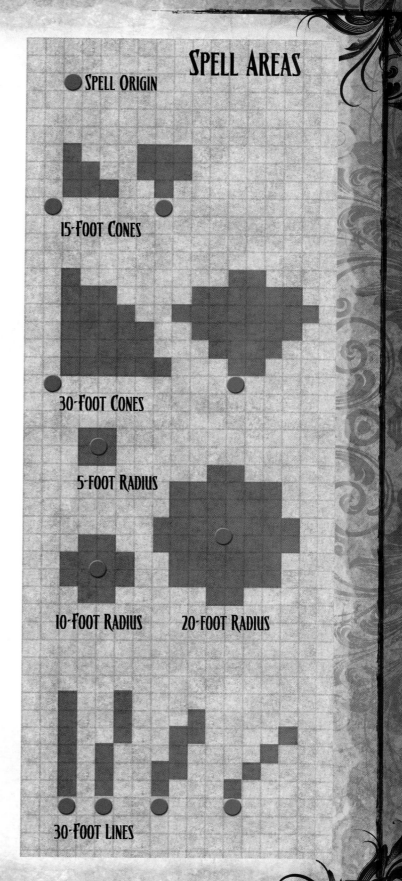

SPELL AREAS

● **SPELL ORIGIN**

15-FOOT CONES

30-FOOT CONES

5-FOOT RADIUS

10-FOOT RADIUS   **20-FOOT RADIUS**

30-FOOT LINES

TABLE 9-2: ITEMS AFFECTED BY MAGICAL ATTACKS

Order*	Item
1st	Shield
2nd	Armor
3rd	Magic helmet, hat, or headband
4th	Item in hand (including weapon, wand, or the like)
5th	Magic cloak
6th	Stowed or sheathed weapon
7th	Magic bracers
8th	Magic clothing
9th	Magic jewelry (including rings)
10th	Anything else

* In order of most likely to least likely to be affected.

time is up, the magic goes away and the spell ends. If a spell's duration is variable, the duration is rolled secretly so the caster doesn't know how long the spell will last.

Instantaneous: The spell energy comes and goes the instant the spell is cast, though the consequences might be long-lasting.

Permanent: The energy remains as long as the effect does. This means the spell is vulnerable to *dispel magic*.

Concentration: The spell lasts as long as you concentrate on it. Concentrating to maintain a spell is a standard action that does not provoke attacks of opportunity. Anything that could break your concentration when casting a spell can also break your concentration while you're maintaining one, causing the spell to end. See concentration on page 206.

You can't cast a spell while concentrating on another one. Some spells last for a short time after you cease concentrating.

Subjects, Effects, and Areas: If the spell affects creatures directly, the result travels with the subjects for the spell's duration. If the spell creates an effect, the effect lasts for the duration. The effect might move or remain still. Such an effect can be destroyed prior to when its duration ends. If the spell affects an area, then the spell stays with that area for its duration.

Creatures become subject to the spell when they enter the area and are no longer subject to it when they leave.

Touch Spells and Holding the Charge: In most cases, if you don't discharge a touch spell on the round you cast it, you can hold the charge (postpone the discharge of the spell) indefinitely. You can make touch attacks round after round until the spell is discharged. If you cast another spell, the touch spell dissipates.

Some touch spells allow you to touch multiple targets as part of the spell. You can't hold the charge of such a spell; you must touch all targets of the spell in the same round that you finish casting the spell.

Discharge: Occasionally a spells lasts for a set duration or until triggered or discharged.

(D) Dismissible: If the duration line ends with "(D)," you can dismiss the spell at will. You must be within range of the spell's effect and must speak words of dismissal, which are usually a modified form of the spell's verbal component. If the spell has no verbal component, you can dismiss the effect with a gesture. Dismissing a spell is a standard action that does not provoke attacks of opportunity.

A spell that depends on concentration is dismissible by its very nature, and dismissing it does not take an action, since all you have to do to end the spell is to stop concentrating on your turn.

Saving Throw

Usually a harmful spell allows a target to make a saving throw to avoid some or all of the effect. The saving throw entry in a spell description defines which type of saving throw the spell allows and describes how saving throws against the spell work.

Negates: The spell has no effect on a subject that makes a successful saving throw.

Partial: The spell has an effect on its subject. A successful saving throw means that some lesser effect occurs.

Half: The spell deals damage, and a successful saving throw halves the damage taken (round down).

None: No saving throw is allowed.

Disbelief: A successful save lets the subject ignore the spell's effect.

(object): The spell can be cast on objects, which receive saving throws only if they are magical or if they are attended (held, worn, grasped, or the like) by a creature resisting the spell, in which case the object uses the creature's saving throw bonus unless its own bonus is greater. This notation does not mean that a spell can be cast only on objects. Some spells of this sort can be cast on creatures or objects. A magic item's saving throw bonuses are each equal to 2 + 1/2 the item's caster level.

(harmless): The spell is usually beneficial, not harmful, but a targeted creature can attempt a saving throw if it desires.

Saving Throw Difficulty Class: A saving throw against your spell has a DC of 10 + the level of the spell + your bonus for the relevant ability (Intelligence for a wizard, Charisma for a bard, paladin, or sorcerer, or Wisdom for a cleric, druid, or ranger). A spell's level can vary depending on your class. Always use the spell level applicable to your class.

Succeeding on a Saving Throw: A creature that successfully saves against a spell that has no obvious physical effects feels a hostile force or a tingle, but cannot deduce the exact nature of the attack. Likewise,

if a creature's saving throw succeeds against a targeted spell, you sense that the spell has failed. You do not sense when creatures succeed on saves against effect and area spells.

Automatic Failures and Successes: A natural 1 (the d20 comes up 1) on a saving throw is always a failure, and the spell may cause damage to exposed items (see Items Surviving after a Saving Throw, below). A natural 20 (the d20 comes up 20) is always a success.

Voluntarily Giving up a Saving Throw: A creature can voluntarily forego a saving throw and willingly accept a spell's result. Even a character with a special resistance to magic can suppress this quality.

Items Surviving after a Saving Throw: Unless the descriptive text for the spell specifies otherwise, all items carried or worn by a creature are assumed to survive a magical attack. If a creature rolls a natural 1 on its saving throw against the effect, however, an exposed item is harmed (if the attack can harm objects). Refer to Table 9–2: Items Affected by Magical Attacks. Determine which four objects carried or worn by the creature are most likely to be affected and roll randomly among them. The randomly determined item must

make a saving throw against the attack form and take whatever damage the attack dealt.

If the selected item is not carried or worn and is not magical, it does not get a saving throw. It simply is dealt the appropriate damage.

Spell Resistance

Spell resistance is a special defensive ability. If your spell is being resisted by a creature with spell resistance, you must make a caster level check (1d20 + caster level) at least equal to the creature's spell resistance for the spell to affect that creature. The defender's spell resistance is like an Armor Class against magical attacks. Include any adjustments to your caster level to this caster level check.

The Spell Resistance entry and the descriptive text of a spell description tell you whether spell resistance protects creatures from the spell. In many cases, spell resistance applies only when a resistant creature is targeted by the spell, not when a resistant creature encounters a spell that is already in place.

The terms "object" and "harmless" mean the same thing for spell resistance as they do for saving throws. A creature with spell resistance must voluntarily lower the resistance (a standard action) in order to be affected by such spells without forcing the caster to make a caster level check.

Descriptive Text

This portion of a spell description details what the spell does and how it works. If one of the previous entries in the description includes "see text," this is where the explanation is found.

ARCANE SPELLS

Wizards, sorcerers, and bards cast arcane spells. Compared to divine spells, arcane spells are more likely to produce dramatic results.

Spell Slots: The various character class tables show how many spells of each level a character can cast per day. These openings for daily spells are called spell slots. A spellcaster always has the option to fill a higher-level spell slot with a lower-level spell. A spellcaster who lacks a high enough ability score to cast spells that would otherwise be his due still gets the slots but must fill them with spells of lower levels.

Preparing Wizard Spells

A wizard's level limits the number of spells he can prepare and cast. His high Intelligence score might allow him to prepare a few extra spells. He can prepare the same spell more than once, but each preparation counts as one spell toward his daily limit. To prepare a spell, the wizard must have an Intelligence score of at least 10 + the spell's level.

Rest: To prepare his daily spells, a wizard must first sleep for 8 hours. The wizard does not have to slumber for every minute of the time, but he must refrain from movement, combat, spellcasting, skill use, conversation, or any other fairly demanding physical or mental task during the rest period. If his rest is interrupted, each interruption adds 1 hour to the total amount of time he has to rest in order to clear his mind, and he must have at least 1 hour of uninterrupted rest immediately prior to preparing his spells. If the character does not need to sleep for some reason, he still must have 8 hours of restful calm before preparing any spells.

Recent Casting Limit/Rest Interruptions: If a wizard has cast spells recently, the drain on his resources reduces his capacity to prepare new spells. When he prepares spells for the coming day, all the spells he has cast within the last 8 hours count against his daily limit.

Preparation Environment: To prepare any spell, a wizard must have enough peace, quiet, and comfort to allow for proper concentration. The wizard's surroundings need not be luxurious, but they must be free from distractions. Exposure to inclement weather prevents the necessary concentration, as does any injury or failed saving throw

the character might experience while studying. Wizards also must have access to their spellbooks to study from and sufficient light to read them. There is one major exception: a wizard can prepare a *read magic* spell even without a spellbook.

Spell Preparation Time: After resting, a wizard must study his spellbook to prepare any spells that day. If he wants to prepare all his spells, the process takes 1 hour. Preparing some smaller portion of his daily capacity takes a proportionally smaller amount of time, but always at least 15 minutes, the minimum time required to achieve the proper mental state.

Spell Selection and Preparation: Until he prepares spells from his spellbook, the only spells a wizard has available to cast are the ones that he already had prepared from the previous day and has not yet used. During the study period, he chooses which spells to prepare. If a wizard already has spells prepared (from the previous day) that he has not cast, she can abandon some or all of them to make room for new spells.

When preparing spells for the day, a wizard can leave some of these spell slots open. Later during that day, he can repeat the preparation process as often as he likes, time and circumstances permitting. During these extra sessions of preparation, the wizard can fill these unused spell slots. He cannot, however, abandon a previously prepared spell to replace it with another one or fill a slot that is empty because he has cast a spell in the meantime. That sort of preparation requires a mind fresh from rest. Like the first session of the day, this preparation takes at least 15 minutes, and it takes longer if the wizard prepares more than one-quarter of his spells.

Prepared Spell Retention: Once a wizard prepares a spell, it remains in his mind as a nearly cast spell until he uses the prescribed components to complete and trigger it or until he abandons it. Certain other events, such as the effects of magic items or special attacks from monsters, can wipe a prepared spell from a character's mind.

Death and Prepared Spell Retention: If a spellcaster dies, all prepared spells stored in his mind are wiped away. Potent magic (such as *raise dead*, *resurrection*, or *true resurrection*) can recover the lost energy when it recovers the character.

Arcane Magical Writings

To record an arcane spell in written form, a character uses complex notation that describes the magical forces involved in the spell. The writer uses the same system no matter what her native language or culture. However, each character uses the system in his own way. Another person's magical writing remains incomprehensible to even the most powerful wizard until he takes time to study and decipher it.

To decipher an arcane magical writing (such as a single spell in another's spellbook or on a scroll), a character must make a Spellcraft check (DC 20 + the spell's level). If the skill check fails, the character cannot attempt to read that particular spell again until the next day. A *read magic* spell automatically deciphers magical writing without a skill check. If the person who created the magical writing is on hand to help the reader, success is also automatic.

Once a character deciphers a particular piece of magical writing, he does not need to decipher it again. Deciphering magical writing allows the reader to identify the spell and gives some idea of its effects (as explained in the spell description). If the magical writing is a scroll and the reader can cast arcane spells, he can attempt to use the scroll.

Wizard Spells and Borrowed Spellbooks

A wizard can use a borrowed spellbook to prepare a spell he already knows and has recorded in his own spellbook, but preparation success is not assured. First, the wizard must decipher the writing in the book (see Arcane Magical Writings, above). Once a spell from another spellcaster's book is deciphered, the reader must make a Spellcraft check (DC 15 + spell's level) to prepare the spell. If the check succeeds, the wizard can prepare the spell. He must repeat the check to prepare the spell again, no matter how many times he has prepared it before. If the check fails, he cannot try to prepare the spell from the same source again until the next day. However, as explained above, he does not need to repeat a check to decipher the writing.

Adding Spells to a Wizard's Spellbook

Wizards can add new spells to their spellbooks through several methods. A wizard can only learn new spells that belong to the wizard spell lists.

Spells Gained at a New Level: Wizards perform a certain amount of spell research between adventures. Each time a character attains a new wizard level, he gains two spells of his choice to add to his spellbook. The two free spells must be of spell levels he can cast.

Spells Copied from Another's Spellbook or a Scroll: A wizard can also add a spell to his book whenever he encounters one on a magic scroll or in another wizard's spellbook. No matter what the spell's source, the wizard must first decipher the magical writing (see Arcane Magical Writings). Next, he must spend 1 hour studying the spell. At the end of the hour, he must make a Spellcraft check (DC 15 + spell's level). A wizard who has specialized in a school of spells gains a +2 bonus on the Spellcraft check if the new spell is from his specialty school. If the check succeeds, the wizard understands the spell and can copy it into his spellbook (see Writing a New Spell into a Spellbook). The process leaves a spellbook that was copied from unharmed, but a spell successfully copied from a magic scroll disappears from the parchment.

If the check fails, the wizard cannot understand or copy the spell. He cannot attempt to learn or copy that spell again until one week has passed. If the spell was from a scroll, a failed Spellcraft check does not cause the spell to vanish.

In most cases, wizards charge a fee for the privilege of copying spells from their spellbooks. This fee is usually equal to half the cost to write the spell into a spellbook (see Writing a New Spell into a Spellbook). Rare and unique spells might cost significantly more.

Independent Research: A wizard can also research a spell independently, duplicating an existing spell or creating an entirely new one. The cost to research a new spell, and the time required, are left up to GM discretion, but it should probably take at least 1 week and cost at least 1,000 gp per level of the spell to be researched. This should also require a number of Spellcraft and Knowledge (arcana) checks.

Writing a New Spell into a Spellbook

Once a wizard understands a new spell, he can record it into his spellbook.

Time: The process takes 1 hour per spell level. Cantrips (0 levels spells) take 30 minutes to record.

Space in the Spellbook: A spell takes up one page of the spellbook per spell level. Even a 0-level spell (cantrip) takes one page. A spellbook has 100 pages.

Materials and Costs: The cost for writing a new spell into a spellbook depends on the level of the spell, as noted on the following table. Note that a wizard does not have to pay these costs in time or gold for spells he gains for free at each new level.

Spell Level	Writing Cost	Spell Level	Writing Cost
0	5 gp	5	250 gp
1	10 gp	6	360 gp
2	40 gp	7	490 gp
3	90 gp	8	640 gp
4	160 gp	9	810 gp

Replacing and Copying Spellbooks

A wizard can use the procedure for learning a spell to reconstruct a lost spellbook. If he already has a particular spell prepared, he can write it directly into a new book at the same cost required to write a spell into a spellbook. The process wipes the prepared spell from his mind, just as casting it would. If he does not have the spell prepared, he can prepare it from a borrowed spellbook and then write it into a new book.

Duplicating an existing spellbook uses the same procedure as replacing it, but the task is much easier. The time requirement and cost per spell are halved.

Selling a Spellbook

Captured spellbooks can be sold for an amount equal to half the cost of purchasing and inscribing the spells within.

Sorcerers and Bards

Sorcerers and bards cast arcane spells, but they do not use spellbooks or prepare spells. Their class level limits the number of spells she can cast (see these class descriptions). Her high Charisma score might allow her to cast a few extra spells. A member of either class must have a Charisma score of at least 10 + the spell's level to cast the spell.

Daily Readying of Spells: Each day, sorcerers and bards must focus their minds on the task of casting their spells. A sorcerer or bard needs 8 hours of rest (just like a wizard), after which she spends 15 minutes concentrating. (A bard must sing, recite, or play an instrument of some kind while concentrating.) During this period, the sorcerer or bard readies her mind to cast her daily allotment of spells. Without such a period to refresh herself, the character does not regain the spell slots she used up the day before.

Recent Casting Limit: Any spells cast within the last 8 hours count against the sorcerer's or bard's daily limit.

Adding Spells to a Sorcerer's or Bard's Repertoire: A sorcerer or bard gains spells each time she attains a new level in her class and never gains spells any other way. When your sorcerer or bard gains a new level, consult Table 3–4 or Table 3–15 to learn how many spells from the appropriate spell list she now knows. With permission from the GM, sorcerers and bards can also select the spells they gain from new and unusual spells that they come across while adventuring.

🌿 DIVINE SPELLS

Clerics, druids, experienced paladins, and experienced rangers can cast divine spells. Unlike arcane spells, divine spells draw power from a divine source. Clerics gain spell power from deities or from divine forces. The divine force of nature powers druid and ranger spells, and the divine forces of law and good power paladin spells. Divine spells tend to focus on healing and protection and are less flashy, destructive, and disruptive than arcane spells.

Preparing Divine Spells

Divine spellcasters prepare their spells in largely the same manner as wizards do, but with a few differences. The relevant ability for most divine spells is Wisdom (Charisma for paladins). To prepare a divine spell, a character must have a Wisdom score (or Charisma score for paladins) of 10 + the spell's level. Likewise, bonus spells are based on Wisdom.

Time of Day: A divine spellcaster chooses and prepares spells ahead of time, but unlike a wizard, does not require a period of rest to prepare spells. Instead, the character chooses a particular time of day to pray and receive spells. The time is usually associated with some daily event. If some event prevents a character from praying at the proper time, she must do so as soon as possible. If the character does not stop to pray for spells at the first opportunity, she must wait until the next day to prepare spells.

Spell Selection and Preparation: A divine spellcaster selects and prepares spells ahead of time through prayer and meditation at a particular time of day. The time required to prepare spells is the same as it is for a wizard (1 hour), as is the requirement for a relatively peaceful environment. When preparing spells for the day, a divine spellcaster can leave some of her spell slots open. Later during that day, she can repeat the preparation process as often as she likes. During these extra sessions of preparation, she can fill these unused spell slots. She cannot, however, abandon a previously prepared spell to replace it with another one or fill a slot that is empty because she has cast a spell in the meantime. Like the first session of the day, this preparation takes at least 15 minutes, and it takes longer if she prepares more than one-quarter of her spells.

Divine spellcasters do not require spellbooks. However, a divine spellcaster's spell selection is limited to the spells on the list for her class. Clerics, druids, paladins, and rangers have separate spell lists. A cleric also has access to two domains determined during character creation. Each domain gives her access to a number of special abilities and bonus spells.

Spell Slots: The character class tables show how many spells of each level each can cast per day. These openings for daily spells are called spell slots. A spellcaster always has the option to fill a higher-level spell slot with a lower-level spell. A spellcaster who lacks a high enough ability score to cast spells that would otherwise be her due still gets the slots but must fill them with spells of lower levels.

Recent Casting Limit: As with arcane spells, at the time of preparation any spells cast within the previous 8 hours count against the number of spells that can be prepared.

Spontaneous Casting of Cure and Inflict Spells: A good cleric (or a cleric of a good deity) can spontaneously cast a cure spell in place of a prepared spell of the same level or higher, but not in place of a bonus domain spell. An evil cleric (or a cleric of an evil deity) can spontaneously cast an inflict spell in place of a prepared spell (that is not a domain spell) of the same level or higher. Each neutral cleric of a neutral deity spontaneously casts either cure spells like a good cleric or inflict spells like an evil one, depending on which option the player chooses when creating the character. The divine energy of the spell that the cure or inflict spell substitutes for is converted into the cure or inflict spell as if that spell had been prepared all along.

Spontaneous Casting of *Summon Nature's Ally* Spells: A druid can spontaneously cast *summon nature's ally* in place of a prepared spell of the same level or higher. The divine energy of the spell that the summon spell substitutes for is converted as if that spell had been prepared all along.

Divine Magical Writings

Divine spells can be written and deciphered like arcane spells (see Arcane Magical Writings). A Spellcraft check can decipher divine magical writing and identify it. Only characters who have the spell (in its divine form) on their class spell list can cast a divine spell from a scroll.

New Divine Spells

Divine spellcasters gain new spells as follows.

Spells Gained at a New Level: Characters who can cast divine spells undertake a certain amount of study between adventures. Each time such a character receives a new level of divine spells, she learns all of the spells from that level automatically.

Independent Research: A divine spellcaster can also research a spell independently, much as an arcane spellcaster can. Only the creator of such a spell can prepare and cast it, unless she decides to share it with others.

SPECIAL ABILITIES

A number of classes and creatures gain the use of special abilities, many of which function like spells.

Spell-Like Abilities: Usually, a spell-like ability works just like the spell of that name. A spell-like ability has no verbal, somatic, or material component, nor does it require a focus. The user activates it mentally. Armor never affects a spell-like ability's use, even if the ability resembles an arcane spell with a somatic component.

A spell-like ability has a casting time of 1 standard action unless noted otherwise in the ability or spell description. In all other ways, a spell-like ability functions just like a spell.

Spell-like abilities are subject to spell resistance and *dispel magic*. They do not function in areas where magic is suppressed or negated. Spell-like abilities cannot be used to counterspell, nor can they be counterspelled.

If a character class grants a spell-like ability that is not based on an actual spell, the ability's effective spell level is equal to the highest-level class spell the character can cast, and is cast at the class level the ability is gained.

Supernatural Abilities: These can't be disrupted in combat and generally don't provoke attacks of opportunity. They aren't subject to spell resistance, counterspells, or *dispel magic*, and don't function in antimagic areas.

Extraordinary Abilities: These abilities cannot be disrupted in combat, as spells can, and they generally do not provoke attacks of opportunity. Effects or areas that negate or disrupt magic have no effect on extraordinary abilities. They are not subject to dispelling, and they function normally in an *antimagic field*. Indeed, extraordinary abilities do not qualify as magical, though they may break the laws of physics.

Natural Abilities: This category includes abilities a creature has because of its physical nature. Natural abilities are those not otherwise designated as extraordinary, supernatural, or spell-like.

10 SPELLS

Eerie in their silence, another wave of the dead-eyed, tentacle-faced hounds charged, barely kept at bay by Kyra's lethal scimitar. The otherworldly things had already quieted cocky Valeros, dragging him away for some terrible purpose amid a litany of colorful curses.

Her mind racing, Seoni grasped for clues as to what these horrors were, where they had come from, and what they could possibly want. Yet for all her questions, the sorceress took comfort in the one thing she knew for certain: like every other foe she had ever faced, these things still knew how to burn.

There are hundreds of spells available to spellcasters in the Pathfinder Roleplaying Game—this chapter begins with the spell lists for all of the game's spellcasting classes. An ^M or ^F appearing at the end of a spell's name in the spell lists denotes a spell with a material or focus component, respectively, that is not normally included in a spell component pouch.

Order of Presentation: In the spell lists and the short descriptions that follow them, the spells are presented in alphabetical order by name except for those belonging to certain spell chains. When a spell's name begins with "lesser," "greater," or "mass," the spell is alphabetized under the second word of the spell name instead.

Hit Dice: The term "Hit Dice" is used synonymously with "character levels" for effects that affect a specific number of Hit Dice of creatures. Creatures with Hit Dice only from their race, not from classes, still have character levels equal to their Hit Dice.

Caster Level: A spell's power often depends on caster level, which is defined as the caster's class level for the purpose of casting a particular spell. A creature with no classes has a caster level equal to its Hit Dice unless otherwise specified. The word "level" in the short descriptions that follow always refers to caster level.

Creatures and Characters: The words "creature" and "character" are used synonymously in the short descriptions.

BARD SPELLS

0-Level Bard Spells

Dancing Lights: Creates torches or other lights.
Daze: Humanoid creature of 4 HD or less loses next action.
Detect Magic: Detects spells and magic items within 60 ft.
Flare: Dazzles one creature (–1 on attack rolls).
Ghost Sound: Figment sounds.
Know Direction: You discern north.
Light: Object shines like a torch.
Lullaby: Makes subject drowsy: –5 on Perception checks, –2 on Will saves against *sleep*.
Mage Hand: 5-pound telekinesis.
Mending: Makes minor repairs on an object.
Message: Whisper conversation at distance.
Open/Close: Opens or closes small or light things.
Prestidigitation: Performs minor tricks.
Read Magic: Read scrolls and spellbooks.
Resistance: Subject gains +1 on saving throws.
Summon Instrument: Summons one musical instrument.

1st-Level Bard Spells

Alarm: Wards an area for 2 hours/level.
Animate Rope: Makes a rope move at your command.
Cause Fear: One creature of 5 HD or less flees for 1d4 rounds.
Charm Person: Makes one person your friend.

Comprehend Languages: You understand all languages.
Confusion, Lesser: One creature is *confused* for 1 round.
Cure Light Wounds: Cures 1d8 damage + 1/level (max +5).
Detect Secret Doors: Reveals hidden doors within 60 ft.
Disguise Self: Changes your appearance.
Erase: Mundane or magical writing vanishes.
Expeditious Retreat: Your base land speed increases by 30 ft.
Feather Fall: Objects or creatures fall slowly.
Grease: Makes 10-ft. square or one object slippery.
Hideous Laughter: Subject loses actions for 1 round/ level.
Hypnotism: Fascinates 2d4 HD of creatures.
Identify: Gives +10 bonus to identify magic items.
Magic Aura: Alters object's magic aura.
Magic Mouth^M: Objects speaks once when triggered.
Obscure Object: Masks object against *scrying*.
Remove Fear: Suppresses fear or gives +4 on saves against fear for one subject + one per four levels.
Silent Image: Creates minor illusion of your design.
Sleep: Puts 4 HD of creatures into magical slumber.
Summon Monster I: Summons extraplanar creature to fight for you.
Undetectable Alignment: Conceals alignment for 24 hours.
Unseen Servant: Invisible force obeys your commands.
Ventriloquism: Throws voice for 1 min./level.

2nd-Level Bard Spells

Alter Self: Assume form of a Small or Medium humanoid.
Animal Messenger: Sends a Tiny animal to a specific place.
Animal Trance: Fascinates 2d6 HD of animals.
Blindness/Deafness: Makes subject blind or deaf.
Blur: Attacks miss subject 20% of the time.
Calm Emotions: Calms creatures, negating emotion effects.
Cat's Grace: Subject gains +4 to Dex for 1 min./level.
Cure Moderate Wounds: Cures 2d8 damage + 1/level (max +10).
Darkness: 20-ft. radius of supernatural shadow.
Daze Monster: Living creature of 6 HD or less loses next action.
Delay Poison: Stops poison from harming target for 1 hour/level.
Detect Thoughts: Allows "listening" to surface thoughts.
Eagle's Splendor: Subject gains +4 to Cha for 1 min./level.
Enthrall: Captivates all within 100 ft. + 10 ft./level.
Fox's Cunning: Subject gains +4 to Int for 1 min./level.
Glitterdust: Blinds creatures, outlines invisible creatures.
Heroism: Gives +2 on attack rolls, saves, skill checks.
Hold Person: Paralyzes one humanoid for 1 round/level.
Hypnotic Pattern: Fascinates (2d4 + level) HD of creatures.
Invisibility: Subject is invisible for 1 min./level or until it attacks.
Locate Object: Senses direction toward object (specific or type).
Minor Image: As *silent image*, plus some sound.
Mirror Image: Creates decoy duplicates of you (1d4 + 1 per three levels, max 8).
Misdirection: Misleads divinations for one creature or object.
Pyrotechnics: Turns fire into blinding light or choking smoke.
Rage: Gives +2 to Str and Con, +1 on Will saves, –2 to AC.

Scare: Panics creatures of less than 6 HD.

Shatter: Sonic vibration damages objects or crystalline creatures.

Silence: Negates sound in 20-ft. radius.

Sound Burst: Deals 1d8 sonic damage and may stun subjects.

Suggestion: Compels subject to follow stated course of action.

Summon Monster II: Summons extraplanar creature to fight for you.

Summon Swarm: Summons swarm of bats, rats, or spiders.

Tongues: Speak and understand any language.

Whispering Wind: Sends a short message 1 mile/level.

3rd-Level Bard Spells

Blink: You randomly vanish and reappear for 1 round/level.

Charm Monster: Makes monster believe it is your ally.

Clairaudience/Clairvoyance: Hear or see at a distance for 1 min./level.

Confusion: Subjects behave oddly for 1 round/level.

Crushing Despair: Subjects take –2 on attack rolls, damage rolls, saves, and checks.

Cure Serious Wounds: Cures 3d8 damage + 1/level (max +15).

Daylight: 60-ft. radius of bright light.

Deep Slumber: Puts 10 HD of creatures to sleep.

Dispel Magic: Cancels one magical spell or effect.

Displacement: Attacks miss subject 50% of the time.

Fear: Subjects within cone flee for 1 round/level.

Gaseous Form: Subject becomes insubstantial and can fly slowly.

Geas, Lesser: Commands subject of 7 HD or less.

Glibness: You gain +20 bonus on Bluff checks, and your lies can escape magical discernment.

Good Hope: Subjects gain +2 on attack rolls, damage rolls, saves, and checks.

Haste: One creature/level moves faster, receives +1 on attack rolls, AC, and Reflex saves.

Illusory Script^M: Only select creatures can read text.

Invisibility Sphere: Makes everyone within 10 feet invisible.

Major Image: As *silent image*, plus sound, smell, and thermal effects.

Phantom Steed: Magic horse appears for 1 hour/level.

Remove Curse: Frees object or person from curse.

Scrying^F: Spies on subject from a distance.

Sculpt Sound: Creates new sounds or changes existing ones into new sounds.

Secret Page: Changes one page to hide its real content.

See Invisibility: Reveals invisible creatures or objects.

Sepia Snake Sigil^M: Creates a snake-shaped text symbol that immobilizes reader.

Slow: One subject/level takes only one action/round, –1 to AC, Reflex saves, and attack rolls.

Speak with Animals: You can communicate with animals.

Summon Monster III: Summons extraplanar creature to fight for you.

Tiny Hut: Creates shelter for 10 creatures.

4th-Level Bard Spells

Break Enchantment: Frees subjects from enchantments, transmutations, and curses.

Cure Critical Wounds: Cures 4d8 damage + 1/level (max +20).

Detect Scrying: Alerts you to magical eavesdropping.

Dimension Door: Teleports you a short distance.

Dominate Person: Controls humanoid telepathically.

Freedom of Movement: Subject moves normally despite impediments to restrict movement.

Hallucinatory Terrain: Makes one type of terrain appear like another (field as forest, or the like).

Hold Monster: As *hold person*, but any creature.

Invisibility, Greater: As *invisibility*, but subject can attack and stay invisible.

Legend Lore^MF: Lets you learn tales about a person, place, or thing.

Locate Creature: Indicates direction to known creature.

Modify Memory: Changes 5 minutes of subject's memories.

Neutralize Poison: Immunizes subject against poison, detoxifies venom in or on subject.

Rainbow Pattern: Lights fascinate 24 HD of creatures.

Repel Vermin: Insects, spiders, and other vermin stay 10 ft. away.

Secure Shelter: Creates sturdy cottage.

Shadow Conjuration: Mimics conjuration below 4th level, but only 20% real.

Shout: Deafens all within cone and deals 5d6 sonic damage.

Speak with Plants: You can talk to plants and plant creatures.

Summon Monster IV: Summons extraplanar creature to fight for you.

Zone of Silence: Keeps eavesdroppers from overhearing you.

5th-Level Bard Spells

Cure Light Wounds, Mass: Cures 1d8 damage + 1/level, affects 1 subject/level.

Dispel Magic, Greater: Works as *dispel magic*, but can affect multiple targets.

Dream: Sends message to anyone sleeping.

False Vision^M: Fools scrying with an illusion.

Heroism, Greater: Gives +4 bonus on attack rolls, saves, skill checks; immunity to fear; temporary hp.

Mind Fog: Subjects in fog get –10 to Wis and Will checks.

Mirage Arcana: As *hallucinatory terrain*, plus structures.

Mislead: Turns you invisible and creates illusory double.

Nightmare: Sends vision dealing 1d10 damage, fatigue.

Persistent Image: As *major image*, but no concentration required.

Seeming: Changes appearance of one person per two levels.

Shadow Evocation: Mimics evocation of lower than 5th level, but only 20% real.

Shadow Walk: Step into shadow to travel rapidly.

Song of Discord: Forces targets to attack each other.

Suggestion, Mass: As *suggestion*, affects subject/level.

Summon Monster V: Summons extraplanar creature to fight for you.

6th-Level Bard Spells

Analyze Dweomer[F]: Reveals magical aspects of subject.

Animate Objects: Objects attack your foes.

Cat's Grace, Mass: As *cat's grace*, affects 1 subject/level.

Charm Monster, Mass: As *charm monster*, but all within 30 ft.

Cure Moderate Wounds, Mass: Cures 2d8 damage + 1/level, affects 1 subject/level.

Eagle's Splendor, Mass: As *eagle's splendor*, affects 1 subject/level.

Eyebite: Target becomes panicked, sickened, and/or comatose.

Find the Path: Shows most direct way to a location.

Fox's Cunning, Mass: As *fox's cunning*, affects 1 subject/level.

Geas/Quest: As *lesser geas*, but affects any creature.

Heroes' Feast: Food for one creature/level cures and grants combat bonuses.

Irresistible Dance: Forces subject to dance.

Permanent Image: Permanent illusion, includes sight, sound, smell, and thermal effects.

Programmed Image[M]: As *major image*, plus triggered by event.

Project Image[M]: Illusory double can talk and cast spells.

Scrying, Greater: As *scrying*, but faster and longer.

Shout, Greater: Devastating yell deals 10d6 sonic damage; stuns creatures.

Summon Monster VI: Summons extraplanar creature to fight for you.

Sympathetic Vibration: Deals 2d10 damage/round to freestanding structure.

Veil: Changes appearance of group of creatures.

CLERIC SPELLS

0-Level Cleric Spells (Orisons)

Bleed: Cause a stabilized creature to resume dying.

Create Water: Creates 2 gallons/level of pure water.

Detect Magic: Detects spells and magic items within 60 ft.

Detect Poison: Detects poison in one creature or object.

Guidance: +1 on one attack roll, saving throw, or skill check.

Light: Object shines like a torch.

Mending: Makes minor repairs on an object.

Purify Food and Drink: Purifies 1 cu. ft./level of food or water.

Read Magic: Read scrolls and spellbooks.

Resistance: Subject gains +1 on saving throws.

Stabilize: Cause a dying creature to stabilize.

Virtue: Subject gains 1 temporary hp.

1st-Level Cleric Spells

Bane: Enemies take –1 on attack rolls and saves against fear.

Bless: Allies gain +1 on attack rolls and saves against fear.

Bless Water[M]: Makes holy water.

Cause Fear: One creature of 5 HD or less flees for 1d4 rounds.

Command: One subject obeys selected command for 1 round.

Comprehend Languages: You understand all spoken and written languages.

Cure Light Wounds: Cures 1d8 damage + 1/level (max +5).

Curse Water[M]: Makes unholy water.

Deathwatch: Reveals how near death subjects within 30 ft. are.

Detect Chaos/Evil/Good/Law: Reveals creatures, spells, or objects of selected alignment.

Detect Undead: Reveals undead within 60 ft.

Divine Favor: You gain +1 per three levels on attack and damage rolls.

Doom: One subject takes –2 on attack rolls, damage rolls, saves, and checks.

Endure Elements: Exist comfortably in hot or cold regions.

Entropic Shield: Ranged attacks against you have 20% miss chance.

Hide from Undead: Undead can't perceive one subject/level.

Inflict Light Wounds: Touch deals 1d8 damage +1/level (max +5).

Magic Stone: Three stones gain +1 on attack, deal 1d6 +1 damage.

Magic Weapon: Weapon gains +1 bonus.

Obscuring Mist: Fog surrounds you.

Protection from Chaos/Evil/Good/Law: +2 to AC and saves, plus additional protection against selected alignment.

Remove Fear: Suppresses fear or gives +4 on saves against fear for one subject + one per four levels.

Sanctuary: Opponents can't attack you, and you can't attack.

Shield of Faith: Aura grants +2 or higher deflection bonus.

Summon Monster I: Summons extraplanar creature to fight for you.

2nd-Level Cleric Spells

Aid: +1 on attack rolls and saves against fear, 1d8 temporary hp +1/level (max +10).

Align Weapon: Weapon becomes good, evil, lawful, or chaotic.

Augury[MF]: Learns whether an action will be good or bad.

Bear's Endurance: Subject gains +4 to Con for 1 min./level.

Bull's Strength: Subject gains +4 to Str for 1 min./level.

Calm Emotions: Calms creatures, negating emotion effects.

Consecrate[M]: Fills area with positive energy, weakening undead.

Cure Moderate Wounds: Cures 2d8 damage + 1/level (max +10).

Darkness: 20-ft. radius of supernatural shadow.

Death Knell: Kills dying creature; you gain 1d8 temporary hp, +2 to Str, and +1 caster level.

Delay Poison: Stops poison from harming target for 1 hour/level.

Desecrate[M]: Fills area with negative energy, making undead stronger.

Eagle's Splendor: Subject gains +4 to Cha for 1 min./level.

Enthrall: Captivates all within 100 ft. + 10 ft./level.

Find Traps: Notice traps as a rogue does.

Gentle Repose: Preserves one corpse.

Hold Person: Paralyzes one humanoid for 1 round/level.

Inflict Moderate Wounds: Touch attack, 2d8 damage + 1/level (max +10).

Make Whole: Repairs an object.

Owl's Wisdom: Subject gains +4 to Wis for 1 min./level.

Remove Paralysis: Frees creatures from paralysis or *slow* effect.

Resist Energy: Ignores 10 (or more) points of damage/attack from specified energy type.

Restoration, Lesser: Dispels magical ability penalty or repairs 1d4 ability damage.

Shatter: Sonic vibration damages objects or crystalline creatures.

Shield Other^F: You take half of subject's damage.

Silence: Negates sound in 20-ft. radius.

Sound Burst: Deals 1d8 sonic damage to subjects; may stun them.

Spiritual Weapon: Magic weapon attacks on its own.

Status: Monitors condition, position of allies.

Summon Monster II: Summons extraplanar creature to fight for you.

Undetectable Alignment: Conceals alignment for 24 hours.

Zone of Truth: Subjects within range cannot lie.

3rd-Level Cleric Spells

Animate Dead^M: Creates undead skeletons and zombies.

Bestow Curse: –6 to an ability score; –4 on attack rolls, saves, and checks; or 50% chance of losing each action.

Blindness/Deafness: Makes subject blinded or deafened.

Contagion: Infects subject with chosen disease.

Continual Flame^M: Makes a permanent, heatless light.

Create Food and Water: Feeds three humans (or one horse)/level.

Cure Serious Wounds: Cures 3d8 damage + 1/level (max +15).

Daylight: 60-ft. radius of bright light.

Deeper Darkness: Object sheds supernatural shadow in 60-ft. radius.

Dispel Magic: Cancels one magical spell or effect.

Glyph of Warding^M: Inscription harms those who pass it.

Helping Hand: Ghostly hand leads subject to you.

Inflict Serious Wounds: Touch attack, 3d8 damage + 1/level (max +15).

Invisibility Purge: Dispels invisibility within 5 ft./level.

Locate Object: Senses direction toward object (specific or type).

Magic Circle against Chaos/Evil/Good/Law: As *protection* spells, but 10-ft. radius and 10 min./level.

Magic Vestment: Armor or shield gains +1 enhancement per four levels.

Meld into Stone: You and your gear merge with stone.

Obscure Object: Masks object against scrying.

Prayer: Allies get +1 bonus on most rolls, enemies –1 penalty.

Protection from Energy: Absorb 12 points/level of damage from one kind of energy.

Remove Blindness/Deafness: Cures normal or magical blindness or deafness.

Remove Curse: Frees object or person from curse.

Remove Disease: Cures all diseases affecting subject.

Searing Light: Ray deals 1d8/two levels damage (more against undead).

Speak with Dead: Corpse answers one question/two levels.

Stone Shape: Sculpts stone into any shape.

Summon Monster III: Summons extraplanar creature to fight for you.

Water Breathing: Subjects can breathe underwater.

Water Walk: Subject treads on water as if solid.

Wind Wall: Deflects arrows, smaller creatures, and gases.

4th-Level Cleric Spells

Air Walk: Subject treads on air as if solid (climb or descend at 45-degree angle).

Chaos Hammer: Harms and slows lawful creatures (1d8 damage/2 levels).

Control Water: Raises or lowers bodies of water.

Cure Critical Wounds: Cures 4d8 damage + 1/level (max +20).

Death Ward: Grants bonuses against death spells and negative energy.

Dimensional Anchor: Bars extradimensional movement.

Discern Lies: Reveals deliberate falsehoods.

Dismissal: Forces a creature to return to native plane.

Divination^M: Provides useful advice for specific proposed actions.

Divine Power: You gain attack bonuses and 1 hp/level.

Freedom of Movement: Subject moves normally despite impediments to movement.

Giant Vermin: Turns centipedes, scorpions, or spiders into giant vermin.

Holy Smite: Harms and possibly blinds evil creatures (1d8 damage/2 levels).

Imbue with Spell Ability: Transfer spells to subject.

Inflict Critical Wounds: Touch attack, 4d8 damage + 1/level (max +20).

Magic Weapon, Greater: Weapon gains +1 bonus/four levels (max +5).

Neutralize Poison: Immunizes subject against poison, detoxifies venom in or on subject.

Order's Wrath: Harms and dazes chaotic creatures (1d8 damage/2 levels).

Planar Ally, Lesser^M: Exchange services with a 6 HD extraplanar creature.

Poison: Touch deals 1d3 Con damage 1/round for 6 rounds.

Repel Vermin: Insects, spiders, and other vermin stay 10 ft. away.

Restoration^M: Restores level and ability score drains.

Sending: Delivers short message anywhere, instantly.

Spell Immunity: Subject is immune to one spell per 4 levels.

Summon Monster IV: Summons extraplanar creature to fight for you.

Tongues: Speak and understand any language.

Unholy Blight: Harms and sickens good creatures (1d8 damage/2 levels).

5th-Level Cleric Spells

Atonement^{FM}: Removes burden of misdeeds from subject and reverses magical alignment change.

Break Enchantment: Frees subjects from enchantments, transmutations, and curses.

Breath of Life: Cures 5d8 damage + 1/level and restores life to recently slain creatures.

Command, Greater: As *command,* but affects one subject/level.

Commune^M: Deity answers one yes-or-no question/level.

Cure Light Wounds, Mass: Cures 1d8 damage + 1/level, affects 1 subject/level.

Dispel Chaos/Evil/Good/Law: +4 bonus against attacks.

Disrupting Weapon: Melee weapon destroys undead.

Flame Strike: Smites foes with divine fire (1d6/level damage).

Hallow^M: Designates location as holy.

Inflict Light Wounds, Mass: Deals 1d8 damage + 1/level, affects 1 subject/level.

Insect Plague: Wasp swarms attack creatures.

Mark of Justice: Designates action that triggers *curse* on subject.

Plane Shift^F: As many as 8 subjects travel to another plane.

Raise Dead^M: Restores life to subject who died as long as one day/level ago.

Righteous Might: Your size increases, and you gain bonuses in combat.

Scrying^F: Spies on subject from a distance.

Slay Living: Touch attack deals 12d6 + 1 per level.

Spell Resistance: Subject gains SR 12 + level.

Summon Monster V: Summons extraplanar creature to fight for you.

Symbol of Pain^M: Triggered rune wracks nearby creatures with pain.

Symbol of Sleep^M: Triggered rune puts nearby creatures into catatonic slumber.

True Seeing^M: Lets you see all things as they really are.

Unhallow^M: Designates location as unholy.

Wall of Stone: Creates a stone wall that can be shaped.

6th-Level Cleric Spells

Animate Objects: Objects attack your foes.

Antilife Shell: 10-ft.-radius field hedges out living creatures.

Banishment: Banishes 2 HD/level of extraplanar creatures.

Bear's Endurance, Mass: As *bear's endurance,* affects 1 subject/level.

Blade Barrier: Wall of blades deals 1d6/level damage.

Bull's Strength, Mass: As *bull's strength,* affects 1 subject/level.

Create Undead^M: Create ghasts, ghouls, mohrgs, or mummies.

Cure Moderate Wounds, Mass: Cures 2d8 damage + 1/level, affects 1 subject/level.

Dispel Magic, Greater: As *dispel magic,* but with multiple targets.

Eagle's Splendor, Mass: As *eagle's splendor,* affects 1 subject/level.

Find the Path: Shows most direct way to a location.

Forbiddance^M: Blocks planar travel, damages creatures of different alignment.

Geas/Quest: As *lesser geas,* but affects any creature.

Glyph of Warding, Greater^M: As *glyph of warding,* but up to 10d8 damage or 6th-level spell.

Harm: Deals 10 points/level damage to target.

Heal: Cures 10 points/level damage, all diseases and mental conditions.

Heroes' Feast: Food for one creature/level cures and grants combat bonuses.

Inflict Moderate Wounds, Mass: Deals 2d8 damage + 1/level, affects 1 subject/level.

Owl's Wisdom, Mass: As *owl's wisdom,* affects 1 subject/level.

Planar Ally^M: As *lesser planar ally,* but up to 12 HD.

Summon Monster VI: Summons extraplanar creature to fight for you.

Symbol of Fear^M: Triggered rune panics nearby creatures.

Symbol of Persuasion^M: Triggered rune charms nearby creatures.

Undeath to Death^M: Destroys 1d4 HD/level undead (max. 20d4).

Wind Walk: You and your allies turn vaporous and travel fast.

Word of Recall: Teleports you back to designated place.

7th-Level Cleric Spells

Blasphemy: Kills, paralyzes, weakens, or dazes nonevil subjects.

Control Weather: Changes weather in local area.

Cure Serious Wounds, Mass: Cures 3d8 damage + 1/level, affects 1 subject/level.

Destruction^F: Kills subject and destroys remains.

Dictum: Kills, paralyzes, staggers, or deafens nonlawful targets.

Ethereal Jaunt: You become ethereal for 1 round/level.

Holy Word: Kills, paralyzes, blinds, or deafens nongood subjects.

Inflict Serious Wounds, Mass: Deals 3d8 damage + 1/level, affects 1 subject/level.

Refuge^M: Alters item to transport its possessor to you.

Regenerate: Subject's severed limbs grow back, cures 4d8 damage +1/level (max +35).

Repulsion: Creatures can't approach you.

Restoration, Greater^M: As *restoration,* plus restores all levels and ability scores.

Resurrection^M: Fully restore dead subject.

Scrying, Greater: As *scrying,* but faster and longer.

Summon Monster VII: Summons extraplanar creature to fight for you.

Symbol of Stunning^M: Triggered rune stuns nearby creatures.

Symbol of Weakness^M: Triggered rune weakens nearby creatures.

Word of Chaos: Kills, confuses, stuns, or deafens nonchaotic subjects.

8th-Level Cleric Spells

Antimagic Field: Negates magic within 10 ft.

Cloak of Chaos^F: +4 to AC, +4 resistance, and SR 25 against lawful spells.

Create Greater Undead^M: Create shadows, wraiths, spectres, or devourers.

Cure Critical Wounds, Mass: Cures 4d8 damage + 1/level for many creatures.

Dimensional Lock: Teleportation and interplanar travel blocked for 1 day/level.

Discern Location: Reveals exact location of creature or object.

Earthquake: Intense tremor shakes 80-ft. radius.

Fire Storm: Deals 1d6/level fire damage.

Holy Aura[F]: +4 to AC, +4 resistance, and SR 25 against evil spells.

Inflict Critical Wounds, Mass: Deals 4d8 damage + 1/level, affects 1 subject/level.

Planar Ally, Greater[M]: As *lesser planar ally,* but up to 18 HD.

Shield of Law[F]: +4 to AC, +4 resistance, and SR 25 against chaotic spells.

Spell Immunity, Greater: As *spell immunity,* but up to 8th-level spells.

Summon Monster VIII: Summons extraplanar creature to fight for you.

Symbol of Death[M]: Triggered rune kills nearby creatures.

Symbol of Insanity[M]: Triggered rune renders nearby creatures insane.

Unholy Aura[F]: +4 to AC, +4 resistance, and SR 25 against good spells.

9th-Level Cleric Spells

Astral Projection[M]: Projects you and others onto Astral Plane.

Energy Drain: Subject gains 2d4 negative levels.

Etherealness: Travel to Ethereal Plane with companions.

Gate[M]: Connects two planes for travel or summoning.

Heal, Mass: As *heal,* but affects 1 subject/level.

Implosion: Inflict 10 damage/level to one creature/round.

Miracle[M]: Requests a deity's intercession.

Soul Bind[F]: Traps newly dead soul to prevent *resurrection.*

Storm of Vengeance: Storm rains acid, lightning, and hail.

Summon Monster IX: Summons extraplanar creature to fight for you.

True Resurrection[M]: As *resurrection,* plus remains aren't needed.

DRUID SPELLS

0-Level Druid Spells (Orisons)

Create Water: Creates 2 gallons/level of pure water.

Detect Magic: Detects spells and magic items within 60 ft.

Detect Poison: Detects poison in one creature or object.

Flare: Dazzles one creature (–1 penalty on attack rolls).

Guidance: +1 on one attack roll, saving throw, or skill check.

Know Direction: You discern north.

Light: Object shines like a torch.

Mending: Makes minor repairs on an object.

Purify Food and Drink: Purifies 1 cu. ft./level of food or water.

Read Magic: Read scrolls and spellbooks.

Resistance: Subject gains +1 bonus on saving throws.

Stabilize: Cause a dying creature to stabilize.

Virtue: Subject gains 1 temporary hp.

1st-Level Druid Spells

Calm Animals: Calms 2d4 + level HD of animals.

Charm Animal: Makes one animal your friend.

Cure Light Wounds: Cures 1d8 damage + 1/level (max +5).

Detect Animals or Plants: Detects kinds of animals or plants.

Detect Snares and Pits: Reveals natural or primitive traps.

Endure Elements: Exist comfortably in hot or cold regions.

Entangle: Plants entangle everyone in 40-ft. radius.

Faerie Fire: Outlines subjects with light, canceling *blur,* concealment, and the like.

Goodberry: 2d4 berries each cure 1 hp (max 8 hp/24 hours).

Hide from Animals: Animals can't perceive one subject/level.

Jump: Subject gets bonus on Acrobatics checks.

Longstrider: Your speed increases by 10 ft.

Magic Fang: One natural weapon of subject creature gets +1 on attack and damage rolls.

Magic Stone: Three stones gain +1 on attack rolls, deal 1d6+1 damage.

Obscuring Mist: Fog surrounds you.

Pass without Trace: One subject/level leaves no tracks.

Produce Flame: 1d6 damage + 1/level, touch or thrown.

Shillelagh: Cudgel or quarterstaff becomes +1 weapon (2d6 damage) for 1 min./level.

Speak with Animals: You can communicate with animals.

Summon Nature's Ally I: Summons creature to fight.

2nd-Level Druid Spells

Animal Messenger: Sends a Tiny animal to a specific place.

Animal Trance: Fascinates 2d6 HD of animals.

Barkskin: Grants +2 (or higher) enhancement to natural armor.

Bear's Endurance: Subject gains +4 to Con for 1 min./level.

Bull's Strength: Subject gains +4 to Str for 1 min./level.

Cat's Grace: Subject gains +4 to Dex for 1 min./level.

Chill Metal: Cold metal damages those who touch it.

Delay Poison: Stops poison from harming subject for 1 hour/level.

Fire Trap[M]: Opened object deals 1d4 + 1/level damage.

Flame Blade: Touch attack deals 1d8 + 1/two levels damage.

Flaming Sphere: Rolling ball of fire deals 3d6 fire damage.

Fog Cloud: Fog obscures vision.

Gust of Wind: Blows away or knocks down smaller creatures.

Heat Metal: Makes metal so hot it damages those who touch it.

Hold Animal: Paralyzes one animal for 1 round/level.

Owl's Wisdom: Subject gains +4 to Wis for 1 min./level.

Reduce Animal: Shrinks one willing animal.

Resist Energy: Ignores 10 or more points of damage per attack from specified energy type.

Restoration, Lesser: Dispels magical ability penalty or repairs 1d4 ability damage.

Soften Earth and Stone: Turns stone to clay, or dirt to sand or mud.

Spider Climb: Grants ability to walk on walls and ceilings.

Summon Nature's Ally II: Summons creature to fight.

Summon Swarm: Summons swarm of bats, rats, or spiders.

Tree Shape: You look exactly like a tree for 1 hour/level.

Warp Wood: Bends wood.

Wood Shape: Reshapes wooden objects to suit you.

3rd-Level Druid Spells

Call Lightning: Calls down lightning bolts (3d6 per bolt) from sky.

Contagion: Infects subject with chosen disease.

Cure Moderate Wounds: Cures 2d8 damage + 1/level (max +10).

Daylight: 60-ft. radius of bright light.

Diminish Plants: Reduces size or blights the growth of normal plants.

Dominate Animal: One animal obeys your silent mental commands and orders.

Magic Fang, Greater: One natural weapon gets + 1/four levels (max +5).

Meld into Stone: You and your gear merge with stone.

Neutralize Poison: Immunizes subject against poison, detoxifies venom in or on subject.

Plant Growth: Grows vegetation, improves crops.

Poison: Touch deals 1d3 Con damage 1/round for 6 rounds.

Protection from Energy: Absorbs 12 points/level of damage from one kind of energy.

Quench: Extinguishes fires.

Remove Disease: Cures all diseases affecting subject.

Sleet Storm: Hampers vision and movement.

Snare: Creates a magic booby trap.

Speak with Plants: You can talk to plants and plant creatures.

Spike Growth: Creatures in area take 1d4 damage, may be slowed.

Stone Shape: Sculpts stone into any shape.

Summon Nature's Ally III: Summons creature to fight.

Water Breathing: Subjects can breathe underwater.

Wind Wall: Deflects arrows, smaller creatures, and gases.

4th-Level Druid Spells

Air Walk: Subject treads on air as if solid (climb or descend at 45-degree angle).

Antiplant Shell: Keeps animated plants at bay.

Blight: Withers one plant or deals 1d6/level damage to plant creature.

Command Plants: Sways the actions of plant creatures.

Control Water: Raises or lowers bodies of water.

Cure Serious Wounds: Cures 3d8 damage + 1/level (max +15).

Dispel Magic: Cancels one magical spell or effect.

Flame Strike: Smites foes with divine fire (1d6/level damage).

Freedom of Movement: Subject moves normally despite impediments to movement.

Giant Vermin: Turns centipedes, scorpions, or spiders into giant vermin.

Ice Storm: Hail deals 5d6 damage in cylinder 40 ft. across.

Reincarnate: Brings dead subject back in a random body.

Repel Vermin: Insects, spiders, and other vermin stay 10 ft. away.

Rusting Grasp: Your touch corrodes iron and alloys.

Scrying^F: Spies on subject from a distance.

Spike Stones: Creatures in area take 1d8 damage, may also be slowed.

Summon Nature's Ally IV: Summons creature to fight.

5th-Level Druid Spells

Animal Growth: One animal doubles in size.

Atonement^FM: Removes burden of misdeeds from subject.

Awaken^M: Animal or tree gains human intellect.

Baleful Polymorph: Transforms subject into harmless animal.

Call Lightning Storm: As *call lightning*, but 5d6 damage per bolt.

Commune with Nature: Learn about terrain for 1 mile/level.

Control Winds: Changes wind direction and speed.

Cure Critical Wounds: Cures 4d8 damage + 1/level (max +20).

Death Ward: Grants bonuses against death spells and negative energy.

Hallow^M: Designates location as holy.

Insect Plague: Wasp swarms attack creatures.

Stoneskin^M: Grants DR 10/adamantine.

Summon Nature's Ally V: Summons creature to fight.

Transmute Mud to Rock: Transforms two 10-ft. cubes per level.

Transmute Rock to Mud: Transforms two 10-ft. cubes per level.

Tree Stride: Step from one tree to another far away.

Unhallow^M: Designates location as unholy.

Wall of Fire: Deals 2d4 fire damage out to 10 ft. and 1d4 out to 20 ft. Passing through wall deals 2d6 damage +1/level.

Wall of Thorns: Thorns damage anyone who tries to pass.

6th-Level Druid Spells

Antilife Shell: 10-ft.-radius field hedges out living creatures.

Bear's Endurance, Mass: As *bear's endurance*, affects 1 subject/level.

Bull's Strength, Mass: As *bull's strength*, affects 1 subject/level.

Cat's Grace, Mass: As *cat's grace*, affects one subject/level.

Cure Light Wounds, Mass: Cures 1d8 damage + 1/level, affects 1 subject/level.

Dispel Magic, Greater: As *dispel magic*, but with multiple targets.

Find the Path: Shows most direct way to a location.

Fire Seeds: Acorns and berries become grenades and bombs.

Ironwood: Magic wood is as strong as steel.

Liveoak: Oak becomes treant guardian.

Move Earth: Digs trenches and builds hills.

Owl's Wisdom, Mass: As *owl's wisdom*, affects 1 subject/level.

Repel Wood: Pushes away wooden objects.

Spellstaff: Stores one spell in wooden quarterstaff.

Stone Tell: Talk to natural or worked stone.

Summon Nature's Ally VI: Summons creature to fight.

Transport via Plants: Move instantly from one plant to another of the same kind.

Wall of Stone: Creates a stone wall that can be shaped.

7th-Level Druid Spells

Animate Plants: One or more plants animate and fight for you.

Changestaff: Your staff becomes a treant on command.

Control Weather: Changes weather in local area.

Creeping Doom: Swarms of centipedes attack at your command.

Cure Moderate Wounds, Mass: Cures 2d8 damage + 1/level, affects 1 subject/level.

Fire Storm: Deals 1d6/level fire damage.

Heal: Cures 10 points/level damage, all diseases and mental conditions.

Scrying, Greater: As *scrying*, but faster and longer.

Summon Nature's Ally VII: Summons creature to fight.

Sunbeam: Beam blinds and deals 4d6 damage.

Transmute Metal to Wood: Metal within 40 ft. becomes wood.

True Seeing[M]**:** Lets you see all things as they really are.

Wind Walk: You and your allies turn vaporous and travel fast.

8th-Level Druid Spells

Animal Shapes: One ally/level polymorphs into chosen animal.

Control Plants: Controls actions of one or more plant creatures.

Cure Serious Wounds, Mass: Cures 3d8 damage + 1/level, affects 1 subject/level.

Earthquake: Intense tremor shakes 80-ft.-radius.

Finger of Death: Deals 10 damage/level to one subject.

Repel Metal or Stone: Pushes away metal and stone.

Reverse Gravity: Objects and creatures fall upward.

Summon Nature's Ally VIII: Summons creature to fight.

Sunburst: Blinds all within 10 ft., deals 6d6 damage.

Whirlwind: Cyclone deals damage and can pick up creatures.

Word of Recall: Teleports you back to designated place.

9th-Level Druid Spells

Antipathy: Object or location affected by spell repels certain creatures.

Cure Critical Wounds, Mass: Cures 4d8 damage + 1/level for many creatures.

Elemental Swarm: Summons multiple elementals.

Foresight: "Sixth sense" warns of impending danger.

Regenerate: Subject's severed limbs grow back, cures 4d8 damage +1/level (max +35).

Shambler: Creates 1d4+2 shambling mounds to fight for you.

Shapechange[F]**:** Transforms you into certain creatures, and you can change forms once per round.

Storm of Vengeance: Storm rains acid, lightning, and hail.

Summon Nature's Ally IX: Summons creature to fight.

Sympathy[M]**:** Object or location attracts certain creatures.

PALADIN SPELLS

1st-Level Paladin Spells

Bless: Allies gain +1 on attack rolls and saves against fear.

Bless Water[M]**:** Makes holy water.

Bless Weapon: Weapon strikes true against evil foes.

Create Water: Creates 2 gallons/level of pure water.

Cure Light Wounds: Cures 1d8 damage + 1/level (max +5).

Detect Poison: Detects poison in one creature or small object.

Detect Undead: Reveals undead within 60 ft.

Divine Favor: You gain +1 per three levels on attack and damage rolls.

Endure Elements: Exist comfortably in hot or cold regions.

Magic Weapon: Weapon gains +1 bonus.

Protection from Chaos/Evil: +2 to AC and saves, plus additional protection against selected alignment.

Read Magic: Read scrolls and spellbooks.

Resistance: Subject gains +1 on saving throws.

Restoration, Lesser: Dispels magical ability penalty or repairs 1d4 ability damage.

Virtue: Subject gains 1 temporary hp.

2nd-Level Paladin Spells

Bull's Strength: Subject gains +4 to Str for 1 min./level.

Delay Poison: Stops poison from harming subject for 1 hour/level.

Eagle's Splendor: Subject gains +4 to Cha for 1 min./level.

Owl's Wisdom: Subject gains +4 to Wis for 1 min./level.

Remove Paralysis: Frees one or more creatures from paralysis or slow effect.

Resist Energy: Ignores 10 or more points of damage per attack from specified energy type.

Shield Other[F]**:** You take half of subject's damage.

Undetectable Alignment: Conceals alignment from magical detection for 24 hours.

Zone of Truth: Subjects within range cannot lie.

3rd-Level Paladin Spells

Cure Moderate Wounds: Cures 2d8 damage +1/level (max. +10).

Daylight: 60-ft. radius of bright light.

Discern Lies: Reveals deliberate falsehoods.

Dispel Magic: Cancels one magical spell or effect.

Heal Mount: As *heal* on horse or other special mount.

Magic Circle against Chaos/Evil: As *protection from chaos*, but 10-ft. radius and 10 min./level.

Magic Weapon, Greater: Weapon gains +1 bonus/four levels (max +5).

Prayer: Allies get +1 bonus on most rolls, enemies –1 penalty.

Remove Blindness/Deafness: Cures normal or magical blindness or deafness.

Remove Curse: Frees object or person from curse.

4th-Level Paladin Spells

Break Enchantment: Frees subjects from enchantments, transmutations, and curses.

Cure Serious Wounds: Cures 3d8 damage + 1/level (max +15).

Death Ward: Grants bonuses against death spells and negative energy.

Dispel Chaos: +4 bonus against attacks by chaotic creatures.

Dispel Evil: +4 bonus against attacks by evil creatures.

Holy Sword: Weapon becomes +5, deals +2d6 damage against evil.

Mark of Justice: Designates action that triggers *curse* on subject.

Neutralize Poison: Immunizes subject against poison, detoxifies venom in or on subject.

Restoration[M]**:** Restores level and ability score drains.

RANGER SPELLS

1st-Level Ranger Spells

Alarm: Wards an area for 2 hours/level.

Animal Messenger: Sends a Tiny animal to a specific place.

Calm Animals: Calms 2d4 + level HD of animals.

Charm Animal: Makes one animal your friend.

Delay Poison: Stops poison from harming subject for 1 hour/level.

Detect Animals or Plants: Detects kinds of animals or plants.

Detect Poison: Detects poison in one creature or object.

Detect Snares and Pits: Reveals natural or primitive traps.

Endure Elements: Exist comfortably in hot or cold regions.

Entangle: Plants entangle everyone in 40-ft. radius.

Hide from Animals: Animals can't perceive one subject/level.

Jump: Subject gets bonus on Acrobatics checks.

Longstrider: Your base speed increases by 10 ft.

Magic Fang: One natural weapon of subject creature gets +1 on attack and damage rolls.

Pass without Trace: One subject/level leaves no tracks.

Read Magic: Read scrolls and spellbooks.

Resist Energy: Ignores 10 (or more) points of damage/attack from specified energy type.

Speak with Animals: You can communicate with animals.

Summon Nature's Ally I: Summons creature to fight for you.

2nd-Level Ranger Spells

Barkskin: Grants +2 (or higher) enhancement to natural armor.

Bear's Endurance: Subject gains +4 to Con for 1 min./level.

Cat's Grace: Subject gains +4 to Dex for 1 min./level.

Cure Light Wounds: Cures 1d8 damage + 1/level (max +5).

Hold Animal: Paralyzes one animal for 1 round/level.

Owl's Wisdom: Subject gains +4 to Wis for 1 min./level.

Protection from Energy: Absorbs 12 points/level of damage from one kind of energy.

Snare: Creates a magic booby trap.

Speak with Plants: You can talk to plants and plant creatures.

Spike Growth: Creatures in area take 1d4 damage, may be slowed.

Summon Nature's Ally II: Summons creature to fight for you.

Wind Wall: Deflects arrows, smaller creatures, and gases.

3rd-Level Ranger Spells

Command Plants: Sway the actions of plant creatures.

Cure Moderate Wounds: Cures 2d8 damage +1/level (max. +10).

Darkvision: See 60 ft. in total darkness.

Diminish Plants: Reduces size or blights growth of normal plants.

Magic Fang, Greater: One natural weapon gets + 1/four levels (max. +5).

Neutralize Poison: Immunizes subject against poison, detoxifies venom in or on subject.

Plant Growth: Grows vegetation, improves crops.

Reduce Animal: Shrinks one willing animal.

Remove Disease: Cures all diseases affecting subject.

Repel Vermin: Insects, spiders, and other vermin stay 10 ft. away.

Summon Nature's Ally III: Summons creature to fight for you.

Tree Shape: You look exactly like a tree for 1 hour/level.

Water Walk: Subject treads on water as if solid.

4th-Level Ranger Spells

Animal Growth: One animal doubles in size.

Commune with Nature: Learn about terrain for 1 mile/level.

Cure Serious Wounds: Cures 3d8 damage + 1/level (max +15).

Freedom of Movement: Subject moves normally despite impediments to movement.

Nondetection^M: Hides subject from divination, scrying.

Summon Nature's Ally IV: Summons creature to fight for you.

Tree Stride: Step from one tree to another far away.

SORCERER/WIZARD SPELLS

0-Level Sorcerer/Wizard Spells (Cantrips)

Abjuration

Resistance: Subject gains +1 on saving throws.

Conjuration

Acid Splash: Orb deals 1d3 acid damage.

Divination

Detect Magic: Detects all spells and magic items within 60 ft.

Detect Poison: Detects poison in one creature or small object.

Read Magic: Read scrolls and spellbooks.

Enchantment

Daze: A single humanoid creature with 4 HD or less loses its next action.

Evocation

Dancing Lights: Creates torches or other lights.

Flare: Dazzles one creature (–1 on attack rolls).

Light: Object shines like a torch.

Ray of Frost: Ray deals 1d3 cold damage.

Illusion

Ghost Sound: Figment sounds.

Necromancy

Bleed: Cause a stabilized creature to resume dying.

Disrupt Undead: Deals 1d6 damage to one undead.

Touch of Fatigue: Touch attack fatigues target.

Transmutation

Mage Hand: 5-pound telekinesis.

Mending: Makes minor repairs on an object.

Message: Whisper conversation at distance.

Open/Close: Opens or closes small or light things.

Universal

Arcane Mark: Inscribes a personal rune on an object or creature (visible or invisible).

Prestidigitation: Performs minor tricks.

1st-Level Sorcerer/Wizard Spells

Abjuration

Alarm: Wards an area for 2 hours/level.

Endure Elements: Exist comfortably in hot or cold regions.

Hold Portal: Holds door shut.

Protection from Chaos/Evil/Good/Law: +2 to AC and saves, plus additional protection against selected alignment.

Shield: Invisible disc gives +4 to AC, blocks *magic missiles*.

Conjuration

Grease: Makes 10-ft. square or one object slippery.

Mage Armor: Gives subject +4 armor bonus.

Mount: Summons riding horse for 2 hours/level.

Obscuring Mist: Fog surrounds you.

Summon Monster I: Summons extraplanar creature to fight for you.

Unseen Servant: Invisible force obeys your commands.

Divination

Comprehend Languages: You understand all spoken and written languages.

Detect Secret Doors: Reveals hidden doors within 60 ft.

Detect Undead: Reveals undead within 60 ft.

Identify: Gives +10 bonus to identify magic items.

True Strike: +20 on your next attack roll.

Enchantment

Charm Person: Makes one person your friend.

Hypnotism: Fascinates 2d4 HD of creatures.

Sleep: Puts 4 HD of creatures into magical slumber.

Evocation

Burning Hands: 1d4/level fire damage (max 5d4).

Floating Disk: Creates 3-ft.-diameter horizontal disk that holds 100 lbs./level.

Magic Missile: 1d4+1 damage; +1 missile per two levels above 1st (max 5).

Shocking Grasp: Touch delivers 1d6/level electricity damage (max 5d6).

Illusion

Color Spray: Knocks unconscious, blinds, and/or stuns weak creatures.

Disguise Self: Changes your appearance.

Magic Aura: Alters object's magic aura.

Silent Image: Creates minor illusion of your design.

Ventriloquism: Throws voice for 1 min./level.

Necromancy

Cause Fear: One creature of 5 HD or less flees for 1d4 rounds.

Chill Touch: One touch/level deals 1d6 damage and possibly 1 Str damage.

Ray of Enfeeblement: Ray causes 1d6 Str penalty + 1 per 2 levels.

Transmutation

Animate Rope: Makes a rope move at your command.

Enlarge Person: Humanoid creature doubles in size.

Erase: Mundane or magical writing vanishes.

Expeditious Retreat: Your base speed increases by 30 ft.

Feather Fall: Objects or creatures fall slowly.

Jump: Subject gets bonus on Acrobatics checks.

Magic Weapon: Weapon gains +1 bonus.

Reduce Person: Humanoid creature halves in size.

2nd-Level Sorcerer/Wizard Spells

Abjuration

Arcane Lock^M: Magically locks a portal or chest.

Obscure Object: Masks object against scrying.

Protection from Arrows: Subject gains DR 10/magic against ranged attacks.

Resist Energy: Ignores first 10 (or more) points of damage per attack from specified energy type.

Conjuration

Acid Arrow: Ranged touch attack; 2d4 damage for 1 round + 1 round/three levels.

Fog Cloud: Fog obscures vision.

Glitterdust: Blinds creatures, outlines invisible creatures.

Summon Monster II: Summons extraplanar creature to fight for you.

Summon Swarm: Summons swarm of bats, rats, or spiders.

Web: Fills 20-ft.-radius spread with sticky spiderwebs that can grapple foes and impair movement.

Divination

Detect Thoughts: Allows "listening" to surface thoughts.

Locate Object: Senses direction toward object (specific or type).

See Invisibility: Reveals invisible creatures or objects.

Enchantment

Daze Monster: Living creature of 6 HD or less loses its next action.

Hideous Laughter: Subject loses actions for 1 round/level.

Touch of Idiocy: Subject takes 1d6 penalty to Int, Wis, and Cha.

Evocation

Continual Flame[M]: Makes a permanent, heatless light.

Darkness: 20-ft. radius of supernatural shadow.

Flaming Sphere: Rolling ball of fire deals 3d6 fire damage.

Gust of Wind: Blows away or knocks down smaller creatures.

Scorching Ray: Ranged touch attack deals 4d6 fire damage, +1 ray/four levels (max 3).

Shatter: Sonic energy damages objects or crystalline creatures.

Illusion

Blur: Attacks miss subject 20% of the time.

Hypnotic Pattern: Fascinates 2d4 + level HD of creatures.

Invisibility: Subject is invisible for 1 min./level or until it attacks.

Magic Mouth[M]: Object speaks once when triggered.

Minor Image: As *silent image*, plus some sound.

Mirror Image: Creates decoy duplicates of you.

Misdirection: Misleads divinations for 1 creature or object.

Phantom Trap[M]: Makes item seem trapped.

Necromancy

Blindness/Deafness: Makes subject blinded or deafened.

Command Undead: Undead creature obeys your commands.

False Life: Gain 1d10 temporary hp + 1/level (max +10).

Ghoul Touch: Paralyzes one subject, which exudes stench that makes those nearby sickened.

Scare: Frightens creatures of less than 6 HD.

Spectral Hand: Creates disembodied glowing hand to deliver touch attacks.

Transmutation

Alter Self: Assume form of a Small or Medium humanoid.

Bear's Endurance: Subject gains +4 to Con for 1 min./level.

Bull's Strength: Subject gains +4 to Str for 1 min./level.

Cat's Grace: Subject gains +4 to Dex for 1 min./level.

Darkvision: See 60 ft. in total darkness.

Eagle's Splendor: Subject gains +4 to Cha for 1 min./level.

Fox's Cunning: Subject gains +4 to Int for 1 min./level.

Knock: Opens locked or magically sealed door.

Levitate: Subject moves up and down at your direction.

Make Whole: Repairs an object.

Owl's Wisdom: Subject gains +4 to Wis for 1 min./level.

Pyrotechnics: Turns fire into blinding light or thick smoke.

Rope Trick: As many as eight creatures hide in extradimensional space.

Spider Climb: Grants ability to walk on walls and ceilings.

Whispering Wind: Sends a short message 1 mile/level.

3rd-Level Sorcerer/Wizard Spells

Abjuration

Dispel Magic: Cancels one magical spell or effect.

Explosive Runes: Deals 6d6 damage when read.

Magic Circle against Chaos/Evil/Good/Law: As *protection* spells, but 10-ft. radius and 10 min./level.

Nondetection[M]: Hides subject from divination, scrying.

Protection from Energy: Absorbs 12 points/level of damage from one kind of energy.

Conjuration

Phantom Steed: Magic horse appears for 1 hour/level.

Sepia Snake Sigil[M]: Creates text symbol that immobilizes reader.

Sleet Storm: Hampers vision and movement.

Stinking Cloud: Nauseating vapors, 1 round/level.

Summon Monster III: Summons extraplanar creature to fight for you.

Divination

Arcane Sight: Magical auras become visible to you.

Clairaudience/Clairvoyance: Hear or see at a distance for 1 min./level.

Tongues: Speak and understand any language.

Enchantment

Deep Slumber: Puts 10 HD of creatures to sleep.

Heroism: Gives +2 bonus on attack rolls, saves, skill checks.

Hold Person: Paralyzes one humanoid for 1 round/level.

Rage: Gives +2 to Str and Con, +1 on Will saves, −2 to AC.

Suggestion: Compels a subject to follow stated course of action.

Evocation

Daylight: 60-ft. radius of bright light.

Fireball: 1d6 damage per level, 20-ft. radius.

Lightning Bolt: Electricity deals 1d6/level damage.

Tiny Hut: Creates shelter for 10 creatures.

Wind Wall: Deflects arrows, smaller creatures, and gases.

Illusion

Displacement: Attacks miss subject 50% of the time.

Illusory Script[M]: Only select creatures can read text.

Invisibility Sphere: Makes everyone within 10 ft. invisible.

Major Image: As *silent image*, plus sound, smell and thermal effects.

Necromancy

Gentle Repose: Preserves one corpse.

Halt Undead: Immobilizes undead for 1 round/level.

Ray of Exhaustion: Ray makes subject exhausted.

Vampiric Touch: Touch deals 1d6 damage per two levels; caster gains damage as temporary hp.

Transmutation

Beast Shape I: You take the form and some of the powers of a Small or Medium animal.

Blink: You randomly vanish and reappear for 1 round per level.

Flame Arrow: Arrows deal +1d6 fire damage.

Fly: Subject flies at speed of 60 ft.

Gaseous Form: Subject becomes insubstantial and can fly slowly.

Haste: One creature/level moves faster, +1 on attack rolls, AC, and Reflex saves.

Keen Edge: Doubles normal weapon's threat range.

Magic Weapon, Greater: Weapon gains +1 bonus/four levels (max +5).

Secret Page: Changes one page to hide its real content.

Shrink Item: Object shrinks to one-sixteenth size.

Slow: One subject/level takes only one action/round, –1 to AC, Reflex saves, and attack rolls.

Water Breathing: Subjects can breathe underwater.

4th-Level Sorcerer/Wizard Spells

Abjuration

Dimensional Anchor: Bars extradimensional movement.

Fire Trap^M**:** Opened object deals 1d4 damage + 1/level.

Globe of Invulnerability, Lesser: Stops 1st- through 3rd-level spell effects.

Remove Curse: Frees object or person from curse.

Stoneskin^M**:** Grants DR 10/adamantine.

Conjuration

Black Tentacles: Tentacles grapple all creatures within a 20-ft. spread.

Dimension Door: Teleports you a short distance.

Minor Creation: Creates one cloth or wood object.

Secure Shelter: Creates sturdy cottage.

Solid Fog: Blocks vision and slows movement.

Summon Monster IV: Summons extraplanar creature to fight for you.

Divination

Arcane Eye: Invisible floating eye moves 30 ft./round.

Detect Scrying: Alerts you to magical eavesdropping

Locate Creature: Indicates direction to familiar creature.

Scrying^F**:** Spies on subject from a distance.

Enchantment

Charm Monster: Makes monster believe it is your ally.

Confusion: Subjects behave oddly for 1 round/level.

Crushing Despair: Subjects take –2 on attack rolls, damage rolls, saves, and checks.

Geas, Lesser: Commands subject of 7 HD or less.

Evocation

Fire Shield: Creatures attacking you take fire damage; you're protected from heat or cold.

Ice Storm: Hail deals 5d6 damage in cylinder 40 ft. across.

Resilient Sphere: Force globe protects but traps one subject.

Shout: Deafens all within cone and deals 5d6 sonic damage.

Wall of Fire: Deals 2d4 fire damage out to 10 ft. and 1d4 out to 20 ft. Passing through wall deals 2d6 damage + 1/level.

Wall of Ice: *Ice plane* creates wall or *hemisphere* creates dome.

Illusion

Hallucinatory Terrain: Makes one type of terrain appear like another (field as forest, or the like).

Illusory Wall: Wall, floor, or ceiling looks real, but anything can pass through.

Invisibility, Greater: As *invisibility,* but subject can attack and stay invisible.

Phantasmal Killer: Fearsome illusion kills subject or deals 3d6 damage.

Rainbow Pattern: Lights fascinate 24 HD of creatures.

Shadow Conjuration: Mimics conjuration below 4th level, but only 20% real.

Necromancy

Animate Dead^M**:** Creates undead skeletons and zombies out of corpses.

Bestow Curse: –6 to an ability score; –4 on attack rolls, saves, and checks; or 50% chance of losing each action.

Contagion: Infects subject with chosen disease.

Enervation: Subject gains 1d4 negative levels.

Fear: Subjects within cone flee for 1 round/level.

Transmutation

Beast Shape II: You take the form and some of the powers of a Tiny or Large animal.

Elemental Body I: Turns you into a Small elemental.

Enlarge Person, Mass: 1 humanoid creature/level doubles in size.

Mnemonic Enhancer^F**:** *Wizard only.* Prepare extra spells or retain one just cast.

Reduce Person, Mass: As *reduce person,* but affects 1 humanoid creature/level.

Stone Shape: Sculpts stone into any shape.

5th-Level Sorcerer/Wizard Spells

Abjuration

Break Enchantment: Frees subjects from enchantments, transmutations, and curses.

Dismissal: Forces a creature to return to its native plane.

Mage's Private Sanctum: Prevents anyone from viewing or scrying an area for 24 hours.

Conjuration

Cloudkill: Kills 3 HD or less; 4–6 HD save or die, 6+ HD take Con damage.

Mage's Faithful Hound: Phantom dog can guard a location and attack intruders.

Major Creation: As *minor creation,* plus stone and metal.

Planar Binding, Lesser: Traps extraplanar creature of 6 HD or less until it performs a task.

Secret Chest[F]**:** Hides expensive chest on Ethereal Plane; you retrieve it at will.

Summon Monster V: Summons extraplanar creature to fight for you.

Teleport: Instantly transports you as far as 100 miles per level.

Wall of Stone: Creates a stone wall that can be shaped.

Divination

Contact Other Plane: Lets you ask question of extraplanar entity.

Prying Eyes: 1d4 + 1/level floating eyes scout for you.

Telepathic Bond: Link lets allies communicate.

Enchantment

Dominate Person: Controls humanoid telepathically.

Feeblemind: Subject's Int and Cha drop to 1.

Hold Monster: As *hold person,* but any creature.

Mind Fog: Subjects in fog get –10 to Wis and Will checks.

Symbol of Sleep[M]**:** Triggered rune puts nearby creatures into catatonic slumber.

Evocation

Cone of Cold: 1d6/level cold damage.

Interposing Hand: Hand provides cover against 1 opponent.

Sending: Delivers short message anywhere, instantly.

Wall of Force: Wall is immune to damage.

Illusion

Dream: Sends message to anyone sleeping.

False Vision[M]**:** Fools scrying with an illusion.

Mirage Arcana: As *hallucinatory terrain,* plus structures.

Nightmare: Sends vision dealing 1d10 damage, fatigue.

Persistent Image: As *major image,* but with no concentration required.

Seeming: Changes appearance of 1 person per 2 levels.

Shadow Evocation: Mimics evocation below 5th level, but only 20% real.

Necromancy

Blight: Withers one plant or deals 1d6/level damage to plant creature.

Magic Jar[F]**:** Enables possession of another creature.

Symbol of Pain[M]**:** Triggered rune wracks creatures with pain.

Waves of Fatigue: Several targets become fatigued.

Transmutation

Animal Growth: One animal doubles in size.

Baleful Polymorph: Turns subject into harmless animal.

Beast Shape III: You take the form of a Diminutive or Huge animal, or Small or Medium magical beast.

Elemental Body II: Turns you into a Medium elemental.

Fabricate[M]**:** Transforms raw materials into finished items.

Overland Flight: You fly at a speed of 40 ft. and can hustle over long distances.

Passwall: Creates passage through wood or stone wall.

Plant Shape I: Turns you into a Small or Medium plant.

Polymorph: Gives one willing subject a new form.

Telekinesis: Moves object, attacks creature, or hurls object or creature.

Transmute Mud to Rock: Transforms two 10-ft. cubes per level.

Transmute Rock to Mud: Transforms two 10-ft. cubes per level.

Universal

Permanency[M]**:** Makes certain spells permanent.

6th-Level Sorcerer/Wizard Spells

Abjuration

Antimagic Field: Negates magic within 10 ft.

Dispel Magic, Greater: As *dispel magic,* but with multiple targets.

Globe of Invulnerability: As *lesser globe of invulnerability,* plus 4th-level spell effects.

Guards and Wards: Array of magic effects protect area.

Repulsion[F]**:** Creatures can't approach you.

Conjuration

Acid Fog: Fog deals acid damage.

Planar Binding: As *lesser planar binding,* but up to 12 HD.

Summon Monster VI: Summons extraplanar creature to fight for you.

Wall of Iron[M]**:** 30 hp/four levels; can topple onto foes.

Divination

Analyze Dweomer[F]**:** Reveals magical aspects of subject.

Legend Lore[MF]**:** Lets you learn tales about a person, place, or thing.

True Seeing[M]**:** Lets you see all things as they really are.

Enchantment

Geas/Quest: As *lesser geas,* but affects any creature.

Heroism, Greater: Gives +4 bonus on attack rolls, saves, skill checks; immunity to fear; temporary hp.

Suggestion, Mass: As *suggestion,* affects 1 subject/level.

Symbol of Persuasion[M]**:** Triggered rune charms creatures.

Evocation

Chain Lightning: 1d6/level damage and 1 secondary bolt/level.
ContingencyF: Sets trigger condition for another spell.
Forceful Hand: Hand pushes creatures away.
Freezing Sphere: Freezes water or deals cold damage.

Illusion

Mislead: Turns you invisible and creates illusory double.
Permanent Image: Permanent illusion, includes sight, sound, smell, and thermal effects.
Programmed ImageM: As *major image*, but triggered by event.
Shadow Walk: Step into shadow to travel rapidly.
Veil: Changes appearance of a group of creatures.

Necromancy

Circle of DeathM: Kills 1d4/level HD of creatures.
Create UndeadM: Raises ghouls, ghasts, mummies, or mohrgs from physical remains.
Eyebite: Target becomes panicked, sickened, and comatose.
Symbol of FearM: Triggered rune panics nearby creatures.
Undeath to DeathM: Destroys 1d4/level HD of undead (max. 20d4).

Transmutation

Bear's Endurance, Mass: As *bear's endurance*, affects one subject/level.
Beast Shape IV: You take the form of a Diminutive to Huge animal or a Tiny to Large magical beast.
Bull's Strength, Mass: As *bull's strength*, affects 1 subject per level.
Cat's Grace, Mass: As *cat's grace*, affects 1 subject/level.
Control Water: Raises or lowers bodies of water.
Disintegrate: Reduces one creature or object to dust.
Eagle's Splendor, Mass: As *eagle's splendor*, 1 subject/level.
Elemental Body III: Turns you into a Large elemental.
Flesh to Stone: Turns subject creature into statue.
Form of the Dragon I: Turns you into a Medium dragon.
Fox's Cunning, Mass: As *fox's cunning*, affects 1 subject/ level.
Mage's Lucubration: *Wizard only.* Recalls spell of 5th level or lower.
Move Earth: Digs trenches and builds hills.
Owl's Wisdom, Mass: As *owl's wisdom*, affects 1 subject/level.
Plant Shape II: Turns you into a Large plant creature.
Stone to Flesh: Restores petrified creature.
TransformationM: You gain combat bonuses.

7th-Level Sorcerer/Wizard Spells

Abjuration

Banishment: Banishes 2 HD/level of extraplanar creatures.
Sequester: Subject is invisible to sight and scrying; renders creature comatose.
Spell TurningM: Reflect 1d4+6 spell levels back at caster.

Conjuration

Instant SummonsM: Prepared object appears in your hand.
Mage's Magnificent MansionF: Door leads to extradimensional mansion.
Phase Door: Creates an invisible passage through a barrier.
Plane ShiftF: As many as eight subjects travel to another plane.
Summon Monster VII: Summons extraplanar creature to fight for you.
Teleport, Greater: As *teleport*, but no range limit and no off-target arrival.
Teleport Object: As *teleport*, but affects a touched object.

Divination

Arcane Sight, Greater: As *arcane sight*, but also reveals magic effects on creatures and objects.
Scrying, Greater: As *scrying*, but faster and longer.
VisionM: As *legend lore*, but quicker.

Enchantment

Hold Person, Mass: As *hold person*, but all within 30 ft.
Insanity: Subject suffers continuous *confusion*.
Power Word Blind: Blinds creature with 200 hp or less.
Symbol of StunningM: Triggered rune stuns creatures.

Evocation

Delayed Blast Fireball: 1d6/level fire damage; you can postpone blast for up to 5 rounds.
ForcecageM: Cube or cage of force imprisons all inside.
Grasping Hand: Hand provides cover, pushes, or grapples.
Mage's SwordF: Floating magic blade strikes opponents.
Prismatic Spray: Rays hit subjects with variety of effects.

Illusion

Invisibility, Mass: As *invisibility*, but affects all in range.
Project Image: Illusory double can talk and cast spells.
Shadow Conjuration, Greater: As *shadow conjuration*, but up to 6th level and 60% real.
SimulacrumM: Creates partially real double of a creature.

Necromancy

Control Undead: Undead don't attack you while under your command.
Finger of Death: Deals 10 damage/level to one subject.
Symbol of WeaknessM: Triggered rune weakens creatures.
Waves of Exhaustion: Several targets become exhausted.

Transmutation

Control Weather: Changes weather in local area.
Elemental Body IV: Turns you into a Huge elemental.
Ethereal Jaunt: You become ethereal for 1 round/level.
Form of the Dragon II: Turns you into a Large dragon.
Giant Form I: Turns you into a Large giant.

Plant Shape III: Turns you into a Huge plant.

Polymorph, Greater: Gives one willing subject a new, more powerful form.

Reverse Gravity: Objects and creatures fall upward.

Statue: Subject can become a statue at will.

Universal

Limited Wish^M: Alters reality (within limits).

8th-Level Sorcerer/Wizard Spells

Abjuration

Dimensional Lock: Teleportation and interplanar travel blocked for 1 day/level.

Mind Blank: Subject is protected from mental/emotional magic and scrying.

Prismatic Wall: Wall's colors have array of effects.

Protection from Spells^{MF}: Confers +8 resistance bonus.

Conjuration

Incendiary Cloud: Cloud deals 6d6 fire damage/round.

Maze: Traps subject in extradimensional maze.

Planar Binding, Greater: As *lesser planar binding,* but up to 18 HD.

Summon Monster VIII: Summons extraplanar creature to fight for you.

Trap the Soul^M: Imprisons subject within gem.

Divination

Discern Location: Reveals exact location of creature or object.

Moment of Prescience: You gain +1/level insight bonus on single attack roll, check, or save.

Prying Eyes, Greater: As *prying eyes,* but eyes have *true seeing.*

Enchantment

Antipathy: Object or location affected by spell repels certain creatures.

Binding^M: Utilizes an array of techniques to imprison a creature.

Charm Monster, Mass: As *charm monster,* but all within 30 ft.

Demand: As *sending,* plus you can send *suggestion.*

Irresistible Dance: Forces subject to dance.

Power Word Stun: Stuns creature with 150 hp or less.

Symbol of Insanity^M: Triggered rune renders nearby creatures insane.

Sympathy^M: Object or location attracts certain creatures.

Evocation

Clenched Fist: Large hand provides cover, pushes, or attacks your foes.

Polar Ray: Ranged touch attack deals 1d6/level cold damage and 1d4 points of Dexterity drain.

Shout, Greater: Devastating yell deals 10d6 sonic damage; stuns creatures.

Sunburst: Blinds all within 10 ft., deals 6d6 damage.

Telekinetic Sphere: As *resilient sphere,* but you move the sphere telekinetically.

Illusion

Scintillating Pattern: Twisting colors *confuse,* stun, or render unconscious.

Screen: Illusion hides area from vision and scrying.

Shadow Evocation, Greater: As *shadow evocation,* but up to 7th level and 60% real.

Necromancy

Clone^{MF}: Duplicate awakens when original dies.

Create Greater Undead^M: Creates shadows, wraiths, spectres, or devourers.

Horrid Wilting: Deals 1d6/level damage within 30 ft.

Symbol of Death^M: Triggered rune kills nearby creatures.

Transmutation

Form of the Dragon III: Turns you into a Huge dragon.

Giant Form II: Turns you into a Huge giant.

Iron Body: Your body becomes living iron.

Polymorph Any Object: Changes a subject into anything else.

Temporal Stasis^M: Puts subject into suspended animation.

9th-Level Sorcerer/Wizard Spells

Abjuration

Freedom: Releases creature from *imprisonment.*

Imprisonment: Entombs subject beneath the earth.

Mage's Disjunction: Dispels magic, disenchants magic items.

Prismatic Sphere: As *prismatic wall,* but surrounds on all sides.

Conjuration

Gate^M: Connects two planes for travel or summoning.

Refuge^M: Alters item to transport its possessor to your abode.

Summon Monster IX: Summons extraplanar creature to fight for you.

Teleportation Circle^M: Teleports creatures inside circle.

Divination

Foresight: "Sixth sense" warns of impending danger.

Enchantment

Dominate Monster: As *dominate person,* but any creature.

Hold Monster, Mass: As *hold monster,* but all within 30 ft.

Power Word Kill: Kills one creature with 100 hp or less.

Evocation

Crushing Hand: Large hand provides cover, pushes, or crushes your foes.

Meteor Swarm: Four exploding spheres each deal 6d6 fire damage.

Illusion

Shades: As *shadow conjuration*, but up to 8th level and 80% real.

Weird: As *phantasmal killer*, but affects all within 30 ft.

Necromancy

Astral ProjectionM: Projects you and companions onto Astral Plane.

Energy Drain: Subject gains 2d4 negative levels.

Soul BindF: Traps newly dead soul to prevent *resurrection*.

Wail of the Banshee: Deals 10 damage/level to 1 creature/level.

Transmutation

Etherealness: Travel to Ethereal Plane with companions.

ShapechangeF: Transforms you into certain creatures, and lets you change forms once per round.

Time Stop: You act freely for 1d4+1 rounds.

Universal

WishM: As *limited wish*, but with fewer limits.

SPELLS

The following spells are presented in alphabetical order, with the exception of those whose names begin with "greater," "lesser," or "mass" (see Order of Presentation on page 224).

ACID ARROW

School conjuration (creation) [acid]; **Level** sorcerer/wizard 2

Casting Time 1 standard action

Components V, S, M (rhubarb leaf and an adder's stomach), F (a dart)

Range long (400 ft. + 40 ft./level)

Effect one arrow of acid

Duration 1 round + 1 round per three levels

Saving Throw none; **Spell Resistance** no

An arrow of acid springs from your hand and speeds to its target. You must succeed on a ranged touch attack to hit your target. The arrow deals 2d4 points of acid damage with no splash damage. For every three caster levels you possess, the acid, unless neutralized, lasts another round (to a maximum of 6 additional rounds at 18th level), dealing another 2d4 points of damage in each round.

ACID FOG

School conjuration (creation) [acid]; **Level** sorcerer/wizard 6

Casting Time 1 standard action

Components V, S, M (powdered peas and an animal hoof)

Range medium (100 ft. + 10 ft./level)

Effect fog spreads in 20-ft. radius, 20 ft. high

Duration 1 round/level

Saving Throw none; **Spell Resistance** no

Acid fog creates a billowing mass of misty vapors like the *solid fog* spell. In addition to slowing down creatures and obscuring sight, this spell's vapors are highly acidic. Each round on your turn, starting when you cast the spell, the fog deals 2d6 points of acid damage to each creature and object within it.

ACID SPLASH

School conjuration (creation) [acid]; **Level** sorcerer/wizard 0

Casting Time 1 standard action

Components V, S

Range close (25 ft. + 5 ft./2 levels)

Effect one missile of acid

Duration instantaneous

Saving Throw none; **Spell Resistance** no

You fire a small orb of acid at the target. You must succeed on a ranged touch attack to hit your target. The orb deals 1d3 points of acid damage. This acid disappears after 1 round.

AID

School enchantment (compulsion) [mind-affecting]; **Level** cleric 2

Casting Time 1 standard action

Components V, S, DF

Range touch

Target living creature touched

Duration 1 min./level

Saving Throw none; **Spell Resistance** yes (harmless)

Aid grants the target a +1 morale bonus on attack rolls and saves against fear effects, plus temporary hit points equal to 1d8 + caster level (to a maximum of 1d8+10 temporary hit points at caster level 10th).

AIR WALK

School transmutation [air]; **Level** cleric 4, druid 4

Casting Time 1 standard action

Components V, S, DF

Range touch

Target creature (Gargantuan or smaller) touched

Duration 10 min./level

Saving Throw none; **Spell Resistance** yes (harmless)

The subject can tread on air as if walking on solid ground. Moving upward is similar to walking up a hill. The maximum upward or downward angle possible is 45 degrees, at a rate equal to half the air walker's normal speed.

A strong wind (21+ miles per hour) can push the subject along or hold it back. At the end of a creature's turn each round, the wind blows the air walker 5 feet for each 5 miles per hour of wind speed. The creature may be subject to additional penalties in exceptionally strong or turbulent winds, such as loss of control over movement or physical damage from being buffeted about.

Should the spell duration expire while the subject is still aloft, the magic fails slowly. The subject floats downward 60 feet per round for 1d6 rounds. If it reaches the ground in that amount of time, it lands safely. If not, it falls the rest of the distance, taking 1d6 points of damage per 10 feet of fall. Since dispelling a spell effectively ends it, the subject also descends in this way if the *air walk* spell is dispelled, but not if it is negated by an *antimagic field*.

You can cast *air walk* on a specially trained mount so it can be ridden through the air. You can train a mount to move with the aid of *air walk* (counts as a trick; see Handle Animal skill) with 1 week of work and a DC 25 Handle Animal check.

ALARM

School abjuration; **Level** bard 1, ranger 1, sorcerer/wizard 1
Casting Time 1 standard action
Components V, S, F/DF (a tiny bell and a piece of very fine silver wire)
Range close (25 ft. + 5 ft./2 levels)
Area 20-ft.-radius emanation centered on a point in space
Duration 2 hours/level (D)
Saving Throw none; **Spell Resistance** no

Alarm creates a subtle ward on an area you select. Once the spell effect is in place, it thereafter sounds a mental or audible alarm each time a creature of Tiny or larger size enters the warded area or touches it. A creature that speaks the password (determined by you at the time of casting) does not set off the *alarm*. You decide at the time of casting whether the *alarm* will be mental or audible in nature.

Mental Alarm: A mental *alarm* alerts you (and only you) so long as you remain within 1 mile of the warded area. You note a single mental "ping" that awakens you from normal sleep but does not otherwise disturb concentration. A *silence* spell has no effect on a mental *alarm*.

Audible Alarm: An audible *alarm* produces the sound of a hand bell, and anyone within 60 feet of the warded area can hear it clearly. Reduce the distance by 10 feet for each interposing closed door and by 20 feet for each substantial interposing wall.

In quiet conditions, the ringing can be heard faintly as far as 180 feet away. The sound lasts for 1 round. Creatures within a *silence* spell cannot hear the ringing.

Ethereal or astral creatures do not trigger the *alarm*.

Alarm can be made permanent with a *permanency* spell.

ALIGN WEAPON

School transmutation [see text]; **Level** cleric 2
Casting Time 1 standard action
Components V, S, DF
Range touch
Target weapon touched or 50 projectiles (all of which must be together at the time of casting)
Duration 1 min./level
Saving Throw Will negates (harmless, object); **Spell Resistance** yes (harmless, object)

Align weapon makes a weapon chaotic, evil, good, or lawful, as you choose. A weapon that is aligned can bypass the damage reduction of certain creatures. This spell has no effect on a weapon that already has an alignment.

You can't cast this spell on a natural weapon, such as an unarmed strike. When you make a weapon chaotic, evil, good, or lawful, *align weapon* is a chaotic, evil, good, or lawful spell, respectively.

ALTER SELF

School transmutation (polymorph); **Level** bard 2, sorcerer/wizard 2
Casting Time 1 standard action
Components V, S, M (a piece of the creature whose form you plan to assume)
Range personal
Target you
Duration 1 min./level (D)

When you cast this spell, you can assume the form of any Small or Medium creature of the humanoid type. If the form you assume has any of the following abilities, you gain the listed ability: darkvision 60 feet, low-light vision, scent, and swim 30 feet.

Small creature: If the form you take is that of a Small humanoid, you gain a +2 size bonus to your Dexterity.

Medium creature: If the form you take is that of a Medium humanoid, you gain a +2 size bonus to your Strength.

ANALYZE DWEOMER

School divination; **Level** bard 6, sorcerer/wizard 6
Casting Time 1 standard action
Components V, S, F (a ruby and gold lens worth 1,500 gp)
Range close (25 ft. + 5 ft./2 levels)
Targets one object or creature per caster level
Duration 1 round/level (D)
Saving Throw none or Will negates, see text; **Spell Resistance** no

You can observe magical auras. Each round, you may examine a single creature or object that you can see as a free action. In the case of a magic item, you learn its functions (including any curse effects), how to activate its functions (if appropriate), and how many charges are left (if it uses charges). In the case of an object or creature with active spells cast upon it, you learn each spell, its effect, and its caster level.

An attended object may attempt a Will save to resist this effect if its holder so desires. If the save succeeds, you learn nothing about the object except what you can discern by looking at it. An object that makes its save cannot be affected by any other *analyze dweomer* spells for 24 hours.

Analyze dweomer does not function when used on an artifact.

ANIMAL GROWTH

School transmutation; **Level** druid 5, ranger 4, sorcerer/wizard 5
Casting Time 1 standard action
Components V, S
Range medium (100 ft. + 10 ft./level)
Target one animal (Gargantuan or smaller)
Duration 1 min./level
Saving Throw Fortitude negates; **Spell Resistance** yes

The target animal grows to twice its normal size and eight times its normal weight. This alteration changes the animal's size category to the next largest, grants it a +8 size bonus to Strength and a +4 size bonus to Constitution (and thus an extra 2 hit points per HD), and imposes a −2 size penalty to Dexterity.

The creature's existing natural armor bonus increases by 2. The size change also affects the animal's modifier to AC, attack rolls, and its base damage. The animal's space and reach change as appropriate to the new size, but its speed does not change. If insufficient room is available for the desired growth, the creature attains the maximum possible size and may make a Strength check (using its increased Strength) to burst any enclosures in the process. If it fails, it is constrained without harm by the materials enclosing it—the spell cannot be used to crush a creature by increasing its size.

All equipment worn or carried by the animal is similarly enlarged by the spell, though this change has no effect on the magical properties of any such equipment.

Any enlarged item that leaves the enlarged creature's possession instantly returns to its normal size.

The spell gives no means of command over an enlarged animal.

Multiple magical effects that increase size do not stack.

ANIMAL MESSENGER

School enchantment (compulsion) [mind-affecting]; **Level** bard 2, druid 2, ranger 1

Casting Time 1 minute

Components V, S, M (a morsel of food the animal likes)

Range close (25 ft. + 5 ft./2 levels)

Target one Tiny animal

Duration 1 day/level

Saving Throw none; see text; **Spell Resistance** yes

You compel a Tiny animal to go to a spot you designate. The most common use for this spell is to get an animal to carry a message to your allies. The animal cannot be one tamed or trained by someone else, including such creatures as familiars and animal companions.

Using some type of food desirable to the animal as a lure, you call the animal to you. It advances and awaits your bidding. You can mentally impress on the animal a certain place well known to you or an obvious landmark. The directions must be simple, because the animal depends on your knowledge and can't find a destination on its own. You can attach a small item or note to the messenger. The animal then goes to the designated location and waits there until the duration of the spell expires, whereupon it resumes its normal activities.

During this period of waiting, the messenger allows others to approach it and remove any scroll or token it carries. The intended recipient gains no special ability to communicate with the animal or read any attached message (if it's written in a language he doesn't know, for example).

ANIMAL SHAPES

School transmutation (polymorph); **Level** druid 8

Casting Time 1 standard action

Components V, S, DF

Range close (25 ft. + 5 ft./2 levels)

Targets up to one willing creature per level, all within 30 ft. of each other.

Duration 1 hour/level (D)

Saving Throw none, see text; **Spell Resistance** yes (harmless)

As *beast shape III*, except you change the form of up to one willing creature per caster level into an animal of your choice; the spell has no effect on unwilling creatures. All creatures must take the same kind of animal form. Recipients remain in the animal form until the spell expires or until you dismiss it for all recipients. In addition, an individual subject may choose to resume its normal form as a full-round action; doing so ends the spell for that subject alone.

ANIMAL TRANCE

School enchantment (compulsion) [mind-affecting, sonic]; **Level** bard 2, druid 2

Casting Time 1 standard action

Components V, S

Range close (25 ft. + 5 ft./2 levels)

Targets animals or magical beasts with Intelligence 1 or 2

Duration concentration

Saving Throw Will negates; **Spell Resistance** yes

Your swaying motions and music (or singing, or chanting) compel animals and magical beasts to do nothing but watch you. Only a creature with an Intelligence score of 1 or 2 can be fascinated by this spell. Roll 2d6 to determine the total number of HD worth of creatures that you fascinate. The closest targets are selected first until no more targets within range can be affected.

ANIMATE DEAD

School necromancy [evil]; **Level** cleric 3, sorcerer/wizard 4

Casting Time 1 standard action

Components V, S, M (an onyx gem worth at least 25 gp per Hit Die of the undead)

Range touch

Targets one or more corpses touched

Duration instantaneous

Saving Throw none; **Spell Resistance** no

This spell turns corpses into undead skeletons or zombies (see the *Pathfinder RPG Bestiary*) that obey your spoken commands.

The undead can be made to follow you, or they can be made to remain in an area and attack any creature (or just a specific kind of creature) entering the place. They remain animated until they are destroyed. A destroyed skeleton or zombie can't be animated again.

Regardless of the type of undead you create with this spell, you can't create more HD of undead than twice your caster level with a single casting of *animate dead*. The *desecrate* spell doubles this limit.

The undead you create remain under your control indefinitely. No matter how many times you use this spell, however, you can control only 4 HD worth of undead creatures per caster level. If you exceed this number, all the newly created creatures fall under your control, and any excess undead from previous castings become uncontrolled. You choose which creatures are released. Undead you control through the Command Undead feat do not count toward this limit.

Skeletons: A skeleton can be created only from a mostly intact corpse or skeleton. The corpse must have bones. If a skeleton is made from a corpse, the flesh falls off the bones.

Zombies: A zombie can be created only from a mostly intact corpse. The corpse must be that of a creature with a physical anatomy.

ANIMATE OBJECTS

School transmutation; **Level** bard 6, cleric 6
Casting Time 1 standard action
Components V, S
Range medium (100 ft. + 10 ft./level)
Targets one Small object per caster level; see text
Duration 1 round/level
Saving Throw none; **Spell Resistance** no

You imbue inanimate objects with mobility and a semblance of life. Each such animated object then immediately attacks whomever or whatever you initially designate.

An animated object can be of any nonmagical material. You may animate one Small or smaller object or a corresponding number of larger objects as follows: A Medium object counts as two Small or smaller objects, a Large object as four, a Huge object as eight, a Gargantuan object as 16, and a Colossal object as 32. You can change the designated target or targets as a move action, as if directing an active spell. See the *Pathfinder RPG Bestiary* for the statistics of animated objects.

This spell cannot affect objects carried or worn by a creature.

Animate objects can be made permanent with a *permanency* spell.

ANIMATE PLANTS

School transmutation; **Level** druid 7
Casting Time 1 standard action
Components V
Range close (25 ft. + 5 ft./2 levels)
Targets one Large plant per three caster levels or all plants within range; see text
Duration 1 round/level or 1 hour/level; see text
Saving Throw none; **Spell Resistance** no

You imbue inanimate plants with mobility and a semblance of life. Each animated plant then immediately attacks whomever or whatever you initially designate as though it were an animated object of the appropriate size category. You may animate one Large or smaller plant, or a number of larger plants as follows: a Huge plant counts as two Large or smaller plants, a Gargantuan plant as four, and a Colossal plant as eight. You can change the designated target or targets as a move action, as if directing an active spell.

Use the statistics for animated objects (see *Pathfinder RPG Bestiary*), except that plants smaller than Large don't have hardness.

Animate plants cannot affect plant creatures, nor does it affect nonliving vegetable material.

Entangle: Alternatively, you may imbue all plants within range with a degree of mobility, which allows them to entwine around creatures in the area. This usage of the spell duplicates the effect of an *entangle* spell. Spell resistance does not keep creatures from being entangled. This effect lasts 1 hour per caster level.

ANIMATE ROPE

School transmutation; **Level** bard 1, sorcerer/wizard 1
Casting Time 1 standard action
Components V, S
Range medium (100 ft. + 10 ft./level)
Target one rope-like object, length up to 50 ft. + 5 ft./level; see text
Duration 1 round/level
Saving Throw none; **Spell Resistance** no

You can animate a nonliving rope-like object. The maximum length assumes a rope with a 1-inch diameter. Reduce the maximum length by 50% for every additional inch of thickness, and increase it by 50% for each reduction of the rope's diameter by half.

The possible commands are "coil" (form a neat, coiled stack), "coil and knot," "loop," "loop and knot," "tie and knot," and the opposites of all of the above ("uncoil," and so forth). You can give one command each round as a move action, as if directing an active spell.

The rope can enwrap only a creature or an object within 1 foot of it—it does not snake outward—so it must be thrown near the intended target. Doing so requires a successful ranged touch attack roll (range increment 10 feet). A typical 1-inch-diameter hemp rope has 2 hit points, AC 10, and requires a DC 23 Strength check to burst it. The rope does not deal damage, but it can be used as a trip line or to cause a single opponent that fails a Reflex saving throw to become entangled. A creature capable of spellcasting that is bound by this spell must make a concentration check with a DC of 15 + the spell's level to cast a spell. An entangled creature can slip free with a DC 20 Escape Artist check.

The rope itself and any knots tied in it are not magical.

The spell cannot affect objects carried or worn by a creature.

ANTILIFE SHELL

School abjuration; **Level** cleric 6, druid 6
Components V, S, DF
Casting Time 1 round
Range 10 ft.
Area 10-ft.-radius emanation, centered on you
Duration 1 min./level (D)
Saving Throw none; **Spell Resistance** yes

You bring into being a mobile, hemispherical energy field that prevents the entrance of most types of living creatures.

The effect hedges out animals, aberrations, dragons, fey, humanoids, magical beasts, monstrous humanoids, oozes, plants, and vermin, but not constructs, outsiders, or undead.

This spell may be used only defensively, not aggressively. Forcing an abjuration barrier against creatures that the spell keeps at bay collapses the barrier.

ANTIMAGIC FIELD

School abjuration; **Level** cleric 8, sorcerer/wizard 6
Casting Time 1 standard action

Components V, S, M/DF (pinch of powdered iron or iron filings)
Range 10 ft.
Area 10-ft.-radius emanation, centered on you
Duration 10 min./level (D)
Saving Throw none; **Spell Resistance** see text

An invisible barrier surrounds you and moves with you. The space within this barrier is impervious to most magical effects, including spells, spell-like abilities, and supernatural abilities. Likewise, it prevents the functioning of any magic items or spells within its confines.

An *antimagic field* suppresses any spell or magical effect used within, brought into, or cast into the area, but does not dispel it. Time spent within an *antimagic field* counts against the suppressed spell's duration.

Summoned creatures of any type wink out if they enter an *antimagic field*. They reappear in the same spot once the field goes away. Time spent winked out counts normally against the duration of the conjuration that is maintaining the creature. If you cast *antimagic field* in an area occupied by a summoned creature that has spell resistance, you must make a caster level check (1d20 + caster level) against the creature's spell resistance to make it wink out. (The effects of instantaneous conjurations are not affected by an *antimagic field* because the conjuration itself is no longer in effect, only its result.)

A normal creature can enter the area, as can normal missiles. Furthermore, while a magic sword does not function magically within the area, it is still a sword (and a masterwork sword at that). The spell has no effect on golems and other constructs that are imbued with magic during their creation process and are thereafter self-supporting (unless they have been summoned, in which case they are treated like any other summoned creatures). Elementals, undead, and outsiders are likewise unaffected unless summoned. These creatures' spell-like or supernatural abilities may be temporarily nullified by the field. *Dispel magic* does not remove the field.

Two or more *antimagic fields* sharing any of the same space have no effect on each other. Certain spells, such as *wall of force, prismatic sphere,* and *prismatic wall,* remain unaffected by *antimagic field.* Artifacts and deities are unaffected by mortal magic such as this.

Should a creature be larger than the area enclosed by the barrier, any part of it that lies outside the barrier is unaffected by the field.

ANTIPATHY

School enchantment (compulsion) [mind-affecting]; **Level** druid 9, sorcerer/wizard 8
Casting Time 1 hour
Components V, S, M/DF (a lump of alum soaked in vinegar)
Range close (25 ft. + 5 ft./2 levels)
Target one location (up to a 10-ft. cube/level) or one object
Duration 2 hours/level (D)
Saving Throw Will partial; **Spell Resistance** yes

You cause an object or location to emanate magical vibrations that repel either a specific kind of intelligent creature or creatures of a particular alignment, as defined by you. The kind of creature to be affected must be named specifically. A creature subtype is not specific enough. Likewise, the specific alignment to be repelled must be named.

Creatures of the designated kind or alignment feel an urge to leave the area or to avoid the affected item.

A compulsion forces them to abandon the area or item, shunning it and never willingly returning to it while the spell is in effect. A creature that makes a successful saving throw can stay in the area or touch the item but feels uncomfortable doing so. This distracting discomfort reduces the creature's Dexterity score by 4 points.

Antipathy counters and dispels *sympathy.*

ANTIPLANT SHELL

School abjuration; **Level** druid 4
Casting Time 1 standard action
Components V, S, DF
Range 10 ft.
Area 10-ft.-radius emanation, centered on you
Duration 1 min./level (D)
Saving Throw none; **Spell Resistance** yes

The *antiplant shell* spell creates an invisible, mobile barrier that keeps all creatures within the shell protected from attacks by plant creatures or animated plants. As with many abjuration spells, forcing the barrier against creatures that the spell keeps at bay strains and collapses the field.

ARCANE EYE

School divination (scrying); **Level** sorcerer/wizard 4
Casting Time 10 minutes
Components V, S, M (a bit of bat fur)
Range unlimited
Effect magical sensor
Duration 1 min./level (D)
Saving Throw none; **Spell Resistance** no

You create an invisible magical sensor that sends you visual information. You can create the *arcane eye* at any point you can see, but it can then travel outside your line of sight without hindrance. An *arcane eye* travels at 30 feet per round (300 feet per minute) if viewing an area ahead as a human would (primarily looking at the floor) or 10 feet per round (100 feet per minute) if examining the ceiling and walls as well as the floor ahead. It sees exactly as you would see if you were there.

The eye can travel in any direction as long as the spell lasts. Solid barriers block its passage, but it can pass through a hole or space as small as 1 inch in diameter. The eye can't enter another plane of existence, even through a *gate* or similar magical portal.

You must concentrate to use an *arcane eye.* If you do not concentrate, the eye is inert until you again concentrate.

ARCANE LOCK

School abjuration; **Level** sorcerer/wizard 2
Casting Time 1 standard action
Components V, S, M (gold dust worth 25 gp)

Range touch

Target door, chest, or portal touched, up to 30 sq. ft./level in size

Duration permanent

Saving Throw none; **Spell Resistance** no

An *arcane lock* spell cast upon a door, chest, or portal magically locks it. You can freely pass your own *arcane lock* without affecting it. If the locked object has a lock, the DC to open that lock increases by 10 while it remains attached to the object. If the object does not have a lock, this spell creates one that can only be opened with a DC 20 Disable Device skill check. A door or object secured with this spell can be opened only by breaking in or with a successful *dispel magic* or *knock* spell. Add 10 to the normal DC to break open a door or portal affected by this spell. A *knock* spell does not remove an *arcane lock*; it only suppresses the effect for 10 minutes.

ARCANE MARK

School universal; **Level** sorcerer/wizard 0

Casting Time 1 standard action

Components V, S

Range touch

Effect one personal rune or mark, all of which must fit within 1 sq. ft.

Duration permanent

Saving Throw none; **Spell Resistance** no

This spell allows you to inscribe your personal rune or mark, which can consist of no more than six characters. The writing can be visible or invisible. An *arcane mark* spell enables you to etch the rune upon any substance without harm to the material upon which it is placed. If an invisible mark is made, a *detect magic* spell causes it to glow and be visible, though not necessarily understandable.

See invisibility, true seeing, a *gem of seeing,* or a *robe of eyes* likewise allows the user to see an invisible *arcane mark.* A *read magic* spell reveals the words, if any. The mark cannot be dispelled, but it can be removed by the caster or by an *erase* spell.

If an *arcane mark* is placed on a living being, the effect gradually fades in about a month.

Arcane mark must be cast on an object prior to casting *instant summons* on the same object (see that spell description for details).

ARCANE SIGHT

School divination; **Level** sorcerer/wizard 3

Casting Time 1 standard action

Components V, S

Range personal

Target you

Duration 1 min./level (D)

This spell makes your eyes glow blue and allows you to see magical auras within 120 feet of you. The effect is similar to that of a *detect magic* spell, but *arcane sight* does not require concentration and discerns aura location and power more quickly.

You know the location and power of all magical auras within your sight. An aura's power depends on a spell's functioning level or an item's caster level, as noted in the description of the *detect magic* spell. If the items or creatures bearing the auras are in line of sight, you can make Spellcraft skill checks to determine the school of magic involved in each. (Make one check per aura; DC 15 + spell level, or 15 + half caster level for a nonspell effect.)

If you concentrate on a specific creature within 120 feet of you as a standard action, you can determine whether it has any spellcasting or spell-like abilities, whether these are arcane or divine (spell-like abilities register as arcane), and the strength of the most powerful spell or spell-like ability the creature currently has available for use.

As with *detect magic,* you can use this spell to identify the properties of magic items, but not artifacts.

Arcane sight can be made permanent with a *permanency* spell.

ARCANE SIGHT, GREATER

School divination; **Level** sorcerer/wizard 7

This spell functions like *arcane sight,* except that you automatically know which spells or magical effects are active upon any individual or object you see.

Unlike *arcane sight,* this spell cannot be made permanent with a *permanency* spell.

ASTRAL PROJECTION

School necromancy; **Level** cleric 9, sorcerer/wizard 9

Casting Time 30 minutes

Components V, S, M (jacinth worth 1,000 gp)

Range touch

Targets you plus one additional willing creature touched per two caster levels

Duration see text

Saving Throw none; **Spell Resistance** yes

By freeing your spirit from your physical body, this spell allows you to project an astral body onto another plane altogether. You can bring the astral forms of other willing creatures with you, provided that these subjects are linked in a circle with you at the time of the casting. These fellow travelers are dependent upon you and must accompany you at all times. If something happens to you during the journey, your companions are stranded wherever you left them.

You project your astral self onto the Astral Plane, leaving your physical body behind on the Material Plane in a state of suspended animation. The spell projects an astral copy of you and all you wear or carry onto the Astral Plane. Since the Astral Plane touches upon other planes, you can travel astrally to any of these other planes as you will. To enter one, you leave the Astral Plane, forming a new physical body (and equipment) on the plane of existence you have chosen to enter.

While you are on the Astral Plane, your astral body is connected at all times to your physical body by an incorporeal silver cord. If the cord is broken, you are killed, astrally and physically. Luckily, very few things can destroy a silver cord. When a second body is formed on a different plane, the silver cord remains invisibly attached to the new body. If the second body or the astral form is slain, the cord simply returns to your body where it rests on the Material Plane, thereby reviving it from its state of suspended animation. This is a traumatic affair, however, and you gain two permanent negative levels if your second body or astral form is slain. Although astral projections are able to function on the Astral Plane, their actions affect only creatures existing on the Astral Plane; a physical body must be materialized on other planes.

You and your companions may travel through the Astral Plane indefinitely. Your bodies simply wait behind in a state of suspended animation until you choose to return your spirits to them. The spell lasts until you desire to end it, or until it is terminated by some outside means, such as *dispel magic* cast upon either the physical body or the astral form, the breaking of the silver cord, or the destruction of your body back on the Material Plane (which kills you).

When this spell ends, your astral body and all of its gear, vanishes.

ATONEMENT

School abjuration; **Level** cleric 5, druid 5
Casting Time 1 hour
Components V, S, M (burning incense), F (a set of prayer beads or other prayer device worth at least 500 gp), DF
Range touch
Target living creature touched
Duration instantaneous
Saving Throw none; **Spell Resistance** yes

This spell removes the burden of misdeeds from the subject. The creature seeking atonement must be truly repentant and desirous of setting right its misdeeds. If the atoning creature committed the evil act unwittingly or under some form of compulsion, *atonement* operates normally at no cost to you. However, in the case of a creature atoning for deliberate misdeeds, you must intercede with your deity (requiring you to expend 2,500 gp in rare incense and offerings). *Atonement* may be cast for one of several purposes, depending on the version selected.

Reverse Magical Alignment Change: If a creature has had its alignment magically changed, *atonement* returns its alignment to its original status at no additional cost.

Restore Class: A paladin, or other class, who has lost her class features due to violating the alignment restrictions of her class may have her class features restored by this spell.

Restore Cleric or Druid Spell Powers: A cleric or druid who has lost the ability to cast spells by incurring the anger of her deity may regain that ability by seeking *atonement* from another cleric of the same deity or another druid. If the transgression was intentional, the casting cleric must expend 2,500 gp in rare incense and offerings for her god's intercession.

Redemption or Temptation: You may cast this spell upon a creature of an opposing alignment in order to offer it a chance to change its alignment to match yours. The prospective subject must be present for the entire casting process. Upon completion of the spell, the subject freely chooses whether it retains its original alignment or acquiesces to your offer and changes to your alignment. No duress, compulsion, or magical influence can force the subject to take advantage of the opportunity offered if it is unwilling to abandon its

old alignment. This use of the spell does not work on outsiders or any creature incapable of changing its alignment naturally.

Though the spell description refers to evil acts, *atonement* can be used on any creature that has performed acts against its alignment, regardless of the actual alignment in question.

Note: Normally, changing alignment is up to the player. This use of *atonement* offers a method for a character to change his or her alignment drastically, suddenly, and definitively.

AUGURY

School divination; **Level** cleric 2
Casting Time 1 minute
Components V, S, M (incense worth at least 25 gp), F (a set of marked sticks or bones worth at least 25 gp)
Range personal
Target you
Duration instantaneous

An *augury* can tell you whether a particular action will bring good or bad results for you in the immediate future.

The base chance for receiving a meaningful reply is 70% + 1% per caster level, to a maximum of 90%; this roll is made secretly. A question may be so straightforward that a successful result is automatic, or so vague as to have no chance of success. If the *augury* succeeds, you get one of four results:

- Weal (if the action will probably bring good results).
- Woe (for bad results).
- Weal and woe (for both).
- Nothing (for actions that don't have especially good or bad results).

If the spell fails, you get the "nothing" result. A cleric who gets the "nothing" result has no way to tell whether it was the consequence of a failed or successful *augury*.

The *augury* can see into the future only about half an hour, so anything that might happen after that does not affect the result. Thus, the result might not take into account the long-term consequences of a contemplated action. All *auguries* cast by the same person about the same topic use the same die result as the first casting.

AWAKEN

School transmutation; **Level** druid 5
Casting Time 24 hours
Components V, S, M (herbs and oils worth 2,000 gp), DF
Range touch
Target animal or tree touched
Duration instantaneous
Saving Throw Will negates; **Spell Resistance** yes

You awaken a tree or animal to human-like sentience. To succeed, you must make a Will save (DC 10 + the animal's current HD, or the HD the tree will have once awakened). The awakened animal or tree is friendly toward you. You have no special empathy or connection with a creature you awaken, although it serves you in specific tasks or endeavors if you communicate your desires to

it. If you cast *awaken* again, any previously awakened creatures remain friendly to you, but they no longer undertake tasks for you unless it is in their best interests.

An awakened tree has characteristics as if it were an animated object (see the *Pathfinder RPG Bestiary*), except that it gains the plant type and its Intelligence, Wisdom, and Charisma scores are each 3d6. An awakened plant gains the ability to move its limbs, roots, vines, creepers, and so forth, and it has senses similar to a human's.

An awakened animal gets 3d6 Intelligence, +1d3 Charisma, and +2 HD. Its type becomes magical beast (augmented animal). An awakened animal can't serve as an animal companion, familiar, or special mount.

An awakened tree or animal can speak one language that you know, plus one additional language that you know per point of Intelligence bonus (if any). This spell does not function on an animal or plant with an Intelligence greater than 2.

BALEFUL POLYMORPH

School transmutation (polymorph); **Level** druid 5, sorcerer/wizard 5
Casting Time 1 standard action
Components V, S
Range close (25 ft. + 5 ft./2 levels)
Target one creature
Duration permanent
Saving Throw: Fortitude negates, Will partial, see text; **Spell Resistance:** yes

As *beast shape III*, except that you change the subject into a Small or smaller animal of no more than 1 HD. If the new form would prove fatal to the creature, such as an aquatic creature not in water, the subject gets a +4 bonus on the save.

If the spell succeeds, the subject must also make a Will save. If this second save fails, the creature loses its extraordinary, supernatural, and spell-like abilities, loses its ability to cast spells (if it had the ability), and gains the alignment, special abilities, and Intelligence, Wisdom, and Charisma scores of its new form in place of its own. It still retains its class and level (or HD), as well as all benefits deriving therefrom (such as base attack bonus, base save bonuses, and hit points). It retains any class features (other than spellcasting) that aren't extraordinary, supernatural, or spell-like abilities.

Any polymorph effects on the target are automatically dispelled when a target fails to resist the effects of *baleful polymorph*, and as long as *baleful polymorph* remains in effect, the target cannot use other polymorph spells or effects to assume a new form. Incorporeal or gaseous creatures are immune to *baleful polymorph*, and a creature with the shapechanger subtype can revert to its natural form as a standard action.

BANE

School enchantment (compulsion) [fear, mind-affecting]; **Level** cleric 1
Casting Time 1 standard action
Components V, S, DF
Range 50 ft.
Area 50-ft.-radius burst, centered on you
Duration 1 min./level
Saving Throw Will negates; **Spell Resistance** yes

Bane fills your enemies with fear and doubt. Each affected creature takes a –1 penalty on attack rolls and a –1 penalty on saving throws against fear effects. *Bane* counters and dispels *bless*.

BANISHMENT

School abjuration; **Level** cleric 6, sorcerer/wizard 7
Casting Time 1 standard action
Components V, S, F (see text)
Range close (25 ft. + 5 ft./2 levels)
Targets one or more extraplanar creatures, no two of which can be more than 30 ft. apart
Duration instantaneous
Saving Throw Will negates; **Spell Resistance** yes

A *banishment* spell is a more powerful version of the *dismissal* spell. It enables you to force extraplanar creatures out of your home plane. As many as 2 Hit Dice of creatures per caster level can be banished.

You can improve the spell's chance of success by presenting at least one object or substance that the target hates, fears, or otherwise opposes. For each such object or substance, you gain a +1 bonus on your caster level check to overcome the target's spell resistance (if any), and the saving throw DC increases by 2.

Certain rare items might work twice as well as a normal item for the purpose of the bonuses (each providing a +2 bonus on the caster level check against spell resistance and increasing the save DC by 4).

BARKSKIN

School transmutation; **Level** druid 2, ranger 2
Casting Time 1 standard action
Components V, S, DF
Range touch
Target living creature touched
Duration 10 min./level
Saving Throw none; **Spell Resistance** yes (harmless)

Barkskin toughens a creature's skin. The effect grants a +2 enhancement bonus to the creature's existing natural armor bonus. This enhancement bonus increases by 1 for every three caster levels above 3rd, to a maximum of +5 at 12th level.

The enhancement bonus provided by *barkskin* stacks with the target's natural armor bonus, but not with other enhancement bonuses to natural armor. A creature without natural armor has an effective natural armor bonus of +0.

BEAR'S ENDURANCE

School transmutation; **Level** cleric 2, druid 2, ranger 2, sorcerer/wizard 2
Casting Time 1 standard action
Components V, S, M/DF (a few hairs, or a pinch of dung, from a bear)
Range touch
Target creature touched
Duration 1 min./level
Saving Throw Will negates (harmless); **Spell Resistance** yes

The affected creature gains greater vitality and stamina. The spell grants the subject a +4 enhancement bonus to Constitution, which adds the usual benefits to hit points, Fortitude saves, Constitution checks, and so forth. Hit points gained by a temporary increase in Constitution score are not temporary hit points. They go away when the subject's Constitution drops back to normal. They are not lost first as temporary hit points are.

BEAR'S ENDURANCE, MASS

School transmutation; **Level** cleric 6, druid 6, sorcerer/wizard 6
Range close (25 ft. + 5 ft./2 levels)
Targets one creature/level, no two of which can be more than 30 ft. apart

Mass bear's endurance works like *bear's endurance*, except that it affects multiple creatures.

BEAST SHAPE I

School transmutation (polymorph); **Level** sorcerer/wizard 3
Casting Time 1 standard action
Components V, S, M (a piece of the creature whose form you plan to assume)
Range personal
Target you
Duration 1 min./level (D)

When you cast this spell, you can assume the form of any Small or Medium creature of the animal type. If the form you assume has any of the following abilities, you gain the listed ability: climb 30 feet, fly 30 feet (average maneuverability), swim 30 feet, darkvision 60 feet, low-light vision, and scent.

Small animal: If the form you take is that of a Small animal, you gain a +2 size bonus to your Dexterity and a +1 natural armor bonus.

Medium animal: If the form you take is that of a Medium animal, you gain a +2 size bonus to your Strength and a +2 natural armor bonus.

BEAST SHAPE II

School transmutation (polymorph); **Level** sorcerer/wizard 4
This spell functions as *beast shape I*, except that it also allows you to assume the form of a Tiny or Large creature of the animal type. If the form you assume has any of the following abilities, you gain the listed ability: climb 60 feet, fly 60 feet (good maneuverability), swim 60 feet, darkvision 60 feet, low-light vision, scent, grab, pounce, and trip.

Tiny animal: If the form you take is that of a Tiny animal, you gain a +4 size bonus to your Dexterity, a −2 penalty to your Strength, and a +1 natural armor bonus.

Large animal: If the form you take is that of a Large animal, you gain a +4 size bonus to your Strength, a −2 penalty to your Dexterity, and a +4 natural armor bonus.

BEAST SHAPE III

School transmutation (polymorph); **Level** sorcerer/wizard 5
This spell functions as *beast shape II*, except that it also allows you to assume the form of a Diminutive or Huge creature of the animal type. This spell also allows you to take on the form of a Small or Medium creature of the magical beast type. If the form you assume has any of the following abilities, you gain the listed ability: burrow 30 feet, climb 90 feet, fly 90 feet (good maneuverability), swim 90 feet, blindsense 30 feet, darkvision 60 feet, low-light vision, scent, constrict, ferocity, grab, jet, poison, pounce, rake, trample, trip, and web.

Diminutive animal: If the form you take is that of a Diminutive animal, you gain a +6 size bonus to your Dexterity, a −4 penalty to your Strength, and a +1 natural armor bonus.

Huge animal: If the form you take is that of a Huge animal, you gain a +6 size bonus to your Strength, a −4 penalty to your Dexterity, and a +6 natural armor bonus.

Small magical beast: If the form you take is that of a Small magical beast, you gain a +4 size bonus to your Dexterity, and a +2 natural armor bonus.

Medium magical beast: If the form you take is that of a Medium magical beast, you gain a +4 size bonus to your Strength, and a +4 natural armor bonus.

BEAST SHAPE IV

School transmutation (polymorph); **Level** sorcerer/wizard 6
This spell functions as *beast shape III* except that it also allows you to assume the form of a Tiny or Large creature of the magical beast type. If the form you assume has any of the following abilities, you gain the listed ability: burrow 60 feet, climb 90 feet, fly 120 feet (good maneuverability), swim 120 feet, blindsense 60 feet, darkvision 90 feet, low-light vision, scent, tremorsense 60 feet, breath weapon, constrict, ferocity, grab, jet, poison, pounce, rake, rend, roar, spikes, trample, trip, and web. If the creature has immunity or resistance to any elements, you gain resistance 20 to those elements. If the creature has vulnerability to an element, you gain that vulnerability.

Tiny magical beast: If the form you take is that of a Tiny magical beast, you gain a −2 penalty to your Strength, a +8 size bonus to your Dexterity, and a +3 natural armor bonus.

Large magical beast: If the form you take is that of a Large magical beast, you gain a +6 size bonus to your Strength, a −2 penalty on your Dexterity, a +2 size bonus to your Constitution, and a +6 natural armor bonus.

BESTOW CURSE

School necromancy; **Level** cleric 3, sorcerer/wizard 4
Casting Time 1 standard action
Components V, S
Range touch
Target creature touched
Duration permanent
Saving Throw Will negates; **Spell Resistance** yes

You place a curse on the subject. Choose one of the following.

- −6 decrease to an ability score (minimum 1).
- −4 penalty on attack rolls, saves, ability checks, and skill checks.
- Each turn, the target has a 50% chance to act normally; otherwise, it takes no action.

You may also invent your own curse, but it should be no more powerful than those described above.

The curse bestowed by this spell cannot be dispelled, but it can be removed with a *break enchantment*, *limited wish*, *miracle*, *remove curse*, or *wish* spell.

Bestow curse counters *remove curse*.

BINDING

School enchantment (compulsion) [mind-affecting]; **Level** sorcerer/wizard 8

Casting Time 1 minute

Components V, S, M (opals worth 500 gp per HD of the target creature, plus other components as specified below)

Range close (25 ft. + 5 ft./2 levels)

Target one living creature

Duration see text (D)

Saving Throw Will negates; see text; **Spell Resistance** yes

A *binding* spell creates a magical restraint to hold a creature. The target gets an initial saving throw only if its Hit Dice equal at least half your caster level.

You may have as many as six assistants help you with the spell. For each assistant who casts *suggestion*, your caster level for this casting of *binding* increases by 1. For each assistant who casts *dominate animal*, *dominate person*, or *dominate monster*, your caster level for this casting of *binding* increases by a number equal to a third of that assistant's level, provided that the spell's target is appropriate for a *binding* spell. Since the assistants' spells are cast simply to improve your caster level for the purpose of the *binding* spell, saving throws and spell resistance against the assistants' spells are irrelevant. Your caster level determines whether the target gets an initial Will saving throw and how long the *binding* lasts. All *binding* spells are dismissible.

Regardless of the version of *binding* you cast, you can specify triggering conditions that end the spell and release the creature whenever they occur. These triggers can be as simple or elaborate as you desire, but the condition must be reasonable and have a likelihood of coming to pass. The conditions can be based on a creature's name, identity, or alignment, but otherwise must be based on observable actions or qualities. Intangibles such as level, class, Hit Dice, or hit points don't qualify. Once the spell is cast, its triggering conditions cannot be changed. Setting a release condition increases the save DC (assuming a saving throw is allowed) by 2.

If you cast any of the first three versions of *binding* (those with limited durations), you may cast additional *binding* spells to prolong the effect, overlapping the durations. If you do so, the target gets a saving throw at the end of the first spell's duration, even if your caster level was high enough to disallow an initial saving throw. If the creature's save succeeds, all *binding* spells it has received are broken.

The *binding* spell has six versions. Choose one of the following versions when you cast the spell.

Chaining: The subject is confined by restraints that generate an *antipathy* spell affecting all creatures who approach the subject, except you. The duration is 1 year per caster level. The subject of this form of *binding* is confined to the spot it occupied when it received the spell. Casting this version requires a chain that is long enough to wrap around the creature three times.

Slumber: This version causes the subject to become comatose for as long as 1 year per caster level. The subject does not need to eat or drink while slumbering, nor does it age. This form of *binding* is slightly easier to resist. Reduce the spell's save DC by 1. Casting this version requires a jar of sand or rose petals. This is a sleep effect.

Bound Slumber: This combination of chaining and slumber lasts for as long as 1 month per caster level. Reduce the save DC by 2. Casting this version requires both a long chain and a jar of sand or rose petals. This is a sleep effect.

Hedged Prison: The subject is transported to or otherwise brought within a confined area from which it cannot wander by any means. This effect is permanent. Reduce the save DC by 3. Casting this version requires a tiny golden cage worth 100 gp that is consumed when the spell is cast.

Metamorphosis: The subject assumes *gaseous form*, except for its head or face. It is held harmless in a jar or other container, which may be transparent if you so choose. The creature remains aware of its surroundings and can speak, but it cannot leave the container, attack, or use any of its powers or abilities. The *binding* is permanent. The subject does not need to breathe, eat, or drink while metamorphosed, nor does it age. Reduce the save DC by 4.

Minimus Containment: The subject is shrunk to a height of 1 inch or less and held within some gem, jar, or similar object. The *binding* is permanent. The subject does not need to breathe, eat, or drink while contained, nor does it age. Reduce the save DC by 4.

You can't dispel a *binding* spell with *dispel magic* or a similar effect, though an *antimagic field* or *mage's disjunction* affects it normally. A bound extraplanar creature cannot be sent back to its home plane by *dismissal*, *banishment*, or a similar effect.

BLACK TENTACLES

School conjuration (creation); **Level** sorcerer/wizard 4

Casting Time 1 standard action

Components V, S, M (octopus or squid tentacle)

Range medium (100 ft. + 10 ft./level)

Area 20-ft.-radius spread

Duration 1 round/level (D)

Saving Throw: none; **Spell Resistance**: no

This spell causes a field of rubbery black tentacles to appear, burrowing up from the floor and reaching for any creature in the area.

Every creature within the area of the spell is the target of a combat maneuver check made to grapple each round at the beginning of your turn, including the round that *black tentacles* is cast. Creatures that enter the area of effect are also automatically attacked. The tentacles do not provoke attacks of opportunity. When determining the tentacles' CMB, the tentacles use your caster level as their base attack bonus and receive a +4 bonus due to their Strength and a +1 size bonus. Roll only once for the entire spell effect each round and apply the result to all creatures in the area of effect.

If the tentacles succeed in grappling a foe, that foe takes 1d6+4 points of damage and gains the grappled condition. Grappled opponents cannot move without first breaking the grapple. All other movement is prohibited unless the creature breaks the grapple first. The *black tentacles* spell receives a +5 bonus on grapple checks made against opponents it is already grappling, but cannot move foes or pin foes. Each round that *black tentacles* succeeds on a grapple check, it deals an additional 1d6+4 points of damage. The CMD of *black tentacles*, for the purposes of escaping the grapple, is equal to 10 + its CMB.

The tentacles created by this spell cannot be damaged, but they can be dispelled as normal. The entire area of effect is considered difficult terrain while the tentacles last.

BLADE BARRIER

School evocation [force]; **Level** cleric 6

Casting Time 1 standard action

Components V, S

Range medium (100 ft. + 10 ft./level)

Effect wall of whirling blades up to 20 ft. long/level, or a ringed wall of whirling blades with a radius of up to 5 ft. per two levels; either form is 20 ft. high

Duration 1 min./level (D)

Saving Throw Reflex half or Reflex negates; see text; **Spell Resistance** yes

An immobile, vertical curtain of whirling blades shaped of pure force springs into existence. Any creature passing through the wall takes 1d6 points of damage per caster level (maximum 15d6), with a Reflex save for half damage.

If you evoke the barrier so that it appears where creatures are, each creature takes damage as if passing through the wall. Each such creature can avoid the wall (ending up on the side of its choice) and thus take no damage by making a successful Reflex save.

A *blade barrier* provides cover (+4 bonus to AC, +2 bonus on Reflex saves) against attacks made through it.

BLASPHEMY

School evocation [evil, sonic]; **Level** cleric 7

Casting Time 1 standard action

Components V

Range 40 ft.

Area nonevil creatures in a 40-ft.-radius spread centered on you

Duration instantaneous

Saving Throw Will partial; **Spell Resistance** yes

Any nonevil creature within the area of a *blasphemy* spell suffers the following ill effects.

HD	Effect
Equal to caster level	Dazed
Up to caster level −1	Weakened, dazed
Up to caster level −5	Paralyzed, weakened, dazed
Up to caster level −10	Killed, paralyzed, weakened, dazed

The effects are cumulative and concurrent. A successful Will save reduces or eliminates these effects. Creatures affected by multiple effects make only one save and apply the result to all the effects.

Dazed: The creature can take no actions for 1 round, though it defends itself normally. Save negates.

Weakened: The creature's Strength score decreases by 2d6 points for 2d4 rounds. Save for half.

Paralyzed: The creature is paralyzed and helpless for 1d10 minutes. Save reduces the paralyzed effect to 1 round.

Killed: Living creatures die. Undead creatures are destroyed. Save negates. If the save is successful, the creature instead takes 3d6 points of damage + 1 point per caster level (maximum +25).

Furthermore, if you are on your home plane when you cast this spell, nonevil extraplanar creatures within the area are instantly banished back to their home planes. Creatures so banished cannot return for at least 24 hours. This effect takes place regardless of whether the creatures hear the *blasphemy* or not. The banishment effect allows a Will save (at a −4 penalty) to negate.

Creatures whose Hit Dice exceed your caster level are unaffected by *blasphemy*.

BLEED

School necromancy; **Level** cleric 0, sorcerer/wizard 0

Casting Time 1 standard action

Components V, S

Range close (25 ft. + 5 ft./2 levels)

Target one living creature

Duration instantaneous

Saving Throw: Will negates; **Spell Resistance**: yes

You cause a living creature that is below 0 hit points but stabilized to resume dying. Upon casting this spell, you target a living creature that has −1 or fewer hit points. That creature begins dying, taking 1 point of damage per round. The creature can be stabilized later normally. This spell causes a creature that is dying to take 1 point of damage.

BLESS

School enchantment (compulsion) [mind-affecting]; **Level** cleric 1, paladin 1

Casting Time 1 standard action

Components V, S, DF

Range 50 ft.

Area The caster and all allies within a 50-ft. burst, centered on the caster

Duration 1 min./level

Saving Throw none; **Spell Resistance** yes (harmless)

Bless fills your allies with courage. Each ally gains a +1 morale bonus on attack rolls and on saving throws against fear effects.

Bless counters and dispels *bane*.

BLESS WATER

School transmutation [good]; **Level** cleric 1, paladin 1

Casting Time 1 minute

Components V, S, M (5 pounds of powdered silver worth 25 gp)

Range touch

Target flask of water touched

Duration instantaneous

Saving Throw Will negates (object); **Spell Resistance** yes (object)

This transmutation imbues a flask (1 pint) of water with positive energy, turning it into holy water (see page 160).

BLESS WEAPON

School transmutation; **Level** paladin 1

Casting Time 1 standard action

Components V, S

Range touch

Target weapon touched

Duration 1 min./level

Saving Throw none; **Spell Resistance** no

This transmutation makes a weapon strike true against evil foes. The weapon is treated as having a +1 enhancement bonus for the purpose of bypassing the DR of evil creatures or striking evil incorporeal creatures (though the spell doesn't grant an actual enhancement bonus). The weapon also becomes good-aligned, which means it can bypass the DR of certain creatures. (This effect overrides and suppresses any other alignment the weapon might have.) Individual arrows or bolts can be transmuted, but affected projectile weapons (such as bows) don't confer the benefit to the projectiles they shoot.

In addition, all critical hit rolls against evil foes are automatically successful, so every threat is a critical hit. This last effect does not apply to any weapon that already has a magical effect related to critical hits, such as a *keen* weapon or a *vorpal sword*.

BLINDNESS/DEAFNESS

School necromancy; **Level** bard 2, cleric 3, sorcerer/wizard 2

Casting Time 1 standard action

Components V

Range medium (100 ft. + 10 ft./level)

Target one living creature

Duration permanent (D)

Saving Throw Fortitude negates; **Spell Resistance** yes

You call upon the powers of unlife to render the subject blinded or deafened, as you choose.

BLINK

School transmutation; **Level** bard 3, sorcerer/wizard 3

Casting Time 1 standard action

Components V, S

Range personal

Target you

Duration 1 round/level (D)

You "blink" quickly back and forth between the Material Plane and the Ethereal Plane and look as though you're winking in and out of reality at random. *Blink* has several effects, as follows.

Physical attacks against you have a 50% miss chance, and the Blind-Fight feat doesn't help opponents, since you're ethereal and not merely invisible. If the attack is capable of striking ethereal creatures, the miss chance is only 20% (for concealment).

If the attacker can see invisible creatures, the miss chance is also only 20%. (For an attacker who can both see and strike ethereal creatures, there is no miss chance.) Likewise, your own attacks have a 20% miss chance, since you sometimes go ethereal just as you are about to strike.

Any individually targeted spell has a 50% chance to fail against you while you're blinking unless your attacker can target invisible, ethereal creatures. Your own spells have a 20% chance to activate just as you go ethereal, in which case they typically do not affect the Material Plane (but they might affect targets on the Ethereal Plane).

While blinking, you take only half damage from area attacks (but full damage from those that extend onto the Ethereal Plane). Although you are only partially visible, you are not considered invisible and targets retain their Dexterity bonus to AC against your attacks. You do receive a +2 bonus on attack rolls made against enemies that cannot see invisible creatures.

You take only half damage from falling, since you fall only while you are material.

While blinking, you can step through (but not see through) solid objects. For each 5 feet of solid material you walk through, there is a 50% chance that you become material. If this occurs, you are shunted off to the nearest open space and take 1d6 points of damage per 5 feet so traveled.

Since you spend about half your time on the Ethereal Plane, you can see and even attack ethereal creatures. You interact with ethereal creatures roughly the same way you interact with material ones.

An ethereal creature is invisible, incorporeal, and capable of moving in any direction, even up or down. As an incorporeal creature, you can move through solid objects, including living creatures.

An ethereal creature can see and hear the Material Plane, but everything looks gray and insubstantial. Sight and hearing on the Material Plane are limited to 60 feet.

Force effects and abjurations affect you normally. Their effects extend onto the Ethereal Plane from the Material Plane, but not vice versa. An ethereal creature can't attack material creatures, and spells you cast while ethereal affect only other ethereal things. Certain material creatures or objects have attacks or effects that work on the Ethereal Plane. Treat other ethereal creatures and objects as material.

BLIGHT

School necromancy; **Level** druid 4, sorcerer/wizard 5

Casting Time 1 standard action

Components V, S, DF

Range touch

Target plant touched

Duration instantaneous

Saving Throw Fortitude half; see text; **Spell Resistance** yes

This spell withers a single plant of any size. An affected plant creature takes 1d6 points of damage per level (maximum 15d6) and may attempt a Fortitude saving throw for half damage. A plant that isn't a creature doesn't receive a save and immediately withers and dies.

This spell has no effect on the soil or surrounding plant life.

BLUR

School illusion (glamer); **Level** bard 2, sorcerer/wizard 2
Casting Time 1 standard action
Components V
Range touch
Target creature touched
Duration 1 min./level (D)
Saving Throw Will negates (harmless); **Spell Resistance** yes (harmless)

The subject's outline appears blurred, shifting, and wavering. This distortion grants the subject concealment (20% miss chance).

A *see invisibility* spell does not counteract the *blur* effect, but a *true seeing* spell does.

Opponents that cannot see the subject ignore the spell's effect (though fighting an unseen opponent carries penalties of its own).

BREAK ENCHANTMENT

School abjuration; **Level** bard 4, cleric 5, paladin 4, sorcerer/wizard 5
Casting Time 1 minute
Components V, S
Range close (25 ft. + 5 ft./2 levels)
Targets up to one creature per level, all within 30 ft. of each other
Duration instantaneous
Saving Throw see text; **Spell Resistance** no

This spell frees victims from enchantments, transmutations, and curses. *Break enchantment* can reverse even an instantaneous effect. For each such effect, you make a caster level check (1d20 + caster level, maximum +15) against a DC of 11 + caster level of the effect. Success means that the creature is free of the spell, curse, or effect. For a cursed magic item, the DC is equal to the DC of the curse.

If the spell is one that cannot be dispelled by *dispel magic* or *stone to flesh*, *break enchantment* works only if that spell is 5th level or lower.

If the effect comes from a permanent magic item, *break enchantment* does not remove the curse from the item, but it does free the victim from the item's effects.

BREATH OF LIFE

School conjuration (healing); **Level** cleric 5
Casting Time 1 standard action
Components V, S
Range touch
Target creature touched
Duration instantaneous
Saving Throw Will negates (harmless) or Will half, see text; **Spell Resistance** yes (harmless) or yes, see text

This spell cures 5d8 points of damage + 1 point per caster level (maximum +25).

Unlike other spells that heal damage, *breath of life* can bring recently slain creatures back to life. If cast upon a creature that has died within 1 round, apply the healing from this spell to the creature. If the healed creature's hit point total is at a negative amount less than its Constitution score, it comes back to life and stabilizes at its new hit point total. If the creature's hit point total is at a negative amount equal to or greater than its Constitution score, the creature remains dead. Creatures brought back to life through *breath of life* gain a temporary negative level that lasts for 1 day.

Creatures slain by death effects cannot be saved by *breath of life*.

Like cure spells, *breath of life* deals damage to undead creatures rather than curing them, and cannot bring them back to life.

BULL'S STRENGTH

School transmutation; **Level** cleric 2, druid 2, paladin 2, sorcerer/wizard 2
Casting Time 1 standard action
Components V, S, M/DF (a few hairs, or a pinch of dung, from a bull)
Range touch
Target creature touched
Duration 1 min./level
Saving Throw Will negates (harmless); **Spell Resistance** yes (harmless)

The subject becomes stronger. The spell grants a +4 enhancement bonus to Strength, adding the usual benefits to melee attack rolls, melee damage rolls, and other uses of the Strength modifier.

BULL'S STRENGTH, MASS

School transmutation; **Level** cleric 6, druid 6, sorcerer/wizard 6
Range close (25 ft. + 5 ft./2 levels)
Targets one creature/level, no two of which can be more than 30 ft. apart

This spell functions like *bull's strength*, except that it affects multiple creatures.

BURNING HANDS

School evocation [fire]; **Level** sorcerer/wizard 1
Casting Time 1 standard action
Components V, S
Range 15 ft.
Area cone-shaped burst
Duration instantaneous
Saving Throw Reflex half; **Spell Resistance** yes

A cone of searing flame shoots from your fingertips. Any creature in the area of the flames takes 1d4 points of fire damage per caster level (maximum 5d4). Flammable materials burn if the flames touch them. A character can extinguish burning items as a full-round action.

CALL LIGHTNING

School evocation [electricity]; **Level** druid 3
Casting Time 1 round
Components V, S

Range medium (100 ft. + 10 ft./level)

Effect one or more 30-ft.-long vertical lines of lightning

Duration 1 min./level

Saving Throw Reflex half; **Spell Resistance** yes

Immediately upon completion of the spell, and once per round thereafter, you may call down a 5-foot-wide, 30-foot-long, vertical bolt of lightning that deals 3d6 points of electricity damage. The bolt of lightning flashes down in a vertical stroke at whatever target point you choose within the spell's range (measured from your position at the time). Any creature in the target square or in the path of the bolt is affected.

You need not call a bolt of lightning immediately; other actions, even spellcasting, can be performed first. Each round after the first you may use a standard action (concentrating on the spell) to call a bolt. You may call a total number of bolts equal to your caster level (maximum 10 bolts).

If you are outdoors and in a stormy area—a rain shower, clouds and wind, hot and cloudy conditions, or even a tornado (including a whirlwind formed by a djinni or an air elemental of at least Large size)—each bolt deals 3d10 points of electricity damage instead of 3d6.

This spell functions indoors or underground but not underwater.

CALL LIGHTNING STORM

School evocation [electricity]; **Level** druid 5

Range long (400 ft. + 40 ft./level)

This spell functions like *call lightning*, except that each bolt deals 5d6 points of electricity damage (or 5d10 if created outdoors in a stormy area), and you may call a maximum of 15 bolts.

CALM ANIMALS

School enchantment (compulsion) [mind-affecting]; **Level** druid 1, ranger 1

Casting Time 1 standard action

Components V, S

Range close (25 ft. + 5 ft./2 levels)

Targets animals within 30 ft. of each other

Duration 1 min./level

Saving Throw Will negates; **Spell Resistance** yes

This spell soothes and quiets animals, rendering them docile and harmless. Only ordinary animals (those with Intelligence scores of 1 or 2) can be affected by this spell. All the subjects must be of the same kind, and no two may be more than 30 feet apart. The maximum number of HD of animals you can affect is equal to 2d4 + caster level.

The affected creatures remain where they are and do not attack or flee. They are not helpless and defend themselves normally if attacked. Any threat breaks the spell on the threatened creatures.

CALM EMOTIONS

School enchantment (compulsion) [mind-affecting]; **Level** bard 2, cleric 2

Casting Time 1 standard action

Components V, S, DF

Range medium (100 ft. + 10 ft./level)

Area creatures in a 20-ft.-radius spread

Duration concentration, up to 1 round/level (D)

Saving Throw Will negates; **Spell Resistance** yes

This spell calms agitated creatures. You have no control over the affected creatures, but *calm emotions* can stop raging creatures from fighting or joyous ones from reveling. Creatures so affected cannot take violent actions (although they can defend themselves) or do anything destructive. Any aggressive action against or damage dealt to a calmed creature immediately breaks the spell on all calmed creatures.

This spell automatically suppresses (but does not dispel) any morale bonuses granted by spells such as *bless, good hope,* and *rage,* and also negates a bard's ability to inspire courage or a barbarian's rage ability. It also suppresses any fear effects and removes the *confused* condition from all targets. While the spell lasts, a suppressed spell, condition, or effect has no effect. When the *calm emotions* spell ends, the original spell or effect takes hold of the creature again, provided that its duration has not expired in the meantime.

CAT'S GRACE

School transmutation; **Level** bard 2, druid 2, ranger 2, sorcerer/wizard 2

Casting Time 1 standard action

Components V, S, M (pinch of cat fur)

Range touch

Target creature touched

Duration 1 min./level

Saving Throw Will negates (harmless); **Spell Resistance** yes

The transmuted creature becomes more graceful, agile, and coordinated. The spell grants a +4 enhancement bonus to Dexterity, adding the usual benefits to AC, Reflex saves, and other uses of the Dexterity modifier.

CAT'S GRACE, MASS

School transmutation; **Level** bard 6, druid 6, sorcerer/wizard 6

Range close (25 ft. + 5 ft./2 levels)

Targets one creature/level, no two of which can be more than 30 ft. apart

This spell functions like *cat's grace,* except that it affects multiple creatures.

CAUSE FEAR

School necromancy [fear, mind-affecting]; **Level** bard 1, cleric 1, sorcerer/wizard 1

Casting Time 1 standard action

Components V, S

Range close (25 ft. + 5 ft./2 levels)

Target one living creature with 5 or fewer HD

Duration 1d4 rounds or 1 round; see text

Saving Throw Will partial; **Spell Resistance** yes

The affected creature becomes frightened. If the subject succeeds on

a Will save, it is shaken for 1 round. Creatures with 6 or more HD are immune to this effect. *Cause fear* counters and dispels *remove fear*.

CHAIN LIGHTNING

School evocation [electricity]; **Level** sorcerer/wizard 6

Casting Time 1 standard action

Components V, S, F (a bit of fur; a piece of amber, glass, or a crystal rod; plus one silver pin per caster level)

Range long (400 ft. + 40 ft./level)

Targets one primary target, plus one secondary target/level (each of which must be within 30 ft. of the primary target)

Duration instantaneous

Saving Throw Reflex half; **Spell Resistance** yes

This spell creates an electrical discharge that begins as a single stroke commencing from your fingertips. Unlike *lightning bolt*, *chain lightning* strikes one object or creature initially, then arcs to other targets.

The bolt deals 1d6 points of electricity damage per caster level (maximum 20d6) to the primary target. After it strikes, lightning can arc to a number of secondary targets equal to your caster level (maximum 20). The secondary bolts each strike one target and deal as much damage as the primary bolt.

Each target can attempt a Reflex saving throw for half damage. The Reflex DC to halve the damage of the secondary bolts is 2 lower than the DC to halve the damage of the primary bolt. You choose secondary targets as you like, but they must all be within 30 feet of the primary target, and no target can be struck more than once. You can choose to affect fewer secondary targets than the maximum.

CHANGESTAFF

School transmutation; **Level** druid 7

Casting Time 1 round

Components V, S, F (a quarterstaff that has been carved and polished for 28 days)

Range touch

Target your touched staff

Duration 1 hour/level (D)

Saving Throw none; **Spell Resistance** no

You change a specially prepared quarterstaff into a Huge treant-like creature (see the *Pathfinder RPG Bestiary*), about 24 feet tall.

When you plant the end of the staff in the ground and speak a special command to conclude the casting of the spell, your staff turns into a creature that looks and fights just like a treant. The staff-treant defends you and obeys any spoken commands. However, it is by no means a true treant; it cannot converse with actual treants or control trees. If the staff-treant is reduced to 0 or fewer hit points, it crumbles to powder and the staff is destroyed. Otherwise, the staff returns to its normal form when the spell duration expires (or when the spell is dismissed), and it can be used as the focus for another casting of the spell. The staff-treant is always at full strength when created, despite any wounds it may have incurred the last time it appeared.

CHAOS HAMMER

School evocation [chaotic]; **Level** cleric 4
Casting Time 1 standard action
Components V, S
Range medium (100 ft. + 10 ft./level)
Area 20-ft.-radius burst
Duration instantaneous (1d6 rounds); see text
Saving Throw Will partial; see text; **Spell Resistance** yes

You unleash chaotic power to smite your enemies. The power takes the form of a multicolored explosion of leaping, ricocheting energy. Only lawful and neutral (not chaotic) creatures are harmed by the spell.

The spell deals 1d8 points of damage per two caster levels (maximum 5d8) to lawful creatures (or 1d6 points of damage per caster level, maximum 10d6, to lawful outsiders) and slows them for 1d6 rounds (see the *slow* spell). A successful Will save reduces the damage by half and negates the slow effect.

The spell deals only half damage against creatures who are neither lawful nor chaotic, and they are not slowed. Such a creature can reduce the damage by half again (down to one-quarter) with a successful Will save.

CHARM ANIMAL

School enchantment (charm) [mind-affecting]; **Level** druid 1, ranger 1
Target one animal

This spell functions like *charm person*, except that it affects a creature of the animal type.

CHARM MONSTER

School enchantment (charm) [mind-affecting]; **Level** bard 3, sorcerer/wizard 4
Target one living creature
Duration 1 day/level

This spell functions like *charm person*, except that the effect is not restricted by creature type or size.

CHARM MONSTER, MASS

School enchantment (charm) [mind-affecting]; **Level** bard 6, sorcerer/wizard 8
Components V
Targets One or more creatures, no two of which can be more than 30 ft. apart
Duration 1 day/level

This spell functions like *charm monster*, except that *mass charm monster* affects a number of creatures whose combined HD do not exceed twice your level, or at least one creature regardless of HD. If there are more potential targets than you can affect, you choose them one at a time until you must choose a creature with too many HD to affect.

CHARM PERSON

School enchantment (charm) [mind-affecting]; **Level** bard 1, sorcerer/wizard 1
Casting Time 1 standard action
Components V, S
Range close (25 ft. + 5 ft./2 levels)
Target one humanoid creature
Duration 1 hour/level
Saving Throw Will negates; **Spell Resistance** yes

This charm makes a humanoid creature regard you as its trusted friend and ally (treat the target's attitude as friendly). If the creature is currently being threatened or attacked by you or your allies, however, it receives a +5 bonus on its saving throw.

The spell does not enable you to control the charmed person as if it were an automaton, but it perceives your words and actions in the most favorable way. You can try to give the subject orders, but you must win an opposed Charisma check to convince it to do anything it wouldn't ordinarily do. (Retries are not allowed.) An affected creature never obeys suicidal or obviously harmful orders, but it might be convinced that something very dangerous is worth doing. Any act by you or your apparent allies that threatens the charmed person breaks the spell. You must speak the person's language to communicate your commands, or else be good at pantomiming.

CHILL METAL

School transmutation [cold]; **Level** druid 2
Casting Time 1 standard action
Components V, S, DF
Range close (25 ft. + 5 ft./2 levels)
Target metal equipment of one creature per two levels, no two of which can be more than 30 ft. apart; or 25 lbs. of metal/level, none of which can be more than 30 ft. away from any of the rest
Duration 7 rounds
Saving Throw Will negates (object); **Spell Resistance** yes (object)

Chill metal makes metal extremely cold. Unattended, nonmagical metal gets no saving throw. Magical metal is allowed a saving throw against the spell. An item in a creature's possession uses the creature's saving throw bonus unless its own is higher.

A creature takes cold damage if its equipment is chilled. It takes full damage if its armor, shield, or weapon is affected. The creature takes minimum damage (1 point or 2 points; see the table) if it's not wearing or wielding such an item.

On the first round of the spell, the metal becomes chilly and uncomfortable to touch but deals no damage. The same effect also occurs on the last round of the spell's duration. During the second (and also the next-to-last) round, icy coldness causes pain and damage. In the third, fourth, and fifth rounds, the metal is freezing cold, and causes more damage, as shown on the table below.

Round	Metal Temperature	Damage
1	Cold	None
2	Icy	1d4 points
3–5	Freezing	2d4 points
6	Icy	1d4 points
7	Cold	None

Any heat intense enough to damage the creature negates cold damage from the spell (and vice versa) on a point-for-point basis. Underwater, *chill metal* deals no damage, but ice immediately forms around the affected metal, making it float if unattended.

Chill metal counters and dispels *heat metal*.

CHILL TOUCH

School necromancy; **Level** sorcerer/wizard 1
Casting Time 1 standard action
Components V, S
Range touch
Targets creature or creatures touched (up to one/level)
Duration instantaneous
Saving Throw Fortitude partial or Will negates; see text; **Spell Resistance** yes

A touch from your hand, which glows with blue energy, disrupts the life force of living creatures. Each touch channels negative energy that deals 1d6 points of damage. The touched creature also takes 1 point of Strength damage unless it makes a successful Fortitude saving throw. You can use this melee touch attack up to one time per level.

An undead creature you touch takes no damage of either sort, but it must make a successful Will saving throw or flee as if panicked for 1d4 rounds + 1 round per caster level.

CIRCLE OF DEATH

School necromancy [death]; **Level** sorcerer/wizard 6
Casting Time 1 standard action
Components V, S, M (a crushed black pearl worth 500 gp)
Range medium (100 ft. + 10 ft./level)
Area several living creatures within a 40-ft.-radius burst
Duration instantaneous
Saving Throw Fortitude negates; **Spell Resistance** yes

Circle of death snuffs out the life force of living creatures, killing them instantly. The spell slays 1d4 HD worth of living creatures per caster level (maximum 20d4). Creatures with the fewest HD are affected first; among creatures with equal HD, those who are closest to the burst's point of origin are affected first. No creature of 9 or more HD can be affected, and HD that are not sufficient to affect a creature are wasted.

CLAIRAUDIENCE/CLAIRVOYANCE

School divination (scrying); **Level** bard 3, sorcerer/wizard 3
Casting Time 10 minutes
Components V, S, F/DF (a small horn or a glass eye)
Range long (400 ft. + 40 ft./level)
Effect magical sensor
Duration 1 min./level (D)
Saving Throw none; **Spell Resistance** no

Clairaudience/clairvoyance creates an invisible magical sensor at a specific location that enables you to hear or see (your choice) almost as if you were there. You don't need line of sight or line of effect, but the locale must be known—a place familiar to you, or an obvious one. Once you have selected the locale, the sensor doesn't move, but you can rotate it in all directions to view the area as desired. Unlike other scrying spells, this spell does not allow magically or supernaturally enhanced senses to work through it. If the chosen locale is magically dark, you see nothing. If it is naturally pitch black, you can see in a 10-foot radius around the center of the spell's effect. *Clairaudience/clairvoyance* functions only on the plane of existence you are currently occupying.

CLENCHED FIST

School evocation [force]; **Level** sorcerer/wizard 8
Components V, S, F/DF (a leather glove)

This spell functions like *interposing hand*, except that the hand can also push or strike one opponent that you select. The floating hand can move as far as 60 feet and can attack in the same round. Since this hand is directed by you, its ability to notice or attack invisible or concealed creatures is no better than yours.

The hand attacks once per round, and its attack bonus equals your caster level + your Intelligence, Wisdom, or Charisma modifier (for a wizard, cleric, or sorcerer, respectively) + 11 for the hand's Strength score (33), – 1 for being Large. The hand deals 1d8+11 points of damage on each attack, and any creature struck must make a Fortitude save (against this spell's save DC) or be stunned for 1 round. Directing the spell to a new target is a move action.

The *clenched fist* can also interpose itself as *interposing hand* does, or it can bull rush an opponent as *forceful hand* does. Its CMB for bull rush checks uses your caster level in place of its base attack bonus, with a +11 bonus for its Strength score and a +1 bonus for being Large.

CLOAK OF CHAOS

School abjuration [chaotic]; **Level** cleric 8
Casting Time 1 standard action
Components V, S, F (a tiny reliquary worth 500 gp)
Range 20 ft.
Targets one creature/level in a 20-ft.-radius burst centered on you
Duration 1 round/level (D)
Saving Throw see text; **Spell Resistance** yes (harmless)

A random pattern of color surrounds the subjects, protecting them from attacks, granting them resistance to spells cast by lawful creatures, and causing lawful creatures that strike the subjects to become *confused*. This abjuration has four effects.

First, each warded creature gains a +4 deflection bonus to AC and a +4 resistance bonus on saves. Unlike *protection from law*, the benefit of this spell applies against all attacks, not just against attacks by lawful creatures.

Second, each warded creature gains spell resistance 25 against lawful spells and spells cast by lawful creatures.

Third, the abjuration protects from possession and mental influence, just as *protection from law* does.

Finally, if a lawful creature succeeds on a melee attack against a warded creature, the offending attacker is *confused* for 1 round (Will save negates, as with the *confusion* spell, but against the save DC of *cloak of chaos*).

CLONE

School necromancy; **Level** sorcerer/wizard 8
Casting Time 10 minutes
Components V, S, M (laboratory supplies worth 1,000 gp), F (special laboratory equipment costing 500 gp)
Range 0 ft.
Effect one clone
Duration instantaneous
Saving Throw none; **Spell Resistance** no

This spell makes an inert duplicate of a creature. If the original individual has been slain, its soul immediately transfers to the clone, creating a replacement (provided that the soul is free and willing to return). The original's physical remains, should they still exist, become inert and cannot thereafter be restored to life. If the original creature has reached the end of its natural life span (that is, it has died of natural causes), any cloning attempt fails.

To create the duplicate, you must have a piece of flesh (not hair, nails, scales, or the like) with a volume of at least 1 cubic inch that was taken from the original creature's living body. The piece of flesh need not be fresh, but it must be kept from rotting. Once the spell is cast, the duplicate must be grown in a laboratory for 2d4 months.

When the clone is completed, the original's soul enters it immediately, if that creature is already dead. The clone is physically identical to the original and possesses the same personality and memories as the original. In other respects, treat the clone as if it were the original character raised from the dead, including its gaining of two permanent negative levels, just as if it had been hit by an energy-draining creature. If the subject is 1st level, it takes 2 points of Constitution drain instead (if this would reduce its Con to 0 or less, it can't be cloned). If the original creature gained permanent negative levels since the flesh sample was taken, the clone gains these negative levels as well.

The spell duplicates only the original's body and mind, not its equipment. A duplicate can be grown while the original still lives, or when the original soul is unavailable, but the resulting body is merely a soulless bit of inert flesh which rots if not preserved.

CLOUDKILL

School conjuration (creation); **Level** sorcerer/wizard 5
Casting Time 1 standard action
Components V, S
Range medium (100 ft. + 10 ft./level)
Effect cloud spreads in 20-ft. radius, 20 ft. high
Duration 1 min./level
Saving Throw Fortitude partial; see text; **Spell Resistance** no

This spell generates a bank of fog, similar to a *fog cloud*, except that its vapors are yellowish green and poisonous. These vapors automatically kill any living creature with 3 or fewer HD (no save). A living creature with 4 to 6 HD is slain unless it succeeds on a Fortitude save (in which case it takes 1d4 points of Constitution damage on your turn each round while in the cloud).

A living creature with more than 6 HD takes 1d4 points of Constitution damage on your turn each round while in the cloud (a successful Fortitude save halves this damage). Holding one's breath doesn't help, but creatures immune to poison are unaffected by the spell.

Unlike a *fog cloud*, the *cloudkill* moves away from you at 10 feet per round, rolling along the surface of the ground.

Figure out the cloud's new spread each round based on its new point of origin, which is 10 feet farther away from the point of origin where you cast the spell.

Because the vapors are heavier than air, they sink to the lowest level of the land, even pouring down den or sinkhole openings. It cannot penetrate liquids, nor can it be cast underwater.

COLOR SPRAY

School illusion (pattern) [mind-affecting]; **Level** sorcerer/wizard 1
Casting Time 1 standard action
Components V, S, M (red, yellow, and blue powder or colored sand)
Range 15 ft.
Area cone-shaped burst
Duration instantaneous; see text
Saving Throw Will negates; **Spell Resistance** yes

A vivid cone of clashing colors springs forth from your hand, causing creatures to become stunned, perhaps also blinded, and possibly knocking them unconscious. Each creature within the cone is affected according to its HD.

2 HD or less: The creature is unconscious, blinded, and stunned for 2d4 rounds, then blinded and stunned for 1d4 rounds, and then stunned for 1 round. (Only living creatures are knocked unconscious.)

3 or 4 HD: The creature is blinded and stunned for 1d4 rounds, then stunned for 1 round.

5 or more HD: The creature is stunned for 1 round.

Sightless creatures are not affected by *color spray*.

COMMAND

School enchantment (compulsion) [language-dependent, mind-affecting]; **Level** cleric 1
Casting Time 1 standard action

Components V
Range close (25 ft. + 5 ft./2 levels)
Target one living creature
Duration 1 round
Saving Throw Will negates; **Spell Resistance** yes

You give the subject a single command, which it obeys to the best of its ability at its earliest opportunity. You may select from the following options.

Approach: On its turn, the subject moves toward you as quickly and directly as possible for 1 round. The creature may do nothing but move during its turn, and it provokes attacks of opportunity for this movement as normal.

Drop: On its turn, the subject drops whatever it is holding. It can't pick up any dropped item until its next turn.

Fall: On its turn, the subject falls to the ground and remains prone for 1 round. It may act normally while prone but takes any appropriate penalties.

Flee: On its turn, the subject moves away from you as quickly as possible for 1 round. It may do nothing but move during its turn, and it provokes attacks of opportunity for this movement as normal.

Halt: The subject stands in place for 1 round. It may not take any actions but is not considered helpless.

If the subject can't carry out your command on its next turn, the spell automatically fails.

COMMAND, GREATER

School enchantment (compulsion) [language-dependent, mind-affecting]; **Level** cleric 5
Targets one creature/level, no two of which can be more than 30 ft. apart
Duration 1 round/level

This spell functions like *command*, except that up to one creature per level may be affected, and the activities continue beyond 1 round. At the start of each commanded creature's action after the first, it gets another Will save to attempt to break free from the spell. Each creature must receive the same command.

COMMAND PLANTS

School transmutation; **Level** druid 4, ranger 3
Casting Time 1 standard action
Components V
Range close (25 ft. + 5 ft./2 levels)
Targets up to 2 HD/level of plant creatures, no two of which can be more than 30 ft. apart
Duration 1 day/level
Saving Throw Will negates; **Spell Resistance** yes

This spell allows you some degree of control over one or more plant creatures. Affected plant creatures can understand you, and they perceive your words and actions in the most favorable way (treat their attitude as friendly). They will not attack you while the spell lasts. You can try to give a subject orders, but you must win an opposed Charisma check to convince it to do anything it wouldn't ordinarily do. (Retries are not

allowed.) A commanded plant never obeys suicidal or obviously harmful orders, but it might be convinced that something very dangerous is worth doing.

You can affect a number of plant creatures whose combined level or HD do not exceed twice your level.

COMMAND UNDEAD

School necromancy; **Level** sorcerer/wizard 2
Casting Time 1 standard action
Components V, S, M (a shred of raw meat and a splinter of bone)
Range close (25 ft. + 5 ft./2 levels)
Target one undead creature
Duration 1 day/level
Saving Throw Will negates; see text; **Spell Resistance** yes

This spell allows you a degree of control over an undead creature. If the subject is intelligent, it perceives your words and actions favorably (treat its attitude as friendly). It will not attack you while the spell lasts. You can give the subject orders, but you must win an opposed Charisma check to convince it to do anything it wouldn't ordinarily do. Retries are not allowed. An intelligent commanded undead never obeys suicidal or obviously harmful orders, but it might be convinced that something very dangerous is worth doing.

A nonintelligent undead creature gets no saving throw against this spell. When you control a mindless being, you can communicate only basic commands, such as "come here," "go there," "fight," "stand still," and so on. Nonintelligent undead won't resist suicidal or obviously harmful orders.

Any act by you or your apparent allies that threatens the commanded undead (regardless of its Intelligence) breaks the spell.

Your commands are not telepathic. The undead creature must be able to hear you.

COMMUNE

School divination; **Level** cleric 5
Casting Time 10 minutes
Components V, S, M (holy or unholy water and incense worth 500 gp), DF
Range personal
Target you
Duration 1 round/level

You contact your deity—or agents thereof—and ask questions that can be answered by a simple yes or no. (A cleric of no particular deity contacts a philosophically allied deity.) You are allowed one such question per caster level. The answers given are correct within the limits of the entity's knowledge. "Unclear" is a legitimate answer, because powerful beings of the Outer Planes are not necessarily omniscient. In cases where a one-word answer would be misleading or contrary to the deity's interests, a short phrase (five words or less) may be given as an answer instead.

The spell, at best, provides information to aid character decisions. The entities contacted structure their answers to further their own purposes. If you lag, discuss the answers, or go off to do anything else, the spell ends.

COMMUNE WITH NATURE

School divination; **Level** druid 5, ranger 4
Casting Time 10 minutes
Components V, S
Range personal
Target you
Duration instantaneous

You become one with nature, attaining knowledge of the surrounding territory. You instantly gain knowledge of as many as three facts from among the following subjects: the ground or terrain, plants, minerals, bodies of water, people, general animal population, presence of woodland creatures, presence of powerful unnatural creatures, or even the general state of the natural setting.

In outdoor settings, the spell operates in a radius of 1 mile per caster level. In natural underground settings—caves, caverns, and the like—the spell is less powerful, and its radius is limited to 100 feet per caster level. The spell does not function where nature has been replaced by construction or settlement, such as in dungeons and towns.

COMPREHEND LANGUAGES

School divination; **Level** bard 1, cleric 1, sorcerer/wizard 1
Casting Time 1 standard action
Components V, S, M/DF (pinch of soot and salt)
Range personal
Target you
Duration 10 min./level

You can understand the spoken words of creatures or read otherwise incomprehensible written messages. The ability to read does not necessarily impart insight into the material, merely its literal meaning. The spell enables you to understand or read an unknown language, not speak or write it.

Written material can be read at the rate of one page (250 words) per minute. Magical writing cannot be read, though the spell reveals that it is magical. This spell can be foiled by certain warding magic (such as the *secret page* and *illusory script* spells). It does not decipher codes or reveal messages concealed in otherwise normal text.

Comprehend languages can be made permanent with a *permanency* spell.

CONE OF COLD

School evocation [cold]; **Level** sorcerer/wizard 5
Casting Time 1 standard action
Components V, S, M (a small crystal or glass cone)
Range 60 ft.
Area cone-shaped burst
Duration instantaneous
Saving Throw Reflex half; **Spell Resistance** yes

Cone of cold creates an area of extreme cold, originating at your hand and extending outward in a cone. It drains heat, dealing 1d6 points of cold damage per caster level (maximum 15d6).

CONFUSION

School enchantment (compulsion) [mind-affecting]; **Level** bard 3, sorcerer/wizard 4
Casting Time 1 standard action
Components V, S, M/DF (three nutshells)
Range medium (100 ft. + 10 ft./level)
Targets all creatures in a 15-ft.-radius burst
Duration 1 round/level
Saving Throw Will negates; **Spell Resistance** yes

This spell causes confusion in the targets, making them unable to determine their actions. Roll on the following table at the start of each subject's turn each round to see what it does in that round.

d%	Behavior
01–25	Act normally
26–50	Do nothing but babble incoherently
51–75	Deal 1d8 points of damage + Str modifier to self with item in hand
76–100	Attack nearest creature (for this purpose, a familiar counts as part of the subject's self)

A confused character who can't carry out the indicated action does nothing but babble incoherently. Attackers are not at any special advantage when attacking a confused character. Any confused character who is attacked automatically attacks its attackers on its next turn, as long as it is still confused when its turn comes. Note that a confused character will not make attacks of opportunity against any creature that it is not already devoted to attacking (either because of its most recent action or because it has just been attacked).

CONFUSION, LESSER

School enchantment (compulsion) [mind-affecting]; **Level** bard 1
Casting Time 1 standard action
Components V, S, DF
Range close (25 ft. + 5 ft./2 levels)
Target one living creature
Duration 1 round
Saving Throw Will negates; **Spell Resistance** yes

This spell causes a single creature to become confused for 1 round.

CONSECRATE

School evocation [good]; **Level** cleric 2
Casting Time 1 standard action
Components V, S, M (a vial of holy water and 25 gp worth of silver dust), DF
Range close (25 ft. + 5 ft./2 levels)
Area 20-ft.-radius emanation
Duration 2 hours/level
Saving Throw none; **Spell Resistance** no

This spell blesses an area with positive energy. The DC to resist positive channeled energy within this area gains a +3 sacred bonus. Every undead creature entering a consecrated area suffers

CONTACT OTHER PLANE

Plane Contacted	Avoid Int/ Cha Decrease	True Answer	Don't Know	Lie	Random Answer
Elemental Plane	DC 7/1 week	01–34	35–62	63–83	84–100
Positive/Negative Energy Plane	DC 8/1 week	01–39	40–65	66–86	87–100
Astral Plane	DC 9/1 week	01–44	45–67	68–88	89–100
Outer Plane, demigod	DC 10/2 weeks	01–49	50–70	71–91	92–100
Outer Plane, lesser deity	DC 12/3 weeks	01–60	61–75	76–95	96–100
Outer Plane, intermediate deity*	DC 14/4 weeks	01–73	74–81	82–98	99–100
Outer Plane, greater deity	DC 16/5 weeks	01–88	89–90	91–99	100

* When contacting the Outer Planes of the Pathfinder Chronicles setting, refer to the intermediate deity line of this table

minor disruption, suffering a –1 penalty on attack rolls, damage rolls, and saves. Undead cannot be created within or summoned into a consecrated area. If the consecrated area contains an altar, shrine, or other permanent fixture dedicated to your deity, pantheon, or aligned higher power, the modifiers given above are doubled (+6 sacred bonus to positive channeled energy DCs, –2 penalties for undead in the area).

You cannot consecrate an area with a similar fixture of a deity other than your own patron. Instead, the *consecrate* spell curses the area, cutting off its connection with the associated deity or power. This secondary function, if used, does not also grant the bonuses and penalties relating to undead, as given above.

Consecrate counters and dispels *desecrate*.

CONTACT OTHER PLANE

School divination; **Level** sorcerer/wizard 5

Casting Time 10 minutes

Components V

Range personal

Target you

Duration concentration

You send your mind to another plane of existence (an Elemental Plane or some plane farther removed) in order to receive advice and information from powers there. See the accompanying table for possible consequences and results of the attempt. The powers reply in a language you understand, but they resent such contact and give only brief answers to your questions. All questions are answered with "yes," "no," "maybe," "never," "irrelevant," or some other one-word answer.

You must concentrate on maintaining the spell (a standard action) in order to ask questions at the rate of one per round. A question is answered by the power during the same round. You may ask one question for every two caster levels.

Contact with minds far removed from your home plane increases the probability that you will incur a decrease in Intelligence and Charisma due to your brain being overwhelmed, but also increases the chance of the power knowing the answer and answering correctly. Once the Outer Planes are reached, the power of the deity contacted determines the effects. (Random results obtained from the table are subject to the personalities of individual deities.) On rare occasions, this divination may be blocked by an act of certain deities or forces.

Avoid Int/Cha Decrease: You must succeed on an Intelligence check against this DC to avoid a decrease in Intelligence and Charisma. If the check fails, your Intelligence and Charisma scores each fall to 8 for the stated duration, and you become unable to cast arcane spells. You cannot take 10 on this check. If you lose Intelligence and Charisma, the effect strikes as soon as the first question is asked, and no answer is received. If a successful contact is made, roll d% to determine the type of answer you gain.

True Answer: You get a true, one-word answer. Questions that cannot be answered in this way are answered randomly.

Don't Know: The entity tells you that it doesn't know.

Lie: The entity intentionally lies to you.

Random Answer: The entity tries to lie but doesn't know the answer, so it makes one up.

CONTAGION

School necromancy [evil]; **Level** cleric 3, druid 3, sorcerer/wizard 4

Casting Time 1 standard action

Components V, S

Range touch

Target living creature touched

Duration instantaneous

Saving Throw Fortitude negates; **Spell Resistance** yes

The subject contracts one of the following diseases: blinding sickness, bubonic plague, cackle fever, filth fever, leprosy, mindfire, red ache, shakes, or slimy doom. The disease is contracted immediately (the onset period does not apply). Use the disease's listed frequency and save DC to determine further effects. For more information on these diseases, see page 557.

CONTINGENCY

School evocation; **Level** sorcerer/wizard 6

Casting Time at least 10 minutes; see text

Components V, S, M (quicksilver and an eyelash of a spell-using creature), F (ivory statuette of you worth 1,500 gp)

Range personal

Target you

Duration 1 day/level (D) or until discharged

You can place another spell upon your person so that it comes into effect under some condition you dictate when casting *contingency*. The *contingency* spell and the companion spell are cast at the same time. The 10-minute casting time is the minimum total for both castings; if the companion spell has a casting time longer than 10 minutes, use that instead. You must pay any costs associated with the companion spell when you cast *contingency*.

The spell to be brought into effect by the *contingency* must be one that affects your person and be of a spell level no higher than one-third your caster level (rounded down, maximum 6th level).

The conditions needed to bring the spell into effect must be clear, although they can be general. In all cases, the *contingency* immediately brings into effect the companion spell, the latter being "cast" instantaneously when the prescribed circumstances occur. If complicated or convoluted conditions are prescribed, the whole spell combination (*contingency* and the companion magic) may fail when triggered. The companion spell occurs based solely on the stated conditions, regardless of whether you want it to.

You can use only one *contingency* spell at a time; if a second is cast, the first one (if still active) is dispelled.

CONTINUAL FLAME

School evocation [light]; **Level** cleric 3, sorcerer/wizard 2

Casting Time 1 standard action

Components V, S, M (ruby dust worth 50 gp)

Range touch

Target object touched

Effect magical, heatless flame

Duration permanent

Saving Throw none; **Spell Resistance** no

A flame, equivalent in brightness to a torch, springs forth from an object that you touch. The effect looks like a regular flame, but it creates no heat and doesn't use oxygen. A *continual flame* can be covered and hidden but not smothered or quenched.

Light spells counter and dispel darkness spells of an equal or lower level.

CONTROL PLANTS

School transmutation; **Level** druid 8

Casting Time 1 standard action

Components V, S, DF

Range close (25 ft. + 5 ft./2 levels)

Targets up to 2 HD/level of plant creatures, no two of which can be more than 30 ft. apart

Duration 1 min./level

Saving Throw Will negates; **Spell Resistance** no

This spell enables you to control the actions of one or more plant creatures for a short period of time. You command the creatures by voice and they understand you, no matter what language you speak. Even if vocal communication is impossible, the controlled plants do not attack you. At the end of the spell, the subjects revert to their normal behavior.

Suicidal or self-destructive commands are simply ignored.

CONTROL UNDEAD

School necromancy; **Level** sorcerer/wizard 7

Casting Time 1 standard action

Components V, S, M (a piece of bone and a piece of raw meat)

Range close (25 ft. + 5 ft./2 levels)

Targets up to 2 HD/level of undead creatures, no two of which can be more than 30 ft. apart

Duration 1 min./level

Saving Throw Will negates; **Spell Resistance** yes

This spell enables you to control undead creatures for a short period of time. You command them by voice and they understand you, no matter what language you speak. Even if vocal communication is impossible, the controlled undead do not attack you. At the end of the spell, the subjects revert to their normal behavior.

Intelligent undead creatures remember that you controlled them, and they may seek revenge after the spell's effects end.

CONTROL WATER

School transmutation [water]; **Level** cleric 4, druid 4, sorcerer/wizard 6

Casting Time 1 standard action

Components V, S, M/DF (a pinch of dust for *lower water* or a drop of water for *raise water*)

Range long (400 ft. + 40 ft./level)

Area water in a volume of 10 ft./level by 10 ft./level by 2 ft./level (S)

Duration 10 min./level (D)

Saving Throw none; see text; **Spell Resistance** no

This spell has two different applications, both of which control water in different ways. The first version of this spell causes water in the area to swiftly evaporate or to sink into the ground below, lowering the water's depth. The second version causes the water to surge and rise, increasing its overall depth and possibly flooding nearby areas.

Lower Water: This causes water or similar liquid to reduce its depth by as much as 2 feet per caster level (to a minimum depth of 1 inch). The water is lowered within a squarish depression whose sides are up to caster level × 10 feet long. In extremely large and deep bodies of water, such as a deep ocean, the spell creates a whirlpool that sweeps ships and similar craft downward, putting them at risk and rendering them unable to leave by normal movement for the duration of the spell. When cast on water elementals and other water-based creatures, this spell acts as a *slow* spell (Will negates). The spell has no effect on other creatures.

Raise Water: This causes water or similar liquid to rise in height, just as the *lower water* version causes it to lower. Boats raised in this way slide down the sides of the hump that the spell creates. If the area affected by the spell includes riverbanks, a beach, or other land nearby, the water can spill over onto dry land.

With either version of this spell, you may reduce one horizontal dimension by half and double the other horizontal dimension to change the overall area of effect.

CONTROL WEATHER

School transmutation; **Level** cleric 7, druid 7, sorcerer/wizard 7
Casting Time 10 minutes; see text
Components V, S
Range 2 miles
Area 2-mile-radius circle, centered on you; see text
Duration 4d12 hours; see text
Saving Throw none; **Spell Resistance** no

You change the weather in the local area. It takes 10 minutes to cast the spell and an additional 10 minutes for the effects to manifest. You can call forth weather appropriate to the climate and season of the area you are in. You can also use this spell to cause the weather in the area to become calm and normal for the season.

Season	Possible Weather
Spring	Tornado, thunderstorm, sleet storm, or hot weather
Summer	Torrential rain, heat wave, or hailstorm
Autumn	Hot or cold weather, fog, or sleet
Winter	Frigid cold, blizzard, or thaw
Late winter or early spring	Hurricane-force winds

You control the general tendencies of the weather, such as the direction and intensity of the wind. You cannot control specific applications of the weather—where lightning strikes, for example, or the exact path of a tornado. The weather continues as you left it for the duration, or until you use a standard action to designate a new kind of weather (which fully manifests itself 10 minutes later). Contradictory conditions are not possible simultaneously.

Control weather can do away with atmospheric phenomena (naturally occurring or otherwise) as well as create them.

A druid casting this spell doubles the duration and affects a circle with a 3-mile radius.

CONTROL WINDS

School transmutation [air]; **Level** druid 5
Casting Time 1 standard action
Components V, S
Range 40 ft./level
Area 40 ft./level radius cylinder 40 ft. high
Duration 10 min./level
Saving Throw Fortitude negates; **Spell Resistance** no

You alter wind force in the area surrounding you. You can make the wind blow in a certain direction or manner, increase its strength, or decrease its strength. The new wind direction and strength persist until the spell ends or until you choose to alter your handiwork, which requires concentration. You may create an "eye" of calm air up to 80 feet in diameter at the center of the area if you so desire, and you may choose to limit the area to any cylindrical area less than your full limit.

Wind Direction: You may choose one of four basic wind patterns to function over the spell's area.

- A downdraft blows from the center outward in equal strength in all directions.
- An updraft blows from the outer edges in toward the center in equal strength from all directions, veering upward before impinging on the eye in the center.
- Rotation causes the winds to circle the center in clockwise or counterclockwise fashion.
- A blast simply causes the winds to blow in one direction across the entire area from one side to the other.

Wind Strength: For every three caster levels, you can increase or decrease wind strength by one level. Each round on your turn, a creature in the wind must make a Fortitude save or suffer the effect of being in the windy area. See Chapter 13 for more details.

Strong winds (21+ mph) make sailing difficult.

A severe wind (31+ mph) causes minor ship and building damage.

A windstorm (51+ mph) drives most flying creatures from the skies, uproots small trees, knocks down light wooden structures, tears off roofs, and endangers ships.

Hurricane force winds (75+ mph) destroy wooden buildings, uproot large trees, and cause most ships to founder.

A tornado (175+ mph) destroys all nonfortified buildings and often uproots large trees.

CREATE FOOD AND WATER

School conjuration (creation); **Level** cleric 3
Casting Time 10 minutes
Components V, S
Range close (25 ft. + 5 ft./2 levels)
Effect food and water to sustain three humans or one horse/level for 24 hours
Duration 24 hours; see text
Saving Throw none; **Spell Resistance** no

The food that this spell creates is simple fare of your choice—highly nourishing, if rather bland. Food so created decays and becomes inedible after 24 hours, although it can be kept fresh for another 24 hours by casting a *purify food and water* spell on it. The water created by this spell is just like clean rain water, and it doesn't go bad as the food does.

CREATE GREATER UNDEAD

School necromancy [evil]; **Level** cleric 8, sorcerer/wizard 8
This spell functions like *create undead*, except that you can create more powerful and intelligent sorts of undead: shadows, wraiths, spectres, and devourers (see the *Pathfinder RPG Bestiary*). The type or types of undead created is based on caster level, as shown below.

Caster Level	Undead Created
15th or lower	Shadow
16th–17th	Wraith
18th–19th	Spectre
20th or higher	Devourer

CREATE UNDEAD

School necromancy [evil]; **Level** cleric 6, sorcerer/wizard 6

Casting Time 1 hour

Components V, S, M (a clay pot filled with grave dirt and an onyx gem worth at least 50 gp per HD of the undead to be created)

Range close (25 ft. + 5 ft./2 levels)

Target one corpse

Duration instantaneous

Saving Throw none; **Spell Resistance** no

A much more potent spell than *animate dead*, this evil spell allows you to infuse a dead body with negative energy to create more powerful sorts of undead: ghouls, ghasts, mummies, and mohrgs (see the *Pathfinder RPG Bestiary*). The type or types of undead you can create are based on your caster level, as shown in the table below.

Caster Level	Undead Created
11th or lower	Ghoul
12th–14th	Ghast
15th–17th	Mummy
18th or higher	Mohrg

You may create less powerful undead than your level would allow if you choose. Created undead are not automatically under the control of their animator. If you are capable of commanding undead, you may attempt to command the undead creature as it forms.

This spell must be cast at night.

CREATE WATER

School conjuration (creation) [water]; **Level** cleric 0, druid 0, paladin 1

Casting Time 1 standard action

Components V, S

Range close (25 ft. + 5 ft./2 levels)

Effect up to 2 gallons of water/level

Duration instantaneous

Saving Throw none; **Spell Resistance** no

This spell generates wholesome, drinkable water, just like clean rain water. Water can be created in an area as small as will actually contain the liquid, or in an area three times as large—possibly creating a downpour or filling many small receptacles. This water disappears after 1 day if not consumed.

Note: Conjuration spells can't create substances or objects within a creature. Water weighs about 8 pounds per gallon. One cubic foot of water contains roughly 8 gallons and weighs about 60 pounds.

CREEPING DOOM

School conjuration (summoning); **Level** druid 7

Casting Time 1 standard action

Components V, S

Range close (25 ft. + 5 ft./2 levels)/100 ft.; see text

Effect four swarms of insects

Duration 1 round/level

Saving Throw Fortitude partial, see text; **Spell Resistance** no

This spell summons four massive swarms of biting and stinging insects. These swarms appear adjacent to one another, but can be directed to move independently. Treat these swarms as centipede swarms (see the *Pathfinder RPG Bestiary*) with the following adjustments. The swarms have 60 hit points each and deal 4d6 points of damage with their swarm attack. The save to resist their poison and distraction effects is equal to the save DC of this spell. Creatures caught in multiple swarms only take damage and make saves once.

You may summon the swarms so that they share the area of other creatures. As a standard action, you can command any number of the swarms to move toward any target within 100 feet of you. You cannot command any swarm to move more than 100 feet away from you, and if you move more than 100 feet from any swarm, that swarm remains stationary, attacking any creatures in its area (but can be commanded again if you move within 100 feet).

CRUSHING DESPAIR

School enchantment (compulsion) [mind-affecting]; **Level** bard 3, sorcerer/wizard 4

Casting Time 1 standard action

Components V, S, M (a single tear)

Range 30 ft.

Area cone-shaped burst

Duration 1 min./level

Saving Throw Will negates; **Spell Resistance** yes

An invisible cone of despair causes great sadness in the subjects. Each affected creature takes a –2 penalty on attack rolls, saving throws, ability checks, skill checks, and weapon damage rolls.

Crushing despair counters and dispels *good hope*.

CRUSHING HAND

School evocation [force]; **Level** sorcerer/wizard 9

This spell functions as *interposing hand*, except that it can also grapple one opponent as *grasping hand*. Its CMB and CMD for grapple checks use your caster level in place of its base attack bonus, with a +12 bonus for its Strength score (35) and a +1 bonus for being Large (its Dexterity is 10, granting no bonus to the CMD). A *crushing hand* deals 2d6+12 points of damage on each successful grapple check against an opponent. The *crushing hand* can instead be directed to bull rush a target (as *forceful hand*), using the same bonuses outlined above, or it can be directed to interpose itself, as *interposing hand* does.

CURE CRITICAL WOUNDS

School conjuration (healing); **Level** bard 4, cleric 4, druid 5

This spell functions like *cure light wounds*, except that it cures 4d8 points of damage + 1 point per caster level (maximum +20).

CURE CRITICAL WOUNDS, MASS

School conjuration (healing); **Level** cleric 8, druid 9

This spell functions like *mass cure light wounds*, except that it cures 4d8 points of damage + 1 point per caster level (maximum +40).

CURE LIGHT WOUNDS

School conjuration (healing); **Level** bard 1, cleric 1, druid 1, paladin 1, ranger 2

Casting Time 1 standard action

Components V, S

Range touch

Target creature touched

Duration instantaneous

Saving Throw Will half (harmless); see text; **Spell Resistance** yes (harmless); see text

When laying your hand upon a living creature, you channel positive energy that cures 1d8 points of damage + 1 point per caster level (maximum +5). Since undead are powered by negative energy, this spell deals damage to them instead of curing their wounds. An undead creature can apply spell resistance, and can attempt a Will save to take half damage.

CURE LIGHT WOUNDS, MASS

School conjuration (healing); **Level** bard 5, cleric 5, druid 6

Casting Time 1 standard action

Components V, S

Range close (25 ft. + 5 ft./2 levels)

Target one creature/level, no two of which can be more than 30 ft. apart

Duration instantaneous

Saving Throw Will half (harmless) or Will half; see text; **Spell Resistance** yes (harmless) or yes; see text

You channel positive energy to cure 1d8 points of damage + 1 point per caster level (maximum +25) on each selected creature. Like other cure spells, *mass cure light wounds* deals damage to undead in its area rather than curing them. Each affected undead may attempt a Will save for half damage.

CURE MODERATE WOUNDS

School conjuration (healing); **Level** bard 2, cleric 2, druid 3, paladin 3, ranger 3

This spell functions like *cure light wounds*, except that it cures 2d8 points of damage + 1 point per caster level (maximum +10).

CURE MODERATE WOUNDS, MASS

School conjuration (healing); **Level** bard 6, cleric 6, druid 7

This spell functions like *mass cure light wounds*, except that it cures 2d8 points of damage + 1 point per caster level (maximum +30).

CURE SERIOUS WOUNDS

School conjuration (healing); **Level** bard 3, cleric 3, druid 4, paladin 4, ranger 4

This spell functions like *cure light wounds*, except that it cures 3d8 points of damage + 1 point per caster level (maximum +15).

CURE SERIOUS WOUNDS, MASS

School conjuration (healing); **Level** cleric 7, druid 8

This spell functions like *mass cure light wounds*, except that it cures 3d8 points of damage + 1 point per caster level (maximum +35).

CURSE WATER

School necromancy [evil]; **Level** cleric 1

Casting Time 1 minute

Components V, S, M (5 lbs. of powdered silver worth 25 gp)

Range touch

Target flask of water touched

Duration instantaneous

Saving Throw Will negates (object); **Spell Resistance** yes (object)

This spell imbues a flask (1 pint) of water with negative energy, turning it into unholy water (see Chapter 6). Unholy water damages good outsiders the way holy water damages undead and evil outsiders.

DANCING LIGHTS

School evocation [light]; **Level** bard 0, sorcerer/wizard 0

Casting Time 1 standard action

Components V, S

Range medium (100 ft. + 10 ft./level)

Effect Up to four lights, all within a 10-ft.-radius area

Duration 1 minute (D)

Saving Throw none; **Spell Resistance** no

Depending on the version selected, you create up to four lights that resemble lanterns or torches (and cast that amount of light), or up to four glowing spheres of light (which look like will-o'-wisps), or one faintly glowing, vaguely humanoid shape. The *dancing lights* must stay within a 10-foot-radius area in relation to each other but otherwise move as you desire (no concentration required): forward or back, up or down, straight or turning corners, or the like. The lights can move up to 100 feet per round. A light winks out if the distance between you and it exceeds the spell's range.

You can only have one *dancing lights* spell active at any one time. If you cast this spell while another casting is still in effect, the previous casting is dispelled. If you make this spell permanent, it does not count against this limit.

Dancing lights can be made permanent with a *permanency* spell.

DARKNESS

School evocation [darkness]; **Level** bard 2, cleric 2, sorcerer/wizard 2

Casting Time 1 standard action

Components V, M/DF (bat fur and a piece of coal)

Range touch

Target object touched

Duration 1 min./level (D)

Saving Throw none; **Spell Resistance** no

This spell causes an object to radiate darkness out to a 20-foot radius. This darkness causes the illumination level in the area to drop one step, from bright light to normal light, from normal light to dim light, or from dim light to darkness. This spell has no effect in an area that is already dark. Creatures with light

vulnerability or sensitivity take no penalties in normal light. All creatures gain concealment (20% miss chance) in dim light. All creatures gain total concealment (50% miss chance) in darkness. Creatures with darkvision can see in an area of dim light or darkness without penalty. Nonmagical sources of light, such as torches and lanterns, do not increase the light level in an area of darkness. Magical light sources only increase the light level in an area if they are of a higher spell level than *darkness*.

If *darkness* is cast on a small object that is then placed inside or under a lightproof covering, the spell's effect is blocked until the covering is removed.

This spell does not stack with itself. *Darkness* can be used to counter or dispel any light spell of equal or lower spell level.

DARKVISION

School transmutation; **Level** ranger 3, sorcerer/wizard 2
Casting Time 1 standard action
Components V, S, M (either a pinch of dried carrot or an agate)
Range touch
Target creature touched
Duration 1 hour/level
Saving Throw Will negates (harmless); **Spell Resistance** yes (harmless)

The subject gains the ability to see 60 feet even in total darkness. Darkvision is black and white only but otherwise like normal sight.

Darkvision can be made permanent with a *permanency* spell.

DAYLIGHT

School evocation [light]; **Level** bard 3, cleric 3, druid 3, paladin 3, sorcerer/wizard 3
Casting Time 1 standard action
Components V, S
Range touch
Target object touched
Duration 10 min./level (D)
Saving Throw none; **Spell Resistance** no

You touch an object when you cast this spell, causing the object to shed bright light in a 60-foot radius. This illumination increases the light level for an additional 60 feet by one step (darkness becomes dim light, dim light becomes normal light, and normal light becomes bright light). Creatures that take penalties in bright light take them while within the 60-foot radius of this magical light. Despite its name, this spell is not the equivalent of daylight for the purposes of creatures that are damaged or destroyed by such light.

If *daylight* is cast on a small object that is then placed inside or under a light-proof covering, the spell's effects are blocked until the covering is removed.

Daylight brought into an area of magical darkness (or vice versa) is temporarily negated, so that the otherwise prevailing light conditions exist in the overlapping areas of effect.

Daylight counters or dispels any darkness spell of equal or lower level, such as *darkness*.

DAZE

School enchantment (compulsion) [mind-affecting]; **Level** bard 0, sorcerer/wizard 0
Casting Time 1 standard action
Components V, S, M (a pinch of wool or similar substance)
Range close (25 ft. + 5 ft./2 levels)
Target one humanoid creature of 4 HD or less
Duration 1 round
Saving Throw Will negates; **Spell Resistance** yes

This spell clouds the mind of a humanoid creature with 4 or fewer Hit Dice so that it takes no actions. Humanoids of 5 or more HD are not affected. A dazed subject is not stunned, so attackers get no special advantage against it. After a creature has been dazed by this spell, it is immune to the effects of this spell for 1 minute.

DAZE MONSTER

School enchantment (compulsion) [mind-affecting]; **Level** bard 2, sorcerer/wizard 2
Range medium (100 ft. + 10 ft./level)
Target one living creature of 6 HD or less

This spell functions like *daze*, but it can affect any one living creature of any type. Creatures of 7 or more HD are not affected.

DEATH KNELL

School necromancy [death, evil]; **Level** cleric 2
Casting Time 1 standard action
Components V, S
Range touch
Target living creature touched
Duration instantaneous/10 minutes per HD of subject; see text
Saving Throw Will negates; **Spell Resistance** yes

You draw forth the ebbing life force of a creature and use it to fuel your own power. Upon casting this spell, you touch a living creature that has −1 or fewer hit points. If the subject fails its saving throw, it dies, and you gain 1d8 temporary hit points and a +2 enhancement bonus to Strength. Additionally, your effective caster level goes up by +1, improving spell effects dependent on caster level. This increase in effective caster level does not grant you access to more spells. These effects last for 10 minutes per HD of the subject creature.

DEATH WARD

School necromancy; **Level** cleric 4, druid 5, paladin 4
Casting Time 1 standard action
Components V, S, DF
Range touch
Target living creature touched
Duration 1 min./level
Saving Throw Will negates (harmless); **Spell Resistance** yes (harmless)

The subject gains a +4 morale bonus on saves against all death spells and magical death effects. The subject is granted a save to negate such effects even if one is not normally allowed.

The subject is immune to energy drain and any negative energy effects, including channeled negative energy.

This spell does not remove negative levels that the subject has already gained, but it does remove the penalties from negative levels for the duration of its effect.

Death ward does not protect against other sorts of attacks, even if those attacks might be lethal.

DEATHWATCH

School necromancy; **Level** cleric 1
Casting Time 1 standard action
Components V, S
Range 30 ft.
Area cone-shaped emanation
Duration 10 min./level
Saving Throw none; **Spell Resistance** no

Using the powers of necromancy, you can determine the condition of creatures near death within the spell's range. You instantly know whether each creature within the area is dead, fragile (alive and wounded, with 3 or fewer hit points left), fighting off death (alive with 4 or more hit points), healthy, undead, or neither alive nor dead (such as a construct). *Deathwatch* sees through any spell or ability that allows creatures to feign death.

DEEP SLUMBER

School enchantment (compulsion) [mind-affecting]; **Level** bard 3, sorcerer/wizard 3
Range close (25 ft. + 5 ft./2 levels)

This spell functions like *sleep*, except that it affects 10 HD of targets.

DEEPER DARKNESS

School evocation [darkness]; **Level** cleric 3
Duration 10 min./level (D)

This spell functions as *darkness*, except that objects radiate darkness in a 60-foot radius and the light level is lowered by two steps. Bright light becomes dim light and normal light becomes darkness. Areas of dim light and darkness become supernaturally dark. This functions like darkness, but even creatures with darkvision cannot see within the spell's confines.

This spell does not stack with itself. *Deeper darkness* can be used to counter or dispel any light spell of equal or lower spell level.

DELAY POISON

School conjuration (healing); **Level** bard 2, cleric 2, druid 2, paladin 2, ranger 1
Casting Time 1 standard action
Components V, S, DF
Range touch
Target creature touched
Duration 1 hour/level
Saving Throw Fortitude negates (harmless); **Spell Resistance** yes (harmless)

The subject becomes temporarily immune to poison. Any poison in its system or any poison to which it is exposed during the spell's duration does not affect the subject until the spell's duration has expired. *Delay poison* does not cure any damage that poison may have already done.

DELAYED BLAST FIREBALL

School evocation [fire]; **Level** sorcerer/wizard 7
Duration 5 rounds or less; see text

This spell functions like *fireball*, except that it is more powerful and can detonate up to 5 rounds after the spell is cast. The burst of flame deals 1d6 points of fire damage per caster level (maximum 20d6). The glowing bead created by *delayed blast fireball* can detonate immediately if you desire, or you can choose to delay the burst for as many as 5 rounds. You select the amount of delay upon completing the spell, and that time cannot change once it has been set unless someone touches the bead. If you choose a delay, the glowing bead sits at its destination until it detonates. A creature can pick up and hurl the bead as a thrown weapon (range increment 10 feet). If a creature handles and moves the bead within 1 round of its detonation, there is a 25% chance that the bead detonates while being handled.

DEMAND

School enchantment (compulsion) [mind-affecting]; **Level** sorcerer/wizard 8
Saving Throw Will partial; **Spell Resistance** yes

This spell functions like *sending*, but the message can also contain a *suggestion* (see the *suggestion* spell), which the subject does its best to carry out. A successful Will save negates the *suggestion* effect but not the contact itself. The *demand*, if received, is understood even if the subject's Intelligence score is as low as 1. If the message is impossible or meaningless according to the circumstances that exist for the subject at the time the *demand* is issued, the message is understood but the *suggestion* is ineffective.

The *demand*'s message to the creature must be 25 words or less, including the *suggestion*. The creature can also give a short reply immediately.

DESECRATE

School evocation [evil]; **Level** cleric 2
Casting Time 1 standard action
Component V, S, M (a vial of unholy water and 25 gp worth (5 pounds) of silver dust, all of which must be sprinkled around the area), DF
Range close (25 ft. + 5 ft./2 levels)
Area 20-ft.-radius emanation
Duration 2 hours/level
Saving Throw none; **Spell Resistance** yes

This spell imbues an area with negative energy. The DC to resist negative channeled energy within this area gains a +3 profane bonus. Every undead creature entering a *desecrated* area gains a +1 profane bonus on all attack rolls, damage rolls, and saving throws. An undead creature created within or summoned into such an area gains +1 hit points per HD.

DETECT CHAOS/EVIL/GOOD/LAW

Creature/Object	None	Faint	Aura Power Moderate	Strong	Overwhelming
Aligned creature[1] (HD)	4 or lower	5–10	11–25	26–50	51 or higher
Aligned Undead (HD)	—	2 or lower	3–8	9–20	21 or higher
Aligned outsider (HD)	—	1 or lower	2–4	5–10	11 or higher
Cleric or paladin of an aligned deity[2] (class levels)	—	1	2–4	5–10	11 or higher
Aligned magic item or spell (caster level)	5th or lower	6th–10th	11th–15th	16th–20th	21st or higher

1 Except for undead and outsiders, which have their own entries on the table.

2 Some characters who are not clerics may radiate an aura of equivalent power. The class description will indicate whether this applies.

If the *desecrated* area contains an altar, shrine, or other permanent fixture dedicated to your deity or aligned higher power, the modifiers given above are doubled (+6 profane bonus to negative channeled energy DCs, +2 profane bonus and +2 hit points per HD for undead created in the area).

Furthermore, anyone who casts *animate dead* within this area may create as many as double the normal amount of undead (that is, 4 HD per caster level rather than 2 HD per caster level).

If the area contains an altar, shrine, or other permanent fixture of a deity, a pantheon, or higher power other than your patron, the *desecrate* spell instead curses the area, cutting off its connection with the associated deity or power. This secondary function, if used, does not also grant the bonuses and penalties relating to undead, as given above.

Desecrate counters and dispels *consecrate*.

DESTRUCTION

School necromancy [death]; **Level** cleric 7

Casting Time 1 standard action

Components V, S, F (holy or unholy symbol costing 500 gp)

Range close (25 ft. + 5 ft./2 levels)

Target one creature

Duration instantaneous

Saving Throw Fortitude partial; **Spell Resistance** yes

This spell instantly delivers 10 points of damage per caster level. If the spell slays the target, it consumes the remains utterly in holy (or unholy) fire (but not its equipment or possessions). If the target's Fortitude saving throw succeeds, it instead takes 10d6 points of damage. The only way to restore life to a character who has failed to save against this spell (and was slain) is to use *true resurrection*, a carefully worded *wish* spell followed by *resurrection*, or *miracle*.

DETECT ANIMALS OR PLANTS

School divination; **Level** druid 1, ranger 1

Casting Time 1 standard action

Components V, S

Range long (400 ft. + 40 ft./level)

Area cone-shaped emanation

Duration concentration, up to 10 min./level (D)

Saving Throw none; **Spell Resistance** no

You can detect a particular kind of animal or plant in a cone emanating out from you in whatever direction you face. You must think of a kind of animal or plant when using the spell, but you can change the animal or plant kind each round. The amount of information revealed depends on how long you search a particular area or focus on a specific kind of animal or plant.

1st Round: Presence or absence of that kind of animal or plant in the area.

2nd Round: Number of individuals of the specified kind in the area and the condition of the healthiest specimen.

3rd Round: The condition (see below) and location of each individual present. If an animal or a plant is outside your line of sight, then you discern its direction but not its exact location.

Conditions: For purposes of this spell, the categories of condition are as follows:

Normal: Has at least 90% of full normal hit points, free of disease.

Fair: 30% to 90% of full normal hit points remaining.

Poor: Less than 30% of full normal hit points remaining, afflicted with a disease, or suffering from a debilitating injury.

Weak: 0 or fewer hit points remaining, afflicted with a disease that has reduced an ability score to 5 or less, or crippled.

If a creature falls into more than one category, the spell indicates the weaker of the two.

Each round you can turn to detect a kind of animal or plant in a new area. The spell can penetrate barriers, but 1 foot of stone, 1 inch of common metal, a thin sheet of lead, or 3 feet of wood or dirt blocks it.

DETECT CHAOS

School divination; **Level** cleric 1

This spell functions like *detect evil*, except that it detects the auras of chaotic creatures, clerics of chaotic deities, chaotic spells, and chaotic magic items, and you are vulnerable to an overwhelming chaotic aura if you are lawful.

DETECT EVIL

School divination; **Level** cleric 1

Casting Time 1 standard action

Component V, S, DF

Range 60 ft.

Area cone-shaped emanation

Duration concentration, up to 10 min./ level (D)
Saving Throw none; **Spell Resistance** no

You can sense the presence of evil. The amount of information revealed depends on how long you study a particular area or subject.

1st Round: Presence or absence of evil.

2nd Round: Number of evil auras (creatures, objects, or spells) in the area and the power of the most potent evil aura present.

If you are of good alignment, and the strongest evil aura's power is overwhelming (see below), and the HD or level of the aura's source is at least twice your character level, you are stunned for 1 round and the spell ends.

3rd Round: The power and location of each aura. If an aura is outside your line of sight, then you discern its direction but not its exact location.

Aura Power: An evil aura's power depends on the type of evil creature or object that you're detecting and its HD, caster level, or (in the case of a cleric) class level; see the table on the previous page. If an aura falls into more than one strength category, the spell indicates the stronger of the two.

Lingering Aura: An evil aura lingers after its original source dissipates (in the case of a spell) or is destroyed (in the case of a creature or magic item). If *detect evil* is cast and directed at such a location, the spell indicates an aura strength of dim (even weaker than a faint aura). How long the aura lingers at this dim level depends on its original power:

Original Strength	Duration of Lingering Aura
Faint	1d6 rounds
Moderate	1d6 minutes
Strong	1d6 × 10 minutes
Overwhelming	1d6 days

Animals, traps, poisons, and other potential perils are not evil, and as such this spell does not detect them. Creatures with actively evil intents count as evil creatures for the purpose of this spell.

Each round, you can turn to detect evil in a new area. The spell can penetrate barriers, but 1 foot of stone, 1 inch of common metal, a thin sheet of lead, or 3 feet of wood or dirt blocks it.

DETECT GOOD

School divination; **Level** cleric 1

This spell functions like *detect evil*, except that it detects the auras of good creatures, clerics or paladins of good deities, good spells, and good magic items, and you are vulnerable to an overwhelming good aura if you are evil.

DETECT LAW

School divination; **Level** cleric 1

This spell functions like *detect evil*, except that it detects the auras of lawful creatures, clerics of lawful deities, lawful spells, and lawful magic items, and you are vulnerable to an overwhelming lawful aura if you are chaotic.

DETECT MAGIC

School divination; **Level** bard 0, cleric 0, druid 0, sorcerer/wizard 0
Casting Time 1 standard action
Component: V, S
Range 60 ft.
Area cone-shaped emanation
Duration concentration, up to 1 min./level (D)
Saving Throw none; **Spell Resistance** no

You detect magical auras. The amount of information revealed depends on how long you study a particular area or subject.

1st Round: Presence or absence of magical auras.

2nd Round: Number of different magical auras and the power of the most potent aura.

3rd Round: The strength and location of each aura. If the items or creatures bearing the auras are in line of sight, you can make Knowledge (arcana) skill checks to determine the school of magic involved in each. (Make one check per aura: DC 15 + spell level, or 15 + 1/2 caster level for a nonspell effect.) If the aura emanates from a magic item, you can attempt to identify its properties (see Spellcraft).

Magical areas, multiple types of magic, or strong local magical emanations may distort or conceal weaker auras.

Aura Strength: An aura's power depends on a spell's functioning spell level or an item's caster level; see the accompanying table. If an aura falls into more than one category, *detect magic* indicates the stronger of the two.

Lingering Aura: A magical aura lingers after its original source dissipates (in the case of a spell) or is destroyed (in the case of a magic item). If *detect magic* is cast and directed at such a location, the spell indicates an aura strength of dim (even weaker than a faint aura). How long the aura lingers at this dim level depends on its original power:

Original Strength	Duration of Lingering Aura
Faint	1d6 rounds
Moderate	1d6 minutes
Strong	1d6 × 10 minutes
Overwhelming	1d6 days

DETECT MAGIC

Spell or Object	Faint	Moderate	Aura Power Strong	Overwhelming
Functioning spell (spell level)	3rd or lower	4th–6th	7th–9th	10th+ (deity-level)
Magic item (caster level)	5th or lower	6th–11th	12th–20th	21st+ (artifact)

Outsiders and elementals are not magical in themselves, but if they are summoned, the conjuration spell registers. Each round, you can turn to detect magic in a new area. The spell can penetrate barriers, but 1 foot of stone, 1 inch of common metal, a thin sheet of lead, or 3 feet of wood or dirt blocks it.

Detect magic can be made permanent with a *permanency* spell.

DETECT POISON

School divination; **Level** cleric 0, druid 0, paladin 1, ranger 1, sorcerer/wizard 0

Casting Time 1 standard action

Components V, S

Range close (25 ft. + 5 ft./2 levels)

Target or Area one creature, one object, or a 5-ft. cube

Duration instantaneous

Saving Throw none; **Spell Resistance** no

You determine whether a creature, object, or area has been poisoned or is poisonous. You can determine the exact type of poison with a DC 20 Wisdom check. A character with the Craft (alchemy) skill may try a DC 20 Craft (alchemy) check if the Wisdom check fails, or may try the Craft (alchemy) check prior to the Wisdom check. The spell can penetrate barriers, but 1 foot of stone, 1 inch of common metal, a thin sheet of lead, or 3 feet of wood or dirt blocks it.

DETECT SCRYING

School divination; **Level** bard 4, sorcerer/wizard 4

Casting Time 1 standard action

Components V, S, M (a piece of mirror and a miniature brass hearing trumpet)

Range 40 ft.

Area 40-ft.-radius emanation centered on you

Duration 24 hours

Saving Throw none; **Spell Resistance** no

You immediately become aware of any attempt to observe you by means of a divination (scrying) spell or effect. The spell's area radiates from you and moves as you move. You know the location of every magical sensor within the spell's area.

If the scrying attempt originates within the area, you also know its location; otherwise, you and the scrier immediately make opposed caster level checks (1d20 + caster level). If you at least match the scrier's result, you get a visual image of the scrier and an accurate sense of his direction and distance from you.

DETECT SECRET DOORS

School divination; **Level** bard 1, sorcerer/wizard 1

Casting Time 1 standard action

Components V, S

Range 60 ft.

Area cone-shaped emanation

Duration concentration, up to 1 min./level (D)

Saving Throw none; **Spell Resistance** no

You can detect secret doors, compartments, caches, and so forth.

Only passages, doors, or openings that have been specifically constructed to escape detection are detected by this spell. The amount of information revealed depends on how long you study a particular area or subject.

1st Round: Presence or absence of secret doors.

2nd Round: Number of secret doors and the location of each. If an aura is outside your line of sight, then you discern its direction but not its exact location.

Each Additional Round: The mechanism or trigger for one particular secret portal closely examined by you. Each round, you can turn to detect secret doors in a new area. The spell can penetrate barriers, but 1 foot of stone, 1 inch of common metal, a thin sheet of lead, or 3 feet of wood or dirt blocks it.

DETECT SNARES AND PITS

School divination; **Level** druid 1, ranger 1

Casting Time 1 standard action

Components V, S

Range 60 ft.

Area cone-shaped emanation

Duration concentration, up to 10 min./level (D)

Saving Throw none; **Spell Resistance** no

You can detect simple pits, deadfalls, and snares as well as mechanical traps constructed of natural materials. The spell does not detect complex traps, including trapdoor traps.

Detect snares and pits does detect certain natural hazards—quicksand (a snare), a sinkhole (a pit), or unsafe walls of natural rock (a deadfall). It does not reveal other potentially dangerous conditions. The spell does not detect magic traps (except those that operate by pit, deadfall, or snaring; see the spell *snare*), nor mechanically complex ones, nor those that have been rendered safe or inactive.

The amount of information revealed depends on how long you study a particular area.

1st Round: Presence or absence of hazards.

2nd Round: Number of hazards and the location of each. If a hazard is outside your line of sight, then you discern its direction but not its exact location.

Each Additional Round: The general type and trigger for one particular hazard closely examined by you.

Each round, you can turn to examine a new area. The spell can penetrate barriers, but 1 foot of stone, 1 inch of common metal, a thin sheet of lead, or 3 feet of wood or dirt blocks it.

DETECT THOUGHTS

School divination [mind-affecting]; **Level** bard 2, sorcerer/wizard 2

Casting Time 1 standard action

Components V, S, F/DF (a copper piece)

Range 60 ft.

Area cone-shaped emanation

Duration concentration, up to 1 min./level (D)

Saving Throw Will negates; see text; **Spell Resistance** no

You detect surface thoughts. The amount of information revealed depends on how long you study a particular area or subject.

1st Round: Presence or absence of thoughts (from conscious creatures with Intelligence scores of 1 or higher).

2nd Round: Number of thinking minds and the Intelligence score of each. If the highest Intelligence is 26 or higher (and at least 10 points higher than your own Intelligence score), you are stunned for 1 round and the spell ends. This spell does not let you determine the location of the thinking minds if you can't see the creatures whose thoughts you are detecting.

3rd Round: Surface thoughts of any mind in the area. A target's Will save prevents you from reading its thoughts, and you must cast *detect thoughts* again to have another chance. Creatures of animal intelligence (Int 1 or 2) have simple, instinctual thoughts.

Each round, you can turn to detect thoughts in a new area. The spell can penetrate barriers, but 1 foot of stone, 1 inch of common metal, a thin sheet of lead, or 3 feet of wood or dirt blocks it.

DETECT UNDEAD

School divination; **Level** cleric 1, paladin 1, sorcerer/wizard 1
Casting Time 1 standard action
Components V, S, M/DF (earth from a grave)
Range 60 ft.
Area cone-shaped emanation
Duration concentration, up to 1 minute/ level (D)
Saving Throw none; **Spell Resistance** no

You can detect the aura that surrounds undead creatures. The amount of information revealed depends on how long you study a particular area.

1st Round: Presence or absence of undead auras.

2nd Round: Number of undead auras in the area and the strength of the strongest undead aura present. If you are of good alignment, and the strongest undead aura's strength is overwhelming (see below), and the creature has HD of at least twice your character level, you are stunned for 1 round and the spell ends.

3rd Round: The strength and location of each undead aura. If an aura is outside your line of sight, then you discern its direction but not its exact location.

Aura Strength: The strength of an undead aura is determined by the HD of the undead creature, as given on the table below.

Lingering Aura: An undead aura lingers after its original source is destroyed. If *detect undead* is cast and directed at such a location, the spell indicates an aura strength of dim (even weaker than a faint aura). How long the aura lingers at this dim level depends on its original power, as given on the table below.

HD	Strength	Lingering Aura Duration
1 or lower	Faint	1d6 rounds
2–4	Moderate	1d6 minutes
5–10	Strong	1d6 × 10 minutes
11 or higher	Overwhelming	1d6 days

Each round, you can turn to detect undead in a new area. The spell can penetrate barriers, but 1 foot of stone, 1 inch of common metal, a thin sheet of lead, or 3 feet of wood or dirt blocks it.

DICTUM

School evocation [lawful, sonic]; **Level** cleric 7
Casting Time 1 standard action
Components V
Range 40 ft.
Area nonlawful creatures in a 40-ft.-radius spread centered on you
Duration instantaneous
Saving Throw none or Will negates; see text; **Spell Resistance** yes

Any nonlawful creature within the area of a *dictum* spell suffers the following ill effects.

HD	Effect
Equal to caster level	Deafened
Up to caster level −1	Staggered, deafened
Up to caster level −5	Paralyzed, staggered, deafened
Up to caster level −10	Killed, paralyzed, staggered, deafened

The effects are cumulative and concurrent. A successful Will save reduces or eliminates these effects. Creatures affected by multiple effects make only one save and apply the result to all the effects.

Deafened: The creature is deafened for 1d4 rounds. Save negates.

Staggered: The creature is staggered for 2d4 rounds. Save reduces the staggered effect to 1d4 rounds.

Paralyzed: The creature is paralyzed and helpless for 1d10 minutes. Save reduces the paralyzed effect to 1 round.

Killed: Living creatures die. Undead creatures are destroyed. Save negates. If the save is successful, the creature instead takes 3d6 points of damage + 1 point per caster level (maximum +25).

Furthermore, if you are on your home plane when you cast this spell, nonlawful extraplanar creatures within the area are instantly banished back to their home planes. Creatures so banished cannot return for at least 24 hours. This effect takes place regardless of whether the creatures hear the *dictum* or not. The banishment effect allows a Will save (at a −4 penalty) to negate.

Creatures whose Hit Dice exceed your caster level are unaffected by *dictum*.

DIMENSION DOOR

School conjuration (teleportation); **Level** bard 4, sorcerer/wizard 4
Casting Time 1 standard action
Components V
Range long (400 ft. + 40 ft./level)
Target you and touched objects or other touched willing creatures
Duration instantaneous
Saving Throw none and Will negates (object); **Spell Resistance** no and yes (object)

You instantly transfer yourself from your current location to any other spot within range. You always arrive at exactly the spot desired—whether by simply visualizing the area or by stating direction. After using this spell, you can't take any other actions until your next turn. You can bring along objects as long as their weight doesn't exceed your maximum load. You may also bring

one additional willing Medium or smaller creature (carrying gear or objects up to its maximum load) or its equivalent per three caster levels. A Large creature counts as two Medium creatures, a Huge creature counts as two Large creatures, and so forth. All creatures to be transported must be in contact with one another, and at least one of those creatures must be in contact with you.

If you arrive in a place that is already occupied by a solid body, you and each creature traveling with you take 1d6 points of damage and are shunted to a random open space on a suitable surface within 100 feet of the intended location.

If there is no free space within 100 feet, you and each creature traveling with you take an additional 2d6 points of damage and are shunted to a free space within 1,000 feet. If there is no free space within 1,000 feet, you and each creature travelling with you take an additional 4d6 points of damage and the spell simply fails.

DIMENSIONAL ANCHOR

School abjuration; **Level** cleric 4, sorcerer/wizard 4
Casting Time 1 standard action
Components V, S
Range medium (100 ft. + 10 ft./level)
Effect ray
Duration 1 min./level
Saving Throw none; **Spell Resistance** yes (object)

A green ray springs from your hand. You must make a ranged touch attack to hit the target. Any creature or object struck by the ray is covered with a shimmering emerald field that completely blocks extradimensional travel. Forms of movement barred by a *dimensional anchor* include *astral projection, blink, dimension door, ethereal jaunt, etherealness, gate, maze, plane shift, shadow walk, teleport,* and similar spell-like abilities. The spell also prevents the use of a *gate* or *teleportation circle* for the duration of the spell.

A *dimensional anchor* does not interfere with the movement of creatures already in ethereal or astral form when the spell is cast, nor does it block extradimensional perception or attack forms. Also, *dimensional anchor* does not prevent summoned creatures from disappearing at the end of a summoning spell.

DIMENSIONAL LOCK

School abjuration; **Level** cleric 8, sorcerer/wizard 8
Casting Time 1 standard action
Components V, S
Range medium (100 ft. + 10 ft./level)
Area 20-ft.-radius emanation centered on a point in space
Duration 1 day/level
Saving Throw none; **Spell Resistance** yes

You create a shimmering emerald barrier that completely blocks extradimensional travel. Forms of movement barred include *astral projection, blink, dimension door, ethereal jaunt, etherealness, gate, maze, plane shift, shadow walk, teleport,* and similar spell-like abilities. Once *dimensional lock* is in place, extradimensional travel into or out of the area is not possible.

A *dimensional lock* does not interfere with the movement of creatures already in ethereal or astral form when the spell is cast, nor does it block extradimensional perception or attack forms. Also, the spell does not prevent summoned creatures from disappearing at the end of a summoning spell.

DIMINISH PLANTS

School transmutation; **Level** druid 3, ranger 3
Casting Time 1 standard action
Components V, S, DF
Range see text
Target or Area see text
Duration instantaneous
Saving Throw none; **Spell Resistance** no

This spell has two versions.

Prune Growth: This version of the spell causes normal vegetation within long range (400 feet + 40 feet per level) to shrink to about one-third normal size, becoming untangled and less bushy. The affected vegetation appears to have been carefully pruned and trimmed. This version of *diminish plants* automatically dispels any spells or effects that enhance plants, such as *entangle, plant growth,* and *wall of thorns.*

At your option, the area can be a 100-foot-radius circle, a 150-foot-radius semicircle, or a 200-foot-radius quarter-circle. You may also designate portions of the area that are not affected.

Stunt Growth: This version of the spell targets all normal plants within a range of 1/2 mile, reducing their potential productivity over the course of the following year to half normal.

This spell has no effect on plant creatures.

DISCERN LIES

School divination; **Level** cleric 4, paladin 3
Casting Time 1 standard action
Components V, S, DF
Range close (25 ft. + 5 ft./2 levels)
Targets one creature/level, no two of which can be more than 30 ft. apart
Duration concentration, up to 1 round/level
Saving Throw Will negates; **Spell Resistance** no

Each round, you concentrate on one target, who must be within range. You know if the target deliberately and knowingly speaks a lie by discerning disturbances in its aura caused by lying. The spell does not reveal the truth, uncover unintentional inaccuracies, or necessarily reveal evasions.

Each round, you may concentrate on a different target.

DISCERN LOCATION

School divination; **Level** cleric 8, sorcerer/wizard 8
Casting Time 10 minutes
Components V, S, DF
Range unlimited
Target one creature or object
Duration instantaneous

Saving Throw none; **Spell Resistance** no

A *discern location* spell is among the most powerful means of locating creatures or objects. Nothing short of a *mind blank* spell or the direct intervention of a deity keeps you from learning the exact location of a single individual or object. *Discern location* circumvents normal means of protection from scrying or location. The spell reveals the name of the creature or object's location (place, name, business name, building name, or the like), community, county (or similar political division), country, continent, and the plane of existence where the target lies.

To find a creature with the spell, you must have seen the creature or have some item that once belonged to it. To find an object, you must have touched it at least once.

DISGUISE SELF

School illusion (glamer); **Level** bard 1, sorcerer/wizard 1
Casting Time 1 standard action
Components V, S
Range personal
Target you
Duration 10 min./level (D)

You make yourself—including clothing, armor, weapons, and equipment—look different. You can seem 1 foot shorter or taller, thin, fat, or in between. You cannot change your creature type (although you can appear as another subtype). Otherwise, the extent of the apparent change is up to you. You could add or obscure a minor feature or look like an entirely different person or gender.

The spell does not provide the abilities or mannerisms of the chosen form, nor does it alter the perceived tactile (touch) or audible (sound) properties of you or your equipment. If you use this spell to create a disguise, you get a +10 bonus on the Disguise check. A creature that interacts with the glamer gets a Will save to recognize it as an illusion.

DISINTEGRATE

School transmutation; **Level** sorcerer/wizard 6
Casting Time 1 standard action
Components V, S, M/DF (a lodestone and a pinch of dust)
Range medium (100 ft. + 10 ft./level)
Effect ray
Duration instantaneous
Saving Throw Fortitude partial (object); **Spell Resistance** yes

A thin, green ray springs from your pointing finger. You must make a successful ranged touch attack to hit. Any creature struck by the ray takes 2d6 points of damage per caster level (to a maximum of 40d6). Any creature reduced to 0 or fewer hit points by this spell is entirely disintegrated, leaving behind only a trace of fine dust. A disintegrated creature's equipment is unaffected.

When used against an object, the ray simply disintegrates as much as a 10-foot cube of nonliving matter. Thus, the spell disintegrates only part of any very large object or structure targeted.

The ray affects even objects constructed entirely of force, such as *forceful hand* or a *wall of force*, but not magical effects such as a *globe of invulnerability* or an *antimagic field*.

A creature or object that makes a successful Fortitude save is partially affected, taking only 5d6 points of damage. If this damage reduces the creature or object to 0 or fewer hit points, it is entirely disintegrated.

Only the first creature or object struck can be affected; that is, the ray affects only one target per casting.

DISMISSAL

School abjuration; **Level** cleric 4, sorcerer/wizard 5
Casting Time 1 standard action
Components V, S, DF
Range close (25 ft. + 5 ft./2 levels)
Target one extraplanar creature
Duration instantaneous
Saving Throw Will negates; see text; **Spell Resistance** yes

This spell forces an extraplanar creature back to its proper plane if it fails a Will save. If the spell is successful, the creature is instantly whisked away, but there is a 20% chance of actually sending the subject to a plane other than its own.

DISPEL CHAOS

School abjuration [lawful]; **Level** cleric 5, paladin 4

This spell functions like *dispel evil*, except that you are surrounded by constant, blue lawful energy, and the spell affects chaotic creatures and spells rather than evil ones.

DISPEL EVIL

School abjuration [good]; **Level** cleric 5, paladin 4
Casting Time 1 standard action
Components V, S, DF
Range touch
Target or Targets you and a touched evil creature from another plane, or you and an enchantment or evil spell on a touched creature or object
Duration 1 round/level or until discharged, whichever comes first
Saving Throw see text; **Spell Resistance** see text

Shimmering, white holy energy surrounds you. This energy has three effects.

First, you gain a +4 deflection bonus to AC against attacks by evil creatures.

Second, on making a successful melee touch attack against an evil creature from another plane, you can choose to drive that creature back to its home plane. The creature can negate the effects with a successful Will save (spell resistance applies). This use discharges and ends the spell.

Third, with a touch you can automatically dispel any one enchantment spell cast by an evil creature or any one evil spell. Spells that can't be dispelled by *dispel magic* also can't be dispelled by *dispel evil*. Saving throws and spell resistance do not apply to this effect. This use discharges and ends the spell.

DISPEL GOOD

School abjuration [evil]; **Level** cleric 5

This spell functions like *dispel evil*, except that you are surrounded by dark, wavering unholy energy, and the spell affects good creatures and spells rather than evil ones.

DISPEL LAW

School abjuration [chaotic]; **Level** cleric 5

This spell functions like *dispel evil*, except that you are surrounded by flickering, yellow chaotic energy, and the spell affects lawful creatures and spells rather than evil ones.

DISPEL MAGIC

School abjuration; **Level** bard 3, cleric 3, druid 4, paladin 3, sorcerer/wizard 3
Casting Time 1 standard action
Components V, S
Range medium (100 ft. + 10 ft./level)
Target or Area one spellcaster, creature, or object
Duration instantaneous
Saving Throw none; **Spell Resistance** no

You can use *dispel magic* to end one ongoing spell that has been cast on a creature or object, to temporarily suppress the magical abilities of a magic item, or to counter another spellcaster's spell. A dispelled spell ends as if its duration had expired. Some spells, as detailed in their descriptions, can't be defeated by *dispel magic*. *Dispel magic* can dispel (but not counter) spell-like effects just as it does spells. The effect of a spell with an instantaneous duration can't be dispelled, because the magical effect is already over before the *dispel magic* can take effect.

You choose to use *dispel magic* in one of two ways: a targeted dispel or a counterspell.

Targeted Dispel: One object, creature, or spell is the target of the *dispel magic* spell. You make one dispel check (1d20 + your caster level) and compare that to the spell with highest caster level (DC = 11 + the spell's caster level). If successful, that spell ends. If not, compare the same result to the spell with the next highest caster level. Repeat this process until you have dispelled one spell affecting the target, or you have failed to dispel every spell.

For example, a 7th-level caster casts *dispel magic*, targeting a creature affected by *stoneskin* (caster level 12th) and *fly* (caster level 6th). The caster level check results in a 19. This check is not high enough to end the *stoneskin* (which would have required a 23 or higher), but it is high enough to end the *fly* (which only required a 17). Had the dispel check resulted in a 23 or higher, the *stoneskin* would have been dispelled, leaving the *fly* intact. Had the dispel check been a 16 or less, no spells would have been affected.

You can also use a targeted dispel to specifically end one spell affecting the target or one spell affecting an area (such as a *wall of fire*). You must name the specific spell effect to be targeted in this way. If your caster level check is equal to or higher than the DC of that spell, it ends. No other spells or effects on the target are dispelled if your check is not high enough to end the targeted effect.

If you target an object or creature that is the effect of an ongoing spell (such as a monster summoned by *summon monster*), you make a dispel check to end the spell that conjured the object or creature.

If the object that you target is a magic item, you make a dispel check against the item's caster level (DC = 11 + the item's caster level). If you succeed, all the item's magical properties are suppressed for 1d4 rounds, after which the item recovers its magical properties. A suppressed item becomes nonmagical for the duration of the effect. An interdimensional opening (such as a *bag of holding*) is temporarily closed. A magic item's physical properties are unchanged: A suppressed magic sword is still a sword (a masterwork sword, in fact). Artifacts and deities are unaffected by mortal magic such as this.

You automatically succeed on your dispel check against any spell that you cast yourself.

Counterspell: When *dispel magic* is used in this way, the spell targets a spellcaster and is cast as a counterspell. Unlike a true counterspell, however, *dispel magic* may not work; you must make a dispel check to counter the other spellcaster's spell.

DISPEL MAGIC, GREATER

School abjuration; **Level** bard 5, cleric 6, druid 6, sorcerer/wizard 6
Target or Area one spellcaster, creature, or object; or a 20-ft.-radius burst

This spell functions like *dispel magic*, except that it can end more than one spell on a target and it can be used to target multiple creatures.

You choose to use *greater dispel magic* in one of three ways: a targeted dispel, area dispel, or a counterspell:

Targeted Dispel: This functions as a targeted *dispel magic*, but it can dispel one spell for every four caster levels you possess, starting with the highest level spells and proceeding to lower level spells.

Additionally, *greater dispel magic* has a chance to dispel any effect that *remove curse* can remove, even if *dispel magic* can't dispel that effect. The DC of this check is equal to the curse's DC.

Area Dispel: When *greater dispel magic* is used in this way, the spell affects everything within a 20-foot-radius burst. Roll one dispel check and apply that check to each creature in the area, as if targeted by *dispel magic*. For each object within the area that is the target of one or more spells, apply the dispel check as with creatures. Magic items are not affected by an area dispel.

For each ongoing area or effect spell whose point of origin is within the area of the *greater dispel magic* spell, apply the dispel check to dispel the spell. For each ongoing spell whose area overlaps that of the *greater dispel magic* spell, apply the dispel check to end the effect, but only within the overlapping area.

If an object or creature that is the effect of an ongoing spell (such as a monster summoned by *summon monster*) is in the area, apply the dispel check to end the spell that conjured that object or creature (returning it whence it came) in addition to attempting to dispel one spell targeting the creature or object.

You may choose to automatically succeed on dispel checks against any spell that you have cast.

Counterspell: This functions as *dispel magic*, but you receive a +4 bonus on your dispel check to counter the other spellcaster's spell.

DISPLACEMENT

School illusion (glamer); **Level** bard 3, sorcerer/wizard 3

Casting Time 1 standard action

Components V, M (a small loop of leather)

Range touch

Target creature touched

Duration 1 round/level (D)

Saving Throw Will negates (harmless); **Spell Resistance** yes (harmless)

The subject of this spell appears to be about 2 feet away from its true location. The creature benefits from a 50% miss chance as if it had total concealment. Unlike actual total concealment, *displacement* does not prevent enemies from targeting the creature normally. *True seeing* reveals its true location and negates the miss chance.

DISRUPT UNDEAD

School necromancy; **Level** sorcerer/wizard 0

Casting Time 1 standard action

Components V, S

Range close (25 ft. + 5 ft./2 levels)

Effect ray

Duration instantaneous

Saving Throw none; **Spell Resistance** yes

You direct a ray of positive energy. You must make a ranged touch attack to hit, and if the ray hits an undead creature, it deals 1d6 points of damage to it.

DISRUPTING WEAPON

School transmutation; **Level** cleric 5

Casting Time 1 standard action

Components V, S

Range touch

Targets one melee weapon

Duration 1 round/level

Saving Throw Will negates (harmless, object); see text; **Spell Resistance** yes (harmless, object)

This spell makes a melee weapon deadly to undead. Any undead creature with HD equal to or less than your caster level must succeed on a Will save or be destroyed utterly if struck in combat with this weapon. Spell resistance does not apply against the destruction effect.

DIVINATION

School divination; **Level** cleric 4

Casting Time 10 minutes

Components V, S, M (incense and an appropriate offering worth 25 gp)

Range personal

Target you

Duration instantaneous

Similar to *augury* but more powerful, a *divination* spell can provide you with a useful piece of advice in reply to a question concerning a specific goal, event, or activity that is to occur within 1 week. The advice granted by the spell can be as simple as a short phrase, or it might take the form of a cryptic rhyme or omen. If your party doesn't act on the information, the conditions may change so that the information is no longer useful. The base chance for a correct *divination* is 70% + 1% per caster level, to a maximum of 90%. If the die roll fails, you know the spell failed, unless specific magic yielding false information is at work.

As with *augury*, multiple *divinations* about the same topic by the same caster use the same dice result as the first *divination* spell and yield the same answer each time.

DIVINE FAVOR

School evocation; **Level** cleric 1, paladin 1

Casting Time 1 standard action

Components V, S, DF

Range personal

Target you

Duration 1 minute

Calling upon the strength and wisdom of a deity, you gain a +1 luck bonus on attack and weapon damage rolls for every three caster levels you have (at least +1, maximum +3). The bonus doesn't apply to spell damage.

DIVINE POWER

School evocation; **Level** cleric 4

Casting Time 1 standard action

Components V, S, DF

Range personal

Target you

Duration 1 round/level

Calling upon the divine power of your patron, you imbue yourself with strength and skill in combat. You gain a +1 luck bonus on attack rolls, weapon damage rolls, Strength checks, and Strength-based skill checks for every three caster levels you have (maximum +6). You also gain 1 temporary hit point per caster level. Whenever you make a full-attack action, you can make an additional attack at your full base attack bonus, plus any appropriate modifiers. This additional attack is not cumulative with similar effects, such as *haste* or weapons with the *speed* special ability.

DOMINATE ANIMAL

School enchantment (compulsion) [mind-affecting]; **Level** druid 3

Casting Time 1 round

Components V, S

Range close (25 ft. + 5 ft./2 levels)

Target one animal

Duration 1 round/level

Saving Throw Will negates; **Spell Resistance** yes

This spell allows you to enchant the targeted animal and direct it with simple commands such as "Attack," "Run," and "Fetch." Suicidal or self-destructive commands (including an order to attack a creature two or more size categories larger than the dominated animal) are simply ignored.

Dominate animal establishes a mental link between you and the subject creature. The animal can be directed by silent mental command as long as it remains in range. You need not see the creature to control it. You do not receive direct sensory input from the creature, but you know what it is experiencing. Because you are directing the animal with your own intelligence, it may be able to undertake actions normally beyond its own comprehension. You need not concentrate exclusively on controlling the creature unless you are trying to direct it to do something it normally couldn't do. Changing your instructions or giving a dominated creature a new command is the equivalent of redirecting a spell, so it is a move action.

DOMINATE MONSTER

School enchantment (compulsion) [mind-affecting]; **Level** sorcerer/wizard 9

Target one creature

This spell functions like *dominate person*, except that the spell is not restricted by creature type.

DOMINATE PERSON

School enchantment (compulsion) [mind-affecting]; **Level** bard 4, sorcerer/wizard 5

Casting Time 1 round

Components V, S

Range close (25 ft. + 5 ft./2 levels)

Target one humanoid

Duration 1 day/level

Saving Throw Will negates; **Spell Resistance** yes

You can control the actions of any humanoid creature through a telepathic link that you establish with the subject's mind.

If you and the subject have a common language, you can generally force the subject to perform as you desire, within the limits of its abilities. If no common language exists, you can communicate only basic commands, such as "Come here," "Go there," "Fight," and "Stand still." You know what the subject is experiencing, but you do not receive direct sensory input from it, nor can it communicate with you telepathically.

Once you have given a dominated creature a command, it continues to attempt to carry out that command to the exclusion of all other activities except those necessary for day-to-day survival (such as sleeping, eating, and so forth). Because of this limited range of activity, a Sense Motive check against DC 15 (rather than DC 25) can determine that the subject's behavior is being influenced by an enchantment effect (see the Sense Motive skill description).

Changing your orders or giving a dominated creature a new command is a move action.

By concentrating fully on the spell (a standard action), you can receive full sensory input as interpreted by the mind of the subject, though it still can't communicate with you. You can't actually see through the subject's eyes, so it's not as good as being there yourself, but you still get a good idea of what's going on.

Subjects resist this control, and any subject forced to take actions against its nature receives a new saving throw with a +2 bonus. Obviously self-destructive orders are not carried out. Once control is established, the range at which it can be exercised is unlimited, as long as you and the subject are on the same plane. You need not see the subject to control it.

If you don't spend at least 1 round concentrating on the spell each day, the subject receives a new saving throw to throw off the domination.

Protection from evil or a similar spell can prevent you from exercising control or using the telepathic link while the subject is so warded, but such an effect does not automatically dispel it.

DOOM

School necromancy [fear, mind-affecting]; **Level** cleric 1

Casting Time 1 standard action

Components V, S, DF

Range medium (100 ft. + 10 ft./level)

Target one living creature

Duration 1 min./level

Saving Throw Will negates; **Spell Resistance** yes

This spell fills a single subject with a feeling of horrible dread that causes it to become shaken.

DREAM

School illusion (phantasm) [mind-affecting]; **Level** bard 5, sorcerer/wizard 5

Casting Time 1 minute

Components V, S

Range unlimited

Target one living creature touched

Duration see text

Saving Throw none; **Spell Resistance** yes

You, or a messenger you touch, send a message to others in the form of a dream. At the beginning of the spell, you must name the recipient or identify him or her by some title that leaves no doubt as to identity. The messenger then enters a trance, appears in the intended recipient's dream, and delivers the message. The message can be of any length, and the recipient remembers it perfectly upon waking. The communication is one-way. The recipient cannot ask questions or offer information, nor can the messenger gain any information by observing the dreams of the recipient.

Once the message is delivered, the messenger's mind returns instantly to its body. The duration of the spell is the time required for the messenger to enter the recipient's dream and deliver the message.

If the recipient is awake when the spell begins, the messenger can choose to wake up (ending the spell) or remain in the trance. The messenger can remain in the trance until the recipient goes to sleep, then enter the recipient's dream and deliver the message as normal. A messenger that is disturbed during the trance comes awake, ending the spell.

Creatures who don't sleep or don't dream cannot be contacted by this spell.

The messenger is unaware of its own surroundings or of the activities around it while in the trance. It is defenseless both physically and mentally (always failing any saving throw) while in the trance.

EAGLE'S SPLENDOR

School transmutation; **Level** bard 2, cleric 2, paladin 2, sorcerer/wizard 2

Casting Time 1 standard action

Components V, S, M/DF (feathers or droppings from an eagle)

Range touch

Target creature touched

Duration 1 min./level

Saving Throw Will negates (harmless); **Spell Resistance** yes

The transmuted creature becomes more poised, articulate, and personally forceful. The spell grants a +4 enhancement bonus to Charisma, adding the usual benefits to Charisma-based skill checks and other uses of the Charisma modifier. Bards, paladins, and sorcerers (and other spellcasters who rely on Charisma) affected by this spell do not gain any additional bonus spells for the increased Charisma, but the save DCs for spells they cast while under this spell's effect do increase.

EAGLE'S SPLENDOR, MASS

School transmutation; **Level** bard 6, cleric 6, sorcerer/wizard 6

Range close (25 ft. + 5 ft./2 levels)

Target One creature/level, no two of which can be more than 30 ft. apart

This spell functions like *eagle's splendor*, except that it affects multiple creatures.

EARTHQUAKE

School evocation [earth]; **Level** cleric 8, druid 8

Casting Time 1 standard action

Components V, S, DF

Range long (400 ft. + 40 ft./level)

Area 80-ft.-radius spread (S)

Duration 1 round

Saving Throw see text; **Spell Resistance** no

When you cast *earthquake*, an intense but highly localized tremor rips the ground. The powerful shockwave created by this spell knocks creatures down, collapses structures, opens cracks in the ground, and more. The effect lasts for 1 round, during which time creatures on the ground can't move or attack. A spellcaster on the ground must make a concentration check (DC 20 + spell level)

or lose any spell he or she tries to cast. The earthquake affects all terrain, vegetation, structures, and creatures in the area. The specific effect of an *earthquake* spell depends on the nature of the terrain where it is cast.

Cave, Cavern, or Tunnel: The roof collapses, dealing 8d6 points of damage to any creature caught under the cave-in (Reflex DC 15 half) and pinning that creature beneath the rubble (see below). An *earthquake* cast on the roof of a very large cavern could also endanger those outside the actual area but below the falling debris and rubble.

Cliffs: Earthquake causes a cliff to crumble, creating a landslide that travels horizontally as far as it falls vertically. Any creature in the path takes 8d6 points of bludgeoning damage (Reflex DC 15 half) and is pinned beneath the rubble (see below).

Open Ground: Each creature standing in the area must make a DC 15 Reflex save or fall down. Fissures open in the earth, and every creature on the ground has a 25% chance to fall into one (Reflex DC 20 to avoid a fissure). The fissures are 40 feet deep. At the end of the spell, all fissures grind shut. Treat all trapped creatures as if they were in the bury zone of an avalanche, trapped without air (see Chapter 13 for more details).

Structure: Any structure standing on open ground takes 100 points of damage, enough to collapse a typical wooden or masonry building, but not a structure built of stone or reinforced masonry. Hardness does not reduce this damage, nor is it halved as damage dealt to objects normally is. Any creature caught inside a collapsing structure takes 8d6 points of bludgeoning damage (Reflex DC 15 half) and is pinned beneath the rubble (see below).

River, Lake, or Marsh: Fissures open under the water, draining away the water from that area and forming muddy ground. Soggy marsh or swampland becomes quicksand for the duration of the spell, sucking down creatures and structures. Each creature in the area must make a DC 15 Reflex save or sink down in the mud and quicksand. At the end of the spell, the rest of the body of water rushes in to replace the drained water, possibly drowning those caught in the mud.

Pinned Beneath Rubble: Any creature pinned beneath rubble takes 1d6 points of nonlethal damage per minute while pinned. If a pinned character falls unconscious, he or she must make a DC 15 Constitution check or take 1d6 points of lethal damage each minute thereafter until freed or dead.

ELEMENTAL BODY I

School transmutation (polymorph); **Level** sorcerer/wizard 4

Casting Time 1 standard action

Components V, S, M (the element you plan to assume)

Range personal

Target you

Duration 1 min/level (D)

When you cast this spell, you can assume the form of a Small air, earth, fire, or water elemental (see the *Pathfinder RPG Bestiary*). The abilities you gain depend upon the type of elemental into which you change. Elemental abilities based on size, such as burn, vortex, and whirlwind, use the size of the elemental you transform into to determine their effect.

Air elemental: If the form you take is that of a Small air elemental, you gain a +2 size bonus to your Dexterity and a +2 natural armor bonus. You also gain fly 60 feet (perfect), darkvision 60 feet, and the ability to create a whirlwind.

Earth elemental: If the form you take is that of a Small earth elemental, you gain a +2 size bonus to your Strength and a +4 natural armor bonus. You also gain darkvision 60 feet and the ability to earth glide.

Fire elemental: If the form you take is that of a Small fire elemental, you gain a +2 size bonus to your Dexterity and a +2 natural armor bonus. You gain darkvision 60 feet, resist fire 20, vulnerability to cold, and the burn ability.

Water elemental: If the form you take is that of a Small water elemental, you gain a +2 size bonus to your Constitution and a +4 natural armor bonus. You also gain swim 60 feet, darkvision 60 feet, the ability to create a vortex, and the ability to breathe water.

ELEMENTAL BODY II

School transmutation (polymorph); **Level** sorcerer/wizard 5
This spell functions as *elemental body I*, except that it also allows you to assume the form of a Medium air, earth, fire, or water elemental. The abilities you gain depend upon the elemental.

Air elemental: As *elemental body I* except that you gain a +4 size bonus to your Dexterity and a +3 natural armor bonus.

Earth elemental: As *elemental body I* except that you gain a +4 size bonus to your Strength and a +5 natural armor bonus.

Fire elemental: As *elemental body I* except that you gain a +4 size bonus to your Dexterity and a +3 natural armor bonus.

Water elemental: As *elemental body I* except that you gain a +4 size bonus to your Constitution and a +5 natural armor bonus.

ELEMENTAL BODY III

School transmutation (polymorph); **Level** sorcerer/wizard 6
This spell functions as *elemental body II*, except that it also allows you to assume the form of a Large air, earth, fire, or water elemental. The abilities you gain depend upon the type of elemental into which you change. You are also immune to bleed damage, critical hits, and sneak attacks while in elemental form.

Air elemental: As *elemental body I* except that you gain a +2 size bonus to your Strength, +4 size bonus to your Dexterity, and a +4 natural armor bonus.

Earth elemental: As *elemental body I* except that you gain a +6 size bonus to your Strength, a −2 penalty on your Dexterity, and a +2 size bonus to your Constitution, and a +6 natural armor bonus.

Fire elemental: As *elemental body I* except that you gain a +4 size bonus to your Dexterity, a +2 size bonus to your Constitution, and a +4 natural armor bonus.

Water elemental: As *elemental body I* except that you gain a +2 size bonus to your Strength, a −2 penalty on your Dexterity, a +6 size bonus to your Constitution, and a +6 natural armor bonus.

ELEMENTAL BODY IV

School transmutation (polymorph); **Level** sorcerer/wizard 7

This spell functions as *elemental body III*, except that it also allows you to assume the form of a Huge air, earth, fire, or water elemental. The abilities you gain depend upon the type of elemental into which you change. You are also immune to bleed damage, critical hits, and sneak attacks while in elemental form and gain DR 5/—.

Air elemental: As *elemental body I* except that you gain a +4 size bonus to your Strength, +6 size bonus to your Dexterity, and a +4 natural armor bonus. You also gain fly 120 feet (perfect).

Earth elemental: As *elemental body I* except that you gain a +8 size bonus to your Strength, a −2 penalty on your Dexterity, a +4 size bonus to your Constitution, and a +6 natural armor bonus.

Fire elemental: As *elemental body I* except that you gain a +6 size bonus to your Dexterity, a +4 size bonus to your Constitution, and a +4 natural armor bonus.

Water elemental: As *elemental body I* except that you gain a +4 size bonus to your Strength, a −2 penalty on your Dexterity, a +8 size bonus to your Constitution, and a +6 natural armor bonus. You also gain swim 120 feet.

ELEMENTAL SWARM

School conjuration (summoning) [see text]; **Level** druid 9
Casting Time 10 minutes
Components V, S
Range medium (100 ft. + 10 ft./level)
Effect two or more summoned creatures, no two of which can be more than 30 ft. apart
Duration 10 min./level (D)
Saving Throw none; **Spell Resistance** no

This spell opens a portal to an Elemental Plane and summons elementals from it. A druid can choose any plane (Air, Earth, Fire, or Water); a cleric opens a portal to the plane matching his domain.

When the spell is complete, 2d4 Large elementals appear. Ten minutes later, 1d4 Huge elementals appear. Ten minutes after that, one greater elemental appears. Each elemental has maximum hit points per HD. Once these creatures appear, they serve you for the duration of the spell.

The elementals obey you explicitly and never attack you, even if someone else manages to gain control over them. You do not need to concentrate to maintain control over the elementals. You can dismiss them singly or in groups at any time.

When you use a summoning spell to summon an air, earth, fire, or water creature, it is a spell of that type.

ENDURE ELEMENTS

School abjuration; **Level** cleric 1, druid 1, paladin 1, ranger 1, sorcerer/wizard 1
Casting Time 1 standard action
Components V, S
Range touch
Target creature touched
Duration 24 hours
Saving Throw Will negates (harmless); **Spell Resistance** yes (harmless)

A creature protected by *endure elements* suffers no harm from being in a hot or cold environment. It can exist comfortably in conditions between −50 and 140 degrees Fahrenheit without having to make Fortitude saves. The creature's equipment is likewise protected.

Endure elements doesn't provide any protection from fire or cold damage, nor does it protect against other environmental hazards such as smoke, lack of air, and so forth.

ENERGY DRAIN

School necromancy; **Level** cleric 9, sorcerer/wizard 9
Saving Throw Fortitude partial; see text for *enervation*

This spell functions like *enervation*, except that the creature struck gains 2d4 temporary negative levels. Twenty-four hours after gaining them, the subject must make a Fortitude saving throw (DC = *energy drain* spell's save DC) for each negative level. If the save succeeds, that negative level is removed. If it fails, that negative level becomes permanent.

An undead creature struck by the ray gains 2d4 × 5 temporary hit points for 1 hour.

ENERVATION

School necromancy; **Level** sorcerer/wizard 4
Casting Time 1 standard action
Components V, S
Range close (25 ft. + 5 ft./2 levels)
Effect ray of negative energy
Duration instantaneous
Saving Throw none; **Spell Resistance** yes

You point your finger and fire a black ray of negative energy that suppresses the life force of any living creature it strikes. You must make a ranged touch attack to hit. If you hit, the subject gains 1d4 temporary negative levels (see Appendix 1). Negative levels stack.

Assuming the subject survives, it regains lost levels after a number of hours equal to your caster level (maximum 15 hours). Usually, negative levels have a chance of becoming permanent, but the negative levels from *enervation* don't last long enough to do so.

An undead creature struck by the ray gains 1d4 × 5 temporary hit points for 1 hour.

ENLARGE PERSON

School transmutation; **Level** sorcerer/wizard 1
Casting Time 1 round

Components V, S, M (powdered iron)

Range close (25 ft. + 5 ft./2 levels)

Target one humanoid creature

Duration 1 min./level (D)

Saving Throw Fortitude negates; **Spell Resistance** yes

This spell causes instant growth of a humanoid creature, doubling its height and multiplying its weight by 8. This increase changes the creature's size category to the next larger one. The target gains a +2 size bonus to Strength, a –2 size penalty to Dexterity (to a minimum of 1), and a –1 penalty on attack rolls and AC due to its increased size.

A humanoid creature whose size increases to Large has a space of 10 feet and a natural reach of 10 feet. This spell does not change the target's speed.

If insufficient room is available for the desired growth, the creature attains the maximum possible size and may make a Strength check (using its increased Strength) to burst any enclosures in the process. If it fails, it is constrained without harm by the materials enclosing it—the spell cannot be used to crush a creature by increasing its size.

All equipment worn or carried by a creature is similarly enlarged by the spell. Melee weapons affected by this spell deal more damage (see page 145). Other magical properties are not affected by this spell. Any *enlarged* item that leaves an enlarged creature's possession (including a projectile or thrown weapon) instantly returns to its normal size. This means that thrown and projectile weapons deal their normal damage. Magical properties of enlarged items are not increased by this spell.

Multiple magical effects that increase size do not stack.

Enlarge person counters and dispels *reduce person*.

Enlarge person can be made permanent with a *permanency* spell.

ENLARGE PERSON, MASS

School transmutation; **Level** sorcerer/wizard 4

Target One humanoid creature/level, no two of which can be more than 30 ft. apart

This spell functions like *enlarge person*, except that it affects multiple creatures.

ENTANGLE

School transmutation; **Level** druid 1, ranger 1

Casting Time 1 standard action

Components V, S, DF

Range long (400 ft. + 40 ft./level)

Area plants in a 40-ft.-radius spread

Duration 1 min./level (D)

Saving Throw: Reflex partial; see text; **Spell Resistance:** no

This spell causes tall grass, weeds, and other plants to wrap around creatures in the area of effect or those that enter the area. Creatures that fail their save gain the entangled condition. Creatures that make their save can move as normal, but those that remain in the area must save again at the end of your turn. Creatures that move into the area must save immediately. Those that fail must end their

movement and gain the entangled condition. Entangled creatures can attempt to break free as a move action, making a Strength or Escape Artist check. The DC for this check is equal to the DC of the spell. The entire area of effect is considered difficult terrain while the effect lasts.

If the plants in the area are covered in thorns, those in the area take 1 point of damage each time they fail a save against the *entangle* or fail a check made to break free. Other effects, depending on the local plants, might be possible at GM discretion.

ENTHRALL

School enchantment (charm) [language dependent, mind-affecting, sonic]; **Level** bard 2, cleric 2

Casting Time 1 round

Components V, S

Range medium (100 ft. + 10 ft./level)

Targets any number of creatures

Duration 1 hour or less

Saving Throw Will negates; see text; **Spell Resistance** yes

If you have the attention of a group of creatures, you can use this spell to hold them enthralled. To cast the spell, you must speak or sing without interruption for 1 full round. Thereafter, those affected give you their undivided attention, ignoring their surroundings. They are considered to have an attitude of friendly while under the effect of the spell. Any potentially affected creature of a race or religion unfriendly to yours gets a +4 bonus on the saving throw.

A target with 4 or more HD or with a Wisdom score of 16 or higher remains aware of its surroundings and has an attitude of indifferent. It gains a new saving throw if it witnesses actions that it opposes.

The effect lasts as long as you speak or sing, to a maximum of 1 hour. Those enthralled by your words take no action while you speak or sing and for 1d3 rounds thereafter while they discuss the topic or performance. Those entering the area during the performance must also successfully save or become enthralled. The speech ends (but the 1d3-round delay still applies) if you lose concentration or do anything other than speak or sing.

If those not enthralled have unfriendly or hostile attitudes toward you, they can collectively make a Charisma check to try to end the spell by jeering and heckling. For this check, use the Charisma bonus of the creature with the highest Charisma in the group; others may make Charisma checks to assist. The heckling ends the spell if this check result beats your Charisma check result. Only one such challenge is allowed per use of the spell.

If any member of the audience is attacked or subjected to some other overtly hostile act, the spell ends and the previously enthralled members become immediately unfriendly toward you. Each creature with 4 or more HD or with a Wisdom score of 16 or higher becomes hostile.

ENTROPIC SHIELD

School abjuration; **Level** cleric 1

Casting Time 1 standard action

Components V, S
Range personal
Target you
Duration 1 min./level (D)

A magical field appears around you, glowing with a chaotic blast of multicolored hues. This field deflects incoming arrows, rays, and other ranged attacks. Each ranged attack directed at you for which the attacker must make an attack roll has a 20% miss chance (similar to the effects of concealment). Other attacks that simply work at a distance are not affected.

ERASE

School transmutation; **Level** bard 1, sorcerer/wizard 1
Casting Time 1 standard action
Components V, S
Range close (25 ft. + 5 ft./2 levels)
Target one scroll or two pages
Duration instantaneous
Saving Throw see text; **Spell Resistance** no

Erase removes writings of either magical or mundane nature from a scroll or from one or two pages of paper, parchment, or similar surfaces. With this spell, you can remove *explosive runes*, a *glyph of warding*, a *sepia snake sigil*, or an *arcane mark*, but not *illusory script* or a *symbol* spell. Nonmagical writing is automatically erased if you touch it and no one else is holding it. Otherwise, the chance of erasing nonmagical writing is 90%.

Magic writing must be touched to be erased, and you also must succeed on a caster level check (1d20 + caster level) against DC 15. A natural 1 is always a failure on this check. If you fail to erase *explosive runes*, a *glyph of warding*, or a *sepia snake sigil*, you accidentally activate that writing instead.

ETHEREAL JAUNT

School transmutation; **Level** cleric 7, sorcerer/wizard 7
Casting Time 1 standard action
Components V, S
Range personal
Target you
Duration 1 round/level (D)

You become ethereal, along with your equipment. For the duration of the spell, you are in the Ethereal Plane, which overlaps the Material Plane. When the spell expires, you return to material existence.

An ethereal creature is invisible, insubstantial, and capable of moving in any direction, even up or down, albeit at half normal speed. As an insubstantial creature, you can move through solid objects, including living creatures. An ethereal creature can see and hear on the Material Plane, but everything looks gray and ephemeral. Sight and hearing onto the Material Plane are limited to 60 feet.

Force effects and abjurations affect an ethereal creature normally. Their effects extend onto the Ethereal Plane from the Material Plane, but not vice versa. An ethereal creature can't attack material creatures, and spells you cast while ethereal affect only other ethereal things. Certain material creatures or objects have attacks or effects that work on the Ethereal Plane.

Treat other ethereal creatures and ethereal objects as if they were material.

If you end the spell and become material while inside a material object (such as a solid wall), you are shunted off to the nearest open space and take 1d6 points of damage per 5 feet that you so travel.

ETHEREALNESS

School transmutation; **Level** cleric 9, sorcerer/wizard 9
Range touch; see text
Targets you and one other touched creature per three levels
Duration 1 min./level (D)
Spell Resistance yes

This spell functions like *ethereal jaunt*, except that you and other willing creatures joined by linked hands (along with their equipment) become ethereal. Besides yourself, you can bring one creature per three caster levels to the Ethereal Plane. Once ethereal, the subjects need not stay together.

When the spell expires, all affected creatures on the Ethereal Plane return to material existence.

EXPEDITIOUS RETREAT

School transmutation; **Level** bard 1, sorcerer/wizard 1
Casting Time 1 standard action
Components V, S
Range personal
Target you
Duration 1 min./level (D)

This spell increases your base land speed by 30 feet. This adjustment is treated as an enhancement bonus. There is no effect on other modes of movement, such as burrow, climb, fly, or swim. As with any effect that increases your speed, this spell affects your jumping distance (see the Acrobatics skill).

EXPLOSIVE RUNES

School abjuration [force]; **Level** sorcerer/wizard 3
Casting Time 1 standard action
Components V, S
Range touch
Target one touched object weighing no more than 10 lbs.
Duration permanent until discharged (D)
Saving Throw see text; **Spell Resistance** yes

You trace mystic runes upon a book, map, scroll, or similar object bearing written information. The *explosive runes* detonate when read, dealing 6d6 points of force damage. Anyone next to the *explosive runes* (close enough to read them) takes the full damage with no saving throw; any other creature within 10 feet of the *explosive runes* is entitled to a Reflex save for half damage. The object on which the *explosive runes* were written also takes full damage (no saving throw).

You and any characters you specifically instruct can read the protected writing without triggering the *explosive runes*. Likewise,

you can remove the *explosive runes* whenever desired. Another creature can remove them with a successful *dispel magic* or *erase* spell, but attempting to dispel or erase the *explosive runes* and failing to do so triggers the explosion.

Magic traps such as *explosive runes* are hard to detect and disable. A character with the trapfinding class feature (only) can use Disable Device to thwart *explosive runes*. The DC to find magic traps using Perception and to disable them is 25 + spell level, or 28 for *explosive runes*.

EYEBITE

School necromancy; **Level** bard 6, sorcerer/wizard 6

Casting Time 1 standard action

Components V, S

Range close (25 ft. + 5 ft./2 levels)

Target one living creature

Duration 1 round/level

Saving Throw: Fortitude negates; **Spell Resistance:** yes

Each round, you can target a single living creature, striking it with waves of power. Depending on the target's HD, this attack has as many as three effects.

HD	Effect
10 or more	Sickened
5–9	Panicked, sickened
4 or less	Comatose, panicked, sickened

The effects are cumulative and concurrent.

Sickened: Sudden pain and fever sweeps over the subject's body. A creature affected by this spell remains sickened for 10 minutes per caster level. The effects cannot be negated by a *remove disease* or *heal* spell, but a *remove curse* is effective.

Panicked: The subject becomes panicked for 1d4 rounds. Even after the panic ends, the creature remains shaken for 10 minutes per caster level, and it automatically becomes panicked again if it comes within sight of you during that time. This is a fear effect.

Comatose: The subject falls into a catatonic coma for 10 minutes per caster level. During this time, it cannot be awakened by any means short of dispelling the effect. This is not a *sleep* effect, and thus elves are not immune to it.

You must spend a swift action each round after the first to target a foe.

FABRICATE

School transmutation; **Level** sorcerer/wizard 5

Casting Time see text

Components V, S, M (the original material, which costs the same amount as the raw materials required to craft the item to be created)

Range close (25 ft. + 5 ft./2 levels)

Target up to 10 cu. ft./level; see text

Duration instantaneous

Saving Throw none; **Spell Resistance** no

You convert material of one sort into a product that is of the same material. Creatures or magic items cannot be created or transmuted by the *fabricate* spell. The quality of items made by this spell is commensurate with the quality of material used as the basis for the new fabrication. If you work with a mineral, the target is reduced to 1 cubic foot per level instead of 10 cubic feet.

You must make an appropriate Craft check to fabricate articles requiring a high degree of craftsmanship.

Casting requires 1 round per 10 cubic feet of material to be affected by the spell.

FAERIE FIRE

School evocation [light]; **Level** druid 1

Casting Time 1 standard action

Components V, S, DF

Range long (400 ft. + 40 ft./level)

Area creatures and objects within a 5-ft.-radius burst

Duration 1 min./level (D)

Saving Throw none; **Spell Resistance** yes

A pale glow surrounds and outlines the subjects. Outlined subjects shed light as candles. Creatures outlined by *faerie fire* take a –20 penalty on all Stealth checks. Outlined creatures do not benefit from the concealment normally provided by darkness (though a 2nd-level or higher magical *darkness* effect functions normally), *blur*, *displacement*, *invisibility*, or similar effects. The light is too dim to have any special effect on undead or dark-dwelling creatures vulnerable to light. The *faerie fire* can be blue, green, or violet, according to your choice at the time of casting. The *faerie fire* does not cause any harm to the objects or creatures thus outlined.

FALSE LIFE

School necromancy; **Level** sorcerer/wizard 2

Casting Time 1 standard action

Components V, S, M (a drop of blood)

Range personal

Target you

Duration 1 hour/level or until discharged; see text

You harness the power of unlife to grant yourself a limited ability to avoid death. While this spell is in effect, you gain temporary hit points equal to 1d10 + 1 per caster level (maximum +10).

FALSE VISION

School illusion (glamer); **Level** bard 5, sorcerer/wizard 5

Casting Time 1 standard action

Components V, S, M (crushed jade worth 250 gp)

Range touch

Area 40-ft.-radius emanation

Duration 1 hour/level (D)

Saving Throw none; **Spell Resistance** no

This spell creates a subtle illusion, causing any divination (scrying) spell used to view anything within the area of this spell to instead receive a false image (as the *major image* spell), as defined by you at the time of casting. As long as the duration lasts, you can concentrate to change the image as desired. While you aren't concentrating, the image remains static.

FEAR

School necromancy [fear, mind-affecting]; **Level** bard 3, sorcerer/wizard 4
Casting Time 1 standard action
Components V, S, M (the heart of a hen or a white feather)
Range 30 ft.
Area cone-shaped burst
Duration 1 round/level or 1 round; see text
Saving Throw Will partial; **Spell Resistance** yes

An invisible cone of terror causes each living creature in the area to become panicked unless it succeeds on a Will save. If cornered, a panicked creature begins cowering. If the Will save succeeds, the creature is shaken for 1 round.

FEATHER FALL

School transmutation; **Level** bard 1, sorcerer/wizard 1
Casting Time 1 immediate action
Components V
Range close (25 ft. + 5 ft./2 levels)
Targets one Medium or smaller freefalling object or creature/level, no two of which may be more than 20 ft. apart
Duration until landing or 1 round/level
Saving Throw Will negates (harmless) or Will negates (object); **Spell Resistance** yes (object)

The affected creatures or objects fall slowly. *Feather fall* instantly changes the rate at which the targets fall to a mere 60 feet per round (equivalent to the end of a fall from a few feet), and the subjects take no damage upon landing while the spell is in effect. When the spell duration expires, a normal rate of falling resumes.

The spell affects one or more Medium or smaller creatures (including gear and carried objects up to each creature's maximum load) or objects, or the equivalent in larger creatures: a Large creature or object counts as two Medium creatures or objects, a Huge creature or object counts as four Medium creatures or objects, and so forth.

This spell has no special effect on ranged weapons unless they are falling quite a distance. If the spell is cast on a falling item, the object does half normal damage based on its weight, with no bonus for the height of the drop.

Feather fall works only upon free-falling objects. It does not affect a sword blow or a charging or flying creature.

FEEBLEMIND

School enchantment (compulsion) [mind-affecting]; **Level** sorcerer/wizard 5
Casting Time 1 standard action
Components V, S, M (a handful of clay, crystal, or glass spheres)
Range medium (100 ft. + 10 ft./level)
Target one creature
Duration instantaneous
Saving Throw Will negates; see text; **Spell Resistance** yes

Target creature's Intelligence and Charisma scores each drop to 1. The affected creature is unable to use Intelligence- or Charisma-based skills, cast spells, understand language, or communicate coherently. Still, it knows who its friends are and can follow them and even protect them. The subject remains in this state until a *heal*, *limited wish*, *miracle*, or *wish* spell is used to cancel the effect of the *feeblemind*. A creature that can cast arcane spells, such as a sorcerer or a wizard, takes a –4 penalty on its saving throw.

FIND THE PATH

School divination; **Level** bard 6, cleric 6, druid 6
Casting Time 3 rounds
Components V, S, F (a set of divination counters)
Range personal or touch
Target you or creature touched
Duration 10 min./level
Saving Throw none or Will negates (harmless); **Spell Resistance** no or yes (harmless)

The recipient of this spell can find the shortest, most direct physical route to a prominent specified destination, such as a city, keep, lake, or dungeon. The locale can be outdoors or underground, as long as it is prominent. For example, a hunter's cabin is not prominent enough, but a logging camp is. *Find the path* works with respect to locations, not objects or creatures at a locale. The location must be on the same plane as the subject at the time of casting.

The spell enables the subject to sense the correct direction that will eventually lead it to its destination, indicating at appropriate times the exact path to follow or physical actions to take. For example, the spell enables the subject to sense what cavern corridor to take when a choice presents itself. The spell ends when the destination is reached or the duration expires, whichever comes first. *Find the path* can be used to remove the subject and its companions from the effect of a *maze* spell in a single round, specifying the destination as "outside the maze." This divination is keyed to the recipient, not its companions, and its effect does not predict or allow for the actions of creatures (including guardians) who might take action to oppose the caster as he follows the path revealed by this spell.

FIND TRAPS

School divination; **Level** cleric 2
Casting Time 1 standard action
Components V, S
Range personal
Target you
Duration 1 min./level

You gain intuitive insight into the workings of traps. You gain an insight bonus equal to 1/2 your caster level (maximum +10) on Perception checks made to find traps while the spell is in effect. You receive a check to notice traps within 10 feet of you, even if

you are not actively searching for them. Note that *find traps* grants no ability to disable the traps that you may find.

FINGER OF DEATH

School necromancy [death]; **Level** druid 8, sorcerer/wizard 7
Casting Time 1 standard action
Components V, S
Range close (25 ft. + 5 ft./2 levels)
Target one creature
Duration instantaneous
Saving Throw Fortitude partial; **Spell Resistance** yes

This spell instantly delivers 10 points of damage per caster level. If the target's Fortitude saving throw succeeds, it instead takes 3d6 points of damage + 1 point per caster level. The subject might die from damage even if it succeeds on its saving throw.

FIRE SEEDS

School conjuration (creation) [fire]; **Level** druid 6
Casting Time 1 standard action
Components V, S, M (acorns or holly berries)
Range touch
Targets up to four acorns or up to eight holly berries
Duration 10 min./level or until used
Saving Throw none or Reflex half; see text; **Spell Resistance** no

Depending on the version of *fire seeds* you choose, you turn acorns into splash weapons that you or another character can throw, or you turn holly berries into bombs that you can detonate on command.

Acorn Grenades: As many as four acorns turn into special thrown splash weapons. An acorn grenade has a range increment of 20 feet. A ranged touch attack roll is required to strike the intended target. Together, the acorns are capable of dealing 1d4 points of fire damage per caster level (maximum 20d4) divided among the acorns as you wish. No acorn can deal more than 10d4 points of damage.

Each acorn grenade explodes upon striking any hard surface. In addition to its regular fire damage, all creatures adjacent to the explosion take 1 point of fire damage per die of the explosion. This explosion of fire ignites any combustible materials adjacent to the target.

Holly Berry Bombs: You turn as many as eight holly berries into special bombs. The holly berries are usually placed by hand, since they are too light to make effective thrown weapons (they can be tossed only 5 feet). If you are within 200 feet and speak a word of command, each berry instantly bursts into flame, causing 1d8 points of fire damage + 1 point per caster level to every creature in a 5-foot-radius burst and igniting any combustible materials within 5 feet. A creature in the area that makes a successful Reflex saving throw takes only half damage.

FIRE SHIELD

School evocation [fire or cold]; **Level** sorcerer/wizard 4
Casting Time 1 standard action
Components V, S, M (phosphorus for the *warm shield*; a firefly or glowworm for the *chill shield*)
Range personal
Target you
Duration 1 round/level (D)

This spell wreathes you in flame and causes damage to each creature that attacks you in melee. The flames also protect you from either cold-based or fire-based attacks, depending on if you choose cool or warm flames for your *fire shield*.

Any creature striking you with its body or a handheld weapon deals normal damage, but at the same time the attacker takes 1d6 points of damage + 1 point per caster level (maximum +15). This damage is either cold damage (if you choose a *chill shield*) or fire damage (if you choose a *warm shield*). If the attacker has spell resistance, it applies to this effect. Creatures wielding melee weapons with reach are not subject to this damage if they attack you.

When casting this spell, you appear to immolate yourself, but the flames are thin and wispy, increasing the light level within 10 feet by one step, up to normal light. The color of the flames is blue or green if the *chill shield* is cast, violet or red if the *warm shield* is employed. The special powers of each version are as follows.

Chill Shield: The flames are cool to the touch. You take only half damage from fire-based attacks. If such an attack allows a Reflex save for half damage, you take no damage on a successful saving throw.

Warm Shield: The flames are warm to the touch. You take only half damage from cold-based attacks. If such an attack allows a Reflex save for half damage, you take no damage on a successful saving throw.

FIRE STORM

School evocation [fire]; **Level** cleric 8, druid 7
Casting Time 1 standard action
Components V, S
Range medium (100 ft. + 10 ft./level)
Area two 10-ft. cubes per level (S)
Duration instantaneous
Saving Throw Reflex half; **Spell Resistance** yes

When a *fire storm* spell is cast, the whole area is shot through with sheets of roaring flame. The raging flames do not harm natural vegetation, ground cover, or any plant creatures in the area that you wish to exclude from damage. Any other creature within the area takes 1d6 points of fire damage per caster level (maximum 20d6). Creatures that fail their Reflex save catch on fire, taking 4d6 points of fire damage each round until the flames are extinguished. Extinguishing the flames is a full-round action that requires a DC 20 Reflex save.

FIRE TRAP

School abjuration [fire]; **Level** druid 2, sorcerer/wizard 4
Casting Time 10 minutes
Components V, S, M (gold dust worth 25 gp)
Range touch
Target object touched

Duration permanent until discharged (D)
Saving Throw Reflex half; see text; **Spell Resistance** yes

Fire trap creates a fiery explosion when an intruder opens the item that the trap protects. A *fire trap* spell can ward any object that can be opened and closed.

When casting *fire trap*, you select a point on the object as the spell's center. When someone other than you opens the object, a fiery explosion fills the area within a 5-foot radius around the spell's center. The flames deal 1d4 points of fire damage + 1 point per caster level (maximum +20). The item protected by the trap is not harmed by this explosion.

A fire-trapped item cannot have a second closure or warding spell placed on it. A *knock* spell does not bypass a *fire trap*. An unsuccessful *dispel magic* spell does not detonate the spell. Underwater, this ward deals half damage and creates a large cloud of steam.

You can use the fire-trapped object without discharging it, as can any individual to whom the object was specifically attuned when cast. Attuning a fire-trapped object to an individual usually involves setting a password that you can share with friends.

Magic traps such as *fire trap* are hard to detect and disable. A character with trapfinding can use the Perception skill to find a *fire trap* and Disable Device to thwart it. The DC in each case is 25 + spell level (DC 27 for a druid's *fire trap* or DC 29 for the arcane version).

FIREBALL

School evocation [fire]; **Level** sorcerer/wizard 3
Casting Time 1 standard action
Components V, S, M (a ball of bat guano and sulfur)
Range long (400 ft. + 40 ft./level)
Area 20-ft.-radius spread
Duration instantaneous
Saving Throw Reflex half; **Spell Resistance** yes

A *fireball* spell generates a searing explosion of flame that detonates with a low roar and deals 1d6 points of fire damage per caster level (maximum 10d6) to every creature within the area. Unattended objects also take this damage. The explosion creates almost no pressure.

You point your finger and determine the range (distance and height) at which the *fireball* is to burst. A glowing, pea-sized bead streaks from the pointing digit and, unless it impacts upon a material body or solid barrier prior to attaining the prescribed range, blossoms into the *fireball* at that point. An early impact results in an early detonation. If you attempt to send the bead through a narrow passage, such as through an arrow slit, you must "hit" the opening with a ranged touch attack, or else the bead strikes the barrier and detonates prematurely.

The *fireball* sets fire to combustibles and damages objects in the area. It can melt metals with low melting points, such as lead, gold, copper, silver, and bronze. If the damage caused to an interposing barrier shatters or breaks through it, the *fireball* may continue beyond the barrier if the area permits; otherwise it stops at the barrier just as any other spell effect does.

FLAME ARROW

School transmutation [fire]; **Level** sorcerer/wizard 3
Casting Time 1 standard action
Components V, S, M (a drop of oil and a small piece of flint)
Range close (25 ft. + 5 ft./2 levels)
Target fifty projectiles, all of which must be together at the time of casting
Duration 10 min./level
Saving Throw none; **Spell Resistance** no

This spell allows you to turn ammunition (such as arrows, crossbow bolts, shuriken, and sling stones) into fiery projectiles. Each piece of ammunition deals an extra 1d6 points of fire damage to any target it hits. A flaming projectile can easily ignite a flammable object or structure, but it won't ignite a creature it strikes.

FLAME BLADE

School evocation [fire]; **Level** druid 2
Casting Time 1 standard action
Components V, S, DF
Range 0 ft.
Effect sword-like beam
Duration 1 min./level (D)
Saving Throw none; **Spell Resistance** yes

A 3-foot-long, blazing beam of red-hot fire springs forth from your hand. You wield this blade-like beam as if it were a scimitar. Attacks with the *flame blade* are melee touch attacks. The blade deals 1d8 points of fire damage + 1 point per two caster levels (maximum +10). Since the blade is immaterial, your Strength modifier does not apply to the damage. A *flame blade* can ignite combustible materials such as parchment, straw, dry sticks, and cloth.

FLAME STRIKE

School evocation [fire]; **Level** cleric 5, druid 4
Casting Time 1 standard action
Components V, S, DF
Range medium (100 ft. + 10 ft./level)
Area cylinder (10-ft. radius, 40-ft. high)
Duration instantaneous
Saving Throw Reflex half; **Spell Resistance** yes

A *flame strike* evokes a vertical column of divine fire. The spell deals 1d6 points of damage per caster level (maximum 15d6). Half the damage is fire damage, but the other half results directly from divine power and is therefore not subject to being reduced by resistance to fire-based attacks.

FLAMING SPHERE

School evocation [fire]; **Level** druid 2, sorcerer/wizard 2
Casting Time 1 standard action
Components V, S, M/DF (tallow, brimstone, and powdered iron)
Range medium (100 ft. + 10 ft./level)
Effect 5-ft.-diameter sphere

Duration 1 round/level

Saving Throw Reflex negates; **Spell Resistance** yes

A burning globe of fire rolls in whichever direction you point and burns those it strikes. It moves 30 feet per round. As part of this movement, it can ascend or jump up to 30 feet to strike a target. If it enters a space with a creature, it stops moving for the round and deals 3d6 points of fire damage to that creature, though a successful Reflex save negates that damage. A *flaming sphere* rolls over barriers less than 4 feet tall. It ignites flammable substances it touches and illuminates the same area as a torch would.

The sphere moves as long as you actively direct it (a move action for you); otherwise, it merely stays at rest and burns. It can be extinguished by any means that would put out a normal fire of its size. The surface of the sphere has a spongy, yielding consistency and so does not cause damage except by its flame. It cannot push aside unwilling creatures or batter down large obstacles. A *flaming sphere* winks out if it exceeds the spell's range.

FLARE

School evocation [light]; **Level** bard 0, druid 0, sorcerer/wizard 0

Casting Time 1 standard action

Components V

Range close (25 ft. + 5 ft./2 levels)

Effect burst of light

Duration instantaneous

Saving Throw Fortitude negates; **Spell Resistance** yes

This cantrip creates a burst of light. If you cause the light to burst in front of a single creature, that creature is dazzled for 1 minute unless it makes a successful Fortitude save. Sightless creatures, as well as creatures already dazzled, are not affected by *flare*.

FLESH TO STONE

School transmutation; **Level** sorcerer/wizard 6

Casting Time 1 standard action

Components V, S, M (lime, water, and earth)

Range medium (100 ft. + 10 ft./level)

Target one creature

Duration instantaneous

Saving Throw Fortitude negates; **Spell Resistance** yes

The subject, along with all its carried gear, turns into a mindless, inert statue. If the statue resulting from this spell is broken or damaged, the subject (if ever returned to its original state) has similar damage or deformities. The creature is not dead, but it does not seem to be alive either when viewed with spells such as *deathwatch*.

Only creatures made of flesh are affected by this spell.

FLOATING DISK

School evocation [force]; **Level** sorcerer/wizard 1

Casting Time 1 standard action

Components V, S, M (a drop of mercury)

Range close (25 ft. + 5 ft./2 levels)

Effect 3-ft.-diameter disk of force

Duration 1 hour/level

Saving Throw none; **Spell Resistance** no

You create a slightly concave, circular plane of force that follows you about and carries loads for you. The disk is 3 feet in diameter and 1 inch deep at its center. It can hold 100 pounds of weight per caster level. If used to transport a liquid, its capacity is 2 gallons. The disk floats approximately 3 feet above the ground at all times and remains level. It floats along horizontally within spell range and will accompany you at a rate of no more than your normal speed each round. If not otherwise directed, it maintains a constant interval of 5 feet between itself and you. The disk winks out of existence when the spell duration expires. The disk also winks out if you move beyond its range or try to take the disk more than 3 feet away from the surface beneath it. When the disk winks out, whatever it was supporting falls to the surface beneath it.

FLY

School transmutation; **Level** sorcerer/wizard 3

Casting Time 1 standard action

Components V, S, F (a wing feather)

Range touch

Target creature touched

Duration 1 min./level

Saving Throw Will negates (harmless); **Spell Resistance** yes (harmless)

The subject can fly at a speed of 60 feet (or 40 feet if it wears medium or heavy armor, or if it carries a medium or heavy load). It can ascend at half speed and descend at double speed, and its maneuverability is good. Using a *fly* spell requires only as much concentration as walking, so the subject can attack or cast spells normally. The subject of a *fly* spell can charge but not run, and it cannot carry aloft more weight than its maximum load, plus any armor it wears. The subject gains a bonus on Fly skill checks equal to 1/2 your caster level.

Should the spell duration expire while the subject is still aloft, the magic fails slowly. The subject floats downward 60 feet per round for 1d6 rounds. If it reaches the ground in that amount of time, it lands safely. If not, it falls the rest of the distance, taking 1d6 points of damage per 10 feet of fall. Since dispelling a spell effectively ends it, the subject also descends safely in this way if the *fly* spell is dispelled, but not if it is negated by an *antimagic field*.

FOG CLOUD

School conjuration (creation); **Level** druid 2, sorcerer/wizard 2

Casting Time 1 standard action

Components V, S

Range medium (100 ft. + 10 ft. level)

Effect fog spreads in 20-ft. radius

Duration 10 min./level

Saving Throw none; **Spell Resistance** no

A bank of fog billows out from the point you designate. The fog obscures all sight, including darkvision, beyond 5 feet. A creature within 5 feet has concealment (attacks have a 20% miss chance). Creatures farther away have total concealment (50% miss chance, and the attacker can't use sight to locate the target).

A moderate wind (11+ mph) disperses the fog in 4 rounds; a strong wind (21+ mph) disperses the fog in 1 round.

The spell does not function underwater.

FORBIDDANCE

School abjuration; **Level** cleric 6
Casting Time 6 rounds
Components V, S, M (holy water and incense worth 1,500 gp, plus 1,500 gp per 60-foot cube), DF
Range medium (100 ft. + 10 ft./level)
Area 60-ft. cube/level (S)
Duration permanent
Saving Throw see text; **Spell Resistance** yes

Forbiddance seals an area against all planar travel into or within it. This includes all teleportation spells (such as *dimension door* and *teleport)*, plane shifting, astral travel, ethereal travel, and all summoning spells. Such effects simply fail automatically.

In addition, it damages entering creatures whose alignments are different from yours. The effect on those attempting to enter the warded area is based on their alignment relative to yours (see below). A creature inside the area when the spell is cast takes no damage unless it exits the area and attempts to reenter, at which time it is affected as normal.

Alignments identical: No effect. The creature may enter the area freely (although not by planar travel).

Alignments different with respect to either law/chaos or good/evil: The creature takes 6d6 points of damage. A successful Will save halves the damage, and spell resistance applies.

Alignments different with respect to both law/chaos and good/evil: The creature takes 12d6 points of damage. A successful Will save halves the damage, and spell resistance applies.

At your option, the abjuration can include a password, in which case creatures of alignments different from yours can avoid the damage by speaking the password as they enter the area. You must select this option (and the password) at the time of casting. Adding a password requires the burning of additional rare incenses worth at least 1,000 gp, plus 1,000 gp per 60-foot cube.

Dispel magic does not dispel a *forbiddance* effect unless the dispeller's level is at least as high as your caster level.

You can't have multiple overlapping *forbiddance* effects. In such a case, the more recent effect stops at the boundary of the older effect.

FORCECAGE

School evocation [force]; **Level** sorcerer/wizard 7
Casting Time 1 standard action
Components V, S, M (ruby dust worth 500 gp)
Range close (25 ft. + 5 ft./2 levels)
Area barred cage (20-ft. cube) or windowless cell (10-ft. cube)
Duration 1 round/level (D)
Saving Throw Reflex negates; **Spell Resistance** no

This spell creates an immobile, invisible cubical prison composed of either bars of force or solid walls of force (your choice).

Creatures within the area are caught and contained unless they are too big to fit inside, in which case the spell automatically fails. Teleportation and other forms of astral travel provide a means of escape, but the force walls or bars extend into the Ethereal Plane, blocking ethereal travel.

Like a *wall of force*, a *forcecage* resists *dispel magic*, although a *mage's disjunction* still functions. The walls of a *forcecage* can be damaged by spells as normal, except for *disintegrate*, which automatically destroys it. The walls of a *forcecage* can be damaged by weapons and supernatural abilities, but they have a Hardness of 30 and a number of hit points equal to 20 per caster level. Contact with a *sphere of annihilation* or *rod of cancellation* instantly destroys a *forcecage*.

Barred Cage: This version of the spell produces a 20-foot cube made of bands of force (similar to a *wall of force* spell) for bars. The bands are a half-inch wide, with half-inch gaps between them. Any creature capable of passing through such a small space can escape; others are confined within the barred cage. You can't attack a creature in a barred cage with a weapon unless the weapon can fit between the gaps. Even against such weapons (including arrows and similar ranged attacks), a creature in the barred cage has cover. All spells and breath weapons can pass through the gaps in the bars.

Windowless Cell: This version of the spell produces a 10-foot cube with no way in and no way out. Solid walls of force form its six sides.

FORCEFUL HAND

School evocation [force]; **Level** sorcerer/wizard 6

This spell functions as *interposing hand*, except that it can also pursue and bull rush one opponent you select. The *forceful hand* gets one bull rush attack per round. This attack does not provoke an attack of opportunity. Its CMB for bull rush checks uses your caster level in place of its base attack bonus, with a +8 bonus for its Strength score (27), and a +1 bonus for being Large. The hand always moves with the opponent to push them back as far as possible. It has no movement limit for this purpose. Directing the spell to a new target is a move action. *Forceful hand* prevents the opponent from moving closer to you without first succeeding on a bull rush attack, moving both the *forceful* hand and the target closer to you. The *forceful hand* can instead be directed to interpose itself, as *interposing hand* does.

FORESIGHT

School divination; **Level** druid 9, sorcerer/wizard 9
Casting Time 1 standard action
Components V, S, M/DF (a hummingbird's feather)
Range personal or touch
Target see text
Duration 10 min./level
Saving Throw none or Will negates (harmless); **Spell Resistance** no or yes (harmless)

This spell grants you a powerful sixth sense in relation to yourself

or another. Once *foresight* is cast, you receive instantaneous warnings of impending danger or harm to the subject of the spell. You are never surprised or flat-footed. In addition, the spell gives you a general idea of what action you might take to best protect yourself and gives you a +2 insight bonus to AC and on Reflex saves. This insight bonus is lost whenever you would lose a Dexterity bonus to AC.

When another creature is the subject of the spell, you receive warnings about that creature. You must communicate what you learn to the other creature for the warning to be useful, and the creature can be caught unprepared in the absence of such a warning. Shouting a warning, yanking a person back, and even telepathically communicating (via an appropriate spell) can all be accomplished before some danger befalls the subject, provided you act on the warning without delay. The subject, however, does not gain the insight bonus to AC and Reflex saves.

FORM OF THE DRAGON I

School transmutation (polymorph); **Level** sorcerer/wizard 6
Casting Time 1 standard action
Components V, S, M (a scale of the dragon type you plan to assume)
Range personal
Target you
Duration 1 min./level (D)
Saving Throw see text; **Spell Resistance** no
You become a Medium chromatic or metallic dragon (see the *Pathfinder RPG Bestiary*). You gain a +4 size bonus to Strength, a +2 size bonus to Constitution, a +4 natural armor bonus, fly 60 feet (poor), darkvision 60 feet, a breath weapon, and resistance to one element. You also gain one bite (1d8), two claws (1d6), and two wing attacks (1d4). Your breath weapon and resistance depend on the type of dragon. You can only use the breath weapon once per casting of this spell. All breath weapons deal 6d8 points of damage and allow a Reflex save for half damage. In addition, some of the dragon types grant additional abilities, as noted below.

Black dragon: 60-foot line of acid, resist acid 20, swim 60 feet
Blue dragon: 60-foot line of electricity, resist electricity 20, burrow 20 feet
Green dragon: 30-foot cone of acid, resist acid 20, swim 40 feet
Red dragon: 30-foot cone of fire, resist fire 30, vulnerability to cold
White dragon: 30-foot cone of cold, resist cold 20, swim 60 feet, vulnerability to fire
Brass dragon: 60-foot line of fire, resist fire 20, burrow 30 feet, vulnerability to cold
Bronze dragon: 60-foot line of electricity, resist electricity 20, swim 60 feet
Copper dragon: 60-foot line of acid, resist acid 20, *spider climb* (always active)
Gold dragon: 30-foot cone of fire, resist fire 20, swim 60 feet
Silver dragon: 30-foot cone of cold, resist cold 30, vulnerability to fire

FORM OF THE DRAGON II

School transmutation (polymorph); **Level** sorcerer/wizard 7
This spell functions as *form of the dragon I* except that it also allows you to assume the form of a Large chromatic or metallic dragon. You gain the following abilities: a +6 size bonus to Strength, a +4 size bonus to Constitution, a +6 natural armor bonus, fly 90 feet (poor), darkvision 60 feet, a breath weapon, DR 5/magic, and resistance to one element. You also gain one bite (2d6), two claws (1d8), two wing attacks (1d6), and one tail slap attack (1d8). You can only use the breath weapon twice per casting of this spell, and you must wait 1d4 rounds between uses. All breath weapons deal 8d8 points of damage and allow a Reflex save for half damage. Line breath weapons increase to 80-foot lines and cones increase to 40-foot cones.

FORM OF THE DRAGON III

School transmutation (polymorph); **Level** sorcerer/wizard 8
This spell functions as *form of the dragon II* save that it also allows you to take the form of a Huge chromatic or metallic dragon. You gain the following abilities: a +10 size bonus to Strength, a +8 size bonus to Constitution, a +8 natural armor bonus, fly 120 feet (poor), blindsense 60 feet, darkvision 120 feet, a breath weapon, DR 10/magic, frightful presence (DC equal to the DC for this spell), and immunity to one element (of the same type *form of the dragon I* grants resistance to). You also gain one bite (2d8), two claws (2d6), two wing attacks (1d8), and one tail slap attack (2d6). You can use the breath weapon as often as you like, but you must wait 1d4 rounds between uses. All breath weapons deal 12d8 points of damage and allow a Reflex save for half damage. Line breath weapons increase to 100-foot lines and cones increase to 50-foot cones.

FOX'S CUNNING

School transmutation; **Level** bard 2, sorcerer/wizard 2
Casting Time 1 standard action
Components V, S, M/DF (hairs or dung from a fox)
Range touch
Target creature touched
Duration 1 min./level
Saving Throw Will negates (harmless); **Spell Resistance** yes
The target becomes smarter. The spell grants a +4 enhancement bonus to Intelligence, adding the usual benefits to Intelligence-based skill checks and other uses of the Intelligence modifier. Wizards (and other spellcasters who rely on Intelligence) affected by this spell do not gain any additional bonus spells for the increased Intelligence, but the save DCs for spells they cast while under this spell's effect do increase. This spell doesn't grant extra skill ranks.

FOX'S CUNNING, MASS

School transmutation; **Level** bard 6, sorcerer/wizard 6
Range close (25 ft. + 5 ft./2 levels)

Target one creature/level, no two of which can be more than 30 ft. apart

This spell functions like *fox's cunning*, except that it affects multiple creatures.

FREEDOM

School abjuration; **Level** sorcerer/wizard 9

Casting Time 1 standard action

Components V, S

Range close (25 ft. + 5 ft./2 levels) or see text

Target one creature

Duration instantaneous

Saving Throw Will negates (harmless); **Spell Resistance** yes

The subject is freed from spells and effects that restrict movement, including *binding*, *entangle*, grappling, *imprisonment*, *maze*, paralysis, petrification, pinning, *sleep*, *slow*, stunning, *temporal stasis*, and *web*. To free a creature from *imprisonment* or *maze*, you must know its name and background, and you must cast this spell at the spot where it was entombed or banished into the *maze*.

FREEDOM OF MOVEMENT

School abjuration; **Level** bard 4, cleric 4, druid 4, ranger 4

Casting Time 1 standard action

Components V, S, M (a leather strip bound to the target), DF

Range personal or touch

Target you or creature touched

Duration 10 min./level

Saving Throw Will negates (harmless); **Spell Resistance** yes (harmless)

This spell enables you or a creature you touch to move and attack normally for the duration of the spell, even under the influence of magic that usually impedes movement, such as paralysis, *solid fog*, *slow*, and *web*. All combat maneuver checks made to grapple the target automatically fail. The subject automatically succeeds on any combat maneuver checks and Escape Artist checks made to escape a grapple or a pin.

The spell also allows the subject to move and attack normally while underwater, even with slashing weapons such as axes and swords or with bludgeoning weapons such as flails, hammers, and maces, provided that the weapon is wielded in the hand rather than hurled. The *freedom of movement* spell does not, however, grant water breathing.

FREEZING SPHERE

School evocation [cold]; **Level** sorcerer/wizard 6

Casting Time 1 standard action

Components V, S, F (a small crystal sphere)

Range long (400 ft. + 40 ft./level)

Target, Effect, or Area see text

Duration instantaneous or 1 round/level; see text

Saving Throw Reflex half; see text; **Spell Resistance** yes

Freezing sphere creates a frigid globe of cold energy that streaks from your fingertips to the location you select, where it explodes in a 40-foot-radius burst, dealing 1d6 points of cold damage per caster level (maximum 15d6) to each creature in the area. A creature of the water subtype instead takes 1d8 points of cold damage per caster level (maximum 15d8) and is staggered for 1d4 rounds.

If the *freezing sphere* strikes a body of water or a liquid that is principally water (not including water-based creatures), it freezes the liquid to a depth of 6 inches in a 40-foot radius. This ice lasts for 1 round per caster level. Creatures that were swimming on the surface of a targeted body of water become trapped in the ice. Attempting to break free is a full-round action. A trapped creature must make a DC 25 Strength check or a DC 25 Escape Artist check to do so.

You can refrain from firing the globe after completing the spell, if you wish. Treat this as a touch spell for which you are holding the charge. You can hold the charge for as long as 1 round per level, at the end of which time the *freezing sphere* bursts centered on you (and you receive no saving throw to resist its effect). Firing the globe in a later round is a standard action.

GASEOUS FORM

School transmutation; **Level** bard 3, sorcerer/wizard 3

Casting Time 1 standard action

Components S, M/DF (a bit of gauze and a wisp of smoke)

Range touch

Target willing corporeal creature touched

Duration 2 min./level (D)

Saving Throw none; **Spell Resistance** no

The subject and all its gear become insubstantial, misty, and translucent. Its material armor (including natural armor) becomes worthless, though its size, Dexterity, deflection bonuses, and armor bonuses from force effects still apply. The subject gains DR 10/magic and becomes immune to poison, sneak attacks, and critical hits. It can't attack or cast spells with verbal, somatic, material, or focus components while in gaseous form. This does not rule out the use of certain spells that the subject may have prepared using the feats Silent Spell, Still Spell, and Eschew Materials. The subject also loses supernatural abilities while in gaseous form. If it has a touch spell ready to use, that spell is discharged harmlessly when the *gaseous form* spell takes effect.

A gaseous creature can't run, but it can fly at a speed of 10 feet and automatically succeeds on all Fly skill checks. It can pass through small holes or narrow openings, even mere cracks, with all it was wearing or holding in its hands, as long as the spell persists. The creature is subject to the effects of wind, and it can't enter water or other liquid. It also can't manipulate objects or activate items, even those carried along with its gaseous form. Continuously active items remain active, though in some cases their effects may be moot.

GATE

School conjuration (creation or calling); **Level** cleric 9, sorcerer/wizard 9

Casting Time 1 standard action

Components V, S, M (see text)

Range medium (100 ft. + 10 ft./level)

Effect see text

Duration instantaneous or concentration (up to 1 round/level); see text

Saving Throw none; **Spell Resistance** no

Casting a *gate* spell has two effects. First, it creates an interdimensional connection between your plane of existence and a plane you specify, allowing travel between those two planes in either direction.

Second, you may then call a particular individual or kind of being through the *gate*.

The *gate* itself is a circular hoop or disk from 5 to 20 feet in diameter (caster's choice) oriented in the direction you desire when it comes into existence (typically vertical and facing you). It is a two-dimensional window looking into the plane you specified when casting the spell, and anyone or anything that moves through is shunted instantly to the other side.

A *gate* has a front and a back. Creatures moving through the *gate* from the front are transported to the other plane; creatures moving through it from the back are not.

Planar Travel: As a mode of planar travel, a *gate* spell functions much like a *plane shift* spell, except that the *gate* opens precisely at the point you desire (a creation effect). Deities and other beings who rule a planar realm can prevent a *gate* from opening in their presence or personal demesnes if they so desire. Travelers need not join hands with you—anyone who chooses to step through the portal is transported. A *gate* cannot be opened to another point on the same plane; the spell works only for interplanar travel.

You may hold the *gate* open only for a brief time (no more than 1 round per caster level), and you must concentrate on doing so, or else the interplanar connection is severed.

Calling Creatures: The second effect of the *gate* spell is to call an extraplanar creature to your aid (a calling effect). By naming a particular being or kind of being as you cast the spell, you cause the *gate* to open in the immediate vicinity of the desired creature and pull the subject through, willing or unwilling. Deities and unique beings are under no compulsion to come through the *gate*, although they may choose to do so of their own accord. This use of the spell creates a *gate* that remains open just long enough to transport the called creatures. This use of the spell has a material cost of 10,000 gp in rare incense and offerings. This cost is in addition to any cost that must be paid to the called creatures.

If you choose to call a kind of creature instead of a known individual, you may call either a single creature or several creatures. In either case, their total HD cannot exceed twice your caster level. In the case of a single creature, you can control it if its HD does not exceed your caster level. A creature with more HD than your caster level can't be controlled. Deities and unique beings cannot be controlled in any event. An uncontrolled being acts as it pleases, making the calling of such creatures rather dangerous. An uncontrolled being may return to its home plane at any time.

If you choose to exact a longer or more involved form of service from a called creature, you must offer some fair trade in return for that service. The service exacted must be reasonable with respect

to the promised favor or reward; see the *lesser planar ally* spell for appropriate rewards. Some creatures may want their payment in "livestock" rather than in coin, which could involve complications. Immediately upon completion of the service, the being is transported to your vicinity, and you must then and there turn over the promised reward. After this is done, the creature is instantly freed to return to its own plane.

Failure to fulfill the promise to the letter results in your being subjected to service by the creature or by its liege and master, at the very least. At worst, the creature or its kin may attack you.

Note: When you use a calling spell such as *gate* to call an air, chaotic, earth, evil, fire, good, lawful, or water creature, it becomes a spell of that type.

GEAS/QUEST

School enchantment (compulsion) [language-dependent, mind-affecting]; **Level** bard 6, cleric 6, sorcerer/wizard 6

Casting Time 10 minutes

Target one living creature

Saving Throw none; **Spell Resistance** yes

This spell functions similarly to *lesser geas*, except that it affects a creature of any HD and allows no saving throw.

If the subject is prevented from obeying the *geas/quest* for 24 hours, it takes a –3 penalty to each of its ability scores. Each day, another –3 penalty accumulates, up to a total of –12. No ability score can be reduced to less than 1 by this effect. The ability score penalties are removed 24 hours after the subject resumes obeying the *geas/quest*.

A *remove curse* spell ends a *geas/quest* spell only if its caster level is at least two higher than your caster level. *Break enchantment* does not end a *geas/quest*, but *limited wish*, *miracle*, and *wish* do.

Bards, sorcerers, and wizards usually refer to this spell as *geas*, while clerics call the same spell *quest*.

GEAS, LESSER

School enchantment (compulsion) [language-dependent, mind-affecting]; **Level** bard 3, sorcerer/wizard 4

Casting Time 1 round

Components V

Range close (25 ft. + 5 ft./2 levels)

Target one living creature with 7 HD or less

Duration 1 day/level or until discharged (D)

Saving Throw Will negates; **Spell Resistance** yes

A *lesser geas* places a magical command on a creature to carry out some service or to refrain from some action or course of activity, as desired by you. The creature must have 7 or fewer HD and be able to understand you. While a *geas* cannot compel a creature to kill itself or perform acts that would result in certain death, it can cause almost any other course of activity.

The *geased* creature must follow the given instructions until the *geas* is completed, no matter how long it takes.

If the instructions involve some open-ended task that the recipient cannot complete through his own actions, the spell remains in effect for a maximum of 1 day per caster level. A clever recipient can subvert some instructions.

If the subject is prevented from obeying the *lesser geas* for 24 hours, it takes a –2 penalty to each of its ability scores. Each day, another –2 penalty accumulates, up to a total of –8. No ability score can be reduced to less than 1 by this effect. The ability score penalties are removed 24 hours after the subject resumes obeying the *lesser geas*.

A *lesser geas* (and all ability score penalties) can be ended by *break enchantment*, *limited wish*, *remove curse*, *miracle*, or *wish*. *Dispel magic* does not affect a *lesser geas*.

GENTLE REPOSE

School necromancy; **Level** cleric 2, sorcerer/wizard 3
Casting Time 1 standard action
Components V, S, M/DF (salt and a copper piece for each of the corpse's eyes)
Range touch
Target corpse touched
Duration 1 day/level
Saving Throw Will negates (object); **Spell Resistance** yes (object)

You preserve the remains of a dead creature so that they do not decay. Doing so effectively extends the time limit on raising that creature from the dead (see *raise dead*). Days spent under the influence of this spell don't count against the time limit. Additionally, this spell makes transporting a slain (and thus decaying) comrade less unpleasant.

The spell also works on severed body parts and the like.

GHOST SOUND

School illusion (figment); **Level** bard 0, sorcerer/wizard 0
Casting Time 1 standard action
Components V, S, M (a bit of wool or a small lump of wax)
Range close (25 ft. + 5 ft./2 levels)
Effect illusory sounds
Duration 1 round/level (D)
Saving Throw Will disbelief; **Spell Resistance** no

Ghost sound allows you to create a volume of sound that rises, recedes, approaches, or remains at a fixed place. You choose what type of sound *ghost sound* creates when casting it and cannot thereafter change the sound's basic character.

The volume of sound created depends on your level. You can produce as much noise as four normal humans per caster level (maximum 40 humans). Thus, talking, singing, shouting, walking, marching, or running sounds can be created. The noise a *ghost sound* spell produces can be virtually any type of sound within the volume limit. A horde of rats running and squeaking is about the same volume as eight humans running and shouting. A roaring lion is equal to the noise from 16 humans, while a roaring dragon is equal to the noise from 32 humans. Anyone who hears a *ghost sound* receives a Will save to disbelieve.

Ghost sound can enhance the effectiveness of a *silent image* spell.

Ghost sound can be made permanent with a *permanency* spell.

GHOUL TOUCH

School necromancy; **Level** sorcerer/wizard 2
Casting Time 1 standard action
Components V, S, M (cloth from a ghoul or earth from a ghoul's lair)
Range touch
Target living humanoid touched
Duration 1d6+2 rounds
Saving Throw Fortitude negates; **Spell Resistance** yes

Imbuing you with negative energy, this spell allows you to paralyze a single living humanoid for the duration of the spell with a successful melee touch attack.

A paralyzed subject exudes a carrion stench that causes all living creatures (except you) in a 10-foot-radius spread to become sickened (Fortitude negates). A *neutralize poison* spell removes the effect from a sickened creature, and creatures immune to poison are unaffected by the stench. This is a poison effect.

GIANT FORM I

School transmutation (polymorph); **Level** sorcerer/wizard 7
Casting Time 1 standard action
Components V, S, M (a piece of the creature whose form you plan to assume)
Range personal
Target you
Duration 1 min./level (D)

When you cast this spell you can assume the form of any Large humanoid creature of the giant subtype (see the *Pathfinder RPG Bestiary*). Once you assume your new form, you gain the following abilities: a +6 size bonus to Strength, a –2 penalty to Dexterity, a +4 size bonus to Constitution, a +4 natural armor bonus, and low-light vision. If the form you assume has any of the following abilities, you gain the listed ability: darkvision 60 feet, rend (2d6 damage), regeneration 5, rock catching, and rock throwing (range 60 feet, 2d6 damage). If the creature has immunity or resistance to any energy, you gain resistance 20 to that energy. If the creature has vulnerability to an energy, you gain that vulnerability.

GIANT FORM II

School Transmutation (polymorph); **Level** sorcerer/wizard 8

This spell functions as *giant form I* except that it also allows you to assume the form of any Huge creature of the giant subtype. You gain the following abilities: a +8 size bonus to Strength, a –2 penalty to Dexterity, a +6 size bonus to Constitution, a +6 natural armor bonus, low-light vision, and a +10 foot enhancement bonus to your speed. If the form you assume has any of the following abilities, you gain the listed ability: swim 60 feet, darkvision 60 feet, rend (2d8 damage), regeneration 5, rock catching, and rock throwing (range 120 feet, 2d10 damage). If the creature has immunity or resistance to any energy, you gain that immunity or resistance. If the creature has vulnerability to an energy, you gain that vulnerability.

GIANT VERMIN

School transmutation; **Level** cleric 4, druid 4

Casting Time 1 standard action

Components V, S, DF

Range close (25 ft. + 5 ft./2 levels)

Targets 1 or more vermin, no two of which can be more than 30 ft. apart

Duration 1 min./level

Saving Throw none; **Spell Resistance** yes

You turn a number of normal-sized centipedes, scorpions, or spiders into their giant counterparts (see the *Pathfinder RPG Bestiary*). Only one type of vermin can be transmuted (so a single casting cannot affect both a centipede and a spider). The number of vermin which can be affected by this spell depends on your caster level, as noted on the table below.

Giant vermin created by this spell do not attempt to harm you, but your control of such creatures is limited to simple commands ("Attack," "Defend," "Stop," and so forth). Orders to attack a certain creature when it appears or guard against a particular occurrence are too complex for the vermin to understand. Unless commanded to do otherwise, the giant vermin attack whomever or whatever is near them.

Caster Level	Centipedes	Scorpions	Spiders
9th or lower	3	1	2
10th–13th	4	2	3
14th–17th	6	3	4
18th–19th	8	4	5
20th or higher	12	6	8

GLIBNESS

School transmutation; **Level** bard 3

Casting Time 1 standard action

Components S

Range personal

Target you

Duration 10 min./level (D)

Your speech becomes fluent and more believable, causing those who hear you to believe every word you say. You gain a +20 bonus on Bluff checks made to convince another of the truth of your words. This bonus doesn't apply to other uses of the Bluff skill, such as feinting in combat, creating a diversion to hide, or communicating a hidden message via innuendo.

If a magical effect is used against you that would detect your lies or force you to speak the truth, the user of the effect must succeed on a caster level check (1d20 + caster level) against a DC of 15 + your caster level to succeed. Failure means the effect does not detect your lies or force you to speak only the truth.

GLITTERDUST

School conjuration (creation); **Level** bard 2, sorcerer/wizard 2

Casting Time 1 standard action

Components V, S, M (ground mica)

Range medium (100 ft. + 10 ft./level)

Area creatures and objects within 10-ft.-radius spread

Duration 1 round/level

Save Will negates (blinding only); **SR** no

A cloud of golden particles covers everyone and everything in the area, causing creatures to become blinded and visibly outlining invisible things for the duration of the spell. All within the area are covered by the dust, which cannot be removed and continues to sparkle until it fades. Each round at the end of their turn blinded creatures may attempt new saving throws to end the blindness effect.

Any creature covered by the dust takes a –40 penalty on Stealth checks.

GLOBE OF INVULNERABILITY

School abjuration; **Level** sorcerer/wizard 6

This spell functions like *lesser globe of invulnerability*, except that it also excludes 4th-level spells and spell-like effects.

GLOBE OF INVULNERABILITY, LESSER

School abjuration; **Level** sorcerer/wizard 4

Casting Time 1 standard action

Components V, S, M (a glass or crystal bead)

Range 10 ft.

Area 10-ft.-radius spherical emanation, centered on you

Duration 1 round/level (D)

Saving Throw none; **Spell Resistance** no

An immobile, faintly shimmering magical sphere surrounds you and excludes all spell effects of 3rd level or lower. The area or effect of any such spells does not include the area of the *lesser globe of invulnerability*. Such spells fail to affect any target located within the globe. Excluded effects include spell-like abilities and spells or spell-like effects from items. Any type of spell, however, can be cast through or out of the magical globe. Spells of 4th level and higher are not affected by the globe, nor are spells already in effect when the globe is cast. The globe can be brought down by a *dispel magic* spell. You can leave and return to the globe without penalty.

Note that spell effects are not disrupted unless their effects enter the globe, and even then they are merely suppressed, not dispelled.

If a given spell has more than one level depending on which character class is casting it, use the level appropriate to the caster to determine whether *lesser globe of invulnerability* stops it.

GLYPH OF WARDING

School abjuration; **Level** cleric 3

Casting Time 10 minutes

Components V, S, M (powdered diamond worth 200 gp)

Range touch

Target or Area object touched or up to 5 sq. ft./level

Duration permanent until discharged (D)

Saving Throw see text; **Spell Resistance** no (object) and yes; see text

This powerful inscription harms those who enter, pass, or open the warded area or object. A *glyph of warding* can guard a bridge or passage, ward a portal, trap a chest or box, and so on.

You set all of the conditions of the ward. Typically, any creature entering the warded area or opening the warded object without speaking a password (which you set when casting the spell) is subject to the magic it stores. Alternatively or in addition to a password trigger, glyphs can be set according to physical characteristics (such as height or weight) or creature type, subtype, or kind. Glyphs can also be set with respect to good, evil, law, or chaos, or to pass those of your religion. They cannot be set according to class, HD, or level. Glyphs respond to invisible creatures normally but are not triggered by those who travel past them ethereally. Multiple glyphs cannot be cast on the same area. However, if a cabinet has three different drawers, each can be separately warded.

When casting the spell, you weave a tracery of faintly glowing lines around the warding sigil. A glyph can be placed to conform to any shape up to the limitations of your total square footage. When the spell is completed, the glyph and tracery become nearly invisible.

Glyphs cannot be affected or bypassed by such means as physical or magical probing, though they can be dispelled. *Mislead*, *polymorph*, and *nondetection* (and similar magical effects) can fool a glyph, though nonmagical disguises and the like can't. *Read magic* allows you to identify a *glyph of warding* with a DC 13 Knowledge (arcana) check. Identifying the glyph does not discharge it and allows you to know the basic nature of the glyph (version, type of damage caused, what spell is stored).

Note: Magic traps such as *glyph of warding* are hard to detect and disable. While any character can use Perception to find a glyph, only a character with the trapfinding class feature can use Disable Device to disarm it. The DC in each case is 25 + spell level, or 28 for *glyph of warding*.

Depending on the version selected, a glyph either blasts the intruder or activates a spell.

Blast Glyph: A *blast glyph* deals 1d8 points of damage per two caster levels (maximum 5d8) to the intruder and to all within 5 feet of him or her. This damage is acid, cold, fire, electricity, or sonic (caster's choice, made at time of casting). Each creature affected can attempt a Reflex save to take half damage. Spell resistance applies against this effect.

Spell Glyph: You can store any harmful spell of 3rd level or lower that you know. All level-dependent features of the spell are based on your caster level at the time of casting the glyph. If the spell has a target, it targets the intruder. If the spell has an area or an amorphous effect, the area or effect is centered on the intruder. If the spell summons creatures, they appear as close as possible to the intruder and attack. Saving throws and spell resistance operate as normal, except that the DC is based on the level of the spell stored in the glyph.

GLYPH OF WARDING, GREATER

School abjuration; **Level** cleric 6

This spell functions like *glyph of warding*, except that a *greater blast glyph* deals up to 10d8 points of damage, and a *greater spell glyph* can store a spell of 6th level or lower.

Read magic allows you to identify a *greater glyph of warding* with a DC 16 Spellcraft check.

Material Component: You trace the glyph with incense, which must first be sprinkled with powdered diamond worth at least 400 gp.

GOODBERRY

School transmutation; **Level** druid 1
Casting Time 1 standard action
Components V, S, DF
Range touch
Targets 2d4 fresh berries touched
Duration 1 day/level
Saving Throw none; **Spell Resistance** yes

Casting *goodberry* makes 2d4 freshly picked berries magical. You (as well as any other druid of 3rd or higher level) can immediately discern which berries are affected. Each transmuted berry provides nourishment as if it were a normal meal for a Medium creature. The berry also cures 1 point of damage when eaten, subject to a maximum of 8 points of such curing in any 24-hour period.

GOOD HOPE

School enchantment (compulsion) [mind-affecting]; **Level** bard 3
Casting Time 1 standard action
Components V, S
Range medium (100 ft. + 10 ft./level)
Targets one living creature/level, no two of which may be more than 30 ft. apart
Duration 1 min./level
Saving Throw Will negates (harmless); **Spell Resistance** yes (harmless)

This spell instills powerful hope in the subjects. Each affected creature gains a +2 morale bonus on saving throws, attack rolls, ability checks, skill checks, and weapon damage rolls.

Good hope counters and dispels *crushing despair*.

GRASPING HAND

School evocation [force]; **Level** sorcerer/wizard 7

This spell functions as *interposing hand*, except that it can also grapple one opponent you select. The *grasping hand* gets one grapple attack per round. This attack does not provoke an attack of opportunity. Its CMB and CMD for grapple checks use your caster level in place of its base attack bonus, with a +10 bonus for its Strength (31) score and a +1 bonus for being Large (its Dexterity is 10, granting no bonus on the Combat Maneuver Defense). The hand holds but does not harm creatures that it grapples. Directing the spell to a new target is a move action. The *grasping hand* can instead be directed to bull rush a target, using the same bonuses outlined above, or it can be directed to interpose itself, as *interposing hand* does.

GREASE

School conjuration (creation); **Level** bard 1, sorcerer/wizard 1
Casting Time 1 standard action
Components V, S, M (butter)
Range close (25 ft. + 5 ft./2 levels)

Target one object or 10-ft. square

Duration 1 min./level (D)

Save see text; **SR** no

A *grease* spell covers a solid surface with a layer of slippery grease. Any creature in the area when the spell is cast must make a successful Reflex save or fall. A creature can walk within or through the area of grease at half normal speed with a DC 10 Acrobatics check. Failure means it can't move that round (and must then make a Reflex save or fall), while failure by 5 or more means it falls (see the Acrobatics skill for details). Creatures that do not move on their turn do not need to make this check and are not considered flat-footed.

The spell can also be used to create a greasy coating on an item. Material objects not in use are always affected by this spell, while an object wielded or employed by a creature requires its bearer to make a Reflex saving throw to avoid the effect. If the initial saving throw fails, the creature immediately drops the item. A saving throw must be made in each round that the creature attempts to pick up or use the *greased* item. A creature wearing *greased* armor or clothing gains a +10 circumstance bonus on Escape Artist checks and combat maneuver checks made to escape a grapple, and to their CMD to avoid being grappled.

GREATER (SPELL NAME)

Any spell whose name begins with *greater* is alphabetized in this chapter according to the spell name. Thus, the description of a *greater* spell appears near the description of the spell on which it is based. Spell chains that have *greater* spells in them include those based on the spells *arcane sight*, *command*, *dispel magic*, *glyph of warding*, *invisibility*, *magic fang*, *magic weapon*, *planar ally*, *planar binding*, *polymorph*, *prying eyes*, *restoration*, *scrying*, *shadow conjuration*, *shadow evocation*, *shout*, and *teleport*.

GUARDS AND WARDS

School abjuration; **Level** sorcerer/wizard 6

Casting Time 30 minutes

Components V, S, M (burning incense, a small measure of brimstone and oil, a knotted string, and a small amount of blood), F (a small silver rod)

Range anywhere within the area to be warded

Area up to 200 sq. ft./level (S)

Duration 2 hours/level (D)

Saving Throw see text; **Spell Resistance** see text

This powerful spell is primarily used to defend a stronghold or fortress by creating a number of magical wards and effects. The ward protects 200 square feet per caster level. The warded area can be as much as 20 feet high, and shaped as you desire. You can ward several stories of a stronghold by dividing the area among them; you must be somewhere within the area to be warded to cast the spell. The spell creates the following magical effects within the warded area.

Fog: Fog fills all corridors, obscuring all sight, including darkvision, beyond 5 feet. A creature within 5 feet has concealment (attacks have a 20% miss chance). Creatures farther away have total concealment (50% miss chance, and the attacker cannot use sight to locate the target). Saving Throw: none. Spell Resistance: no.

Arcane Locks: All doors in the warded area are *arcane locked*. Saving Throw: none. Spell Resistance: no.

Webs: Webs fill all stairs from top to bottom. These strands are identical with those created by the *web* spell, except that they regrow in 10 minutes if they are burned or torn away while the *guards and wards* spell lasts. Saving Throw: Reflex negates; see text for *web*. Spell Resistance: no.

Confusion: Where there are choices in direction—such as a corridor intersection or side passage—a minor *confusion*-type effect functions so as to make it 50% probable that intruders believe they are going in the opposite direction from the one they actually chose. This is a mind-affecting effect. Saving Throw: none. Spell Resistance: yes.

Lost Doors: One door per caster level is covered by a *silent image* to appear as if it were a plain wall. Saving Throw: Will disbelief (if interacted with). Spell Resistance: no.

In addition, you can place your choice of one of the following five magical effects.

1. *Dancing lights* in four corridors. You can designate a simple program that causes the lights to repeat as long as the *guards and wards* spell lasts. Saving Throw: none. Spell Resistance: no.

2. A *magic mouth* in two places. Saving Throw: none. Spell Resistance: no.

3. A *stinking cloud* in two places. The vapors appear in the places you designate; they return within 10 minutes if dispersed by wind while the *guards and wards* spell lasts. Saving Throw: Fortitude negates; see text for *stinking cloud*. Spell Resistance: no.

4. A *gust of wind* in one corridor or room. Saving Throw: Fortitude negates. Spell Resistance: yes.

5. A *suggestion* in one place. You select an area of up to 5 feet square, and any creature who enters or passes through the area receives the *suggestion* mentally. Saving Throw: Will negates. Spell Resistance: yes.

The whole warded area radiates strong magic of the abjuration school. A *dispel magic* cast on a specific effect, if successful, removes only that effect. A successful *mage's disjunction* destroys the entire *guards and wards* effect.

GUIDANCE

School divination; **Level** cleric 0, druid 0

Casting Time 1 standard action

Components V, S

Range touch

Target creature touched

Duration 1 minute or until discharged

Saving Throw Will negates (harmless); **Spell Resistance** yes

This spell imbues the subject with a touch of divine guidance. The creature gets a +1 competence bonus on a single attack roll, saving throw, or skill check. It must choose to use the bonus before making the roll to which it applies.

GUST OF WIND

School evocation [air]; **Level** druid 2, sorcerer/wizard 2
Casting Time 1 standard action
Components V, S
Range 60 ft.
Effect line-shaped gust of severe wind emanating out from you to the extreme of the range
Duration 1 round
Saving Throw Fortitude negates; **Spell Resistance** yes

This spell creates a severe blast of air (approximately 50 mph) that originates from you, affecting all creatures in its path. All flying creatures in this area take a −4 penalty on Fly skill checks. Tiny or smaller flying creatures must make a DC 25 Fly skill check or be blown back 2d6 × 10 feet and take 2d6 points of damage. Small or smaller flying creatures must make a DC 20 Fly skill check to move against the force of the wind.

A Tiny or smaller creature on the ground is knocked down and rolled 1d4 × 10 feet, taking 1d4 points of nonlethal damage per 10 feet.

Small creatures are knocked prone by the force of the wind.

Medium or smaller creatures are unable to move forward against the force of the wind unless they succeed at a DC 15 Strength check.

Large or larger creatures may move normally within a *gust of wind* effect.

This spell can't move a creature beyond the limit of it's range.

Any creature, regardless of size, takes a −4 penalty on ranged attacks and Perception checks in the area of a *gust of wind*.

The force of the gust automatically extinguishes candles, torches, and similar unprotected flames. It causes protected flames, such as those in lanterns, to dance wildly and has a 50% chance to extinguish those lights.

In addition to the effects noted, a *gust of wind* can do anything that a sudden blast of wind would be expected to do. It can create a stinging spray of sand or dust, fan a large fire, overturn delicate awnings or hangings, heel over a small boat, and blow gases or vapors to the edge of its range.

Gust of wind can be made permanent with a *permanency* spell.

HALLOW

School evocation [good]; **Level** cleric 5, druid 5
Casting Time 24 hours
Components V, S, M (herbs, oils, and incense worth at least 1,000 gp, plus 1,000 gp per level of the spell to be included in the *hallowed* area), DF
Range touch
Area 40-ft. radius emanating from the touched point
Duration instantaneous
Saving Throw see text; **Spell Resistance** see text

Hallow makes a particular site, building, or structure a holy site. This has four major effects.

First, the site is warded by a *magic circle against evil* effect.

Second, the DC to resist positive channeled energy within this area gains a +4 sacred bonus and the DC to resist negative energy is reduced by 4. Spell resistance does not apply to this effect. This provision does not apply to the druid version of the spell.

Third, any dead body interred in a *hallowed* site cannot be turned into an undead creature.

Finally, you can fix a single spell effect to the *hallowed* site. The spell effect lasts for 1 year and functions throughout the entire site, regardless of the normal duration and area or effect. You may designate whether the effect applies to all creatures, creatures who share your faith or alignment, or creatures who adhere to another faith or alignment. At the end of the year, the chosen effect lapses, but it can be renewed or replaced simply by casting *hallow* again.

Spell effects that may be tied to a *hallowed* site include *aid, bane, bless, cause fear, darkness, daylight, death ward, deeper darkness, detect evil, detect magic, dimensional anchor, discern lies, dispel magic, endure elements, freedom of movement, invisibility purge, protection from energy, remove fear, resist energy, silence, tongues,* and *zone of truth.* Saving throws and spell resistance might apply to these spells' effects. (See the individual spell descriptions for details.)

An area can receive only one *hallow* spell (and its associated spell effect) at a time. *Hallow* counters but does not dispel *unhallow*.

HALLUCINATORY TERRAIN

School illusion (glamer); **Level** bard 4, sorcerer/wizard 4
Casting Time 10 minutes
Components V, S, M (a stone, a twig, and a green leaf)
Range long (400 ft. + 40 ft./level)
Area one 30-ft. cube/level (S)
Duration 2 hours/level (D)
Saving Throw Will disbelief (if interacted with); **Spell Resistance** no

You make natural terrain look, sound, and smell like some other sort of natural terrain. Structures, equipment, and creatures within the area are not hidden or changed in appearance.

HALT UNDEAD

School necromancy; **Level** sorcerer/wizard 3
Casting Time 1 standard action
Components V, S, M (a pinch of sulfur and powdered garlic)
Range medium (100 ft. + 10 ft./level)
Targets up to three undead creatures, no two of which can be more than 30 ft. apart
Duration 1 round/level
Saving Throw Will negates (see text); **Spell Resistance** yes

This spell renders as many as three undead creatures immobile. A nonintelligent undead creature gets no saving throw; an intelligent undead creature does. If the spell is successful, it renders the undead creature immobile for the duration of the spell (similar to the effect of *hold person* on a living creature). The effect is broken if the *halted* creatures are attacked or take damage.

HARM

School necromancy; **Level** cleric 6
Casting Time 1 standard action

Components V, S
Range touch
Target creature touched
Duration instantaneous
Saving Throw Will half; see text; **Spell Resistance** yes

Harm charges a subject with negative energy that deals 10 points of damage per caster level (to a maximum of 150 points at 15th level). If the creature successfully saves, *harm* deals half this amount. *Harm* cannot reduce the target's hit points to less than 1.

If used on an undead creature, *harm* acts like *heal*.

HASTE

School transmutation; **Level** bard 3, sorcerer/wizard 3
Casting Time 1 standard action
Components V, S, M (a shaving of licorice root)
Range close (25 ft. + 5 ft./2 levels)
Targets one creature/level, no two of which can be more than
    30 ft. apart
Duration 1 round/level
Saving Throw Fortitude negates (harmless); **Spell Resistance**
    yes (harmless)

The transmuted creatures move and act more quickly than normal. This extra speed has several effects.

When making a full attack action, a hasted creature may make one extra attack with one natural or manufactured weapon. The attack is made using the creature's full base attack bonus, plus any modifiers appropriate to the situation. (This effect is not cumulative with similar effects, such as that provided by a *speed* weapon, nor does it actually grant an extra action, so you can't use it to cast a second spell or otherwise take an extra action in the round.)

A hasted creature gains a +1 bonus on attack rolls and a +1 dodge bonus to AC and Reflex saves. Any condition that makes you lose your Dexterity bonus to Armor Class (if any) also makes you lose dodge bonuses.

All of the hasted creature's modes of movement (including land movement, burrow, climb, fly, and swim) increase by 30 feet, to a maximum of twice the subject's normal speed using that form of movement. This increase counts as an enhancement bonus, and it affects the creature's jumping distance as normal for increased speed. Multiple *haste* effects don't stack. *Haste* dispels and counters *slow*.

HEAL

School conjuration (healing); **Level** cleric 6, druid 7
Casting Time 1 standard action
Components V, S
Range touch
Target creature touched
Duration instantaneous
Saving Throw Will negates (harmless); **Spell Resistance** yes (harmless)

Heal enables you to channel positive energy into a creature to wipe away injury and afflictions. It immediately ends any and all of the following adverse conditions affecting the target: ability

damage, blinded, confused, dazed, dazzled, deafened, diseased, exhausted, fatigued, feebleminded, insanity, nauseated, poisoned, sickened, and stunned. It also cures 10 hit points of damage per level of the caster, to a maximum of 150 points at 15th level.

Heal does not remove negative levels or restore permanently drained ability score points.

If used against an undead creature, *heal* instead acts like *harm*.

HEAL, MASS

School conjuration (healing); **Level** cleric 9
Range close (25 ft. + 5 ft./2 levels)
Targets one or more creatures, no two of which can be more than
    30 ft. apart

This spell functions like *heal*, except as noted above. The maximum number of hit points restored to each creature is 250.

HEAL MOUNT

School conjuration (healing); **Level** paladin 3
Casting Time 1 standard action
Components V, S
Range touch
Target your mount touched
Duration instantaneous
Saving Throw Will negates (harmless); **Spell Resistance** yes (harmless)

This spell functions like *heal*, but it affects only the paladin's special mount (typically a horse).

HEAT METAL

School transmutation [fire]; **Level** druid 2
Casting Time 1 standard action
Components V, S, DF
Range close (25 ft. + 5 ft./2 levels)
Target metal equipment of one creature per two levels, no two of
    which can be more than 30 ft. apart; or 25 lbs. of metal/level, all
    of which must be within a 30-ft. circle
Duration 7 rounds
Saving Throw Will negates (object); **Spell Resistance** yes (object)

Heat metal causes metal objects to become red-hot. Unattended, nonmagical metal gets no saving throw. Magical metal is allowed a saving throw against the spell. An item in a creature's possession uses the creature's saving throw bonus unless its own is higher.

A creature takes fire damage if its equipment is heated. It takes full damage if its armor, shield, or weapon is affected. The creature takes minimum damage (1 point or 2 points; see the table) if it's not wearing or wielding such an item.

On the first round of the spell, the metal becomes warm and uncomfortable to touch but deals no damage. The same effect also occurs on the last round of the spell's duration. During the second (and also the next-to-last) round, intense heat causes pain and damage. In the third, fourth, and fifth rounds, the metal is searing hot, and causes more damage, as shown on the table presented on the following page.

Round	Metal Temperature	Damage
1	Warm	None
2	Hot	1d4 points
3–5	Searing	2d4 points
6	Hot	1d4 points
7	Warm	None

Any cold intense enough to damage the creature negates fire damage from the spell (and vice versa) on a point-for-point basis. If cast underwater, *heat metal* deals half damage and boils the surrounding water.

Heat metal counters and dispels *chill metal*.

HELPING HAND

School evocation; **Level** cleric 3

Casting Time 1 standard action

Components V, S, DF

Range 5 miles

Effect ghostly hand

Duration 1 hour/level

Saving Throw none; **Spell Resistance** no

You create the ghostly image of a hand, which you can send to find a creature within 5 miles. The hand then beckons to that creature and leads it to you if the creature is willing to follow.

When the spell is cast, you specify a person (or any creature) by physical description, which can include race, gender, and appearance but not ambiguous factors such as level, alignment, or class. When the description is done, the hand streaks off in search of a subject that fits the description. The amount of time it takes to find the subject depends on how far away he is, as detailed on the following table.

Distance	Time to Locate
100 ft. or less	1 round
1,000 ft.	1 minute
1 mile	10 minutes
2 miles	1 hour
3 miles	2 hours
4 miles	3 hours
5 miles	4 hours

Once the hand locates the subject, it beckons the creature to follow it. If the subject does so, the hand points in your direction, indicating the most direct, feasible route. The hand hovers 10 feet in front of the subject, moving before it at a speed of as much as 240 feet per round. Once the hand leads the subject back to you, it disappears.

The subject is not compelled to follow the hand or act in any particular way toward you. If the subject chooses not to follow, the hand continues to beckon for the duration of the spell, then disappears. If the spell expires while the subject is en route to you, the hand disappears; the subject must then rely on its own devices to locate you.

If more than one subject in a 5-mile radius meets the description, the hand locates the closest creature. If that creature refuses to follow the hand, the hand does not seek out a second subject.

If, at the end of 4 hours of searching, the hand has found no subject that matches the description within 5 miles, it returns to you, displays an outstretched palm (indicating that no such creature was found), and disappears.

The ghostly hand has no physical form. It is invisible to anyone except you and a potential subject. It cannot engage in combat or execute any other task aside from locating a subject and leading it back to you. The hand can't pass through solid objects but can ooze through small cracks and slits. The hand cannot travel more than 5 miles from the spot it appeared when you cast the spell.

HEROES' FEAST

School conjuration [creation]; **Level** bard 6, cleric 6

Casting Time 10 minutes

Components V, S, DF

Range close (25 ft. + 5 ft./2 levels)

Effect feast for one creature/level

Duration 1 hour plus 12 hours; see text

Saving Throw none; **Spell Resistance** no

You bring forth a great feast, including a magnificent table, chairs, service, and food and drink. The feast takes 1 hour to consume, and the beneficial effects do not set in until this hour is over. Every creature partaking of the feast is cured of all sickness and nausea, receives the benefits of both *neutralize poison* and *remove disease*, and gains 1d8 temporary hit points + 1 point per two caster levels (maximum +10) after imbibing the nectar-like beverage that is part of the feast. The ambrosial food grants each creature that partakes a +1 morale bonus on attack rolls and Will saves and a +4 morale bonus on saving throws against poison and fear effects for 12 hours.

If the feast is interrupted for any reason, the spell is ruined and all effects of the spell are negated.

HEROISM

School enchantment (compulsion) [mind-affecting]; **Level** bard 2, sorcerer/wizard 3

Casting Time 1 standard action

Components V, S

Range touch

Target creature touched

Duration 10 min./level

Saving Throw Will negates (harmless); **Spell Resistance** yes (harmless)

This spell imbues a single creature with great bravery and morale in battle. The target gains a +2 morale bonus on attack rolls, saves, and skill checks.

HEROISM, GREATER

School enchantment (compulsion) [mind-affecting]; **Level** bard 5, sorcerer/wizard 6

Duration 1 min./level

This spell functions like *heroism*, except the creature gains a +4 morale bonus on attack rolls, saves, and skill checks, immunity to fear effects, and temporary hit points equal to your caster level (maximum 20).

HIDE FROM ANIMALS

School abjuration; **Level** druid 1, ranger 1

Casting Time 1 standard action

Components S, DF

Range touch

Targets one creature touched/level

Duration 10 min./level (D)

Saving Throw Will negates (harmless); **Spell Resistance** yes

Animals cannot sense the warded creatures. Even extraordinary or supernatural sensory capabilities, such as blindsense, blindsight, scent, and tremorsense, cannot detect or locate warded creatures. Animals simply act as though the warded creatures are not there. If a warded character touches an animal or attacks any creature, even with a spell, the spell ends for all recipients.

HIDE FROM UNDEAD

School abjuration; **Level** cleric 1

Casting Time 1 standard action

Components V, S, DF

Range touch

Targets one touched creature/level

Duration 10 min./level (D)

Saving Throw Will negates (harmless); see text; **Spell Resistance** yes

Undead cannot see, hear, or smell creatures warded by this spell. Even extraordinary or supernatural sensory capabilities, such as blindsense, blindsight, scent, and tremorsense, cannot detect or locate warded creatures. Nonintelligent undead creatures (such as skeletons or zombies) are automatically affected and act as though the warded creatures are not there. An intelligent undead creature gets a single Will saving throw. If it fails, the subject can't see any of the warded creatures. If it has reason to believe unseen opponents are present, however, it can attempt to find or strike them. If a warded creature attempts to channel positive energy, turn or command undead, touches an undead creature, or attacks any creature (even with a spell), the spell ends for all recipients.

HIDEOUS LAUGHTER

School enchantment (compulsion) [mind-affecting]; **Level** bard 1, sorcerer/wizard 2

Casting Time 1 standard action

Components V, S, M (tiny fruit tarts and a feather)

Range close (25 ft. + 5 ft./2 levels)

Target one creature; see text

Duration 1 round/level

Saving Throw Will negates; **Spell Resistance** yes

This spell afflicts the subject with uncontrollable laughter. It collapses into gales of manic laughter, falling prone. The subject can take no actions while laughing, but is not considered helpless.

On the creature's next turn, it may attempt a new saving throw to end the effect. If successful, the effect ends and the creature is treated as if it spent a full-round action on its turn.

A creature with an Intelligence score of 2 or lower is not affected. A creature whose type is different from the caster's receives a +4 bonus on its saving throw, because humor doesn't "translate" well.

HOLD ANIMAL

School enchantment (compulsion) [mind-affecting]; **Level** druid 2, ranger 2

Components: V, S

Target one animal

This spell functions like *hold person*, except that it affects an animal instead of a humanoid.

HOLD MONSTER

School enchantment (compulsion) [mind-affecting]; **Level** bard 4, sorcerer/wizard 5

Components: V, S, M/DF (one hard metal bar or rod, which can be as small as a three-penny nail)

Target one living creature

This spell functions like *hold person*, except that it affects any living creature that fails its Will save.

HOLD MONSTER, MASS

School enchantment (compulsion) [mind-affecting]; **Level** sorcerer/wizard 9

Targets one or more creatures, no two of which can be more than 30 ft. apart

This spell functions like *hold person*, except that it affects multiple creatures and holds any living creature that fails its Will save.

HOLD PERSON

School enchantment (compulsion) [mind-affecting]; **Level** bard 2, cleric 2, sorcerer/wizard 3

Casting Time 1 standard action

Components V, S, F/DF (a small, straight piece of iron)

Range medium (100 ft. + 10 ft./level)

Target one humanoid creature

Duration 1 round/level (D); see text

Saving Throw Will negates; see text; **Spell Resistance** yes

The subject becomes paralyzed and freezes in place. It is aware and breathes normally but cannot take any actions, even speech. Each round on its turn, the subject may attempt a new saving throw to end the effect. This is a full-round action that does not provoke attacks of opportunity. A winged creature who is paralyzed cannot flap its wings and falls. A swimmer can't swim and may drown.

HOLD PERSON, MASS

School enchantment (compulsion) [mind-affecting]; **Level** sorcerer/wizard 7

Targets one or more humanoid creatures, no two of which can be more than 30 ft. apart

This spell functions like *hold person*, except as noted above.

HOLD PORTAL

School abjuration; **Level** sorcerer/wizard 1

Casting Time 1 standard action

Component V

Range medium (100 ft. + 10 ft./level)

Target one portal, up to 20 sq. ft./level

Duration 1 min./level (D)

Saving Throw none; **Spell Resistance** no

This spell magically holds shut a door, gate, window, or shutter of wood, metal, or stone. The magic affects the portal just as if it were securely closed and normally locked. A *knock* spell or a successful *dispel magic* spell can negate a *hold portal* spell.

Add 5 to the normal DC for forcing open a portal affected by this spell.

HOLY AURA

School abjuration [good]; **Level** cleric 8

Casting Time 1 standard action

Components V, S, F (a tiny reliquary worth 500 gp)

Range 20 ft.

Targets one creature/level in a 20-ft.-radius burst centered on you

Duration 1 round/level (D)

Saving Throw see text; **Spell Resistance** yes (harmless)

A brilliant divine radiance surrounds the subjects, protecting them from attacks, granting them resistance to spells cast by evil creatures, and causing evil creatures to become blinded when they strike the subjects. This abjuration has four effects.

First, each warded creature gains a +4 deflection bonus to AC and a +4 resistance bonus on saves. Unlike *protection from evil*, this benefit applies against all attacks, not just against attacks by evil creatures.

Second, each warded creature gains spell resistance 25 against evil spells and spells cast by evil creatures.

Third, the abjuration protects the recipient from possession and mental influence, just as *protection from evil* does.

Finally, if an evil creature succeeds on a melee attack against a creature warded by a *holy aura*, the offending attacker is blinded (Fortitude save negates, as *blindness/deafness*, but against *holy aura's* save DC).

HOLY SMITE

School evocation [good]; **Level** cleric 4

Casting Time 1 standard action

Components V, S

Range medium (100 ft. + 10 ft./level)

Area 20-ft.-radius burst

Duration instantaneous (1 round); see text

Saving Throw Will partial; see text; **Spell Resistance** yes

You draw down holy power to smite your enemies. Only evil and neutral creatures are harmed by the spell; good creatures are unaffected.

The spell deals 1d8 points of damage per two caster levels (maximum 5d8) to each evil creature in the area (or 1d6 points of damage per caster level, maximum 10d6, to an evil outsider) and causes it to become blinded for 1 round. A successful Will saving throw reduces damage to half and negates the blinded effect.

The spell deals only half damage to creatures who are neither good nor evil, and they are not blinded. Such a creature can reduce that damage by half (down to one-quarter of the roll) with a successful Will save.

HOLY SWORD

School evocation [good]; **Level** paladin 4

Casting Time 1 standard action

Components V, S

Range touch

Target melee weapon touched

Duration 1 round/level

Saving Throw none; **Spell Resistance** no

This spell allows you to channel holy power into your sword, or any other melee weapon you choose. The weapon acts as a +5 *holy weapon* (+5 enhancement bonus on attack and damage rolls, extra 2d6 damage against evil opponents). It also emits a *magic circle against evil* effect (as the spell). If the *magic circle* ends, the sword creates a new one on your turn as a free action. The spell is automatically canceled 1 round after the weapon leaves your hand. You cannot have more than one *holy sword* at a time.

If this spell is cast on a magic weapon, the powers of the spell supercede any that the weapon normally has, rendering the normal enhancement bonus and powers of the weapon inoperative for the duration of the spell. This spell is not cumulative with *bless weapon* or any other spell that might modify the weapon in any way. This spell does not work on artifacts. A masterwork weapon's bonus to attack does not stack with an enhancement bonus to attack.

HOLY WORD

School evocation [good, sonic]; **Level** cleric 7

Casting Time 1 standard action

Components V

Range 40 ft.

Area nongood creatures in a 40-ft.-radius spread centered on you

Duration instantaneous

Saving Throw Will partial; **Spell Resistance** yes

Any nongood creature within the area of a *holy word* spell suffers the following ill effects.

HD	Effect
Equal to caster level	Deafened
Up to caster level −1	Blinded, deafened
Up to caster level −5	Paralyzed, blinded, deafened
Up to caster level −10	Killed, paralyzed, blinded, deafened

The effects are cumulative and concurrent. A successful Will save reduces or eliminates these effects. Creatures affected by multiple effects make only one save and apply the result to all the effects.

Deafened: The creature is deafened for 1d4 rounds. Save negates.

Blinded: The creature is blinded for 2d4 rounds. Save reduces the blinded effect to 1d4 rounds.

Paralyzed: The creature is paralyzed and helpless for 1d10 minutes. Save reduces the paralyzed effect to 1 round.

Killed: Living creatures die. Undead creatures are destroyed. Save negates. If the save is successful, the creature instead takes 3d6 points of damage + 1 point per caster level (maximum +25).

Furthermore, if you are on your home plane when you cast this spell, nongood extraplanar creatures within the area are instantly banished back to their home planes. Creatures so banished cannot return for at least 24 hours. This effect takes place regardless of whether the creatures hear the *holy word* or not. The banishment effect allows a Will save (at a –4 penalty) to negate.

Creatures whose HD exceed your caster level are unaffected by *holy word*.

HORRID WILTING

School necromancy; **Level** sorcerer/wizard 8

Casting Time 1 standard action

Components V, S, M/DF (a bit of sponge)

Range long (400 ft. + 40 ft./level)

Targets living creatures, no two of which can be more than 60 ft. apart

Duration instantaneous

Saving Throw Fortitude half; **Spell Resistance** yes

This spell evaporates moisture from the body of each subject living creature, causing flesh to wither and crack and crumble to dust. This deals 1d6 points of damage per caster level (maximum 20d6). This spell is especially devastating to water elementals and plant creatures, which instead take 1d8 points of damage per caster level (maximum 20d8).

HYPNOTIC PATTERN

School illusion (pattern) [mind-affecting]; **Level** bard 2, sorcerer/wizard 2

Casting Time 1 standard action

Components V (bard only), S, M (a stick of incense or a crystal rod); see text

Range medium (100 ft. + 10 ft./level)

Effect colorful lights in a 10-ft.-radius spread

Duration Concentration + 2 rounds

Saving Throw Will negates; **Spell Resistance** yes

A twisting pattern of subtle, shifting colors weaves through the air, fascinating creatures within it. Roll 2d4 and add your caster level (maximum 10) to determine the total number of HD of creatures affected. Creatures with the fewest HD are affected first; and, among creatures with equal HD, those who are closest to the spell's point of origin are affected first. HD that are not sufficient to affect a creature are wasted. Affected creatures become fascinated by the pattern of colors. Sightless creatures are not affected.

A wizard or sorcerer need not utter a sound to cast this spell, but a bard must perform as a verbal component.

HYPNOTISM

School enchantment (compulsion) [mind-affecting]; **Level** bard 1, sorcerer/wizard 1

Casting Time 1 round

Components V, S

Range close (25 ft. + 5 ft./2 levels)

Area several living creatures, no two of which may be more than 30 ft. apart

Duration 2d4 rounds (D)

Saving Throw Will negates; **Spell Resistance** yes

Your gestures and droning incantation fascinate nearby creatures, causing them to stop and stare blankly at you. In addition, you can use their rapt attention to make your suggestions and requests seem more plausible. Roll 2d4 to see how many total HD of creatures you affect. Creatures with fewer HD are affected before creatures with more HD. Only creatures that can see or hear you are affected, but they do not need to understand you to be fascinated.

If you use this spell in combat, each target gains a +2 bonus on its saving throw. If the spell affects only a single creature not in combat at the time, the saving throw has a penalty of –2.

While the subject is fascinated by this spell, it reacts as though it were two steps more friendly in attitude. This allows you to make a single request of the affected creature (provided you can communicate with it). The request must be brief and reasonable. Even after the spell ends, the creature retains its new attitude toward you, but only with respect to that particular request.

A creature that fails its saving throw does not remember that you enspelled it.

ICE STORM

School evocation [cold]; **Level** druid 4, sorcerer/wizard 4

Casting Time 1 standard action

Components V, S, M/DF (dust and water)

Range long (400 ft. + 40 ft./level)

Area cylinder (20-ft. radius, 40 ft. high)

Duration 1 round/level (D)

Saving Throw none; **Spell Resistance** yes

Great magical hailstones pound down upon casting this spell, dealing 3d6 points of bludgeoning damage and 2d6 points of cold damage to every creature in the area. This damage only occurs once, when the spell is cast. For the remaining duration of the spell, heavy snow and sleet rains down in the area. Creatures inside this area take a –4 penalty on Perception skill checks and the entire area is treated as difficult terrain. At the end of the duration, the snow and hail disappear, leaving no aftereffects (other than the damage dealt).

IDENTIFY

School divination; **Level** bard 1, sorcerer/wizard 1

Casting Time 1 standard action

Components V, S, M (wine stirred with an owl's feather)

Range 60 ft.

Area cone-shaped emanation

Duration 3 rounds/level (D)

Saving Throw: none; **Spell Resistance:** no

This spell functions as *detect magic*, except that it gives you a +10 enhancement bonus on Spellcraft checks made to identify the properties and command words of magic items in your possession. This spell does not allow you to identify artifacts.

ILLUSORY SCRIPT

School illusion (phantasm) [mind-affecting]; **Level** bard 3, sorcerer/wizard 3

Casting Time 1 minute per page

Components V, S, M (lead-based ink worth 50 gp)

Range touch

Target one touched object weighing no more than 10 lbs.

Duration one day/level (D)

Saving Throw Will negates; see text; **Spell Resistance** yes

You write instructions or other information on parchment, paper, or any suitable writing material. The *illusory script* appears to be some form of foreign or magical writing. Only the person (or people) designated by you at the time of the casting can read the writing; it's unintelligible to any other character.

Any unauthorized creature attempting to read the script triggers a potent illusory effect and must make a saving throw. A successful saving throw means the creature can look away with only a mild sense of disorientation. Failure means the creature is subject to a *suggestion* implanted in the script by you at the time the *illusory script* spell was cast. The *suggestion* lasts only 30 minutes. Typical *suggestions* include "Close the book and leave," "Forget the existence of this note," and so forth. If successfully dispelled by *dispel magic*, the *illusory script* and its secret message disappear. The hidden message can be read by a combination of the *true seeing* spell with the *read magic* or *comprehend languages* spell.

ILLUSORY WALL

School illusion (figment); **Level** sorcerer/wizard 4

Casting Time 1 standard action

Components V, S

Range close (25 ft. + 5 ft./2 levels)

Effect image 1 ft. by 10 ft. by 10 ft.

Duration permanent

Saving Throw Will disbelief (if interacted with); **Spell Resistance** no

This spell creates the illusion of a wall, floor, ceiling, or similar surface. It appears absolutely real when viewed, but physical objects can pass through it without difficulty. When the spell is used to hide pits, traps, or normal doors, any detection abilities that do not require sight work normally. Touch or a probing search reveals the true nature of the surface, though such measures do not cause the illusion to disappear. Although the caster can see through his *illusory wall*, other creatures cannot, even if they succeed at their will save (but they do learn that it is not real).

IMBUE WITH SPELL ABILITY

School evocation; **Level** cleric 4

Casting Time 10 minutes

Components V, S, DF

Range touch

Target creature touched; see text

Duration permanent until discharged (D)

Saving Throw Will negates (harmless); **Spell Resistance** yes (harmless)

You transfer some of your currently prepared spells, and the ability to cast them, to another creature. Only a creature with an Intelligence score of at least 5 and a Wisdom score of at least 9 can receive this boon. Only cleric spells from the schools of abjuration, divination, and conjuration (healing) can be transferred. The number and level of spells that the subject can be granted depends on its Hit Dice; even multiple castings of *imbue with spell ability* can't exceed this limit.

HD of Recipient	Spells Imbued
2 or lower	One 1st-level spell
3–4	One or two 1st-level spells
5 or higher	One or two 1st-level spells and one 2nd-level spell

The transferred spell's variable characteristics (range, duration, area, and the like) function according to your level, not the level of the recipient.

Once you cast *imbue with spell ability*, you cannot prepare a new 4th-level spell to replace it until the recipient uses the imbued spells or is slain, or until you dismiss the *imbue with spell ability* spell. In the meantime, you remain responsible to your deity or your principles for the use to which the spell is put. If the number of 4th-level spells you can cast decreases, and that number drops below your current number of active *imbue with spell ability* spells, the more recently cast imbued spells are dispelled.

To cast a spell with a verbal component, the subject must be able to speak. To cast a spell with a somatic component, it must be able to move freely. To cast a spell with a material component or focus, it must have the materials or focus.

IMPLOSION

School evocation; **Level** cleric 9

Casting Time 1 standard action

Components V, S

Range close (25 ft. + 5 ft./2 levels)

Target one corporeal creature/round

Duration concentration (up to 1 round per 2 levels)

Saving Throw Fortitude negates; **Spell Resistance** yes

This spell causes a destructive resonance in a corporeal creature's body. Each round you concentrate (including the first), you can cause one creature to collapse in on itself, inflicting 10 points of damage per caster level. If you break concentration, the spell immediately ends, though any implosions that have already happened remain in effect. You can target a particular creature only once with each casting of the spell. Implosion has no effect on creatures in *gaseous form* or on incorporeal creatures.

IMPRISONMENT

School abjuration; **Level** sorcerer/wizard 9
Casting Time 1 standard action
Components V, S
Range touch
Target creature touched
Duration instantaneous
Saving Throw Will negates; see text; **Spell Resistance** yes

When you cast *imprisonment* and touch a creature, it is entombed in a state of suspended animation (see the *temporal stasis* spell) in a small sphere far beneath the surface of the ground. The subject remains there unless a *freedom* spell is cast at the locale where the imprisonment took place. Magical search by a *crystal ball*, a *locate object* spell, or some other similar divination does not reveal the fact that a creature is imprisoned, but *discern location* does. A *wish* or *miracle* spell will not free the recipient, but will reveal where it is entombed. If you know the target's name and some facts about its life, the target takes a −4 penalty on its save.

INCENDIARY CLOUD

School conjuration (creation) [fire]; **Level** sorcerer/wizard 8
Casting Time 1 standard action
Components V, S
Range medium (100 ft. + 10 ft./level)
Area cloud spreads in 20-ft. radius, 20 ft. high
Duration 1 round/level (D)
Saving Throw: Reflex half, see text; **Spell Resistance:** no

An *incendiary cloud* spell creates a cloud of roiling smoke shot through with white-hot embers. The smoke obscures all sight as a *fog cloud* does. In addition, the white-hot embers within the cloud deal 6d6 points of fire damage to everything within the cloud on your turn each round. All targets can make Reflex saves each round to take half damage.

As with a *cloudkill* spell, the smoke moves away from you at 10 feet per round. Figure out the smoke's new spread each round based on its new point of origin, which is 10 feet farther away from where you were when you cast the spell. By concentrating, you can make the cloud move as much as 60 feet each round. Any portion of the cloud that would extend beyond your maximum range dissipates harmlessly, reducing the remainder's spread thereafter.

As with *fog cloud*, wind disperses the smoke, and the spell can't be cast underwater.

INFLICT CRITICAL WOUNDS

School necromancy; **Level** cleric 4

This spell functions like *inflict light wounds*, except that you deal 4d8 points of damage + 1 point per caster level (maximum +20).

INFLICT CRITICAL WOUNDS, MASS

School necromancy; **Level** cleric 8

This spell functions like *mass inflict light wounds*, except that it deals 4d8 points of damage + 1 point per caster level (maximum +40).

INFLICT LIGHT WOUNDS

School necromancy; **Level** cleric 1
Casting Time 1 standard action
Components V, S
Range touch
Target creature touched
Duration instantaneous
Saving Throw Will half; **Spell Resistance** yes

When laying your hand upon a creature, you channel negative energy that deals 1d8 points of damage + 1 point per caster level (maximum +5).

Since undead are powered by negative energy, this spell cures such a creature of a like amount of damage, rather than harming it.

INFLICT LIGHT WOUNDS, MASS

School necromancy; **Level** cleric 5
Casting Time 1 standard action
Components V, S
Range close (25 ft. + 5 ft./2 levels)
Target one creature/level, no two of which can be more than 30 ft. apart
Duration instantaneous
Saving Throw Will half; **Spell Resistance** yes

Negative energy spreads out in all directions from the point of origin, dealing 1d8 points of damage + 1 point per caster level (maximum +25) to nearby living enemies.

Like other *inflict* spells, *mass inflict light wounds* cures undead in its area rather than damaging them. A cleric capable of spontaneously casting *inflict* spells can also spontaneously cast *mass inflict* spells.

INFLICT MODERATE WOUNDS

School necromancy; **Level** cleric 2

This spell functions like *inflict light wounds*, except that you deal 2d8 points of damage + 1 point per caster level (maximum +10).

INFLICT MODERATE WOUNDS, MASS

School necromancy; **Level** cleric 6

This spell functions like *mass inflict light wounds*, except that it deals 2d8 points of damage + 1 point per caster level (maximum +30).

INFLICT SERIOUS WOUNDS

School necromancy; **Level** cleric 3

This spell functions like *inflict light wounds*, except that you deal 3d8 points of damage + 1 point per caster level (maximum +15).

INFLICT SERIOUS WOUNDS, MASS

School necromancy; **Level** cleric 7

This spell functions like *mass inflict light wounds*, except that it deals 3d8 points of damage + 1 point per caster level (maximum +35).

INSANITY

School enchantment (compulsion) [mind-affecting]; **Level** sorcerer/wizard 7

Casting Time 1 standard action

Components V, S

Range medium (100 ft. + 10 ft./level)

Target one living creature

Duration instantaneous

Saving Throw Will negates; **Spell Resistance** yes

The affected creature suffers from a continuous *confusion* effect, as the spell.

Remove curse does not remove *insanity*. *Greater restoration, heal, limited wish, miracle,* or *wish* can restore the creature.

INSECT PLAGUE

School conjuration (summoning); **Level** cleric 5, druid 5

Casting Time 1 round

Components V, S, DF

Range long (400 ft. + 40 ft./level)

Effect one swarm of wasps per three levels, each of which must be adjacent to at least one other swarm

Duration 1 min./level

Saving Throw none; **Spell Resistance** no

You summon a number of swarms of wasps (one per three levels, to a maximum of six swarms at 18th level, see the *Pathfinder RPG Bestiary*). The swarms must be summoned so that each one is adjacent to at least one other swarm (that is, the swarms must fill one contiguous area). You may summon the wasp swarms so that they share the area of other creatures. Each swarm attacks any creatures occupying its area. The swarms are stationary after being summoned, and won't pursue creatures that flee.

INSTANT SUMMONS

School conjuration (summoning); **Level** sorcerer/wizard 7

Casting Time 1 standard action

Components V, S, M (sapphire worth 1,000 gp)

Range see text

Target one object weighing 10 lbs. or less whose longest dimension is 6 ft. or less

Duration permanent until discharged

Saving Throw none; **Spell Resistance** no

You call some nonliving item directly to your hand from virtually any location.

First, you must place your *arcane mark* on the item. Then you cast this spell, which magically and invisibly inscribes the name of the item on a sapphire worth at least 1,000 gp. Thereafter, you can summon the item by speaking a special word (set by you when the spell is cast) and crushing the gem. The item appears instantly in your hand. Only you can use the gem in this way.

If the item is in the possession of another creature, the spell does not work, but you know who the possessor is and roughly where that creature is located when the summons occurs.

The inscription on the gem is invisible. It is also unreadable, except by means of a *read magic* spell, to anyone but you.

The item can be summoned from another plane, but only if no other creature has claimed ownership of it.

INTERPOSING HAND

School evocation [force]; **Level** sorcerer/wizard 5

Casting Time 1 standard action

Components V, S, F (a soft glove)

Range medium (100 ft. + 10 ft./level)

Effect 10-ft. hand

Duration 1 round/level (D)

Saving Throw none; **Spell Resistance** yes

Interposing hand creates a Large magic hand that appears between you and one opponent. This floating, disembodied hand then moves to remain between the two of you, regardless of where you move or how the opponent tries to get around it, providing cover (+4 AC) for you against that opponent. Nothing can fool the hand—it sticks with the selected opponent in spite of *darkness*, invisibility, polymorphing, or any other attempt at hiding or disguise. The hand does not pursue an opponent, however.

An *interposing hand* is 10 feet long and about that wide with its fingers outstretched. It has as many hit points as you do when you're undamaged, and is AC 20 (–1 size, +11 natural). It takes damage as a normal creature, but most magical effects that don't cause damage do not affect it.

The hand never provokes attacks of opportunity from opponents. It cannot push through a *wall of force* or enter an *antimagic field*, but it suffers the full effect of a *prismatic wall* or *prismatic sphere*. The hand makes saving throws as its caster.

Disintegrate or a successful *dispel magic* destroys it.

Any creature weighing 2,000 pounds or less that tries to push past the hand is slowed to half its normal speed. The hand cannot reduce the speed of a creature weighing more than 2,000 pounds, but it still affects the creature's attacks.

Directing the spell to a new target is a move action.

INVISIBILITY

School illusion (glamer); **Level** bard 2, sorcerer/wizard 2

Casting Time 1 standard action

Components V, S, M/DF (an eyelash encased in gum arabic)

Range personal or touch

Target you or a creature or object weighing no more than 100 lbs./level

Duration 1 min./level (D)

Saving Throw Will negates (harmless) or Will negates (harmless, object); **Spell Resistance** yes (harmless) or yes (harmless, object)

The creature or object touched becomes invisible. If the recipient is a creature carrying gear, that vanishes, too. If you cast the spell on someone else, neither you nor your allies can see the subject, unless you can normally see invisible things or you employ magic to do so.

Items dropped or put down by an invisible creature become visible; items picked up disappear if tucked into the clothing or pouches worn by the creature. Light, however, never becomes invisible, although a source of light can become so (thus, the effect is that of a light with no visible source). Any part of an item that the subject carries but that extends more than 10 feet from it becomes visible.

Of course, the subject is not magically silenced, and certain other conditions can render the recipient detectable (such as swimming in water or stepping in a puddle). If a check is required, a stationary invisible creature has a +40 bonus on its Stealth checks. This bonus is reduced to +20 if the creature is moving. The spell ends if the subject attacks any creature. For purposes of this spell, an attack includes any spell targeting a foe or whose area or effect includes a foe. Exactly who is a foe depends on the invisible character's perceptions. Actions directed at unattended objects do not break the spell. Causing harm indirectly is not an attack. Thus, an invisible being can open doors, talk, eat, climb stairs, summon monsters and have them attack, cut the ropes holding a rope bridge while enemies are on the bridge, remotely trigger traps, open a portcullis to release attack dogs, and so forth. If the subject attacks directly, however, it immediately becomes visible along with all its gear. Spells such as *bless* that specifically affect allies but not foes are not attacks for this purpose, even when they include foes in their area.

Invisibility can be made permanent (on objects only) with a *permanency* spell.

INVISIBILITY, GREATER

School illusion (glamer); **Level** bard 4, sorcerer/wizard 4
Components: V, S
Target you or creature touched
Duration 1 round/level (D)
Saving Throw Will negates (harmless)

This spell functions like *invisibility*, except that it doesn't end if the subject attacks.

INVISIBILITY, MASS

School illusion (glamer); **Level** sorcerer/wizard 7
Range long (400 ft. + 40 ft./level)
Targets any number of creatures, no two of which can be more than 180 ft. apart

This spell functions like *invisibility*, except that the effect moves with the group and is broken when anyone in the group attacks. Individuals in the group cannot see each other. The spell is broken for any individual who moves more than 180 feet from the nearest member of the group. If only two individuals are affected, the one moving away from the other one loses its invisibility. If both are

moving away from each other, they both become visible when the distance between them exceeds 180 feet.

INVISIBILITY PURGE

School evocation; **Level** cleric 3
Casting Time 1 standard action
Components V, S
Range personal
Target you
Duration 1 min./level (D)

You surround yourself with a sphere of power with a radius of 5 feet per caster level that negates all forms of invisibility.

Anything invisible becomes visible while in the area.

INVISIBILITY SPHERE

School illusion (glamer); **Level** bard 3, sorcerer/wizard 3
Components: V, S, M
Area 10-ft.-radius emanation around the creature

This spell functions like *invisibility*, except that this spell confers invisibility upon all creatures within 10 feet of the recipient at the time the spell is cast. The center of the effect is mobile with the recipient.

Those affected by this spell can see each other and themselves as if unaffected by the spell. Any affected creature moving out of the area becomes visible, but creatures moving into the area after the spell is cast do not become invisible. Affected creatures (other than the recipient) who attack negate the invisibility only for themselves. If the spell recipient attacks, the *invisibility sphere* ends.

IRON BODY

School transmutation; **Level** sorcerer/wizard 8
Casting Time 1 standard action
Components V, S, M/DF (a piece of iron from an iron golem, a hero's armor, or a war machine)
Range personal
Target you
Duration 1 min./level (D)

This spell transforms your body into living iron, which grants you several powerful resistances and abilities. You gain damage reduction 15/adamantine. You are immune to blindness, critical hits, ability score damage, deafness, disease, drowning, electricity, poison, stunning, and all spells or attacks that affect your physiology or respiration, because you have no physiology or respiration while this spell is in effect. You take only half damage from acid and fire. However, you also become vulnerable to all special attacks that affect iron golems (see the *Pathfinder RPG Bestiary*).

You gain a +6 enhancement bonus to your Strength score, but you take a –6 penalty to Dexterity as well (to a minimum Dexterity score of 1), and your speed is reduced to half normal. You have an arcane spell failure chance of 35% and a –6 armor check penalty, just as if you were clad in full plate armor. You cannot drink (and thus can't use potions) or play wind instruments.

Your unarmed attack deals damage equal to a club sized for you (1d4 for Small characters or 1d6 for Medium characters), and you are considered armed when making unarmed attacks.

Your weight increases by a factor of 10, causing you to sink in water like a stone. However, you could survive the lack of air at the bottom of the ocean—at least until the spell duration expires.

IRONWOOD

School transmutation; **Level** druid 6
Casting Time 1 minute/lb. created
Components V, S, F (wood to be transformed)
Range 0 ft.
Effect an *ironwood* object weighing up to 5 lbs./level
Duration 1 day/level (D)
Saving Throw none; **Spell Resistance** no

Ironwood is a magical substance created by druids from normal wood. While remaining natural wood in almost every way, *ironwood* is as strong, heavy, and resistant to fire as steel. Spells that affect metal or iron do not function on *ironwood*. Spells that affect wood do affect *ironwood*, although *ironwood* does not burn. Using this spell with *wood shape* or a wood-related Craft check, you can fashion wooden items that function as steel items. Thus, wooden plate armor and wooden swords can be created that are as durable as their normal steel counterparts. These items are freely usable by druids.

Further, if you make only half as much *ironwood* as the spell would normally allow, any weapon, shield, or suit of armor so created is treated as a magic item with a +1 enhancement bonus.

IRRESISTIBLE DANCE

School enchantment (compulsion) [mind-affecting]; **Level** bard 6, sorcerer/wizard 8
Casting Time 1 standard action
Components V
Range touch
Target living creature touched
Duration 1d4+1 rounds
Saving Throw Will partial; **Spell Resistance** yes

The subject feels an undeniable urge to dance and begins doing so, complete with foot shuffling and tapping. The spell effect makes it impossible for the subject to do anything other than caper and prance in place. The effect imposes a –4 penalty to Armor Class and a –10 penalty on Reflex saves, and it negates any AC bonus granted by a shield the target holds. The dancing subject provokes attacks of opportunity each round on its turn. A successful Will save reduces the duration of this effect to 1 round.

JUMP

School transmutation; **Level** druid 1, ranger 1, sorcerer/wizard 1
Casting Time 1 standard action
Components V, S, M (a grasshopper's hind leg)
Range touch
Target creature touched
Duration 1 min./level (D)

Saving Throw Will negates (harmless); **Spell Resistance** yes

The subject gets a +10 enhancement bonus on Acrobatics checks made to attempt high jumps or long jumps. The enhancement bonus increases to +20 at caster level 5th, and to +30 (the maximum) at caster level 9th.

KEEN EDGE

School transmutation; **Level** sorcerer/wizard 3
Casting Time 1 standard action
Components V, S
Range close (25 ft. + 5 ft./2 levels)
Targets one weapon or 50 projectiles, all of which must be together at the time of casting
Duration 10 min./level
Saving Throw Will negates (harmless, object); **Spell Resistance** yes (harmless, object)

This spell makes a weapon magically keen, improving its ability to deal telling blows. This transmutation doubles the threat range of the weapon. A threat range of 20 becomes 19–20, a threat range of 19–20 becomes 17–20, and a threat range of 18–20 becomes 15–20. The spell can be cast only on piercing or slashing weapons. If cast on arrows or crossbow bolts, the *keen edge* on a particular projectile ends after one use, whether or not the missile strikes its intended target. Treat shuriken as arrows, rather than as thrown weapons, for the purpose of this spell.

Multiple effects that increase a weapon's threat range (such as the *keen* special weapon property and the Improved Critical feat) don't stack. You can't cast this spell on a natural weapon, such as a claw.

KNOCK

School transmutation; **Level** sorcerer/wizard 2
Casting Time 1 standard action
Components V
Range medium (100 ft. + 10 ft./level)
Target one door, box, or chest with an area of up to 10 sq. ft./level
Duration instantaneous; see text
Saving Throw none; **Spell Resistance** no

Knock opens stuck, barred, or locked doors, as well as those subject to *hold portal* or *arcane lock*. When you complete the casting of this spell, make a caster level check against the DC of the lock with a +10 bonus. If successful, *knock* opens up to two means of closure. This spell opens secret doors, as well as locked or trick-opening boxes or chests. It also loosens welds, shackles, or chains (provided they serve to hold something shut). If used to open an *arcane locked* door, the spell does not remove the *arcane lock* but simply suspends its functioning for 10 minutes. In all other cases, the door does not relock itself or become stuck again on its own. *Knock* does not raise barred gates or similar impediments (such as a portcullis), nor does it affect ropes, vines, and the like. The effect is limited by the area. Each casting can undo as many as two means of preventing access.

KNOW DIRECTION

School divination; **Level** bard 0, druid 0
Casting Time 1 standard action
Components V, S
Range personal
Target you
Duration instantaneous

When you cast this spell, you instantly know the direction of north from your current position. The spell is effective in any environment in which "north" exists, but it may not work in extraplanar settings. Your knowledge of north is correct at the moment of casting, but you can get lost again within moments if you don't find some external reference point to help you keep track of direction.

LEGEND LORE

School divination; **Level** bard 4, sorcerer/wizard 6
Casting Time see text
Components V, S, M (incense worth 250 gp), F (four pieces of ivory worth 50 gp each)
Range personal
Target you
Duration see text

Legend lore brings to your mind legends about an important person, place, or thing. If the person or thing is at hand, or if you are in the place in question, the casting time is only 1d4 × 10 minutes. If you have only detailed information on the person, place, or thing, the casting time is 1d10 days, and the resulting lore is less complete and specific (though it often provides enough information to help you find the person, place, or thing, thus allowing a better *legend lore* result next time). If you know only rumors, the casting time is 2d6 weeks, and the resulting lore is vague and incomplete (though it often directs you to more detailed information, thus allowing a better *legend lore* result next time).

During the casting, you cannot engage in other than routine activities: eating, sleeping, and so forth. When completed, the divination brings legends (if any) about the person, place, or things to your mind. These may be legends that are still current, legends that have been forgotten, or even information that has never been generally known. If the person, place, or thing is not of legendary importance, you gain no information. As a rule of thumb, characters who are 11th level and higher are "legendary," as are the sorts of creatures they contend with, the major magic items they wield, and the places where they perform their key deeds.

LESSER (SPELL NAME)

Any spell whose name begins with *lesser* is alphabetized in this chapter according to the spell name. Thus, the description of a *lesser* spell appears near the description of the spell on which it is based. Spell chains that have *lesser* spells in them include those based on the spells *confusion*, *geas*, *globe of invulnerability*, *planar ally*, *planar binding*, and *restoration*.

LEVITATE

School transmutation; **Level** sorcerer/wizard 2
Casting Time 1 standard action
Components V, S, F (a leather loop or golden wire bent into a cup shape)
Range personal or close (25 ft. + 5 ft./2 levels)
Target you or one willing creature or one object (total weight up to 100 lbs./level)
Duration 1 min./level (D)
Saving Throw none; **Spell Resistance** no

Levitate allows you to move yourself, another creature, or an object up and down as you wish. A creature must be willing to be levitated, and an object must be unattended or possessed by a willing creature. You can mentally direct the recipient to move up or down as much as 20 feet each round; doing so is a move action. You cannot move the recipient horizontally, but the recipient could clamber along the face of a cliff, for example, or push against a ceiling to move laterally (generally at half its base land speed).

A levitating creature that attacks with a melee or ranged weapon finds itself increasingly unstable; the first attack has a −1 penalty on attack rolls, the second −2, and so on, to a maximum penalty of −5. A full round spent stabilizing allows the creature to begin again at −1.

LIGHT

School evocation [light]; **Level** bard 0, cleric 0, druid 0, sorcerer/wizard 0
Casting Time 1 standard action
Components V, M/DF (a firefly)
Range touch
Target object touched
Duration 10 min./level
Saving Throw none; **Spell Resistance** no

This spell causes a touched object to glow like a torch, shedding normal light in a 20-foot radius from the point touched, and increasing the light level for an additional 20 feet by one step, up to normal light (darkness becomes dim light, and dim light becomes normal light). In an area of normal or bright light, this spell has no effect. The effect is immobile, but it can be cast on a movable object.

You can only have one *light* spell active at any one time. If you cast this spell while another casting is still in effect, the previous casting is dispelled. If you make this spell permanent (through *permanency* or a similar effect), it does not count against this limit. *Light* can be used to counter or dispel any darkness spell of equal or lower spell level.

LIGHTNING BOLT

School evocation [electricity]; **Level** sorcerer/wizard 3
Casting Time 1 standard action
Components V, S, M (fur and a glass rod)
Range 120 ft.
Area 120-ft. line
Duration instantaneous
Saving Throw Reflex half; **Spell Resistance** yes

You release a powerful stroke of electrical energy that deals 1d6 points of electricity damage per caster level (maximum 10d6) to each creature within its area. The bolt begins at your fingertips.

The *lightning bolt* sets fire to combustibles and damages objects in its path. It can melt metals with a low melting point, such as lead, gold, copper, silver, or bronze. If the damage caused to an interposing barrier shatters or breaks through it, the bolt may continue beyond the barrier if the spell's range permits; otherwise, it stops at the barrier just as any other spell effect does.

LIMITED WISH

School universal; **Level** sorcerer/wizard 7
Casting Time 1 standard action
Components V, S, M (diamond worth 1,500 gp)
Range see text
Target, Effect, Area see text
Duration see text
Saving Throw none, see text; **Spell Resistance** yes

A *limited wish* lets you create nearly any type of effect. For example, a *limited wish* can do any of the following things.

- Duplicate any sorcerer/wizard spell of 6th level or lower, provided the spell does not belong to one of your opposition schools.
- Duplicate any non-sorcerer/wizard spell of 5th level or lower, provided the spell does not belong to one of your opposition schools.
- Duplicate any sorcerer/wizard spell of 5th level or lower, even if it belongs to one of your opposition schools.
- Duplicate any non-sorcerer/wizard spell of 4th level or lower, even if it belongs to one of your opposition schools.
- Undo the harmful effects of many spells, such as *geas/quest* or *insanity*.
- Produce any other effect whose power level is in line with the above effects, such as a single creature automatically hitting on its next attack or taking a –7 penalty on its next saving throw.

A duplicated spell allows saving throws and spell resistance as normal, but the save DC is for a 7th-level spell. When a *limited wish* spell duplicates a spell with a material component that costs more than 1,000 gp, you must provide that component (in addition to the 1,500 gp diamond component for this spell).

LIVEOAK

School transmutation; **Level** druid 6
Casting Time 10 minutes
Components V, S
Range touch
Target tree touched
Duration 1 day/level (D)
Saving Throw none; **Spell Resistance** no

This spell turns an oak tree into a protector or guardian. The spell can only be cast on a single tree at a time; while *liveoak* is in effect, you can't cast it again on another tree. *Liveoak* must be cast on a healthy, Huge oak. A triggering phrase of up to one word per caster level is placed on the targeted oak. The *liveoak* spell triggers the tree into animating as a treant.

If *liveoak* is dispelled, the tree takes root immediately wherever it happens to be. If released by you, the tree tries to return to its original location before taking root.

LOCATE CREATURE

School divination; **Level** bard 4, sorcerer/wizard 4
Components V, S, M (fur from a bloodhound)
Duration 10 min./level

This spell functions like *locate object,* except this spell locates a known creature. You slowly turn and sense when you are facing in the direction of the creature to be located, provided it is within range. You also know in which direction the creature is moving, if any.

The spell can locate a creature of a specific kind or a specific creature known to you. It cannot find a creature of a certain type. To find a kind of creature, you must have seen such a creature up close (within 30 feet) at least once.

Running water blocks the spell. It cannot detect objects. It can be fooled by *mislead, nondetection,* and *polymorph* spells.

LOCATE OBJECT

School divination; **Level** bard 2, cleric 3, sorcerer/wizard 2
Casting Time 1 standard action
Components V, S, F/DF (a forked twig)
Range long (400 ft. + 40 ft./level)
Area circle, centered on you, with a radius of 400 ft. + 40 ft./level
Duration 1 min./level
Saving Throw none; **Spell Resistance** no

You sense the direction of a well-known or clearly visualized object. You can search for general items, in which case you locate the nearest of its kind if more than one is within range. Attempting to find a certain item requires a specific and accurate mental image; if the image is not close enough to the actual object, the spell fails. You cannot specify a unique item unless you have observed that particular item firsthand (not through divination).

The spell is blocked by even a thin sheet of lead. Creatures cannot be found by this spell. *Polymorph any object* and *nondetection* fool it.

LONGSTRIDER

School transmutation; **Level** druid 1, ranger 1
Casting Time 1 standard action
Components V, S, M (a pinch of dirt)
Range personal
Target you
Duration 1 hour/level (D)

This spell gives you a +10 foot enhancement bonus to your base speed. It has no effect on other modes of movement, such as burrow, climb, fly, or swim.

LULLABY

School enchantment (compulsion) [mind-affecting]; **Level** bard 0
Casting Time 1 standard action
Components V, S

Range medium (100 ft. + 10 ft./level)

Area living creatures within a 10-ft.-radius burst

Duration concentration + 1 round/level (D)

Saving Throw Will negates; **Spell Resistance** yes

Any creature within the area that fails a Will save becomes drowsy and inattentive, taking a –5 penalty on Perception checks and a –2 penalty on Will saves against *sleep* effects while the *lullaby* is in effect. *Lullaby* lasts for as long as the caster concentrates, plus up to 1 round per caster level thereafter.

MAGE ARMOR

School conjuration (creation) [force]; **Level** sorcerer/wizard 1

Casting Time 1 standard action

Components V, S, F (a piece of cured leather)

Range touch

Target creature touched

Duration 1 hour/level (D)

Saving Throw Will negates (harmless); **Spell Resistance** no

An invisible but tangible field of force surrounds the subject of a *mage armor* spell, providing a +4 armor bonus to AC.

Unlike mundane armor, *mage armor* entails no armor check penalty, arcane spell failure chance, or speed reduction. Since *mage armor* is made of force, incorporeal creatures can't bypass it the way they do normal armor.

MAGE HAND

School transmutation; **Level** bard 0, sorcerer/wizard 0

Casting Time 1 standard action

Components V, S

Range close (25 ft. + 5 ft./2 levels)

Target one nonmagical, unattended object weighing up to 5 lbs.

Duration concentration

Saving Throw none; **Spell Resistance** no

You point your finger at an object and can lift it and move it at will from a distance. As a move action, you can propel the object as far as 15 feet in any direction, though the spell ends if the distance between you and the object ever exceeds the spell's range.

MAGE'S DISJUNCTION

School abjuration; **Level** sorcerer/wizard 9

Casting Time 1 standard action

Components V

Range close (25 ft. + 5 ft./2 levels)

Area all magical effects and magic items within a 40-ft.-radius burst, or one magic item (see text)

Duration 1 minute/level

Saving Throw Will negates (object); **Spell Resistance** no

All magical effects and magic items within the radius of the spell, except for those that you carry or touch, are disjoined. That is, spells and spell-like effects are unraveled and destroyed completely (ending the effect as a *dispel magic* spell does), and each permanent magic item must make a successful Will save or be turned into a normal item for the duration of this spell.

An item in a creature's possession uses its own Will save bonus or its possessor's Will save bonus, whichever is higher. If an item's saving throw results in a natural 1 on the die, the item is destroyed instead of being suppressed.

You also have a 1% chance per caster level of destroying an *antimagic field*. If the *antimagic field* survives the *disjunction*, no items within it are disjoined.

You can also use this spell to target a single item. The item gets a Will save at a –5 penalty to avoid being permanently destroyed. Even artifacts are subject to *mage's disjunction*, though there is only a 1% chance per caster level of actually affecting such powerful items. If successful, the artifact's power unravels, and it is destroyed (with no save). If an artifact is destroyed, you must make a DC 25 Will save or permanently lose all spellcasting abilities. These abilities cannot be recovered by mortal magic, not even *miracle* or *wish*. Destroying artifacts is a dangerous business, and it is 95% likely to attract the attention of some powerful being who has an interest in or connection with the device.

MAGE'S FAITHFUL HOUND

School conjuration (creation); **Level** sorcerer/wizard 5

Casting Time 1 standard action

Components V, S, M (a tiny silver whistle, a piece of bone, and a thread)

Range close (25 ft. + 5 ft./2 levels)

Effect phantom watchdog

Duration 1 hour/caster level or until discharged, then 1 round/caster level; see text

Saving Throw none; **Spell Resistance** no

You conjure up a phantom watchdog that is invisible to everyone but yourself. It then guards the area where it was conjured (it does not move). The hound immediately starts barking loudly if any Small or larger creature approaches within 30 feet of it. (Those within 30 feet of the hound when it is conjured may move about in the area, but if they leave and return, they activate the barking.) The hound sees invisible and ethereal creatures. It does not react to figments, but it does react to shadow illusions.

If an intruder approaches to within 5 feet of the hound, the dog stops barking and delivers a vicious bite (+10 attack bonus, 2d6+3 points of piercing damage) once per round. The dog also gets the bonuses appropriate to an invisible creature (see *invisibility*).

The dog is considered ready to bite intruders, so it delivers its first bite on the intruder's turn. Its bite is the equivalent of a magic weapon for the purpose of damage reduction. The hound cannot be attacked, but it can be dispelled.

The spell lasts for 1 hour per caster level, but once the hound begins barking, it lasts only 1 round per caster level. If you are ever more than 100 feet distant from the hound, the spell ends.

MAGE'S LUCUBRATION

School transmutation; **Level** wizard 6

Casting Time 1 standard action

Components V, S

Range personal

Target you

Duration instantaneous

You instantly prepare any one spell of 5th level or lower that you have used during the past 24 hours. The spell must have been actually cast during that period. The chosen spell is stored in your mind as through prepared in the normal fashion.

If the recalled spell requires material components, you must provide them. The recovered spell is not usable until the material components are available.

MAGE'S MAGNIFICENT MANSION

School conjuration (creation); **Level** sorcerer/wizard 7

Casting Time 1 standard action

Components V, S, F (a miniature ivory door, a piece of polished marble, and a silver spoon, each worth 5 gp)

Range close (25 ft. + 5 ft./2 levels)

Effect extradimensional mansion, up to three 10-ft. cubes/level (S)

Duration 2 hours/level (D)

Saving Throw none; **Spell Resistance** no

You conjure up an extradimensional dwelling that has a single entrance on the plane from which the spell was cast. The entry point looks like a faint shimmering in the air that is 4 feet wide and 8 feet high. Only those you designate may enter the mansion, and the portal is shut and made invisible behind you when you enter. You may open it again from your own side at will. Once observers have passed beyond the entrance, they are in a magnificent foyer with numerous chambers beyond. The atmosphere is clean, fresh, and warm.

You can create any floor plan you desire to the limit of the spell's effect. The place is furnished and contains sufficient foodstuffs to serve a nine-course banquet to a dozen people per caster level. A staff of near-transparent servants (as many as two per caster level), liveried and obedient, wait upon all who enter. The servants function as *unseen servant* spells except that they are visible and can go anywhere in the mansion.

Since the place can be entered only through its special portal, outside conditions do not affect the mansion, nor do conditions inside it pass to the plane beyond.

MAGE'S PRIVATE SANCTUM

School abjuration; **Level** sorcerer/wizard 5

Casting Time 10 minutes

Components V, S, M (a sheet of lead, a piece of glass, a wad of cotton, and powdered chrysolite)

Range close (25 ft. + 5 ft./2 levels)

Area 30-ft. cube/level (S)

Duration 24 hours (D)

Saving Throw none; **Spell Resistance** no

This spell ensures privacy. Anyone looking into the area from outside sees only a dark, foggy mass. Darkvision cannot penetrate it. No sounds, no matter how loud, can escape the area, so nobody can eavesdrop from outside. Those inside can see out normally.

Divination (scrying) spells cannot perceive anything within the area, and those within are immune to *detect thoughts*. The ward prevents speech between those inside and those outside (because it blocks sound), but it does not prevent other communication, such as a *sending* or *message* spell, or telepathic communication, such as that between a wizard and his familiar.

The spell does not prevent creatures or objects from moving into and out of the area.

Mage's private sanctum can be made permanent with a *permanency* spell.

MAGE'S SWORD

School evocation [force]; **Level** sorcerer/wizard 7

Casting Time 1 standard action

Components V, S, F (a miniature platinum sword worth 250 gp)

Range close (25 ft. + 5 ft./2 levels)

Effect one sword

Duration 1 round/level (D)

Saving Throw none; **Spell Resistance** yes

This spell brings into being a shimmering, sword-like plane of force. The sword strikes at any opponent within its range, as you desire, starting in the round that you cast the spell. The sword attacks its designated target once each round on your turn. Its attack bonus is equal to your caster level + your Intelligence bonus or your Charisma bonus (for wizards or sorcerers, respectively) with an additional +3 enhancement bonus. As a force effect, it can strike ethereal and incorporeal creatures. It deals 4d6+3 points of force damage, with a threat range of 19–20 and a critical multiplier of ×2.

The sword always strikes from your direction. It does not get a bonus for flanking or help a combatant get one. If the sword goes beyond the spell range from you, goes out of your sight, or you are not directing it, it returns to you and hovers.

Each round after the first, you can use a standard action to switch the sword to a new target. If you do not, the sword continues to attack the previous round's target.

The sword cannot be attacked or harmed by physical attacks, but *dispel magic*, *disintegrate*, a *sphere of annihilation*, or a *rod of cancellation* affects it. The sword's AC is 13 (10, +0 size bonus for Medium object, +3 deflection bonus).

If an attacked creature has spell resistance, the resistance is checked the first time *mage's sword* strikes it. If the sword is successfully resisted, the spell is dispelled. If not, the sword has its normal full effect on that creature for the duration of the spell.

MAGIC AURA

School illusion (glamer); **Level** bard 1, sorcerer/wizard 1

Casting Time 1 standard action

Components V, S, F (a small square of silk that must be passed over the object that receives the aura)

Range touch

Target one touched object weighing up to 5 lbs./level

Duration 1 day/level (D)

Saving Throw none; see text; **Spell Resistance** no

You alter an item's aura so that it registers to *detect* spells (and spells with similar capabilities) as though it were nonmagical, or a magic item of a kind you specify, or the subject of a spell you specify. If the object bearing *magic aura* has *identify* cast on it or is similarly examined, the examiner recognizes that the aura is false and detects the object's actual qualities if he succeeds on a Will save. Otherwise, he believes the aura and no amount of testing reveals what the true magic is.

If the targeted item's own aura is exceptionally powerful (if it is an artifact, for instance), *magic aura* doesn't work.

Note: A magic weapon, shield, or suit of armor must be a masterwork item, so a sword of average make, for example, looks suspicious if it has a magical aura.

MAGIC CIRCLE AGAINST CHAOS

School abjuration [lawful]; **Level** cleric 3, paladin 3, sorcerer/wizard 3

This spell functions like *magic circle against evil*, except that it is similar to *protection from chaos* instead of *protection from evil*, and it can imprison a nonlawful called creature.

MAGIC CIRCLE AGAINST EVIL

School abjuration [good]; **Level** cleric 3, paladin 3, sorcerer/wizard 3

Casting Time 1 standard action

Components V, S, M/DF (a 3-ft.-diameter circle of powdered silver)

Range touch

Area 10-ft.-radius emanation from touched creature

Duration 10 min./level

Saving Throw Will negates (harmless); **Spell Resistance** no; see text

All creatures within the area gain the effects of a *protection from evil* spell, and evil summoned creatures cannot enter the area either. Creatures in the area, or who later enter the area, receive only one attempt to suppress effects that are controlling them. If successful, such effects are suppressed as long as they remain in the area. Creatures that leave the area and come back are not protected. You must overcome a creature's spell resistance in order to keep it at bay (as in the third function of *protection from evil*), but the deflection and resistance bonuses and the protection from mental control apply regardless of enemies' spell resistance.

This spell has an alternative version that you may choose when casting it. A *magic circle against evil* can be focused inward rather than outward. When focused inward, the spell binds a nongood called creature (such as those called by the *lesser planar binding*, *planar binding*, and *greater planar binding* spells) for a maximum of 24 hours per caster level, provided that you cast the spell that calls the creature within 1 round of casting the *magic circle*. The creature cannot cross the circle's boundaries. If a creature too large to fit into the spell's area is the subject of the spell, the spell acts as a normal *protection from evil* spell for that creature only.

A *magic circle* leaves much to be desired as a trap. If the circle of powdered silver laid down in the process of spellcasting is broken, the effect immediately ends. The trapped creature can do nothing that disturbs the circle, directly or indirectly, but other creatures can. If the called creature has spell resistance, it can test the trap once a day. If you fail to overcome its spell resistance, the creature breaks free, destroying the circle. A creature capable of any form of dimensional travel (*astral projection, blink, dimension door, etherealness, gate, plane shift, shadow walk, teleport,* and similar abilities) can simply leave the circle through such means. You can prevent the creature's extradimensional escape by casting a *dimensional anchor* spell on it, but you must cast the spell before the creature acts. If you are successful, the *anchor* effect lasts as long as the *magic circle* does. The creature cannot reach across the *magic circle*, but its ranged attacks (ranged weapons, spells, magical abilities, and the like) can. The creature can attack any target it can reach with its ranged attacks except for the circle itself.

You can add a special diagram (a two-dimensional bounded figure with no gaps along its circumference, augmented with various magical sigils) to make the *magic circle* more secure. Drawing the diagram by hand takes 10 minutes and requires a DC 20 Spellcraft check. You do not know the result of this check. If the check fails, the diagram is ineffective. You can take 10 when drawing the diagram if you are under no particular time pressure to complete the task. This task also takes 10 full minutes. If time is no factor at all, and you devote 3 hours and 20 minutes to the task, you can take 20.

A successful diagram allows you to cast a *dimensional anchor* spell on the *magic circle* during the round before casting any summoning spell. The *anchor* holds any called creatures in the *magic circle* for 24 hours per caster level. A creature cannot use its spell resistance against a *magic circle* prepared with a diagram, and none of its abilities or attacks can cross the diagram. If the creature tries a Charisma check to break free of the trap (see the *lesser planar binding* spell), the DC increases by 5. The creature is immediately released if anything disturbs the diagram—even a straw laid across it. The creature itself cannot disturb the diagram either directly or indirectly, as noted above.

This spell is not cumulative with *protection from evil* and vice versa.

MAGIC CIRCLE AGAINST GOOD

School abjuration [evil]; **Level** cleric 3, sorcerer/wizard 3

This spell functions like *magic circle against evil*, except that it is similar to *protection from good* instead of *protection from evil*, and it can imprison a nonevil called creature.

MAGIC CIRCLE AGAINST LAW

School abjuration [chaotic]; **Level** cleric 3, sorcerer/wizard 3

This spell functions like *magic circle against evil*, except that it is similar to *protection from law* instead of *protection from evil*, and it can imprison a nonchaotic called creature.

MAGIC FANG

School transmutation; **Level** druid 1, ranger 1

Casting Time 1 standard action

Components V, S, DF
Range touch
Target living creature touched
Duration 1 min./level
Saving Throw Will negates (harmless); **Spell Resistance** yes (harmless)

Magic fang gives one natural weapon or unarmed strike of the subject a +1 enhancement bonus on attack and damage rolls. The spell can affect a slam attack, fist, bite, or other natural weapon. The spell does not change an unarmed strike's damage from nonlethal damage to lethal damage.

Magic fang can be made permanent with a *permanency* spell.

MAGIC FANG, GREATER

School transmutation; **Level** druid 3, ranger 3
Range close (25 ft. + 5 ft./2 levels)
Target one living creature
Duration 1 hour/level

This spell functions like *magic fang*, except that the enhancement bonus on attack and damage rolls is +1 per four caster levels (maximum +5). This bonus does not allow a natural weapon or unarmed strike to bypass damage reduction aside from magic.

Alternatively, you may imbue all of the creature's natural weapons with a +1 enhancement bonus (regardless of your caster level).

Greater magic fang can be made permanent with a *permanency* spell.

MAGIC JAR

School necromancy; **Level** sorcerer/wizard 5
Casting Time 1 standard action
Components V, S, F (a gem or crystal worth at least 100 gp)
Range medium (100 ft. + 10 ft./level)
Target one creature
Duration 1 hour/level or until you return to your body
Saving Throw Will negates; see text; **Spell Resistance** yes

By casting *magic jar*, you place your soul in a gem or large crystal (known as the *magic jar*), leaving your body lifeless. Then you can attempt to take control of a nearby body, forcing its soul into the *magic jar*. You may move back to the jar (thereby returning the trapped soul to its body) and attempt to possess another body. The spell ends when you send your soul back to your own body, leaving the receptacle empty. To cast the spell, the *magic jar* must be within spell range and you must know where it is, though you do not need line of sight or line of effect to it. When you transfer your soul upon casting, your body is, as near as anyone can tell, dead.

While in the *magic jar*, you can sense and attack any life force within 10 feet per caster level (and on the same plane of existence). You do need line of effect from the jar to the creatures. You cannot determine the exact creature types or positions of these creatures. In a group of life forces, you can sense a difference of 4 or more HD between one creature and another and can determine whether a life force is powered by positive or negative energy. (Undead creatures are powered by negative energy. Only sentient undead creatures have, or are, souls.)

You could choose to take over either a stronger or a weaker creature, but which particular stronger or weaker creature you attempt to possess is determined randomly.

Attempting to possess a body is a full-round action. It is blocked by *protection from evil* or a similar ward. You possess the body and force the creature's soul into the *magic jar* unless the subject succeeds on a Will save. Failure to take over the host leaves your life force in the *magic jar*, and the target automatically succeeds on further saving throws if you attempt to possess its body again.

If you are successful, your life force occupies the host body, and the host's life force is imprisoned in the *magic jar*. You keep your Intelligence, Wisdom, Charisma, level, class, base attack bonus, base save bonuses, alignment, and mental abilities. The body retains its Strength, Dexterity, Constitution, hit points, natural abilities, and automatic abilities. A body with extra limbs does not allow you to make more attacks (or more advantageous two-weapon attacks) than normal. You can't choose to activate the body's extraordinary or supernatural abilities. The creature's spells and spell-like abilities do not stay with the body.

As a standard action, you can shift freely from a host to the *magic jar* if within range, sending the trapped soul back to its body. The spell ends when you shift from the jar to your own body.

If the host body is slain, you return to the *magic jar*, if within range, and the life force of the host departs (it is dead). If the host body is slain beyond the range of the spell, both you and the host die. Any life force with nowhere to go is treated as slain.

If the spell ends while you are in the *magic jar*, you return to your body (or die if your body is out of range or destroyed). If the spell ends while you are in a host, you return to your body (or die, if it is out of range of your current position), and the soul in the *magic jar* returns to its body (or dies if it is out of range). Destroying the receptacle ends the spell, and the spell can be dispelled at either the *magic jar* or the host's location.

MAGIC MISSILE

School evocation [force]; **Level** sorcerer/wizard 1
Casting Time 1 standard action
Components V, S
Range medium (100 ft. + 10 ft./level)
Targets up to five creatures, no two of which can be more than 15 ft. apart
Duration instantaneous
Saving Throw none; **Spell Resistance** yes

A missile of magical energy darts forth from your fingertip and strikes its target, dealing 1d4+1 points of force damage.

The missile strikes unerringly, even if the target is in melee combat, so long as it has less than total cover or total concealment. Specific parts of a creature can't be singled out. Objects are not damaged by the spell.

For every two caster levels beyond 1st, you gain an additional missile—two at 3rd level, three at 5th, four at 7th, and the maximum of five missiles at 9th level or higher. If you shoot multiple missiles, you can have them strike a single creature or several creatures.

A single missile can strike only one creature. You must designate targets before you check for spell resistance or roll damage.

MAGIC MOUTH

School illusion (glamer); **Level** bard 1, sorcerer/wizard 2

Casting Time 1 standard action

Components V, S, M (a small bit of honeycomb and jade dust worth 10 gp)

Range close (25 ft. + 5 ft./2 levels)

Target one creature or object

Duration permanent until discharged

Saving Throw Will negates (object); **Spell Resistance** yes (object)

This spell imbues the chosen object or creature with an enchanted mouth that suddenly appears and speaks its message the next time a specified event occurs. The message, which must be 25 or fewer words long, can be in any language known by you and can be delivered over a period of 10 minutes. The mouth cannot utter verbal components, use command words, or activate magical effects. It does, however, move according to the words articulated; if it were placed upon a statue, the mouth of the statue would move and appear to speak. *Magic mouth* can also be placed upon a tree, rock, or any other object or creature.

The spell functions when specific conditions are fulfilled according to your command as set in the spell. Commands can be as general or as detailed as desired, although only visual and audible triggers can be used. Triggers react to what appears to be the case. Disguises and illusions can fool them. Normal darkness does not defeat a visual trigger, but magical *darkness* or *invisibility* does. Silent movement or magical *silence* defeats audible triggers. Audible triggers can be keyed to general types of noises or to a specific noise or spoken word. Actions can serve as triggers if they are visible or audible. A *magic mouth* cannot distinguish alignment, level, Hit Dice, or class except by external garb.

The range limit of a trigger is 15 feet per caster level, so a 6th-level caster can command a *magic mouth* to respond to triggers as far as 90 feet away. Regardless of range, the mouth can respond only to visible or audible triggers and actions in line of sight or within hearing distance.

Magic mouth can be made permanent with a *permanency* spell.

MAGIC STONE

School transmutation; **Level** cleric 1, druid 1

Casting Time 1 standard action

Components V, S, DF

Range touch

Targets up to three pebbles touched

Duration 30 minutes or until discharged

Saving Throw Will negates (harmless, object); **Spell Resistance** yes (harmless, object)

You transmute as many as three pebbles, which can be no larger than sling bullets, so that they strike with great force when thrown or slung. If hurled, they have a range increment of 20 feet. If slung, treat them as sling bullets (range increment 50 feet). The spell gives them a +1 enhancement bonus on attack and damage rolls. The user of the stones makes a normal ranged attack. Each stone that hits deals 1d6+1 points of damage (including the spell's enhancement bonus), or 2d6+2 points against undead.

MAGIC VESTMENT

School transmutation; **Level** cleric 3

Casting Time 1 standard action

Components V, S, DF

Range touch

Target armor or shield touched

Duration 1 hour/level

Saving Throw Will negates (harmless, object); **Spell Resistance** yes (harmless, object)

You imbue a suit of armor or a shield with an enhancement bonus of +1 per four caster levels (maximum +5 at 20th level).

An outfit of regular clothing counts as armor that grants no AC bonus for the purpose of this spell.

MAGIC WEAPON

School transmutation; **Level** cleric 1, paladin 1, sorcerer/wizard 1

Casting Time 1 standard action

Components V, S, DF

Range touch

Target weapon touched

Duration 1 min./level

Saving Throw Will negates (harmless, object); **Spell Resistance** yes (harmless, object)

Magic weapon gives a weapon a +1 enhancement bonus on attack and damage rolls. An enhancement bonus does not stack with a masterwork weapon's +1 bonus on attack rolls.

You can't cast this spell on a natural weapon, such as an unarmed strike (instead, see *magic fang*). A monk's unarmed strike is considered a weapon, and thus it can be enhanced by this spell.

MAGIC WEAPON, GREATER

School transmutation; **Level** cleric 4, paladin 3, sorcerer/wizard 3

Casting Time 1 standard action

Components V, S, M/DF (powdered lime and carbon)

Range close (25 ft. + 5 ft./2 levels)

Target one weapon or 50 projectiles (all of which must be together at the time of casting)

Duration 1 hour/level

Saving Throw Will negates (harmless, object); **Spell Resistance** yes (harmless, object)

This spell functions like *magic weapon*, except that it gives a weapon an enhancement bonus on attack and damage rolls of +1 per four caster levels (maximum +5). This bonus does not allow a weapon to bypass damage reduction aside from magic.

Alternatively, you can affect as many as 50 arrows, bolts, or bullets.

The projectiles must be of the same kind, and they have to be together (in the same quiver or other container). Projectiles, but not thrown weapons, lose their transmutation after they are used. Treat shuriken as projectiles, rather than as thrown weapons, for the purpose of this spell.

MAJOR CREATION

School conjuration (creation); **Level** sorcerer/wizard 5
Casting Time: 10 minutes
Range close (25 ft. + 5 ft./2 levels)
Duration see text

This spell functions like *minor creation*, except that you can also create an object of mineral nature: stone, crystal, metal, or the like. The duration of the created item varies with its relative hardness and rarity, as indicated on the following table.

Hardness and Rarity Examples	Duration
Vegetable matter	2 hr./level
Stone, crystal, base metals	1 hr./level
Precious metals	20 min./level
Gems	10 min./level
Rare metal*	1 round/level

* Includes adamantine, alchemical silver, and mithral. You can't use major creation to create a cold iron item.

MAJOR IMAGE

School illusion (figment); **Level** bard 3, sorcerer/wizard 3
Duration Concentration + 3 rounds

This spell functions like *silent image*, except that sound, smell, and thermal illusions are included in the spell effect. While concentrating, you can move the image within the range.

The image disappears when struck by an opponent unless you cause the illusion to react appropriately.

MAKE WHOLE

School transmutation; **Level** cleric 2, sorcerer/wizard 2
Range close (25 ft. + 5 ft./2 levels)
Target one object of up to 10 cu. ft./level or one construct creature of any size

This spell functions as *mending*, except that it repairs 1d6 points of damage per level when cast on an object or construct creature (maximum 5d6).

Make whole can fix destroyed magic items (at 0 hit points or less), and restores the magic properties of the item if your caster level is at least twice that of the item. Items with charges (such as wands) and single-use items (such as potions and scrolls) cannot be repaired in this way. When *make whole* is used on a construct creature, the spell bypasses any immunity to magic as if the spell did not allow spell resistance.

MARK OF JUSTICE

School necromancy; **Level** cleric 5, paladin 4

Casting Time 10 minutes

Components V, S, DF

Range touch

Target creature touched

Duration permanent; see text

Saving Throw none; **Spell Resistance** yes

You mark a subject and state some behavior on the part of the subject that will activate the mark. When activated, the mark curses the subject. Typically, you designate some sort of undesirable behavior that activates the mark, but you can pick any act you please. The effect of the mark is identical with the effect of *bestow curse*.

Since this spell takes 10 minutes to cast and involves writing on the target, you can cast it only on a creature that is willing or restrained.

Like the effect of *bestow curse*, a *mark of justice* cannot be dispelled, but it can be removed with a *break enchantment*, *limited wish*, *miracle*, *remove curse*, or *wish* spell. *Remove curse* works only if its caster level is equal to or higher than your *mark of justice* caster level. These restrictions apply regardless of whether the mark has activated.

MASS (SPELL NAME)

Any spell whose name begins with *mass* is alphabetized in this chapter according to the spell name. Thus, the description of a *mass* spell appears near the description of the spell on which it is based. Spell chains that have *mass* spells in them include those based on the spells *bear's endurance*, *bull's strength*, *cat's grace*, *charm monster*, *cure critical wounds*, *cure light wounds*, *cure moderate wounds*, *cure serious wounds*, *eagle's splendor*, *enlarge person*, *fox's cunning*, *heal*, *hold monster*, *hold person*, *inflict critical wounds*, *inflict light wounds*, *inflict moderate wounds*, *inflict serious wounds*, *invisibility*, *owl's wisdom*, *reduce person*, and *suggestion*.

MAZE

School conjuration (teleportation); **Level** sorcerer/wizard 8

Casting Time 1 standard action

Components V, S

Range close (25 ft. + 5 ft./2 levels)

Target one creature

Duration see text

Saving Throw none; **Spell Resistance** yes

You banish the subject into an extradimensional labyrinth. Each round on its turn, it may attempt a DC 20 Intelligence check to escape the labyrinth as a full-round action. If the subject doesn't escape, the maze disappears after 10 minutes, freeing the subject.

On escaping or leaving the maze, the subject reappears where it had been when the *maze* spell was cast. If this location is filled with a solid object, the subject appears in the nearest open space. Spells and abilities that move a creature within a plane, such as *teleport* and *dimension door*, do not help a creature escape a *maze* spell, although a *plane shift* spell allows it to exit to whatever plane is designated in that spell. Minotaurs are not affected by this spell.

MELD INTO STONE

School transmutation [earth]; **Level** cleric 3, druid 3

Casting Time 1 standard action

Components V, S, DF

Range personal

Target you

Duration 10 min./level

Meld into stone enables you to meld your body and possessions into a single block of stone. The stone must be large enough to accommodate your body in all three dimensions. When the casting is complete, you and not more than 100 pounds of nonliving gear merge with the stone. If either condition is violated, the spell fails and is wasted.

While in the stone, you remain in contact, however tenuous, with the face of the stone through which you melded. You remain aware of the passage of time and can cast spells on yourself while hiding in the stone. Nothing that goes on outside the stone can be seen, but you can still hear what happens around you. Minor physical damage to the stone does not harm you, but its partial destruction (to the extent that you no longer fit within it) expels you and deals you 5d6 points of damage. The stone's complete destruction expels you and slays you instantly unless you make a DC 18 Fortitude save. Even if you make your save, you still take 5d6 points of damage.

Any time before the duration expires, you can step out of the stone through the surface that you entered. If the spell's duration expires or the effect is dispelled before you voluntarily exit the stone, you are violently expelled and take 5d6 points of damage.

The following spells harm you if cast upon the stone that you are occupying. *Stone to flesh* expels you and deals you 5d6 points of damage. *Stone shape* deals 3d6 points of damage but does not expel you. *Transmute rock to mud* expels you and then slays you instantly unless you make a DC 18 Fortitude save, in which case you are merely expelled. Finally, *passwall* expels you without damage.

MENDING

School transmutation; **Level** bard 0, cleric 0, druid 0, sorcerer/wizard 0

Casting Time 10 minutes

Components V, S

Range 10 ft.

Target one object of up to 1 lb./level

Duration instantaneous

Saving Throw: Will negates (harmless, object); **Spell Resistance:** yes (harmless, object)

This spell repairs damaged objects, restoring 1d4 hit points to the object. If the object has the broken condition, this condition is removed if the object is restored to at least half its original hit points. All of the pieces of an object must be present for this spell to function. Magic items can be repaired by this spell, but you must have a caster level equal to or higher than that of the object. Magic items that are destroyed (at 0 hit points or less) can be repaired with this spell, but this spell does not restore their magic abilities. This spell does not affect creatures (including constructs). This spell has no effect on objects that have been warped or otherwise transmuted, but it can still repair damage done to such items.

MESSAGE

School transmutation [language-dependent]; **Level** bard 0, sorcerer/wizard 0

Casting Time 1 standard action

Components V, S, F (a piece of copper wire)

Range medium (100 ft. + 10 ft./level)

Targets one creature/level

Duration 10 min./level

Saving Throw none; **Spell Resistance** no

You can whisper messages and receive whispered replies. Those nearby can hear these messages with a DC 25 Perception check. You point your finger at each creature you want to receive the message. When you whisper, the whispered message is audible to all targeted creatures within range. Magical *silence*, 1 foot of stone, 1 inch of common metal (or a thin sheet of lead), or 3 feet of wood or dirt blocks the spell. The message does not have to travel in a straight line. It can circumvent a barrier if there is an open path between you and the subject, and the path's entire length lies within the spell's range. The creatures that receive the message can whisper a reply that you hear. The spell transmits sound, not meaning; it doesn't transcend language barriers. To speak a message, you must mouth the words and whisper.

METEOR SWARM

School evocation [fire]; **Level** sorcerer/wizard 9

Casting Time 1 standard action

Components V, S

Range long (400 ft. + 40 ft./level)

Area four 40-ft.-radius spreads, see text

Duration instantaneous

Saving Throw none or Reflex half, see text; **Spell Resistance** yes

Meteor swarm is a very powerful and spectacular spell that is similar to *fireball* in many aspects. When you cast it, four 2-foot-diameter spheres spring from your outstretched hand and streak in straight lines to the spots you select. The meteor spheres leave a fiery trail of sparks.

If you aim a sphere at a specific creature, you may make a ranged touch attack to strike the target with the meteor. Any creature struck by a sphere takes 2d6 points of bludgeoning damage (no save) and takes a −4 penalty on the saving throw against the sphere's fire damage (see below). If a targeted sphere misses its target, it simply explodes at the nearest corner of the target's space. You may aim more than one sphere at the same target.

Once a sphere reaches its destination, it explodes in a 40-foot-radius spread, dealing 6d6 points of fire damage to each creature in the area. If a creature is within the area of more than one sphere, it must save separately against each. Despite stemming from separate spheres, all of the fire damage is added together after the saves have been made, and fire resistance is applied only once.

MIND BLANK

School abjuration; **Level** sorcerer/wizard 8

Casting Time 1 standard action

Components V, S

Range close (25 ft. + 5 ft./2 levels)

Target one creature

Duration 24 hours

Saving Throw Will negates (harmless); **Spell Resistance** yes (harmless)

The subject is protected from all devices and spells that gather information about the target through divination magic (such as *detect evil*, *locate creature*, *scry*, and *see invisible*). This spell also grants a +8 resistance bonus on saving throws against all mind-affecting spells and effects. *Mind blank* even foils *limited wish*, *miracle*, and *wish* spells when they are used in such a way as to gain information about the target. In the case of scrying that scans an area the creature is in, such as *arcane eye*, the spell works but the creature simply isn't detected. Scrying attempts that are targeted specifically at the subject do not work at all.

MIND FOG

School enchantment (compulsion) [mind-affecting]; **Level** bard 5, sorcerer/wizard 5

Casting Time 1 standard action

Components V, S

Range medium (100 ft. + 10 ft./level)

Effect fog spreads in 20-ft. radius, 20 ft. high

Duration 30 minutes and 2d6 rounds; see text

Saving Throw Will negates; **Spell Resistance** yes

Mind fog produces a bank of thin mist that weakens the mental resistance of those caught in it. Creatures in the *mind fog* take a −10 penalty on Wisdom checks and Will saves. (A creature that successfully saves against the fog is not affected and need not make further saves even if it remains in the fog.) Affected creatures take the penalty as long as they remain in the fog and for 2d6 rounds thereafter. The fog is stationary and lasts for 30 minutes (or until dispersed by wind).

A moderate wind (11+ mph) disperses the fog in 4 rounds; a strong wind (21+ mph) disperses the fog in 1 round.

The fog is thin and does not significantly hamper vision.

MINOR CREATION

School conjuration (creation); **Level** sorcerer/wizard 4

Casting Time 1 minute

Components V, S, M (a tiny piece of matter of the same sort of item you plan to create with *minor creation*)

Range 0 ft.

Effect unattended, nonmagical object of nonliving plant matter, up to 1 cu. ft./level

Duration 1 hour/level (D)

Saving Throw none; **Spell Resistance** no

You create a nonmagical, unattended object of nonliving vegetable matter. The volume of the item created cannot exceed 1 cubic foot per caster level. You must succeed on an appropriate Craft skill check to make a complex item.

Attempting to use any created object as a material component causes the spell to fail.

MINOR IMAGE

School illusion (figment); **Level** bard 2, sorcerer/wizard 2
Duration concentration + 2 rounds
This spell functions like *silent image*, except that *minor image* includes some minor sounds but not understandable speech.

MIRACLE

School evocation; **Level** cleric 9
Casting Time 1 standard action
Components V, S; see text
Range see text
Target, Effect, or Area see text
Duration see text
Saving Throw see text; **Spell Resistance** yes
You don't so much cast a *miracle* as request one. You state what you would like to have happen and request that your deity (or the power you pray to for spells) intercede.

A *miracle* can do any of the following things.

- Duplicate any cleric spell of 8th level or lower.
- Duplicate any other spell of 7th level or lower.
- Undo the harmful effects of certain spells, such as *feeblemind* or *insanity*.
- Have any effect whose power level is in line with the above effects.

Alternatively, a cleric can make a very powerful request. Casting such a *miracle* costs the cleric 25,000 gp in powdered diamond because of the powerful divine energies involved. Examples of especially powerful *miracles* of this sort could include the following:

- Swinging the tide of a battle in your favor by raising fallen allies to continue fighting.
- Moving you and your allies, with all your and their gear, from one plane to a specific locale through planar barriers with no chance of error.
- Protecting a city from an earthquake, volcanic eruption, flood, or other major natural disaster.

In any event, a request that is out of line with the deity's (or alignment's) nature is refused.

A duplicated spell allows saving throws and spell resistance as normal, but the save DCs are as for a 9th-level spell. When a *miracle* spell duplicates a spell with a material component that costs more than 100 gp, you must provide that component.

MIRAGE ARCANA

School illusion (glamer); **Level** bard 5, sorcerer/wizard 5
Casting Time 1 standard action
Components V, S

Area one 20-ft. cube/level (S)
Duration concentration + 1 hour/level (D)
This spell functions like *hallucinatory terrain*, except that it enables you to make any area appear to be something other than it is. The illusion includes audible, visual, tactile, and olfactory elements. Unlike *hallucinatory terrain*, the spell can alter the appearance of structures (or add them where none are present). Still, it can't disguise, conceal, or add creatures (though creatures within the area might hide themselves within the illusion just as they can hide themselves within a real location).

MIRROR IMAGE

School illusion (figment); **Level** bard 2, sorcerer/wizard 2
Casting Time 1 standard action
Components V, S
Range personal
Target you
Duration 1 min./level
This spell creates a number of illusory doubles of you that inhabit your square. These doubles make it difficult for enemies to precisely locate and attack you.

When *mirror image* is cast, 1d4 images plus one image per three caster levels (maximum eight images total) are created. These images remain in your space and move with you, mimicking your movements, sounds, and actions exactly. Whenever you are attacked or are the target of a spell that requires an attack roll, there is a possibility that the attack targets one of your images instead. If the attack is a hit, roll randomly to see whether the selected target is real or a figment. If it is a figment, the figment is destroyed. If the attack misses by 5 or less, one of your figments is destroyed by the near miss. Area spells affect you normally and do not destroy any of your figments. Spells and effects that do not require an attack roll affect you normally and do not destroy any of your figments. Spells that require a touch attack are harmlessly discharged if used to destroy a figment.

An attacker must be able to see the figments to be fooled. If you are invisible or the attacker is blind, the spell has no effect (although the normal miss chances still apply).

MISDIRECTION

School illusion (glamer); **Level** bard 2, sorcerer/wizard 2
Casting Time 1 standard action
Components V, S
Range close (25 ft. + 5 ft./2 levels)
Target one creature or object, up to a 10-ft. cube in size
Duration 1 hour/level
Saving Throw none or Will negates; see text; **Spell Resistance** no
By means of this spell, you misdirect the information from divination spells that reveal auras (*detect evil, detect magic, discern lies*, and the like). On casting the spell, you choose another object within range. For the duration of the spell, the subject of *misdirection* is detected as if it were the other object. Neither the subject nor the other object gets a saving throw against this

effect. Detection spells provide information based on the second object rather than on the actual target of the detection unless the caster of the detection succeeds on a Will save. For instance, you could make yourself detect as a tree if one were within range at casting: not evil, not lying, not magical, neutral in alignment, and so forth. This spell does not affect other types of divination magic (*augury*, *detect thoughts*, *clairaudience/clairvoyance*, and the like).

MISLEAD

School illusion (figment, glamer); **Level** bard 5, sorcerer/wizard 6
Casting Time 1 standard action
Components S
Range close (25 ft. + 5 ft./2 levels)
Target/Effect you/one illusory double
Duration 1 round/level (D) and concentration + 3 rounds; see text
Saving Throw none or Will disbelief (if interacted with); see text; **Spell Resistance** no

You become invisible (as *greater invisibility*, a glamer), and at the same time, an illusory double of you (as *major image*, a figment) appears. You are then free to go elsewhere while your double moves away. The double appears within range but thereafter moves as you direct it (which requires concentration beginning on the first round after the casting). You can make the figment appear superimposed perfectly over your own body so that observers don't notice an image appearing and you turning invisible. You and the figment can then move in different directions. The double moves at your speed and can talk and gesture as if it were real, but it cannot attack or cast spells, though it can pretend to do so.

The illusory double lasts as long as you concentrate upon it, plus 3 additional rounds. After you cease concentration, the illusory double continues to carry out the same activity until the duration expires. The *greater invisibility* lasts for 1 round per level, regardless of concentration.

MNEMONIC ENHANCER

School transmutation; **Level** wizard 4
Casting Time 10 minutes
Components V, S, M (a piece of string, and ink consisting of squid secretion mixed with black dragon's blood), F (an ivory plaque worth 50 gp)
Range personal
Target you
Duration instantaneous

Casting this spell allows you to prepare additional spells or retain spells recently cast. Pick one of these two versions when the spell is cast.

Prepare: You prepare up to three additional levels of spells. A cantrip counts as 1/2 level for this purpose. You prepare and cast these spells normally.

Retain: You retain any spell of 3rd level or lower that you had cast up to 1 round before you started casting the *mnemonic enhancer*. This restores the previously cast spell to your mind.

In either event, the spell or spells prepared or retained fade after 24 hours (if not cast).

MODIFY MEMORY

School enchantment (compulsion) [mind-affecting]; **Level** bard 4
Casting Time 1 round; see text
Components V, S
Range close (25 ft. + 5 ft./2 levels)
Target one living creature
Duration permanent
Saving Throw Will negates; **Spell Resistance** yes

You reach into the subject's mind and modify as many as 5 minutes of its memories in one of the following ways.

- Eliminate all memory of an event the subject actually experienced. This spell cannot negate *charm*, *geas/quest*, *suggestion*, or similar spells.
- Allow the subject to recall with perfect clarity an event it actually experienced.
- Change the details of an event the subject actually experienced.
- Implant a memory of an event the subject never experienced.

Casting the spell takes 1 round. If the subject fails to save, you proceed with the spell by spending as much as 5 minutes (a period of time equal to the amount of memory you want to modify) visualizing the memory you wish to modify in the subject. If your concentration is disturbed before the visualization is complete, or if the subject is ever beyond the spell's range during this time, the spell is lost.

A modified memory does not necessarily affect the subject's actions, particularly if it contradicts the creature's natural inclinations. An illogical modified memory is dismissed by the creature as a bad dream, too much wine, or another similar excuse.

MOMENT OF PRESCIENCE

School divination; **Level** sorcerer/wizard 8
Casting Time 1 standard action
Components V, S
Range personal
Target you
Duration 1 hour/level or until discharged

This spell grants you a sixth sense. Once during the spell's duration, you may choose to use its effect. This spell grants you an insight bonus equal to your caster level (maximum +25) on any single attack roll, combat maneuver check, opposed ability or skill check, or saving throw. Alternatively, you can apply the insight bonus to your AC against a single attack (even if flat-footed). Activating the effect doesn't take an action; you can even activate it on another character's turn. You must choose to use the *moment of prescience* before you make the roll it is to modify. Once used, the spell ends. You can't have more than one *moment of prescience* active on you at the same time.

MOUNT

School conjuration (summoning); **Level** sorcerer/wizard 1
Casting Time 1 round

Components V, S, M (a bit of horse hair)
Range close (25 ft. + 5 ft./2 levels)
Effect one mount
Duration 2 hours/level (D)
Saving Throw none; **Spell Resistance** no

You summon a horse or a pony (your choice) to serve you as a mount (see the *Pathfinder RPG Bestiary*). The steed serves willingly and well. The mount comes with a bit and bridle and a riding saddle.

MOVE EARTH

School transmutation [earth]; **Level** druid 6, sorcerer/wizard 6
Casting Time see text
Components V, S, M (clay, loam, sand, and an iron blade)
Range long (400 ft. + 40 ft./level)
Area dirt in an area up to 750 ft. square and up to 10 ft. deep (S)
Duration instantaneous
Saving Throw none; **Spell Resistance** no

Move earth moves dirt (clay, loam, sand, and soil), possibly collapsing embankments, moving hillocks, shifting dunes, and so forth.

In no event can rock formations be collapsed or moved. The area to be affected determines the casting time. For every 150-foot square (up to 10 feet deep), casting takes 10 minutes. The maximum area, 750 feet by 750 feet, takes 4 hours and 10 minutes to move.

This spell does not violently break the surface of the ground. Instead, it creates wavelike crests and troughs, with the earth reacting with glacial fluidity until the desired result is achieved. Trees, structures, rock formations, and such are mostly unaffected except for changes in elevation and relative topography.

The spell cannot be used for tunneling and is generally too slow to trap or bury creatures. Its primary use is for digging or filling moats or for adjusting terrain contours before a battle.

This spell has no effect on earth creatures.

NEUTRALIZE POISON

School conjuration (healing); **Level** bard 4, cleric 4, druid 3, paladin 4, ranger 3
Casting Time 1 standard action
Components V, S, M/DF (charcoal)
Range touch
Target creature or object of up to 1 cu. ft./level touched
Duration instantaneous or 10 min./level; see text
Saving Throw Will negates (harmless, object); **Spell Resistance** yes (harmless, object)

You detoxify any sort of venom in the creature or object touched. If the target is a creature, you must make a caster level check (1d20 + caster level) against the DC of each poison affecting the target. Success means that the poison is neutralized. A cured creature suffers no additional effects from the poison, and any temporary effects are ended, but the spell does not reverse instantaneous effects, such as hit point damage, temporary ability damage, or effects that don't go away on their own.

This spell can instead neutralize the poison in a poisonous creature or object for 10 minutes per level, at the caster's option. If cast on a creature, the creature receives a Will save to negate the effect.

NIGHTMARE

School illusion (phantasm) [mind-affecting, evil]; **Level** bard 5, sorcerer/wizard 5
Casting Time 10 minutes
Components V, S
Range unlimited
Target one living creature
Duration instantaneous
Saving Throw Will negates; see text; **Spell Resistance** yes

You send a hideous and unsettling phantasmal vision to a specific creature that you name or otherwise specifically designate.

The *nightmare* prevents restful sleep and causes 1d10 points of damage. The *nightmare* leaves the subject fatigued and unable to regain arcane spells for the next 24 hours.

The difficulty of the save depends on your knowledge the subject and the physical connection (if any) you have to that creature.

Knowledge	Will Save Modifier
None*	+10
Secondhand (you have heard of the subject)	+5
Firsthand (you have met the subject)	+0
Familiar (you know the subject well)	−5

*You must have some sort of connection to a creature of which you have no knowledge.

Connection	Will Save Modifier
Likeness or picture	−2
Possession or garment	−4
Body part, lock of hair, bit of nail, etc.	−10

Dispel evil cast on the subject while you are casting the spell dispels the *nightmare* and causes you to be stunned for 10 minutes per caster level of the *dispel evil*.

If the recipient is awake when the spell begins, you can choose to cease casting (ending the spell) or to enter a trance until the recipient goes to sleep, whereupon you become alert again and complete the casting. If you are disturbed during the trance, you must succeed on a concentration check as if you were in the midst of casting a spell or the spell ends.

If you choose to enter a trance, you are not aware of your surroundings or the activities around you while in the trance.

You are defenseless, both physically and mentally, while in the trance. (You always fail Reflex and Will saving throws, for example.)

Creatures who don't sleep (such as outsiders) or dream are immune to this spell.

NONDETECTION

School abjuration; **Level** ranger 4, sorcerer/wizard 3
Casting Time 1 standard action
Components V, S, M (diamond dust worth 50 gp)
Range touch
Target creature or object touched
Duration 1 hour/level
Saving Throw Will negates (harmless, object); **Spell Resistance** yes (harmless, object)

The warded creature or object becomes difficult to detect by divination spells such as *clairaudience/clairvoyance*, *locate object*, and *detect* spells. *Nondetection* also prevents location by such magic items as *crystal ball*s. If a divination is attempted against the warded creature or item, the caster of the divination must succeed on a caster level check (1d20 + caster level) against a DC of 11 + the caster level of the spellcaster who cast *nondetection*. If you cast *nondetection* on yourself or on an item currently in your possession, the DC is 15 + your caster level.

If cast on a creature, *nondetection* wards the creature's gear as well as the creature itself.

OBSCURE OBJECT

School abjuration; **Level** bard 1, cleric 3, sorcerer/wizard 2
Casting Time 1 standard action
Components V, S, M/DF (chameleon skin)
Range touch
Target one object touched of up to 100 lbs./level
Duration 8 hours (D)
Saving Throw Will negates (object); **Spell Resistance** yes (object)

This spell hides an object from location by divination (scrying) effects, such as the *scrying* spell or a *crystal ball*. Such an attempt automatically fails (if the divination is targeted on the object) or fails to perceive the object (if the divination is targeted on a nearby location, object, or person).

OBSCURING MIST

School conjuration (creation); **Level** cleric 1, druid 1, sorcerer/wizard 1
Casting Time 1 standard action
Components V, S
Range 20 ft.
Effect cloud spreads in 20-ft. radius from you, 20 ft. high
Duration 1 min./level (D)
Saving Throw none; **Spell Resistance** no

A misty vapor arises around you. It is stationary. The vapor obscures all sight, including darkvision, beyond 5 feet. A creature 5 feet away has concealment (attacks have a 20% miss chance). Creatures farther away have total concealment (50% miss chance, and the attacker cannot use sight to locate the target).

A moderate wind (11+ mph), such as from a *gust of wind* spell, disperses the fog in 4 rounds. A strong wind (21+ mph) disperses the fog in 1 round. A *fireball*, *flame strike*, or similar spell burns away the fog in the explosive or fiery spell's area. A *wall of fire* burns away the fog in the area into which it deals damage.

This spell does not function underwater.

OPEN/CLOSE

School transmutation; **Level** bard 0, sorcerer/wizard 0
Casting Time 1 standard action
Components V, S, F (a brass key)
Range close (25 ft. + 5 ft./2 levels)
Target object weighing up to 30 lbs. or portal that can be opened or closed
Duration instantaneous
Saving Throw Will negates (object); **Spell Resistance** yes (object)

You can open or close (your choice) a door, chest, box, window, bag, pouch, bottle, barrel, or other container. If anything resists this activity (such as a bar on a door or a lock on a chest), the spell fails. In addition, the spell can only open and close things weighing 30 pounds or less. Thus, doors, chests, and similar objects sized for enormous creatures may be beyond this spell's ability to affect.

ORDER'S WRATH

School evocation [lawful]; **Level** cleric 4
Casting Time 1 standard action
Components V, S
Range medium (100 ft. + 10 ft./level)
Area nonlawful creatures within a burst that fills a 30-ft. cube
Duration instantaneous (1 round); see text
Saving Throw Will partial; see text; **Spell Resistance** yes

You channel lawful power to smite enemies. The power takes the form of a three-dimensional grid of energy. Only chaotic and neutral (not lawful) creatures are harmed by the spell.

The spell deals 1d8 points of damage per two caster levels (maximum 5d8) to chaotic creatures (or 1d6 points of damage per caster level, maximum 10d6, to chaotic outsiders) and causes them to be dazed for 1 round. A successful Will save reduces the damage to half and negates the daze effect.

The spell deals only half damage to creatures who are neither chaotic nor lawful, and they are not dazed. They can reduce the damage in half again (down to one-quarter of the roll) with a successful Will save.

OVERLAND FLIGHT

School transmutation; **Level** sorcerer/wizard 5
Components: V, S
Range personal
Target you
Duration 1 hour/level

This spell functions like a *fly* spell, except you can fly at a speed of 40 feet (30 feet if wearing medium or heavy armor, or if carrying a medium or heavy load) with a bonus on Fly skill checks equal to half your caster level. When using this spell for long-distance

movement, you can hustle without taking nonlethal damage (a forced march still requires Constitution checks). This means you can cover 64 miles in an 8-hour period of flight (or 48 miles at a speed of 30 feet).

OWL'S WISDOM

School transmutation; **Level** cleric 2, druid 2, paladin 2, ranger 2, sorcerer/wizard 2

Casting Time 1 standard action

Components V, S, M/DF (feathers or droppings from an owl)

Range touch

Target creature touched

Duration 1 min./level

Saving Throw Will negates (harmless); **Spell Resistance** yes

The transmuted creature becomes wiser. The spell grants a +4 enhancement bonus to Wisdom, adding the usual benefit to Wisdom-related skills. Clerics, druids, and rangers (and other Wisdom-based spellcasters) who receive *owl's wisdom* do not gain any additional bonus spells for the increased Wisdom, but the save DCs for their spells increase.

OWL'S WISDOM, MASS

School transmutation; **Level** cleric 6, druid 6, sorcerer/wizard 6

Range close (25 ft. + 5 ft./2 levels)

Target one creature/level, no two of which can be more than 30 ft. apart

This spell functions like *owl's wisdom*, except that it affects multiple creatures.

PASSWALL

School transmutation; **Level** sorcerer/wizard 5

Casting Time 1 standard action

Components V, S, M (sesame seeds)

Range touch

Effect 5-ft.-by-8-ft. opening, 10 ft. deep plus 5 ft. deep per three additional levels

Duration 1 hour/level (D)

Saving Throw none; **Spell Resistance** no

You create a passage through wooden, plaster, or stone walls, but not through metal or other harder materials. The passage is 10 feet deep plus an additional 5 feet deep per three caster levels above 9th (15 feet at 12th, 20 feet at 15th, and a maximum of 25 feet deep at 18th level). If the wall's thickness is more than the depth of the passage created, then a single *passwall* simply makes a niche or short tunnel. Several *passwall* spells can then form a continuing passage to breach very thick walls. When *passwall* ends, creatures within the passage are ejected out the nearest exit. If someone dispels the *passwall* or you dismiss it, creatures in the passage are ejected out the far exit, if there is one, or out the sole exit if there is only one.

PASS WITHOUT TRACE

School transmutation; **Level** druid 1, ranger 1

Casting Time 1 standard action

Components V, S, DF

Range touch

Targets one creature/level touched

Duration 1 hour/level (D)

Saving Throw Will negates (harmless); **Spell Resistance** yes (harmless)

The subject or subjects of this spell do not leave footprints or a scent trail while moving. Tracking the subjects is impossible by nonmagical means.

PERMANENCY

School universal; **Level** sorcerer/wizard 5

Casting Time 2 rounds

Components V, S, M (see tables below)

Range see text

Target see text

Duration permanent; see text

Saving Throw none; **Spell Resistance** no

This spell makes the duration of certain other spells permanent. You first cast the desired spell and then follow it with the *permanency* spell.

Depending on the spell, you must be of a minimum caster level and must expend a specific gp value of diamond dust as a material component.

You can make the following spells permanent in regard to yourself.

Spell	Minimum Caster Level	GP Cost
Arcane sight	11th	7,500 gp
Comprehend languages	9th	2,500 gp
Darkvision	10th	5,000 gp
Detect magic	9th	2,500 gp
Read magic	9th	2,500 gp
See invisibility	10th	5,000 gp
Tongues	11th	7,500 gp

You cannot cast these spells on other creatures. This application of *permanency* can be dispelled only by a caster of higher level than you were when you cast the spell.

In addition to personal use, *permanency* can be used to make the following spells permanent on yourself, another creature, or an object (as appropriate).

Spell	Minimum Caster Level	GP Cost
Enlarge person	9th	2,500 gp
Magic fang	9th	2,500 gp
Magic fang, greater	11th	7,500 gp
Reduce person	9th	2,500 gp
Resistance	9th	2,500 gp
*Telepathic bond**	13th	12,500 gp

*Only bonds two creatures per casting of *permanency*.

Additionally, the following spells can be cast upon objects or areas only and rendered permanent.

Spell	Minimum Caster Level	GP Cost
Alarm	9th	2,500 gp
Animate objects	14th	15,000 gp
Dancing lights	9th	2,500 gp
Ghost sound	9th	2,500 gp
Gust of wind	11th	7,500 gp
Invisibility	10th	5,000 gp
Mage's private sanctum	13th	12,500 gp
Magic mouth	10th	5,000 gp
Phase door	15th	17,500 gp
Prismatic sphere	17th	22,500 gp
Prismatic wall	16th	20,000 gp
Shrink item	11th	7,500 gp
Solid fog	12th	10,000 gp
Stinking cloud	11th	7,500 gp
Symbol of death	16th	20,000 gp
Symbol of fear	14th	15,000 gp
Symbol of insanity	16th	20,000 gp
Symbol of pain	13th	12,500 gp
Symbol of persuasion	14th	15,000 gp
Symbol of sleep	16th	20,000 gp
Symbol of stunning	15th	17,500 gp
Symbol of weakness	15th	17,500 gp
Teleportation circle	17th	22,500 gp
Wall of fire	12th	10,000 gp
Wall of force	13th	12,500 gp
Web	10th	5,000 gp

Spells cast on other targets are vulnerable to *dispel magic* as normal. The GM may allow other spells to be made permanent.

PERMANENT IMAGE

School illusion (figment); **Level** bard 6, sorcerer/wizard 6
Effect figment that cannot extend beyond a 20-ft. cube + one 10-ft. cube/level (S)
Duration permanent (D)
This spell functions like *silent image,* except that the figment includes visual, auditory, olfactory, and thermal elements, and the spell is permanent. By concentrating, you can move the image within the limits of the range, but it is static while you are not concentrating.

PERSISTENT IMAGE

School illusion (figment); **Level** bard 5, sorcerer/wizard 5
Duration 1 min./level (D)
This spell functions like *silent image,* except that the figment includes visual, auditory, olfactory, and thermal components, and the figment follows a script determined by you. The figment follows that script without your having to concentrate on it. The illusion can include intelligible speech if you wish.

PHANTASMAL KILLER

School illusion (phantasm) [fear, mind-affecting]; **Level** sorcerer/ wizard 4

Casting Time 1 standard action
Components V, S
Range medium (100 ft. + 10 ft./level)
Target one living creature
Duration instantaneous
Saving Throw Will disbelief, then Fortitude partial; see text; **Spell Resistance** yes
You create a phantasmal image of the most fearsome creature imaginable to the subject simply by forming the fears of the subject's subconscious mind into something that its conscious mind can visualize: this most horrible beast. Only the spell's subject can see the *phantasmal killer.* You see only a vague shape. The target first gets a Will save to recognize the image as unreal. If that save fails, the phantasm touches the subject, and the subject must succeed on a Fortitude save or die from fear. Even if the Fortitude save is successful, the subject takes 3d6 points of damage.

If the subject of a *phantasmal killer* attack succeeds in disbelieving and possesses telepathy or is wearing a *helm of telepathy,* the beast can be turned upon you. You must then disbelieve it or become subject to its deadly fear attack.

PHANTOM STEED

School conjuration (creation); **Level** bard 3, sorcerer/wizard 3
Casting Time 10 minutes
Components V, S
Range 0 ft.
Effect one quasi-real, horselike creature
Duration 1 hour/level (D)
Saving Throw none; **Spell Resistance** no
You conjure a Large, quasi-real, horselike creature (the exact coloration can be customized as you wish). It can be ridden only by you or by the one person for whom you specifically created the mount. A phantom steed has a black head and body, gray mane and tail, and smoke-colored, insubstantial hooves that make no sound. It has what seems to be a saddle, bit, and bridle. It does not fight, but animals shun it and refuse to attack it.

The mount is AC 18 (–1 size, +4 natural armor, +5 Dex) and 7 hit points + 1 hit point per caster level. If it loses all its hit points, the phantom steed disappears. A phantom steed has a speed of 20 feet per two caster levels, to a maximum of 100 feet at 10th level. It can bear its rider's weight plus up to 10 pounds per caster level.

These mounts gain certain powers according to caster level. A mount's abilities include those of mounts of lower caster levels.

8th Level: The mount can ride over sandy, muddy, or even swampy ground without difficulty or decrease in speed.

10th Level: The mount can use *water walk* at will (as the spell, no action required to activate this ability).

12th Level: The mount can use *air walk* at will (as the spell, no action required to activate this ability) for up to 1 round at a time, after which it falls to the ground.

14th Level: The mount can fly at its speed with a bonus on Fly skill checks equal to your caster level.

PHANTOM TRAP

School illusion (glamer); **Level** sorcerer/wizard 2

Casting Time 1 standard action

Components V, S, M (special dust worth 50 gp)

Range touch

Target object touched

Duration permanent (D)

Saving Throw none; **Spell Resistance** no

This spell makes a lock or other small mechanism seem to be trapped to anyone who can detect traps. You place the spell upon any small mechanism or device, such as a lock, hinge, hasp, cork, cap, or ratchet. Any character able to detect traps, or who uses any spell or device enabling trap detection, is certain a real trap exists. Of course, the effect is illusory and nothing happens if the trap is "sprung"; its primary purpose is to frighten away thieves or make them waste precious time.

If another *phantom trap* is active within 50 feet when the spell is cast, the casting fails.

PHASE DOOR

School conjuration (creation); **Level** sorcerer/wizard 7

Casting Time 1 standard action

Components V

Range touch

Effect ethereal 5-ft.-by-8-ft. opening, 10 ft. deep + 5 ft. deep per three levels

Duration one usage per two levels

Saving Throw none; **Spell Resistance** no

This spell creates an ethereal passage through wooden, plaster, or stone walls, but not other materials. The *phase door* is invisible and inaccessible to all creatures except you, and only you can use the passage. You disappear when you enter the *phase door* and appear when you exit. If you desire, you can take one other creature (Medium or smaller) through the door. This counts as two uses of the door. The door does not allow light, sound, or spell effects through it, nor can you see through it without using it. Thus, the spell can provide an escape route, though certain creatures, such as phase spiders, can follow with ease. A *gem of true seeing* or similar magic reveals the presence of a *phase door* but does not allow its use.

A *phase door* is subject to *dispel magic*. If anyone is within the passage when it is dispelled, he is harmlessly ejected just as if he were inside a *passwall* effect.

You can allow other creatures to use the *phase door* by setting some triggering condition for the door. Such conditions can be as simple or elaborate as you desire. They can be based on a creature's name, identity, or alignment, but otherwise must be based on observable actions or qualities. Intangibles such as level, class, HD, and hit points don't qualify.

Phase door can be made permanent with a *permanency* spell.

PLANAR ALLY

School conjuration (calling) [see text for *lesser planar ally*];

Level cleric 6

Components V, S, M (offerings worth 1,250 gp plus payment), DF

Effect one or two called outsiders, totaling no more than 12 HD, which cannot be more than 30 ft. apart when they appear

This spell functions like *lesser planar ally*, except you may call a single creature of 12 HD or less, or two creatures of the same kind whose HD total no more than 12. The creatures agree to help you and request your return payment together.

PLANAR ALLY, GREATER

School conjuration (calling) [see text for *lesser planar ally*];

Level cleric 8

Components V, S, M (offerings worth 2,500 gp plus payment), DF

Effect up to three called outsiders, totaling no more than 18 HD, no two of which can be more than 30 ft. apart when they appear.

This spell functions like *lesser planar ally*, except that you may call a single creature of 18 HD or less, or up to three creatures of the same kind whose Hit Dice total no more than 18. The creatures agree to help you and request your return payment together.

PLANAR ALLY, LESSER

School conjuration (calling) [see text]; **Level** cleric 4

Casting Time 10 minutes

Components V, S, M (offerings worth 500 gp plus payment, see text), DF

Range close (25 ft. + 5 ft./2 levels)

Effect one called outsider of 6 HD or less

Duration instantaneous

Saving Throw none; **Spell Resistance** no

By casting this spell, you request your deity to send you an outsider (of 6 HD or less) of the deity's choice. If you serve no particular deity, the spell is a general plea answered by a creature sharing your philosophical alignment. If you know an individual creature's name, you may request that individual by speaking the name during the spell (though you might get a different creature anyway).

You may ask the creature to perform one task in exchange for a payment from you. Tasks might range from the simple to the complex. You must be able to communicate with the creature called in order to bargain for its services.

The creature called requires a payment for its services. This payment can take a variety of forms, from donating gold or magic items to an allied temple, to a gift given directly to the creature, to some other action on your part that matches the creature's alignment and goals. Regardless, this payment must be made before the creature agrees to perform any services. The bargaining takes at least 1 round, so any actions by the creature begin in the round after it arrives.

A task taking up to 1 minute per caster level requires a payment of 100 gp per HD of the creature called. For a task taking up to 1 hour per caster level, the creature requires a payment of 500 gp per HD. A long-term task, one requiring up to 1 day per caster level, requires a payment of 1,000 gp per HD.

A nonhazardous task requires only half the indicated payment,

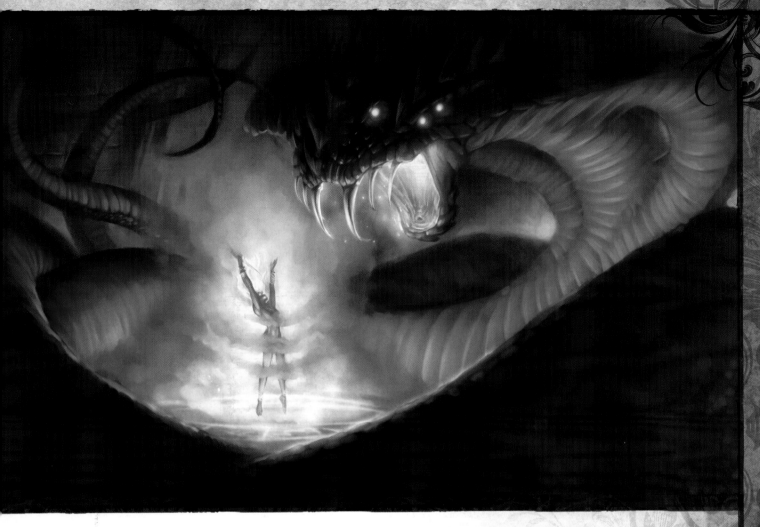

while an especially hazardous task might require a greater gift. Few if any creatures will accept a task that seems suicidal (remember, a called creature actually dies when it is killed, unlike a summoned creature). However, if the task is strongly aligned with the creature's ethos, it may halve or even waive the payment.

At the end of its task, or when the duration bargained for expires, the creature returns to its home plane (after reporting back to you, if appropriate and possible).

Note: When you use a calling spell that calls an air, chaotic, earth, evil, fire, good, lawful, or water creature, it is a spell of that type.

PLANAR BINDING

School conjuration (calling) [see text for *lesser planar binding*];
   Level sorcerer/wizard 6
Components: V, S
Targets up to three elementals or outsiders, totaling no more than 12 HD, no two of which can be more than 30 ft. apart when they appear

This spell functions like *lesser planar binding*, except that you may call a single creature of 12 HD or less, or up to three creatures of the same kind whose Hit Dice total no more than 12. Each creature gets a saving throw, makes an independent attempt to escape, and must be individually persuaded to aid you.

PLANAR BINDING, GREATER

School conjuration (calling) [see text for *lesser planar binding*];
   Level: sorcerer/wizard 8
Components: V, S
Targets up to three elementals or outsiders, totaling no more than 18 HD, no two of which can be more than 30 ft. apart when they appear.

This spell functions like *lesser planar binding*, except that you may call a single creature of 18 HD or less, or up to three creatures of the same kind whose Hit Dice total no more than 18. Each creature gets a saving throw, makes an independent attempt to escape, and must be individually persuaded to aid you.

PLANAR BINDING, LESSER

School conjuration (calling) [see text]; **Level** sorcerer/wizard 5
Casting Time 10 minutes
Components V, S
Range close (25 ft. + 5 ft./2 levels); see text

Target one elemental or outsider with 6 HD or less
Duration instantaneous
Saving Throw Will negates; **Spell Resistance** no and yes; see text

Casting this spell attempts a dangerous act: to lure a creature from another plane to a specifically prepared trap, which must lie within the spell's range. The called creature is held in the trap until it agrees to perform one service in return for its freedom.

To create the trap, you must use a *magic circle* spell, focused inward. The kind of creature to be bound must be known and stated. If you wish to call a specific individual, you must use that individual's proper name in casting the spell.

The target creature is allowed a Will saving throw. If the saving throw succeeds, the creature resists the spell. If the saving throw fails, the creature is immediately drawn to the trap (spell resistance does not keep it from being called). The creature can escape from the trap by successfully pitting its spell resistance against your caster level check, by dimensional travel, or with a successful Charisma check (DC 15 + 1/2 your caster level + your Charisma modifier). It can try each method once per day. If it breaks loose, it can flee or attack you. A *dimensional anchor* cast on the creature prevents its escape via dimensional travel. You can also employ a calling diagram (see *magic circle against evil*) to make the trap more secure.

If the creature does not break free of the trap, you can keep it bound for as long as you dare. You can attempt to compel the creature to perform a service by describing the service and perhaps offering some sort of reward. You make a Charisma check opposed by the creature's Charisma check. The check is assigned a bonus of +0 to +6 based on the nature of the service and the reward. If the creature wins the opposed check, it refuses service. New offers, bribes, and the like can be made or the old ones reoffered every 24 hours. This process can be repeated until the creature promises to serve, until it breaks free, or until you decide to get rid of it by means of some other spell. Impossible demands or unreasonable commands are never agreed to. If you ever roll a natural 1 on the Charisma check, the creature breaks free of the spell's effect and can escape or attack you.

Once the requested service is completed, the creature need only to inform you to be instantly sent back whence it came. The creature might later seek revenge. If you assign some open-ended task that the creature cannot complete through its own actions, the spell remains in effect for a maximum of 1 day per caster level, and the creature gains an immediate chance to break free (with the same chance to resist as when it was trapped). Note that a clever recipient can subvert some instructions.

When you use a calling spell to call an air, chaotic, earth, evil, fire, good, lawful, or water creature, it is a spell of that type.

PLANE SHIFT

School conjuration (teleportation); **Level** cleric 5, sorcerer/wizard 7
Casting Time 1 standard action
Components V, S, F (a forked metal rod attuned to the plane of travel)
Range touch
Target creature touched, or up to eight willing creatures joining hands
Duration instantaneous
Saving Throw Will negates; **Spell Resistance** yes

You move yourself or some other creature to another plane of existence or alternate dimension. If several willing persons link hands in a circle, as many as eight can be affected by the *plane shift* at the same time. Precise accuracy as to a particular arrival location on the intended plane is nigh impossible. From the Material Plane, you can reach any other plane, though you appear 5 to 500 miles (5d%) from your intended destination. *Plane shift* transports creatures instantaneously and then ends. The creatures need to find other means if they are to travel back (including casting *plane shift* again).

PLANT GROWTH

School transmutation; **Level** druid 3, ranger 3
Casting Time 1 standard action
Components V, S, DF
Range see text
Target or Area see text
Duration instantaneous
Saving Throw none; **Spell Resistance** no

Plant growth has different effects depending on the version chosen.

Overgrowth: This effect causes normal vegetation (grasses, briars, bushes, creepers, thistles, trees, vines, and so on) within long range (400 feet + 40 feet per caster level) to become thick and overgrown. The plants entwine to form a thicket or jungle that creatures must hack or force a way through. Speed drops to 5 feet, or 10 feet for Large or larger creatures. The area must have brush and trees in it for this spell to take effect. If this spell is cast on an area that is already affected by any spell or effect that enhances plants, such as *entangle* or *wall of thorns*, any DC involved with these spells is increased by 4. This bonus is granted for 1 day after the casting of *plant growth*.

At your option, the area can be a 100-foot-radius circle, a 150-foot-radius semicircle, or a 200-foot-radius quarter circle.

You may designate places within the area that are not affected.

Enrichment: This effect targets plants within a range of a half-mile, raising their potential productivity over the course of the next year to one-third above normal.

Plant growth counters *diminish plants*.

This spell has no effect on plant creatures.

PLANT SHAPE I

School transmutation (polymorph); **Level** sorcerer/wizard 5
Casting Time 1 standard action
Components V, S, M (a piece of the creature whose form you plan to assume)
Range personal
Target you
Duration 1 min./level (D)

When you cast this spell you can assume the form of any Small or

Medium creature of the plant type (see the *Pathfinder RPG Bestiary*). If the form you assume has any of the following abilities, you gain the listed ability: darkvision 60 feet, low-light vision, constrict, grab, and poison. If the form you assume does not possess the ability to move, your speed is reduced to 5 feet and you lose all other forms of movement. If the creature has vulnerability to an element, you gain that vulnerability.

Small plant: If the form you take is that of a Small plant, you gain a +2 size bonus to your Constitution and a +2 natural armor bonus.

Medium plant: If the form you take is that of a Medium plant, you gain a +2 size bonus to your Strength, a +2 size bonus to your Constitution, and a +2 natural armor bonus.

PLANT SHAPE II

School transmutation (polymorph); **Level** sorcerer/wizard 6
This spell functions as *plant shape I* except that it also allows you to assume the form of a Large creature of the plant type. If the creature has immunity or resistance to any elements, you gain resistance 20 to those elements. If the creature has vulnerability to an element, you gain that vulnerability.

Large plant: If the form you take is that of a Large plant, you gain a +4 size bonus to your Strength, a +2 size bonus to your Constitution, and a +4 natural armor bonus.

PLANT SHAPE III

School transmutation (polymorph); **Level** sorcerer/wizard 7
This spell functions as *plant shape II* except that it also allows you to assume the form of a Huge creature of the plant type. If the form you assume has any of the following abilities, you gain the listed ability: DR, regeneration 5, and trample.

Huge plant: If the form you take is that of a Huge plant, you gain a +8 size bonus to your Strength, a −2 penalty to your Dexterity, a +4 size bonus to your Constitution, and a +6 natural armor bonus.

POISON

School necromancy; **Level** cleric 4, druid 3
Casting Time 1 standard action
Components V, S, DF
Range touch
Target living creature touched
Duration instantaneous; see text
Saving Throw Fortitude negates; see text; **Spell Resistance** yes
Calling upon the venomous powers of natural predators, you infect the subject with a horrible poison by making a successful melee touch attack. This poison deals 1d3 Constitution damage per round for 6 rounds. Poisoned creatures can make a Fortitude save each round to negate the damage and end the affliction.

POLAR RAY

School evocation [cold]; **Level** sorcerer/wizard 8
Casting Time 1 standard action
Components V, S, F (a white ceramic cone or prism)
Range medium (100 ft. + 10 ft./level)
Effect ray
Duration instantaneous
Saving Throw none; **Spell Resistance** yes
A blue-white ray of freezing air and ice springs from your hand. You must succeed on a ranged touch attack with the ray to deal damage to a target. The ray deals 1d6 points of cold damage per caster level (maximum 25d6) and 1d4 points of Dexterity drain.

POLYMORPH

School transmutation (polymorph); **Level** sorcerer/wizard 5
Casting Time 1 standard action
Components V, S, M (a piece of the creature whose form you choose)
Range touch
Target living creature touched
Duration 1 min/level (D)
Saving Throw Will negates (harmless); **Spell Resistance** yes (harmless)
This spell transforms a willing creature into an animal, humanoid or elemental of your choosing; the spell has no effect on unwilling creatures, nor can the creature being targeted by this spell influence the new form assumed (apart from conveying its wishes, if any, to you verbally).

If you use this spell to cause the target to take on the form of an animal, the spell functions as *beast shape II*. If the form is that of an elemental, the spell functions as *elemental body I*. If the form is that of a humanoid, the spell functions as *alter self*. The subject may choose to resume its normal form as a full-round action; doing so ends the spell for that subject.

POLYMORPH, GREATER

School transmutation (polymorph); **Level** sorcerer/wizard 7
This spell functions as *polymorph* except that it allows the creature to take on the form of a dragon, magical beast, or plant creature. If you use this spell to cause the target to take on the form of an animal or magical beast, it functions as *beast shape IV*. If the form is that of an elemental, the spell functions as *elemental body III*. If the form is that of a humanoid, the spell functions as *alter self*. If the form is that of a plant, the spell functions as *plant shape II*. If the form is that of a dragon, the spell functions as *form of the dragon I*. The subject may choose to resume its normal form as a full-round action; doing so ends the spell.

POLYMORPH ANY OBJECT

School transmutation (polymorph); **Level** sorcerer/wizard 8
Casting Time 1 standard action
Components V, S, M/DF (mercury, gum arabic, and smoke)
Range close (25 ft. + 5 ft./2 levels)
Target one creature, or one nonmagical object of up to 100 cu. ft./level
Duration see text
Saving Throw Fortitude negates (object); see text; **Spell Resistance** yes (object)
This spell functions like *greater polymorph*, except that it

changes one object or creature into another. You can use this spell to transform all manner of objects and creatures into new forms—you aren't limited to transforming a living creature into another living form. The duration of the spell depends on how radical a change is made from the original state to its transmuted state. The duration is determined by using the following guidelines.

Changed Subject Is...	Increase to Duration Factor*
Same kingdom (animal, vegetable, mineral)	+5
Same class (mammals, fungi, metals, etc.)	+2
Same size	+2
Related (twig is to tree, wolf fur is to wolf, etc.)	+2
Same or lower Intelligence	+2

*Add all that apply. Look up the total on the next table.

Duration Factor	Duration	Example
0	20 minutes	Pebble to human
2	1 hour	Marionette to human
4	3 hours	Human to marionette
5	12 hours	Lizard to manticore
6	2 days	Sheep to wool coat
7	1 week	Shrew to manticore
9+	Permanent	Manticore to shrew

If the target of the spell does not have physical ability scores (Strength, Dexterity, or Constitution), this spell grants a base score of 10 to each missing ability score. If the target of the spell does not have mental ability scores (Intelligence, Wisdom, or Charisma), this spell grants a score of 5 to such scores. Damage taken by the new form can result in the injury or death of the polymorphed creature. In general, damage occurs when the new form is changed through physical force. A nonmagical object cannot be made into a magic item with this spell. Magic items aren't affected by this spell.

This spell cannot create material of great intrinsic value, such as copper, silver, gems, silk, gold, platinum, mithral, or adamantine. It also cannot reproduce the special properties of cold iron in order to overcome the damage reduction of certain creatures.

This spell can also be used to duplicate the effects of *baleful polymorph, greater polymorph, flesh to stone, stone to flesh, transmute mud to rock, transmute metal to wood,* or *transmute rock to mud.*

POWER WORD BLIND

School enchantment (compulsion) [mind-affecting]; **Level** sorcerer/wizard 7

Casting Time 1 standard action

Components V

Range close (25 ft. + 5 ft./2 levels)

Target one creature with 200 hp or less

Duration see text

Saving Throw none; **Spell Resistance** yes

You utter a single word of power that causes a creature to become blinded, whether the creature can hear the word or not. The

duration of the spell depends on the target's current hit point total. Any creature that currently has 201 or more hit points is unaffected.

Hit Points	Duration
50 or less	Permanent
51–100	1d4+1 minutes
101–200	1d4+1 rounds

POWER WORD KILL

School enchantment (compulsion) [death, mind-affecting]; **Level** sorcerer/wizard 9

Casting Time 1 standard action

Components V

Range close (25 ft. + 5 ft./2 levels)

Target one living creature with 100 hp or less

Duration instantaneous

Saving Throw none; **Spell Resistance** yes

You utter a single word of power that instantly kills one creature of your choice, whether the creature can hear the word or not. Any creature that currently has 101 or more hit points is unaffected by *power word kill.*

POWER WORD STUN

School enchantment (compulsion) [mind-affecting]; **Level** sorcerer/wizard 8

Casting Time 1 standard action

Components V

Range close (25 ft. + 5 ft./2 levels)

Target one creature with 150 hp or less

Duration See text

Saving Throw none; **Spell Resistance** yes

You utter a single word of power that instantly causes one creature of your choice to become stunned, whether the creature can hear the word or not. The duration of the spell depends on the target's current hit point total. Any creature that currently has 151 or more hit points is unaffected by *power word stun.*

Hit Points	Duration
50 or less	4d4 rounds
51–100	2d4 rounds
101–150	1d4 rounds

PRAYER

School enchantment (compulsion) [mind-affecting]; **Level** cleric 3, paladin 3

Casting Time 1 standard action

Components V, S, DF

Range 40 ft.

Area all allies and foes within a 40-ft.-radius burst centered on you

Duration 1 round/level

Saving Throw none; **Spell Resistance** yes

You bring special favor upon yourself and your allies while bringing disfavor to your enemies. You and each of your allies gain a +1 luck bonus on attack rolls, weapon damage rolls, saves, and skill checks, while each of your foes takes a –1 penalty on such rolls.

PRESTIDIGITATION

School universal; **Level** bard 0, sorcerer/wizard 0
Casting Time 1 standard action
Components V, S
Range 10 ft.
Target, Effect, or Area see text
Duration 1 hour
Saving Throw see text; **Spell Resistance** no

Prestidigitations are minor tricks that novice spellcasters use for practice. Once cast, a *prestidigitation* spell enables you to perform simple magical effects for 1 hour. The effects are minor and have severe limitations. A prestidigitation can slowly lift 1 pound of material. It can color, clean, or soil items in a 1-foot cube each round. It can chill, warm, or flavor 1 pound of nonliving material. It cannot deal damage or affect the concentration of spellcasters. *Prestidigitation* can create small objects, but they look crude and artificial. The materials created by a *prestidigitation* spell are extremely fragile, and they cannot be used as tools, weapons, or spell components. Finally, *prestidigitation* lacks the power to duplicate any other spell effects. Any actual change to an object (beyond just moving, cleaning, or soiling it) persists only 1 hour.

PRISMATIC SPHERE

School abjuration; **Level** sorcerer/wizard 9
Components: V
Range 10 ft.
Effect 10-ft.-radius sphere centered on you

This spell functions like *prismatic wall*, except you conjure up an immobile, opaque globe of shimmering, multicolored light that surrounds you and protects you from all forms of attack. The sphere flashes in all colors of the visible spectrum.

The sphere's *blindness* effect on creatures with less than 8 HD lasts 2d4 × 10 minutes.

You can pass into and out of the *prismatic sphere* and remain near it without harm. When you're inside it, however, the sphere blocks any attempt to project something through the sphere (including spells). Other creatures that attempt to attack you or pass through suffer the effects of each color, one at a time.

Typically, only the upper hemisphere of the globe exists, since you are at the center of the sphere, so the lower half is usually occluded by the floor surface you are standing on.

The colors of the sphere have the same effects as the colors of a *prismatic wall*.

Prismatic sphere can be made permanent with a *permanency* spell.

PRISMATIC SPRAY

School evocation; **Level** sorcerer/wizard 7

Casting Time 1 standard action
Components V, S
Range 60 ft.
Area cone-shaped burst
Duration instantaneous
Saving Throw see text; **Spell Resistance** yes

This spell causes seven shimmering, multicolored beams of light to spray from your hand. Each beam has a different power. Creatures in the area of the spell with 8 HD or less are automatically blinded for 2d4 rounds. Every creature in the area is randomly struck by one or more beams, which have additional effects.

1d8	Color of Beam	
1	Red	20 points fire damage (Reflex half)
2	Orange	40 points acid damage (Reflex half)
3	Yellow	80 points electricity damage (Reflex half)
4	Green	Poison (Frequency 1/rd. for 6 rd.; Init. effect death; Sec. effect 1 Con/rd.; Cure 2 consecutive Fort saves)*
5	Blue	*Flesh to stone* (Fortitude negates)
6	Indigo	Insane, as insanity spell (Will negates)
7	Violet	Sent to another plane (Will negates)
8	Struck by two rays	Roll twice more, ignoring any "8" results

* See poisons on page 557.

PRISMATIC WALL

School abjuration; **Level** sorcerer/wizard 8
Casting Time 1 standard action
Components V, S
Range close (25 ft. + 5 ft./2 levels)
Effect wall 4 ft./level wide, 2 ft./level high
Duration 10 min./level (D)
Saving Throw see text; **Spell Resistance** see text

Prismatic wall creates a vertical, opaque wall—a shimmering, multicolored plane of light that protects you from all forms of attack. The wall flashes with seven colors, each of which has a distinct power and purpose. The wall is immobile, and you can pass through and remain near the wall without harm. Any other creature with less than 8 HD that is within 20 feet of the wall is blinded by the colors for 2d4 rounds if it looks at the wall.

The wall's maximum proportions are 4 feet wide per caster level and 2 feet high per caster level. A *prismatic wall* spell cast to materialize in a space occupied by a creature is disrupted, and the spell is wasted.

Each color in the wall has a special effect. The accompanying table shows the seven colors of the wall, the order in which they appear, their effects on creatures trying to attack you or pass through the wall, and the magic needed to negate each color.

The wall can be destroyed, color by color, in consecutive order, by casting the specified spells on the wall; however, the first color must

PRISMATIC WALL

Order	Color	Effect of Color	Negated by
1st	Red	Stops nonmagical ranged weapons. Deals 20 points of fire damage (Reflex half).	*Cone of cold*
2nd	Orange	Stops magical ranged weapons. Deals 40 points of acid damage (Reflex half).	*Gust of wind*
3rd	Yellow	Stops poisons, gases, and petrification. Deals 80 points of electricity damage (Reflex half).	*Disintegrate*
4th	Green	Stops breath weapons. Poison (frequency: 1/rd. for 6 rd.; init. effect: death, sec. effect: 1 Con/rd.; cure 2 consecutive Fort saves).	*Passwall*
5th	Blue	Stops divination and mental attacks. Turned to stone (Fortitude negates).	*Magic missile*
6th	Indigo	Stops all spells. Will save or become insane (as *insanity* spell).	*Daylight*
7th	Violet	Energy field destroys all objects and effects.* Creatures sent to another plane (Will negates).	*Dispel magic* or *greater dispel magic*

* The violet effect makes the special effects of the other six colors redundant, but these six effects are included here because certain magic items can create prismatic effects one color at a time, and spell resistance might render some colors ineffective (see above).

be brought down before the second can be affected, and so on. A *rod of cancellation* or a *mage's disjunction* spell destroys a *prismatic wall*, but an *antimagic field* fails to penetrate it. *Dispel magic* and *greater dispel magic* can only be used on the wall once all the other colors have been destroyed. Spell resistance is effective against a *prismatic wall*, but the caster level check must be repeated for each color present.

Prismatic wall can be made permanent with a *permanency* spell.

PRODUCE FLAME

School evocation [fire]; **Level** druid 1
Casting Time 1 standard action
Components V, S
Range 0 ft.
Effect flame in your palm
Duration 1 min./level (D)
Saving Throw none; **Spell Resistance** yes

Flames as bright as a torch appear in your open hand. The flames harm neither you nor your equipment.

In addition to providing illumination, the flames can be hurled or used to touch enemies. You can strike an opponent with a melee touch attack, dealing fire damage equal to 1d6 + 1 point per caster level (maximum +5). Alternatively, you can hurl the flames up to 120 feet as a thrown weapon. When doing so, you attack with a ranged touch attack (with no range penalty) and deal the same damage as with the melee attack. No sooner do you hurl the flames than a new set appears in your hand. Each attack you make reduces the remaining duration by 1 minute. If an attack reduces the remaining duration to 0 minutes or less, the spell ends after the attack resolves.

This spell does not function underwater.

PROGRAMMED IMAGE

School illusion (figment); **Level** bard 6, sorcerer/wizard 6

Components V, S, M (fleece and jade dust worth 25 gp)
Effect visual figment that cannot extend beyond a 20-ft. cube + one 10-ft. cube/level (S)
Duration permanent until triggered, then 1 round/level

This spell functions like *silent image*, except that this spell's figment activates when a specific condition occurs. The figment includes visual, auditory, olfactory, and thermal elements, including intelligible speech.

You set the triggering condition (which may be a special word) when casting the spell. The event that triggers the illusion can be as general or as specific and detailed as desired but must be based on an audible, tactile, olfactory, or visual trigger. The trigger cannot be based on some quality not normally obvious to the senses, such as alignment. See *magic mouth* for more details about such triggers.

PROJECT IMAGE

School illusion (shadow); **Level** bard 6, sorcerer/wizard 7
Casting Time 1 standard action
Components V, S, M (a small replica of you worth 5 gp)
Range medium (100 ft. + 10 ft./level)
Effect one shadow duplicate
Duration 1 round/level (D)
Saving Throw Will disbelief (if interacted with); **Spell Resistance** no

You tap energy from the Plane of Shadow to create a quasi-real, illusory version of yourself. The projected image looks, sounds, and smells like you but is intangible. The projected image mimics your actions (including speech) unless you direct it to act differently (which is a move action).

You can see through its eyes and hear through its ears as if you were standing where it is, and during your turn you can switch from using its senses to using your own, or back again, as a free action. While you are using its senses, your body is considered blinded and deafened.

If you desire, any spell you cast whose range is touch or greater can originate from the projected image instead of from you. The projected image can't cast any spells on itself except for illusion spells. The spells affect other targets normally, despite originating from the projected image.

Objects are affected by the projected image as if they had succeeded on their Will save. You must maintain line of effect to the projected image at all times. If your line of effect is obstructed, the spell ends. If you use *dimension door, teleport, plane shift,* or a similar spell that breaks your line of effect, even momentarily, the spell ends.

PROTECTION FROM ARROWS

School abjuration; **Level** sorcerer/wizard 2
Casting Time 1 standard action
Components V, S, F (a piece of tortoiseshell or turtle shell)
Range touch
Target creature touched
Duration 1 hour/level or until discharged
Saving Throw Will negates (harmless); **Spell Resistance** yes (harmless)
The warded creature gains resistance to ranged weapons. The subject gains damage reduction 10/magic against ranged weapons. This spell doesn't grant you the ability to damage creatures with similar damage reduction. Once the spell has prevented a total of 10 points of damage per caster level (maximum 100 points), it is discharged.

PROTECTION FROM CHAOS

School abjuration [lawful]; **Level** cleric 1, paladin 1, sorcerer/wizard 1
This spell functions like *protection from evil*, except that the deflection and resistance bonuses apply to attacks made by chaotic creatures. The target receives a new saving throw against control by chaotic creatures and chaotic summoned creatures cannot touch the target.

PROTECTION FROM ENERGY

School abjuration; **Level** cleric 3, druid 3, ranger 2, sorcerer/wizard 3
Casting Time 1 standard action
Components V, S, DF
Range touch
Target creature touched
Duration 10 min./level or until discharged
Saving Throw Fortitude negates (harmless); **Spell Resistance** yes (harmless)
Protection from energy grants temporary immunity to the type of energy you specify when you cast it (acid, cold, electricity, fire, or sonic). When the spell absorbs 12 points per caster level of energy damage (to a maximum of 120 points at 10th level), it is discharged.

Protection from energy overlaps (and does not stack with) *resist energy*. If a character is warded by *protection from energy* and *resist energy,* the *protection* spell absorbs damage until its power is exhausted.

PROTECTION FROM EVIL

School abjuration [good]; **Level** cleric 1, paladin 1, sorcerer/wizard 1
Casting Time 1 standard action
Components V, S, M/DF
Range touch
Target creature touched
Duration 1 min./level (D)
Saving Throw Will negates (harmless); **Spell Resistance** no; see text
This spell wards a creature from attacks by evil creatures, from mental control, and from summoned creatures. It creates a magical barrier around the subject at a distance of 1 foot. The barrier moves with the subject and has three major effects.

First, the subject gains a +2 deflection bonus to AC and a +2 resistance bonus on saves. Both these bonuses apply against attacks made or effects created by evil creatures.

Second, the subject immediately receives another saving throw (if one was allowed to begin with) against any spells or effects that possess or exercise mental control over the creature (including enchantment [charm] effects and enchantment [compulsion] effects such as *charm person, command,* and *dominate person*). This saving throw is made with a +2 morale bonus, using the same DC as the original effect. If successful, such effects are suppressed for the duration of this spell. The effects resume when the duration of this spell expires. While under the effects of this spell, the target is immune to any new attempts to possess or exercise mental control over the target. This spell does not expel a controlling life force (such as a ghost or spellcaster using *magic jar*), but it does prevent them from controlling the target. This second effect only functions against spells and effects created by evil creatures or objects, subject to GM discretion.

Third, the spell prevents bodily contact by evil summoned creatures. This causes the natural weapon attacks of such creatures to fail and the creatures to recoil if such attacks require touching the warded creature. Summoned creatures that are not evil are immune to this effect. The protection against contact by summoned creatures ends if the warded creature makes an attack against or tries to force the barrier against the blocked creature. Spell resistance can allow a creature to overcome this protection and touch the warded creature.

PROTECTION FROM GOOD

School abjuration [evil]; **Level** cleric 1, sorcerer/wizard 1
This spell functions like *protection from evil*, except that the deflection and resistance bonuses apply to attacks made by good creatures. The target receives a new saving throw against control by good creatures and good summoned creatures cannot touch the target.

PROTECTION FROM LAW

School abjuration [chaotic]; **Level** cleric 1, sorcerer/wizard 1
This spell functions like *protection from evil*, except that the deflection and resistance bonuses apply to attacks made by lawful creatures. The target receives a new saving throw against control by lawful creatures and lawful summoned creatures cannot touch the target.

PROTECTION FROM SPELLS

School abjuration; **Level** sorcerer/wizard 8

Casting Time 1 standard action

Components V, S, M (diamond worth 500 gp), F (One 1,000 gp diamond per target. Each subject must carry the gem for the duration of the spell. If a subject loses the gem, the spell ceases to affect him.)

Range touch

Targets up to one creature touched per four levels

Duration 10 min./level

Saving Throw Will negates (harmless); **Spell Resistance** yes (harmless)

The subject gains a +8 resistance bonus on saving throws against spells and spell-like abilities (but not against supernatural and extraordinary abilities).

PRYING EYES

School divination; **Level** sorcerer/wizard 5

Casting Time 1 minute

Components V, S, M (a handful of crystal marbles)

Range 1 mile

Effect 10 or more levitating eyes

Duration 1 hour/level; see text (D)

Saving Throw none; **Spell Resistance** no

You create a number of semitangible, visible magical orbs (called "eyes") equal to 1d4 + your caster level. These eyes move out, scout around, and return as you direct them when casting the spell. Each eye can see 120 feet (normal vision only) in all directions.

While the individual eyes are quite fragile, they're small and difficult to spot. Each eye is a Fine construct, about the size of a small apple, that has 1 hit point, AC 18 (+8 bonus for its size), flies at a speed of 30 feet with a +20 bonus on Fly skill checks and a +16 bonus on Stealth skill checks. It has a Perception modifier equal to your caster level (maximum +15) and is subject to illusions, darkness, fog, and any other factors that affect your ability to receive visual information about your surroundings. An eye traveling in darkness must find its way by touch.

When you create the eyes, you specify instructions you want them to follow in a command of no more than 25 words. Any knowledge you possess is known by the eyes as well.

In order to report their findings, the eyes must return to your hand. Each replays in your mind all it has seen during its existence. It takes an eye 1 round to replay 1 hour of recorded images. After relaying its findings, an eye disappears.

If an eye ever gets more than 1 mile away from you, it instantly ceases to exist. However, your link with the eye is such that you won't know if the eye was destroyed because it wandered out of range or because of some other event.

The eyes exist for up to 1 hour per caster level or until they return to you. *Dispel magic* can destroy eyes. Roll separately for each eye caught in an area dispel. Of course, if an eye is sent into darkness, it could hit a wall or similar obstacle and destroy itself.

PRYING EYES, GREATER

School divination; **Level** sorcerer/wizard 8

This spell functions like *prying eyes*, except that the eyes can see all things as they actually are, just as if they had *true seeing* with a range of 120 feet. Thus, they can navigate darkened areas at normal speed. Also, a *greater prying eye*'s maximum Perception modifier is +25 instead of +15.

PURIFY FOOD AND DRINK

School transmutation; **Level** cleric 0, druid 0

Casting Time 1 standard action

Components V, S

Range 10 ft.

Target 1 cu. ft./level of contaminated food and water

Duration instantaneous

Saving Throw Will negates (object); **Spell Resistance** yes (object)

This spell makes spoiled, rotten, diseased, poisonous, or otherwise contaminated food and water pure and suitable for eating and drinking. This spell does not prevent subsequent natural decay or spoilage. Unholy water and similar food and drink of significance is spoiled by *purify food and drink*, but the spell has no effect on creatures of any type nor upon magic potions. Water weighs about 8 pounds per gallon. One cubic foot of water contains roughly 8 gallons and weighs about 60 pounds.

PYROTECHNICS

School transmutation; **Level** bard 2, sorcerer/wizard 2

Casting Time 1 standard action

Components V, S, M (one fire source)

Range long (400 ft. + 40 ft./level)

Target one fire source, up to a 20-ft. cube

Duration 1d4+1 rounds, or 1d4+1 rounds after creatures leave the smoke cloud; see text

Saving Throw Will negates or Fortitude negates; see text; **Spell Resistance** yes or no; see text

Pyrotechnics turns a fire into a burst of blinding fireworks or a thick cloud of choking smoke, depending on your choice. The spell uses one fire source, which is immediately extinguished. A fire so large that it exceeds a 20-foot cube is only partly extinguished. Magical fires are not extinguished, although a fire-based creature used as a source takes 1 point of damage per caster level.

Fireworks: The fireworks are a flashing, fiery, momentary burst of glowing, colored aerial lights. This effect causes creatures within 120 feet of the fire source to become blinded for 1d4+1 rounds (Will negates). These creatures must have line of sight to the fire to be affected. Spell resistance can prevent blindness.

Smoke Cloud: A stream of smoke billows out from the fire, forming a choking cloud that spreads 20 feet in all directions and lasts for 1 round per caster level. All sight, even darkvision, is ineffective in or through the cloud. All within the cloud take −4 penalties to Strength and Dexterity (Fortitude negates). These effects last for 1d4+1 rounds after the cloud dissipates or after the creature leaves the area of the cloud. Spell resistance does not apply.

QUENCH

School transmutation; **Level** druid 3

Casting Time 1 standard action

Components V, S, DF

Range medium (100 ft. + 10 ft./level)

Area or Target one 20-ft. cube/level (S) or one fire-based magic item

Duration instantaneous

Saving Throw none or Will negates (object); **Spell Resistance** no or yes (object)

Quench is often used to put out forest fires and other conflagrations. It extinguishes all nonmagical fires in its area. The spell also dispels any fire spells in its area, though you must succeed on a dispel check (1d20 +1 per caster level, maximum +15) against each spell to dispel it. The DC to dispel such spells is 11 + the caster level of the fire spell.

Each creature with the fire subtype within the area of a *quench* spell takes 1d6 points of damage per caster level (maximum 10d6, no save allowed).

Alternatively, you can target the spell on a single magic item that creates or controls flame. The item loses all its fire-based magical abilities for 1d4 hours unless it succeeds on a Will save. Artifacts are immune to this effect.

RAGE

School enchantment (compulsion) [mind-affecting]; **Level** bard 2, sorcerer/wizard 3

Casting Time 1 standard action

Components V, S

Range medium (100 ft. + 10 ft./level)

Targets one willing living creature per three levels, no two of which may be more than 30 ft. apart

Duration concentration + 1 round/level (D)

Saving Throw none; **Spell Resistance** yes

Each affected creature gains a +2 morale bonus to Strength and Constitution, a +1 morale bonus on Will saves, and a –2 penalty to AC. The effect is otherwise identical with a barbarian's rage except that the subjects aren't fatigued at the end of the rage.

RAINBOW PATTERN

School illusion (pattern) [mind-affecting]; **Level** bard 4, sorcerer/wizard 4

Casting Time 1 standard action

Components V (bard only), S, M (a piece of phosphor), F (a crystal prism); see text

Range medium (100 ft. + 10 ft./level)

Effect colorful lights with a 20-ft.-radius spread

Duration Concentration +1 round/level (D)

Saving Throw Will negates; **Spell Resistance** yes

A glowing, rainbow-hued pattern of interweaving colors fascinates those within it. *Rainbow pattern* fascinates a maximum of 24 HD of creatures. Creatures with the fewest HD are affected first. Among creatures with equal HD, those who are closest to the spell's point of origin are affected first. An affected creature that fails its saves is fascinated by the pattern.

With a simple gesture (a free action), you can make the *rainbow pattern* move up to 30 feet per round (moving its effective point of origin). All fascinated creatures follow the moving rainbow of light, trying to remain within the effect. Fascinated creatures who are restrained and removed from the pattern still try to follow it. If the pattern leads its subjects into a dangerous area, each fascinated creature gets a second save. If the view of the lights is completely blocked, creatures who can't see them are no longer affected.

The spell does not affect sightless creatures.

RAISE DEAD

School conjuration (healing); **Level** cleric 5

Casting Time 1 minute

Components V, S, M (diamond worth 5,000 gp), DF

Range touch

Target dead creature touched

Duration instantaneous

Saving Throw none, see text; **Spell Resistance** yes (harmless)

You restore life to a deceased creature. You can raise a creature that has been dead for no longer than 1 day per caster level. In addition, the subject's soul must be free and willing to return. If the subject's soul is not willing to return, the spell does not work; therefore, a subject that wants to return receives no saving throw.

Coming back from the dead is an ordeal. The subject of the spell gains two permanent negative levels when it is raised, just as if it had been hit by an energy-draining creature. Negative levels equal to or greater than the creature's Hit Dice are instead applied as Constitution drain (if this would reduce its Con to 0 or less, it can't be raised). A character who died with spells prepared has a 50% chance of losing any given spell upon being raised. A spellcasting creature that doesn't prepare spells (such as a sorcerer) has a 50% chance of losing any given unused spell slot as if it had been used to cast a spell.

A raised creature has a number of hit points equal to its current HD. Any ability scores damaged to 0 are raised to 1. Normal poison and normal disease are cured in the process of raising the subject, but magical diseases and curses are not undone. While the spell closes mortal wounds and repairs lethal damage of most kinds, the body of the creature to be raised must be whole. Otherwise, missing parts are still missing when the creature is brought back to life. None of the dead creature's equipment or possessions are affected in any way by this spell.

A creature who has been turned into an undead creature or killed by a death effect can't be raised by this spell. Constructs, elementals, outsiders, and undead creatures can't be raised. The spell cannot bring back a creature that has died of old age.

RAY OF ENFEEBLEMENT

School necromancy; **Level** sorcerer/wizard 1

Casting Time 1 standard action

Components V, S

Range close (25 ft. + 5 ft./2 levels)

Effect ray

Duration 1 round/level

Saving Throw Fortitude half; **Spell Resistance** yes

A coruscating ray springs from your hand. You must succeed on a ranged touch attack to strike a target. The subject takes a penalty to Strength equal to 1d6+1 per two caster levels (maximum 1d6+5). The subject's Strength score cannot drop below 1. A successful Fortitude save reduces this penalty by half. This penalty does not stack with itself. Apply the highest penalty instead.

RAY OF EXHAUSTION

School necromancy; **Level** sorcerer/wizard 3

Casting Time 1 standard action

Components V, S, M (a drop of sweat)

Range close (25 ft. + 5 ft./2 levels)

Effect ray

Duration 1 min./level

Saving Throw Fortitude partial; see text; **Spell Resistance** yes

A black ray projects from your pointing finger. You must succeed on a ranged touch attack with the ray to strike a target.

The subject is immediately exhausted for the spell's duration. A successful Fortitude save means the creature is only fatigued.

A character that is already fatigued instead becomes exhausted.

This spell has no effect on a creature that is already exhausted. Unlike normal exhaustion or fatigue, the effect ends as soon as the spell's duration expires.

RAY OF FROST

School evocation [cold]; **Level** sorcerer/wizard 0

Casting Time 1 standard action

Components V, S

Range close (25 ft. + 5 ft./2 levels)

Effect ray

Duration instantaneous

Saving Throw none; **Spell Resistance** yes

A ray of freezing air and ice projects from your pointing finger. You must succeed on a ranged touch attack with the ray to deal damage to a target. The ray deals 1d3 points of cold damage.

READ MAGIC

School divination; **Level** bard 0, cleric 0, druid 0, paladin 1, ranger 1, sorcerer/wizard 0

Casting Time 1 standard action

Components V, S, F (a clear crystal or mineral prism)

Range personal

Target you

Duration 10 min./level

You can decipher magical inscriptions on objects—books, scrolls, weapons, and the like—that would otherwise be unintelligible. This deciphering does not normally invoke the magic contained in the writing, although it may do so in the case of a cursed or trapped scroll. Furthermore, once the spell is cast and you have read the magical inscription, you are thereafter able to read that particular writing without recourse to the use of *read magic*. You can read at the rate of one page (250 words) per minute. The spell allows you to identify a *glyph of warding* with a DC 13 Spellcraft check, a *greater glyph of warding* with a DC 16 Spellcraft check, or any *symbol* spell with a Spellcraft check (DC 10 + spell level).

Read magic can be made permanent with a *permanency* spell.

REDUCE ANIMAL

School transmutation; **Level** druid 2, ranger 3

Casting Time 1 standard action

Components V, S

Range touch

Target one willing animal of Small, Medium, Large, or Huge size

Duration 1 hour/level (D)

Saving Throw none; **Spell Resistance** no

This spell functions like *reduce person*, except that it affects a single willing animal. Reduce the damage dealt by the animal's natural attacks as appropriate for its new size (see Chapter 6 how to adjust damage for size).

REDUCE PERSON

School transmutation; **Level** sorcerer/wizard 1

Casting Time 1 round

Components V, S, M (a pinch of powdered iron)

Range close (25 ft. + 5 ft./2 levels)

Target one humanoid creature

Duration 1 min./level (D)

Saving Throw Fortitude negates; **Spell Resistance** yes

This spell causes instant diminution of a humanoid creature, halving its height, length, and width and dividing its weight by 8. This decrease changes the creature's size category to the next smaller one. The target gains a +2 size bonus to Dexterity, a −2 size penalty to Strength (to a minimum of 1), and a +1 bonus on attack rolls and AC due to its reduced size.

A Small humanoid creature whose size decreases to Tiny has a space of 2-1/2 feet and a natural reach of 0 feet (meaning that it must enter an opponent's square to attack). A Large humanoid creature whose size decreases to Medium has a space of 5 feet and a natural reach of 5 feet. This spell doesn't change the target's speed.

All equipment worn or carried by a creature is similarly reduced by the spell.

Melee and projectile weapons deal less damage. Other magical properties are not affected by this spell. Any *reduced* item that leaves the *reduced* creature's possession (including a projectile or thrown weapon) instantly returns to its normal size. This means that thrown weapons deal their normal damage (projectiles deal damage based on the size of the weapon that fired them).

Multiple magical effects that reduce size do not stack. *Reduce person* counters and dispels *enlarge person*.

Reduce person can be made permanent with a *permanency* spell.

REDUCE PERSON, MASS

School transmutation; **Level** sorcerer/wizard 4

Target one humanoid creature/level, no two of which can be more than 30 ft. apart

This spell functions like *reduce person*, except that it affects multiple creatures.

REFUGE

School conjuration (teleportation); **Level** cleric 7, sorcerer/wizard 9

Casting Time 1 standard action

Components V, S, M (a prepared object worth 1,500 gp)

Range touch

Target object touched

Duration permanent until discharged

Saving Throw none; **Spell Resistance** no

When you cast this spell, you create powerful magic in a specially prepared object. This object contains the power to instantly transport its possessor across any distance within the same plane to your abode. Once the item is so enhanced, you must give it willingly to a creature and at the same time inform it of a command word to be spoken when the item is used. To make use of the item, the subject speaks the command word at the same time that it rends or breaks the item (a standard action). When this is done, the individual and all objects it is wearing and carrying (to a maximum of the character's heavy load) are instantly transported to your abode. No other creatures are affected (aside from a familiar or animal companion that is touching the subject).

You can alter the spell when casting it so that it transports you to within 10 feet of the possessor of the item when it is broken and the command word spoken. You will have a general idea of the location and situation of the item possessor at the time the *refuge* spell is discharged, but once you decide to alter the spell in this fashion, you have no choice whether or not to be transported.

REGENERATE

School conjuration (healing); **Level** cleric 7, druid 9

Casting Time 3 full rounds

Components V, S, DF

Range touch

Target living creature touched

Duration instantaneous

Saving Throw Fortitude negates (harmless); **Spell Resistance** yes (harmless)

The subject's severed body members (fingers, toes, hands, feet, arms, legs, tails, or even heads of multiheaded creatures), broken bones, and ruined organs grow back. After the spell is cast, the physical regeneration is complete in 1 round if the severed members are present and touching the creature. It takes 2d10 rounds otherwise.

Regenerate also cures 4d8 points of damage + 1 point per caster level (maximum +35), rids the subject of exhaustion and fatigue, and eliminates all nonlethal damage the subject has taken. It has no effect on nonliving creatures (including undead).

REINCARNATE

School transmutation; **Level** druid 4

Casting Time 10 minutes

Components V, S, DF, M (oils worth 1,000 gp)

Range touch

Target dead creature touched

Duration instantaneous

Saving Throw none, see text; **Spell Resistance** yes (harmless)

With this spell, you bring back a dead creature in another body, provided that its death occurred no more than 1 week before the casting of the spell and the subject's soul is free and willing to return. If the subject's soul is not willing to return, the spell does not work; therefore, a subject that wants to return receives no saving throw.

Since the dead creature is returning in a new body, all physical ills and afflictions are repaired. The condition of the remains is not a factor. So long as some small portion of the creature's body still exists, it can be reincarnated, but the portion receiving the spell must have been part of the creature's body at the time of death. The magic of the spell creates an entirely new young adult body for the soul to inhabit from the natural elements at hand. This process takes 1 hour to complete. When the body is ready, the subject is reincarnated.

A reincarnated creature recalls the majority of its former life and form. It retains any class abilities, feats, or skill ranks it formerly possessed. Its class, base attack bonus, base save bonuses, and hit points are unchanged. Strength, Dexterity, and Constitution scores depend partly on the new body. First eliminate the subject's racial adjustments (since it is no longer necessarily of his previous race) and then apply the adjustments found below to its remaining ability scores. The subject of the spell gains two permanent negative levels when it is reincarnated. Negative levels equal to or greater than the creature's Hit Dice are instead applied as Constitution drain (if this would reduce its Con to 0 or less, it can't be reincarnated). A character who died with spells prepared has a 50% chance of losing any given spell upon being reincarnated. A spellcasting creature that doesn't prepare spells (such as a sorcerer) has a 50% chance of losing any given unused spell slot as if it had been used to cast a spell.

It's possible for the change in the subject's ability scores to make it difficult for it to pursue its previous character class. If this is the case, the subject is advised to become a multiclass character.

For a humanoid creature, the new incarnation is determined using the table on the next page. For nonhumanoid creatures, a similar table of creatures of the same type should be created.

A creature that has been turned into an undead creature or killed by a death effect can't be returned to life by this spell. Constructs, elementals, outsiders, and undead creatures can't be reincarnated. The spell can bring back a creature that has died of old age.

d%	Incarnation	Str	Dex	Con
01	Bugbear	+4	+2	+2
02–13	Dwarf	+0	+0	+2
14–25	Elf	+0	+2	−2
26	Gnoll	+4	+0	+2
27–38	Gnome	−2	+0	+2
39–42	Goblin	−2	+2	+0
43–52	Half-elf	+0	+2	+0
53–62	Half-orc	+2	+0	+0
63–74	Halfling	−2	+2	+0
75–89	Human	+0	+0	+2
90–93	Kobold	−4	+2	−2
94	Lizardfolk	+2	+0	+2
95–98	Orc	+4	+0	+0
99	Troglodyte	+0	−2	+4
100	Other (GM's choice)	?	?	?

The reincarnated creature gains all abilities associated with its new form, including forms of movement and speeds, natural armor, natural attacks, extraordinary abilities, and the like, but it doesn't automatically speak the language of the new form.

A *wish* or a *miracle* spell can restore a reincarnated character to his or her original form.

REMOVE BLINDNESS/DEAFNESS

School conjuration (healing); **Level** cleric 3, paladin 3
Casting Time 1 standard action
Components V, S
Range touch
Target creature touched
Duration instantaneous
Saving Throw Fortitude negates (harmless); **Spell Resistance** yes (harmless)
Remove blindness/deafness cures blindness or deafness (your choice), whether the effect is normal or magical in nature. The spell does not restore ears or eyes that have been lost, but it repairs them if they are damaged.

Remove blindness/deafness counters and dispels *blindness/deafness*.

REMOVE CURSE

School abjuration; **Level** bard 3, cleric 3, paladin 3, sorcerer/wizard 4
Casting Time 1 standard action
Components V, S
Range touch
Target creature or object touched
Duration instantaneous
Saving Throw Will negates (harmless); **Spell Resistance** yes (harmless)
Remove curse can remove all curses on an object or a creature. If the target is a creature, you must make a caster level check (1d20 + caster level) against the DC of each curse affecting the target. Success means that the curse is removed. *Remove curse* does not remove the curse from a cursed shield, weapon, or suit of armor, although a successful caster level check enables the creature afflicted with any such cursed item to remove and get rid of it.

Remove curse counters and dispels *bestow curse*.

REMOVE DISEASE

School conjuration (healing); **Level** cleric 3, druid 3, ranger 3
Casting Time 1 standard action
Components V, S
Range touch
Target creature touched
Duration instantaneous
Saving Throw Fortitude negates (harmless); **Spell Resistance** yes (harmless)
Remove disease can cure all diseases from which the subject is suffering. You must make a caster level check (1d20 + caster level) against the DC of each disease affecting the target. Success means that the disease is cured. The spell also kills some hazards and parasites, including green slime and others.

Since the spell's duration is instantaneous, it does not prevent reinfection after a new exposure to the same disease at a later date.

REMOVE FEAR

School abjuration; **Level** bard 1, cleric 1
Casting Time 1 standard action
Components V, S
Range close (25 ft. + 5 ft./2 levels)
Targets one creature plus one additional creature per four levels, no two of which can be more than 30 ft. apart
Duration 10 minutes; see text
Saving Throw Will negates (harmless); **Spell Resistance** yes (harmless)
You instill courage in the subject, granting it a +4 morale bonus against fear effects for 10 minutes. If the subject is under the influence of a fear effect when receiving the spell, that effect is suppressed for the duration of the spell.

Remove fear counters and dispels *cause fear*.

REMOVE PARALYSIS

School conjuration (healing); **Level** cleric 2, paladin 2
Casting Time 1 standard action
Components V, S
Range close (25 ft. + 5 ft./2 levels)
Targets up to four creatures, no two of which can be more than 30 ft. apart
Duration instantaneous
Saving Throw Will negates (harmless); **Spell Resistance** yes (harmless)
You can free one or more creatures from the effects of temporary paralysis or related magic, including spells and effects that cause a creature to gain the staggered condition. If the spell is cast on one creature, the paralysis is negated. If cast on two creatures, each receives another save with a +4 resistance bonus against the effect that afflicts it. If cast on three or four creatures, each receives another save with a +2 resistance bonus.

The spell does not restore ability scores reduced by penalties, damage, or drain.

REPEL METAL OR STONE

School abjuration [earth]; **Level** druid 8
Casting Time 1 standard action
Components V, S
Range 60 ft.
Area 60-ft. line from you
Duration 1 round/level (D)
Saving Throw none; **Spell Resistance** no

This spell creates waves of invisible energy that roll forth from you. All metal or stone objects in the path of the spell are pushed away from you to the limit of the range. Fixed metal or stone objects larger than 3 inches in diameter and loose objects weighing more than 500 pounds are not affected. Anything else, including animated objects, small boulders, and creatures in metal armor, moves back. Fixed objects 3 inches in diameter or smaller bend or break, and the pieces move with the wave of energy. Objects affected by the spell are repelled at the rate of 40 feet per round.

Objects such as metal armor, swords, and the like are pushed back, dragging their bearers with them. Even magic items with metal components are repelled, although an *antimagic field* blocks the effects. A creature being dragged by an item it is carrying can let go. A creature being dragged by a shield can loose it as a move action and drop it as a free action.

The waves of energy continue to sweep down the set path for the spell's duration. After you cast the spell, the path is set, and you can then do other things or go elsewhere without affecting the spell's power.

REPEL VERMIN

School abjuration; **Level** bard 4, cleric 4, druid 4, ranger 3
Casting Time 1 standard action
Components V, S, DF
Range 10 ft.
Area 10-ft.-radius emanation centered on you
Duration 10 min./level (D)
Saving Throw none or Will negates; see text; **Spell Resistance** yes

An invisible barrier holds back vermin. A vermin with HD of less than one-third your level cannot penetrate the barrier.

A vermin with HD of one-third your level or more can penetrate the barrier if it succeeds on a Will save. Even so, crossing the barrier deals the vermin 2d6 points of damage, and pressing against the barrier causes pain, which deters most vermin.

REPEL WOOD

School transmutation; **Level** druid 6
Casting Time 1 standard action
Components V, S
Range 60 ft.
Area 60-ft. line-shaped emanation from you
Duration 1 min./level (D)
Saving Throw none; **Spell Resistance** no

Waves of energy roll forth from you, moving in the direction that you determine, causing all wooden objects in the path of the spell to be pushed away from you to the limit of the range. Wooden objects larger than 3 inches in diameter that are fixed firmly are not affected, but loose objects are. Objects 3 inches in diameter or smaller that are fixed in place splinter and break, and the pieces move with the wave of energy. Objects affected by the spell are repelled at the rate of 40 feet per round.

Objects such as wooden shields, spears, wooden weapon shafts and hafts, and arrows and bolts are pushed back, dragging those carrying them along. A creature being dragged by an item it is carrying can let go. A creature being dragged by a shield can loose it as a move action and drop it as a free action. If a spear is planted (set) in a way that prevents this forced movement, it splinters. Even magic items with wooden sections are repelled, although an *antimagic field* blocks the effects.

The waves of energy continue to sweep down the set path for the spell's duration. After you cast the spell, the path is set, and you can then do other things or go elsewhere without affecting the spell's power.

REPULSION

School abjuration; **Level** cleric 7, sorcerer/wizard 6
Casting Time 1 standard action
Components V, S, F/DF (a pair of canine statuettes worth 50 gp)
Range up to 10 ft./level
Area up to 10-ft.-radius/level emanation centered on you
Duration 1 round/level (D)
Saving Throw Will negates; **Spell Resistance** yes

An invisible, mobile field surrounds you and prevents creatures from approaching you. You decide how big the field is at the time of casting (to the limit your level allows). Any creature within or entering the field must attempt a save. If it fails, it becomes unable to move toward you for the duration of the spell. Repelled creatures' actions are not otherwise restricted. They can fight other creatures and can cast spells and attack you with ranged weapons. If you move closer to an affected creature, nothing happens. The creature is not forced back. The creature is free to make melee attacks against you if you come within reach. If a repelled creature moves away from you and then tries to turn back toward you, it cannot move any closer if it is still within the spell's area.

RESILIENT SPHERE

School evocation [force]; **Level** sorcerer/wizard 4
Casting Time 1 standard action
Components V, S, F (a crystal sphere)
Range close (25 ft. + 5 ft./2 levels)
Effect 1-ft.-diameter/level sphere, centered around a creature
Duration 1 min./level (D)
Saving Throw Reflex negates; **Spell Resistance** yes

A globe of shimmering force encloses a creature, provided the creature is small enough to fit within the diameter of the sphere. The sphere contains its subject for the spell's duration. The sphere functions as a *wall of force*, except that it can be negated by *dispel magic*. A subject inside the sphere can breathe normally.

The sphere cannot be physically moved either by people outside it or by the struggles of those within.

RESISTANCE

School abjuration; **Level** bard 0, cleric 0, druid 0, paladin 1, sorcerer/wizard 0
Casting Time 1 standard action
Components V, S, M/DF (a miniature cloak)
Range touch
Target creature touched
Duration 1 minute
Saving Throw Will negates (harmless); **Spell Resistance** yes (harmless)

You imbue the subject with magical energy that protects it from harm, granting it a +1 resistance bonus on saves.

Resistance can be made permanent with a *permanency* spell.

RESIST ENERGY

School abjuration; **Level** cleric 2, druid 2, paladin 2, ranger 1, sorcerer/wizard 2
Casting Time 1 standard action
Components V, S, DF
Range touch
Target creature touched
Duration 10 min./level
Saving Throw Fortitude negates (harmless); **Spell Resistance** yes (harmless)

This abjuration grants a creature limited protection from damage of whichever one of five energy types you select: acid, cold, electricity, fire, or sonic. The subject gains resist energy 10 against the energy type chosen, meaning that each time the creature is subjected to such damage (whether from a natural or magical source), that damage is reduced by 10 points before being applied to the creature's hit points. The value of the energy resistance granted increases to 20 points at 7th level and to a maximum of 30 points at 11th level. The spell protects the recipient's equipment as well.

Resist energy absorbs only damage. The subject could still suffer unfortunate side effects.

Resist energy overlaps (and does not stack with) *protection from energy*. If a character is warded by *protection from energy* and *resist energy*, the *protection* spell absorbs damage until its power is exhausted.

RESTORATION

School conjuration (healing); **Level** cleric 4, paladin 4
Casting Time 3 rounds
Components V, S, M (diamond dust worth 100 gp or 1,000 gp, see text)
Range touch
Target creature touched
Duration instantaneous
Saving Throw Will negates (harmless); **Spell Resistance** yes (harmless)

This spell functions like *lesser restoration*, except that it also dispels temporary negative levels or one permanent negative level. If this spell is used to dispel a permanent negative level, it has a material component of diamond dust worth 1,000 gp. This spell cannot be used to dispel more than one permanent negative level possessed by a target in a 1-week period.

Restoration cures all temporary ability damage, and it restores all points permanently drained from a single ability score (your choice if more than one is drained). It also eliminates any fatigue or exhaustion suffered by the target.

RESTORATION, GREATER

School conjuration (healing); **Level** cleric 7
Components V, S, M (diamond dust worth 5,000 gp)

This spell functions like *lesser restoration*, except that it dispels all permanent and temporary negative levels afflicting the healed creature. *Greater restoration* also dispels all magical effects penalizing the creature's abilities, cures all temporary ability damage, and restores all points permanently drained from all ability scores. It also eliminates fatigue and exhaustion, and removes all forms of insanity, confusion, and similar mental effects.

RESTORATION, LESSER

School conjuration (healing); **Level** cleric 2, druid 2, paladin 1
Casting Time 3 rounds
Components V, S
Range touch
Target creature touched
Duration instantaneous
Saving Throw Will negates (harmless); **Spell Resistance** yes (harmless)

Lesser restoration dispels any magical effects reducing one of the subject's ability scores or cures 1d4 points of temporary ability damage to one of the subject's ability scores. It also eliminates any fatigue suffered by the character, and improves an exhausted condition to fatigued. It does not restore permanent ability drain.

RESURRECTION

School conjuration (healing); **Level** cleric 7
Components V, S, M (diamond worth 10,000 gp), DF

This spell functions like *raise dead*, except that you are able to restore life and complete strength to any deceased creature.

The condition of the remains is not a factor. So long as some small portion of the creature's body still exists, it can be resurrected, but the portion receiving the spell must have been part of the creature's body at the time of death. (The remains of a creature hit by a *disintegrate* spell count as a small portion of its body.) The creature can have been dead no longer than 10 years per caster level.

Upon completion of the spell, the creature is immediately restored to full hit points, vigor, and health, with no loss of prepared spells. The subject of the spell gains one permanent negative level when it is raised, just as if it had been hit by an energy-draining creature. If the subject is 1st level, it takes 2 points of Constitution drain instead (if this would reduce its Con to 0 or less, it can't be resurrected).

You can resurrect someone killed by a death effect or someone who has been turned into an undead creature and then destroyed.

You cannot resurrect someone who has died of old age. Constructs, elementals, outsiders, and undead creatures can't be resurrected.

REVERSE GRAVITY

School transmutation; **Level** druid 8, sorcerer/wizard 7

Casting Time 1 standard action

Components V, S, M/DF (lodestone and iron filings)

Range medium (100 ft. + 10 ft./level)

Area up to one 10-ft. cube/level (S)

Duration 1 round/level (D)

Saving Throw none; see text; **Spell Resistance** no

This spell reverses gravity in an area, causing unattached objects and creatures in the area to fall upward and reach the top of the area in 1 round. If a solid object (such as a ceiling) is encountered in this fall, falling objects and creatures strike it in the same manner as they would during a normal downward fall. If an object or creature reaches the top of the area without striking anything, it remains there, oscillating slightly, until the spell ends. At the end of the spell duration, affected objects and creatures fall downward.

Provided it has something to hold onto, a creature caught in the area can attempt a Reflex save to secure itself when the spell strikes. Creatures who can fly or levitate can keep themselves from falling.

RIGHTEOUS MIGHT

School transmutation; **Level** cleric 5

Casting Time 1 standard action

Components V, S, DF

Range personal

Target you

Duration 1 round/level (D)

Your height immediately doubles, and your weight increases by a factor of eight. This increase changes your size category to the next larger one. You gain a +4 size bonus to Strength and Constitution and take a –2 penalty to your Dexterity. You gain a +2 enhancement bonus to your natural armor. You gain DR 5/evil (if you normally channel positive energy) or DR 5/good (if you normally channel negative energy). At 15th level, this DR becomes 10/evil or 10/good (the maximum). Your size modifier for AC and attacks changes as appropriate to your new size category. This spell doesn't change your speed. Determine space and reach as appropriate to your new size.

If insufficient room is available for the desired growth, you attain the maximum possible size and may make a Strength check (using your increased Strength) to burst any enclosures in the process (see Chapter 7 for rules on breaking objects). If you fail, you are constrained without harm by the materials enclosing you—the spell cannot crush you by increasing your size.

All equipment you wear or carry is similarly enlarged by the spell. Melee weapons deal more damage. Other magical properties are not affected by this spell. Any enlarged item that leaves your possession (including a projectile or thrown weapon) instantly returns to its normal size. This means that thrown and projectile weapons deal their normal damage. Magical effects that increase size do not stack.

ROPE TRICK

School transmutation; **Level** sorcerer/wizard 2

Casting Time 1 standard action

Components V, S, M (powdered corn and a twisted loop of parchment)

Range touch

Target one touched piece of rope from 5 ft. to 30 ft. long

Duration 1 hour/level (D)

Saving Throw none; **Spell Resistance** no

When this spell is cast upon a piece of rope from 5 to 30 feet long, one end of the rope rises into the air until the whole rope hangs perpendicular to the ground, as if affixed at the upper end. The upper end is, in fact, fastened to an extradimensional space that is outside the usual multiverse of extradimensional spaces. Creatures in the extradimensional space are hidden, beyond the reach of spells (including divinations), unless those spells work across planes. The space holds as many as eight creatures (of any size). The rope cannot be removed or hidden. The rope can support up to 16,000 pounds. A weight greater than that can pull the rope free.

Spells cannot be cast across the extradimensional interface, nor can area effects cross it. Those in the extradimensional space can see out of it as if a 3-foot-by-5-foot window were centered on the rope. The window is invisible, and even creatures that can see the window can't see through it. Anything inside the extradimensional space drops out when the spell ends. The rope can be climbed by only one person at a time. The *rope trick* spell enables climbers to reach a normal place if they do not climb all the way to the extradimensional space.

RUSTING GRASP

School transmutation; **Level** druid 4

Casting Time 1 standard action

Components V, S, DF

Range touch

Target one nonmagical ferrous object (or the volume of the object within 3 ft. of the touched point) or one ferrous creature

Duration see text

Saving Throw none; **Spell Resistance** no

Any iron or iron alloy item you touch crumbles into rust. If the item is so large that it cannot fit within a 3-foot radius, a 3-foot-radius volume of the metal is rusted and destroyed. Magic items made of metal are immune to this spell.

You may employ *rusting grasp* in combat with a successful melee touch attack. *Rusting grasp* used in this way instantaneously destroys 1d6 points of AC gained from metal armor (to the maximum amount of protection the armor offers) through corrosion.

Weapons in use by an opponent targeted by the spell are more difficult to grasp. You must succeed on a melee touch attack against the weapon. A metal weapon that is hit is destroyed. Striking at an opponent's weapon provokes an attack of opportunity. Also, you must touch the weapon and not the other way around.

Against a ferrous creature, *rusting grasp* instantaneously deals 3d6 points of damage + 1 per caster level (maximum +15) per

successful attack. The spell lasts for 1 round per level, and you can make one melee touch attack per round.

SANCTUARY

School abjuration; **Level** cleric 1
Casting Time 1 standard action
Components V, S, DF
Range touch
Target creature touched
Duration 1 round/level
Saving Throw Will negates; **Spell Resistance** no

Any opponent attempting to directly attack the warded creature, even with a targeted spell, must attempt a Will save. If the save succeeds, the opponent can attack normally and is unaffected by that casting of the spell. If the save fails, the opponent can't follow through with the attack, that part of its action is lost, and it can't directly attack the warded creature for the duration of the spell. Those not attempting to attack the subject remain unaffected. This spell does not prevent the warded creature from being attacked or affected by area of effect spells. The subject cannot attack without breaking the spell but may use nonattack spells or otherwise act.

SCARE

School necromancy [fear, mind-affecting]; **Level** bard 2, sorcerer/ wizard 2
Casting Time 1 standard action
Components V, S, M (a bone from an undead creature)
Range medium (100 ft. + 10 ft./level)
Targets one living creature per three levels, no two of which can be more than 30 ft. apart
Duration 1 round/level or 1 round; see text for *cause fear*
Saving Throw Will partial; **Spell Resistance** yes

This spell functions like *cause fear*, except that it causes all targeted creatures of less than 6 HD to become frightened.

SCINTILLATING PATTERN

School illusion (pattern) [mind-affecting]; **Level** sorcerer/wizard 8
Casting Time 1 standard action
Components V, S, M (a crystal prism)
Range close (25 ft. + 5 ft./2 levels)
Effect colorful lights in a 20-ft.-radius spread
Duration concentration + 2 rounds
Saving Throw none; **Spell Resistance** yes

A twisting pattern of coruscating colors weaves through the air, affecting creatures within. The spell affects a total number of HD of creatures equal to your caster level (maximum 20). Creatures with the fewest HD are affected first, and among creatures with equal HD, those who are closest to the spell's point of origin are affected first. HD that are not sufficient to affect a creature are wasted. The spell affects each subject according to its HD.

6 or less: Unconscious for 1d4 rounds, then stunned for 1d4 rounds, and then *confused* for 1d4 rounds. (Treat an unconscious result as stunned for nonliving creatures.)

7 to 12: Stunned for 1d4 rounds, then *confused* for an additional 1d4 rounds.

13 or more: *Confused* for 1d4 rounds.

Sightless creatures are not affected by *scintillating pattern*.

SCORCHING RAY

School evocation [fire]; **Level** sorcerer/wizard 2
Casting Time 1 standard action
Components V, S
Range close (25 ft. + 5 ft./2 levels)
Effect one or more rays
Duration instantaneous
Saving Throw none; **Spell Resistance** yes
You blast your enemies with a searing beam of fire. You may fire one ray, plus one additional ray for every four levels beyond 3rd (to a maximum of three rays at 11th level). Each ray requires a ranged touch attack to hit and deals 4d6 points of fire damage. The rays may be fired at the same or different targets, but all rays must be aimed at targets within 30 feet of each other and fired simultaneously.

SCREEN

School illusion (glamer); **Level** sorcerer/wizard 8
Casting Time 10 minutes
Components V, S
Range close (25 ft. + 5 ft./2 levels)
Area 30-ft. cube/level (S)
Duration 24 hours
Saving Throw none or Will disbelief (if interacted with); see text;
 Spell Resistance no
This spell creates a powerful protection from scrying and observation. When casting the spell, you dictate what will and will not be observed in the spell's area. The illusion created must be stated in general terms. Once the conditions are set, they cannot be changed. Attempts to scry the area automatically detect the image stated by you with no save allowed. Sight and sound are appropriate to the illusion created. Direct observation may allow a save (as per a normal illusion), if there is cause to disbelieve what is seen. Even entering the area does not cancel the illusion or necessarily allow a save, assuming that hidden beings take care to stay out of the way of those affected by the illusion.

SCRYING

School divination (scrying); **Level** bard 3, cleric 5, druid 4, sorcerer/wizard 4
Casting Time 1 hour
Components V, S, M/DF (a pool of water), F (a silver mirror worth 1,000 gp)
Range see text
Effect magical sensor
Duration 1 min./level
Saving Throw Will negates; **Spell Resistance** yes
You can observe a creature at any distance. If the subject succeeds on a Will save, the spell fails. The difficulty of the save depends on how well your knowledge of the subject and what sort of physical connection (if any) you have to that creature. Furthermore, if the subject is on another plane, it gets a +5 bonus on its Will save.

Knowledge	Will Save Modifier
None*	+10
Secondhand (you have heard of the subject)	+5
Firsthand (you have met the subject)	+0
Familiar (you know the subject well)	−5

*You must have some sort of connection (see below) to a creature of which you have no knowledge.

Connection	Will Save Modifier
Likeness or picture	−2
Possession or garment	−4
Body part, lock of hair, bit of nail, etc.	−10

If the save fails, you can see and hear the subject and its surroundings (approximately 10 feet in all directions of the subject). If the subject moves, the sensor follows at a speed of up to 150 feet.

As with all divination (scrying) spells, the sensor has your full visual acuity, including any magical effects. In addition, the following spells have a 5% chance per caster level of operating through the sensor: *detect chaos*, *detect evil*, *detect good*, *detect law*, *detect magic*, and *message*.

If the save succeeds, you can't attempt to scry on that subject again for at least 24 hours.

SCRYING, GREATER

School divination (scrying); **Level** bard 6, cleric 7, druid 7, sorcerer/wizard 7
Casting Time 1 standard action
Components V, S
Duration 1 hour/level
This spell functions like *scrying*, except as noted above. Additionally, all of the following spells function reliably through the sensor: *detect chaos*, *detect evil*, *detect good*, *detect law*, *detect magic*, *message*, *read magic*, and *tongues*.

SCULPT SOUND

School transmutation; **Level** bard 3

Casting Time 1 standard action

Components V, S

Range close (25 ft. + 5 ft./2 levels)

Targets one creature or object/level, no two of which can be more than 30 ft. apart

Duration 1 hour/level (D)

Saving Throw Will negates (object); **Spell Resistance** yes (object)

You can change the sounds that creatures or objects make. You can create sounds where none exist, deaden sounds, or transform sounds into other sounds. All affected creatures or objects must be transmuted in the same way. Once the transmutation is made, you cannot change it. You can change the qualities of sounds but cannot create words with which you are unfamiliar yourself.

A spellcaster whose voice is changed dramatically is unable to cast spells with verbal components.

SEARING LIGHT

School evocation; **Level** cleric 3

Casting Time 1 standard action

Components V, S

Range medium (100 ft. + 10 ft./level)

Effect ray

Duration instantaneous

Saving Throw none; **Spell Resistance** yes

Focusing divine power like a ray of the sun, you project a blast of light from your open palm. You must succeed on a ranged touch attack to strike your target. A creature struck by this ray of light takes 1d8 points of damage per two caster levels (maximum 5d8). An undead creature takes 1d6 points of damage per caster level (maximum 10d6), and an undead creature particularly vulnerable to bright light takes 1d8 points of damage per caster level (maximum 10d8). A construct or inanimate object takes only 1d6 points of damage per two caster levels (maximum 5d6).

SECRET CHEST

School conjuration (summoning); **Level** sorcerer/wizard 5

Casting Time 10 minutes

Components V, S, F (the chest and its replica)

Range see text

Target one chest and up to 1 cu. ft. of goods/caster level

Duration 60 days or until discharged

Saving Throw none; **Spell Resistance** no

You hide a chest on the Ethereal Plane for as long as 60 days and can retrieve it at will. The chest can contain up to 1 cubic foot of material per caster level (regardless of the chest's actual size, which is about 3 feet by 2 feet by 2 feet). If any living creatures are in the chest, there is a 75% chance that the spell simply fails. Once the chest is hidden, you can retrieve it by concentrating (a standard action), and it appears next to you.

The chest must be exceptionally well crafted and expensive, constructed for you by master crafters. The cost of such a chest is never less than 5,000 gp. Once it is constructed, you must make a tiny replica (of the same materials and perfect in every detail) so that the miniature of the chest appears to be a perfect copy. (The replica costs 50 gp.) The chests are nonmagical and can be fitted with locks, wards, and so on, just as any normal chest can be.

To hide the chest, you cast the spell while touching both the chest and the replica. The chest vanishes into the Ethereal Plane. You need the replica to recall the chest. After 60 days, there is a cumulative chance of 5% per day that the chest is irretrievably lost. If the miniature of the chest is lost or destroyed, there is no way, even with a *wish* spell, that the large chest can be summoned back, although an extraplanar expedition might be mounted to find it.

Living things in the chest eat, sleep, and age normally, and they die if they run out of food, air, water, or whatever they need to survive.

SECRET PAGE

School transmutation; **Level** bard 3, sorcerer/wizard 3

Casting Time 10 minutes

Components V, S, M (powdered herring scales and a vial of will-o'-wisp essence)

Range touch

Target page touched, up to 3 sq. ft. in size

Duration permanent

Saving Throw none; **Spell Resistance** no

Secret page alters the contents of a page so that it appears to be something entirely different. The text of a spell can be changed to show another spell of equal or lower level known by the caster. This spell cannot be used to change a spell contained on a scroll, but it can be used to hide a scroll. *Explosive runes* or *sepia snake sigil* can be cast upon the *secret page*.

A *comprehend languages* spell alone cannot reveal a *secret page*'s contents. You are able to reveal the original contents by speaking a special word. You can then peruse the actual page and return it to its *secret page* form at will. You can also remove the spell by double repetition of the special word. A *detect magic* spell reveals dim magic on the page in question but does not reveal its true contents. *True seeing* reveals the presence of the hidden material but does not reveal the contents unless cast in combination with *comprehend languages*. A *secret page* spell can be dispelled, and the hidden writings can be destroyed by means of an *erase* spell.

SECURE SHELTER

School conjuration (creation); **Level** bard 4, sorcerer/wizard 4

Casting Time 10 minutes

Components V, S, M (a chip of stone, sand, a drop of water, and a wood splinter)

Range close (25 ft. + 5 ft./2 levels)

Effect 20-ft.-square structure

Duration 2 hours/level (D)

Saving Throw none; **Spell Resistance** no

You conjure a sturdy cottage or lodge made of material that is common in the area where the spell is cast. The floor is level, clean, and dry. The lodging resembles a normal cottage, with a sturdy door, two shuttered windows, and a small fireplace.

The shelter must be heated as a normal dwelling, and extreme heat adversely affects it and its occupants. The dwelling does, however, provide considerable security otherwise—it is as strong as a normal stone building, regardless of its material composition. The dwelling resists flames and fire as if it were stone. It is impervious to normal missiles (but not the sort cast by siege engines or giants).

The door, shutters, and even chimney are secure against intrusion, the former two being secured with *arcane lock* and the latter by an iron grate at the top and a narrow flue. In addition, these three areas are protected by an *alarm* spell. Finally, an *unseen servant* is conjured to provide service to you for the duration of the shelter.

The *secure shelter* contains crude furnishings—eight bunks, a trestle table, eight stools, and a writing desk.

SEE INVISIBILITY

School divination; **Level** bard 3, sorcerer/wizard 2
Casting Time 1 standard action
Components V, S, M (talc and powdered silver)
Range personal
Target you
Duration 10 min./level (D)
You can see any objects or beings that are invisible within your range of vision, as well as any that are ethereal, as if they were normally visible. Such creatures are visible to you as translucent shapes, allowing you easily to discern the difference between visible, invisible, and ethereal creatures.

The spell does not reveal the method used to obtain invisibility. It does not reveal illusions or enable you to see through opaque objects. It does not reveal creatures who are simply hiding, concealed, or otherwise hard to see.

See invisibility can be made permanent with a *permanency* spell.

SEEMING

School illusion (glamer); **Level** bard 5, sorcerer/wizard 5
Casting Time 1 standard action
Components V, S
Range close (25 ft. + 5 ft./2 levels)
Targets one creature per two levels, no two of which can be more than 30 ft. apart
Duration 12 hours (D)
Saving Throw Will negates or Will disbelief (if interacted with); **Spell Resistance** yes or no; see text
This spell functions like *disguise self*, except that you can change the appearance of other people as well. Affected creatures resume their normal appearances if slain. Unwilling targets can negate the spell's effect on them by making Will saves or with spell resistance.

SENDING

School evocation; **Level** cleric 4, sorcerer/wizard 5
Casting Time 10 minutes
Components V, S, M/DF (fine copper wire)

Range see text
Target one creature
Duration 1 round; see text
Saving Throw none; **Spell Resistance** no
You contact a particular creature with which you are familiar and send a short message of 25 words or less to the subject. The subject recognizes you if it knows you. It can answer in like manner immediately. A creature with an Intelligence score as low as 1 can understand the *sending*, though the subject's ability to react is limited as normal by its Intelligence. Even if the *sending* is received, the subject is not obligated to act upon it in any manner.

If the creature in question is not on the same plane of existence as you are, there is a 5% chance that the *sending* does not arrive. (Local conditions on other planes may worsen this chance considerably.)

SEPIA SNAKE SIGIL

School conjuration (creation) [force]; **Level** bard 3, sorcerer/wizard 3
Casting Time 10 minutes
Components V, S, M (powdered amber worth 500 gp and a snake scale)
Range touch
Target one touched book or written work
Duration permanent or until discharged; until released or 1d4 days + 1 day/level; see text
Saving Throw Reflex negates; **Spell Resistance** no
You cause a small symbol to appear in the text of a written work. The text containing the symbol must be at least 25 words long. When anyone reads the text containing the symbol, the *sepia snake sigil* springs into being, transforming into a large sepia serpent that strikes at the reader, provided there is line of effect between the symbol and the reader.

Simply seeing the enspelled text is not sufficient to trigger the spell; the subject must deliberately read it. The target is entitled to a save to evade the snake's strike. If it succeeds, the *sepia snake* dissipates in a flash of brown light accompanied by a puff of dun-colored smoke and a loud noise. If the target fails its save, it is engulfed in a shimmering amber field of force and immobilized until released, either at your command or when 1d4 days + 1 day per caster level have elapsed.

While trapped in the amber field of force, the subject does not age, breathe, grow hungry, sleep, or regain spells. It is preserved in a state of suspended animation, unaware of its surroundings. It can be damaged by outside forces (and perhaps even killed), since the field provides no protection against physical injury. However, a dying subject does not lose hit points or become stable until the spell ends.

The hidden sigil cannot be detected by normal observation, and *detect magic* reveals only that the entire text is magical.

A *dispel magic* can remove the sigil. An *erase* spell destroys the entire page of text.

Sepia snake sigil can be cast in combination with other spells that hide or garble text, such as *secret page*.

SEQUESTER

School abjuration; **Level** sorcerer/wizard 7

Casting Time 1 standard action

Components V, S, M (a basilisk eyelash and gum arabic)

Range touch

Target one willing creature or object (up to a 2-ft. cube/level) touched

Duration 1 day/level (D)

Saving Throw none or Will negates (object); **Spell Resistance** no or yes (object)

When cast, this spell prevents divination spells from detecting or locating the target and also renders the affected target invisible (as the *invisibility* spell). The spell does not prevent the subject from being discovered through tactile means or through the use of devices. Creatures affected by *sequester* become comatose and are effectively in a state of suspended animation until the spell ends.

Note: The Will save prevents an attended or magical object from being *sequestered*. There is no save to see the *sequestered* creature or object or to detect it with a divination spell.

SHADES

School illusion (shadow); **Level** sorcerer/wizard 9

This spell functions like *shadow conjuration,* except that it mimics conjuration spells of 8th level or lower. The illusory conjurations created deal four-fifths (80%) damage to nonbelievers, and nondamaging effects are 80% likely to work against nonbelievers.

SHADOW CONJURATION

School illusion (shadow); **Level** bard 4, sorcerer/wizard 4

Casting Time 1 standard action

Components V, S

Range see text

Effect see text

Duration see text

Saving Throw Will disbelief (if interacted with); varies; see text; **Spell Resistance** yes; see text

You use material from the Plane of Shadow to shape quasi-real illusions of one or more creatures, objects, or forces. *Shadow conjuration* can mimic any sorcerer or wizard conjuration (summoning) or conjuration (creation) spell of 3rd level or lower.

Shadow conjurations are only one-fifth (20%) as strong as the real things, though creatures who believe the *shadow conjurations* to be real are affected by them at full strength. Any creature that interacts with the spell can make a Will save to recognize its true nature.

Spells that deal damage have normal effects unless the affected creature succeeds on a Will save. Each disbelieving creature takes only one-fifth (20%) damage from the attack. If the disbelieved attack has a special effect other than damage, that effect is only 20% likely to occur. Regardless of the result of the save to disbelieve, an affected creature is also allowed any save that the spell being simulated allows, but the save DC is set according to *shadow conjuration's* level (4th) rather than the spell's normal level. In addition, any effect created by *shadow conjuration* allows spell resistance, even if the spell it is simulating does not. Shadow

objects or substances have normal effects except against those who disbelieve them. Against disbelievers, they are 20% likely to work.

A shadow creature has one-fifth the hit points of a normal creature of its kind (regardless of whether it's recognized as shadowy). It deals normal damage and has all normal abilities and weaknesses. Against a creature that recognizes it as a shadow creature, however, the shadow creature's damage is one-fifth (20%) normal, and all special abilities that do not deal lethal damage are only 20% likely to work. (Roll for each use and each affected character separately.) Furthermore, the shadow creature's AC bonuses are just one-fifth as large.

A creature that succeeds on its save sees the *shadow conjurations* as transparent images superimposed on vague, shadowy forms. Objects automatically succeed on their Will saves against this spell.

SHADOW CONJURATION, GREATER

School illusion (shadow); **Level** sorcerer/wizard 7

This spell functions like *shadow conjuration,* except that it duplicates any sorcerer or wizard conjuration (summoning) or conjuration (creation) spell of 6th level or lower. The illusory conjurations created deal three-fifths (60%) damage to nonbelievers, and nondamaging effects are 60% likely to work against nonbelievers.

SHADOW EVOCATION

School illusion (shadow); **Level** bard 5, sorcerer/wizard 5

Casting Time 1 standard action

Components V, S

Range see text

Effect see text

Duration see text

Saving Throw Will disbelief (if interacted with); **Spell Resistance** yes

You tap energy from the Plane of Shadow to cast a quasi-real, illusory version of a sorcerer or wizard evocation spell of 4th level or lower. Spells that deal damage have normal effects unless an affected creature succeeds on a Will save. Each disbelieving creature takes only one-fifth damage from the attack. If the disbelieved attack has a special effect other than damage, that effect is one-fifth as strong (if applicable) or only 20% likely to occur. If recognized as a *shadow evocation,* a damaging spell deals only one-fifth (20%) damage. Regardless of the result of the save to disbelieve, an affected creature is also allowed any save (or spell resistance) that the spell being simulated allows, but the save DC is set according to *shadow evocation's* level (5th) rather than the spell's normal level.

Nondamaging effects have normal effects except against those who disbelieve them. Against disbelievers, they have no effect.

Objects automatically succeed on their Will saves against this spell.

SHADOW EVOCATION, GREATER

School illusion (shadow); **Level** sorcerer/wizard 8

This spell functions like *shadow evocation,* except that it enables you to create partially real, illusory versions of sorcerer or wizard evocation spells of 7th level or lower. If recognized as a *greater shadow evocation,* a spell only has three-fifths (60%) the normal affect (if applicable) or is only 60% likely to occur.

SHADOW WALK

School illusion (shadow); **Level** bard 5, sorcerer/wizard 6
Casting Time 1 standard action
Components V, S
Range touch
Targets up to one touched creature/level
Duration 1 hour/level (D)
Saving Throw Will negates; **Spell Resistance** yes

To use the *shadow walk* spell, you must be in an area of dim light. You and any creature you touch are then transported along a coiling path of shadowstuff to the edge of the Material Plane where it borders the Plane of Shadow. The effect is largely illusory, but the path is quasi-real. You can take more than one creature along with you (subject to your level limit), but all must be touching each other.

In the region of shadow, you move at a rate of 50 miles per hour, moving normally on the borders of the Plane of Shadow but much more rapidly relative to the Material Plane. Thus, you can use this spell to travel rapidly by stepping onto the Plane of Shadow, moving the desired distance, and then stepping back onto the Material Plane.

Because of the blurring of reality between the Plane of Shadow and the Material Plane, you can't make out details of the terrain or areas you pass over during transit, nor can you predict perfectly where your travel will end. It's impossible to judge distances accurately, making the spell virtually useless for scouting or spying. Furthermore, when the spell effect ends, you are shunted 1d10 × 100 feet in a random horizontal direction from your desired endpoint. If this would place you within a solid object, you are shunted 1d10 × 1,000 feet in the same direction. If this would still place you within a solid object, you (and any creatures with you) are shunted to the nearest empty space available, but the strain of this activity renders each creature fatigued (no save).

Shadow walk can also be used to travel to other planes that border on the Plane of Shadow, but this usage requires the transit of the Plane of Shadow to arrive at a border with another plane of reality. The transit of the Plane of Shadow requires 1d4 hours.

Any creatures touched by you when *shadow walk* is cast also make the transition to the borders of the Plane of Shadow.

They may opt to follow you, wander off through the plane, or stumble back into the Material Plane (50% chance for either of the latter results if they are lost or abandoned by you). Creatures unwilling to accompany you into the Plane of Shadow receive a Will saving throw, negating the effect if successful.

SHAMBLER

School conjuration (creation); **Level** druid 9
Casting Time 1 standard action
Components V, S
Range medium (100 ft. + 10 ft./level)
Effect three or more shambling mounds, no two of which can be more than 30 ft. apart; see text
Duration 7 days or 7 months (D); see text
Saving Throw none; **Spell Resistance** no

The *shambler* spell creates 1d4+2 shambling mounds with the advanced template (see the *Pathfinder RPG Bestiary*). The creatures willingly aid you in combat or battle, perform a specific mission, or serve as bodyguards. The creatures remain with you for 7 days unless you dismiss them. If the shamblers are created only for guard duty, however, the duration of the spell is 7 months. In this case, the shamblers can only be ordered to guard a specific site or location. Shamblers summoned to guard duty cannot move outside the spell's range, which is measured from the point where each first appeared. You can only have one *shambler* spell in effect at one time. If you cast this spell while another casting is still in effect, the previous casting is dispelled. The shamblers have resistance to fire as normal shambling mounds do only if the terrain where they are summoned is rainy, marshy, or damp.

SHAPECHANGE

School transmutation (polymorph); **Level** druid 9, sorcerer/wizard 9
Casting Time 1 standard action
Components V, S, F (jade circlet worth 1,500 gp)
Range personal
Target you
Duration 10 min./level (D)

This spell allows you to take the form of a wide variety of creatures. This spell can function as *alter self, beast shape IV, elemental body IV, form of the dragon III, giant form II,* and *plant shape III* depending on what form you take. You can change form once each round as a free action. The change takes place either immediately before your regular action or immediately after it, but not during the action.

SHATTER

School evocation [sonic]; **Level** bard 2, cleric 2, sorcerer/wizard 2
Casting Time 1 standard action
Components V, S, M/DF (a chip of mica)
Range close (25 ft. + 5 ft./2 levels)
Area or Target 5-ft.-radius spread; or one solid object or one crystalline creature
Duration instantaneous
Saving Throw Will negates (object); Will negates (object) or Fortitude half; see text; **Spell Resistance** yes

Shatter creates a loud, ringing noise that breaks brittle, nonmagical objects; sunders a single solid, nonmagical object; or damages a crystalline creature.

Used as an area attack, *shatter* destroys nonmagical objects of crystal, glass, ceramic, or porcelain. All such unattended objects within a 5-foot radius of the point of origin are smashed into dozens of pieces by the spell. Objects weighing more than 1 pound per your level are not affected, but all other objects of the appropriate composition are shattered.

Alternatively, you can target *shatter* against a single solid nonmagical object, regardless of composition, weighing up to 10 pounds per caster level. Targeted against a crystalline creature (of

any weight), *shatter* deals 1d6 points of sonic damage per caster level (maximum 10d6), with a Fortitude save for half damage.

SHIELD

School abjuration [force]; **Level** sorcerer/wizard 1

Casting Time 1 standard action

Components V, S

Range personal

Target you

Duration 1 min./level (D)

Shield creates an invisible shield of force that hovers in front of you. It negates *magic missile* attacks directed at you. The disk also provides a +4 shield bonus to AC. This bonus applies against incorporeal touch attacks, since it is a force effect. The *shield* has no armor check penalty or arcane spell failure chance.

SHIELD OF FAITH

School abjuration; **Level** cleric 1

Casting Time 1 standard action

Components V, S, M (parchment with a holy text written on it)

Range touch

Target creature touched

Duration 1 min./level

Saving Throw Will negates (harmless); **Spell Resistance** yes (harmless)

This spell creates a shimmering, magical field around the target that averts and deflects attacks. The spell grants the subject a +2 deflection bonus to AC, with an additional +1 to the bonus for every six levels you have (maximum +5 deflection bonus at 18th level).

SHIELD OF LAW

School abjuration [lawful]; **Level** cleric 8

Casting Time 1 standard action

Components V, S, F (a reliquary worth 500 gp)

Range 20 ft.

Targets one creature/level in a 20-ft.-radius burst centered on you

Duration 1 round/level (D)

Saving Throw see text; **Spell Resistance** yes (harmless)

A dim, blue glow surrounds the subjects, protecting them from attacks, granting them resistance to spells cast by chaotic creatures, and *slowing* chaotic creatures when they strike the subjects. This abjuration has four effects.

First, each warded creature gains a +4 deflection bonus to AC and a +4 resistance bonus on saves. Unlike *protection from chaos*, this benefit applies against all attacks, not just against attacks by chaotic creatures.

Second, a warded creature gains spell resistance 25 against chaotic spells and spells cast by chaotic creatures.

Third, the abjuration protects you from possession and mental influence, just as *protection from chaos* does.

Finally, if a chaotic creature succeeds on a melee attack against a warded creature, the attacker is *slowed* (Will save negates, as the *slow* spell, but against *shield of law's* save DC).

SHIELD OTHER

School abjuration; **Level** cleric 2, paladin 2

Casting Time 1 standard action

Components V, S, F (a pair of platinum rings worth 50 gp worn by both you and the target)

Range close (25 ft. + 5 ft./2 levels)

Target one creature

Duration 1 hour/level (D)

Saving Throw Will negates (harmless); **Spell Resistance** yes (harmless)

This spell wards the subject and creates a mystic connection between you and the subject so that some of its wounds are transferred to you. The subject gains a +1 deflection bonus to AC and a +1 resistance bonus on saves. Additionally, the subject takes only half damage from all wounds and attacks (including those dealt by special abilities) that deal hit point damage. The amount of damage not taken by the warded creature is taken by you. Forms of harm that do not involve hit points, such as *charm* effects, temporary ability damage, level draining, and death effects, are not affected. If the subject suffers a reduction of hit points from a lowered Constitution score, the reduction is not split with you because it is not hit point damage. When the spell ends, subsequent damage is no longer divided between the subject and you, but damage already split is not reassigned to the subject.

If you and the subject of the spell move out of range of each other, the spell ends.

SHILLELAGH

School transmutation; **Level** druid 1

Casting Time 1 standard action

Components V, S, DF

Range touch

Target one touched nonmagical oak club or quarterstaff

Duration 1 min./level

Saving Throw Will negates (object); **Spell Resistance** yes (object)

Your own nonmagical club or quarterstaff becomes a weapon with a +1 enhancement bonus on attack and damage rolls. A quarterstaff gains this enhancement for both ends of the weapon. It deals damage as if it were two size categories larger (a Small club or quarterstaff so transmuted deals 1d8 points of damage, a Medium 2d6, and a Large 3d6), +1 for its enhancement bonus. These effects only occur when the weapon is wielded by you. If you do not wield it, the weapon behaves as if unaffected by this spell.

SHRINK ITEM

School transmutation; **Level** sorcerer/wizard 3

Casting Time 1 standard action

Components V, S

Range touch

Target one touched object of up to 2 cu. ft./level

Duration 1 day/level; see text

Saving Throw Will negates (object); **Spell Resistance** yes (object)

You are able to shrink one nonmagical item (if it is within the size limit) to 1/16 of its normal size in each dimension (to about 1/4,000 the original volume and mass). This change effectively reduces the object's size by four categories. Optionally, you can also change its now shrunken composition to a clothlike one. Objects changed by a *shrink item* spell can be returned to normal composition and size merely by tossing them onto any solid surface or by a word of command from the original caster. Even a burning fire and its fuel can be shrunk by this spell. Restoring the shrunken object to its normal size and composition ends the spell.

Shrink item can be made permanent with a *permanency* spell, in which case the affected object can be shrunk and expanded an indefinite number of times, but only by the original caster.

SHOCKING GRASP

School evocation [electricity]; **Level** sorcerer/wizard 1
Casting Time 1 standard action
Components V, S
Range touch
Target creature or object touched
Duration instantaneous
Saving Throw none; **Spell Resistance** yes

Your successful melee touch attack deals 1d6 points of electricity damage per caster level (maximum 5d6). When delivering the jolt, you gain a +3 bonus on attack rolls if the opponent is wearing metal armor (or is carrying a metal weapon or is made of metal).

SHOUT

School evocation [sonic]; **Level** bard 4, sorcerer/wizard 4
Casting Time 1 standard action
Components V
Range 30 ft.
Area cone-shaped burst
Duration instantaneous
Saving Throw Fortitude partial or Reflex negates (object); see text; **Spell Resistance** yes (object)

You emit an ear-splitting yell that deafens and damages creatures in its path. Any creature within the area is deafened for 2d6 rounds and takes 5d6 points of sonic damage. A successful save negates the deafness and reduces the damage by half. Any exposed brittle or crystalline object or crystalline creature takes 1d6 points of sonic damage per caster level (maximum 15d6). An affected creature is allowed a Fortitude save to reduce the damage by half, and a creature holding fragile objects can negate damage to them with a successful Reflex save. A *shout* spell cannot penetrate a *silence* spell.

SHOUT, GREATER

School evocation [sonic]; **Level** bard 6, sorcerer/wizard 8 **Components**: V, S, F (a metal or ivory horn)
Range 60 ft.
Saving Throw Fortitude partial or Reflex negates (object); see text

This spell functions like *shout*, except that the cone deals 10d6 points of sonic damage (or 1d6 points of sonic damage per caster level, maximum 20d6, against exposed brittle or crystalline

objects or crystalline creatures). It also causes creatures to be stunned for 1 round and deafened for 4d6 rounds. A creature in the area of the cone can negate the stunning and halve both the damage and the duration of the deafness with a successful Fortitude save. A creature holding vulnerable objects can attempt a Reflex save to negate the damage to those objects.

SILENCE

School illusion (glamer); **Level** bard 2, cleric 2
Casting Time 1 round
Components V, S
Range long (400 ft. + 40 ft./level)
Area 20-ft.-radius emanation centered on a creature, object, or point in space
Duration 1 round/level (D)
Saving Throw: Will negates; see text or none (object); **Spell Resistance:** yes; see text or no (object)

Upon the casting of this spell, complete silence prevails in the affected area. All sound is stopped: Conversation is impossible, spells with verbal components cannot be cast, and no noise whatsoever issues from, enters, or passes through the area. The spell can be cast on a point in space, but the effect is stationary unless cast on a mobile object. The spell can be centered on a creature, and the effect then radiates from the creature and moves as it moves. An unwilling creature can attempt a Will save to negate the spell and can use spell resistance, if any. Items in a creature's possession or magic items that emit sound receive the benefits of saves and spell resistance, but unattended objects and points in space do not. Creatures in an area of a *silence* spell are immune to sonic or language-based attacks, spells, and effects.

SILENT IMAGE

School illusion (figment); **Level** bard 1, sorcerer/wizard 1
Casting Time 1 standard action
Components V, S, F (a bit of fleece)
Range long (400 ft. + 40 ft./level)
Effect visual figment that cannot extend beyond four 10-ft. cubes + one 10-ft. cube/level (S)
Duration concentration
Saving Throw Will disbelief (if interacted with); **Spell Resistance** no

This spell creates the visual illusion of an object, creature, or force, as visualized by you. The illusion does not create sound, smell, texture, or temperature. You can move the image within the limits of the size of the effect.

SIMULACRUM

School illusion (shadow); **Level** sorcerer/wizard 7
Casting Time 12 hours
Components V, S, M (ice sculpture of the target plus powdered rubies worth 500 gp per HD of the simulacrum)
Range 0 ft.
Effect one duplicate creature
Duration instantaneous

Saving Throw none; **Spell Resistance** no

Simulacrum creates an illusory duplicate of any creature. The duplicate creature is partially real and formed from ice or snow. It appears to be the same as the original, but it has only half of the real creature's levels or HD (and the appropriate hit points, feats, skill ranks, and special abilities for a creature of that level or HD). You can't create a simulacrum of a creature whose HD or levels exceed twice your caster level. You must make a Disguise check when you cast the spell to determine how good the likeness is. A creature familiar with the original might detect the ruse with a successful Perception check (opposed by the caster's Disguise check) or a DC 20 Sense Motive check.

At all times, the simulacrum remains under your absolute command. No special telepathic link exists, so command must be exercised in some other manner. A simulacrum has no ability to become more powerful. It cannot increase its level or abilities. If reduced to 0 hit points or otherwise destroyed, it reverts to snow and melts instantly into nothingness. A complex process requiring at least 24 hours, 100 gp per hit point, and a fully equipped magical laboratory can repair damage to a simulacrum.

SLAY LIVING

School necromancy [death]; **Level** cleric 5

Casting Time 1 standard action

Components V, S

Range touch

Target living creature touched

Duration instantaneous

Saving Throw Fortitude partial; **Spell Resistance** yes

You can attempt to slay any one living creature. When you cast this spell, your hand seethes with eerie dark fire. You must succeed on a melee touch attack to touch the target. The target takes 12d6 points of damage + 1 point per caster level. If the target's Fortitude saving throw succeeds, it instead takes 3d6 points of damage + 1 point per caster level. The subject might die from damage even if it succeeds on its saving throw.

SLEEP

School enchantment (compulsion) [mind-affecting]; **Level** bard 1, sorcerer/wizard 1

Casting Time 1 round

Components V, S, M (fine sand, rose petals, or a live cricket)

Range medium (100 ft. + 10 ft./level)

Area one or more living creatures within a 10-ft.-radius burst

Duration 1 min./level

Saving Throw Will negates; **Spell Resistance** yes

A *sleep* spell causes a magical slumber to come upon 4 HD of creatures. Creatures with the fewest HD are affected first. Among creatures with equal HD, those who are closest to the spell's point of origin are affected first. HD that are not sufficient to affect a creature are wasted. Sleeping creatures are helpless. Slapping or wounding awakens an affected creature, but normal noise does not. Awakening a creature is a standard action (an application of the aid another action). *Sleep* does not target unconscious creatures, constructs, or undead creatures.

SLEET STORM

School conjuration (creation) [cold]; **Level** druid 3, sorcerer/wizard 3

Casting Time 1 standard action

Components V, S, M/DF (dust and water)

Range long (400 ft. + 40 ft./level)

Area cylinder (40-ft. radius, 20 ft. high)

Duration 1 round/level

Saving Throw none; **Spell Resistance** no

Driving sleet blocks all sight (even darkvision) within it and causes the ground in the area to be icy. A creature can walk within or through the area of sleet at half normal speed with a DC 10 Acrobatics check. Failure means it can't move in that round, while failure by 5 or more means it falls (see the Acrobatics skill for details).

The sleet extinguishes torches and small fires.

SLOW

School transmutation; **Level** bard 3, sorcerer/wizard 3

Casting Time 1 standard action

Components V, S, M (a drop of molasses)

Range close (25 ft. + 5 ft./2 levels)

Targets one creature/level, no two of which can be more than 30 ft. apart

Duration 1 round/level

Saving Throw Will negates; **Spell Resistance** yes

An affected creature moves and attacks at a drastically slowed rate. Creatures affected by this spell are staggered and can take only a single move action or standard action each turn, but not both (nor may it take full-round actions). Additionally, it takes a −1 penalty on attack rolls, AC, and Reflex saves. A *slowed* creature moves at half its normal speed (round down to the next 5-foot increment), which affects the creature's jumping distance as normal for decreased speed.

Multiple *slow* effects don't stack. *Slow* counters and dispels *haste*.

SNARE

School transmutation; **Level** druid 3, ranger 2

Casting Time 3 rounds

Components V, S, DF

Range touch

Target touched nonmagical circle of vine, rope, or thong with a 2 ft. diameter + 2 ft./level

Duration Until triggered or broken

Saving Throw none; **Spell Resistance** no

This spell enables you to make a snare that functions as a magic trap. The snare can be made from any supple vine, a thong, or a rope. When you cast *snare* upon it, the cordlike object blends with its surroundings (DC 23 Perception check for a character with the trapfinding ability to locate). One end of the snare is tied in a loop that contracts around one or more of the limbs of any creature stepping inside the circle.

If a strong and supple tree is nearby, the snare can be fastened to it. The spell causes the tree to bend, straightening when the loop is triggered, dealing 1d6 points of damage to the creature trapped and lifting it off the ground by the trapped limb or limbs. If no such tree is available, the cordlike object tightens around the creature, dealing no damage but causing it to be entangled.

The snare is magical. To escape, a trapped creature must make a DC 23 Escape Artist check or a DC 23 Strength check that is a full-round action. The snare has AC 7 and 5 hit points. A successful escape from the snare breaks the loop and ends the spell.

SOFTEN EARTH AND STONE

School transmutation [earth]; **Level** druid 2
Casting Time 1 standard action
Components V, S, DF
Range close (25 ft. + 5 ft./2 levels)
Area 10-ft. square/level; see text
Duration instantaneous
Saving Throw none; **Spell Resistance** no

When this spell is cast, all natural, undressed earth or stone in the spell's area is softened. Wet earth becomes thick mud, dry earth becomes loose sand or dirt, and stone becomes soft clay that is easily molded or chopped. You affect a 10-foot square area to a depth of 1 to 4 feet, depending on the toughness or resilience of the ground at that spot. Magical, enchanted, dressed, or worked stone cannot be affected. Earth or stone creatures are not affected.

A creature in mud must succeed on a Reflex save or be caught for 1d2 rounds and unable to move, attack, or cast spells. A creature that succeeds on its save can move through the mud at half speed, and it can't run or charge. Loose dirt is not as troublesome as mud, but all creatures in the area can move at only half their normal speed and can't run or charge over the surface. Stone softened into clay does not hinder movement, but it does allow characters to cut, shape, or excavate areas they may not have been able to affect before.

While this spell does not affect dressed or worked stone, cavern ceilings or vertical surfaces such as cliff faces can be affected. Usually, this causes a moderate collapse or landslide as the loosened material peels away from the face of the wall or roof and falls (treat as a cave-in with no bury zone, see Chapter 13).

A moderate amount of structural damage can be dealt to a manufactured structure by softening the ground beneath it, causing it to settle. However, most well-built structures will only be damaged by this spell, not destroyed.

SOLID FOG

School conjuration (creation); **Level** sorcerer/wizard 4
Components: V, S, M (powdered peas and an animal hoof)
Duration 1 min./level
Spell Resistance no

This spell functions like *fog cloud*, but in addition to obscuring sight, the *solid fog* is so thick that it impedes movement. Creatures moving through a *solid fog* move at half their normal

speed and take a –2 penalty on all melee attack and melee damage rolls. The vapors prevent effective ranged weapon attacks (except for magic rays and the like). A creature or object that falls into *solid fog* is slowed so that each 10 feet of vapor that it passes through reduces the falling damage by 1d6. A creature cannot take a 5-foot-step while in *solid fog. Solid fog*, and effects that work like *solid fog*, do not stack with each other in terms of slowed movement and attack penalties.

Unlike normal fog, only a severe wind (31+ mph) disperses these vapors, and it does so in 1 round.

Solid fog can be made permanent with a *permanency* spell. A permanent *solid fog* dispersed by wind reforms in 10 minutes.

SONG OF DISCORD

School enchantment (compulsion) [mind-affecting, sonic]; **Level** bard 5
Casting Time 1 standard action
Components V, S
Range medium (100 ft. + 10 ft./level)
Area creatures within a 20-ft.-radius spread
Duration 1 round/level
Saving Throw Will negates; **Spell Resistance** yes

This spell causes those within the area to turn on each other rather than attack their foes. Each affected creature has a 50% chance to attack the nearest target each round. (Roll to determine each creature's behavior every round at the beginning of its turn.) A creature that does not attack its nearest neighbor is free to act normally for that round. Creatures forced by a *song of discord* to attack their fellows employ all methods at their disposal, choosing their deadliest spells and most advantageous combat tactics. They do not, however, harm targets that have fallen unconscious.

SOUL BIND

School necromancy; **Level** cleric 9, sorcerer/wizard 9
Casting Time 1 standard action
Components V, S, F (see text)
Range close (25 ft. + 5 ft./2 levels)
Target corpse
Duration permanent
Saving Throw Will negates; **Spell Resistance** no

You draw the soul from a newly dead body and imprison it in a black sapphire gem. The subject must have been dead no more than 1 round per caster level. The soul, once trapped in the gem, cannot be returned through *clone, raise dead, reincarnation, resurrection, true resurrection,* or even a *miracle* or a *wish*. Only by destroying the gem or dispelling the spell on the gem can one free the soul (which is then still dead).

The focus for this spell is a black sapphire of at least 1,000 gp value for every HD possessed by the creature whose soul is to be bound. If the gem is not valuable enough, it shatters when the binding is attempted. (While creatures have no concept of level or HD as such, the value of the gem needed to trap an individual can be researched.)

SOUND BURST

School evocation [sonic]; **Level** bard 2, cleric 2

Casting Time 1 standard action

Components V, S, F/DF (a musical instrument)

Range close (25 ft. + 5 ft./2 levels)

Area 10-ft.-radius spread

Duration instantaneous

Saving Throw Fortitude partial; **Spell Resistance** yes

You blast an area with a tremendous cacophony. Every creature in the area takes 1d8 points of sonic damage and must succeed on a Fortitude save to avoid being stunned for 1 round. Creatures that cannot hear are not stunned but are still damaged.

SPEAK WITH ANIMALS

School divination; **Level** bard 3, druid 1, ranger 1

Casting Time 1 standard action

Components V, S

Range personal

Target you

Duration 1 min./level

You can ask questions of and receive answers from animals, but the spell doesn't make them any more friendly than normal. Wary and cunning animals are likely to be terse and evasive, while the more stupid ones make inane comments. If an animal is friendly toward you, it may do some favor or service for you.

SPEAK WITH DEAD

School necromancy [language-dependent]; **Level** cleric 3

Casting Time 10 minutes

Components V, S, DF

Range 10 ft.

Target one dead creature

Duration 1 min./level

Saving Throw Will negates; see text; **Spell Resistance** no

You grant the semblance of life to a corpse, allowing it to answer questions. You may ask one question per two caster levels. The corpse's knowledge is limited to what it knew during life, including the languages it spoke. Answers are brief, cryptic, or repetitive, especially if the creature would have opposed you in life.

If the dead creature's alignment was different from yours, the corpse gets a Will save to resist the spell as if it were alive. If successful, the corpse can refuse to answer your questions or attempt to deceive you, using Bluff. The corpse can only speak about what it knew in life. It cannot answer any questions that pertain to events that occurred after its death.

If the corpse has been subject to *speak with dead* within the past week, the new spell fails. You can cast this spell on a corpse that has been deceased for any amount of time, but the body must be mostly intact to be able to respond. A damaged corpse may be able to give partial answers or partially correct answers, but it must at least have a mouth in order to speak at all. This spell does not affect a corpse that has been turned into an undead creature.

SPEAK WITH PLANTS

School divination; **Level** bard 4, druid 3, ranger 2

Casting Time 1 standard action

Components V, S

Range personal

Target you

Duration 1 min./level

You can communicate with normal plants and plant creatures, and can ask questions of and receive answers from them. A normal plant's sense of its surroundings is limited, so it won't be able to give (or recognize) detailed descriptions of creatures or answer questions about events outside its immediate vicinity. The spell doesn't make plant creatures any more friendly or cooperative than normal. Furthermore, wary and cunning plant creatures are likely to be terse and evasive, while the more stupid ones may make inane comments. If a plant creature is friendly, it may do some favor or service for you.

SPECTRAL HAND

School necromancy; **Level** sorcerer/wizard 2

Casting Time 1 standard action

Components V, S

Range medium (100 ft. + 10 ft./level)

Effect one spectral hand

Duration 1 min./level (D)

Saving Throw none; **Spell Resistance** no

A ghostly hand shaped from your life force materializes and moves as you desire, allowing you to deliver low-level, touch range spells at a distance. On casting the spell, you lose 1d4 hit points that return when the spell ends (even if it is dispelled), but not if the hand is destroyed. (The hit points can be healed as normal.) For as long as the spell lasts, any touch range spell of 4th level or lower that you cast can be delivered by the *spectral hand*. The spell gives you a +2 bonus on your melee touch attack roll, and attacking with the hand counts normally as an attack. The hand always strikes from your direction. The hand cannot flank targets like a creature can. After it delivers a spell, or if it goes beyond the spell range or goes out of your sight, the hand returns to you and hovers.

The hand is incorporeal and thus cannot be harmed by normal weapons. It has improved evasion (half damage on a failed Reflex save and no damage on a successful save), your save bonuses, and an AC of 22 (+8 size, +4 natural armor). Your Intelligence modifier applies to the hand's AC as if it were the hand's Dexterity modifier. The hand has 1 to 4 hit points, the same number that you lost in creating it.

SPELL IMMUNITY

School abjuration; **Level** cleric 4

Casting Time 1 standard action

Components V, S, DF

Range touch

Target creature touched

Duration 10 min./level

Saving Throw Will negates (harmless); **Spell Resistance** yes (harmless)

The warded creature is immune to the effects of one specified spell for every four levels you have. The spells must be of 4th level or lower. The warded creature effectively has unbeatable spell resistance regarding the specified spell or spells. Naturally, that immunity doesn't protect a creature from spells for which spell resistance doesn't apply. *Spell immunity* protects against spells, spell-like effects of magic items, and innate spell-like abilities of creatures. It does not protect against supernatural or extraordinary abilities, such as breath weapons or gaze attacks.

Only a particular spell can be protected against, not a certain domain or school of spells or a group of spells that are similar in effect. A creature can have only one *spell immunity* or *greater spell immunity* spell in effect on it at a time.

SPELL IMMUNITY, GREATER

School abjuration; **Level** cleric 8
This spell functions like *spell immunity*, except the immunity applies to spells of 8th level or lower. A creature can have only one *spell immunity* or *greater spell immunity* spell in effect on it at a time.

SPELL RESISTANCE

School abjuration; **Level** cleric 5
Casting Time 1 standard action
Components V, S, DF
Range touch
Target creature touched
Duration 1 min./level
Saving Throw Will negates (harmless); **Spell Resistance** yes (harmless)
The target gains spell resistance equal to 12 + your caster level.

SPELLSTAFF

School transmutation; **Level** druid 6
Casting Time 10 minutes
Components V, S, F (the staff that stores the spell)
Range touch
Target wooden quarterstaff touched
Duration permanent until discharged (D)
Saving Throw Will negates (object); **Spell Resistance** yes (object)
You store one spell that you can normally cast in a wooden quarterstaff. Only one such spell can be stored in a staff at a given time, and you cannot have more than one *spellstaff* at any given time. You can cast a spell stored within a staff just as though it were among those you had prepared, but it does not count against your normal allotment for a given day. You use up any applicable material components required to cast the spell when you store it in the *spellstaff*.

SPELL TURNING

School abjuration; **Level** sorcerer/wizard 7
Casting Time 1 standard action
Components V, S, M/DF (a small silver mirror)
Range personal
Target you

Duration until expended or 10 min./level
Spells and spell-like effects targeted on you are turned back upon the original caster. The abjuration turns only spells that have you as a target. Effect and area spells are not affected. *Spell turning* also fails to stop touch range spells. From seven to ten (1d4+6) spell levels are affected by the turning. The exact number is rolled secretly.

When you are targeted by a spell of higher level than the amount of spell turning you have left, that spell is partially turned. Subtract the amount of spell turning left from the spell level of the incoming spell, then divide the result by the spell level of the incoming spell to see what fraction of the effect gets through. For damaging spells, you and the caster each take a fraction of the damage. For nondamaging spells, each of you has a proportional chance to be the one who is affected. If you and a spellcasting attacker are both warded by *spell turning* effects in operation, a resonating field is created. Roll randomly to determine the result.

d%	Effect
01–70	Spell drains away without effect.
71–80	Spell affects both of you equally at full effect.
81–97	Both turning effects are rendered nonfunctional for 1d4 minutes.
98–100	Both of you go through a rift into another plane.

SPIDER CLIMB

School transmutation; **Level** druid 2, sorcerer/wizard 2
Casting Time 1 standard action
Components V, S, M (a live spider)
Range touch
Target creature touched
Duration 10 min./level
Saving Throw Will negates (harmless); **Spell Resistance** yes (harmless)
The subject can climb and travel on vertical surfaces or even traverse ceilings as well as a spider does. The affected creature must have its hands free to climb in this manner. The subject gains a climb speed of 20 feet and a +8 racial bonus on Climb skill checks; furthermore, it need not make Climb checks to traverse a vertical or horizontal surface (even upside down). A *spider climbing* creature retains its Dexterity bonus to Armor Class (if any) while climbing, and opponents get no special bonus to their attacks against it. It cannot, however, use the run action while climbing.

SPIKE GROWTH

School transmutation; **Level** druid 3, ranger 2
Casting Time 1 standard action
Components V, S, DF
Range medium (100 ft. + 10 ft./level)
Area one 20-ft. square/level
Duration 1 hour/level (D)
Saving Throw Reflex partial; **Spell Resistance** yes
Any ground-covering vegetation in the spell's area becomes very

hard and sharply pointed without changing its appearance.

In areas of bare earth, roots and rootlets act in the same way. Typically, *spike growth* can be cast in any outdoor setting except open water, ice, heavy snow, sandy desert, or bare stone. Any creature moving on foot into or through the spell's area takes 1d4 points of piercing damage for each 5 feet of movement through the spiked area.

Any creature that takes damage from this spell must also succeed on a Reflex save or suffer injuries to its feet and legs that slow its land speed by half. This speed penalty lasts for 24 hours or until the injured creature receives a *cure* spell (which also restores lost hit points). Another character can remove the penalty by taking 10 minutes to dress the injuries and succeeding on a Heal check against the spell's save DC.

Magic traps are hard to detect. A character with trapfinding can use the Perception skill to find a *spike growth*. The DC is 25 + spell level, or DC 28 for *spike growth* (or DC 27 for *spike growth* cast by a ranger). *Spike growth* can't be disabled with the Disable Device skill.

SPIKE STONES

School transmutation [earth]; **Level** druid 4
Casting Time 1 standard action
Components V, S, DF
Range medium (100 ft. + 10 ft./level)
Area one 20-ft. square/level
Duration 1 hour/level (D)
Saving Throw Reflex partial; **Spell Resistance** yes

Rocky ground, stone floors, and similar surfaces shape themselves into long, sharp points that blend into the background.

Spike stones impede progress through an area and deal damage. Any creature moving on foot into or through the spell's area moves at half speed. In addition, each creature moving through the area takes 1d8 points of piercing damage for each 5 feet of movement through the spiked area.

Any creature that takes damage from this spell must also succeed on a Reflex save to avoid injuries to its feet and legs. A failed save causes the creature's speed to be reduced to half normal for 24 hours or until the injured creature receives a *cure* spell (which also restores lost hit points). Another character can remove the penalty by taking 10 minutes to dress the injuries and succeeding on a Heal check against the spell's save DC.

Magic traps such as *spike stones* are hard to detect. A character with trapfinding can use the Perception skill to find *spike stones*. The DC is 25 + spell level, or DC 29 for *spike stones*. *Spike stones* is a magic trap that can't be disabled with the Disable Device skill.

SPIRITUAL WEAPON

School evocation [force]; **Level** cleric 2
Casting Time 1 standard action
Components V, S, DF
Range medium (100 ft. + 10 ft./level)
Effect magic weapon of force
Duration 1 round/level (D)

Saving Throw none; **Spell Resistance** yes

A weapon made of force appears and attacks foes at a distance, as you direct it, dealing 1d8 force damage per hit, + 1 point per three caster levels (maximum +5 at 15th level). The weapon takes the shape of a weapon favored by your deity or a weapon with some spiritual significance or symbolism to you (see below) and has the same threat range and critical multipliers as a real weapon of its form. It strikes the opponent you designate, starting with one attack in the round the spell is cast and continuing each round thereafter on your turn. It uses your base attack bonus (possibly allowing it multiple attacks per round in subsequent rounds) plus your Wisdom modifier as its attack bonus. It strikes as a spell, not as a weapon, so for example, it can damage creatures that have damage reduction. As a force effect, it can strike incorporeal creatures without the reduction in damage associated with incorporeality. The weapon always strikes from your direction. It does not get a flanking bonus or help a combatant get one. Your feats or combat actions do not affect the weapon. If the weapon goes beyond the spell range, if it goes out of your sight, or if you are not directing it, the weapon returns to you and hovers.

Each round after the first, you can use a move action to redirect the weapon to a new target. If you do not, the weapon continues to attack the previous round's target. On any round that the weapon switches targets, it gets one attack. Subsequent rounds of attacking that target allow the weapon to make multiple attacks if your base attack bonus would allow it to. Even if the *spiritual weapon* is a ranged weapon, use the spell's range, not the weapon's normal range increment, and switching targets still is a move action.

A *spiritual weapon* cannot be attacked or harmed by physical attacks, but *dispel magic*, *disintegrate*, a *sphere of annihilation*, or a *rod of cancellation* affects it. A *spiritual weapon's* AC against touch attacks is 12 (10 + size bonus for Tiny object).

If an attacked creature has spell resistance, you make a caster level check (1d20 + caster level) against that spell resistance the first time the *spiritual weapon* strikes it. If the weapon is successfully resisted, the spell is dispelled. If not, the weapon has its normal full effect on that creature for the duration of the spell.

The weapon that you get is often a force replica of your deity's own personal weapon. A cleric without a deity gets a weapon based on his alignment. A neutral cleric without a deity can create a *spiritual weapon* of any alignment, provided he is acting at least generally in accord with that alignment at the time. The weapons associated with each alignment are as follows: chaos (battleaxe), evil (light flail), good (warhammer), law (longsword).

STABILIZE

School conjuration (healing); **Level** cleric 0, druid 0
Casting Time 1 standard action
Components V, S
Range close (25 ft. + 5 ft./2 levels)
Target one living creature
Duration instantaneous

Saving Throw: Will negates (harmless); **Spell Resistance:** yes (harmless)

Upon casting this spell, you target a living creature that has −1 or fewer hit points. That creature is automatically stabilized and does not lose any further hit points. If the creature later takes damage, it continues dying normally.

STATUE

School transmutation; **Level** sorcerer/wizard 7

Casting Time 1 round

Components V, S, M (lime, sand, and a drop of water stirred by an iron spike)

Range touch

Target creature touched

Duration 1 hour/level (D)

Saving Throw Will negates (harmless); **Spell Resistance** yes (harmless)

A *statue* spell turns the subject to solid stone, along with any garments and equipment worn or carried. In statue form, the subject gains hardness 8. The subject retains its own hit points. The subject can see, hear, and smell normally, but it does not need to eat or breathe. Feeling is limited to those sensations that can affect the granite-hard substance of the individual's body. Chipping is equal to a mere scratch, but breaking off one of the statue's arms constitutes serious damage. The subject of a *statue* spell can return to its normal state, act, and then return instantly to the statue state (a free action) if it so desires as long as the spell duration is in effect.

STATUS

School divination; **Level** cleric 2

Casting Time 1 standard action

Components V, S

Range touch

Targets one living creature touched per three levels

Duration 1 hour/level

Saving Throw Will negates (harmless); **Spell Resistance** yes (harmless)

When you need to keep track of comrades who may get separated, *status* allows you to mentally monitor their relative positions and general condition. You are aware of direction and distance to the creatures and any conditions affecting them: unharmed, wounded, disabled, staggered, unconscious, dying, nauseated, panicked, stunned, poisoned, diseased, confused, or the like. Once the spell has been cast upon the subjects, the distance between them and the caster does not affect the spell as long as they are on the same plane of existence. If a subject leaves the plane, or if it dies, the spell ceases to function for it.

STINKING CLOUD

School conjuration (creation); **Level** sorcerer/wizard 3

Casting Time 1 standard action

Components V, S, M (a rotten egg or cabbage leaves)

Range medium (100 ft. + 10 ft./level)

Effect cloud spreads in 20-ft. radius, 20 ft. high

Duration 1 round/level

Saving Throw Fortitude negates; see text; **Spell Resistance** no

Stinking cloud creates a bank of fog like that created by *fog cloud*, except that the vapors are nauseating. Living creatures in the cloud become nauseated. This condition lasts as long as the creature is in the cloud and for 1d4+1 rounds after it leaves. (Roll separately for each nauseated character.) Any creature that succeeds on its save but remains in the cloud must continue to save each round on your turn. This is a poison effect.

Stinking cloud can be made permanent with a *permanency* spell. A permanent *stinking cloud* dispersed by wind reforms in 10 minutes.

STONE SHAPE

School transmutation [earth]; **Level** cleric 3, druid 3, sorcerer/wizard 4

Casting Time 1 standard action

Components V, S, M/DF (soft clay)

Range touch

Target stone or stone object touched, up to 10 cu. ft. + 1 cu. ft./level

Duration instantaneous

Saving Throw none; **Spell Resistance** no

You can form an existing piece of stone into any shape that suits your purpose. While it's possible to make crude coffers, doors, and so forth with *stone shape*, fine detail isn't possible. There is a 30% chance that any shape including moving parts simply doesn't work.

STONESKIN

School abjuration; **Level** druid 5, sorcerer/wizard 4

Casting Time 1 standard action

Components V, S, M (granite and diamond dust worth 250 gp)

Range touch

Target creature touched

Duration 10 min./level or until discharged

Saving Throw Will negates (harmless); **Spell Resistance** yes (harmless)

The warded creature gains resistance to blows, cuts, stabs, and slashes. The subject gains DR 10/adamantine. It ignores the first 10 points of damage each time it takes damage from a weapon, though an adamantine weapon bypasses the reduction. Once the spell has prevented a total of 10 points of damage per caster level (maximum 150 points), it is discharged.

STONE TELL

School divination; **Level** druid 6

Casting Time 10 minutes

Components V, S, DF

Range personal

Target you

Duration 1 min./level

You gain the ability to speak with stones, which relate to you who or what has touched them as well as revealing what is covered or concealed behind or under them. The stones relate complete descriptions if asked. A stone's perspective, perception, and knowledge may prevent the stone from providing the details you are looking for. You can speak with natural or worked stone.

STONE TO FLESH

School transmutation; **Level** sorcerer/wizard 6

Casting Time 1 standard action

Components V, S, M (a drop of blood mixed with earth)

Range medium (100 ft. + 10 ft./level)

Target one petrified creature or a cylinder of stone from 1 ft. to 3 ft. in diameter and up to 10 ft. long

Duration instantaneous

Saving Throw Fortitude negates (object); see text; **Spell Resistance** yes

This spell restores a petrified creature to its normal state, restoring life and goods. The creature must make a DC 15 Fortitude save to survive the process. Any petrified creature, regardless of size, can be restored. The spell also can convert a mass of stone into a fleshy substance. Such flesh is inert and lacking a vital life force unless a life force or magical energy is available. For example, this spell would turn an animated stone statue into an animated flesh statue, but an ordinary statue would become a mass of inert flesh in the shape of the statue. You can affect an object that fits within a cylinder from 1 foot to 3 feet in diameter and up to 10 feet long or a cylinder of up to those dimensions in a larger mass of stone.

STORM OF VENGEANCE

School conjuration (summoning); **Level** cleric 9, druid 9

Casting Time 1 round

Components V, S

Range long (400 ft. + 40 ft./level)

Effect 360-ft.-radius storm cloud

Duration concentration (maximum 10 rounds) (D)

Saving Throw see text; **Spell Resistance** yes

You create a huge black storm cloud in the air. Each creature under the cloud must succeed on a Fortitude save or be deafened for 1d4 × 10 minutes. Each round you continue to concentrate, the spell generates additional effects as noted below. Each effect occurs on your turn.

2nd Round: Acid rains down in the area, dealing 1d6 points of acid damage (no save).

3rd Round: You call six bolts of lightning down from the cloud. You decide where the bolts strike. No two bolts may be directed at the same target. Each bolt deals 10d6 points of electricity damage. A creature struck can attempt a Reflex save for half damage.

4th Round: Hailstones rain down in the area, dealing 5d6 points of bludgeoning damage (no save).

5th through 10th Rounds: Violent rain and wind gusts reduce visibility. The rain obscures all sight, including darkvision, beyond 5 feet. A creature 5 feet away has concealment (attacks have a 20% miss chance). Creatures farther away have total concealment (50% miss chance, and the attacker cannot use sight to locate the target). Speed is reduced by three-quarters.

Ranged attacks within the area of the storm are impossible. Spells cast within the area are disrupted unless the caster succeeds on a Concentration check against a DC equal to the *storm of vengeance*'s save DC + the level of the spell the caster is trying to cast.

SUGGESTION

School enchantment (compulsion) [language-dependent, mind-affecting]; **Level** bard 2, sorcerer/wizard 3

Casting Time 1 standard action

Components V, M (a snake's tongue and a honeycomb)

Range close (25 ft. + 5 ft./2 levels)

Target one living creature

Duration 1 hour/level or until completed

Saving Throw Will negates; **Spell Resistance** yes

You influence the actions of the target creature by suggesting a course of activity (limited to a sentence or two). The *suggestion* must be worded in such a manner as to make the activity sound reasonable. Asking the creature to do some obviously harmful act automatically negates the effect of the spell.

The suggested course of activity can continue for the entire duration. If the suggested activity can be completed in a shorter time, the spell ends when the subject finishes what it was asked to do. You can instead specify conditions that will trigger a special activity during the duration. If the condition is not met before the spell duration expires, the activity is not performed.

A very reasonable *suggestion* causes the save to be made with a penalty (such as –1 or –2).

SUGGESTION, MASS

School enchantment (compulsion) [language-dependent, mind-affecting]; **Level** bard 5, sorcerer/wizard 6

Range medium (100 ft. + 10 ft./level)

Targets one creature/level, no two of which can be more than 30 ft. apart

This spell functions like *suggestion*, except that it can affect more creatures. The same *suggestion* applies to all these creatures.

SUMMON INSTRUMENT

School conjuration (summoning); **Level** bard 0

Casting Time 1 round

Components V, S

Range 0 ft.

Effect one summoned handheld musical instrument

Duration 1 min./level (D)

Saving Throw none; **Spell Resistance** no

This spell summons one handheld musical instrument of your choice. This instrument appears in your hands or at your feet (your choice). The instrument is typical for its type. Only one instrument appears per casting, and it will play only for you. You can't summon an instrument too large to be held in two hands. The summoned instrument disappears at the end of this spell.

SUMMON MONSTER I

School conjuration (summoning) [see text]; **Level** bard 1, cleric 1, sorcerer/wizard 1

Casting Time 1 round

Components V, S, F/DF (a tiny bag and a small candle)

Range close (25 ft. + 5 ft./2 levels)

TABLE 10-1: SUMMON MONSTER

1st Level	Subtype
Dire rat*	—
Dog*	—
Dolphin*	—
Eagle*	—
Fire beetle*	—
Frog, poison*	—
Pony (horse)*	—
Viper (snake)*	—

2nd Level	Subtype
Ant, giant (worker)*	—
Elemental (Small)	Elemental
Giant centipede*	—
Giant frog*	—
Giant spider*	—
Goblin dog*	—
Horse*	—
Hyena*	—
Lemure (devil)	Evil, Lawful
Octopus*	—
Squid*	—
Wolf*	—

3rd Level	Subtype
Ant, giant (soldier)*	—
Ape*	—
Aurochs (herd animal)*	—
Boar*	—
Cheetah*	—
Constrictor snake*	—
Crocodile*	—
Dire bat*	—
Dretch (demon)	Chaotic, Evil
Electric eel*	—
Lantern archon	Good, Lawful
Leopard (cat)*	—
Monitor lizard*	—
Shark*	—
Wolverine*	—

4th Level	Subtype
Ant, giant (drone)*	—
Bison (herd animal)*	—
Deinonychus (dinosaur)*	—
Dire ape*	—
Dire boar*	—
Dire wolf*	—
Elemental (Medium)	Elemental
Giant scorpion*	—
Giant wasp*	—

	Subtype
Grizzly bear*	—
Hell hound	Evil, Lawful
Hound archon	Good, Lawful
Lion*	—
Mephit (any)	Elemental
Pteranodon (dinosaur)*	—
Rhinoceros*	—

5th Level	Subtype
Ankylosaurus (dinosaur)*	—
Babau (demon)	Chaotic, Evil
Bearded devil	Evil, Lawful
Bralani azata	Chaotic, Good
Dire lion*	—
Elemental (Large)	Elemental
Giant moray eel*	—
Kyton	Evil, Lawful
Orca (dolphin)*	—
Salamander	Evil
Woolly rhinoceros*	—
Xill	Evil, Lawful

6th Level	Subtype
Dire bear*	—
Dire tiger*	—
Elasmosaurus (dinosaur)*	—
Elemental (Huge)	Elemental
Elephant*	—
Erinyes (devil)	Evil, Lawful
Giant octopus*	—
Invisible stalker	Air
Lillend azata	Chaotic, Good
Shadow demon	Chaotic, Evil
Succubus (demon)	Chaotic, Evil
Triceratops (dinosaur)*	—

7th Level	Subtype
Bebilith	Chaotic, Evil
Bone devil	Evil, Lawful
Brachiosaurus (dinosaur)*	—
Dire crocodile*	—
Dire shark*	—
Elemental (greater)	Elemental
Giant squid*	—
Mastodon (elephant)*	—
Roc*	—
Tyrannosaurus (dinosaur)*	—
Vrock (demon)	Chaotic, Evil

TABLE 10-1: SUMMON MONSTER

8th Level	Subtype
Barbed devil	Evil, Lawful
Elemental (elder)	Elemental
Hezrou (demon)	Chaotic, Evil

9th Level	Subtype
Astral Deva (angel)	Good
Ghaele azata	Chaotic, Good
Glabrezu (demon)	Chaotic, Evil
Ice devil	Evil, Lawful
Nalfeshnee (demon)	Chaotic, Evil
Trumpet archon	Good, Lawful

* This creature is summoned with the celestial template if you are good, or the fiendish template if you are evil; you may choose either if you are neutral.

Effect one summoned creature
Duration 1 round/level (D)
Saving Throw none; **Spell Resistance** no

This spell summons an extraplanar creature (typically an outsider, elemental, or magical beast native to another plane). It appears where you designate and acts immediately, on your turn. It attacks your opponents to the best of its ability. If you can communicate with the creature, you can direct it not to attack, to attack particular enemies, or to perform other actions. The spell conjures one of the creatures from the 1st Level list on Table 10–1. You choose which kind of creature to summon, and you can choose a different one each time you cast the spell.

A summoned monster cannot summon or otherwise conjure another creature, nor can it use any teleportation or planar travel abilities. Creatures cannot be summoned into an environment that cannot support them. Creatures summoned using this spell cannot use spells or spell-like abilities that duplicate spells with expensive material components (such as *wish*).

When you use a summoning spell to summon a creature with an alignment or elemental subtype, it is a spell of that type. Creatures on Table 10–1 marked with an "*" are summoned with the celestial template, if you are good, and the fiendish template, if you are evil. If you are neutral, you may choose which template to apply to the creature. Creatures marked with an "*" always have an alignment that matches yours, regardless of their usual alignment. Summoning these creatures makes the summoning spell's type match your alignment.

SUMMON MONSTER II

School conjuration (summoning); **Level** bard 2, cleric 2, sorcerer/wizard 2

This spell functions like *summon monster I*, except that you can summon one creature from the 2nd-level list or 1d3 creatures of the same kind from the 1st-level list.

SUMMON MONSTER III

School conjuration (summoning); **Level** bard 3, cleric 3, sorcerer/wizard 3

This spell functions like *summon monster I*, except that you can summon one creature from the 3rd-level list, 1d3 creatures of the same kind from the 2nd-level list, or 1d4+1 creatures of the same kind from the 1st-level list.

SUMMON MONSTER IV

School conjuration (summoning); **Level** bard 4, cleric 4, sorcerer/wizard 4

This spell functions like *summon monster I*, except that you can summon one creature from the 4th-level list, 1d3 creatures of the same kind from the 3rd-level list, or 1d4+1 creatures of the same kind from a lower-level list.

SUMMON MONSTER V

School conjuration (summoning); **Level** bard 5, cleric 5, sorcerer/wizard 5

This spell functions like *summon monster I*, except that you can summon one creature from the 5th-level list, 1d3 creatures of the same kind from the 4th-level list, or 1d4+1 creatures of the same kind from a lower-level list.

SUMMON MONSTER VI

School conjuration (summoning); **Level** bard 6, cleric 6, sorcerer/wizard 6

This spell functions like *summon monster I*, except you can summon one creature from the 6th-level list, 1d3 creatures of the same kind from the 5th-level list, or 1d4+1 creatures of the same kind from a lower-level list.

SUMMON MONSTER VII

School conjuration (summoning); **Level** cleric 7, sorcerer/wizard 7

This spell functions like *summon monster I*, except that you can summon one creature from the 7th-level list, 1d3 creatures of the same kind from the 6th-level list, or 1d4+1 creatures of the same kind from a lower-level list.

SUMMON MONSTER VIII

School conjuration (summoning); **Level** cleric 8, sorcerer/wizard 8

This spell functions like *summon monster I*, except that you can summon one creature from the 8th-level list, 1d3 creatures of the same kind from the 7th-level list, or 1d4+1 creatures of the same kind from a lower-level list.

SUMMON MONSTER IX

School conjuration (summoning); **Level** cleric 9, sorcerer/wizard 9

This spell functions like *summon monster I*, except that you can summon one creature from the 9th-level list, 1d3 creatures of the same kind from the 8th-level list, or 1d4+1 creatures of the same kind from a lower-level list.

TABLE 10-2: SUMMON NATURE'S ALLY

1st Level	Subtype
Dire rat	—
Dolphin	—
Dog	—
Eagle	—
Frog, poison	—
Giant centipede	—
Fire beetle	—
Mite (gremlin)	—
Pony (horse)	—
Stirge	—
Viper (snake)	—

2nd Level	Subtype
Ant, giant (worker)	—
Elemental (Small)	Elemental
Giant frog	—
Giant spider	—
Goblin dog	—
Horse	—
Hyena	—
Octopus	—
Squid	—
Wolf	—

3rd Level	Subtype
Ant, giant (soldier)	—
Ape	—
Aurochs (herd animal)	—
Boar	—
Cheetah	—
Constrictor snake	—
Crocodile	—
Dire bat	—
Electric eel	—
Giant crab	—
Leopard (cat)	—
Monitor lizard	—
Shark	—
Wolverine	—

4th Level	Subtype
Ant, giant (drone)	—
Bison (herd animal)	—
Deinonychus (dinosaur)	—
Dire ape	—
Dire boar	—
Dire wolf	—
Elemental (Medium)	Elemental
Giant scorpion	—
Giant stag beetle	—
Giant wasp	—
Griffon	—
Grizzly bear	—
Lion	—
Mephit (any)	Elemental
Owlbear	—
Pteranodon (dinosaur)	—
Rhinoceros	—
Satyr	—
Tiger	—

5th Level	Subtype
Ankylosaurus (dinosaur)	—
Cyclops	—
Dire lion	—
Elemental (Large)	Elemental
Ettin	—
Giant moray eel	—
Girallon	—
Manticore	—
Orca (dolphin)	—
Woolly rhinoceros	—

6th Level	Subtype
Bulette	—
Dire bear	—
Dire tiger	—
Elasmosaurus (dinosaur)	—
Elemental (Huge)	Elemental
Elephant	—
Giant octopus	—
Hill giant	—
Stegosaurus (dinosaur)	—
Stone giant	Earth
Triceratops (dinosaur)	—

7th Level	Subtype
Brachiosaurus (dinosaur)	—
Dire crocodile	—
Dire shark	—
Elemental (greater)	Elemental
Fire giant	Fire
Frost giant	Cold
Giant squid	—
Mastodon (elephant)	—
Roc	—
Tyrannosaurus (dinosaur)	—

8th Level	Subtype
Cloud giant	Air
Elemental (elder)	Elemental
Purple worm	—

9th Level	Subtype
Pixie (w/*irresistible dance* and sleep arrows)	—
Storm giant	—

SUMMON NATURE'S ALLY I

School conjuration (summoning); **Level** druid 1, ranger 1

Casting Time 1 round

Components V, S, DF

Range close (25 ft. + 5 ft./2 levels)

Effect one summoned creature

Duration 1 round/level (D)

Saving Throw none; **Spell Resistance** no

This spell summons to your side a natural creature (typically an animal, fey, magical beast, outsider with the elemental subtype, or a giant). The summoned ally appears where you designate and acts immediately, on your turn. It attacks your opponents to the best of its ability. If you can communicate with the creature, you can direct it not to attack, to attack particular enemies, or to perform other actions as you command.

A summoned monster cannot summon or otherwise conjure another creature, nor can it use any teleportation or planar travel abilities. Creatures cannot be summoned into an environment that cannot support them. Creatures summoned using this spell cannot use spells or spell-like abilities that duplicate spells that have expensive material components (such as *wish*).

The spell conjures one of the creatures from the 1st Level list on Table 10–2. You choose which kind of creature to summon, and you can change that choice each time you cast the spell. All the creatures on the table are neutral unless otherwise noted.

When you use a summoning spell to summon a creature with an alignment or elemental subtype, it is a spell of that type. All creatures summoned with this spell without alignment subtypes have an alignment that matches yours, regardless of their usual alignment. Summoning these creatures makes the summoning spell's type match your alignment.

SUMMON NATURE'S ALLY II

School conjuration (summoning); **Level** druid 2, ranger 2

This spell functions as *summon nature's ally I*, except that you summon one 2nd-level creature or 1d3 1st-level creatures of the same kind.

SUMMON NATURE'S ALLY III

School conjuration (summoning) [see text]; **Level** druid 3, ranger 3

This spell functions like *summon nature's ally I*, except that you can summon one 3rd-level creature, 1d3 2nd-level creatures of the same kind, or 1d4+1 1st-level creatures of the same kind.

SUMMON NATURE'S ALLY IV

School conjuration (summoning) [see text]; **Level** druid 4, ranger 4

This spell functions like *summon nature's ally I*, except that you can summon one 4th-level creature, 1d3 3rd-level creatures of the same kind, or 1d4+1 lower-level creatures of the same kind.

SUMMON NATURE'S ALLY V

School conjuration (summoning) [see text]; **Level** druid 5

This spell functions like *summon nature's ally I*, except that you can summon one 5th-level creature, 1d3 4th-level creatures of the same kind, or 1d4+1 lower-level creatures of the same kind.

SUMMON NATURE'S ALLY VI

School conjuration (summoning) [see text]; **Level** druid 6

This spell functions like *summon nature's ally I*, except that you can summon one 6th-level creature, 1d3 5th-level creatures of the same kind, or 1d4+1 lower-level creatures of the same kind.

SUMMON NATURE'S ALLY VII

School conjuration (summoning) [see text]; **Level** druid 7

This spell functions like *summon nature's ally I*, except that you can summon one 7th-level creature, 1d3 6th-level creatures of the same kind, or 1d4+1 lower-level creatures of the same kind.

SUMMON NATURE'S ALLY VIII

School conjuration (summoning) [see text]; **Level** druid 8

This spell functions like *summon nature's ally I*, except that you can summon one 8th-level creature, 1d3 7th-level creatures of the same kind, or 1d4+1 lower-level creatures of the same kind.

SUMMON NATURE'S ALLY IX

School conjuration (summoning) [see text]; **Level** druid 9

This spell functions like *summon nature's ally I*, except that you can summon one 9th-level creature, 1d3 8th-level creatures of the same kind, or 1d4+1 lower-level creatures of the same kind.

SUMMON SWARM

School conjuration (summoning); **Level** bard 2, druid 2, sorcerer/wizard 2

Casting Time 1 round

Components V, S, M/DF (a square of red cloth)

Range close (25 ft. + 5 ft./2 levels)

Effect one swarm of bats, rats, or spiders

Duration concentration + 2 rounds

Saving Throw none; **Spell Resistance** no

You summon a swarm of bats, rats, or spiders (your choice), which attacks all other creatures within its area. (You may summon the swarm so that it shares the area of other creatures.) If no living creatures are within its area, the swarm attacks or pursues the nearest creature as best it can. The caster has no control over its target or direction of travel.

SUNBEAM

School evocation [light]; **Level** druid 7

Casting Time 1 standard action

Components V, S, DF

Range 60 ft.

Area line from your hand

Duration 1 round/level or until all beams are exhausted

Saving Throw Reflex negates and Reflex half; see text; **Spell Resistance** yes

For the duration of this spell, you can use a standard action to evoke a dazzling beam of intense light each round. You can call forth one beam per three caster levels (maximum six beams at 18th level). The spell ends when its duration runs out or your allotment of beams is exhausted.

Each creature in the beam is blinded and takes 4d6 points of damage. Any creatures to which sunlight is harmful or unnatural take double damage. A successful Reflex save negates the blindness and reduces the damage by half.

An undead creature caught within the beam takes 1d6 points of damage per caster level (maximum 20d6), or half damage if a Reflex save is successful. In addition, the beam results in the destruction of any undead creature specifically harmed by bright light if it fails its save.

The ultraviolet light generated by the spell deals damage to fungi, mold, oozes, and slimes just as if they were undead creatures.

SUNBURST

School evocation [light]; **Level** druid 8, sorcerer/wizard 8
Casting Time 1 standard action
Components V, S, M/DF (sunstone and fire source)
Range long (400 ft. + 40 ft./level)
Area 80-ft.-radius burst
Duration instantaneous
Saving Throw Reflex partial; see text; **Spell Resistance** yes

Sunburst causes a globe of searing radiance to explode silently from a point you select. All creatures in the globe are blinded and take 6d6 points of damage. A creature to which sunlight is harmful or unnatural takes double damage. A successful Reflex save negates the blindness and reduces the damage by half.

An undead creature caught within the globe takes 1d6 points of damage per caster level (maximum 25d6), or half damage if a Reflex save is successful. In addition, the burst results in the destruction of any undead creature specifically harmed by bright light if it fails its save.

The ultraviolet light generated by the spell deals damage to fungi, mold, oozes, and slimes just as if they were undead creatures.

Sunburst dispels any darkness spells of lower than 9th level within its area.

SYMBOL OF DEATH

School necromancy [death]; **Level** cleric 8, sorcerer/wizard 8
Casting Time 10 minutes
Components V, S, M (mercury and phosphorus, plus powdered diamond and opal worth 5,000 gp each)
Range 0 ft.; see text
Effect one symbol
Duration see text
Saving Throw Fortitude negates; **Spell Resistance** yes

This spell allows you to scribe a potent rune of power upon a surface. When triggered, a *symbol of death* kills one or more creatures within 60 feet of the symbol (treat as a burst) whose combined total current hit points do not exceed 150. The *symbol of death* affects the closest creatures first, skipping creatures with too many hit points to affect. Once triggered, the *symbol* becomes active and glows, lasting for 10 minutes per caster level or until it has affected 150 hit points' worth of creatures, whichever comes first. A creature that enters the area while the *symbol of death* is active is subject to its effect, whether or not that creature was in the area when it was triggered. A creature need save against the *symbol* only once as long as it remains within the area, though if it leaves the area and returns while the *symbol* is still active, it must save again.

Until it is triggered, the *symbol of death* is inactive (though visible and legible at a distance of 60 feet). To be effective, a *symbol of death* must always be placed in plain sight and in a prominent location. Covering or hiding the rune renders the *symbol of death* ineffective, unless a creature removes the covering, in which case the *symbol of death* works normally.

As a default, a *symbol of death* is triggered whenever a creature does one or more of the following, as you select: looks at the rune; reads the rune; touches the rune; passes over the rune; or passes through a portal bearing the rune. Regardless of the trigger method or methods chosen, a creature more than 60 feet from a *symbol of death* can't trigger it (even if it meets one or more of the triggering conditions, such as reading the rune). Once the spell is cast, a *symbol of death*'s triggering conditions cannot be changed.

In this case, "reading" the rune means any attempt to study it, identify it, or fathom its meaning. Throwing a cover over a *symbol of death* to render it inoperative triggers it if the symbol reacts to touch. You can't use a *symbol of death* offensively; for instance, a touch-triggered *symbol of death* remains untriggered if an item bearing the *symbol of death* is used to touch a creature. Likewise, a *symbol of death* cannot be placed on a weapon and set to activate when the weapon strikes a foe.

You can also set special triggering limitations of your own. These can be as simple or elaborate as you desire. Special conditions for triggering a *symbol of death* can be based on a creature's name, identity, or alignment, but otherwise must be based on observable actions or qualities. Intangibles such as level, class, HD, and hit points don't qualify.

When scribing a *symbol of death*, you can specify a password or phrase that prevents a creature using it from triggering the symbol's effect. Anyone using the password remains immune to that particular rune's effects so long as the creature remains within 60 feet of the rune. If the creature leaves the radius and returns later, it must use the password again.

You also can attune any number of creatures to the *symbol of death*, but doing this can extend the casting time. Attuning one or two creatures takes negligible time, and attuning a small group (as many as 10 creatures) extends the casting time to 1 hour. Attuning a large group (as many as 25 creatures) takes 24 hours. Attuning larger groups takes an additional 24 hours per 25 creatures. Any creature attuned to a *symbol of death* cannot trigger it and is immune to its effects, even if within its radius when it is triggered. You are automatically considered attuned to your own *symbols of death*, and thus always ignore the effects and cannot inadvertently trigger them.

Read magic allows you to identify a *symbol* with a Spellcraft check (DC 10 + the *symbol*'s spell level). Of course, if the *symbol* is set to be

triggered by reading it, this will trigger the symbol.

A *symbol of death* can be removed by a successful *dispel magic* targeted solely on the rune. An *erase* spell has no effect on a *symbol of death*. Destruction of the surface where a *symbol of death* is inscribed destroys the *symbol* but also triggers it.

Symbol of death can be made permanent with a *permanency* spell. A permanent *symbol of death* that is disabled or has affected its maximum number of hit points becomes inactive for 10 minutes, but then can be triggered again as normal.

Note: Magic traps such as *symbol of death* are hard to detect and disable. While any character can use Perception to find a symbol, only a character with the trapfinding class feature can use Disable Device to disarm it. The DC in each case is 25 + spell level, or 33 for *symbol of death*.

SYMBOL OF FEAR

School necromancy [fear, mind-affecting]; **Level** cleric 6, sorcerer/wizard 6

Components V, S, M (mercury and phosphorus, plus powdered diamond and opal worth a total of 1,000 gp)

Saving Throw Will negates

This spell functions like *symbol of death*, except that all creatures within 60 feet of the *symbol of fear* instead become panicked for 1 round per caster level.

Note: Magic traps such as *symbol of fear* are hard to detect and disable. While any character can use Perception to find a symbol, only a character with the trapfinding class feature can use Disable Device to disarm it. The DC in each case is 25 + spell level, or 31 for *symbol of fear*.

SYMBOL OF INSANITY

School enchantment (compulsion) [mind-affecting]; **Level** cleric 8, sorcerer/wizard 8

Components V, S, M (mercury and phosphorus, plus powdered diamond and opal worth a total of 5,000 gp)

Saving Throw Will negates

This spell functions like *symbol of death*, except that all creatures within the radius of the *symbol of insanity* instead become permanently insane (as the *insanity* spell).

Unlike *symbol of death*, symbol of insanity has no hit point limit; once triggered, a *symbol of insanity* simply remains active for 10 minutes per caster level.

Note: Magic traps such as *symbol of insanity* are hard to detect and disable. While any character can use Perception to find a symbol, only a character with the trapfinding class feature can use Disable Device to disarm it. The DC in each case is 25 + spell level, or 33 for *symbol of insanity*.

SYMBOL OF PAIN

School necromancy [evil]; **Level** cleric 5, sorcerer/wizard 5

Components V, S, M (mercury and phosphorus, plus powdered diamond and opal worth a total of 1,000 gp)

This spell functions like *symbol of death*, except that each creature within the radius of a *symbol of pain* instead suffers wracking pains that impose a −4 penalty on attack rolls, skill checks, and ability checks. These effects last for 1 hour after the creature moves

farther than 60 feet from the symbol.

Unlike *symbol of death*, *symbol of pain* has no hit point limit; once triggered, a *symbol of pain* simply remains active for 10 minutes per caster level.

Note: Magic traps such as *symbol of pain* are hard to detect and disable. While any character can use Perception to find a symbol, only a character with the trapfinding class feature can use Disable Device to disarm it. The DC in each case is 25 + spell level, or 30 for *symbol of pain*.

SYMBOL OF PERSUASION

School enchantment (charm) [mind-affecting]; **Level** cleric 6, sorcerer/wizard 6

Components V, S, M (mercury and phosphorus, plus powdered diamond and opal worth a total of 5,000 gp)

Saving Throw Will negates

This spell functions like *symbol of death*, except that all creatures within the radius of a *symbol of persuasion* instead become charmed by the caster (as the *charm monster* spell) for 1 hour per caster level.

Unlike *symbol of death*, *symbol of persuasion* has no hit point limit; once triggered, a *symbol of persuasion* simply remains active for 10 minutes per caster level.

Note: Magic traps such as *symbol of persuasion* are hard to detect and disable. While any character can use Perception to find a symbol, only a character with the trapfinding class feature can use Disable Device to disarm it. The DC in each case is 25 + spell level, or 31 for *symbol of persuasion*.

SYMBOL OF SLEEP

School enchantment (compulsion) [mind-affecting]; **Level** cleric 5, sorcerer/wizard 5

Components V, S, M (mercury and phosphorus, plus powdered diamond and opal worth a total of 1,000 gp)

Saving Throw Will negates

This spell functions like *symbol of death*, except that all creatures of 10 HD or less within 60 feet of the *symbol of sleep* instead fall into a catatonic slumber for 3d6 × 10 minutes. Unlike with the *sleep* spell, sleeping creatures cannot be awakened by nonmagical means before this time expires.

Unlike *symbol of death*, *symbol of sleep* has no hit point limit; once triggered, a *symbol of sleep* simply remains active for 10 minutes per caster level.

Note: Magic traps such as *symbol of sleep* are hard to detect and disable. While any character can use Perception to find a symbol, only a character with the trapfinding class feature can use Disable Device to disarm it. The DC in each case is 25 + spell level, or 30 for *symbol of sleep*.

SYMBOL OF STUNNING

School enchantment (compulsion) [mind-affecting]; **Level** cleric 7, sorcerer/wizard 7

Components V, S, M (mercury and phosphorus, plus powdered diamond and opal worth a total of 5,000 gp)

Saving Throw Will negates

This spell functions like *symbol of death*, except that all creatures within 60 feet of a *symbol of stunning* instead become stunned for 1d6 rounds.

Note: Magic traps such as *symbol of stunning* are hard to detect and disable. While any character can use Perception to find a symbol, only a character with the trapfinding class feature can use Disable Device to disarm it. The DC in each case is 25 + spell level, or 32 for *symbol of stunning*.

SYMBOL OF WEAKNESS

School necromancy; **Level** cleric 7, sorcerer/wizard 7
Components V, S, M (mercury and phosphorus, plus powdered diamond and opal worth a total of 5,000 gp)
This spell functions like *symbol of death*, except that every creature within 60 feet of a *symbol of weakness* instead suffers crippling weakness that deals 3d6 points of Strength damage.

Unlike *symbol of death*, *symbol of weakness* has no hit point limit; once triggered, a *symbol of weakness* simply remains active for 10 minutes per caster level. A creature can only be affected by this symbol once.

Note: Magic traps such as *symbol of weakness* are hard to detect and disable. While any character can use Perception to find a symbol, only a character with the trapfinding class feature can use Disable Device to disarm it. The DC in each case is 25 + spell level, or 32 for *symbol of weakness*.

SYMPATHETIC VIBRATION

School evocation [sonic]; **Level** bard 6
Casting Time 10 minutes
Components V, S, F (a tuning fork)
Range touch
Target one freestanding structure
Duration up to 1 round/level
Saving Throw none; see text; **Spell Resistance** yes
By attuning yourself to a freestanding structure, you can create a damaging vibration within it. Once it begins, the vibration deals 2d10 points of damage per round to the target structure, bypassing hardness. You can choose at the time of casting to limit the duration of the spell; otherwise it lasts for 1 round per level. If the spell is cast upon a target that is not freestanding, the surrounding stone dissipates the effect and no damage occurs.

Sympathetic vibration cannot affect creatures (including constructs). Since a structure is an unattended object, it gets no saving throw to resist the effect.

SYMPATHY

School enchantment (compulsion) [mind-affecting]; **Level** druid 9, sorcerer/wizard 8
Casting Time 1 hour
Components V, S, M (a drop of honey and crushed pearls worth 1,500 gp)
Range close (25 ft. + 5 ft./2 levels)
Target one location (up to a 10-ft. cube/level) or one object
Duration 2 hours/level (D)

Saving Throw Will negates; see text; **Spell Resistance** yes
You cause an object or location to emanate magical vibrations that attract either a specific kind of intelligent creature or creatures of a particular alignment, as defined by you. The particular kind of creature to be affected must be named specifically. A creature subtype is not specific enough. Likewise, the specific alignment must be named.

Creatures of the specified kind or alignment feel elated and pleased to be in the area or desire to touch or possess the object. The compulsion to stay in the area or touch the object is overpowering. If the save is successful, the creature is released from the enchantment, but a subsequent save must be made 1d6 × 10 minutes later. If this save fails, the affected creature attempts to return to the area or object.

Sympathy counters and dispels *antipathy*.

TELEKINESIS

School transmutation; **Level** sorcerer/wizard 5
Casting Time 1 standard action
Components V, S
Range long (400 ft. + 40 ft./level)
Target or Targets see text
Duration concentration (up to 1 round/level) or instantaneous; see text
Saving Throw Will negates (object) or none; see text; **Spell Resistance** yes (object); see text
You move objects or creatures by concentrating on them. Depending on the version selected, the spell can provide a gentle, sustained force, perform a variety of combat maneuvers, or exert a single short, violent thrust.

Sustained Force: A sustained force moves an object weighing no more than 25 pounds per caster level (maximum 375 pounds at 15th level) up to 20 feet per round. A creature can negate the effect on an object it possesses with a successful Will save or with spell resistance.

This version of the spell can last 1 round per caster level, but it ends if you cease concentration. The weight can be moved vertically, horizontally, or in both directions. An object cannot be moved beyond your range. The spell ends if the object is forced beyond the range. If you cease concentration for any reason, the object falls or stops.

An object can be telekinetically manipulated as if with one hand. For example, a lever or rope can be pulled, a key can be turned, an object rotated, and so on, if the force required is within the weight limitation. You might even be able to untie simple knots, though delicate activities such as these require DC 15 Intelligence checks.

Combat Maneuver: Alternatively, once per round, you can use *telekinesis* to perform a bull rush, disarm, grapple (including pin), or trip. Resolve these attempts as normal, except that they don't provoke attacks of opportunity, you use your caster level in place of your Combat Maneuver Bonus, and you add your Intelligence modifier (if a wizard) or Charisma modifier (if a sorcerer) in place of your Strength or Dexterity modifier. No save is allowed against these attempts, but spell resistance applies normally. This version of the spell can last 1 round per caster level, but it ends if you cease concentration.

Violent Thrust: Alternatively, the spell energy can be spent in a single round. You can hurl one object or creature per caster level (maximum 15) that are within range and all within 10 feet of each other toward any target within 10 feet per level of all the objects. You can hurl up to a total weight of 25 pounds per caster level (maximum 375 pounds at 15th level).

You must succeed on attack rolls (one per creature or object thrown) to hit the target with the items, using your base attack bonus + your Intelligence modifier (if a wizard) or Charisma modifier (if a sorcerer). Weapons cause standard damage (with no Strength bonus; note that arrows or bolts deal damage as daggers of their size when used in this manner). Other objects cause damage ranging from 1 point per 25 pounds (for less dangerous objects) to 1d6 points of damage per 25 pounds (for hard, dense objects). Objects and creatures that miss their target land in a square adjacent to the target.

Creatures who fall within the weight capacity of the spell can be hurled, but they are allowed Will saves (and spell resistance) to negate the effect, as are those whose held possessions are targeted by the spell.

If a telekinesed creature is hurled against a solid surface, it takes damage as if it had fallen 10 feet (1d6 points).

TELEKINETIC SPHERE

School evocation [force]; **Level** sorcerer/wizard 8
Casting Time 1 standard action
Components V, S, M (a crystal sphere and a pair of small magnets)
Range close (25 ft. + 5 ft./2 levels)
Effect 1-ft.-diameter/level sphere, centered around creatures or objects
Duration 1 min./level (D)
Saving Throw Reflex negates (object); **Spell Resistance** yes (object)

This spell functions like *resilient sphere,* but the creatures or objects caught inside the globe created by the spell are made nearly weightless. Anything contained within a *telekinetic sphere* weighs only one-sixteenth of its normal weight. You can telekinetically lift anything in the sphere that normally weighs 5,000 pounds or less. The telekinetic control extends from you out to medium range (100 feet + 10 feet per caster level) after the sphere has succeeded in encapsulating its contents.

You can move the sphere, along with the objects and creatures it contains that weigh a total of 5,000 pounds or less, by concentrating on the sphere. You can begin moving a sphere in the round after casting the spell. If you concentrate on doing so (a standard action), you can move the sphere as much as 30 feet in a round. If you cease concentrating, the sphere does not move in that round (if on a level surface) or descends at its falling rate (if aloft) until it reaches a level surface. You can resume concentrating on your next turn or any later turn during the spell's duration.

The sphere falls at a rate of only 60 feet per round, which is not fast enough to cause damage to the contents of the sphere.

You can move the sphere telekinetically even if you are in it.

TELEPATHIC BOND

School divination; **Level** sorcerer/wizard 5
Casting Time 1 standard action
Components V, S, M (two eggshells from two different creatures)
Range close (25 ft. + 5 ft./2 levels)
Targets you plus one willing creature per three levels, no two of which can be more than 30 ft. apart
Duration 10 min./level (D)
Saving Throw none; **Spell Resistance** no

You forge a telepathic bond among yourself and a number of willing creatures, each of which must have an Intelligence score of 3 or higher. Each creature included in the link is linked to all the others. The creatures can communicate telepathically through the bond regardless of language. No special power or influence is established as a result of the bond. Once the bond is formed, it works over any distance (although not from one plane to another).

If desired, you may leave yourself out of the telepathic bond forged. This decision must be made at the time of casting.

Telepathic bond can be made permanent with a *permanency* spell, though it only bonds two creatures per casting of *permanency*.

TELEPORT

School conjuration (teleportation); **Level** sorcerer/wizard 5
Casting Time 1 standard action
Components V
Range personal and touch
Target you and touched objects or other touched willing creatures
Duration instantaneous
Saving Throw none and Will negates (object); **Spell Resistance** no and yes (object)

This spell instantly transports you to a designated destination, which may be as distant as 100 miles per caster level. Interplanar travel is not possible. You can bring along objects as long as their weight doesn't exceed your maximum load. You may also bring one additional willing Medium or smaller creature (carrying gear or objects up to its maximum load) or its equivalent per three caster levels. A Large creature counts as two Medium creatures, a Huge creature counts as four Medium creatures, and so forth. All creatures to be transported must be in contact with one another, and at least one of those creatures must be in contact with you. As with all spells where the range is personal and the target is you, you need not make a saving throw, nor is spell resistance applicable to you. Only objects held or in use (attended) by another person receive saving throws and spell resistance.

You must have some clear idea of the location and layout of the destination. The clearer your mental image, the more likely the teleportation works. Areas of strong physical or magical energy may make teleportation more hazardous or even impossible.

To see how well the teleportation works, roll d% and consult the table at the end of this spell. Refer to the following information for definitions of the terms on the table.

Familiarity: "Very familiar" is a place where you have been very often and where you feel at home. "Studied carefully" is a place you know well, either because you can currently physically see it or you've been there often. "Seen casually" is a place that you have seen more than once but with which you are not very familiar. "Viewed once" is a place that you have seen once, possibly using magic such as *scrying*.

"False destination" is a place that does not truly exist or if you are teleporting to an otherwise familiar location that no longer exists as such or has been so completely altered as to no longer be familiar to you. When traveling to a false destination, roll 1d20+80 to obtain results on the table, rather than rolling d%, since there is no real destination for you to hope to arrive at or even be off target from.

On Target: You appear where you want to be.

Off Target: You appear safely a random distance away from the destination in a random direction. Distance off target is d% of the distance that was to be traveled. The direction off target is determined randomly.

Similar Area: You wind up in an area that's visually or thematically similar to the target area. Generally, you appear in the closest similar place within range. If no such area exists within the spell's range, the spell simply fails instead.

Mishap: You and anyone else teleporting with you have gotten "scrambled." You each take 1d10 points of damage, and you reroll on the chart to see where you wind up. For these rerolls, roll 1d20+80. Each time "Mishap" comes up, the characters take more damage and must reroll.

Familiarity	On Target	Off Target	Similar Area	Mishap
Very familiar	01–97	98–99	100	—
Studied carefully	01–94	95–97	98–99	100
Seen casually	01–88	89–94	95–98	99–100
Viewed once	01–76	77–88	89–96	97–100
False destination	—	—	81–92	93–100

TELEPORT, GREATER

School conjuration (teleportation); **Level** sorcerer/wizard 7
This spell functions like *teleport,* except that there is no range limit and there is no chance you arrive off target. In addition, you need not have seen the destination, but in that case you must have at least a reliable description of the place to which you are teleporting. If you attempt to teleport with insufficient information (or with misleading information), you disappear and simply reappear in your original location. Interplanar travel is not possible.

TELEPORT OBJECT

School conjuration (teleportation); **Level** sorcerer/wizard 7
Range touch
Target one touched object of up to 50 lbs./level and 3 cu. ft./level
Saving Throw Will negates (object); **Spell Resistance** yes (object)
This spell functions like *teleport,* except that it teleports an object, not you. Creatures and magical forces cannot be teleported.

If desired, the target object can be sent to a distant location on the Ethereal Plane. In this case, the point from which the object was teleported remains faintly magical until the item is retrieved. A successful targeted *dispel magic* spell cast on that point brings the vanished item back from the Ethereal Plane.

TELEPORTATION CIRCLE

School conjuration (teleportation); **Level** sorcerer/wizard 9
Casting Time 10 minutes
Components V, M (amber dust to cover circle worth 1,000 gp)
Range 0 ft.
Effect 5-ft.-radius circle that teleports those who activate it
Duration 10 min./level (D)
Saving Throw none; **Spell Resistance** yes
You create a circle on the floor or other horizontal surface that teleports, as *greater teleport,* any creature who stands on it to a designated spot. Once you designate the destination for the circle, you can't change it. The spell fails if you attempt to set the circle to teleport creatures into a solid object, to a place with which you are not familiar and have no clear description, or to another plane.

The circle itself is subtle and nearly impossible to notice. If you intend to keep creatures from activating it accidentally, you need to mark the circle in some way.

Teleportation circle can be made permanent with a *permanency* spell. A permanent *teleportation circle* that is disabled becomes inactive for 10 minutes, then can be triggered again as normal.

Magic traps such as *teleportation circle* are hard to detect and disable. A character with the trapfinding class feature can use Disable Device to disarm magic traps. The DC in each case is 25 + spell level, or 34 in the case of *teleportation circle.*

TEMPORAL STASIS

School transmutation; **Level** sorcerer/wizard 8
Casting Time 1 standard action
Components V, S, M (powdered diamond, emerald, ruby, and sapphire dust worth 5,000 gp)
Range touch
Target creature touched
Duration permanent
Saving Throw Fortitude negates; **Spell Resistance** yes
You must succeed on a melee touch attack. You place the subject into a state of suspended animation. For the creature, time ceases to flow, and its condition becomes fixed. The creature does not grow older. Its body functions virtually cease, and no force or effect can harm it. This state persists until the magic is removed (such as by a successful *dispel magic* spell or a *freedom* spell).

TIME STOP

School transmutation; **Level** sorcerer/wizard 9
Casting Time 1 standard action
Components V
Range personal
Target you
Duration 1d4+1 rounds (apparent time); see text

This spell seems to make time cease to flow for everyone but you. In fact, you speed up so greatly that all other creatures seem frozen, though they are actually still moving at their normal speeds. You are free to act for 1d4+1 rounds of apparent time. Normal and magical fire, cold, gas, and the like can still harm you. While the *time stop* is in effect, other creatures are invulnerable to your attacks and spells; you cannot target such creatures with any attack or spell. A spell that affects an area and has a duration longer than the remaining duration of the *time stop* have their normal effects on other creatures once the *time stop* ends. Most spellcasters use the additional time to improve their defenses, summon allies, or flee from combat.

You cannot move or harm items held, carried, or worn by a creature stuck in normal time, but you can affect any item that is not in another creature's possession.

You are undetectable while *time stop* lasts. You cannot enter an area protected by an *antimagic field* while under the effect of *time stop*.

TINY HUT

School evocation [force]; **Level** bard 3, sorcerer/wizard 3
Casting Time 1 standard action
Components V, S, M (a small crystal bead)
Range 20 ft.
Effect 20-ft.-radius sphere centered on your location
Duration 2 hours/level (D)
Saving Throw none; **Spell Resistance** no

You create an unmoving, opaque sphere of force of any color you desire around yourself. Half the sphere projects above the ground, and the lower hemisphere passes through the ground. As many as nine other Medium creatures can fit into the field with you; they can freely pass into and out of the hut without harming it. However, if you remove yourself from the hut, the spell ends.

The temperature inside the hut is 70° F if the exterior temperature is between 0° and 100° F. An exterior temperature below 0° or above 100° lowers or raises the interior temperature on a 1-degree-for-1 basis. The hut also provides protection against the elements, such as rain, dust, and sandstorms. The hut withstands any wind of less than hurricane force, but a hurricane (75+ mph wind speed) or greater force destroys it.

The interior of the hut is a hemisphere. You can illuminate it dimly upon command or extinguish the light as desired. Although the force field is opaque from the outside, it is transparent from within. Missiles, weapons, and most spell effects can pass through the hut without affecting it, although the occupants cannot be seen from outside the hut (they have total concealment).

TONGUES

School divination; **Level** bard 2, cleric 4, sorcerer/wizard 3
Casting Time 1 standard action
Components V, M/DF (a clay model of a ziggurat)
Range touch
Target creature touched
Duration 10 min./level
Saving Throw Will negates (harmless); **Spell Resistance** no

This spell grants the creature touched the ability to speak and understand the language of any intelligent creature, whether it is a racial tongue or a regional dialect. The subject can speak only one language at a time, although it may be able to understand several languages. *Tongues* does not enable the subject to speak with creatures who don't speak. The subject can make itself understood as far as its voice carries. This spell does not predispose any creature addressed toward the subject in any way.

Tongues can be made permanent with a *permanency* spell.

TOUCH OF FATIGUE

School necromancy; **Level** sorcerer/wizard 0
Casting Time 1 standard action
Components V, S, M (a drop of sweat)
Range touch
Target creature touched
Duration 1 round/level
Saving Throw Fortitude negates; **Spell Resistance** yes

You channel negative energy through your touch, fatiguing the target. You must succeed on a touch attack to strike a target. The subject is immediately fatigued for the spell's duration.

This spell has no effect on a creature that is already fatigued. Unlike with normal fatigue, the effect ends as soon as the spell's duration expires.

TOUCH OF IDIOCY

School enchantment (compulsion) [mind-affecting]; **Level** sorcerer/wizard 2
Casting Time 1 standard action
Components V, S
Range touch
Target living creature touched
Duration 10 min./level
Saving Throw no; **Spell Resistance** yes

With a touch, you reduce the target's mental faculties. Your successful melee touch attack applies a 1d6 penalty to the target's Intelligence, Wisdom, and Charisma scores. This penalty can't reduce any of these scores below 1.

This spell's effect may make it impossible for the target to cast some or all of its spells, if the requisite ability score drops below the minimum required to cast spells of that level.

TRANSFORMATION

School transmutation; **Level** sorcerer/wizard 6
Casting Time 1 standard action
Components V, S, M (a *potion of bull's strength*, which you drink and whose effects are subsumed by the spell effects)
Range personal
Target you
Duration 1 round/level

You become a fighting machine—stronger, tougher, faster, and more skilled in combat. Your mindset changes so that you relish combat and you can't cast spells, even from magic items.

You gain a +4 enhancement bonus to Strength, Dexterity, and Constitution, a +4 natural armor bonus to AC, a +5 competence bonus on Fortitude saves, and proficiency with all simple and martial weapons. Your base attack bonus equals your character level (which may give you multiple attacks).

You lose your spellcasting ability, including your ability to use spell activation or spell completion magic items, just as if the spells were no longer on your class list.

TRANSMUTE METAL TO WOOD

School transmutation; **Level** druid 7
Casting Time 1 standard action
Components V, S, DF
Range long (400 ft. + 40 ft./level)
Area all metal objects within a 40-ft.-radius burst
Duration instantaneous
Saving Throw none; **Spell Resistance** yes (object; see text)

This spell enables you to change all metal objects within its area to wood. Weapons, armor, and other metal objects carried by creatures are affected as well. A magic object made of metal effectively has spell resistance equal to 20 + its caster level against this spell. Artifacts cannot be transmuted. Weapons converted from metal to wood take a –2 penalty on attack and damage rolls. The armor bonus of any armor converted from metal to wood is reduced by 2. Weapons changed by this spell splinter and break on any natural attack roll of 1 or 2, and armor changed by this spell loses an additional point of armor bonus every time it is struck with a natural attack roll of 19 or 20.

Only *limited wish, miracle, wish,* or similar magic can restore a transmuted object to its metallic state.

TRANSMUTE MUD TO ROCK

School transmutation [earth]; **Level** druid 5, sorcerer/wizard 5
Casting Time 1 standard action
Components V, S, M/DF (sand, lime, and water)
Range medium (100 ft. + 10 ft./level)
Area up to two 10-ft. cubes/level (S)
Duration permanent
Saving Throw see text; **Spell Resistance** no

This spell permanently transforms normal mud or quicksand of any depth into soft stone (sandstone or a similar mineral).

Any creature in the mud is allowed a Reflex save to escape before the area is hardened to stone.

Transmute mud to rock counters and dispels *transmute rock to mud.*

TRANSMUTE ROCK TO MUD

School transmutation [earth]; **Level** druid 5, sorcerer/wizard 5
Casting Time 1 standard action
Components V, S, M/DF (clay and water)
Range medium (100 ft. + 10 ft./level)
Area up to two 10-ft. cubes/level (S)
Duration permanent; see text
Saving Throw see text; **Spell Resistance** no

This spell turns natural, uncut, or unworked rock of any sort into an equal volume of mud. Magical stone is not affected by the spell. The depth of the mud created cannot exceed 10 feet. A creature unable to levitate, fly, or otherwise free itself from the mud sinks until hip- or chest-deep, reducing its speed to 5 feet and causing a –2 penalty on attack rolls and AC. Brush or similar material thrown atop the mud can support creatures able to climb on top of it. Creatures large enough to walk on the bottom can wade through the area at a speed of 5 feet.

If *transmute rock to mud* is cast upon the ceiling of a cavern or tunnel, the mud falls to the floor and spreads out in a pool at a depth of 5 feet. The falling mud and the ensuing cave-in deal 8d6 points of bludgeoning damage to anyone caught directly beneath the targeted area, or half damage to those who succeed on Reflex saves.

Castles and large stone buildings are generally immune to the effect of the spell, since *transmute rock to mud* can't affect worked stone and doesn't reach deep enough to undermine such buildings' foundations. However, small buildings or structures often rest upon foundations shallow enough to be damaged or even partially toppled by this spell.

The mud remains until a successful *dispel magic* or *transmute mud to rock* spell restores its substance—but not necessarily its form. Evaporation turns the mud to normal dirt over a period of days. The exact time depends on exposure to the sun, wind, and normal drainage.

Transmute rock to mud counters and dispels *transmute mud to rock.*

TRANSPORT VIA PLANTS

School conjuration (teleportation); **Level** druid 6
Casting Time 1 standard action
Components V, S
Range unlimited
Target you and touched objects or other touched willing creatures
Duration 1 round
Saving Throw none; **Spell Resistance** no

You can enter any normal plant (equal to your size or larger) and pass any distance to a plant of the same kind in a single round, regardless of the distance separating the two. The plants must be alive. The destination plant need not be familiar to you. If you are uncertain of the location of a particular kind of destination plant, you need merely designate direction and distance and the *transport via plants* spell moves you as close as possible to the desired location. If a particular destination plant is desired but the plant is not living, the spell fails and you are ejected from the entry plant.

You can bring along objects as long as their weight doesn't exceed your maximum load. You may also bring one additional willing Medium or smaller creature (carrying gear or objects up to its maximum load) or its equivalent per three caster levels. Use the following equivalents to determine the maximum number of larger creatures you can bring along: a Large creature counts as two Medium creatures, a Huge creature counts as four Medium

creatures, and so forth. All creatures to be transported by the spell must be in physical contact with one another, and at least one of those creatures must be in contact with you.

You can't use this spell to travel through plant creatures.

The destruction of an occupied plant slays you and any creatures you have brought along, and ejects the bodies and all carried objects from it.

TRAP THE SOUL

School conjuration (summoning); **Level** sorcerer/wizard 8
Casting Time 1 standard action or see text
Components V, S, M (gem worth 1,000 gp per HD of the trapped creature)
Range close (25 ft. + 5 ft./2 levels)
Target one creature
Duration permanent; see text
Saving Throw see text; **Spell Resistance** yes; see text

Trap the soul forces a creature's life force (and its material body) into a gem. The gem holds the trapped entity indefinitely or until the gem is broken and the life force is released, which allows the material body to reform. If the trapped creature is a powerful creature from another plane, it can be required to perform a service immediately upon being freed. Otherwise, the creature can go free once the gem imprisoning it is broken.

Depending on the version selected, the spell can be triggered in one of two ways.

Spell Completion: First, the spell can be completed by speaking its final word as a standard action as if you were casting a regular spell at the subject. This allows spell resistance (if any) and a Will save to avoid the effect. If the creature's name is spoken as well, any spell resistance is ignored and the save DC increases by 2. If the save or spell resistance is successful, the gem shatters.

Trigger Object: The second method is far more insidious, for it tricks the subject into accepting a trigger object inscribed with the final spell word, automatically placing the creature's soul in the trap. To use this method, both the creature's name and the trigger word must be inscribed on the trigger object when the gem is enspelled. A *sympathy* spell can also be placed on the trigger object. As soon as the subject picks up or accepts the trigger object, its life force is automatically transferred to the gem without the benefit of spell resistance or a save.

TREE SHAPE

School transmutation; **Level** druid 2, ranger 3
Casting Time 1 standard action
Components V, S, DF
Range personal
Target you
Duration 1 hour/level (D)

This spell allows you to assume the form of a Large living tree or shrub or a Large dead tree trunk with a small number of limbs. The exact type of tree, as well as its appearance, is completely under your control. Even the closest inspection cannot reveal that the tree in question is actually a magically concealed creature. To all normal tests you are, in fact, a tree or shrub, although a *detect magic* spell reveals a faint transmutation on the tree. While in tree form, you can observe all that transpires around you just as if you were in your normal form, and your hit points and save bonuses remain unaffected. You gain a +10 natural armor bonus to AC but have an effective Dexterity score of 0 and a speed of 0 feet. You are immune to critical hits while in tree form. All clothing and gear carried or worn changes with you. You can dismiss *tree shape* as a free action (instead of as a standard action).

TREE STRIDE

School conjuration (teleportation); **Level** druid 5, ranger 4
Casting Time 1 standard action
Components V, S, DF
Range personal
Target you
Duration 1 hour/level or until expended; see text

When you cast this spell, you gain the ability to step into a tree, magically infusing yourself with the plant. Once within a tree, you can teleport from that particular tree to another tree. The trees you enter must be of the same kind, must be living, and must have girth at least equal to yours. By moving into an oak tree (for example), you instantly know the location of all other oak trees within transport range (see below) and may choose whether you want to pass into one or simply step back out of the tree you moved into. You may choose to pass to any tree of the appropriate kind within the transport range as shown on the following table.

Type of Tree	Transport Range
Oak, ash, yew	3,000 feet
Elm, linden	2,000 feet
Other deciduous	1,500 feet
Any coniferous	1,000 feet

You may move into a tree up to one time per caster level (passing from one tree to another counts only as moving into one tree). The spell lasts until the duration expires or you exit a tree. Each transport is a full-round action.

You can, at your option, remain within a tree without transporting yourself, but you are forced out when the spell ends. If the tree in which you are concealed is chopped down or burned, you are slain if you do not exit before the process is complete.

TRUE RESURRECTION

School conjuration (healing); **Level** cleric 9
Casting Time: 10 minutes
Components V, S, DF, M (diamond worth 25,000 gp)

This spell functions like *raise dead*, except that you can resurrect a creature that has been dead for as long as 10 years per caster level. This spell can even bring back creatures whose bodies have been destroyed, provided that you unambiguously identify the deceased in some fashion (reciting the deceased's time and place of birth or death is the most common method).

Upon completion of the spell, the creature is immediately restored to full hit points, vigor, and health, with no negative levels (or Constitution points) and all of the prepared spells possessed by the creature when it died.

You can revive someone killed by a death effect or someone who has been turned into an undead creature and then destroyed. This spell can also resurrect elementals or outsiders, but it can't resurrect constructs or undead creatures.

Even *true resurrection* can't restore to life a creature who has died of old age.

TRUE SEEING

School divination; **Level** cleric 5, druid 7, sorcerer/wizard 6
Casting Time 1 standard action
Components V, S, M (an eye ointment that costs 250 gp)
Range touch
Target creature touched
Duration 1 min./level
Saving Throw Will negates (harmless); **Spell Resistance** yes (harmless)

You confer on the subject the ability to see all things as they actually are. The subject sees through normal and magical darkness, notices secret doors hidden by magic, sees the exact locations of creatures or objects under *blur* or *displacement* effects, sees invisible creatures or objects normally, sees through illusions, and sees the true form of polymorphed, changed, or transmuted things. Further, the subject can focus its vision to see into the Ethereal Plane (but not into extradimensional spaces). The range of *true seeing* conferred is 120 feet.

True seeing, however, does not penetrate solid objects. It in no way confers X-ray vision or its equivalent. It does not negate concealment, including that caused by fog and the like. *True seeing* does not help the viewer see through mundane disguises, spot creatures who are simply hiding, or notice secret doors hidden by mundane means. In addition, the spell effects cannot be further enhanced with known magic, so one cannot use *true seeing* through a *crystal ball* or in conjunction with *clairaudience/clairvoyance*.

TRUE STRIKE

School divination; **Level** sorcerer/wizard 1
Casting Time 1 standard action
Components V, F (small wooden replica of an archery target)
Range personal
Target you
Duration see text

You gain temporary, intuitive insight into the immediate future during your next attack. Your next single attack roll (if it is made before the end of the next round) gains a +20 insight bonus. Additionally, you are not affected by the miss chance that applies to attackers trying to strike a concealed target.

UNDEATH TO DEATH

School necromancy; **Level** cleric 6, sorcerer/wizard 6
Components: V, S, M/DF (diamond powder worth 500 gp)

Area several undead creatures within a 40-ft.-radius burst
Saving Throw Will negates

This spell functions like *circle of death*, except that it destroys undead creatures as noted above.

UNDETECTABLE ALIGNMENT

School abjuration; **Level** bard 1, cleric 2, paladin 2
Casting Time 1 standard action
Components V, S
Range close (25 ft. + 5 ft./2 levels)
Target one creature or object
Duration 24 hours
Saving Throw Will negates (object); **Spell Resistance** yes (object)

An *undetectable alignment* spell conceals the alignment of an object or a creature from all forms of divination.

UNHALLOW

School evocation [evil]; **Level** cleric 5, druid 5
Casting Time 24 hours
Components V, S, M (herbs, oils, and incense worth at least 1,000 gp, plus 1,000 gp per level of the spell to be tied to the *unhallowed* area)
Range touch
Area 40-ft. radius emanating from the touched point
Duration instantaneous
Saving Throw see text; **Spell Resistance** see text

Unhallow makes a particular site, building, or structure an unholy site. This has three major effects.

First, the site or structure is guarded by a *magic circle against good* effect.

Second, the DC to resist negative channeled energy within the spell's area of effect gains a +4 profane bonus and the DC to resist positive energy is reduced by 4. Spell resistance does not apply to this effect. This provision does not apply to the druid version of the spell.

Finally, you may choose to fix a single spell effect to the *unhallowed* site. The spell effect lasts for 1 year and functions throughout the entire site, regardless of its normal duration and area or effect. You may designate whether the effect applies to all creatures, creatures that share your faith or alignment, or creatures that adhere to another faith or alignment. At the end of the year, the chosen effect lapses, but it can be renewed or replaced simply by casting *unhallow* again.

Spell effects that may be tied to an *unhallowed* site include *aid, bane, bless, cause fear, darkness, daylight, death ward, deeper darkness, detect magic, detect good, dimensional anchor, discern lies, dispel magic, endure elements, freedom of movement, invisibility purge, protection from energy, remove fear, resist energy, silence, tongues,* and *zone of truth.*

Saving throws and spell resistance might apply to these spells' effects. (See the individual spell descriptions for details.)

An area can receive only one *unhallow* spell (and its associated spell effect) at a time.

Unhallow counters but does not dispel *hallow*.

UNHOLY AURA

School abjuration [evil]; **Level** cleric 8

Casting Time 1 standard action

Components V, S, F (a tiny reliquary worth 500 gp)

Range 20 ft.

Targets one creature/level in a 20-ft.-radius burst centered on you

Duration 1 round/level (D)

Saving Throw see text; **Spell Resistance** yes (harmless)

A malevolent darkness surrounds the subjects, protecting them from attacks, granting them resistance to spells cast by good creatures, and weakening good creatures when they strike the subjects. This abjuration has four effects.

First, each warded creature gains a +4 deflection bonus to AC and a +4 resistance bonus on saves. Unlike the effect of *protection from good*, this benefit applies against all attacks, not just against attacks by good creatures.

Second, a warded creature gains SR 25 against good spells and spells cast by good creatures.

Third, the abjuration protects the subjects from possession and mental influence, just as *protection from good* does.

Finally, if a good creature succeeds on a melee attack against a warded creature, the offending attacker takes 1d6 points of Strength damage (Fortitude negates).

UNHOLY BLIGHT

School evocation [evil]; **Level** cleric 4

Casting Time 1 standard action

Components V, S

Range medium (100 ft. + 10 ft./level)

Area 20-ft.-radius spread

Duration instantaneous (1d4 rounds); see text

Saving Throw Will partial; **Spell Resistance** yes

You call up unholy power to smite your enemies. The power takes the form of a cold, cloying miasma of greasy darkness. Only good and neutral (not evil) creatures are harmed by the spell.

The spell deals 1d8 points of damage per two caster levels (maximum 5d8) to a good creature (or 1d6 per caster level, maximum 10d6, to a good outsider) and causes it to be sickened for 1d4 rounds. A successful Will save reduces damage to half and negates the sickened effect. The effects cannot be negated by *remove disease* or *heal*, but *remove curse* is effective.

The spell deals only half damage to creatures who are neither evil nor good, and they are not sickened. Such a creature can reduce the damage by half again (down to one-quarter) with a successful Will save.

UNSEEN SERVANT

School conjuration (creation); **Level** bard 1, sorcerer/wizard 1

Casting Time 1 standard action

Components V, S, M (a piece of string and a bit of wood)

Range close (25 ft. + 5 ft./2 levels)

Effect one invisible, mindless, shapeless servant

Duration 1 hour/level

Saving Throw none; **Spell Resistance** no

An *unseen servant* is an invisible, mindless, shapeless force that performs simple tasks at your command. It can run and fetch things, open unstuck doors, and hold chairs, as well as clean and mend. The servant can perform only one activity at a time, but it repeats the same activity over and over again if told to do so as long as you remain within range. It can open only normal doors, drawers, lids, and the like. It has an effective Strength score of 2 (so it can lift 20 pounds or drag 100 pounds). It can trigger traps and such, but it can exert only 20 pounds of force, which is not enough to activate certain pressure plates and other devices. It can't perform any task that requires a skill check with a DC higher than 10 or that requires a check using a skill that can't be used untrained. This servant cannot fly, climb, or even swim (though it can walk on water). Its base speed is 15 feet.

The servant cannot attack in any way; it is never allowed an attack roll. It cannot be killed, but it dissipates if it takes 6 points of damage from area attacks. (It gets no saves against attacks.) If you attempt to send it beyond the spell's range (measured from your current position), the servant ceases to exist.

VAMPIRIC TOUCH

School necromancy; **Level** sorcerer/wizard 3

Casting Time 1 standard action

Components V, S

Range touch

Target living creature touched

Duration instantaneous/1 hour; see text

Saving Throw none; **Spell Resistance** yes

You must succeed on a melee touch attack. Your touch deals 1d6 points of damage per two caster levels (maximum 10d6). You gain temporary hit points equal to the damage you deal. You can't gain more than the subject's current hit points + the subject's Constitution score (which is enough to kill the subject). The temporary hit points disappear 1 hour later.

VEIL

School illusion (glamer); **Level** bard 6, sorcerer/wizard 6

Casting Time 1 standard action

Components V, S

Range long (400 ft. + 40 ft./level)

Targets one or more creatures, no two of which can be more than 30 ft. apart

Duration concentration + 1 hour/level (D)

Saving Throw Will negates; see text; **Spell Resistance** yes; see text

You instantly change the appearance of the subjects and then maintain that appearance for the spell's duration. You can make the subjects appear to be anything you wish. The subjects look, feel, and smell just like the creatures the spell makes them resemble. Affected creatures resume their normal appearances if slain. You must succeed on a Disguise check to duplicate the appearance of a specific individual. This spell gives you a +10 bonus on the check.

Unwilling targets can negate the spell's effect on them by making Will saves or with spell resistance. Those who interact with the subjects can attempt Will disbelief saves to see through the glamer, but spell resistance doesn't help.

VENTRILOQUISM

School illusion (figment); **Level** bard 1, sorcerer/wizard 1

Casting Time 1 standard action

Components V, F (parchment rolled into cone)

Range close (25 ft. + 5 ft./2 levels)

Effect intelligible sound, usually speech

Duration 1 min./level (D)

Saving Throw Will disbelief (if interacted with); **Spell Resistance** no

You can make your voice (or any sound that you can normally make vocally) seem to issue from someplace else. You can speak in any language you know. With respect to such voices and sounds, anyone who hears the sound and rolls a successful save recognizes it as illusory (but still hears it).

VIRTUE

School transmutation; **Level** cleric 0, druid 0, paladin 1

Casting Time 1 standard action

Components V, S, DF

Range touch

Target creature touched

Duration 1 min.

Saving Throw none; **Spell Resistance** yes (harmless)

With a touch, you infuse a creature with a tiny surge of life, granting the subject 1 temporary hit point.

VISION

School divination; **Level** sorcerer/wizard 7

Casting Time 1 standard action

This spell functions like *legend lore*, except that it works more quickly and produces some strain on you. You pose a question about some person, place, or object, then cast the spell. If the person or object is at hand or if you are in the place in question, you receive a vision about it by succeeding on a caster level check (1d20 + 1 per caster level; maximum +25) against DC 20. If only detailed information on the person, place, or object is known, the DC is 25, and the information gained is incomplete. If only rumors are known, the DC is 30, and the information gained is vague. After this spell is complete, you are fatigued.

WAIL OF THE BANSHEE

School necromancy [death, sonic]; **Level** sorcerer/wizard 9

Casting Time 1 standard action

Components V

Range close (25 ft. + 5 ft./2 levels)

Target one living creature/level within a 40-ft.-radius spread

Duration instantaneous

Saving Throw Fortitude negates; **Spell Resistance** yes

When you cast this spell, you emit a terrible, soul-chilling scream that possibly kills creatures that hear it (except for yourself). The spell affects up to one creature per caster level, inflicting 10 points of damage per caster level. Creatures closest to the point of origin are affected first.

WALL OF FIRE

School evocation [fire]; **Level** druid 5, sorcerer/wizard 4

Casting Time 1 standard action

Components V, S, M/DF (a piece of phosphor)

Range medium (100 ft. + 10 ft./level)

Effect opaque sheet of flame up to 20 ft. long/level or a ring of fire with a radius of up to 5 ft./two levels; either form 20 ft. high

Duration concentration + 1 round/level

Saving Throw none; **Spell Resistance** yes

An immobile, blazing curtain of shimmering violet fire springs into existence. One side of the wall, selected by you, sends forth waves of heat, dealing 2d4 points of fire damage to creatures within 10 feet and 1d4 points of fire damage to those past 10 feet but within 20 feet. The wall deals this damage when it appears, and to all creatures in the area on your turn each round. In addition, the wall deals 2d6 points of fire damage + 1 point of fire damage per caster level (maximum +20) to any creature passing through it. The wall deals double damage to undead creatures.

If you evoke the wall so that it appears where creatures are, each creature takes damage as if passing through the wall. If any 5-foot length of wall takes 20 points or more of cold damage in 1 round, that length goes away. (Do not divide cold damage by 2, as normal for objects.)

Wall of fire can be made permanent with a *permanency* spell. A permanent *wall of fire* that is extinguished by cold damage becomes inactive for 10 minutes, then reforms at normal strength.

WALL OF FORCE

School evocation [force]; **Level** sorcerer/wizard 5

Casting Time 1 standard action

Components V, S, M (powdered quartz)

Range close (25 ft. + 5 ft./2 levels)

Effect wall whose area is up to one 10-ft. square/level

Duration 1 round /level (D)

Saving Throw none; **Spell Resistance** no

A *wall of force* creates an invisible wall of pure force. The wall cannot move and is not easily destroyed. A *wall of force* is immune to *dispel magic*, although a *mage's disjunction* can still dispel it. A *wall of force* can be damaged by spells as normal, except for *disintegrate*, which automatically destroys it. It can be damaged by weapons and supernatural abilities, but a *wall of force* has hardness 30 and a number of hit points equal to 20 per caster level. Contact with a *sphere of annihilation* or *rod of cancellation* instantly destroys a *wall of force*.

Breath weapons and spells cannot pass through a *wall of force* in either direction, although *dimension door, teleport,* and similar

effects can bypass the barrier. It blocks ethereal creatures as well as material ones (though ethereal creatures can usually circumvent the wall by going around it, through material floors and ceilings). Gaze attacks can operate through a *wall of force*.

The caster can form the wall into a flat, vertical plane whose area is up to one 10-foot square per level. The wall must be continuous and unbroken when formed. If its surface is broken by any object or creature, the spell fails.

Wall of force can be made permanent with a *permanency* spell.

WALL OF ICE

School evocation [cold]; **Level** sorcerer/wizard 4

Casting Time 1 standard action

Components V, S, M (a piece of quartz or rock crystal)

Range medium (100 ft. + 10 ft./level)

Effect anchored plane of ice, up to one 10-ft. square/level, or hemisphere of ice with a radius of up to 3 ft. + 1 ft./level

Duration 1 min./level

Saving Throw Reflex negates; see text; **Spell Resistance** yes

This spell creates an anchored plane of ice or a hemisphere of ice, depending on the version selected. A *wall of ice* cannot form in an area occupied by physical objects or creatures. Its surface must be smooth and unbroken when created. Any creature adjacent to the wall when it

is created may attempt a Reflex save to disrupt the wall as it is being formed. A successful save indicates that the spell automatically fails. Fire can melt a *wall of ice*, and it deals full damage to the wall (instead of the normal half damage taken by objects). Suddenly melting a *wall of ice* creates a great cloud of steamy fog that lasts for 10 minutes.

Ice Plane: A sheet of strong, hard ice appears. The wall is 1 inch thick per caster level. It covers up to a 10-foot-square area per caster level (so a 10th-level wizard can create a *wall of ice* 100 feet long and 10 feet high, a wall 50 feet long and 20 feet high, or any other combination of length and height that does not exceed 1,000 square feet). The plane can be oriented in any fashion as long as it is anchored. A vertical wall need only be anchored on the floor, while a horizontal or slanting wall must be anchored on two opposite sides.

Each 10-foot square of wall has 3 hit points per inch of thickness. Creatures can hit the wall automatically. A section of wall whose hit points drop to 0 is breached. If a creature tries to break through the wall with a single attack, the DC for the Strength check is 15 + caster level.

Even when the ice has been broken through, a sheet of frigid air remains. Any creature stepping through it (including the one who broke through the wall) takes 1d6 points of cold damage + 1 point per caster level (no save).

Hemisphere: The wall takes the form of a hemisphere whose

maximum radius is 3 feet + 1 foot per caster level. The *hemisphere* is as hard to break through as the *ice plane* form, but it does not deal damage to those who go through a breach.

WALL OF IRON

School conjuration (creation); **Level** sorcerer/wizard 6

Casting Time 1 standard action

Components V, S, M (a small iron sheet plus gold dust worth 50 gp)

Range medium (100 ft. + 10 ft./level)

Effect iron wall whose area is up to one 5-ft. square/level; see text

Duration instantaneous

Saving Throw see text; **Spell Resistance** no

You cause a flat, vertical iron wall to spring into being. The wall inserts itself into any surrounding nonliving material if its area is sufficient to do so. The wall cannot be conjured so that it occupies the same space as a creature or another object. It must always be a flat plane, though you can shape its edges to fit the available space.

A *wall of iron* is 1 inch thick per four caster levels. You can double the wall's area by halving its thickness. Each 5-foot square of the wall has 30 hit points per inch of thickness and hardness 10. A section of wall whose hit points drop to 0 is breached. If a creature tries to break through the wall with a single attack, the DC for the Strength check is 25 + 2 per inch of thickness.

If you desire, the wall can be created vertically resting on a flat surface but not attached to the surface, so that it can be tipped over to fall on and crush creatures beneath it. The wall is 50% likely to tip in either direction if left unpushed. Creatures can push the wall in one direction rather than letting it fall randomly. A creature must make a DC 40 Strength check to push the wall over. Creatures with room to flee the falling wall may do so by making successful Reflex saves. Any Large or smaller creature that fails takes 10d6 points of damage while fleeing from the wall. The wall cannot crush Huge and larger creatures.

Like any iron wall, this wall is subject to rust, perforation, and other natural phenomena. Iron created by this spell is not suitable for use in the creation of other objects and cannot be sold.

WALL OF STONE

School conjuration (creation) [earth]; **Level** cleric 5, druid 6, sorcerer/wizard 5

Casting Time 1 standard action

Components V, S, M/DF (a small block of granite)

Range medium (100 ft. + 10 ft./level)

Effect stone wall whose area is up to one 5-ft. square/level (S)

Duration instantaneous

Saving Throw see text; **Spell Resistance** no

This spell creates a wall of rock that merges into adjoining rock surfaces. A *wall of stone* is 1 inch thick per four caster levels and composed of up to one 5-foot square per level. You can double the wall's area by halving its thickness. The wall cannot be conjured so that it occupies the same space as a creature or another object.

Unlike a *wall of iron*, you can create a *wall of stone* in almost any shape you desire. The wall created need not be vertical, nor rest upon any firm foundation; however, it must merge with and be solidly supported by existing stone. It can be used to bridge a chasm, for instance, or as a ramp. For this use, if the span is more than 20 feet, the wall must be arched and buttressed. This requirement reduces the spell's area by half. The wall can be crudely shaped to allow crenellations, battlements, and so forth by likewise reducing the area.

Like any other stone wall, this one can be destroyed by a *disintegrate* spell or by normal means such as breaking and chipping. Each 5-foot square of the wall has hardness 8 and 15 hit points per inch of thickness. A section of wall whose hit points drop to 0 is breached. If a creature tries to break through the wall with a single attack, the DC for the Strength check is 20 + 2 per inch of thickness.

It is possible, but difficult, to trap mobile opponents within or under a wall of stone, provided the wall is shaped so it can hold the creatures. Creatures can avoid entrapment with successful Reflex saves.

WALL OF THORNS

School conjuration (creation); **Level** druid 5

Casting Time 1 standard action

Components V, S

Range medium (100 ft. + 10 ft./level)

Effect wall of thorny brush, up to one 10-ft. cube/level (S)

Duration 10 min./level (D)

Saving Throw none; **Spell Resistance** no

A *wall of thorns* spell creates a barrier of very tough, pliable, tangled brush bearing needle-sharp thorns as long as a human's finger. Any creature forced into or attempting to move through a *wall of thorns* takes piercing damage per round of movement equal to 25 minus the creature's AC. Dexterity and dodge bonuses to AC do not count for this calculation. (Creatures with an AC of 25 or higher, without considering Dexterity and dodge bonuses, take no damage from contact with the wall.)

You can make the wall as thin as 5 feet thick, which allows you to shape the wall as a number of 10-by-10-by-5-foot blocks equal to twice your caster level. This has no effect on the damage dealt by the thorns, but any creature attempting to break through takes that much less time to force its way through the barrier.

Creatures can force their way slowly through the wall by making a Strength check as a full-round action. For every 5 points by which the check exceeds 20, a creature moves 5 feet (up to a maximum distance equal to its normal land speed). Of course, moving or attempting to move through the thorns incurs damage as described above. A creature trapped in the thorns can choose to remain motionless in order to avoid taking any more damage.

Any creature within the area of the spell when it is cast takes damage as if it had moved into the wall and is caught inside. In order to escape, it must attempt to push its way free, or it can wait until the spell ends. Creatures with the ability to pass through overgrown areas unhindered can pass through a *wall of thorns* at normal speed without taking damage.

A *wall of thorns* can be breached by slow work with edged weapons. Chopping away at the wall creates a safe passage 1 foot deep for every 10 minutes of work. Normal fire cannot harm the barrier, but magical fire burns it away in 10 minutes.

WARP WOOD

School transmutation; **Level** druid 2

Casting Time 1 standard action

Components V, S

Range close (25 ft. + 5 ft./2 levels)

Target 1 Small wooden object/level, all within a 20-ft. radius

Duration instantaneous

Saving Throw Will negates (object); **Spell Resistance** yes (object)

You cause wood to bend and warp, permanently destroying its straightness, form, and strength. A warped door springs open (or becomes stuck, requiring a Strength check to open, at your option). A boat or ship springs a leak. Warped ranged weapons are useless. A warped melee weapon causes a –4 penalty on attack rolls.

You may warp one Small or smaller object or its equivalent per caster level. A Medium object counts as two Small objects, a Large object as four, a Huge object as eight, a Gargantuan object as 16, and a Colossal object as 32.

Alternatively, you can unwarp wood (effectively warping it back to normal) with this spell. *Make whole*, on the other hand, does no good in repairing a warped item.

You can combine multiple consecutive *warp wood* spells to warp (or unwarp) an object that is too large for you to warp with a single spell. Until the object is completely warped, it suffers no ill effects.

WATER BREATHING

School transmutation; **Level** cleric 3, druid 3, sorcerer/wizard 3

Casting Time 1 standard action

Components V, S, M/DF (short reed or piece of straw)

Range touch

Target living creatures touched

Duration 2 hours/level; see text

Saving Throw Will negates (harmless); **Spell Resistance** yes (harmless)

The transmuted creatures can breathe water freely. Divide the duration evenly among all the creatures you touch. The spell does not make creatures unable to breathe air.

WATER WALK

School transmutation [water]; **Level** cleric 3, ranger 3

Casting Time 1 standard action

Components V, S, DF

Range touch

Targets one touched creature/level

Duration 10 min./level (D)

Saving Throw Will negates (harmless); **Spell Resistance** yes (harmless)

The transmuted creatures can tread on any liquid as if it were firm ground. Mud, oil, snow, quicksand, running water, ice, and even lava can be traversed easily, since the subjects' feet hover an inch or two above the surface. Creatures crossing molten lava still take damage from the heat because they are near it. The subjects can walk, run, charge, or otherwise move across the surface as if it were normal ground.

If the spell is cast underwater (or while the subjects are partially or wholly submerged in whatever liquid they are in), the subjects are borne toward the surface at 60 feet per round until they can stand on it.

WAVES OF EXHAUSTION

School necromancy; **Level** sorcerer/wizard 7

Casting Time 1 standard action

Components V, S

Range 60 ft.

Area cone-shaped burst

Duration instantaneous

Saving Throw no; **Spell Resistance** yes

Waves of negative energy cause all living creatures in the spell's area to become exhausted. This spell has no effect on a creature that is already exhausted.

WAVES OF FATIGUE

School necromancy; **Level** sorcerer/wizard 5

Casting Time 1 standard action

Components V, S

Range 30 ft.

Area cone-shaped burst

Duration instantaneous

Saving Throw no; **Spell Resistance** yes

Waves of negative energy render all living creatures in the spell's area fatigued. This spell has no effect on a creature that is already fatigued.

WEB

School conjuration (creation); **Level** sorcerer/wizard 2

Casting Time 1 standard action

Components V, S, M (spider web)

Range medium (100 ft. + 10 ft./level)

Effect webs in a 20-ft.-radius spread

Duration 10 min./level (D)

Saving Throw Reflex negates; see text; **Spell Resistance** no

Web creates a many-layered mass of strong, sticky strands. These strands trap those caught in them. The strands are similar to spiderwebs but far larger and tougher. These masses must be anchored to two or more solid and diametrically opposed points or else the web collapses upon itself and disappears. Creatures caught within a web become grappled by the sticky fibers. Attacking a creature in a web doesn't cause you to become grappled.

Anyone in the effect's area when the spell is cast must make a Reflex save. If this save succeeds, the creature is inside the web but is otherwise unaffected. If the save fails, the creature gains the grappled condition, but can break free by making a combat maneuver check or Escape Artist check as a standard action against the DC of this spell. The entire area of the web is considered difficult terrain. Anyone moving through the webs must make a combat maneuver check or Escape Artist check as part of their move action, with a DC equal to the spell's DC. Creatures that fail lose their movement and become grappled in the first square of webbing that they enter.

If you have at least 5 feet of web between you and an opponent, it provides cover. If you have at least 20 feet of web between you, it provides total cover.

The strands of a *web* spell are flammable. A *flaming weapon* can slash them away as easily as a hand brushes away cobwebs. Any fire can set the webs alight and burn away one 5-foot square in 1 round. All creatures within flaming webs take 2d4 points of fire damage from the flames.

Web can be made permanent with a *permanency* spell. A permanent web that is damaged (but not destroyed) regrows in 10 minutes.

WEIRD

School illusion (phantasm) [fear, mind-affecting]; **Level** sorcerer/wizard 9

Targets any number of creatures, no two of which can be more than 30 ft. apart

This spell functions like *phantasmal killer*, except it can affect more than one creature. Only the affected creatures see the phantasmal creatures attacking them, though you see the attackers as shadowy shapes.

If a subject's Fortitude save succeeds, it still takes 3d6 points of damage and is stunned for 1 round. The subject also takes 1d4 points of Strength damage.

WHIRLWIND

School evocation [air]; **Level** druid 8

Casting Time 1 standard action

Components V, S, DF

Range long (400 ft. + 40 ft./level)

Effect cyclone 10 ft. wide at base, 30 ft. wide at top, and 30 ft. tall

Duration 1 round/level (D)

Saving Throw Reflex negates; see text; **Spell Resistance** yes

This spell creates a powerful cyclone of raging wind that moves through the air, along the ground, or over water at a speed of 60 feet per round. You can concentrate on controlling the cyclone's every movement or specify a simple program. Directing the cyclone's movement or changing its programmed movement is a standard action for you. The cyclone always moves during your turn. If the cyclone exceeds the spell's range, it moves in a random, uncontrolled fashion for 1d3 rounds and then dissipates. (You can't regain control of the cyclone, even if it comes back within range.)

Any Large or smaller creature that comes in contact with the spell effect must succeed on a Reflex save or take 3d6 points of damage. A Medium or smaller creature that fails its first save must succeed on a second one or be picked up bodily by the cyclone and held suspended in its powerful winds, taking 1d8 points of damage each round on your turn with no save allowed. You may direct the cyclone to eject any carried creatures whenever you wish, depositing the hapless souls wherever the cyclone happens to be when they are released.

WHISPERING WIND

School transmutation [air]; **Level** bard 2, sorcerer/wizard 2

Casting Time 1 standard action

Components V, S

Range 1 mile/level

Area 10-ft.-radius spread

Duration no more than 1 hour/level or until discharged (destination is reached)

Saving Throw none; **Spell Resistance** no

You send a message or sound on the wind to a designated spot. The *whispering wind* travels to a specific location within range that is familiar to you, provided that it can find a way to the location. A *whispering wind* is as gentle and unnoticed as a zephyr until it reaches the location. It then delivers its whisper-quiet message or other sound. Note that the message is delivered regardless of whether anyone is present to hear it. The wind then dissipates.

You can prepare the spell to bear a message of no more than 25 words, cause the spell to deliver other sounds for 1 round, or merely have the *whispering wind* seem to be a faint stirring of the air. You can likewise cause the *whispering wind* to move as slowly as 1 mile per hour or as quickly as 1 mile per 10 minutes.

When the spell reaches its objective, it swirls and remains in place until the message is delivered. As with *magic mouth*, *whispering wind* cannot speak verbal components, use command words, or activate magical effects.

WIND WALK

School transmutation [air]; **Level** cleric 6, druid 7

Casting Time 1 standard action

Components V, S, DF

Range touch

Targets you and one touched creature per three levels

Duration 1 hour/level (D); see text

Saving Throw no and Will negates (harmless); **Spell Resistance** no and yes (harmless)

You alter the substance of your body to a cloudlike vapor (as the *gaseous form* spell) and move through the air, possibly at great speed. You can take other creatures with you, each of which acts independently.

Normally, a wind walker flies at a speed of 10 feet with perfect maneuverability. If desired by the subject, a magical wind wafts a wind walker along at up to 600 feet per round (60 mph) with poor maneuverability. Wind walkers are not invisible but rather appear misty and translucent. If fully clothed in white, they are 80% likely to be mistaken for clouds, fog, vapors, or the like.

A wind walker can regain its physical form as desired and later resume the cloud form. Each change to and from vaporous form takes 5 rounds, which counts toward the duration of the spell (as does any time spent in physical form). As noted above, you can dismiss the spell, and you can even dismiss it for individual wind walkers and not others.

For the last minute of the spell's duration, a wind walker in cloud

form automatically descends 60 feet per round (for a total of 600 feet), though it may descend faster if it wishes. This descent serves as a warning that the spell is about to end.

WIND WALL

School evocation [air]; **Level** cleric 3, druid 3, ranger 2, sorcerer/wizard 3

Casting Time 1 standard action

Components V, S, M/DF (a tiny fan and an exotic feather)

Range medium (100 ft. + 10 ft./level)

Effect wall up to 10 ft./level long and 5 ft./level high (S)

Duration 1 round/level

Saving Throw none; see text; **Spell Resistance** yes

An invisible vertical curtain of wind appears. It is 2 feet thick and of considerable strength. It is a roaring blast sufficient to blow away any bird smaller than an eagle, or tear papers and similar materials from unsuspecting hands. (A Reflex save allows a creature to maintain its grasp on an object.) Tiny and Small flying creatures cannot pass through the barrier. Loose materials and cloth garments fly upward when caught in a *wind wall*. Arrows and bolts are deflected upward and miss, while any other normal ranged weapon passing through the wall has a 30% miss chance. (A giant-thrown boulder, a siege engine projectile, and other massive ranged weapons are not affected.) Gases, most gaseous breath weapons, and creatures in *gaseous form* cannot pass through the wall (although it is no barrier to incorporeal creatures).

While the wall must be vertical, you can shape it in any continuous path along the ground that you like. It is possible to create cylindrical or square *wind walls* to enclose specific points.

WISH

School universal; **Level** sorcerer/wizard 9

Casting Time 1 standard action

Components V, S, M (diamond worth 25,000 gp)

Range see text

Target, Effect, Area see text

Duration see text

Saving Throw none, see text; **Spell Resistance** yes

Wish is the mightiest spell a wizard or sorcerer can cast. By simply speaking aloud, you can alter reality to better suit you. Even *wish*, however, has its limits. A *wish* can produce any one of the following effects.

- Duplicate any sorcerer/wizard spell of 8th level or lower, provided the spell does not belong to one of your opposition schools.
- Duplicate any non-sorcerer/wizard spell of 7th level or lower, provided the spell does not belong to one of your opposition schools.
- Duplicate any sorcerer/wizard spell of 7th level or lower, even if it belongs to one of your opposition schools.
- Duplicate any non-sorcerer/wizard spell of 6th level or lower, even if it belongs to one of your opposition schools.
- Undo the harmful effects of many other spells, such as *geas/quest* or *insanity*.

- Grant a creature a +1 inherent bonus to an ability score. Two to five *wish* spells cast in immediate succession can grant a creature a +2 to +5 inherent bonus to an ability score (two *wishes* for a +2 inherent bonus, three *wishes* for a +3 inherent bonus, and so on). Inherent bonuses are instantaneous, so they cannot be dispelled. *Note*: An inherent bonus may not exceed +5 for a single ability score, and inherent bonuses to a particular ability score do not stack, so only the best one applies.
- Remove injuries and afflictions. A single *wish* can aid one creature per caster level, and all subjects are cured of the same kind of affliction. For example, you could heal all the damage you and your companions have taken, or remove all poison effects from everyone in the party, but not do both with the same *wish*.
- Revive the dead. A *wish* can bring a dead creature back to life by duplicating a *resurrection* spell. A *wish* can revive a dead creature whose body has been destroyed, but the task takes two *wishes*: one to recreate the body and another to infuse the body with life again. A *wish* cannot prevent a character who was brought back to life from gaining a permanent negative level.
- Transport travelers. A *wish* can lift one creature per caster level from anywhere on any plane and place those creatures anywhere else on any plane regardless of local conditions. An unwilling target gets a Will save to negate the effect, and spell resistance (if any) applies.
- Undo misfortune. A *wish* can undo a single recent event. The *wish* forces a reroll of any roll made within the last round (including your last turn). Reality reshapes itself to accommodate the new result. For example, a *wish* could undo an opponent's successful save, a foe's successful critical hit (either the attack roll or the critical roll), a friend's failed save, and so on. The reroll, however, may be as bad as or worse than the original roll. An unwilling target gets a Will save to negate the effect, and spell resistance (if any) applies.

You may try to use a *wish* to produce greater effects than these, but doing so is dangerous. (The *wish* may pervert your intent into a literal but undesirable fulfillment or only a partial fulfillment, at the GM's discretion.)

Duplicated spells allow saves and spell resistance as normal (but save DCs are for 9th-level spells).

When a *wish* duplicates a spell with a material component that costs more than 10,000 gp, you must provide that component (in addition to the 25,000 gp diamond component for this spell).

WOOD SHAPE

School transmutation; **Level** druid 2

Casting Time 1 standard action

Components V, S, DF

Range touch

Target one touched piece of wood no larger than 10 cu. ft. + 1 cu. ft./level

Duration instantaneous

Saving Throw Will negates (object); **Spell Resistance** yes (object)

Wood shape enables you to form one existing piece of wood into any shape that suits your purpose. While it is possible to make crude coffers, doors, and so forth, fine detail isn't possible. There is a 30% chance that any shape that includes moving parts simply doesn't work.

WORD OF RECALL

School conjuration (teleportation); **Level** cleric 6, druid 8
Casting Time 1 standard action
Components V
Range unlimited
Target you and touched objects or other willing creatures
Duration instantaneous
Saving Throw none or Will negates (harmless, object); **Spell Resistance** no or yes (harmless, object)

Word of recall teleports you instantly back to your sanctuary when the word is uttered. You must designate the sanctuary when you prepare the spell, and it must be a very familiar place. The actual point of arrival is a designated area no larger than 10 feet by 10 feet. You can be transported any distance within a plane but cannot travel between planes. You can transport, in addition to yourself, any objects you carry, as long as their weight doesn't exceed your maximum load. You may also bring one additional willing Medium or smaller creature (carrying gear or objects up to its maximum load) or its equivalent per three caster levels. A Large creature counts as two Medium creatures, a Huge creature counts as two Large creatures, and so forth. All creatures to be transported must be in contact with one another, and at least one of those creatures must be in contact with you. Exceeding this limit causes the spell to fail.

An unwilling creature can't be teleported by *word of recall*. Likewise, a creature's Will save (or spell resistance) prevents items in its possession from being teleported. Unattended, nonmagical objects receive no saving throw.

WORD OF CHAOS

School evocation [chaotic, sonic]; **Level** cleric 7
Casting Time 1 standard action
Components V
Range 40 ft.
Area nonchaotic creatures in a 40-ft.-radius spread centered on you
Duration instantaneous
Saving Throw none or Will negates; see text; **Spell Resistance** yes

Any nonchaotic creature within the area of a *word of chaos* spell suffers the following ill effects, depending on their HD.

HD	Effect
Equal to caster level	Deafened
Up to caster level –1	Stunned, deafened
Up to caster level –5	Confused, stunned, deafened
Up to caster level –10	Killed, confused, stunned, deafened

The effects are cumulative and concurrent. A successful Will save reduces or eliminates these effects. Creatures affected by multiple effects make only one save and apply the result to all the effects.

Deafened: The creature is deafened for 1d4 rounds. Save negates.

Stunned: The creature is stunned for 1 round. Save negates.

Confused: The creature is confused for 1d10 minutes. This is a mind-affecting enchantment effect. Save reduces the confused effect to 1 round.

Killed: Living creatures die. Undead creatures are destroyed. Save negates. If the save is successful, the creature instead takes 3d6 points of damage + 1 point per caster level (maximum +25).

Furthermore, if you are on your home plane when you cast this spell, nonchaotic extraplanar creatures within the area are instantly banished back to their home planes. Creatures so banished cannot return for at least 24 hours. This effect takes place regardless of whether the creatures hear the *word of chaos* or not. The banishment effect allows a Will save (at a –4 penalty) to negate.

Creatures whose HD exceed your caster level are unaffected by *word of chaos*.

ZONE OF SILENCE

School illusion (glamer); **Level** bard 4
Casting Time 1 round
Components V, S
Range personal
Area 5-ft.-radius emanation centered on you
Duration 1 hour/level (D)

By casting *zone of silence*, you manipulate sound waves in your immediate vicinity so that you and those within the spell's area can converse normally, yet no one outside can hear your voices or any other noises from within, including language-dependent or sonic spell effects. This effect is centered on you and moves with you. Anyone who enters the zone immediately becomes subject to its effects, but those who leave are no longer affected. Note, however, that a successful DC 20 Linguistics check to read lips can still reveal what's said inside a *zone of silence*.

ZONE OF TRUTH

School enchantment (compulsion) [mind-affecting]; **Level** cleric 2, paladin 2
Casting Time 1 standard action
Components V, S, DF
Range close (25 ft. + 5 ft./2 levels)
Area 20-ft.-radius emanation
Duration 1 min./level
Saving Throw Will negates; **Spell Resistance** yes

Creatures within the emanation area (or those who enter it) can't speak any deliberate and intentional lies. Each potentially affected creature is allowed a save to avoid the effects when the spell is cast or when the creature first enters the emanation area. Affected creatures are aware of this enchantment. Therefore, they may avoid answering questions to which they would normally respond with a lie, or they may be evasive as long as they remain within the boundaries of the truth. Creatures who leave the area are free to speak as they choose.

11 Prestige Classes

The towering bebilith hissed in delight as its razor-sharp pincers struck. With horrifying speed, it began tearing Amiri's armor apart, peeling her like an orange.

Seltyiel had figured the beast would go for her first—that was why he'd waited to strike. He ducked under the creature's legs, delivering a devastating blow to its belly. He grinned in triumph as his blade sank home, feeling his magic swell up inside him. Entrails had hardly begun slopping into the dirt before he sent a devastating cone of cold up into the raw, open wound.

Prestige classes allow characters to become truly exceptional, gaining powers beyond the ken of their peers. Unlike the core classes, characters must meet specific requirements before they can take their first level of a prestige class. If a character does not meet the requirements for a prestige class before gaining any benefits of that level, that character cannot take that prestige class. Characters that take levels in prestige classes do not gain any favored class bonuses for those levels.

This chapter presents 10 prestige classes for you to choose from, and other prestige classes appear in other Pathfinder products. Some prestige classes are quite focused and heavy on flavor that might not be compatible with your campaign—consult with your GM before you start to work toward qualifying for a prestige class to make sure that the class is allowed.

The prestige classes presented in this chapter are summarized below.

Arcane Archer: An arcane spellcaster who draws upon ancient elven traditions to infuse his arrows with potent magical power.

Arcane Trickster: A troublemaker and a scoundrel who uses arcane magic to enhance her thievery and trickery.

Assassin: A remorseless murderer who kills for money and the sheer thrill of death-dealing.

Dragon Disciple: An arcane spellcaster who has embraced his latent draconic heritage and, over the course of training and devotion, undergoes a partial transformation into a dragon.

Duelist: A swashbuckling swordfighter who relies upon grace, poise, and acrobatics to win the day.

Eldritch Knight: An arcane spellcaster who augments his magical skills with combat to create a deadly combination of weapons and magic.

Loremaster: A spellcaster who devotes his life to research and rumination upon the mysteries of the world.

Mystic Theurge: Equally devoted to divine and arcane magic, the mystic theurge combines both magical traditions into one incredibly diverse class.

Pathfinder Chronicler: An explorer at heart, the Pathfinder chronicler travels to distant, exotic lands to expand her knowledge of the world.

Shadowdancer: A mysterious adventurer who walks the boundaries between the real world and the realm of shadows, and who can command shadows to do her bidding.

Definitions of Terms

Here are definitions of some terms used in this section.

Core Class: One of the standard eleven classes found in Chapter 3.

Caster Level: Generally equal to the number of class levels (see below) in a spellcasting class. Some prestige classes add caster levels to an existing class.

Character Level: The total level of the character, which is the sum of all class levels held by that character.

Class Level: The level of a character in a particular class. For a character with levels in only one class, class level and character level are the same.

ARCANE ARCHER

Many who seek to perfect the use of the bow sometimes pursue the path of the arcane archer. Arcane archers are masters of ranged combat, as they possess the ability to strike at targets with unerring accuracy and can imbue their arrows with powerful spells. Arrows fired by arcane archers fly at weird and uncanny angles to strike at foes around corners, and can pass through solid objects to hit enemies that cower behind such cover. At the height of their power, arcane archers can fell even the most powerful foes with a single, deadly shot.

Those who have trained as both rangers and wizards excel as arcane archers, although other multiclass combinations are not unheard of. Arcane archers may be found wherever elves travel, but not all are allies of the elves. Many, particularly half-elven arcane archers, use elven traditions solely for their own gain, or worse, against the elves whose very traditions they adhere to.

Role: Arcane archers deal death from afar, winnowing down opponents while their allies rush into hand-to-hand combat. With their capacity to unleash hails of arrows on the enemy, they represent the pinnacle of ranged combat.

Alignment: Arcane archers can be of any alignment. Elf or half-elf arcane archers tend to be free-spirited and are rarely lawful. Similarly, it is uncommon for elven arcane archers to be evil, and overall the path of the arcane archer is more often pursued by good or neutral characters.

Hit Die: d10.

Requirements

To qualify to become an arcane archer, a character must fulfill all the following criteria.

Base Attack Bonus: +6.

Feats: Point Blank Shot, Precise Shot, Weapon Focus (longbow or shortbow).

Spells: Ability to cast 1st-level arcane spells.

Class Skills

The arcane archer's class skills (and the key ability for each skill) are Perception (Wis), Ride (Dex), Stealth (Dex), and Survival (Wis).

Skill Ranks Per Level: 4 + Int modifier.

Class Features

All of the following are class features of the arcane archer prestige class.

Weapon and Armor Proficiency: An arcane archer is proficient with all simple and martial weapons, light armor, medium armor, and shields.

Spells per Day: At the indicated levels, an arcane archer gains new spells per day as if he had also gained a level in an arcane spellcasting class he belonged to before adding the prestige class. He does not, however, gain other benefits a character of that class would have gained, except for additional spells per day, spells known (if he is a spontaneous spellcaster), and an increased effective level of spellcasting. If a character had more than one arcane spellcasting class before becoming an arcane archer, he must decide to which class he adds the new level for purposes of determining spells per day.

Enhance Arrows (Su): At 1st level, every nonmagical arrow an arcane archer nocks and lets fly becomes magical, gaining a +1 enhancement bonus. Unlike magic weapons created by normal means, the archer need not spend gold pieces to accomplish this task. However, an archer's magic arrows only function for him.

In addition, the arcane archer's arrows gain a number of additional qualities as he gains additional levels. The elemental, elemental burst, and aligned qualities can be changed once per day, when the arcane archer prepares spells or, in the case of spontaneous spellcasters, after 8 hours of rest.

At 3rd level, every nonmagical arrow fired by an arcane archer gains one of the following elemental themed weapon qualities: *flaming*, *frost*, or *shock*.

At 5th level, every nonmagical arrow fired by an arcane archer gains the *distance* weapon quality.

At 7th level, every nonmagical arrow fired by an arcane archer gains one of the following elemental burst weapon qualities: *flaming burst*, *icy burst*, or *shocking burst*. This ability replaces the ability gained at 3rd level.

At 9th level, every nonmagical arrow fired by an arcane archer gains one of the following aligned weapon qualities: *anarchic*, *axiomatic*, *holy*, or *unholy*. The arcane archer cannot choose an ability that is the opposite of his alignment (for example, a lawful good arcane archer could not choose *anarchic* or *unholy* as his weapon quality).

The bonuses granted by a magic bow apply as normal to

TABLE 11-1: ARCANE ARCHER

Level	Base Attack Bonus	Fort Save	Ref Save	Will Save	Special	Spells per Day
1st	+1	+1	+1	+0	Enhance arrows (magic)	—
2nd	+2	+1	+1	+1	Imbue arrow	+1 level of existing class
3rd	+3	+2	+2	+1	Enhance arrows (elemental)	+1 level of existing class
4th	+4	+2	+2	+1	Seeker arrow	+1 level of existing class
5th	+5	+3	+3	+2	Enhance arrows (*distance*)	—
6th	+6	+3	+3	+2	Phase arrow	+1 level of existing class
7th	+7	+4	+4	+2	Enhance arrows (elemental burst)	+1 level of existing class
8th	+8	+4	+4	+3	Hail of arrows	+1 level of existing class
9th	+9	+5	+5	+3	Enhance arrows (aligned)	—
10th	+10	+5	+5	+3	Arrow of death	+1 level of existing class

arrows that have been enhanced with this ability. Only the larger enhancement bonus applies. Duplicate abilities do not stack.

Imbue Arrow (Su): At 2nd level, an arcane archer gains the ability to place an area spell upon an arrow. When the arrow is fired, the spell's area is centered where the arrow lands, even if the spell could normally be centered only on the caster. This ability allows the archer to use the bow's range rather than the spell's range. A spell cast in this way uses its standard casting time and the arcane archer can fire the arrow as part of the casting. The arrow must be fired during the round that the casting is completed or the spell is wasted. If the arrow misses, the spell is wasted.

Seeker Arrow (Su): At 4th level, an arcane archer can launch an arrow at a target known to him within range, and the arrow travels to the target, even around corners. Only an unavoidable obstacle or the limit of the arrow's range prevents the arrow's flight. This ability negates cover and concealment modifiers, but otherwise the attack is rolled normally. Using this ability is a standard action (and shooting the arrow is part of the action). An arcane archer can use this ability once per day at 4th level, and one additional time per day for every two levels beyond 4th, to a maximum of four times per day at 10th level.

Phase Arrow (Su): At 6th level, an arcane archer can launch an arrow once per day at a target known to him within range, and the arrow travels to the target in a straight path, passing through any nonmagical barrier or wall in its way. (Any magical barrier stops the arrow.) This ability negates cover, concealment, armor, and shield modifiers, but otherwise the attack is rolled normally. Using this ability is a standard action (and shooting the arrow is part of the action). An arcane archer can use this ability once per day at 6th level, and one additional time per day for every two levels beyond 6th, to a maximum of three times per day at 10th level.

Hail of Arrows (Su): In lieu of his regular attacks, once per day an arcane archer of 8th level or higher can fire an arrow at each and every target within range, to a maximum of one target for every arcane archer level she has earned. Each attack uses the archer's primary attack bonus, and each enemy may only be targeted by a single arrow.

Arrow of Death (Su): At 10th level, an arcane archer can create a special type of *slaying arrow* that forces the target, if damaged by the arrow's attack, to make a Fortitude save or be slain immediately. The DC of this save is equal to 20 + the arcane archer's Charisma modifier. It takes 1 day to make a *slaying arrow*, and the arrow only functions for the arcane archer who created it. The *slaying arrow* lasts no longer than 1 year, and the archer can only have one such arrow in existence at a time.

ARCANE TRICKSTER

Few can match the guile and craftiness of arcane tricksters. These prodigious thieves blend the subtlest aspects of the arcane with the natural cunning of the bandit and the scoundrel, using spells to enhance their natural thieving abilities. Arcane tricksters can pick locks, disarm traps, and lift purses from a safe distance using their magical legerdemain, and as often as not seek humiliation as a goal to triumph over their foes than more violent solutions.

The path to becoming an arcane trickster is a natural progression for rogues who have supplemented their talents for theft with the study of the arcane. Multiclass rogue/sorcerers and rogue/bards are the most common arcane tricksters, although other combinations are possible. Arcane tricksters are most often found in large, cosmopolitan cities where their talents for magical larceny can be most effectively put to use, prowling the streets and stealing from the unwary.

Role: With their mastery of magic, arcane tricksters can make for even more subtle or confounding opponents than standard rogues. Ranged legerdemain enhances their skill as thieves, and their ability to make sneak attacks without flanking or as part of a spell can make arcane tricksters formidable damage-dealers.

Alignment: All arcane tricksters have a penchant for mischief and thievery, and are therefore never lawful. Although they sometimes acquire their magical abilities through the studious path of wizardry, their magical aptitude more often stems from a sorcerous bloodline. As such, many arcane tricksters are of a chaotic alignment.

Hit Die: d6.

Requirements

To qualify to become an arcane trickster, a character must fulfill all of the following criteria.

Alignment: Any nonlawful.

Skills: Disable Device 4 ranks, Escape Artist 4 ranks, Knowledge (arcana) 4 ranks.

Spells: Ability to cast *mage hand* and at least one arcane spell of 2nd level or higher.

Special: Sneak attack +2d6.

Class Skills

The arcane trickster's class skills (and the key ability for each skill) are Acrobatics (Dex), Appraise (Int), Bluff (Cha), Climb (Str), Diplomacy (Cha), Disable Device (Int), Disguise (Cha), Escape Artist (Dex), Knowledge (all skills taken individually) (Int), Perception (Wis), Sense Motive (Wis), Sleight of Hand (Dex), Spellcraft (Int), Stealth (Dex), and Swim (Str).

Skill Ranks Per Level: 4 + Int modifier.

TABLE 11-2: ARCANE TRICKSTER

Level	Base Attack Bonus	Fort Save	Ref Save	Will Save	Special	Spells per Day
1st	+0	+0	+1	+1	Ranged legerdemain	+1 level of existing class
2nd	+1	+1	+1	+1	Sneak attack +1d6	+1 level of existing class
3rd	+1	+1	+2	+2	Impromptu sneak attack 1/day	+1 level of existing class
4th	+2	+1	+2	+2	Sneak attack +2d6	+1 level of existing class
5th	+2	+2	+3	+3	Tricky spells 3/day	+1 level of existing class
6th	+3	+2	+3	+3	Sneak attack +3d6	+1 level of existing class
7th	+3	+2	+4	+4	Impromptu sneak attack 2/day, Tricky spells 4/day	+1 level of existing class
8th	+4	+3	+4	+4	Sneak attack +4d6	+1 level of existing class
9th	+4	+3	+5	+5	Invisible thief, Tricky spells 5/day	+1 level of existing class
10th	+5	+3	+5	+5	Sneak attack +5d6, surprise spells	+1 level of existing class

Class Features

All of the following are class features of the arcane trickster prestige class.

Weapon and Armor Proficiency: Arcane tricksters gain no proficiency with any weapon or armor.

Spells per Day: When a new arcane trickster level is gained, the character gains new spells per day as if she had also gained a level in a spellcasting class she belonged to before adding the prestige class. She does not, however, gain other benefits a character of that class would have gained, except for additional spells per day, spells known (if she is a spontaneous spellcaster), and an increased effective level of spellcasting. If a character had more than one spellcasting class before becoming an arcane trickster, she must decide to which class she adds the new level for purposes of determining spells per day.

Ranged Legerdemain (Su): An arcane trickster can use Disable Device and Sleight of Hand at a range of 30 feet. Working at a distance increases the normal skill check DC by 5, and an arcane trickster cannot take 10 on this check. Any object to be manipulated must weigh 5 pounds or less. She can only use this ability if she has at least 1 rank in the skill being used.

Sneak Attack: This is exactly like the rogue ability of the same name. The extra damage dealt increases by +1d6 every other level (2nd, 4th, 6th, 8th, and 10th). If an arcane trickster gets a sneak attack bonus from another source, the bonuses on damage stack.

Impromptu Sneak Attack (Ex): Beginning at 3rd level, once per day an arcane trickster can declare one melee or ranged attack she makes to be a sneak attack (the target can be no more than 30 feet distant if the impromptu sneak attack is a ranged attack). The target of an impromptu

sneak attack loses any Dexterity bonus to AC, but only against that attack. The power can be used against any target, but creatures that are not subject to critical hits take no extra damage (though they still lose any Dexterity bonus to AC against the attack).

At 7th level, an arcane trickster can use this ability twice per day.

Tricky Spells (Su): Starting at 5th level, an arcane trickster can cast her spells without their somatic or verbal components, as if using the Still Spell and Silent Spell feats. Spells cast using this ability do not increase in spell level or casting time. She can use this ability 3 times per day at 5th level and one additional time per every two levels thereafter, to a maximum of 5 times per day at 9th level. The arcane trickster decides to use this ability at the time of casting.

Invisible Thief (Su): At 9th level, an arcane trickster can become invisible, as if under the effects of *greater invisibility*, as a free action. She can remain invisible for a number of rounds per day equal to her arcane trickster level. Her caster level for this effect is equal to her caster level. These rounds need not be consecutive.

Surprise Spells: At 10th level, an arcane trickster can add her sneak attack damage to any spell that deals damage, if the targets are flat-footed. This additional damage only applies to spells that deal hit point damage, and the additional damage is of the same type as the spell. If the spell allows a saving throw to negate or halve the damage, it also negates or halves the sneak attack damage.

ASSASSIN

A mercenary undertaking his task with cold, professional detachment, the assassin is equally adept at espionage, bounty hunting, and terrorism. At his core, an assassin is an artisan, and his medium is death. Trained in a variety of killing techniques, assassins are among the most feared classes.

While nearly any class is capable of becoming an assassin, rogues suit the part more than any other, from both an ability viewpoint and an ideological one. Though they make excellent allies during combat, assassins excel in more clandestine situations, and the best assassins are the ones the victims never knew existed.

Role: Assassins tend to be loners by nature, seeing companions as liabilities at best. Sometimes an assassin's missions put him in the company of adventurers for long stretches at a time, but few people are comfortable trusting a professional assassin to watch their backs in a fight, and are more likely to let the emotionless killer scout ahead or help prepare ambushes.

Alignment: Due to its necessary selfishness and callous indifference toward taking lives, the assassin class attracts those with evil alignments more than any others. Because the profession requires a degree of self-discipline, chaotic characters are ill suited to becoming these shadowy killers. Neutral characters sometimes become assassins, frequently thinking of themselves as simple professionals performing a job, yet the nature of their duties inevitably pushes them toward an evil alignment.

Hit Die: d8.

Requirements

To qualify to become an assassin, a character must fulfill all the following criteria.

Alignment: Any evil.

Skills: Disguise 2 ranks, Stealth 5 ranks.

Special: The character must kill someone for no other reason than to become an assassin.

Class Skills

The assassin's class skills (and the key ability for each skill) are Acrobatics (Dex), Bluff (Cha), Climb (Str), Diplomacy (Cha), Disable Device (Int), Disguise (Cha), Escape Artist (Dex), Intimidate (Cha), Linguistics (Int), Perception (Wis), Sense Motive (Wis), Sleight of Hand (Dex), Stealth (Dex), Swim (Str), and Use Magic Device (Cha).

Skill Ranks Per Level: 4 + Int modifier.

Class Features

All of the following are class features of the assassin prestige class.

Weapon and Armor Proficiency: Assassins are proficient with the crossbow (hand, light, or heavy), dagger (any type), dart, rapier, sap, shortbow (normal and composite), and short sword. Assassins are proficient with light armor but not with shields.

Sneak Attack: This is exactly like the rogue ability of the same name. The extra damage dealt increases by +1d6 every other level (1st, 3rd, 5th, 7th, and 9th). If an assassin gets a sneak attack bonus from another source, the bonuses on damage stack.

Death Attack (Ex): If an assassin studies his victim for 3 rounds and then makes a sneak attack with a melee weapon that successfully deals damage, the sneak attack has the additional effect of possibly either paralyzing or killing the target (assassin's choice). Studying the victim is a standard action. The death attack fails if the target detects the assassin or recognizes the assassin as an enemy (although the attack might still be a sneak attack if the target is denied his Dexterity bonus to his Armor Class or is flanked). If the victim of such a death attack fails a Fortitude save (DC 10 + the assassin's class level + the assassin's Int modifier) against the kill effect, she dies. If the saving throw fails against the paralysis effect, the victim is rendered helpless and unable to act for 1d6 rounds plus 1 round per level of the assassin.

TABLE 11-3: ASSASSIN

Level	Base Attack Bonus	Fort Save	Ref Save	Will Save	Special
1st	+0	+0	+1	+0	Sneak attack +1d6, death attack, poison use
2nd	+1	+1	+1	+1	+1 save bonus against poison, uncanny dodge
3rd	+2	+1	+2	+1	Sneak attack +2d6
4th	+3	+1	+2	+1	+2 save bonus against poison, hidden weapons, true death
5th	+3	+2	+3	+2	Improved uncanny dodge, Sneak attack +3d6
6th	+4	+2	+3	+2	+3 save bonus against poison, quiet death
7th	+5	+2	+4	+2	Sneak attack +4d6
8th	+6	+3	+4	+3	+4 save bonus against poison, hide in plain sight
9th	+6	+3	+5	+3	Sneak attack +5d6, swift death
10th	+7	+3	+5	+3	+5 save bonus against poison, angel of death

If the victim's saving throw succeeds, the attack is just a normal sneak attack. Once the assassin has completed the 3 rounds of study, he must make the death attack within the next 3 rounds.

If a death attack is attempted and fails (the victim makes her save) or if the assassin does not launch the attack within 3 rounds of completing the study, 3 new rounds of study are required before he can attempt another death attack.

Poison Use: Assassins are trained in the use of poison and cannot accidentally poison themselves when applying poison to a blade (see Poison, page 557).

Save Bonus against Poison: At 2nd level, the assassin gains a +1 saving throw bonus against poisons. This bonus increase by +1 every two levels.

Uncanny Dodge (Ex): At 2nd level, an assassin cannot be caught flat-footed, even if the attacker is invisible. He still loses his Dexterity bonus to AC if immobilized. An assassin with this ability can still lose his Dexterity bonus to AC if an opponent successfully uses the feint action against him.

If an assassin already has uncanny dodge from a different class, he automatically gains improved uncanny dodge instead.

Hidden Weapons (Ex): At 4th level, an assassin becomes a master at hiding weapons on his body. He adds his assassin level to all Sleight of Hand skill checks made to prevent others from noticing them.

True Death (Su): Starting at 4th level, anyone slain by an assassin's death attack becomes more difficult to bring back from the dead. Spellcasters attempting to bring a creature back from the dead using *raise dead* or similar magic must make a caster level check with a DC equal to 15 + the assassin's level or the spell fails and the material component is wasted. Casting *remove curse* the round before attempting to bring the creature back from the dead negates this chance. The DC of the *remove curse* is 10 + the assassin's level.

Improved Uncanny Dodge (Ex): At 5th level and higher, an assassin can no longer be flanked. This defense

denies a rogue the ability to sneak attack the assassin by flanking him, unless the attacker has at least four more rogue levels than the target has assassin levels.

If a character already has uncanny dodge from another class, the levels from the classes that grant uncanny dodge stack to determine the minimum rogue level required to flank the character.

Quiet Death (Ex): At 6th level, whenever an assassin kills a creature using his death attack during a surprise round, he can also make a Stealth check, opposed by Perception checks of those in the vicinity to prevent them from identifying him as the assailant. If successful, those nearby might not even notice that the target is dead for a few moments, allowing the assassin to avoid detection.

Hide in Plain Sight (Su): At 8th level, an assassin can use the Stealth skill even while being observed. As long as he is within 10 feet of an area of dim light, an assassin can hide himself from view in the open without having anything to actually hide behind. He cannot, however, hide in his own shadow.

Swift Death (Ex): At 9th level, once per day, an assassin can make a death attack against a foe without studying the foe beforehand. He must still sneak attack his foe using a melee weapon that deals damage.

Angel of Death (Su): At 10th level, the assassin becomes a master of death. Once per day, when the assassin makes a successful death attack, he can cause the target's body to crumble to dust. This prevents *raise dead* and *resurrection* (although *true resurrection* works as normal). The assassin must declare the use of this ability before the attack is made. If the attack misses or the target successfully saves against the death attack, this ability is wasted with no effect.

DRAGON DISCIPLE

As some of the most ancient, powerful, and capricious creatures in existence, dragons occasionally enter into trysts with unsuspecting mortals or sire offspring with exceptional individuals. Likewise, the great power wielded by these creatures has long intrigued wizards and alchemists who have sought various magical methods to infuse their bodies with draconic power. As a result, the blood of dragons runs through the veins of many races. For some, this heritage manifests as a sorcerous bloodline and a predilection for magic; for others, however, the power of their draconic ancestors becomes an obsession.

Spellcasters who embrace their draconic heritage and learn to channel their abilities can become dragon disciples, fearsome warriors who possess not only the repertoire of an accomplished sorcerer but also the ability to unleash the furious power of dragons upon their foes. As dragon disciples discover the power of their forebears, they can learn to breathe fire, take flight on leathery wings, and—at the pinnacle of their abilities—assume the form of a dragon. Although they are rare, dragon disciples can be found in any land where dragons interact with mortals.

Role: With the magic of a spellcasting class at their disposal, dragon disciples can assume the typical role of a magic-user, hampering the movement of the enemy and hurling damage-dealing spells at their opponents. Dragon disciples' draconic abilities, however, make these versatile spellcasters even more formidable, as they use their breath weapons and flight to destroy their foes directly.

Alignment: Dragon disciples can be of any alignment, although they tend to be more chaotic than lawful. Those dragon disciples that assume the traits of chromatic dragons, such as bestial white and fearsome red dragons, have a proclivity for evil. Conversely, those that take after the metallic dragons, such as stoic brass and chivalric gold dragons, are often of good alignments.

Hit Die: d12.

Requirements

To qualify to become a dragon disciple, a character must fulfill all the following criteria.

TABLE 11-4: DRAGON DISCIPLE

Level	Base Attack Bonus	Fort Save	Ref Save	Will Save	Special	Spells per Day
1st	+0	+1	+0	+1	Blood of dragons, natural armor increase (+1)	—
2nd	+1	+1	+1	+1	Ability boost (Str +2), bloodline feat, dragon bite	+1 level of existing arcane spellcasting class
3rd	+2	+2	+1	+2	Breath weapon	+1 level of existing arcane spellcasting class
4th	+3	+2	+1	+2	Ability boost (Str +2), natural armor increase (+1)	+1 level of existing arcane spellcasting class
5th	+3	+3	+2	+3	Blindsense 30 ft., bloodline feat	—
6th	+4	+3	+2	+3	Ability boost (Con +2)	+1 level of existing arcane spellcasting class
7th	+5	+4	+2	+4	Dragon form (1/day), natural armor increase (+1)	+1 level of existing arcane spellcasting class
8th	+6	+4	+3	+4	Ability boost (Int +2), bloodline feat	+1 level of existing arcane spellcasting class
9th	+6	+5	+3	+5	Wings	—
10th	+7	+5	+3	+5	Blindsense 60 ft., Dragon form (2/day)	+1 level of existing arcane spellcasting class

Race: Any nondragon.

Skills: Knowledge (arcana) 5 ranks.

Languages: Draconic.

Spellcasting: Ability to cast 1st-level arcane spells without preparation. If the character has sorcerer levels, he must have the draconic bloodline. If the character gains levels of sorcerer after taking this class, he must take the draconic bloodline.

Class Skills

The dragon disciple's class skills (and the key ability for each skill) are Diplomacy (Cha), Escape Artist (Dex), Fly (Dex), Knowledge (all skills taken individually) (Int), Perception (Wis), and Spellcraft (Int).

Skill Ranks Per Level: 2 + Int modifier.

Class Features

All of the following are class features of the dragon disciple prestige class.

Weapon and Armor Proficiency: Dragon disciples gain no proficiency with any weapon or armor.

Spells per Day: At the indicated levels, a dragon disciple gains new spells per day as if he had also gained a level in an arcane spellcasting class he belonged to before adding the prestige class. He does not, however, gain other benefits a character of that class would have gained, except for additional spells per day, spells known (if he is a spontaneous spellcaster), and an increased effective level of spellcasting. If a character had more than one arcane spellcasting class before becoming a dragon disciple, he must decide to which class he adds the new level for purposes of determining spells per day.

Blood of Dragons: A dragon disciple adds his level to his sorcerer levels when determining the powers gained from his bloodline. If the dragon disciple does not have levels of sorcerer, he instead gains bloodline powers of the draconic bloodline, using his dragon disciple level as his sorcerer level to determine the bonuses gained. He must choose a dragon type upon gaining his first level in this class and that type must be the same as his sorcerer type. This ability does not grant bonus spells to a sorcerer unless he possesses spell slots of an appropriate level. Such bonus spells are automatically granted if the sorcerer gains spell slots of the spell's level.

Natural Armor Increase (Ex): As his skin thickens, a dragon disciple takes on more and more of his progenitor's physical aspect. At 1st, 4th, and 7th level, a dragon disciple gains an increase to the character's existing natural armor (if any), as indicated on Table 11–4. These armor bonuses stack.

Ability Boost (Ex): As a dragon disciple gains levels in this prestige class, his ability scores increase as noted on Table 11–4. These increases stack and are gained as if through level advancement.

Bloodline Feat: Upon reaching 2nd level, and every three levels thereafter, a dragon disciple receives one bonus feat,

chosen from the draconic bloodline's bonus feat list (see page 75).

Dragon Bite (Ex): At 2nd level, whenever the dragon disciple uses his bloodline to grow claws, he also gains a bite attack. This is a primary natural attack that deals 1d6 points of damage (1d4 if the dragon disciple is Small), plus 1–1/2 times the dragon disciple's Strength modifier. Upon reaching 6th level, this bite also deals 1d6 points of energy damage. The type of damage dealt is determined by the dragon disciple's bloodline.

Breath Weapon (Su): At 3rd level, a dragon disciple gains the breath weapon bloodline power, even if his level does not yet grant that power. Once his level is high enough to grant this ability through the bloodline, the dragon disciple gains an additional use of his breath weapon each day. The type and shape of the breath weapon depends on the type of dragon selected by the dragon disciple, as detailed under the Draconic sorcerer bloodline description (see page 75).

Blindsense (Ex): At 5th level, the dragon disciple gains blindsense with a range of 30 feet. Using nonvisual senses the dragon disciple notices things he cannot see. He usually does not need to make Perception checks to notice and pinpoint the location of creatures within range of his blindsense ability, provided that he has line of effect (see page 215) to that creature.

Any opponent the dragon disciple cannot see still has total concealment against him, and the dragon disciple still has the normal miss chance when attacking foes that have concealment. Visibility still affects the movement of a creature with blindsense. A creature with blindsense is still denied its Dexterity bonus to Armor Class against attacks from creatures it cannot see. At 10th level, the range of this ability increases to 60 feet.

Dragon Form (Sp): At 7th level, a dragon disciple can assume the form of a dragon. This ability works like *form of the dragon I*. At 10th level, this ability functions as *form of the dragon II* and the dragon disciple can use this ability twice per day. His caster level for this effect is equal to his effective sorcerer levels for his draconic bloodline. Whenever he casts *form of the dragon*, he must assume the form of a dragon of the same type as his bloodline.

Wings (Su): At 9th level, a dragon disciple gains the wings bloodline power, even if his level does not yet grant this ability through the bloodline, the dragon disciple's speed increases to 90 feet.

DUELIST

Duelists represent the pinnacle of elegant swordplay. They move with a grace unmatched by most foes, parrying blows and countering attacks with swift thrusts of their blades. They may wear armor, but generally eschew such bulky protection as their grace allows them to dodge their opponents with ease. While others flounder on treacherous terrain, duelists charge nimbly across the battlefield, leaping and tumbling into the fray. They thrive in melee, where their skill with the blade allows them to make sudden attacks against clumsy foes and to cripple opponents with particularly well-placed thrusts of the blade.

The path to the duelist is natural for rogues and bards, as those classes do not rely on armor for defense, although nearly as many duelists come from the ranks of fighters and rangers. They are often found in those regions that possess elaborate rules and etiquette for battle.

Role: The abilities of duelists complement those rogues or bards who wish to accentuate their fighting prowess but, because of their lack of heavy armor, are afraid to leap into combat. Duelists fight in the forefront alongside fighters, barbarians, and other melee combatants, deftly avoiding the blades of their opponents while expertly targeting their vulnerabilities.

Alignment: Duelists can be of any alignment, although since most hail from backgrounds as rogues or bards, they tend to eschew lawful behavior. Lawful duelists are not unheard of, however, and such duelists often adhere to a strict code of honor, refusing to attack unarmed or obviously inferior opponents.

Hit Die: d10.

Requirements

To qualify to become a duelist, a character must fulfill all the following criteria.

Base Attack Bonus: +6.

Skills: Acrobatics 2 ranks, Perform 2 ranks. **Feats:** Dodge, Mobility, Weapon Finesse.

Class Skills

The duelist's class skills (and the key ability for each skill) are Acrobatics (Dex), Bluff (Cha), Escape Artist (Dex), Perception (Wis), Perform (Cha), and Sense Motive (Wis).

Skill Ranks Per Level: 4 + Int modifier.

Class Features

All of the following are class features of the duelist prestige class.

Weapon and Armor Proficiency: The duelist is proficient with all simple and martial weapons. Duelists are proficient with light armor but not with shields.

Canny Defense (Ex): When wearing light or no armor and not using a shield, a duelist adds 1 point of Intelligence bonus (if any) per duelist class level as a dodge bonus to her Armor Class while wielding a melee weapon. If a duelist is caught flat-footed or otherwise denied her Dexterity bonus, she also loses this bonus.

TABLE 11-5: DUELIST

Level	Base Attack Bonus	Fort Save	Ref Save	Will Save	Special
1st	+1	+0	+1	+0	Canny defense, precise strike
2nd	+2	+1	+1	+1	Improved reaction +2, parry
3rd	+3	+1	+2	+1	Enhanced mobility
4th	+4	+1	+2	+1	Combat Reflexes, grace
5th	+5	+2	+3	+2	Riposte
6th	+6	+2	+3	+2	Acrobatic charge
7th	+7	+2	+4	+2	Elaborate defense
8th	+8	+3	+4	+3	Improved reaction +4
9th	+9	+3	+5	+3	Deflect Arrows, no retreat
10th	+10	+3	+5	+3	Crippling critical

Precise Strike (Ex): A duelist gains the ability to strike precisely with a light or one-handed piercing weapon, adding her duelist level to her damage roll.

When making a precise strike, a duelist cannot attack with a weapon in her other hand or use a shield. A duelist's precise strike only works against living creatures with discernible anatomies. Any creature that is immune to critical hits is also immune to a precise strike, and any item or ability that protects a creature from critical hits also protects a creature from a precise strike.

Improved Reaction (Ex): At 2nd level, a duelist gains a +2 bonus on initiative checks. At 8th level, the bonus increases to +4. This bonus stacks with the benefit provided by the Improved Initiative feat.

Parry (Ex): At 2nd level, a duelist learns to parry the attacks of other creatures, causing them to miss. Whenever the duelist takes a full attack action with a light or one-handed piercing weapon, she can elect not to take one of her attacks. At any time before her next turn, she can attempt to parry an attack against her or an adjacent ally as an immediate action. To parry the attack, the duelist makes an attack roll, using the same bonuses as the attack she chose to forego during her previous action. If her attack roll is greater than the roll of the attacking creature, the attack automatically misses. For each size category that the attacking creature is larger than the duelist, the duelist takes a –4 penalty on her attack roll. The duelist also takes a –4 penalty when attempting to parry an attack made against an adjacent ally. The duelist must declare the use of this ability after the attack is announced, but before the roll is made.

Enhanced Mobility (Ex): Starting at 3rd level, when wearing light or no armor and not using a shield, a duelist gains an additional +4 bonus to AC against attacks of opportunity caused when she moves out of a threatened square.

Combat Reflexes: At 4th level, a duelist gains the benefit of the Combat Reflexes feat when using a light or one-handed piercing weapon.

Grace (Ex): At 4th level, a duelist gains an additional +2 competence bonus on all Reflex saving throws. This ability functions for a duelist only when she is wearing light or no armor and not using a shield.

Riposte (Ex): Starting at 5th level, a duelist can make an attack of opportunity against any creature whose attack she successfully parries, so long as the creature she is attacking is within reach.

Acrobatic Charge (Ex): At 6th level, a duelist gains the ability to charge in situations where others cannot. She may charge over difficult terrain that normally slows movement. Depending on the circumstance, she may still need to make appropriate checks to successfully move over the terrain.

Elaborate Defense (Ex): At 7th level and higher, if a duelist chooses to fight defensively or use total defense in melee combat, she gains an additional +1 dodge bonus to AC for every 3 levels of duelist she has attained.

Deflect Arrows: At 9th level, a duelist gains the benefit of the Deflect Arrows feat when using a light or one-handed piercing weapon. The duelist does not need a free hand to use this feat.

No Retreat (Ex): At 9th level, enemies adjacent to the duelist that take a withdraw action provoke an attack of opportunity from the duelist.

Crippling Critical (Ex): When you confirm a critical hit using a light or one-handed piercing weapon, you can apply one of the following penalties in addition to the damage dealt: reduce all of the target's speeds by 10 feet (minimum 5 feet), 1d4 points of Strength or Dexterity damage, −4 penalty on all saving throws, −4 penalty to Armor Class, or 2d6 points of bleed damage. These penalties last for 1 minute, except for ability damage, which must be healed normally, and bleed damage, which continues until the target receives magic healing or a DC 15 Heal skill check.

ELDRITCH KNIGHT

Fearsome warriors and spellcasters, eldritch knights are rare among magic-users in their ability to wade into battle alongside fighters, barbarians, and other martial classes. Those who must face eldritch knights in combat fear them greatly, for their versatility on the battlefield is tremendous; against heavily armed and armored opponents they may level crippling spells, while opposing spellcasters meet their ends on an eldritch knight's blade.

Because the road to becoming an eldritch knight requires both martial prowess and arcane power, eldritch knights almost always begin their paths as multiclassed characters, such as fighter/wizards or ranger/sorcerers. They may be found wherever studies of the arcane are as prevalent as martial training.

Role: Eldritch knights blend the abilities of fighting classes and spellcasters, hurling magic at the enemy one moment and hewing down their opponents with steel the next. They are just as comfortable fighting in the thick of combat as they are casting spells at foes while remaining safely behind their compatriots. Their versatility makes them valuable allies when the nature of an upcoming battle is unclear.

Alignment: The road to becoming an eldritch knight is as varied as the paths leading to apprenticeship under a wizard or a career as a soldier, and eldritch knights can therefore be of any alignment. Maintaining a balance between studies of arcane lore and martial techniques requires great discipline, however, and for that reason many favor lawful alignments.

Hit Die: d10.

Requirements

To qualify to become an eldritch knight, a character must fulfill all the following criteria.

Weapon Proficiency: Must be proficient with all martial weapons.

Spells: Able to cast 3rd-level arcane spells.

Class Skills

The eldritch knight's class skills (and the key ability for each skill) are Climb (Str), Knowledge (arcana) (Int), Knowledge (nobility) (Int), Linguistics (Int), Ride (Dex), Sense Motive (Wis), Spellcraft (Int), and Swim (Str).

Skill Ranks Per Level: 2 + Int modifier.

Class Features

All of the following are features of the eldritch knight prestige class.

TABLE 11–6: ELDRITCH KNIGHT

Level	Base Attack Bonus	Fort Save	Ref Save	Will Save	Special	Spells per Day
1st	+1	+1	+0	+0	Bonus combat feat, diverse training	—
2nd	+2	+1	+1	+1	—	+1 level of existing arcane spellcasting class
3rd	+3	+2	+1	+1	—	+1 level of existing arcane spellcasting class
4th	+4	+2	+1	+1	—	+1 level of existing arcane spellcasting class
5th	+5	+3	+2	+2	Bonus combat feat	+1 level of existing arcane spellcasting class
6th	+6	+3	+2	+2	—	+1 level of existing arcane spellcasting class
7th	+7	+4	+2	+2	—	+1 level of existing arcane spellcasting class
8th	+8	+4	+3	+3	—	+1 level of existing arcane spellcasting class
9th	+9	+5	+3	+3	Bonus combat feat	+1 level of existing arcane spellcasting class
10th	+10	+5	+3	+3	Spell critical	+1 level of existing arcane spellcasting class

Weapon and Armor Proficiency: Eldritch knights gain no proficiency with any weapon or armor.

Bonus Feat: At 1st level, an eldritch knight may choose a bonus combat feat. This is in addition to the feats that a character of any class normally gets from advancing levels. The character must still meet any prerequisites for these bonus feats. An eldritch knight gains an additional combat feat at 5th and 9th level.

Diverse Training: An eldritch knight adds his level to any levels of fighter he might have for the purpose of meeting the prerequisites for feats (if he has no fighter levels, treat his eldritch knight levels as levels of fighter). He also adds his level to any levels in an arcane spellcasting class for the purpose of meeting the prerequisites for feats.

Spells per Day: At the indicated levels, an eldritch knight gains new spells per day as if he had also gained a level in an arcane spellcasting class he belonged to before adding the prestige class. He does not, however, gain any other benefit a character of that class would have gained, except for additional spells per day, spells known (if he is a spontaneous spellcaster), and an increased effective level of spellcasting. If a character had more than one arcane spellcasting class before becoming an eldritch knight, he must decide to which class he adds the new level for purposes of determining spells per day.

Spell Critical (Su): At 10th level, whenever an eldritch knight successfully confirms a critical hit, he can cast a spell as a swift action. The spell must include the target of the attack as one of its targets or in its area of effect. Casting this spell does not provoke an attack of opportunity. The caster must still meet all of the spell's components and must roll for arcane spell failure if necessary.

LOREMASTER

The loremaster is a gatherer and keeper of secrets. He is often obsessed by the written word, with cryptic and arcane lore serving as his devoted mistress. Holding to the adage that knowledge is power, the loremaster often forsakes material wealth and personal glory for rare or unusual information, an endless quest that brings him ever closer to his unattainable goal: perfection through edification. Often rejecting what he views as the pointless affectations and transitory pleasures of his short-sighted neighbors, the loremaster believes that the only worthwhile goal in life is the acquisition of intellectual might. After all, wealth is spent, passions fade, and the power of the body is limited by age, while the mind's capacity to grow greater with time is infinite.

The loremaster class holds little appeal for non-spellcasters—indeed, before one can devote a life to the studies and traditions of the loremaster, a character must first master several spells of the school of divination. Most loremasters begin their paths as clerics or wizards, but any character capable of casting enough divination spells can, eventually, become a loremaster.

Role: Loremasters' lives are spent in study, research, and fieldwork. While the first two lend themselves to the loremaster's reputation as a bookish recluse, the latter oftentimes forces a loremaster to seek out the aid of adventurers who, through a mutually beneficial arrangement, might provide a degree of protection to the scholar while he seeks whatever knowledge he is after. For his part, the loremaster provides a wealth of information and arcane firepower to a party. Some loremasters actively deride those of their kind who fear to leave the safety of the temple or library, pointing out that only old lore can be discovered in books—new lore must be sought out in the world. These more active loremasters might join up with an adventuring party for the benefit of the journey, content with whatever knowledge might be picked up along the way.

Alignment: Most loremasters cannot be bothered with distracting and pointless philosophies such as ethics, and so tend to be neutral, neutral good, or neutral evil.

Hit Die: d6.

Requirements

To qualify to become a loremaster, a character must fulfill all the following criteria.

Skills: Knowledge (any two) 7 ranks in each.

Feats: Any three metamagic or item creation feats, plus Skill Focus (Knowledge [any individual Knowledge skill]).

Spells: Able to cast seven different divination spells, one of which must be 3rd level or higher.

Class Skills

The loremaster's class skills (and the key ability for each skill) are Appraise (Int), Diplomacy (Cha), Handle Animals (Cha), Heal (Wis), Knowledge (all skills taken individually) (Int), Linguistics (Int), Perform (Cha), Spellcraft (Int), and Use Magic Device (Cha).

Skill Ranks Per Level: 4 + Int modifier.

Class Features

All of the following are Class Features of the loremaster prestige class.

Weapon and Armor Proficiency: Loremasters gain no proficiency with any weapon or armor.

Spells per Day/Spells Known: When a new loremaster level is gained, the character gains new spells per day as if he had also gained a level in a spellcasting class he belonged to before adding the prestige class. He does not, however, gain other benefits a character of that class would have gained, except for additional spells per day, spells known (if he is a spontaneous spellcaster), and an increased effective level of spellcasting. If a character had more than one spellcasting class before becoming a loremaster, he must decide to which class he adds the new level for purposes of determining spells per day.

Secret: At 1st level and every two levels higher than 1st (3rd, 5th, 7th, and 9th), the loremaster chooses one secret from the Loremaster Secrets table. His level plus Intelligence modifier determines which secrets he can choose. He can't choose the same secret twice.

Lore: At 2nd level, a loremaster adds half his level to all Knowledge skill checks and may make such checks untrained. The bonuses gained from this ability stack with those gained from Bardic Knowledge.

Bonus Languages: A loremaster can learn any new language at 4th and 8th level.

Greater Lore (Ex): At 6th level, a loremaster gains the ability to understand magic items. Whenever a loremaster examines a magic item to determine its properties, he gains a +10 circumstance bonus on his Spellcraft skill check.

True Lore (Ex): At 10th level, a loremaster's knowledge becomes vast indeed. Once per day a loremaster can use his knowledge to gain the effect of a *legend lore* spell or an *analyze dweomer* spell. If used to create a *legend lore* effect, this ability has a casting time of 1 minute, regardless of how much information is already known about the subject in question.

TABLE 11-7: LOREMASTER

Level	Base Attack Bonus	Fort Save	Ref Save	Will Save	Special	Spells per Day
1st	+0	+0	+0	+1	Secret	+1 level of existing class
2nd	+1	+1	+1	+1	Lore	+1 level of existing class
3rd	+1	+1	+1	+2	Secret	+1 level of existing class
4th	+2	+1	+1	+2	Bonus language	+1 level of existing class
5th	+2	+2	+2	+3	Secret	+1 level of existing class
6th	+3	+2	+2	+3	Greater lore	+1 level of existing class
7th	+3	+2	+2	+4	Secret	+1 level of existing class
8th	+4	+3	+3	+4	Bonus language	+1 level of existing class
9th	+4	+3	+3	+5	Secret	+1 level of existing class
10th	+5	+3	+3	+5	True lore	+1 level of existing class

LOREMASTER SECRETS

Level + Int Modifier	Secret Effect
1 Instant mastery	4 ranks of a skill in which the character has no ranks
2 Secret health	Toughness bonus feat
3 Secrets of inner strength	+2 bonus on Will saves
4 The lore of true stamina	+2 bonus on Fortitude saves
5 Secret knowledge of avoidance	+2 bonus on Reflex saves
6 Weapon trick	+1 bonus on attack rolls
7 Dodge trick	+1 dodge bonus to AC
8 Applicable knowledge	Any one feat
9 Newfound arcana	1 bonus 1st-level spell*
10 More newfound arcana	1 bonus 2nd-level spell*

* As if gained through having a high ability score.

MYSTIC THEURGE

Mystic theurges place no boundaries on their magical abilities and find no irreconcilable paradox in devotion to the arcane as well as the divine. They seek magic in all of its forms, finding no reason or logic in denying themselves instruction by limiting their knowledge to one stifling paradigm, though many are simply hungry for limitless power. No matter what their motivations, mystic theurges believe that perception is reality, and through the divine forces and astral energies of the multiverse, that perception can be used to manipulate and control not only the nature of this reality, but destiny itself.

Mystic theurges are drawn from multiclass spellcasters who can already cast both arcane and divine spells, and the powers that they gain increase their mastery over both.

Role: The mystic theurge is a powerful component for any party, supplying magic for attack, defense, and healing. Mystic theurges travel the world in search of arcane and holy artifacts, magical lore, or divine revelations, and most have no qualms about teaming up with groups of adventurers so long as that group's goals do not directly conflict with their own.

Alignment: The motivations of a mystic theurge rarely stem from a sense of altruism or philanthropy, so most tend to be neutral, neutral good, or neutral evil. Lawful mystic theurges, whether good, neutral, or evil, are rarer, and often use their powers for either the benefit—or control—of society. Chaotic mystic theurges are rarer still, as the calling generally requires great personal discipline.

Hit Die: d6.

Requirements

To qualify to become a mystic theurge, a character must fulfill all the following criteria.

Skills: Knowledge (arcana) 3 ranks, Knowledge (religion) 3 ranks.

Spells: Able to cast 2nd-level divine spells and 2nd-level arcane spells.

Class Skills

The mystic theurge's class skills (and the key ability for each skill) are Knowledge (arcana) (Int), Knowledge (religion) (Int), Sense Motive (Wis), and Spellcraft (Int).

Skill Ranks Per Level: 2 + Int modifier.

Class Features

All of the following are features of the mystic theurge prestige class.

Weapon and Armor Proficiency: Mystic theurges gain no proficiency with any weapon or armor.

Spells per Day: When a new mystic theurge level is gained, the character gains new spells per day as if he had also gained a level in any one arcane spellcasting class he belonged to before he added the prestige class

and any one divine spellcasting class he belonged to previously. He does not, however, gain other benefits a character of that class would have gained. This essentially means that he adds the level of mystic theurge to the level of whatever other arcane spellcasting class and divine spellcasting class the character has, then determines spells per day, spells known, and caster level accordingly. If a character had more than one arcane spellcasting class or more than one divine spellcasting class before he became a mystic theurge, he must decide to which class he adds each level of mystic theurge for the purpose of determining spells per day.

Combined Spells (Su): A mystic theurge can prepare and cast spells from one of his spellcasting classes using the available slots from any of his other spellcasting classes. Spells prepared or cast in this way take up a slot one level higher than they originally occupied. This ability cannot be used to cast a spell at a lower level if that spell exists on both spell lists. At 1st level, a mystic theurge can prepare 1st-level spells from one of his spellcasting classes using the 2nd-level slots of the other spellcasting class. Every two levels thereafter, the level of spells that can be cast in this way increases by one, to a maximum of 5th-level spells at 9th level (these spells would take up 6th-level spell slots). The components of these spells do not change, but they otherwise follow the rules for the spellcasting class used to cast the spell.

Spontaneous spellcasters can only select spells that they have prepared that day using non-spontaneous classes for this ability, even if the spells have already been cast. For example, a cleric/sorcerer/mystic theurge can use this ability to spontaneously cast a *bless* spell using a 2nd-level sorcerer spell slot, if the character had a prepared *bless* spell using a 1st-level cleric spell slot, even if that spell had already been cast that day.

Spell Synthesis (Su): At 10th level, a mystic theurge can cast two spells, one from each of his spellcasting classes, using one action. Both of the spells must have the same casting time. The mystic theurge can make any decisions concerning the spells independently. Any target affected by both of the spells takes a –2 penalty on saves made against each spell. The mystic theurge receives a +2 bonus on caster level checks made to overcome spell resistance with these two spells. A mystic theurge may use this ability once per day.

PATHFINDER CHRONICLER

Brave explorers and scavengers of lost or forgotten knowledge, Pathfinder chroniclers are quintessential adventurers, exploring the world for esoteric truths, magical and mundane relics and artifacts, and new and mysterious vistas, be they wonderful or terrible. For some, this journey is purely about the wealth, for others the glory of discovery, and still more are stirred by the irresistible drive to uncover the bones of the ages and legends of forgotten epochs in an effort to chronicle the deeds of yesterday, today, and tomorrow.

The Pathfinder chronicler class attracts any who see the world as a great mystery to be unraveled, and thus has a diverse and varied following, from fighters and bards to wizards and clerics, and everything in between. However, due to their role as historians and preservers of posterity,

Table 11-8: Mystic Theurge

Level	Base Attack Bonus	Fort Save	Ref Save	Will Save	Special	Spells per Day
1st	+0	+0	+0	+1	Combined spells (1st)	+1 level of existing arcane spellcasting class/ +1 level of existing divine spellcasting class
2nd	+1	+1	+1	+1		+1 level of existing arcane spellcasting class/ +1 level of existing divine spellcasting class
3rd	+1	+1	+1	+2	Combined spells (2nd)	+1 level of existing arcane spellcasting class/ +1 level of existing divine spellcasting class
4th	+2	+1	+1	+2		+1 level of existing arcane spellcasting class/ +1 level of existing divine spellcasting class
5th	+2	+2	+2	+3	Combined spells (3rd)	+1 level of existing arcane spellcasting class/ +1 level of existing divine spellcasting class
6th	+3	+2	+2	+3		+1 level of existing arcane spellcasting class/ +1 level of existing divine spellcasting class
7th	+3	+2	+2	+4	Combined spells (4th)	+1 level of existing arcane spellcasting class/ +1 level of existing divine spellcasting class
8th	+4	+3	+3	+4		+1 level of existing arcane spellcasting class/ +1 level of existing divine spellcasting class
9th	+4	+3	+3	+5	Combined spells (5th)	+1 level of existing arcane spellcasting class/ +1 level of existing divine spellcasting class
10th	+5	+3	+3	+5	Spell synthesis	+1 level of existing arcane spellcasting class/ +1 level of existing divine spellcasting class

hopefuls must be literate and scholarly—for Pathfinder chroniclers are more than mere treasure hunters.

Role: The Pathfinder chronicler's missions often thrust her into the role of party leader, and adventures typically result from, and revolve around, his endless quests.

Alignment: A Pathfinder chronicler's alignment largely determines her motivations. Good characters tend to view their missions as noble ventures, neutral characters seek to preserve knowledge for knowledge's sake, and evil characters are driven by an urge to accumulate wealth and add to their own glory.

Hit Dice: d8.

Requirements

To qualify to become a Pathfinder chronicler, a character must fulfill all the following criteria.

Skills: Linguistics 3 ranks, Perform (oratory) 5 ranks, Profession (scribe) 5 ranks.

Special: Must have authored or scribed something (other than a magical scroll or other device) for which another person (not a PC) paid at least 50 gp.

Class Skills

The Pathfinder chronicler's class skills (and the key ability for each skill) are Appraise (Int), Bluff (Cha), Diplomacy (Cha), Disguise (Cha), Escape Artist (Dex), Intimidate (Cha), Knowledge (all skills, taken individually) (Int), Linguistics (Int), Perception (Wis), Perform (Cha), Ride (Dex), Sense Motive (Wis), Sleight of Hand (Dex), Survival (Wis), and Use Magic Device (Cha).

Skill Ranks Per Level: 8 + Int modifier.

Class Features

The following are class features of the Pathfinder chronicler prestige class.

Weapon and Armor Proficiency: Pathfinder chroniclers gain no proficiency with any weapon or armor

Bardic Knowledge (Ex): This ability is identical to the bard class feature of the same name, and levels in this class stack with levels in any other class that grants a similar ability.

Deep Pockets (Ex): A Pathfinder chronicler collects items as well as lore, picking up small amounts of this or that throughout her travels. As a result, she may carry unspecified equipment worth up to 100 gp per class level. This can be any kind of gear that can reasonably fit into a backpack, including potions and scrolls (but not any other sort of magic item). As a full-round action, the chronicler may dig through her pockets to retrieve an item she specifies at that time, deducting its value from the allocated amount of cost. This item cannot weigh more than 10 pounds. When the total remaining cost reaches 0, the chronicler can retrieve no more items until she refills her deep pockets by spending a few hours and an amount of gold to bring her total up to 100 gp per class level.

In addition, if she takes 1 hour to pack her gear each day, she gains a +4 bonus to Strength to determine her

light encumbrance. This does not affect her maximum carrying capacity. The efficient distribution of weight simply encumbers her less than the same amount of weight normally should. Finally, the Pathfinder chronicler gains a +4 bonus on Sleight of Hand checks made to conceal small objects on her person.

Master Scribe (Ex): A Pathfinder chronicler adds her class level as a bonus on all Linguistics and Profession (scribe) checks, as well as Use Magic Device checks involving scrolls or other written magical items. A Pathfinder chronicler can make Linguistics checks to decipher text as a full-round action and can always take 10 on Linguistics and Profession (scribe) checks, even if distracted or endangered.

Live to Tell the Tale (Ex): At 2nd level, once per day per two class levels, a Pathfinder chronicler can attempt a new saving throw against any ongoing condition against which she failed a saving throw in a previous round, even if the effect is normally

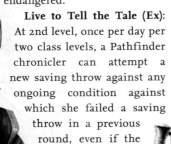

permanent. This ability has no effect on conditions that do not allow saving throws or against instantaneous effects.

Pathfinding (Ex): Beginning at 2nd level, a Pathfinder chronicler develops an excellent sense of direction and skill at leading others through difficult terrain or by following ancient maps. A Pathfinder chronicler gains a +5 bonus on Survival checks made to avoid becoming lost and to Intelligence checks to escape a *maze* spell. In addition, she always uses the "road or trail" overland movement modifier even when in trackless terrain, whether on foot or mounted. With a DC 15 Survival check, the Pathfinder chronicler can extend this benefit to one companion per class level.

Bardic Performance (Su): At 3rd level, a Pathfinder chronicler gains this ability, which functions like the bard class feature of the same name, except that the chronicler's effective bard level is 2 lower than her class level. Levels in this class stack with levels in any other class that grants a similar ability to determine her effective bard level.

Improved Aid (Ex): Starting at 3rd level, a Pathfinder chronicler using the aid another action grants a +4 bonus, rather than the normal +2.

Epic Tales (Su): A 4th-level Pathfinder chronicler can inscribe a tale so evocative and so moving that it conveys the effects of bardic performance through the written word. To create an epic tale requires the Pathfinder chronicler to expend a number of rounds of her bardic performance ability equal to twice the duration of the epic tale (maximum duration of 10 rounds), and any relevant Perform skill check is made with Profession (scribe) instead. An epic tale affects only the reader, but it grants all the benefits that would normally apply for hearing a performance. A Pathfinder chronicler may apply the effects of any feats that affect bardic performance to her epic tales. An epic tale retains its supernatural potency for 1 day per class level. It requires 1 hour to inscribe, a full-round action to activate, and a duration equal to 1/2 the number of bardic performance rounds expended during its creation. Once activated, an epic tale's magic is consumed.

Whispering Campaign (Ex): Pathfinder chroniclers influence the world through their control of information and ability to shape public perception. At 5th level, as a special use of bardic performance, the Pathfinder chronicler can create the effect of a *doom* spell as cast by a sorcerer of her class level by denouncing a creature in person. This is a language-dependent effect.

Alternatively, the chronicler can denounce a particular target (an individual or a definable group of creatures) to others. This form of bardic music creates the effect of the *enthrall* spell, but at the end of the performance all creatures who failed to save shift their attitude toward the target of the oration by one step (in the direction of the Pathfinder chronicler's choice) for 1 day per class level.

TABLE 11-9: PATHFINDER CHRONICLER

Level	Base Attack Bonus	Fort Save	Ref Save	Will Save	Special
1st	+0	+0	+1	+1	Bardic knowledge, deep pockets, master scribe
2nd	+1	+1	+1	+1	Live to tell the tale, pathfinding
3rd	+2	+1	+2	+2	Bardic performance, improved aid
4th	+3	+1	+2	+2	Epic tales
5th	+3	+2	+3	+3	Whispering campaign
6th	+4	+2	+3	+3	Inspired action (move)
7th	+5	+2	+4	+4	Call down the legends
8th	+6	+3	+4	+4	Greater epic tales
9th	+6	+3	+5	+5	Inspired action (standard)
10th	+7	+3	+5	+5	Lay of the exalted dead

Inspire Action (Su): As a special use of bardic performance, a 6th-level Pathfinder chronicler can exhort any one ally within hearing to a sudden surge of action, allowing her ally to immediately take an extra move action. This does not count against the ally's number of actions on his own turn.

At 9th level, she can enable an ally to immediately take a standard action instead.

Call Down the Legends (Su): At 7th level, once per week as a full-round action, a Pathfinder chronicler can summon 2d4 4th-level human barbarians, as if she used a bronze *horn of Valhalla*; these summoned barbarians serve her with complete loyalty. The barbarians are constructs, not actual people (although they seem to be). They arrive with the normal starting equipment for barbarians (see page 454) and attack anyone the chronicler designates.

Greater Epic Tales (Su): At 8th level, the Pathfinder chronicler's written word gains power. This ability functions like the chronicler's epic tales ability, except that if read aloud, the bardic performance takes effect as if the author had used the ability, but the effects are targeted by the reader and use the reader's Charisma score where applicable.

Lay of the Exalted Dead (Su): Once per week as a full-round action, a 10th-level Pathfinder chronicler can summon 1d4+1 5th-level human barbarians, as if she used an iron *horn of Valhalla*. The summoned barbarians serve her with complete and unquestioning loyalty. They are constructs, with the incorporeal subtype (they take 50% of the damage from corporeal sources, and no damage from nonmagical sources). They arrive wearing +2 *studded leather* and wielding +1 *ghost touch greataxes* (allowing them to deal full damage to corporeal creatures) and attack anyone the chronicler designates. To the chronicler and their allies, these exalted dead appear like a noble troop of spectral warriors. Her enemies, however, behold the terrible wrath of the ancient heroes and must succeed at Will saves or become shaken for 1 round per summoned barbarian (DC 15 + the Pathfinder chronicler's Charisma modifier).

SHADOWDANCER

Civilized folk have always feared the night, barring themselves behind doors or comforting themselves with bonfires when the shadows grow long, rightfully wary of the creatures that prowl the darkness. Yet long ago, some learned that the best way to conquer an enemy is to embrace it. These were the first shadowdancers.

Shadowdancers exist in the boundary between light and darkness, where they weave together the shadows to become half-seen artists of deception. Unbound by any specified morality or traditional code, shadowdancers encompass a wide variety of adventuring types who have seen the value of the dark. Spellcasters use their abilities to safely cast spells from hiding and then move quickly away, while classes devoted to hand-to-hand combat enjoy the ability to attack foes with the element of surprise. Some even take the name of their kind quite literally, becoming eerie and mysterious performers and dancers, though more often the temptation presented by their talents with deception and infiltration causes shadowdancers to turn to lives of thievery.

Role: Shadowdancers adventure for a wide variety of reasons. Many adventuring parties find shadowdancers valuable members of their teams due to their incredible stealth and ability to surprise enemies with lightning-quick attacks where they're least expected. For this reason, their services are often sought out by those groups in need of scouts or spies.

Alignment: Because of their nature as visually duplicitous tricksters, shadowdancers do not fit comfortably into the lawful category, as many use their talents to avoid the eyes of legitimate authority. Yet though they are allies of darkness, shadowdancers are neither inherently evil nor predisposed to good. To them, the darkness is simply the darkness, without any of the usual moral connotations made by the unenlightened.

Hit Die: d8.

Table 11-10: Shadowdancer

Level	Base Attack Bonus	Fort Save	Ref Save	Will Save	Special
1st	+0	+0	+1	+0	Hide in plain sight
2nd	+1	+1	+1	+1	Evasion, darkvision, uncanny dodge
3rd	+2	+1	+2	+1	Rogue talent, shadow illusion, summon shadow
4th	+3	+1	+2	+1	Shadow call, shadow jump 40 ft.
5th	+3	+2	+3	+2	Defensive roll, improved uncanny dodge
6th	+4	+2	+3	+2	Rogue talent, shadow jump 80 ft.
7th	+5	+2	+4	+2	Slippery mind
8th	+6	+3	+4	+3	shadow jump 160 ft., shadow power
9th	+6	+3	+5	+3	Rogue talent
10th	+7	+3	+5	+3	Improved evasion, shadow jump 320 ft., shadow master

Requirements

To qualify to become a shadowdancer, a character must fulfill all the following criteria.

Skills: Stealth 5 ranks, Perform (dance) 2 ranks.
Feats: Combat Reflexes, Dodge, Mobility.

Class Skills

The shadowdancer's class skills (and the key ability for each skill) are Acrobatics (Dex), Bluff (Cha), Diplomacy (Cha), Disguise (Cha), Escape Artist (Dex), Perception (Wis), Perform (Cha), Sleight of Hand (Dex), and Stealth (Dex).

Skill Ranks Per Level: 6 + Int modifier.

Class Features

All of the following are features of the shadowdancer prestige class.

Weapon and Armor Proficiency: Shadowdancers are proficient with the club, crossbow (hand, light, or heavy), dagger (any type), dart, mace, morningstar, quarterstaff, rapier, sap, shortbow (normal and composite), and short sword. Shadowdancers are proficient with light armor but not with shields.

Hide in Plain Sight (Su): A shadowdancer can use the Stealth skill even while being observed. As long as she is within 10 feet of an area of dim light, a shadowdancer can hide herself from view in the open without anything to actually hide behind. She cannot, however, hide in her own shadow.

Evasion (Ex): At 2nd level, a shadowdancer gains evasion. If exposed to any effect that normally allows her to attempt a Reflex saving throw for half damage, she takes no damage with a successful saving throw. The evasion ability can only be used if the shadowdancer is wearing light armor or no armor.

Darkvision (Ex): At 2nd level, a shadowdancer gains darkvision out to a range of 60 feet. If she already has darkvision, the range increases by 30 feet.

Uncanny Dodge (Ex): At 2nd level, a shadowdancer cannot be caught flat-footed, even if the attacker is invisible. He still loses her Dexterity bonus to AC if immobilized. A shadowdancer with this ability can still lose his Dexterity bonus to AC if an opponent successfully uses the feint action against him.

If a shadowdancer already has uncanny dodge from a different class, he automatically gains improved uncanny dodge instead (see page 393).

Rogue Talent: At 3rd level, and every three levels thereafter, a shadowdancer gains a special ability that allows her to confound her foes. This functions as the rogue talent class feature. A shadowdancer cannot select an individual talent more than once. If a shadowdancer has the advanced talents rogue class feature, she can chose from the advanced talents list instead.

Shadow Illusion (Sp): When a shadowdancer reaches 3rd level, she can create visual illusions. This ability functions as *silent image*, using the shadowdancer's level as the caster level. A shadowdancer can use this ability once per day for every two shadowdancer levels she has attained. The DC for this ability is Charisma-based.

Summon Shadow (Su): At 3rd level, a shadowdancer can summon a shadow, an undead shade. Unlike a normal shadow, this shadow's alignment matches that of the shadowdancer, and the creature cannot create spawn. The summoned shadow receives a +4 bonus on Will saves made to halve the damage from positive channeled energy and the shadow cannot be turned or commanded. This shadow serves as a companion to the shadowdancer and can communicate intelligibly with the shadowdancer. This shadow has a number of hit points equal to half the shadowdancer's total. The shadow uses the shadowdancer's base attack bonus and base save bonuses. Otherwise, this shadow is identical to the shadow found in the *Pathfinder RPG Bestiary*.

If a shadow companion is destroyed, or the shadowdancer chooses to dismiss it, the shadowdancer must attempt a DC

15 Fortitude save. If the saving throw fails, the shadowdancer gains one permanent negative level. A successful saving throw avoids this negative level. A destroyed or dismissed shadow companion cannot be replaced for 30 days.

Shadow Call (Sp): At 4th level, a shadowdancer can create creatures and effects out of raw shadow. This ability functions as *shadow conjuration,* using the shadowdancer's level as the caster level. A shadowdancer can use this ability once per day at 4th level, plus one additional time per day for every two levels attained beyond 4th (2/day at 6th level, 3/day at 8th level, and 4/day at 10th level). Upon reaching 10th level, this ability functions as *greater shadow conjuration.* The DC for this ability is Charisma-based.

Shadow Jump (Su): At 4th level, a shadowdancer gains the ability to travel between shadows as if by means of a *dimension door* spell. The limitation is that the magical transport must begin and end in an area with at least some dim light. A shadowdancer can jump up to a total of 40 feet each day in this way; this may be a single jump of 40 feet or four jumps of 10 feet each. Every two levels higher than 4th, the distance a shadowdancer can jump each day doubles (80 feet at 6th, 160 feet at 8th, and 320 feet at 10th). This amount can be split among many jumps, but each one, no matter how small, counts as a 10-foot increment.

Defensive Roll (Ex): Starting at 5th level, once per day, a shadowdancer can attempt to avoid a lethal blow. This functions as the rogue's advanced talent of the same name.

Improved Uncanny Dodge (Ex): At 5th level and higher, shadowdancer can no longer be flanked. This defense denies a rogue the ability to sneak attack the shadowdancer by flanking her, unless the attacker has at least four more rogue levels than the target has shadowdancer levels.

If a character already has uncanny dodge from another class, the levels from the classes that grant uncanny dodge stack to determine the minimum rogue level required to flank the character.

Slippery Mind (Ex): At 7th level, a shadowdancer becomes resilient to enchantment spells. This functions as the rogue's advanced talent of the same name.

Shadow Power (Sp): At 8th level, a shadowdancer can use raw shadow to damage her foes. This ability functions as *shadow evocation,* using the shadowdancer's level as the caster level. A shadowdancer can use this ability once per day at 8th level, and one additional time per day upon reaching 10th level. The DC for this ability is Charisma-based.

Improved Evasion (Ex): This ability, gained at 10th level, works like evasion (see above). A shadowdancer takes no damage at all on successful saving throws against attacks that allow a Reflex saving throw for half damage. What's more, she takes only half damage even if she fails her saving throw.

Shadow Master (Su): At 10th level, whenever a shadowdancer is in an area of dim light, she gains DR 10/— and a +2 luck bonus on all saving throws. In addition, whenever she successfully scores a critical hit against a foe who is in an area of dim light, that foe is blinded for 1d6 rounds.

12 GAMEMASTERING

A soulless moon shone down upon the jagged coast, its pale light making the autumn wind's icy claws all the more chilling. Rising like some grim lighthouse, the old mansion teetered upon the cliff, the groans of its moldering timbers barely muffled by the crashing of waves upon the rocks below. Leaves rustled in the shadows, as did a faint scraping in the night beyond. Suddenly, an ominous light flickered to life high in one window. The villagers' tales said that the masters of the house were long dead, but perhaps they had once again returned home.

It's one thing to play a character on an adventure. It's quite another to run the adventure as a Game Master. It's a lot more work, sure, but it can be a lot more rewarding to create an entire world for your friends to explore.

But what exactly *is* a Game Master?

Storyteller: First and foremost, the Game Master is a storyteller. He presents the world and its characters to the players of the game, and it is through the GM that the players interact with them. The Game Master must be able to craft stories and to translate them into a verbal medium.

Entertainer: A Game Master must also be a master at improvisation. He has to be ready to handle anything that his players want to do, to resolve situations and issue rulings quickly enough to keep the pace of the game going at an entertaining clip. A Game Master is on stage, and his players are his audience.

Judge: The Game Master must be the arbiter of everything that occurs in the game. All rule books, including this one, are his tools, but his word is the law. He must not antagonize the players or work to impede their ability to enjoy the game, yet neither should he favor them and coddle them. He should be impartial, fair, and consistent in his administration of the rules.

Inventor: The Game Master's job does not end when the game session does. He must be an inventor as well. By creating NPCs, plots, magic items, spells, worlds, deities, monsters, and everything else, he propels his game's evolution forward, constantly elevating his campaign into something greater.

Player: Just because he's playing dozens of characters during the course of a session doesn't make him any less a player than the others who sit at the table.

STARTING A CAMPAIGN

Before you run a game, you need to know what kind of game you'll be running. Whether you write out the plans for the coming session in a dozen notebooks, scribble down ideas and key NPC stat blocks on a bunch of sticky notes or your computer, or just have a vague idea of a plot and a few names in your head, you'll need to prepare parts of your adventure before the game begins. Some GMs enjoy the challenge of presenting a "sandbox" for the players to explore at their whim, but even then you need to know what kind of things are in that sandbox for the PCs to encounter. And as a general rule, everything you can prepare before the game begins will save you time making decisions during the game. Even more important, preparation beforehand allows you to maintain consistency—few things ruin the suspension of disbelief more for a group of discerning players than having the Game Master call the local innkeeper "Radimus" one session and "Penelope" the next. Preparing for your

adventure beforehand can help you maintain innkeeper gender identities and so much more!

Of course, the backbone of any campaign is the adventures that comprise it, be they an intricately connected series of plots and storylines or an open-ended sandbox of possibility. But where do these adventures come from? There are, essentially, two sources for adventures. You can build your own from scratch, or you can run a published adventure. Both options have different pros and cons, and you certainly don't have to limit yourself to only one choice for the duration of a campaign.

PUBLISHED ADVENTURES

Published adventures are your friend. As a Game Master, you're going to be spending a lot of time as it is preparing for games—and when you don't have time to come up with an adventure, a published adventure can be a godsend. By studying how published adventures are put together, you can hone your own adventure-creating skills. And by running a published adventure for your group, you leave the details of invention and creation to the adventure writer, giving you time to focus on the game play itself.

The most important thing to remember when using a published adventure, though, is that the writer of the adventure doesn't know your group the way *you* know your group. If you know your players are particularly paranoid and assume all helpful NPCs are out to get them, then a published adventure about a kindly cleric who's actually a shapechanged demon probably won't work well for your group. Feel free to change published adventures as you see fit, either while you're reading them or during play. If, for example, one of your players has written into his character's backstory that his father was killed by an orc warlord and he became an adventurer to someday get revenge on that orc, go ahead and change the hobgoblin warlord in the adventure into an orc. Adapting adventures to your group and your play style in this manner is an important part of running published adventures, since it customizes the experience to your group and makes it all the more enjoyable.

Paizo Publishing offers a large variety of published adventures in its Pathfinder Modules line and complete campaigns in the form of its monthly Pathfinder Adventure Path installments. To learn more about these valuable GM resources, please visit **paizo.com**.

BUILDING AN ADVENTURE

There are countless ways to build an adventure. The classic method is to simply write everything out beforehand. While this does get everything you need to know about the adventure down on paper, it's an awful lot of work. If you're the only person who'll ever be running the adventure, it's okay to simply outline the plot, draw a map of the adventure site, create encounters and stat blocks, and have at it. An adventure need not look like much more than a shopping list—you only really need to write down what you can't easily remember come game time.

One important tip to remember about adventure writing—you're not writing a story. The main characters of the adventure should be the players, and they're missing from the tale when you prepare the adventure. Instead, think of the adventure as an outline for a script. You can have an idea in your head of how things will work out, but if you avoid making assumptions about what your characters will do in the adventure and instead just focus on creating the building blocks of the adventure (such as room descriptions, NPC motivations, stat blocks, and the like), you'll be much more capable of reacting to the unexpected when the PCs do their thing.

Whatever you decide to do in your adventure, there are three elements that, if you prepare them beforehand, will save you a lot of time and anguish in the end—stat blocks, encounters, and treasure.

Stat Blocks

One of the most complex parts of the game is the stat block. Every NPC, every monster, and every timid little forest creature in the campaign world has its own stat block. This isn't to say, of course, that you need to generate a stat block for every creature that appears in your adventure, but you should certainly generate stat blocks for all of the important NPCs and monsters with whom you expect the PCs to interact. The *Pathfinder RPG Bestiary* provides more than 300 pre-made monster stat blocks for use in adventures, and that's just the beginning—you can use stat blocks from other monster bestiaries or adventures just as easily in your game. One good trick is to copy a stat block onto a 3×5 card or into a small document you can easily bring up on your computer during the game—you can keep these cards and documents forever to reuse them as needed.

Think of stat blocks as shorthand versions of character sheets. For a sample stat block, see page 455 of this book—definitions for the various abbreviations in the stat block can be found on pages 11–13. For a more detailed description of how to read a stat block or additional examples of what a stat block looks like, consult the *Pathfinder RPG Bestiary*.

Designing Encounters

The heart of any adventure is its encounters. An encounter is any event that puts a specific problem before the PCs that they must solve. Most encounters present combat with monsters or hostile NPCs, but there are many other types—a trapped corridor, a political interaction with a suspicious king, a dangerous passage

TABLE 12-1: ENCOUNTER DESIGN

Difficulty	Challenge Rating Equals...
Easy	APL −1
Average	APL
Challenging	APL +1
Hard	APL +2
Epic	APL +3

over a rickety rope bridge, an awkward argument with a friendly NPC who suspects a PC has betrayed him, or anything that adds drama to the game. Brain-teasing puzzles, roleplaying challenges, and skill checks are all classic methods for resolving encounters, but the most complex encounters to build are the most common ones—combat encounters.

When designing a combat encounter, you first decide what level of challenge you want your PCs to face, then follow the steps outlined below.

Step 1—Determine APL: Determine the average level of your player characters—this is their Average Party Level (APL for short). You should round this value to the nearest whole number (this is one of the few exceptions to the round down rule). Note that these encounter creation guidelines assume a group of four or five PCs. If your group contains six or more players, add one to their average level. If your group contains three or fewer players, subtract one from their average level. For example, if your group consists of six players, two of which are 4th level and four of which are 5th level, their APL is 6th (28 total levels, divided by six players, rounding up, and adding one to the final result).

Step 2—Determine CR: Challenge Rating (or CR) is a convenient number used to indicate the relative danger presented by a monster, trap, hazard, or other encounter—the higher the CR, the more dangerous the encounter. Refer to Table 12–1 to determine the Challenge Rating your group should face, depending on the difficulty of the challenge you want and the group's APL.

Step 3—Build the Encounter: Determine the total XP award for the encounter by looking it up by its CR on Table 12–2. This gives you an "XP budget" for the encounter. Every creature, trap, and hazard is worth an amount of XP determined by its CR, as noted on Table 12–2. To build your encounter, simply add creatures, traps, and hazards whose combined XP does not exceed the total XP budget for your encounter. It's easiest to add the highest CR challenges to the encounter first, filling out the remaining total with lesser challenges.

For example, let's say you want your group of six 8th-level PCs to face a challenging encounter against a group of gargoyles (each CR 4) and their stone giant boss (CR 8). The PCs have an APL of 9, and table 12–1 tells you that a challenging encounter for your APL 9

Table 12-2: Experience Point Awards

CR	Total XP	1–3	4–5	6+
		Individual XP		
1/8	50	15	15	10
1/6	65	20	15	10
1/4	100	35	25	15
1/3	135	45	35	25
1/2	200	65	50	35
1	400	135	100	65
2	600	200	150	100
3	800	265	200	135
4	1,200	400	300	200
5	1,600	535	400	265
6	2,400	800	600	400
7	3,200	1,070	800	535
8	4,800	1,600	1,200	800
9	6,400	2,130	1,600	1,070
10	9,600	3,200	2,400	1,600
11	12,800	4,270	3,200	2,130
12	19,200	6,400	4,800	3,200
13	25,600	8,530	6,400	4,270
14	38,400	12,800	9,600	6,400
15	51,200	17,100	12,800	8,530
16	76,800	25,600	19,200	12,800
17	102,400	34,100	25,600	17,100
18	153,600	51,200	38,400	25,600
19	204,800	68,300	51,200	34,100
20	307,200	102,000	76,800	51,200
21	409,600	137,000	102,400	68,300
22	614,400	205,000	153,600	102,400
23	819,200	273,000	204,800	137,000
24	1,228,800	410,000	307,200	204,800
25	1,638,400	546,000	409,600	273,000

Table 12-3: High CR Equivalencies

Number of Creatures	Equal to...
1 Creature	CR
2 Creatures	CR +2
3 Creatures	CR +3
4 Creatures	CR +4
6 Creatures	CR +5
8 Creatures	CR +6
12 Creatures	CR +7
16 Creatures	CR +8

group is a CR 10 encounter—worth 9,600 XP according to Table 12–2. At CR 8, the stone giant is worth 4,800 XP, leaving you with another 4,800 points in your XP budget for the gargoyles. Gargoyles are CR 4 each, and thus worth 1,200 XP apiece, meaning that the encounter can support four gargoyles in its XP budget. You could further refine the encounter by including only three gargoyles, leaving you with 1,200 XP to spend on a trio of Small earth elemental servants (at CR 1, each is worth 400 XP) to further aid the stone giant.

Adding NPCs: Creatures whose Hit Dice are solely a factor of their class levels and not a feature of their race, such as all of the PC races detailed in Chapter 2, are factored into combats a little differently than normal monsters or monsters with class levels. A creature that possesses class levels, but does not have any racial Hit Dice, is factored in as a creature with a CR equal to its class levels –1. A creature that only possesses non-player class levels (such as a warrior or adept—see page 448) is factored in as a creature with a CR equal to its class levels –2. If this reduction would reduce a creature's CR to below 1, its CR drops one step on the following progression for each step below 1 this reduction would make: 1/2, 1/3, 1/4, 1/6, 1/8.

High CR Encounters: The XP values for high-CR encounters can seem quite daunting. Table 12–3 provides some simple formulas to help you manage these large numbers. When using a large number of identical creatures, this chart can help simplify the math by combining them into one CR, making it easier to find their total XP value. For example, using this chart, four CR 8 creatures (worth 4,800 XP each) are equivalent to a CR 12 creature (worth 19,200 XP).

Ad Hoc CR Adjustments: While you can adjust a specific monster's CR by advancing it, applying templates, or giving it class levels (rules for all three of these options appear in the *Pathfinder RPG Bestiary*), you can also adjust an encounter's difficulty by applying ad hoc adjustments to the encounter or creature itself. Listed here are three additional ways you can alter an encounter's difficulty.

Favorable Terrain for the PCs: An encounter against a monster that's out of its favored element (like a yeti encountered in a sweltering cave with lava, or an enormous dragon encountered in a tiny room) gives the PCs an advantage. Build the encounter as normal, but when you award experience for the encounter, do so as if the encounter were one CR lower than its actual CR.

Unfavorable Terrain for the PCs: Monsters are designed with the assumption that they are encountered in their favored terrain—encountering a water-breathing aboleth in an underwater area does not increase the CR for that encounter, even though none of the PCs breathe water. If, on the other hand, the terrain impacts the encounter significantly (such as an encounter against a creature with blindsight in an area that suppresses all light), you can, at your option, increase the effective XP award as if the encounter's CR were one higher.

NPC Gear Adjustments: You can significantly increase or decrease the power level of an NPC with class levels by adjusting the NPC's gear. The combined value of an NPC's

TABLE 12-4: CHARACTER WEALTH BY LEVEL

PC Level*	Wealth
2	1,000 gp
3	3,000 gp
4	6,000 gp
5	10,500 gp
6	16,000 gp
7	23,500 gp
8	33,000 gp
9	46,000 gp
10	62,000 gp
11	82,000 gp
12	108,000 gp
13	140,000 gp
14	185,000 gp
15	240,000 gp
16	315,000 gp
17	410,000 gp
18	530,000 gp
19	685,000 gp
20	880,000 gp

* For 1st-level PCs, see table 6–1 in Chapter 6.

TABLE 12-5: TREASURE VALUES PER ENCOUNTER

Average Party Level	Treasure per Encounter		
	Slow	Medium	Fast
1	170 gp	260 gp	400 gp
2	350 gp	550 gp	800 gp
3	550 gp	800 gp	1,200 gp
4	750 gp	1,150 gp	1,700 gp
5	1,000 gp	1,550 gp	2,300 gp
6	1,350 gp	2,000 gp	3,000 gp
7	1,750 gp	2,600 gp	3,900 gp
8	2,200 gp	3,350 gp	5,000 gp
9	2,850 gp	4,250 gp	6,400 gp
10	3,650 gp	5,450 gp	8,200 gp
11	4,650 gp	7,000 gp	10,500 gp
12	6,000 gp	9,000 gp	13,500 gp
13	7,750 gp	11,600 gp	17,500 gp
14	10,000 gp	15,000 gp	22,000 gp
15	13,000 gp	19,500 gp	29,000 gp
16	16,500 gp	25,000 gp	38,000 gp
17	22,000 gp	32,000 gp	48,000 gp
18	28,000 gp	41,000 gp	62,000 gp
19	35,000 gp	53,000 gp	79,000 gp
20	44,000 gp	67,000 gp	100,000 gp

gear is given in Chapter 14 on Table 14–9. A classed NPC encountered with no gear should have his CR reduced by 1 (provided that loss of gear actually hampers the NPC), while a classed NPC that instead has gear equivalent to that of a PC (as listed on Table 12–4) has a CR of 1 higher than his actual CR. Be careful awarding NPCs this extra gear, though—especially at high levels, where you can blow out your entire adventure's treasure budget in one fell swoop!

Awarding Experience

Pathfinder Roleplaying Game characters advance in level by defeating monsters, overcoming challenges, and completing adventures—in so doing, they earn experience points (XP for short). Although you can award experience points as soon as a challenge is overcome, this can quickly disrupt the flow of game play. It's easier to simply award experience points at the end of a game session—that way, if a character earns enough XP to gain a level, he won't disrupt the game while he levels up his character. He can instead take the time between game sessions to do that.

Keep a list of the CRs of all the monsters, traps, obstacles, and roleplaying encounters the PCs overcome. At the end of each session, award XP to each PC that participated. Each monster, trap, and obstacle awards a set amount of XP, as determined by its CR, regardless of the level of the party in relation to the challenge, although you should never bother awarding XP for challenges that have a CR of 10 or more lower than the APL. Pure roleplaying encounters generally have a CR equal to the average level of the party (although particularly easy or difficult roleplaying encounters might be one higher or lower). There are two methods for awarding XP. While one is more exact, it requires a calculator for ease of use. The other is slightly more abstract.

Exact XP: Once the game session is over, take your list of defeated CR numbers and look up the value of each CR on Table 12–2 under the "Total XP" column. Add up the XP values for each CR and then divide this total by the number of characters—each character earns an amount of XP equal to this number.

Abstract XP: Simply add up the individual XP awards listed for a group of the appropriate size. In this case, the division is done for you—you need only total up all the awards to determine how many XP to award to each PC.

Story Awards: Feel free to award Story Awards when players conclude a major storyline or make an important accomplishment. These awards should be worth double the amount of experience points for a CR equal to the APL. Particularly long or difficult story arcs might award even more, at your discretion as GM.

Placing Treasure

As PCs gain levels, the amount of treasure they carry and use increases as well. The Pathfinder Roleplaying Game assumes that all PCs of equivalent level have roughly equal amounts of treasure and magic items. Since the primary income for a PC derives from treasure and loot gained from adventuring, it's important to moderate the wealth and hoards you place in your adventures. To aid in placing treasure, the amount of treasure and magic items the PCs receive for their adventures is tied to the Challenge Rating of the encounters they face—the higher an encounter's CR, the more treasure it can award.

Table 12–4 lists the amount of treasure each PC is expected to have at a specific level. Note that this table assumes a standard fantasy game. Low-fantasy games might award only half this value, while high-fantasy games might double the value. It is assumed that some of this treasure is consumed in the course of an adventure (such as potions and scrolls), and that some of the less useful items are sold for half value so more useful gear can be purchased.

Table 12–4 can also be used to budget gear for characters starting above 1st level, such as a new character created to replace a dead one. Characters should spend no more than half their total wealth on any single item. For a balanced approach, PCs that are built after 1st level should spend no more than 25% of their wealth on weapons, 25% on armor and protective devices, 25% on other magic items, 15% on disposable items like potions, scrolls, and wands, and 10% on ordinary gear and coins. Different character types might spend their wealth differently than these percentages suggest; for example, arcane casters might spend very little on weapons but a great deal more on other magic items and disposable items.

Table 12–5 lists the amount of treasure each encounter should award based on the average level of the PCs and the speed of the campaign's XP progression (slow, medium, or fast). Easy encounters should award treasure one level lower than the PCs' average level. Challenging, hard, and epic encounters should award treasure one, two, or three levels higher than the PCs' average level, respectively. If you are running a low-fantasy game, cut these values in half. If you are running a high-fantasy game, double these values.

Encounters against NPCs typically award three times the treasure a monster-based encounter awards, due to NPC gear. To compensate, make sure the PCs face off against a pair of additional encounters that award little in the way of treasure. Animals, plants, constructs, mindless undead, oozes, and traps are great "low treasure" encounters. Alternatively, if the PCs face a number of creatures with little or no treasure, they should have the opportunity to acquire a number of significantly more valuable objects sometime in the near future to make up for the imbalance. As a general rule, PCs should not own any magic item worth more than half their total character wealth, so make sure to check before awarding expensive magic items.

Building a Treasure Hoard

While it's often enough to simply tell your players they've found 5,000 gp in gems and 10,000 gp in jewelry, it's generally more interesting to give details. Giving treasure a personality can not only help the verisimilitude of your game, but can sometimes trigger new adventures. The information on the following pages can help you randomly determine types of additional treasure— suggested values are given for many of the objects, but feel free to assign values to the objects as you see fit. It's easiest to place the expensive items first—if you wish, you can even randomly roll magic items, using the tables in Chapter 15, to determine what sort of items are present in the hoard. Once you've consumed a sizable portion of the hoard's value, the remainder can simply be loose coins or nonmagical treasure with values arbitrarily assigned as you see fit.

Coins: Coins in a treasure hoard can consist of copper, silver, gold, and platinum pieces—silver and gold are the most common, but you can divide the coinage as you wish. Coins and their value relative to each other are described at the start of Chapter 6.

Gems: Although you can assign any value to a gemstone, some are inherently more valuable than others. Use the value categories below (and their associated gemstones) as guidelines when assigning values to gemstones.

Low-Quality Gems (10 gp): agates; azurite; blue quartz; hematite; lapis lazuli; malachite; obsidian; rhodochrosite; tigereye; turquoise; freshwater (irregular) pearl

Semi-Precious Gems (50 gp): bloodstone; carnelian; chalcedony; chrysoprase; citrine; jasper; moonstone; onyx; peridot; rock crystal (clear quartz); sard; sardonyx; rose, smoky, or star rose quartz; zircon

Medium Quality Gemstones (100 gp): amber; amethyst; chrysoberyl; coral; red or brown-green garnet; jade; jet; white, golden, pink, or silver pearl; red, red-brown, or deep green spinel; tourmaline

High Quality Gemstones (500 gp): alexandrite; aquamarine; violet garnet; black pearl; deep blue spinel; golden yellow topaz

Jewels (1,000 gp): emerald; white, black, or fire opal; blue sapphire; fiery yellow or rich purple corundum; blue or black star sapphire

Grand Jewels (5,000 gp or more): clearest bright green emerald; diamond; jacinth; ruby

Nonmagical Treasures: This expansive category includes jewelry, fine clothing, trade goods, alchemical items, masterwork objects, and more. Unlike gemstones, many of these objects have set values, but you can always increase an object's value by having it be bejeweled or of particularly fine craftsmanship. This increase in cost doesn't grant additional abilities—a gem-encrusted masterwork cold iron scimitar worth 40,000 gp functions the same as a typical masterwork cold iron scimitar worth the base price of 330 gp. Listed below are numerous examples of several types of nonmagical treasures, along with typical values.

Fine Artwork (100 gp or more): Although some artwork is composed of precious materials, the value of most paintings, sculptures, works of literature, fine clothing, and the like come from their skill and craftsmanship. Artwork is often bulky or cumbersome to move and fragile to boot, making salvage an adventure in and of itself.

Jewelry, Minor (50 gp): This category includes relatively small pieces of jewelry crafted from materials like brass, bronze, copper, ivory, or even exotic woods, sometimes set with tiny or flawed low-quality gems. Minor jewelry includes rings, bracelets, and earrings.

Jewelry, Normal (100–500 gp): Most jewelry is made of silver, gold, jade, or coral, often ornamented with semi-precious or even medium-quality gemstones. Normal jewelry includes all types of minor jewelry plus armbands, necklaces, and brooches.

Jewelry, Precious (500 gp or more): Truly precious jewelry is crafted from gold, mithral, platinum, or similar rare metals. Such objects include normal jewelry types plus crowns, scepters, pendants, and other large items.

Masterwork Tools (100–300 gp): This category includes masterwork weapons, armor, and skill kits—see Chapter 6 for more details and costs for these items.

Mundane Gear (up to 1,000 gp): There are many valuable items of mundane or alchemical nature detailed in Chapter 6 that can be utilized as treasure. Most of the alchemical items are portable and valuable, but other objects like locks, holy symbols, spyglasses, fine wine, or fine clothing work well as interesting bits of treasure. Trade goods can even serve as treasure—10 pounds of saffron, for example, is worth 150 gp.

Treasure Maps and Other Intelligence (variable): Items like treasure maps, deeds to ships and homes, lists of informants or guard rosters, passwords, and the like can also make fun items of treasure—you can set the value of such items at any amount you wish, and often they can serve double-duty as adventure seeds.

Magic Items: Of course, the discovery of a magic item is the true prize for any adventurer. You should take care with the placement of magic items in a hoard—it's generally more satisfying for many players to find a magic item rather than purchase it, so there's no crime in placing items that happen to be those your players can use! An extensive list of magic items (and their costs) is given in Chapter 15.

Although you should generally place items with careful consideration of their likely effects on your campaign, it can be fun and save time to generate magic items in a treasure hoard randomly. You can "purchase" random die rolls of magic items for a treasure

hoard at the following prices, subtracting the indicated amount from your treasure budget and then rolling on the appropriate column on table 15–2 in Chapter 15 to determine what item is in the treasure hoard. Take care with this approach, though! It's easy, through the luck (or unluck) of the dice to bloat your game with too much treasure or deprive it of the same. Random magic item placement should always be tempered with good common sense by the GM.

Magic Item Category	Average Value
Minor Item	1,000 gp
Medium Item	10,000 gp
Major Item	40,000 gp

PREPARING FOR THE GAME

Your job as Game Master begins well before the game session does. Your most important duty before a game is, of course, to prepare for that game. This means reading up on the adventure you'll be running (or perhaps even designing the adventure), preparing any props or handouts you might need to give the PCs, prepping the play area for guests, and so on. In the days leading up to the game, you should resolve any out-of-game issues that your players have—email is a great way to do this, since it creates its own written record you can use to add to your campaign journal (see page 403). This includes helping players level up their characters; answering questions they may have about using non-core rules and supplements for spells, feats, and the like; and providing them with answers to questions they have about the game world.

For example, say one of your PCs is searching for his missing sister, who was abducted years ago by a thieves' guild. You can drop in clues about this sister in the game, but between games, the PC might want to spend a few days investigating a lead in the local underworld or at the City Hall of Records. Personal quests like these are a great way for a player to build his character's history and personality, but they can get in the way of gaming when other players are at the table. If you can't afford to spend one-on-one time with players, handling these side-quests via email is a great way to take care of the situation.

You should also ensure that all of the players can make the game, and if not all of them can, decide if the game should be canceled or not. There are few things more frustrating than realizing that half your group can't play, especially if some of the players had to drive a long way to reach the game. If a player is absent, decide what happens to his PC. Can someone else play him? Does he gain experience and treasure as usual?

Make sure that accommodations are met. If your game session's going to last a long time, think about where folks can go for lunch or dinner—if you're planning on providing food, make sure it's ready to go before the game begins. Many tables organize responsibilities among the players—if a GM hosts the game at his house, the players might split up the task of providing drinks, snacks, or meals. Try to use common sense here—while it's tempting to load up with potato chips and soda pop, gaming is no excuse for poor health! Of course, if your home is not the hosting site for the game, that doesn't let you off the hook. You as GM are the organizing force for the gathering—you're technically throwing the party, and it's your responsibility to see that your players have a comfortable, enjoyable place to game, otherwise the game itself will suffer.

DURING THE GAME

The bulk of this book provides the rules you need to adjudicate the game and run things, but there are many other problems and events that can come up that require you to think quickly before they become disruptive. Listed here are several of the more common speed bumps and problems that you'll invariably be called upon to handle during the game.

Cheating and Fudging: We all know that cheating is bad. But sometimes, as a GM, you might find yourself in a situation where cheating might improve the game. We prefer to call this "fudging" rather than cheating, and while you should try to avoid it when you can, you are the law in your world, and you shouldn't feel bound by the dice. A GM should be impartial and fair, and in theory, that's what random dice results help support. Some players have trouble putting trust in their GM, but dice

offer something that's irrefutable and truly non-partisan (as long as the dice aren't doctored or loaded, of course). Still, it's no good if a single roll of the dice would result in a premature end to your campaign, or a character's death when they did everything right.

Likewise, don't feel bound to the predetermined plot of an encounter or the rules as written. Feel free to adjust the results or interpret things creatively—especially in cases where you as the GM made a poor assumption to begin with. For example, you might design an encounter against a band of werewolves, only to realize too late that none of the PCs have silver weapons and therefore can't hurt them. In this case, it's okay to cheat and say that these werewolves are hurt by normal weapons, or to have the town guard (armed with silver arrows) show up at the last minute to save the PCs. As long as you can keep such developments to a minimum, these on-the-spot adjustments can even enhance the game—so the town guard saved the PCs, but now that they have, it can give you leverage over the PCs to send them on their next quest as repayment to the guards!

Divine Intervention: The literary term for it is *deus ex machina*—"god from the machine." This is what happens in a story when a plot device manifests in an unexpected (and usually unsatisfying) way to resolve a story element, typically in a way that renders the actions of the main characters meaningless. Even great authors use *deus ex machina* to resolve stories now and then, so don't be afraid to use it in your game if things are looking grim. The town guard rushing in to save the PCs from the werewolves in the previous paragraph is an excellent example of *deus ex machina*, but so is the old classic of "divine intervention." In this case, the PCs are faced with an impossible situation and you, as the GM, change the situation so that they can now achieve their goals, perhaps after a PC begs for aid from his deity.

You can quantify divine interventions, if you wish, at the start of a campaign. Tell every player that they get a fixed number of interventions during the campaign (it's often best to limit this to just one such intervention). Thereafter, the PC can use this divine intervention to save himself or the party, perhaps by preventing an effect that would otherwise cause a character's death, or to suddenly manifest an escape from a deathtrap. You, as the GM, have full power over how the intervention resolves, of course, so players won't be able to use divine intervention to bypass plot elements you know they can handle—if a player tries this, simply tell him that his request for intervention is denied and that he can save his intervention for when it's truly needed.

GM Fiat: The GM is the law of the game. His reading of the rules should be respected and adhered to. It's easy to get hung up on complicated aspects of the game during play, but the game is never enhanced by long, drawn-out arguments over these complications between players and GM. When complications involving rules interpretations occur, listen to the player and make the decision as quickly as you can on how to resolve the situation. If the rule in question isn't one you're familiar with, you can go with the player's interpretation but with the knowledge that after the game you'll read up on the rules and, with the next session, will have an official ruling in play. Alternatively, you can simply rule that something works in a way that helps the story move on, despite the most logical or impassioned arguments from the players. Even then, you owe it to your players to spend time after the game researching the rule to make sure your ruling was fair— and if not, make amends the next game as necessary.

One handy rule to keep under your belt is the Fiat Rule—simply grant a player a +2 or a –2 bonus or penalty to a die roll if no one at the table is precisely sure how a situation might be handled by the rules. For example, a character who attempts to trip an iron golem in a room where the floor is magnetized could gain a +2 bonus on his attempt at your discretion, since the magnetic pull exerted by the floor helps pull the golem down.

Handling PC Death: Eventually, through bad luck or bad tactics, a player character is going to die in your game. Other events, such as petrification, paralysis, sleep, and stunning can have a similar effect on the game as PC death, and the following advice should apply to those effects as well.

When a PC dies, his player no longer has any input into the game (unless he has a cohort or other allied NPC he can start playing). That player has to sit at the table quietly, watching and waiting while everyone else continues to have fun with the game. In some cases, the effect is only temporary, with another player able to step in to restore the PC to life (or cure his petrification, remove his paralysis, or whatever), but nevertheless, when a player stops playing the game because his character's been removed from the action, you as a GM have a problem on your hands.

When such an event occurs, keep going with the game; try to resolve the current conflict or combat as quickly as possible so that the players can move on to addressing the problem of their dead ally. If there's no way to restore the dead PC to life and the party needs to retreat to the city to pay for a resurrection, don't delay that event by forcing the PCs to endure additional wandering monsters; just gloss over the return to civilization as best you can so you can get the unlucky player back into the game as quickly as you can. A PC death is often a great time to end the session, in fact, since you can then handle the resurrection details out of game via email.

If the player of a dead character prefers instead to move on to a new character, let him create his new character at the table. In this case, that player need not sit around bored—the act of creating a new character is involving

CAMPAIGN JOURNAL

All Game Masters should keep a campaign journal. This can be a simple folder containing stacks of paper, a three-ring binder, a PDA, a computer, a tablet, a notebook, or anything else that you can keep notes in. Use this journal to record your thoughts and ideas related to the game as they happen, before, during, and after the game session. As you continue to run campaigns, you'll doubtless need to expand your journal. Periodically, you should back up your journal, perhaps by copying the contents to a computer and saving them to a DVD, or maybe just by photocopying the contents and stashing the copy in a safe place. Nothing's more frustrating than losing 3 years of campaign notes due to a crashed hard drive or a natural disaster!

enough that you can continue to run the game for the surviving PCs, after all. Once the player's new character is done, let the other players take a 5 or 10 minute break while you step aside to talk to the player and learn about his new character, and to work with the player on a way to introduce the new character into the game as quickly and seamlessly as possible.

One other thing that PC death can do is bloat surviving player treasure. If your group simply splits up the dead PC's gear or sells it, the surviving players can become obscenely over-geared for their level. If this doesn't bother you, you should at least work to ensure that the new PC has gear equal in power to that now possessed by the rest of the party. It's usually a much easier solution to simply assume that the old PC's gear goes away, either being buried with his body or sent on to his surviving kin. One pretty handy way to solve the situation is to introduce the player's new character as a prisoner that the PCs rescue, and to have the old PC's gear be given to the new PC to equip him for the remainder of the adventure. Of course, this isn't always a graceful solution, but it can be a good one to keep treasure levels under control until the new PC can sell off parts of his old character's gear to purchase new gear. In this situation, consider letting the PC get full resale value for his gear, since you don't want to penalize him for losing a character by saddling him with half the gear he used to have.

Rolling Dice: Some GMs prefer to roll all of their dice in front of the players, letting the results fall where they may. Others prefer to make all rolls behind a screen, hiding the results from the PCs so that, if they need to, they can fudge the dice results to make the game do what they want. Neither way is the "correct" way; choose whichever you wish, or even mix and match as feels right for you.

The only time you should not reveal the results of a die roll to the player character is when knowledge of the roll's result would give the player knowledge he shouldn't have.

A good example of this is saving throws against effects that the player shouldn't necessarily realize his character has been exposed to (such as a disease or a subtle, long-acting poison).

Troublesome Players: Play the game long enough and eventually you'll find yourself with a troublemaking player—it's just an unfortunate fact of any pastime that involves multiple people interacting in a team-oriented event. To a certain extent, you can rely on other players to help mediate problems with a troublemaker, but sometimes you'll need to step in and ask the player in question to cease his inappropriate behavior. Don't be afraid to ask the troublemaker to leave the game session if he won't correct his behavior after a polite but firm request. If tempers are running hot among multiple players, don't hesitate to call the game session early and break up, giving the players time to cool down and get over the event.

CAMPAIGN TIPS

So now you have an adventure or two ready for your players to experience. While you can certainly keep these adventures as separate entities, and perhaps even have your players make new characters each time you start a new adventure, the Pathfinder Roleplaying Game assumes that your players will keep their same characters as they go from adventure to adventure, growing more powerful as they accumulate experience and treasure.

So, what happens between adventures? What is the world that those adventures take place in? Who lives there, and what do NPCs who don't take part in the adventures do? The answers to these questions and more comprise your world, or setting, and the specific progression of adventures your PCs undertake in this setting is known as a campaign.

Many published campaign settings exist—the *Pathfinder Chronicles Campaign Setting* is the assumed setting for most games that use the Pathfinder Roleplaying Game rules, but it is by no means the only one. Dozens of publishers offer intriguing and detailed settings to choose from—you can even use settings from games that use rules quite different than those presented in this book, or settings that are inspired by or lifted directly from a favorite series of books or movies. But for some, the most rewarding part of being a Game Master is the act of creating your own campaign setting and running it for your players.

The act of creating a campaign is no less daunting than creating a world. It can quickly become overwhelming, especially when you start to consider all of the areas you'll need to become an expert at. If your world has multiple moons, how does that affect tides? If you choose a specific shape for your main continent, what does that do to trade winds? Where do the deserts go, and where do the swamps go? How many rivers is too many? What impact would a technologically advanced nation of warriors have on the neighboring shamanistic barbarians? Does your world have chocolate and coffee and avocados? What's the tallest mountain in your world, and why is it the tallest? Are there salmon and trout in your world, and if there's not, what do the bears eat instead? If you have a nation modeled on ancient Japan, does that mean you need to learn Japanese in order to name NPCs who live there? Is there gunpowder in your world, and if not, why not? Is the world's core molten? If it's not, how would that impact your world's magnetosphere—would there still be a north pole? How much does a longsword weigh if your campaign world is half the size of Earth? What happens if your campaign world is shaped like a ring?

For these reasons, it's generally best to assume an Earth-like baseline for your first campaign world. Another handy tip is to avoid detailing everything at once. Staying just one step ahead of your players is often all you need to do—if you know that the first adventure they'll be going on is an exploration of an abandoned fort, don't worry about detailing anything but the surrounding 5-mile area, along with, perhaps, a small village for them to start the adventure in. If you know that the second adventure's going to be in a haunted mine in the mountains, you then have as long as it takes the PCs to explore that abandoned fort to detail the area between your first village and the badlands to the east where the mine's located. By creating only what you need to run the next few games, you slowly but surely build a larger whole, while at the same time maintaining your sanity.

Yet still, the lure of building an entire campaign setting is great. In a lot of ways, creating your own world is like an entirely different game in and of itself—a Game Master thus gets to play the game more often than his players, since when the actual session isn't going, the GM gets to design cities and evil temples and nations and dungeons and monsters to his heart's content. The *Pathfinder Gamemastery Guide* provides a wealth of advanced advice and tools you can use to build your campaign world, but the remainder of this chapter covers a number of different topics to aid you. These topics barely scratch the surface of the implications and ideas you'll be facing when creating your own campaign world, but they can get you started.

Cost of Living

An adventurer's primary source of income is treasure, and his primary purchases are tools and items he needs to continue adventuring—spell components, weapons, magic items, potions, and the like. Yet what about things like food? Rent? Taxes? Bribes? Idle purchases?

You can certainly handle these minor expenditures in detail during play, but tracking every time a PC pays for a room, buys water, or pays a gate tax can swiftly become obnoxious and tiresome. If you're not really into tracking these minor costs of living, you can choose to simply ignore these small payments. A more realistic and easier-to-use method is to have PCs pay a recurring cost of living tax. At the start of every game month, a PC must pay an amount of gold equal to the lifestyle bracket he wishes to live in—if he can't afford his desired bracket, he drops down to the first one he can afford.

Destitute (0 gp/month): The PC is homeless and lives in the wilderness or on the streets. A destitute character must track every purchase, and may need to resort to Survival checks or theft to feed himself.

Poor (3 gp/month): The PC lives in common rooms of taverns, with his parents, or in some other communal situation—this is the lifestyle of most untrained laborers and commoners. He need not track purchases of meals or taxes that cost 1 sp or less.

Average (10 gp/month): The PC lives in his own apartment, small house, or similar location—this is the lifestyle of most trained or skilled experts or warriors. He can secure any nonmagical item worth 1 gp or less from his home in 1d10 minutes, and need not track purchases of common meals or taxes that cost 1 gp or less.

Wealthy (100 gp/month): The PC has a sizable home or a nice suite of rooms in a fine inn. He can secure any nonmagical item worth 5 gp or less from his belongings in his home in 1d10 minutes, and need only track purchases of meals or taxes in excess of 10 gp.

Extravagant (1,000 gp/month): The PC lives in a mansion, castle, or other extravagant home—he might even own the building in question. This is the lifestyle of most aristocrats. He can secure any nonmagical item worth 25 gp or less from his belongings in his home in 1d10 minutes. He need only track purchases of meals or taxes in excess of 100 gp.

Monstrous Characters

You should decide on how exotic your world is at the start. The Pathfinder Roleplaying Game assumes a baseline that all PCs, and thus the majority of the civilized world's NPCs, are of one of the seven races presented in Chapter 2. You might want to narrow those choices—perhaps there are only humans in your world, or perhaps one or more of the races in Chapter 2 are rare enough to be nearly legends on

ALTERNATIVE RACES

Only more experienced GMs should consider allowing players to play anything other than the races presented in Chapter 2, but if you want to start experimenting, the following races from the *Pathfinder RPG Bestiary* are good choices for races that are close in power to those listed in Chapter 2.

- Aasimar
- Goblin
- Hobgoblin
- Kobold
- Merfolk
- Mite
- Orc
- Tengu
- Tiefling

The following races are somewhat more powerful, due to the fact that they possess racial Hit Dice, exceptional ability score modifiers, natural attacks, or other unusual abilities. These races are intended as monstrous foes, not as PC races, and if you allow players to play one of these creatures, you should allow characters who pick from the list above or from the seven core races to start play at 2nd level.

- Boggard
- Bugbear
- Dark Creeper
- Drow
- Duergar
- Gnoll
- Lizardfolk
- Morlock
- Svirfneblin

their own. In these cases, you should inform your players that their choices for races are reduced, as appropriate.

On the other end of things, perhaps your world is much more extravagant than the implied world. In this case, you might allow your players to play characters of races other than those detailed in Chapter 2. The *Pathfinder RPG Bestiary* has many non-standard races to choose from, but you should note that most of these are significantly more powerful than those presented in Chapter 2. Any race that grants racial Hit Dice is probably too potent a choice for most campaigns. As a general guideline, you should advise your players to choose races of roughly equal power, using a creature's racial HD (not its CR) as a general guideline. Characters who wish instead to play standard races should be allowed to start at higher level, so that their total HD match the highest HD held by a non-standard race in the party.

ENDING THE CAMPAIGN

In the Pathfinder Roleplaying Game, 20th level represents the top end of power most mortals can hope to achieve, yet this certainly doesn't mean that your campaign needs to go all the way to 20th level. If you aren't running an open-ended campaign where the PCs set the pace and the goals, you should pick a level at which you wish the campaign's story arc to end. Talk this over with your players to make sure you're picking a level range that they're comfortable with as well. Note that you can also extend or shorten the length of a campaign by selecting a slow or fast XP progression. If you choose to run a campaign with a level cap of lower than 20th, consider placing your new level cap at a point where it feels like the last level achievable is something worthy. Odd-numbered levels are generally better than even-numbered ones, since most spellcasters achieve a new level of spell on odd-numbered levels. Multiples of 5 are good as well, since these multiples represent the last level before a new iterative attack. Stopping at 9th level is a good choice, since that allows the players to achieve capstone abilities like a bard's inspire greatness, a druid's venom immunity, a sorcerer's 3rd bloodline power, and *teleport* and *raise dead* as capstone spells. Likewise, 13th level works well, giving capstone abilities like a monk's spell resistance or spells like *greater teleport*, *limited wish*, and *resurrection*. Setting level caps of lower than 20th allows you to use them as soft limits—if your campaign's story arc goes beyond what you'd originally planned, your players can continue to gain levels and new abilities beyond what you estimated. Since the classes presented in Chapter 3 don't have additional rules provided beyond 20th level, setting a campaign arc to end at 20th level requires great timing and, invariably, some manipulation on your part as GM to make sure the story winds up before the PCs reach enough XP to theoretically hit 21st level.

Beyond 20th Level

Although Chapter 3 doesn't describe what happens after 20th level, this isn't to say that there are no resources available to you should you wish to continue your campaign on to 21st level and beyond. Rules for epic-level play like this exist in numerous products that are compatible with the Pathfinder Roleplaying Game, although in many cases these alternative rules can provide unanticipated problems. For example, if your campaign world is populated by creatures and villains who, at the upper limit of power, can challenge a 20th-level character, where will epic-level PCs go for challenges? You might be looking at creating an entirely new campaign setting, one set on different planes, planets, or dimensions from the one where your players spent their first 20 levels, and that's a lot of work.

Paizo Publishing may eventually publish rules to take your game into these epic realms, but if you can't wait and would rather not use existing open content rules for epic-level play, you can use the following brief guidelines to continue beyond 20th level. Note that these guidelines aren't robust enough to keep the game vibrant and interesting on their own for much longer past 20th level, but they should do in a pinch for a campaign that needs, say, 22 or 23 experience levels to wrap up. Likewise, you can use these rules to create super-powerful NPCs for 20th-level characters to face.

Experience Points: To gain a level beyond 20th, a character must double the experience points needed to achieve the previous level. Thus, assuming the medium XP progression, a 20th-level character needs 2,100,000 XP to become 21st level, since he needed 1,050,000 XP to reach 20th level from 19th. He'd then need 4,200,000 XP to reach 22nd level, 8,400,000 XP to reach 23rd, and so on.

Scaling Powers: Hit dice, base attack bonuses, and saving throws continue to increase at the same rate beyond 20th level, as appropriate for the class in question. Note that no character can have more than 4 attacks based on its base attack bonus. Note also that, before long, the difference between good saving throws and poor saving throws becomes awkwardly large—the further you get from 20th level, the more noticeable this difference grows, and for high-level characters, bolstering their poor saving throws should become increasingly important. Class abilities that have a set, increasing rate, such as a barbarian's damage reduction, a fighter's bonus feats and weapon training, a paladin's smite evil, or a rogue's sneak attack continue to progress at the appropriate rate.

Spells: A spellcaster's caster level continues to increase by one for each level beyond 20th level. Every odd-numbered level, a spellcaster gains access to a new level of spell one above his previous maximum level, gaining one spell slot in that new level. These spell slots can be used to prepare or cast spells adjusted by metamagic feats or any known spell of lower levels. Every even-numbered level, a spellcaster gains additional spell slots equal to the highest level spell he can currently cast. He can split these new slots any way he wants among the slots he currently has access to.

For example, a 21st-level wizard gains a single 10th-level spell slot, in which he can prepare any spell of level 1st through 9th, or in which he can prepare a metamagic spell that results in an effective spell level of 10 (such as extended *summon monster IX*, or quickened *disintegrate*). At 22nd level he gains 10 spell-levels' worth of new spell slots, and can gain 10 1st-level spells per day, two 5th-level spells per day, one 7th-level and one 3rd-level spell per day, or one more 10th-level spell per day. At 23rd level, he gains a single 11th-level spell slot, and so on.

Spellcasters who have a limited number of spells known (such as bards and sorcerers) can opt out of the benefits they gain (either a new level of spells or a number of spell slots) for that level and in exchange learn two more spells of any level they can currently cast.

You might want to further adjust the rate of spell level gain for classes (like paladins and rangers) who gain spells more slowly than more dedicated spellcaster classes.

Multiclassing/Prestige Classes: The simplest way to progress beyond 20th level is to simply multiclass or take levels in a prestige class, in which case you gain all of the abilities of the new class level normally. This effectively treats 20th level as a hard limit for class level, but not as a hard limit for total character level.

13 Environment

The frantic mercenary clambered out of the sewer drain onto the street, but barely had time to yell "Run!" to the crowd before the grate—and the street itself—exploded behind him. The roaring, filthy otyugh had not balked at the narrow exit point, and as stone and wagon and bystander went flying, panic bloomed.

From the safety of the tavern's rooftop patio, Lord Vashten sadly nodded at the chaos below as he turned to his esteemed guest, the Countess Lianna.

"And that, my dear, is the trouble with adventurers. Never the good sense to keep mayhem where it belongs."

From the lifeless desert to the trap-filled dungeon, the environment helps to define the world. Bringing these settings to life can help create a vibrant and immersive experience.

This chapter contains rules to help the GM adjudicate the game world, including rules for dungeons and their features, traps, various types of terrain, and environmental hazards.

DUNGEONS

Of all the strange places that an adventurer might explore, none is deadlier than the dungeon. These labyrinths, full of deadly traps, hungry monsters, and priceless treasure, test every skill a character possesses. These rules can apply to dungeons of any type, from the wreck of a sunken ship to a vast cave complex.

Types of Dungeons

The four basic dungeon types are defined by their current status. Many dungeons are variations on these basic types or combinations of more than one of them. Sometimes old dungeons are used again and again by different inhabitants for different purposes.

Ruined Structure: Once occupied, this place is now abandoned (completely or in part) by its original creator or creators, and other creatures have wandered in. Many subterranean creatures look for abandoned underground constructions in which to make their lairs. Any traps that might exist have probably been set off, but wandering beasts might very well be common.

Occupied Structure: This type of dungeon is still in use. Creatures (usually intelligent) live there, although they might not be the dungeon's creators. An occupied structure might be a home, a fortress, a temple, an active mine, a prison, or a headquarters. This type of dungeon is less likely to have traps or wandering beasts, and more likely to have organized guards—both on watch and on patrol. Traps or wandering beasts that might be encountered are usually under the control of the occupants. Occupied structures have furnishings to suit the inhabitants, as well as decorations, supplies, and the ability for occupants to move around. The inhabitants might have a communication system, and they almost certainly control an exit to the outside.

Some dungeons are partially occupied and partially empty or in ruins. In such cases, the occupants are typically not the original builders, but instead a group of intelligent creatures that have set up their base, lair, or fortification within an abandoned dungeon.

Safe Storage: When people want to protect something, they sometimes bury it underground. Whether the item they want to protect is a fabulous treasure, a forbidden artifact, or the dead body of an important figure, these valuable objects are placed within a dungeon and surrounded by barriers, traps, and guardians.

The safe storage dungeon is the most likely to have traps but the least likely to have wandering beasts. This type of dungeon is normally built for function rather than appearance, but sometimes it has ornamentation in the form of statuary or painted walls. This is particularly true of the tombs of important people.

Sometimes, however, a vault or a crypt is constructed in such a way as to house living guardians. The problem with this strategy is that something must be done to keep the creatures alive between intrusion attempts. Magic is usually the best solution to provide food and water for these creatures. Builders of vaults or tombs often use undead creatures or constructs, both of which have no need for sustenance or rest, to guard their dungeons. Magic traps can attack intruders by summoning monsters into the dungeon that disappear when their task is done.

Natural Cavern Complex: Underground caves provide homes for all sorts of subterranean monsters. Created naturally and connected by labyrinthine tunnel systems, these caverns lack any sort of pattern, order, or decoration. With no intelligent force behind its construction, this type of dungeon is the least likely to have traps or even doors.

Fungi of all sorts thrive in caves, sometimes growing in huge forests of mushrooms and puffballs. Subterranean predators prowl these forests, looking for weaker creatures feeding upon the fungi. Some varieties of fungus give off a phosphorescent glow, providing a natural cavern complex with its own limited light source. In other areas, a *daylight* spell or similar magical effect can provide enough light for green plants to grow.

Natural cavern complexes often connect with other types of dungeons, the caves having been discovered when the manufactured dungeons were delved. A cavern complex can connect two otherwise unrelated dungeons, sometimes creating a strange mixed environment. A natural cavern complex joined with another dungeon often provides a route by which subterranean creatures find their way into a manufactured dungeon and populate it.

Dungeon Terrain

The following rules cover the basics of terrain that can be found in a dungeon.

Walls

Masonry walls—stones piled on top of each other, usually but not always held in place with mortar—often divide dungeons into corridors and chambers. Dungeon walls can also be hewn from solid rock, leaving them with a rough, chiseled look. Still other dungeon walls can be the smooth, unblemished stone of a naturally occurring cave. Dungeon walls are difficult to break down or through, but they're generally easy to climb.

TABLE 13-1: WALLS

Wall Type	Typical Thickness	Break DC	Hardness	Hit Points[1]	Climb DC
Masonry	1 ft.	35	8	90 hp	20
Superior masonry	1 ft.	35	8	90 hp	25
Reinforced masonry	1 ft.	45	8	180 hp	20
Hewn stone	3 ft.	50	8	540 hp	25
Unworked stone	5 ft.	65	8	900 hp	15
Iron	3 in.	30	10	90 hp	25
Paper	Paper-thin	1	—	1 hp	30
Wooden	6 in.	20	5	60 hp	21
Magically treated[2]	—	+20	×2	×2[3]	—

1 Per 10-foot-by-10-foot section.

2 This modifier can be applied to any of the other wall types.

3 Or an additional 50 hit points, whichever is greater.

Masonry Walls: The most common kind of dungeon wall, masonry walls are usually at least 1 foot thick. Often, these ancient walls sport cracks and crevices, and sometimes dangerous slimes or small monsters live in these areas and wait for prey. Masonry walls stop all but the loudest noises. It takes a DC 20 Climb check to travel along a masonry wall.

Superior Masonry Walls: Sometimes masonry walls are better built (smoother, with tighter-fitting stones and less cracking), and occasionally these superior walls are covered with plaster or stucco. Covered walls often bear paintings, carved reliefs, or other decoration. Superior masonry walls are no more difficult to destroy than regular masonry walls but are more difficult to climb (DC 25).

Reinforced Masonry Walls: These are masonry walls with iron bars on one or both sides of the wall, or placed within the wall to strengthen it. The hardness of a reinforced wall remains the same, but its hit points are doubled and the Strength check DC to break through it is increased by 10.

Hewn Stone Walls: Such walls usually result when a chamber or passage is tunneled out from solid rock. The rough surface of a hewn wall frequently provides minuscule ledges where fungus grows and fissures where vermin, bats, and subterranean snakes live. When such a wall has an "other side" (meaning it separates two chambers in the dungeon), the wall is usually at least 3 feet thick; anything thinner risks collapsing from the weight of all the stone overhead. It takes a DC 25 Climb check to climb a hewn stone wall.

Unworked Stone Walls: These surfaces are uneven and rarely flat. They are smooth to the touch but filled with tiny holes, hidden alcoves, and ledges at various heights. They're also usually wet or at least damp, since it's water that most frequently creates natural caves. When such a wall has an "other side," the wall is usually at least 5 feet thick. It takes a DC 15 Climb check to move along an unworked stone wall.

Iron Walls: These walls are placed within dungeons around important places, such as vaults.

Paper Walls: Paper walls are placed as screens to block line of sight, but nothing more.

Wooden Walls: Wooden walls often exist as recent additions to older dungeons, used to create animal pens, storage bins, and temporary structures, or just to make a number of smaller rooms out of a larger one.

Magically Treated Walls: These walls are stronger than average, with a greater hardness, more hit points, and a higher break DC. Magic can usually double the hardness and hit points of a wall and add up to 20 to the break DC. A magically treated wall also gains a saving throw against spells that could affect it, with the save bonus equaling 2 + 1/2 the caster level of the magic reinforcing the wall. Creating a magic wall requires the Craft Wondrous Item feat and the expenditure of 1,500 gp for each 10-foot-by-10-foot wall section.

Walls with Arrow Slits: Walls with arrow slits can be made of any durable material but are most commonly masonry, hewn stone, or wood. Such a wall allows defenders to fire arrows or crossbow bolts at intruders from behind the safety of the wall. Archers behind arrow slits have improved cover that gives them a +8 bonus to Armor Class, a +4 bonus on Reflex saves, and the benefits of the improved evasion class feature.

Floors

As with walls, dungeon floors come in many types.

Flagstone: Like masonry walls, flagstone floors are made of fitted stones. They are usually cracked and only somewhat level. Slime and mold grows in the cracks. Sometimes water runs in rivulets between the stones or sits in stagnant puddles. Flagstone is the most common dungeon floor.

Uneven Flagstone: Over time, some floors can become so uneven that a DC 10 Acrobatics check is required to run or charge across the surface. Failure means the character

can't move that round. Floors as treacherous as this should be the exception, not the rule.

Hewn Stone Floors: Rough and uneven, hewn floors are usually covered with loose stones, gravel, dirt, or other debris. A DC 10 Acrobatics check is required to run or charge across such a floor. Failure means the character can still act, but can't run or charge in this round.

Light Rubble: Small chunks of debris litter the ground. Light rubble adds 2 to the DC of Acrobatics checks.

Dense Rubble: The ground is covered with debris of all sizes. It costs 2 squares of movement to enter a square with dense rubble. Dense rubble adds 5 to the DC of Acrobatics checks, and it adds 2 to the DC of Stealth checks.

Smooth Stone Floors: Finished and sometimes even polished, smooth floors are found only in dungeons made by capable and careful builders.

Natural Stone Floors: The floor of a natural cave is as uneven as the walls. Caves rarely have flat surfaces of any great size. Rather, their floors have many levels. Some adjacent floor surfaces might vary in elevation by only a foot, so that moving from one to the other is no more difficult than negotiating a stair step, but in other places the floor might suddenly drop off or rise up several feet or more, requiring Climb checks to get from one surface to the other. Unless a path has been worn and well marked in the floor of a natural cave, it takes 2 squares of movement to enter a square with a natural stone floor, and the DC of Acrobatics checks increases by 5. Running and charging are impossible, except along paths.

Slippery: Water, ice, slime, or blood can make any of the dungeon floors described in this section more treacherous. Slippery floors increase the DC of Acrobatics checks by 5.

Grate: A grate often covers a pit or an area lower than the main floor. Grates are usually made from iron, but large ones can also be made from iron-bound timbers. Many grates have hinges to allow access to what lies below (such grates can be locked like any door), while others are permanent and designed to not move. A typical 1-inch-thick iron grate has 25 hit points, hardness 10, and a DC of 27 for Strength checks to break through it or tear it loose.

Ledge: Ledges allow creatures to walk above some lower area. They often circle around pits, run along underground streams, form balconies around large rooms, or provide a place for archers to stand while firing upon enemies below. Narrow ledges (12 inches wide or less) require those moving along them to make Acrobatics checks. Failure results in the moving character falling off the ledge. Ledges sometimes have railings along the wall. In such a case, characters gain a +5 circumstance bonus on Acrobatics checks to move along the ledge. A character who is next to a railing gains a +2 circumstance bonus to his CMD to avoid being bull rushed off the edge.

Ledges can also have low walls 2 to 3 feet high along their edges. Such walls provide cover against attackers within 30 feet on the other side of the wall, as long as the target is closer to the low wall than the attacker is.

Transparent Floor: Transparent floors, made of reinforced glass or magic materials (even a *wall of force*), allow a dangerous setting to be viewed safely from above. Transparent floors are sometimes placed over lava pools, arenas, monster dens, and torture chambers. They can be used by defenders to watch key areas for intruders.

Sliding Floors: A sliding floor is a type of trap door, designed to be moved and thus reveal something that lies beneath it. A typical sliding floor moves so slowly that anyone standing on one can avoid falling into the gap it creates, assuming there's somewhere else to go. If such a floor slides quickly enough that there's a chance of a character falling into whatever lies beneath—a spiked pit, a vat of burning oil, or a pool filled with sharks—then it's a trap.

Trap Floors: Some floors are designed to become suddenly dangerous. With the application of just the right amount of weight, or the pull of a lever somewhere nearby, spikes protrude from the floor, gouts of steam or flame shoot up from hidden holes, or the entire floor tilts. These strange floors are sometimes found in arenas, designed to make combats more exciting and deadly. Construct these floors as you would any other trap.

Doors

Doors in dungeons are much more than mere entrances and exits. Often they can be encounters all by themselves. Dungeon doors come in three basic types: wooden, stone, and iron.

Wooden Doors: Constructed of thick planks nailed together, sometimes bound with iron for strength (and to reduce swelling from dungeon dampness), wooden doors are the most common type. Wooden doors come in varying strengths: simple, good, and strong. Simple doors (break DC 15) are not meant to keep out motivated attackers. Good doors (break DC 18), while sturdy and long-lasting, are still not meant to take much punishment. Strong doors (break DC 25) are bound in iron and are a sturdy barrier to those attempting to get past them. Iron hinges fasten the door to its frame, and typically a circular pull-ring in the center is there to help open it. Sometimes, instead of a pull-ring, a door has an iron pull-bar on one or both sides of the door to serve as a handle. In inhabited dungeons, these doors are usually well-maintained (not stuck) and unlocked, although important areas are locked up if possible.

Stone: Carved from solid blocks of stone, these heavy, unwieldy doors are often built so that they pivot when opened, although dwarves and other skilled craftsfolk are able to fashion hinges strong enough to hold up a

TABLE 13-2: DOORS

Door Type	Typical Thickness	Hardness	Hit Points	Break DC Stuck	Break DC Locked
Simple wooden	1 in.	5	10 hp	13	15
Good wooden	1-1/2 in.	5	15 hp	16	18
Strong wooden	2 in.	5	20 hp	23	25
Stone	4 in.	8	60 hp	28	28
Iron	2 in.	10	60 hp	28	28
Portcullis, wooden	3 in	5	30 hp	25*	25*
Portcullis, iron	2 in.	10	60 hp	25*	25*
Lock	—	15	30 hp	—	—
Hinge	—	10	30 hp	—	—

* DC to lift. Use appropriate door figure for breaking.

stone door. Secret doors concealed within a stone wall are usually stone doors. Otherwise, such doors stand as tough barriers protecting something important beyond. Thus, they are often locked or barred.

Iron: Rusted but sturdy, iron doors in a dungeon are hinged like wooden doors. These doors are the toughest form of nonmagical door. They are usually locked or barred.

Breaking Doors: Dungeon doors might be locked, trapped, reinforced, barred, magically sealed, or sometimes just stuck. All but the weakest characters can eventually knock down a door with a heavy tool such as a sledgehammer, and a number of spells and magic items give characters an easy way around a locked door.

Attempts to literally chop down a door with a slashing or bludgeoning weapon use the hardness and hit points given in Table 13-2. When assigning a DC to an attempt to knock a door down, use the following as guidelines.

DC 10 or Lower: a door just about anyone can break open.

DC 11–15: a door that a strong person could break with one try and an average person might be able to break with one try.

DC 16–20: a door that almost anyone could break, given time.

DC 21–25: a door that only a strong or very strong person has a hope of breaking, probably not on the first try.

DC 26 or Higher: a door that only an exceptionally strong person has a hope of breaking.

Locks: Dungeon doors are often locked, and thus the Disable Device skill comes in very handy. Locks are usually built into the door, either on the edge opposite the hinges or right in the middle of the door. Built-in locks either control an iron bar that juts out of the door and into the wall of its frame, or else a sliding iron bar or heavy wooden bar that rests behind the entire door. By contrast, padlocks are not built-in but usually run through two rings, one on the door and the other on the wall. More complex locks, such as combination locks and puzzle locks, are usually built into the door itself. Because such keyless locks are larger and more complex, they are typically only found in sturdy doors (strong wooden, stone, or iron doors).

The Disable Device DC to pick a lock often falls within the range of 20 to 30, although locks with lower or higher DCs can exist. A door can have more than one lock, each of which must be unlocked separately. Locks are often trapped, usually with poison needles that extend out to prick a rogue's finger.

Breaking a lock is sometimes quicker than breaking the whole door. If a PC wants to whack at a lock with a weapon, treat the typical lock as having hardness 15 and 30 hit points. A lock can only be broken if it can be attacked separately from the door, which means that a built-in lock is immune to this sort of treatment. In an occupied dungeon, every locked door should have a key somewhere.

A special door might have a lock with no key, instead requiring that the right combination of nearby levers must be manipulated or the right symbols must be pressed on a keypad in the correct sequence to open the door.

Stuck Doors: Dungeons are often damp, and sometimes doors get stuck, particularly wooden doors. Assume that about 10% of wooden doors and 5% of non-wooden doors are stuck. These numbers can be doubled (to 20% and 10%, respectively) for long-abandoned or neglected dungeons.

Barred Doors: When characters try to bash down a barred door, it's the quality of the bar that matters, not the material the door is made of. It takes a DC 25 Strength check to break through a door with a wooden bar, and a DC 30 Strength check if the bar is made of iron. Characters can attack the door and destroy it instead, leaving the bar hanging in the now-open doorway.

Magic Seals: Spells such as *arcane lock* can discourage passage through a door. A door with an *arcane lock* spell on it is considered locked even if it doesn't have a physical lock. It takes a *knock* spell, a *dispel magic* spell, or a successful Strength check to open such a door.

Hinges: Most doors have hinges, but sliding doors do not. They usually have tracks or grooves instead, allowing them to slide easily to one side.

Standard Hinges: These hinges are metal, joining one edge of the door to the door frame or wall. Remember that the door swings open toward the side with the hinges. (So, if the hinges are on the PCs' side, the door opens toward them; otherwise it opens away from them.) Adventurers can take the hinges apart one at a time with successful Disable Device checks (assuming the hinges are on their side of the door, of course). Such a task has a DC of 20 because most hinges are rusted or stuck. Breaking a hinge is difficult. Most have hardness 10 and 30 hit points. The break DC for a hinge is the same as for breaking down the door.

Nested Hinges: These hinges are much more complex than ordinary hinges, and are found only in areas of excellent construction. These hinges are built into the wall and allow the door to swing open in either direction. PCs can't get at the hinges to fool with them unless they break through the door frame or wall. Nested hinges are typically found on stone doors but sometimes on wooden or iron doors as well.

Pivots: Pivots aren't really hinges at all, but simple knobs jutting from the top and bottom of the door that fit into holes in the door frame, allowing the door to spin. The advantages of pivots are that they can't be dismantled like hinges and they're simple to make. The disadvantage is that since the door pivots on its center of gravity (typically in the middle), nothing larger than half the door's width can fit through without squeezing. Doors with pivots are usually stone and often quite wide to overcome this disadvantage. Another solution is to place the pivot toward one side and have the door be thicker at that end and thinner toward the other end so that it opens more like a normal door. Secret doors in walls often turn on pivots, since the lack of hinges makes it easier to hide the door's presence. Pivots also allow objects such as bookcases to be used as secret doors.

Secret Doors: Disguised as a bare patch of wall (or floor or ceiling), a bookcase, a fireplace, or a fountain, a secret door leads to a secret passage or room. Someone examining the area finds a secret door, if one exists, on a successful Perception check (DC 20 for a typical secret door to DC 30 for a well-hidden secret door).

Many secret doors require special methods of opening, such as hidden buttons or pressure plates. Secret doors can open like normal doors, or they might pivot, slide, sink, rise, or even lower like a drawbridge to permit access. Builders might put a secret door low near the floor or high in a wall, making it difficult to find or reach. Wizards and sorcerers have a spell, *phase door*, that allows them to create a magic secret door that only they can use.

Magic Doors: Enchanted by the original builders, a door might speak to explorers, warning them away. It might be protected from harm, increasing its hardness or giving it more hit points as well as an improved saving throw bonus against *disintegrate* and similar spells. A magic door might not lead into the space behind it, but instead might be a portal to a faraway place or even another plane of existence. Other magic doors might require passwords or special keys to open them.

Portcullises: These special doors consist of iron or thick, ironbound wooden shafts that descend from recesses in the ceilings above archways. Sometimes a portcullis has crossbars that create a grid, sometimes not. Typically raised by means of a winch or a capstan, a portcullis can be dropped quickly, and the shafts end in spikes to discourage anyone from standing underneath (or from attempting to dive under it as it drops). Once it is dropped, a portcullis locks, unless it is so large that no normal person could lift it anyway. In any event, lifting a typical portcullis requires a DC 25 Strength check.

Walls, Doors, and Detect Spells

Stone walls, iron walls, and iron doors are usually thick enough to block most detect spells, such as *detect thoughts*. Wooden walls, wooden doors, and stone doors are usually not thick enough to do so. A secret stone door built into a wall and as thick as the wall itself (at least 1 foot) does block most detect spells.

Stairs

Stairs are the most common means of traveling up and down within a dungeon. A character can move up or down stairs as part of their movement without penalty, but they cannot run on them. Increase the DC of any Acrobatics skill check made on stairs by 4. Some stairs are particularly steep and are treated as difficult terrain.

Cave-Ins and Collapses (CR 8)

Cave-ins and collapsing tunnels are extremely dangerous. Not only do dungeon explorers face the danger of being crushed by tons of falling rock, but even if they survive they might be buried beneath a pile of rubble or cut off from the only known exit. A cave-in buries anyone in the middle of the collapsing area, and then sliding debris damages anyone in the periphery of the collapse. A typical corridor subject to a cave-in might have a bury zone with a 15-foot radius and a 10-foot-wide slide zone extending beyond the bury zone. A weakened ceiling can be spotted with a DC 20 Knowledge (engineering) or DC 20 Craft (stonemasonry) check. Remember that Craft checks can be made untrained as Intelligence checks. A dwarf can make such a check if he simply passes within 10 feet of a weakened ceiling.

A weakened ceiling might collapse when subjected to a major impact or concussion. A character can cause a cave-in by destroying half the pillars holding up the ceiling.

Characters in the bury zone of a cave-in take 8d6 points of damage, or half that amount if they make a DC 15 Reflex save. They are subsequently buried. Characters in the slide zone take 3d6 points of damage, or no damage at all if they make a DC 15 Reflex save. Characters in the slide zone who fail their saves are buried.

Characters take 1d6 points of nonlethal damage per minute while buried. If such a character falls unconscious, he must make a DC 15 Constitution check each minute. If it fails, he takes 1d6 points of lethal damage each minute until freed or dead.

Characters who aren't buried can dig out their friends. In 1 minute, using only her hands, a character can clear rocks and debris equal to five times her heavy load limit. The amount of loose stone that fills a 5-foot-by-5-foot area weighs 1 ton (2,000 pounds). Armed with an appropriate tool, such as a pick, crowbar, or shovel,

a digger can clear loose stone twice as quickly as by hand. A buried character can attempt to free himself with a DC 25 Strength check.

Slimes, Molds, and Fungi

In a dungeon's damp, dark recesses, molds and fungi thrive. For purposes of spells and other special effects, all slimes, molds, and fungi are treated as plants. Like traps, dangerous slimes and molds have CRs, and characters earn XP for encountering them.

A form of glistening organic sludge coats almost anything that remains in the damp and dark for too long. This kind of slime, though it might be repulsive, is not dangerous. Molds and fungi flourish in dark, cool, damp places. While some are as inoffensive as the normal dungeon slime, others are quite dangerous. Mushrooms, puffballs, yeasts, mildew, and other sorts of bulbous, fibrous, or flat patches of fungi can be found throughout most dungeons. They are usually inoffensive, and some are even edible (although most are unappealing or odd-tasting).

Brown Mold (CR 2): Brown mold feeds on warmth, drawing heat from anything around it. It normally comes in patches 5 feet in diameter, and the temperature is always cold in a 30-foot radius around it. Living creatures within 5 feet of it take 3d6 points of nonlethal cold damage. Fire brought within 5 feet of brown mold causes the mold to instantly double in size. Cold damage, such as from a *cone of cold*, instantly destroys it.

Green Slime (CR 4): This dungeon peril is a dangerous variety of normal slime. Green slime devours flesh and organic materials on contact and is even capable of dissolving metal. Bright green, wet, and sticky, it clings to walls, floors, and ceilings in patches, reproducing as it consumes organic matter. It drops from walls and ceilings when it detects movement (and possible food) below.

A single 5-foot square of green slime deals 1d6 points of Constitution damage per round while it devours flesh. On the first round of contact, the slime can be scraped off a creature (destroying the scraping device), but after that it must be frozen, burned, or cut away (dealing damage to the victim as well). Anything that deals cold or fire damage, sunlight, or a *remove disease* spell destroys a patch of green slime. Against wood or metal, green slime deals 2d6 points of damage per round, ignoring metal's hardness but not that of wood. It does not harm stone.

Phosphorescent Fungus: This strange underground fungus gives off a soft violet glow that illuminates underground caverns and passages as well as a candle does. Rare patches of fungus illuminate as well as a torch does.

Shrieker: This human-sized purple mushroom emits a piercing sound that lasts for 1d3 rounds whenever there is movement or a light source within 10 feet. This shriek makes it impossible to hear any other sound within 50 feet. The sound attracts nearby creatures that are disposed to investigate it. Some creatures that live near shriekers learn that this noise means there is food or an intruder nearby.

Yellow Mold (CR 6): If disturbed, a 5-foot square of this mold bursts forth with a cloud of poisonous spores. All within 10 feet of the mold must make a DC 15 Fortitude save or take 1d3 points of Constitution damage. Another DC 15 Fortitude save is required once per round for the next 5 rounds, to avoid taking 1d3 points of Constitution damage each round. A successful Fortitude save ends this effect. Fire destroys yellow mold, and sunlight renders it dormant.

TRAPS

Traps are a common danger in dungeon environments. From gouts of white-hot flame to hails of poisoned darts, traps can serve to protect valuable treasure or stop intruders from proceeding.

Elements of a Trap

All traps—mechanical or magical—have the following elements: CR, type, Perception DC, Disable Device DC, trigger, reset, and effect. Some traps might also include optional elements, such as poison or a bypass. These characteristics are described below.

Type

A trap can be either mechanical or magical in nature.

Mechanical: Dungeons are frequently equipped with deadly mechanical (nonmagical) traps. A trap typically is defined by its location and triggering conditions, how hard it is to spot before it goes off, how much damage it deals, and whether or not the characters receive a saving throw to mitigate its effects. Traps that attack with arrows, sweeping blades, and other types of weaponry make normal attack rolls, with specific attack bonuses dictated by the trap's design. A mechanical trap can be constructed by a PC through successful use of the Craft (traps) skill (see Designing a Trap on page 423 and the skill description on page 91).

Creatures that succeed on a Perception check detect a trap before it is triggered. The DC of this check depends on the trap itself. Success generally indicates that the creature has detected the mechanism that activates the trap, such as a pressure plate, odd gears attached to a door handle, and the like. Beating this check by 5 or more also gives some indication of what the trap is designed to do.

Magic: Many spells can be used to create dangerous traps. Unless the spell or item description states otherwise, assume the following to be true.

- A successful Perception check (DC 25 + spell level) detects a magic trap before it goes off.
- Magic traps permit a saving throw in order to avoid the effect (DC 10 + spell level × 1.5).
- Magic traps may be disarmed by a character with the trapfinding class feature with a successful Disable Device skill check (DC 25 + spell level). Other characters have no chance to disarm a magic trap with a Disable Device check.

Magic traps are further divided into spell traps and magic device traps. Magic device traps initiate spell effects when activated, just as wands, rods, rings, and other magic items do. Creating a magic device trap requires the Craft Wondrous Item feat.

Spell traps are simply spells that themselves function as traps. Creating a spell trap requires the services of a character who can cast the needed spell or spells, who is usually either the character creating the trap or an NPC spellcaster hired for that purpose.

Perception and Disable Device DCs

The builder sets the Perception and Disable Device DCs for a mechanical trap. For a magic trap, the values depend on the highest-level spell used.

Mechanical Trap: The base DC for both Perception and Disable Device checks is 20. Raising or lowering either of these DCs affects the CR (Table 13–3).

Magic Trap: The DC for both Perception and Disable Device checks is equal to 25 + the spell level of the highest-level spell used. Only characters with the trapfinding class feature can attempt a Disable Device check involving a magic trap.

Trigger

A trap's trigger determines how it is sprung.

Location: A location trigger springs a trap when someone stands in a particular square.

Proximity: This trigger activates the trap when a creature approaches within a certain distance of it. A proximity trigger differs from a location trigger in that the creature need not be standing in a particular square. Creatures that are flying can spring a trap with a proximity trigger but not one with a location trigger. Mechanical proximity triggers are extremely sensitive to the slightest change in the air. This makes them useful only in places such as crypts, where the air is unusually still.

The proximity trigger used most often for magic device traps is the *alarm* spell. Unlike when the spell is cast, an *alarm* spell used as a trigger can have an area that's no larger than the area the trap is meant to protect.

Some magic device traps have special proximity triggers that activate only when certain kinds of creatures approach. For example, a *detect good* spell can serve as a proximity trigger on an evil altar, springing the attached trap only when someone of good alignment gets close enough to it.

Sound: This trigger springs a magic trap when it detects any sound. A sound trigger functions like an ear and has a +15 bonus on Perception checks. A successful Stealth check, magical *silence*, and other effects that would negate hearing defeat it. A trap with a sound trigger requires the casting of *clairaudience* during its construction.

Visual: This trigger for magic traps works like an actual eye, springing the trap whenever it "sees" something. A trap with a visual trigger requires the casting of *arcane eye*, *clairvoyance*, or *true seeing* during its construction. Sight range and the Perception bonus conferred on the trap depend on the spell chosen, as shown.

Spell	Sight Range	Perception Bonus
Arcane eye	Line of sight (unlimited range)	+20
Clairvoyance	One preselected location	+15
True seeing	Line of sight (up to 120 ft.)	+30

If you want the trap to see in the dark, you must either choose the *true seeing* option or add *darkvision* to the trap as well. (*Darkvision* limits the trap's sight range in the dark to 60 feet.) If invisibility, disguises, or illusions can fool the spell being used, they can fool the visual trigger as well.

Touch: A touch trigger, which springs the trap when touched, is one of the simplest kinds of trigger to construct. This trigger may be physically attached to the part of the mechanism that deals the damage or it may not. You can make a magic touch trigger by adding *alarm* to the trap and reducing the area of the effect to cover only the trigger spot.

Timed: This trigger periodically springs the trap after a certain duration has passed.

Spell: All spell traps have this kind of trigger. The appropriate spell descriptions explain the trigger conditions for traps that contain spell triggers.

Duration

Unless otherwise stated, most traps have a duration of instantaneous; once triggered, they have their effect and then stop functioning. Some traps have a duration measured in rounds. Such traps continue to have their listed effect each round at the top of the initiative order (or whenever they were activated, if they were triggered during combat).

Reset

A reset element is the set of conditions under which a trap becomes ready to trigger again. Resetting a trap

usually takes only a minute or so. For a trap with a more difficult reset method, you should set the time and labor required.

No Reset: Short of completely rebuilding the trap, there's no way to trigger it more than once. Spell traps have no reset element.

Repair: To get the trap functioning again, you must repair it. Repairing a mechanical trap requires a Craft (traps) check against a DC equal to the one for building it. The cost for raw materials is one-fifth of the trap's original market price. To calculate how long it takes to fix a trap, use the same calculations you would for building it, but use the cost of the raw materials required for repair in place of the market price.

Manual: Resetting the trap requires someone to move the parts back into place. This is the kind of reset element most mechanical traps have.

Automatic: The trap resets itself, either immediately or after a timed interval.

Bypass (Optional Element)

If the builder of a trap wants to be able to move past the trap after it is created or placed, it's a good idea to build in a bypass mechanism: something that temporarily disarms the trap. Bypass elements are typically used only with mechanical traps; spell traps usually have built-in allowances for the caster to bypass them.

Lock: A lock bypass requires a DC 30 Disable Device check to open.

Hidden Switch: A hidden switch requires a DC 25 Perception check to locate.

Hidden Lock: A hidden lock combines the features above, requiring a DC 25 Perception check to locate and a DC 30 Disable Device check to open.

Effect

The effect of a trap is what happens to those who spring it. This often takes the form of either damage or a spell effect, but some traps have special effects. A trap usually either makes an attack roll or forces a saving throw to avoid it. Occasionally a trap uses both of these options, or neither (see Never Miss).

Pits: These are holes (covered or not) that characters can fall into, causing them to take damage. A pit needs no attack roll, but a successful Reflex save (DC set by the builder) avoids it. Other save-dependent mechanical traps also fall into this category. Falling into a pit deals 1d6 points of damage per 10 feet of depth.

Pits in dungeons come in three basic varieties: uncovered, covered, and chasms. Pits and chasms can be defeated by judicious application of the Acrobatics skill, the Climb skill, or various mechanical or magical means.

Uncovered pits and natural chasms serve mainly to discourage intruders from going a certain way, although they cause much grief to characters who stumble into them in the dark, and they can greatly complicate nearby melee.

Covered pits are much more dangerous. They can be detected with a DC 20 Perception check, but only if the character is taking the time to carefully examine the area before walking across it. A character who fails to detect a covered pit is still entitled to a DC 20 Reflex save to avoid falling into it. If she was running or moving recklessly at the time, however, she gets no saving throw and falls automatically.

Trap coverings can be as simple as piled refuse (straw, leaves, sticks, garbage), a large rug, or an actual trap door concealed to appear as a normal part of the floor. Such a trap door usually swings open when enough weight (usually about 50 to 80 pounds) is placed upon it. Devious trap builders sometimes design trap doors so they spring back shut after they open. The trap door might lock once it's back in place, leaving the stranded character well and truly trapped. Opening such a trap door is just as difficult as opening a regular door (assuming the trapped character can reach it), and a DC 13 Strength check is needed to keep a spring-loaded door open.

Pit traps often have something nastier than just a hard floor at the bottom. A trap designer might put spikes, monsters, or a pool of acid, lava, or even water at the bottom. For rules on pit spikes and other such add-ons, see the Miscellaneous Trap Features section.

Monsters sometimes live in pits. Any monster that can fit into the pit might have been placed there by the dungeon's designer, or might simply have fallen in and not been able to climb back out.

A secondary trap, mechanical or magical, at the bottom of a pit can be particularly deadly. Activated by a falling victim, the secondary trap attacks the already injured character when she's least ready for it.

Ranged Attack Traps: These traps fling darts, arrows, spears, or the like at whomever activated the trap. The builder sets the attack bonus. A ranged attack trap can be configured to simulate the effect of a composite bow with a high Strength rating, which provides the trap with a bonus on damage equal to its Strength rating. These traps deal whatever damage their ammunition normally does. If a trap is constructed with a high Strength rating, it has a corresponding bonus on damage.

Melee Attack Traps: These traps feature such obstacles as sharp blades that emerge from walls and stone blocks that fall from ceilings. Once again, the builder sets the attack bonus. These traps deal the same damage as the melee weapons they "wield." In the case of a falling stone block, you can assign any amount of bludgeoning damage you like, but remember that whoever resets the trap has to lift that stone back into place.

A melee attack trap can be constructed with a built-in bonus on damage rolls, just as if the trap itself had a high Strength score.

Spell Traps: Spell traps produce the spell's effect. Like all spells, a spell trap that allows a saving throw has a save DC of 10 + spell level + caster's relevant ability modifier.

Magic Device Traps: These traps produce the effects of any spells included in their construction, as described in the appropriate entries. If the spell in a magic device trap allows a saving throw, its save DC is (10 + spell level) × 1.5. Some spells make attack rolls instead.

Special: Some traps have miscellaneous features that produce special effects, such as drowning for a water trap or ability damage for poison. Saving throws and damage depend on the poison or are set by the builder, as appropriate.

Miscellaneous Trap Features

Some traps include optional features that can make them considerably more deadly. The most common features are discussed below.

Alchemical Item: Mechanical traps might incorporate alchemical devices or other special substances or items, such as tanglefoot bags, alchemist's fire, thunderstones, and the like. Some such items mimic spell effects. If the item mimics a spell effect, it increases the CR as shown on Table 13–3: CR Modifiers for Mechanical Traps.

Gas: With a gas trap, the danger is in the inhaled poison it delivers. Traps employing gas usually have the never miss and onset delay features.

Liquid: Any trap that involves a danger of drowning is in this category. Traps employing liquid usually have the never miss and onset delay features.

Multiple Targets: Traps with this feature can affect more than one character.

Never Miss: When the entire dungeon wall moves to crush you, your quick reflexes won't help, since the wall can't possibly miss. A trap with this feature has neither an attack bonus nor a saving throw to avoid, but it does have an onset delay. Most traps involving liquid or gas are of the never miss variety.

Onset Delay: An onset delay is the amount of time between when the trap is sprung and when it deals damage. A never miss trap always has an onset delay.

Poison: Traps that employ poison are deadlier than their nonpoisonous counterparts, so they have correspondingly higher CRs. To determine the CR modifier for a given poison, consult Table 13–3. Only injury, contact, and inhaled poisons are suitable for traps; ingested types are

not. Some traps simply deal the poison's damage. Others deal damage with ranged or melee attacks as well. See page 557 for more information on poison.

Pit Spikes: Treat spikes at the bottom of a pit as daggers, each with a +10 attack bonus. The damage bonus for each spike is +1 per 10 feet of pit depth (to a maximum of +5). Each character who falls into the pit is attacked by 1d4 spikes. This damage is in addition to any damage from the fall itself, and the statistics presented above are merely the most common variant—some traps might have far more dangerous spikes at their bottom. Pit spikes add to the average damage of the trap (see Average Damage, below).

Pit Bottom: If something other than spikes waits at the bottom of a pit, it's best to treat that as a separate trap (see Multiple Traps) with a location trigger that activates on any significant impact, such as a falling character.

Touch Attack: This feature applies to any trap that needs only a successful touch attack (melee or ranged) to hit.

SAMPLE TRAPS

The following sample traps represent just some of the possibilities when constructing traps to challenge the player characters.

ARROW TRAP — CR 1
Type mechanical; **Perception** DC 20; **Disable Device** DC 20

EFFECTS

Trigger touch; **Reset** none
Effect Atk +15 ranged (1d8+1/×3)

PIT TRAP — CR 1
Type mechanical; **Perception** DC 20; **Disable Device** DC 20

EFFECTS

Trigger location; **Reset** manual
Effect 20-ft.-deep pit (2d6 falling damage); DC 20 Reflex avoids; multiple targets (all targets in a 10-ft.-square area)

POISONED DART TRAP — CR 1
Type mechanical; **Perception** DC 20; **Disable Device** DC 20

EFFECTS

Trigger touch; **Reset** none
Effect Atk +10 ranged (1d3 plus greenblood oil)

SWINGING AXE TRAP — CR 1
Type mechanical; **Perception** DC 20; **Disable Device** DC 20

EFFECTS

Trigger location; **Reset** manual
Effect Atk +10 melee (1d8+1/×3); multiple targets (all targets in a 10-ft. line)

BURNING HANDS TRAP — CR 2
Type magic; **Perception** DC 26; **Disable Device** DC 26

EFFECTS

Trigger proximity (*alarm*); **Reset** none
Effect spell effect (*burning hands*, 2d4 fire damage, DC 11 Reflex save for half damage); multiple targets (all targets in a 15-ft. cone)

JAVELIN TRAP — CR 2
Type mechanical; **Perception** DC 20; **Disable Device** DC 20

EFFECTS

Trigger location; **Reset** none
Effect Atk +15 ranged (1d6+6)

SPIKED PIT TRAP — CR 2
Type mechanical; **Perception** DC 20; **Disable Device** DC 20

EFFECTS

Trigger location; **Reset** manual
Effect 10-ft.-deep pit (1d6 falling damage); pit spikes (Atk +10 melee, 1d4 spikes per target for 1d4+2 damage each); DC 20 Reflex avoids; multiple targets (all targets in a 10-ft.-square area)

ACID ARROW TRAP — CR 3
Type magic; **Perception** DC 27; **Disable Device** DC 27

EFFECTS

Trigger proximity (*alarm*); **Reset** none
Effect spell effect (*acid arrow*, Atk +2 ranged touch, 2d4 acid damage for 4 rounds)

CAMOUFLAGED PIT TRAP — CR 3
Type mechanical; **Perception** DC 25; **Disable Device** DC 20

EFFECTS

Trigger location; **Reset** manual
Effect 30-ft.-deep pit (3d6 falling damage); DC 20 Reflex avoids; multiple targets (all targets in a 10-ft.-square area)

ELECTRICITY ARC TRAP — CR 4
Type mechanical; **Perception** DC 25; **Disable Device** DC 20

EFFECTS

Trigger touch; **Reset** none
Effect electricity arc (4d6 electricity damage, DC 20 Reflex save for half damage); multiple targets (all targets in a 30-ft. line)

WALL SCYTHE TRAP — CR 4
Type mechanical; **Perception** DC 20; **Disable Device** DC 20

EFFECTS

Trigger location; **Reset** automatic reset
Effect Atk +20 melee (2d4+6/×4)

FALLING BLOCK TRAP — CR 5
Type mechanical; **Perception** DC 20; **Disable Device** DC 20

EFFECTS

Trigger location; **Reset** manual
Effect Atk +15 melee (6d6); multiple targets (all targets in a 10-ft. square)

FIREBALL TRAP — CR 5

Type magic; **Perception** DC 28; **Disable Device** DC 28

EFFECTS

Trigger proximity (*alarm*); **Reset** none
Effect spell effect (*fireball*, 6d6 fire damage, DC 14 Reflex save for half damage); multiple targets (all targets in a 20-ft.-radius burst)

FLAME STRIKE TRAP — CR 6

Type magic; **Perception** DC 30; **Disable Device** DC 30

EFFECTS

Trigger proximity (*alarm*); **Reset** none
Effect spell effect (*flame strike*, 8d6 fire damage, DC 17 Reflex save for half damage); multiple targets (all targets in a 10-ft.-radius cylinder)

WYVERN ARROW TRAP — CR 6

Type mechanical; **Perception** DC 20; **Disable Device** DC 20

EFFECTS

Trigger location; **Reset** none
Effect Atk +15 ranged (1d6 plus wyvern poison/×3)

FROST FANGS TRAP — CR 7

Type mechanical; **Perception** DC 25; **Disable Device** DC 20

EFFECTS

Trigger location; **Duration** 3 rounds; **Reset** none
Effect jets of freezing water (3d6 cold damage, DC 20 Reflex save for half damage); multiple targets (all targets in a 40-ft.-square chamber)

SUMMON MONSTER VI TRAP — CR 7

Type magic; **Perception** DC 31; **Disable Device** DC 31

EFFECTS

Trigger proximity (*alarm*); **Reset** none
Effect spell effect (*summon monster VI*, summons 1d3 Large elementals or 1 Huge elemental)

CAMOUFLAGED SPIKED PIT TRAP — CR 8

Type mechanical; **Perception** DC 25; **Disable Device** DC 20

EFFECTS

Trigger location; **Reset** manual
Effect 50-ft.-deep pit (5d6 falling damage); pit spikes (Atk +15 melee, 1d4 spikes per target for 1d6+5 damage each); DC 20 Reflex avoids; multiple targets (all targets in a 10-ft.-square area)

INSANITY MIST TRAP — CR 8

Type mechanical; **Perception** DC 25; **Disable Device** DC 20

EFFECTS

Trigger location; **Reset** repair
Effect poison gas (insanity mist); never miss; onset delay (1 round); multiple targets (all targets in a 10-ft.-by-10-ft. room)

HAIL OF ARROWS TRAP — CR 9

Type mechanical; **Perception** DC 25; **Disable Device** DC 25

EFFECTS

Trigger visual (*arcane eye*); **Reset** repair
Effect Atk +20 ranged (6d6); multiple targets (all targets in a 20-ft. line)

SHOCKING FLOOR TRAP — CR 9

Type magic; **Perception** DC 26; **Disable Device** DC 26

EFFECTS

Trigger proximity (*alarm*); **Duration** 1d6 rounds; **Reset** none
Effect spell effect (*shocking grasp*, Atk +9 melee touch [4d6 electricity damage]); multiple targets (all targets in a 40-ft.-square room)

ENERGY DRAIN TRAP — CR 10

Type magic; **Perception** DC 34; **Disable Device** DC 34

EFFECTS

Trigger visual (*true seeing*); **Reset** none
Effect spell effect (*energy drain*, Atk +10 ranged touch, 2d4 temporary negative levels, DC 23 Fortitude negates after 24 hours)

CHAMBER OF BLADES TRAP — CR 10

Type mechanical; **Perception** DC 25; **Disable Device** DC 20

EFFECTS

Trigger location; **Duration** 1d4 rounds; **Reset** repair
Effect Atk +20 melee (3d8+3); multiple targets (all targets in a 20-ft.-square chamber)

CONE OF COLD TRAP — CR 11

Type magic; **Perception** DC 30; **Disable Device** DC 30

EFFECTS

Trigger proximity (*alarm*); **Reset** none
Effect spell effect (*cone of cold*, 15d6 cold damage, DC 17 Reflex save for half damage); multiple targets (all targets in a 60-ft. cone)

POISONED PIT TRAP — CR 12

Type mechanical; **Perception** DC 25; **Disable Device** DC 20

EFFECTS

Trigger location; **Reset** manual
Effect 50-ft.-deep pit (5d6 falling damage); pit spikes (Atk +15 melee, 1d4 spikes per target for 1d6+5 damage each plus poison [shadow essence]); DC 25 Reflex avoids; multiple targets (all targets in a 10-ft.-square area)

MAXIMIZED FIREBALL TRAP — CR 13

Type magic; **Perception** DC 31; **Disable Device** DC 31

EFFECTS

Trigger proximity (*alarm*); **Reset** none
Effect spell effect (*fireball*, 60 fire damage, DC 14 Reflex save for half damage); multiple targets (all targets in a 20-ft.-radius burst)

HARM TRAP — CR 14

Type magic; **Perception** DC 31; **Disable Device** DC 31

EFFECTS

Trigger touch; **Reset** none

Effect spell effect (*harm*, +6 melee touch, 130 damage, DC 19 Will save for half, cannot be reduced to less than 1 hit point)

CRUSHING STONE TRAP — CR 15

Type mechanical; **Perception** DC 30; **Disable Device** DC 20

EFFECTS

Trigger location; **Reset** manual

Effect Atk +15 melee (16d6); multiple targets (all targets in a 10-ft. square)

EMPOWERED DISINTEGRATE TRAP — CR 16

Type magic; **Perception** DC 33; **Disable Device** DC 33

EFFECTS

Trigger sight (*true seeing*); **Reset** none

Effect spell effect (empowered *disintegrate*, +9 ranged touch, 30d6 damage plus 50%, DC 19 Fort save reduces the damage to 5d6 plus 50%)

LIGHTNING BOLT GALLERY TRAP — CR 17

Type magic; **Perception** DC 29; **Disable Device** DC 29

EFFECTS

Trigger proximity (*alarm*); **Duration** 1d6 rounds; **Reset** none

Effect spell effect (heightened *lighting bolt*, 8d6 electricity damage, DC 16 Reflex save for half); multiple targets (all targets in a 60-ft.-square chamber)

DEADLY SPEAR TRAP — CR 18

Type mechanical; **Perception** DC 30; **Disable Device** DC 30

EFFECTS

Trigger sight (*true seeing*); **Reset** manual

Effect Atk +20 ranged (1d8+6 plus black lotus extract)

METEOR SWARM TRAP — CR 19

Type magic; **Perception** DC 34; **Disable Device** DC 34

EFFECTS

Trigger sight (*true seeing*); **Reset** none

Effect spell effect (meteor swarm, 4 meteors at separate targets, +9 ranged touch, 2d6 plus 6d6 fire [–4 save on a hit], DC 23 Reflex save for half fire damage, 18d6 fire damage from other meteors, DC 23 Reflex save for half damage); multiple targets (four targets, no two of which can be more than 40 ft. apart)

DESTRUCTION TRAP — CR 20

Type magic; **Perception** DC 34; **Disable Device** DC 34

EFFECTS

Trigger proximity (*alarm*); **Reset** none

Effect spell effect (heightened *destruction*, 190 damage, DC 23 Fortitude save reduces damage to 10d6)

TABLE 13-3: CR MODIFIERS FOR MECHANICAL TRAPS

Feature	CR Modifier
Perception DC	
15 or lower	−1
16–20	—
21–25	+1
26–29	+2
30 or higher	+3
Disable Device DC	
15 or lower	−1
16–20	—
21–25	+1
26–29	+2
30 or higher	+3
Reflex Save DC (Pit or Other Save-Dependent Trap)	
15 or lower	−1
16–20	—
21–25	+1
26–29	+2
30 or higher	+3
Attack Bonus (Melee or Ranged Attack Trap)	
+0 or lower	−2
+1 to +5	−1
+6 to +10	—
+11 to +15	+1
+16 to +20	+2
Touch attack	+1
Damage/Effect	
Average damage	+1 per 10 points of average damage
Miscellaneous Features	
Alchemical device	Level of spell mimicked
Automatic reset	+1
Liquid	+5
Multiple targets (non-damage)	+1
Never miss	+2
Proximity or visual trigger	+1

Poison	CR of poison	Poison	CR of poison
Black adder venom	+1	Malyass root paste	+3
Black lotus extract	+8	Medium spider venom	+2
Bloodroot	+1	Nitharit	+4
Blue whinnis	+1	Purple worm poison	+4
Burnt othur fumes	+6	Sassone leaf residue	+3
Deathblade	+5	Shadow essence	+3
Dragon bile	+6	Small centipede poison	+1
Giant wasp poison	+3	Terinav root	+5
Greenblood oil	+1	Ungol dust	+3
Insanity mist	+4	Wyvern poison	+5
Large scorpion venom	+3		

Designing a Trap

Designing new traps is a simple process. Start by deciding what type of trap you want to create.

Mechanical Traps: Simply select the elements you want the trap to have and add up the adjustments to the trap's Challenge Rating that those elements require (see Table 13–3) to arrive at the trap's final CR. From the CR you can derive the DC of the Craft (traps) checks a character must make to construct the trap (see page 424).

Magic Traps: As with mechanical traps, decide what elements you want and then determine the CR of the resulting trap (see Table 13–4). If a player character wants to design and construct a magic trap, he, or an ally, must have the Craft Wondrous Item feat. In addition, he must be able to cast the spell or spells that the trap requires—or he must be able to hire an NPC to cast the spells for him.

Challenge Rating of a Trap

To calculate the Challenge Rating of a trap, add all the CR modifiers (see Table 13–3 or Table 13–4) to the base CR for the trap type.

Mechanical Trap: The base CR for a mechanical trap is 0. If your final CR is 0 or lower, add features until you get a CR of 1 or higher.

Magic Trap: For a spell trap or magic device trap, the base CR is 1. The highest-level spell used modifies the CR (see Table 13–4).

Average Damage: If a trap (mechanical or magical) does hit point damage, calculate the average damage for a successful hit and round that value to the nearest multiple of 10. If the trap is designed to hit more than one target, multiply this value by 2. If the trap is designed to deal damage over a number of rounds, multiply this value by the number of rounds the trap will be active (or the average number of rounds, if the duration is variable). Use this value to adjust the Challenge Rating of the trap, as indicated on Table 13–3. Damage from poison does not count toward this value, but extra damage from pit spikes and multiple attacks does.

For a magic trap, only one modifier applies to the CR—either the level of the highest-level spell used in the trap, or the average damage figure, whichever is larger.

Multiple Traps: If a trap is really two or more connected traps that affect approximately the same area, determine the CR of each one separately.

Multiple Dependent Traps: If one trap depends on the success of the other (that is, you can avoid the second trap by not falling victim to the first), characters earn XP for both traps by defeating the first one, regardless if the second one is also sprung.

Multiple Independent Traps: If two or more traps act independently (they do not depend on one another to activate), characters only earn XP for traps that they defeat.

TABLE 13-4: CR MODIFIERS FOR MAGIC TRAPS

Feature	CR Modifier
Highest-level spell effect	+ Spell level
Damaging spell effect	+1 per 10 points of average damage

Mechanical Trap Cost

The cost of a mechanical trap is 1,000 gp × the trap's Challenge Rating. If the trap uses spells in its trigger or reset, add those costs separately. If the trap cannot be reset, divide the cost in half. If the trap has an automatic reset, increase the cost by half (+50%). Particularly simple traps, such as pit traps, might have a greatly reduced cost, subject to GM discretion. Such traps might cost as little as 250 gp × the trap's Challenge Rating.

After you've determined the cost by Challenge Rating, add the price of any alchemical items or poison you incorporated into the trap. If the trap uses one of these elements and has an automatic reset, multiply the poison or alchemical item cost by 20 to provide an adequate supply of doses.

Multiple Traps: If a trap is really two or more connected traps, determine the final cost of each separately, then add those values together. This holds for both multiple dependent and multiple independent traps.

Magic Device Trap Cost

Building a magic device trap involves the expenditure of gp and requires the services of a spellcaster. Table 13–5 summarizes the cost information for magic device traps. If the trap uses more than one spell (for instance, a sound or visual trigger spell in addition to the main spell effect), the builder must pay for them all (except *alarm*, which is free unless it must be cast by an NPC).

The costs derived from Table 13–5 assume that the builder is casting the necessary spells himself (or perhaps some other PC is providing the spells for free). If an NPC spellcaster must be hired to cast them, those costs must be factored in as well (see Chapter 6).

A magic device trap takes 1 day to construct per 500 gp of its cost.

Spell Trap Cost

A spell trap has a cost only if the builder must hire an NPC spellcaster to cast it.

Craft DCs for Mechanical Traps

Once you know the Challenge Rating of a trap, determine the Craft (traps) DC by referring to the values and modifiers given on Table 13–6.

Making the Checks: To determine how much progress a character makes on building a trap each week, that character

TABLE 13-5: COST MODIFIERS FOR MAGIC DEVICE TRAPS

Feature	Cost Modifier
Alarm spell used in trigger	—
One-Shot Trap	
Each spell used	+50 gp × caster level × spell level
Material components	+ Material component costs
Automatic Reset Trap	
Each spell used	+500 gp × caster level × spell level
Material components	+ Material component costs × 100

TABLE 13-6: CRAFT (TRAPS) DCS

Trap CR	Base Craft (Traps) DC
1–5	20
6–10	25
11–15	30
16+	35

Additional Components	Modifier to Craft (Traps) DC
Proximity trigger	+5
Automatic reset	+5

makes a Craft (traps) check. See the Craft skill description for details on Craft checks and the circumstances that can affect them.

WILDERNESS

Outside the safety of city walls, the wilderness is a dangerous place, and many adventurers have gotten lost in its trackless wilds or fallen victim to deadly weather. The following rules give you guidelines on running adventures in a wilderness setting.

Getting Lost

There are many ways to get lost in the wilderness. Following an obvious road, trail, or feature such as a stream or shoreline prevents most from becoming lost, but travelers striking off cross-country might become disoriented—especially in conditions of poor visibility or in difficult terrain.

Poor Visibility: Anytime characters cannot see at least 60 feet due to reduced visibility conditions, they might become lost. Characters traveling through fog, snow, or a downpour might easily lose the ability to see any landmarks not in their immediate vicinity. Similarly, characters traveling at night might be at risk, too, depending on the quality of their light sources, the amount of moonlight, and whether they have darkvision or low-light vision.

Difficult Terrain: Any character in forest, moor, hill, or mountain terrain might become lost if he moves away from a trail, road, stream, or other obvious path or track. Forests are especially dangerous because they obscure far-off landmarks and make it hard to see the sun or stars.

Chance to Get Lost: If conditions exist that make getting lost a possibility, the character leading the way must succeed on a Survival check or become lost. The difficulty of this check varies based on the terrain, the visibility conditions, and whether or not the character has a map of the area being traveled through. Refer to the table below and use the highest DC that applies.

Terrain	Survival DC
Desert or plains	14
Forest	16
Moor or hill	10
Mountain	12
Open sea	18
Urban, ruins, or dungeon	8

Situation	Check Modifier
Proper navigational tools (map, sextant)	+4
Poor visibility	−4

A character with at least 5 ranks in Knowledge (geography) or Knowledge (local) pertaining to the area being traveled through gains a +2 bonus on this check.

Check once per hour (or portion of an hour) spent in local or overland movement to see if travelers have become lost. In the case of a party moving together, only the character leading the way makes the check.

Effects of Being Lost: If a party becomes lost, it is no longer certain of moving in the direction it intended to travel. Randomly determine the direction in which the party actually travels during each hour of local or overland movement. The characters' movement continues to be random until they blunder into a landmark they can't miss, or until they recognize that they are lost and make an effort to regain their bearings.

Recognizing You're Lost: Once per hour of random travel, each character in the party may attempt a Survival check (DC 20, –1 per hour of random travel) to recognize that he is no longer certain of his direction of travel. Some circumstances might make it obvious that the characters are lost.

Setting a New Course: Determining the correct direction of travel once a party has become lost requires a Survival check (DC 15, +2 per hour of random travel). If a character fails this check, he chooses a random direction as the "correct" direction for resuming travel.

Once the characters are traveling along their new course, correct or incorrect, they might get lost again. If the conditions still make it possible for travelers to become lost, check once per hour of travel as described above to see

if the party maintains its new course or begins to move at random again.

Conflicting Directions: It's possible that several characters may attempt to determine the right direction to proceed after becoming lost. Make a Survival check for each character in secret, then tell the players whose characters succeeded the correct direction in which to travel, and tell the players whose characters failed a random direction they think is right, with no indication who is correct.

Regaining Your Bearings: There are several ways for characters to find their way after becoming lost. First, if the characters successfully set a new course and follow it to the destination they're trying to reach, they're not lost anymore. Second, the characters, through random movement, might run into an unmistakable landmark. Third, if conditions suddenly improve—the fog lifts or the sun comes up—lost characters may attempt to set a new course, as described above, with a +4 bonus on the Survival check.

Forest Terrain

Forest terrain can be divided into three categories: sparse, medium, and dense. An immense forest could have all three categories within its borders, with more sparse terrain at the outer edge of the forest and dense forest at its heart.

The table below describes in general terms how likely it is that a given square has a terrain element in it.

	Category of Forest		
	Sparse	Medium	Dense
Typical trees	50%	70%	80%
Massive trees	—	10%	20%
Light undergrowth	50%	70%	50%
Heavy undergrowth	—	20%	50%

Trees: The most important terrain element in a forest is the trees, obviously. A creature standing in the same square as a tree gains partial cover, which grants a +2 bonus to Armor Class and a +1 bonus on Reflex saves. The presence of a tree doesn't otherwise affect a creature's fighting space, because it's assumed that the creature is using the tree to its advantage when it can. The trunk of a typical tree has AC 4, hardness 5, and 150 hp. A DC 15 Climb check is sufficient to climb a tree. Medium and dense forests have massive trees as well. These trees take up an entire square and provide cover to anyone behind them. They have AC 3, hardness 5, and 600 hp. Like their smaller counterparts, it takes a DC 15 Climb check to climb them.

Undergrowth: Vines, roots, and short bushes cover much of the ground in a forest. A space covered with light undergrowth costs 2 squares of movement to move into, and provides concealment. Undergrowth increases the DC of Acrobatics and Stealth checks by 2 because the leaves and branches get in the way. Heavy undergrowth costs 4 squares of movement to move into and provides concealment with a 30% miss chance (instead of the usual 20%). It increases the DC of Acrobatics checks by 5. Heavy undergrowth is easy to hide in, granting a +5 circumstance bonus on Stealth checks. Running and charging are impossible. Squares with undergrowth are often clustered together. Undergrowth and trees aren't mutually exclusive; it's common for a 5-foot square to have both a tree and undergrowth.

Forest Canopy: It's common for elves and other forest dwellers to live on raised platforms far above the surface floor. These wooden platforms often have rope bridges between them. To get to the treehouses, characters ascend the trees' branches (Climb DC 15), use rope ladders (Climb DC 0), or take pulley elevators (which can be made to rise a number of feet equal to a Strength check, made each round as a full-round action). Creatures on platforms or branches in a forest canopy are considered to have cover when fighting creatures on the ground, and in medium or dense forests they have concealment as well.

Other Forest Terrain Elements: Fallen logs generally stand about 3 feet high and provide cover just as low walls do. They cost 5 feet of movement to cross. Forest streams average 5 to 10 feet wide and no more than 5 feet deep. Pathways wind through most forests, allowing normal movement and providing neither cover nor concealment. These paths are less common in dense forests, but even unexplored forests have occasional game trails.

Stealth and Detection in a Forest: In a sparse forest, the maximum distance at which a Perception check for detecting the nearby presence of others can succeed is 3d6 × 10 feet. In a medium forest, this distance is 2d8 × 10 feet, and in a dense forest it is 2d6 × 10 feet.

Because any square with undergrowth provides concealment, it's usually easy for a creature to use the Stealth skill in the forest. Logs and massive trees provide cover, which also makes hiding possible.

The background noise in the forest makes Perception checks that rely on sound more difficult, increasing the DC of the check by 2 per 10 feet, not 1.

Forest Fires (CR 6)

Most campfire sparks ignite nothing, but if conditions are dry, winds are strong, or the forest floor is dried out and flammable, a forest fire can result. Lightning strikes often set trees ablaze and start forest fires in this way. Whatever the cause of the fire, travelers can get caught in the conflagration.

A forest fire can be spotted from as far away as 2d6 × 100 feet by a character who makes a Perception check, treating the fire as a Colossal creature (reducing the DC by 16). If all characters fail their Perception checks, the fire moves closer to them. They automatically see it when it closes to half the original distance. With proper elevation, the smoke from a forest fire can be spotted as far as 10 miles away.

Characters who are blinded or otherwise unable to make Perception checks can feel the heat of the fire (and thus automatically "spot" it) when it is 100 feet away.

The leading edge of a fire (the downwind side) can advance faster than a human can run (assume 120 feet per round for winds of moderate strength). Once a particular portion of the forest is ablaze, it remains so for 2d4 × 10 minutes before dying to a smoking wasteland. Characters overtaken by a forest fire might find the leading edge of the fire advancing away from them faster than they can keep up, trapping them deeper and deeper within its grasp.

Within the bounds of a forest fire, a character faces three dangers: heat damage, catching on fire, and smoke inhalation.

Heat Damage: Getting caught within a forest fire is even worse than being exposed to extreme heat (see Heat Dangers on page 444). Breathing the air causes a character to take 1d6 points of fire damage per round (no save). In addition, a character must make a Fortitude save every 5 rounds (DC 15, +1 per previous check) or take 1d4 points of nonlethal damage. A character who holds his breath can avoid the lethal damage, but not the nonlethal damage. Those wearing heavy clothing or any sort of armor take a –4 penalty on their saving throws. Those wearing metal armor or who come into contact with very hot metal are affected as if by a *heat metal* spell.

Catching on Fire: Characters engulfed in a forest fire are at risk of catching on fire when the leading edge of the fire overtakes them, and continue to be at risk once per minute thereafter. See Catching on Fire on page 444.

Smoke Inhalation: Forest fires naturally produce a great deal of smoke. A character who breathes heavy smoke must make a Fortitude save each round (DC 15, +1 per previous check) or spend that round choking and coughing. A character who chokes for 2 consecutive rounds takes 1d6 points of nonlethal damage. Smoke also provides concealment to characters within it.

Marsh Terrain

Two categories of marsh exist: relatively dry moors and watery swamps. Both are often bordered by lakes (described in Aquatic Terrain), which are effectively a third category of terrain found in marshes.

	Marsh Category	
	Moor	Swamp
Shallow bog	20%	40%
Deep bog	5%	20%
Light undergrowth	30%	20%
Heavy undergrowth	10%	20%

Bogs: If a square is part of a shallow bog, it has deep mud or standing water of about 1 foot in depth. It costs 2 squares of movement to move into a square with a shallow bog, and the DC of Acrobatics checks in such a square increases by 2.

A square that is part of a deep bog has roughly 4 feet of standing water. It costs Medium or larger creatures 4 squares of movement to move into a square with a deep bog, or characters can swim if they wish. Small or smaller creatures must swim to move through a deep bog. Tumbling is impossible in a deep bog.

The water in a deep bog provides cover for Medium or larger creatures. Smaller creatures gain improved cover (+8 bonus to AC, +4 bonus on Reflex saves). Medium or larger creatures can crouch as a move action to gain this improved cover. Creatures with this improved cover take a –10 penalty on attacks against creatures that aren't underwater.

Deep bog squares are usually clustered together and surrounded by an irregular ring of shallow bog squares.

Both shallow and deep bogs increase the DC of Stealth checks by 2.

Undergrowth: The bushes, rushes, and other tall grasses in marshes function as undergrowth does in a forest. A square that is part of a bog does not also have undergrowth.

Quicksand: Patches of quicksand present a deceptively solid appearance (appearing as undergrowth or open land) that might trap careless characters. A character approaching a patch of quicksand at a normal pace is entitled to a DC 15 Survival check to spot the danger before stepping in, but charging or running characters don't have a chance to detect a hidden patch before blundering into it. A typical patch of quicksand is 20 feet in diameter; the momentum of a charging or running character carries him 1d2 × 5 feet into the quicksand.

Effects of Quicksand: Characters in quicksand must make a DC 10 Swim check every round to simply tread water in place, or a DC 15 Swim check to move 5 feet in whatever direction is desired. If a trapped character fails this check by 5 or more, he sinks below the surface and begins to drown whenever he can no longer hold his breath (see the Swim skill description in Chapter 4).

Characters below the surface of quicksand may swim back to the surface with a successful Swim check (DC 15, +1 per consecutive round of being under the surface).

Rescue: Pulling out a character trapped in quicksand can be difficult. A rescuer needs a branch, spear haft, rope, or similar tool that enables him to reach the victim with one end of it. Then he must make a DC 15 Strength check to successfully pull the victim, and the victim must make a DC 10 Strength check to hold onto the branch, pole, or rope. If both checks succeed, the victim is pulled 5 feet closer to safety. If the victim fails to hold on, he must make a DC 15 Swim check immediately to stay above the surface.

Hedgerows: Common in moors, hedgerows are tangles of stones, soil, and thorny bushes. Narrow hedgerows function as low walls, and it takes 3 squares of movement to cross them. Wide hedgerows are more than 5 feet tall and take up entire squares. They provide total cover, just as a wall does. It takes 4 squares of movement to move through a square with a wide hedgerow; creatures that succeed on a DC 10 Climb check need only 2 squares of movement to move through the square.

Other Marsh Terrain Elements: Some marshes, particularly swamps, have trees just as forests do, usually clustered in small stands. Paths lead across many marshes, winding to avoid bog areas. As in forests, paths allow normal movement and don't provide the concealment that undergrowth does.

Stealth and Detection in a Marsh: In a marsh, the maximum distance at which a Perception check for detecting the nearby presence of others can succeed is 6d6 × 10 feet. In a swamp, this distance is 2d8 × 10 feet.

Undergrowth and deep bogs provide plentiful concealment, so it's easy to use Stealth in a marsh.

Hills Terrain

A hill can exist in most other types of terrain, but hills can also dominate the landscape. Hills terrain is divided into two categories: gentle hills and rugged hills. Hills terrain often serves as a transition zone between rugged terrain such as mountains and flat terrain such as plains.

	Hills Category	
	Gentle Hills	Rugged Hills
Gradual slope	75%	40%
Steep slope	20%	50%
Cliff	5%	10%
Light undergrowth	15%	15%

Gradual Slope: This incline isn't steep enough to affect movement, but characters gain a +1 bonus on melee attacks against foes downhill from them.

Steep Slope: Characters moving uphill (to an adjacent square of higher elevation) must spend 2 squares of movement to enter each square of steep slope. Characters running or charging downhill (moving to an adjacent square of lower elevation) must succeed on a DC 10 Acrobatics check upon entering the first steep slope square. Mounted characters make a DC 10 Ride check instead. Characters who fail this check stumble and must end their movement 1d2 × 5 feet later. Characters who fail by 5 or more fall prone in the square where they end their movement. A steep slope increases the DC of Acrobatics checks by 2.

Cliff: A cliff typically requires a DC 15 Climb check to scale and is 1d4 × 10 feet tall, although the needs of your map might mandate a taller cliff. A cliff isn't perfectly vertical, taking up 5-foot squares if it's less than 30 feet tall and 10-foot squares if it's 30 feet or taller.

Light Undergrowth: Sagebrush and other scrubby bushes grow on hills, although they rarely cover the landscape. Light undergrowth provides concealment and increases the DC of Acrobatics and Stealth checks by 2.

Other Hills Terrain Elements: Trees aren't out of place in hills terrain, and valleys often have active streams (5 to 10 feet wide and no more than 5 feet deep) or dry streambeds (treat as a trench 5 to 10 feet across) in them. If you add a stream or streambed, remember that water always flows downhill.

Stealth and Detection in Hills: In gentle hills, the maximum distance at which a Perception check for detecting the nearby presence of others can succeed is 2d10 × 10 feet. In rugged hills, this distance is 2d6 × 10 feet.

Hiding in hills terrain can be difficult if there isn't undergrowth around. A hilltop or ridge provides enough cover to hide from anyone below the hilltop or ridge.

Mountain Terrain

The three mountain terrain categories are alpine meadows, rugged mountains, and forbidding mountains. As characters ascend into a mountainous area, they're likely to face each terrain category in turn, beginning with alpine meadows, extending through rugged mountains, and reaching forbidding mountains near the summit.

Mountains have an important terrain element, the rock wall, that is marked on the border between squares rather than taking up squares itself.

	Mountain Category		
	Alpine Meadow	Rugged	Forbidding
Gradual slope	50%	25%	15%
Steep slope	40%	55%	55%
Cliff	10%	15%	20%
Chasm	—	5%	10%
Light undergrowth	20%	10%	—
Scree	—	20%	30%
Dense rubble	—	20%	30%

Gradual and Steep Slopes: These function as described in Hills Terrain.

Cliff: These terrain elements also function like their hills terrain counterparts, but they're typically 2d6 × 10 feet tall. Cliffs taller than 80 feet take up 20 feet of horizontal space.

Chasm: Usually formed by natural geological processes, chasms function like pits in a dungeon setting. Chasms aren't hidden, so characters won't fall into them by accident (although bull rushes are another story). A typical chasm is 2d4 × 10 feet deep, at least 20 feet long, and anywhere from 5 feet to 20 feet wide. It takes a DC 15 Climb check to climb out of a chasm. In forbidding mountain terrain, chasms are typically 2d8 × 10 feet deep.

Light Undergrowth: This functions as described in Forest Terrain.

Scree: A field of shifting gravel, scree doesn't affect speed, but it can be treacherous on a slope. The DC of Acrobatics checks increases by 2 if there's scree on a gradual slope and by 5 if there's scree on a steep slope. The DC of Stealth checks increases by 2 if the scree is on a slope of any kind.

Dense Rubble: The ground is covered with rocks of all sizes. It costs 2 squares of movement to enter a square with dense rubble. The DC of Acrobatics checks on dense rubble increases by 5, and the DC of Stealth checks increases by 2.

Rock Wall: A vertical plane of stone, rock walls require DC 25 Climb checks to ascend. A typical rock wall is 2d4 × 10 feet tall in rugged mountains and 2d8 × 10 feet tall in forbidding mountains. Rock walls are drawn on the edges of squares, not in the squares themselves.

Cave Entrance: Found in cliff and steep slope squares and next to rock walls, cave entrances are typically between 5 and 20 feet wide and 5 feet deep. A cave could be anything from a simple chamber to the entrance to an elaborate dungeon. Caves used as monster lairs typically have 1d3 rooms that are 1d4 × 10 feet across.

Other Mountain Terrain Features: Most alpine meadows begin above the treeline, so trees and other forest elements are rare in the mountains. Mountain terrain can include active streams (5 to 10 feet wide and no more than 5 feet deep) and dry streambeds (treat as a trench 5 to 10 feet across). Particularly high-altitude areas tend to be colder than the lowland areas that surround them, so they might be covered in ice sheets (described in Desert Terrain).

Stealth and Detection in Mountains: As a guideline, the maximum distance in mountain terrain at which a Perception check for detecting the nearby presence of others can succeed is 4d10 × 10 feet. Certain peaks and ridgelines afford much better vantage points, of course, and twisting valleys and canyons have much shorter spotting distances. Because there's little vegetation to

obstruct line of sight, the specifics on your map are your best guide for the range at which an encounter could begin. As in hills terrain, a ridge or peak provides enough cover to hide from anyone below the high point.

It's easier to hear faraway sounds in the mountains. The DC of Perception checks that rely on sound increase by 1 per 20 feet between listener and source, not per 10 feet.

Avalanches (CR 7)

The combination of high peaks and heavy snowfalls means that avalanches are a deadly peril in many mountainous areas. While avalanches of snow and ice are common, it's also possible to have an avalanche of rock and soil.

An avalanche can be spotted from as far away as 1d10 × 500 feet by a character who makes a DC 20 Perception check, treating the avalanche as a Colossal creature. If all characters fail their Perception checks to determine the encounter distance, the avalanche moves closer to them, and they automatically become aware of it when it closes to half the original distance. It's possible to hear an avalanche coming even if you can't see it. Under optimum conditions (no other loud noises occurring), a character who makes a DC 15 Perception check can hear the avalanche or landslide when it is 1d6 × 500 feet away. This check might have a DC of 20, 25, or higher in conditions where hearing is difficult (such as in the middle of a thunderstorm).

A landslide or avalanche consists of two distinct areas: the bury zone (in the direct path of the falling debris) and the slide zone (the area the debris spreads out to encompass). Characters in the bury zone always take damage from the avalanche; characters in the slide zone might be able to get out of the way. Characters in the bury zone take 8d6 points of damage, or half that amount if they make a DC 15 Reflex save. They are subsequently buried. Characters in the slide zone take 3d6 points of damage, or no damage if they make a DC 15 Reflex save. Those who fail their saves are buried.

Buried characters take 1d6 points of nonlethal damage per minute. If a buried character falls unconscious, he must make a DC 15 Constitution check or take 1d6 points of lethal damage each minute thereafter until freed or dead. See Cave-Ins and Collapses on page 415 for rules on digging out buried characters.

The typical avalanche has a width of 1d6 × 100 feet, from one edge of the slide zone to the opposite edge. The bury zone in the center of the avalanche is half as wide as the avalanche's full width.

To determine the precise location of characters in the path of an avalanche, roll 1d6 × 20; the result is the number of feet from the center of the path taken by the bury zone to the center of the party's location. Avalanches of snow and ice advance at a speed of 500 feet per round, while rock and soil avalanches travel at a speed of 250 feet per round.

Mountain Travel

High altitude travel can be extremely fatiguing—and sometimes deadly—to creatures that aren't used to it. Cold becomes extreme, and the lack of oxygen in the air can wear down even the most hardy of warriors.

Acclimated Characters: Creatures accustomed to high altitude generally fare better than lowlanders. Any creature with an Environment entry that includes mountains is considered native to the area and acclimated to the high altitude. Characters can also acclimate themselves by living at high altitude for a month. Characters who spend more than two months away from the mountains must reacclimate themselves when they return. Undead, constructs, and other creatures that do not breathe are immune to altitude effects.

Altitude Zones: In general, mountains present three possible altitude bands: low pass, low peak/high pass, and high peak.

Low Pass (lower than 5,000 feet): Most travel in low mountains takes place in low passes, a zone consisting largely of alpine meadows and forests. Travelers might find the going difficult (which is reflected in the movement modifiers for traveling through mountains), but the altitude itself has no game effect.

Low Peak or High Pass (5,000 to 15,000 feet): Ascending to the highest slopes of low mountains, or most normal travel through high mountains, falls into this category. All non-acclimated creatures labor to breathe in the thin air at this altitude. Characters must succeed on a Fortitude save each hour (DC 15, +1 per previous check) or be fatigued. The fatigue ends when the character descends to an altitude with more air. Acclimated characters do not have to attempt the Fortitude save.

High Peak (more than 15,000 feet): The highest mountains exceed 15,000 feet in height. At these elevations, creatures are subject to both high altitude fatigue (as described above) and altitude sickness, whether or not they're acclimated to high altitudes. Altitude sickness represents long-term oxygen deprivation, and affects mental and physical ability scores. After each 6-hour period a character spends at an altitude of over 15,000

feet, he must succeed on a Fortitude save (DC 15, +1 per previous check) or take 1 point of damage to all ability scores. Creatures acclimated to high altitude receive a +4 competence bonus on their saving throws to resist high altitude effects and altitude sickness, but eventually even seasoned mountaineers must abandon these dangerous elevations.

Desert Terrain

Desert terrain exists in warm, temperate, and cold climates, but all deserts share one common trait: little rain. The three categories of desert terrain are tundra (cold desert), rocky deserts (often temperate), and sandy deserts (often warm).

Tundra differs from the other desert categories in two important ways. Because snow and ice cover much of the landscape, it's easy to find water. During the height of summer, the permafrost thaws to a depth of a foot or so, turning the landscape into a vast field of mud. The muddy tundra affects movement and skill use as the shallow bogs described in Marsh Terrain, although there's little standing water.

The table below describes terrain elements found in each of the three desert categories. The terrain elements on this table are mutually exclusive; for instance, a square of tundra might contain either light undergrowth or an ice sheet, but not both.

	Desert Category		
	Tundra	Rocky	Sandy
Light undergrowth	15%	5%	5%
Ice sheet	25%	—	—
Light rubble	5%	30%	10%
Dense rubble	—	30%	5%
Sand dunes	—	—	50%

Light Undergrowth: Consisting of scrubby, hardy bushes and cacti, light undergrowth functions as described for other terrain types.

Ice Sheet: The ground is covered with slippery ice. It costs 2 squares of movement to enter a square covered by an ice sheet, and the DC of Acrobatics checks there increases by 5. A DC 10 Acrobatics check is required to run or charge across an ice sheet.

Light Rubble: Small rocks are strewn across the ground, making nimble movement more difficult. The DC of Acrobatics checks increases by 2.

Dense Rubble: This terrain feature consists of more and larger stones. It costs 2 squares of movement to enter a square with dense rubble. The DC of Acrobatics checks increases by 5, and the DC of Stealth checks increases by 2.

Sand Dunes: Created by the action of wind on sand, dunes function as hills that move. If the wind is strong and consistent, a sand dune can move several hundred feet in a week's time. Sand dunes can cover hundreds of squares. They always have a gentle slope pointing in the direction of the prevailing wind and a steep slope on the leeward side.

Other Desert Terrain Features: Tundra is sometimes bordered by forests, and the occasional tree isn't out of place in the cold wastes. Rocky deserts have towers and mesas consisting of flat ground surrounded on all sides by cliffs and steep slopes (as described in Mountain Terrain). Sandy deserts sometimes have quicksand; this functions as described in Marsh Terrain, although desert quicksand is a waterless mixture of fine sand and dust. All desert terrain is crisscrossed with dry streambeds (treat as trenches 5 to 15 feet wide) that fill with water on the rare occasions when rain falls.

Stealth and Detection in the Desert: In general, the maximum distance in desert terrain at which a Perception check for detecting the nearby presence of others can succeed is 6d6 × 20 feet; beyond this distance, elevation changes and heat distortion in warm deserts makes sight-based Perception impossible. The presence of dunes in sandy deserts limits spotting distance to 6d6 × 10 feet. The scarcity of undergrowth or other elements that offer concealment or cover makes using Stealth more difficult.

Sandstorms

A sandstorm reduces visibility to 1d10 × 5 feet and provides a –4 penalty on Perception checks. A sandstorm deals 1d3 points of nonlethal damage per hour to any creatures caught in the open, and leaves a thin coating of sand in its wake. Driving sand creeps in through all but the most secure seals and seams, chafing skin and contaminating carried gear.

Plains Terrain

Plains come in three categories: farms, grasslands, and battlefields. Farms are common in settled areas, while grasslands represent untamed plains. The battlefields where large armies clash are temporary places, usually reclaimed by natural vegetation or the farmer's plow. Battlefields represent a third terrain category because adventurers tend to spend a lot of time there, not because they're particularly prevalent.

The table below shows the proportions of terrain elements in the different categories of plains. On a farm, light undergrowth represents most mature grain crops, so farms growing vegetable crops will have less light undergrowth, as will all farms during the time between harvest and a few months after planting.

The terrain elements in the table below are mutually exclusive.

	Plains Category		
	Farm	Grassland	Battlefield
Light undergrowth	40%	20%	10%
Heavy undergrowth	—	10%	—
Light rubble	—	—	10%
Trench	5%	—	5%
Berm	—	—	5%

Undergrowth: Whether they're crops or natural vegetation, the tall grasses of the plains function like light undergrowth in a forest. Particularly thick bushes form patches of heavy undergrowth that dot the landscape in grasslands.

Light Rubble: On the battlefield, light rubble usually represents something that was destroyed: the ruins of a building or the scattered remnants of a stone wall, for example. It functions as described in the Desert Terrain section.

Trench: Often dug before a battle to protect soldiers, a trench functions as a low wall, except that it provides no cover against adjacent foes. It costs 2 squares of movement to leave a trench, but it costs nothing extra to enter one. Creatures outside a trench who make a melee attack against a creature inside the trench gain a +1 bonus on melee attacks because they have higher ground. In farm terrain, trenches are generally irrigation ditches.

Berm: A common defensive structure, a berm is a low, earthen wall that slows movement and provides a measure of cover. Put a berm on the map by drawing two adjacent rows of steep slope (described in Hills Terrain), with the edges of the berm on the downhill side. Thus, a character crossing a 2-square berm will travel uphill for 1 square, then downhill for 1 square. Two square berms provide cover as low walls for anyone standing behind them. Larger berms provide the low wall benefit for anyone standing 1 square downhill from the top of the berm.

Fences: Wooden fences are generally used to contain livestock or impede oncoming soldiers. It costs an extra square of movement to cross a wooden fence. A stone fence provides a measure of cover as well, functioning as low walls. Mounted characters can cross a fence without slowing their movement if they succeed on a DC 15 Ride check. If the check fails, the steed crosses the fence, but the rider falls out of the saddle.

Other Plains Terrain Features: Occasional trees dot the landscape in many plains, although on battlefields they're often felled to provide raw material for siege engines (described in Urban Features). Hedgerows (described in Marsh Terrain) are found in plains as well. Streams, generally 5 to 20 feet wide and 5 to 10 feet deep, are commonplace.

Stealth and Detection in Plains: In plains terrain, the maximum distance at which a Perception check for

detecting the nearby presence of others can succeed is 6d6 × 40 feet, although the specifics of your map might restrict line of sight. Cover and concealment are not uncommon, so a good place of refuge is often nearby, if not right at hand.

Aquatic Terrain

Aquatic terrain is the least hospitable to most PCs, because they can't breathe there. Aquatic terrain doesn't offer the variety that land terrain does. The ocean floor holds many marvels, including undersea analogues of any of the terrain elements described earlier in this section, but if characters find themselves in the water because they were bull rushed off the deck of a pirate ship, the tall kelp beds hundreds of feet below them don't matter. Accordingly, these rules simply divide aquatic terrain into two categories: flowing water (such as streams and rivers) and non-flowing water (such as lakes and oceans).

Flowing Water: Large, placid rivers move at only a few miles per hour, so they function as still water for most purposes. But some rivers and streams are swifter; anything floating in them moves downstream at a speed of 10 to 40 feet per round. The fastest rapids send swimmers bobbing downstream at 60 to 90 feet per round. Fast rivers are always at least rough water (Swim DC 15), and whitewater rapids are stormy water (Swim DC 20). If a character is in moving water, move her downstream the indicated distance at the end of her turn. A character trying to maintain her position relative to the riverbank can spend some or all of her turn swimming upstream.

Swept Away: Characters swept away by a river moving 60 feet per round or faster must make DC 20 Swim checks every round to avoid going under. If a character gets a check result of 5 or more over the minimum necessary, she arrests her motion by catching a rock, tree limb, or bottom snag—she is no longer being carried along by the flow of the water. Escaping the rapids by reaching the bank requires three DC 20 Swim checks in a row. Characters arrested by a rock, limb, or snag can't escape under their own power unless they strike out into the water and attempt to swim their way clear. Other characters can rescue them as if they were trapped in quicksand (described in Marsh Terrain).

Non-Flowing Water: Lakes and oceans simply require a swim speed or successful Swim checks to move through (DC 10 in calm water, DC 15 in rough water, DC 20 in stormy water). Characters need a way to breathe if they're underwater; failing that, they risk drowning. When underwater, characters can move in any direction.

Stealth and Detection Underwater: How far you can see underwater depends on the water's clarity. As a guideline, creatures can see 4d8 × 10 feet if the water is clear, and

1d8 × 10 feet if it's murky. Moving water is always murky, unless it's in a particularly large, slow-moving river.

It's hard to find cover or concealment to hide underwater (except along the sea floor).

Invisibility: An invisible creature displaces water and leaves a visible, body-shaped "bubble" where the water was displaced. The creature still has concealment (20% miss chance), but not total concealment (50% miss chance).

Underwater Combat

Land-based creatures can have considerable difficulty when fighting in water. Water affects a creature's attack rolls, damage, and movement. In some cases a creature's opponents might get a bonus on attacks. The effects are summarized on Table 13–7. They apply whenever a character is swimming, walking in chest-deep water, or walking along the bottom of a body of water.

Ranged Attacks Underwater: Thrown weapons are ineffective underwater, even when launched from land. Attacks with other ranged weapons take a –2 penalty on attack rolls for every 5 feet of water they pass through, in addition to the normal penalties for range.

Attacks from Land: Characters swimming, floating, or treading water on the surface, or wading in water at least chest deep, have improved cover (+8 bonus to AC, +4 bonus on Reflex saves) from opponents on land. Land-bound opponents who have *freedom of movement* effects ignore this cover when making melee attacks against targets in the water. A completely submerged creature has total cover against opponents on land unless those opponents have *freedom of movement* effects. Magical effects are unaffected except for those that require attack rolls (which are treated like any other effects) and fire effects.

Fire: Nonmagical fire (including alchemist's fire) does not burn underwater. Spells or spell-like effects with the fire descriptor are ineffective underwater unless the caster makes a caster level check (DC 20 + spell level). If the check succeeds, the spell creates a bubble of steam instead of its usual fiery effect, but otherwise the spell works as described. A supernatural fire effect is ineffective underwater unless its description states otherwise. The surface of a body of water blocks line of effect for any fire spell. If the caster has made the caster level check to make the fire spell usable underwater, the surface still blocks the spell's line of effect.

Spellcasting Underwater: Casting spells while submerged can be difficult for those who cannot breathe underwater. A creature that cannot breathe water must make a concentration check (DC 15 + spell level) to cast a spell underwater (this is in addition to the caster level check to successfully cast a fire spell underwater). Creatures that can breathe water are unaffected and can cast spells normally. Some spells might function differently underwater, subject to GM discretion.

TABLE 13-7: COMBAT ADJUSTMENTS UNDERWATER

Condition	Attack/Damage Slashing or Bludgeoning	Piercing	Movement	Off Balance?[1]
Freedom of movement	normal/normal	normal/normal	normal	No
Has a swim speed	−2/half	normal	normal	No
Successful Swim check	−2/half[2]	normal	quarter or half[3]	No
Firm footing[4]	−2/half[2]	normal	half	No
None of the above	−2/half[2]	−2/half	normal	Yes

1 Creatures flailing about in the water (usually because they failed their Swim checks) have a hard time fighting effectively. An off-balance creature loses its Dexterity bonus to Armor Class, and opponents gain a +2 bonus on attacks against it.

2 A creature without *freedom of movement* effects or a swim speed makes grapple checks underwater at a −2 penalty, but deals damage normally when grappling.

3 A successful Swim check lets a creature move one-quarter its speed as a move action or one-half its speed as a full-round action.

4 Creatures have firm footing when walking along the bottom, braced against a ship's hull, or the like. A creature can only walk along the bottom if it wears or carries enough gear to weigh itself down: at least 16 pounds for Medium creatures, twice that for each size category larger than Medium, and half that for each size category smaller than Medium.

Floods

In many wilderness areas, river floods are a common occurrence.

In spring, an enormous snowmelt can engorge the streams and rivers it feeds. Other catastrophic events such as massive rainstorms or the destruction of a dam can create floods as well.

During a flood, rivers become wider, deeper, and swifter. Assume that a river rises by 1d10+10 feet during the spring flood, and its width increases by a factor of 1d4 × 50%. Fords might disappear for days, bridges might be swept away, and even ferries might not be able to manage the crossing of a flooded river. A river in flood makes Swim checks one category harder (calm water becomes rough, and rough water becomes stormy). Rivers also become 50% swifter.

URBAN ADVENTURES

At first glance, a city is much like a dungeon, made up of walls, doors, rooms, and corridors. Adventures that take place in cities have two salient differences from their dungeon counterparts, however. Characters have greater access to resources, and they must contend with law enforcement.

Access to Resources: Unlike in dungeons and the wilderness, characters can buy and sell gear quickly in a city. A large city or metropolis probably has high-level NPCs and experts in obscure fields of knowledge who can provide assistance and decipher clues. And when the PCs are battered and bruised, they can retreat to the comfort of a room at an inn.

The freedom to retreat and ready access to the marketplace means that the players have a greater degree of control over the pacing of an urban adventure.

Law Enforcement: The other key distinctions between adventuring in a city and delving into a dungeon is that

a dungeon is, almost by definition, a lawless place where the only law is that of the jungle: kill or be killed. A city, on the other hand, is held together by a code of laws, many of which are explicitly designed to prevent the sort of killing and looting that adventurers engage in all the time. Even so, most cities' laws recognize monsters as a threat to the stability the city relies on, and prohibitions about murder rarely apply to monsters such as aberrations or evil outsiders. Most evil humanoids, however, are typically protected by the same laws that protect all the citizens of the city. Having an evil alignment is not a crime (except in some severely theocratic cities, perhaps, with the magical power to back up the law); only evil deeds are against the law. Even when adventurers encounter an evildoer in the act of perpetrating some heinous evil upon the populace of the city, the law tends to frown on the sort of vigilante justice that leaves the evildoer dead or otherwise unable to testify at a trial.

Weapon and Spell Restrictions

Different cities have different laws about such issues as carrying weapons in public and restricting spellcasters.

The city's laws might not affect all characters equally. A monk isn't hampered at all by a law about peace-bonding weapons, but a cleric is reduced to a fraction of his power if all holy symbols are confiscated at the city's gates.

Urban Features

Walls, doors, poor lighting, and uneven footing: in many ways a city is much like a dungeon. Some special considerations for an urban setting are covered below.

Walls and Gates

Many cities are surrounded by walls. A typical small city wall is a fortified stone wall 5 feet thick and 20 feet high. Such a wall is fairly smooth, requiring a DC 30 Climb check to scale. The walls are crenellated on one side to provide a low wall for the guards atop it, and there is just barely room for guards to walk along the top of the wall. A typical small city wall has AC 3, hardness 8, and 450 hp per 10-foot section.

A typical large city wall is 10 feet thick and 30 feet high, with crenellations on both sides for the guards on top of the wall. It is likewise smooth, requiring a DC 30 Climb check to scale. Such a wall has AC 3, hardness 8, and 720 hp per 10-foot section.

A typical metropolis wall is 15 feet thick and 40 feet tall. It has crenellations on both sides and often has a tunnel and small rooms running through its interior. Metropolis walls have AC 3, hardness 8, and 1,170 hp per 10-foot section.

Unlike smaller cities, metropolises often have interior walls as well as surrounding walls—either old walls that the city has outgrown, or walls dividing individual districts from each other. Sometimes these walls are as large and thick as the outer walls, but more often they have the characteristics of a large city's or small city's walls.

Watchtowers: Some city walls are adorned with watchtowers set at irregular intervals. Few cities have enough guards to keep someone constantly stationed at every tower, unless the city is expecting attack from outside. The towers provide a superior view of the surrounding countryside as well as a point of defense against invaders.

Watchtowers are typically 10 feet higher than the wall they adjoin, and their diameter is 5 times the thickness of the wall. Arrow slits line the outer sides of the upper stories of a tower, and the top is crenellated like the surrounding walls are. In a small tower (25 feet in diameter adjoining a 5-foot-thick wall), a simple ladder typically connects the tower's stories and its roof. In a larger tower, stairs serve that purpose.

Heavy wooden doors, reinforced with iron and bearing good locks (Disable Device DC 30), block entry to a tower, unless the tower is in regular use. As a rule, the captain of the guard keeps the keys to the towers secured on her person, and second copies are in the city's inner fortress or barracks.

Gates: A typical city gate is a gatehouse with two portcullises and murder holes above the space between them. In towns and some small cities, the primary entry is through iron double doors set into the city wall.

Gates are usually open during the day and locked or barred at night. Usually, one gate lets in travelers after sunset and is staffed by guards who will open it for someone who seems honest, presents proper papers, or offers a large enough bribe (depending on the city and the guards).

Guards and Soldiers

A city typically has full-time military personnel equal to 1% of its adult population, in addition to militia or conscript soldiers equal to 5% of the population. The full-time soldiers are city guards responsible for maintaining order within the city, similar to the role of modern police, and (to a lesser extent) for defending the city from outside assault. Conscript soldiers are called up to serve in case of an attack on the city.

A typical city guard force works on three 8-hour shifts, with 30% of the force on a day shift (8 a.m. to 4 p.m.), 35% on an evening shift (4 p.m. to 12 a.m.), and 35% on a night shift (12 a.m. to 8 a.m.). At any given time, 80% of the guards on duty are on the streets patrolling, while the remaining 20% are stationed at various posts throughout the city where they can respond to nearby alarms. At least one such guard post is present within each neighborhood of a city (each neighborhood consisting of several districts).

The majority of a city guard force is made up of warriors, mostly 1st level. Officers include higher-level warriors, fighters, a fair number of clerics, and wizards or sorcerers, as well as multiclass fighter/spellcasters.

Siege Engines

Siege engines are large weapons, temporary structures, or pieces of equipment traditionally used in besieging castles or fortresses.

Siege engines are treated as difficult devices if someone tries to disable them using Disable Device. This takes 2d4 rounds and requires a DC 20 Disable Device check. Siege engines are typically made out of wood and have an AC of 3 (–5 Dex, –2 size), a Hardness of 5, and 80 hit points. Siege engines made up of a different material might have different values. Some siege engines are armored as well. Treat the siege engine as a Huge creature to determine the cost of such armor. Siege engines can be crafted as masterwork and enchanted as magic weapons, adding bonuses on attack rolls to the checks made to hit with the siege engine. A masterwork siege engine costs 300 gp more than the listed price. Enchanting a siege engine costs twice the normal amount. For example, a +1 *flaming heavy catapult*, armored with full plate, would have an AC of 11 and would cost 23,100 gp (800 gp base + 6,000 gp for the armor + 300 gp masterwork + 16,000 gp for the enhancements).

Catapult, Heavy: A heavy catapult is a massive engine capable of throwing rocks or heavy objects with great force. Because the catapult throws its payload in a high arc, it can hit squares out of its line of sight. To fire a heavy catapult, the crew chief makes a special check against DC 15 using only his base attack bonus, Intelligence modifier, range increment penalty, and the appropriate modifiers from the lower section of Table 13–8. If the check succeeds, the catapult stone hits the square the catapult was aimed at, dealing the indicated damage to any object or character in the square. Characters who succeed on a DC 15 Reflex save take half damage. Once a catapult stone hits a square,

TABLE 13-8: SIEGE ENGINES

Item	Cost	Damage	Critical	Range Increment	Typical Crew
Catapult, heavy	800 gp	6d6	—	200 ft. (100 ft. minimum)	4
Catapult, light	550 gp	4d6	—	150 ft. (100 ft. minimum)	2
Ballista	500 gp	3d8	19–20	120 ft.	1
Ram	1,000 gp	3d6*	—	—	10
Siege tower	2,000 gp	—	—	—	20

* See description for special rules.

CATAPULT ATTACK MODIFIERS

Condition	Modifier
No line of sight to target square	–6
Successive shots (crew can see where most recent misses landed)	Cumulative +2 per previous miss (maximum +10)
Successive shots (crew can't see where most recent misses landed, but observer is providing feedback)	Cumulative +1 per previous miss (maximum +5)

subsequent shots hit the same square unless the catapult is reaimed or the wind changes direction or speed.

If a catapult stone misses, roll 1d8 to determine where it lands. This determines the misdirection of the throw, with 1 being back toward the catapult and 2 through 8 counting clockwise around the target square. Finally, count 1d4 squares away from the target square for every range increment of the attack.

Loading a catapult requires a series of full-round actions. It takes a DC 15 Strength check to winch the throwing arm down; most catapults have wheels to allow up to two crew members to use the aid another action, assisting the main winch operator. A DC 15 Profession (siege engineer) check latches the arm into place, and then another DC 15 Profession (siege engineer) check loads the catapult ammunition. It takes four full-round actions to reaim a heavy catapult (multiple crew members can perform these full-round actions in the same round, so it would take a crew of four only 1 round to reaim the catapult).

A heavy catapult takes up a space 15 feet across.

Catapult, Light: This is a smaller, lighter version of the heavy catapult. It functions as the heavy catapult, except that it takes a DC 10 Strength check to winch the arm into place, and only two full-round actions are required to reaim the catapult.

A light catapult takes up a space 10 feet across.

Ballista: A ballista is essentially a Huge heavy crossbow fixed in place. Its size makes it hard for most creatures to aim it. Thus, a Medium creature takes a –4

penalty on attack rolls when using a ballista, and a Small creature takes a –6 penalty. It takes a creature smaller than Large two full-round actions to reload the ballista after firing.

A ballista takes up a space 5 feet across.

Ram: This heavy pole is sometimes suspended from a movable scaffold that allows the crew to swing it back and forth against objects. As a full-round action, the character closest to the front of the ram makes an attack roll against the AC of the construction, applying the –4 penalty for lack of proficiency. It's not possible to be proficient with this device. In addition to the damage given on Table 13–8, up to nine other characters holding the ram can add their Strength modifiers to the ram's damage, if they devote an attack action to doing so. It takes at least one Huge or larger creature, two

Large creatures, four Medium creatures, or eight Small creatures to swing a ram.

A ram is typically 30 feet long. In a battle, the creatures wielding the ram stand in two adjacent columns of equal length, with the ram between them.

Siege Tower: This device is a massive wooden tower on wheels or rollers that can be rolled up against a wall to allow attackers to scale the tower and thus get to the top of the wall with cover. The wooden walls are usually 1 foot thick.

A typical siege tower takes up a space 15 feet across. The creatures inside push it at a base land speed of 10 feet (and a siege tower can't run). The eight creatures pushing on the ground floor have total cover, and those on higher floors get improved cover and can fire through arrow slits.

City Streets

Typical city streets are narrow and twisting. Most streets average 15 to 20 feet wide, while alleys range from 10 feet wide to only 5 feet. Cobblestones in good condition allow normal movement, but roads in poor repair and heavily rutted dirt streets are considered light rubble, increasing the DC of Acrobatics checks by 2.

Some cities have no larger thoroughfares, particularly cities that gradually grew from small settlements to larger cities. Cities that are planned, or perhaps have suffered a major fire that allowed authorities to construct new roads through formerly inhabited areas, might have a few larger streets through town. These main roads are 25 feet wide—offering room for wagons to pass each other—with 5-foot-wide sidewalks on either side.

Crowds: Urban streets are often full of people going about their daily lives. In most cases, it isn't necessary to put every 1st-level commoner on the map when a fight breaks out on the city's main thoroughfare. Instead, just indicate which squares on the map contain crowds. If crowds see something obviously dangerous, they'll move away at 30 feet per round at initiative count 0. It takes 2 squares of movement to enter a square with crowds. The crowds provide cover for anyone who does so, enabling a Stealth check and providing a bonus to Armor Class and on Reflex saves.

Directing Crowds: It takes a DC 15 Diplomacy check or DC 20 Intimidate check to convince a crowd to move in a particular direction, and the crowd must be able to hear or see the character making the attempt. It takes a full-round action to make the Diplomacy check, but only a free action to make the Intimidate check.

If two or more characters are trying to direct a crowd in different directions, they make opposed Diplomacy or Intimidate checks to determine to whom the crowd listens. The crowd ignores everyone if none of the characters' check results beat the DCs given above.

Above and Beneath the Streets

Rooftops: Getting to a roof usually requires climbing a wall (see the Walls section), unless the character can reach a roof by jumping down from a higher window, balcony, or bridge. Flat roofs, common only in warm climates (as accumulated snow can cause a flat roof to collapse), are easy to run across. Moving along the peak of a pitched roof requires a DC 20 Acrobatics check. Moving on an angled roof surface without changing altitude (moving parallel to the peak, in other words) requires a DC 15 Acrobatics check. Moving up and down across the peak of a roof requires a DC 10 Acrobatics check.

Eventually a character runs out of roof, requiring a long jump across to the next roof or down to the ground. The distance to the closest roof is usually 1d3 × 5 feet horizontally, but the next roof is equally likely to be 5 feet higher, 5 feet lower, or the same height. Use the guidelines in the Acrobatics skill (a horizontal jump's peak height is one-fourth of the horizontal distance) to determine whether a character can make a jump.

Sewers: To get into the sewers, most characters open a grate (a full-round action) and jump down 10 feet. Sewers are built exactly like dungeons, except that they're much more likely to have floors that are slippery or covered with water. Sewers are also similar to dungeons in terms of creatures liable to be encountered therein. Some cities were built atop the ruins of older civilizations, so their sewers sometimes lead to treasures and dangers from a bygone age.

City Buildings

Most city buildings fall into three categories. The majority of buildings in the city are two to five stories high, built side-by-side to form long rows separated by secondary or main streets. These row houses usually have businesses on the ground floor, with offices or apartments above.

Inns, successful businesses, and large warehouses—as well as millers, tanners, and other businesses that require extra space—are generally large, free-standing buildings with up to five stories.

Finally, small residences, shops, warehouses, or storage sheds are simple, one-story wooden buildings, especially if they're in poorer neighborhoods.

Most city buildings are made of a combination of stone or clay brick (on the lower one or two stories) and timbers (for the upper stories, interior walls, and floors). Roofs are a mixture of boards, thatch, and slates, sealed with pitch. A typical lower-story wall is 1 foot thick, with AC 3, hardness 8, 90 hp, and a Climb DC of 25. Upper-story walls are 6 inches thick, with AC 3, hardness 5, 60 hp, and a Climb DC of 21. Exterior doors on most buildings are good wooden doors that are usually kept locked, except on public buildings such as shops and taverns.

City Lights

If a city has main thoroughfares, they are lined with lanterns hanging at a height of 7 feet from building awnings. These lanterns are spaced 60 feet apart, so their illumination is all but continuous. Secondary streets and alleys are not lit; it is common for citizens to hire lantern-bearers when going out after dark.

Alleys can be dark places even in daylight, thanks to the shadows of the tall buildings that surround them. A dark alley in daylight is rarely dark enough to afford true concealment, but it can lend a +2 circumstance bonus on Stealth checks.

WEATHER

Weather can play an important role in an adventure.

Table 13–9 can be used as a simple local weather table. Terms on that table are defined as follows.

Calm: Wind speeds are light (0 to 10 mph).

Cold: Between 0° and 40° Fahrenheit during the day, 10 to 20 degrees colder at night.

Cold Snap: Lowers temperature by −10° F.

Downpour: Treat as rain (see Precipitation, below), but conceals as fog. Can create floods. A downpour lasts for 2d4 hours.

Heat Wave: Raises temperature by +10° F.

Hot: Between 85° and 110° Fahrenheit during the day, 10 to 20 degrees colder at night.

Moderate: Between 40° and 60° Fahrenheit during the day, 10 to 20 degrees colder at night.

Powerful Storm (Windstorm/Blizzard/Hurricane/Tornado): Wind speeds are over 50 mph (see Table 13–10). In addition, blizzards are accompanied by heavy snow (1d3 feet), and hurricanes are accompanied by downpours. Windstorms last for 1d6 hours. Blizzards last for 1d3 days. Hurricanes can last for up to a week, but their major impact on characters comes in a 24-to-48-hour period when the center of the storm moves through their area. Tornadoes are very short-lived (1d6 × 10 minutes), typically forming as part of a thunderstorm system.

Precipitation: Roll d% to determine whether the precipitation is fog (01–30), rain/snow (31–90), or sleet/hail (91–00). Snow and sleet occur only when the temperature is 30° Fahrenheit or below. Most precipitation lasts for 2d4 hours. By contrast, hail lasts for only 1d20 minutes but usually accompanies 1d4 hours of rain.

Storm (Duststorm/Snowstorm/Thunderstorm): Wind speeds are severe (30 to 50 mph) and visibility is cut by three-quarters. Storms last for 2d4–1 hours. See Storms, below, for more details.

Warm: Between 60° and 85° Fahrenheit during the day, 10 to 20 degrees colder at night.

Windy: Wind speeds are moderate to strong (10 to 30 mph); see Table 13–10.

Rain, Snow, Sleet, and Hail

Bad weather frequently slows or halts travel and makes it virtually impossible to navigate from one spot to another. Torrential downpours and blizzards obscure vision as effectively as a dense fog.

Most precipitation is rain, but in cold conditions it can manifest as snow, sleet, or hail. Precipitation of any kind followed by a cold snap in which the temperature dips from above freezing to 30° F or below might produce ice.

Rain: Rain reduces visibility ranges by half, resulting in a –4 penalty on Perception checks. It has the same effect on flames, ranged weapon attacks, and Perception checks as severe wind.

Snow: Falling snow has the same effects on visibility, ranged weapon attacks, and skill checks as rain, and it costs 2 squares of movement to enter a snow-covered square. A day of snowfall leaves 1d6 inches of snow on the ground.

Heavy Snow: Heavy snow has the same effects as normal snowfall but also restricts visibility as fog does (see Fog). A day of heavy snow leaves 1d4 feet of snow on the ground, and it costs 4 squares of movement to enter a square covered with heavy snow. Heavy snow accompanied by strong or severe winds might result in snowdrifts 1d4 × 5 feet deep, especially in and around objects big enough to deflect the wind—a cabin or a large tent, for instance. There is a 10% chance that a heavy snowfall is accompanied by lightning (see Thunderstorm). Snow has the same effect on flames as moderate wind.

Sleet: Essentially frozen rain, sleet has the same effect as rain while falling (except that its chance to extinguish protected flames is 75%) and the same effect as snow once on the ground.

Hail: Hail does not reduce visibility, but the sound of falling hail makes sound-based Perception checks more difficult (–4 penalty). Sometimes (5% chance) hail can become large enough to deal 1 point of lethal damage (per storm) to anything in the open. Once on the ground, hail has the same effect on movement as snow.

Storms

The combined effects of precipitation (or dust) and wind that accompany all storms reduce visibility ranges by three-quarters, imposing a –8 penalty on Perception checks. Storms make ranged weapon attacks impossible, except for those using siege weapons, which have a –4 penalty on attack rolls. They automatically extinguish candles, torches, and similar unprotected flames. They cause protected flames, such as those of lanterns, to dance wildly and have a 50% chance to extinguish these lights. See Table 13–10 for possible consequences to creatures caught outside without shelter during such a storm. Storms are divided into the following three types.

Duststorm (CR 3): These desert storms differ from other storms in that they have no precipitation. Instead, a duststorm blows fine grains of sand that obscure vision, smother unprotected flames, and can even choke protected flames (50% chance). Most duststorms are accompanied by severe winds and leave behind a deposit of 1d6 inches of sand. There is a 10% chance for a greater duststorm to be accompanied by windstorm-magnitude winds (see Table 13–10). These greater duststorms deal 1d3 points of nonlethal damage each round to anyone caught out in the open without shelter and also pose a choking hazard (see Drowning, except that a character with a scarf or similar protection across her mouth and nose does not begin to choke until after a number of rounds equal to 10 + her Constitution score). Greater duststorms leave 2d3–1 feet of fine sand in their wake.

Snowstorm: In addition to the wind and precipitation common to other storms, snowstorms leave 1d6 inches of snow on the ground afterward.

Thunderstorm: In addition to wind and precipitation (usually rain, but sometimes also hail), thunderstorms are accompanied by lightning that can pose a hazard to characters without proper shelter (especially those in metal armor). As a rule of thumb, assume one bolt per minute for a 1-hour period at the center of the storm. Each bolt causes between 4d8 and 10d8 points of electricity damage. One in 10 thunderstorms is accompanied by a tornado.

Powerful Storms: Very high winds and torrential precipitation reduce visibility to zero, making Perception checks and all ranged weapon attacks impossible. Unprotected flames are automatically extinguished, and protected flames have a 75% chance of being doused. Creatures caught in the area must make a Fortitude save or face the effects based on the size of the creature (see Table 13–10). Powerful storms are divided into the following four types.

Windstorm: While accompanied by little or no precipitation, windstorms can cause considerable damage simply through the force of their winds.

Blizzard: The combination of high winds, heavy snow (typically 1d3 feet), and bitter cold make blizzards deadly for all who are unprepared for them.

TABLE 13-9: RANDOM WEATHER

d%	Weather	Cold Climate	Temperate Climate[1]	Desert
01–70	Normal weather	Cold, calm	Normal for season[2]	Hot, calm
71–80	Abnormal weather	Heat wave (01–30) or cold snap (31–100)	Heat wave (01–50) or cold snap (51–100)	Hot, windy
81–90	Inclement weather	Precipitation (snow)	Precipitation (normal for season)	Hot, windy
91–99	Storm	Snowstorm	Thunderstorm, snowstorm	Duststorm
100	Powerful storm	Blizzard	Windstorm, blizzard, hurricane, tornado	Downpour

1 Temperate includes forests, hills, marshes, mountains, plains, and warm aquatic environments.

2 Winter is cold, summer is warm, spring and autumn are temperate. Marsh regions are slightly warmer in winter.

TABLE 13-10: WIND EFFECTS

Wind Force	Wind Speed	Ranged Attacks Normal/Siege Weapons[1]	Checked Size[2]	Blown Away Size[3]	Fly Penalty
Light	0–10 mph	—/—	—	—	—
Moderate	11–20 mph	—/—	—	—	—
Strong	21–30 mph	–2/—	Tiny	—	–2
Severe	31–50 mph	–4/—	Small	Tiny	–4
Windstorm	51–74 mph	Impossible/–4	Medium	Small	–8
Hurricane	75–174 mph	Impossible/–8	Large	Medium	–12
Tornado	175–300 mph	Impossible/impossible	Huge	Large	–16

1 The siege weapon category includes ballista and catapult attacks as well as boulders tossed by giants.

2 *Checked Size*: Creatures of this size or smaller are unable to move forward against the force of the wind unless they succeed on a DC 10 Strength check (if on the ground) or a DC 20 Fly skill check if airborne.

3 *Blown Away Size*: Creatures on the ground are knocked prone and rolled 1d4 × 10 feet, taking 1d4 points of nonlethal damage per 10 feet, unless they make a DC 15 Strength check. Flying creatures are blown back 2d6 × 10 feet and take 2d6 points of nonlethal damage due to battering and buffeting, unless they succeed on a DC 25 Fly skill check.

Hurricane: In addition to very high winds and heavy rain, hurricanes are accompanied by floods. Most adventuring activity is impossible under such conditions.

Tornado: In addition to incredibly high winds, tornadoes can severely injure and kill those that get pulled into their funnels.

Fog

Whether in the form of a low-lying cloud or a mist rising from the ground, fog obscures all sight beyond 5 feet, including darkvision. Creatures 5 feet away have concealment (attacks by or against them have a 20% miss chance).

Winds

The wind can create a stinging spray of sand or dust, fan a large fire, keel over a small boat, and blow gases or vapors away. If powerful enough, it can even knock characters down (see Table 13–10), interfere with ranged attacks, or impose penalties on some skill checks.

Light Wind: A gentle breeze, having little or no game effect.

Moderate Wind: A steady wind with a 50% chance of extinguishing small, unprotected flames, such as candles.

Strong Wind: Gusts that automatically extinguish unprotected flames (candles, torches, and the like). Such gusts impose a –2 penalty on ranged attack rolls and on Perception checks.

Severe Wind: In addition to automatically extinguishing any unprotected flames, winds of this magnitude cause protected flames (such as those of lanterns) to dance wildly and have a 50% chance of extinguishing these lights. Ranged weapon attacks and Perception checks are at a –4 penalty. This is the velocity of wind produced by a *gust of wind* spell.

Windstorm: Powerful enough to bring down branches if not whole trees, windstorms automatically extinguish unprotected flames and have a 75% chance of blowing out protected flames, such as those of lanterns. Ranged weapon attacks are impossible, and even siege weapons have a –4 penalty on attack rolls. Perception checks that rely on sound are at a –8 penalty due to the howling of the wind.

Hurricane-Force Wind: All flames are extinguished. Ranged attacks are impossible (except with siege weapons, which have a –8 penalty on attack rolls). Perception checks based on sound are impossible: all characters can hear is the roaring of the wind. Hurricane-force winds often fell trees.

Tornado (CR 10): All flames are extinguished. All ranged attacks are impossible (even with siege weapons), as are sound-based Perception checks. Instead of being blown away (see Table 13–10), characters in close proximity to a tornado who fail their Fortitude saves are sucked toward the tornado. Those who come in contact with the actual funnel cloud are picked up and whirled around for 1d10 rounds, taking 6d6 points of damage per round, before being violently expelled (falling damage might apply). While a tornado's rotational speed can be as great as 300 mph, the funnel itself moves forward at an average of 30 mph (roughly 250 feet per round). A tornado uproots trees, destroys buildings, and causes similar forms of major destruction.

THE PLANES

While endless adventure awaits out in the game—there are other worlds beyond these—other continents, other planets, other galaxies. Yet even beyond this existence of countless planets exist more worlds—entirely different dimensions of reality known as the planes of existence. Except for rare linking points that allow travel between them, each plane is effectively its own universe with its own natural laws. Collectively, the entirety of these other dimensions and planes is known as the Great Beyond.

Although the number of planes is limited only by imagination, they can all be categorized into five general types: the Material Plane, the transitive planes, the Inner Planes, the Outer Planes, and the countless demiplanes.

Material Plane: The Material Plane tends to be the most Earth-like of all planes and operates under the same set of natural laws that our own real world does. The "size" of the Material Plane depends upon the campaign—it might conform only to the single world on which your game is set, or it might encompass an entire universe of planets, moons, stars, and galaxies. The Material Plane is the default plane for the Pathfinder Roleplaying Game.

Transitive Planes: Transitive planes have one important common characteristic: they "overlap" with other planes, and as such can be used to travel between these overlapping realities. These planes have the strongest regular interaction with the Material Plane and are often accessed by using various spells. They have native inhabitants as well. Example transitive planes include the following.

Astral Plane: A silvery void that connects the Material and Inner Planes to the Outer Planes, the astral plane is the medium through which the souls of the departed travel to the afterlife. A traveler in the Astral Plane sees the plane as a vast empty void periodically dotted with tiny motes of physical reality calved off of the countless planes it overlaps. Powerful spellcasters utilize the Astral Plane for a tiny fraction of a second when they teleport, or they can use it to travel between planes with spells like *astral projection.*

Ethereal Plane: The Ethereal Plane is a ghostly realm that exists as a buffer between the Material Plane and the Shadow Plane, overlapping each. A traveler in the Ethereal plane experiences the real world as if the world were an insubstantial ghost, and can move through solid objects without being seen in the real world. Strange creatures dwell in the Ethereal Plane, as well as ghosts and dreams, many of which can sometimes extend their influence into the real world in mysterious and terrifying ways. Powerful spellcasters utilize the Ethereal Plane with spells like *blink, etherealness,* and *ethereal jaunt.*

Shadow Plane: The eerie and deadly Shadow Plane is a grim, colorless "duplicate" of the Material Plane. It overlaps with the Material Plane but is smaller in size, and is in many ways a warped and mocking "reflection" of the Material Plane, one infused with negative energy (see Inner Planes) and serving as home for strange monsters like undead shadows and worse. Powerful spellcasters utilize the Shadow Plane to swiftly travel immense distances on the Material Plane with *shadow walk,* or draw upon the mutable essence of the Shadow Plane to create quasi-real effects and creatures with spells like *shadow evocation* or *shades.*

Inner Planes: The Inner Planes contain the building blocks of reality—it's easiest to envision these planes as "containing" the Material Plane, but they do not overlap with the Material Plane as do the transitive planes. Each Inner Plane is made up of a single type of energy or element that overwhelms all others. The natives of a particular Inner Plane are made of the same energy or element as the plane itself. Example Inner Planes include the following.

Elemental Planes: The four classic Inner Planes are the Plane of Air, the Plane of Earth, the Plane of Fire, and the Plane of Water—it is from these planes that the creatures known as elementals hail, yet they house many other strange denizens as well, such as the genie races, strange metal-eating xorns, unseen invisible stalkers, and mischievous mephits.

Energy Planes: Two energy planes exist—the Positive Energy Plane (from which the animating spark of life hails) and the Negative Energy Plane (from which the sinister taint of undeath hails). Energy from both planes infuses reality, the ebb and flow of this energy running through all creatures to bear them along the journey from birth to death. Clerics utilize power from these planes when they channel energy.

Outer Planes: Beyond the realm of the mortal world, beyond the building blocks of reality, lie the Outer Planes. Vast beyond imagining, it is to these realms that the souls of the dead travel, and it is upon these realms in which the gods themselves hold court. Each of the Outer Planes has an alignment, representing a particular moral or ethical outlook, and the natives of each plane

tend to behave in agreement with that plane's alignment. The Outer Planes are also the final resting place of souls from the Material Plane, whether that final rest takes the form of calm introspection or eternal damnation. The denizens of the Outer Planes form the mythologies of civilization, comprising angels and demons, titans and devils, and countless other incarnations of possibility. Each campaign world should have different Outer Planes to match its themes and needs, but classic Outer Planes include lawful good Heaven, the chaos and evil of the Abyss, the regimented lawful evil of Hell, and the capricious freedom and joys of chaotic good Elysium. Powerful spellcasters can contact the Outer Planes for advice or guidance with spells like *commune* and *contact outer plane*, or can conjure allies with spells like *planar ally* or *summon monster*.

Demiplanes: This catchall category covers all extradimensional spaces that function like planes but have measurable size and limited access. Other kinds of planes are theoretically infinite in size, but a demiplane might be only a few hundred feet across. There are countless demiplanes adrift in reality, and while most are connected to the Astral Plane and Ethereal Plane, some are cut off entirely from the transitive planes and can only be accessed by well-hidden portals or obscure magic spells.

Layered Planes

Infinities may be broken into smaller infinities, and planes into smaller, related planes. These layers are effectively separate planes of existence, and each layer can have its own features and qualities. Layers are connected to each other through a variety of planar gates, natural vortices, paths, and shifting borders.

Access to a layered plane from elsewhere usually happens on the first layer of the plane, which can be either the top or bottom layer, depending on the specific plane. Most fixed access points (such as portals and natural vortices) reach this layer, which makes it the gateway for other layers of the plane. The *plane shift* spell generally deposits the spellcaster on the first layer of the plane.

How Planes Interact

Two planes that are separate do not overlap or directly connect to each other. They are like planets in different orbits. The only way to get from one separate plane to the other is to go through a third plane, such as a Transitive Plane.

Coterminous Planes: Planes that touch at specific points are coterminous. Where they touch, a connection exists, and travelers can leave one reality behind and enter the other.

Coexistent Planes: If a link between two planes can be created at any point, the two planes are coexistent. These planes overlap each other completely. A coexistent plane can be reached from anywhere on the plane it overlaps. When moving on a coexistent plane, it is often possible to see into or interact with the plane with which it coexists.

ENVIRONMENTAL RULES

Environmental hazards specific to one kind of terrain are described in the Wilderness section. Environmental hazards common to more than one setting are detailed below.

Acid Effects

Corrosive acids deals 1d6 points of damage per round of exposure except in the case of total immersion (such as in a vat of acid), which deals 10d6 points of damage per round. An attack with acid, such as from a hurled vial or a monster's spittle, counts as a round of exposure.

The fumes from most acids are inhaled poisons. Those who are adjacent to a large body of acid must make a DC 13 Fortitude save or take 1 point of Constitution damage each round. This poison does not have a frequency, a creature is safe as soon as it moves away from the acid.

Creatures immune to acid's caustic properties might still drown in it if they are totally immersed (see Drowning).

Cold Dangers

Cold and exposure deal nonlethal damage to the victim. A character cannot recover from the damage dealt by a cold environment until she gets out of the cold and warms up again. Once a character has taken an amount of nonlethal damage equal to her total hit points, any further damage from a cold environment is lethal damage.

An unprotected character in cold weather (below 40° F) must make a Fortitude save each hour (DC 15, +1 per previous check) or take 1d6 points of nonlethal damage. A character who has the Survival skill may receive a bonus on this saving throw and might be able to apply this bonus to other characters as well (see the skill description).

In conditions of severe cold or exposure (below 0° F), an unprotected character must make a Fortitude save once every 10 minutes (DC 15, +1 per previous check), taking 1d6 points of nonlethal damage on each failed save. A character who has the Survival skill may receive a bonus on this saving throw and might be able to apply this bonus to other characters as well. Characters wearing a cold weather outfit only need check once per hour for cold and exposure damage.

A character who takes any nonlethal damage from cold or exposure is beset by frostbite or hypothermia (treat her as fatigued). These penalties end when the character recovers the nonlethal damage she took from the cold and exposure.

Extreme cold (below –20° F) deals 1d6 points of lethal damage per minute (no save). In addition, a character must make a Fortitude save (DC 15, +1 per previous check) or take 1d4 points of nonlethal damage.

Ice Effects

Characters walking on ice must spend 2 squares of movement to enter a square covered by ice, and the DC for Acrobatics checks increases by +5. Characters in prolonged contact with ice might run the risk of taking damage from severe cold.

Darkness

Darkvision allows many characters and monsters to see perfectly well without any light at all, but characters with normal or low-light vision can be rendered completely blind by putting out the lights. Torches or lanterns can be blown out by sudden gusts of subterranean wind, magical light sources can be dispelled or countered, or magical traps might create fields of impenetrable darkness.

In many cases, some characters or monsters might be able to see while others are blinded. For purposes of the following points, a blinded creature is one who simply can't see through the surrounding darkness.

Creatures blinded by darkness lose the ability to deal extra damage due to precision (for example, via sneak attack or a duelist's precise strike ability).

Blind creatures must make a DC 10 Acrobatics skill check to move faster than half speed. Creatures that fail this check fall prone. Blinded creatures can't run or charge.

All opponents have total concealment from a blinded creature, so the blinded creature has a 50% miss chance in combat. A blinded creature must first pinpoint the location of an opponent in order to attack the right square; if the blinded creature launches an attack without pinpointing its foe, it attacks a random square within its reach. For ranged attacks or spells against a foe whose location is not pinpointed, roll to determine which adjacent square the blinded creature is facing; its attack is directed at the closest target that lies in that direction.

A blinded creature loses its Dexterity modifier to AC (if positive) and takes a –2 penalty to AC.

A blinded creature takes a –4 penalty on Perception checks and most Strength- and Dexterity-based skill checks, including any with an armor check penalty. A creature blinded by darkness automatically fails any skill check relying on vision.

Creatures blinded by darkness cannot use gaze attacks and are immune to gaze attacks.

A creature blinded by darkness can make a Perception check as a free action each round in order to locate foes (DC equal to opponents' Stealth checks). A successful check lets a blinded character hear an unseen creature "over there somewhere." It's almost impossible to pinpoint the location of an unseen creature. A Perception check that beats the DC by 20 reveals the unseen creature's square (but the unseen creature still has total concealment from the blinded creature).

A blinded creature can grope about to find unseen creatures. A character can make a touch attack with his hands or a weapon into two adjacent squares using a standard action. If an unseen target is in the designated square, there is a 50% miss chance on the touch attack. If successful, the groping character deals no damage but has pinpointed the unseen creature's current location. If the unseen creature moves, its location is once again unknown.

If a blinded creature is struck by an unseen foe, the blinded character pinpoints the location of the creature that struck him (until the unseen creature moves, of course). The only exception is if the unseen creature has a reach greater than 5 feet (in which case the blinded character knows the location of the unseen opponent, but has not pinpointed him) or uses a ranged attack (in which case the blinded character knows the general direction of the foe, but not his location).

A creature with the scent ability automatically pinpoints unseen creatures within 5 feet of its location.

Falling

Creatures that fall take 1d6 points of damage per 10 feet fallen, to a maximum of 20d6. Creatures that take lethal damage from a fall land in a prone position.

If a character deliberately jumps instead of merely slipping or falling, the damage is the same but the first 1d6 is nonlethal damage. A DC 15 Acrobatics check allows the character to avoid any damage from the first 10 feet fallen and converts any damage from the second 10 feet to nonlethal damage. Thus, a character who slips from a ledge 30 feet up takes 3d6 damage. If the same character deliberately jumps, he takes 1d6 points of nonlethal damage and 2d6 points of lethal damage. And if the character leaps down with a successful Acrobatics check, he takes only 1d6 points of nonlethal damage and 1d6 points of lethal damage from the plunge.

Falls onto yielding surfaces (soft ground, mud) also convert the first 1d6 of damage to nonlethal damage.

TABLE 13-11: DAMAGE FROM FALLING OBJECTS

Object Size	Damage
Tiny or smaller	1d6
Small	2d6
Medium	3d6
Large	4d6
Huge	6d6
Gargantuan	8d6
Colossal	10d6

This reduction is cumulative with reduced damage due to deliberate jumps and the Acrobatics skill.

A character cannot cast a spell while falling, unless the fall is greater than 500 feet or the spell is an immediate action, such as *feather fall*. Casting a spell while falling requires a concentration check with a DC equal to 20 + the spell's level. Casting *teleport* or a similar spell while falling does not end your momentum, it just changes your location, meaning that you still take falling damage, even if you arrive atop a solid surface.

Falling into Water: Falls into water are handled somewhat differently. If the water is at least 10 feet deep, the first 20 feet of falling do no damage. The next 20 feet do nonlethal damage (1d3 per 10-foot increment). Beyond that, falling damage is lethal damage (1d6 per additional 10-foot increment).

Characters who deliberately dive into water take no damage on a successful DC 15 Swim check or DC 15 Acrobatics check, so long as the water is at least 10 feet deep for every 30 feet fallen. The DC of the check, however, increases by 5 for every 50 feet of the dive.

Falling Objects

Just as characters take damage when they fall more than 10 feet, so too do they take damage when they are hit by falling objects.

Objects that fall upon characters deal damage based on their size and the distance they have fallen. Table 13-11 determines the amount of damage dealt by an object based on its size. Note that this assumes that the object is made of dense, heavy material, such as stone. Objects made of lighter materials might deal as little as half the listed damage, subject to GM discretion. For example, a Huge boulder that hits a character deals 6d6 points of damage, whereas a Huge wooden wagon might deal only 3d6 damage. In addition, if an object falls less than 30 feet, it deals half the listed damage. If an object falls more than 150 feet, it deals double the listed damage. Note that a falling object takes the same amount of damage as it deals.

Dropping an object on a creature requires a ranged touch attack. Such attacks generally have a range increment of 20 feet. If an object falls on a creature

(instead of being thrown), that creature can make a DC 15 Reflex save to halve the damage if he is aware of the object. Falling objects that are part of a trap use the trap rules instead of these general guidelines.

Heat Dangers

Heat deals nonlethal damage that cannot be recovered from until the character gets cooled off (reaches shade, survives until nightfall, gets doused in water, is targeted by *endure elements*, and so forth). Once a character has taken an amount of nonlethal damage equal to her total hit points, any further damage from a hot environment is lethal damage.

A character in very hot conditions (above 90° F) must make a Fortitude saving throw each hour (DC 15, +1 for each previous check) or take 1d4 points of nonlethal damage. Characters wearing heavy clothing or armor of any sort take a –4 penalty on their saves. A character with the Survival skill may receive a bonus on this saving throw and might be able to apply this bonus to other characters as well (see the skill description). Characters reduced to unconsciousness begin taking lethal damage (1d4 points per hour).

In severe heat (above 110° F), a character must make a Fortitude save once every 10 minutes (DC 15, +1 for each previous check) or take 1d4 points of nonlethal damage. Characters wearing heavy clothing or armor of any sort take a –4 penalty on their saves. A character with the Survival skill may receive a bonus on this saving throw and might be able to apply this bonus to other characters as well (see the Survival skill in Chapter 4). Characters reduced to unconsciousness begin taking lethal damage (1d4 points per each 10-minute period).

A character who takes any nonlethal damage from heat exposure now suffers from heatstroke and is fatigued. These penalties end when the character recovers from the nonlethal damage she took from the heat.

Extreme heat (air temperature over 140° F, fire, boiling water, lava) deals lethal damage. Breathing air in these temperatures deals 1d6 points of fire damage per minute (no save). In addition, a character must make a Fortitude save every 5 minutes (DC 15, +1 per previous check) or take 1d4 points of nonlethal damage. Those wearing heavy clothing or any sort of armor take a –4 penalty on their saves.

Boiling water deals 1d6 points of scalding damage, unless the character is fully immersed, in which case it deals 10d6 points of damage per round of exposure.

Catching on Fire

Characters exposed to burning oil, bonfires, and non-instantaneous magic fires might find their clothes, hair, or equipment on fire. Spells with an instantaneous duration don't normally set a character on fire, since the heat and flame from these come and go in a flash.

Characters at risk of catching fire are allowed a DC 15 Reflex save to avoid this fate. If a character's clothes or hair catch fire, he takes 1d6 points of damage immediately. In each subsequent round, the burning character must make another Reflex saving throw. Failure means he takes another 1d6 points of damage that round. Success means that the fire has gone out—that is, once he succeeds on his saving throw, he's no longer on fire.

A character on fire may automatically extinguish the flames by jumping into enough water to douse himself. If no body of water is at hand, rolling on the ground or smothering the fire with cloaks or the like permits the character another save with a +4 bonus.

Those whose clothes or equipment catch fire must make DC 15 Reflex saves for each item. Flammable items that fail take the same amount of damage as the character.

Lava Effects

Lava or magma deals 2d6 points of fire damage per round of exposure, except in the case of total immersion (such as when a character falls into the crater of an active volcano), which deals 20d6 points of fire damage per round.

Damage from lava continues for 1d3 rounds after exposure ceases, but this additional damage is only half of that dealt during actual contact (that is, 1d6 or 10d6 points per round). Immunity or resistance to fire serves as an immunity or resistance to lava or magma. A creature immune or resistant to fire might still drown if completely immersed in lava (see Drowning).

Smoke Effects

A character who breathes heavy smoke must make a Fortitude save each round (DC 15, +1 per previous check) or spend that round choking and coughing. A character who chokes for 2 consecutive rounds takes 1d6 points of nonlethal damage. Smoke obscures vision, giving concealment (20% miss chance) to characters within it.

Starvation and Thirst

Characters might find themselves without food or water and with no means to obtain them. In normal climates, Medium characters need at least a gallon of fluids and about a pound of decent food per day to avoid starvation. (Small characters need half as much.) In very hot climates, characters need two or three times as much water to avoid dehydration.

A character can go without water for 1 day plus a number of hours equal to his Constitution score. After this time, the character must make a Constitution check each hour (DC 10, +1 for each previous check) or take 1d6 points of nonlethal damage. Characters that take an amount of nonlethal damage equal to their total hit points begin to take lethal damage instead.

A character can go without food for 3 days, in growing discomfort. After this time, the character must make a Constitution check each day (DC 10, +1 for each previous check) or take 1d6 points of nonlethal damage. Characters that take an amount of nonlethal damage equal to their total hit points begin to take lethal damage instead.

Characters who have taken nonlethal damage from lack of food or water are fatigued. Nonlethal damage from thirst or starvation cannot be recovered until the character gets food or water, as needed—not even magic that restores hit points heals this damage.

Suffocation

A character who has no air to breathe can hold her breath for 2 rounds per point of Constitution. If a character takes a standard or full-round action, the remaining duration that the character can hold her breath is reduced by 1 round. After this period of time, the character must make a DC 10 Constitution check in order to continue holding her breath. The check must be repeated each round, with the DC increasing by +1 for each previous success.

When the character fails one of these Constitution checks, she begins to suffocate. In the first round, she falls unconscious (0 hit points). In the following round, she drops to −1 hit points and is dying. In the third round, she suffocates.

Slow Suffocation: A Medium character can breathe easily for 6 hours in a sealed chamber measuring 10 feet on a side. After that time, the character takes 1d6 points of nonlethal damage every 15 minutes. Each additional Medium character or significant fire source (a torch, for

example) proportionally reduces the time the air will last. Once rendered unconscious through the accumulation of nonlethal damage, the character begins to take lethal damage at the same rate. Small characters consume half as much air as Medium characters.

Water Dangers

Any character can wade in relatively calm water that isn't over his head, no check required. Similarly, swimming in calm water only requires Swim skill checks with a DC of 10. Trained swimmers can just take 10. Remember, however, that armor or heavy gear makes any attempt at swimming much more difficult (see the Swim skill description).

By contrast, fast-moving water is much more dangerous. Characters must make a successful DC 15 Swim check or a DC 15 Strength check to avoid going under. On a failed check, the character takes 1d3 points of nonlethal damage per round (1d6 points of lethal damage if flowing over rocks and cascades).

Very deep water is not only generally pitch black, posing a navigational hazard, but worse, deals water pressure damage of 1d6 points per minute for every 100 feet the character is below the surface. A successful Fortitude save (DC 15, +1 for each previous check) means the diver takes no damage in that minute. Very cold water deals 1d6 points of nonlethal damage from hypothermia per minute of exposure.

Drowning

Any character can hold her breath for a number of rounds equal to twice her Constitution score. If a character takes a standard or full-round action, the remaining duration that the character can hold her breath is reduced by 1 round. After this period of time, the character must make a DC 10 Constitution check every round in order to continue holding her breath. Each round, the DC increases by 1.

When the character finally fails her Constitution check, she begins to drown. In the first round, she falls unconscious (0 hp). In the following round, she drops to −1 hit points and is dying. In the third round, she drowns.

Unconscious characters must begin making Constitution checks immediately upon being submerged (or upon becoming unconscious if the character was conscious when submerged). Once she fails one of these checks, she immediately drops to −1 (or loses 1 additional hit point, if her total is below −1). On the following round, she drowns.

It is possible to drown in substances other than water, such as sand, quicksand, fine dust, and silos full of grain.

14 Creating NPCs

Panic filled the streets as a star streaked from the sky, falling in defiance of all nature's laws. In that moment there was only anarchy. Amid gasps and cries, parents raced home to protect their families. Opportunistic scoundrels shattered storefront glass. Cowards cursed and fled. Heroes raced to gain a better vantage. And all the while a chorus of distant shouts cried out to the deities, proclaimed the end times, and called for a semblance of order. In the moments before its terrible crash, the light of that dying star revealed the true nature of all it shone upon, and afterward no one would ever be the same.

Aside from the players, every other person encountered in the game world is a nonplayer character (NPC). These characters are designed and controlled by the GM to fill every role from noble king to simple baker. While some of these characters use player classes, most rely upon basic NPC classes, allowing them to be easily generated. The following rules govern all of the NPC classes and include information on generating quick NPCs for an evening's game.

ADEPT

Alignment: Any.
Hit Die: d6.

Class Skills

The adept's class skills (and the key ability for each skill) are Craft (Int), Handle Animal (Cha), Heal (Wis), Knowledge (all skills taken individually) (Int), Profession (Wis), Spellcraft (Int), and Survival (Wis).

Skill Ranks per Level: 2 + Int modifier.

Class Features

All of the following are class features of the adept NPC class.

Weapon and Armor Proficiency: Adepts are skilled with all simple weapons. Adepts are not proficient with any type of armor or shield.

Spells: An adept casts divine spells, which are drawn from the adept spell list. Like a cleric, an adept must choose and prepare her spells in advance. Unlike a cleric, an adept cannot spontaneously cast *cure* or *inflict* spells.

To prepare or cast a spell, an adept must have a Wisdom score equal to at least 10 + the spell level. The Difficulty Class for a saving throw against an adept's spell is 10 + the spell level + the adept's Wisdom modifier.

Adepts, unlike wizards, do not acquire their spells from books or scrolls, nor do they prepare them through study. Instead, they meditate or pray for their spells, receiving them as divine inspiration or through their own strength of faith. Each adept must choose a time each day during which she must spend an hour in quiet contemplation or supplication to regain her daily allotment of spells. Time spent resting has no effect on whether an adept can prepare spells.

Like other spellcasters, an adept can cast only a certain number of spells of each spell level per day. Her base daily spell allotment is given on Table 14–1. In addition, she receives bonus spells per day if she has a high Wisdom score.

Where Table 14–1 indicates that the adept gets 0 spells per day of a given spell level, she gains only the bonus spells she would be entitled to based on her Wisdom score for that spell level.

Each adept has a particular holy symbol (as a divine focus) depending on the adept's magical tradition.

TABLE 14-1: ADEPT

NPC Level	Base Attack Bonus	Fort Save	Ref Save	Will Save	Special	Spells per Day					
						0	1st	2nd	3rd	4th	5th
1st	+0	+0	+0	+2		3	1	—	—	—	—
2nd	+1	+0	+0	+3	Summon familiar	3	1	—	—	—	—
3rd	+1	+1	+1	+3		3	2	—	—	—	—
4th	+2	+1	+1	+4		3	2	0	—	—	—
5th	+2	+1	+1	+4		3	2	1	—	—	—
6th	+3	+2	+2	+5		3	2	1	—	—	—
7th	+3	+2	+2	+5		3	3	2	—	—	—
8th	+4	+2	+2	+6		3	3	2	0	—	—
9th	+4	+3	+3	+6		3	3	2	1	—	—
10th	+5	+3	+3	+7		3	3	2	1	—	—
11th	+5	+3	+3	+7		3	3	3	2	—	—
12th	+6/+1	+4	+4	+8		3	3	3	2	0	—
13th	+6/+1	+4	+4	+8		3	3	3	2	1	—
14th	+7/+2	+4	+4	+9		3	3	3	2	1	—
15th	+7/+2	+5	+5	+9		3	3	3	3	2	—
16th	+8/+3	+5	+5	+10		3	3	3	3	2	0
17th	+8/+3	+5	+5	+10		3	3	3	3	2	1
18th	+9/+4	+6	+6	+11		3	3	3	3	2	1
19th	+9/+4	+6	+6	+11		3	3	3	3	3	2
20th	+10/+5	+6	+6	+12		3	3	3	3	3	2

Summon Familiar: At 2nd level, an adept can call a familiar, just as a wizard can using the arcane bond ability.

Adept Spell List

Adepts choose their spells from the following list.

0 Level: *create water, detect magic, ghost sound, guidance, light, mending, purify food and drink, read magic, stabilize, touch of fatigue.*

1st Level: *bless, burning hands, cause fear, command, comprehend languages, cure light wounds, detect chaos, detect evil, detect good, detect law, endure elements, obscuring mist, protection from chaos, protection from evil, protection from good, protection from law, sleep.*

2nd Level: *aid, animal trance, bear's endurance, bull's strength, cat's grace, cure moderate wounds, darkness, delay poison, invisibility, mirror image, resist energy, scorching ray, see invisibility, web.*

3rd Level: *animate dead, bestow curse, contagion, continual flame, cure serious wounds, daylight, deeper darkness, lightning bolt, neutralize poison, remove curse, remove disease, tongues.*

4th Level: *cure critical wounds, minor creation, polymorph, restoration, stoneskin, wall of fire.*

5th Level: *baleful polymorph, break enchantment, commune, heal, major creation, raise dead, true seeing, wall of stone.*

ARISTOCRAT

Alignment: Any.
Hit Die: d8.

Class Skills

The aristocrat's class skills (and the key ability for each skill) are Appraise (Int), Bluff (Cha), Craft (Int), Diplomacy (Cha), Disguise (Cha), Handle Animal (Cha), Intimidate (Cha), Knowledge (all skills taken individually) (Int), Linguistics (Int), Perception (Wis), Perform (Cha), Profession (Wis), Ride (Dex), Sense Motive (Wis), Survival (Wis), and Swim (Str).

Skill Ranks per Level: 4 + Int modifier.

Class Features

The following is a class feature of the aristocrat NPC class.

Weapon and Armor Proficiency: The aristocrat is proficient in the use of all simple and martial weapons and with all types of armor and shields.

COMMONER

Alignment: Any.
Hit Die: d6.

Class Skills

The commoner's class skills (and the key ability for each skill) are Climb (Str), Craft (Int), Handle Animal (Cha), Perception (Wis), Profession (Wis), Ride (Dex), and Swim (Str).

Skill Ranks per Level: 2 + Int modifier.

Class Features

The following is a class feature of the commoner NPC class.

Weapon and Armor Proficiency: The commoner is proficient with one simple weapon. He is not proficient with any other weapons, nor is he proficient with any type of armor or shield.

TABLE 14-2: ARISTOCRAT

NPC Level	Base Attack Bonus	Fort Save	Ref Save	Will Save
1st	+0	+0	+0	+2
2nd	+1	+0	+0	+3
3rd	+2	+1	+1	+3
4th	+3	+1	+1	+4
5th	+3	+1	+1	+4
6th	+4	+2	+2	+5
7th	+5	+2	+2	+5
8th	+6/+1	+2	+2	+6
9th	+6/+1	+3	+3	+6
10th	+7/+2	+3	+3	+7
11th	+8/+3	+3	+3	+7
12th	+9/+4	+4	+4	+8
13th	+9/+4	+4	+4	+8
14th	+10/+5	+4	+4	+9
15th	+11/+6/+1	+5	+5	+9
16th	+12/+7/+2	+5	+5	+10
17th	+12/+7/+2	+5	+5	+10
18th	+13/+8/+3	+6	+6	+11
19th	+14/+9/+4	+6	+6	+11
20th	+15/+10/+5	+6	+6	+12

TABLE 14-3: COMMONER

NPC Level	Base Attack Bonus	Fort Save	Ref Save	Will Save
1st	+0	+0	+0	+0
2nd	+1	+0	+0	+0
3rd	+1	+1	+1	+1
4th	+2	+1	+1	+1
5th	+2	+1	+1	+1
6th	+3	+2	+2	+2
7th	+3	+2	+2	+2
8th	+4	+2	+2	+2
9th	+4	+3	+3	+3
10th	+5	+3	+3	+3
11th	+5	+3	+3	+3
12th	+6/+1	+4	+4	+4
13th	+6/+1	+4	+4	+4
14th	+7/+2	+4	+4	+4
15th	+7/+2	+5	+5	+5
16th	+8/+3	+5	+5	+5
17th	+8/+3	+5	+5	+5
18th	+9/+4	+6	+6	+6
19th	+9/+4	+6	+6	+6
20th	+10/+5	+6	+6	+6

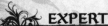

EXPERT

Alignment: Any.
Hit Die: d8.

Class Skills

The expert can choose any 10 skills to be class skills.
Skill Ranks per Level: 6 + Int modifier.

Class Features

The following is a class feature of the expert NPC class.
Weapon and Armor Proficiency: The expert is proficient in the use of all simple weapons and with light armor, but not with any type of shield.

WARRIOR

Alignment: Any.
Hit Die: d10.

Class Skills

The warrior's class skills (and the key ability for each skill) are Climb (Str), Craft (Int), Handle Animal (Cha), Intimidate (Cha), Profession (Wis), Ride (Dex), and Swim (Str).
Skill Ranks per Level: 2 + Int modifier.

Class Features

The following is a class feature of the warrior NPC class.

Weapon and Armor Proficiency: The warrior is proficient in the use of all simple and martial weapons and with all types of armor and shields.

CREATING NPCS

The world that the player characters inhabit should be full of rich and vibrant characters with whom they can interact. While most need little more than names and general descriptions, some require complete statistics, such as town guards, local clerics, and wizened sages. The PCs might find themselves in combat with these characters, either against them or as allies. Alternatively the PCs might find themselves relying on the skills and abilities of the NPCs. In either case, the process for creating these NPCs can be performed in seven simple steps.

Step 1: The Basics

The first step in making an NPC is to determine its basic role in your campaign. This includes its race, class, and basic concept.

Step 2: Determine Ability Scores

Once the character's basic concept has been determined, its ability scores must be assigned. Apply the NPC's racial modifiers after the scores have been assigned. For every four levels the NPC has attained, increase one of its scores by 1. If the NPC possesses levels in a PC class, it is

TABLE 14-4: EXPERT

NPC Level	Base Attack Bonus	Fort Save	Ref Save	Will Save
1st	+0	+0	+0	+2
2nd	+1	+0	+0	+3
3rd	+2	+1	+1	+3
4th	+3	+1	+1	+4
5th	+3	+1	+1	+4
6th	+4	+2	+2	+5
7th	+5	+2	+2	+5
8th	+6/+1	+2	+2	+6
9th	+6/+1	+3	+3	+6
10th	+7/+2	+3	+3	+7
11th	+8/+3	+3	+3	+7
12th	+9/+4	+4	+4	+8
13th	+9/+4	+4	+4	+8
14th	+10/+5	+4	+4	+9
15th	+11/+6/+1	+5	+5	+9
16th	+12/+7/+2	+5	+5	+10
17th	+12/+7/+2	+5	+5	+10
18th	+13/+8/+3	+6	+6	+11
19th	+14/+9/+4	+6	+6	+11
20th	+15/+10/+5	+6	+6	+12

TABLE 14-5: WARRIOR

NPC Level	Base Attack Bonus	Fort Save	Ref Save	Will Save
1st	+1	+2	+0	+0
2nd	+2	+3	+0	+0
3rd	+3	+3	+1	+1
4th	+4	+4	+1	+1
5th	+5	+4	+1	+1
6th	+6/+1	+5	+2	+2
7th	+7/+2	+5	+2	+2
8th	+8/+3	+6	+2	+2
9th	+9/+4	+6	+3	+3
10th	+10/+5	+7	+3	+3
11th	+11/+6/+1	+7	+3	+3
12th	+12/+7/+2	+8	+4	+4
13th	+13/+8/+3	+8	+4	+4
14th	+14/+9/+4	+9	+4	+4
15th	+15/+10/+5	+9	+5	+5
16th	+16/+11/+6/+1	+10	+5	+5
17th	+17/+12/+7/+2	+10	+5	+5
18th	+18/+13/+8/+3	+11	+6	+6
19th	+19/+14/+9/+4	+11	+6	+6
20th	+20/+15/+10/+5	+12	+6	+6

considered a heroic NPC and receives better ability scores. These scores can be assigned in any order.

Basic NPCs: The ability scores for a basic NPC are: 13, 12, 11, 10, 9, and 8.

Heroic NPCs: The ability scores for a heroic NPC are: 15, 14, 13, 12, 10, and 8.

Preset Ability Scores: Instead of assigning the scores, you can use Table 14–6 to determine the NPC's ability scores, adjusting them as necessary to fit. Use the Melee NPC ability scores for characters whose primary role involves melee combat, such as barbarians, fighters, monks, paladins, rangers, and warriors. The Ranged NPC ability scores are for characters that fight with ranged weapons or use their Dexterity to hit, such as fighters, rangers, and rogues. Use the Divine NPC ability scores for characters with divine spellcasting capabilities, such as adepts, clerics, and druids. The Arcane NPC ability scores should be used by characters with arcane spellcasting capabilities, such as bards, sorcerers, and wizards. Finally, the Skill NPC ability scores should be used for characters that focus on skill use, such as aristocrats, bards, commoners, experts, and rogues. Some NPCs might not fit into one of these categories and should have custom ability scores.

Step 3: Skills

To assign skills precisely, total up the number of skill ranks possessed by the character and assign them normally.

Remember that the number of ranks in an individual skill that a character can possess is limited by his total HD.

For simpler skill generation, refer to Table 14–8 to determine the total number of skill selections the NPC possesses. After selecting that number of skills, mostly from the class skills lists of the NPC's class, the NPC receives a number of ranks in each skill equal to his level.

If the NPC has two classes, start by selecting skills for the class with the fewest number of skill selections. The NPC receives a number of ranks in those skills equal to his total character level. Next, find the difference in the number of selections between the first class and the other class possessed by the NPC. Select that number of new skills and give the NPC a number of ranks in those skills equal to his level in the second class. For example, a human fighter 3/monk 4 with a +1 Intelligence modifier can select four skills for his fighter class (since it receives fewer selections). These four skills each have seven ranks (equal to his total level). Next, he selects a number of skills equal to the difference between the fighter and the monk classes, in this case two skills. These two skills each have four ranks (his monk level).

If the NPC has three or more classes, you must use the precise method for determining his skills.

Once all of the NPC's ranks have been determined, assign class skill bonuses and apply the bonus or penalty from the NPC's relevant ability score.

Step 4: Feats

After skills have been determined, the next step is to assign the NPC's feats. Start by assigning all of the feats granted through class abilities. Next, assign the feats garnered from the NPC's total character level (one feat for every two levels beyond 1st). Remember that humans receive an additional feat at 1st level. For simplified feat choices, select feats from the lists provided for the following character types.

Arcane Caster: Arcane Strike, Combat Casting, Eschew Materials, Greater Spell Focus, Greater Spell Penetration, Improved Initiative, Iron Will, item creation feats (all), Lightning Reflexes, metamagic feats (all), Spell Focus, Spell Mastery, Spell Penetration, and Toughness.

Divine Caster (With Channeling): Alignment Channel, Channel Smite, Combat Casting, Command Undead, Elemental Channel, Extra Channel, Improved Initiative, Improved Channel, Iron Will, item creation feats (all), metamagic feats (all), Power Attack, Selective Channeling, Spell Focus, Spell Penetration, Toughness, and Turn Undead.

Divine Caster (Without Channeling): Cleave, Combat Casting, Eschew Materials, Improved Initiative, Iron Will, item creation feats (all), Lightning Reflexes, metamagic feats (all), Natural Spell, Power Attack, Spell Focus, Spell Penetration, Toughness, and Weapon Focus.

Melee (Finesse Fighter): Combat Expertise, Combat Reflexes, Dazzling Display, Deadly Stroke, Dodge, Greater Vital Strike, Improved Disarm, Improved Feint, Improved Trip, Improved Vital Strike, Mobility, Spring Attack, Shatter Defenses, Vital Strike, Weapon Finesse, and Whirlwind Attack.

Melee (Unarmed Fighter): Combat Reflexes, Deflect Arrows, Dodge, Gorgon's Fist, Improved Grapple, Improved Initiative, Improved Unarmed Strike, Medusa's Wrath, Mobility, Scorpion Style, Snatch Arrows, Spring Attack, Stunning Fist, and Weapon Focus.

Melee (Mounted): Improved Critical, Improved Initiative, Mounted Combat, Power Attack, Ride-By Attack, Skill Focus (Ride), Spirited Charge, Toughness, Trample, and Weapon Focus.

Melee (Sword and Shield Fighter): Cleave, Great Cleave, Great Fortitude, Greater Vital Strike, Improved Bull Rush, Improved Critical, Improved Initiative, Improved Vital Strike, Power Attack, Shield Focus, Shield Master, Shield Slam, Two-Weapon Fighting, Vital Strike, and Weapon Focus.

Melee (Two-Handed Fighter): Cleave, Great Cleave, Great Fortitude, Greater Vital Strike, Improved Bull Rush, Improved Critical, Improved Initiative, Improved Sunder, Improved Vital Strike, Power Attack, Vital Strike, and Weapon Focus.

Melee (Two-Weapon Fighter): Combat Reflexes, Dodge, Double Slice, Greater Two-Weapon Fighting, Greater Vital Strike, Improved Critical, Improved Initiative, Improved Two-Weapon Fighting, Improved Vital Strike, Two-Weapon Defense, Two-Weapon Fighting, Two-Weapon Rend, Vital Strike, and Weapon Focus.

Ranged: Deadly Aim, Far Shot, Greater Vital Strike, Improved Initiative, Improved Vital Strike, Manyshot, Pinpoint Targeting, Point Blank Shot, Precise Shot, Rapid Reload, Rapid Shot, Shot on the Run, Vital Strike, and Weapon Focus.

Skill (most NPC classes): Armor Proficiency (all), Great Fortitude, Improved Initiative, Iron Will, Lightning Reflexes, Martial Weapon Proficiency, Run, Shield Proficiency, Skill Focus, and Toughness.

TABLE 14-6: NPC ABILITY SCORES

Ability	Melee NPC		Ranged NPC		Divine NPC		Arcane NPC		Skill NPC	
Score	Basic	Heroic	Basic	Heroic	Basic	Heroic	Basic	Heroic	Basic	Heroic
Strength	13	15	11	13	10	12	8	8	10	12
Dexterity	11	13	13	15	8	8	12	14	12	14
Constitution	12	14	12	14	12	14	10	12	11	13
Intelligence	9	10	10	12	9	10	13*	15*	13	15
Wisdom	10	12	9	10	13	15	9	10	8	8
Charisma	8	8	8	8	11	13	11*	13*	9	10

* If the arcane caster's spellcasting relies on Charisma, exchange these scores with one another.

TABLE 14-7: RACIAL ABILITY ADJUSTMENTS

Ability Score	Dwarf	Elf	Gnome	Half-Elf*	Half-Orc*	Halfling	Human*
Strength	—	—	−2	—	—	−2	—
Dexterity	—	+2	—	—	—	+2	—
Constitution	+2	−2	+2	—	—	—	—
Intelligence	—	+2	—	—	—	—	—
Wisdom	+2	—	—	—	—	—	—
Charisma	−2	—	+2	—	—	+2	—

* Half-elves, half-orcs, and humans receive a +2 bonus to one ability score of your choice.

TABLE 14-8: NPC SKILL SELECTIONS

PC Class	Skill Selections*	NPC Class	Skill Selections*
Barbarian	4 + Int Mod	Adept	2 + Int Mod
Bard	6 + Int Mod	Aristocrat	4 + Int Mod
Cleric	2 + Int Mod	Commoner	2 + Int Mod
Druid	4 + Int Mod	Expert	6 + Int Mod
Fighter	2 + Int Mod	Warrior	2 + Int Mod
Monk	4 + Int Mod		
Paladin	2 + Int Mod		
Ranger	6 + Int Mod		
Rogue	8 + Int Mod		
Sorcerer	2 + Int Mod		
Wizard	2 + Int Mod		

* Humans receive one additional skill selection.

Step 5: Class Features

After determining feats, the next step is to fill in all the class features possessed by the NPC. This is the time to make decisions about the NPC's spell selection, rage powers, rogue talents, and other class-based abilities.

When it comes to spells, determine how many spell selections you need to make for each level. Choose a variety of spells for the highest two levels of spells possessed by the NPC. For all other levels, stick to a few basic spells, prepared multiple times (if possible). If this NPC is slated to appear in only one encounter (such as a combat), leaving off lower-level spells entirely is an acceptable way to speed up generation, especially if the NPC is unlikely to cast those spells. You can always choose a few during play if they are needed.

Step 6: Gear

After recording all of the NPC's class features, the next step is to outfit the character with gear appropriate to his level. Note that NPCs receive less gear than PCs of an equal level. If an NPC is a recurring character, his gear should be selected carefully. Use the total gp value found on Table 14–9 to determine how much gear he should carry. NPCs that are only scheduled to appear once can have a simpler gear selection. Table 14–9 includes a number of categories to make it easier to select an NPC's gear. When outfitting the character, spend the listed amount on each category by purchasing as few items as possible. Leftover gold from any category can be spent on any other category. Funds left over at the end represent coins and jewelry carried by the character.

Note that these values are approximate and based on the values for a campaign using the medium experience progression and a normal treasure allotment. If your campaign is using the fast experience progression, treat your NPCs as one level higher when determining their gear. If your campaign is using the slow experience progression, treat the NPCs as one level lower when determining their gear. If your campaign

Table 14–9: NPC Gear

Basic Level	Heroic Level	Total gp Value	Weapons	Protection	Magic	Limited Use	Gear
1	—	260 gp	50 gp	130 gp	—	40 gp	40 gp
2	1	390 gp	100 gp	150 gp	—	40 gp	100 gp
3	2	780 gp	350 gp	200 gp	—	80 gp	150 gp
4	3	1,650 gp	650 gp	800 gp	—	100 gp	200 gp
5	4	2,400 gp	900 gp	1,000 gp	—	300 gp	200 gp
6	5	3,450 gp	1,400 gp	1,400 gp	—	450 gp	200 gp
7	6	4,650 gp	2,350 gp	1,650 gp	—	450 gp	200 gp
8	7	6,000 gp	2,700 gp	2,000 gp	500 gp	600 gp	200 gp
9	8	7,800 gp	3,000 gp	2,500 gp	1,000 gp	800 gp	500 gp
10	9	10,050 gp	3,500 gp	3,000 gp	2,000 gp	1,050 gp	500 gp
11	10	12,750 gp	4,000 gp	4,000 gp	3,000 gp	1,250 gp	500 gp
12	11	16,350 gp	6,000 gp	4,500 gp	4,000 gp	1,350 gp	500 gp
13	12	21,000 gp	8,500 gp	5,500 gp	5,000 gp	1,500 gp	500 gp
14	13	27,000 gp	9,000 gp	8,000 gp	7,000 gp	2,500 gp	500 gp
15	14	34,800 gp	12,000 gp	10,500 gp	9,000 gp	2,800 gp	500 gp
16	15	45,000 gp	17,000 gp	13,500 gp	11,000 gp	3,000 gp	500 gp
17	16	58,500 gp	19,000 gp	18,000 gp	16,000 gp	4,000 gp	1,500 gp
18	17	75,000 gp	24,000 gp	23,000 gp	20,000 gp	6,500 gp	1,500 gp
19	18	96,000 gp	30,000 gp	28,000 gp	28,000 gp	8,000 gp	2,000 gp
20	19	123,000 gp	40,000 gp	35,000 gp	35,000 gp	11,000 gp	2,000 gp
—	20	159,000 gp	55,000 gp	40,000 gp	44,000 gp	18,000 gp	2,000 gp

is high fantasy, double these values. Reduce them by half if your campaign is low fantasy. If the final value of an NPC's gear is a little over or under these amounts, that's okay.

Weapons: This includes normal, masterwork, and magic weapons, as well as magic staves and wands used by spellcasters to harm their enemies. For example, a *wand of scorching ray* would count as a weapon, but a *staff of life* would count as a piece of magic gear.

Protection: This category includes armor and shields, as well as any magic item that augments a character's Armor Class or saving throws.

Magic: This category includes all other permanent magic items. Most rings, rods, and wondrous items fit into this category.

Limited Use: Items that fall into this category include alchemical items, potions, scrolls, and wands with few charges. Charged wondrous items fall into this grouping as well.

Gear: Use the amount in this category to purchase standard nonmagical gear for the character. In most cases, this equipment can be omitted during creation and filled in as needed during play. You can assume that the character has whatever gear is needed for him to properly use his skills and class abilities. This category can also include jewelry, gems, or loose coins that the NPC might have on his person.

Step 7: Details

Once you have assigned all of the NPC's gear, all that remains is to fill out the details. Determine the character's attack and damage bonuses, CMB, CMD, initiative modifier, and Armor Class. If the character's magic items affect his skills or ability scores, make sure to take those changes into account. Determine the character's total hit points by assuming the average result. Finally, fill out any other important details, such as name, alignment, religion, and a few personality traits to round him out.

Example: Kiramor, the Forest Shadow

Looking over your notes for the evening's game, you discover that you need a mysterious forest character for the PCs to interact with on their way to town. If things go poorly, they might have to fight him. Since your party consists of 4th-level characters, you decide to make this forest guardian an elven ranger 4/rogue 2. You want him to be skilled at fighting with ranged weapons, but you also want him to be competent with a rapier. Taking this into account, you use the heroic ability scores for a ranged NPC found on Table 14–6. Since he is an elf, you apply the racial modifiers to Dexterity, Constitution, and Intelligence. Since he is 6th level, you put his bonus attribute point gained at 4th level into his Dexterity, raising it up to 18. Moving on to skills, you see that

KIRAMOR, THE FOREST SHADOW

Male elf ranger 4/rogue 2

N Medium humanoid (elf)

Init +4 (+6 in forests); **Senses** low-light vision; Perception +11
(+13 in forests)

DEFENSE

AC 18, touch 14, flat-footed 14
(+4 armor, +4 Dex)

hp 39 (4d10+2d8+6)

Fort +6, **Ref** +12, **Will** +2; +2 against enchantment

Defensive Abilities evasion; **Immune** sleep

OFFENSE

Spd 30 ft.

Melee mwk rapier +10 (1d6+1/18–20)

Ranged +1 longbow +10 (1d8+1/×3)

Ranged +1 longbow +8/+8 (1d8+1/×3)

Special Attacks favored enemy (humanoid [orc]), favored terrain
(forest), rogue talents (bleeding attack), sneak attack (1d6)

STATISTICS

Str 13, **Dex** 18, **Con** 12, **Int** 14, **Wis** 10, **Cha** 8

Base Atk +5; **CMB** +6; **CMD** 20

Feats Deadly Aim, Endurance, Point Blank Shot, Rapid Shot,
Weapon Finesse

Skills Acrobatics +13, Climb +10, Escape Artist +9, Heal +9,
Knowledge (geography) +11, Knowledge (nature) +11,
Perception +11 (+13 in forests), Stealth +13, Survival +9 (+11
following tracks), Swim +6

Languages Common, Elven, Orc, Sylvan

SQ nature bond (wolf), track, trapfinding +1

Combat Gear potion of cure moderate wounds, potion of
invisibility; **Other Gear** +1 longbow with 40 arrows, mwk
rapier, +1 studded leather armor, gear and coins worth 200 gp

rangers receive fewer skill selections than rogues, so
you start by selecting skills for the ranger. You add two
for his Intelligence modifier for a total of eight skills
at six ranks each. After selecting these eight skills, you
move on to the rogue skills. The difference between the
ranger and the rogue is two, meaning that you can select
two more skills, with two ranks in each. After selecting
his skills, you move on to his feats. Starting with his
class feats, you select Rapid Shot as his ranger combat
style feat. In addition, the forest guardian receives three
additional feats for his class levels. Since you want him
to be skilled at archery, most of these feats come from
the ranged list, including Deadly Aim and Point Blank
Shot. To ensure that he is good with a rapier, you spend
his final feat selection on Weapon Finesse. Next you
note all of his class and racial features, making whatever
selections are necessary, such as favored enemy, favored
terrain, hunter's bond, and rogue talents. Moving on to
gear, you assign gear using the line for a 6th-level heroic

NPC, giving him a +1 longbow, a masterwork rapier, +1
studded leather armor, a potion of invisibility, a potion of
cure moderate wounds, and a pack full of nonmagic gear.
Although he has a bit more gp in weapons than the
chart allows, he has spent a bit less in armor, roughly
balancing him out. With your task nearly completed,
you add all of his statistics and details, naming him
Kiramor. Your forest shadow is then ready to face off
against the PCs.

15 Magic Items

With a tremendous crash, a tree toppled to the ground, another victim of the dragon's wrath. The beast hissed, caustic vapors swirling through its ivory teeth as it roared a furious challenge to the monk and barbarian, enraged at their intrusion. Amiri grinned in delight. She'd found the magical dragonbane sword only minutes ago in the overgrown temple, and here, as if drawn to its doom, was a wyrm ready to test its blade. The shield maidens would sing of Amiri's sword and their triumph this day, but first they had to survive...

From the common *potion of cure light wounds* to the mighty *holy avenger*, magic items are valuable tools used by heroes and villains alike. This chapter contains a wide variety of items to enhance any character.

Magic items are divided into categories: armor, weapons, potions, rings, rods, scrolls, staves, wands, and wondrous items. In addition, some magic items are cursed or intelligent. Finally, a few magic items are of such rarity and power that they are considered to belong to a category of their own—artifacts. Artifacts are classified in turn as minor (extremely rare but not one-of-a-kind items) or major (each one unique and incredibly potent).

Magic Items and Detect Magic

When *detect magic* identifies a magic item's school of magic, this information refers to the school of the spell placed within the potion, scroll, or wand, or the prerequisite given for the item. The description of each item provides its aura strength and the school to which it belongs.

If more than one spell is given as a prerequisite, use the highest-level spell. If no spells are included in the prerequisites, use the following default guidelines.

Item Nature	School
Armor and protection items	Abjuration
Weapons or offensive items	Evocation
Bonus to ability score, skill check, etc.	Transmutation

USING ITEMS

To use a magic item, it must be activated, although sometimes activation simply means putting a ring on your finger. Some items, once donned, function constantly. In most cases, though, using an item requires a standard action that does not provoke attacks of opportunity. By contrast, spell completion items are treated like spells in combat and do provoke attacks of opportunity.

Activating a magic item is a standard action unless the item description indicates otherwise. However, the casting time of a spell is the time required to activate the same power in an item, regardless of the type of magic item, unless the item description specifically states otherwise.

The four ways to activate magic items are described below.

Spell Completion: This is the activation method for scrolls. A scroll is a spell that is mostly finished. The preparation is done for the caster, so no preparation time is needed beforehand as with normal spellcasting. All that's left to do is perform the finishing parts of the spellcasting (the final gestures, words, and so on). To use a spell completion item safely, a character must be of high enough level in the right class to cast the spell already. If he can't already cast the spell, there's a chance he'll make a mistake. Activating a spell completion item is a standard action (or the spell's casting time, whichever is longer) and provokes attacks of opportunity exactly as casting a spell does.

Spell Trigger: Spell trigger activation is similar to spell completion, but it's even simpler. No gestures or spell finishing is needed, just a special knowledge of spellcasting that an appropriate character would know, and a single word that must be spoken. Spell trigger items can be used by anyone whose class can cast the corresponding spell. This is the case even for a character who can't actually cast spells, such as a 3rd-level paladin. The user must still determine what spell is stored in the item before she can activate it. Activating a spell trigger item is a standard action and does not provoke attacks of opportunity.

Command Word: If no activation method is suggested either in the magic item description or by the nature of the item, assume that a command word is needed to activate it. Command word activation means that a character speaks the word and the item activates. No other special knowledge is needed.

A command word can be a real word, but when this is the case, the holder of the item runs the risk of activating the item accidentally by speaking the word in normal conversation. More often, the command word is some seemingly nonsensical word, or a word or phrase from an ancient language no longer in common use. Activating a command word magic item is a standard action and does not provoke attacks of opportunity.

Sometimes the command word to activate an item is written right on the item. Occasionally, it might be hidden within a pattern or design engraved on, carved into, or built into the item, or the item might bear a clue to the command word.

The Knowledge (arcana) and Knowledge (history) skills might be useful in helping to identify command words or deciphering clues regarding them. A successful check against DC 30 is needed to come up with the word itself. If that check is failed, succeeding on a second check (DC 25) might provide some insight into a clue. The spells *detect magic, identify,* and *analyze dweomer* all reveal command words if the properties of the item are successfully identified.

Use Activated: This type of item simply has to be used in order to activate it. A character has to drink a potion, swing a sword, interpose a shield to deflect a blow in combat, look through a lens, sprinkle dust, wear a ring, or don a hat. Use activation is generally straightforward and self-explanatory.

Many use-activated items are objects that a character wears. Continually functioning items are practically always items that one wears. A few must simply be in the character's possession (meaning on his person). However, some items made for wearing must still be activated. Although this activation sometimes requires a command word (see above), usually it means mentally willing the activation to happen. The description of an item states whether a command word is needed in such a case.

Unless stated otherwise, activating a use-activated magic item is either a standard action or not an action at all and does not provoke attacks of opportunity, unless the use involves performing an action that provokes an attack of opportunity in itself. If the use of the item takes time before a magical effect occurs, then use activation is a standard action. If the item's activation is subsumed in its use and takes no extra time use, activation is not an action at all.

Use activation doesn't mean that if you use an item, you automatically know what it can do. You must know (or at least guess) what the item can do and then use the item in order to activate it, unless the benefit of the item comes automatically, such as from drinking a potion or swinging a sword.

Size and Magic Items

When an article of magic clothing or jewelry is discovered, most of the time size shouldn't be an issue. Many magic garments are made to be easily adjustable, or they adjust themselves magically to the wearer. Size should not keep characters of various kinds from using magic items.

There may be rare exceptions, especially with race-specific items.

Armor and Weapon Sizes: Armor and weapons that are found at random have a 30% chance of being Small (01–30), a 60% chance of being Medium (31–90), and a 10% chance of being any other size (91–100).

MAGIC ITEMS ON THE BODY

Many magic items need to be donned by a character who wants to employ them or benefit from their abilities. It's possible for a creature with a humanoid-shaped body to wear as many as 15 magic items at the same time. However, each of those items must be worn on (or over) a particular part of the body, known as a "slot."

A humanoid-shaped body can be decked out in magic gear consisting of one item from each of the following groups, keyed to which slot on the body the item is worn.

Armor: suits of armor.

Belts: belts and girdles.

Body: robes and vestments.

Chest: mantles, shirts, and vests.

Eyes: eyes, glasses, and goggles.

Feet: boots, shoes, and slippers.

Hands: gauntlets and gloves.

Head: circlets, crowns, hats, helms, and masks.

Headband: headbands and phylacteries.

Neck: amulets, brooches, medallions, necklaces, periapts, and scarabs.

Ring (up to two): rings.

Shield: shields.

Shoulders: capes and cloaks.

Wrist: bracelets and bracers.

Of course, a character may carry or possess as many items of the same type as he wishes. However, additional items beyond those in the slots listed above have no effect.

Some items can be worn or carried without taking up a slot on a character's body. The description of an item indicates when an item has this property.

SAVING THROWS AGAINST MAGIC ITEM POWERS

Magic items produce spells or spell-like effects. For a saving throw against a spell or spell-like effect from a magic item, the DC is 10 + the level of the spell or effect + the ability modifier of the minimum ability score needed to cast that level of spell.

Staves are an exception to the rule. Treat the saving throw as if the wielder cast the spell, including caster level and all modifiers to save DCs.

Most item descriptions give saving throw DCs for various effects, particularly when the effect has no exact spell equivalent (making its level otherwise difficult to determine quickly).

DAMAGING MAGIC ITEMS

A magic item doesn't need to make a saving throw unless it is unattended, it is specifically targeted by the effect, or its wielder rolls a natural 1 on his save. Magic items should always get a saving throw against spells that might deal damage to them—even against attacks from which a nonmagical item would normally get no chance to save. Magic items use the same saving throw bonus for all saves, no matter what the type (Fortitude, Reflex, or Will). A magic item's saving throw bonus equals 2 + 1/2 its caster level (rounded down). The only exceptions to this are intelligent magic items, which make Will saves based on their own Wisdom scores.

Magic items, unless otherwise noted, take damage as nonmagical items of the same sort. A damaged magic item continues to function, but if it is destroyed, all its magical power is lost. Magic items that take damage in excess of half their total hit points, but not more than their total hit points, gain the broken condition, and might not function properly (see the Appendix).

Repairing Magic Items

Repairing a magic item requires material components equal to half the cost to create the item, and requires half the time. The *make whole* spell can also repair a damaged (or even a destroyed) magic item—if the caster is high enough level.

Charges, Doses, and Multiple Uses

Many items, particularly wands and staves, are limited in power by the number of charges they hold. Normally, charged items have 50 charges at most (10 for staves). If such an item is found as a random part of a treasure, roll d% and divide by 2 to determine the number of charges left (round

down, minimum 1). If the item has a maximum number of charges other than 50, roll randomly to determine how many charges are left.

Prices listed are always for fully charged items. (When an item is created, it is fully charged.) For an item that's worthless when its charges run out (which is the case for almost all charged items), the value of the partially used item is proportional to the number of charges left. For an item that has usefulness in addition to its charges, only part of the item's value is based on the number of charges left.

PURCHASING MAGIC ITEMS

Magic items are valuable, and most major cities have at least one or two purveyors of magic items, from a simple potion merchant to a weapon smith that specializes in magic swords. Of course, not every item in this book is available in every town.

The following guidelines are presented to help GMs determine what items are available in a given community. These guidelines assume a setting with an average level of magic. Some cities might deviate wildly from these baselines, subject to GM discretion. The GM should keep a list of what items are available from each merchant and should replenish the stocks on occasion to represent new acquisitions.

The number and types of magic items available in a community depend upon its size. Each community has a base value associated with it (see Table 15–1). There is a 75% chance that any item of that value or lower can be found for sale with little effort in that community. In addition, the community has a number of other items for sale. These items are randomly determined and are broken down by category (minor, medium, or major). After determining the number of items available in each category, refer to Table 15–2 to determine the type of each item (potion, scroll, ring, weapon, etc.) before moving on to the individual charts to determine the exact item. Reroll any items that fall below the community's base value.

If you are running a campaign with low magic, reduce the base value and the number of items in each community by half. Campaigns with little or no magic might not have magic items for sale at all. GMs running these sorts of campaigns should make some adjustments to the challenges faced by the characters due to their lack of magic gear.

Campaigns with an abundance of magic items might have communities with twice the listed base value and random items available. Alternatively, all communities might count as one size category larger for the purposes of what items are available. In a campaign with very common magic, all magic items might be available for purchase in a metropolis.

Nonmagical items and gear are generally available in a community of any size unless the item is particularly expensive, such as full plate, or made of an unusual material, such as an adamantine longsword. These items should follow

the base value guidelines to determine their availability, subject to GM discretion.

MAGIC ITEM DESCRIPTIONS

Each general type of magic item gets an overall description, followed by descriptions of specific items.

General descriptions include notes on activation, random generation, and other material. The AC, hardness, hit points, and break DC are given for typical examples of some magic items. The AC assumes that the item is unattended and includes a –5 penalty for the item's effective Dexterity of 0. If a creature holds the item, use the creature's Dexterity modifier in place of the –5 penalty.

Some individual items, notably those that just store spells, don't get full-blown descriptions. Reference the spell's description for details, modified by the form of the item (potion, scroll, wand, and so on). Assume that the spell is cast at the minimum level required to cast it.

Items with full descriptions have their powers detailed, and each of the following topics is covered in notational form as part of its entry.

Aura: Most of the time, a *detect magic* spell reveals the school of magic associated with a magic item and the strength of the aura an item emits. This information (when applicable) is given at the beginning of the item's notational entry. See the *detect magic* spell description for details.

Caster Level (CL): The next item in a notational entry gives the caster level of the item, indicating its relative power. The caster level determines the item's saving throw bonus, as well as range or other level-dependent aspects of the powers of the item (if variable). It also determines the level that must be contended with should the item come under the effect of a *dispel magic* spell or similar situation.

For potions, scrolls, and wands, the creator can set the caster level of an item at any number high enough to cast the stored spell but not higher than her own caster level. For other magic items, the caster level is determined by the item itself.

Slot: Most magic items can only be utilized if worn or wielded in their proper slots. If the item is stowed or placed elsewhere, it does not function. If the slot lists "none," the item must be held or otherwise carried to function.

Price: This is the cost, in gold pieces, to purchase the item, if it is available for sale. Generally speaking, magic items can be sold by PCs for half this value.

Weight: This is the weight of an item. When a weight figure is not given, the item has no weight worth noting (for purposes of determining how much of a load a character can carry).

Description: This section of a magic item describes the item's powers and abilities. Potions, scrolls, staves, and wands refer to various spells as part of their descriptions (see Chapter 10 for details on these spells).

Construction: With the exception of artifacts, most magic items can be built by a spellcaster with the appropriate feats and prerequisites. This section describes those prerequisites.

Requirements: Certain requirements must be met in order for a character to create a magic item. These include feats, spells, and miscellaneous requirements such as level, alignment, and race or kind.

A spell prerequisite may be provided by a character who has prepared the spell (or who knows the spell, in the case of a sorcerer or bard), or through the use of a spell completion or spell trigger magic item or a spell-like ability that produces the desired spell effect. For each day that passes in the creation process, the creator must expend one spell completion item or one charge from a spell trigger item if either of those objects is used to supply a prerequisite.

It is possible for more than one character to cooperate in the creation of an item, with each participant providing one or more of the prerequisites. In some cases, cooperation may even be necessary.

If two or more characters cooperate to create an item, they must agree among themselves who will be considered the creator for the purpose of determinations where the creator's level must be known.

Cost: This is the cost in gold pieces to create the item. Generally this cost is equal to half the price of an item, but additional material components might increase this number. The cost to create includes the costs derived from the base cost plus the costs of the components.

ARMOR

In general, magic armor protects the wearer to a greater extent than nonmagical armor. Magic armor bonuses are enhancement bonuses, never rise above +5, and stack with regular armor bonuses (and with shield and magic shield enhancement bonuses). All magic armor is also masterwork armor, reducing armor check penalties by 1.

In addition to an enhancement bonus, armor may have special abilities. Special abilities usually count as additional bonuses for determining the market value of an item, but do not improve AC. A suit of armor cannot have an effective bonus (enhancement plus special ability bonus equivalents, including from character abilities and spells) higher than +10. A suit of armor with a special ability must also have at least a +1 enhancement bonus.

A suit of armor or a shield may be made of an unusual material. Roll d%: 01–95 indicates that the item is of a standard sort, and 96–100 indicates that it is made of a special material (see Chapter 6).

Armor is always created so that if the type of armor comes with a pair of boots, a helm, or a set of gauntlets, these pieces can be switched for other magic boots, helms, or gauntlets.

TABLE 15-1: AVAILABLE MAGIC ITEMS

Community Size	Base Value	Minor	Medium	Major
Thorp	50 gp	1d4 items	—	—
Hamlet	200 gp	1d6 items	—	—
Village	500 gp	2d4 items	1d4 items	—
Small town	1,000 gp	3d4 items	1d6 items	—
Large town	2,000 gp	3d4 items	2d4 items	1d4 items
Small city	4,000 gp	4d4 items	3d4 items	1d6 items
Large city	8,000 gp	4d4 items	3d4 items	2d4 items
Metropolis	16,000 gp	*	4d4 items	3d4 items

* In a metropolis, nearly all minor magic items are available.

TABLE 15-2: RANDOM MAGIC ITEM GENERATION

Minor	Medium	Major	Item
01–04	01–10	01–10	Armor and shields
05–09	11–20	11–20	Weapons
10–44	21–30	21–25	Potions
45–46	31–40	26–35	Rings
—	41–50	36–45	Rods
47–81	51–65	46–55	Scrolls
—	66–68	56–75	Staves
82–91	69–83	76–80	Wands
92–100	84–100	81–100	Wondrous items

TABLE 15-3: ARMOR AND SHIELDS

Minor	Medium	Major	Item	Base Price
01–60	01–05	—	+1 shield	1,000 gp
61–80	06–10	—	+1 armor	1,000 gp
81–85	11–20	—	+2 shield	4,000 gp
86–87	21–30	—	+2 armor	4,000 gp
—	31–40	01–08	+3 shield	9,000 gp
—	41–50	09–16	+3 armor	9,000 gp
—	51–55	17–27	+4 shield	16,000 gp
—	56–57	28–38	+4 armor	16,000 gp
—	—	39–49	+5 shield	25,000 gp
—	—	50–57	+5 armor	25,000 gp
—	—	—	+6 armor/shield[1]	36,000 gp
—	—	—	+7 armor/shield[1]	49,000 gp
—	—	—	+8 armor/shield[1]	64,000 gp
—	—	—	+9 armor/shield[1]	81,000 gp
—	—	—	+10 armor/shield[1]	100,000 gp
88–89	58–60	58–60	Specific armor[2]	—
90–91	61–63	61–63	Specific shield[3]	—
92–100	64–100	64–100	Special ability and roll again[2,3]	—

1 Armor and shields can't have enhancement bonuses higher than +5. Use these lines to determine price when special abilities are added in.

2 Roll on Table 15–6.

3 Roll on Table 15–7.

Caster Level for Armor and Shields: The caster level of a magic shield or magic armor with a special ability is given in the item description. For an item with only an enhancement bonus, the caster level is three times the enhancement bonus. If an item has both an enhancement bonus and a special ability, the higher of the two caster level requirements must be met.

Shields: Shield enhancement bonuses stack with armor enhancement bonuses. Shield enhancement bonuses do not act as attack or damage bonuses when the shield is used in a shield bash. The *bashing* special ability, however, does grant a +1 bonus on attack and damage rolls (see the special ability description).

A shield could be built that also acted as a magic weapon, but the cost of the enhancement bonus on attack rolls would need to be added into the cost of the shield and its enhancement bonus to AC.

As with armor, special abilities built into the shield add to the market value in the form of additions to the bonus of the shield, although they do not improve AC. A shield cannot have an effective bonus (enhancement plus special ability bonus equivalents) higher than +10. A shield with a special ability must also have at least a +1 enhancement bonus.

Activation: Usually a character benefits from magic armor and shields in exactly the way a character benefits from nonmagical armor and shields: by wearing them. If armor or a shield has a special ability that the user needs to activate, then the user usually needs to utter the command word (a standard action).

Armor for Unusual Creatures: The cost of armor for nonhumanoid creatures, as well as for creatures who are neither Small nor Medium, varies (see Chapter 6). The cost of the masterwork quality and any magical enhancement remains the same.

Magic Armor and Shield Special Ability Descriptions

Most magic armor and shields only have enhancement bonuses. Such items can also have one or more of the special abilities detailed below. Armor or a shield with a special ability must have at least a +1 enhancement bonus.

Animated: As a move action, an *animated shield* can be loosed to defend its wielder on its own. For the following 4 rounds, the shield grants its bonus to the one who loosed it and then drops. While animated, the shield provides its shield bonus and the bonuses from all of the other shield special abilities it possesses, but it cannot take actions on its own, such as those provided by the *bashing* and *blinding* abilities. It can, however, use special abilities that do not require an action to function, such as *arrow deflection* and *reflecting*. While animated, a shield shares the same space as the activating character and accompanies the character who activated it, even if the character moves by magical means. A character with an *animated shield* still takes any

penalties associated with shield use, such as armor check penalty, arcane spell failure chance, and nonproficiency. If the wielder who loosed it has an unoccupied hand, she can grasp it to end its animation as a free action. Once a shield has been retrieved, it cannot be animated again for at least 4 rounds. This property cannot be added to a tower shield.

Strong transmutation; CL 12th; Craft Magic Arms and Armor, *animate objects*; Price +2 bonus.

Arrow Catching: A shield with this ability attracts ranged weapons to it. It has a deflection bonus of +1 against ranged weapons because projectiles and thrown weapons veer toward it. Additionally, any projectile or thrown weapon aimed at a target within 5 feet of the shield's wearer diverts from its original target and targets the shield's bearer instead. If the wielder has total cover relative to the attacker, the projectile or thrown weapon is not diverted. Additionally, those attacking the wearer with ranged weapons ignore any miss chances that would normally apply. Projectiles and thrown weapons that have an enhancement bonus higher than the shield's base AC bonus are not diverted to the wearer (but the shield's deflection bonus still applies against these weapons). The wielder can activate or deactivate this ability with a command word.

Moderate abjuration; CL 8th; Craft Magic Arms and Armor, *entropic shield*; Price +1 bonus.

Arrow Deflection: This shield protects the wielder as if he had the Deflect Arrows feat. Once per round when he would normally be struck by a ranged weapon, he can make a DC 20 Reflex save. If the ranged weapon (or piece of ammunition) has an enhancement bonus, the DC increases by that amount. If he succeeds, the shield deflects the weapon. He must be aware of the attack and not flat-footed. Attempting to deflect a ranged weapon doesn't count as an action. Exceptional ranged weapons, such as boulders hurled by giants or *acid arrows*, can't be deflected.

Faint abjuration; CL 5th; Craft Magic Arms and Armor, *shield*; Price +2 bonus.

Bashing: A shield with this special ability is designed to perform a shield bash. A *bashing shield* deals damage as if it were a weapon of two size categories larger (a Medium light shield thus deals 1d6 points of damage and a Medium heavy shield deals 1d8 points of damage). The shield acts as a +1 weapon when used to bash. Only light and heavy shields can have this ability.

Moderate transmutation; CL 8th; Craft Magic Arms and Armor, *bull's strength*; Price +1 bonus.

Blinding: A shield with this ability flashes with a brilliant light up to twice per day upon command of the wielder. Except for the wielder, anyone within 20 feet must make a DC 14 Reflex save or be blinded for 1d4 rounds.

Moderate evocation; CL 7th; Craft Magic Arms and Armor, *searing light*; Price +1 bonus.

Energy Resistance: A suit of armor or a shield with this property protects against one type of energy (acid, cold, electricity, fire, or sonic) and is designed with patterns

TABLE 15-4: ARMOR SPECIAL ABILITIES

Minor	Medium	Major	Special Ability	Base Price Modifier
01–25	01–05	01–03	Glamered	+2,700 gp
26–32	06–08	04	Fortification, light	+1 bonus[1]
33–52	09–11	—	Slick	+3,750 gp
53–92	12–17	—	Shadow	+3,750 gp
93–96	18–19	—	Spell resistance (13)	+2 bonus[1]
97	20–29	05–07	Slick, improved	+15,000 gp
98–99	30–49	08–13	Shadow, improved	+15,000 gp
—	50–74	14–28	Energy resistance	+18,000 gp
—	75–79	29–33	Ghost touch	+3 bonus[1]
—	80–84	34–35	Invulnerability	+3 bonus[1]
—	85–89	36–40	Fortification, moderate	+3 bonus[1]
—	90–94	41–42	Spell resistance (15)	+3 bonus[1]
—	95–99	43	Wild	+3 bonus[1]
—	—	44–48	Slick, greater	+33,750 gp
—	—	49–58	Shadow, greater	+33,750 gp
—	—	59–83	Energy resistance, improved	+42,000 gp
—	—	84–88	Spell resistance (17)	+4 bonus[1]
—	—	89	Etherealness	+49,000 gp
—	—	90	Undead controlling	+49,000 gp
—	—	91–92	Fortification, heavy	+5 bonus[1]
—	—	93–94	Spell resistance (19)	+5 bonus[1]
—	—	95–99	Energy resistance, greater	+66,000 gp
100	100	100	Roll twice again[2]	—

1 Add to enhancement bonus on Table 15–3 to determine total market price.

2 If you roll a special ability twice, only one counts. If you roll two versions of the same special ability, use the better.

TABLE 15-5: SHIELD SPECIAL ABILITIES

Minor	Medium	Major	Special Ability	Base Price Modifier
01–20	01–10	01–05	Arrow catching	+1 bonus[1]
21–40	11–20	06–08	Bashing	+1 bonus[2]
41–50	21–25	09–10	Blinding	+1 bonus[1]
51–75	26–40	11–15	Fortification, light	+1 bonus[1]
76–92	41–50	16–20	Arrow deflection	+2 bonus[1]
93–97	51–57	21–25	Animated	+2 bonus[1]
98–99	58–59	—	Spell resistance (13)	+2 bonus[1]
—	60–79	26–41	Energy resistance	+18,000 gp
—	80–85	42–46	Ghost touch	+3 bonus[1]
—	86–95	47–56	Fortification, moderate	+3 bonus[1]
—	96–98	57–58	Spell resistance (15)	+3 bonus[1]
—	99	59	Wild	+3 bonus[1]
—	—	60–84	Energy resistance, improved	+42,000 gp
—	—	85–86	Spell resistance (17)	+4 bonus[1]
—	—	87	Undead controlling	+49,000 gp
—	—	88–91	Fortification, heavy	+5 bonus[1]
—	—	92–93	Reflecting	+5 bonus[1]
—	—	94	Spell resistance (19)	+5 bonus[1]
—	—	95–99	Energy resistance, greater	+66,000 gp
100	100	100	Roll twice again[2]	—

1 Add to enhancement bonus on Table 15–3 to determine total market price.

2 If you roll a special ability twice, only one counts. If you roll two versions of the same special ability, use the better.

depicting the element it protects against. The armor absorbs the first 10 points of energy damage per attack that the wearer would normally take (similar to the *resist energy* spell).

Faint abjuration; CL 3rd; Craft Magic Arms and Armor, *resist energy*; Price +18,000 gp.

Energy Resistance, Improved: As *energy resistance*, except it absorbs the first 20 points of energy damage per attack.

Moderate abjuration; CL 7th; Craft Magic Arms and Armor, *resist energy*; Price +42,000 gp.

Energy Resistance, Greater: As *energy resistance*, except it absorbs the first 30 points of energy damage per attack.

Moderate abjuration; CL 11th; Craft Magic Arms and Armor, *resist energy*; Price +66,000 gp.

Etherealness: On command, this ability allows the wearer of the armor to become ethereal (as the *ethereal jaunt* spell) once per day. The character can remain ethereal for as long as desired, but once he returns to normal, he cannot become ethereal again that day.

Strong transmutation; CL 13th; Craft Magic Arms and Armor, *ethereal jaunt*; Price +49,000 gp.

Fortification: This suit of armor or shield produces a magical force that protects vital areas of the wearer more effectively. When a critical hit or sneak attack is scored on the wearer, there is a chance that the critical hit or sneak attack is negated and damage is instead rolled normally.

Fortification Type	Chance for Normal Damage	Base Price Modifier
Light	25%	+1 bonus
Moderate	50%	+3 bonus
Heavy	75%	+5 bonus

Strong abjuration; CL 13th; Craft Magic Arms and Armor, *limited wish* or *miracle*; Price varies (see above).

Ghost Touch: This armor or shield seems almost translucent. Both its enhancement bonus and its armor bonus count against the attacks of corporeal and incorporeal creatures. It can be picked up, moved, and worn by corporeal and incorporeal creatures alike. Incorporeal creatures gain the armor's or shield's enhancement bonus

TABLE 15-6: SPECIFIC ARMORS

Minor	Medium	Major	Specific Armor	Market Price
01–50	01–25	—	Mithral shirt	1,100 gp
51–80	26–45	—	Dragonhide plate	3,300 gp
81–100	46–57	—	Elven chain	5,150 gp
—	58–67	—	Rhino hide	5,165 gp
—	68–82	01–10	Adamantine breastplate	10,200 gp
—	83–97	11–20	Dwarven plate	16,500 gp
—	98–100	21–32	Banded mail of luck	18,900 gp
—	—	33–50	Celestial armor	22,400 gp
—	—	51–60	Plate armor of the deep	24,650 gp
—	—	61–75	Breastplate of command	25,400 gp
—	—	76–90	Mithral full plate of speed	26,500 gp
—	—	91–100	Demon armor	52,260 gp

against both corporeal and incorporeal attacks, and they can still pass freely through solid objects.

Strong transmutation; CL 15th; Craft Magic Arms and Armor, *etherealness*; Price +3 bonus.

Glamered: Upon command, a suit of *glamered armor* changes shape and appearance to assume the form of a normal set of clothing. The armor retains all its properties (including weight) when it is so disguised. Only a *true seeing* spell or similar magic reveals the true nature of the armor when disguised.

Moderate illusion; CL 10th; Craft Magic Arms and Armor, *disguise self*; Price +2,700 gp.

Invulnerability: This suit of armor grants the wearer damage reduction 5/magic.

Strong abjuration and evocation (if *miracle* is used); CL 18th; Craft Magic Arms and Armor, *stoneskin*, *wish* or *miracle*; Price +3 bonus.

Reflecting: This shield seems like a highly polished mirror. Its surface is completely reflective. Once per day, it can be called on to reflect a spell back at its caster exactly like the *spell turning* spell.

Strong abjuration; CL 14th; Craft Magic Arms and Armor, *spell turning*; Price +5 bonus.

Shadow: This armor blurs the wearer whenever she tries to hide, while also dampening the sound around her, granting a +5 competence bonus on Stealth checks. The armor's armor check penalty still applies normally.

Faint illusion; CL 5th; Craft Magic Arms and Armor, *invisibility*, *silence*; Price +3,750 gp.

Shadow, Improved: As *shadow*, except it grants a +10 competence bonus on Stealth checks.

Moderate illusion; CL 10th; Craft Magic Arms and Armor, *invisibility*, *silence*; Price +15,000 gp.

Shadow, Greater: As *shadow*, except it grants a +15 competence bonus on Stealth checks.

Strong illusion; CL 15th; Craft Magic Arms and Armor, *invisibility*, *silence*; Price +33,750 gp.

Slick: *Slick* armor seems coated at all times with a slightly greasy oil. It provides a +5 competence bonus on its wearer's Escape Artist checks. The armor's armor check penalty still applies normally.

Faint conjuration; CL 4th; Craft Magic Arms and Armor, *grease*; Price +3,750 gp.

Slick, Improved: As *slick*, except it grants a +10 competence bonus on Escape Artist checks.

Moderate conjuration; CL 10th; Craft Magic Arms and Armor, *grease*; Price +15,000 gp.

Slick, Greater: As *slick*, except it grants a +15 competence bonus on Escape Artist checks.

Strong conjuration; CL 15th; Craft Magic Arms and Armor, *grease*; Price +33,750 gp.

Spell Resistance: This property grants the armor's wearer spell resistance while the armor is worn. The spell resistance can be 13, 15, 17, or 19, depending on the armor.

Strong abjuration; CL 15th; Craft Magic Arms and Armor, *spell resistance*; Price +2 bonus (SR 13), +3 bonus (SR 15), +4 bonus (SR 17), or +5 bonus (SR 19).

Undead Controlling: *Undead controlling* armor or shields often have skeletal or other grisly decorations or flourishes to their decor. They let the user control up to 26 HD of undead per day, as the *control undead* spell. At dawn each day, the wearer loses control of any undead still under his sway. Armor or a shield with this ability appears to be made of bone; this feature is entirely decorative and has no other effect on the armor.

Strong necromancy; CL 13th; Craft Magic Arms and Armor, *control undead*; Price +49,000 gp.

Wild: The wearer of a suit of armor or a shield with this ability preserves his armor bonus (and any enhancement bonus) while in a wild shape. Armor and shields with this ability usually appear to be covered in leaf patterns. While the wearer is in a wild shape, the armor cannot be seen.

Moderate transmutation; CL 9th; Craft Magic Arms and Armor, *baleful polymorph*; Price +3 bonus.

Specific Armors

ADAMANTINE BREASTPLATE

Aura no aura (nonmagical); **CL** —

Slot armor; **Price** 10,200 gp; **Weight** 30 lbs.

DESCRIPTION

This nonmagical breastplate is made of adamantine, giving its wearer damage reduction of 2/—.

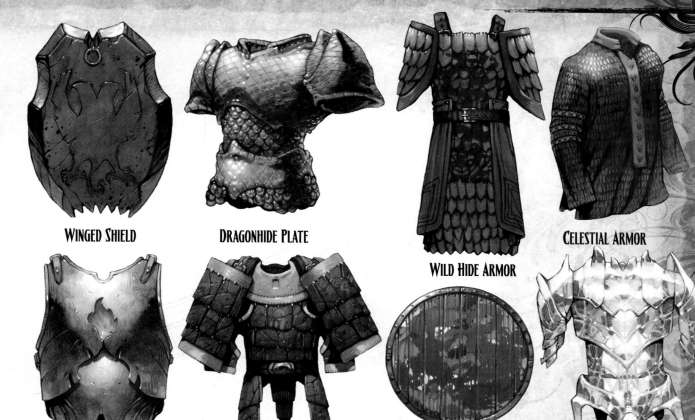

WINGED SHIELD

DRAGONHIDE PLATE

WILD HIDE ARMOR

CELESTIAL ARMOR

BREASTPLATE OF COMMAND

DWARVEN PLATE

CASTER'S SHIELD

MITHRAL FULL PLATE OF SPEED

BANDED MAIL OF LUCK

Aura strong enchantment; **CL** 12th

Slot armor; **Price** 18,900 gp; **Weight** 35 lbs.

DESCRIPTION

Ten 100-gp gems adorn this +3 *banded mail*. Once per week, the armor allows its wearer to require that an attack roll made against him be rerolled. He must take whatever consequences come from the second roll. The wearer's player must decide whether to have the attack roll rerolled before damage is rolled.

CONSTRUCTION

Requirements Craft Magic Arms and Armor, *bless*; **Cost** 9,650 gp

BREASTPLATE OF COMMAND

Aura strong enchantment; **CL** 15th

Slot armor; **Price** 25,400 gp; **Weight** 30 lbs.

DESCRIPTION

This +2 *breastplate* bestows a commanding aura upon its wearer. The wearer gains a +2 competence bonus on all Charisma checks, including Charisma-based skill checks. The wearer also gains a +2 competence bonus to his Leadership score. Friendly troops within 360 feet of the user become braver than normal, gaining a +2 resistance bonus on saving throws against fear. Since the effect arises in great part from the distinctiveness of the armor, it does not function if the wearer hides or conceals herself in any way.

CONSTRUCTION

Requirements Craft Magic Arms and Armor, *mass charm monster*; **Cost** 12,875 gp

CELESTIAL ARMOR

Aura faint transmutation [good]; **CL** 5th

Slot armor; **Price** 22,400 gp; **Weight** 20 lbs.

DESCRIPTION

This bright silver or gold +3 *chainmail* is so fine and light that it can be worn under normal clothing without betraying its presence. It has a maximum Dexterity bonus of +8, an armor check penalty of −2, and an arcane spell failure chance of 15%. It is considered light armor and allows the wearer to use *fly* on command (as the spell) once per day.

CONSTRUCTION

Requirements Craft Magic Arms and Armor, *fly*, creator must be good; **Cost** 11,350 gp

DEMON ARMOR

Aura strong necromancy [evil]; **CL** 13th

Slot armor; **Price** 52,260 gp; **Weight** 50 lbs.

DESCRIPTION

This plate armor is fashioned to make the wearer appear to be a demon. The helmet is shaped to look like a horned demon

head, and its wearer looks out of the open, tooth-filled mouth. This +4 *full plate* allows the wearer to make claw attacks that deal 1d10 points of damage, strike as +1 weapons, and afflict the target as if she had been struck by a *contagion* spell (Fortitude DC 14 negates). Use of *contagion* requires a normal melee attack with the claws. The "claws" are built into the armor's vambraces and gauntlets, and cannot be disarmed.

A suit of *demon armor* is infused with evil, and as a result it bestows one negative level on any nonevil creature wearing it. This negative level persists as long as the armor is worn and disappears when the armor is removed. The negative level cannot be overcome in any way (including *restoration* spells) while the armor is worn.

CONSTRUCTION

Requirements Craft Magic Arms and Armor, *contagion*; **Cost** 26,955 gp

DWARVEN PLATE

Aura no aura (nonmagical); **CL** —

Slot armor; **Price** 16,500 gp; **Weight** 50 lbs.

DESCRIPTION

This full plate is made of adamantine, giving its wearer damage reduction of 3/—.

DRAGONHIDE PLATE

Aura no aura (nonmagical); **CL** —

Slot armor; **Price** 3,300 gp; **Weight** 50 lbs.

DESCRIPTION

This suit of full plate is made of dragonhide, rather than metal, so druids can wear it. It is otherwise identical to masterwork full plate.

ELVEN CHAIN

Aura no aura (nonmagical); **CL** —

Slot armor; **Price** 5,150 gp; **Weight** 20 lbs.

DESCRIPTION

This extremely light chainmail is made of very fine mithral links. This armor is treated, in all ways, like light armor, including when determining proficiency. The armor has an arcane spell failure chance of 20%, a maximum Dexterity bonus of +4, and an armor check penalty of −2.

MITHRAL FULL PLATE OF SPEED

Aura faint transmutation; **CL** 5th

Slot armor; **Price** 26,500 gp; **Weight** 25 lbs.

DESCRIPTION

As a free action, the wearer of this fine set of +1 *mithral full plate* can activate it, enabling him to act as though affected by a *haste* spell for up to 10 rounds each day. The duration of the *haste* effect need not be consecutive rounds.

The armor has an arcane spell failure chance of 25%, a maximum Dexterity bonus of +3, and an armor check penalty of −3. It is considered medium armor, except that you must be proficient in heavy armor to avoid taking nonproficiency penalties.

CONSTRUCTION

Requirements Craft Magic Arms and Armor, *haste*; **Cost** 18,500 gp

MITHRAL SHIRT

Aura no aura (nonmagical); **CL** —

Slot armor; **Price** 1,100 gp; **Weight** 10 lbs.

DESCRIPTION

This extremely light chain shirt is made of very fine mithral links. The armor has an arcane spell failure chance of 10%, a maximum Dexterity bonus of +6, and no armor check penalty. It is considered light armor.

PLATE ARMOR OF THE DEEP

Aura moderate abjuration; **CL** 11th

Slot armor; **Price** 24,650 gp; **Weight** 50 lbs.

DESCRIPTION

This +1 *full plate* is decorated with a wave and fish motif. Although the armor remains as heavy and bulky as normal full plate, the wearer of *plate armor of the deep* is treated as unarmored for purposes of Swim checks. The wearer can breathe underwater and can converse with any water-breathing creature with a language.

CONSTRUCTION

Requirements Craft Magic Arms and Armor, *freedom of movement*, *tongues*, *water breathing*; **Cost** 13,150 gp

RHINO HIDE

Aura moderate transmutation; **CL** 9th

Slot armor; **Price** 5,165 gp; **Weight** 25 lbs.

DESCRIPTION

This +2 *hide armor* is made from rhinoceros hide. In addition to granting a +2 enhancement bonus to AC, it has a −1 armor check penalty and deals an additional 2d6 points of damage on any successful charge attack made by the wearer, including a mounted charge.

CONSTRUCTION

Requirements Craft Magic Arms and Armor, *bull's strength*; **Cost** 2,665 gp

Specific Shields

ABSORBING SHIELD

Aura strong transmutation; **CL** 17th

Slot shield; **Price** 50,170 gp; **Weight** 15 lbs.

DESCRIPTION

This +1 *heavy steel shield* is made of metal, but its color is flat black that seems to absorb light. Once every 2 days, on command, it can *disintegrate* an object that it touches, as the spell but requiring a melee touch attack. This effect only functions as an attack—it can't be activated to target a creature or weapon as it strikes the shield.

CONSTRUCTION

Requirements Craft Magic Arms and Armor, *disintegrate*; **Cost** 25,170 gp

CASTER'S SHIELD

Aura moderate abjuration; **CL** 6th

Slot shield; **Price** 3,153 gp (plus the value of the scroll spell if one is currently scribed); **Weight** 5 lbs.

DESCRIPTION

This +1 *light wooden shield* has a leather strip on the back on which a spellcaster can scribe a single spell as on a scroll. A spell so scribed requires half the normal cost in raw materials. The strip cannot accommodate spells of higher than 3rd level. The strip is reusable.

A random *caster's shield* has a 50% chance of having a single medium scroll spell on it. The spell is divine (01–80 on d%) or arcane (81–100). A *caster's shield* has a 5% arcane spell failure chance.

CONSTRUCTION

Requirements Craft Magic Arms and Armor, Scribe Scroll, creator must be at least 6th level; **Cost** 1,653 gp

DARKWOOD BUCKLER

Aura no aura (nonmagical); **CL** —

Slot shield; **Price** 203 gp; **Weight** 2.5 lbs.

DESCRIPTION

This nonmagical light wooden shield is made out of darkwood. It has no enhancement bonus, but its construction material makes it lighter than a normal wooden shield. It has no armor check penalty.

DARKWOOD SHIELD

Aura no aura (nonmagical); **CL** —

Slot shield; **Price** 257 gp; **Weight** 5 lbs.

DESCRIPTION

This nonmagical heavy wooden shield is made out of darkwood. It has no enhancement bonus, but its construction material makes it lighter than a normal wooden shield. It has no armor check penalty.

LION'S SHIELD

Aura moderate conjuration; **CL** 10th

Slot shield; **Price** 9,170 gp; **Weight** 15 lbs.

DESCRIPTION

This +2 *heavy steel shield* is fashioned to appear to be a roaring lion's head. Three times per day as a free action, the lion's head can be commanded to attack (independently of the shield wearer), biting with the wielder's base attack bonus (including multiple attacks, if the wielder has them) and dealing 2d6 points of damage. This attack is in addition to any actions performed by the wielder.

CONSTRUCTION

Requirements Craft Magic Arms and Armor, *summon nature's ally IV*; **Cost** 4,670 gp

MITHRAL HEAVY SHIELD

Aura no aura (nonmagical); **CL** —

Slot shield; **Price** 1,020 gp; **Weight** 5 lbs.

DESCRIPTION

This heavy shield is made of mithral and thus is much lighter than a standard steel shield. It has a 5% arcane spell failure chance and no armor check penalty.

TABLE 15–7: SPECIFIC SHIELDS

Minor	Medium	Major	Specific Shield	Market Price
01–30	01–20	—	Darkwood buckler	203 gp
31–80	21–45	—	Darkwood shield	257 gp
81–95	46–70	—	Mithral heavy shield	1,020 gp
96–100	71–85	01–20	*Caster's shield*	3,153 gp
—	86–90	21–40	*Spined shield*	5,580 gp
—	91–95	41–60	*Lion's shield*	9,170 gp
—	96–100	61–90	*Winged shield*	17,257 gp
—	—	91–100	*Absorbing shield*	50,170 gp

SPINED SHIELD

Aura moderate evocation; **CL** 6th

Slot shield; **Price** 5,580 gp; **Weight** 15 lbs.

DESCRIPTION

This +1 *heavy steel shield* is covered in spines. It acts as a normal spiked shield. On command up to three times per day, the shield's wearer can fire one of the shield's spines. A fired spine has a +1 enhancement bonus, a range increment of 120 feet, and deals 1d10 points of damage (19–20/x2). Fired spines regenerate each day.

CONSTRUCTION

Requirements Craft Magic Arms and Armor, *magic missile*; **Cost** 2,875 gp

WINGED SHIELD

Aura faint transmutation; **CL** 5th

Slot shield; **Price** 17,257 gp; **Weight** 10 lbs.

DESCRIPTION

This heavy wooden shield has a +3 enhancement bonus. Arching bird wings are carved into the face of the shield. Once per day, it can be commanded to *fly* (as the spell), carrying the wielder. The shield can carry up to 133 pounds and move at 60 feet per round, or up to 266 pounds and move at 40 feet per round.

CONSTRUCTION

Requirements Craft Magic Arms and Armor, *fly*; **Cost** 8,707 gp

WEAPONS

A magic weapon is enhanced to strike more truly and deliver more damage. Magic weapons have enhancement bonuses ranging from +1 to +5. They apply these bonuses to both attack and damage rolls when used in combat. All magic weapons are also masterwork weapons, but their masterwork bonuses on attack rolls do not stack with their enhancement bonuses on attack rolls.

Weapons come in two basic categories: melee and ranged. Some of the weapons listed as melee weapons can also be used as ranged weapons. In this case, their enhancement bonuses apply to both melee and ranged attacks.

Some magic weapons have special abilities. Special abilities count as additional bonuses for determining the market value of the item, but do not modify attack or damage bonuses

TABLE 15-8: WEAPONS

Minor	Medium	Major	Weapon Bonus	Base Price[1]
01–70	01–10	—	+1	2,000 gp
71–85	11–29	—	+2	8,000 gp
—	30–58	01–20	+3	18,000 gp
—	59–62	21–38	+4	32,000 gp
—	—	39–49	+5	50,000 gp
—	—	—	+6[2]	72,000 gp
—	—	—	+7[2]	98,000 gp
—	—	—	+8[2]	128,000 gp
—	—	—	+9[2]	162,000 gp
—	—	—	+10[2]	200,000 gp
86–90	63–68	50–63	Specific weapon[3]	—
91–100	69–100	64–100	Special ability and roll again[4]	—

1 For ammunition, this price is for 50 arrows, bolts, or bullets.
2 A weapon can't have an enhancement bonus higher than +5. Use these lines to determine price when special abilities are added in.
3 See Table 15–11.
4 See Table 15–9 for melee weapons and Table 15–10 for ranged weapons.

(except where specifically noted). A single weapon cannot have a modified bonus (enhancement bonus plus special ability bonus equivalents, including from character abilities and spells) higher than +10. A weapon with a special ability must also have at least a +1 enhancement bonus. Weapons cannot possess the same special ability more than once.

Weapons or ammunition can be made of an unusual material. Roll d%: 01–95 indicates that the item is of a standard sort, and 96–100 indicates that it is made of a special material (see Chapter 6).

Caster Level for Weapons: The caster level of a weapon with a special ability is given in the item description. For an item with only an enhancement bonus and no other abilities, the caster level is three times the enhancement bonus. If an item has both an enhancement bonus and a special ability, the higher of the two caster level requirements must be met.

Additional Damage Dice: Some magic weapons deal additional dice of damage. Unlike other modifiers to damage, additional dice of damage are not multiplied when the attacker scores a critical hit.

Ranged Weapons and Ammunition: The enhancement bonus from a ranged weapon does not stack with the enhancement bonus from ammunition. Only the higher of the two enhancement bonuses applies.

Ammunition fired from a projectile weapon with an enhancement bonus of +1 or higher is treated as a magic weapon for the purpose of overcoming damage reduction. Similarly, ammunition fired from a projectile weapon with an alignment gains the alignment of that projectile weapon.

Magic Ammunition and Breakage: When a magic arrow, crossbow bolt, or sling bullet misses its target, there is a 50% chance it breaks or is otherwise rendered useless. A magic arrow, bolt, or bullet that successfully hits a target is automatically destroyed after it delivers its damage.

Light Generation: Fully 30% of magic weapons shed light equivalent to a *light* spell. These glowing weapons are quite obviously magical. Such a weapon can't be concealed when drawn, nor can its light be shut off. Some of the specific weapons detailed below always or never glow, as defined in their descriptions.

Hardness and Hit Points: Each +1 of a magic weapon's enhancement bonus adds +2 to its hardness and +10 to its hit points. See also Table 7–12 on page 175.

Activation: Usually a character benefits from a magic weapon in the same way a character benefits from a mundane weapon—by wielding (attacking with) it. If a weapon has a special ability that the user needs to activate, then the user usually needs to utter a command word (a standard action). A character can activate the special abilities of 50 pieces of ammunition at the same time, assuming each piece has identical abilities.

Magic Weapons and Critical Hits: Some weapon special abilities and some specific weapons have an extra effect on a critical hit. This special effect also functions against creatures not normally subject to critical hits. On a successful critical roll, apply the special effect, but do not multiply the weapon's regular damage.

Weapons for Unusually Sized Creatures: The cost of weapons for creatures who are neither Small nor Medium varies (see Chapter 6). The cost of the masterwork quality and any magical enhancement remains the same.

Special Qualities: Roll d%. A 01–30 result indicates that the item sheds light, 31–45 indicates that something (a design, inscription, or the like) provides a clue to the weapon's function, and 46–100 indicates no special qualities.

Magic Weapon Special Ability Descriptions

A weapon with a special ability must also have at least a +1 enhancement bonus.

Anarchic: An *anarchic* weapon is infused with the power of chaos. It makes the weapon chaotically aligned and thus bypasses the corresponding damage reduction. It deals an extra 2d6 points of damage against all creatures of lawful alignment. It bestows one permanent negative level (see page 562) on any lawful creature attempting to wield it. The negative level remains as long as the weapon is in hand and disappears when the weapon is no longer wielded. This negative level cannot be overcome in any way (including *restoration* spells) while the weapon is wielded.

Moderate evocation [chaotic]; CL 7th; Craft Magic Arms and Armor, *chaos hammer*, creator must be chaotic; Price +2 bonus.

Axiomatic: An *axiomatic* weapon is infused with lawful power. It makes the weapon law-aligned and thus bypasses the corresponding damage reduction. It deals an extra 2d6 points of damage against chaotic creatures. It bestows one

TABLE 15-9: MELEE WEAPON SPECIAL ABILITIES

Minor	Medium	Major	Special Ability	Base Price Modifier[1]
01–10	01–06	01–03	Bane	+1 bonus
11–17	07–12	—	Defending	+1 bonus
18–27	13–19	04–06	Flaming	+1 bonus
28–37	20–26	07–09	Frost	+1 bonus
38–47	27–33	10–12	Shock	+1 bonus
48–56	34–38	13–15	Ghost touch	+1 bonus
57–67	39–44	—	Keen[2]	+1 bonus
68–71	45–48	16–19	Ki focus	+1 bonus
72–75	49–50	—	Merciful	+1 bonus
76–82	51–54	20–21	Mighty cleaving	+1 bonus
83–87	55–59	22–24	Spell storing	+1 bonus
88–91	60–63	25–28	Throwing	+1 bonus
92–95	64–65	29–32	Thundering	+1 bonus
96–99	66–69	33–36	Vicious	+1 bonus
—	70–72	37–41	Anarchic	+2 bonus
—	73–75	42–46	Axiomatic	+2 bonus
—	76–78	47–49	Disruption[3]	+2 bonus
—	79–81	50–54	Flaming burst	+2 bonus
—	82–84	55–59	Icy burst	+2 bonus
—	85–87	60–64	Holy	+2 bonus
—	88–90	65–69	Shocking burst	+2 bonus
—	91–93	70–74	Unholy	+2 bonus
—	94–95	75–78	Wounding	+2 bonus
—	—	79–83	Speed	+3 bonus
—	—	84–86	Brilliant energy	+4 bonus
—	—	87–88	Dancing	+4 bonus
—	—	89–90	Vorpal[2]	+5 bonus
100	96–100	91–100	Roll again twice[4]	—

1 Add to enhancement bonus on Table 15–8 to determine total market price.

2 Piercing or slashing weapons only (slashing only for vorpal). Reroll if randomly generated for a bludgeoning weapon.

3 Bludgeoning weapons only. Reroll if randomly generated for a piercing or slashing weapon.

4 Reroll if you get a duplicate special ability, an ability incompatible with an ability that you've already rolled, or if the extra ability puts you over the +10 limit. A weapon's enhancement bonus and special ability bonus equivalents can't total more than +10.

TABLE 15-10: RANGED WEAPON SPECIAL ABILITIES

Minor	Medium	Major	Special Ability	Base Price Modifier[1]
01–12	01–08	01–04	Bane[2]	+1 bonus
13–25	09–16	05–08	Distance	+1 bonus
26–40	17–28	09–12	Flaming[2]	+1 bonus
41–55	29–40	13–16	Frost[2]	+1 bonus
56–60	41–42	—	Merciful[2]	+1 bonus
61–68	43–47	17–21	Returning	+1 bonus
69–83	48–59	22–25	Shock[2]	+1 bonus
84–93	60–64	26–27	Seeking	+1 bonus
94–99	65–68	28–29	Thundering[2]	+1 bonus
—	69–71	30–34	Anarchic[2]	+2 bonus
—	72–74	35–39	Axiomatic[2]	+2 bonus
—	75–79	40–49	Flaming burst[2]	+2 bonus
—	80–82	50–54	Holy[2]	+2 bonus
—	83–87	55–64	Icy burst[2]	+2 bonus
—	88–92	65–74	Shocking burst[2]	+2 bonus
—	93–95	75–79	Unholy[2]	+2 bonus
—	—	80–84	Speed	+3 bonus
—	—	85–90	Brilliant energy	+4 bonus
100	96–100	91–100	Roll again twice[3]	—

1 Add to enhancement bonus on Table 15–8 to determine total market price.

2 Bows, crossbows, and slings crafted with this ability bestow this power upon their ammunition.

3 Reroll if you get a duplicate special ability, an ability incompatible with an ability that you've already rolled, or if the extra ability puts you over the +10 limit. A weapon's enhancement bonus and special ability bonus equivalents can't total more than +10.

permanent negative level (see page 562) on any chaotic creature attempting to wield it. The negative level remains as long as the weapon is in hand and disappears when the weapon is no longer wielded. This negative level cannot be overcome in any way (including *restoration* spells) while the weapon is wielded.

Moderate evocation [lawful]; CL 7th; Craft Magic Arms and Armor, *order's wrath*, creator must be lawful; Price +2 bonus.

Bane: A *bane* weapon excels against certain foes. Against a designated foe, the weapon's enhancement bonus is +2 better than its actual bonus. It also deals an extra 2d6 points of damage against the foe. To randomly determine a weapon's designated foe, roll on the following table.

d%	Designated Foe
01–05	Aberrations
06–09	Animals
10–16	Constructs
17–22	Dragons
23–27	Fey
28–60	Humanoids (pick one subtype)
61–65	Magical beasts
66–70	Monstrous humanoids
71–72	Oozes
73–88	Outsiders (pick one subtype)
89–90	Plants
91–98	Undead
99–100	Vermin

Moderate conjuration; CL 8th; Craft Magic Arms and Armor, *summon monster I*; Price +1 bonus.

Brilliant Energy: A *brilliant energy* weapon has its significant portion transformed into light, although this does not modify the item's weight. It always gives off light as a torch (20-foot radius). A *brilliant energy* weapon ignores nonliving matter. Armor and shield bonuses to AC (including any enhancement bonuses to that armor) do not count against it because the weapon passes through armor. (Dexterity, deflection, dodge, natural armor, and other such bonuses still apply.) A *brilliant energy* weapon cannot harm undead, constructs, and objects. This property can only be applied to melee weapons, thrown weapons, and ammunition.

Strong transmutation; CL 16th; Craft Magic Arms and Armor, *gaseous form, continual flame*; Price +4 bonus.

Dancing: As a standard action, a *dancing* weapon can be loosed to attack on its own. It fights for 4 rounds using the base attack bonus of the one who loosed it and then drops. While dancing, it cannot make attacks of opportunity, and the person who activated it is not considered armed with the weapon. The weapon is considered wielded or attended by the creature for all maneuvers and effects that target items. While dancing, the weapon shares the same space as the activating character and can attack adjacent foes (weapons with reach can attack opponents up to 10 feet away). The *dancing* weapon accompanies the person who activated it everywhere, whether she moves by physical or magical means. If the wielder who loosed it has an unoccupied hand, she can grasp it while it is attacking on its own as a free action; when so retrieved, the weapon can't dance (attack on its own) again for 4 rounds.

Strong transmutation; CL 15th; Craft Magic Arms and Armor, *animate objects*; Price +4 bonus.

Defending: A *defending* weapon allows the wielder to transfer some or all of the weapon's enhancement bonus to his AC as a bonus that stacks with all others. As a free action, the wielder chooses how to allocate the weapon's enhancement bonus at the start of his turn before using the weapon, and the bonus to AC lasts until his next turn.

Moderate abjuration; CL 8th; Craft Magic Arms and Armor, *shield* or *shield of faith*; Price +1 bonus.

Disruption: A *disruption* weapon is the bane of all undead. Any undead creature struck in combat must succeed on a DC 14 Will save or be destroyed. A *disruption* weapon must be a bludgeoning melee weapon.

Strong conjuration; CL 14th; Craft Magic Arms and Armor, *heal*; Price +2 bonus.

Distance: This special ability can only be placed on a ranged weapon. A *distance* weapon has double the range increment of other weapons of its kind.

Moderate divination; CL 6th; Craft Magic Arms and Armor, *clairaudience/clairvoyance*; Price +1 bonus.

Flaming: Upon command, a *flaming* weapon is sheathed in fire that deals an extra 1d6 points of fire damage on a

successful hit. The fire does not harm the wielder. The effect remains until another command is given.

Moderate evocation; CL 10th; Craft Magic Arms and Armor and *flame blade, flame strike,* or *fireball*; Price +1 bonus.

Flaming Burst: A *flaming burst* weapon functions as a *flaming* weapon that also explodes with flame upon striking a successful critical hit. The fire does not harm the wielder. In addition to the extra fire damage from the *flaming* ability (see above), a *flaming burst* weapon deals an extra 1d10 points of fire damage on a successful critical hit. If the weapon's critical multiplier is ×3, add an extra 2d10 points of fire damage instead, and if the multiplier is ×4, add an extra 3d10 points of fire damage.

Even if the *flaming* ability is not active, the weapon still deals its extra fire damage on a successful critical hit.

Strong evocation; CL 12th; Craft Magic Arms and Armor and *flame blade, flame strike,* or *fireball*; Price +2 bonus.

Frost: Upon command, a *frost* weapon is sheathed in icy cold that deals an extra 1d6 points of cold damage on a successful hit. The cold does not harm the wielder. The effect remains until another command is given.

Moderate evocation; CL 8th; Craft Magic Arms and Armor, *chill metal* or *ice storm*; Price +1 bonus.

Ghost Touch: A *ghost touch* weapon deals damage normally against incorporeal creatures, regardless of its bonus. An incorporeal creature's 50% reduction in damage from corporeal sources does not apply to attacks made against it with *ghost touch* weapons. The weapon can be picked up and moved by an incorporeal creature at any time. A manifesting ghost can wield the weapon against corporeal foes. Essentially, a *ghost touch* weapon counts as both corporeal or incorporeal.

Moderate conjuration; CL 9th; Craft Magic Arms and Armor, *plane shift*; Price +1 bonus.

Holy: A *holy* weapon is imbued with holy power. This power makes the weapon good-aligned and thus bypasses the corresponding damage reduction. It deals an extra 2d6 points of damage against all creatures of evil alignment. It bestows one permanent negative level on any evil creature attempting to wield it. The negative level remains as long as the weapon is in hand and disappears when the weapon is no longer wielded. This negative level cannot be overcome in any way (including by *restoration* spells) while the weapon is wielded.

Moderate evocation [good]; CL 7th; Craft Magic Arms and Armor, *holy smite*, creator must be good; Price +2 bonus.

Icy Burst: An *icy burst* weapon functions as a *frost* weapon that also explodes with frost upon striking a successful critical hit. The frost does not harm the wielder. In addition to the extra damage from the *frost* ability, an *icy burst* weapon deals an extra 1d10 points of cold damage on a successful critical hit. If the weapon's critical multiplier is ×3, add an extra 2d10 points of cold damage instead, and if the multiplier is ×4, add an extra 3d10 points.

Even if the *frost* ability is not active, the weapon still deals its extra cold damage on a successful critical hit.

Moderate evocation; CL 10th; Craft Magic Arms and Armor, *chill metal* or *ice storm*; Price +2 bonus.

Keen: This ability doubles the threat range of a weapon. Only piercing or slashing melee weapons can be *keen*. If you roll this property randomly for an inappropriate weapon, reroll. This benefit doesn't stack with any other effect that expands the threat range of a weapon (such as the *keen edge* spell or the Improved Critical feat).

Moderate transmutation; CL 10th; Craft Magic Arms and Armor, *keen edge*; Price +1 bonus.

Ki Focus: The magic weapon serves as a channel for the wielder's ki, allowing her to use her special ki attacks through the weapon as if they were unarmed attacks. These attacks include the monk's ki strike, quivering palm, and the Stunning Fist feat (including any condition that the monk can apply using this feat). Only melee weapons can have the *ki focus* ability.

Moderate transmutation; CL 8th; Craft Magic Arms and Armor, creator must be a monk; Price +1 bonus.

Merciful: The weapon deals an extra 1d6 points of damage, and all damage it deals is nonlethal damage. On command, the weapon suppresses this ability until told to resume it (allowing it to deal lethal damage, but without any bonus damage from this ability).

Faint conjuration; CL 5th; Craft Magic Arms and Armor, *cure light wounds*; Price +1 bonus.

Mighty Cleaving: A *mighty cleaving* weapon allows a wielder using the Cleave feat to make one additional attack if the first attack hits, as long as the next foe is adjacent to the first and also within reach. This additional attack cannot be against the first foe. Only melee weapons can be *mighty cleaving* weapons.

Moderate evocation; CL 8th; Craft Magic Arms and Armor, *divine power*; Price +1 bonus.

Returning: This special ability can only be placed on a weapon that can be thrown. A *returning* weapon flies through the air back to the creature that threw it. It returns to the thrower just before the creature's next turn (and is therefore ready to use again in that turn). Catching a *returning* weapon when it comes back is a free action. If the character can't catch it, or if the character has moved since throwing it, the weapon drops to the ground in the square from which it was thrown.

Moderate transmutation; CL 7th; Craft Magic Arms and Armor, *telekinesis*; Price +1 bonus.

Seeking: Only ranged weapons can have the *seeking* ability. The weapon veers toward its target, negating any miss chances that would otherwise apply, such as from concealment. The wielder still has to aim the weapon at the right square. Arrows mistakenly shot into an empty space, for example, do not veer and hit invisible enemies, even if they are nearby.

Strong divination; CL 12th; Craft Magic Arms and Armor, *true seeing*; Price +1 bonus.

TABLE 15-11: SPECIFIC WEAPONS

Minor	Medium	Major	Specific Weapon	Market Price
01–15	—	—	Sleep arrow	132 gp
16–25	—	—	Screaming bolt	267 gp
26–45	—	—	Silver dagger, masterwork	322 gp
46–65	—	—	Cold iron longsword, masterwork	330 gp
66–75	01–09	—	Javelin of lightning	1,500 gp
76–80	10–15	—	Slaying arrow	2,282 gp
81–90	16–24	—	Adamantine dagger	3,002 gp
91–100	25–33	—	Adamantine battleaxe	3,010 gp
—	34–37	—	Slaying arrow (greater)	4,057 gp
—	38–40	—	Shatterspike	4,315 gp
—	41–46	—	Dagger of venom	8,302 gp
—	47–51	—	Trident of warning	10,115 gp
—	52–57	01–04	Assassin's dagger	10,302 gp
—	58–62	05–07	Shifter's sorrow	12,780 gp
—	63–66	08–09	Trident of fish command	18,650 gp
—	67–74	10–13	Flame tongue	20,715 gp
—	75–79	14–17	Luck blade (0 wishes)	22,060 gp
—	80–86	18–24	Sword of subtlety	22,310 gp
—	87–91	25–31	Sword of the planes	22,315 gp
—	92–95	32–37	Nine lives stealer	23,057 gp
—	96–98	38–42	Oathbow	25,600 gp
—	99–100	43–46	Sword of life stealing	25,715 gp
—	—	47–51	Mace of terror	38,552 gp
—	—	52–57	Life-drinker	40,320 gp
—	—	58–62	Sylvan scimitar	47,315 gp
—	—	63–67	Rapier of puncturing	50,320 gp
—	—	68–73	Sun blade	50,335 gp
—	—	74–79	Frost brand	54,475 gp
—	—	80–84	Dwarven thrower	60,312 gp
—	—	85–91	Luck blade (1 wish)	62,360 gp
—	—	92–95	Mace of smiting	75,312 gp
—	—	96–97	Luck blade (2 wishes)	102,660 gp
—	—	98–99	Holy avenger	120,630 gp
—	—	100	Luck blade (3 wishes)	142,960 gp

Shock: Upon command, a *shock* weapon is sheathed in crackling electricity that deals an extra 1d6 points of electricity damage on a successful hit. The electricity does not harm the wielder. The effect remains until another command is given.

Moderate evocation; CL 8th; Craft Magic Arms and Armor, *call lightning* or *lightning bolt*; Price +1 bonus.

Shocking Burst: A *shocking burst* weapon functions as a *shock* weapon that explodes with electricity upon striking a successful critical hit. The electricity does not harm the wielder. In addition to the extra electricity damage from the *shock* ability, a *shocking burst* weapon deals an extra 1d10 points of electricity damage on a successful critical hit. If the weapon's critical

multiplier is ×3, add an extra 2d10 points of electricity damage instead, and if the multiplier is ×4, add an extra 3d10 points.

Even if the *shock* ability is not active, the weapon still deals its extra electricity damage on a successful critical hit.

Moderate evocation; CL 10th; Craft Magic Arms and Armor, *call lightning* or *lightning bolt*; Price +2 bonus.

Speed: When making a full-attack action, the wielder of a *speed* weapon may make one extra attack with it. The attack uses the wielder's full base attack bonus, plus any modifiers appropriate to the situation. (This benefit is not cumulative with similar effects, such as a *haste* spell.)

Moderate transmutation; CL 7th; Craft Magic Arms and Armor, *haste*; Price +3 bonus.

Spell Storing: A *spell storing* weapon allows a spellcaster to store a single targeted spell of up to 3rd level in the weapon. (The spell must have a casting time of 1 standard action.) Anytime the weapon strikes a creature and the creature takes damage from it, the weapon can immediately cast the spell on that creature as a free action if the wielder desires. (This special ability is an exception to the general rule that casting a spell from an item takes at least as long as casting that spell normally.) Once the spell has been cast from the weapon, a spellcaster can cast any other targeted spell of up to 3rd level into it. The weapon magically imparts to the wielder the name of the spell currently stored within it. A randomly rolled *spell storing* weapon has a 50% chance to have a spell stored in it already.

Strong evocation (plus aura of stored spell); CL 12th; Craft Magic Arms and Armor, creator must be a caster of at least 12th level; Price +1 bonus.

Throwing: This ability can only be placed on a melee weapon. A melee weapon crafted with this ability gains a range increment of 10 feet and can be thrown by a wielder proficient in its normal use.

Faint transmutation; CL 5th; Craft Magic Arms and Armor, *magic stone*; Price +1 bonus.

Thundering: A *thundering* weapon creates a cacophonous roar like thunder upon striking a successful critical hit. The sonic energy does not harm the wielder. A *thundering* weapon deals an extra 1d8 points of sonic damage on a successful critical hit. If the weapon's critical multiplier is ×3, add an extra 2d8 points of sonic damage instead, and if the multiplier is ×4, add an extra 3d8 points of sonic damage. Subjects dealt critical hits by a *thundering* weapon must make a DC 14 Fortitude save or be deafened permanently.

Faint necromancy; CL 5th; Craft Magic Arms and Armor, *blindness/deafness*; Price +1 bonus.

Unholy: An *unholy* weapon is imbued with unholy power. This power makes the weapon evil-aligned and thus bypasses the corresponding damage reduction. It deals an extra 2d6 points of damage against all creatures of good alignment. It bestows one permanent negative level on any good creature attempting to wield it. The negative level remains as long as the weapon is in hand and disappears when the weapon is no longer wielded. This negative level cannot be overcome in any way (including *restoration* spells) while the weapon is wielded.

Moderate evocation [evil]; CL 7th; Craft Magic Arms and Armor, *unholy blight*, creator must be evil; Price +2 bonus.

Vicious: When a *vicious* weapon strikes an opponent, it creates a flash of disruptive energy that resonates between the opponent and the wielder. This energy deals an extra 2d6 points of damage to the opponent and 1d6 points of damage to the wielder. Only melee weapons can be *vicious*.

Moderate necromancy; CL 9th; Craft Magic Arms and Armor, *enervation*; Price +1 bonus.

Vorpal: This potent and feared ability allows the weapon to sever the heads of those it strikes. Upon a roll of natural 20 (followed by a successful roll to confirm the critical hit), the weapon severs the opponent's head (if it has one) from its body. Some creatures, such as many aberrations and all oozes, have no heads. Others, such as golems and undead creatures other than vampires, are not affected by the loss of their heads. Most other creatures, however, die when their heads are cut off. A *vorpal* weapon must be a slashing melee weapon. If you roll this property randomly for an inappropriate weapon, reroll.

Strong necromancy and transmutation; CL 18th; Craft Magic Arms and Armor, *circle of death*, *keen edge*; Price +5 bonus.

Wounding: A *wounding* weapon deals 1 point of bleed damage when it hits a creature. Multiple hits from a wounding weapon increase the bleed damage. Bleeding creatures take the bleed damage at the start of their turns. Bleeding can be stopped by a DC 15 Heal check or through the application of any spell that cures hit point damage. A critical hit does not multiply the bleed damage. Creatures immune to critical hits are immune to the bleed damage dealt by this weapon.

Moderate evocation; CL 10th; Craft Magic Arms and Armor, *bleed*; Price +2 bonus.

Specific Weapons

ADAMANTINE BATTLEAXE

Aura no aura (nonmagical); **CL** —
Slot none; **Price** 3,010 gp; **Weight** 6 lbs.

DESCRIPTION

This nonmagical axe is made out of adamantine. As a masterwork weapon, it has a +1 enhancement bonus on attack rolls.

ADAMANTINE DAGGER

Aura no aura (nonmagical); **CL** —
Slot none; **Price** 3,002 gp; **Weight** 1 lb.

DESCRIPTION

This nonmagical dagger is made out of adamantine. As a masterwork weapon, it has a +1 enhancement bonus on attack rolls.

ASSASSIN'S DAGGER

Aura moderate necromancy; **CL** 9th
Slot none; **Price** 10,302 gp; **Weight** 1 lb.

DESCRIPTION

This wicked-looking, curved *+2 dagger* provides a +1 bonus to the DC of a Fortitude save forced by the death attack of an assassin.

CONSTRUCTION

Requirements Craft Magic Arms and Armor, *slay living*; **Cost** 5,302 gp

DAGGER OF VENOM

Aura faint necromancy; **CL** 5th

Slot none; **Price** 8,302 gp; **Weight** 1 lb.

DESCRIPTION

This black *+1 dagger* has a serrated edge. It allows the wielder to use a *poison* effect (as the spell, save DC 14) upon a creature struck by the blade once per day. The wielder can decide to use the power after he has struck. Doing so is a free action, but the *poison* effect must be invoked in the same round that the dagger strikes.

CONSTRUCTION

Requirements Craft Magic Arms and Armor, *poison*; **Cost** 4,302 gp

DWARVEN THROWER

Aura moderate evocation; **CL** 10th

Slot none; **Price** 60,312 gp; **Weight** 5 lbs.

DESCRIPTION

This weapon functions as a *+2 warhammer* in the hands of most users. Yet in the hands of a dwarf, the warhammer gains an additional +1 enhancement bonus (for a total enhancement bonus of +3) and gains the *returning* special ability. It can be hurled with a 30-foot range increment. When hurled, a *dwarven thrower* deals an extra 2d8 points of damage against creatures of the giant subtype or an extra 1d8 points of damage against any other target.

CONSTRUCTION

Requirements Craft Magic Arms and Armor, creator must be a dwarf of at least 10th level; **Cost** 30,312 gp

FLAME TONGUE

Aura strong evocation; **CL** 12th

Slot none; **Price** 20,715 gp; **Weight** 4 lbs.

DESCRIPTION

This is a *+1 flaming burst longsword*. Once per day, the sword can blast forth a fiery ray at any target within 30 feet as a ranged touch attack. The ray deals 4d6 points of fire damage on a successful hit.

CONSTRUCTION

Requirements Craft Magic Arms and Armor, *scorching ray* and *fireball*, *flame blade*, or *flame strike*; **Cost** 10,515 gp

FROST BRAND

Aura strong evocation; **CL** 14th

Slot none; **Price** 54,475 gp; **Weight** 8 lbs.

DESCRIPTION

This *+3 frost greatsword* sheds light as a torch when the temperature drops below 0° F. At such times it cannot be concealed when drawn, nor can its light be shut off. Its wielder is protected from fire; the sword absorbs the first 10 points of fire damage each round that the wielder would otherwise take.

A *frost brand* extinguishes all nonmagical fires in a 20-foot radius. As a standard action, it can also dispel lasting fire spells, but not instantaneous effects. You must succeed on a dispel check (1d20 +14) against each spell to dispel it. The DC to dispel such spells is 11 + the caster level of the fire spell.

CONSTRUCTION

Requirements Craft Magic Arms and Armor, *ice storm*, *dispel magic*, *protection from energy*; **Cost** 27,375 gp and 5 sp

HOLY AVENGER

Aura strong abjuration; **CL** 18th

Slot none; **Price** 120,630 gp; **Weight** 4 lbs.

DESCRIPTION

This *+2 cold iron longsword* becomes a *+5 holy cold iron longsword* in the hands of a paladin.

This sacred weapon provides spell resistance of 5 + the paladin's level to the wielder and anyone adjacent to her. It also enables the paladin to use *greater dispel magic* (once per round as a standard action) at the class level of the paladin. Only the area dispel is possible, not the targeted dispel or counterspell versions of *greater dispel magic*.

CONSTRUCTION

Requirements Craft Magic Arms and Armor, *holy aura*, creator must be good; **Cost** 60,630 gp

JAVELIN OF LIGHTNING

Aura faint evocation; **CL** 5th

Slot none; **Price** 1,500 gp; **Weight** 2 lbs.

DESCRIPTION

This javelin becomes a 5d6 *lightning bolt* when thrown (Reflex DC 14 half). It is consumed in the attack.

CONSTRUCTION

Requirements Craft Magic Arms and Armor, *lightning bolt*; **Cost** 750 gp

LIFE-DRINKER

Aura strong necromancy; **CL** 13th

Slot none; **Price** 40,320 gp; **Weight** 12 lbs.

DESCRIPTION

This *+1 greataxe* is favored by undead and constructs, who do not suffer its drawback. A life-drinker bestows two negative levels on its target whenever it deals damage, just as if its target had been struck by an undead creature. One day after being struck, subjects must make a DC 16 Fortitude save for each negative level or the negative levels become permanent.

Each time a *life-drinker* deals damage to a foe, it also bestows one negative level on the wielder. Any negative levels gained by the wielder in this fashion lasts for 1 hour.

CONSTRUCTION

Requirements Craft Magic Arms and Armor, *enervation*; **Cost** 20,320 gp

LONGSWORD, COLD IRON MASTERWORK

Aura no aura (nonmagical); **CL** —

Slot none; **Price** 330 gp; **Weight** 4 lbs.

DESCRIPTION

This nonmagical longsword is crafted out of cold iron. As a masterwork weapon, it has a +1 enhancement bonus on attack rolls.

LUCK BLADE

Aura strong evocation; **CL** 17th

Slot none; **Price** 22,060 gp (0 *wishes*), 62,360 gp (1 *wish*), 102,660 gp (2 *wishes*), 142,960 gp (3 *wishes*); **Weight** 2 lbs.

DESCRIPTION

This +2 *short sword* gives its possessor a +1 luck bonus on all saving throws. Its possessor also gains the power of good fortune, usable once per day. This extraordinary ability allows its possessor to reroll one roll that she just made, before the results are revealed. She must take the result of the reroll, even if it's worse than the original roll. In addition, a luck blade may contain up to three *wishes* (when randomly rolled, a luck blade holds 1d4–1 *wishes*, minimum 0). When the last *wish* is used, the sword remains a +2 *short sword*, still grants the +1 luck bonus, and still grants its reroll power.

CONSTRUCTION

Requirements Craft Magic Arms and Armor, *wish* or *miracle*; **Cost** 11,185 gp (0 wishes), 43,835 gp (1 wish), 76,485 gp (2 wishes), 109,135 gp (3 wishes).

MACE OF SMITING

Aura moderate transmutation; **CL** 11th

Slot none; **Price** 75,312 gp; **Weight** 8 lbs.

DESCRIPTION

This +3 *adamantine heavy mace* has a +5 enhancement bonus against constructs, and a successful critical hit dealt to a construct completely destroys the construct (no saving throw). A critical hit dealt to an outsider deals ×4 damage rather than ×2.

CONSTRUCTION

Requirements Craft Magic Arms and Armor, *disintegrate*; **Cost** 39,312 gp

MACE OF TERROR

Aura strong necromancy; **CL** 13th

Slot none; **Price** 38,552 gp; **Weight** 8 lbs.

DESCRIPTION

This weapon usually appears to be a particularly frightening-looking iron or steel mace. On command, this +2 *heavy mace* causes the wielder's clothes and appearance to transform into an illusion of darkest horror such that living creatures in a 30-foot cone become panicked as if by a *fear* spell (Will DC 16 partial). Those who fail take a –2 morale penalty on saving throws, and they flee from the wielder. The wielder may use this ability up to three times per day.

CONSTRUCTION

Requirements Craft Magic Arms and Armor, *fear*; **Cost** 19,432 gp

NINE LIVES STEALER

Aura strong necromancy [evil]; **CL** 13th

Slot none; **Price** 23,057 gp; **Weight** 4 lbs.

DESCRIPTION

This longsword always performs as a +2 *longsword*, but it also has the power to draw the life force from an opponent. It can do this nine times before the ability is lost. At that point, the sword becomes a simple +2 *longsword* (with a faint evil aura). A critical hit must be dealt for the sword's death-dealing ability to function, and this weapon has no effect on creatures not subject to critical hits. The victim is entitled to a DC 20 Fortitude save to avoid death. If the save is successful, the sword's death-dealing ability does not function, no use of the ability is expended, and normal critical damage is determined. This sword is evil, and any good character attempting to wield it gains two negative levels. These negative levels remain as long as the sword is in hand and disappear when the sword is no longer wielded. These negative levels never result in actual level loss, but they cannot be overcome in any way (including *restoration* spells) while the sword is wielded.

CONSTRUCTION

Requirements Craft Magic Arms and Armor, *finger of death*; **Cost** 11,528 gp 5 sp.

OATHBOW

Aura strong evocation; **CL** 15th

Slot none; **Price** 25,600 gp; **Weight** 3 lbs.

DESCRIPTION

Of elven make, this white +2 *composite longbow* (+2 Str bonus) whispers, "Swift defeat to my enemies" in Elven when nocked and pulled. Once per day, if the archer swears aloud to slay her target (a free action), the bow's whisper becomes the shout "Death to those who have wronged me!" Against such a sworn enemy, the bow has a +5 enhancement bonus, and arrows launched from it deal an additional 2d6 points of damage (and ×4 on a critical hit instead of the normal ×3). After an enemy has been sworn, the bow is treated as only a masterwork weapon against all foes other than the sworn enemy, and the archer takes a –1 penalty on attack rolls with any weapon other than the *oathbow*. These bonuses and penalties last for 7 days or until the sworn enemy is slain or destroyed by the wielder of the *oathbow*, whichever comes first.

The *oathbow* may only have one sworn enemy at a time. Once the wielder swears to slay a target, he cannot make a new oath until he has slain that target or 7 days have passed. Even if the wielder slays the sworn enemy on the same day that he makes the oath, he cannot activate the *oathbow's* special power again until 24 hours have passed from the time he made the oath.

CONSTRUCTION

Requirements Craft Magic Arms and Armor, creator must be an elf; **Cost** 13,100 gp

RAPIER OF PUNCTURING

Aura strong necromancy; **CL** 13th

Slot none; **Price** 50,320 gp; **Weight** 2 lbs.

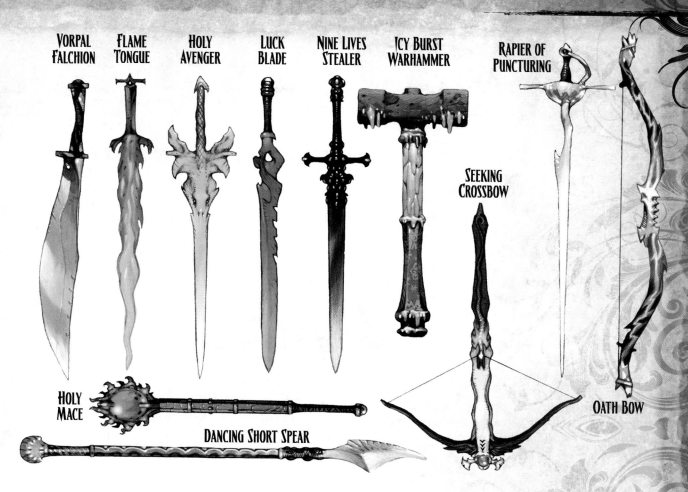

VORPAL FALCHION · **FLAME TONGUE** · **HOLY AVENGER** · **LUCK BLADE** · **NINE LIVES STEALER** · **ICY BURST WARHAMMER** · **RAPIER OF PUNCTURING**

SEEKING CROSSBOW

OATH BOW

HOLY MACE

DANCING SHORT SPEAR

DESCRIPTION

Three times per day, this +2 *wounding rapier* allows the wielder to make a touch attack with the weapon that deals 1d6 points of Constitution damage by draining blood. Creatures immune to critical hits are immune to the Constitution damage dealt by this weapon.

CONSTRUCTION

Requirements Craft Magic Arms and Armor, *harm*; **Cost** 25,320 gp

SCREAMING BOLT

Aura faint enchantment; **CL** 5th

Slot none; **Price** 267 gp; **Weight** 1/10 lb.

DESCRIPTION

These +2 *bolts* scream when fired, forcing all enemies of the wielder within 20 feet of the path of the bolt to succeed on a DC 14 Will save or become shaken. This is a mind-affecting fear effect.

CONSTRUCTION

Requirements Craft Magic Arms and Armor, *doom*; **Cost** 137 gp

SHATTERSPIKE

Aura strong evocation; **CL** 13th

Slot none; **Price** 4,315 gp; **Weight** 4 lbs.

DESCRIPTION

This intimidating weapon appears to be a longsword with multiple hooks, barbs, and serrations along the blade, excellent for catching and sundering a foe's weapon. Wielders without the Improved Sunder feat use a *shatterspike* as a +1 *longsword* only. Wielders with the Improved Sunder feat instead use *shatterspike* as a +4 *longsword* when attempting to sunder an opponent's weapon. *Shatterspike* can damage weapons with an enhancement bonus of +4 or lower.

CONSTRUCTION

Requirements Str 13, Craft Magic Arms and Armor, Improved Sunder, Power Attack, *shatter*; **Cost** 2,315 gp

SHIFTER'S SORROW

Aura strong transmutation; **CL** 15th

Slot none; **Price** 12,780 gp; **Weight** 10 lbs.

DESCRIPTION

This +1/+1 *two-bladed sword* has blades of alchemical silver. The weapon deals an extra 2d6 points of damage against any creature with the shapechanger subtype. When a shapechanger or a creature in an alternate form (such as a druid using wild shape) is struck by the weapon, it must make a DC 15 Will save or return to its natural form.

CONSTRUCTION

Requirements Craft Magic Arms and Armor, *baleful polymorph*; **Cost** 6,780 gp

82–84	Outsiders, good
85–87	Outsiders, lawful
88	Outsiders, water
89–90	Plants
91–98	Undead
99–100	Vermin

SILVER DAGGER, MASTERWORK

Aura no aura (nonmagical); **CL** —

Slot none; **Price** 322 gp; **Weight** 1 lb.

DESCRIPTION

As a masterwork weapon, this alchemical silver dagger has a +1 enhancement bonus on attack rolls (but not to damage rolls).

SLAYING ARROW

Aura strong necromancy; **CL** 13th

Slot none; **Price** 2,282 gp (*slaying arrow*) or 4,057 gp (*greater slaying arrow*); **Weight** 1/10 lb.

DESCRIPTION

This *+1 arrow* is keyed to a particular type or subtype of creature. If it strikes such a creature, the target must make a DC 20 Fortitude save or take 50 points of damage. Note that even creatures normally exempt from Fortitude saves (undead and constructs) are subject to this attack. When keyed to a living creature, this is a death effect (and thus *death ward* protects a target). To determine the type or subtype of creature the arrow is keyed to, roll on the table below.

A *greater slaying arrow* functions just like a normal *slaying arrow*, but the DC to avoid the death effect is 23 and the arrow deals 100 points of damage if the saving throw is failed.

CONSTRUCTION

Requirements Craft Magic Arms and Armor, *finger of death* (*slaying arrow*) or heightened *finger of death* (*greater slaying arrow*); **Cost** 1,144 gp 5 sp (*slaying arrow*) or 2,032 gp (*greater slaying arrow*)

d%	Designated Type or Subtype
01–05	Aberrations
06–09	Animals
10–16	Constructs
17–27	Dragons
28–32	Fey
33	Humanoids, aquatic
34–35	Humanoids, dwarf
36–37	Humanoids, elf
38–44	Humanoids, giant
45	Humanoids, gnoll
46	Humanoids, gnome
47–49	Humanoids, goblinoid
50	Humanoids, halfling
51–54	Humanoids, human
55–57	Humanoids, reptilian
58–60	Humanoids, orc
61–65	Magical beasts
66–70	Monstrous humanoids
71–72	Oozes
73	Outsiders, air
74–76	Outsiders, chaotic
77	Outsiders, earth
78–80	Outsiders, evil
81	Outsiders, fire

SLEEP ARROW

Aura faint enchantment; **CL** 5th

Slot none; **Price** 132 gp; **Weight** 1/10 lb.

DESCRIPTION

This *+1 arrow* is painted white and has white fletching. If it strikes a foe so that it would normally deal damage, it instead bursts into magical energy that deals nonlethal damage (in the same amount as would lethal damage) and forces the target to make a DC 11 Will save or fall asleep.

CONSTRUCTION

Requirements Craft Magic Arms and Armor, *sleep*; **Cost** 70 gp

SUN BLADE

Aura moderate evocation; **CL** 10th

Slot none; **Price** 50,335 gp; **Weight** 2 lbs.

DESCRIPTION

This sword is the size of a bastard sword. However, a *sun blade* is wielded as if it were a short sword with respect to weight and ease of use. In other words, the weapon appears to all viewers to be a bastard sword, and deals bastard sword damage, but the wielder feels and reacts as if the weapon were a short sword. Any individual able to use either a bastard sword or a short sword with proficiency is proficient in the use of a *sun blade*. Likewise, Weapon Focus and Weapon Specialization in short sword and bastard sword apply equally, but the benefits of those feats do not stack.

In normal combat, the glowing golden blade of the weapon is equal to a *+2 bastard sword*. Against evil creatures, its enhancement bonus is +4. Against Negative Energy Plane creatures or undead creatures, the sword deals double damage (and ×3 on a critical hit instead of the usual ×2).

The blade also has a special sunlight power. Once per day, the wielder can swing the blade vigorously above his head while speaking a command word. The *sun blade* then sheds a bright yellow radiance that acts like bright light and affects creatures susceptible to light as if it were natural sunlight. The radiance begins shining in a 10-foot radius around the sword wielder and extends outward at 5 feet per round for 10 rounds thereafter, to create a globe of light with a 60-foot radius. When the wielder stops swinging, the radiance fades to a dim glow that persists for another minute before disappearing entirely. All *sun blades* are of good alignment, and any evil creature attempting to wield one gains one negative level. The negative level remains as long as the sword is in hand and disappears when the sword is no longer wielded. This negative level cannot be overcome in any way (including by *restoration* spells) while the sword is wielded.

CONSTRUCTION

Requirements Craft Magic Arms and Armor, *daylight*, creator must be good; **Cost** 25,335 gp

SWORD OF LIFE STEALING

Aura strong necromancy; **CL** 17th

Slot none; **Price** 25,715 gp; **Weight** 4 lbs.

DESCRIPTION

This black iron +2 *longsword* bestows a negative level when it deals a critical hit. The sword wielder gains 1d6 temporary hit points each time a negative level is bestowed on another. These temporary hit points last for 24 hours. One day after being struck, subjects must make a DC 16 Fortitude save for each negative level gained or they become permanent.

CONSTRUCTION

Requirements Craft Magic Arms and Armor, *enervation*; **Cost** 13,015 gp

SWORD OF THE PLANES

Aura strong evocation; **CL** 15th

Slot none; **Price** 22,315 gp; **Weight** 4 lbs.

DESCRIPTION

This longsword has an enhancement bonus of +1 on the Material Plane, but on any Elemental Plane its enhancement bonus increases to +2. The +2 enhancement bonus also applies whenever the weapon is used against creatures native to the Elemental Plane. It operates as a +3 *longsword* on the Astral Plane and the Ethereal Plane, or when used against opponents native to either of those planes. On any other plane, or against any outsider, it functions as a +4 *longsword*.

CONSTRUCTION

Requirements Craft Magic Arms and Armor, *plane shift*; **Cost** 11,315 gp

SWORD OF SUBTLETY

Aura moderate illusion; **CL** 7th

Slot none; **Price** 22,310 gp; **Weight** 2 lbs.

DESCRIPTION

A +1 *short sword* with a thin, dull gray blade, this weapon provides a +4 bonus on its wielder's attack and damage rolls when he is making a sneak attack with it.

CONSTRUCTION

Requirements Craft Magic Arms and Armor, *blur*; **Cost** 11,310 gp

SYLVAN SCIMITAR

Aura moderate evocation; **CL** 11th

Slot none; **Price** 47,315 gp; **Weight** 4 lbs.

DESCRIPTION

This +3 *scimitar*, when used outdoors in a temperate climate, grants its wielder the use of the Cleave feat and deals an extra 1d6 points of damage.

CONSTRUCTION

Requirements Craft Magic Arms and Armor, *divine power* or creator must be a 7th-level druid; **Cost** 23,815 gp

TRIDENT OF FISH COMMAND

Aura moderate enchantment; **CL** 7th

Slot none; **Price** 18,650 gp; **Weight** 4 lbs.

DESCRIPTION

The magical properties of this +1 *trident* with a 6-foot-long haft enable its wielder to charm up to 14 HD of aquatic animals as per the spell *charm animals* (Will DC 16 negates, animals get a +5 bonus if currently under attack by the wielder or his allies), no two of which can be more than 30 feet apart. The wielder can use this effect up to three times per day. The wielder can communicate with the animals as if using a *speak with animals* spell. Animals making their saving throws are free of control, but they will not approach within 10 feet of the trident.

CONSTRUCTION

Requirements Craft Magic Arms and Armor, *charm animals*, *speak with animals*; **Cost** 9,482 gp and 5 sp

TRIDENT OF WARNING

Aura moderate divination; **CL** 7th

Slot none; **Price** 10,115 gp; **Weight** 4 lbs.

DESCRIPTION

A weapon of this type enables its wielder to determine the location, depth, kind, and number of aquatic predators within 680 feet. A *trident of warning* must be grasped and pointed in order for the character using it to gain such information, and it requires 1 round to scan a hemisphere with a radius of 680 feet. The weapon is otherwise a +2 *trident*.

CONSTRUCTION

Requirements Craft Magic Arms and Armor, *locate creature*; **Cost** 5,215 gp

POTIONS

A potion is a magic liquid that produces its effect when imbibed. Potions vary incredibly in appearance. Magic oils are similar to potions, except that oils are applied externally rather than imbibed. A potion or oil can be used only once. It can duplicate the effect of a spell of up to 3rd level that has a casting time of less than 1 minute and targets one or more creatures or objects. The price of a potion is equal to the level of the spell × the creator's caster level × 50 gp. If the potion has a material component cost, it is added to the base price and cost to create. Table 15–12 gives sample prices for potions created at the lowest possible caster level for each spellcasting class. Note that some spells appear at different levels for different casters. The level of such spells depends on the caster brewing the potion.

Potions are like spells cast upon the imbiber. The character taking the potion doesn't get to make any decisions about the effect—the caster who brewed the potion has already done so. The drinker of a potion is both the effective target and the caster of the effect (though the potion indicates the caster level, the drinker still controls the effect).

The person applying an oil is the effective caster, but the object is the target.

TABLE 15–12: POTIONS

Minor	Medium	Major	Spell Level	Caster Level
01–20	—	—	0	1st
21–60	01–20	—	1st	1st
61–100	21–60	01–20	2nd	3rd
—	61–100	21–100	3rd	5th

POTION COSTS

Spell Level	Cleric, Druid, Wizard	Sorcerer	Bard	Paladin, Ranger
0	25 gp	25 gp	25 gp	—
1st	50 gp	50 gp	50 gp	50 gp
2nd	300 gp	400 gp	400 gp	400 gp
3rd	750 gp	900 gp	1,050 gp	1,050 gp

Physical Description: A typical potion or oil consists of 1 ounce of liquid held in a ceramic or glass vial fitted with a tight stopper. The stoppered container is usually no more than 1 inch wide and 2 inches high. The vial has AC 13, 1 hit point, hardness 1, and a break DC of 12.

Identifying Potions: In addition to the standard methods of identification, PCs can sample from each container they find to attempt to determine the nature of the liquid inside with a Perception check. The DC of this check is equal to 15 + the spell level of the potion (although this DC might be higher for rare or unusual potions).

Activation: Drinking a potion or applying an oil requires no special skill. The user merely removes the stopper and swallows the potion or smears on the oil. The following rules govern potion and oil use.

Drinking a potion or using an oil is a standard action. The potion or oil takes effect immediately. Using a potion or oil provokes attacks of opportunity. An enemy may direct an attack of opportunity against the potion or oil container rather than against the character. A successful attack of this sort can destroy the container, preventing the character from drinking the potion or applying the oil.

A creature must be able to swallow a potion or smear on an oil. Because of this, incorporeal creatures cannot use potions or oils. Any corporeal creature can imbibe a potion or use an oil.

A character can carefully administer a potion to an unconscious creature as a full-round action, trickling the liquid down the creature's throat. Likewise, it takes a full-round action to apply an oil to an unconscious creature.

RINGS

Rings bestow magical powers upon their wearers. Only a rare few have charges—most magic rings are permanent and potent magic items. Anyone can use a ring.

A character can only effectively wear two magic rings. A third magic ring doesn't work if the wearer is already wearing two magic rings.

Physical Description: Rings have no appreciable weight. Although exceptions exist that are crafted from glass or bone, the vast majority of rings are forged from metal—usually precious metals such as gold, silver, and platinum. A ring has AC 13, 2 hit points, hardness 10, and a break DC of 25.

Activation: A ring's ability is usually activated by a spoken command word (a standard action that does not provoke attacks of opportunity) or its effects work continually. Some rings have unusual activations, as mentioned in the ring's specific description.

Special Qualities: Roll d%. A result of 01 indicates the ring is intelligent, 02–31 indicates that something (a design, inscription, or the like) provides a clue to its function, and 32–100 indicates no special qualities. Intelligent items have extra abilities and sometimes extraordinary powers and special purposes (see page 532). Rings with charges can never be intelligent.

RING OF ANIMAL FRIENDSHIP

Aura faint enchantment; **CL** 3rd

Slot ring; **Price** 10,800 gp; **Weight** —

DESCRIPTION

A *ring of animal friendship* always bears some sort of animal-like design in its craftsmanship. On command, this ring affects an animal as if the wearer had cast *charm animal*.

CONSTRUCTION

Requirements Forge Ring, *charm animal*; **Cost** 5,400 gp

RING OF BLINKING

Aura moderate transmutation; **CL** 7th

Slot ring; **Price** 27,000 gp; **Weight** —

DESCRIPTION

On command, this ring makes the wearer blink, as the *blink* spell.

CONSTRUCTION

Requirements Forge Ring, *blink*; **Cost** 13,500 gp

RING OF CHAMELEON POWER

Aura faint illusion; **CL** 3rd

Slot ring; **Price** 12,700 gp; **Weight** —

DESCRIPTION

As a free action, the wearer of this ring can gain the ability to magically blend in with the surroundings. This provides a +10 competence bonus on her Stealth checks. As a standard action, she can also use the spell *disguise self* as often as she wants.

CONSTRUCTION

Requirements Forge Ring, *disguise self*, *invisibility*; **Cost** 6,350 gp

RING OF CLIMBING

Aura faint transmutation; **CL** 5th

Slot ring; **Price** 2,500 gp; **Weight** —

DESCRIPTION

This ring is actually a magic leather cord that ties around a finger. It continually grants the wearer a +5 competence bonus on Climb checks.

CONSTRUCTION

Requirements Forge Ring, creator must have 5 ranks in the Climb skill; **Cost** 1,250 gp

RING OF CLIMBING, IMPROVED

Aura faint transmutation; **CL** 5th

Slot ring; **Price** 10,000 gp; **Weight** —

DESCRIPTION

As a *ring of climbing*, except it grants a +10 competence bonus on its wearer's Climb checks.

CONSTRUCTION

Requirements Forge Ring, creator must have 10 ranks in the Climb skill; **Cost** 5,000 gp

RING OF COUNTERSPELLS

Aura moderate evocation; **CL** 11th

Slot ring; **Price** 4,000 gp; **Weight** —

DESCRIPTION

This ring might seem to be a *ring of spell storing* upon first examination. However, while it allows a single spell of 1st through 6th level to be cast into it, that spell cannot be cast out of the ring again. Instead, should that spell ever be cast upon the wearer, the spell is immediately countered, as a counterspell action, requiring no action (or even knowledge) on the wearer's part. Once so used, the spell cast within the ring is gone. A new spell (or the same one as before) may be placed into it again.

CONSTRUCTION

Requirements Forge Ring, *imbue with spell ability*; **Cost** 2,000 gp

RING OF DJINNI CALLING

Aura strong conjuration; **CL** 17th

Slot ring; **Price** 125,000 gp; **Weight** —

DESCRIPTION

One of the many rings of fable, this "genie" ring is useful indeed. It serves as a special *gate* by means of which a specific djinni (see the *Pathfinder RPG Bestiary*) can be called from the Plane of Air. When the ring is rubbed (a standard action), the call goes out, and the djinni appears on the next round. The djinni faithfully obeys and serves the wearer of the ring, but never for more than 1 hour per day. If the djinni of the ring is ever killed, the ring becomes nonmagical and worthless.

CONSTRUCTION

Requirements Forge Ring, *gate*; **Cost** 62,500 gp

RING OF ELEMENTAL COMMAND

Aura strong conjuration; **CL** 15th

Slot ring; **Price** 200,000 gp; **Weight** —

DESCRIPTION

All four kinds of *elemental command* rings are very powerful. Each

TABLE 15-13: RINGS

Minor	Medium	Major	Ring	Market Price
01–18	—	—	Protection +1	2,000 gp
19–28	—	—	Feather falling	2,200 gp
29–36	—	—	Sustenance	2,500 gp
37–44	—	—	Climbing	2,500 gp
45–52	—	—	Jumping	2,500 gp
53–60	—	—	Swimming	2,500 gp
61–70	01–05	—	Counterspells	4,000 gp
71–75	06–08	—	Mind shielding	8,000 gp
76–80	09–18	—	Protection +2	8,000 gp
81–85	19–23	—	Force shield	8,500 gp
86–90	24–28	—	Ram, the	8,600 gp
—	29–34	—	Climbing, improved	10,000 gp
—	35–40	—	Jumping, improved	10,000 gp
—	41–46	—	Swimming, improved	10,000 gp
91–93	47–50	—	Animal friendship	10,800 gp
94–96	51–56	01–02	Energy resistance, minor	12,000 gp
97–98	57–61	—	Chameleon power	12,700 gp
99–100	62–66	—	Water walking	15,000 gp
—	67–71	03–07	Protection +3	18,000 gp
—	72–76	08–10	Spell storing, minor	18,000 gp
—	77–81	11–15	Invisibility	20,000 gp
—	82–85	16–19	Wizardry (I)	20,000 gp
—	86–90	20–25	Evasion	25,000 gp
—	91–93	26–28	X-ray vision	25,000 gp
—	94–97	29–32	Blinking	27,000 gp
—	98–100	33–39	Energy resistance, major	28,000 gp
—	—	40–49	Protection +4	32,000 gp
—	—	50–55	Wizardry (II)	40,000 gp
—	—	56–60	Freedom of movement	40,000 gp
—	—	61–63	Energy resistance, greater	44,000 gp
—	—	64–65	Friend shield (pair)	50,000 gp
—	—	66–70	Protection +5	50,000 gp
—	—	71–74	Shooting stars	50,000 gp
—	—	75–79	Spell storing	50,000 gp
—	—	80–83	Wizardry (III)	70,000 gp
—	—	84–86	Telekinesis	75,000 gp
—	—	87–88	Regeneration	90,000 gp
—	—	89–91	Spell turning	100,000 gp
—	—	92–93	Wizardry (IV)	100,000 gp
—	—	94	Three wishes	120,000 gp
—	—	95	Djinni calling	125,000 gp
—	—	96	Elemental command (air)	200,000 gp
—	—	97	Elemental command (earth)	200,000 gp
—	—	98	Elemental command (fire)	200,000 gp
—	—	99	Elemental command (water)	200,000 gp
—	—	100	Spell storing, major	200,000 gp

appears to be nothing more than a lesser magic ring until fully activated (by meeting a special condition, such as single-handedly slaying an elemental of the appropriate type or exposure to a sacred material of the appropriate element), but each has certain other powers as well as the following common properties.

Elementals of the plane to which the ring is attuned can't attack the wearer, or even approach within 5 feet of him. If the wearer desires, he may forego this protection and instead attempt to charm the elemental (as *charm monster*, Will DC 17 negates). If the charm attempt fails, however, absolute protection is lost and no further attempt at charming can be made.

Creatures from the plane to which the ring is attuned who attack the wearer take a –1 penalty on their attack rolls. The ring wearer makes applicable saving throws against the extraplanar creature's attacks with a +2 resistance bonus. He gains a +4 morale bonus on all attack rolls against such creatures. Any weapon he uses bypasses the damage reduction of such creatures, regardless of any qualities the weapon may or may not have.

The wearer of the ring is able to converse with creatures from the plane to which his ring is attuned. These creatures recognize that he wears the ring, and show a healthy respect for the wearer if alignments are similar. If alignments are opposed, creatures fear the wearer if he is strong. If he is weak, they hate and desire to slay him.

The possessor of a *ring of elemental command* takes a saving throw penalty as follows:

Element	Saving Throw Penalty
Air	–2 against earth-based effects
Earth	–2 against air- or electricity-based effects
Fire	–2 against water- or cold-based effects
Water	–2 against fire-based effects

In addition to the powers described above, each specific ring gives its wearer the following abilities according to its kind.

Ring of Elemental Command (Air)
- *Feather fall* (unlimited use, wearer only)
- *Resist energy (electricity)* (unlimited use, wearer only)
- *Gust of wind* (twice per day)
- *Wind wall* (unlimited use)
- *Air walk* (once per day, wearer only)
- *Chain lightning* (once per week)

The ring appears to be a *ring of feather falling* until a certain condition is met to activate its full potential. It must be reactivated each time a new wearer acquires it.

Ring of Elemental Command (Earth)
- *Meld into stone* (unlimited use, wearer only)
- *Soften earth and stone* (unlimited use)
- *Stone shape* (twice per day)
- *Stoneskin* (once per week, wearer only)
- *Passwall* (twice per week)
- *Wall of stone* (once per day)

The ring appears to be a *ring of meld into stone* (allowing the wearer to cast *meld into stone* at will) until the established condition is met.

Ring of Elemental Command (Fire)
- *Resist energy (fire)* (as a *major ring of energy resistance [fire]*)
- *Burning hands* (unlimited use)
- *Flaming sphere* (twice per day)
- *Pyrotechnics* (twice per day)
- *Wall of fire* (once per day)
- *Flame strike* (twice per week)

The ring appears to be a *major ring of energy resistance (fire)* until the established condition is met.

Ring of Elemental Command (Water)
- *Water walk* (unlimited use)
- *Create water* (unlimited use)
- *Water breathing* (unlimited use)
- *Wall of ice* (once per day)
- *Ice storm* (twice per week)
- *Control water* (twice per week)

The ring appears to be a *ring of water walking* until the established condition is met.

CONSTRUCTION

Requirements Forge Ring, *summon monster VI*, all appropriate spells; **Cost** 100,000 gp

RING OF ENERGY RESISTANCE

Aura faint (minor) or moderate (major or greater) abjuration; **CL** 3rd (minor), 7th (major), or 11th (greater)

Slot ring; **Price** 12,000 gp (minor), 28,000 gp (major), 44,000 gp (greater); **Weight** —

DESCRIPTION

This ring continually protects the wearer from damage from one type of energy—acid, cold, electricity, fire, or sonic (chosen by the creator of the item; determine randomly if found as part of a treasure hoard). Each time the wearer would normally take such damage, subtract the ring's resistance value from the damage dealt.

A *minor ring of energy resistance* grants 10 points of resistance. A *major ring of energy resistance* grants 20 points of resistance. A *greater ring of energy resistance* grants 30 points of resistance.

CONSTRUCTION

Requirements Forge Ring, *resist energy*; **Cost** 6,000 gp (minor), 14,000 gp (major), 22,000 gp (greater)

RING OF EVASION

Aura moderate transmutation; **CL** 7th

Slot ring; **Price** 25,000 gp; **Weight** —

DESCRIPTION

This ring continually grants the wearer the ability to avoid damage as if she had evasion. Whenever she makes a Reflex saving throw to determine whether she takes half damage, a successful save results in no damage.

CONSTRUCTION

Requirements Forge Ring, *jump*; **Cost** 12,500 gp

RING OF FEATHER FALLING

Aura faint transmutation; **CL** 1st

Slot ring; **Price** 2,200 gp; **Weight** —

DESCRIPTION

This ring is crafted with a feather pattern all around its edge. It acts exactly like a *feather fall* spell, activated immediately if the wearer falls more than 5 feet.

CONSTRUCTION

Requirements Forge Ring, *feather fall*; **Cost** 1,100 gp

RING OF FORCE SHIELD

Aura moderate evocation; **CL** 9th

Slot ring; **Price** 8,500 gp; **Weight** —

DESCRIPTION

An iron band, this simple ring generates a shield-sized (and shield-shaped) *wall of force* that stays with the ring and can be wielded by the wearer as if it were a heavy shield (+2 AC). This special creation has no armor check penalty or arcane spell failure chance since it is weightless and encumbrance-free. It can be activated and deactivated at will as a free action.

CONSTRUCTION

Requirements Forge Ring, *wall of force*; **Cost** 4,250 gp

RING OF FREEDOM OF MOVEMENT

Aura moderate abjuration; **CL** 7th

Slot ring; **Price** 40,000 gp; **Weight** —

DESCRIPTION

This gold ring allows the wearer to act as if continually under the effect of a *freedom of movement* spell.

CONSTRUCTION

Requirements Forge Ring, *freedom of movement*; **Cost** 20,000 gp

RING OF FRIEND SHIELD

Aura moderate abjuration; **CL** 10th

Slot ring; **Price** 50,000 gp (for a pair); **Weight** —

DESCRIPTION

These curious rings always come in pairs. A *friend shield* ring without its mate is useless. Either wearer of one of a pair of the rings can, at any time, command his ring to cast a *shield other* spell with the wearer of the mated ring as the recipient. This effect has no range limitation.

CONSTRUCTION

Requirements Forge Ring, *shield other*; **Cost** 25,000 gp

RING OF INVISIBILITY

Aura faint illusion; **CL** 3rd

Slot ring; **Price** 20,000 gp; **Weight** —

DESCRIPTION

By activating this simple silver ring, the wearer can benefit from *invisibility*, as the spell.

CONSTRUCTION

Requirements Forge Ring, *invisibility*; **Cost** 10,000 gp

RING OF JUMPING

Aura faint transmutation; **CL** 2nd

Slot ring; **Price** 2,500 gp; **Weight** —

DESCRIPTION

This ring continually allows the wearer to leap about, providing a +5 competence bonus on all his Acrobatics checks made to make high or long jumps.

CONSTRUCTION

Requirements Forge Ring, creator must have 5 ranks in the Acrobatics skill; **Cost** 1,250 gp

RING OF JUMPING, IMPROVED

Aura moderate transmutation; **CL** 7th

Slot ring; **Price** 10,000 gp; **Weight** —

DESCRIPTION

As a *ring of jumping*, except it grants a +10 competence bonus on its wearer's Acrobatics checks made to make high or long jumps.

CONSTRUCTION

Requirements Forge Ring, creator must have 10 ranks in the Acrobatics skill; **Cost** 5,000 gp

RING OF MIND SHIELDING

Aura faint abjuration; **CL** 3rd

Slot ring; **Price** 8,000 gp; **Weight** —

DESCRIPTION

This ring is usually of fine workmanship and wrought from heavy gold. The wearer is continually immune to *detect thoughts*, *discern lies*, and any attempt to magically discern her alignment.

CONSTRUCTION

Requirements Forge Ring, *nondetection*; **Cost** 4,000 gp

RING OF PROTECTION

Aura faint abjuration; **CL** 5th

Slot ring; **Price** 2,000 gp (+1), 8,000 gp (+2), 18,000 gp (+3), 32,000 gp (+4), 50,000 gp (+5); **Weight** —

DESCRIPTION

This ring offers continual magical protection in the form of a deflection bonus of +1 to +5 to AC.

CONSTRUCTION

Requirements Forge Ring, *shield of faith*, caster must be of a level at least three times the bonus of the ring; **Cost** 1,000 gp (+1), 4,000 gp (+2), 9,000 gp (+3), 16,000 gp (+4), 25,000 gp (+5)

RING OF THE RAM

Aura moderate transmutation; **CL** 9th

Slot ring; **Price** 8,600 gp; **Weight** —

DESCRIPTION

The *ring of the ram* is an ornate ring forged of hard metal, usually iron or an iron alloy. It has the head of a ram as its device. The wearer can command the ring to give forth a ram-like force, manifested by a

vaguely discernible shape that resembles the head of a ram or a goat. This force strikes a single target, dealing 1d6 points of damage if 1 charge is expended, 2d6 points if 2 charges are used, or 3d6 points if 3 charges (the maximum) are used. Treat this as a ranged attack with a 50-foot maximum range and no penalties for distance.

The force of the blow is considerable, and those struck by the ring are subject to a bull rush if within 30 feet of the ring-wearer. The ram is Large and uses the ring's caster level as its base attack bonus with a Strength of 25. This gives the ram a Combat Maneuver Bonus of +17. The ram gains a +1 bonus on the bull rush attempt if 2 charges are expended, or +2 if 3 charges are expended.

In addition to its attack mode, the *ring of the ram* also has the power to open doors as if it were a character with Strength 25. This expends 1 charge. If 2 charges are expended, the effect is equivalent to a character with Strength 27. If 3 charges are expended, the effect is that of a character with Strength 29.

A newly created ring has 50 charges. When all the charges are expended, the ring becomes a nonmagical item.

CONSTRUCTION

Requirements Forge Ring, *bull's strength, telekinesis*; **Cost** 4,300 gp

RING OF REGENERATION

Aura strong conjuration; **CL** 15th

Slot ring; **Price** 90,000 gp; **Weight** —

DESCRIPTION

This white gold ring is generally set with a large green sapphire. When worn, the ring continually allows a living wearer to heal 1 point of damage per round and an equal amount of nonlethal damage. In addition, he is immune to bleed damage while wearing a *ring of regeneration*. If the wearer loses a limb, an organ, or any other body part while wearing this ring, the ring *regenerates* it as the spell. In either case, only damage taken while wearing the ring is regenerated.

CONSTRUCTION

Requirements Forge Ring, *regenerate*; **Cost** 45,000 gp

RING OF SHOOTING STARS

Aura strong evocation; **CL** 12th

Slot ring; **Price** 50,000 gp; **Weight** —

DESCRIPTION

This ring has two modes of operation: one for being in dim light or outdoors at night, and a second one when the wearer is underground or indoors at night.

During the night, under the open sky or in areas of shadow or darkness, the *ring of shooting stars* can perform the following functions on command.

- *Dancing lights* (once per hour)
- *Light* (twice per night)
- Ball lightning (special, once per night)
- Shooting stars (special, three per week)

The first special function, ball lightning, releases one to four balls of lightning (ring wearer's choice). These glowing globes resemble *dancing lights*, and the ring wearer controls them similarly (see the *dancing lights* spell description). The spheres have a 120-foot range and a duration of 4 rounds. They can be moved at 120 feet per round. Each sphere is about 3 feet in diameter, and any creature who comes within 5 feet of one causes its charge to dissipate, taking electricity damage in the process according to the number of balls created.

Number of Balls	Damage per Ball
1 lightning ball	4d6 points of electricity damage
2 lightning balls	3d6 points of electricity damage each
3 lightning balls	2d6 points of electricity damage each
4 lightning balls	1d6 points of electricity damage each

Once the ball lightning function is activated, the balls can be released at any time before the sun rises. Multiple balls can be released in the same round.

The second special function produces three shooting stars that can be released from the ring each week, simultaneously or one at a time. They impact for 12 points of damage and spread (as a *fireball*) in a 5-foot-radius sphere for 24 points of fire damage.

Any creature struck by a shooting star takes full damage from impact plus full fire damage from the spread unless it makes a DC 13 Reflex save. Creatures not struck but within the spread ignore the impact damage and take only half damage from the fire spread on a successful DC 13 Reflex save. Range is 70 feet, at the end of which the shooting star explodes unless it strikes a creature or object before that. A shooting star always follows a straight line, and any creature in its path must make a save or be hit by the projectile.

Indoors at night, or underground, the *ring of shooting stars* has the following properties.

- *Faerie fire* (twice per day)
- Spark shower (special, once per day)

The spark shower is a flying cloud of sizzling purple sparks that fan out from the ring for a distance of 20 feet in an arc 10 feet wide. Creatures within this area take 2d8 points of damage each if not wearing metal armor or carrying a metal weapon. Those wearing metal armor and/or carrying a metal weapon take 4d8 points of damage.

CONSTRUCTION

Requirements Forge Ring, *faerie fire, fireball, light, lightning bolt*; **Cost** 25,000 gp

RING OF SPELL STORING, MINOR

Aura faint evocation; **CL** 5th

Slot ring; **Price** 18,000 gp; **Weight** —

DESCRIPTION

A *minor ring of spell storing* contains up to three levels of spells (either divine or arcane, or even a mix of both spell types) that the wearer can cast. Each spell has a caster level equal to the minimum level needed to cast that spell. The user need not provide any material components or focus to cast the spell, and there is no arcane spell failure chance for wearing armor (because the ring wearer need not gesture). The activation time for the ring is the same as the casting time for the relevant spell, with a minimum of 1 standard action.

For a randomly generated ring, treat it as a scroll to determine what spells are stored in it. If you roll a spell that would put the ring over the three-level limit, ignore that roll; the ring has no more spells in it.

A spellcaster can cast any spells into the ring, so long as the total spell levels do not add up to more than three. Metamagic versions of spells take up storage space equal to their spell level modified by the metamagic feat. A spellcaster can use a scroll to put a spell into the *minor ring of spell storing*.

The ring magically imparts to the wearer the names of all spells currently stored within it.

CONSTRUCTION

Requirements Forge Ring, *imbue with spell ability*; **Cost** 9,000 gp

RING OF SPELL STORING

Aura moderate evocation; **CL** 9th

Slot ring; **Price** 50,000 gp; **Weight** —

DESCRIPTION

As the *minor ring of spell storing*, except it holds up to 5 levels of spells.

CONSTRUCTION

Requirements Forge Ring, *imbue with spell ability*; **Cost** 25,000 gp

RING OF SPELL STORING, MAJOR

Aura strong evocation; **CL** 17th

Slot ring; **Price** 200,000 gp; **Weight** —

DESCRIPTION

As the *minor ring of spell storing*, except it holds up to 10 levels of spells.

CONSTRUCTION

Requirements Forge Ring, *imbue with spell ability*; **Cost** 100,000 gp

RING OF SPELL TURNING

Aura strong abjuration; **CL** 13th

Slot ring; **Price** 100,000 gp; **Weight** —

DESCRIPTION

Up to three times per day on command, this simple platinum band automatically reflects the next nine levels of spells cast at the wearer, exactly as if *spell turning* had been cast upon him.

CONSTRUCTION

Requirements Forge Ring, *spell turning*; **Cost** 50,000 gp

RING OF SUSTENANCE

Aura faint conjuration; **CL** 5th

Slot ring; **Price** 2,500 gp; **Weight** —

DESCRIPTION

This ring continually provides its wearer with life-sustaining nourishment. The ring also refreshes the body and mind, so that its wearer needs only sleep 2 hours per day to gain the benefit of 8 hours of sleep. This allows a spellcaster that requires rest to prepare spells to do so after only 2 hours, but this does not allow a spellcaster to prepare spells more than once per day. The ring must be worn for a full week before it begins to work. If it is removed, the owner must wear it for another week to reattune it to himself.

CONSTRUCTION

Requirements Forge Ring, *create food and water*; **Cost** 1,250 gp

RING OF SWIMMING

Aura faint transmutation; **CL** 2nd

Slot ring; **Price** 2,500 gp; **Weight** —

DESCRIPTION

This silver ring usually has fish-like designs and motifs etched into the band. It continually grants the wearer a +5 competence bonus on Swim checks.

CONSTRUCTION

Requirements Forge Ring, creator must have 5 ranks in the Swim skill; **Cost** 1,250 gp

RING OF SWIMMING, IMPROVED

Aura moderate transmutation; **CL** 7th

Slot ring; **Price** 10,000 gp; **Weight** —

DESCRIPTION

As a *ring of swimming*, except it grants a +10 competence bonus on its wearer's Swim checks.

CONSTRUCTION

Requirements Forge Ring, creator must have 10 ranks in the Swim skill; **Cost** 5,000 gp

RING OF TELEKINESIS

Aura moderate transmutation; **CL** 9th

Slot ring; **Price** 75,000 gp; **Weight** —

DESCRIPTION

This ring allows the caster to use the spell *telekinesis* on command.

CONSTRUCTION

Requirements Forge Ring, *telekinesis*; **Cost** 37,500 gp

RING OF THREE WISHES

Aura strong universal or evocation (if *miracle* is used); **CL** 20th

Slot ring; **Price** 120,000 gp; **Weight** —

DESCRIPTION

This ring is set with three rubies. Each ruby stores a *wish* spell, activated by the ring. When a *wish* is used, that ruby disappears. For a randomly generated ring, roll 1d3 to determine the remaining number of rubies. When all the *wishes* are used, the ring becomes a nonmagical item.

CONSTRUCTION

Requirements Forge Ring, *wish* or *miracle*; **Cost** 97,500 gp

RING OF WATER WALKING

Aura moderate transmutation; **CL** 9th

Slot ring; **Price** 15,000 gp; **Weight** —

DESCRIPTION

This ring is often made of coral or bluish metal decorated with wave motifs. It allows the wearer to continually utilize the effects of the spell *water walk*.

CONSTRUCTION

Requirements Forge Ring, *water walk*; **Cost** 7,500 gp

RING OF WIZARDRY

Aura moderate (*wizardry I*) or strong (*wizardry II–IV*) (no school);
CL 11th (*I*), 14th (*II*), 17th (*III*), 20th (*IV*)

Slot ring; **Price** 20,000 gp (I), 40,000 gp (II), 70,000 gp (III),
100,000 gp (IV); **Weight** —

DESCRIPTION

This special ring comes in four kinds (*ring of wizardry I*, *ring of wizardry II*, *ring of wizardry III*, and *ring of wizardry IV*), all of them useful only to arcane spellcasters. The wearer's arcane spells per day are doubled for one specific spell level. A *ring of wizardry I* doubles 1st-level spells, a *ring of wizardry II* doubles 2nd-level spells, a *ring of wizardry III* doubles 3rd-level spells, and a *ring of wizardry IV* doubles 4th-level spells. Bonus spells from high ability scores or school specialization are not doubled.

CONSTRUCTION

Requirements Forge Ring, *limited wish*; **Cost** 10,000 gp (I),
20,000 gp (II), 35,000 gp (III), 50,000 gp (IV)

RING OF X-RAY VISION

Aura moderate divination; **CL** 6th

Slot ring; **Price** 25,000 gp; **Weight** —

DESCRIPTION

On command, this ring gives its wearer the ability to see into and through solid matter. Vision range is 20 feet, with the viewer seeing as if he were looking at something in normal light even if there is no illumination. X-ray vision can penetrate 1 foot of stone, 1 inch of common metal, or up to 3 feet of wood or dirt. Thicker substances or a thin sheet of lead blocks the vision.

Using the ring is exhausting, causing the wearer 1 point of Constitution damage per minute after the first 10 minutes of use in a single day. The ring must be used in 1-minute increments.

CONSTRUCTION

Requirements Forge Ring, *true seeing*; **Cost** 12,500 gp

RODS

Rods are scepter-like devices that have unique magical powers and do not usually have charges. Anyone can use a rod.

Physical Description: Rods weigh approximately 5 pounds. They range from 2 feet to 3 feet long and are usually made of iron or some other metal. (Many, as noted in their descriptions, can function as light maces or clubs due to their hardy construction.) These sturdy items have AC 9, 10 hit points, hardness 10, and a break DC of 27.

Activation: Details relating to rod use vary from item to item. Unless noted otherwise, you must be holding a rod to use its abilities. See the individual descriptions for specifics.

Special Qualities: Roll d%. A 01 result indicates the rod is intelligent, 02–31 indicates that something (a design, inscription, or the like) provides a clue to its function, and 32–100 indicates no special qualities. Intelligent items have extra abilities and sometimes extraordinary powers and special purposes (see Intelligent Items later in this chapter).

Rods with charges can never be intelligent.

IMMOVABLE ROD

Aura moderate transmutation; **CL** 10th

Slot none; **Price** 5,000 gp; **Weight** 5 lbs.

DESCRIPTION

This rod looks like a flat iron bar with a small button on one end. When the button is pushed (a move action), the rod does not move from where it is, even if staying in place defies gravity. Thus, the owner can lift or place the rod wherever he wishes, push the button, and let go. Several *immovable rods* can even make a ladder when used together (although only two are needed). An *immovable rod* can support up to 8,000 pounds before falling to the ground. If a creature pushes against an *immovable rod*, it must make a DC 30 Strength check to move the rod up to 10 feet in a single round.

CONSTRUCTION

Requirements Craft Rod, *levitate*; **Cost** 2,500 gp

METAMAGIC RODS

Metamagic rods hold the essence of a metamagic feat, allowing the user to apply metamagic effects to spells (but not spell-like abilities) as they are cast. This does not change the spell slot of the altered spell. All the rods described here are use-activated (but casting spells in a threatened area still draws an attack of opportunity). A caster may only use one metamagic rod on any given spell, but it is permissible to combine a rod with metamagic feats possessed by the rod's wielder. In this case, only the feats possessed by the wielder adjust the spell slot of the spell being cast.

Possession of a metamagic rod does not confer the associated feat on the owner, only the ability to use the given feat a specified number of times per day. A sorcerer still must take a full-round action when using a metamagic rod, just as if using a metamagic feat he possesses (except for *quicken metamagic rods*, which can be used as a swift action).

Lesser and Greater Metamagic Rods: Normal metamagic rods can be used with spells of 6th level or lower. Lesser rods can be used with spells of 3rd level or lower, while greater rods can be used with spells of 9th level or lower.

METAMAGIC, EMPOWER

Aura strong (no school); **CL** 17th

Slot none; **Price** 9,000 gp (lesser), 32,500 gp (normal), 73,000 gp
(greater); **Weight** 5 lbs.

DESCRIPTION

The wielder can cast up to three spells per day that are empowered as though using the Empower Spell feat.

CONSTRUCTION

Requirements Craft Rod, Empower Spell; **Cost** 4,500 gp (lesser),
16,250 gp (normal), 36,500 gp (greater)

METAMAGIC, ENLARGE

Aura strong (no school); **CL** 17th

Slot none; **Price** 3,000 gp (lesser), 11,000 gp (normal), 24,500 gp
(greater); **Weight** 5 lbs.

DESCRIPTION

The wielder can cast up to three spells per day that are enlarged as though using the Enlarge Spell feat.

CONSTRUCTION

Requirements Craft Rod, Enlarge Spell; **Cost** 1,500 gp (lesser), 5,500 gp (normal), 12,250 gp (greater)

METAMAGIC, EXTEND

Aura strong (no school); **CL** 17th

Slot none; **Price** 3,000 gp (lesser), 11,000 gp (normal), 24,500 gp (greater); **Weight** 5 lbs.

DESCRIPTION

The wielder can cast up to three spells per day that are extended as though using the Extend Spell feat.

CONSTRUCTION

Requirements Craft Rod, Extend Spell; **Cost** 1,500 gp (lesser), 5,500 gp (normal), 12,250 gp (greater)

METAMAGIC, MAXIMIZE

Aura strong (no school); **CL** 17th

Slot none; **Price** 14,000 gp (lesser), 54,000 gp (normal), 121,500 gp (greater); **Weight** 5 lbs.

DESCRIPTION

The wielder can cast up to three spells per day that are maximized as though using the Maximize Spell feat.

CONSTRUCTION

Requirements Craft Rod, Maximize Spell feat; **Cost** 7,000 gp (lesser), 27,000 gp (normal), 60,750 gp (greater)

METAMAGIC, QUICKEN

Aura strong (no school); **CL** 17th

Slot none; **Price** 35,000 gp (lesser), 75,500 gp (normal), 170,000 gp (greater); **Weight** 5 lbs.

DESCRIPTION

The wielder can cast up to three spells per day that are quickened as though using the Quicken Spell feat.

CONSTRUCTION

Requirements Craft Rod, Quicken Spell; **Cost** 17,500 gp (lesser), 37,750 gp (normal), 85,000 gp (greater)

METAMAGIC, SILENT

Aura strong (no school); **CL** 17th

Slot none; **Price** 3,000 gp (lesser), 11,000 gp (normal), 24,500 gp (greater); **Weight** 5 lbs.

DESCRIPTION

The wielder can cast up to three spells per day without verbal components as though using the Silent Spell feat.

CONSTRUCTION

Requirements Craft Rod, Silent Spell; **Cost** 1,500 gp (lesser), 5,500 gp (normal), 12,250 gp (greater)

ROD OF ABSORPTION

Aura strong abjuration; **CL** 15th

TABLE 15-14: RODS

Medium	Major	Rod	Market Price
01–07	—	Metamagic, Enlarge, lesser	3,000 gp
08–14	—	Metamagic, Extend, lesser	3,000 gp
15–21	—	Metamagic, Silent, lesser	3,000 gp
22–28	—	Immovable	5,000 gp
29–35	—	Metamagic, Empower, lesser	9,000 gp
36–42	—	Metal and mineral detection	10,500 gp
43–53	01–04	Cancellation	11,000 gp
54–57	05–06	Metamagic, Enlarge	11,000 gp
58–61	07–08	Metamagic, Extend	11,000 gp
62–65	09–10	Metamagic, Silent	11,000 gp
66–71	11–14	Wonder	12,000 gp
72–79	15–19	Python	13,000 gp
80–83	—	Metamagic, Maximize, lesser	14,000 gp
84–89	20–21	Flame extinguishing	15,000 gp
90–97	22–25	Viper	19,000 gp
—	26–30	Enemy detection	23,500 gp
—	31–36	Metamagic, Enlarge, greater	24,500 gp
—	37–42	Metamagic, Extend, greater	24,500 gp
—	43–48	Metamagic, Silent, greater	24,500 gp
—	49–53	Splendor	25,000 gp
—	54–58	Withering	25,000 gp
98–99	59–64	Metamagic, Empower	32,500 gp
—	65–69	Thunder and lightning	33,000 gp
100	70–73	Metamagic, Quicken, lesser	35,000 gp
—	74–77	Negation	37,000 gp
—	78–80	Absorption	50,000 gp
—	81–84	Flailing	50,000 gp
—	85–86	Metamagic, Maximize	54,000 gp
—	87–88	Rulership	60,000 gp
—	89–90	Security	61,000 gp
—	91–92	Lordly might	70,000 gp
—	93–94	Metamagic, Empower, greater	73,000 gp
—	95–96	Metamagic, Quicken	75,500 gp
—	97–98	Alertness	85,000 gp
—	99	Metamagic, Maximize, greater	121,500 gp
—	100	Metamagic, Quicken, greater	170,000 gp

Slot none; **Price** 50,000 gp; **Weight** 5 lbs.

DESCRIPTION

This rod absorbs spells or spell-like abilities into itself. The magic absorbed must be a single-target spell or a ray directed at either the character holding the rod or her gear. The rod then nullifies the spell's effect and stores its potential until the wielder releases this energy in the form of spells of her own. She can instantly detect a spell's level as the rod absorbs that spell's energy. Absorption requires no action on the part of the user if the rod is in hand at the time.

A running total of absorbed (and used) spell levels should be kept. The wielder of the rod can use captured spell energy to cast any spell she has prepared, without expending the preparation itself. The only restrictions are that the levels of spell energy stored in

the rod must be equal to or greater than the level of the spell the wielder wants to cast, that any material components required for the spell be present, and that the rod be in hand when casting. For casters such as bards or sorcerers who do not prepare spells, the rod's energy can be used to cast any spell of the appropriate level or levels that they know.

A *rod of absorption* absorbs a maximum of 50 spell levels and can thereafter only discharge any remaining potential it might have. The rod cannot be recharged. The wielder knows the rod's remaining absorbing potential and current amount of stored energy.

To determine the absorption potential remaining in a newly found rod, roll d% and divide the result by 2. Then roll d% again: on a result of 71–100, half the levels already absorbed by the rod are still stored within.

CONSTRUCTION

Requirements Craft Rod, *spell turning*; **Cost** 25,000 gp

ROD OF ALERTNESS

Aura moderate abjuration, divination, enchantment, and evocation; **CL** 11th

Slot none; **Price** 85,000 gp; **Weight** 4 lbs.

DESCRIPTION

This rod is indistinguishable from a +1 *light mace*. It has eight flanges on its mace-like head. The rod bestows a +1 insight bonus on initiative checks. If grasped firmly, the rod enables the holder to use *detect evil, detect good, detect chaos, detect law, detect magic, discern lies, light,* or *see invisibility.* Each different use is a standard action.

If the head of a *rod of alertness* is planted in the ground and the possessor wills it to alertness (a standard action), the rod senses any creatures within 120 feet who intend to harm the possessor. At the same time, the rod creates the effect of a *prayer* spell upon all creatures friendly to the possessor in a 20-foot radius. Immediately thereafter, the rod sends forth a mental alert to these friendly creatures, warning them of any unfriendly creatures within the 120-foot radius. These effects last for 10 minutes, and the rod can perform this function once per day. Last, the rod can be used to simulate the casting of an *animate objects* spell, utilizing any 11 (or fewer) Small objects located roughly around the perimeter of a 5-foot-radius circle centered on the rod when planted in the ground. Objects remain animated for 11 rounds. The rod can perform this function once per day.

CONSTRUCTION

Requirements Craft Rod, *alarm, animate objects, detect chaos, detect evil, detect good, detect law, detect magic, discern lies, light, prayer, see invisibility*; **Cost** 42,500 gp

ROD OF CANCELLATION

Aura strong abjuration; **CL** 17th

Slot none; **Price** 11,000 gp; **Weight** 5 lbs.

DESCRIPTION

This dreaded rod is a bane to magic items, for its touch drains an item of all magical properties. The item touched must make a

DC 23 Will save to prevent the rod from draining it. If a creature is holding it at the time, then the item can use the holder's Will save bonus in place of its own if the holder's is better. In such cases, contact is made by making a melee touch attack roll. Upon draining an item, the rod itself becomes brittle and cannot be used again. Drained items are only restorable by *wish* or *miracle*. If a *sphere of annihilation* and a *rod of cancellation* negate each other, nothing can restore either of them.

CONSTRUCTION

Requirements Craft Rod, *mage's disjunction*; **Cost** 5,500 gp

ROD OF ENEMY DETECTION

Aura moderate divination; **CL** 10th

Slot none; **Price** 23,500 gp; **Weight** 5 lbs.

DESCRIPTION

This device pulses in the wielder's hand and points in the direction of any creature or creatures hostile to the bearer of the device (nearest ones first). These creatures can be invisible, ethereal, hidden, disguised, or in plain sight. Detection range is 60 feet. If the bearer of the rod concentrates for a full round, the rod pinpoints the location of the nearest enemy and indicates how many enemies are within range. The rod can be used to pinpoint three times each day, each use lasting up to 10 minutes. Activating the rod is a standard action.

CONSTRUCTION

Requirements Craft Rod, *true seeing*; **Cost** 11,750 gp

ROD OF FLAILING

Aura moderate enchantment; **CL** 9th

Slot none; **Price** 50,000 gp; **Weight** 5 lbs.

DESCRIPTION

Upon the command of its possessor, the rod activates, changing from a normal-seeming rod to a +3/+3 *dire flail*. The dire flail is a double weapon, which means that each of the weapon's heads can be used to attack. The wielder can gain an extra attack (with the second head) at the cost of making all attacks at a −2 penalty (as if she had the Two-Weapon Fighting feat).

Once per day, the wielder can use a free action to cause the rod to grant her a +4 deflection bonus to Armor Class and a +4 resistance bonus on saving throws for 10 minutes. The rod need not be in weapon form to grant this benefit.

Transforming it into a weapon or back into a rod is a move action.

CONSTRUCTION

Requirements Craft Rod, Craft Magic Arms and Armor, *bless*; **Cost** 25,000 gp

ROD OF FLAME EXTINGUISHING

Aura strong transmutation; **CL** 12th

Slot none; **Price** 15,000 gp; **Weight** 5 lbs.

DESCRIPTION

This rod can extinguish Medium or smaller nonmagical fires with simply a touch (a standard action). For the rod to be effective against other sorts of fires, the wielder must expend 1 or more of the rod's charges.

Extinguishing a Large or larger nonmagical fire, or a magic fire of Medium or smaller (such as that of a *flaming* weapon or a *burning hands* spell), expends 1 charge. Continual magic flames, such as those of a weapon or a fire creature, are suppressed for 6 rounds and flare up again after that time. To extinguish an instantaneous fire spell, the rod must be within the area of the effect and the wielder must have used a ready action, effectively countering the entire spell.

When applied to Large or larger magic fires, such as those caused by *fireball*, *flame strike*, or *wall of fire*, extinguishing the flames expends 2 charges from the rod.

If a *rod of flame extinguishing* is touched to a creature with the fire subtype by making a successful melee touch attack, the rod deals 6d6 points of damage to the creature. This use requires 3 charges.

A *rod of flame extinguishing* has 10 charges when found. Spent charges are renewed every day, so that a wielder can expend up to 10 charges in any 24-hour period.

CONSTRUCTION

Requirements Craft Rod, *pyrotechnics*; **Cost** 7,500 gp

ROD OF LORDLY MIGHT

Aura strong enchantment, evocation, necromancy, and transmutation; **CL** 19th

Slot none; **Price** 70,000 gp; **Weight** 10 lbs.

DESCRIPTION

This rod has functions that are spell-like, and it can also be used as a magic weapon of various sorts. In addition, it has several more mundane uses. The *rod of lordly might* is metal, thicker than other rods, with a flanged ball at one end and six stud-like buttons along its length. Pushing any of the rod's buttons is an action equivalent to drawing a weapon, and the rod weighs 10 pounds.

The following spell-like functions of the rod can each be used once per day.

- *Hold person* upon a touched creature, if the wielder so commands (Will DC 14 negates). The wielder must choose to use this power (a free action) and then succeed on a melee touch attack to activate the power. If the attack fails, the effect is lost.
- *Fear* upon all enemies viewing it, if the wielder so desires (10-foot maximum range, Will DC 16 partial). Invoking this power is a standard action.
- Deal 2d4 hit points of damage to an opponent on a successful touch attack (Will DC 17 half) and cure the wielder of the same amount of damage. The wielder must choose to use this power before attacking, as with *hold person*.

The following functions of the rod have no limit on the number of times they can be employed.

- In its normal form, the rod can be used as a +2 *light mace*.
- When button 1 is pushed, the rod becomes a +1 *flaming longsword*. A blade springs from the ball, with the ball itself becoming the sword's hilt. The weapon stretches to an overall length of 4 feet.
- When button 2 is pushed, the rod becomes a +4 *battleaxe*. A wide

blade springs forth at the ball, and the whole lengthens to 4 feet.

- When button 3 is pushed, the rod becomes a +3 *shortspear* or +3 *longspear*. The spear blade springs forth, and the handle can be lengthened up to 12 feet (wielder's choice) for an overall length ranging from 6 feet to 15 feet. At its 15-foot length, the rod is suitable for use as a lance.

The following other functions of the rod also have no limit on the number of times they can be employed.

- Climbing pole/ladder. When button 4 is pushed, a spike that can anchor in stone is extruded from the ball, while the other end sprouts three sharp hooks. The rod lengthens to anywhere between 5 and 50 feet in a single round, stopping when button 4 is pushed again. Horizontal bars 3 inches long fold out from the sides, 1 foot apart, in staggered progression. The rod is firmly held by the spike and hooks and can bear up to 4,000 pounds. The wielder can retract the pole by pushing button 5.
- The ladder function can be used to force open doors. The wielder plants the rod's base 30 feet or less from the portal to be forced and in line with it, then pushes button 4. The force exerted has a Strength modifier of +12.
- When button 6 is pushed, the rod indicates magnetic north and gives the wielder knowledge of his approximate depth beneath the surface or height above it.

CONSTRUCTION

Requirements Craft Magic Arms and Armor, Craft Rod, *bull's strength*, *fear*, *flame blade*, *hold person*, *inflict light wounds*; **Cost** 35,000 gp

ROD OF METAL AND MINERAL DETECTION

Aura moderate divination; **CL** 9th

Slot none; **Price** 10,500 gp; **Weight** 5 lbs.

DESCRIPTION

This rod is valued by treasure hunters and miners alike, for it pulses and hums in the wielder's hand in the proximity of metal. As the wearer aims the rod, the pulsations grow more noticeable as it points to the largest mass of metal within 30 feet. However, the wielder can concentrate on a specific metal or mineral. If the specific mineral is within 30 feet, the rod points to any places it is located, and the rod wielder knows the approximate quantity as well. If more than one deposit of the specified metal or mineral is within range, the rod points to the largest cache first. Each operation requires a full-round action.

CONSTRUCTION

Requirements Craft Rod, *locate object*; **Cost** 5,250 gp

ROD OF NEGATION

Aura strong varied; **CL** 15th

Slot none; **Price** 37,000 gp; **Weight** 5 lbs.

DESCRIPTION

This device negates the spell or spell-like function or functions of magic items. The wielder points the rod at the magic item, and a pale gray beam shoots forth to touch the target device, attacking as a ray (a ranged touch attack). The ray functions as a *greater dispel magic* spell, except it only affects magic items. To negate instantaneous effects from an item, the rod wielder needs to have a readied action. The dispel check uses the rod's caster level (15th). The target item gets no saving throw, although the rod can't negate artifacts (even minor artifacts). The rod can function three times per day.

CONSTRUCTION

Requirements Craft Rod, *dispel magic*, and *limited wish* or *miracle*; **Cost** 18,500 gp

ROD OF THE PYTHON

Aura moderate transmutation; **CL** 10th

Slot none; **Price** 13,000 gp; **Weight** 10 lbs.

DESCRIPTION

Unlike most rods, one end of this rod curls and twists back on itself in a crook—the tip of this crook sometimes looks like the head of a snake. The rod itself is about 4 feet long and weighs 10 pounds. It strikes as a +1/+1 *quarterstaff*. If the user throws the rod to the ground (a standard action), it grows to become a constrictor snake by the end of the round. The python obeys all commands of the owner. (In animal form, it retains the +1 enhancement bonus on attacks and damage possessed by the rod form.) The serpent returns to rod form (a full-round action) whenever the wielder desires, or whenever it moves farther than 100 feet from the owner. If the snake form is slain, it returns to rod form and cannot be activated again for three days. A *rod of the python* only functions if the possessor is good.

CONSTRUCTION

Requirements Craft Rod, Craft Magic Arms and Armor, *baleful polymorph*, creator must be good; **Cost** 6,500 gp

ROD OF RULERSHIP

Aura strong enchantment; **CL** 20th

Slot none; **Price** 60,000 gp; **Weight** 8 lbs.

DESCRIPTION

This rod looks like a royal scepter worth at least 5,000 gp in materials and workmanship alone. The wielder can command the obedience and fealty of creatures within 120 feet when she activates the device (a standard action). Creatures totaling 300 Hit Dice can be ruled, but creatures with Intelligence scores of 12 or higher are each entitled to a DC 16 Will save to negate the effect. Ruled creatures obey the wielder as if she were their absolute sovereign. Still, if the wielder gives a command that is contrary to the nature of the creatures commanded, the magic is broken. The rod can be used for 500 total minutes before crumbling to dust. This duration need not be continuous.

CONSTRUCTION

Requirements Craft Rod, *mass charm monster*; **Cost** 32,500 gp

ROD OF SECURITY

Aura strong conjuration; **CL** 20th

Slot none; **Price** 61,000 gp; **Weight** 5 lbs.

DESCRIPTION

This item creates a nondimensional space, a pocket paradise. There the rod's possessor and as many as 199 other creatures can stay in complete safety for a period of time, up to 200 days divided by the number of creatures affected. All fractions are rounded down. In this pocket paradise, creatures don't age, and natural healing takes place at twice the normal rate. Fresh water and food (fruits and vegetables only) are in abundance. The climate is comfortable for all creatures involved.

Activating the rod (a standard action) causes the wielder and all creatures touching the rod to be transported instantaneously to the paradise. Members of large groups can hold hands or otherwise maintain physical contact, allowing all connected creatures in a circle or a chain to be affected by the rod. Unwilling creatures get a DC 17 Will save to negate the effect. If such a creature succeeds on its save, other creatures beyond that point in a chain can still be affected by the rod.

When the rod's effect expires, is dismissed, or is dispelled, all the affected creatures instantly reappear in the location they occupied when the rod was activated. If something else occupies the space that a traveler would be returning to, then his body is displaced a sufficient distance to provide the space required for reentry. The rod's possessor can dismiss the effect whenever he wishes before the maximum time period expires, but the rod can only be activated once per week.

CONSTRUCTION

Requirements Craft Rod, *gate*; **Cost** 30,500 gp

ROD OF SPLENDOR

Aura strong conjuration and transmutation; **CL** 12th

Slot none; **Price** 25,000 gp; **Weight** 5 lbs.

DESCRIPTION

The possessor of this fantastically bejeweled rod gains a +4 enhancement bonus to her Charisma score for as long as she holds or carries the item. Once per day, the rod garbs her in magically created clothing of the finest fabrics, plus adornments of furs and jewels.

Apparel created by the magic of the rod remains in existence for 12 hours. However, if the possessor attempts to sell or give away any part of it, use it for a spell component, or the like, all the apparel immediately disappears. The same applies if any of it is forcibly taken from her.

The value of noble garb created by the rod ranges from 7,000 to 10,000 gp (1d4+6 × 1,000 gp)—1,000 gp for the fabric alone, 5,000 gp for the furs, and the rest for the jewel trim (maximum of twenty gems, maximum value 200 gp each).

In addition, the rod has a second special power, usable once per week. Upon command, it creates a palatial tent—a huge pavilion of silk 60 feet across. Inside the tent are temporary furnishings and food suitable to the splendor of the pavilion and sufficient to entertain as many as 100 people. The tent and its trappings last for 1 day. At the end of that time, the tent and all objects associated with it (including any items that were taken out of the tent) disappear.

CONSTRUCTION

Requirements Craft Rod, *eagle's splendor*, *fabricate*, *major creation*; **Cost** 12,500 gp

ROD OF THUNDER AND LIGHTNING

Aura moderate evocation; **CL** 9th

Slot none; **Price** 33,000 gp; **Weight** 5 lbs.

DESCRIPTION

Constructed of iron set with silver rivets, this rod has the properties of a +2 *light mace*. Its other powers are as follows.

- **Thunder:** Once per day, the rod can strike as a *+3 light mace*, and the opponent struck is stunned from the noise of the rod's impact (Fortitude DC 16 negates). Activating this sonic power counts as a free action, and it works if the wielder strikes an opponent within 1 round.
- **Lightning:** Once per day, when the wielder desires, a short spark of electricity can leap forth when the rod strikes an opponent to deal the normal damage for a *+2 light mace* (1d6+2) and an extra 2d6 points of electricity damage. Even when the rod might not score a normal hit in combat, if the roll was good enough to count as a successful melee touch attack, then the 2d6 points of electricity damage still apply. The wielder activates this power as a free action, and it works if he strikes an opponent within 1 round.
- **Thunderclap:** Once per day as a standard action, the wielder can cause the rod to give out a deafening noise, just as a *shout* spell (Fortitude DC 16 partial, 2d6 points of sonic damage, target deafened for 2d6 rounds).
- **Lightning Stroke:** Once per day as a standard action, the wielder can cause the rod to shoot out a 5-foot-wide *lightning bolt* (9d6 points of electricity damage, Reflex DC 16 half) to a range of 200 feet.
- **Thunder and Lightning:** Once per week as a standard action, the wielder of the rod can combine the thunderclap described above with a *lightning bolt*, as in the lightning stroke. The thunderclap affects all within 10 feet of the bolt. The lightning stroke deals 9d6 points of electricity damage (count rolls of 1 or 2 as rolls of 3, for a range of 27 to 54 points), and the thunderclap deals 2d6 points of sonic damage. A single DC 16 Reflex save applies for both effects.

CONSTRUCTION

Requirements Craft Magic Arms and Armor, Craft Rod, *lightning bolt*, *shout*; **Cost** 16,500 gp

ROD OF THE VIPER

Aura moderate necromancy; **CL** 10th

Slot none; **Price** 19,000 gp; **Weight** 5 lbs.

DESCRIPTION

This rod strikes as a +2 *heavy mace*. Once per day, upon command, the head of the rod becomes that of an actual serpent for 10 minutes. During this period, any successful strike with the rod deals its usual damage and also poisons the creature hit. This poison deals 1d3 Constitution damage per round for 6 rounds.

Poisoned creatures can make a DC 16 Fortitude save each round to negate the damage and end the affliction. Multiple hits extend the duration by 3 rounds and increase the DC by +2 for each hit. The rod only functions if its possessor is evil.

CONSTRUCTION

Requirements Craft Rod, Craft Magic Arms and Armor, *poison*, creator must be evil; **Cost** 9,500 gp

ROD OF WITHERING

Aura strong necromancy; **CL** 13th

Slot none; **Price** 25,000 gp; **Weight** 5 lbs.

DESCRIPTION

A *rod of withering* acts as a +1 *light mace* that deals no hit point damage. Instead, the wielder deals 1d4 points of Strength damage and 1d4 points of Constitution damage to any creature she touches with the rod (by making a melee touch attack). If she scores a critical hit, the damage from that hit is permanent ability drain. In either case, the defender negates the effect with a DC 17 Fortitude save.

CONSTRUCTION

Requirements Craft Rod, Craft Magic Arms and Armor, *contagion*; **Cost** 12,500 gp

ROD OF WONDER

Aura moderate enchantment; **CL** 10th

Slot none; **Price** 12,000 gp; **Weight** 5 lbs.

DESCRIPTION

A *rod of wonder* is a strange and unpredictable device that randomly generates any number of weird effects each time it is used. Activating the rod is a standard action. Typical powers of the rod include the following.

d%	Wondrous Effect
01–05	*Slow* target for 10 rounds (Will DC 15 negates).
06–10	*Faerie fire* surrounds the target.
11–15	Deludes wielder for 1 round into believing the rod functions as indicated by a second die roll (no save).
16–20	*Gust of wind*, but at windstorm force (Fortitude DC 14 negates).
21–25	Wielder learns target's surface thoughts (as with *detect thoughts*) for 1d4 rounds (no save).
26–30	*Stinking cloud* appears at 30-ft. range (Fortitude DC 15 negates).
31–33	Heavy rain falls for 1 round in 60-ft. radius centered on rod wielder.
34–36	Summon an animal—a rhino (01–25 on d%), elephant (26–50), or mouse (51–100).
37–46	*Lightning bolt* (70 ft. long, 5 ft. wide), 6d6 damage (Reflex DC 15 half).
47–49	A stream of 600 large butterflies pours forth and flutters around for 2 rounds, blinding everyone within 25 ft. (Reflex DC 14 negates).
50–53	*Enlarge person* on target if within 60 ft. of rod (Fortitude DC 13 negates).

54–58	*Darkness*, 30-ft.-diameter hemisphere, centered 30 ft. away from rod.
59–62	Grass grows in 160-square-ft. area before the rod, or grass existing there grows to 10 times normal size.
63–65	Turn ethereal any nonliving object of up to 1,000 lbs. mass and up to 30 cubic ft. in size.
66–69	Reduce wielder two size categories (no save) for 1 day.
70–79	*Fireball* at target or 100 ft. straight ahead, 6d6 damage (Reflex DC 15 half).
80–84	*Invisibility* covers rod wielder.
85–87	Leaves grow from target if within 60 ft. of rod. These last 24 hours.
88–90	10–40 gems, value 1 gp each, shoot forth in a 30-ft.-long stream. Each gem deals 1 point of damage to any creature in its path: roll 5d4 for the number of hits and divide them among the available targets.
91–95	Shimmering colors dance and play over a 40-ft.-by-30-ft. area in front of rod. Creatures therein are blinded for 1d6 rounds (Fortitude DC 15 negates).
96–97	Wielder (50% chance) or target (50% chance) turns permanently blue, green, or purple (no save).
98–100	*Flesh to stone* (or *stone to flesh* if target is stone already) if target is within 60 ft. (Fortitude DC 18 negates).

CONSTRUCTION

Requirements Craft Rod, *confusion*, creator must be chaotic; **Cost** 6,000 gp

SCROLLS

A scroll is a spell (or collection of spells) that has been stored in written form. A spell on a scroll can be used only once. The writing vanishes from the scroll when the spell is activated. Using a scroll is basically like casting a spell. The price of a scroll is equal to the level of the spell × the creator's caster level × 25 gp. If the scroll has a material component cost, it is added to the base price and cost to create. Table 15–15 gives sample prices for scrolls created at the lowest possible caster level for each spellcasting class. Note that some spells appear at different levels for different casters. The level of such spells depends on the caster scribing the scroll.

Physical Description: A scroll is a heavy sheet of fine vellum or high-quality paper. An area about 8-1/2 inches wide and 11 inches long is sufficient to hold one spell. The sheet is reinforced at the top and bottom with strips of leather slightly longer than the sheet is wide. A scroll holding more than one spell has the same width (about 8-1/2 inches) but is an extra foot or so long for each additional spell. Scrolls that hold three or more spells are usually fitted with reinforcing rods at each end rather than simple strips of leather. A scroll has AC 9, 1 hit point, hardness 0, and a break DC of 8.

To protect it from wrinkling or tearing, a scroll is rolled up from both ends to form a double cylinder. (This also helps the user unroll the scroll quickly.) The scroll is placed in a tube of ivory, jade, leather, metal, or wood. Most scroll cases are inscribed with magic symbols which often identify the owner or the spells stored on the scrolls inside. The symbols sometimes hide magic traps.

Activation: To activate a scroll, a spellcaster must read the spell written on it. This involves several steps and conditions.

Decipher the Writing: The writing on a scroll must be deciphered before a character can use it or know exactly what spell it contains. This requires a *read magic* spell or a successful Spellcraft check (DC 20 + spell level). Deciphering a scroll is a full-round action.

Deciphering a scroll to determine its contents does not activate its magic unless it is a specially prepared cursed scroll. A character can decipher the writing on a scroll in advance so that she can proceed directly to the next step when the time comes to use the scroll.

Activate the Spell: Activating a scroll requires reading the spell from the scroll. The character must be able to see and read the writing on the scroll. Activating a scroll spell requires no material components or focus. (The creator of the scroll provided these when scribing the scroll.) Note that some spells are effective only when cast on an item or items. In such a case, the scroll user must provide the item when activating the spell. Activating a scroll spell is subject to disruption just as casting a normally prepared spell would be. Using a scroll is like casting a spell for purposes of arcane spell failure chance.

To have any chance of activating a scroll spell, the scroll user must meet the following requirements.

- The spell must be of the correct type (arcane or divine). Arcane spellcasters (wizards, sorcerers, and bards) can only use scrolls containing arcane spells, and divine spellcasters (clerics, druids, paladins, and rangers) can only use scrolls containing divine spells. (The type of scroll a character creates is also determined by his class.)
- The user must have the spell on her class list.
- The user must have the requisite ability score.

If the user meets all the requirements noted above, and her caster level is at least equal to the spell's caster level, she can automatically activate the spell without a check. If she meets all three requirements but her own caster level is lower than the scroll spell's caster level, then she has to make a caster level check (DC = scroll's caster level + 1) to cast the spell successfully. If she fails, she must make a DC 5 Wisdom check to avoid a mishap (see Scroll Mishaps). A natural roll of 1 always fails, whatever the modifiers. If the caster level check fails but no mishap occurs, the scroll is not expended. Activating a scroll is a standard action (or the spell's casting time, whichever is longer) and it provokes attacks of opportunity exactly as casting a spell does.

Determine Effect: A spell successfully activated from a scroll works exactly like a spell prepared and cast the normal way. Assume the scroll spell's caster level is always the minimum level required to cast the spell for the character who scribed the scroll, unless the scriber specifically desired otherwise.

The writing for an activated spell disappears from the scroll as the spell is cast.

Scroll Mishaps: When a mishap occurs, the spell on the scroll has a reversed or harmful effect. Possible mishaps are given below.

- A surge of uncontrolled magical energy deals 1d6 points of damage per spell level to the scroll user.
- Spell strikes the scroll user or an ally instead of the intended target, or a random target nearby if the scroll user was the intended recipient.
- Spell takes effect at some random location within spell range.
- Spell's effect on the target is contrary to the spell's normal effect.
- The scroll user suffers some minor but bizarre effect related to the spell in some way. Most such effects should last only as long as the original spell's duration, or 2d10 minutes for instantaneous spells.
- Some innocuous item or items appear in the spell's area.
- Spell has delayed effect. Sometime within the next 1d12 hours, the spell activates. If the scroll user was the intended recipient, the spell takes effect normally. If the user was not the intended recipient, the spell goes off in the general direction of the original recipient or target, up to the spell's maximum range, if the target has moved away.

STAVES

A staff is a long shaft that stores several spells. Unlike wands, which can contain a wide variety of spells, each staff is of a certain kind and holds specific spells. A staff has 10 charges when created.

Physical Description: A typical staff measures anywhere from 4 feet to 7 feet long and is 2 inches to 3 inches thick, weighing about 5 pounds. Most staves are wood, but an exotic few are bone, metal, or even glass. A staff often has a gem or some device at its tip or is shod in metal at one or both ends. Staves are often decorated with carvings or runes. A typical staff is like a walking stick, quarterstaff, or cudgel. It has AC 7, 10 hit points, hardness 5, and a break DC of 24.

Activation: Staves use the spell trigger activation method, so casting a spell from a staff is usually a standard action that doesn't provoke attacks of opportunity. (If the spell being cast has a longer casting time than 1 standard action, however, it takes that long to cast the spell from a staff.) To activate a staff, a character must hold it forth in at least one hand (or whatever passes for a hand, for nonhumanoid creatures).

Special Qualities: Roll d%. A 01–30 result indicates that something (a design, inscription, or the like) provides some clue to the staff's function, and 31–100 indicates no special qualities.

TABLE 15-15: SCROLLS

Minor	Medium	Major	Spell Level	Caster Level
01–05	—	—	0	1st
06–50	—	—	1st	1st
51–95	01–05	—	2nd	3rd
96–100	06–65	—	3rd	5th
—	66–95	01–05	4th	7th
—	96–100	06–50	5th	9th
—	—	51–70	6th	11th
—	—	71–85	7th	13th
—	—	86–95	8th	15th
—	—	96–100	9th	17th

SCROLL COSTS

Spell Level	Cleric, Druid, Wizard	Sorcerer	Bard	Paladin, Ranger
0	12.5 gp	12.5 gp	12.5 gp	—
1st	25 gp	25 gp	25 gp	25 gp
2nd	150 gp	200 gp	200 gp	200 gp
3rd	375 gp	450 gp	525 gp	525 gp
4th	700 gp	800 gp	1,000 gp	1,000 gp
5th	1,125 gp	1,250 gp	1,625 gp	—
6th	1,650 gp	1,800 gp	2,400 gp	—
7th	2,275 gp	2,450 gp	—	—
8th	3,000 gp	3,200 gp	—	—
9th	3,825 gp	4,050 gp	—	—

Using Staves: Staves use the wielder's ability score and relevant feats to set the DC for saves against their spells. Unlike with other sorts of magic items, the wielder can use his caster level when activating the power of a staff if it's higher than the caster level of the staff.

This means that staves are far more potent in the hands of a powerful spellcaster. Because they use the wielder's ability score to set the save DC for the spell, spells from a staff are often harder to resist than those from other magic items, which use the minimum ability score required to cast the spell. Not only are aspects of the spell dependent on caster level (range, duration, and so on) potentially higher, but spells from a staff are also harder to dispel and have a better chance of overcoming a target's spell resistance.

Staves hold a maximum of 10 charges. Each spell cast from a staff consumes one or more charges. When a staff runs out of charges, it cannot be used until it is recharged. Each morning, when a spellcaster prepares spells or regains spell slots, he can also imbue one staff with a portion of his power so long as one or more of the spells cast by the staff is on his spell list and he is capable of casting at least one of the spells. Imbuing a staff with this power restores one charge to the staff, but the caster must forgo one prepared

TABLE 15-16: STAVES

Medium	Major	Staff	Market Price
01–15	01–03	*Charming*	17,600 gp
16–30	04–09	*Fire*	18,950 gp
31–40	10–11	*Swarming insects*	22,800 gp
41–55	12–13	*Size alteration*	26,150 gp
56–75	14–19	*Healing*	29,600 gp
76–90	20–24	*Frost*	41,400 gp
91–95	25–31	*Illumination*	51,500 gp
96–100	32–38	*Defense*	62,000 gp
—	39–45	*Abjuration*	82,000 gp
—	46–50	*Conjuration*	82,000 gp
—	51–55	*Divination*	82,000 gp
—	56–60	*Enchantment*	82,000 gp
—	61–65	*Evocation*	82,000 gp
—	66–70	*Illusion*	82,000 gp
—	71–75	*Necromancy*	82,000 gp
—	76–80	*Transmutation*	82,000 gp
—	81–85	*Earth and stone*	85,800 gp
—	86–90	*Woodlands*	100,400 gp
—	91–95	*Life*	109,400 gp
—	96–98	*Passage*	206,900 gp
—	99–100	*Power*	235,000 gp

spell or spell slot of a level equal to the highest-level spell cast by the staff. For example, a 9th-level wizard with a *staff of fire* could imbue the staff with one charge per day by using up one of his 4th-level spells. A staff cannot gain more than one charge per day and a caster cannot imbue more than one staff per day.

Furthermore, a staff can hold a spell of any level, unlike a wand, which is limited to spells of 4th level or lower. The minimum caster level of a staff is 8th.

STAFF OF ABJURATION

Aura strong abjuration; **CL** 13th

Slot none; **Price** 82,000 gp; **Weight** 5 lbs.

DESCRIPTION

Usually carved from the heartwood of an ancient oak or other large tree, this staff allows use of the following spells:

- *Dispel magic* (1 charge)
- *Resist energy* (1 charge)
- *Shield* (1 charge)
- *Dismissal* (2 charges)
- *Lesser globe of invulnerability* (2 charges)
- *Repulsion* (3 charges)

CONSTRUCTION

Requirements Craft Staff, *dismissal, dispel magic, lesser globe of invulnerability, repulsion, resist energy, shield*; **Cost** 41,000 gp

STAFF OF CHARMING

Aura moderate enchantment; **CL** 8th

Slot none; **Price** 17,600 gp; **Weight** 5 lbs.

DESCRIPTION

Made of twisting wood ornately shaped and carved, this staff allows use of the following spells:

- *Charm person* (1 charge)
- *Charm monster* (2 charges)

CONSTRUCTION

Requirements Craft Staff, *charm person, charm monster*; **Cost** 8,800 gp

STAFF OF CONJURATION

Aura strong conjuration; **CL** 13th

Slot none; **Price** 82,000 gp; **Weight** 5 lbs.

DESCRIPTION

This staff is usually made of ash or walnut and bears ornate carvings of many different kinds of creatures. It allows use of the following spells:

- *Stinking cloud* (1 charge)
- *Summon swarm* (1 charge)
- *Unseen servant* (1 charge)
- *Cloudkill* (2 charges)
- *Minor creation* (2 charges)
- *Summon monster VI* (3 charges)

CONSTRUCTION

Requirements Craft Staff, *cloudkill, minor creation, stinking cloud, summon monster VI, summon swarm, unseen servant*; **Cost** 41,000 gp

STAFF OF DEFENSE

Aura strong abjuration; **CL** 15th

Slot none; **Price** 62,000 gp; **Weight** 5 lbs.

DESCRIPTION

The *staff of defense* is a simple-looking polished wooden staff that throbs with power when held defensively. It allows use of the following spells:

- *Shield* (1 charge)
- *Shield of Faith* (1 charge)
- *Shield other* (1 charge)
- *Shield of law* (3 charges)

CONSTRUCTION

Requirements Craft Staff, *shield, shield of faith, shield of law, shield other*, creator must be lawful; **Cost** 31,000 gp

STAFF OF EARTH AND STONE

Aura moderate transmutation; **CL** 11th

Slot none; **Price** 85,800 gp; **Weight** 5 lbs.

DESCRIPTION

This staff is topped with a fist-sized emerald that gleams with smoldering power. It allows the use of the following spells:

- *Move earth* (1 charge)
- *Passwall* (1 charge)

CONSTRUCTION

Requirements Craft Staff, *move earth, passwall*; **Cost** 42,900 gp

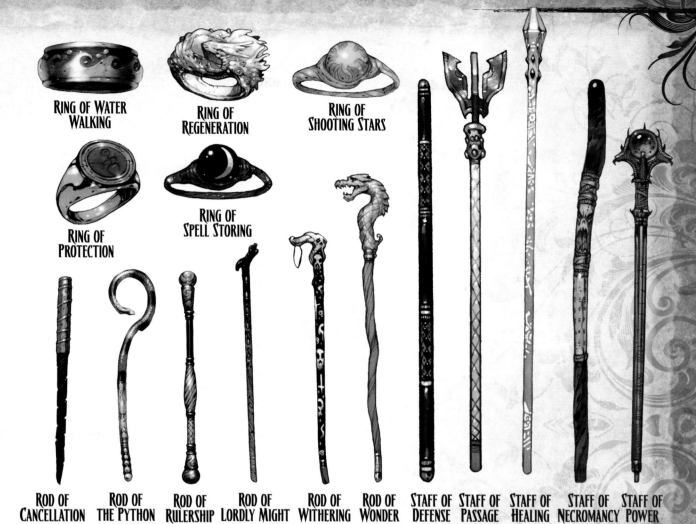

RING OF WATER WALKING

RING OF REGENERATION

RING OF SHOOTING STARS

RING OF PROTECTION

RING OF SPELL STORING

ROD OF CANCELLATION

ROD OF THE PYTHON

ROD OF RULERSHIP

ROD OF LORDLY MIGHT

ROD OF WITHERING

ROD OF WONDER

STAFF OF DEFENSE

STAFF OF PASSAGE

STAFF OF HEALING

STAFF OF NECROMANCY

STAFF OF POWER

STAFF OF DIVINATION

Aura strong divination; **CL** 13th

Slot none; **Price** 82,000 gp; **Weight** 5 lbs.

DESCRIPTION

Made from a supple length of willow, often with a forked tip, this staff allows use of the following spells:

- *Detect secret doors* (1 charge)
- *Locate object* (1 charge)
- *Tongues* (1 charge)
- *Locate creature* (2 charges)
- *Prying eyes* (2 charges)
- *True seeing* (3 charges)

CONSTRUCTION

Requirements Craft Staff, *detect secret doors, locate creature, locate object, prying eyes, tongues, true seeing;* **Cost** 41,000 gp

STAFF OF ENCHANTMENT

Aura strong enchantment; **CL** 13th

Slot none; **Price** 82,000 gp; **Weight** 5 lbs.

DESCRIPTION

Often made from applewood and topped with a clear crystal, this staff allows use of the following spells:

- *Hideous laughter* (1 charge)
- *Sleep* (1 charge)
- *Suggestion* (1 charge)
- *Crushing despair* (2 charges)
- *Mind fog* (2 charges)
- *Mass suggestion* (3 charges)

CONSTRUCTION

Requirements Craft Staff, *crushing despair, hideous laughter, mass suggestion, mind fog, sleep, suggestion;* **Cost** 41,000 gp

STAFF OF EVOCATION

Aura strong evocation; **CL** 13th

Slot none; **Price** 82,000 gp; **Weight** 5 lbs.

DESCRIPTION

This smooth hickory or yew staff allows use of the following spells:

- *Fireball* (1 charge)
- *Magic missile* (1 charge)
- *Shatter* (1 charge)

- *Ice storm* (2 charges)
- *Wall of force* (2 charges)
- *Chain lightning* (3 charges)

CONSTRUCTION

Requirements Craft Staff, *chain lightning, fireball, ice storm, magic missile, shatter, wall of force*; **Cost** 41,000 gp

STAFF OF FIRE

Aura moderate evocation; **CL** 8th

Slot none; **Price** 18,950 gp; **Weight** 5 lbs.

DESCRIPTION

Crafted from bronzewood with brass bindings, this staff allows use of the following spells:

- *Burning hands* (1 charge)
- *Fireball* (2 charges)
- *Wall of fire* (3 charges)

CONSTRUCTION

Requirements Craft Staff, *burning hands, fireball, wall of fire*; **Cost** 9,475 gp

STAFF OF FROST

Aura moderate evocation; **CL** 10th

Slot none; **Price** 41,400 gp; **Weight** 5 lbs.

DESCRIPTION

Tipped on either end with a glistening diamond, this rune-covered staff allows use of the following spells:

- *Ice storm* (1 charge)
- *Wall of ice* (2 charges)
- *Cone of cold* (3 charges)

CONSTRUCTION

Requirements Craft Staff, *cone of cold, ice storm, wall of ice*; **Cost** 20,700 gp

STAFF OF HEALING

Aura moderate conjuration; **CL** 8th

Slot none; **Price** 29,600 gp; **Weight** 5 lbs.

DESCRIPTION

This white ash staff is decorated with inlaid silver runes. It allows use of the following spells:

- *Cure serious wounds* (1 charge)
- *Lesser restoration* (1 charge)
- *Remove blindness/deafness* (2 charges)
- *Remove disease* (3 charges)

CONSTRUCTION

Requirements Craft Staff, *cure serious wounds, lesser restoration, remove blindness/deafness, remove disease*; **Cost** 14,800 gp

STAFF OF ILLUMINATION

Aura strong evocation; **CL** 15th

Slot none; **Price** 51,500 gp; **Weight** 5 lbs.

DESCRIPTION

This staff is usually sheathed in silver and decorated with sunbursts. It allows use of the following spells:

- *Dancing lights* (1 charge)
- *Flare* (1 charge)
- *Daylight* (2 charges)
- *Sunburst* (3 charges)

CONSTRUCTION

Requirements Craft Staff, *dancing lights, daylight, flare, sunburst*; **Cost** 20,750 gp

STAFF OF ILLUSION

Aura strong illusion; **CL** 13th

Slot none; **Price** 82,000 gp; **Weight** 5 lbs.

DESCRIPTION

This staff is made from ebony or other dark wood and carved into an intricately twisted, fluted, or spiral shape. It allows use of the following spells:

- *Disguise self* (1 charge)
- *Major image* (1 charge)
- *Mirror image* (1 charge)
- *Persistent image* (2 charges)
- *Rainbow pattern* (2 charges)
- *Mislead* (3 charges)

CONSTRUCTION

Requirements Craft Staff, *disguise self, major image, mirror image, persistent image, mislead, rainbow pattern*; **Cost** 41,000 gp

STAFF OF LIFE

Aura moderate conjuration; **CL** 11th

Slot none; **Price** 109,400 gp; **Weight** 5 lbs.

DESCRIPTION

A *staff of life* is made of thick polished oak shod in gold and decorated with sinuous runes. This staff allows use of the following spells:

- *Heal* (1 charge)
- *Raise dead* (5 charges)

CONSTRUCTION

Requirements Craft Staff, *heal, raise dead*; **Cost** 79,700 gp

STAFF OF NECROMANCY

Aura strong necromancy; **CL** 13th

Slot none; **Price** 82,000 gp; **Weight** 5 lbs.

DESCRIPTION

This staff is made from ebony or other dark wood and carved with images of bones and skulls mingled with strange spidery runes. It allows use of the following spells:

- *Cause fear* (1 charge)
- *Ghoul touch* (1 charge)
- *Halt undead* (1 charge)
- *Enervation* (2 charges)
- *Waves of fatigue* (2 charges)
- *Circle of death* (3 charges)

CONSTRUCTION

Requirements Craft Staff, *cause fear, circle of death, enervation, ghoul touch, halt undead, waves of fatigue*; **Cost** 41,000 gp

STAFF OF PASSAGE

Aura strong varied; **CL** 17th

Slot none; **Price** 206,900 gp; **Weight** 5 lbs.

DESCRIPTION

This potent item allows use of the following spells:

- *Dimension door* (1 charge)
- *Passwall* (1 charge)
- *Greater teleport* (2 charges)
- *Phase door* (2 charges)
- *Astral projection* (2 charges)

CONSTRUCTION

Requirements Craft Staff, *astral projection, dimension door, greater teleport, passwall, phase door*; **Cost** 115,950 gp

STAFF OF POWER

Aura strong varied; **CL** 15th

Slot none; **Price** 235,000 gp; **Weight** 5 lbs.

DESCRIPTION

The *staff of power* is a very potent magic item with offensive and defensive abilities. It is usually topped with a glistening gem that often burns from within with a flickering red light. The staff allows the use of the following spells:

- *Continual flame* (1 charge)
- *Fireball* (heightened to 5th level) (1 charge)
- *Levitate* (1 charge)
- *Lightning bolt* (heightened to 5th level) (1 charge)
- *Magic missile* (1 charge)
- *Ray of enfeeblement* (heightened to 5th level) (1 charge)
- *Cone of cold* (2 charges)
- *Globe of invulnerability* (2 charges)
- *Hold monster* (2 charges)
- *Wall of force* (in a 10-ft.-diameter hemisphere around the caster only) (2 charges)

The wielder of a *staff of power* gains a +2 luck bonus to AC and on saving throws. The staff is also a +2 *quarterstaff*, and its wielder may use it to smite opponents. If 1 charge is expended (as a free action), the staff causes double damage (×3 on a critical hit) for 1 round.

A *staff of power* can be used for a retributive strike, requiring it to be broken by its wielder. (If this breaking of the staff is purposeful and declared by the wielder, it can be performed as a standard action that does not require the wielder to make a Strength check.) All charges currently in the staff are instantly released in a 30-foot spread. All within 2 squares of the broken staff take points of damage equal to 20 × the number of charges in the staff, those 3 or 4 squares away take 15 ×the number of charges in damage, and those 5 or 6 squares distant take 10 × the number of charges in damage. All those affected can make DC 17 Reflex saves to reduce the damage by half.

The character breaking the staff has a 50% chance of traveling to another plane of existence, but if he does not, the explosive release of spell energy destroys him. Only certain items, including the *staff of the magi* and the *staff of power*, are capable of being used for a retributive strike.

CONSTRUCTION

Requirements Craft Staff, Craft Magic Arms and Armor, *cone of cold, continual flame,* heightened *fireball, globe of invulnerability, hold monster, levitate,* heightened *lightning bolt, magic missile,* heightened *ray of enfeeblement, wall of force;* **Cost** 117,500 gp

STAFF OF SIZE ALTERATION

Aura moderate transmutation; **CL** 8th

Slot none; **Price** 26,150 gp; **Weight** 5 lbs.

DESCRIPTION

This staff of dark wood is relatively more stout and sturdy than most magical staves, with a gnarled and twisted knot of wood at the top end. It allows use of the following spells:

- *Enlarge person* (1 charge)
- *Reduce person* (1 charge)
- *Shrink item* (2 charges)
- *Mass enlarge person* (3 charges)
- *Mass reduce person* (3 charges)

CONSTRUCTION

Requirements Craft Staff, *enlarge person, mass enlarge person, mass reduce person, reduce person, shrink item;* **Cost** 13,075 gp

STAFF OF SWARMING INSECTS

Aura moderate conjuration; **CL** 9th

Slot none; **Price** 22,800 gp; **Weight** 5 lbs.

DESCRIPTION

Made of twisted darkwood covered with knots and nodules resembling crawling insects (which occasionally seem to move), this staff allows use of the following spells:

- *Summon swarm* (1 charge)
- *Insect plague* (3 charges)

CONSTRUCTION

Requirements Craft Staff, *insect plague, summon swarm;* **Cost** 11,400 gp

STAFF OF TRANSMUTATION

Aura strong transmutation; **CL** 13th

Slot none; **Price** 82,000 gp; **Weight** 5 lbs.

DESCRIPTION

This staff is generally carved from or decorated with petrified wood or fossilized bone, each etched with tiny but complex runes. It allows use of the following spells:

- *Alter self* (1 charge)
- *Blink* (1 charge)
- *Expeditious retreat* (1 charge)
- *Baleful polymorph* (2 charges)
- *Polymorph* (2 charges)
- *Disintegrate* (3 charges)

CONSTRUCTION

Requirements Craft Staff, *alter self, baleful polymorph, blink, disintegrate, expeditious retreat, polymorph;* **Cost** 41,000 gp

STAFF OF THE WOODLANDS

Aura strong varied; **CL** 13th

Slot none; **Price** 100,400 gp; **Weight** 5 lbs.

DESCRIPTION

Appearing to have grown naturally into its shape, this oak, ash, or yew staff allows use of the following spells:

- *Charm animal* (1 charge)
- *Speak with animals* (1 charge)
- *Barkskin* (2 charges)
- *Summon nature's ally VI* (3 charges)
- *Wall of thorns* (3 charges)
- *Animate plants* (4 charges)

The staff may be used as a weapon, functioning as a +2 *quarterstaff*. The *staff of the woodlands* also allows its wielder to cast *pass without trace* at will, with no charge cost. These two attributes continue to function after all the charges are expended.

CONSTRUCTION

Requirements Craft Magic Arms and Armor, Craft Staff, *animate plants, barkskin, charm animal, pass without trace, speak with animals, summon nature's ally VI, wall of thorns*; **Cost** 50,500 gp

WANDS

A wand is a thin baton that contains a single spell of 4th level or lower. A wand has 50 charges when created—each charge allows the use of the wand's spell one time. A wand that runs out of charges is just a stick. The price of a wand is equal to the level of the spell × the creator's caster level × 750 gp. If the wand has a material component cost, it is added to the base price and cost to create once for each charge (50 × material component cost). Table 15–17 gives sample prices for wands created at the lowest possible caster level for each spellcasting class. Note that some spells appear at different levels for different casters. The level of such spells depends on the caster crafting the wand.

TABLE 15-17: WANDS

Minor	Medium	Major	Spell Level	Caster Level
01–05	—	—	0	1st
06–60	—	—	1st	1st
61–100	01–60	—	2nd	3rd
—	61–100	01–60	3rd	5th
—	—	61–100	4th	7th

WAND COSTS

Spell Level	Cleric, Druid, Wizard	Sorcerer	Bard	Paladin, Ranger
0	375 gp	375 gp	375 gp	—
1st	750 gp	750 gp	750 gp	750 gp
2nd	4,500 gp	6,000 gp	6,000 gp	6,000 gp
3rd	11,250 gp	13,500 gp	15,750 gp	15,750 gp
4th	21,000 gp	24,000 gp	30,000 gp	30,000 gp

Physical Description: A wand is 6 to 12 inches long, 1/4 inch thick, and weighs no more than 1 ounce. Most wands are wood, but some are bone, metal, or even crystal. A typical wand has AC 7, 5 hit points, hardness 5, and a break DC of 16.

Activation: Wands use the spell trigger activation method, so casting a spell from a wand is usually a standard action that doesn't provoke attacks of opportunity. (If the spell being cast has a longer casting time than 1 action, however, it takes that long to cast the spell from a wand.) To activate a wand, a character must hold it in hand (or whatever passes for a hand, for nonhumanoid creatures) and point it in the general direction of the target or area. A wand may be used while grappling or while swallowed whole.

Special Qualities: Roll d%. A 01–30 result indicates that something (a design, inscription, or the like) provides some clue to the wand's function, and 31–100 indicates no special qualities.

WONDROUS ITEMS

This is a catch all category for anything that doesn't fall into the other groups. Anyone can use a wondrous item (unless specified otherwise in the description).

Physical Description: Varies.

Activation: Usually use-activated or command word, but details vary from item to item.

Special Qualities: Roll d%. An 01 result indicates the wondrous item is intelligent, 02–31 indicates that something (a design, inscription, or the like) provides a clue to its function, and 32–100 indicates no special qualities. Intelligent items have extra abilities and sometimes extraordinary powers and special purposes (see Intelligent Items later in this chapter).

Wondrous items with charges can never be intelligent.

AMULET OF MIGHTY FISTS

Aura faint evocation; **CL** 5th

Slot neck; **Price** 4,000 gp (+1), 16,000 gp (+2), 36,000 gp (+3), 64,000 gp (+4), 100,000 gp (+5); **Weight** —

DESCRIPTION

This amulet grants an enhancement bonus of +1 to +5 on attack and damage rolls with unarmed attacks and natural weapons.

Alternatively, this amulet can grant melee weapon special abilities, so long as they can be applied to unarmed attacks. See Table 15–9 for a list of abilities. Special abilities count as additional bonuses for determining the market value of the item, but do not modify attack or damage bonuses. An *amulet of mighty fists* cannot have a modified bonus (enhancement bonus plus special ability bonus equivalents) higher than +5. An *amulet of mighty fists* does not need to have a +1 enhancement bonus to grant a melee weapon special ability.

CONSTRUCTION

Requirements Craft Wondrous Item, *greater magic fang*, creator's caster level must be at least three times the amulet's bonus, plus any requirements of the melee weapon special abilities; **Cost** 2,000 gp (+1), 8,000 gp (+2), 18,000 gp (+3), 32,000 gp (+4), 50,000 gp (+5)

TABLE 15-18: MINOR WONDROUS ITEMS

d%	Item	Market Price
01	Feather token, anchor	50 gp
02	Universal solvent	50 gp
03	Elixir of love	150 gp
04	Unguent of timelessness	150 gp
05	Feather token, fan	200 gp
06	Dust of tracelessness	250 gp
07	Elixir of hiding	250 gp
08	Elixir of tumbling	250 gp
09	Elixir of swimming	250 gp
10	Elixir of vision	250 gp
11	Silversheen	250 gp
12	Feather token, bird	300 gp
13	Feather token, tree	400 gp
14	Feather token, swan boat	450 gp
15	Elixir of truth	500 gp
16	Feather token, whip	500 gp
17	Dust of dryness	850 gp
18	Hand of the mage	900 gp
19	Bracers of armor +1	1,000 gp
20	Cloak of resistance +1	1,000 gp
21	Pearl of power, 1st-level spell	1,000 gp
22	Phylactery of faithfulness	1,000 gp
23	Salve of slipperiness	1,000 gp
24	Elixir of fire breath	1,100 gp
25	Pipes of the sewers	1,150 gp
26	Dust of illusion	1,200 gp
27	Brooch of shielding	1,500 gp
28	Necklace of fireballs type I	1,650 gp
29	Dust of appearance	1,800 gp
30	Hat of disguise	1,800 gp
31	Pipes of sounding	1,800 gp
32	Efficient quiver	1,800 gp
33	Amulet of natural armor +1	2,000 gp
34	Handy haversack	2,000 gp
35	Horn of fog	2,000 gp
36	Elemental gem	2,250 gp
37	Robe of bones	2,400 gp
38	Sovereign glue	2,400 gp
39	Bag of holding type I	2,500 gp
40	Boots of elvenkind	2,500 gp
41	Boots of the winterlands	2,500 gp
42	Candle of truth	2,500 gp
43	Cloak of elvenkind	2,500 gp
44	Eyes of the eagle	2,500 gp
45	Goggles of minute seeing	2,500 gp
46	Scarab, golembane	2,500 gp
47	Necklace of fireballs type II	2,700 gp
48	Stone of alarm	2,700 gp
49	Bead of force	3,000 gp
50	Chime of opening	3,000 gp
51	Horseshoes of speed	3,000 gp
52	Rope of climbing	3,000 gp
53	Bag of tricks, gray	3,400 gp
54	Dust of disappearance	3,500 gp
55	Lens of detection	3,500 gp
56	Vestment, druid's	3,750 gp
57	Figurine of wondrous power, silver raven	3,800 gp
58	Amulet of mighty fists +1	4,000 gp
59	Belt of giant strength +2	4,000 gp
60	Belt of incredible dexterity +2	4,000 gp
61	Belt of mighty constitution +2	4,000 gp
62	Bracers of armor +2	4,000 gp
63	Cloak of resistance +2	4,000 gp
64	Gloves of arrow snaring	4,000 gp
65	Headband of alluring charisma +2	4,000 gp
66	Headband of inspired wisdom +2	4,000 gp
67	Headband of vast intelligence +2	4,000 gp
68	Ioun stone, clear spindle	4,000 gp
69	Restorative ointment	4,000 gp
70	Marvelous pigments	4,000 gp
71	Pearl of power, 2nd-level spell	4,000 gp
72	Stone salve	4,000 gp
73	Necklace of fireballs type III	4,350 gp
74	Circlet of persuasion	4,500 gp
75	Slippers of spider climbing	4,800 gp
76	Incense of meditation	4,900 gp
77	Bag of holding type II	5,000 gp
78	Bracers of archery, lesser	5,000 gp
79	Ioun stone, dusty rose prism	5,000 gp
80	Helm of comprehend languages and read magic	5,200 gp
81	Vest of escape	5,200 gp
82	Eversmoking bottle	5,400 gp
83	Sustaining spoon	5,400 gp
84	Necklace of fireballs type IV	5,400 gp
85	Boots of striding and springing	5,500 gp
86	Wind fan	5,500 gp
87	Necklace of fireballs type V	5,850 gp
88	Horseshoes of a zephyr	6,000 gp
89	Pipes of haunting	6,000 gp
90	Gloves of swimming and climbing	6,250 gp
91	Crown of blasting, minor	6,480 gp
92	Horn of goodness/evil	6,500 gp
93	Robe of useful items	7,000 gp
94	Boat, folding	7,200 gp
95	Cloak of the manta ray	7,200 gp
96	Bottle of air	7,250 gp
97	Bag of holding type III	7,400 gp
98	Periapt of health	7,400 gp
99	Boots of levitation	7,500 gp
100	Harp of charming	7,500 gp

Table 15-19: Medium Wondrous Items

d%	Item	Market Price	d%	Item	Market Price
01	Amulet of natural armor +2	8,000 gp	51	Belt of might constitution +4	16,000 gp
02	Golem manual, flesh	8,000 gp	52	Belt of physical perfection +2	16,000 gp
03	Hand of glory	8,000 gp	53	Boots, winged	16,000 gp
04	Ioun stone, deep red sphere	8,000 gp	54	Bracers of armor +4	16,000 gp
05	Ioun stone, incandescent blue sphere	8,000 gp	55	Cloak of resistance +4	16,000 gp
06	Ioun stone, pale blue rhomboid	8,000 gp	56	Headband of alluring charisma +4	16,000 gp
07	Ioun stone, pink and green sphere	8,000 gp	57	Headband of inspired wisdom +4	16,000 gp
08	Ioun stone, pink rhomboid	8,000 gp	58	Headband of mental superiority +2	16,000 gp
09	Ioun stone, scarlet and blue sphere	8,000 gp	59	Headband of vast intelligence +4	16,000 gp
10	Deck of illusions	8,100 gp	60	Pearl of power, 4th-level spell	16,000 gp
11	Necklace of fireballs type VI	8,100 gp	61	Scabbard of keen edges	16,000 gp
12	Candle of invocation	8,400 gp	62	Figurine of wondrous power, golden lions	16,500 gp
13	Robe of blending	8,400 gp	63	Chime of interruption	16,800 gp
14	Bag of tricks, rust	8,500 gp	64	Broom of flying	17,000 gp
15	Necklace of fireballs type VII	8,700 gp	65	Figurine of wondrous power, marble elephant	17,000 gp
16	Bracers of armor +3	9,000 gp	66	Amulet of natural armor +3	18,000 gp
17	Cloak of resistance +3	9,000 gp	67	Ioun stone, iridescent spindle	18,000 gp
18	Decanter of endless water	9,000 gp	68	Bracelet of friends	19,000 gp
19	Necklace of adaptation	9,000 gp	69	Carpet of flying, 5 ft. by 5 ft.	20,000 gp
20	Pearl of power, 3rd-level spell	9,000 gp	70	Horn of blasting	20,000 gp
21	Figurine of wondrous power, serpentine owl	9,100 gp	71	Ioun stone, pale lavender ellipsoid	20,000 gp
22	Strand of prayer beads, lesser	9,600 gp	72	Ioun stone, pearly white spindle	20,000 gp
23	Bag of holding type IV	10,000 gp	73	Portable hole	20,000 gp
24	Belt of physical might +2	10,000 gp	74	Stone of good luck (luckstone)	20,000 gp
25	Figurine of wondrous power, bronze griffon	10,000 gp	75	Figurine of wondrous power, ivory goats	21,000 gp
26	Figurine of wondrous power, ebony fly	10,000 gp	76	Rope of entanglement	21,000 gp
27	Glove of storing	10,000 gp	77	Golem manual, stone	22,000 gp
28	Headband of mental prowess +2	10,000 gp	78	Mask of the skull	22,000 gp
29	Ioun stone, dark blue rhomboid	10,000 gp	79	Mattock of the titans	23,348 gp
30	Cape of the mountebank	10,800 gp	80	Crown of blasting, major	23,760 gp
31	Phylactery of negative channeling	11,000 gp	81	Cloak of displacement, minor	24,000 gp
32	Phylactery of positive channeling	11,000 gp	82	Helm of underwater action	24,000 gp
33	Gauntlet of rust	11,500 gp	83	Bracers of archery, greater	25,000 gp
34	Boots of speed	12,000 gp	84	Bracers of armor +5	25,000 gp
35	Goggles of night	12,000 gp	85	Cloak of resistance +5	25,000 gp
36	Golem manual, clay	12,000 gp	86	Eyes of doom	25,000 gp
37	Medallion of thoughts	12,000 gp	87	Pearl of power, 5th-level spell	25,000 gp
38	Blessed book	12,500 gp	88	Maul of the titans	25,305 gp
39	Gem of brightness	13,000 gp	89	Cloak of the bat	26,000 gp
40	Lyre of building	13,000 gp	90	Iron bands of binding	26,000 gp
41	Robe, Monk's	13,000 gp	91	Cube of frost resistance	27,000 gp
42	Cloak of arachnida	14,000 gp	92	Helm of telepathy	27,000 gp
43	Belt of dwarvenkind	14,900 gp	93	Periapt of proof against poison	27,000 gp
44	Periapt of wound closure	15,000 gp	94	Robe of scintillating colors	27,000 gp
45	Pearl of the sirines	15,300 gp	95	Manual of bodily health +1	27,500 gp
46	Figurine of wondrous power, onyx dog	15,500 gp	96	Manual of gainful exercise +1	27,500 gp
47	Amulet of mighty fists +2	16,000 gp	97	Manual of quickness in action +1	27,500 gp
48	Bag of tricks, tan	16,000 gp	98	Tome of clear thought +1	27,500 gp
49	Belt of giant strength +4	16,000 gp	99	Tome of leadership and influence +1	27,500 gp
50	Belt of incredible dexterity +4	16,000 gp	100	Tome of understanding +1	27,500 gp

TABLE 15-20: MAJOR WONDROUS ITEMS

d%	Item	Market Price	d%	Item	Market Price
01	Dimensional shackles	28,000 gp	51	Cube of force	62,000 gp
02	Figurine of wondrous power, obsidian steed	28,500 gp	52	Amulet of mighty fists +4	64,000 gp
03	Drums of panic	30,000 gp	53	Belt of physical perfection +4	64,000 gp
04	Ioun stone, orange prism	30,000 gp	54	Bracers of armor +8	64,000 gp
05	Ioun stone, pale green prism	30,000 gp	55	Headband of mental superiority +4	64,000 gp
06	Lantern of revealing	30,000 gp	56	Pearl of power, 8th-level spell	64,000 gp
07	Amulet of natural armor +4	32,000 gp	57	Crystal ball with telepathy	70,000 gp
08	Amulet of proof against detection and location	35,000 gp	58	Horn of blasting, greater	70,000 gp
09	Carpet of flying, 5 ft. by 10 ft.	35,000 gp	59	Pearl of power, two spells	70,000 gp
10	Golem manual, iron	35,000 gp	60	Helm of teleportation	73,500 gp
11	Amulet of mighty fists +3	36,000 gp	61	Gem of seeing	75,000 gp
12	Belt of giant strength +6	36,000 gp	62	Robe of the archmagi	75,000 gp
13	Belt of incredible dexterity +6	36,000 gp	63	Mantle of faith	76,000 gp
14	Belt of mighty constitution +6	36,000 gp	64	Crystal ball with true seeing	80,000 gp
15	Bracers of armor +6	36,000 gp	65	Pearl of power, 9th-level spell	81,000 gp
16	Headband of alluring charisma +6	36,000 gp	66	Well of many worlds	82,000 gp
17	Headband of inspired wisdom +6	36,000 gp	67	Manual of bodily health +3	82,500 gp
18	Headband of vast intelligence +6	36,000 gp	68	Manual of gainful exercise +3	82,500 gp
19	Ioun stone, vibrant purple prism	36,000 gp	69	Manual of quickness in action +3	82,500 gp
20	Pearl of power, 6th-level spell	36,000 gp	70	Tome of clear thought +3	82,500 gp
21	Scarab of protection	38,000 gp	71	Tome of leadership and influence +3	82,500 gp
22	Belt of physical might +4	40,000 gp	72	Tome of understanding +3	82,500 gp
23	Headband of mental prowess +4	40,000 gp	73	Apparatus of the crab	90,000 gp
24	Ioun stone, lavender and green ellipsoid	40,000 gp	74	Belt of physical might +6	90,000 gp
25	Ring gates	40,000 gp	75	Headband of mental prowess +6	90,000 gp
26	Crystal ball	42,000 gp	76	Mantle of spell resistance	90,000 gp
27	Golem manual, stone guardian	44,000 gp	77	Mirror of opposition	92,000 gp
28	Strand of prayer beads	45,800 gp	78	Strand of prayer beads, greater	95,800 gp
29	Orb of storms	48,000 gp	79	Amulet of mighty fists +5	100,000 gp
30	Boots of teleportation	49,000 gp	80	Manual of bodily health +4	110,000 gp
31	Bracers of armor +7	49,000 gp	81	Manual of gainful exercise +4	110,000 gp
32	Pearl of power, 7th-level spell	49,000 gp	82	Manual of quickness in action +4	110,000 gp
33	Amulet of natural armor +5	50,000 gp	83	Tome of clear thought +4	110,000 gp
34	Cloak of displacement, major	50,000 gp	84	Tome of leadership and influence +4	110,000 gp
35	Crystal ball with see invisibility	50,000 gp	85	Tome of understanding +4	110,000 gp
36	Horn of Valhalla	50,000 gp	86	Amulet of the planes	120,000 gp
37	Crystal ball with detect thoughts	51,000 gp	87	Robe of eyes	120,000 gp
38	Wings of flying	54,000 gp	88	Helm of brilliance	125,000 gp
39	Cloak of etherealness	55,000 gp	89	Manual of bodily health +5	137,500 gp
40	Instant fortress	55,000 gp	90	Manual of gainful exercise +5	137,500 gp
41	Manual of bodily health +2	55,000 gp	91	Manual of quickness in action +5	137,500 gp
42	Manual of gainful exercise +2	55,000 gp	92	Tome of clear thought +5	137,500 gp
43	Manual of quickness in action +2	55,000 gp	93	Tome of leadership and influence +5	137,500 gp
44	Tome of clear thought +2	55,000 gp	94	Tome of understanding +5	137,500 gp
45	Tome of leadership and influence +2	55,000 gp	95	Belt of physical perfection +6	144,000 gp
46	Tome of understanding +2	55,000 gp	96	Headband of mental superiority +6	144,000 gp
47	Eyes of charming	56,000 gp	97	Efreeti bottle	145,000 gp
48	Robe of stars	58,000 gp	98	Cubic gate	164,000 gp
49	Carpet of flying, 10 ft. by 10 ft.	60,000 gp	99	Iron flask	170,000 gp
50	Darkskull	60,000 gp	100	Mirror of life trapping	200,000 gp

AMULET OF NATURAL ARMOR

Aura faint transmutation; **CL** 5th

Slot neck; **Price** 2,000 gp (+1), 8,000 gp (+2), 18,000 gp (+3), 32,000 gp (+4), or 50,000 gp (+5); **Weight** —

DESCRIPTION

This amulet, usually crafted from bone or beast scales, toughens the wearer's body and flesh, giving him an enhancement bonus to his natural armor from +1 to +5, depending on the kind of amulet.

CONSTRUCTION

Requirements Craft Wondrous Item, *barkskin*, creator's caster level must be at least three times the amulet's bonus; **Cost** 1,000 gp (+1), 4,000 gp (+2), 9,000 gp (+3), 16,000 gp (+4), 25,000 gp (+5)

AMULET OF THE PLANES

Aura strong conjuration; **CL** 15th

Slot neck; **Price** 120,000 gp; **Weight** —

DESCRIPTION

This device usually appears to be a black circular amulet, although any character looking closely at it sees a dark, moving swirl of color. The amulet allows its wearer to utilize *plane shift*. However, this is a difficult item to master. The user must make a DC 15 Intelligence check in order to get the amulet to take her to the plane (and the specific location on that plane) that she wants. If she fails, the amulet transports her and all those traveling with her to a random location on that plane (01–60 on d%) or to a random plane (61–100).

CONSTRUCTION

Requirements Craft Wondrous Item, *plane shift*; **Cost** 60,000 gp

AMULET OF PROOF AGAINST DETECTION AND LOCATION

Aura moderate abjuration; **CL** 8th

Slot neck; **Price** 35,000 gp; **Weight** —

DESCRIPTION

This silver amulet protects the wearer from scrying and magical location just as a *nondetection* spell does. If a divination spell is attempted against the wearer, the caster of the divination must succeed on a caster level check (1d20 + caster level) against a DC of 23 (as if the wearer had cast *nondetection* on herself).

CONSTRUCTION

Requirements Craft Wondrous Item, *nondetection*; **Cost** 17,500 gp

APPARATUS OF THE CRAB

Aura strong evocation and transmutation; **CL** 19th

Slot none; **Price** 90,000 gp; **Weight** 500 lbs.

DESCRIPTION

At first glance, an inactive *apparatus of the crab* appears to be a large, sealed iron barrel big enough to hold two Medium creatures. Close examination, and a DC 20 Perception check, reveals a secret catch that opens a hatch at one end. Anyone who crawls inside finds 10 (unlabeled) levers and seating for two Medium or Small occupants. These levers allow those inside to activate and control the apparatus's movements and actions.

Lever (1d10)	Lever Function
1	Extend/retract legs and tail
2	Uncover/cover forward porthole
3	Uncover/cover side portholes
4	Extend/retract pincers and feelers
5	Snap pincers
6	Move forward/backward
7	Turn left/right
8	Open/close "eyes" with *continual flame* inside
9	Rise/sink in water
10	Open/close hatch

Operating a lever is a full-round action, and no lever may be operated more than once per round. However, since two characters can fit inside, the apparatus can move and attack in the same round. The device can function in water up to 900 feet deep. It holds enough air for a crew of two to survive 1d4+1 hours (twice as long for a single occupant). When activated, the apparatus looks something like a giant lobster.

When active, an *apparatus of the crab* has the following characteristics: **hp** 200; **hardness** 15; **Spd** 20 ft., swim 20 ft.; **AC** 20 (−1 size, +11 natural); **Attack** 2 pincers +12 melee (2d8); **CMB** +14; **CMD** 24.

CONSTRUCTION

Requirements Craft Wondrous Item, *animate objects*, *continual flame*, creator must have 8 ranks in Knowledge (engineering); **Cost** 45,000 gp

BAG OF HOLDING

Aura moderate conjuration; **CL** 9th

Slot none; **Price** see below; **Weight** see below

DESCRIPTION

This appears to be a common cloth sack about 2 feet by 4 feet in size. The *bag of holding* opens into a nondimensional space: its inside is larger than its outside dimensions. Regardless of what is put into the bag, it weighs a fixed amount. This weight, and the limits in weight and volume of the bag's contents, depend on the bag's type, as shown on the table below.

Bag	Bag Weight	Contents Limit	Contents Volume Limit	Market Price
Type I	15 lbs.	250 lbs.	30 cubic ft.	2,500 gp
Type II	25 lbs.	500 lbs.	70 cubic ft.	5,000 gp
Type III	35 lbs.	1,000 lbs.	150 cubic ft.	7,400 gp
Type IV	60 lbs.	1,500 lbs.	250 cubic ft.	10,000 gp

If a *bag of holding* is overloaded, or if sharp objects pierce it (from inside or outside), the bag immediately ruptures and is ruined, and all contents are lost forever. If a *bag of holding* is turned inside out, all of its contents spill out, unharmed, but the bag must be put right before it can be used again. If living creatures are placed within the bag, they can survive for up to 10 minutes, after which time they suffocate. Retrieving a specific item from a *bag of holding* is a move action, unless the bag contains more than an ordinary backpack would hold, in which case retrieving a specific item is a full-round action. Magic items placed inside the bag do not offer any benefit to the character carrying the bag.

If a *bag of holding* is placed within a *portable hole,* a rift to the Astral Plane is torn in the space: bag and hole alike are sucked into the void and forever lost. If a *portable hole* is placed within a *bag of holding,* it opens a gate to the Astral Plane: the hole, the bag, and any creatures within a 10-foot radius are drawn there, destroying the *portable hole* and *bag of holding* in the process.

CONSTRUCTION

Requirements Craft Wondrous Item, *secret chest;* **Cost** 1,250 gp (type I), 2,500 gp (type II), 3,700 gp (type III), 5,000 gp (type IV)

BAG OF TRICKS

Aura faint (gray or rust) or moderate (tan) conjuration; **CL** 3rd (gray), 5th (rust), 9th (tan)

Slot none; **Price** 3,400 gp (gray); 8,500 gp (rust); 16,000 gp (tan)

DESCRIPTION

This small sack appears empty. Anyone reaching into the bag feels a small, fuzzy ball. If the ball is removed and tossed up to 20 feet away, it turns into an animal. The animal serves the character who drew it from the bag for 10 minutes (or until slain or ordered back into the bag), at which point it disappears. It can follow any of the commands described in the Handle Animal skill. Each of the three kinds of *bags of tricks* produces a different set of animals. Use the following tables to determine what animals can be drawn out of each.

The heavy horse appears with harness and tack and accepts the character who drew it from the bag as a rider.

Animals produced are always random, and only one may exist at a time. Up to 10 animals can be drawn from the bag each week, but no more than two per day. Statistics for these animals can be found in the *Pathfinder RPG Bestiary.*

CONSTRUCTION

Requirements Craft Wondrous Item, *summon nature's ally II* (gray), *summon nature's ally III* (rust), or *summon nature's ally V* (tan); **Cost** 1,700 gp (gray); 4,250 gp (rust); 8,000 gp (tan)

Gray Bag		Rust Bag		Tan Bag	
d%	Animal	d%	Animal	d%	Animal
01–30	Bat	01–30	Wolverine	01–30	Grizzly bear
31–60	Rat	31–60	Wolf	31–60	Lion
61–75	Cat	61–85	Boar	61–80	Heavy horse
76–90	Weasel	86–100	Leopard	81–90	Tiger
91–100	Riding dog			91–100	Rhinoceros

BEAD OF FORCE

Aura moderate evocation; **CL** 10th

Slot none; **Price** 3,000 gp; **Weight** —

DESCRIPTION

This small black sphere appears to be a lusterless pearl. A *bead*

EXTRADIMENSIONAL SPACES

A number of spells and magic items utilize extradimensional spaces, such as *rope trick,* a *bag of holding,* a *handy haversack,* and a *portable hole.* These spells and magic items create a tiny pocket space that does not exist in any dimension. Such items do not function, however, inside another extradimensional space. If placed inside such a space, they cease to function until removed from the extradimensional space. For example, if a *bag of holding* is brought into a *rope trick,* the contents of the *bag of holding* become inaccessible until the *bag of holding* is taken outside the *rope trick.* The only exception to this is when a *bag of holding* and a *portable hole* interact, forming a rift to the Astral Plane, as noted in their descriptions.

of force can be thrown up to 60 feet with no range penalties. Upon sharp impact, the bead explodes, sending forth a burst that deals 5d6 points of force damage to all creatures within a 10-foot radius.

Once thrown, a *bead of force* functions like a *resilient sphere* spell (Reflex DC 16 negates) with a radius of 10 feet and a duration of 10 minutes. A globe of shimmering force encloses a creature, provided the latter is small enough to fit within the diameter of the sphere. The sphere contains its subject for the spell's duration. The sphere is not subject to damage of any sort except from a *rod of cancellation,* a *rod of negation, disintegrate,* or a targeted *dispel magic* spell. These effects destroy the sphere without harm to the subject. Nothing can pass through the sphere, inside or out, though the subject can breathe normally. The subject may struggle, but the globe cannot be physically moved either by people outside it or by the struggles of those within. The explosion completely consumes the bead, making this a one-use item.

CONSTRUCTION

Requirements Craft Wondrous Item, *resilient sphere;* **Cost** 1,500 gp

BELT OF DWARVENKIND

Aura strong divination; **CL** 12th

Slot belt; **Price** 14,900 gp; **Weight** 1 lb.

DESCRIPTION

This belt gives the wearer a +4 competence bonus on Charisma checks and Charisma-based skill checks as they relate to dealing with dwarves, a +2 competence bonus on similar checks when dealing with gnomes and halflings, and a –2 competence penalty on similar checks when dealing with anyone else. The wearer can understand, speak, and read Dwarven. If the wearer is not a dwarf, he gains 60-foot darkvision, dwarven stonecunning, a +2 enhancement bonus to Constitution, and a +2 resistance bonus on saves against poison, spells, and spell-like effects.

CONSTRUCTION

Requirements Craft Wondrous Item, *tongues,* creator must be a dwarf; **Cost** 7,450 gp

BELT OF GIANT STRENGTH

Aura moderate transmutation; **CL** 8th

Slot belt; **Weight** 1 lb.; **Price** 4,000 gp (+2), 16,000 gp (+4), 36,000 gp (+6)

DESCRIPTION

This belt is a thick leather affair, often decorated with huge metal buckles. The belt grants the wearer an enhancement bonus to Strength of +2, +4, or +6. Treat this as a temporary ability bonus for the first 24 hours the belt is worn.

CONSTRUCTION

Requirements Craft Wondrous Item, *bull's strength*; **Cost** 2,000 gp (+2), 8,000 gp (+4), 18,000 gp (+6)

BELT OF INCREDIBLE DEXTERITY

Aura moderate transmutation; **CL** 8th

Slot belt; **Weight** 1 lb.; **Price** 4,000 gp (+2), 16,000 gp (+4), 36,000 gp (+6)

DESCRIPTION

This belt has a large silver buckle, usually depicting the image of a tiger. The belt grants the wearer an enhancement bonus to Dexterity of +2, +4, or +6. Treat this as a temporary ability bonus for the first 24 hours the belt is worn.

CONSTRUCTION

Requirements Craft Wondrous Item, *cat's grace*; **Cost** 2,000 gp (+2), 8,000 gp (+4), 18,000 gp (+6)

BELT OF MIGHTY CONSTITUTION

Aura moderate transmutation; **CL** 8th

Slot belt; **Weight** 1 lb.; **Price** 4,000 gp (+2), 16,000 gp (+4), 36,000 gp (+6)

DESCRIPTION

This belt's golden buckle depicts a bear. The belt grants the wearer an enhancement bonus to Constitution of +2, +4, or +6. Treat this as a temporary ability bonus for the first 24 hours the belt is worn.

CONSTRUCTION

Requirements Craft Wondrous Item, *bear's endurance*; **Cost** 2,000 gp (+2), 8,000 gp (+4), 18,000 gp (+6)

BELT OF PHYSICAL MIGHT

Aura strong transmutation; **CL** 12th

Slot belt; **Weight** 1 lb.; **Price** 10,000 gp (+2), 40,000 gp (+4), 90,000 gp (+6)

DESCRIPTION

This belt has a large steel buckle, usually depicting the image of a giant. The belt grants the wearer an enhancement bonus to two physical ability scores (Strength, Dexterity, or Constitution) of +2, +4, or +6. Treat this as a temporary ability bonus for the first 24 hours the belt is worn. These bonuses are chosen when the belt is created and cannot be changed.

CONSTRUCTION

Requirements Craft Wondrous Item, *bear's endurance*, *bull's strength*, and/or *cat's grace*; **Cost** 5,000 gp (+2), 20,000 gp (+4), 45,000 gp (+6)

BELT OF PHYSICAL PERFECTION

Aura strong transmutation; **CL** 16th

Slot belt; **Weight** 1 lb.; **Price** 16,000 gp (+2), 64,000 gp (+4), 144,000 gp (+6)

DESCRIPTION

This belt has a large platinum buckle, usually depicting the image of a titan. The belt grants the wearer an enhancement bonus to all physical ability scores (Strength, Dexterity, and Constitution) of +2, +4, or +6. Treat this as a temporary ability bonus for the first 24 hours the belt is worn.

CONSTRUCTION

Requirements Craft Wondrous Item, *bear's endurance*, *bull's strength*, *cat's grace*; **Cost** 8,000 gp (+2), 32,000 gp (+4), 77,000 gp (+6)

BLESSED BOOK

Aura moderate transmutation; **CL** 7th

Slot none; **Price** 12,500 gp; **Weight** 1 lb.

DESCRIPTION

This well-made tome is always of small size, typically no more than 12 inches tall, 8 inches wide, and 1 inch thick. All such books are durable, waterproof, bound with iron overlaid with silver, and locked.

A wizard can fill the 1,000 pages of a *blessed book* with spells without paying the material cost. This book is never found as randomly generated treasure with spells already inscribed in it.

CONSTRUCTION

Requirements Craft Wondrous Item, *secret page*; **Cost** 6,250 gp

BOAT, FOLDING

Aura moderate transmutation; **CL** 6th

Slot none; **Price** 7,200 gp; **Weight** 4 lbs.

DESCRIPTION

A *folding boat* looks like a small wooden box about 12 inches long, 6 inches wide, and 6 inches deep when it is inactive. In this mode, it can be used to store items just like any other box. Yet when the proper command word is given, the box unfolds itself rapidly in the space of a single round to form a boat 10 feet long, 4 feet wide, and 2 feet in depth. A second command word causes it to unfold even further into a ship 24 feet long, 8 feet wide, and 6 feet deep. The *folding boat* cannot unfold if there isn't enough open space for it to occupy once unfolded. Any objects formerly stored in the box now rest inside the boat or ship.

In its smaller form, the boat has one pair of oars, an anchor, a mast, and a lateen sail. In its larger form, the boat has a deck, single rowing seats, five sets of oars, a rudder, an anchor, a deck cabin, and a mast with a square sail. The boat can hold 4 people comfortably, while the ship carries 15 with ease.

A third word of command causes the boat or ship to fold itself into a box once again, but only when it is unoccupied.

CONSTRUCTION

Requirements Craft Wondrous Item, *fabricate*, creator must have 2 ranks in the Craft (ships) skill; **Cost** 3,600 gp

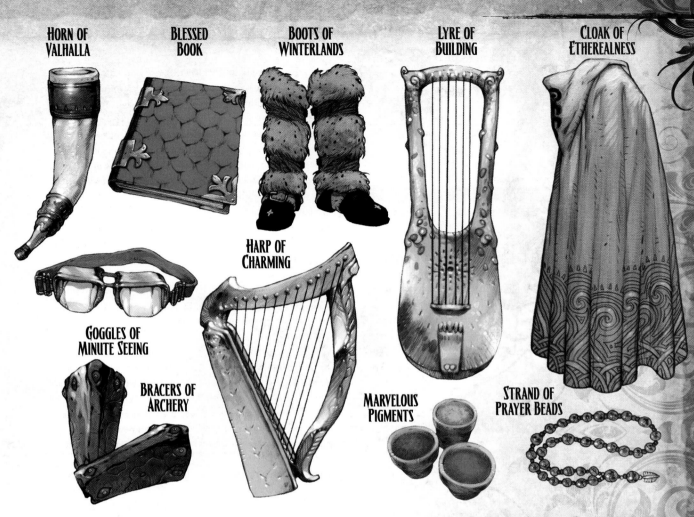

HORN OF VALHALLA

BLESSED BOOK

BOOTS OF WINTERLANDS

LYRE OF BUILDING

CLOAK OF ETHEREALNESS

GOGGLES OF MINUTE SEEING

HARP OF CHARMING

BRACERS OF ARCHERY

MARVELOUS PIGMENTS

STRAND OF PRAYER BEADS

BOOTS OF ELVENKIND

Aura faint transmutation; **CL** 5th

Slot feet; **Price** 2,500 gp; **Weight** 1 lb.

DESCRIPTION

These soft boots enable the wearer to move nimbly about in virtually any surroundings, granting a +5 competence bonus on Acrobatics checks.

CONSTRUCTION

Requirements Craft Wondrous Item, creator must be an elf; **Cost** 1,250 gp

BOOTS OF LEVITATION

Aura faint transmutation; **CL** 3rd

Slot feet; **Price** 7,500 gp; **Weight** 1 lb.

DESCRIPTION

These soft leather boots are incredibly light and comfortable, with thin soles reinforced by strips of tough hide that provide an unexpected amount of support and protection to the foot. On command, these boots allow the wearer to levitate as if she had cast *levitate* on herself.

CONSTRUCTION

Requirements Craft Wondrous Item, *levitate*; **Cost** 3,750 gp

BOOTS OF SPEED

Aura moderate transmutation; **CL** 10th

Slot feet; **Price** 12,000 gp; **Weight** 1 lb.

DESCRIPTION

As a free action, the wearer can click her heels together, letting her act as though affected by a *haste* spell for up to 10 rounds each day. The *haste* effect's duration need not be consecutive rounds.

CONSTRUCTION

Requirements Craft Wondrous Item, *haste*; **Cost** 6,000 gp

BOOTS OF STRIDING AND SPRINGING

Aura faint transmutation; **CL** 3rd

Slot feet; **Price** 5,500 gp; **Weight** 1 lb.

DESCRIPTION

These boots increase the wearer's base land speed by 10 feet. In addition to this striding ability (considered an enhancement bonus), these boots allow the wearer to make great leaps. She can jump with a +5 competence bonus on Acrobatics checks.

CONSTRUCTION

Requirements Craft Wondrous Item, *longstrider*, creator must have 5 ranks in the Acrobatics skill; **Cost** 2,750 gp

BOOTS OF TELEPORTATION

Aura moderate conjuration; **CL** 9th

Slot feet; **Price** 49,000 gp; **Weight** 3 lbs.

DESCRIPTION

Any character wearing this footwear may *teleport* three times per day, exactly as if he had cast the spell of the same name.

CONSTRUCTION

Requirements Craft Wondrous Item, *teleport*; **Cost** 24,500 gp

BOOTS OF THE WINTERLANDS

Aura faint abjuration and transmutation; **CL** 5th

Slot feet; **Price** 2,500 gp; **Weight** 1 lb.

DESCRIPTION

This footgear bestows many powers upon the wearer. First, he is able to travel across snow at his normal speed, leaving no tracks. Second, the boots also enable him to travel at normal speed across the most slippery ice (horizontal surfaces only, not vertical or sharply slanted ones) without falling or slipping. Finally, *boots of the winterlands* warm the wearer, as if he were affected by an *endure elements* spell.

CONSTRUCTION

Requirements Craft Wondrous Item, *cat's grace, endure elements, pass without trace*; **Cost** 1,250 gp

BOOTS, WINGED

Aura moderate transmutation; **CL** 8th

Slot feet; **Price** 16,000 gp; **Weight** 1 lb.

DESCRIPTION

These boots appear to be ordinary footgear. On command, they sprout wings at the heel and let the wearer fly, without having to maintain concentration, as if affected by a *fly* spell (including a +4 bonus on Fly skill checks). He can fly three per times day for up to 5 minutes per flight.

CONSTRUCTION

Requirements Craft Wondrous Item, *fly*; **Cost** 8,000 gp

BOTTLE OF AIR

Aura moderate transmutation; **CL** 7th

Slot none; **Price** 7,250 gp; **Weight** 2 lbs.

DESCRIPTION

This item appears to be a normal glass bottle with a cork. When taken to any airless environment, it retains air within it at all times, continually renewing its contents. This means that a character can draw air out of the bottle to breathe. The bottle can even be shared by multiple characters who pass it around. Breathing out of the bottle is a standard action, but a character so doing can then act for as long as she can hold her breath.

CONSTRUCTION

Requirements Craft Wondrous Item, *water breathing*; **Cost** 3,625 gp

BRACELET OF FRIENDS

Aura strong conjuration; **CL** 15th

Slot wrists; **Price** 19,000 gp; **Weight** —

DESCRIPTION

This silver charm bracelet has four charms upon it when created. The owner may designate one person known to him to be keyed to each charm. (This designation takes a standard action, but once done it lasts forever or until changed.) When a charm is grasped and the name of the keyed individual is spoken, that person is called to the spot (a standard action) along with his gear, as long as the owner and the called person are on the same plane. The keyed individual knows who is calling, and the *bracelet of friends* only functions on willing travelers. Once a charm is activated, it disappears. Charms separated from the bracelet are worthless. A bracelet found with fewer than four charms is worth 25% less for each missing charm.

CONSTRUCTION

Requirements Craft Wondrous Item, *refuge*; **Cost** 9,500 gp

BRACERS OF ARCHERY, GREATER

Aura moderate transmutation; **CL** 8th

Slot wrists; **Price** 25,000 gp; **Weight** 1 lb.

DESCRIPTION

These wristbands look like normal protective wear. The bracers empower the wearer to use any bow (not including crossbows) as if she were proficient in its use. If she already has proficiency with any type of bow, she gains a +2 competence bonus on attack rolls and a +1 competence bonus on damage rolls whenever using that type of bow. Both bracers must be worn for the magic to be effective.

CONSTRUCTION

Requirements Craft Wondrous Item, Craft Magic Arms and Armor, crafter must be proficient with a longbow or shortbow; **Cost** 12,500 gp

BRACERS OF ARCHERY, LESSER

Aura faint transmutation; **CL** 4th

Slot wrists; **Price** 5,000 gp; **Weight** 1 lb.

DESCRIPTION

These wristbands function as *greater bracers of archery*, except that they grant a +1 competence bonus on attack rolls and no bonus on damage rolls.

CONSTRUCTION

Requirements Craft Wondrous Item, Craft Magic Arms and Armor, crafter must be proficient with a longbow or shortbow; **Cost** 2,500 gp

BRACERS OF ARMOR

Aura moderate conjuration; **CL** 7th

Slot wrists; **Price** 1,000 gp (+1), 4,000 gp (+2), 9,000 gp (+3), 16,000 gp (+4), 25,000 gp (+5), 36,000 gp (+6), 49,000 gp (+7), 64,000 gp (+8); **Weight** 1 lb.

DESCRIPTION

These items appear to be wrist or arm guards. They surround the wearer with an invisible but tangible field of force, granting him an armor bonus of +1 to +8, just as though he were wearing armor. Both bracers must be worn for the magic to be effective.

Alternatively, *bracers of armor* can be enchanted with armor special abilities. See Table 15–4 for a list of abilities. Special abilities usually count as additional bonuses for determining the market value of an item, but do not improve AC. *Bracers of armor* cannot have a modified bonus (armor bonus plus armor special ability bonus equivalents) higher than +8. *Bracers of armor* must have at least a +1 armor bonus to grant an armor special ability. *Bracers of armor* cannot have any armor special abilities that add a flat gp amount to their cost. *Bracers of armor* and ordinary armor do not stack. If a creature receives a larger armor bonus from another source, the *bracers of armor* cease functioning and do not grant their armor bonus or their armor special abilities. If the *bracers of armor* grant a larger armor bonus, the other source of armor ceases functioning.

CONSTRUCTION

Requirements Craft Wondrous Item, *mage armor*, creator's caster level must be at least two times that of the bonus placed in the bracers, plus any requirements of the armor special abilities; **Cost** 500 gp (+1), 2,000 gp (+2), 4,500 gp (+3), 8,000 gp (+4), 12,500 gp (+5), 18,000 gp (+6), 24,500 gp (+7), 32,000 gp (+8)

BROOCH OF SHIELDING

Aura faint abjuration; **CL** 1st

Slot neck; **Price** 1,500 gp; **Weight** —

DESCRIPTION

This appears to be a piece of silver or gold jewelry used to fasten a cloak or cape. In addition to this mundane task, it can absorb *magic missiles* of the sort generated by the spell or spell-like ability. A brooch can absorb up to 101 points of damage from *magic missiles* before it melts and becomes useless.

CONSTRUCTION

Requirements Craft Wondrous Item, *shield*; **Cost** 750 gp

BROOM OF FLYING

Aura moderate transmutation; **CL** 9th

Slot none; **Price** 17,000 gp; **Weight** 3 lbs.

DESCRIPTION

This broom is able to fly through the air as if affected by an *overland flight* spell (+4 on Fly skill checks) for up to 9 hours per day (split up as its owner desires). The broom can carry 200 pounds and fly at a speed of 40 feet, or up to 400 pounds at a speed at 30 feet. In addition, the broom can travel alone to any destination named by the owner as long as she has a good idea of the location and layout of that destination. It flies to its owner from as far away as 300 yards when she speaks the command word. The *broom of flying* has a speed of 40 feet when it has no rider.

CONSTRUCTION

Requirements Craft Wondrous Item, *overland flight*, *permanency*; **Cost** 8,500 gp

CANDLE OF INVOCATION

Aura strong conjuration; **CL** 17th

Slot none; **Price** 8,400 gp; **Weight** 1/2 lb.

DESCRIPTION

Each of these special tapers is dedicated to one of the nine alignments. Simply burning the candle generates a favorable aura for the individual if the candle's alignment matches that of the character. Characters of the same alignment as the burning candle add a +2 morale bonus on attack rolls, saving throws, and skill checks while within 30 feet of the flame.

A cleric whose alignment matches the candle's operates as if two levels higher for purposes of determining spells per day if he burns the candle during or just prior to his spell preparation time. He can even cast spells normally unavailable to him as if he were of that higher level, but only so long as the candle continues to burn. Except in special cases (see below), a candle burns for 4 hours. It is possible to extinguish the candle simply by blowing it out, so users often place it in a lantern to protect it from drafts and the like. Doing this doesn't interfere with its magical properties.

In addition, burning a candle also allows the owner to cast a *gate* spell, the respondent being of the same alignment as the candle, but the taper is immediately consumed in the process.

CONSTRUCTION

Requirements Craft Wondrous Item, *gate*, creator must be same alignment as candle created; **Cost** 4,200 gp

CANDLE OF TRUTH

Aura faint enchantment; **CL** 3rd

Slot none; **Price** 2,500 gp; **Weight** 1/2 lb.

DESCRIPTION

This white tallow candle, when burned, calls into place a *zone of truth* spell (Will DC 13 negates) in a 5-foot radius centered on the candle. The zone lasts for 1 hour, while the candle burns. If the candle is snuffed before that time, the effect is canceled and the candle ruined.

CONSTRUCTION

Requirements Craft Wondrous Item, *zone of truth*; **Cost** 1,250 gp

CAPE OF THE MOUNTEBANK

Aura moderate conjuration; **CL** 9th

Slot shoulders; **Price** 10,800 gp; **Weight** 1 lb.

DESCRIPTION

On command, this bright red and gold cape allows the wearer to use the magic of the *dimension door* spell once per day. When he disappears, he leaves behind a cloud of smoke, appearing in a similar fashion at his destination.

CONSTRUCTION

Requirements Craft Wondrous Item, *dimension door*; **Cost** 5,400 gp

CARPET OF FLYING

Aura moderate transmutation; **CL** 10th

Slot none; **Price** varies; **Weight** —

DESCRIPTION

This rug is able to fly through the air as if affected by an *overland flight* spell of unlimited duration. The size, carrying capacity, and speed of the different *carpets of flying* are shown on the table

below. Beautifully and intricately made, each carpet has its own command word to activate it—if the device is within voice range, the command word activates it, whether the speaker is on the rug or not. The carpet is then controlled by spoken directions.

Size	Capacity	Speed	Weight	Market Price
5 ft. by 5 ft.	200 lbs.	40 ft.	8 lbs.	20,000 gp
5 ft. by 10 ft.	400 lbs.	40 ft.	10 lbs.	35,000 gp
10 ft. by 10 ft.	800 lbs.	40 ft.	15 lbs.	60,000 gp

A *carpet of flying* can carry up to double its capacity, but doing so reduces its speed to 30 feet. A *carpet of flying* can hover without making a Fly skill check and gives a +5 bonus to other Fly checks.

CONSTRUCTION

Requirements Craft Wondrous Item, *overland flight*; **Cost** 10,000 gp (5 ft. by 5 ft.), 17,500 gp (5 ft. by 10 ft.), 30,000 gp (10 ft. by 10 ft.)

CHIME OF INTERRUPTION

Aura moderate evocation; **CL** 7th

Slot none; **Price** 16,800 gp; **Weight** 1 lb.

DESCRIPTION

This instrument can be struck once every 10 minutes, and its resonant tone lasts for 3 full minutes.

While the chime is resonating, no spell requiring a verbal component can be cast within a 30-foot radius of it unless the caster can make a concentration check (DC 15 + the spell's level).

CONSTRUCTION

Requirements Craft Wondrous Item, *shout*; **Cost** 8,400 gp

CHIME OF OPENING

Aura moderate transmutation; **CL** 11th

Slot none; **Price** 3,000 gp; **Weight** 1 lb.

DESCRIPTION

A *chime of opening* is a hollow mithral tube about 1 foot long. When struck, it sends forth magical vibrations that cause locks, lids, doors, valves, and portals to open. The device functions against normal bars, shackles, chains, bolts, and so on. A *chime of opening* also automatically dispels a *hold portal* spell or even an *arcane lock* cast by a wizard of lower than 15th level.

The chime must be pointed at the item or gate to be loosed or opened (which must be visible and known to the user). The chime is then struck and a clear tone rings forth. The wielder can make a caster level check against the lock or binding, using the chime's caster level of 11th. The DC of this check is equal to the Disable Device DC to open the lock or binding. Each sounding only opens one form of locking, so if a chest is chained, padlocked, locked, and *arcane locked*, it takes four successful uses of a *chime of opening* to get it open. A *silence* spell negates the power of the device. A brand-new chime can be used a total of 10 times before it cracks and becomes useless.

CONSTRUCTION

Requirements Craft Wondrous Item, *knock*; **Cost** 1,500 gp

CIRCLET OF PERSUASION

Aura faint transmutation; **CL** 5th

Slot head; **Price** 4,500 gp; **Weight** —

DESCRIPTION

This silver headband grants a +3 competence bonus on the wearer's Charisma-based checks.

CONSTRUCTION

Requirements Craft Wondrous Item, *eagle's splendor*; **Cost** 2,250 gp

CLOAK OF ARACHNIDA

Aura moderate conjuration and transmutation; **CL** 6th

Slot shoulders; **Price** 14,000 gp; **Weight** 1 lb.

DESCRIPTION

This black garment, embroidered with a web-like pattern in silk, gives the wearer the ability to climb as if a *spider climb* spell had been placed upon her. In addition, the cloak grants her immunity to entrapment by *web* spells or webs of any sort; she can actually move in webs at half her normal speed. Once per day, the wearer of this cloak can cast *web*. She also gains a +2 luck bonus on all Fortitude saves against poison from spiders.

CONSTRUCTION

Requirements Craft Wondrous Item, *spider climb, web*; **Cost** 7,000 gp

CLOAK OF THE BAT

Aura moderate transmutation; **CL** 7th

Slot shoulders; **Price** 26,000 gp; **Weight** 1 lb.

DESCRIPTION

Fashioned of dark brown or black cloth, this cloak bestows a +5 competence bonus on Stealth checks. The wearer is also able to hang upside down from the ceiling like a bat.

By holding the edges of the garment, the wearer is able to *fly* as per the spell (including a +7 bonus on Fly skill checks). If he desires, the wearer can actually polymorph himself into an ordinary bat and fly accordingly (as *beast shape III*). All possessions worn or carried are part of the transformation. Flying, either with the cloak or in bat form, can be accomplished only in darkness (either under the night sky or in a lightless or near-lightless environment underground). Either of the flying powers is usable for up to 7 minutes at a time, but after a flight of any duration the cloak cannot bestow any flying power for a like period of time.

CONSTRUCTION

Requirements Craft Wondrous Item, *beast shape III, fly*; **Cost** 13,000 gp

CLOAK OF DISPLACEMENT, MAJOR

Aura moderate illusion; **CL** 7th

Slot shoulders; **Price** 50,000 gp; **Weight** 1 lb.

DESCRIPTION

This item appears to be a normal cloak, but on command its magical properties distort and warp light waves. This displacement works just like the *displacement* spell and lasts for a total of 15 rounds per day, which the wearer can divide up as she sees fit.

CONSTRUCTION

Requirements Craft Wondrous Item, Extend Spell, *displacement*; **Cost** 25,000 gp

CLOAK OF DISPLACEMENT, MINOR

Aura faint illusion; **CL** 3rd

Slot shoulders; **Price** 24,000 gp; **Weight** 1 lb.

DESCRIPTION

This item appears to be a normal cloak, but when worn by a character, its magical properties distort and warp light waves. This displacement works similar to the *blur* spell, granting a 20% miss chance on attacks against the wearer. It functions continually.

CONSTRUCTION

Requirements Craft Wondrous Item, *blur*; **Cost** 12,000 gp

CLOAK OF ELVENKIND

Aura faint illusion; **CL** 3rd

Slot shoulders; **Price** 2,500 gp; **Weight** 1 lb.

DESCRIPTION

When this plain gray cloak is worn with the hood drawn up around the head, the wearer gains a +5 competence bonus on Stealth checks.

CONSTRUCTION

Requirements Craft Wondrous Item, *invisibility*, creator must be an elf; **Cost** 1,250 gp

CLOAK OF ETHEREALNESS

Aura strong transmutation; **CL** 15th

Slot shoulders; **Price** 55,000 gp; **Weight** 1 lb.

DESCRIPTION

This silvery gray cloak seems to absorb light rather than be illuminated by it. On command, the cloak makes its wearer ethereal (as the *ethereal jaunt* spell). The effect is dismissible. The cloak works for a total of up to 10 minutes per day. This duration need not be continuous, but it must be used in 1 minute increments.

CONSTRUCTION

Requirements Craft Wondrous Item, *ethereal jaunt*; **Cost** 27,500 gp

CLOAK OF THE MANTA RAY

Aura moderate transmutation; **CL** 9th

Slot shoulders; **Price** 7,200 gp; **Weight** 1 lb.

DESCRIPTION

This cloak appears to be made of leather until the wearer enters salt water. At that time, the *cloak of the manta ray* adheres to the individual, and he appears nearly identical to a manta ray (as the *beast shape II* spell, except that it allows only manta ray form). He gains a +3 natural armor bonus, the ability to breathe underwater, and a swim speed of 60 feet, like a real manta ray.

The cloak does allow the wearer to attack with a manta ray's tail spine, dealing 1d6 points of damage. This attack can be used in addition to any other attack the character has, using his highest melee attack bonus. The wearer can release his arms from the cloak without sacrificing underwater movement if so desired.

CONSTRUCTION

Requirements Craft Wondrous Item, *beast shape II*, *water breathing*; **Cost** 3,600 gp

CLOAK OF RESISTANCE

Aura faint abjuration; **CL** 5th

Slot shoulders; **Price** 1,000 gp (+1), 4,000 gp (+2), 9,000 gp (+3), 16,000 gp (+4), 25,000 gp (+5); **Weight** 1 lb.

DESCRIPTION

These garments offer magic protection in the form of a +1 to +5 resistance bonus on all saving throws (Fortitude, Reflex, and Will).

CONSTRUCTION

Requirements Craft Wondrous Item, resistance, creator's caster level must be at least three times the cloak's bonus; **Cost** 500 gp (+1), 2,000 gp (+2), 4,500 gp (+3), 8,000 gp (+4), 12,500 gp (+5)

CROWN OF BLASTING, MINOR

Aura moderate evocation; **CL** 6th

Slot head; **Price** 6,480 gp; **Weight** 1 lb.

DESCRIPTION

On command, this simple golden crown projects a blast of *searing light* (3d8 points of damage) once per day.

CONSTRUCTION

Requirements Craft Wondrous Item, *searing light*; **Cost** 3,240 gp

CROWN OF BLASTING, MAJOR

Aura strong evocation; **CL** 17th

Slot head; **Price** 23,760 gp; **Weight** 1 lb.

DESCRIPTION

On command, this elaborate golden crown projects a blast of *searing light* (5d8 maximized for 40 points of damage) once per day.

CONSTRUCTION

Requirements Craft Wondrous Item, Maximize Spell, *searing light*; **Cost** 11,880 gp

CRYSTAL BALL

Aura moderate divination; **CL** 10th

Slot none; **Price** varies; **Weight** 7 lbs.

DESCRIPTION

This is the most common form of scrying device, a crystal sphere about 6 inches in diameter. So well-known are these items that many so-called oracles or fortune-tellers use similar appearing (but completely non-magical) replicas of these items to ply their trades. A character can use a magical *crystal ball* to see over virtually any distance or into other planes of existence, as with the spell *scrying* (Will DC 16 negates). A *crystal ball* can be used multiple times per day, but the DC to resist its power decreases by 1 for each additional use.

Certain *crystal balls* have additional powers that can be used through the *crystal ball* on the target viewed.

Crystal Ball Type	Market Price
Crystal ball	42,000 gp
Crystal ball with *see invisibility*	50,000 gp
Crystal ball with *detect thoughts* (Will DC 13 negates)	51,000 gp
Crystal ball with *telepathy**	70,000 gp
Crystal ball with *true seeing*	80,000 gp

* The viewer is able to send and receive silent mental messages with the person appearing in the crystal ball. Once per day, the character may attempt to implant a *suggestion* (as the spell, Will DC 14 negates) as well.

CONSTRUCTION

Requirements Craft Wondrous Item, *scrying* (plus any additional spells put into item); **Cost** 21,000 gp (standard), 25,000 (with *see invisibility*), 25,500 gp (with *detect thoughts*), 35,000 gp (with *telepathy*), 40,000 gp (with *true seeing*)

CUBE OF FORCE

Aura moderate evocation; **CL** 10th

Slot none; **Price** 62,000 gp; **Weight** 1/2 lb.

DESCRIPTION

This device is just under an inch across and can be made of ivory, bone, or any hard mineral. Typically, each of the cube's faces are polished smooth, but sometimes they are etched with runes. The device enables its possessor to put up a special cube made up of 6 individual *wall of force* spells, 10 feet on a side around her person. This cubic screen moves with the character and is impervious to the attack forms mentioned on the table below. The cube has 36 charges when fully charged—charges used are automatically renewed each day. The possessor presses one face of the cube to activate a particular type of screen or to deactivate the device. Each effect costs a certain number of charges to maintain for every minute (or portion of a minute) it is in operation. Also, when an effect is active, the possessor's speed is limited to the maximum value given on the table.

When the *cube of force* is active, attacks dealing more than 30 points of damage drain 1 charge for every 10 points of damage beyond 30 that they deal. The charge cost to maintain each of the cube's six walls is summarized below.

Cube Face	Charge Cost per Minute	Max. Speed	Effect
1	1	30 ft.	Keeps out gases, wind, etc.
2	2	20 ft.	Keeps out nonliving matter
3	3	15 ft.	Keeps out living matter
4	4	10 ft.	Keeps out magic
5	6	10 ft.	Keeps out all things
6	0	As normal	Deactivates

Spells that affect the integrity of the screen also drain extra charges. These spells cannot be cast into or out of the cube.

Attack Form	Extra Charges
Disintegrate	6
Horn of blasting	6
Passwall	3
Phase door	5
Prismatic spray	7
Wall of fire	2

CONSTRUCTION

Requirements Craft Wondrous Item, *wall of force*; **Cost** 31,000 gp

CUBE OF FROST RESISTANCE

Aura faint abjuration; **CL** 5th

Slot none; **Price** 27,000 gp; **Weight** 2 lbs.

DESCRIPTION

This cube is activated or deactivated by pressing one side. When activated, it creates a cube-shaped area 10 feet on a side centered on the possessor (or on the cube itself, if the item is later placed on a surface). The temperature within this area is always at least 65° F. The field absorbs all cold-based attacks. However, if the field is subjected to more than 50 points of cold damage in 1 round (from one or multiple attacks), it collapses and cannot be reactivated for 1 hour. If the field absorbs more than 100 points of cold damage in a 10-round period, the cube is destroyed.

CONSTRUCTION

Requirements Craft Wondrous Item, *protection from energy*; **Cost** 13,500 gp

CUBIC GATE

Aura strong conjuration; **CL** 13th

Slot none; **Price** 164,000 gp; **Weight** 2 lbs.

DESCRIPTION

This potent magical item is a small cube fashioned from carnelian. Each of the six sides of the cube is keyed to a different plane of existence or dimension, one of which is the Material Plane. The character creating the item chooses the planes to which the other five sides are keyed.

If a side of the *cubic gate* is pressed once, it opens a *gate* to a random point on the plane keyed to that side. There is a 10% chance per minute that an outsider from that plane (determine randomly) comes through it looking for food, fun, or trouble. Pressing the side a second time closes the *gate*. It is impossible to open more than one *gate* at a time.

If a side is pressed twice in quick succession, the character so doing is transported to a random point on the other plane, along with all creatures in adjacent squares. The other creatures may avoid this fate by succeeding on DC 23 Will saves.

CONSTRUCTION

Requirements Craft Wondrous Item, *plane shift*; **Cost** 82,000 gp

DARKSKULL

Aura moderate evocation [evil]; **CL** 9th

Slot none; **Price** 60,000 gp; **Weight** 5 lbs.

DESCRIPTION

This skull, carved from ebony, is wholly evil. Wherever the skull goes, the area around it is treated as though an *unhallow* spell had been cast with the skull as the touched point of origin. Each *darkskull* has a single spell effect tied to it. This spell is from the standard list given in the *unhallow* spell description, and it cannot be changed.

CONSTRUCTION

Requirements Craft Wondrous Item, *unhallow*, creator must be evil; **Cost** 30,000 gp

DECANTER OF ENDLESS WATER

Aura moderate transmutation; **CL** 9th

Slot none; **Price** 9,000 gp; **Weight** 2 lbs.

DESCRIPTION

If the stopper is removed from this ordinary-looking flask and a command word spoken, an amount of fresh or salt water pours out. Separate command words determine the type of water as well as the volume and velocity.

- "Stream" pours out 1 gallon per round.
- "Fountain" produces a 5-foot-long stream at 5 gallons per round.
- "Geyser" produces a 20-foot-long, 1-foot-wide stream at 30 gallons per round.

The geyser effect exerts considerable pressure, requiring the holder to make a DC 12 Strength check to avoid being knocked down each round the effect is maintained. In addition, the powerful force of the geyser deals 1d4 points of damage per round to a creature that is subjected to it. The geyser can only affect one target per round, but the user can direct the beam of water without needing to make an attack role to strike the target since the geyser's constant flow allows for ample opportunity to aim. Creatures with the fire subtype take 2d4 points of damage per round from the geyser rather than 1d4. The command word must be spoken to stop it.

CONSTRUCTION

Requirements Craft Wondrous Item, *control water*; **Cost** 4,500 gp

DECK OF ILLUSIONS

Aura moderate illusion; **CL** 6th

Slot none; **Price** 8,100 gp; **Weight** 1/2 lb.

DESCRIPTION

This set of parchment cards is usually found in an ivory, leather, or wooden box. A full deck consists of 34 cards. When a card is drawn at random and thrown to the ground, a *major image* of a creature is formed. The figment lasts until dispelled. The illusory creature cannot move more than 30 feet away from where the card landed, but otherwise moves and acts as if it were real. At all times it obeys the desires of the character who drew the card. When the illusion is dispelled, the card becomes blank and cannot be used again. If the card is picked up, the illusion is automatically and instantly dispelled. The cards in a deck and the illusions they bring forth are summarized on the following table. (Use one of the first two columns to simulate the contents of a full deck using either ordinary playing cards or tarot cards.)

Playing Card	Tarot Card	Creature
Ace of hearts	IV. The Emperor	Red dragon
King of hearts	Knight of swords	Male human fighter and four guards
Queen of hearts	Queen of staves	Female human wizard
Jack of hearts	King of staves	Male human druid
Ten of hearts	VII. The Chariot	Cloud giant
Nine of hearts	Page of staves	Ettin
Eight of hearts	Ace of cups	Bugbear
Two of hearts	Five of staves	Goblin

Playing Card	Tarot Card	Creature
Ace of diamonds	III. The Empress	Glabrezu (demon)
King of diamonds	Two of cups	Male elf wizard and female apprentice
Queen of diamonds	Queen of swords	Half-elf ranger
Jack of diamonds	XIV. Temperance	Harpy
Ten of diamonds	Seven of staves	Male half-orc barbarian
Nine of diamonds	Four of pentacles	Ogre mage
Eight of diamonds	Ace of pentacles	Gnoll
Two of diamonds	Six of pentacles	Kobold

Playing Card	Tarot Card	Creature
Ace of spades	II. The High Priestess	Lich
King of spades	Three of staves	Three human clerics
Queen of spades	Four of cups	Medusa
Jack of spades	Knight of pentacles	Male dwarf paladin
Ten of spades	Seven of swords	Frost giant
Nine of spades	Three of swords	Troll
Eight of spades	Ace of swords	Hobgoblin
Two of spades	Five of cups	Goblin

Playing Card	Tarot Card	Creature
Ace of clubs	VIII. Strength	Iron golem
King of clubs	Page of pentacles	Three halfling rogues
Queen of clubs	Ten of cups	Pixie
Jack of clubs	Nine of pentacles	Half-elf bard
Ten of clubs	Nine of staves	Hill giant
Nine of clubs	King of swords	Ogre
Eight of clubs	Ace of staves	Orc
Two of clubs	Five of cups	Kobold

Playing Card	Tarot Card	Creature
Joker	Two of pentacles	Illusion of deck's owner
Joker (trademark)	Two of staves	Illusion of deck's owner (sex reversed)

A randomly generated deck is usually complete (11–100 on d%), but may be discovered (01–10) with 1d20 of its cards missing. If cards are missing, reduce the price by a corresponding amount.

CONSTRUCTION

Requirements Craft Wondrous Item, *major image*; **Cost** 4,050 gp

DIMENSIONAL SHACKLES

Aura moderate abjuration; **CL** 11th

Slot wrists; **Price** 28,000 gp; **Weight** 5 lbs.

DESCRIPTION

These shackles have golden runes traced across their cold iron links. Any creature bound within them is affected as if a *dimensional anchor* spell were cast upon it (no save). They fit any Small to Large creature. The DC to break or slip out of the shackles is 30.

CONSTRUCTION

Requirements Craft Wondrous Item, *dimensional anchor*; **Cost** 14,000 gp

DRUMS OF PANIC

Aura moderate necromancy; **CL** 7th

Slot none; **Price** 30,000 gp; **Weight** 10 lbs. for the pair.

DESCRIPTION

These drums are kettle drums (hemispheres about 1-1/2 feet in diameter on stands). They come in pairs and are unremarkable in appearance. If both of the pair are sounded, all creatures within 120 feet (with the exception of those within a 20-foot-radius safe zone around the drums) are affected as by a *fear* spell (Will DC 16 partial). *Drums of panic* can be used once per day.

CONSTRUCTION

Requirements Craft Wondrous Item, *fear*; **Cost** 15,000 gp

DUST OF APPEARANCE

Aura faint conjuration; **CL** 5th

Slot none; **Price** 1,800 gp; **Weight** —

DESCRIPTION

This powder appears to be a very fine, very light metallic dust. A single handful of this substance flung into the air coats objects within a 10-foot radius, making them visible even if they are invisible. It likewise negates the effects of *blur* and *displacement*. In this, it works just like the *faerie fire* spell. The dust also reveals figments, mirror images, and projected images for what they are. A creature coated with the dust takes a –30 penalty on its Stealth checks. The dust's effect lasts for 5 minutes.

Dust of appearance is typically stored in small silk packets or hollow bone tubes.

CONSTRUCTION

Requirements Craft Wondrous Item, *glitterdust*; **Cost** 900 gp

DUST OF DISAPPEARANCE

Aura moderate illusion; **CL** 7th

Slot none; **Price** 3,500 gp; **Weight** —

DESCRIPTION

This dust looks like *dust of appearance* and is typically stored in the same manner. A creature or object touched by it becomes invisible (as *greater invisibility*). Normal vision can't see dusted creatures or objects, nor can they be detected by magical means, including *see invisibility* or *invisibility purge*. *Dust of appearance*, however, does reveal people and objects made invisible by *dust of disappearance*. Other factors, such as sound and smell, also allow possible detection.

The *greater invisibility* bestowed by the dust lasts for 2d6 rounds. The invisible creature doesn't know when the duration will end.

CONSTRUCTION

Requirements Craft Wondrous Item, *greater invisibility*; **Cost** 1,750 gp

DUST OF DRYNESS

Aura moderate transmutation; **CL** 11th

Slot none; **Price** 850 gp; **Weight** —

DESCRIPTION

This special dust has many uses. If it is thrown into water, a volume of as much as 100 gallons is instantly transformed into nothingness, and the dust becomes a marble-sized pellet, floating or resting where it was thrown. If this pellet is hurled, it breaks and releases the same volume of water. The dust affects only water (fresh, salt, alkaline), not other liquids.

If the dust is employed against an outsider with the elemental and water subtypes, the creature must make a DC 18 Fortitude save or be destroyed. The dust deals 5d6 points of damage to the creature even if its saving throw succeeds.

CONSTRUCTION

Requirements Craft Wondrous Item, *control water*; **Cost** 425 gp

DUST OF ILLUSION

Aura moderate illusion; **CL** 6th

Slot none; **Price** 1,200 gp; **Weight** —

DESCRIPTION

This unremarkable powder resembles chalk dust or powdered graphite. Stare at it, however, and the dust changes color and form. Put *dust of illusion* on a creature, and that creature is affected as if by a *disguise self* glamer, with the individual who sprinkles the dust envisioning the illusion desired. An unwilling target is allowed a DC 11 Reflex save to avoid the dust. The glamer lasts for 2 hours.

CONSTRUCTION

Requirements Craft Wondrous Item, *disguise self*; **Cost** 600 gp

DUST OF TRACELESSNESS

Aura faint transmutation; **CL** 3rd

Slot none; **Price** 250 gp; **Weight** —

DESCRIPTION

This normal-seeming dust is actually a magic powder that can conceal the passage of its possessor and his companions. Tossing a handful of this dust into the air causes a chamber of up to 100 square feet of floor space to become as dusty, dirty, and cobweb-laden as if it had been abandoned and disused for a decade.

A handful of dust sprinkled along a trail causes evidence of the passage of as many as a dozen men and horses to be obliterated for 250 feet back into the distance. The results of the dust are instantaneous, and no magical aura lingers afterward from this use of the dust. Survival checks made to track a quarry across an area affected by this dust have a DC 20 higher than normal.

CONSTRUCTION

Requirements Craft Wondrous Item, *pass without trace*; **Cost** 125 gp

EFFICIENT QUIVER

Aura moderate conjuration; **CL** 9th

Slot none; **Price** 1,800 gp; **Weight** 2 lbs.

DESCRIPTION

This appears to be a typical arrow container capable of holding about 20 arrows. It has three distinct portions, each with a nondimensional space allowing it to store far more than would normally be possible. The first and smallest one can contain up to 60 objects of the same general size and shape as an arrow. The second slightly longer compartment holds up to 18 objects of the same general size and shape as a javelin. The third and longest portion of the case contains as many as six objects of the same general size and shape as a bow (spears, staves, or the like). Once the owner has filled it, the quiver can quickly produce any item she wishes that is within the quiver, as if from a regular quiver or scabbard. The *efficient quiver* weighs the same no matter what's placed inside it.

CONSTRUCTION

Requirements Craft Wondrous Item, *secret chest*; **Cost** 900 gp

EFREETI BOTTLE

Aura strong conjuration; **CL** 14th

Slot none; **Price** 145,000 gp; **Weight** 1 lb.

DESCRIPTION

This item is typically fashioned of brass or bronze, with a lead stopper bearing special seals. Periodically, a thin stream of bitter-smelling smoke issues from the bottle's top. The bottle can be opened once per day. When opened, the efreeti (see the *Pathfinder RPG Bestiary*) imprisoned within issues from the bottle instantly amid a cloud of noxious smoke. There is a 10% chance (01–10 on d%) that the efreeti is insane and attacks immediately upon being released. There is also a 10% chance (91–100) that the efreeti of the bottle grants three *wishes*. In either case, afterward the efreeti disappears forever, and the bottle becomes nonmagical. The other 80% of the time (11–90), the inhabitant of the bottle loyally serves the character for up to 10 minutes per day (or until the efreeti's death), doing as she commands. Roll each day the bottle is opened for that day's effect.

CONSTRUCTION

Requirements Craft Wondrous Item, *planar binding*; **Cost** 72,500 gp

ELEMENTAL GEM

Aura moderate conjuration; **CL** 11th

Slot none; **Price** 2,250 gp; **Weight** —

DESCRIPTION

An elemental gem comes in one of four different varieties. Each contains a conjuration spell attuned to a specific elemental plane (Air, Earth, Fire, or Water).

When the gem is crushed, smashed, or broken (a standard action), a Large elemental appears as if summoned by a *summon nature's ally* spell. The elemental is under the control of the creature that broke the gem.

The coloration of the gem varies with the type of elemental it summons. Air elemental gems are transparent, earth elemental gems are light brown, fire elemental gems are reddish orange, and water elemental gems are blue-green.

CONSTRUCTION

Requirements Craft Wondrous Item, *summon monster V* or *summon nature's ally V*; **Cost** 1,125 gp

ELIXIR OF FIRE BREATH

Aura moderate evocation; **CL** 11th

Slot none; **Price** 1,100 gp; **Weight** —

DESCRIPTION

This strange bubbling elixir bestows upon the drinker the ability to spit gouts of flame. He can breathe fire up to three times, each time dealing 4d6 points of fire damage to a single target up to 25 feet away. The victim can attempt a DC 13 Reflex save for half damage. Unused blasts of fire dissipate 1 hour after the liquid is consumed.

CONSTRUCTION

Requirements Craft Wondrous Item, *scorching ray*; **Cost** 550 gp

ELIXIR OF HIDING

Aura faint illusion; **CL** 5th

Slot none; **Price** 250 gp; **Weight** —

DESCRIPTION

A character drinking this liquid gains an intuitive ability to sneak and hide (+10 competence bonus on Stealth checks for 1 hour).

CONSTRUCTION

Requirements Craft Wondrous Item, *invisibility*; **Cost** 125 gp

ELIXIR OF LOVE

Aura faint enchantment; **CL** 4th

Slot none; **Price** 150 gp; **Weight** —

DESCRIPTION

This sweet-tasting liquid causes the character drinking it to become enraptured with the first creature she sees after consuming the draft (as *charm person*—the drinker must be a humanoid of Medium or smaller size, Will DC 14 negates). The charm effect wears off in 1d3 hours.

CONSTRUCTION

Requirements Craft Wondrous Item, *charm person*; **Cost** 75 gp

ELIXIR OF SWIMMING

Aura faint transmutation; **CL** 2nd

Slot none; **Price** 250 gp; **Weight** —

DESCRIPTION

This elixir bestows swimming ability. An almost imperceptible magic sheath surrounds the drinker, allowing him to glide through the water easily (+10 competence bonus on Swim checks for 1 hour).

CONSTRUCTION

Requirements Craft Wondrous Item, creator must have 5 ranks in the Swim skill; **Cost** 125 gp

ELIXIR OF TRUTH

Aura faint enchantment; **CL** 5th

Slot none; **Price** 500 gp; **Weight** —

DESCRIPTION

This elixir forces the drinker it to say nothing but the truth for 10 minutes (Will DC 13 negates). She must answer any questions put to her in that time, but with each question she can make a separate DC 13 Will save. If one of these secondary saves is successful, she doesn't break free of the truth-compelling enchantment but also doesn't have to answer that particular question (if she does answer, she must tell the truth). No more than one question can be asked each round. This is a mind-affecting compulsion enchantment.

CONSTRUCTION

Requirements Craft Wondrous Item, *zone of truth*; **Cost** 250 gp

ELIXIR OF TUMBLING

Aura faint transmutation; **CL** 5th

Slot none; **Price** 250 gp; **Weight** —

DESCRIPTION

This draught of liquid grants the drinker the ability to tumble about, avoiding attacks and moving carefully across nearly any surface, granting a +10 competence bonus on Acrobatics checks for 1 hour.

CONSTRUCTION

Requirements Craft Wondrous Item, *cat's grace*; **Cost** 125 gp

ELIXIR OF VISION

Aura faint divination; **CL** 2nd

Slot none; **Price** 250 gp; **Weight** —

DESCRIPTION

Drinking this elixir grants the imbiber the ability to notice acute details with great accuracy (+10 competence bonus on Perception checks for 1 hour).

CONSTRUCTION

Requirements Craft Wondrous Item, *true seeing*; **Cost** 125 gp

EVERSMOKING BOTTLE

Aura faint transmutation; **CL** 3rd

Slot none; **Price** 5,400 gp; **Weight** 1 lb.

DESCRIPTION

This metal urn is identical in appearance to an *efreeti bottle*, except that it does nothing but smoke. The amount of smoke is great if the stopper is pulled out, pouring from the bottle and totally obscuring vision across a 50-foot spread in 1 round. If the bottle is left unstoppered, the smoke billows out another 10 feet per round until it has covered a 100-foot radius. This area remains smoke-filled until the *eversmoking bottle* is stoppered.

The bottle must be resealed by a command word, after which the smoke dissipates normally. A moderate wind (11+ mph) disperses the smoke in 4 rounds; a strong wind (21+ mph) disperses the smoke in 1 round.

CONSTRUCTION

Requirements Craft Wondrous Item, *pyrotechnics*; **Cost** 2,700 gp

EYES OF CHARMING

Aura moderate enchantment; **CL** 7th

Slot eyes; **Price** 56,000 gp for a pair; **Weight** —

DESCRIPTION

These two crystal lenses fit over the user's eyes. The wearer is able to use *charm person* (one target per round) merely by meeting a target's gaze. Those failing a DC 16 Will save are charmed as per the spell. Both lenses must be worn for the magic item to take effect.

CONSTRUCTION

Requirements Craft Wondrous Item, Heighten Spell, *charm person*; **Cost** 28,000 gp

EYES OF DOOM

Aura moderate necromancy; **CL** 11th

Slot eyes; **Price** 25,000 gp; **Weight** —

DESCRIPTION

These crystal lenses fit over the user's eyes, enabling him to cast *doom* upon those around him (one target per round) as a gaze attack, except that the wearer must take a standard action, and those merely looking at the wearer are not affected. Those failing a DC 11 Will save are affected as by the *doom* spell. The wearer also gains the additional power of a continual *deathwatch* effect and can use *fear* (Will DC 16 partial) as a normal gaze attack once per week. Both lenses must be worn for the magic item to take effect.

CONSTRUCTION

Requirements Craft Wondrous Item, *doom, deathwatch, fear*; **Cost** 12,500 gp

EYES OF THE EAGLE

Aura faint divination; **CL** 3rd

Slot eyes; **Price** 2,500 gp; **Weight** —

DESCRIPTION

These items are made of special crystal and fit over the eyes of the wearer. These lenses grant a +5 competence bonus on Perception checks. Wearing only one of the pair causes a character to become dizzy and stunned for 1 round. Both lenses must be worn for the magic item to take effect.

CONSTRUCTION

Requirements Craft Wondrous Item, *clairaudience/clairvoyance*; **Cost** 1,250 gp

FEATHER TOKEN

Aura strong conjuration; **CL** 12th

Slot none; **Price** 50 gp (anchor), 300 gp (bird), 200 gp (fan), 450 gp (swan boat), 400 gp (tree), 500 gp (whip); **Weight** —

DESCRIPTION

Each of these items is a small feather that has a power to suit a special need. The kinds of tokens are described below. Each token is usable once. A particular feather token has no specific features to identify it unless its magic aura is viewed—even tokens with identical powers can be wildly different in appearance.

Anchor: A token that creates an anchor that moors a craft in water so as to render it immobile for up to 1 day.

Bird: A token that creates a small bird that can be used to deliver a small written message unerringly to a designated target. The token lasts as long as it takes to carry the message.

Fan: A token that forms a huge flapping fan, causing a breeze of sufficient strength to propel one ship (about 25 mph). This wind is not cumulative with existing wind speed. The token can, however, be used to lessen existing winds, creating an area of relative calm or lighter winds (but wave size in a storm is not affected). The fan can be used for up to 8 hours. It does not function on land.

Swan Boat: A token that forms a swan-like boat capable of moving on water at a speed of 60 feet. It can carry eight horses and gear, 32 Medium characters, or any equivalent combination. The boat lasts for 1 day.

Tree: A token that causes a great oak to spring into being (5-foot-diameter trunk, 60-foot height, 40-foot top diameter). This is an instantaneous effect.

Whip: A token that forms into a huge leather whip and wields itself against any opponent desired just like a *dancing weapon*. The weapon has a +10 base attack bonus, does 1d6+1 points of nonlethal damage, has a +1 enhancement bonus on attack and damage rolls, and a makes a free grapple attack (with a +15 bonus on its combat maneuver checks) if it hits. The whip lasts no longer than 1 hour.

CONSTRUCTION

Requirements Craft Wondrous Item, *major creation*; **Cost** 25 gp (anchor), 150 gp (bird), 100 gp (fan), 225 gp (swan boat), 200 gp (tree), 250 gp (whip)

FIGURINES OF WONDROUS POWER

Aura varies; **CL** varies

Slot none; **Price** 10,000 gp (bronze griffon), 10,000 gp (ebony fly), 16,500 gp (golden lions), 21,000 gp (ivory goats), 17,000 gp (marble elephant), 28,500 gp (obsidian steed), 15,500 gp (onyx dog), 9,100 gp (serpentine owl), 3,800 gp (silver raven); **Weight** 1 lb.

DESCRIPTION

Each of the several kinds of *figurines of wondrous power* appears to be a miniature statuette of a creature an inch or so high (with one exception). When the figurine is tossed down and the correct command word spoken, it becomes a living creature of normal size (except when noted otherwise below). The creature obeys and serves its owner. Unless stated otherwise, the creature understands Common but does not speak.

If a *figurine of wondrous power* is broken or destroyed in its statuette form, it is forever ruined. All magic is lost, its power departed. If slain in animal form, the figurine simply reverts to a statuette that can be used again at a later time.

Bronze Griffon: When animated, a bronze griffon acts in all ways like a normal griffon under the command of its possessor (see the *Pathfinder RPG Bestiary*). The item can be used twice per week for up to 6 hours per use. When 6 hours have passed or when the

command word is spoken, the bronze griffon once again becomes a tiny statuette. Moderate transmutation; CL 11th; Craft Wondrous Item, *animate objects*.

Ebony Fly: When animated, an ebony fly is the size of a pony and has all the statistics of a pegasus but can make no attacks. The item can be used three times per week for up to 12 hours per use. When 12 hours have passed or when the command word is spoken, the ebony fly again becomes a tiny statuette. Moderate transmutation; CL 11th; Craft Wondrous Item, *animate objects*.

Golden Lions: These figurines come in pairs. They become normal adult male lions. If slain in combat, the lions cannot be brought back from statuette form for 1 full week. Otherwise, they can be used once per day for up to 1 hour. They enlarge and shrink upon speaking the command word. Moderate transmutation; CL 11th; Craft Wondrous Item, *animate objects*.

Ivory Goats: These figurines come in threes. Each goat of this trio looks slightly different from the others, and each has a different function:

- *The Goat of Traveling*: This statuette provides a speedy and enduring mount equal to that of a heavy horse in every way except appearance. The goat can travel for a maximum of 1 day each week—continuously or in any combination of periods totaling 24 hours. At this point, or when the command word is uttered, it returns to its statuette form for no less than 1 day before it can again be used.

- *The Goat of Travail*: This statuette becomes an enormous creature, larger than a bull, with the statistics of a nightmare (see the *Pathfinder RPG Bestiary*) except for the addition of a pair of wicked horns of exceptional size (damage 1d8+4 for each horn). If it is charging to attack, it may only use its horns (but add 6 points of damage to each successful attack in that round). It can be called to life just once per month for up to 12 hours at a time.

- *The Goat of Terror*: When called upon with the proper command word, this statuette becomes a destrier-like mount with the statistics of a light horse. However, its rider can employ the goat's horns as weapons (one horn as a *+3 heavy lance*, the other as a *+5 longsword*). When ridden in an attack against an opponent, the goat of terror radiates *fear* as the spell in a 30-foot radius (Will DC 16 partial). It can be used once every 2 weeks for up to 3 hours per use. Moderate transmutation; CL 11th; Craft Wondrous Item, *animate objects*.

Marble Elephant: This is the largest of the figurines, the statuette being about the size of a human hand. Upon utterance of the command word, a marble elephant grows to the size and specifications of a true elephant. The animal created from the statuette is fully obedient to the figurine's owner, serving as a beast of burden, a mount, or a combatant. The statuette can be used four times per month for up to 24 hours at a time. Moderate transmutation; CL 11th; Craft Wondrous Item, *animate objects*.

Obsidian Steed: This figurine appears to be a small, shapeless lump of black stone. Only careful inspection reveals that it vaguely resembles some form of quadruped. On command, the near-formless piece of obsidian becomes a fantastic mount. Treat it as

a heavy horse with the following additional powers usable once per round at will: *overland flight*, *plane shift*, and *ethereal jaunt*. The steed allows itself to be ridden, but if the rider is of good alignment, the steed is 10% likely per use to carry him to the lower planes and then return to its statuette form. The statuette can be used once per week for one continuous period of up to 24 hours. Note that when an obsidian steed becomes ethereal or plane shifts, its rider and his gear follow suit. Thus, the user can travel to other planes via this means. Strong conjuration and transmutation; CL 15th; Craft Wondrous Item, *animate objects*, *etherealness*, *fly*, *plane shift*.

Onyx Dog: When commanded, this statuette changes into a creature with the same properties as a riding dog except that it is endowed with an Intelligence of 8, can communicate in Common, and has exceptional olfactory and visual abilities. It has the scent ability and adds +4 on its Perception checks. It has 60-foot darkvision, and it can *see invisibility*. An onyx dog can be used once per week for up to 6 hours. It obeys only its owner. Moderate transmutation; CL 11th; Craft Wondrous Item, *animate objects*.

Serpentine Owl: This figurine becomes either a normal-sized horned owl or a giant owl (use the stats for the giant eagle) according to the command word used. The transformation can take place once per day, with a maximum duration of 8 continuous hours. However, after three transformations into giant owl form, the statuette loses all its magical properties. The owl communicates with its owner by telepathic means, informing her of all it sees and hears. Moderate transmutation; CL 11th; Craft Wondrous Item, *animate objects*.

Silver Raven: This silver figurine turns into a raven on command (but it retains its metallic consistency, which gives it hardness 10). Another command sends it off into the air, bearing a message just like a creature affected by an *animal messenger* spell. If not commanded to carry a message, the raven obeys the commands of its owner, although it has no special powers or telepathic abilities. It can maintain its nonfigurine status for only 24 hours per week, but the duration need not be continuous. Moderate enchantment and transmutation; CL 6th; Craft Wondrous Item, *animal messenger*, *animate objects*.

CONSTRUCTION

Requirements Craft Wondrous Item, *animate objects*, additional spells, see text; **Cost** 5,000 gp (bronze griffon), 5,000 gp (ebony fly), 8,250 gp (golden lions), 10,500 gp (ivory goats), 8,500 gp (marble elephant), 14,250 gp (obsidian steed), 7,750 gp (onyx dog), 4,550 gp (serpentine owl), 1,900 gp (silver raven)

GAUNTLET OF RUST

Aura moderate transmutation; **CL** 7th

Slot hands; **Price** 11,500 gp; **Weight** 2 lbs.

DESCRIPTION

This single metal gauntlet looks rusted and pitted but is actually quite powerful. Once per day, it can affect an object as with the *rusting grasp* spell. It also completely protects the wearer and her gear from rust (magical or otherwise), including the attack of a rust monster.

CONSTRUCTION

Requirements Craft Wondrous Item, *rusting grasp*; **Cost** 5,750 gp

GEM OF BRIGHTNESS

Aura moderate evocation; **CL** 6th

Slot none; **Price** 13,000 gp; **Weight** —

DESCRIPTION

This crystal appears to be a long, rough prism. Upon utterance of a command word, though, the gem's facets suddenly grow highly polished as the crystal emits bright light of one of three sorts.

- One command word causes the gem to shed light as a hooded lantern. This use of the gem does not expend any charges, and it continues to emit light until this command word is spoken a second time to extinguish the illumination.
- Another command word causes the *gem of brightness* to send out a bright ray 1 foot in diameter and 50 feet long. This strikes as a ranged touch attack, and any creature struck by this beam is blinded for 1d4 rounds unless it makes a DC 14 Fortitude save. This use of the gem expends 1 charge.
- The third command word causes the gem to flare in a blinding flash of light that fills a 30-foot cone. Although this glare lasts but a moment, any creature within the cone must make a DC 14 Fortitude save or be blinded for 1d4 rounds. This use expends 5 charges.

A newly created *gem of brightness* has 50 charges. When all its charges are expended, the gem becomes nonmagical and its facets grow cloudy with a fine network of cracks.

CONSTRUCTION

Requirements Craft Wondrous Item, *daylight*; **Cost** 6,500 gp

GEM OF SEEING

Aura moderate divination; **CL** 10th

Slot none; **Price** 75,000 gp; **Weight** —

DESCRIPTION

This finely cut and polished stone is indistinguishable from an ordinary jewel in appearance. When it is gazed through, a *gem of seeing* enables the user to see as though she were affected by the *true seeing* spell. A *gem of seeing* can be used for as many as 30 minutes a day, in increments of 5 minutes. These increments do not need to be consecutive.

CONSTRUCTION

Requirements Craft Wondrous Item, *true seeing*; **Cost** 37,500 gp

GLOVES OF ARROW SNARING

Aura faint abjuration; **CL** 3rd

Slot hands; **Price** 4,000 gp; **Weight** —

DESCRIPTION

Once worn, these snug gloves seem to meld with the hands, becoming almost invisible to casual observation. Twice per day, the wearer can act as if he had the Snatch Arrows feat (see Chapter 5 for details), even if he does not meet the prerequisites for the feat. Both gloves must be worn for the magic to be effective, and at least one hand must be free to take advantage of the magic.

CONSTRUCTION

Requirements Craft Wondrous Item, *shield*; **Cost** 2,000 gp

GLOVE OF STORING

Aura moderate transmutation; **CL** 6th

Slot hands; **Price** 10,000 gp (one glove); **Weight** —

DESCRIPTION

This device is a single leather glove. On command, one item held in the hand wearing the glove disappears. The item can weigh no more than 20 pounds and must be able to be held in one hand. While stored, the item has negligible weight. With a snap of the fingers wearing the glove, the item reappears. A glove can only store one item at a time. Storing or retrieving the item is a free action. The item is shrunk down so small within the palm of the glove that it cannot be seen. Spell durations are not suppressed, but continue to expire. If the glove's effect is suppressed or dispelled, the stored item appears instantly. A *glove of storing* uses up your entire hands slot. You may not use another item (even another *glove of storing*) that also uses the hands slot.

CONSTRUCTION

Requirements Craft Wondrous Item, *shrink item*; **Cost** 5,000 gp

GLOVES OF SWIMMING AND CLIMBING

Aura faint transmutation; **CL** 5th

Slot hands; **Price** 6,250 gp; **Weight** —

DESCRIPTION

These apparently normal lightweight gloves grant a +5 competence bonus on Swim checks and Climb checks. Both gloves must be worn for the magic to be effective.

CONSTRUCTION

Requirements Craft Wondrous Item, *bull's strength*, *cat's grace*; **Cost** 3,125 gp

GOGGLES OF MINUTE SEEING

Aura faint divination; **CL** 3rd

Slot eyes; **Price** 2,500 gp; **Weight** —

DESCRIPTION

The lenses of this item are made of special crystal. When placed over the eyes of the wearer, the lenses enable her to see much better than normal at distances of 1 foot or less, granting her a +5 competence bonus on Disable Device checks. Both lenses must be worn for the magic to be effective.

CONSTRUCTION

Requirements Craft Wondrous Item, *true seeing*; **Cost** 1,250 gp

GOGGLES OF NIGHT

Aura faint transmutation; **CL** 3rd

Slot eyes; **Price** 12,000 gp; **Weight** —

DESCRIPTION

The lenses of this item are made of dark crystal. Even though the lenses are opaque, when placed over the eyes of the wearer, they enable him to see normally and also grant him 60-foot darkvision. Both lenses must be worn for the magic to be effective.

CONSTRUCTION

Requirements Craft Wondrous Item, *darkvision*; **Cost** 6,000 gp

GOLEM MANUAL

Aura varies; **CL** varies

Slot none; **Price** 12,000 gp (clay), 8,000 gp (flesh), 35,000 gp (iron), 22,000 gp (stone), 44,000 gp (stone guardian); **Weight** 5 lbs.

DESCRIPTION

A *golem manual* contains information, incantations, and magical power that help a character to craft a golem (see the *Pathfinder RPG Bestiary*). The instructions therein grant a +5 competence bonus on skill checks made to craft the golem's body. Each manual also holds the prerequisite spells needed for a specific golem (although these spells can only be used to create a golem and cannot be copied), effectively granting the builder use of the Craft Construct feat during the construction of the golem, and an increase to her caster level for the purpose of crafting a golem.

The spells included in a *golem manual* require a spell trigger activation and can be activated only to assist in the construction of a golem. The cost of the book does not include the cost of constructing the golem's body. Once the golem is finished, the writing in the manual fades and the book is consumed in flames. When the book's ashes are sprinkled upon the golem, it becomes fully animated.

Clay Golem Manual: The book contains *animate objects, bless, commune, prayer,* and *resurrection*. The reader may treat her caster level as two levels higher than normal for the purpose of crafting a clay golem. Moderate conjuration, divination, enchantment, and transmutation; CL 11th; Craft Construct, creator must be caster level 11th, *animate objects, commune, prayer, resurrection*.

Flesh Golem Manual: The book contains *animate dead, bull's strength, geas/quest,* and *limited wish*. The reader may treat her caster level as one level higher than normal for the purpose of crafting a flesh golem. Moderate enchantment, necromancy [evil], and transmutation; CL 8th; Craft Construct, creator must be caster level 8th, *animate dead, bull's strength, geas/quest, limited wish*.

Iron Golem Manual: The book contains *cloudkill, geas/quest, limited wish,* and *polymorph any object*. The reader may treat her caster level as four levels higher than normal for the purpose of crafting a iron golem. Strong conjuration, enchantment, and transmutation; CL 16th; Craft Construct, creator must be caster level 16th, *cloudkill, geas/quest, limited wish, polymorph any object*.

Stone Golem Manual: The book contains *antimagic field, geas/quest, limited wish,* and *symbol of stunning*. The reader may treat her caster level as three levels higher than normal for the purpose of crafting a stone golem. Strong abjuration and enchantment; CL 14th; Craft Construct, creator must be caster level 14th, *antimagic field, geas/quest, limited wish, symbol of stunning*.

Stone Golem Guardian Manual: The book contains *antimagic field, discern location, geas/quest, limited wish, shield,* and *symbol of stunning*. The reader may treat her caster level as three levels higher than normal for the purpose of crafting a stone golem shield guardian. Strong abjuration and enchantment; CL 16th; Craft Construct, creator must be caster level 16th, *antimagic field, discern location, geas/quest, limited wish, shield,* and *symbol of stunning*.

CONSTRUCTION

Requirements Craft Construct, caster must be of a specific level, additional spells; **Cost** 6,000 gp (clay), 4,000 gp (flesh), 17,500 gp (iron), 11,000 gp (stone), 22,000 gp (stone guardian)

HAND OF GLORY

Aura faint varied; **CL** 5th

Slot neck; **Price** 8,000 gp; **Weight** 2 lbs.

DESCRIPTION

This mummified human hand hangs by a leather cord around a character's neck (taking up space as a magic necklace would). If a magic ring is placed on one of the fingers of the hand, the wearer benefits from the ring as if wearing it herself, and it does not count against her two-ring limit. The hand can wear only one ring at a time. Even without a ring, the hand itself allows its wearer to use *daylight* and *see invisibility* each once per day.

CONSTRUCTION

Requirements Craft Wondrous Item, *animate dead, daylight, see invisibility*; **Cost** 4,000 gp

HAND OF THE MAGE

Aura faint transmutation; **CL** 2nd

Slot neck; **Price** 900 gp; **Weight** 2 lbs.

DESCRIPTION

This mummified elf hand hangs by a golden chain around a character's neck (taking up space as a magic necklace would). It allows the wearer to utilize the spell *mage hand* at will.

CONSTRUCTION

Requirements Craft Wondrous Item, *mage hand*; **Cost** 450 gp

HANDY HAVERSACK

Aura moderate conjuration; **CL** 9th

Slot none; **Price** 2,000 gp; **Weight** 5 lbs.

DESCRIPTION

A backpack of this sort appears to be well made, well used, and quite ordinary. It is constructed of finely tanned leather, and the straps have brass hardware and buckles. It has two side pouches, each of which appears large enough to hold about a quart of material. In fact, each is like a *bag of holding* and can actually hold material of as much as 2 cubic feet in volume or 20 pounds in weight. The large central portion of the pack can contain up to 8 cubic feet or 80 pounds of material. Even when so filled, the backpack always weighs only 5 pounds.

While such storage is useful enough, the pack has an even greater power. When the wearer reaches into it for a specific item, that item is always on top. Thus, no digging around and fumbling is ever necessary to find what a haversack contains. Retrieving any specific item from a haversack is a move action, but it does not provoke the attacks of opportunity that retrieving a stored item usually does.

CONSTRUCTION

Requirements Craft Wondrous Item, *secret chest*; **Cost** 1,000 gp

HARP OF CHARMING

Aura faint enchantment; **CL** 5th

Slot none; **Price** 7,500 gp; **Weight** 5 lbs.

DESCRIPTION

This beautiful and intricately carved harp can be held comfortably in one hand, but both hands are required to utilize its magic. When played, a *harp of charming* enables the performer to work one *suggestion* (as the spell, Will DC 14 negates) into the music for each 10 minutes of playing if he can succeed on a DC 14 Perform (string instruments) check. If the check fails, the audience cannot be affected by any further performances from the harpist for 24 hours.

CONSTRUCTION

Requirements Craft Wondrous Item, *suggestion*; **Cost** 3,750 gp

HAT OF DISGUISE

Aura faint illusion; **CL** 1st

Slot head; **Price** 1,800 gp; **Weight** —

DESCRIPTION

This apparently normal hat allows its wearer to alter her appearance as with a *disguise self* spell. As part of the disguise, the hat can be changed to appear as a comb, ribbon, headband, cap, coif, hood, helmet, and so on.

CONSTRUCTION

Requirements Craft Wondrous Item, *disguise self*; **Cost** 900 gp

HEADBAND OF ALLURING CHARISMA

Aura moderate transmutation; **CL** 8th

Slot headband; **Price** 4,000 gp (+2), 16,000 gp (+4), 36,000 gp (+6); **Weight** 1 lb.

DESCRIPTION

This attractive silver headband is decorated with a number of small red and orange gemstones. The headband grants the wearer an enhancement bonus to Charisma of +2, +4, or +6. Treat this as a temporary ability bonus for the first 24 hours the headband is worn.

CONSTRUCTION

Requirements Craft Wondrous Item, *eagle's splendor*; **Cost** 2,000 gp (+2), 8,000 gp (+4), 18,000 gp (+6)

HEADBAND OF INSPIRED WISDOM

Aura moderate transmutation; **CL** 8th

Slot headband; **Price** 4,000 gp (+2), 16,000 gp (+4), 36,000 gp (+6); **Weight** 1 lb.

DESCRIPTION

This simple bronze headband is decorated with an intricate pattern of small green gemstones. The headband grants the wearer an enhancement bonus to Wisdom of +2, +4, or +6. Treat this as a temporary ability bonus for the first 24 hours the headband is worn.

CONSTRUCTION

Requirements Craft Wondrous Item, *owl's wisdom*; **Cost** 2,000 gp (+2), 8,000 gp (+4), 18,000 gp (+6)

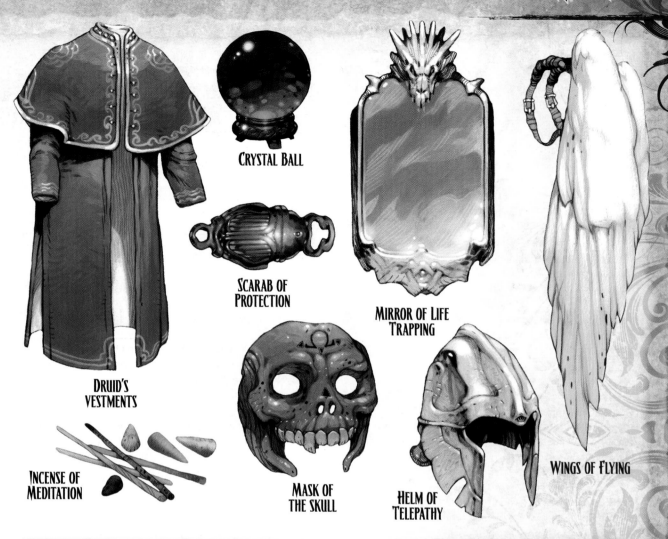

DRUID'S
VESTMENTS

CRYSTAL BALL

SCARAB OF
PROTECTION

MIRROR OF LIFE
TRAPPING

INCENSE OF
MEDITATION

MASK OF
THE SKULL

HELM OF
TELEPATHY

WINGS OF FLYING

HEADBAND OF MENTAL PROWESS

Aura strong transmutation; **CL** 12th

Slot headband; **Price** 10,000 gp (+2), 40,000 gp (+4), 90,000 gp (+6); **Weight** 1 lb.

DESCRIPTION

This simple copper headband has a small yellow gem set so that when it rests upon the forehead of the wearer, the yellow gem sits perched on the wearer's brow as if it were a third eye in the middle of his forehead. Often, the headband contains additional designs to further accentuate the appearance of a third, crystal eye.

The headband grants the wearer an enhancement bonus to two mental ability scores (Intelligence, Wisdom, or Charisma) of +2, +4, or +6. Treat this as a temporary ability bonus for the first 24 hours the headband is worn. These bonuses are chosen when the headband is created and cannot be changed. If the headband grants a bonus to Intelligence, it also grants skill ranks as a *headband of vast intelligence*.

CONSTRUCTION

Requirements Craft Wondrous Item, *eagle's splendor*, *fox's cunning*, and/or *owl's wisdom*; **Cost** 5,000 gp (+2), 20,000 gp (+4), 45,000 gp (+6)

HEADBAND OF MENTAL SUPERIORITY

Aura strong transmutation; **CL** 16th

Slot headband; **Price** 16,000 gp (+2), 64,000 gp (+4), 144,000 gp (+6); **Weight** 1 lb.

DESCRIPTION

This ornate headband is decorated with numerous small white gemstones. The headband grants the wearer an enhancement bonus to all mental ability scores (Intelligence, Wisdom, and Charisma) of +2, +4, or +6. Treat this as a temporary ability bonus for the first 24 hours the headband is worn. The headband also grants skill ranks as a *headband of vast intelligence*.

CONSTRUCTION

Requirements Craft Wondrous Item, *eagle's splendor*, *fox's cunning*, *owl's wisdom*; **Cost** 8,000 gp (+2), 32,000 gp (+4), 77,000 gp (+6)

HEADBAND OF VAST INTELLIGENCE

Aura moderate transmutation; **CL** 8th

Slot headband; **Price** 4,000 gp (+2), 16,000 gp (+4), 36,000 gp (+6); **Weight** 1 lb.

DESCRIPTION

This intricate gold headband is decorated with several small blue and deep purple gemstones. The headband grants the wearer an enhancement bonus to Intelligence of +2, +4, or +6. Treat this as a temporary ability bonus for the first 24 hours the headband is worn. A *headband of vast intelligence* has one skill associated with it per +2 bonus it grants. After being worn for 24 hours, the headband grants a number of skill ranks in those skills equal to the wearer's total Hit Dice. These ranks do not stack with the ranks a creature already possesses. These skills are chosen when the headband is created. If no skill is listed, the headband is assumed to grant skill ranks in randomly determined Knowledge skills.

CONSTRUCTION

Requirements Craft Wondrous Item, *fox's cunning*; **Cost** 2,000 gp (+2), 8,000 gp (+4), 18,000 gp (+6)

HELM OF BRILLIANCE

Aura strong varied; **CL** 13th

Slot head; **Price** 125,000 gp; **Weight** 3 lbs.

DESCRIPTION

This normal-looking helm takes its true form and manifests its powers when the user dons it and speaks the command word. Made of brilliant silver and polished steel, a newly created helm is set with large magic gems: 10 diamonds, 20 rubies, 30 fire opals, and 40 opals. When struck by bright light, the helm scintillates and sends forth reflective rays in all directions from its crown-like, gem-tipped spikes. The jewels' functions are as follows:

- Diamond: *Prismatic spray* (save DC 20)
- Ruby: *Wall of fire*
- Fire opal: *Fireball* (10d6, Reflex DC 20 half)
- Opal: *Daylight*

The helm may be used once per round, but each gem can perform its spell-like power just once. Until all its jewels are depleted, a *helm of brilliance* also has the following magical properties when activated.

- It emanates a bluish light when undead are within 30 feet. This light causes 1d6 points of damage per round to all such creatures within that range.
- The wearer may command any weapon he wields to become a *flaming weapon*. This is in addition to whatever abilities the weapon may already have (unless the weapon already is a *flaming weapon*). The command takes 1 round to take effect.
- The helm provides fire resistance 30. This protection does not stack with similar protection from other sources.

Once all its jewels have lost their magic, the helm loses its powers and the gems turn to worthless powder. Removing a jewel destroys it.

If a creature wearing the helm is damaged by magical fire (after the fire protection is taken into account) and fails an additional DC 15 Will save, the remaining gems on the helm overload and detonate. Remaining diamonds become *prismatic sprays* that each randomly target a creature within range (possibly the wearer),

rubies become straight-line *walls of fire* extending outward in a random direction from the helm wearer, and fire opals become *fireballs* centered on the helm wearer. The opals and the helm itself are destroyed.

CONSTRUCTION

Requirements Craft Wondrous Item, *detect undead, fireball, flame blade, daylight, prismatic spray, protection from energy, wall of fire*; **Cost** 62,500 gp

HELM OF COMPREHEND LANGUAGES AND READ MAGIC

Aura faint divination; **CL** 4th

Slot head; **Price** 5,200 gp; **Weight** 3 lbs.

DESCRIPTION

Appearing as a normal helmet, a *helm of comprehend languages and read magic* grants its wearer the ability to understand the spoken words of any creature and to read text in any language and any magical writing. The wearer gains a +5 competence bonus on Linguistics checks to understand messages written in incomplete, archaic, or exotic forms. Note that understanding a magical text does not necessarily imply spell use.

CONSTRUCTION

Requirements Craft Wondrous Item, *comprehend languages, read magic*; **Cost** 2,600 gp

HELM OF TELEPATHY

Aura faint divination and enchantment; **CL** 5th

Slot head; **Price** 27,000 gp; **Weight** 3 lbs.

DESCRIPTION

This pale metal or ivory helm covers much of the head when worn. The wearer can use *detect thoughts* at will. Furthermore, he can send a telepathic message to anyone whose surface thoughts he is reading (allowing two-way communication). Once per day, the wearer of the helm can implant a *suggestion* (as the spell, Will DC 14 negates) along with his telepathic message.

CONSTRUCTION

Requirements Craft Wondrous Item, *detect thoughts, suggestion*; **Cost** 13,500 gp

HELM OF TELEPORTATION

Aura moderate conjuration; **CL** 9th

Slot head; **Price** 73,500 gp; **Weight** 3 lbs.

DESCRIPTION

A character wearing this device may *teleport* three times per day, exactly as if he had cast the spell of the same name.

CONSTRUCTION

Requirements Craft Wondrous Item, *teleport*; **Cost** 36,750 gp

HELM OF UNDERWATER ACTION

Aura faint transmutation; **CL** 5th

Slot head; **Price** 24,000 gp; **Weight** 3 lbs.

DESCRIPTION

The wearer of this helmet can see underwater. Drawing the small lenses in compartments on either side into position before the

HORN OF VALHALLA

d%	Type of Horn	Barbarians Summoned	Prerequisite
01–40	Silver	2d4+2, 2nd-level	None
41–75	Brass	2d4+1, 3rd-level	Spellcaster level 1st
76–90	Bronze	2d4, 4th-level	Proficiency with all martial weapons or bardic performance ability
91–100	Iron	1d4+1, 5th-level	Proficiency with all martial weapons or bardic performance ability

wearer's eyes activates the visual properties of the helm, allowing her to see five times farther than water and light conditions would allow for normal human vision. (Weeds, obstructions, and the like block vision in the usual manner.) If the command word is spoken, the *helm of underwater action* gives the wearer a 30-foot swim speed and creates a globe of air around the wearer's head and maintains it until the command word is spoken again, enabling her to breathe freely.

CONSTRUCTION

Requirements Craft Wondrous Item, *water breathing*; **Cost** 12,000 gp

HORN OF BLASTING

Aura moderate evocation; **CL** 7th

Slot none; **Price** 20,000 gp; **Weight** 1 lb.

DESCRIPTION

This horn appears to be a normal trumpet. It can be sounded as a normal horn, but if the command word is spoken and the instrument is then played, it deals 5d6 points of sonic damage to creatures within a 40-foot cone and causes them to be deafened for 2d6 rounds (a DC 16 Fortitude save reduces the damage by half and negates the deafening). Crystalline objects and creatures take 7d6 points of sonic damage, with no save unless they're held, worn, or carried by creatures (Fortitude DC 16 negates).

If a *horn of blasting* is used magically more than once in a given day, there is a 20% cumulative chance with each extra use that it explodes and deals 10d6 points of sonic damage to the person sounding it.

CONSTRUCTION

Requirements Craft Wondrous Item, *shout*; **Cost** 10,000 gp

HORN OF BLASTING, GREATER

Aura strong evocation; **CL** 16th

Slot none; **Price** 70,000 gp; **Weight** 1 lb.

DESCRIPTION

This horn functions as a *horn of blasting*, except that it deals 10d6 points of sonic damage, stuns creatures for 1 round, and deafens them for 4d6 rounds (a DC 19 Fortitude reduces the damage by half and negates the stunning and deafening). Crystalline objects take 16d6 points of sonic damage as described for the *horn of blasting*. A *greater horn of blasting* also has a 20% cumulative chance of exploding for each usage beyond the first each day.

CONSTRUCTION

Requirements Craft Wondrous Item, *greater shout*; **Cost** 35,000 gp

HORN OF FOG

Aura faint conjuration; **CL** 3rd

Slot none; **Price** 2,000 gp; **Weight** 1 lb.

DESCRIPTION

This small bugle allows its possessor to blow forth a thick cloud of heavy fog similar to that of an *obscuring mist* spell. The fog covers a 10-foot square next to the horn blower each round that the user continues to blow the horn; a fog cloud travels 10 feet each round in a straight line from the emanation point unless blocked by something substantial such as a wall. The device makes a deep, foghorn-like noise, with the note dropping abruptly to a lower register at the end of each blast. The fog dissipates after 3 minutes. A moderate wind (11+ mph) disperses the fog in 4 rounds; a strong wind (21+ mph) disperses the fog in 1 round.

CONSTRUCTION

Requirements Craft Wondrous Item, *obscuring mist*; **Cost** 1,000 gp

HORN OF GOODNESS/EVIL

Aura moderate abjuration; **CL** 6th

Slot none; **Price** 6,500 gp; **Weight** 1 lb.

DESCRIPTION

This trumpet adapts itself to its owner, so it produces either a good or an evil effect depending on the owner's alignment. If the owner is neither good nor evil, the horn has no power whatsoever. If he is good, then blowing the horn has the effect of a *magic circle against evil*. If he is evil, then blowing the horn has the effect of a *magic circle against good*. In either case, this ward lasts for 1 hour. The horn can be blown once per day.

CONSTRUCTION

Requirements Craft Wondrous Item, *magic circle against good*, *magic circle against evil*; **Cost** 3,250 gp

HORN OF VALHALLA

Aura strong conjuration; **CL** 13th

Slot none; **Price** 50,000 gp; **Weight** 2 lbs.

DESCRIPTION

This magic instrument comes in four varieties. Each appears to be normal until someone speaks its command word and blows the horn. Then the horn summons a number of human barbarians to fight for the character who summoned them. Each horn can be blown just once every 7 days. Roll d% and refer to the table above to see what type of horn is found. The horn's type determines what barbarians are summoned and what prerequisite is needed to use the horn. Any character who uses a *horn of Valhalla* but

doesn't have the prerequisite is attacked by the barbarians she herself summoned.

Summoned barbarians are constructs, not actual people (though they seem to be); they arrive with the starting equipment for barbarians. They attack anyone the possessor of the horn commands them to fight until they or their opponents are slain or until 1 hour has elapsed, whichever comes first.

CONSTRUCTION

Requirements Craft Wondrous Item, *summon monster VI*; **Cost** 25,000 gp

HORSESHOES OF SPEED

Aura faint transmutation; **CL** 3rd
Slot feet; **Price** 3,000 gp; **Weight** 12 lbs. (for four)
DESCRIPTION

These iron shoes come in sets of four like ordinary horseshoes. When affixed to an animal's hooves, they increase the animal's base land speed by 30 feet; this counts as an enhancement bonus. As with other effects that increase speed, jumping distances increase proportionally (see Chapter 4). All four shoes must be worn by the same animal for the magic to be effective.

CONSTRUCTION

Requirements Craft Wondrous Item, *haste*; **Cost** 1,500 gp

HORSESHOES OF A ZEPHYR

Aura faint transmutation; **CL** 3rd
Slot feet; **Price** 6,000 gp; **Weight** 4 lbs. (for four).
DESCRIPTION

These four iron shoes are affixed like normal horseshoes. They allow a horse to travel without actually touching the ground. The horse must still run above (always around 4 inches above) a roughly horizontal surface. This means that non-solid or unstable surfaces can be crossed, and that movement is possible without leaving tracks on any sort of ground. The horse moves at its normal base land speed. All four shoes must be worn by the same animal for the magic to be effective.

CONSTRUCTION

Requirements Craft Wondrous Item, *levitate*; **Cost** 3,000 gp

INCENSE OF MEDITATION

Aura moderate enchantment; **CL** 7th
Slot none; **Price** 4,900 gp; **Weight** 1 lb.
DESCRIPTION

This small rectangular block of sweet-smelling incense is visually indistinguishable from nonmagical incense until lit. When it is burned, the special fragrance and pearly hued smoke of this special incense are recognizable by anyone making a DC 15 Spellcraft check.

When a divine spellcaster lights a block of *incense of meditation* and then spends 8 hours praying and meditating nearby, the incense enables him to prepare all his spells as though affected by the Maximize Spell feat. However, all the spells prepared in this way are at their normal level, not at three levels higher (as with the regular metamagic feat).

Each block of incense burns for 8 hours, and the effects persist for 24 hours.

CONSTRUCTION

Requirements Craft Wondrous Item, Maximize Spell, *bless*; **Cost** 2,450 gp

INSTANT FORTRESS

Aura strong conjuration; **CL** 13th
Slot none; **Price** 55,000 gp; **Weight** 1 lb.
DESCRIPTION

This metal cube is small, but when activated by speaking a command word it grows to form a tower 20 feet square and 30 feet high, with arrow slits on all sides and a crenellated battlement atop it. The metal walls extend 10 feet into the ground, rooting it to the spot and preventing it from being tipped over. The fortress has a small door that opens only at the command of the owner of the fortress—even *knock* spells can't open the door.

The adamantine walls of an *instant fortress* have 100 hit points and hardness 20. The fortress cannot be repaired except by a *wish* or a *miracle*, which restores 50 points of damage taken.

The fortress springs up in just 1 round, with the door facing the device's owner. The door opens and closes instantly at his command. People and creatures nearby (except the owner) must be careful not to be caught by the fortress's sudden growth. Anyone so caught takes 10d10 points of damage (Reflex DC 19 half).

The fortress is deactivated by speaking a command word (different from the one used to activate it). It cannot be deactivated unless it is empty.

CONSTRUCTION

Requirements Craft Wondrous Item, *mage's magnificent mansion*; **Cost** 27,500 gp

IOUN STONES

Aura strong varied; **CL** 12th
Slot none; **Price** varies; **Weight** —
DESCRIPTION

These crystalline stones always float in the air and must be within 3 feet of their owner to be of any use. When a character first acquires a stone, she must hold it and then release it, whereupon it takes up a circling orbit 1d3 feet from her head. Thereafter, a stone must be grasped or netted to separate it from its owner. The owner may voluntarily seize and stow a stone (to keep it safe while she is sleeping, for example), but she loses the benefits of the stone during that time. Ioun stones have AC 24, 10 hit points, and hardness 5. The powers of each stone vary depending on its color and shape (see the table).

Regeneration from the pearly white *ioun stone* works like a *ring of regeneration*. It only cures damage taken while the character is using the stone. The pale lavender and lavender-and-green stones work like a *rod of absorption*, but absorbing a spell requires a readied action, and these stones cannot be used to empower spells. Stored spells in the vibrant purple stone must be placed by a spellcaster but

IOUN STONES

Color	Shape	Effect	Market Price
Clear	Spindle	Sustains creature without food or water	4,000 gp
Dusty rose	Prism	+1 insight bonus to AC	5,000 gp
Deep red	Sphere	+2 enhancement bonus to Dexterity	8,000 gp
Incandescent blue	Sphere	+2 enhancement bonus to Wisdom	8,000 gp
Pale blue	Rhomboid	+2 enhancement bonus to Strength	8,000 gp
Pink	Rhomboid	+2 enhancement bonus to Constitution	8,000 gp
Pink and green	Sphere	+2 enhancement bonus to Charisma	8,000 gp
Scarlet and blue	Sphere	+2 enhancement bonus to Intelligence[1]	8,000 gp
Dark blue	Rhomboid	Alertness (as the feat)	10,000 gp
Iridescent	Spindle	Sustains creature without air	18,000 gp
Pale lavender	Ellipsoid	Absorbs spells of 4th level or lower[2]	20,000 gp
Pearly white	Spindle	Regenerate 1 point of damage per 10 minutes	20,000 gp
Pale green	Prism	+1 competence bonus on attack rolls, saves, skill checks, and ability checks	30,000 gp
Orange	Prism	+1 caster level	30,000 gp
Vibrant purple	Prism	Stores three levels of spells, as a *ring of spell storing*	36,000 gp
Lavender and green	Ellipsoid	Absorbs spells of 8th level or lower[3]	40,000 gp

1 This stone has one skill associated with it, as a +2 *headband of vast intelligence*.

2 After absorbing 20 spell levels, the stone burns out and turns to dull gray, forever useless.

3 After absorbing 50 spell levels, the stone burns out and turns dull gray, forever useless.

can be used by anyone (see *ring of minor spell storing*).

CONSTRUCTION

Requirements Craft Wondrous Item, creator must be 12th level; **Cost** half the market price

IRON BANDS OF BINDING

Aura strong evocation; **CL** 13th

Slot none; **Price** 26,000 gp; **Weight** 1 lb.

DESCRIPTION

This potent item appears to be a 3-inch-diameter rusty iron sphere with bandings on the globe.

When the proper command word is spoken and the spherical iron device is hurled at an opponent, the bands expand and then contract to bind the target creature on a successful ranged touch attack. A single Large or smaller creature can be captured thus and held immobile (as if pinned) until the command word is spoken to bring the bands into spherical form again. The creature can break (and destroy) the bands with a DC 30 Strength check or escape them with a DC 30 combat maneuver check or Escape Artist check. *Iron bands of binding* are usable once per day.

CONSTRUCTION

Requirements Craft Wondrous Item, *grasping hand*; **Cost** 13,000 gp

IRON FLASK

Aura strong conjuration; **CL** 20th

Slot none; **Price** 170,000 gp (empty); **Weight** 1 lb.

DESCRIPTION

These special containers are typically inlaid with runes of silver and stoppered by a brass plug bearing a seal engraved with sigils, glyphs, and special symbols. When the user speaks the command word, he can force any creature from another plane into the container, provided that creature fails a DC 19 Will save. The range of this effect is 60 feet. Only one creature at a time can be so contained. Loosing the stopper frees the captured creature.

The command word can be used only once per day.

If the individual freeing the captured creature speaks the command word, the creature can be forced to serve for 1 hour. If freed without the command word, the creature acts according to its natural inclinations. (It usually attacks the user, unless it perceives a good reason not to.) Any attempt to force the same creature into the flask a second time provides it a +2 bonus on its saving throw and makes it hostile. A newly discovered bottle might contain any of the following:

d%	Contents	d%	Contents
01–50	Empty	89	Demon (glabrezu)
51–54	Large air elemental	90	Demon (succubus)
55–58	Invisible stalker	91	Devil (osyluth)
59–62	Large earth elemental	92	Devil (barbazu)
63–66	Xorn	93	Devil (erinyes)
67–70	Large fire elemental	94	Devil (cornugon)
71–74	Salamander	95	Agathion (avoral)
75–78	Large water elemental	96	Azata (ghaele)
79–82	Xill	97	Archon (trumpet)
83–85	Yeth hound	98	Rakshasa
86	Demon (shadow)	99	Demon (balor)
87	Demon (vrock)	100	Devil (pit fiend)
88	Demon (hezrou)		

CONSTRUCTION

Requirements Craft Wondrous Item, *trap the soul*; **Cost** 85,000 gp

LANTERN OF REVEALING

Aura faint evocation; **CL** 5th

Slot none; **Price** 30,000 gp; **Weight** 2 lbs.

DESCRIPTION

This lantern operates as a normal hooded lantern. While it is lit, it also reveals all invisible creatures and objects within 25 feet of it, just like the spell *invisibility purge*.

CONSTRUCTION

Requirements Craft Wondrous Item, *invisibility purge*; **Cost** 15,000 gp

LENS OF DETECTION

Aura moderate divination; **CL** 9th

Slot eyes; **Price** 3,500 gp; **Weight** 1 lb.

DESCRIPTION

This circular prism lets its user detect minute details, granting a +5 competence bonus on Perception checks. It also aids in tracking, adding a +5 competence bonus on Survival checks when tracking. The lens is about 6 inches in diameter and set in a frame with a handle.

CONSTRUCTION

Requirements Craft Wondrous Item, *true seeing*; **Cost** 1,750 gp

LYRE OF BUILDING

Aura moderate transmutation; **CL** 6th

Slot none; **Price** 13,000 gp; **Weight** 5 lbs.

DESCRIPTION

This magical instrument is usually made of gold and inlaid with numerous gems. If the proper chords are struck, a single use of this lyre negates any attacks made against inanimate construction (walls, roof, floor, and so on) within 300 feet. This includes the effects of a *horn of blasting*, a *disintegrate* spell, or an attack from a ram or similar siege weapon. The lyre can be used in this way once per day, with the protection lasting for 30 minutes.

The lyre is also useful with respect to building. Once a week, its strings can be strummed so as to produce chords that magically construct buildings, mines, tunnels, ditches, etc. The effect produced in 30 minutes of playing is equal to the work of 100 humans laboring for 3 days. Each hour after the first, a character playing the lyre must make a DC 18 Perform (string instruments) check. If it fails, she must stop and cannot play the lyre again for this purpose until a week has passed.

CONSTRUCTION

Requirements Craft Wondrous Item, *fabricate*; **Cost** 6,500 gp

MANTLE OF FAITH

Aura strong abjuration [good]; **CL** 20th

Slot chest; **Price** 76,000 gp; **Weight** —

DESCRIPTION

This holy garment, worn over normal clothing, grants damage reduction 5/evil to the character wearing it.

CONSTRUCTION

Requirements Craft Wondrous Item, *stoneskin*; **Cost** 38,000 gp

MANTLE OF SPELL RESISTANCE

Aura moderate abjuration; **CL** 9th

Slot chest; **Price** 90,000 gp; **Weight** —

DESCRIPTION

This garment, worn over normal clothing or armor, grants the wearer spell resistance 21.

CONSTRUCTION

Requirements Craft Wondrous Item, *spell resistance*; **Cost** 45,000 gp

MANUAL OF BODILY HEALTH

Aura strong evocation (if *miracle* is used); **CL** 17th

Slot none; **Price** 27,500 gp (+1), 55,000 gp (+2), 82,500 gp (+3), 110,000 gp (+4), 137,500 gp (+5); **Weight** 5 lbs.

DESCRIPTION

This thick tome contains tips on health and fitness, but entwined within the words is a powerful magical effect. If anyone reads this book, which takes a total of 48 hours over a minimum of 6 days, he gains an inherent bonus from +1 to +5 (depending on the type of manual) to his Constitution score. Once the book is read, the magic disappears from the pages and it becomes a normal book.

CONSTRUCTION

Requirements Craft Wondrous Item, *wish* or *miracle*; **Cost** 26,250 gp (+1), 52,500 gp (+2), 78,750 gp (+3), 105,000 gp (+4), 131,250 gp (+5)

MANUAL OF GAINFUL EXERCISE

Aura strong evocation (if *miracle* is used); **CL** 17th

Slot none; **Price** 27,500 gp (+1), 55,000 gp (+2), 82,500 gp (+3), 110,000 gp (+4), 137,500 gp (+5); **Weight** 5 lbs.

DESCRIPTION

This thick tome contains exercise descriptions and diet suggestions, but entwined within the words is a powerful magical effect. If anyone reads this book, which takes a total of 48 hours over a minimum of 6 days, she gains an inherent bonus from +1 to +5 (depending on the type of manual) to her Strength score. Once the book is read, the magic disappears from the pages and it becomes a normal book.

CONSTRUCTION

Requirements Craft Wondrous Item, *wish* or *miracle*; **Cost** 26,250 gp (+1), 52,500 gp (+2), 78,750 gp (+3), 105,000 gp (+4), 131,250 gp (+5)

MANUAL OF QUICKNESS OF ACTION

Aura strong evocation (if *miracle* is used); **CL** 17th

Slot none; **Price** 27,500 gp (+1), 55,000 gp (+2), 82,500 gp (+3), 110,000 gp (+4), 137,500 gp (+5); **Weight** 5 lbs.

DESCRIPTION

This thick tome contains tips on coordination exercises and balance, but entwined within the words is a powerful magical effect. If anyone reads this book, which takes a total of 48 hours over a minimum of 6 days, he gains an inherent bonus from +1 to +5 (depending on the type of manual) to his Dexterity score. Once the book is read, the magic disappears from the pages and it becomes a normal book.

CONSTRUCTION

Requirements Craft Wondrous Item, *wish* or *miracle*; **Cost** 26,250 gp
(+1), 52,500 gp (+2), 78,750 gp (+3), 105,000 gp (+4), 131,250 gp (+5)

MARVELOUS PIGMENTS

Aura strong conjuration; **CL** 15th
Slot none; **Price** 4,000 gp; **Weight** —

DESCRIPTION

These pigments enable their possessor to create actual, permanent objects simply by depicting their form in two dimensions. The pigments are applied by a stick tipped with bristles, hair, or fur. The emulsion flows from the application to form the desired object as the artist concentrates on the image. One pot of *marvelous pigments* is sufficient to create a 1,000-cubic-foot object by depicting it two-dimensionally over a 100-square-foot surface.

Only normal, inanimate objects can be created. Creatures can't be created. The pigments must be applied to a surface. It takes 10 minutes and a DC 15 Craft (painting) check to depict an object with the pigments. *Marvelous pigments* cannot create magic items. Objects of value depicted by the pigments—precious metals, gems, jewelry, ivory, and so on—appear to be valuable but are really made of tin, lead, glass, brass, bone, and other such inexpensive materials. The user can create normal weapons, armor, and any other mundane item (including foodstuffs) whose value does not exceed 2,000 gp. The effect is instantaneous.

CONSTRUCTION

Requirements Craft Wondrous Item, *major creation*; **Cost** 2,000 gp

MASK OF THE SKULL

Aura strong necromancy and transmutation; **CL** 13th
Slot head; **Price** 22,000 gp; **Weight** 3 lbs.

DESCRIPTION

This fearsome-looking mask of ivory, beaten copper, or pale wood is typically fashioned into the likeness of a human skull with a missing lower jaw, allowing the bottom half of the wearer's face to remain visible when the mask is worn.

Once per day, after it has been worn for at least 1 hour, the mask can be loosed to fly from the wearer's face. It travels up to 50 feet away from the wearer and attacks a target assigned to it. The grinning skull mask makes a touch attack against the target based on the wearer's base attack bonus. If the attack succeeds, the target must make a DC 20 Fortitude save or take 130 points of damage, as if affected by a *finger of death* spell. If the target succeeds on his saving throw, he nevertheless takes 3d6+13 points of damage. After attacking (whether successful or not), the mask flies back to its user. The mask has AC 16, 10 hit points, and hardness 6.

CONSTRUCTION

Requirements Craft Wondrous Item, *animate objects, finger of death, fly;* **Cost** 11,000 gp

MATTOCK OF THE TITANS

Aura strong transmutation; **CL** 16th
Slot none; **Price** 23,348 gp; **Weight** 120 lbs.

DESCRIPTION

This digging tool is 10 feet long. Any creature of at least Huge size can use it to loosen or tumble earth or earthen ramparts (a 10-foot cube every 10 minutes). It also smashes rock (a 10-foot cube per hour). If used as a weapon, it is the equivalent of a Gargantuan +3 *adamantine warhammer*, dealing 4d6 points of base damage.

CONSTRUCTION

Requirements Craft Wondrous Item, Craft Magic Arms and Armor, *move earth;* **Cost** 13,348 gp

MAUL OF THE TITANS

Aura strong evocation; **CL** 15th
Slot none; **Price** 25,305 gp; **Weight** 160 lbs.

DESCRIPTION

This mallet is 8 feet long. If used as a weapon, it is the equivalent of a +3 *greatclub* and deals triple damage against inanimate objects. The wielder must have a Strength of at least 18 to wield it properly. Otherwise, she takes a –4 penalty on attack rolls.

CONSTRUCTION

Requirements Craft Wondrous Item, Craft Magic Arms and Armor, *clenched fist;* **Cost** 12,805 gp

MEDALLION OF THOUGHTS

Aura faint divination; **CL** 5th
Slot neck; **Price** 12,000 gp; **Weight** —

DESCRIPTION

This appears to be a normal pendant disk hung from a neck chain. Usually fashioned from bronze, copper, or silver, the medallion allows the wearer to read the thoughts of others, as with the spell *detect thoughts*.

CONSTRUCTION

Requirements Craft Wondrous Item, *detect thoughts;* **Cost** 6,000 gp

MIRROR OF LIFE TRAPPING

Aura strong abjuration; **CL** 17th
Slot none; **Price** 200,000 gp; **Weight** 50 lbs.

DESCRIPTION

This crystal device is usually about 4 feet square and framed in metal or wood. The frame typically depicts dragons, demons, devils, genies, coiling nagas, or other powerful creatures that are well known for their magical powers. It can be hung or placed on a surface and then activated by giving a command word. The same command word deactivates the mirror. A *mirror of life trapping* has 15 extradimensional compartments within it. Any creature coming within 30 feet of the device and looking at its own reflection must make a DC 23 Will save or be trapped within the mirror in one of the cells. A creature not aware of the nature of the device always sees its own reflection. The probability of a creature seeing its reflection, and thus needing to make the saving throw, drops to 50% if the creature is aware that the mirror traps life and seeks to avoid looking at it (treat as a gaze attack— see the *Pathfinder RPG Bestiary* for rules on gaze attacks).

NECKLACE OF FIREBALLS

Necklace	10d6	9d6	8d6	7d6	6d6	5d6	4d6	3d6	2d6	Market Price
Type I	—	—	—	—	—	1	—	2	—	1,650 gp
Type II	—	—	—	—	1	—	2	—	2	2,700 gp
Type III	—	—	—	1	—	2	—	4	—	4,350 gp
Type IV	—	—	1	—	2	—	2	—	4	5,400 gp
Type V	—	1	—	2	—	2	—	2	—	5,850 gp
Type VI	1	—	2	—	2	—	4	—	—	8,100 gp
Type VII	1	2	—	2	—	2	—	2	—	8,700 gp

When a creature is trapped, it is taken bodily into the mirror. Size is not a factor, but constructs and undead are not trapped, nor are inanimate objects and other nonliving matter. A victim's equipment (including clothing and anything being carried) remains behind. If the mirror's owner knows the right command word, he can call the reflection of any creature trapped within to its surface and engage his powerless prisoner in conversation. Another command word frees the trapped creature. Each pair of command words is specific to each prisoner.

If the mirror's capacity is exceeded, one victim (determined randomly) is set free in order to accommodate the latest one. If the mirror is destroyed (Hardness 1, 5 hit points), all victims currently trapped in it are freed.

CONSTRUCTION

Requirements Craft Wondrous Item, *imprisonment*; **Cost** 100,000 gp

MIRROR OF OPPOSITION

Aura strong necromancy; **CL** 15th

Slot none; **Price** 92,000 gp; **Weight** 45 lbs.

DESCRIPTION

This item resembles a normal mirror about 4 feet long and 3 feet wide. It can be hung or placed on a surface and then activated by speaking a command word. The same command word deactivates the mirror. If a creature sees its reflection in the mirror's surface, an exact duplicate of that creature comes into being. This opposite immediately attacks the original. The duplicate has all the possessions and powers of its original (including magic). Upon the defeat or destruction of either the duplicate or the original, the duplicate and its items disappear completely. The mirror functions up to four times per day. Destroying the mirror (Hardness 1, 5 hit points) causes all of the duplicates to immediately vanish.

CONSTRUCTION

Requirements Craft Wondrous Item, *clone*; **Cost** 46,000 gp

NECKLACE OF ADAPTATION

Aura moderate transmutation; **CL** 7th

Slot neck; **Price** 9,000 gp; **Weight** 1 lb.

DESCRIPTION

This necklace is a heavy chain with a platinum medallion. The magic of the necklace wraps the wearer in a shell of fresh air, making him immune to all harmful vapors and gases (such as *cloudkill* and *stinking cloud* effects, as well as inhaled poisons) and allowing him to breathe, even underwater or in a vacuum.

CONSTRUCTION

Requirements Craft Wondrous Item, *alter self*; **Cost** 4,500 gp

NECKLACE OF FIREBALLS

Aura moderate evocation; **CL** 10th

Slot neck (does not take up slot); **Price** 1,650 gp (type I), 2,700 gp (type II), 4,350 gp (type III), 5,400 gp (type IV), 5,850 gp (type V), 8,100 gp (type VI), 8,700 gp (type VII); **Weight** 1 lb.

DESCRIPTION

This item appears to be a string of beads, sometimes with the ends tied together to form a necklace. (It does not count as an item worn around the neck for the purpose of determining which of a character's worn magic items is effective.) If a character holds it, however, all can see the strand as it really is—a golden chain from which hang a number of golden spheres. The spheres are detachable by the wearer (and only by the wearer), who can easily hurl one of them up to 70 feet. When a sphere arrives at the end of its trajectory, it detonates as a *fireball* spell (Reflex DC 14 half).

Spheres come in different strengths, ranging from those that deal 2d6 points of fire damage to those that deal 10d6. The market price of a sphere is 150 gp for each die of damage it deals.

Each *necklace of fireballs* contains a combination of spheres of various strengths. Some traditional combinations, designated types I through VII, are detailed above.

If the necklace is being worn or carried by a character who fails her saving throw against a magical fire attack, the item must make a saving throw as well (with a save bonus of +7). If the necklace fails to save, all its remaining spheres detonate simultaneously, often with regrettable consequences for the wearer.

CONSTRUCTION

Requirements Craft Wondrous Item, *fireball*; **Cost** 825 gp (type I), 1,350 gp (type II), 2,175 gp (type III), 2,700 gp (type IV), 2,925 gp (type V), 4,050 gp (type VI), 4,350 gp (type VII)

ORB OF STORMS

Aura strong varied; **CL** 18th

Slot none; **Price** 48,000 gp; **Weight** 6 lbs.

DESCRIPTION

This glass sphere is 8 inches in diameter. The possessor can call forth all manner of weather, even supernaturally destructive storms. Once per day, she can call upon the orb to use a *control weather* spell. Once per day on command, she can conjure a *storm of vengeance*. The possessor of the orb is continually protected by an *endure elements* effect.

CONSTRUCTION

Requirements Craft Wondrous Item, *control weather, endure elements, storm of vengeance*; **Cost** 24,000 gp

PEARL OF POWER

Aura strong transmutation; **CL** 17th

Slot none; **Price** 1,000 gp (1st), 4,000 gp (2nd), 9,000 gp (3rd), 16,000 gp (4th), 25,000 gp (5th), 36,000 gp (6th), 49,000 gp (7th), 64,000 gp (8th), 81,000 gp (9th), 70,000 gp (two spells); **Weight** —

DESCRIPTION

This seemingly normal pearl of average size and luster is a potent aid to all spellcasters who prepare spells (clerics, druids, rangers, paladins, and wizards). Once per day on command, a *pearl of power* enables the possessor to recall any one spell that she had prepared and then cast that day. The spell is then prepared again, just as if it had not been cast. The spell must be of a particular level, depending on the pearl. Different pearls exist for recalling one spell per day of each level from 1st through 9th and for the recall of two spells per day (each of a different level, 6th or lower).

CONSTRUCTION

Requirements Craft Wondrous Item, creator must be able to cast spells of the spell level to be recalled; **Cost** 500 gp (1st), 2,000 gp (2nd), 4,500 gp (3rd), 8,000 gp (4th), 12,500 gp (5th), 18,000 gp (6th), 24,500 gp (7th), 32,000 gp (8th), 40,500 gp (9th), 35,000 gp (two spells)

PEARL OF THE SIRINES

Aura moderate abjuration and transmutation; **CL** 8th

Slot none; **Price** 15,300 gp; **Weight** —

DESCRIPTION

This pearl is worth at least 1,000 gp for its beauty alone, yet if it is clasped firmly in hand or held to the breast while the possessor attempts actions related to the pearl's powers, she understands and is able to employ the item.

The pearl enables its possessor to breathe in water as if she were in clean, fresh air. Her swim speed is 60 feet, and she can cast spells and act underwater without hindrance.

CONSTRUCTION

Requirements Craft Wondrous Item, *freedom of movement, water breathing*; **Cost** 8,150 gp

PERIAPT OF HEALTH

Aura faint conjuration; **CL** 5th

Slot neck; **Price** 7,500 gp; **Weight** —

DESCRIPTION

The wearer of this blue gem on a silver chain (worn on the neck) is immune to disease, including supernatural diseases.

CONSTRUCTION

Requirements Craft Wondrous Item, *remove disease*; **Cost** 3,750 gp

PERIAPT OF PROOF AGAINST POISON

Aura faint conjuration; **CL** 5th

Slot neck; **Price** 27,000 gp; **Weight** —

DESCRIPTION

This item is a brilliant-cut black gem on a delicate silver chain meant to be worn about the neck. The wearer is immune to poison, although poisons active when the periapt is first donned still run their course.

CONSTRUCTION

Requirements Craft Wondrous Item, *neutralize poison*; **Cost** 13,500 gp

PERIAPT OF WOUND CLOSURE

Aura moderate conjuration; **CL** 10th

Slot neck; **Price** 15,000 gp; **Weight** —

DESCRIPTION

This stone is bright red and dangles on a gold chain meant to be worn on the neck. The wearer of this periapt automatically becomes stable if his hit points drop below 0 (but not if the damage is enough to kill the wearer). The periapt doubles the wearer's normal rate of healing or allows normal healing of wounds that would not do so normally. Hit point damage caused by bleeding is negated for the wearer of the periapt, but he is still susceptible to damage from bleeding that causes ability damage or drain.

CONSTRUCTION

Requirements Craft Wondrous Item, *heal*; **Cost** 7,500 gp

PHYLACTERY OF FAITHFULNESS

Aura faint divination; **CL** 1st

Slot headband; **Price** 1,000 gp; **Weight** —

DESCRIPTION

This item is a tiny box containing religious scripture. The box is affixed to a leather cord and tied around the forehead, worn so that the box sits upon the wearer's brow. There is no mundane way to determine what function this religious item performs until it is worn. The wearer of a *phylactery of faithfulness* is aware of any action or item that could adversely affect his alignment and his standing with his deity, including magical effects. He acquires this information prior to performing such an action or becoming associated with such an item if he takes a moment to contemplate the act.

CONSTRUCTION

Requirements Craft Wondrous Item, *detect chaos, detect evil, detect good, detect law*; **Cost** 500 gp

PHYLACTERY OF NEGATIVE CHANNELING

Aura moderate necromancy [evil]; **CL** 10th

Slot headband; **Price** 11,000 gp; **Weight** —

DESCRIPTION

This item is a boon to any character able to channel negative energy, increasing the amount of damage dealt to living creatures by +2d6. This also increases the amount of damage healed by undead creatures.

CONSTRUCTION

Requirements Craft Wondrous Item, creator must be a 10th-level cleric; **Cost** 5,500 gp

PHYLACTERY OF POSITIVE CHANNELING

Aura moderate necromancy [good]; **CL** 10th

Slot headband; **Price** 11,000 gp; **Weight** —

DESCRIPTION

This item allows channelers of positive energy to increase the amount of damage dealt to undead creatures by +2d6. This also increases the amount of damage healed by living creatures.

CONSTRUCTION

Requirements Craft Wondrous Item, creator must be a 10th-level cleric; **Cost** 5,500 gp

PIPES OF HAUNTING

Aura faint necromancy; **CL** 4th

Slot none; **Price** 6,000 gp; **Weight** 3 lbs.

DESCRIPTION

This magic item appears to be a small set of pan pipes. When played by a person who succeeds on a DC 15 Perform (wind instruments) check, the pipes create an eerie, spellbinding tune. Those within 30 feet who hear the tune must succeed on a DC 13 Will save or become frightened for 4 rounds. Creatures with 6 or more Hit Dice are unaffected. *Pipes of haunting* can be sounded twice a day.

CONSTRUCTION

Requirements Craft Wondrous Item, *scare*; **Cost** 3,000 gp

PIPES OF THE SEWERS

Aura faint conjuration; **CL** 2nd

Slot none; **Price** 1,150 gp; **Weight** 3 lbs.

DESCRIPTION

If the possessor learns the proper tune, he can use these pipes to attract 1d3 rat swarms if rats are within 400 feet. For each 50-foot distance the rats have to travel, there is a 1-round delay. The piper must continue playing until the rats appear, and when they do so, the piper must make a DC 10 Perform (wind instruments) check. Success means that they obey the piper's telepathic commands so long as he continues to play. Failure indicates that they turn on the piper. If for any reason the piper ceases playing, the rats leave immediately. The Perform DC increases by +5 for each time the rats have been successfully called in a 24-hour period.

If the rats are under the control of another creature, add the HD of the controller to the Perform check DC. Once control is assumed, another check is required each round to maintain it if the other creature is actively seeking to reassert its control.

CONSTRUCTION

Requirements Craft Wondrous Item, *charm animal, summon nature's ally I,* wild empathy ability; **Cost** 575 gp

PIPES OF SOUNDING

Aura faint illusion; **CL** 2nd

Slot none; **Price** 1,800 gp; **Weight** 3 lbs.

DESCRIPTION

When played by a character who has the Perform (wind instruments) skill, these shiny metallic pan pipes create a variety of sounds. The figment sounds are the equivalent of *ghost sound*.

CONSTRUCTION

Requirements Craft Wondrous Item, *ghost sound*; **Cost** 900 gp

PORTABLE HOLE

Aura strong conjuration; **CL** 12th

Slot none; **Price** 20,000 gp; **Weight** —

DESCRIPTION

A *portable hole* is a circle of cloth spun from the webs of a phase spider interwoven with strands of ether and beams of starlight, resulting in a portable extradimensional space. When opened fully, a *portable hole* is 6 feet in diameter, but it can be folded up to be as small as a pocket handkerchief. When spread upon any surface, it causes an extradimensional space 10 feet deep to come into being. This hole can be picked up from inside or out by simply taking hold of the edges of the cloth and folding it up. Either way, the entrance disappears, but anything inside the hole remains, traveling with the item.

The only air in the hole is that which enters when the hole is opened. It contains enough air to supply one Medium creature or two Small creatures for 10 minutes. The cloth does not accumulate weight even if its hole is filled. Each *portable hole* opens on its own particular nondimensional space. If a *bag of holding* is placed within a *portable hole*, a rift to the Astral Plane is torn in that place. Both the bag and the cloth are sucked into the void and forever lost. If a *portable hole* is placed within a *bag of holding*, it opens a gate to the Astral Plane. The hole, the bag, and any creatures within a 10-foot radius are drawn there, the *portable hole* and *bag of holding* being destroyed in the process.

CONSTRUCTION

Requirements Craft Wondrous Item, *plane shift*; **Cost** 10,000 gp

RESTORATIVE OINTMENT

Aura faint conjuration; **CL** 5th

Slot none; **Price** 4,000 gp; **Weight** 1/2 lb.

DESCRIPTION

A jar of this unguent is 3 inches in diameter and 1 inch deep, and contains five applications. Placed upon a poisoned wound or swallowed, the ointment detoxifies any poison (as *neutralize poison* with a +5 bonus on the check). Applied to a diseased area, it removes disease (as *remove disease* with a +5 bonus on the check). Rubbed on a wound, the ointment cures 1d8+5 points of damage (as *cure light wounds*).

CONSTRUCTION

Requirements Craft Wondrous Item, *cure light wounds, neutralize poison, remove disease*; **Cost** 2,000 gp

RING GATES

Aura strong conjuration; **CL** 17th

Slot none; **Price** 40,000 gp; **Weight** 1 lb. each.

DESCRIPTION

These always come in pairs—two iron rings, each about 18 inches in diameter. The rings must be on the same plane of existence and within 100 miles of each other to function. Whatever is put through one ring comes out the other, and up to 100 pounds of material can be transferred each day. (Objects only partially pushed through and then retracted do not count.) This useful device allows for instantaneous transport of items or messages, and even attacks. A character can reach through to grab things near the other ring, or even stab a weapon through if so desired. Alternatively, a character could stick his head through to look around. A spellcaster could even cast a spell through a *ring gate*. A Small character can make a DC 13 Escape Artist check to slip through. Creatures of Tiny, Diminutive, or Fine size can pass through easily. Each ring has an "entry side" and an "exit side," both marked with appropriate symbols.

CONSTRUCTION

Requirements Craft Wondrous Item, *gate*; **Cost** 20,000 gp

ROBE OF THE ARCHMAGI

Aura strong varied; **CL** 14th
Slot body; **Price** 75,000 gp; **Weight** 1 lb.

DESCRIPTION

This normal-appearing garment can be white (01–45 on d%, good alignment), gray (46–75, neither good nor evil alignment), or black (76–100, evil alignment). To most wearers, the robe offers no powers or has no effects unless the wearer's alignment doesn't match that of the robe (see below). Only an arcane spellcaster can fully realize this potent magic item's powers once the robe is donned. These powers are as follows.

- +5 armor bonus to AC.
- Spell resistance 18.
- +4 resistance bonus on all saving throws.
- +2 enhancement bonus on caster level checks made to overcome spell resistance.

As mentioned above, all *robes of the archmagi* are attuned to a specific alignment. If a white robe is donned by an evil character, she immediately gains three permanent negative levels. The same is true with respect to a black robe donned by a good character. An evil or good character who puts on a gray robe, or a neutral character who dons either a white or black robe, gains two permanent negative levels. While these negative levels remain as long as the garment is worn and cannot be overcome in any way (including *restoration* spells), they are immediately removed if the robe is removed.

CONSTRUCTION

Requirements Craft Wondrous Item, *antimagic field*, *mage armor* or *shield of faith*, creator must be of same alignment as robe; **Cost** 37,500 gp

ROBE OF BLENDING

Aura moderate transmutation; **CL** 10th
Slot body; **Price** 8,400 gp; **Weight** 1 lb.

DESCRIPTION

Once per day this simple wool robe allows you to assume the form of another humanoid creature, as if using *alter self*. This change lasts for 1 hour, although you can end it prematurely as a free action. While in this form, you also gain the ability to speak and understand the basic racial languages of your chosen form. For example, if you take the form of an orc, you can speak and understand Orc.

CONSTRUCTION

Requirements Craft Wondrous Item, *alter self*, *tongues*; **Cost** 4,200 gp

ROBE OF BONES

Aura moderate necromancy [evil]; **CL** 6th
Slot body; **Price** 2,400 gp; **Weight** 1 lb.

DESCRIPTION

This sinister item functions much like a *robe of useful items* for the serious necromancer. It appears to be an unremarkable robe, but a character who dons it notes that it is adorned with small embroidered figures representing undead creatures. Only the wearer of the robe can see the embroidery, recognize them for the creatures they become, and detach them. One figure can be detached each round. Detaching a figure causes it to become an actual undead creature (see the list below). The skeleton or zombie is not under the control of the wearer of the robe, but may be subsequently commanded, rebuked, turned, or destroyed. A newly created *robe of bones* always has two embroidered figures of each of the following undead (see the *Pathfinder RPG Bestiary*):

- Human skeleton
- Wolf skeleton
- Heavy horse skeleton
- Fast goblin zombie
- Tough human zombie
- Plague ogre zombie

CONSTRUCTION

Requirements Craft Wondrous Item, *animate dead*; **Cost** 1,200 gp

ROBE OF EYES

Aura moderate divination; **CL** 11th
Slot body; **Price** 120,000 gp; **Weight** 1 lb.

DESCRIPTION

This valuable garment appears to be a normal robe until it is put on. Its wearer is able to see in all directions at the same moment due to scores of visible, magical eye-like patterns that adorn the robe. She also gains 120-foot darkvision.

The *robe of eyes* sees all forms of invisible or ethereal creatures or objects within 120 feet.

The wearer of a *robe of eyes* gains a +10 competence bonus on Perception checks. She retains her Dexterity bonus to AC even when flat-footed, and can't be flanked. She is not able to avert or close her eyes when confronted by a creature with a gaze attack.

A *light* or *continual flame* spell cast directly on a *robe of eyes*

causes it to be blinded for 1d3 minutes. A *daylight* spell blinds it for 2d4 minutes.

CONSTRUCTION

Requirements Craft Wondrous Item, *true seeing*; **Cost** 60,000 gp

ROBE, MONK'S

Aura moderate transmutation; **CL** 10th

Slot body; **Price** 13,000 gp; **Weight** 1 lb.

DESCRIPTION

This simple brown robe, when worn, confers great ability in unarmed combat. If the wearer has levels in monk, her AC and unarmed damage is treated as a monk of five levels higher. If donned by a character with the Stunning Fist feat, the robe lets her make one additional stunning attack per day. If the character is not a monk, she gains the AC and unarmed damage of a 5th-level monk (although she does not add her Wisdom bonus to her AC). This AC bonus functions just like the monk's AC bonus.

CONSTRUCTION

Requirements Craft Wondrous Item, *righteous might* or *transformation*; **Cost** 6,500 gp

ROBE OF SCINTILLATING COLORS

Aura moderate illusion; **CL** 11th

Slot body; **Price** 27,000 gp; **Weight** 1 lb.

DESCRIPTION

The wearer of this robe can cause the garment to display a shifting pattern of incredible hues, color after color cascading from the upper part of the robe to the hem in sparkling rainbows of dazzling light. The colors daze those near the wearer, conceal the wearer, and illuminate the surroundings. It takes 1 full round after the wearer speaks the command word for the colors to start flowing on the robe. The colors create the equivalent of a gaze attack with a 30-foot range. Those who look at the wearer are dazed for 1d4+1 rounds (Will DC 16 negates). This is a mind-affecting pattern effect.

Every round of continuous scintillation of the robe gives the wearer better concealment. The miss chance on attacks against the wearer starts at 10% and increases by 10% each round until it reaches 50% (total concealment).

The robe illuminates a 30-foot radius continuously.

The effect can be used no more than a total of 10 rounds per day.

CONSTRUCTION

Requirements Craft Wondrous Item, *blur*, *rainbow pattern*; **Cost** 13,500 gp

ROBE OF STARS

Aura strong varied; **CL** 15th

Slot body; **Price** 58,000 gp; **Weight** 1 lb.

DESCRIPTION

This garment is typically black or dark blue and embroidered with small white or silver stars. The robe has three magical powers.

- It enables its wearer to travel physically to the Astral Plane, along with all that she is wearing or carrying.
- It gives its wearer a +1 luck bonus on all saving throws.
- Its wearer can use up to six of the embroidered stars on the chest portion of the robe as +5 *shuriken*. The robe grants its wearer proficiency with such weapons. Each shuriken disappears after it is used. The stars are replenished once per month.

CONSTRUCTION

Requirements Craft Wondrous Item, *magic missile*, *astral projection* or *plane shift*; **Cost** 29,000 gp

ROBE OF USEFUL ITEMS

Aura moderate transmutation; **CL** 9th

Slot body; **Price** 7,000 gp; **Weight** 1 lb.

DESCRIPTION

This appears to be an unremarkable robe, but a character who dons it notes that it is adorned with small cloth patches of various shapes. Only the wearer of the robe can see these patches, recognize them for what items they become, and detach them. One patch can be detached each round. Detaching a patch causes it to become an actual item, as indicated below. A newly created *robe of useful items* always has two each of the following patches:

- Dagger
- Bullseye lantern (full and lit)
- Mirror (a highly polished 2-foot-by-4-foot steel mirror) •
- Pole (10-foot length)
- Hempen rope (50-foot coil)
- Sack

In addition, the robe has several other patches. Roll 4d4 for the number of other patches and then roll for each patch on the table below to determine its nature.

d%	Result
01–08	Bag of 100 gold pieces
09–15	Coffer, silver (6 in. by 6 in. by 1 ft.), 500 gp value
16–22	Door, iron (up to 10 ft. wide and 10 ft. high and barred on one side—must be placed upright, attaches and hinges itself)
23–30	Gems, 10 (100 gp value each)
31–44	Ladder, wooden (24 ft. long)
45–51	Mule (with saddle bags)
52–59	Pit, open (10 ft. by 10 ft. by 10 ft.)
60–68	*Potion of cure serious wounds*
69–75	Rowboat (12 ft. long)
76–83	Minor scroll of one randomly determined spell
84–90	War dogs, pair (treat as riding dogs)
91–96	Window (2 ft. by 4 ft., up to 2 ft. deep)
97–100	Portable ram

Multiple items of the same kind are permissible. Once removed, a patch cannot be replaced.

CONSTRUCTION

Requirements Craft Wondrous Item, *fabricate*; **Cost** 3,500 gp

ROPE OF CLIMBING

Aura faint transmutation; **CL** 3rd
Slot none; **Price** 3,000 gp; **Weight** 3 lbs.
DESCRIPTION
A 60-foot-long *rope of climbing* is no thicker than a wand, but it is strong enough to support 3,000 pounds. Upon command, the rope snakes forward, upward, downward, or in any other direction at 10 feet per round, attaching itself securely wherever its owner desires. It can unfasten itself and return in the same manner.

A *rope of climbing* can be commanded to knot or unknot itself. This causes large knots to appear at 1-foot intervals along the rope. Knotting shortens the rope to a 50-foot length until the knots are untied, but lowers the DC of Climb checks while using it by 10. A creature must hold one end of the rope when its magic is invoked.
CONSTRUCTION
Requirements Craft Wondrous Item, *animate rope*; **Cost** 1,500 gp

ROPE OF ENTANGLEMENT

Aura strong transmutation; **CL** 12th
Slot none; **Price** 21,000 gp; **Weight** 5 lbs.
DESCRIPTION
A *rope of entanglement* looks just like any other hempen rope about 30 feet long. Upon command, the rope lashes forward 20 feet or upward 10 feet to entangle a victim. An entangled creature can break free with a DC 20 Strength check or a DC 20 Escape Artist check.

A *rope of entanglement* has AC 22, 12 hit points, hardness 10, and damage reduction 5/slashing. The rope repairs damage to itself at a rate of 1 point per 5 minutes, but if a *rope of entanglement* is severed (all 12 hit points lost to damage), it is destroyed.
CONSTRUCTION
Requirements Craft Wondrous Item, *animate objects, animate rope* or *entangle*; **Cost** 10,500 gp

SALVE OF SLIPPERINESS

Aura moderate conjuration; **CL** 6th
Slot none; **Price** 1,000 gp; **Weight** —
DESCRIPTION
This substance provides a +20 competence bonus on all Escape Artist checks and combat maneuver checks made to escape from a grapple. The salve also grants a +10 competence bonus to the wearer's Combat Maneuver Defense for the purpose of avoiding grapple attempts. In addition, such obstructions as webs (magical or otherwise) do not affect an anointed individual. Magic ropes and the like do not avail against this salve. If it is smeared on a floor or on steps, the area should be treated as a long-lasting *grease* spell. The salve requires 8 hours to wear off normally, or it can be wiped off with an alcohol solution (even wine).

Salve of slipperiness is needed to coat the inside of a container meant to hold *sovereign glue*.

CONSTRUCTION

Requirements Craft Wondrous Item, *grease*; **Cost** 500 gp

SCABBARD OF KEEN EDGES

Aura faint transmutation; **CL** 5th
Slot none; **Price** 16,000 gp; **Weight** 1 lb.
DESCRIPTION
This scabbard can shrink or enlarge to accommodate any knife, dagger, sword, or similar weapon up to and including a greatsword. Up to three times per day on command, the scabbard casts *keen edge* on any blade placed within it.
CONSTRUCTION
Requirements Craft Wondrous Item, *keen edge*; **Cost** 8,000 gp

SCARAB OF PROTECTION

Aura strong abjuration and necromancy; **CL** 18th
Slot neck; **Price** 38,000 gp; **Weight** —
DESCRIPTION
This device appears to be a silver medallion in the shape of a beetle. If it is held for 1 round, an inscription appears on its surface letting the holder know that it is a protective device.

The scarab's possessor gains spell resistance 20. The scarab can also absorb energy-draining attacks, death effects, and negative energy effects. Upon absorbing 12 such attacks, the scarab turns to powder and is destroyed.
CONSTRUCTION
Requirements Craft Wondrous Item, *death ward, spell resistance*; **Cost** 19,000 gp

SCARAB, GOLEMBANE

Aura moderate divination; **CL** 8th
Slot neck; **Price** 2,500 gp; **Weight** —
DESCRIPTION
This beetle-shaped pin enables its wearer to detect any golem within 60 feet, although he must concentrate (a standard action) in order for the detection to take place. A scarab enables its possessor to combat golems with weapons, unarmed attacks, or natural weapons as if those golems had no damage reduction.
CONSTRUCTION
Requirements Craft Wondrous Item, *detect magic,* creator must be at least 10th level; **Cost** 1,250 gp

SILVERSHEEN

Aura faint transmutation; **CL** 5th
Slot none; **Price** 250 gp; **Weight** —
DESCRIPTION
This shimmering paste-like substance can be applied to a weapon as a standard action. It gives the weapon the properties of alchemical silver for 1 hour, replacing the properties of any other special material it might have. One vial coats a single melee weapon or 20 units of ammunition.
CONSTRUCTION
Requirements Craft Wondrous Item; **Cost** 125 gp

SLIPPERS OF SPIDER CLIMBING

Aura faint transmutation; **CL** 4th

Slot feet; **Price** 4,800 gp; **Weight** 1/2 lb.

DESCRIPTION

When worn, a pair of these slippers enables movement on vertical surfaces or even upside down along ceilings, leaving the wearer's hands free. Her climb speed is 20 feet. Severely slippery surfaces—icy, oiled, or greased surfaces—make these slippers useless. The slippers can be used for 10 minutes per day, split up as the wearer chooses (minimum 1 minute per use).

CONSTRUCTION

Requirements Craft Wondrous Item, *spider climb*; **Cost** 2,400 gp

SOVEREIGN GLUE

Aura strong transmutation; **CL** 20th

Slot none; **Price** 2,400 gp (per ounce); **Weight** —

DESCRIPTION

This pale amber substance is thick and viscous. Because of its particular powers, it can be contained only in a flask whose inside has been coated with 1 ounce of *salve of slipperiness*, and each time any of the bonding agent is poured from the flask, a new application of the *salve of slipperiness* must be put in the flask within 1 round to prevent the remaining glue from adhering to the side of the container. A flask of *sovereign glue*, when found, holds anywhere from 1 to 7 ounces of the stuff (1d8–1, minimum 1), with the other ounce of the flask's capacity taken up by the *salve of slipperiness*. One ounce of this adhesive covers 1 square foot of surface, bonding virtually any two substances together in a permanent union. The glue takes 1 round to set. If the objects are pulled apart (a move action) before that time has elapsed, that application of the glue loses its stickiness and is worthless. If the glue is allowed to set, then attempting to separate the two bonded objects has no effect, except when *universal solvent* is applied to the bond. *Sovereign glue* is dissolved by *universal solvent*.

CONSTRUCTION

Requirements Craft Wondrous Item, *make whole*; **Cost** 1,200 gp

STONE OF ALARM

Aura faint abjuration; **CL** 3rd

Slot none; **Price** 2,700 gp; **Weight** 2 lbs.

DESCRIPTION

This stone cube, when given the command word, affixes itself to any object. If that object is touched thereafter by anyone who does not first speak that same command word, the stone emits a piercing screech for 1 hour that can be heard up to a quarter-mile away (assuming no intervening barriers).

CONSTRUCTION

Requirements Craft Wondrous Item, *alarm*; **Cost** 1,350 gp

STONE OF GOOD LUCK (LUCKSTONE)

Aura faint evocation; **CL** 5th

Slot none; **Price** 20,000 gp; **Weight** —

DESCRIPTION

This small bit of agate grants its possessor a +1 luck bonus on saving throws, ability checks, and skill checks.

Construction **Requirements** Craft Wondrous Item, *divine favor*; **Cost** 10,000 gp

STONE SALVE

Aura strong abjuration and transmutation; **CL** 13th

Slot none; **Price** 4,000 gp per ounce; **Weight** —

DESCRIPTION

This ointment has two uses. If an ounce of it is applied to the flesh of a petrified creature, it returns the creature to flesh as the *stone to flesh* spell. If an ounce of it is applied to the flesh of a nonpetrified creature, it protects the creature as a *stoneskin* spell.

CONSTRUCTION

Requirements Craft Wondrous Item, *stone to flesh*, *stoneskin*; **Cost** 2,000 gp

STRAND OF PRAYER BEADS

Aura faint, moderate or strong (many schools); **CL** 1st (*blessing*), 5th (*healing*), 7th (*smiting*), 9th (*karma*), 11th (*wind walking*), 17th (*summons*)

Slot none; **Price** 9,600 gp (lesser), 45,800 gp (standard), 95,800 gp (greater); **Weight** 1/2 lb.

DESCRIPTION

This item appears to be nothing more than a string of prayer beads until the owner casts a divine spell while the beads are carried. Once that occurs, the owner instantly knows the powers of the prayer beads and understands how to activate the strand's special magical beads. Each strand includes two or more special beads, each with a different magic power selected from the following list.

Special Bead Type	Special Bead Ability
Bead of blessing	Wearer can cast *bless*.
Bead of healing	Wearer can cast his choice of *cure serious wounds*, *remove blindness/deafness*, or *remove disease*.
Bead of karma	Wearer casts his spells at +4 caster level. Effect lasts 10 minutes.
Bead of smiting	Wearer can cast *chaos hammer*, *holy smite*, *order's wrath*, or *unholy blight* (Will DC 17 partial).
Bead of summons	Summons a powerful creature of appropriate alignment from the Outer Planes (an angel, devil, etc.) to aid the wearer for 1 day. (If the wearer uses the *bead of summons* to summon a deity's emissary frivolously, the deity takes that character's items and places a *geas* upon him as punishment at the very least.)
Bead of wind walking	Wearer can cast *wind walk*.

A *lesser strand of prayer beads* has a *bead of blessing* and a *bead of healing*. A *strand of prayer beads* has a *bead of healing*, a *bead of karma*, and a *bead of smiting*. A *greater strand of prayer beads* has a *bead of healing*, a *bead of karma*, a *bead of summons*, and a *bead of wind walking*.

Each special bead can be used once per day, except for the *bead of summons*, which works only once and then becomes nonmagical. The *beads of blessing*, *smiting*, and *wind walking* function as spell trigger items; the *beads of karma* and *summons* can be activated by any character capable of casting divine spells. The owner need not hold or wear the *strand of prayer beads* in any specific location, as long as he carries it somewhere on his person.

The power of a special bead is lost if it is removed from the strand. Reduce the price of a strand of prayer beads that is missing one or more beads by the following amounts: *bead of blessing* –600 gp, *bead of healing* –9,000 gp, *bead of karma* –20,000 gp, *bead of smiting* –16,800 gp, *bead of summons* –20,000 gp, *bead of wind walking* –46,800 gp.

CONSTRUCTION

Requirements Craft Wondrous Item and one of the following spells per bead, as appropriate: *bless* (blessing); *cure serious wounds*, *remove blindness/ deafness*, or *remove disease* (healing); *righteous might* (karma); *gate* (summons); *chaos hammer*, *holy smite*, *order's wrath*, or *unholy blight* (smiting), *wind walk* (wind walking); **Cost** 4,800 gp (lesser), 22,900 gp (standard), 47,900 gp (greater)

SUSTAINING SPOON

Aura faint conjuration; **CL** 5th

Slot none; **Price** 5,400 gp; **Weight** —

DESCRIPTION

If this unremarkable appearing utensil is placed in an empty container, the vessel fills with a thick, pasty gruel. Although the gruel tastes like warm, wet cardboard, it is highly nourishing and contains everything necessary to sustain any herbivorous, omnivorous, or carnivorous creature. The spoon can produce sufficient gruel each day to feed up to four humans.

CONSTRUCTION

Requirements Craft Wondrous Item, *create food and water*; **Cost** 2,700 gp

TOME OF CLEAR THOUGHT

Aura strong evocation (if *miracle* is used); **CL** 17th

Slot none; **Price** 27,500 gp (+1), 55,000 gp (+2), 82,500 gp (+3), 110,000 gp (+4), 137,500 gp (+5); **Weight** 5 lbs.

DESCRIPTION

This heavy book contains instruction on improving memory and logic, but entwined within the words is a powerful magical effect. If anyone reads this book, which takes a total of 48 hours over a minimum of 6 days, she gains an inherent bonus from +1 to +5 (depending on the type of tome) to her Intelligence score. Once the book is read, the magic disappears from the pages and it becomes a normal book.

CONSTRUCTION

Requirements Craft Wondrous Item, *miracle* or *wish*; **Cost** 26,250 gp (+1), 52,500 gp (+2), 78,750 gp (+3), 105,000 gp (+4), 131,250 gp (+5)

TOME OF LEADERSHIP AND INFLUENCE

Aura strong evocation (if *miracle* is used); **CL** 17th

Slot none; **Price** 27,500 gp (+1), 55,000 gp (+2), 82,500 gp (+3), 110,000 gp (+4), 137,500 gp (+5); **Weight** 5 lbs.

DESCRIPTION

This ponderous book details suggestions for persuading and inspiring others, but entwined within the words is a powerful magical effect. If anyone reads this book, which takes a total of 48 hours over a minimum of 6 days, he gains an inherent bonus from +1 to +5 (depending on the type of tome) to his Charisma score. Once the book is read, the magic disappears from the pages and it becomes a normal book.

CONSTRUCTION

Requirements Craft Wondrous Item, *miracle* or *wish*; **Cost** 26,250 gp (+1), 52,500 gp (+2), 78,750 gp (+3), 105,000 gp (+4), 131,250 gp (+5)

TOME OF UNDERSTANDING

Aura strong evocation (if *miracle* is used); **CL** 17th

Slot none; **Price** 27,500 gp (+1), 55,000 gp (+2), 82,500 gp (+3), 110,000 gp (+4), 137,500 gp (+5); **Weight** 5 lbs.

DESCRIPTION

This thick book contains tips for improving instinct and perception, but entwined within the words is a powerful magical effect. If anyone reads this book, which takes a total of 48 hours over a minimum of 6 days, she gains an inherent bonus from +1 to +5 (depending on the type of tome) to her Wisdom score. Once the book is read, the magic disappears from the pages and it becomes a normal book.

CONSTRUCTION

Requirements Craft Wondrous Item, *miracle or wish*; **Cost** 26,250 gp (+1), 52,500 gp (+2), 78,750 gp (+3), 105,000 gp (+4), 131,250 gp (+5)

UNGUENT OF TIMELESSNESS

Aura faint transmutation; **CL** 3rd

Slot none; **Price** 150 gp; **Weight** —

DESCRIPTION

When applied to any matter that was once alive, such as wood, paper, or a dead body, this ointment allows that substance to resist the passage of time. Each year of actual time affects the substance as if only a day had passed. The coated object gains a +1 resistance bonus on all saving throws. The unguent never wears off, although it can be magically removed (by dispelling the effect, for instance). One flask contains enough material to coat eight Medium or smaller objects. A Large object counts as two Medium objects, and a Huge object counts as four Medium objects.

CONSTRUCTION

Requirements Craft Wondrous Item, *gentle repose*; **Cost** 75 gp

UNIVERSAL SOLVENT

Aura faint transmutation; **CL** 3rd

Slot none; **Price** 50 gp; **Weight** —

DESCRIPTION

This substance has the unique property of being able to dissolve *sovereign glue*, tanglefoot bags, and all other adhesives. Applying the solvent is a standard action.

CONSTRUCTION

Requirements Craft Wondrous Item, *acid arrow*; **Cost** 25 gp

VEST OF ESCAPE

Aura faint conjuration and transmutation; **CL** 4th

Slot chest; **Price** 5,200 gp; **Weight** —

DESCRIPTION

Hidden within secret pockets of this simple silk vest are magic lockpicks that provide a +4 competence bonus on Disable Device checks. The vest also grants its wearer a +6 competence bonus on Escape Artist checks.

CONSTRUCTION

Requirements Craft Wondrous Item, *knock, grease*; **Cost** 2,600 gp

VESTMENT, DRUID'S

Aura moderate transmutation; **CL** 10th

Slot body; **Price** 3,750 gp; **Weight** —

DESCRIPTION

This light garment is worn over normal clothing or armor. Most such vestments are green, embroidered with plant or animal motifs. When this item is worn by a character with the wild shape ability, the character can use that ability one additional time each day.

CONSTRUCTION

Requirements Craft Wondrous Item, *polymorph* or wild shape ability; **Cost** 1,375 gp

WELL OF MANY WORLDS

Aura strong conjuration; **CL** 17th

Slot none; **Price** 82,000 gp; **Weight** —

DESCRIPTION

This strange, interdimensional device looks just like a *portable hole*. Anything placed within it is immediately cast to another world—a parallel world, another planet, or a different plane (chosen randomly). If the well is moved, it opens to a new plane (also randomly determined). It can be picked up, folded, or rolled, just as a *portable hole* can be. Objects from the world the well touches can come through the opening just as easily—it is a two-way portal.

CONSTRUCTION

Requirements Craft Wondrous Item, *gate*; **Cost** 41,000 gp

WIND FAN

Aura faint evocation; **CL** 5th

Slot none; **Price** 5,500 gp; **Weight** —

DESCRIPTION

A *wind fan* appears to be nothing more than a wood and papyrus or cloth instrument with which to create a cooling breeze. By uttering the command word, its possessor causes the fan to duplicate a *gust of wind* spell. The fan can be used once per day with no risk. If it is used more frequently, there is a 20% cumulative chance per usage during that day that the device tears into useless, nonmagical tatters.

CONSTRUCTION

Requirements Craft Wondrous Item, *gust of wind*; **Cost** 2,750 gp

WINGS OF FLYING

Aura moderate transmutation; **CL** 10th

Slot shoulders; **Price** 54,000 gp; **Weight** 2 lbs.

DESCRIPTION

A pair of these wings might appear to be nothing more than a plain cloak of old, black cloth, or they could be as elegant as a long cape of blue feathers. When the wearer speaks the command word, the cloak turns into a pair of bat or bird wings that empower her to fly with a speed of 60 feet (average maneuverability), also granting a +5 competence bonus on Fly skill checks.

CONSTRUCTION

Requirements Craft Wondrous Item, *fly*; **Cost** 27,000 gp

INTELLIGENT ITEMS

Magic items sometimes have intelligence of their own. Magically imbued with sentience, these items think and feel the same way characters do and should be treated as NPCs. Intelligent items have extra abilities and sometimes extraordinary powers and special purposes. Only permanent magic items (as opposed to single-use items or those with charges) can be intelligent. (This means that potions, scrolls, and wands, among other items, are never intelligent.) In general, less than 1% of magic items have intelligence.

Intelligent items can actually be considered creatures because they have Intelligence, Wisdom, and Charisma scores. Treat them as constructs. Intelligent items often have the ability to illuminate their surroundings at will (as magic weapons do); many cannot see otherwise.

Unlike most magic items, intelligent items can activate their own powers without waiting for a command word from their owner. Intelligent items act during their owner's turn in the initiative order.

Designing an Intelligent Item

Creating a magic item with intelligence follows these simple guidelines. Intelligent items must have an alignment, mental ability scores, languages, senses, and at least one other special ability. These statistics and abilities can be improved during creation, increasing the item's overall cost. Many of these abilities add to an item's Ego score. Intelligent items with high Ego scores are difficult to control and can sometimes take control of their owner, making them dangerous to possess.

An intelligent magic item has a base price increase of 500 gp. When determining the total value of an intelligent item, add this value to the sum of the prices of all of its additional abilities gained through being intelligent, before adding them to the magic item's base price.

Intelligent Item Alignment

Any item with intelligence has an alignment (see Table 15–21). Note that intelligent weapons already have alignments, either stated or by implication. If you're generating a random intelligent weapon, that weapon's alignment must fit with any alignment-oriented special abilities it has.

Any character whose alignment does not correspond to that of the item (except as noted by the asterisks on the table) gains one negative level if he or she so much as picks up the item. Although this negative level never results in actual level loss, it remains as long as the item is in hand and cannot be overcome in any way (including by *restoration* spells). This negative level is cumulative with any other penalties the item might place on inappropriate wielders. Items with Ego scores (see below) of 20 to 29 bestow two negative levels. Items with Ego scores of 30 or higher bestow three negative levels.

Intelligent Item Ability Scores

Intelligent magic items possess all three mental ability scores: Intelligence, Wisdom, and Charisma. Each one of these ability scores begins at a value of 10, but can be increased to as high as 20. Table 15–22 shows the cost to increase one of the item's ability scores. This cost must be paid for each ability score raised above 10. For example, an intelligent magic item with a 15 Intelligence, 12 Wisdom, and 10 Charisma would cost at least 2,400 gp more than the base item (including the 500 gp for being an intelligent item).

Languages Spoken by Item

Like a character, an intelligent item understands Common plus one additional language per point of Intelligence bonus. Choose appropriate languages, taking into account the item's origin and purposes. If the item does not possess speech, it can still read and understand the languages it knows.

Senses and Communication

Every intelligent magic item begins with the ability to see and hear within 30 feet, as well as the ability to communicate empathically with its owner. Empathy only allows the item to encourage or discourage certain actions through urges and emotions. Additional forms of communication and better senses increase the item's cost and Ego score, as noted on Table 15–23.

Empathy (Su): Empathy allows the item to encourage or discourage certain actions by communicating emotions and urges. It does not allow for verbal communication.

Speech (Su): An intelligent item with the capability for speech can talk using any of the languages it knows.

Telepathy (Su): Telepathy allows an intelligent item to communicate with its wielder telepathically, regardless of its

TABLE 15-21: INTELLIGENT ITEM ALIGNMENT

d%	Alignment of Item
01–10	Chaotic good
11–20	Chaotic neutral*
21–35	Chaotic evil
36–45	Neutral evil*
46–55	Lawful evil
56–70	Lawful good
71–80	Lawful neutral*
81–90	Neutral good*
91–100	Neutral

* The item can also be used by any character whose alignment corresponds to the non-neutral portion of the item's alignment.

TABLE 15-22: INTELLIGENT ITEM ABILITY SCORES

Score	Base Price Modifier	Ego Modifier
10	—	—
11	+200 gp	—
12	+500 gp	+1
13	+700 gp	+1
14	+1,000 gp	+2
15	+1,400 gp	+2
16	+2,000 gp	+3
17	+2,800 gp	+3
18	+4,000 gp	+4
19	+5,200 gp	+4
20	+8,000 gp	+5

TABLE 15-23: INTELLIGENT ITEM SENSES AND COMMUNICATION

Ability	Base Price Modifier	Ego Modifier
Empathy	—	—
Speech	+500 gp	—
Telepathy	+1,000 gp	+1
Senses (30 ft.)	—	—
Senses (60 ft.)	+500 gp	—
Senses (120 ft.)	+1,000 gp	—
Darkvision	+500 gp	—
Blindsense	+5,000 gp	+1
Read languages	+1,000 gp	+1
Read magic	+2,000 gp	+1

known languages. The wielder must be touching the item to communicate in this way.

Senses: Senses allow an intelligent magic item to see and hear out to the listed distance. Adding darkvision or blindsense allows the item to use those senses out to the same range as the item's base senses.

Table 15-24: Intelligent Item Powers

d%	Item Power	Base Price Modifier	Ego Modifier
01–10	Item can cast a 0-level spell at will	+1,000 gp	+1
11–20	Item can cast a 1st-level spell 3/day	+1,200 gp	+1
21–25	Item can use *magic aura* on itself at will	+2,000 gp	+1
26–35	Item can cast a 2nd-level spell 1/day	+2,400 gp	+1
36–45	Item has 5 ranks in one skill*	+2,500 gp	+1
46–50	Item can sprout limbs and move with a speed of 10 feet	+5,000 gp	+1
51–55	Item can cast a 3rd-level spell 1/day	+6,000 gp	+1
56–60	Item can cast a 2nd-level spell 3/day	+7,200 gp	+1
61–70	Item has 10 ranks in one skill*	+10,000 gp	+2
71–75	Item can change shape into one other form of the same size	+10,000 gp	+2
76–80	Item can *fly*, as per the spell, at a speed of 30 feet	+10,000 gp	+2
81–85	Item can cast a 4th-level spell 1/day	+11,200 gp	+2
86–90	Item can *teleport* itself 1/day	+15,000 gp	+2
91–95	Item can cast a 3rd-level spell 3/day	+18,000 gp	+2
96–100	Item can cast a 4th-level spell 3/day	+33,600 gp	+2

* Intelligent items can only possess Intelligence-, Wisdom-, or Charisma-based skills, unless they also possess some form of ability to move.

Table 15-25: Intelligent Item Purpose

d%	Purpose	Ego Modifier
01–20	Defeat/slay diametrically opposed alignment*	+2
21–30	Defeat/slay arcane spellcasters (including spellcasting monsters and those that use spell-like abilities)	+2
31–40	Defeat/slay divine spellcasters (including divine entities and servitors)	+2
41–50	Defeat/slay non-spellcasters	+2
51–55	Defeat/slay a particular creature type (see the *bane* special ability for choices)	+2
56–60	Defeat/slay a particular race or kind of creature	+2
61–70	Defend a particular race or kind of creature	+2
71–80	Defeat/slay the servants of a specific deity	+2
81–90	Defend the servants and interests of a specific deity	+2
91–95	Defeat/slay all (other than the item and the wielder)	+2
96–100	Choose one	+2

* The purpose of the neutral (N) version of this item is to preserve the balance by defeating/slaying powerful beings of the extreme alignments (LG, LE, CG, CE).

Table 15-26: Special Purpose Item Dedicated Powers

d%	Dedicated Power	Base Price Modifier	Ego Modifier
01–20	Item can detect any special purpose foes within 60 feet	+10,000 gp	+1
21–35	Item can use a 4th-level spell at will	+56,000 gp	+2
36–50	Wielder gets +2 luck bonus on attacks, saves, and checks	+80,000 gp	+2
51–65	Item can use a 5th-level spell at will	+90,000 gp	+2
66–80	Item can use a 6th-level spell at will	+132,000 gp	+2
81–95	Item can use a 7th-level spell at will	+182,000 gp	+2
96–100	Item can use *true resurrection* on wielder, once per month	+200,000 gp	+2

Read Languages (Ex): The item can read script in any language, regardless of its known languages.

Read Magic (Sp): An intelligent magic item with this ability can read magical writings and scrolls as if through *read magic*. This ability does not allow the magic item to activate scrolls or other items. An intelligent magic item can suppress and resume this ability as a free action.

Intelligent Item Powers

Each intelligent item should possess at least one power, although more powerful items might possess a host of powers. To find the item's specific powers, choose or roll on Table 15–24. All powers function at the direction of the item, although intelligent items generally follow the wishes of their owner. Activating a power or concentrating on an active one is a standard action the item takes. The caster level for these effects is equal to the item's caster level. Save DCs are based off the item's highest mental ability score.

Special Purpose Items

Some intelligent items have special purposes that guide their actions. Intelligent magic items with a special purpose gain a +2 Ego bonus. An item's purpose must suit the type and alignment of the item and should always be treated reasonably. A purpose of "defeat/slay arcane spellcasters" doesn't mean that the sword forces the wielder to kill every wizard she sees. Nor does it mean that the sword believes it is possible to kill every wizard, sorcerer, and bard in the world. It does mean that the item hates arcane spellcasters and wants to bring the local wizards' cabal to ruin, as well as end the rule of a sorcerer-queen in a nearby land. Likewise, a purpose of "defend elves" doesn't mean that if the wielder is an elf, he only wants to help the wielder. It means that the item wants to be used in furthering the cause of elves, stamping out their enemies and aiding their leaders. A purpose of "defeat/slay all" isn't just a matter of self-preservation. It means that the item won't rest (or let its wielder rest) until it places itself above all others.

Table 15–25 has a number of sample purposes that a magic item might possess. If the wielder specifically ignores or goes against an intelligent item's special purpose, the item gains a +4 bonus to its Ego until the wielder cooperates. This is in addition to the +2 Ego bonus gained by items with a special purpose.

Dedicated Powers

A dedicated power operates only when an intelligent item is in pursuit of its special purpose. This determination is always made by the item. It should always be easy and straightforward to see how the ends justify the means. Unlike its other powers, an intelligent item can refuse to use its dedicated powers even if the owner is dominant (see Items Against Characters). The caster level for these effects is equal to the item's caster level. Save DCs are based on the

item's highest mental ability score. See Table 15–26 for a list of dedicated powers.

Item Ego

Ego is a measure of the total power and force of personality that an item possesses. An item's Ego score is the sum of all of its Ego modifiers plus an additional bonus for the cost of the base magic item (excluding the cost of all of the intelligent item enhancements). An item's Ego score helps determine whether the item or the character is dominant in their relationship, as detailed below.

Base Magic Item Value	Ego Modifier
Up to 1,000 gp	—
1,001 gp to 5,000 gp	+1
5,001 gp to 10,000 gp	+2
10,001 gp to 20,000 gp	+3
20,001 gp to 50,000 gp	+4
50,001 gp to 100,000 gp	+6
100,001 gp to 200,000 gp	+8
200,001 gp and higher	+12

Items against Characters

When an item has an Ego of its own, it has a will of its own. The item is absolutely true to its alignment. If the character who possesses the item is not true to that alignment's goals or the item's special purpose, personality conflict—item against character—results. Similarly, any item with an Ego score of 20 or higher always considers itself superior to any character, and a personality conflict results if the possessor does not always agree with the item.

When a personality conflict occurs, the possessor must make a Will saving throw (DC = item's Ego). If the possessor succeeds, she is dominant. If she fails, the item is dominant. Dominance lasts for 1 day or until a critical situation occurs (such as a major battle, a serious threat to either the item or the character, and so on). Should an item gain dominance, it resists the character's desires and demands concessions such as any of the following:

- Removal of associates or items whose alignment or personality is distasteful to the item.
- The character divesting herself of all other magic items or items of a certain type.
- Obedience from the character so the item can direct where they go for its own purposes.
- Immediate seeking out and slaying of creatures hateful to the item.
- Magical protections and devices to safeguard the item from molestation when it is not in use.
- That the character carry the item with her on all occasions.
- That the character relinquish the item to a more suitable possessor due to alignment differences or conduct.

In extreme circumstances, the item can resort to even harsher measures, such as the following:

- Force its possessor into combat.
- Refuse to strike opponents.
- Strike at its wielder or her associates.
- Force its possessor to surrender to an opponent.
- Cause itself to drop from the character's grasp.

Naturally, such actions are unlikely when harmony reigns between the character's and item's alignments or when their purposes and personalities are well matched. Even so, an item might wish to have a lesser character possess it in order to easily establish and maintain dominance over him, or a higher-level possessor so as to better accomplish its goals.

All magic items with personalities desire to play an important role in whatever activity is under way, particularly combat. Such items are natural rivals, even with others of the same alignment. No intelligent item wants to share its wielder with others. An intelligent item is aware of the presence of any other intelligent item within 60 feet, and most intelligent items try their best to mislead or distract their host so that she ignores or destroys the rival. Of course, alignment might change this sort of behavior.

Items with personalities are never totally controlled or silenced by the characters that possess them, even though they may never successfully control their possessors. They may be powerless to force their demands, but most remain undaunted and continue to air their wishes and demands.

CURSED ITEMS

Cursed items are magic items with some sort of potentially negative impact. Occasionally they mix bad with good, forcing characters to make difficult choices. Cursed items are almost never made intentionally. Instead they are the result of rushed work, inexperienced crafters, or a lack of proper components. While many of these items still have functions, they either do not work as intended or come with serious drawbacks. When a magic item creation skill check fails by 5 or more, roll on Table 15–27 to determine the type of curse possessed by the item.

Identifying Cursed Items: Cursed items are identified like any other magic item with one exception: unless the check made to identify the item exceeds the DC by 10 or more, the curse is not detected. If the check is not made by 10 or more, but still succeeds, all that is revealed is the magic item's original intent. If the item is known to be cursed, the nature of the curse can be determined using the standard DC to identify the item.

Removing Cursed Items: While some cursed items can be simply discarded, others force a compulsion upon the user to keep the item, no matter the costs. Others reappear even if discarded or are impossible to throw away. These items can only be discarded after the character or item is targeted by a *remove curse* or similar magic. The DC of the caster level check to undo the curse is equal to 10 + the item's caster level. If the spell is successful, the item can be discarded on the following round, but the curse reasserts itself if the item is used again.

Common Cursed Item Effects

The following are some of the most common cursed item effects. GMs should feel free to invent new cursed item effects to fit specific items.

Delusion: The user believes the item is what it appears to be, yet it actually has no magical power other than to deceive. The user is mentally fooled into thinking the item is functioning and cannot be convinced otherwise without the casting of *remove curse*.

Opposite Effect or Target: These cursed items malfunction, so that either they do the opposite of what the creator intended, or they target the user instead of someone else. The interesting point to keep in mind here is that these items aren't always bad to have. Opposite-effect items include weapons that impose penalties on attack and damage rolls rather than bonuses. Just as a character shouldn't necessarily immediately know what the enhancement bonus of a noncursed magic item is, she shouldn't immediately know that a weapon is cursed. Once she knows, however, the item can be discarded unless some sort of compulsion is placed upon it that compels the wielder to keep and use it. In such cases, a *remove curse* spell is generally needed to get rid of the item.

Intermittent Functioning: The three varieties of intermittent functioning items all function perfectly as intended—at least some of the time. The three varieties are unreliable, dependent, and uncontrolled items.

Unreliable: Each time the item is activated, there is a 5% chance (01–05 on d%) that it does not function.

Dependent: The item only functions in certain situations. To determine the situation, select or roll on the following table.

d%	Situation
01–03	Temperature below freezing
04–05	Temperature above freezing
06–10	During the day
11–15	During the night
16–20	In direct sunlight
21–25	Out of direct sunlight
26–34	Underwater
35–37	Out of water
38–45	Underground
46–55	Aboveground
56–60	Within 10 feet of a random creature type
61–64	Within 10 feet of a random race or kind of creature
65–72	Within 10 feet of an arcane spellcaster
73–80	Within 10 feet of a divine spellcaster

81–85	In the hands of a nonspellcaster
86–90	In the hands of a spellcaster
91–95	In the hands of a creature of a particular alignment
96	In the hands of a creature of a particular gender
97–99	On holy days or during particular astrological events
100	More than 100 miles from a particular site

Uncontrolled: An uncontrolled item occasionally activates at random times. Roll d% every day. On a result of 01–05 the item activates at some random point during that day.

Requirement: Some items have stringent requirements that must be met for them to be usable. To keep an item with this kind of curse functioning, one or more of the following conditions must be met.

- Character must eat twice as much as normal.
- Character must sleep twice as much as normal.
- Character must undergo a specific quest (one time only, and the item functions normally thereafter).
- Character must sacrifice (destroy) 100 gp in valuables per day.
- Character must sacrifice (destroy) 2,000 gp worth of magic items each week.
- Character must swear fealty to a particular noble or to his entire family.
- Character must discard all other magic items.
- Character must worship a particular deity.
- Character must change her name to a specific name. The item only works for characters of that name.
- Character must add a specific class at the next opportunity if not of that class already.
- Character must have a minimum number of ranks in a particular skill.
- Character must sacrifice some part of her life energy (2 points of Constitution) one time. If the character gets the Constitution points back (such as from a *restoration* spell), the item ceases functioning. (The item does not cease functioning if the character receives a Constitution increase caused by level gain, a *wish*, or the use of a magic item.)
- Item must be cleansed with holy water each day.
- Item must be used to kill a living creature each day.
- Item must be bathed in volcanic lava once per month.
- Item must be used at least once a day, or it won't function again for its current possessor.
- Item must draw blood when wielded (weapons only). It can't be put away or exchanged for another weapon until it has scored a hit.
- Item must have a particular spell cast upon it each day (such as *bless*, *atonement*, or *animate objects*).

Requirements are so dependent upon suitability to the item that they should never be determined randomly. An intelligent item with a requirement often imposes its requirement through its personality. If the requirement is not met, the item ceases to function. If it is met, usually the item

TABLE 15-27: COMMON ITEM CURSES

d%	Curse
01–15	Delusion
16–35	Opposite effect or target
36–45	Intermittent functioning
46–60	Requirement
61–75	Drawback
76–90	Completely different effect
91–100	Substitute specific cursed item on Table 15–28

TABLE 15-28: SPECIFIC CURSED ITEMS

d%	Item
01–05	*Incense of obsession*
06–15	*Ring of clumsiness*
16–20	*Amulet of inescapable location*
21–25	*Stone of weight*
26–30	*Bracers of defenselessness*
31–35	*Gauntlets of fumbling*
36–40	*–2 sword, cursed*
41–43	*Armor of rage*
44–46	*Medallion of thought projection*
47–52	*Flask of curses*
53–54	*Dust of sneezing and choking*
55	*Helm of opposite alignment*
56–60	*Potion of poison*
61	*Broom of animated attack*
62–63	*Robe of powerlessness*
64	*Vacuous grimoire*
65–68	*Spear, cursed backbiter*
69–70	*Armor of arrow attraction*
71–72	*Net of snaring*
73–75	*Bag of devouring*
76–80	*Mace of blood*
81–85	*Robe of vermin*
86–88	*Periapt of foul rotting*
89–92	*Sword, berserking*
93–96	*Boots of dancing*
97	*Crystal hypnosis ball*
98	*Necklace of strangulation*
99	*Poisonous cloak*
100	*Scarab of death*

functions for one day before the requirement must be met again (although some requirements are one time only, others monthly, and still others continuous).

Drawback: Items with drawbacks are usually still beneficial to the possessor but carry some negative aspect. Although sometimes drawbacks occur only when the item is used (or held, in the case of some weapons), usually the drawback remains with the character for as long as she has the item.

Unless otherwise indicated, drawbacks remain in effect as long as the item is possessed. The DC to save against any of these effects is usually equal to 10 + the item's caster level.

d%	Drawback
01–04	Character's hair grows 1 inch longer every hour.
05–09	Character either shrinks 6 inches (01–50 on d%) or grows that much taller (51–100). Only happens once.
10–13	Temperature around item is 10° F cooler than normal.
14–17	Temperature around item is 10° F warmer than normal.
18–21	Character's hair color changes.
22–25	Character's skin color changes.
26–29	Character now bears some identifying mark (tattoo, weird glow, or the like).
30–32	Character's gender changes.
33–34	Character's race or kind changes.
35	Character is afflicted with a random disease that cannot be cured.
36–39	Item continually emits a disturbing sound (moaning, weeping, screaming, cursing, insults).
40	Item looks ridiculous (garishly colored, silly shape, glows bright pink).
41–45	Character becomes selfishly possessive.
46–49	Character becomes paranoid about losing the item and afraid of damage occurring to it.
50–51	Character's alignment changes.
52–54	Character must attack nearest creature (5% chance [01–05 on d%] each day).
55–57	Character is stunned for 1d4 rounds once item function is finished (or randomly, 1/day).
58–60	Character's vision is blurry (–2 penalty on attack rolls, saves, and skill checks requiring vision).
61–64	Character gains one negative level.
65	Character gains two negative levels.
66–70	Character must make a Will save each day or take 1 point of Intelligence damage.
71–75	Character must make a Will save each day or take 1 point of Wisdom damage.
76–80	Character must make a Will save each day or take 1 point of Charisma damage.
81–85	Character must make a Fortitude save each day or take 1 point of Constitution damage.
86–90	Character must make a Fortitude save each day or take 1 point of Strength damage.
91–95	Character must make a Fortitude save each day or take 1 point of Dexterity damage.
96	Character is polymorphed into a specific creature (5% chance [01–05 on d%] each day).
97	Character cannot cast arcane spells.
98	Character cannot cast divine spells.
99	Character cannot cast any spells.
100	Either pick one of the above that's appropriate or create a drawback specifically for that item.

 SPECIFIC CURSED ITEMS

Perhaps the most dangerous and insidious of all cursed items are those whose intended functions are completely replaced by a curse. Yet even these items can have their uses, particularly as traps or weapons. The following are provided as specific examples of cursed items. Instead of prerequisites, each cursed item is associated with one or more ordinary magic items whose creation might result in the cursed item. Cursed items can be sold, if the curse is not known to the buyer, as if they were the item they appear to be.

Cursed suits of armor and weapons can come in many forms, and the examples listed here are merely the most common. For example, a *cursed –2 sword*, might appear as a *+3 shortsword* or a *+1 dagger*, with a similar negative instead of the listed –2.

AMULET OF INESCAPABLE LOCATION
Aura moderate abjuration; **CL** 10th
Slot neck; **Weight** 1/2 lb.
DESCRIPTION
This device appears to prevent location, scrying and detection, or influence by *detect thoughts* or telepathy, as per an *amulet of proof against detection and location*. Actually, the amulet gives the wearer a –10 penalty on all saves against divination spells.
CREATION
Magic Items *amulet of proof against detection and location*

ARMOR OF ARROW ATTRACTION
Aura strong abjuration; **CL** 16th
Slot armor; **Weight** 50 lbs.
DESCRIPTION
Magical analysis indicates that this armor is a normal suit of +3 full plate. The armor works normally with regard to melee attacks but actually attracts ranged weapons. The wearer takes a –15 penalty to AC against ranged weapons. The true nature of the armor does not reveal itself until the character is fired upon in earnest.
CREATION
Magic Items *+3 full plate*

ARMOR OF RAGE
Aura strong necromancy; **CL** 16th
Slot armor; **Weight** 50 lbs.
DESCRIPTION
This armor is similar in appearance to *breastplate of command* and functions as a *+1 breastplate*. However, when it is worn, the armor causes the character to take a –4 penalty to Charisma. All unfriendly characters within 300 feet have a +1 morale bonus on attack rolls against her. The effect is not noticeable to the wearer or those affected. In other words, the wearer does not immediately notice that donning the armor is the cause of her problems, nor do foes understand the reason for the depth of their enmity.
CREATION
Magic Items *breastplate of command, +1 breastplate*

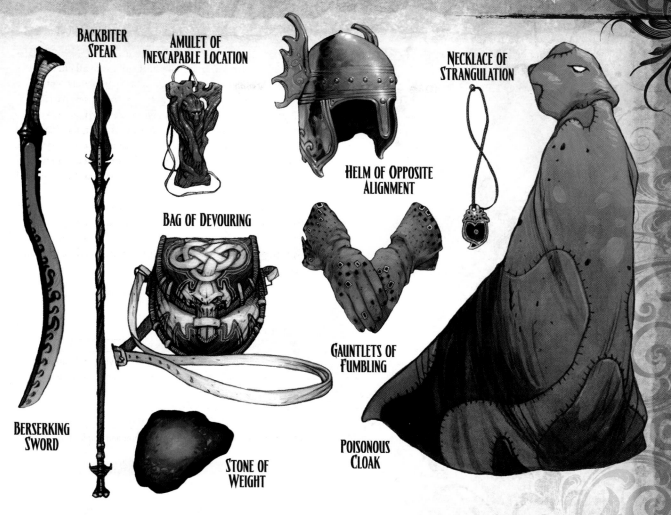

BACKBITER SPEAR

AMULET OF INESCAPABLE LOCATION

NECKLACE OF STRANGULATION

HELM OF OPPOSITE ALIGNMENT

BAG OF DEVOURING

GAUNTLETS OF FUMBLING

BERSERKING SWORD

STONE OF WEIGHT

POISONOUS CLOAK

BAG OF DEVOURING

Aura strong conjuration; **CL** 17th

Slot none; **Weight** 15 lbs.

DESCRIPTION

This bag appears to be an ordinary sack. Detection for magical properties makes it seem as if it were a *bag of holding*. The sack is, however, something entirely different and more insidious. It is—in fact, one of the feeding orifices of an extradimensional creature.

Any substance of animal or vegetable nature is subject to "swallowing" if thrust within the bag. The *bag of devouring* is 90% likely to ignore any initial intrusion, but anytime thereafter that it senses living flesh within (such as if someone reaches into the bag to pull something out), it is 60% likely to close around the offending member and attempt to draw the whole victim in. The bag has a +8 bonus on combat maneuver checks made to grapple. If it pins a creature, it pulls them inside as a free action. The bag has CMD of 18 for those attempting to break free.

The bag can hold up to 30 cubic feet of matter. It acts as a *bag of holding type I*, but each hour it has a 5% cumulative chance of swallowing the contents and then spitting the stuff out in some nonspace or on some other plane. Creatures drawn within are consumed in 1 round. The bag destroys the victim's body and

prevents any form of raising or resurrection that requires part of the corpse. There is a 50% chance that a *wish*, *miracle*, or *true resurrection* spell can restore a devoured victim to life. Check once for each destroyed creature. If the check fails, the creature cannot be brought back to life by mortal magic.

CREATION

Magic Items *bag of holding* (any type)

BOOTS OF DANCING

Aura strong enchantment; **CL** 16th

Slot feet; **Weight** 1 lb.

DESCRIPTION

These boots appear and function as one of the other kinds of magic boots. When the wearer is in (or fleeing from) melee combat, *boots of dancing* impede movement, making him behave as if *irresistible dance* had been cast upon him. Only a *remove curse* spell enables the wearer to be rid of the boots once their true nature is revealed.

CREATION

Magic Items *boots of elvenkind, boots of levitation, boots of speed, boots of striding and springing, boots of teleportation, boots of the winterlands, winged boots*

BRACERS OF DEFENSELESSNESS

Aura strong conjuration; **CL** 16th

Slot wrists; **Weight** 1 lb.

DESCRIPTION

These bejeweled and shining bracers initially appear to be *bracers of armor +5* and actually serve as such until the wearer is attacked in anger by an enemy with a Challenge Rating equal to or greater than her level. At that moment and thereafter, the bracers cause a –5 penalty to AC. Once their curse is activated, *bracers of defenselessness* can be removed only by means of a *remove curse* spell.

CREATION

Magic Items *bracers of armor +5*

BROOM OF ANIMATED ATTACK

Aura moderate transmutation; **CL** 10th

Slot none; **Weight** 3 lbs.

DESCRIPTION

This item is indistinguishable in appearance from a normal broom. It is identical to a *broom of flying* by all tests short of attempted use.

If a creature attempts to fly using the broom, the broom does a loop-the-loop with its hopeful rider, dumping him on his head from 1d4+5 feet off the ground (no falling damage, since the fall is less than 10 feet). The broom then attacks the victim, swatting the victim's face with the straw or twig end and beating him with the handle end. The broom gets two attacks per round with each end (two swats with the straw and two with the handle, for a total of four attacks per round). It attacks with a +5 bonus on each attack roll. The straw end causes a victim to be blinded for 1 round when it hits. The handle deals 1d6 points of damage when it hits. The broom has AC 13, CMD 17, 18 hit points, and hardness 4.

CREATION

Magic Items *broom of flying*

CRYSTAL HYPNOSIS BALL

Aura strong divination; **CL** 17th

Slot none; **Weight** 7 lbs.

DESCRIPTION

This cursed scrying device is indistinguishable, at first glance, from a normal *crystal ball*. However, anyone attempting to use the scrying device becomes fascinated for 1d6 minutes, and a telepathic *suggestion* is implanted in his mind (Will DC 19 negates).

The user of the device believes that the desired creature or scene was viewed, but actually he came under the influence of a powerful wizard, lich, or even some power or being from another plane. Each further use brings the *crystal hypnosis ball* gazer deeper under the influence of the controller, either as a servant or a tool. Note that throughout this time, the user remains unaware of his subjugation.

CREATION

Magic Items *crystal ball*

DUST OF SNEEZING AND CHOKING

Aura moderate conjuration; **CL** 7th

Slot none; **Weight** —

DESCRIPTION

This fine dust appears to be *dust of appearance*. If cast into the air, it causes those within a 20-foot spread to fall into fits of sneezing and coughing. Those failing a DC 15 Fortitude save take 3d6 points of Constitution damage immediately. Those who succeed on this saving throw are nonetheless disabled by choking (treat as stunned) for 5d4 rounds.

CREATION

Magic Items *dust of appearance, dust of tracelessness*

FLASK OF CURSES

Aura moderate conjuration; **CL** 7th

Slot none; **Weight** 2 lbs.

DESCRIPTION

This item looks like an ordinary beaker, bottle, container, decanter, flask, or jug. It may contain a liquid, or it may emit smoke. When the flask is first unstoppered, all within 30 feet must make a DC 17 Will save or be cursed, taking a –2 penalty on attack rolls, saving throws, and skill checks until a *remove curse* spell is cast upon them.

CREATION

Magic Items *decanter of endless water, efreeti bottle, eversmoking bottle, iron flask*

GAUNTLETS OF FUMBLING

Aura moderate transmutation; **CL** 7th

Slot hands; **Weight** 2 lbs.

DESCRIPTION

These gauntlets perform according to their appearance until the wearer finds herself under attack or in a life-and-death situation. At that time, the curse is activated. The wearer becomes fumble-fingered, with a 50% chance each round of dropping anything held in either hand. The gauntlets also lower Dexterity by 2 points. Once the curse is activated, the gloves can be removed only by means of a *remove curse* spell, a *wish*, or a *miracle*.

CREATION

Magic Items *gauntlet of rust, gloves of arrow snatching, glove of storing, gloves of swimming and climbing*

HELM OF OPPOSITE ALIGNMENT

Aura strong transmutation; **CL** 12th

Slot head; **Weight** 3 lbs.

DESCRIPTION

When placed upon the head, this item's curse immediately takes effect (Will DC 15 negates). On a failed save, the alignment of the wearer is radically altered to an alignment as different as possible from the former alignment—good to evil, chaotic to lawful, neutral to some extreme commitment (LE, LG, CE, or CG). Alteration in alignment is mental as well as moral, and the individual changed by the magic thoroughly enjoys his new outlook. A character who succeeds on his save can continue to wear the helmet without suffering the effect of the curse, but if he takes it off and later puts it on again, another save is required.

Only a *wish* or a *miracle* can restore a character's former alignment, and the affected individual does not make any attempt to return to the former alignment. In fact, he views the prospect with horror and avoids it in any way possible. If a character of a class with an alignment requirement is affected, an *atonement* spell is needed as well if the curse is to be obliterated. When a *helm of opposite alignment* has functioned once, it loses its magical properties.

CREATION

Magic Items *hat of disguise, helm of comprehend languages and read magic, helm of telepathy*

INCENSE OF OBSESSION

Aura moderate enchantment; **CL** 6th

Slot none; **Weight** —

DESCRIPTION

These blocks of incense appear to be *incense of meditation*. If meditation is conducted while *incense of obsession* is burning, the user becomes totally confident that her spell ability is superior due to the magic incense. She uses her spells at every opportunity, even when not needed or useless. The user remains obsessed with her abilities and spells until all have been used or cast, or until 24 hours have elapsed.

CREATION

Magic Items *incense of meditation*

MACE OF BLOOD

Aura moderate abjuration; **CL** 8th

Slot none; **Weight** 8 lbs.

DESCRIPTION

This *+3 heavy mace* must be coated in blood every day, or else its bonus fades away until the mace is coated again. The character using this mace must make a DC 13 Will save every day it is within his possession or become chaotic evil.

CREATION

Magic Items *+3 heavy mace*

MEDALLION OF THOUGHT PROJECTION

Aura moderate divination; **CL** 7th

Slot neck; **Weight** —

DESCRIPTION

This device seems like a *medallion of thoughts*, even down to the range at which it functions, except that the thoughts overheard are muffled and distorted, requiring a DC 15 Will save to sort them out. However, while the user thinks she is picking up the thoughts of others, all she is really hearing are figments created by the medallion itself. These illusory thoughts always seem plausible and thus can seriously mislead any who rely upon them. What's worse, unknown to her, the cursed medallion actually broadcasts her thoughts to creatures in the path of the beam, thus alerting them to her presence.

CREATION

Magic Items *medallion of thoughts*

NECKLACE OF STRANGULATION

Aura strong conjuration; **CL** 18th

Slot neck; **Weight** —

DESCRIPTION

A *necklace of strangulation* appears to be a wondrous piece of magical jewelry. When placed on the neck, the necklace immediately tightens, dealing 6 points of damage per round. It cannot be removed by any means short of a *limited wish, wish,* or *miracle* and remains clasped around the victim's throat even after his death. Only when he has decayed to a dry skeleton (after approximately 1 month) does the necklace loosen, ready for another victim.

CREATION

Magic Items *necklace of adaptation, necklace of fireballs, periapt of health, periapt of proof against poison, periapt of wound closure*

NET OF SNARING

Aura moderate evocation; **CL** 8th

Slot none; **Weight** 6 lbs.

DESCRIPTION

This net provides a +3 bonus on attack rolls but can only be used underwater. Underwater, it can be commanded to shoot forth up to 30 feet to trap a creature. If thrown on land, it changes course to target the creature that threw it.

CREATION

Magic Items *+3 net*

PERIAPT OF FOUL ROTTING

Aura moderate abjuration; **CL** 10th

Slot neck; **Weight** —

DESCRIPTION

This engraved gem appears to be of little value. If any character keeps the periapt in her possession for more than 24 hours, she contracts a terrible rotting affliction that permanently drains 1 point of Dexterity, Constitution, and Charisma every week. The periapt (and the affliction) can be removed only by application of a *remove curse* spell followed by a *cure disease* and then a *heal, miracle, limited wish,* or *wish* spell. The rotting can also be countered by crushing a *periapt of health* and sprinkling its dust upon the afflicted character (a full-round action), whereupon the *periapt of foul rotting* likewise crumbles to dust.

CREATION

Magic Items *periapt of health, periapt of proof against poison, periapt of wound closure*

POISONOUS CLOAK

Aura strong abjuration; **CL** 15th

Slot shoulders; **Weight** 1 lb.

DESCRIPTION

This cloak is usually made of a wool, although it can be made of leather. A *detect poison* spell can reveal the presence of poison in the cloak's fabric. The garment can be handled without harm, but as soon as it is actually donned, the wearer takes 4d6 points of Constitution damage unless she succeeds on a DC 28 Fortitude save.

Once donned, a *poisonous cloak* can be removed only with a *remove curse* spell; doing this destroys the magical property of the cloak. If a *neutralize poison* spell is then used, it is possible to revive a dead victim with a *raise dead* or *resurrection spell*.

CREATION

Magic Items *cloak of arachnida, cloak of the bat, cloak of etherealness, cloak of resistance +5, major cloak of displacement*

POTION OF POISON

Aura strong conjuration; **CL** 12th

Slot none; **Weight** —

DESCRIPTION

This potion has lost its beneficial abilities and become a potent poison. This poison deals 1d3 Constitution damage per round for 6 rounds. A poisoned creature can make a DC 14 Fortitude save each round to negate the damage and end the affliction.

CREATION

Magic Items any potion

ROBE OF POWERLESSNESS

Aura strong transmutation; **CL** 13th

Slot body; **Weight** 1 lb.

DESCRIPTION

A *robe of powerlessness* appears to be a magic robe of another sort. As soon as a character dons this garment, she takes a –10 penalty to Strength, as well as to Intelligence, Wisdom, or Charisma, forgetting spells and magic knowledge accordingly. If the character is a spellcaster, the robe targets the character's primary spellcasting score, otherwise it targets Intelligence. The robe can be removed easily, but in order to restore mind and body, the character must receive a *remove curse* spell followed by *heal*.

CREATION

Magic Items *robe of the archmagi, robe of blending, robe of bones, robe of eyes, robe of scintillating colors, robe of stars, robe of useful items*

ROBE OF VERMIN

Aura strong abjuration; **CL** 13th

Slot body; **Weight** 1 lb.

DESCRIPTION

The wearer notices nothing unusual when the robe is donned, and it functions normally. However, as soon as he is in a situation requiring concentration and action against hostile opponents, the true nature of the garment is revealed: the wearer immediately suffers a multitude of bites from the insects that magically infest the garment. He must cease all other activities in order to scratch, shift the robe, and generally show signs of the extreme discomfort caused by the bites and movement of these pests.

The wearer takes a –5 penalty on initiative checks and a –2 penalty on all attack rolls, saves, and skill checks. If he tries to cast a spell, he must make a concentration check (DC 20 + spell level) or lose the spell.

CREATION

Magic Items *robe of the archmagi, robe of blending, robe of bones, robe of eyes, robe of scintillating colors, robe of stars, robe of useful items*

RING OF CLUMSINESS

Aura strong transmutation; **CL** 15th

Slot ring; **Weight** —

DESCRIPTION

This ring operates exactly like a *ring of feather falling*. However, it also makes the wearer clumsy. She takes a –4 penalty to Dexterity and has a 20% chance of spell failure when trying to cast any arcane spell that has a somatic component. (This chance of spell failure stacks with other arcane spell failure chances.)

CREATION

Magic Items *ring of feather falling*

SCARAB OF DEATH

Aura strong abjuration; **CL** 19th

Slot neck; **Weight** —

DESCRIPTION

If this small scarab brooch is held for more than 1 round or carried in a living creature's possessions for 1 minute, it changes into a horrible burrowing beetle-like creature. The thing tears through any leather or cloth, burrows into flesh, and reaches the victim's heart in 1 round, causing death. A DC 25 Reflex save allows the wearer to tear the scarab away before it burrows out of sight, but he still takes 3d6 points of damage. The beetle then returns to its scarab form. Placing the scarab in a container of wood, ceramic, bone, ivory, or metal prevents it from coming to life and allows for long-term storage of the item.

CREATION

Magic Items *amulet of mighty fists, amulet of natural armor, amulet of the planes, amulet of proof against detection and location, brooch of shielding, golembane scarab, scarab of protection*

SPEAR, CURSED BACKBITER

Aura moderate evocation; **CL** 10th

Slot none; **Weight** 3 lbs.

Description This is a +2 *shortspear*, but each time it is used in melee against a foe and the attack roll is a natural 1, it damages its wielder instead of her intended target. When the curse takes effect, the spear curls around to strike its wielder in the back, automatically dealing the damage to the wielder. The curse even functions when the spear is hurled, and in such a case the damage to the hurler is doubled.

CREATION

Magic Items +2 *shortspear*, any magic weapon

STONE OF WEIGHT (LOADSTONE)

Aura faint transmutation; **CL** 5th

Slot none; **Weight** 1 lb.

DESCRIPTION

This dark, polished stone reduces the possessor's base land speed to half of normal. Once picked up, the stone cannot be disposed of by any nonmagical means—if it is thrown away or smashed, it reappears somewhere upon the possessor's person. If a *remove curse* spell is cast upon a *loadstone*, the item may be discarded normally and no longer haunts the individual.

CREATION

Magic Items *ioun stone, stone of alarm, stone of controlling earth elementals, stone of good luck*

SWORD, −2 CURSED

Aura strong evocation; **CL** 15th

Slot none; **Weight** 4 lbs.

DESCRIPTION

This longsword performs well against targets in practice, but when used in combat its wielder takes a −2 penalty on attack rolls.

All damage dealt is also reduced by 2 points, but never below a minimum of 1 point of damage on any successful hit. The sword always forces that character to employ it rather than another weapon. The sword's owner automatically draws it and fights with it even when she meant to draw or ready some other weapon.

CREATION

Magic Items +2 *longsword*, any magic weapon

SWORD, BERSERKING

Aura moderate evocation; **CL** 8th

Slot none; **Weight** 12 lbs.

DESCRIPTION

This sword appears to be a +2 *greatsword*. However, whenever it is used in battle, its wielder goes berserk (gaining all the benefits and drawbacks of the barbarian's rage ability). He attacks the nearest creature and continues to fight until unconscious or dead or until no living thing remains within 30 feet. Although many see this sword as a cursed object, others see it as a boon.

CREATION

Magic Items +2 *greatsword*, any magic weapon

VACUOUS GRIMOIRE

Aura strong enchantment; **CL** 20th

Slot none; **Weight** 2 lbs.

DESCRIPTION

A book of this sort looks like a normal one on some mildly interesting topic. Any character who opens the work and reads so much as a single word therein must make two DC 15 Will saves. The first is to determine if the reader takes 1 point of permanent Intelligence and Charisma drain. The second is to find out if the

reader takes 2 points of permanent Wisdom drain. To destroy the book, it must be burned while *remove curse* is being cast. If the grimoire is placed with other books, its appearance instantly alters to conform to the look of those other works.

CREATION

Magic Items *blessed book, manual of bodily health, manual of gainful exercise, manual of quickness of action, tome of clear thoughts, tome of leadership and influence, tome of understanding*

ARTIFACTS

Artifacts are extremely powerful. Rather than merely another form of magical equipment, they are the sorts of legendary relics that whole campaigns can be based on. Each could be the center of a whole set of adventures—a quest to recover it, a fight against an opponent wielding it, a mission to cause its destruction, and so on.

Unlike normal magic items, artifacts are not easily destroyed. Instead of construction information, each artifact includes one possible means by which it might be destroyed.

Artifacts can never be purchased, nor are they found as part of a random treasure hoard. When placing an artifact in your game, be sure to consider its impact and role. Remember that artifacts are fickle objects, and if they become too much of a nuisance, they can easily disappear or become lost once again.

Minor Artifacts

Minor artifacts are not necessarily unique items. Even so, they are magic items that no longer can be created, at least by common mortal means.

BOOK OF INFINITE SPELLS

Aura strong (all schools); **CL** 18th

Slot none; **Weight** 3 lbs.

DESCRIPTION

This work bestows upon any character of any class the ability to use the spells within its pages. However, any character not already able to use spells gains one negative level for as long as the book is in her possession or while she uses its power. A *book of infinite spells* contains 1d8+22 pages. The nature of each page is determined by a d% roll: 01–50, arcane spell; 51–100, divine spell.

Determine the exact spell randomly.

Once a page is turned, it can never be flipped back—paging through a *book of infinite spells* is a one-way trip. If the book is closed, it always opens again to the page it was on before the book was closed. When the last page is turned, the book vanishes.

Once per day the owner of the book can cast the spell to which the book is opened. If that spell happens to be one that is on the character's class spell list, she can cast it up to four times per day. The pages cannot be ripped out without destroying the book. Similarly, the spells cannot be cast as scroll spells, nor can they be copied into a spellbook—their magic is bound up permanently within the book itself.

The owner of the book need not have the book on her person in order to use its power. The book can be stored in a place of safety

while the owner is adventuring and still allow its owner to cast spells by means of its power.

Each time a spell is cast, there is a chance that the energy connected with its use causes the page to magically turn despite all precautions. The chance of a page turning depends on the spell the page contains and what sort of spellcaster the owner is.

Condition	Chance of Page Turning
Caster employing a spell usable by own class and level	10%
Caster employing a spell not usable by own class and level	20%
Nonspellcaster employing divine spell	25%
Nonspellcaster employing arcane spell	30%

Treat each spell use as if a scroll were being employed, for purposes of determining casting time, spell failure, and so on.

DESTRUCTION

The *book of infinite spells* can be destroyed when the current page contains the *erase* spell, by casting the spell on the book itself.

DECK OF MANY THINGS

Aura strong (all schools); **CL** 20th

Slot none; **Weight** —

DESCRIPTION

A *deck of many things* (both beneficial and malign) is usually found in a box or leather pouch. Each deck contains a number of cards or plaques made of ivory or vellum. Each is engraved with glyphs, characters, and sigils. As soon as one of these cards is drawn from the pack, its magic is bestowed upon the person who drew it, for better or worse.

The character with a *deck of many things* who wishes to draw a card must announce how many cards she will draw before she begins. Cards must be drawn within 1 hour of each other, and a character can never draw from this deck any more cards than she has announced. If the character does not willingly draw her allotted number (or if she is somehow prevented from doing so), the cards flip out of the deck on their own. If the Idiot or Jester is drawn, the possessor of the deck may elect to draw additional cards.

Each time a card is taken from the deck, it is replaced (making it possible to draw the same card twice) unless the draw is the Jester or the Fool, in which case the card is discarded from the pack. A *deck of many things* contains 22 cards. To simulate the magic cards, you may want to use tarot cards, as indicated in the second column of the accompanying table. If no tarot deck is available, substitute ordinary playing cards instead, as indicated in the third column. The effects of each card, summarized on the table, are fully described below.

Balance: The character must change to a radically different alignment. If the character fails to act according to the new alignment, she gains a negative level.

Comet: The character must single-handedly defeat the next hostile monster or monsters encountered, or the benefit is lost. If successful, the character gains enough XP to attain the next experience level.

Donjon: This card signifies imprisonment—either by the *imprisonment* spell or by some powerful being. All gear and spells are stripped from the victim in any case. Draw no more cards.

Euryale: The medusa-like visage of this card brings a curse that only the Fates card or a deity can remove. The –1 penalty on all saving throws is otherwise permanent.

The Fates: This card enables the character to avoid even an instantaneous occurrence if so desired, for the fabric of reality is unraveled and respun. Note that it does not enable something to happen. It can only stop something from happening or reverse a past occurrence. The reversal is only for the character who drew the card; other party members may have to endure the situation.

Flames: Hot anger, jealousy, and envy are but a few of the possible motivational forces for the enmity. The enmity of the outsider can't be ended until one of the parties has been slain. Determine the outsider randomly, and assume that it attacks the character (or plagues her life in some way) within 1d20 days.

Fool: The payment of XP and the redraw are mandatory. This card is always discarded when drawn, unlike all others except the Jester.

Gem: This card indicates wealth. The jewelry is all gold set with gems, each piece worth 2,000 gp, and the gems are worth 1,000 gp each.

Idiot: This card causes the drain of 1d4+1 points of Intelligence immediately. The additional draw is optional.

Jester: This card is always discarded when drawn, unlike all others except the Fool. The redraws are optional.

Key: The magic weapon granted must be one usable by the character. It suddenly appears out of nowhere in the character's hand.

Knight: The fighter appears out of nowhere and serves loyally until death. He or she is of the same race (or kind) and gender as the character. This fighter can be taken as a cohort by a character with the Leadership feat.

Moon: This card bears the image of a moonstone gem with the appropriate number of *wishes* shown as gleams therein; sometimes it depicts a moon with its phase indicating the number of *wishes* (full = four; gibbous = three; half = two; quarter = one). These *wishes* are the same as those granted by the 9th-level wizard spell and must be used within a number of minutes equal to the number received.

Rogue: When this card is drawn, one of the character's NPC friends (preferably a cohort) is totally alienated and made forever hostile. If the character has no cohorts, the enmity of some powerful personage (or community, or religious order) can be substituted. The hatred is secret until the time is ripe for it to be revealed with devastating effect.

Ruin: As implied by its name, when this card is drawn, all nonmagical possessions of the drawer are lost.

Skull: A dread wraith appears. The character must fight it alone—if others help, they get dread wraiths to fight as well. If the character is slain, she is slain forever and cannot be revived, even with a *wish* or a *miracle.*

DECK OF MANY THINGS

Plaque	Tarot Card	Playing Card	Summary of Effect
Balance	XI. Justice	Two of spades	Change alignment instantly.
Comet	Two of swords	Two of diamonds	Defeat the next monster you meet to gain one level.
Donjon	Four of swords	Ace of spades	You are *imprisoned*.
Euryale	Ten of swords	Queen of spades	−1 penalty on all saving throws henceforth.
The Fates	Three of cups	Ace of hearts	Avoid any situation you choose, once.
Flames	XV. The Devil	Queen of clubs	Enmity between you and an outsider.
Fool	0. The Fool	Joker (with trademark)	Lose 10,000 experience points and you must draw again.
Gem	Seven of cups	Two of hearts	Gain your choice of 25 pieces of jewelry or 50 gems.
Idiot	Two of pentacles	Two of clubs	Lose 1d4+1 Intelligence. You may draw again.
Jester	XII. The Hanged Man	Joker (without trademark)	Gain 10,000 XP or two more draws from the deck.
Key	V. The Hierophant	Queen of hearts	Gain a major magic weapon.
Knight	Page of swords	Jack of hearts	Gain the service of a 4th-level fighter.
Moon	XVIII. The Moon	Queen of diamonds	You are granted 1d4 wishes.
Rogue	Five of swords	Jack of spades	One of your friends turns against you.
Ruin	XVI. The Tower	King of spades	Immediately lose all wealth and property.
Skull	XIII. Death	Jack of clubs	Defeat dread wraith or be forever destroyed.
Star	XVII. The Star	Jack of diamonds	Immediately gain a +2 inherent bonus to one ability score.
Sun	XIX. The Sun	King of diamonds	Gain beneficial medium wondrous item and 50,000 XP.
Talons	Queen of pentacles	Ace of clubs	All magic items you possess disappear permanently.
Throne	Four of wands	King of hearts	Gain a +6 bonus on Diplomacy checks plus a small castle.
Vizier	IX. The Hermit	Ace of diamonds	Know the answer to your next dilemma.
The Void	Eight of swords	King of clubs	Body functions, but soul is trapped elsewhere.

Star: The 2 points are added to any ability the character chooses. They cannot be divided among two abilities.

Sun: Roll for a medium wondrous item until a useful item is indicated.

Talons: When this card is drawn, every magic item owned or possessed by the character is instantly and irrevocably lost, except for the deck.

Throne: The character becomes a true leader in people's eyes. The castle gained appears in any open area she wishes (but the decision where to place it must be made within 1 hour).

Vizier: This card empowers the character drawing it with the one-time ability to call upon a source of wisdom to solve any single problem or answer fully any question upon her request. The query or request must be made within 1 year. Whether the information gained can be successfully acted upon is another matter entirely.

The Void: This black card spells instant disaster. The character's body continues to function, as though comatose, but her psyche is trapped in a prison somewhere—in an object on a far plane or planet, possibly in the possession of an outsider. A *wish* or a *miracle* does not bring the character back, instead merely revealing the plane of entrapment. Draw no more cards.

DESTRUCTION

The *deck of many things* can be destroyed by losing it in a wager with a deity of law. The deity must be unaware of the nature of the deck.

PHILOSOPHER'S STONE

Aura strong transmutation; **CL** 20th
Slot none; **Weight** 3 lbs.

DESCRIPTION

This rare substance appears to be an ordinary, sooty piece of blackish rock. If the stone is broken open (break DC 20), a cavity is revealed at the stone's heart. This cavity is lined with a magical type of quicksilver that enables any character with at least 10 ranks in Craft (alchemy) to transmute base metals (iron and lead) into silver and gold. A single *philosopher's stone* can turn up to 5,000 pounds of iron into silver (worth 25,000 gp), or up to 1,000 pounds of lead into gold (worth 50,000 gp). However, the quicksilver becomes unstable once the stone is opened and loses its potency within 24 hours, so all transmutations must take place within that period.

The quicksilver found in the center of the stone may also be put to another use. If mixed with any cure potion while the substance is still potent, it creates a special oil of life that acts as a *true resurrection* spell for any dead body it is sprinkled upon.

DESTRUCTION

The philosopher's stone can be destroyed by being placed in the heel of a titan's boot for at least 1 entire week.

SPHERE OF ANNIHILATION

Aura strong transmutation; **CL** 20th
Slot none; **Weight** —

DESCRIPTION

A *sphere of annihilation* is a globe of absolute blackness 2 feet in diameter. Any matter that comes in contact with a sphere is instantly sucked into the void and utterly destroyed. Only the direct intervention of a deity can restore an annihilated character.

A *sphere of annihilation* is static, resting in some spot as if it were a normal hole. It can be caused to move, however, by mental effort (think of this as a mundane form of *telekinesis*, too weak to move actual objects but a force to which the sphere, being weightless, is sensitive). A character's ability to gain control of a *sphere of annihilation* (or to keep controlling one) is based on the result of a control check against DC 30 (a move action). A control check is 1d20 + character level + character Int modifier. If the check succeeds, the character can move the sphere (perhaps to bring it into contact with an enemy) as a free action.

Control of a sphere can be established from as far away as 40 feet (the character need not approach too closely). Once control is established, it must be maintained by continuing to make control checks (all DC 30) each round. For as long as a character maintains control (does not fail a check) in subsequent rounds, he can control the sphere from a distance of 40 feet + 10 feet per character level. The sphere's speed in a round is 10 feet + 5 feet for every 5 points by which the character's control check result in that round exceeded 30.

If a control check fails, the sphere slides 10 feet in the direction of the character attempting to move it. If two or more creatures vie for control of a *sphere of annihilation*, the rolls are opposed. If none are successful, the sphere slips toward the one who rolled lowest.

See also *talisman of the sphere*.

DESTRUCTION

Should a *gate* spell be cast upon a *sphere of annihilation*, there is a 50% chance (01–50 on d%) that the spell destroys it, a 35% chance (51–85) that the spell does nothing, and a 15% chance (86–100) that a gap is torn in the spatial fabric, catapulting everything within a 180-foot radius into another plane. If a *rod of cancellation* touches a *sphere of annihilation*, they negate each other in a tremendous explosion. Everything within a 60-foot radius takes 2d6 × 10 points of damage. *Dispel magic* and *mage's disjunction* have no effect on a sphere.

STAFF OF THE MAGI

Aura strong (all schools); **CL** 20th

Slot none; **Weight** 5 lbs.

DESCRIPTION

A long wooden staff, shod in iron and inscribed with sigils and runes of all types, this potent artifact contains many spell powers and other functions. Unlike a normal staff, a *staff of the magi* holds 50 charges and cannot be recharged normally. Some of its powers use charges, while others don't. A *staff of the magi* does not lose its powers if it runs out of charges. The following powers do not use charges:

- *Detect magic*
- *Enlarge person* (Fortitude DC 15 negates)
- *Hold portal*
- *Light*
- *Mage armor*
- *Mage hand*

The following powers drain 1 charge per usage:

- *Dispel magic*
- *Fireball* (10d6 damage, Reflex DC 17 half)
- *Ice storm*
- *Invisibility*
- *Knock*
- *Lightning bolt* (10d6 damage, Reflex DC 17 half)
- *Passwall*
- *Pyrotechnics* (Will or Fortitude DC 16 negates)
- *Wall of fire*
- *Web*

These powers drain 2 charges per usage:

- *Monster summoning IX*
- *Plane shift* (Will DC 21 negates)
- *Telekinesis* (400 lbs. maximum weight; Will DC 19 negates)

A *staff of the magi* gives the wielder spell resistance 23. If this is willingly lowered, however, the staff can also be used to absorb arcane spell energy directed at its wielder, as a *rod of absorption* does. Unlike the rod, this staff converts spell levels into charges rather than retaining them as spell energy usable by a spellcaster. If the staff absorbs enough spell levels to exceed its limit of 50 charges, it explodes as if a retributive strike had been performed (see below). The wielder has no idea how many spell levels are cast at her, for the staff does not communicate this knowledge as a *rod of absorption* does. (Thus, absorbing spells can be risky.)

DESTRUCTION

A *staff of the magi* can be broken for a retributive strike. Such an act must be purposeful and declared by the wielder. All charges in the staff are released in a 30-foot spread. All within 10 feet of the broken staff take hit points of damage equal to 8 times the number of charges in the staff, those between 11 feet and 20 feet away take points equal to 6 times the number of charges, and those 21 feet to 30 feet distant take 4 times the number of charges. A DC 23 Reflex save reduces damage by half.

The character breaking the staff has a 50% chance (01–50 on d%) of traveling to another plane of existence, but if she does not (51–100), the explosive release of spell energy destroys her (no saving throw).

TALISMAN OF PURE GOOD

Aura strong evocation [good]; **CL** 18th

Slot none; **Weight** —

DESCRIPTION

A good divine spellcaster who possesses this item can cause a flaming crack to open at the feet of an evil divine spellcaster who is up to 100 feet away. The intended victim is swallowed up forever and sent hurtling to the center of the earth. The wielder of the talisman must be good, and if he is not exceptionally pure in thought and deed, the evil character gains a DC 19 Reflex saving throw to leap away from the crack. Obviously, the target must be standing on solid ground for this item to function.

A *talisman of pure good* has 6 charges. If a neutral (LN, N, CN) divine spellcaster touches one of these stones, he takes 6d6 points of damage per round of contact. If an evil divine spellcaster touches one, he takes 8d6 points of damage per round of contact. All other characters are unaffected by the device.

DESTRUCTION

The *talisman of pure good* can be destroyed by placing it in the mouth of a holy man who died while committing a truly heinous act of his own free will.

TALISMAN OF THE SPHERE

Aura strong transmutation; **CL** 16th

Slot none; **Weight** 1 lb.

DESCRIPTION

This small adamantine loop and handle is typically fitted with a fine adamantine chain so that it can be worn about as a necklace. A *talisman of the sphere* is worse than useless to those unable to cast arcane spells. Characters who cannot cast arcane spells take 5d6 points of damage merely from picking up and holding a talisman of this sort. However, when held by an arcane spellcaster who is concentrating on control of a *sphere of annihilation,* a *talisman of the sphere* doubles the character's modifier on his control check (doubling both his Intelligence bonus and his character level for this purpose).

If the wielder of a talisman establishes control, he need check for maintaining control only every other round thereafter. If control is not established, the sphere moves toward him. Note that while many spells and effects of cancellation have no effect upon a *sphere of annihilation,* the talisman's power of control can be suppressed or canceled.

DESTRUCTION

A *talisman of the sphere* can only be destroyed by throwing the item into a *sphere of annihilation.*

TALISMAN OF ULTIMATE EVIL

Aura strong evocation [evil]; **CL** 18th

Slot none; **Weight** —

DESCRIPTION

An evil divine spellcaster who possesses this item can cause a flaming crack to open at the feet of a good divine spellcaster who is up to 100 feet away. The intended victim is swallowed up forever and sent hurtling to the center of the earth. The wielder of the talisman must be evil, and if she is not exceptionally foul and perverse in the sights of her evil deity, the good character gains a DC 19 Reflex save to leap away from the crack. Obviously, the target must be standing on solid ground for this item to function.

A *talisman of ultimate evil* has 6 charges. If a neutral (LN, N, CN) divine spellcaster touches one of these stones, she takes 6d6 points of damage per round of contact. If a good divine spellcaster touches one, she takes 8d6 points of damage per round of contact. All other characters are unaffected by the device.

DESTRUCTION

If a *talisman of ultimate evil* is given to the newborn child of a redeemed villain, it instantly crumbles to dust.

Major Artifacts

Major artifacts are unique items—only one of each such item exists. These are the most potent of magic items, capable of altering the balance of a campaign. Unlike all other magic items, major artifacts are not easily destroyed. Each should have only a single, specific means of destruction.

AXE OF THE DWARVISH LORDS

Aura strong conjuration and transmutation; **CL** 20th

Slot none; **Weight** 12 lbs.

DESCRIPTION

This is a *+6 keen throwing goblinoid bane dwarven waraxe.* Any dwarf who holds it doubles the range of his or her darkvision. Any nondwarf who grasps the *Axe* takes 4 points of temporary Charisma damage; these points cannot be healed or restored in any way while the *Axe* is held. The current owner of the *Axe* gains a +10 bonus on Craft (armor, jewelry, stonemasonry, traps, and weapons) checks. The wielder of the *Axe* can summon an elder earth elemental (as *summon monster IX;* duration 20 rounds) once per week.

DESTRUCTION

The *Axe of the Dwarvish Lords* rusts away to nothing if it is ever used by a goblin to behead a dwarven king.

CODEX OF THE INFINITE PLANES

Aura overwhelming transmutation; **CL** 30th

Slot none; **Weight** 300 lbs.

DESCRIPTION

The *Codex* is enormous—supposedly, it requires two strong men to lift it. No matter how many pages are turned, another always remains. Anyone opening the *Codex* for the first time is utterly annihilated, as with a *destruction* spell (Fortitude DC 30). Those who survive can peruse its pages and learn its powers, though not without risk. Each day spent studying the *Codex* allows the reader to make a Spellcraft check (DC 50) to learn one of its powers (choose the power learned randomly; add a +1 circumstance bonus on the check per additional day spent reading until a power is learned). However, each day of study also forces the reader to make a Will save (DC 30 + 1 per day of study) to avoid being driven insane (as the *insanity* spell). The powers of the *Codex of the Infinite Planes* are as follows: *astral projection, banishment, elemental swarm, gate, greater planar ally, greater planar binding, plane shift,* and *soul bind.* Each of these spell-like abilities are usable at will by the owner of the *Codex* (assuming that he or she has learned how to access the power). The *Codex of the Infinite Planes* has a caster level of 30th for the purposes of all powers and catastrophes, and all saving throw DCs are 20 + spell level. Activating any power requires a Spellcraft check (DC 40 + twice the spell level of the power; the character can't take 10 on this check). Any failure on either check indicates that a catastrophe befalls the user (roll on the table below for the effect). A character can only incur one catastrophe per power use.

d%	Catastrophe
01–25	**Natural Fury:** An *earthquake* spell centered on the reader strikes every round for 1 minute, and an intensified *storm of vengeance* spell is centered and targeted on the reader.
26–50	**Fiendish Vengeance:** A *gate* opens and 1d3+1 balors, pit fiends, or similar evil outsiders step through and attempt to destroy the owner of the *Codex*.
51–75	**Ultimate Imprisonment:** Reader's soul is captured (as *trap the soul;* no save allowed) in a random gem somewhere on the plane while his or her body is entombed beneath the earth (as *imprisonment*).
76–100	**Death:** The reader utters a *wail of the banshee* and then is subject to a *destruction* spell. This repeats every round for 10 rounds until the reader is dead.

DESTRUCTION

The *Codex of the Infinite Planes* is destroyed if one page is torn out and left on each plane in existence. Note that tearing out a page immediately triggers a catastrophe.

THE ORBS OF DRAGONKIND

Aura strong enchantment; **CL** 20th.

Slot none; **Weight** 5 lbs.

DESCRIPTION

Each of these fabled *Orbs* contains the essence and personality of an ancient dragon of a different variety (one for each of the major ten different chromatic and metallic dragons). The bearer of an *Orb* can, as a standard action, dominate dragons of its particular variety within 500 feet (as *dominate monster*), the dragon being forced to make a DC 25 Will save to resist. Spell resistance is not useful against this effect. Each *Orb of Dragonkind* bestows upon the wielder the AC and saving throw bonuses of the dragon within. These values replace whatever values the character would otherwise have, whether they are better or worse. These values cannot be modified by any means short of ridding the character of the *Orb*. A character possessing an *Orb of Dragonkind* is immune to the breath weapon—but only the breath weapon—of the dragon variety keyed to the *Orb*. Finally, a character possessing an *Orb* can herself use the breath weapon of the dragon in the *Orb* three times per day.

All *Orbs of Dragonkind* can be used to communicate verbally and visually with the possessors of the other *Orbs*. The owner of an *Orb* knows if there are dragons within 10 miles at all times. For dragons of the *Orb's* particular variety, the range is 100 miles. If within 1 mile of a dragon of the *Orb's* variety, the wielder can determine the dragon's exact location and age. The bearer of one of these *Orbs* earns the enmity of dragonkind forever for profiting by draconic enslavement, even if she later loses the item. Each *Orb* also has an individual power that can be invoked once per round at caster level 10th.

* *Black Dragon Orb: Fly.*
* *Blue Dragon Orb: Haste.*
* *Brass Dragon Orb: Teleport.*

* *Bronze Dragon Orb: Scrying* (Will DC 18 negates).
* *Copper Dragon Orb: Suggestion* (Will DC 17 negates).
* *Gold Dragon Orb:* The owner of the gold *Orb* can call upon any power possessed by one of the other *Orbs*—including the dominate and breath weapon abilities but not AC, save bonuses, or breath weapon immunity—but can only use an individual power once per day. She can dominate any other possessor of an *Orb* within 1 mile (Will DC 23 negates).
* *Green Dragon Orb: Spectral hand.*
* *Red Dragon Orb: Wall of fire.*
* *Silver Dragon Orb: Cure critical wounds* (Will DC 18 half).
* *White Dragon Orb: Protection from energy (cold)* (Fortitude DC 17 negates)

DESTRUCTION

An *orb of dragonkind* immediately shatters if it is caught in the breath weapon of a dragon who is a blood relative of the dragon trapped within. This causes everyone within 90 feet to be struck by the breath weapon of that dragon, released as the orb explodes.

THE SHADOWSTAFF

Aura strong conjuration; **CL** 20th.

Slot none; **Weight** 1 lb.

DESCRIPTION

This artifact was crafted ages ago, weaving together wispy strands of shadow into a twisted black staff. The *Shadowstaff* makes the wielder slightly shadowy and incorporeal, granting him a +4 bonus to AC and on Reflex saves (which stacks with any other bonuses). However, in bright light (such as that of the sun, but not a torch) or in absolute darkness, the wielder takes a –2 penalty on all attack rolls, saves, and checks. The *Shadowstaff* also has these powers.

* *Summon Shadows:* Three times per day the staff may summon 2d4 shadows. Immune to turning, they serve the wielder as if called by a *summon monster V* spell cast at 20th level.
* *Summon Nightshade:* Once per month, the staff can summon an advanced shadow demon that serves the wielder as if called by a *summon monster IX* spell cast at 20th level.
* *Shadow Form:* Three times per day the wielder can become a living shadow, with all the movement powers granted by *gaseous form*.
* *Shadow Bolt:* Three times per day the staff can project a ray attack that deals 10d6 points of cold damage to a single target. The shadow bolt has a range of 100 feet.

DESTRUCTION

The *Shadowstaff* fades away to nothingness if it is exposed to true sunlight for a continuous 24 hour period.

MAGIC ITEM CREATION

To create magic items, spellcasters use special feats which allow them to invest time and money in an item's creation. At the end of this process, the spellcaster must make a single skill check (usually Spellcraft, but sometimes another skill) to finish the item. If an item type has multiple possible skills, you choose which skill to make the check with. The DC to create a magic item is 5 + the caster level for the item. Failing this check means that the item does not function and the materials and time are wasted. Failing this check by 5 or more results in a cursed item (see Cursed Items for more information).

Note that all items have prerequisites in their descriptions. These prerequisites must be met for the item to be created. Most of the time, they take the form of spells that must be known by the item's creator (although access through another magic item or spellcaster is allowed). The DC to create a magic item increases by +5 for each prerequisite the caster does not meet. The only exception to this is the requisite item creation feat, which is mandatory. In addition, you cannot create potions, spell-trigger, or spell-completion magic items without meeting their spell prerequisites.

While item creation costs are handled in detail below, note that normally the two primary factors are the caster level of the creator and the level of the spell or spells put into the item. A creator can create an item at a lower caster level than her own, but never lower than the minimum level needed to cast the needed spell. Using metamagic feats, a caster can place spells in items at a higher level than normal.

Magic supplies for items are always half of the base price in gp. For many items, the market price equals the base price. Armor, shields, weapons, and items with value independent of their magically enhanced properties add their item cost to the market price. The item cost does not influence the base price (which determines the cost of magic supplies), but it does increase the final market price.

In addition, some items cast or replicate spells with costly material components. For these items, the market price equals the base price plus an extra price for the spell component costs. The cost to create these items is the magic supplies cost plus the costs for the components. Descriptions of these items include an entry that gives the total cost of creating the item.

The creator also needs a fairly quiet, comfortable, and well-lit place in which to work. Any place suitable for preparing spells is suitable for making items. Creating an item requires 8 hours of work per 1,000 gp in the item's base price (or fraction thereof), with a minimum of at least 8 hours. Potions and scrolls are an exception to this rule; they can take as little as 2 hours to create (if their base price is 250 gp or less). Scrolls and potions whose base price is more than 250 gp, but less than 1,000 gp, take 8 hours to create, just like any other magic item. The character must spend the gold at the beginning of the construction process. Regardless of the time needed for construction, a caster can create no more than one magic item per day. This process can be accelerated to 4 hours of work per 1,000 gp in the item's base price (or fraction thereof) by increasing the DC to create the item by +5.

The caster can work for up to 8 hours each day. He cannot rush the process by working longer each day, but the days need not be consecutive, and the caster can use the rest of his time as he sees fit. If the caster is out adventuring, he can devote 4 hours each day to item creation, although he nets only 2 hours' worth of work. This time is not spent in one continuous period, but rather during lunch, morning preparation, and during watches at night. If time is dedicated to creation, it must be spent in uninterrupted 4-hour blocks. This work is generally done in a controlled environment, where distractions are at a minimum, such as a laboratory or shrine. Work that is performed in a distracting or dangerous environment nets only half the amount of progress (just as with the adventuring caster).

A character can work on only one item at a time. If a character starts work on a new item, all materials used on the under-construction item are wasted.

Magic Item Gold Piece Values

Many factors must be considered when determining the price of new magic items. The easiest way to come up with a price is to compare the new item to an item that is already priced, using that price as a guide. Otherwise, use the guidelines summarized on Table 15–29.

Multiple Similar Abilities: For items with multiple similar abilities that don't take up space on a character's body, use the following formula: Calculate the price of the single most costly ability, then add 75% of the value of the next most costly ability, plus 1/2 the value of any other abilities.

Multiple Different Abilities: Abilities such as an attack roll bonus or saving throw bonus and a spell-like function are not similar, and their values are simply added together to determine the cost. For items that take up a space on a character's body, each additional power not only has no discount but instead has a 50% increase in price.

0-Level Spells: When multiplying spell levels to determine value, 0-level spells should be treated as 1/2 level.

Other Considerations: Once you have a cost figure, reduce that number if either of the following conditions applies:

Item Requires Skill to Use: Some items require a specific skill to get them to function. This factor should reduce the cost about 10%.

Item Requires Specific Class or Alignment to Use: Even more restrictive than requiring a skill, this limitation cuts the price by 30%.

Prices presented in the magic item descriptions (the gold piece value following the item's slot) are the market value, which is generally twice what it costs the creator to make the item.

Since different classes get access to certain spells at different levels, the prices for two characters to make the same item might actually be different. An item is only worth two times what the caster of the lowest possible level can make it for. Calculate the market price based on the lowest possible level caster, no matter who makes the item.

Not all items adhere to these formulas. First and foremost, these few formulas aren't enough to truly gauge the exact differences between items. The price of a magic item may be modified based on its actual worth. The formulas only

TABLE 15-29: ESTIMATING MAGIC ITEM GOLD PIECE VALUES

Effect	Base Price	Example
Ability bonus (enhancement)	Bonus squared × 1,000 gp	*Belt of incredible dexterity +2*
Armor bonus (enhancement)	Bonus squared × 1,000 gp	*+1 chainmail*
Bonus spell	Spell level squared × 1,000 gp	*Pearl of power*
AC bonus (deflection)	Bonus squared × 2,000 gp	*Ring of protection +3*
AC bonus (other)[1]	Bonus squared × 2,500 gp	*Ioun stone (dusty rose prism)*
Natural armor bonus (enhancement)	Bonus squared × 2,000 gp	*Amulet of natural armor +1*
Save bonus (resistance)	Bonus squared × 1,000 gp	*Cloak of resistance +5*
Save bonus (other)[1]	Bonus squared × 2,000 gp	*Stone of good luck*
Skill bonus (competence)	Bonus squared × 100 gp	*Cloak of elvenkind*
Spell resistance	10,000 gp per point over SR 12; SR 13 minimum	*Mantle of spell resistance*
Weapon bonus (enhancement)	Bonus squared × 2,000 gp	*+1 longsword*
Spell Effect	**Base Price**	**Example**
Single use, spell completion	Spell level × caster level × 25 gp	*Scroll of haste*
Single use, use-activated	Spell level × caster level × 50 gp	*Potion of cure light wounds*
50 charges, spell trigger	Spell level × caster level × 750 gp	*Wand of fireball*
Command word	Spell level × caster level × 1,800 gp	*Cape of the mountebank*
Use-activated or continuous	Spell level × caster level × 2,000 gp[2]	*Lantern of revealing*
Special	**Base Price Adjustment**	**Example**
Charges per day	Divide by (5 divided by charges per day)	*Boots of teleportation*
No space limitation[3]	Multiply entire cost by 2	*Ioun stone*
Multiple different abilities	Multiply lower item cost by 1.5	*Helm of brilliance*
Charged (50 charges)	1/2 unlimited use base price	*Ring of the ram*
Component	**Extra Cost**	**Example**
Armor, shield, or weapon	Add cost of masterwork item	*+1 composite longbow*
Spell has material component cost	Add directly into price of item per charge[4]	*Wand of stoneskin*

Spell Level: A 0-level spell is half the value of a 1st-level spell for determining price.

1   Such as a luck, insight, sacred, or profane bonus.

2   If a continuous item has an effect based on a spell with a duration measured in rounds, multiply the cost by 4. If the duration of the spell is 1 minute/level, multiply the cost by 2, and if the duration is 10 minutes/level, multiply the cost by 1.5. If the spell has a 24-hour duration or greater, divide the cost in half.

3   An item that does not take up one of the spaces on a body costs double.

4   If item is continuous or unlimited, not charged, determine cost as if it had 100 charges. If it has some daily limit, determine as if it had 50 charges.

provide a starting point. The pricing of scrolls assumes that, whenever possible, a wizard or cleric created it. Potions and wands follow the formulas exactly. Staves follow the formulas closely, and other items require at least some judgment calls.

Creating Magic Armor

To create magic armor, a character needs a heat source and some iron, wood, or leatherworking tools. He also needs a supply of materials, the most obvious being the armor or the pieces of the armor to be assembled. Armor to be made into magic armor must be masterwork armor, and the masterwork cost is added to the base price to determine final market value. Additional magic supply costs for the materials are subsumed in the cost for creating the magic armor—half the base price of the item.

Creating magic armor has a special prerequisite: The creator's caster level must be at least three times the enhancement bonus of the armor. If an item has both an enhancement bonus and a special ability, the higher of the two caster level requirements must be met. Magic armor or a magic shield must have at least a +1 enhancement bonus to have any armor or shield special abilities.

If spells are involved in the prerequisites for making the armor, the creator must have prepared the spells to be cast (or must know the spells, in the case of a sorcerer or bard) and must provide any material components or focuses the spells require. The act of working on the armor triggers the prepared spells, making them unavailable for casting during each day of the armor's creation. (That is, those spell slots are expended from the caster's currently prepared spells, just as if they had been cast.)

Creating some armor may entail other prerequisites beyond or other than spellcasting. See the individual descriptions for details.

Crafting magic armor requires one day for each 1,000 gp value of the base price.

Item Creation Feat Required: Craft Magic Arms and Armor.

Skill Used in Creation: Spellcraft or Craft (armor).

Creating Magic Weapons

To create a magic weapon, a character needs a heat source and some iron, wood, or leatherworking tools. She also needs a supply of materials, the most obvious being the weapon or the pieces of the weapon to be assembled. Only a masterwork weapon can become a magic weapon, and the masterwork cost is added to the total cost to determine final market value. Additional magic supplies costs for the materials are subsumed in the cost for creating the magic weapon—half the base price of the item based upon the item's total effective bonus.

Creating a magic weapon has a special prerequisite: The creator's caster level must be at least three times the enhancement bonus of the weapon. If an item has both an enhancement bonus and a special ability, the higher of the two caster level requirements must be met. A magic weapon must have at least a +1 enhancement bonus to have any melee or ranged special weapon abilities.

If spells are involved in the prerequisites for making the weapon, the creator must have prepared the spells to be cast (or must know the spells, in the case of a sorcerer or bard) but need not provide any material components or focuses the spells require. The act of working on the weapon triggers the prepared spells, making them unavailable for casting during each day of the weapon's creation. (That is, those spell slots are expended from the caster's currently prepared spells, just as if they had been cast.)

At the time of creation, the creator must decide if the weapon glows or not as a side-effect of the magic imbued within it. This decision does not affect the price or the creation time, but once the item is finished, the decision is binding.

Creating magic double-headed weapons is treated as creating two weapons when determining cost, time, and special abilities.

Creating some weapons may entail other prerequisites beyond or other than spellcasting. See the individual descriptions for details.

Crafting a magic weapon requires 1 day for each 1,000 gp value of the base price.

Item Creation Feat Required: Craft Magic Arms and Armor.

Skill Used in Creation: Spellcraft, Craft (bows) (for magic bows and arrows), or Craft (weapons) (for all other weapons).

Creating Potions

The creator of a potion needs a level working surface and at least a few containers in which to mix liquids, as well as a source of heat to boil the brew. In addition, he needs

POTION BASE COSTS (BY BREWER'S CLASS)

Spell Level	Cleric, Druid, Wizard	Sorcerer	Bard	Paladin, Ranger*
0	25 gp	25 gp	25 gp	—
1st	50 gp	50 gp	50 gp	50 gp
2nd	300 gp	400 gp	400 gp	400 gp
3rd	750 gp	900 gp	1,050 gp	1,050 gp

* Caster level is equal to class level −3.

Prices assume that the potion was made at the minimum caster level. The cost to create a potion is half the base price.

ingredients. The costs for materials and ingredients are subsumed in the cost for brewing the potion: 25 gp × the level of the spell × the level of the caster.

All ingredients and materials used to brew a potion must be fresh and unused. The character must pay the full cost for brewing each potion. (Economies of scale do not apply.)

The imbiber of the potion is both the caster and the target. Spells with a range of personal cannot be made into potions.

The creator must have prepared the spell to be placed in the potion (or must know the spell, in the case of a sorcerer or bard) and must provide any material component or focus the spell requires.

Material components are consumed when he begins working, but a focus is not. (A focus used in brewing a potion can be reused.) The act of brewing triggers the prepared spell, making it unavailable for casting until the character has rested and regained spells. (That is, that spell slot is expended from the caster's currently prepared spells, just as if it had been cast.) Brewing a potion requires 1 day.

Item Creation Feat Required: Brew Potion.

Skill Used in Creation: Spellcraft or Craft (alchemy)

Creating Rings

To create a magic ring, a character needs a heat source. He also needs a supply of materials, the most obvious being a ring or the pieces of the ring to be assembled. The cost for the materials is subsumed in the cost for creating the ring. Ring costs are difficult to determine. Refer to Table 15–29 and use the ring prices in the ring descriptions as a guideline. Creating a ring generally costs half the ring's market price.

Rings that duplicate spells with costly material components add in the value of 50 × the spell's component cost. Having a spell with a costly component as a prerequisite does not automatically incur this cost. The act of working on the ring triggers the prepared spells, making them unavailable for casting during each day of the ring's creation. (That is, those spell slots are expended from the caster's currently prepared spells, just as if they had been cast.)

Creating some rings may entail other prerequisites beyond or other than spellcasting. See the individual descriptions for details.

Scroll Base Costs (By Scriber's Class)

Spell Level	Cleric, Druid, Wizard	Sorcerer	Bard	Paladin, Ranger*
0	12 gp 5 sp	12 gp 5 sp	12 gp 5 sp	—
1st	25 gp	25 gp	25 gp	25 gp
2nd	150 gp	200 gp	200 gp	200 gp
3rd	375 gp	450 gp	525 gp	525 gp
4th	700 gp	800 gp	1,000 gp	1,000 gp
5th	1,125 gp	1,250 gp	1,625 gp	—
6th	1,650 gp	1,800 gp	2,400 gp	—
7th	2,275 gp	2,450 gp	—	—
8th	3,000 gp	3,200 gp	—	—
9th	3,825 gp	4,050 gp	—	—

* Caster level is equal to class level −3.

Prices assume that the scroll was made at the minimum caster level. The cost to create a scroll is half the base price.

Forging a ring requires 1 day for each 1,000 gp of the base price.

Item Creation Feat Required: Forge Ring.

Skill Used in Creation: Spellcraft or Craft (jewelry).

Creating Rods

To create a magic rod, a character needs a supply of materials, the most obvious being a rod or the pieces of the rod to be assembled. The cost for the materials is subsumed in the cost for creating the rod. Rod costs are difficult to determine. Refer to Table 15–29 and use the rod prices in the rod descriptions as a guideline. Creating a rod costs half the market value listed.

If spells are involved in the prerequisites for making the rod, the creator must have prepared the spells to be cast (or must know the spells, in the case of a sorcerer or bard) but need not provide any material components or focuses the spells require. The act of working on the rod triggers the prepared spells, making them unavailable for casting during each day of the rod's creation. (That is, those spell slots are expended from the caster's currently prepared spells, just as if they had been cast.)

Creating some rods may entail other prerequisites beyond or other than spellcasting. See the individual descriptions for details.

Crafting a rod requires 1 day for each 1,000 gp of base price.

Item Creation Feat Required: Craft Rod.

Skill Used in Creation: Spellcraft, Craft (jewelry), Craft (sculptures), or Craft (weapons).

Creating Scrolls

To create a scroll, a character needs a supply of choice writing materials, the cost of which is subsumed in the cost for scribing the scroll: 12.5 gp × the level of the spell × the level of the caster.

All writing implements and materials used to scribe a scroll must be fresh and unused. A character must pay the full cost for scribing each spell scroll no matter how many times she previously has scribed the same spell.

The creator must have prepared the spell to be scribed (or must know the spell, in the case of a sorcerer or bard) and must provide any material component or focus the spell requires. A material component is consumed when she begins writing, but a focus is not. (A focus used in scribing a scroll can be reused.) The act of writing triggers the prepared spell, making it unavailable for casting until the character has rested and regained spells. (That is, that spell slot is expended from the caster's currently prepared spells, just as if it had been cast.)

Scribing a scroll requires 1 day per 1,000 gp of the base price. Although an individual scroll might contain more than one spell, each spell must be scribed as a separate effort, meaning that no more than 1 spell can be scribed in a day.

Item Creation Feat Required: Scribe Scroll.

Skill Used in Creation: Spellcraft, Craft (calligraphy), or Profession (scribe).

Creating Staves

To create a magic staff, a character needs a supply of materials, the most obvious being a staff or the pieces of the staff to be assembled.

The materials cost is subsumed in the cost of creation: 400 gp × the level of the highest-level spell × the level of the caster, plus 75% of the value of the next most costly ability (300 gp × the level of the spell × the level of the caster), plus 1/2 the value of any other abilities (200 gp × the level of the spell × the level of the caster). Staves are always fully charged (10 charges) when created.

If desired, a spell can be placed into the staff at less than the normal cost, but then activating that particular spell drains additional charges from the staff. Divide the cost of the spell by the number of charges it consumes to determine its final price. Note that this does not change the order in which the spells are priced (the highest level spell is still priced first, even if it requires more than one charge to activate). The caster level of all spells in a staff must be the same, and no staff can have a caster level of less than 8th, even if all the spells in the staff are low-level spells.

The creator must have prepared the spells to be stored (or must know the spells, in the case of a sorcerer or bard) and must provide any focus the spells require as well as material component costs sufficient to activate the spell 50 times (divide this amount by the number of charges one use of the spell expends). Material components are consumed when he begins working, but focuses are not. (A focus used in creating a staff can be reused.) The act of working on the staff triggers the prepared spells, making them unavailable for casting during each day of the staff's creation. (That is, those spell slots are expended from the caster's currently prepared spells, just as if they had been cast.)

Creating a few staves may entail other prerequisites beyond spellcasting. See the individual descriptions for details.

Crafting a staff requires 1 day for each 1,000 gp of the base price.

Item Creation Feat Required: Craft Staff.

Skill Used in Creation: Spellcraft, Craft (jewelry), Craft (sculptures), or Profession (woodcutter).

Creating Wands

To create a magic wand, a character needs a small supply of materials, the most obvious being a baton or the pieces of the wand to be assembled. The cost for the materials is subsumed in the cost for creating the wand: 375 gp × the level of the spell × the level of the caster. Wands are always fully charged (50 charges) when created.

The creator must have prepared the spell to be stored (or must know the spell, in the case of a sorcerer or bard) and must provide any focuses the spell requires. Fifty of each needed material component are required (one for each charge). Material components are consumed when work begins, but focuses are not. A focus used in creating a wand can be reused. The act of working on the wand triggers the prepared spell, making it unavailable for casting during each day devoted to the wand's creation. (That is, that spell slot is expended from the caster's currently prepared spells, just as if it had been cast.)

Crafting a wand requires 1 day per each 1,000 gp of the base price.

Item Creation Feat Required: Craft Wand.

Skill Used in Creation: Spellcraft, Craft (jewelry), Craft (sculptures), or Profession (woodcutter).

Creating Wondrous Items

To create a wondrous item, a character usually needs some sort of equipment or tools to work on the item. She also needs a supply of materials, the most obvious being the item itself or the pieces of the item to be assembled. The cost for the materials is subsumed in the cost for creating

Wand Base Costs (By Crafter's Class)

Spell Level	Cleric, Druid, Wizard	Sorcerer	Bard	Paladin, Ranger*
0	375 gp	375 gp	375 gp	—
1st	750 gp	750 gp	750 gp	750 gp
2nd	4,500 gp	6,000 gp	6,000 gp	6,000 gp
3rd	11,250 gp	13,500 gp	15,750 gp	15,750 gp
4th	21,000 gp	24,000 gp	30,000 gp	30,000 gp

* Caster level is equal to class level −3.

Prices assume that the wand was made at the minimum caster level. The cost to create a wand is half the base price.

the item. Wondrous item costs are difficult to determine. Refer to Table 15–29 and use the item prices in the item descriptions as a guideline. Creating an item costs half the market value listed.

If spells are involved in the prerequisites for making the item, the creator must have prepared the spells to be cast (or must know the spells, in the case of a sorcerer or bard) but need not provide any material components or focuses the spells require. The act of working on the item triggers the prepared spells, making them unavailable for casting during each day of the item's creation. (That is, those spell slots are expended from the caster's currently prepared spells, just as if they had been cast.)

Creating some items may entail other prerequisites beyond or other than spellcasting. See the individual descriptions for details.

Crafting a wondrous item requires 1 day for each 1,000 gp of the base price.

Item Creation Feat Required: Craft Wondrous Item.

Skill Used In Creation: Spellcraft or an applicable Craft or Profession skill check.

Adding New Abilities

Sometimes, lack of funds or time make it impossible for a magic item crafter to create the desired item from scratch. Fortunately, it is possible to enhance or build upon an existing magic item. Only time, gold, and the various prerequisites required of the new ability to be added to the magic item restrict the type of additional powers one can place.

The cost to add additional abilities to an item is the same as if the item was not magical, less the value of the original item. Thus, a +1 longsword can be made into a +2 vorpal longsword, with the cost to create it being equal to that of a +2 vorpal sword minus the cost of a +1 longsword.

If the item is one that occupies a specific place on a character's body, the cost of adding any additional ability to that item increases by 50%. For example, if a character adds the power to confer invisibility to her ring of protection +2, the cost of adding this ability is the same as for creating a ring of invisibility multiplied by 1.5.

The following appendices contain rules on special abilities and conditions, as well as a recommended reading for those seeking further inspiration.

APPENDIX 1: SPECIAL ABILITIES

The following special abilities include rules commonly used by a number of creatures, spells, and traps.

Extraordinary Abilities (Ex): Extraordinary abilities are nonmagical. They are, however, not something that just anyone can do or even learn to do without extensive training. Effects or areas that suppress or negate magic have no effect on extraordinary abilities.

Spell-Like Abilities (Sp): Spell-like abilities, as the name implies, are magical abilities that are very much like spells. Spell-like abilities are subject to spell resistance and *dispel magic*. They do not function in areas where magic is suppressed or negated (such as an *antimagic field*). Spell-like abilities can be dispelled, but they cannot be counterspelled or used to counterspell.

Supernatural Abilities (Su): Supernatural abilities are magical but not spell-like. Supernatural abilities are not subject to spell resistance and do not function in areas where magic is suppressed or negated (such as an *antimagic field*). A supernatural ability's effect cannot be dispelled and is not subject to counterspells. See Table 16–1 for a summary of the types of special abilities.

Ability Score Bonuses

Some spells and abilities increase your ability scores. Ability score increases with a duration of 1 day or less give only temporary bonuses. For every two points of increase to a single ability, apply a +1 bonus to the skills and statistics listed with the relevant ability.

Strength: Temporary increases to your Strength score give you a bonus on Strength-based skill checks, melee attack rolls, and weapon damage rolls (if they rely on Strength). The bonus also applies to your Combat Maneuver Bonus (if you are Small or larger) and to your Combat Maneuver Defense.

Dexterity: Temporary increases to your Dexterity score give you a bonus on Dexterity-based skill checks, ranged attack rolls, initiative checks, and Reflex saving throws. The bonus also applies to your Armor Class, your Combat Maneuver Bonus (if you are Tiny or smaller), and your Combat Maneuver Defense.

Constitution: Temporary increases to your Constitution score give you a bonus on your Fortitude saving throws. In addition, multiply your total Hit Dice by this bonus and add that amount to your current and total hit points. When the bonus ends, remove this total from your current and total hit points.

Intelligence: Temporary increases to your Intelligence score give you a bonus on Intelligence-based skill checks. This bonus also applies to any spell DCs based on Intelligence.

Wisdom: Temporary increases to your Wisdom score give you a bonus on Wisdom-based skill checks and Will saving throws. This bonus also applies to any spell DCs based on Wisdom.

Charisma: Temporary increases to your Charisma score give you a bonus on Charisma-based skill checks. This bonus also applies to any spell DCs based on Charisma and the DC to resist your channeled energy.

Permanent Bonuses: Ability bonuses with a duration greater than 1 day actually increase the relevant ability score after 24 hours. Modify all skills and statistics related to that ability. This might cause you to gain skill points, hit points, and other bonuses. These bonuses should be noted separately in case they are removed.

Ability Score Damage, Penalty, and Drain

Diseases, poisons, spells, and other abilities can all deal damage directly to your ability scores. This damage does not actually reduce an ability, but it does apply a penalty to the skills and statistics that are based on that ability.

For every 2 points of damage you take to a single ability, apply a –1 penalty to skills and statistics listed with the relevant ability. If the amount of ability damage you have taken equals or exceeds your ability score, you immediately fall unconscious until the damage is less than your ability score. The only exception to this is your Constitution score. If the damage to your Constitution is equal to or greater than your Constitution score, you die. Unless otherwise noted, damage to your ability scores is healed at the rate of 1 per day to each ability score that has been damaged. Ability damage can be healed through the use of spells, such as *lesser restoration*.

Some spells and abilities cause you to take an ability penalty for a limited amount of time. While in effect, these penalties function just like ability damage, but they cannot cause you to fall unconscious or die. In essence, penalties cannot decrease your ability score to less than 1.

Strength: Damage to your Strength score causes you to take penalties on Strength-based skill checks, melee attack rolls, and weapon damage rolls (if they rely on Strength). The penalty also applies to your Combat Maneuver Bonus (if you are Small or larger) and your Combat Maneuver Defense.

TABLE 16-1: SPECIAL ABILITY TYPES

	Extraordinary	Spell-Like	Supernatural
Dispel	No	Yes	No
Spell resistance	No	Yes	No
Antimagic field	No	Yes	Yes
Attack of opportunity	No	Yes	No

Dispel: Can *dispel magic* and similar spells dispel the effects of abilities of that type?

Spell Resistance: Does spell resistance protect a creature from these abilities?

Antimagic Field: Does an *antimagic field* or similar magic suppress the ability?

Attack of Opportunity: Does using the ability provoke attacks of opportunity the way that casting a spell does?

Dexterity: Damage to your Dexterity score causes you to take penalties on Dexterity-based skill checks, ranged attack rolls, initiative checks, and Reflex saving throws. The penalty also applies to your Armor Class, your Combat Maneuver Bonus (if you are Tiny or smaller), and to your Combat Maneuver Defense.

Constitution: Damage to your Constitution score causes you to take penalties on your Fortitude saving throws. In addition, multiply your total Hit Dice by this penalty and subtract that amount from your current and total hit points. Lost hit points are restored when the damage to your Constitution is healed.

Intelligence: Damage to your Intelligence score causes you to take penalties on Intelligence-based skill checks. This penalty also applies to any spell DCs based on Intelligence.

Wisdom: Damage to your Wisdom score causes you to take penalties on Wisdom-based skill checks and Will saving throws. This penalty also applies to any spell DCs based on Wisdom.

Charisma: Damage to your Charisma score causes you to take penalties on Charisma-based skill checks. This penalty also applies to any spell DCs based off Charisma and the DC to resist your channeled energy.

Ability Drain: Ability drain actually reduces the relevant ability score. Modify all skills and statistics related to that ability. This might cause you to lose skill points, hit points, and other bonuses. Ability drain can be healed through the use of spells such as *restoration*.

Afflictions

From curses to poisons to diseases, there are a number of afflictions that can affect a creature. While each of these afflictions has a different effect, they all function using the same basic system. All afflictions grant a saving throw when they are contracted. If successful, the creature does not suffer from the affliction and does not need to make any further rolls. If the saving throw is a failure, the creature falls victim to the affliction and must deal with its effects.

Afflictions require a creature to make a saving throw after a period of time to avoid taking certain penalties. With most afflictions, if a number of saving throws are made consecutively, the affliction is removed and no further saves are necessary. Some afflictions, usually supernatural ones, cannot be cured through saving throws alone and require the aid of powerful magic to remove. Each affliction is presented as a short block of information to help you better adjudicate its results.

Name: This is the name of the affliction.

Type: This is the type of the affliction, such as curse, disease, or poison. It might also include the means by which it is contracted, such as contact, ingestion, inhalation, injury, spell, or trap.

Save: This gives the type of save necessary to avoid contracting the affliction, as well as the DC of that save. Unless otherwise noted, this is also the save to avoid the affliction's effects once it is contracted, as well as the DC of any caster level checks needed to end the affliction through magic, such as *remove curse* or *neutralize poison*.

Onset: Some afflictions have a variable amount of time before they set in. Creatures that come in contact with an affliction with an onset time must make a saving throw immediately. Success means that the affliction is avoided and no further saving throws must be made. Failure means that the creature has contracted the affliction and must begin making additional saves after the onset period has elapsed. The affliction's effect does not occur until after the onset period has elapsed and then only if further saving throws are failed.

Frequency: This is how often the periodic saving throw must be attempted after the affliction has been contracted (after the onset time, if the affliction has any). While some afflictions last until they are cured, others end prematurely, even if the character is not cured through other means. If an affliction ends after a set amount of time, it will be noted in the frequency. For example, a disease with a frequency of "1/day" lasts until cured, but a poison with a frequency of "1/round for 6 rounds" ends after 6 rounds have passed.

Afflictions without a frequency occur only once, immediately upon contraction (or after the onset time if one is listed).

Effect: This is the effect that the character suffers each time if he fails his saving throw against the affliction. Most afflictions cause ability damage or hit point damage. These effects are cumulative, but they can be cured normally. Other afflictions cause the creature to take penalties or other effects. These effects are sometimes cumulative, with the rest only affecting the creature if it failed its most recent save. Some afflictions have different effects after the first save is failed. These afflictions have an initial effect, which occurs when the first save is failed, and a secondary effect, when additional saves are failed, as noted in the text. Hit point and ability score damage caused by an affliction cannot be healed naturally while the affliction persists.

Cure: This tells you how the affliction is cured. Commonly, this is a number of saving throws that must be made consecutively. Even if the affliction has a limited frequency, it might be cured prematurely if enough saving throws are made. Hit point damage and ability score damage is not removed when an affliction is cured. Such damage must be healed normally. Afflictions without a cure entry can only be cured through powerful spells, such as *neutralize poison* and *remove curse*. No matter how many saving throws are made, these afflictions continue to affect the target.

Example: Valeros has been exposed to the red ache disease. He failed a DC 15 Fortitude save to avoid contracting it, so after the onset period of 1d3 days has passed, he must make another DC 15 Fortitude save to avoid taking 1d6 points of Strength damage. From this point onward, he must make a DC 15 Fortitude save each day (according to the disease's frequency) to avoid further Strength damage. If, on two consecutive days, he makes his Fortitude saves, he is cured of the disease and any damage it caused begins to heal as normal.

Curses

Careless rogues plundering a tomb, drunken heroes insulting a powerful wizard, and foolhardy adventurers who pick up ancient swords all might suffer from curses. These magic afflictions can have a wide variety of effects, from a simple penalty to certain checks to transforming the victim into a toad. Some even cause the afflicted to slowly rot away, leaving nothing behind but dust. Unlike other afflictions, most curses cannot be cured through a number of successful saving throws. Curses can be cured through magic, however, usually via spells such as *remove curse* and *break enchantment*. While some curses cause a progressive deterioration, others inflict a static penalty from the moment they are contracted, neither fading over time nor growing worse. In addition, there are a number of magic items that act like curses. See Chapter 15 for a description of these cursed items.

The following samples present just some of the possibilities when creating curses.

BALEFUL POLYMORPH SPELL
Type curse, spell; **Save** Fortitude DC 17 negates, Will DC 17 partial

Effect transforms target into a lizard; see *baleful polymorph* description

BESTOW CURSE TRAP
Type curse, spell, trap; **Save** Will DC 14

Effect –6 penalty to Strength

CURSE OF THE AGES

Type curse; **Save** Will DC 17
Frequency 1/day
Effect age 1 year

MUMMY ROT

Type curse, disease, injury; **Save** Fortitude DC 16
Onset 1 minute; **Frequency** 1/day
Effect 1d6 Con damage and 1d6 Cha damage; **Cure** mummy rot can only be cured by successfully casting both *remove curse* and *remove disease* within 1 minute of each other.

UNLUCK

Type curse; **Save** Will DC 20 negates, no save to avoid effects
Frequency 1/hour
Effect target must reroll any roll decided by the GM and take the worse result

WEREWOLF LYCANTHROPY

Type curse, injury; **Save** Fortitude DC 15 negates, Will DC 15 to avoid effects
Onset the next full moon; **Frequency** on the night of every full moon or whenever the target is injured
Effect target transforms into a wolf under the GM's control until the next morning

Diseases

From a widespread plague to the bite of a dire rat, disease is a serious threat to common folk and adventurers alike. Diseases rarely have a limited frequency, but most have a lengthy onset time. This onset time can also be variable. Most diseases can be cured by a number of consecutive saving throws or by spells such as *remove disease*.

The following samples represent just some of the possibilities when creating diseases.

BLINDING SICKNESS

Type disease, ingested; **Save** Fortitude DC 16
Onset 1d3 days; **Frequency** 1/day
Effect 1d4 Str damage, if more than 2 Str damage, target must make an additional Fort save or be permanently blinded; **Cure** 2 consecutive saves

BUBONIC PLAGUE

Type disease, injury or inhaled; **Save** Fortitude DC 17
Onset 1 day; **Frequency** 1/day
Effect 1d4 Con damage and 1 Cha damage and target is fatigued; **Cure** 2 consecutive saves

CACKLE FEVER

Type disease, inhaled; **Save** Fortitude DC 16
Onset 1 day; **Frequency** 1/day
Effect 1d6 Wis damage; **Cure** 2 consecutive saves

DEMON FEVER

Type disease, injury; **Save** Fortitude DC 18
Onset 1 day; **Frequency** 1/day
Effect 1d6 Con damage, target must make a second Fort save or 1 point of the damage is drain instead; **Cure** 2 consecutive saves

DEVIL CHILLS

Type disease, injury; **Save** Fortitude DC 14
Onset 1d4 days; **Frequency** 1/day
Effect 1d4 Str damage; **Cure** 3 consecutive saves

FILTH FEVER

Type disease, injury; **Save** Fortitude DC 12
Onset 1d3 days; **Frequency** 1/day
Effect 1d3 Dex damage and 1d3 Con damage; **Cure** 2 consecutive saves

LEPROSY

Type disease, contact, inhaled, or injury; **Save** Fortitude DC 12 negates, Fortitude DC 20 to avoid effects
Onset 2d4 weeks; **Frequency** 1/week
Effect 1d2 Cha damage; **Cure** 2 consecutive saves

MINDFIRE

Type disease, inhaled; **Save** Fortitude DC 12
Onset 1 day; **Frequency** 1/day
Effect 1d4 Int damage; **Cure** 2 consecutive saves

RED ACHE

Type disease, injury; **Save** Fortitude DC 15
Onset 1d3 days; **Frequency** 1/day
Effect 1d6 Str damage; **Cure** 2 consecutive saves

SHAKES

Type disease, contact; **Save** Fortitude DC 13
Onset 1 day; **Frequency** 1/day
Effect 1d8 Dex damage; **Cure** 2 consecutive saves

SLIMY DOOM

Type disease, contact; **Save** Fortitude DC 14
Onset 1 day; **Frequency** 1/day
Effect 1d4 Con damage, target must make a second Fort save or 1 point of the damage is drain instead; **Cure** 2 consecutive saves

Poison

No other affliction is so prevalent as poison. From the fangs of a viper to the ichor-stained assassin's blade, poison is a constant threat. Poisons can be cured by successful saving throws and spells such as *neutralize poison*.

Contact poisons are contracted the moment someone touches the poison with his bare skin. Such poisons can be used as injury poisons. Contact poisons usually have an onset time of 1 minute and a frequency of 1 minute. Ingested poisons are contracted when a creature eats or drinks the poison. Ingested poisons usually have an onset time of 10 minutes and a frequency of 1 minute. Injury poisons are primarily contracted through the attacks of certain creatures and through weapons coated in the toxin. Injury poisons do not usually have an onset time and have a frequency of 1 round. Inhaled poisons are contracted the moment a creature enters an area containing such poisons. Most inhaled poisons fill a volume equal to a 10-foot cube per dose. Creatures can attempt to hold their breaths while inside to avoid inhaling the toxin. Creatures holding their breaths receive a 50% chance of not having to make a Fortitude save each round. See the rules for holding your breath and suffocation in Chapter 13. Note that a character that would normally suffocate while attempting to hold its breath instead begins to breathe normally again.

Unlike other afflictions, multiple doses of the same poison stack. Poisons delivered by injury and contact cannot inflict more than one dose of poison at a time, but inhaled and ingested poisons can inflict multiple doses at once. Each additional dose extends the total duration of the poison (as noted under frequency) by half its total duration. In addition, each dose of poison increases the DC to resist the poison by +2. This increase is cumulative. Multiple doses do not alter the cure conditions of the poison, and meeting these conditions ends the affliction for all the doses. For example, a character is bit three times in the same round by a trio of Medium monstrous spiders, injecting him with three doses of Medium spider venom. The unfortunate character must make a DC 18 Fortitude save for the next 8 rounds. Fortunately, just one successful save cures the character of all three doses of the poison.

Applying poison to a weapon or single piece of ammunition is a standard action. Whenever a character applies or readies a poison for use there is a 5% chance that he exposes himself to the poison and must save against the poison as normal. This does not consume the dose of poison. Whenever a character attacks with a poisoned weapon, if the attack roll results in a natural 1, he exposes himself to the poison. This poison is consumed when the weapon strikes a creature or is touched by the wielder. Characters with the poison use class feature do not risk accidentally poisoning themselves.

Poisons can be made using Craft (alchemy). The DC to make a poison is equal to its Fortitude save DC. Rolling a natural 1 on a Craft skill check while making a poison exposes the crafter to the poison. Crafters with the poison use class feature do not risk poisoning themselves when using Craft to make poison.

The following samples represent just some of the possibilities when creating poisons.

ARSENIC

Type poison, ingested; **Save** Fortitude DC 13
Onset 10 minutes.; **Frequency** 1/minute for 4 minutes
Effect 1d2 Con damage; **Cure** 1 save

BELLADONNA

Type poison, ingested; **Save** Fortitude DC 14
Onset 10 minutes; **Frequency** 1/minute for 6 minutes
Effect 1d2 Str damage, target can attempt one save to cure a lycanthropy affliction contracted in the past hour; **Cure** 1 save

BLACK ADDER VENOM

Type poison, injury; **Save** Fortitude DC 11
Frequency 1/round for 6 rounds
Effect 1d2 Con damage; **Cure** 1 save

BLACK LOTUS EXTRACT

Type poison, contact; **Save** Fortitude DC 20
Onset 1 minute; **Frequency** 1/round for 6 rounds
Effect 1d6 Con damage; **Cure** 2 consecutive saves

BLOODROOT

Type poison, injury; **Save** Fortitude DC 12
Onset 1 round; **Frequency** 1/round for 4 rounds
Effect 1 Con damage and 1 Wis damage; **Cure** 1 save

BLUE WHINNIS

Type poison, injury; **Save** Fortitude DC 14
Frequency 1/round for 2 rounds
Initial Effect 1 Con damage; **Secondary Effect** unconsciousness for 1d3 hours; **Cure** 1 save

BURNT OTHUR FUMES

Type poison, inhaled; **Save** Fortitude DC 18
Frequency 1/round for 6 rounds
Initial Effect 1 Con drain; **Secondary Effect** 1d3 Con damage; **Cure** 2 consecutive saves

DARK REAVER POWDER

Type poison, ingested; **Save** Fortitude DC 18
Onset 10 minutes; **Frequency** 1/minute for 6 minutes
Effect 1d3 Con damage and 1 Str damage; **Cure** 2 consecutive saves

DEATHBLADE

Type poison, injury; **Save** Fortitude DC 20
Frequency 1/round for 6 rounds
Effect 1d3 Con damage; **Cure** 2 consecutive saves

DRAGON BILE

Type poison, contact; **Save** Fortitude DC 26
Frequency 1/round for 6 rounds
Effect 1d3 Str damage

TABLE 16-2: SAMPLE POISONS

Name	Type	Fort DC	Onset	Frequency	Effect	Cure	Cost
Arsenic	ingested	13	10 min.	1/min. for 4 min.	1d2 Con	1 save	120 gp
Belladonna	ingested	14	10 min.	1/min. for 6 min.	1d2 Str, see text	1 save	100 gp
Black adder venom	injury	11	—	1/rd. for 6 rds.	1d2 Con	1 save	120 gp
Black lotus extract	contact	20	1 min.	1/rd. for 6 rds.	1d6 Con	2 saves	4,500 gp
Bloodroot	injury	12	1 rd.	1/rd. for 4 rds.	1 Con and 1 Wis	1 save	100 gp
Blue whinnis	injury	14	—	1/rd. for 2 rds.	1 Con/unconscious 1d3 hours	1 save	120 gp
Burnt othur fumes	inhaled	18	—	1/rd. for 6 rds.	1 Con drain/1d3 Con	2 saves	2,100 gp
Dark reaver powder	ingested	18	10 min.	1/min. for 6 min.	1d3 Con and 1 Str	2 saves	800 gp
Deathblade	injury	20	—	1/rd. for 6 rds.	1d3 Con	2 saves	1,800 gp
Dragon bile	contact	26	—	1/rd. for 6 rds.	1d3 Str	—	1,500 gp
Drow poison	injury	13	—	1/min. for 2 min.	unconscious 1 min./2d4 hours	1 save	75 gp
Giant wasp poison	injury	18	—	1/rd. for 6 rds.	1d2 Dex	1 save	210 gp
Greenblood oil	injury	13	—	1/rd. for 4 rds.	1 Con	1 save	100 gp
Green prismatic poison	spell	varies	—	1/rd. for 6 rds.	Death/1 Con	2 saves	—
Hemlock	ingested	18	10 min.	1/min. for 6 min.	1d6 Dex, see text	2 saves	2,500 gp
Id moss	ingested	14	10 min.	1/min. for 6 min.	1d3 Int	1 save	125 gp
Insanity mist	inhaled	15	—	1/rd. for 6 rds.	1d3 Wis	1 save	1,500 gp
King's sleep	ingested	19	1 day	1/day	1 Con drain	2 saves	5,000 gp
Large scorpion venom	injury	17	—	1/rd. for 6 rds.	1d2 Str	1 save	200 gp
Lich dust	ingested	17	10 min.	1/min. for 6 min.	1d3 Str	2 saves	400 gp
Malyass root paste	contact	16	1 min.	1/min. for 6 min.	1d2 Dex	1 save	250 gp
Medium spider venom	injury	14	—	1/rd. for 4 rds.	1d2 Str	1 save	150 gp
Nightmare vapor	inhaled	20	—	1/rd. for 6 rds.	1 Wis and confused 1 round	2 saves	1,800 gp
Nitharit	contact	13	1 min.	1/min. for 6 min.	1d3 Con	1 save	650 gp
Oil of taggit	ingested	15	1 min.	—	unconscious 1d3 hours	1 save	90 gp
Purple worm poison	injury	24	—	1/rd. for 6 rds.	1d3 Str	2 saves	700 gp
Sassone leaf residue	contact	16	1 min.	1/rd. for 6 rds.	2d12 hp/1 Con	1 save	300 gp
Shadow essence	injury	17	—	1/rd. for 6 rds.	1 Str drain/1d2 Str	1 save	250 gp
Small centipede poison	injury	11	—	1/rd. for 4 rds.	1 Dex	1 save	90 gp
Striped toadstool	ingested	11	10 min.	1/min. for 4 min.	1d3 Wis and 1 Int	1 save	180 gp
Tears of death	contact	22	1 min.	1/rd. for 6 rds.	1d6 Con and paralyzed 1 min.	—	6,500 gp
Terinav root	contact	16	1 min.	1/rd. for 6 rds.	1d3 Dex	1 save	400 gp
Ungol dust	inhaled	15	—	1/rd. for 4 rds.	1 Cha drain/1d2 Cha	1 save	1,000 gp
Wolfsbane	ingested	16	10 min.	1/min. for 6 min.	1d3 Con	1 save	500 gp
Wyvern poison	injury	17	—	1/rd. for 6 rds.	1d4 Con	2 saves	3,000 gp

DROW POISON

Type poison, injury; **Save** Fortitude DC 13

Frequency 1/minute for 2 minutes

Initial Effect unconsciousness for 1 minute; **Secondary Effect** unconsciousness for 2d4 hours; **Cure** 1 save

GIANT WASP POISON

Type poison, injury; **Save** Fortitude DC 18

Frequency 1/round for 6 rounds

Effect 1d2 Dex damage; **Cure** 1 save

GREENBLOOD OIL

Type poison, injury; **Save** Fortitude DC 13

Frequency 1/round for 4 rounds

Effect 1 Con damage; **Cure** 1 save

GREEN PRISMATIC POISON

Type poison, spell; **Save** Fort DC varies by spell

Frequency 1/round for 6 rounds

Initial Effect death; **Secondary Effect** 1 Con damage; **Cure** 2 consecutive saves. See *prismatic sphere*, *prismatic spray*, or *prismatic wall* for more details.

HEMLOCK

Type poison, ingested; **Save** Fortitude DC 18

Onset 10 minutes; **Frequency** 1/minute for 6 minutes

Effect 1d6 Dex damage, creatures reduced to 0 Dexterity suffocate; **Cure** 2 consecutive saves

ID MOSS

Type poison, ingested; **Save** Fortitude DC 14

Onset 10 minutes; **Frequency** 1/minute for 6 minutes
Effect 1d3 Int damage; **Cure** 1 save

INSANITY MIST

Type poison, inhaled; **Save** Fortitude DC 15
Frequency 1/rounds for 6 rounds
Effect 1d3 Wis damage; **Cure** 1 save

KING'S SLEEP

Type poison, ingested; **Save** Fortitude DC 19
Onset 1 day; **Frequency** 1/day
Effect 1 Con drain; **Cure** 2 consecutive saves

LARGE SCORPION VENOM

Type poison, injury; **Save** Fortitude DC 17
Frequency 1/round for 6 rounds
Effect 1d2 Str damage; **Cure** 1 save

LICH DUST

Type poison, ingested; **Save** Fortitude DC 17
Onset 10 minutes; **Frequency** 1/minute for 6 minutes
Effect 1d3 Str damage; **Cure** 2 consecutive saves

MALYASS ROOT PASTE

Type poison, contact; **Save** Fortitude DC 16
Onset 1 minute; **Frequency** 1/minute for 6 minutes
Effect 1d2 Dex damage; **Cure** 1 save

MEDIUM SPIDER VENOM

Type poison, injury; **Save** Fortitude DC 14
Frequency 1/round for 4 rounds
Effect 1d2 Str damage; **Cure** 1 save

NIGHTMARE VAPOR

Type poison, inhaled; **Save** Fortitude DC 20
Frequency 1/round for 6 rounds
Effect 1 Wis damage and confused for 1 round; **Cure** 2 consecutive saves

NITHARIT

Type poison, contact; **Save** Fortitude DC 13
Onset 1 minute; **Frequency** 1/minute for 6 minutes
Effect 1d3 Con damage; **Cure** 1 save

OIL OF TAGGIT

Type poison, ingested; **Save** Fortitude DC 15
Onset 1 minute
Effect unconsciousness for 1d3 hours; **Cure** 1 save

PURPLE WORM POISON

Type poison, injury; **Save** Fortitude DC 24
Frequency 1/round for 6 rounds
Effect 1d3 Str damage; **Cure** 2 consecutive saves

SASSONE LEAF RESIDUE

Type poison, contact; **Save** Fortitude DC 16
Onset 1 minute; **Frequency** 1/minute for 6 minutes
Initial Effect 2d12 hit point damage; **Secondary Effect** 1 Con damage; **Cure** 1 save

SHADOW ESSENCE

Type poison, injury; **Save** Fortitude DC 17
Frequency 1/round for 6 rounds
Initial Effect 1 Str drain; **Secondary Effect** 1d2 Str damage; **Cure** 1 save

SMALL CENTIPEDE POISON

Type poison, injury; **Save** Fortitude DC 11
Frequency 1/round for 4 rounds
Effect 1 Dex damage; **Cure** 1 save

STRIPED TOADSTOOL

Type poison, ingested; **Save** Fortitude DC 11
Onset 10 minutes; **Frequency** 1/minute for 4 minutes
Effect 1d3 Wis damage and 1 Int damage; **Cure** 1 save

TEARS OF DEATH

Type poison, contact; **Save** Fortitude DC 22
Onset 1 minute; **Frequency** 1/minute for 6 minutes
Effect 1d6 Con damage and paralyzed for 1 minute

TERINAV ROOT

Type poison, contact; **Save** Fortitude DC 16
Onset 1 minute; **Frequency** 1/minute for 6 minutes
Effect 1d3 Dex damage; **Cure** 1 save

UNGOL DUST

Type poison, inhaled; **Save** Fortitude DC 15
Frequency 1/round for 4 rounds
Initial Effect 1 Cha drain; **Secondary Effect** 1d2 Cha damage; **Cure** 1 save

WOLFSBANE

Type poison, ingested; **Save** Fortitude DC 16
Onset 10 minute; **Frequency** 1/minute for 6 minutes
Effect 1d3 Con damage; **Cure** 1 save

WYVERN POISON

Type poison, injury; **Save** Fortitude DC 17
Frequency 1/round for 6 rounds
Effect 1d4 Con damage; **Cure** 2 consecutive saves

Blindsight and Blindsense

Some creatures possess blindsight, the extraordinary ability to use a nonvisual sense (or a combination of senses) to operate effectively without vision. Such senses may include sensitivity to vibrations, acute scent, keen hearing, or echolocation. This makes invisibility and concealment (even magical darkness) irrelevant to the creature (though it still can't see ethereal creatures). This ability operates out to a range specified in the creature description.

- Blindsight never allows a creature to distinguish color or visual contrast. A creature cannot read with blindsight.
- Blindsight does not subject a creature to gaze attacks (even though darkvision does).
- Blinding attacks do not penalize creatures that use blindsight.
- Deafening attacks thwart blindsight if it relies on hearing.
- Blindsight works underwater but not in a vacuum.
- Blindsight negates displacement and blur effects.

Blindsense: Other creatures have blindsense, a lesser ability that lets the creature notice things it cannot see, but without the precision of blindsight. The creature with blindsense usually does not need to make Perception checks to notice and locate creatures within range of its blindsense ability, provided that it has line of effect to that creature. Any opponent that cannot be seen has total concealment (50% miss chance) against a creature with blindsense, and the blindsensing creature still has the normal miss chance when attacking foes that have concealment. Visibility still affects the movement of a creature with blindsense. A creature with blindsense is still denied its Dexterity bonus to Armor Class against attacks from creatures it cannot see.

Channel Resistance

Creatures with channel resistance gain a bonus on Will saves made against channeled energy. They add their bonus to any Will saves made to halve the damage and resist the effect.

Charm and Compulsion

Many abilities and spells can cloud the minds of characters and monsters, leaving them unable to tell friend from foe—or worse yet, deceiving them into thinking that their former friends are now their worst enemies. Two general types of enchantments affect characters and creatures: charms and compulsions.

Charming another creature gives the charming character the ability to befriend and suggest courses of action to his minion, but the servitude is not absolute or mindless. Charms of this type include the various *charm* spells and some monster abilities. Essentially, a *charmed* character retains free will but makes choices according to a skewed view of the world.

- A charmed creature doesn't gain any magical ability to understand his new friend's language.
- A charmed character retains his original alignment and allegiances, generally with the exception that he now

regards the charming creature as a dear friend and will give great weight to his suggestions and directions.

- A charmed character fights his former allies only if they threaten his new friend, and even then he uses the least lethal means at his disposal as long as these tactics show any possibility of success (just as he would in a fight with an actual friend).
- A charmed character is entitled to an opposed Charisma check against his master in order to resist instructions or commands that would make him do something he wouldn't normally do even for a close friend. If he succeeds, he decides not to go along with that order but remains charmed.
- A charmed character never obeys a command that is obviously suicidal or grievously harmful to him.
- If the charming creature commands his minion to do something that the influenced character would be violently opposed to, the subject may attempt a new saving throw to break free of the influence altogether.
- A charmed character who is openly attacked by the creature who charmed him or by that creature's apparent allies is automatically freed of the spell or effect.

Compulsion is a different matter altogether. A compulsion overrides the subject's free will in some way or simply changes the way the subject's mind works. A charm makes the subject a friend of the caster; a compulsion makes the subject obey the caster.

Regardless of whether a character is charmed or compelled, he does not volunteer information or tactics that his master doesn't ask for.

Damage Reduction

Some magic creatures have the supernatural ability to instantly heal damage from weapons or ignore blows altogether as though they were invulnerable.

The numerical part of a creature's damage reduction (or DR) is the amount of damage the creature ignores from normal attacks. Usually, a certain type of weapon can overcome this reduction (see Overcoming DR). This information is separated from the damage reduction number by a slash. For example, DR 5/magic means that a creature takes 5 less points of damage from all weapons that are not magic. If a dash follows the slash, then the damage reduction is effective against any attack that does not ignore damage reduction.

Whenever damage reduction completely negates the damage from an attack, it also negates most special effects that accompany the attack, such as injury poison, a monk's stunning, and injury-based disease. Damage reduction does not negate touch attacks, energy damage dealt along with an attack, or energy drains. Nor does it affect poisons or diseases delivered by inhalation, ingestion, or contact.

Attacks that deal no damage because of the target's damage reduction do not disrupt spells.

Spells, spell-like abilities, and energy attacks (even nonmagical fire) ignore damage reduction.

Sometimes damage reduction represents instant healing. Sometimes it represents the creature's tough hide or body. In either case, other characters can see that conventional attacks won't work.

If a creature has damage reduction from more than one source, the two forms of damage reduction do not stack. Instead, the creature gets the benefit of the best damage reduction in a given situation.

Overcoming DR: Damage reduction may be overcome by special materials, magic weapons (any weapon with a +1 or higher enhancement bonus, not counting the enhancement from masterwork quality), certain types of weapons (such as slashing or bludgeoning), and weapons imbued with an alignment.

Ammunition fired from a projectile weapon with an enhancement bonus of +1 or higher is treated as a magic weapon for the purpose of overcoming damage reduction. Similarly, ammunition fired from a projectile weapon with an alignment gains the alignment of that projectile weapon (in addition to any alignment it may already have).

Weapons with an enhancement bonus of +3 or greater can ignore some types of damage reduction, regardless of their actual material or alignment. The following table shows what type of enhancement bonus is needed to overcome some common types of damage reduction.

DR Type	Weapon Enhancement Bonus Equivalent
Cold iron/silver	+3
Adamantine*	+4
Alignment-based	+5

* Note that this does not give the ability to ignore hardness, like an actual adamantine weapon does

Darkvision

Darkvision is the extraordinary ability to see with no light source at all, out to a range specified for the creature. Darkvision is black-and-white only (colors cannot be discerned). It does not allow characters to see anything that they could not see otherwise—invisible objects are still invisible, and illusions are still visible as what they seem to be. Likewise, darkvision subjects a creature to gaze attacks normally. The presence of light does not spoil darkvision.

Death Attacks

In most cases, a death attack allows the victim a Fortitude save to avoid the effect, but if the save fails, the creature takes a large amount of damage, which might cause it to die instantly.

- *Raise dead* doesn't work on someone killed by a death attack or effect.
- Death attacks slay instantly. A victim cannot be made stable and thereby kept alive.
- In case it matters, a dead character, no matter how he died, has hit points equal to or less than his negative Constitution score.
- The spell *death ward* protects against these attacks.

Energy Drain and Negative Levels

Some spells and a number of undead creatures have the ability to drain away life and energy; this dreadful attack results in "negative levels." These cause a character to take a number of penalties.

For each negative level a creature has, it takes a cumulative –1 penalty on all ability checks, attack rolls, combat maneuver checks, Combat Maneuver Defense, saving throws, and skill checks. In addition, the creature reduces its current and total hit points by 5 for each negative level it possesses. The creature is also treated as one level lower for the purpose of level-dependent variables (such as spellcasting) for each negative level possessed. Spellcasters do not lose any prepared spells or slots as a result of negative levels. If a creature's negative levels equal or exceed its total Hit Dice, it dies.

A creature with temporary negative levels receives a new saving throw to remove the negative level each day. The DC of this save is the same as the effect that caused the negative levels.

Some abilities and spells (such as *raise dead*) bestow permanent level drain on a creature. These are treated just like temporary negative levels, but they do not allow a new save each day to remove them. Level drain can be removed through spells like *restoration*. Permanent negative levels remain after a dead creature is restored to life. A creature whose permanent negative levels equal its Hit Dice cannot be brought back to life through spells like *raise dead* and *resurrection* without also receiving a *restoration* spell, cast the round after it is restored to life.

Energy Immunity and Vulnerability

A creature with energy immunity never takes damage from that energy type. Vulnerability means the creature takes half again as much (+50%) damage as normal from that energy type, regardless of whether a saving throw is allowed or if the save is a success or failure.

Energy Resistance

A creature with resistance to energy has the ability (usually extraordinary) to ignore some damage of a certain type per attack, but it does not have total immunity.

Each resistance ability is defined by what energy type it resists and how many points of damage are resisted.

It doesn't matter whether the damage has a mundane or magical source.

When resistance completely negates the damage from an energy attack, the attack does not disrupt a spell. This resistance does not stack with the resistance that a spell might provide.

Fear

Spells, magic items, and certain monsters can affect characters with fear. In most cases, the character makes a Will saving throw to resist this effect, and a failed roll means that the character is shaken, frightened, or panicked.

Shaken: Characters who are shaken take a –2 penalty on attack rolls, saving throws, skill checks, and ability checks.

Frightened: Characters who are frightened are shaken, and in addition they flee from the source of their fear as quickly as they can. They can choose the paths of their flight. Other than that stipulation, once they are out of sight (or hearing) of the source of their fear, they can act as they want. If the duration of their fear continues, however, characters can be forced to flee if the source of their fear presents itself again. Characters unable to flee can fight (though they are still shaken).

Panicked: Characters who are panicked are shaken, and they run away from the source of their fear as quickly as they can, dropping whatever they are holding. Other than running away from the source, their paths are random. They flee from all other dangers that confront them rather than facing those dangers. Once they are out of sight (or hearing) of any source of danger, they can act as they want. Panicked characters cower if they are prevented from fleeing.

Becoming Even More Fearful: Fear effects are cumulative. A shaken character who is made shaken again becomes frightened, and a shaken character who is made frightened becomes panicked instead. A frightened character who is made shaken or frightened becomes panicked instead.

Invisibility

The ability to move about unseen is not foolproof. While they can't be seen, invisible creatures can be heard, smelled, or felt.

Invisibility makes a creature undetectable by vision, including darkvision.

Invisibility does not, by itself, make a creature immune to critical hits, but it does make the creature immune to extra damage from being a ranger's favored enemy and from sneak attacks.

A creature can generally notice the presence of an active invisible creature within 30 feet with a DC 20 Perception check. The observer gains a hunch that "something's there" but can't see it or target it accurately with an attack. It's practically impossible (+20 DC) to pinpoint an invisible creature's location with a Perception check. Even once a character has pinpointed the square that contains an invisible creature, the creature still benefits from total concealment (50% miss chance). There are a number of modifiers that can be applied to this DC if the invisible creature is moving or engaged in a noisy activity.

Invisible Creature is...	Perception DC Modifier
In combat or speaking	–20
Moving at half speed	–5
Moving at full speed	–10
Running or charging	–20
Not moving	+20
Using Stealth	Stealth check +20
Some distance away	+1 per 10 feet
Behind an obstacle (door)	+5
Behind an obstacle (stone wall)	+15

A creature can grope about to find an invisible creature. A character can make a touch attack with his hands or a weapon into two adjacent 5-foot squares using a standard action. If an invisible target is in the designated area, there is a 50% miss chance on the touch attack. If successful, the groping character deals no damage but has successfully pinpointed the invisible creature's current location. If the invisible creature moves, its location, obviously, is once again unknown.

If an invisible creature strikes a character, the character struck knows the location of the creature that struck him (until, of course, the invisible creature moves). The only exception is if the invisible creature has a reach greater than 5 feet. In this case, the struck character knows the general location of the creature but has not pinpointed the exact location.

If a character tries to attack an invisible creature whose location he has pinpointed, he attacks normally, but the invisible creature still benefits from full concealment (and thus a 50% miss chance). A particularly large and slow invisible creature might get a smaller miss chance.

If a character tries to attack an invisible creature whose location he has not pinpointed, have the player choose the space where the character will direct the attack. If the invisible creature is there, conduct the attack normally. If the enemy's not there, roll the miss chance as if it were there and tell him that the character has missed, regardless of the result. That way the player doesn't know whether the attack missed because the enemy's not there or because you successfully rolled the miss chance.

If an invisible character picks up a visible object, the object remains visible. An invisible creature can pick up a small visible item and hide it on his person (tucked in a pocket or behind a cloak) and render it effectively invisible. One could coat an invisible object with flour to at least keep track of its position (until the flour falls off or blows away).

Invisible creatures leave tracks. They can be tracked normally. Footprints in sand, mud, or other soft surfaces can give enemies clues to an invisible creature's location.

An invisible creature in the water displaces water, revealing its location. The invisible creature, however, is still hard to see and benefits from concealment.

A creature with the scent ability can detect an invisible creature as it would a visible one.

A creature with the Blind-Fight feat has a better chance to hit an invisible creature. Roll the miss chance twice, and he misses only if both rolls indicate a miss. (Alternatively, make one 25% miss chance roll rather than two 50% miss chance rolls.)

A creature with blindsight can attack (and otherwise interact with) creatures regardless of invisibility.

An invisible burning torch still gives off light, as does an invisible object with a *light* or similar spell cast upon it.

Ethereal creatures (such as ghosts from the *Pathfinder RPG Bestiary*) are invisible. Since ethereal creatures are not materially present, Perception checks, scent, Blind-Fight, and blindsight don't help locate them. Incorporeal creatures are often invisible. Scent, Blind-Fight, and blindsight don't help creatures find or attack invisible, incorporeal creatures, but Perception checks can help.

Invisible creatures cannot use gaze attacks.

Invisibility does not thwart divination spells.

Since some creatures can detect or even see invisible creatures, it is helpful to be able to hide even when invisible.

Low-Light Vision

Characters with low-light vision have eyes that are so sensitive to light that they can see twice as far as normal in dim light. Low-light vision is color vision. A spellcaster with low-light vision can read a scroll as long as even the tiniest candle flame is next to him as a source of light.

Characters with low-light vision can see outdoors on a moonlit night as well as they can during the day.

Paralysis

Some monsters and spells have the supernatural or spell-like ability to paralyze their victims, immobilizing them through magical means. Paralysis from poison is discussed in the Afflictions section.

A paralyzed character cannot move, speak, or take any physical action. He is rooted to the spot, frozen and helpless. Not even friends can move his limbs. He may take purely mental actions, such as casting a spell with no components.

A winged creature flying in the air at the time that it becomes paralyzed cannot flap its wings and falls. A swimmer can't swim and may drown.

Scent

This extraordinary ability lets a creature detect approaching enemies, sniff out hidden foes, and track by sense of smell.

A creature with the scent ability can detect opponents by sense of smell, generally within 30 feet. If the opponent is upwind, the range is 60 feet. If it is downwind, the range is 15 feet. Strong scents, such as smoke or rotting garbage, can be detected at twice the ranges noted above. Overpowering scents, such as skunk musk or troglodyte stench, can be detected at three times these ranges.

The creature detects another creature's presence but not its specific location. Noting the direction of the scent is a move action. If the creature moves within 5 feet (1 square) of the scent's source, the creature can pinpoint the area that the source occupies, even if it cannot be seen.

A creature with the Survival skill and the scent ability can follow tracks by smell, making a Survival check to find or follow a track. A creature with the scent ability can attempt to follow tracks using Survival untrained. The typical DC for a fresh trail is 10. The DC increases or decreases depending on how strong the quarry's odor is, the number of creatures, and the age of the trail. For each hour that the trail is cold, the DC increases by 2. The ability otherwise follows the rules for the Survival skill in regards to tracking. Creatures tracking by scent ignore the effects of surface conditions and poor visibility.

Creatures with the scent ability can identify familiar odors just as humans do familiar sights.

Water, particularly running water, ruins a trail for air-breathing creatures. Water-breathing creatures that have the scent ability, however, can use it in the water easily.

False, powerful odors can easily mask other scents. The presence of such an odor completely spoils the ability to properly detect or identify creatures, and the base Survival DC to track becomes 20 rather than 10.

Spell Resistance

Spell resistance is the extraordinary ability to avoid being affected by spells. Some spells also grant spell resistance.

To affect a creature that has spell resistance, a spellcaster must make a caster level check (1d20 + caster level) at least equal to the creature's spell resistance. The defender's spell resistance is like an Armor Class against magical attacks. If the caster fails the check, the spell doesn't affect the creature. The possessor does not have to do anything special to use spell resistance. The creature need not even be aware of the threat for its spell resistance to operate.

Only spells and spell-like abilities are subject to spell resistance. Extraordinary and supernatural abilities (including enhancement bonuses on magic weapons) are not. A creature can have some abilities that are subject to spell resistance and some that are not. Even some spells ignore spell resistance; see When Spell Resistance Applies, below.

A creature can voluntarily lower its spell resistance. Doing so is a standard action that does not provoke an attack of opportunity. Once a creature lowers its resistance, it remains down until the creature's next turn. At the beginning of the creature's next turn, the creature's spell resistance automatically returns unless the creature intentionally keeps it down (also a standard action that does not provoke an attack of opportunity).

A creature's spell resistance never interferes with its own spells, items, or abilities.

A creature with spell resistance cannot impart this power to others by touching them or standing in their midst. Only the rarest of creatures and a few magic items have the ability to bestow spell resistance upon another.

Spell resistance does not stack, but rather overlaps.

When Spell Resistance Applies

Each spell includes an entry that indicates whether spell resistance applies to the spell. In general, whether spell resistance applies depends on what the spell does.

Targeted Spells: Spell resistance applies if the spell is targeted at the creature. Some individually targeted spells can be directed at several creatures simultaneously. In such cases, a creature's spell resistance applies only to the portion of the spell actually targeted at that creature. If several different resistant creatures are subjected to such a spell, each checks its spell resistance separately.

Area Spells: Spell resistance applies if the resistant creature is within the spell's area. It protects the resistant creature without affecting the spell itself.

Effect Spells: Most effect spells summon or create something and are not subject to spell resistance. Sometimes, however, spell resistance applies to effect spells, usually to those that act upon a creature more or less directly.

Spell resistance can protect a creature from a spell that's already been cast. Check spell resistance when the creature is first affected by the spell.

Check spell resistance only once for any particular casting of a spell or use of a spell-like ability. If spell resistance fails the first time, it fails each time the creature encounters that same casting of the spell. Likewise, if the spell resistance succeeds the first time, it always succeeds. If the creature has voluntarily lowered its spell resistance and is then subjected to a spell, the creature still has a single chance to resist that spell later, when its spell resistance is back up.

Spell resistance has no effect unless the energy created or released by the spell actually goes to work on the resistant creature's mind or body. If the spell acts on anything else and the creature is affected as a consequence, no roll is required. Spell-resistant creatures can be harmed by a spell when they are not being directly affected.

Spell resistance does not apply if an effect fools the creature's senses or reveals something about the creature.

Magic actually has to be working for spell resistance to apply. Spells that have instantaneous durations but lasting results aren't subject to spell resistance unless the resistant creature is exposed to the spell the instant it is cast.

Successful Spell Resistance

Spell resistance prevents a spell or a spell-like ability from affecting or harming the resistant creature, but it never removes a magical effect from another creature or negates a spell's effect on another creature. Spell resistance prevents a spell from disrupting another spell.

Against an ongoing spell that has already been cast, a failed check against spell resistance allows the resistant creature to ignore any effect the spell might have. The magic continues to affect others normally.

APPENDIX 2: CONDITIONS

If more than one condition affects a character, apply them all. If effects can't combine, apply the most severe effect.

Bleed: A creature that is taking bleed damage takes the listed amount of damage at the beginning of its turn. Bleeding can be stopped by a DC 15 Heal check or through the application of any spell that cures hit point damage (even if the bleed is ability damage). Some bleed effects cause ability damage or even ability drain. Bleed effects do not stack with each other unless they deal different kinds of damage. When two or more bleed effects deal the same kind of damage, take the worse effect. In this case, ability drain is worse than ability damage.

Blinded: The creature cannot see. It takes a −2 penalty to Armor Class, loses its Dexterity bonus to AC (if any), and takes a −4 penalty on most Strength- and Dexterity-based skill checks and on opposed Perception skill checks. All checks and activities that rely on vision (such as reading and Perception checks based on sight) automatically fail. All opponents are considered to have total concealment (50% miss chance) against the blinded character. Blind creatures must make a DC 10 Acrobatics skill check to move faster than half speed. Creatures that fail this check fall prone. Characters who remain blinded for a long time grow accustomed to these drawbacks and can overcome some of them.

Broken: Items that have taken damage in excess of half their total hit points gain the broken condition, meaning they are less effective at their designated task. The broken condition has the following effects, depending upon the item.

- If the item is a weapon, any attacks made with the item suffer a −2 penalty on attack and damage rolls. Such weapons only score a critical hit on a natural 20 and only deal ×2 damage on a confirmed critical hit.

- If the item is a suit of armor or a shield, the bonus it grants to AC is halved, rounding down. Broken armor doubles its armor check penalty on skills.
- If the item is a tool needed for a skill, any skill check made with the item takes a –2 penalty.
- If the item is a wand or staff, it uses up twice as many charges when used.
- If the item does not fit into any of these categories, the broken condition has no effect on its use. Items with the broken condition, regardless of type, are worth 75% of their normal value. If the item is magical, it can only be repaired with a *mending* or *make whole* spell cast by a character with a caster level equal to or higher than the item's. Items lose the broken condition if the spell restores the object to half its original hit points or higher. Non-magical items can be repaired in a similar fashion, or through the Craft skill used to create it. Generally speaking, this requires a DC 20 Craft check and 1 hour of work per point of damage to be repaired. Most craftsmen charge one-tenth the item's total cost to repair such damage (more if the item is badly damaged or ruined).

Confused: A confused creature is mentally befuddled and cannot act normally. A confused creature cannot tell the difference between ally and foe, treating all creatures as enemies. Allies wishing to cast a beneficial spell that requires a touch on a confused creature must succeed on a melee touch attack. If a confused creature is attacked, it attacks the creature that last attacked it until that creature is dead or out of sight.

Roll on the following table at the beginning of each confused subject's turn each round to see what the subject does in that round.

d%	Behavior
01–25	Act normally.
26–50	Do nothing but babble incoherently.
51–75	Deal 1d8 points of damage + Str modifier to self with item in hand.
76–100	Attack nearest creature (for this purpose, a familiar counts as part of the subject's self).

A confused creature who can't carry out the indicated action does nothing but babble incoherently. Attackers are not at any special advantage when attacking a confused creature. Any confused creature who is attacked automatically attacks its attackers on its next turn, as long as it is still confused when its turn comes. Note that a confused creature will not make attacks of opportunity against anything that it is not already devoted to attacking (either because of its most recent action or because it has just been attacked).

Cowering: The character is frozen in fear and can take no actions. A cowering character takes a –2 penalty to Armor Class and loses his Dexterity bonus (if any).

Dazed: The creature is unable to act normally. A dazed creature can take no actions, but has no penalty to AC.

A dazed condition typically lasts 1 round.

Dazzled: The creature is unable to see well because of overstimulation of the eyes. A dazzled creature takes a –1 penalty on attack rolls and sight-based Perception checks.

Dead: The character's hit points are reduced to a negative amount equal to his Constitution score, his Constitution drops to 0, or he is killed outright by a spell or effect. The character's soul leaves his body. Dead characters cannot benefit from normal or magical healing, but they can be restored to life via magic. A dead body decays normally unless magically preserved, but magic that restores a dead character to life also restores the body either to full health or to its condition at the time of death (depending on the spell or device). Either way, resurrected characters need not worry about rigor mortis, decomposition, and other conditions that affect dead bodies.

Deafened: A deafened character cannot hear. He takes a –4 penalty on initiative checks, automatically fails Perception checks based on sound, takes a –4 penalty on opposed Perception checks, and has a 20% chance of spell failure when casting spells with verbal components. Characters who remain deafened for a long time grow accustomed to these drawbacks and can overcome some of them.

Disabled: A character with 0 hit points, or one who has negative hit points but has become stable and conscious, is disabled. A disabled character may take a single move action or standard action each round (but not both, nor can he take full-round actions, but he can still take swift, immediate, and free actions). He moves at half speed. Taking move actions doesn't risk further injury, but performing any standard action (or any other action the GM deems strenuous, including some free actions such as casting a quickened spell) deals 1 point of damage after the completion of the act. Unless the action increased the disabled character's hit points, he is now in negative hit points and dying.

A disabled character with negative hit points recovers hit points naturally if he is being helped. Otherwise, each day he can attempt a DC 10 Constitution check after resting for 8 hours, to begin recovering hit points naturally. The character takes a penalty on this roll equal to his negative hit point total. Failing this check causes the character to lose 1 hit point, but this does not cause the character to become unconscious. Once a character makes this check, he continues to heal naturally and is no longer in danger of losing hit points naturally.

Dying: A dying creature is unconscious and near death. Creatures that have negative hit points and have not stabilized are dying. A dying creature can take no actions. On the character's next turn, after being reduced to negative hit points (but not dead), and on all subsequent turns, the character must make a DC 10 Constitution check to become stable. The character takes a penalty on this roll equal to his negative hit point total. A character that is stable does not need to make this check. A natural 20 on this check is an automatic success. If the character fails this check, he loses 1 hit point. If a dying creature has an amount of negative hit points equal to its Constitution score, it dies.

Energy Drained: The character gains one or more negative levels, which might become permanent. If the subject has at least as many negative levels as Hit Dice, he dies. See Energy Drain and Negative levels on page 562 for more information.

Entangled: The character is ensnared. Being entangled impedes movement, but does not entirely prevent it unless the bonds are anchored to an immobile object or tethered by an opposing force. An entangled creature moves at half speed, cannot run or charge, and takes a –2 penalty on all attack rolls and a –4 penalty to Dexterity. An entangled character who attempts to cast a spell must make a concentration check (DC 15 + spell level) or lose the spell.

Exhausted: An exhausted character moves at half speed, cannot run or charge, and takes a –6 penalty to Strength and Dexterity. After 1 hour of complete rest, an exhausted character becomes fatigued. A fatigued character becomes exhausted by doing something else that would normally cause fatigue.

Fascinated: A fascinated creature is entranced by a supernatural or spell effect. The creature stands or sits quietly, taking no actions other than to pay attention to the fascinating effect, for as long as the effect lasts. It takes a –4 penalty on skill checks made as reactions, such as Perception checks. Any potential threat, such as a hostile creature approaching, allows the fascinated creature a new saving throw against the fascinating effect. Any obvious threat, such as someone drawing a weapon, casting a spell, or aiming a ranged weapon at the fascinated creature, automatically breaks the effect. A fascinated creature's ally may shake it free of the spell as a standard action.

Fatigued: A fatigued character can neither run nor charge and takes a –2 penalty to Strength and Dexterity. Doing anything that would normally cause fatigue causes the fatigued character to become exhausted. After 8 hours of complete rest, fatigued characters are no longer fatigued.

Flat-Footed: A character who has not yet acted during a combat is flat-footed, unable to react normally to the situation. A flat-footed character loses his Dexterity bonus to AC (if any) and cannot make attacks of opportunity.

Frightened: A frightened creature flees from the source of its fear as best it can. If unable to flee, it may fight. A frightened creature takes a –2 penalty on all attack rolls, saving throws, skill checks, and ability checks. A frightened creature can use special abilities, including spells, to flee; indeed, the creature must use such means if they are the only way to escape.

Frightened is like shaken, except that the creature must flee if possible. Panicked is a more extreme state of fear.

Grappled: A grappled creature is restrained by a creature, trap, or effect. Grappled creatures cannot move and take a –4 penalty to Dexterity. A grappled creature takes a –2 penalty on all attack rolls and combat maneuver checks, except those made to grapple or escape a grapple. In addition, grappled creatures can take no action that requires two hands to perform. A grappled character who attempts to cast a spell or use a spell-like ability must make a concentration check (DC 10 + grappler's CMB + spell level, see page 206), or lose the spell. Grappled creatures cannot make attacks of opportunity.

A grappled creature cannot use Stealth to hide from the creature grappling it, even if a special ability, such as hide in plain sight, would normally allow it to do so. If a grappled creature becomes invisible, through a spell or other ability, it gains a +2 circumstance bonus on its CMD to avoid being grappled, but receives no other benefit.

Helpless: A helpless character is paralyzed, held, bound, sleeping, unconscious, or otherwise completely at an opponent's mercy. A helpless target is treated as having a Dexterity of 0 (–5 modifier). Melee attacks against a helpless target get a +4 bonus (equivalent to attacking a prone target). Ranged attacks get no special bonus against helpless targets. Rogues can sneak attack helpless targets.

As a full-round action, an enemy can use a melee weapon to deliver a coup de grace to a helpless foe. An enemy can also use a bow or crossbow, provided he is adjacent to the target. The attacker automatically hits and scores a critical hit. (A rogue also gets his sneak attack damage bonus against a helpless foe when delivering a coup de grace.) If the defender survives, he must make a Fortitude save (DC 10 + damage dealt) or die. Delivering a coup de grace provokes attacks of opportunity.

Creatures that are immune to critical hits do not take critical damage, nor do they need to make Fortitude saves to avoid being killed by a coup de grace.

Incorporeal: Creatures with the incorporeal condition do not have a physical body. Incorporeal creatures are immune to all nonmagical attack forms. Incorporeal creatures take half damage (50%) from magic weapons, spells, spell-like effects, and supernatural effects. Incorporeal creatures take full damage from other incorporeal creatures and effects, as well as all force effects.

Invisible: Invisible creatures are visually undetectable. An invisible creature gains a +2 bonus on attack rolls against a sighted opponent, and ignores its opponent's Dexterity bonus to AC (if any). See Invisibility, under Special Abilities.

Nauseated: Creatures with the nauseated condition experience stomach distress. Nauseated creatures are unable to attack, cast spells, concentrate on spells, or do anything else requiring attention. The only action such a character can take is a single move actions per turn.

Panicked: A panicked creature must drop anything it holds and flee at top speed from the source of its fear, as well as any other dangers it encounters, along a random path. It can't take any other actions. In addition, the creature takes a –2 penalty on all saving throws, skill checks, and ability checks. If cornered, a panicked creature cowers and does not attack, typically using the total defense action in combat. A panicked creature can use special abilities, including spells, to flee; indeed, the creature must use such means if they are the only way to escape.

Panicked is a more extreme state of fear than shaken or frightened.

Paralyzed: A paralyzed character is frozen in place and unable to move or act. A paralyzed character has effective Dexterity and Strength scores of 0 and is helpless, but can take purely mental actions. A winged creature flying in the air at the time that it becomes paralyzed cannot flap its wings and falls. A paralyzed swimmer can't swim and may drown. A creature can move through a space occupied by a paralyzed creature—ally or not. Each square occupied by a paralyzed creature, however, counts as 2 squares to move through.

Petrified: A petrified character has been turned to stone and is considered unconscious. If a petrified character cracks or breaks, but the broken pieces are joined with the body as he returns to flesh, he is unharmed. If the character's petrified body is incomplete when it returns to flesh, the body is likewise incomplete and there is some amount of permanent hit point loss and/or debilitation.

Pinned: A pinned creature is tightly bound and can take few actions. A pinned creature cannot move and is denied its Dexterity bonus. A pinned character also takes an additional –4 penalty to his Armor Class. A pinned creature is limited in the actions that it can take. A pinned creature can always attempt to free itself, usually through a combat maneuver check or Escape Artist check. A pinned creature can take verbal and mental actions, but cannot cast any spells that require a somatic or material component. A pinned character who attempts to cast a spell or use a spell-like ability must make a concentration check (DC 10 + grappler's CMB + spell level) or lose the spell. Pinned is a more severe version of grappled, and their effects do not stack.

Prone: The character is lying on the ground. A prone attacker has a –4 penalty on melee attack rolls and cannot use a ranged weapon (except for a crossbow). A prone defender gains a +4 bonus to Armor Class against ranged attacks, but takes a –4 penalty to AC against melee attacks.

Standing up is a move-equivalent action that provokes an attack of opportunity.

Shaken: A shaken character takes a –2 penalty on attack rolls, saving throws, skill checks, and ability checks. Shaken is a less severe state of fear than frightened or panicked.

Sickened: The character takes a –2 penalty on all attack rolls, weapon damage rolls, saving throws, skill checks, and ability checks.

Stable: A character who was dying but who has stopped losing hit points each round and still has negative hit points is stable. The character is no longer dying, but is still unconscious. If the character has become stable because of aid from another character (such as a Heal check or magical healing), then the character no longer loses hit points. The character can make a DC 10 Constitution check each hour to become conscious and disabled (even though his hit points are still negative). The character takes a penalty on this roll equal to his negative hit point total.

If a character has become stable on his own and hasn't had help, he is still at risk of losing hit points. Each hour he can make a Constitution check to become stable (as a character that has received aid), but each failed check causes him to lose 1 hit point.

Staggered: A staggered creature may take a single move action or standard action each round (but not both, nor can he take full-round actions). A staggered creature can still take free, swift, and immediate actions. A creature with nonlethal damage exactly equal to its current hit points gains the staggered condition.

Stunned: A stunned creature drops everything held, can't take actions, takes a –2 penalty to AC, and loses its Dexterity bonus to AC (if any).

Unconscious: Unconscious creatures are knocked out and helpless. Unconsciousness can result from having negative hit points (but not more than the creature's Constitution score), or from nonlethal damage in excess of current hit points.

APPENDIX 3: INSPIRING READING

The Pathfinder Roleplaying Game and the fantasy RPGs that preceded it took inspiration from the great classics of fantasy fiction. The following list includes those authors and tales that specifically inspired Paizo Publishing in the creation of this version of fantasy RPG rules.

Barker, Clive: *The Hellbound Heart, Imagica, Weaveworld Beowulf* (anonymous)

Blackwood, Algernon: "The Willows," "The Wendigo," et al.

Brackett, Leigh: *The Sword of Rhiannon,* Skaith series, et al.

Burroughs, Edgar Rice: Pellucidar, Mars, and Venus series

Campbell, Ramsey: Ryre the Swordsman series, et al.

Dunsany, Lord: *The King of Elfland's Daughter,* et al.

Farmer, Philip José: World of Tiers series, et al.

Carter, Lin: ed. The Year's Best Fantasy, Flashing Swords

Feist, Raymond: Riftwar saga, et al.

Gygax, Gary: Gord the Rogue series, et al.

Kuttner, Henry: *Elak of Atlantis, The Dark World*

Homer: *The Odyssey*

Howard, Robert E.: Conan series, et al.

Hugo, Victor: *Les Miserables*

King, Stephen: Dark Tower series

Leiber, Fritz: Fafhrd & Gray Mouser series, et al.

Lovecraft, H. P.: Cthulhu Mythos tales, et al.

Machen, Arthur: "The White People," et al.

Martin, George R. R.: Song of Ice and Fire series

Merritt, A.: *The Ship of Ishtar, The Moon Pool*, et al.

Miéville, China: Bas-Lag series

Moorcock, Michael: Elric series, et al.

Moore, C. L.: *Black God's Kiss*

Offutt, Andrew J.: ed. Swords Against Darkness

One Thousand and One Nights (traditional)

Poe, Edgar Allan: "The Fall of the House of Usher," et al.

Saberhagen, Fred: *Changeling Earth*, et al.

Saunders, Charles: Imaro series, et al.

Shakespeare, William: *Macbeth*, et al.

Simmons, Dan: Hyperion series, *The Terror*, et al.

Smith, Clark Ashton: Averoigne and Zothique tales, et al.

Stoker, Bram: *Dracula, Lair of the White Worm*, et al.

Tolkien, J. R. R.: Lord of the Rings trilogy, *The Hobbit*

Vance, Jack: Dying Earth series, et al.

Wagner, Karl Edward: Kane series, ed. Echoes of Valor

Wells, H. G.: *The Time Machine*, et al.

Wellman, Manly Wade: John the Balladeer series, et al.

Zelazny, Roger: Amber series, et al.

APPENDIX 4: GAME AIDS

In addition to a few character sheets and some dice, there are a wide variety of additional tools available to enhance your game. The following game aids can be found at your local game store, or purchased online at **paizo.com**.

Pathfinder Adventure Path: These monthly adventures provide everything a GM needs to run an entire campaign, taking characters from 1st level to the heights of power. Each campaign is divided into six parts, with one adventure in each installment.

Pathfinder Modules: Great for a GM with little time to prepare for a game, each of these modules contains one adventure, suitable for a few sessions of play.

Pathfinder Campaign Setting: These products detail the world of Golarion, the setting for all Pathfinder Adventure Paths and Modules. With these books you can design your own games set in this rich and exciting world.

Pathfinder Roleplaying Game GM Screen: This screen can be placed on the table to allow the GM to keep all of his notes and dice rolls secret. The inside of the screen is packed with useful tables and charts for the GM to easily reference during play.

GameMastery Flip-Mats and *GameMastery Map Packs*: These full-color map products are scaled for use with most miniatures, making combat vibrant and exciting. Flip-Mats are laminated so that you can write on them with nearly any marker. Map Packs include 18 tiles each, allowing you to customize the terrain.

GameMastery Item Cards: Packaged in decks with a wide variety of items, each of these cards has a full-color illustration of a magic item on one side, with a space for customizing the item on the back. Item Cards make sorting through your treasure quick and easy.

GameMastery Critical Hit Deck: Add a dramatic flair to combat with this deck of 52 cards. Each one transforms an ordinary critical hit into an exciting combat effect, from broken bones to severed limbs.

3.5/Pathfinder Conversion PDF: Finally, if you want help in converting a 3.5 product to the Pathfinder RPG, or vice versa, head over to **paizo.com** for this handy conversion guide.

CHARACTER SHEET

CHARACTER NAME _____ ALIGNMENT _____ PLAYER _____

CHARACTER CLASS AND LEVEL _____ DEITY _____ HOMELAND _____

RACE _____ SIZE ___ GENDER ___ AGE ___ HEIGHT ___ WEIGHT ___ HAIR ___ EYES ___

ABILITY NAME	ABILITY SCORE	ABILITY MODIFIER	TEMP ADJUSTMENT	TEMP MODIFIER
STR STRENGTH				
DEX DEXTERITY				
CON CONSTITUTION				
INT INTELLIGENCE				
WIS WISDOM				
CHA CHARISMA				

HP HIT POINTS   TOTAL [ ]   DR [ ]

WOUNDS/CURRENT HP

NONLETHAL DAMAGE

INITIATIVE MODIFIER [ ] = [ ] + [ ]
TOTAL   DEX MODIFIER   MISC MODIFIER

AC ARMOR CLASS [ ] = 10 + [ ] + [ ] + [ ] + [ ] + [ ] + [ ] + [ ]
TOTAL   ARMOR BONUS   SHIELD BONUS   DEX MODIFIER   SIZE MODIFIER   NATURAL ARMOR   DEFLECTION MODIFIER   MISC MODIFIER

TOUCH ARMOR CLASS [ ]   **FLAT-FOOTED** ARMOR CLASS [ ]   MODIFIERS

SAVING THROWS	TOTAL		BASE SAVE		ABILITY MODIFIER		MAGIC MODIFIER		MISC MODIFIER		TEMPORARY MODIFIER	MODIFIERS
FORTITUDE (Constitution)		=		+		+		+		+		
REFLEX (Dexterity)		=		+		+		+		+		
WILL (Wisdom)		=		+		+		+		+		

BASE ATTACK BONUS [ ]   **SPELL RESISTANCE** [ ]

CMB [ ] = [ ] + [ ] + [ ]   MODIFIERS
TOTAL   BASE ATTACK BONUS   STRENGTH MODIFIER   SIZE MODIFIER

CMD [ ] = [ ] + [ ] + [ ] + [ ] + 10
TOTAL   BASE ATTACK BONUS   STRENGTH MODIFIER   DEXTERITY MODIFIER   SIZE MODIFIER

WEAPON		ATTACK BONUS	CRITICAL
TYPE	RANGE	AMMUNITION	DAMAGE

WEAPON		ATTACK BONUS	CRITICAL
TYPE	RANGE	AMMUNITION	DAMAGE

WEAPON		ATTACK BONUS	CRITICAL
TYPE	RANGE	AMMUNITION	DAMAGE

WEAPON		ATTACK BONUS	CRITICAL
TYPE	RANGE	AMMUNITION	DAMAGE

WEAPON		ATTACK BONUS	CRITICAL
TYPE	RANGE	AMMUNITION	DAMAGE

SPEED LAND [ ] FT. [ ] SQ.   BASE SPEED   [ ] FT. [ ] SQ.   WITH ARMOR   TEMP MODIFIERS

[ ] FT.   [ ] FT.   [ ] FT.   [ ] FT.
FLY   MANEUVERABILITY   SWIM   CLIMB   BURROW

SKILLS

SKILL NAMES	TOTAL BONUS	ABILITY MOD.	RANKS	MISC. MOD.
☐ ACROBATICS	___	=DEX	+ ___	+ ___
☐ APPRAISE	___	=INT	+ ___	+ ___
☐ BLUFF	___	=CHA	+ ___	+ ___
☐ CLIMB	___	=STR	+ ___	+ ___
☐ CRAFT _____	___	=INT	+ ___	+ ___
☐ CRAFT _____	___	=INT	+ ___	+ ___
☐ CRAFT _____	___	=INT	+ ___	+ ___
☐ DIPLOMACY	___	=CHA	+ ___	+ ___
☐ DISABLE DEVICE*	___	=DEX	+ ___	+ ___
☐ DISGUISE	___	=CHA	+ ___	+ ___
☐ ESCAPE ARTIST	___	=DEX	+ ___	+ ___
☐ FLY	___	=DEX	+ ___	+ ___
☐ HANDLE ANIMAL*	___	=CHA	+ ___	+ ___
☐ HEAL	___	=WIS	+ ___	+ ___
☐ INTIMIDATE	___	=CHA	+ ___	+ ___
☐ KNOWLEDGE (ARCANA)*	___	=INT	+ ___	+ ___
☐ KNOWLEDGE (DUNGEONEERING)*	___	=INT	+ ___	+ ___
☐ KNOWLEDGE (ENGINEERING)*	___	=INT	+ ___	+ ___
☐ KNOWLEDGE (GEOGRAPHY)*	___	=INT	+ ___	+ ___
☐ KNOWLEDGE (HISTORY)*	___	=INT	+ ___	+ ___
☐ KNOWLEDGE (LOCAL)*	___	=INT	+ ___	+ ___
☐ KNOWLEDGE (NATURE)*	___	=INT	+ ___	+ ___
☐ KNOWLEDGE (NOBILITY)*	___	=INT	+ ___	+ ___
☐ KNOWLEDGE (PLANES)*	___	=INT	+ ___	+ ___
☐ KNOWLEDGE (RELIGION)*	___	=INT	+ ___	+ ___
☐ LINGUISTICS*	___	=INT	+ ___	+ ___
☐ PERCEPTION	___	=WIS	+ ___	+ ___
☐ PERFORM _____	___	=CHA	+ ___	+ ___
☐ PERFORM _____	___	=CHA	+ ___	+ ___
☐ PROFESSION* _____	___	=WIS	+ ___	+ ___
☐ PROFESSION* _____	___	=WIS	+ ___	+ ___
☐ RIDE	___	=DEX	+ ___	+ ___
☐ SENSE MOTIVE	___	=WIS	+ ___	+ ___
☐ SLEIGHT OF HAND*	___	=DEX	+ ___	+ ___
☐ SPELLCRAFT*	___	=INT	+ ___	+ ___
☐ STEALTH	___	=DEX	+ ___	+ ___
☐ SURVIVAL	___	=WIS	+ ___	+ ___
☐ SWIM	___	=STR	+ ___	+ ___
☐ USE MAGIC DEVICE*	___	=CHA	+ ___	+ ___

☑ CLASS SKILL * TRAINED ONLY

CONDITIONAL MODIFIERS:

_____

LANGUAGES:

_____
_____
_____

AC ITEMS

	BONUS	TYPE	CHECK PENALTY	SPELL FAILURE	WEIGHT	PROPERTIES
TOTALS						

SPELLS

SPELLS KNOWN	SPELL SAVE DC	LEVEL	SPELLS PER DAY	BONUS SPELLS
		0		—
		1ST		
		2ND		
		3RD		
		4TH		
		5TH		
		6TH		
		7TH		
		8TH		
		9TH		

CONDITIONAL MODIFIERS

DOMAINS/SPECIALTY SCHOOL

0 ☐☐☐☐☐☐☐☐

1ST ☐☐☐☐☐☐☐☐

2ND ☐☐☐☐☐☐☐☐

3RD ☐☐☐☐☐☐☐☐

4TH ☐☐☐☐☐☐☐☐

5TH ☐☐☐☐☐☐☐☐

6TH ☐☐☐☐☐☐☐☐

7TH ☐☐☐☐☐☐☐☐

8TH ☐☐☐☐☐☐☐☐

9TH ☐☐☐☐☐☐☐☐

GEAR

ITEM	WT.
TOTAL WEIGHT	

LIGHT LOAD		LIFT OVER HEAD	
MEDIUM LOAD		LIFT OFF GROUND	
HEAVY LOAD		DRAG OR PUSH	

MONEY

CP

SP

GP

PP

FEATS

SPECIAL ABILITIES

EXPERIENCE POINTS · NEXT LEVEL

EMPOWER YOUR GAME!

The *Pathfinder RPG Core Rulebook* contains everything you need to get started exploring a dangerous world beset by magic and evil, but your journey gets bigger and better with the exciting optional rulebooks below! Dozens of great adventure modules, complete campaigns, and accessories are also available at your local retailer or online at **paizo.com**, where you'll find a welcoming community of thousands of Pathfinder RPG fans and experts ready to give you a helping hand!

PATHFINDER RPG BESTIARY

This 328-page book presents more than 350 different creatures for use in the Pathfinder Roleplaying Game. Within this tome you'll find fire-breathing dragons and blood-drinking vampires, vile demons and shapechanging werewolves, sadistic goblins and lumbering giants, and so much more! And it doesn't stop there—with full rules for advancing monsters, adapting monsters to different roles, and designing your own unique creations, you'll never be without a band of hideous minions again!

$39.99 • PZO1112 • ISBN 978-1-60125-183-1

PATHFINDER RPG ADVANCED PLAYER'S GUIDE

This 336-page hardcover player reference provides a wealth of new ideas and options for players, including six completely new character classes, expanded rules for the 11 core classes, new feats and combat abilities, fantastic equipment, dozens of new spells, and more! This must-have volume gives players the edge they need to make the most of their characters and ensure they survive to defeat the next monster, claim the next treasure, and form legends of their own that will endure the ages!

$39.99 • PZO1115 • 978-1-60125-246-3

PATHFINDER RPG GAMEMASTERY GUIDE

Packed with invaluable hints and information, this 320-page hardcover rulebook contains everything GMs need to take their games to the next level, from advice on the nuts and bolts of running a session to the greater mysteries of crafting engaging worlds and storylines. Whether you've run one game or a thousand, this book has page after page of secrets to make you sharper, faster, and more creative, while always staying one step ahead of your players.

$39.99 • PZO1114 • 978-1-60125-217-3

PATHFINDER RPG GM SCREEN

This beautiful 4-panel screen—constructed of ultra-high-grade hardcover book stock—features stunning artwork on the player's side and a huge number of charts and tables on the GM side to speed up play and reduce time spent leafing through rulebooks in search of an obscure modifier or result. From skill check Difficulty Classes to two-weapon fighting modifiers, the *Pathfinder RPG GM Screen* gives you the tools you need to keep the game fast and fun.

$14.99 • PZO1113 • ISBN 978-1-60125-216-6

PATHFINDER RPG BESTIARY 2

The newest hardcover rulebook for the smash hit Pathfinder Roleplaying Game presents more than 300 new creatures for all your fantasy RPG needs. From classic creatures like undead dragons, hippogriffs, and the Jabberwock to denizens of the outer planes like daemons, proteans and the all-new aeons, the *Pathfinder RPG Bestiary 2* is packed from cover-to-cover with exciting surprises and fuel for a thousand campaigns!

$39.99 • PZO1116 • 978-1-60125-268-5

PATHFINDER CAMPAIGN SETTING WORLD GUIDE: THE INNER SEA

The exciting world of the Pathfinder Roleplaying Game comes alive in this giant 320-page hardcover campaign setting! This definitive volume contains expanded coverage of the 40+ nations in Golarion's Inner Sea region, from ruin-strewn Varisia in the north to the sweltering jungles of the Mwangi Expanse in the south to crashed sky cities, savage frontier kingdoms, and everything in between. Plus tons of info on Pathfinder's gods, new character abilities, magic items, and more!

$39.99 • 978-1-60125-269-2